T0181103

Lecture Notes in Computer Science 12105

More information about this series at http://www.springer.com/series/7410

Anne Canteaut · Yuval Ishai (Eds.)

Advances in Cryptology – EUROCRYPT 2020

39th Annual International Conference on the Theory
and Applications of Cryptographic Techniques
Zagreb, Croatia, May 10–14, 2020
Proceedings, Part I

 Springer

Editors
Anne Canteaut ⓘ
Équipe-projet COSMIQ
Inria
Paris, France

Yuval Ishai
Computer Science Department
Technion
Haifa, Israel

ISSN 0302-9743   ISSN 1611-3349 (electronic)
Lecture Notes in Computer Science
ISBN 978-3-030-45720-4   ISBN 978-3-030-45721-1 (eBook)
https://doi.org/10.1007/978-3-030-45721-1

LNCS Sublibrary: SL4 – Security and Cryptology

This Springer imprint is published by the registered company Springer Nature Switzerland AG
The registered company address is: Gewerbestrasse 11, 6330 Cham, Switzerland

Preface

Eurocrypt 2020, the 39th Annual International Conference on the Theory and Applications of Cryptographic Techniques, was held in Zagreb, Croatia, during May 10–14, 2020.[1] The conference was sponsored by the International Association for Cryptologic Research (IACR). Lejla Batina (Radboud University, The Netherlands) and Stjepan Picek (Delft University of Technology, The Netherlands) were responsible for the local organization. They were supported by a local organizing team consisting of Marin Golub and Domagoj Jakobovic (University of Zagreb, Croatia). Peter Schwabe acted as the affiliated events chair and Simona Samardjiska helped with the promotion and local organization. We are deeply indebted to all of them for their support and smooth collaboration.

The conference program followed the now established parallel-track system where the works of the authors were presented in two concurrently running tracks. The invited talks and the talks presenting the best paper/best young researcher spanned over both tracks.

We received a total of 375 submissions. Each submission was anonymized for the reviewing process and was assigned to at least three of the 57 Program Committee (PC) members. PC members were allowed to submit at most two papers. The reviewing process included a rebuttal round for all submissions. After extensive deliberations the PC accepted 81 papers. The revised versions of these papers are included in these three volume proceedings, organized topically within their respective track.

The PC decided to give the Best Paper Award to the paper "Optimal Broadcast Encryption from Pairings and LWE" by Shweta Agrawal and Shota Yamada and the Best Young Researcher Award to the paper "Private Information Retrieval with Sublinear Online Time" by Henry Corrigan-Gibbs and Dmitry Kogan. Both papers, together with "Candidate iO from Homomorphic Encryption Schemes" by Zvika Brakerski, Nico Döttling, Sanjam Garg, and Giulio Malavolta, received invitations for the *Journal of Cryptology*.

The program also included invited talks by Alon Rosen, titled "Fine-Grained Cryptography: A New Frontier?", and by Alice Silverberg, titled "Mathematics and Cryptography: A Marriage of Convenience?".

We would like to thank all the authors who submitted papers. We know that the PC's decisions can be very disappointing, especially rejections of very good papers which did not find a slot in the sparse number of accepted papers. We sincerely hope that these works eventually get the attention they deserve.

We are also indebted to the members of the PC and all external reviewers for their voluntary work. The PC work is quite a workload. It has been an honor to work with

---

[1] This preface was written before the conference took place, under the assumption that it will take place as planned in spite of travel restrictions related to the coronavirus.

everyone. The PC's work was simplified by Shai Halevi's submission software and his support, including running the service on IACR servers.

Finally, we thank everyone else – speakers, session chairs, and rump-session chairs – for their contribution to the program of Eurocrypt 2020. We would also like to thank the many sponsors for their generous support, including the Cryptography Research Fund that supported student speakers.

May 2020   Anne Canteaut
                                                                          Yuval Ishai

Eurocrypt 2020

The 39th Annual International Conference on the Theory and Applications of Cryptographic Techniques

Sponsored by *the International Association for Cryptologic Research (IACR)*

May 10–14, 2020
Zagreb, Croatia

General Co-chairs

Lejla Batina   Radboud University, The Netherlands
Stjepan Picek   Delft University of Technology, The Netherlands

Program Co-chairs

Anne Canteaut   Inria, France
Yuval Ishai   Technion, Israel

Program Committee

Divesh Aggarwal	National University of Singapore, Singapore
Benny Applebaum	Tel Aviv University, Israel
Fabrice Benhamouda	Algorand Foundation, USA
Elette Boyle	IDC Herzliya, Israel
Zvika Brakerski	Weizmann Institute of Science, Israel
Anne Broadbent	University of Ottawa, Canada
Nishanth Chandran	MSR India, India
Yilei Chen	Visa Research, USA
Aloni Cohen	Boston University, USA
Ran Cohen	Boston University and Northeastern University, USA
Geoffroy Couteau	CNRS, IRIF, Université de Paris, France
Joan Daemen	Radboud University, The Netherlands
Luca De Feo	IBM Research Zurich, Switzerland
Léo Ducas	CWI Amsterdam, The Netherlands
Maria Eichlseder	Graz University of Technology, Austria
Thomas Eisenbarth	University of Lübeck and WPI, Germany
Thomas Fuhr	ANSSI, France
Romain Gay	Cornell Tech, USA
Benedikt Gierlichs	KU Leuven, Belgium
Rishab Goyal	UT Austin, USA

Vipul Goyal	Carnegie Mellon University, USA
Tim Güneysu	Ruhr-Universität Bochum and DFKI, Germany
Jian Guo	Nanyang Technological University, Singapore
Mohammad Hajiabadi	UC Berkeley, USA
Carmit Hazay	Bar-Ilan University, Israel
Susan Hohenberger	Johns Hopkins University, USA
Pavel Hubáček	Charles University Prague, Czech Republic
Abhishek Jain	Johns Hopkins University, USA
Marc Joye	Zama, France
Bhavana Kanukurthi	IISc Bangalore, India
Nathan Keller	Bar-Ilan University, Israel
Susumu Kiyoshima	NTT Research, USA
Eyal Kushilevitz	Technion, Israel
Gregor Leander	Ruhr-Universität Bochum, Germany
Tancrède Lepoint	Google, USA
Tal Malkin	Columbia University, USA
Alexander May	Ruhr-Universität Bochum, Germany
Bart Mennink	Radboud University, The Netherlands
Kazuhiko Minematsu	NEC Corporation, Japan
María Naya-Plasencia	Inria, France
Ryo Nishimaki	NTT Secure Platform Laboratories, Japan
Cécile Pierrot	Inria and Université de Lorraine, France
Sondre Rønjom	University of Bergen, Norway
Ron Rothblum	Technion, Israel
Alessandra Scafuro	North Carolina State University, USA
Peter Schwabe	Radboud University, The Netherlands
Adam Smith	Boston University, USA
François-Xavier Standaert	KU Leuven, Belgium
Yosuke Todo	NTT Secure Platform Laboratories, Japan
Gilles Van Assche	STMicroelectronics, Belgium
Prashant Nalini Vasudevan	UC Berkeley, USA
Muthuramakrishnan Venkitasubramaniam	University of Rochester, USA
Frederik Vercauteren	KU Leuven, Belgium
Damien Vergnaud	Sorbonne Université and Institut Universitaire de France, France
Eylon Yogev	Technion, Israel
Yu Yu	Shanghai Jiao Tong University, China
Gilles Zémor	Université de Bordeaux, France

External Reviewers

Aysajan Abidin
Ittai Abraham
Thomas Agrikola
Navid Alamati
Nils Albartus
Martin Albrecht
Ghada Almashaqbeh
Joël Alwen
Miguel Ambrona
Ghous Amjad
Nicolas Aragon
Gilad Asharov
Tomer Ashur
Thomas Attema
Nuttapong Attrapadung
Daniel Augot
Florian Bache
Christian Badertscher
Saikrishna
    Badrinarayanan
Shi Bai
Josep Balasch
Foteini Baldimtsi
Marshall Ball
Zhenzhen Bao
James Bartusek
Lejla Batina
Enkhtaivan Batnyam
Carsten Baum
Gabrielle Beck
Christof Beierle
Amos Beimel
Sebastian Berndt
Dan J. Bernstein
Francesco Berti
Ward Beullens
Rishabh Bhadauria
Obbattu Sai Lakshmi
    Bhavana
Jean-Francois Biasse
Begül Bilgin
Nina Bindel
Nir Bitansky

Olivier Blazy
Naresh Boddu
Koen de Boer
Alexandra Boldyreva
Xavier Bonnetain
Carl Bootland
Jonathan Bootle
Adam Bouland
Christina Boura
Tatiana Bradley
Marek Broll
Olivier Bronchain
Ileana Buhan
Mark Bun
Sergiu Bursuc
Benedikt Bünz
Federico Canale
Sébastien Canard
Ran Canetti
Xavier Caruso
Ignacio Cascudo
David Cash
Gaëtan Cassiers
Guilhem Castagnos
Wouter Castryck
Hervé Chabanne
André Chailloux
Avik Chakraborti
Hubert Chan
Melissa Chase
Cong Chen
Hao Chen
Jie Chen
Ming-Shing Chen
Albert Cheu
Jérémy Chotard
Arka Rai Choudhuri
Kai-Min Chung
Michele Ciampi
Benoit Cogliati
Sandro Coretti-Drayton
Jean-Sébastien Coron
Adriana Suarez Corona

Alain Couvreur
Jan-Pieter D'Anvers
Bernardo David
Thomas Decru
Claire Delaplace
Patrick Derbez
Apoorvaa Deshpande
Siemen Dhooghe
Denis Diemert
Itai Dinur
Christoph Dobraunig
Yevgeniy Dodis
Jack Doerner
Jelle Don
Nico Döttling
Benjamin Dowling
John Schank
Markus Duermuth
Orr Dunkelman
Fréderic Dupuis
Iwan Duursma
Sébastien Duval
Stefan Dziembowski
Aner Moshe Ben Efraim
Naomi Ephraim
Thomas Espitau
Andre Esser
Brett Hemenway Falk
Antonio Faonio
Serge Fehr
Patrick Felke
Rex Fernando
Dario Fiore
Ben Fisch
Marc Fischlin
Nils Fleischhacker
Cody Freitag
Benjamin Fuller
Ariel Gabizon
Philippe Gaborit
Steven Galbraith
Chaya Ganesh
Juan Garay

Rachit Garg
Pierrick Gaudry
Nicholas Genise
Essam Ghadafi
Satrajit Ghosh
Kristian Gjøsteen
Aarushi Goel
Junqing Gong
Alonso Gonzalez
Lorenzo Grassi
Jens Groth
Aurore Guillevic
Berk Gulmezoglu
Aldo Gunsing
Chun Guo
Qian Guo
Siyao Guo
Shai Halevi
Shuai Han
Abida Haque
Phil Hebborn
Brett Hemenway
Shoichi Hirose
Dennis Hofheinz
Justin Holmgren
Akinori Hosoyamada
Senyang Huang
Paul Huynh
Kathrin Hövelmanns
Andreas Hülsing
Ilia Iliashenko
Laurent Imbert
Takanori Isobe
Tetsu Iwata
Håkon Jacobsen
Tibor Jager
Aayush Jain
Samuel Jaques
Jéremy Jean
Yanxue Jia
Zhengzhong Jin
Thomas Johansson
Kimmo Järvinen
Saqib Kakvi
Daniel Kales
Seny Kamara

Gabe Kaptchuk
Martti Karvonen
Shuichi Katsumata
Raza Ali Kazmi
Florian Kerschbaum
Dakshita Khurana
Jean Kieffer
Ryo Kikuchi
Eike Kiltz
Sam Kim
Elena Kirshanova
Fuyuki Kitagawa
Dima Kogan
Lisa Kohl
Markulf Kohlweiss
Ilan Komargodski
Yashvanth Kondi
Venkata Koppula
Lucas Kowalczyk
Karel Kral
Ralf Kuesters
Ashutosh Kumar
Ranjit Kumaresan
Srijita Kundu
Peter Kutasp
Thijs Laarhoven
Gijs Van Laer
Russell Lai
Virginie Lallemand
Baptiste Lambin
Julien Lavauzelle
Phi Hung Le
Eysa Lee
Hyung Tae Lee
Jooyoung Lee
Antonin Leroux
Gaëtan Leurent
Xin Li
Xiao Liang
Chengyu Lin
Huijia (Rachel) Lin
Wei-Kai Lin
Eik List
Guozhen Liu
Jiahui Liu
Qipeng Liu

Shengli Liu
Tianren Liu
Pierre Loidreau
Alex Lombardi
Patrick Longa
Sébastien Lord
Julian Loss
George Lu
Atul Luykx
Vadim Lyubashevsky
Fermi Ma
Varun Madathil
Roel Maes
Bernardo Magri
Saeed Mahloujifar
Christian Majenz
Eleftheria Makri
Giulio Malavolta
Mary Maller
Alex Malozemoff
Nathan Manohar
Daniel Masny
Simon Masson
Takahiro Matsuda
Noam Mazor
Audra McMillan
Lauren De Meyer
Peihan Miao
Gabrielle De Micheli
Ian Miers
Brice Minaud
Pratyush Mishra
Ahmad Moghimi
Esfandiar Mohammadi
Victor Mollimard
Amir Moradi
Tal Moran
Andrew Morgan
Mathilde de la Morinerie
Nicky Mouha
Tamer Mour
Pratyay Mukherjee
Marta Mularczyk
Koksal Mus
Pierrick Méaux
Jörn Müller-Quade

Yusuke Naito
Mridul Nandi
Samuel Neves
Ngoc Khanh Nguyen
Anca Nitulescu
Ariel Nof
Sai Lakshmi Bhavana
    Obbattu
Maciej Obremski
Tobias Oder
Frédérique Oggier
Miyako Ohkubo
Mateus de Oliveira
    Oliveira
Tron Omland
Maximilian Orlt
Michele Orrù
Emmanuela Orsini
Morten Øygarden
Ferruh Ozbudak
Carles Padro
Aurel Page
Jiaxin Pan
Omer Paneth
Lorenz Panny
Anat Paskin-Cherniavsky
Alain Passelègue
Sikhar Patranabis
Michaël Peeters
Chris Peikert
Alice Pellet-Mary
Olivier Pereira
Léo Perrin
Edoardo Persichetti
Thomas Peters
George Petrides
Thi Minh Phuong Pham
Duong-Hieu Phan
Krzysztof Pietrzak
Oxana Poburinnaya
Supartha Podder
Bertram Poettering
Antigoni Polychroniadou
Claudius Pott
Bart Preneel
Robert Primas

Luowen Qian
Willy Quach
Ahmadreza Rahimi
Somindu Ramannai
Matthieu Rambaud
Hugues Randriam
Shahram Rasoolzadeh
Divya Ravi
Mariana P. Raykova
Christian Rechberger
Ling Ren
Joost Renes
Leonid Reyzin
Joao Ribeiro
Silas Richelson
Peter Rindal
Francisco
    Rodríguez-Henríquez
Schuyler Rosefield
Mélissa Rossi
Mike Rosulek
Dragos Rotaru
Lior Rotem
Arnab Roy
Paul Rösler
Reihaneh Safavi-Naini
Amin Sakzad
Simona Samardjiska
Antonio Sanso
Yu Sasaki
Pascal Sasdrich
Or Sattath
John Schanck
Sarah Scheffler
Tobias Schneider
Markus Schofnegger
Peter Scholl
Jan Schoone
André Schrottenloher
Sven Schäge
Adam Sealfon
Jean-Pierre Seifert
Gregor Seiler
Sruthi Sekar
Okan Seker
Karn Seth

Yannick Seurin
Ido Shahaf
Ronen Shaltiel
Barak Shani
Sina Shiehian
Omri Shmueli
Jad Silbak
Thierry Simon
Luisa Sinischalchi
Veronika Slivova
Benjamin Smith
Yifan Song
Pratik Soni
Jessica Sorrell
Nicholas Spooner
Akshayaram Srinivasan
Damien Stehlé
Ron Steinfeld
Noah
    Stephens-Davidowitz
Martin Strand
Shifeng Sun
Ridwan Syed
Katsuyuki Takashima
Titouan Tanguy
Stefano Tessaro
Enrico Thomae
Jean-Pierre Tillich
Benjamin Timon
Junichi Tomida
Deniz Toz
Rotem Tsabary
Daniel Tschudi
Yiannis Tselekounis
Yi Tu
Dominique Unruh
Bogdan Ursu
Vinod Vaikuntanathan
Kerem Varici
Philip Vejre
Marloes Venema
Daniele Venturi
Fernando Virdia
Vanessa Vitse
Damian Vizár
Chrysoula Vlachou

Fine-Grained Cryptography: A New Frontier?
(Abstracts of Invited Talk)

Alon Rosen

IDC Herzliya

Abstract. Fine-grained cryptography is concerned with adversaries that are only moderately more powerful than the honest parties. We will survey recent results in this relatively underdeveloped area of study and examine whether the time is ripe for further advances in it.

One approach for weakening the assumptions underlying cryptographic constructions is to require less from them. For instance, rather than requiring a super-polynomial gap between the running time of the honest parties and that of the adversary, one could settle for some fixed polynomial gap. This *fine-grained* approach to cryptography was considered as early as 1974 by Merkle, who relied on a random oracle to construct a key-exchange protocol in which the honest parties run in time $O(n)$, while security holds against $O(n^2)$-time adversaries.

Merkle's scheme demonstrates how in a fine-grained setting, public-key encryption can be obtained from a primitive as unstructured as a random oracle. While the lack of structure renders the scheme less susceptible to cryptanalysis than its traditional counterparts, it does have its limitations. As proved by Barak and Mahmoody in 2009, the quadratic gap in Merkle's construction is optimal. If one were to increase the gap between honest and malicious parties, it will be necessary to rely on structured computational problems.

Structured problems are often computationally easy, and hence are less desirable from a cryptographic standpoint. But they do offer their own advantages. After all, it is the most structured problems within P that admit the only known lower bounds in complexity theory. Could it actually be a structured problem that will give rise to unconditionally secure cryptography?

But even forgoing unconditional security, structure may be used to attain larger than quadratic gaps between honest and malicious parties. For instance, recent advances in fine-grained complexity have increased our confidence in the hardness of a host of problems in P, along with a web of interconnectedness between them. Based on such problems, we now have new candidate proofs of work with any arbitrary fixed polynomial gap between parties.

Could such results be extended to constructing fine-grained one-way functions? This is a necessary step we need to take if we were to bypass the optimality of the gap in

---

Supported by ISF grant No. 1399/17 and by Project PROMETHEUS (780701).

Merkle's key-exchange protocol. Looking even further, suppose we do succeed in our quest. Should we stop there? And what about the foundations? Shouldn't they also be revisited and adapted to the fine-grained setting?

Contents - Part I

Invited Talk

Mathematics and Cryptography: A Marriage of Convenience?
INVITED TALK   3
   Alice Silverberg

Best Paper Awards

Optimal Broadcast Encryption from Pairings and LWE   13
   Shweta Agrawal and Shota Yamada

Private Information Retrieval with Sublinear Online Time   44
   Henry Corrigan-Gibbs and Dmitry Kogan

Obfuscation and Functional Encryption

Candidate iO from Homomorphic Encryption Schemes   79
   Zvika Brakerski, Nico Döttling, Sanjam Garg, and Giulio Malavolta

Indistinguishability Obfuscation Without Maps:
Attacks and Fixes for Noisy Linear FE   110
   Shweta Agrawal and Alice Pellet-Mary

Combiners for Functional Encryption, Unconditionally   141
   Aayush Jain, Nathan Manohar, and Amit Sahai

Impossibility Results for Lattice-Based Functional Encryption Schemes   169
   Akın Ünal

Symmetric Cryptanalysis

Mind the Composition: Birthday Bound Attacks on EWCDMD
and SoKAC21   203
   Mridul Nandi

Improving Key-Recovery in Linear Attacks:
Application to 28-Round PRESENT   221
   Antonio Flórez-Gutiérrez and María Naya-Plasencia

New Slide Attacks on Almost Self-similar Ciphers   250
   Orr Dunkelman, Nathan Keller, Noam Lasry, and Adi Shamir

The Retracing Boomerang Attack   280
    Orr Dunkelman, Nathan Keller, Eyal Ronen, and Adi Shamir

Randomness Extraction

Extracting Randomness from Extractor-Dependent Sources.   313
    Yevgeniy Dodis, Vinod Vaikuntanathan, and Daniel Wichs

How to Extract Useful Randomness from Unreliable Sources   343
    Divesh Aggarwal, Maciej Obremski, João Ribeiro, Luisa Siniscalchi,
    and Ivan Visconti

Low Error Efficient Computational Extractors in the CRS Model   373
    Ankit Garg, Yael Tauman Kalai, and Dakshita Khurana

Symmetric Cryptography I

Tight Time-Space Lower Bounds for Finding Multiple Collision Pairs
and Their Applications.   405
    Itai Dinur

Tight Security Bounds for Double-Block Hash-then-Sum MACs.   435
    Seongkwang Kim, Byeonghak Lee, and Jooyoung Lee

Modeling for Three-Subset Division Property Without Unknown Subset:
Improved Cube Attacks Against Trivium and Grain-128AEAD.   466
    Yonglin Hao, Gregor Leander, Willi Meier, Yosuke Todo,
    and Qingju Wang

Secret Sharing

Blackbox Secret Sharing Revisited: A Coding-Theoretic Approach
with Application to Expansionless Near-Threshold Schemes   499
    Ronald Cramer and Chaoping Xing

Evolving Ramp Secret Sharing with a Small Gap   529
    Amos Beimel and Hussien Othman

Lower Bounds for Leakage-Resilient Secret Sharing   556
    Jesper Buus Nielsen and Mark Simkin

Fault-Attack Security

FRIET: An Authenticated Encryption Scheme with Built-in Fault Detection . . .   581
    Thierry Simon, Lejla Batina, Joan Daemen, Vincent Grosso,
    Pedro Maat Costa Massolino, Kostas Papagiannopoulos,
    Francesco Regazzoni, and Niels Samwel

Fault Template Attacks on Block Ciphers Exploiting Fault Propagation   612
    Sayandeep Saha, Arnab Bag, Debapriya Basu Roy, Sikhar Patranabis,
    and Debdeep Mukhopadhyay

Security of Hedged Fiat–Shamir Signatures Under Fault Attacks   644
    Diego F. Aranha, Claudio Orlandi, Akira Takahashi,
    and Greg Zaverucha

Succinct Proofs

Transparent SNARKs from DARK Compilers   677
    Benedikt Bünz, Ben Fisch, and Alan Szepieniec

SPARKs: Succinct Parallelizable Arguments of Knowledge   707
    Naomi Ephraim, Cody Freitag, Ilan Komargodski, and Rafael Pass

Marlin: Preprocessing zkSNARKs with Universal and Updatable SRS   738
    Alessandro Chiesa, Yuncong Hu, Mary Maller, Pratyush Mishra,
    Noah Vesely, and Nicholas Ward

FRACTAL: Post-quantum and Transparent Recursive Proofs
from Holography   769
    Alessandro Chiesa, Dev Ojha, and Nicholas Spooner

Author Index   795

Contents – Part II

Generic Models

Separate Your Domains: NIST PQC KEMs, Oracle Cloning
and Read-Only Indifferentiability 3
   Mihir Bellare, Hannah Davis, and Felix Günther

On the Memory-Tightness of Hashed ElGamal 33
   Ashrujit Ghoshal and Stefano Tessaro

Blind Schnorr Signatures and Signed ElGamal Encryption in the Algebraic
Group Model 63
   Georg Fuchsbauer, Antoine Plouviez, and Yannick Seurin

On Instantiating the Algebraic Group Model from Falsifiable Assumptions ... 96
   Thomas Agrikola, Dennis Hofheinz, and Julia Kastner

Secure Computation I

Resource-Restricted Cryptography: Revisiting MPC Bounds
in the Proof-of-Work Era 129
   Juan Garay, Aggelos Kiayias, Rafail M. Ostrovsky,
   Giorgos Panagiotakos, and Vassilis Zikas

Efficient Constructions for Almost-Everywhere Secure Computation .. 159
   Siddhartha Jayanti, Srinivasan Raghuraman, and Nikhil Vyas

The Price of Active Security in Cryptographic Protocols 184
   Carmit Hazay, Muthuramakrishnan Venkitasubramaniam,
   and Mor Weiss

Succinct Non-interactive Secure Computation 216
   Andrew Morgan, Rafael Pass, and Antigoni Polychroniadou

Quantum I

Finding Hash Collisions with Quantum Computers by Using Differential
Trails with Smaller Probability than Birthday Bound 249
   Akinori Hosoyamada and Yu Sasaki

Implementing Grover Oracles for Quantum Key Search
on AES and LowMC.   280
   Samuel Jaques, Michael Naehrig, Martin Roetteler,
   and Fernando Virdia

Optimal Merging in Quantum k-xor and k-sum Algorithms   311
   María Naya-Plasencia and André Schrottenloher

On the Quantum Complexity of the Continuous Hidden
Subgroup Problem.   341
   Koen de Boer, Léo Ducas, and Serge Fehr

Foundations

Formalizing Data Deletion in the Context of the Right to Be Forgotten   373
   Sanjam Garg, Shafi Goldwasser, and Prashant Nalini Vasudevan

OptORAMa: Optimal Oblivious RAM.   403
   Gilad Asharov, Ilan Komargodski, Wei-Kai Lin, Kartik Nayak,
   Enoch Peserico, and Elaine Shi

On the Streaming Indistinguishability of a Random Permutation
and a Random Function.   433
   Itai Dinur

Isogeny-Based Cryptography

He Gives C-Sieves on the CSIDH.   463
   Chris Peikert

Quantum Security Analysis of CSIDH.   493
   Xavier Bonnetain and André Schrottenloher

Rational Isogenies from Irrational Endomorphisms   523
   Wouter Castryck, Lorenz Panny, and Frederik Vercauteren

Lattice-Based Cryptography

Hardness of LWE on General Entropic Distributions.   551
   Zvika Brakerski and Nico Döttling

Key-Homomorphic Pseudorandom Functions from LWE
with Small Modulus   576
   Sam Kim

Integral Matrix Gram Root and Lattice Gaussian Sampling Without Floats. . .   608
   Léo Ducas, Steven Galbraith, Thomas Prest, and Yang Yu

Symmetric Cryptography II

TNT: How to Tweak a Block Cipher.   641
  Zhenzhen Bao, Chun Guo, Jian Guo, and Ling Song

On a Generalization of Substitution-Permutation Networks:
The HADES Design Strategy   674
  Lorenzo Grassi, Reinhard Lüftenegger, Christian Rechberger,
  Dragos Rotaru, and Markus Schofnegger

Lightweight Authenticated Encryption Mode Suitable
for Threshold Implementation.   705
  Yusuke Naito, Yu Sasaki, and Takeshi Sugawara

Secure Computation II

PSI from PaXoS: Fast, Malicious Private Set Intersection.   739
  Benny Pinkas, Mike Rosulek, Ni Trieu, and Avishay Yanai

Two-Round Oblivious Transfer from CDH or LPN   768
  Nico Döttling, Sanjam Garg, Mohammad Hajiabadi, Daniel Masny,
  and Daniel Wichs

Private Aggregation from Fewer Anonymous Messages   798
  Badih Ghazi, Pasin Manurangsi, Rasmus Pagh, and Ameya Velingker

Broadcast-Optimal Two-Round MPC.   828
  Ran Cohen, Juan Garay, and Vassilis Zikas

Author Index   859

Contents – Part III

Asymmetric Cryptanalysis

(One) Failure Is Not an Option: Bootstrapping the Search for Failures
in Lattice-Based Encryption Schemes 3
  Jan-Pieter D'Anvers, Mélissa Rossi, and Fernando Virdia

Key Recovery from Gram–Schmidt Norm Leakage in Hash-and-Sign
Signatures over NTRU Lattices............................. 34
  *Pierre-Alain Fouque, Paul Kirchner, Mehdi Tibouchi, Alexandre Wallet,
  and Yang Yu*

An Algebraic Attack on Rank Metric Code-Based Cryptosystems 64
  *Magali Bardet, Pierre Briaud, Maxime Bros, Philippe Gaborit,
  Vincent Neiger, Olivier Ruatta, and Jean-Pierre Tillich*

Low Weight Discrete Logarithm and Subset Sum in $2^{0.65n}$
with Polynomial Memory..................................... 94
  Andre Esser and Alexander May

Verifiable Delay Functions

Continuous Verifiable Delay Functions 125
  Naomi Ephraim, Cody Freitag, Ilan Komargodski, and Rafael Pass

Generic-Group Delay Functions Require Hidden-Order Groups........... 155
  Lior Rotem, Gil Segev, and Ido Shahaf

Signatures

Sigma Protocols for MQ, PKP and SIS, and Fishy Signature Schemes...... 183
  Ward Beullens

Signatures from Sequential-OR Proofs........................... 212
  Marc Fischlin, Patrick Harasser, and Christian Janson

Attribute-Based Encryption

Compact Adaptively Secure ABE from k-Lin: Beyond NC^1
and Towards NL.. 247
  Huijia Lin and Ji Luo

Adaptively Secure ABE for DFA from k-Lin and More   278
    Junqing Gong and Hoeteck Wee

Side-Channel Security

Tornado: Automatic Generation of Probing-Secure Masked
Bitsliced Implementations   311
    Sonia Belaïd, Pierre-Évariste Dagand, Darius Mercadier,
    Matthieu Rivain, and Raphaël Wintersdorff

Side-Channel Masking with Pseudo-Random Generator   342
    Jean-Sébastien Coron, Aurélien Greuet, and Rina Zeitoun

Non-Interactive Zero-Knowledge

Compact NIZKs from Standard Assumptions on Bilinear Maps   379
    Shuichi Katsumata, Ryo Nishimaki, Shota Yamada,
    and Takashi Yamakawa

New Constructions of Statistical NIZKs: Dual-Mode
DV-NIZKs and More   410
    Benoît Libert, Alain Passelègue, Hoeteck Wee, and David J. Wu

Non-interactive Zero-Knowledge in Pairing-Free Groups
from Weaker Assumptions   442
    Geoffroy Couteau, Shuichi Katsumata, and Bogdan Ursu

Public-Key Encryption

Everybody's a Target: Scalability in Public-Key Encryption   475
    Benedikt Auerbach, Federico Giacon, and Eike Kiltz

Security Under Message-Derived Keys: Signcryption in iMessage   507
    Mihir Bellare and Igors Stepanovs

Double-Base Chains for Scalar Multiplications on Elliptic Curves   538
    Wei Yu, Saud Al Musa, and Bao Li

Zero-Knowledge

Stacked Garbling for Disjunctive Zero-Knowledge Proofs   569
    David Heath and Vladimir Kolesnikov

Which Languages Have 4-Round Fully Black-Box Zero-Knowledge
Arguments from One-Way Functions?   599
    Carmit Hazay, Rafael Pass,
    and Muthuramakrishnan Venkitasubramaniam

Statistical ZAPR Arguments from Bilinear Maps.   620
  Alex Lombardi, Vinod Vaikuntanathan, and Daniel Wichs

Statistical ZAP Arguments.   642
  Saikrishna Badrinarayanan, Rex Fernando, Aayush Jain,
  Dakshita Khurana, and Amit Sahai

Statistical Zaps and New Oblivious Transfer Protocols.   668
  Vipul Goyal, Abhishek Jain, Zhengzhong Jin, and Giulio Malavolta

Quantum II

Measure-Rewind-Measure: Tighter Quantum Random Oracle Model
Proofs for One-Way to Hiding and CCA Security.   703
  Veronika Kuchta, Amin Sakzad, Damien Stehlé, Ron Steinfeld,
  and Shi-Feng Sun

Secure Multi-party Quantum Computation with a Dishonest Majority   729
  Yfke Dulek, Alex B. Grilo, Stacey Jeffery, Christian Majenz,
  and Christian Schaffner

Efficient Simulation of Random States and Random Unitaries   759
  Gorjan Alagic, Christian Majenz, and Alexander Russell

Quantum-Access-Secure Message Authentication via Blind-Unforgeability . . .   788
  Gorjan Alagic, Christian Majenz, Alexander Russell, and Fang Song

Author Index   819

Invited Talk

Invited Talk

Mathematics and Cryptography: A Marriage of Convenience?
Invited Talk

Alice Silverberg$^{(\boxtimes)}$

Departments of Mathematics and Computer Science, University of California, Irvine, Irvine, CA, USA
asilverb@uci.edu

Abstract. Mathematics and cryptography have a long history together, with the ups and downs inherent in any long relationship. Whether it is a marriage of convenience or a love match, their progeny have lives of their own and have had an impact on the world. This invited lecture will briefly recall some high points from the past, give speculation and encouragement for the future of this marriage, and give counseling on how to improve communication, resolve conflicts, and play well together, based on personal experience and lessons learned.

1 Introduction

For a number of years, I have been moving within and between the overlapping mathematics and cryptography communities. My background is in number theory, and I became intrigued with cryptography after elliptic curves were introduced to the field. My cryptography-related research includes work on traitor tracing, hierarchical identity based encryption, bilinear and multilinear maps, torus-based cryptography, efficient use of elliptic curves and abelian varieties in cryptography, primality proving, fully homomorphic encryption, and lattices. For the past seven years I've been organizing conferences and workshops designed to bring together mathematicians and cryptographers to work on cryptography questions of common interest. In the talk, I will tell some stories about my adventures, give observations based on my experiences, and share some of what I've learned that I hope will be helpful for others.

I have some specific goals and some general goals for the talk. Specific aims include recalling some of the fruitful interactions between mathematics and cryptography from the past and how they came about, discussing problems for the future, and suggesting productive ways to move forward. Many of the impediments to making full use of mathematics to solve cryptographic questions are social rather than technical. Cultural differences between the fields can lead to obstacles and misunderstanding that delay the progress of science. I will attempt to share some thoughts and ideas for how to move forward in constructive ways.

Supported in part by the Alfred P. Sloan Foundation and by National Science Foundation Grant CNS-1703321.

A. Canteaut and Y. Ishai (Eds.): EUROCRYPT 2020, LNCS 12105, pp. 3–9, 2020.
https://doi.org/10.1007/978-3-030-45721-1_1

I hope that some of these suggestions will also have wider applicability, to our daily lives and our interactions with others.

My more general goals come from a sense that we live in dangerous times. Communication between people is breaking down. Norms for social behavior are changing. The value systems on which we based our decisions and our lives are being called into question. We wonder whether it makes sense to continue working as before, when the problems of the world seem so weighty. In an effort to act locally while thinking globally, in the talk I plan to give some suggestions that I hope will not only help the cryptography and mathematics communities work together, but will also be useful more generally, in working with others or communicating across cultures.

Due to the (necessarily) short time frame I was given to write this paper, there are aspects I was not able to include. In particular, I apologize for the lack of careful referencing. Ideally, I would be setting a good example by giving a complete bibliography of relevant sources, and I regret not having the time to do so. I thank the many people who contributed to the research mentioned below, and I hope they will forgive me for not citing them explicitly.

2   Fruitful Interactions

There is a long history of fruitful interactions between mathematics and cryptography. Much of it involves number theory, a field of mathematics that extends back thousands of years.

One of the most well known mathematical cryptosystems is RSA, from the 1970s, whose security is based on the (presumed) difficulty of factoring products of large prime numbers.

Diffie-Hellman key exchange and El Gamal encryption, while originally based on properties of finite fields and their multiplicative groups, have been extended to make use of other groups, including groups coming from elliptic curves and, more generally, abelian varieties such as Jacobian varieties of hyperelliptic curves.

Understanding and generalizing the mathematics underlying these schemes has led to torus-based cryptography, including the LUC, XTR, and CEILIDH cryptosystems. These cryptosystems can be understood in terms of certain varieties from algebraic geometry that are called algebraic tori, which are themselves generalizations of the multiplicative group of a finite field. The algorithms in these cryptosystems can be reinterpreted as compression and decompression algorithms that allow you to send shorter transmissions for the same security. On the other hand, these compression algorithms can be viewed as telling us that one actually gets less security than had been realized, for discrete log cryptography over extensions of finite fields.

The Weil pairing on elliptic curves was first used destructively in cryptography as an attack on the elliptic curve discrete log problem, and then used constructively in pairing-based cryptography. This seems to me like an area that could have progressed sooner and faster, had there been a longer and deeper tradition of mathematicians and computer scientists working more closely together on cryptographic questions. The interest in pairing-based cryptography led to the introduction into cryptography of other number theoretic pairings, such as what cryptographers call the Tate pairing or the Tate-Lichtenbaum pairing. The use in cryptography of pairings on elliptic curves also led to the construction of identity-based encryption schemes. Work on ways to use abelian varieties to make pairing-based cryptography more efficient led to compression algorithms for points on elliptic curves over a certain class of finite fields, and this in turn led to some of the torus-based cryptography and compression results in finite fields mentioned above.

Lattice-based cryptography, which hopes to survive the advent of quantum computers, comes from a field of number theory that is traditionally called the geometry of numbers. Research in this area makes use of the arithmetic and geometry of algebraic number fields. This thriving area has great potential for future interactions between mathematics and security research.

While both factoring-based cryptography and discrete log-based cryptography, including standard elliptic curve cryptography, are threatened by the potential advent of quantum computers, a possibly quantum-resistant use of elliptic curves was recently discovered. It makes use of isogenies on elliptic curves, and its security is based on the presumed difficulty of actually finding an isogeny between two elliptic curves that have one.

Permeating these themes is the power of mathematics to make or break the security of modern-day cryptography. As alluded to above, the constructive use of mathematics in cryptography has a flip side, namely mathematical cryptanalysis, which has a long history, even before mathematics was used in a serious way to build cryptosystems. As algorithms for solving mathematics problems get better and stronger, cryptography is under threat. All that is needed is a new mathematical idea, for problems that were presumed hard to suddenly become easy. This has the potential to not only make currently used cryptosystems obsolete, but also to reveal our past secrets that we had assumed were secure, potentially including financial, medical, military, or government secrets, for good or ill.

3 Looking Toward the Future

I believe that mathematics and cryptography are no longer just staying together for the sake of the children. They have now committed to each other and to making it work out. Where do they go from here? Next, I give a sampling of problems.

3.1 Computing on Encrypted Data and Fully Homomorphic Encryption

Creating efficient and secure methods to compute on encrypted data, for example with efficient fully homomorphic encryption, is an area where mathematical ideas have been and can continue to be helpful. Efficient and secure fully homomorphic encryption would allow people to calculate aggregate statistics from collections of sensitive data from different sources while maintaining privacy. In the history of fully homomorphic encryption thus far, both the constructions and attacks make use of ideas from both cryptology and mathematics, including the theory of lattices (geometry of numbers) and algebraic number theory.

3.2   Cryptographic Multilinear Maps

Pairing-based cryptography uses bilinear maps, namely, maps

$$G_1 \times G_2 \to G_3$$

that are linear in each input variable, where the G_i are finite groups in which the discrete logarithm problem is believed to be hard. This necessitates the introduction of new hard problems that I would feel more comfortable with if they were better known in and carefully studied by the mathematical community.

A natural generalization is to have more than two inputs. This leads to the open problem of finding cryptographically useful multilinear maps.

The candidate multilinear maps that we have seen so far look very different from what I envisioned when I first started thinking about cryptographic multilinear maps. They don't fall neatly into the original framework. For me, this is one of a number of examples that demonstrate the richness and potential of cryptography. It is a field in which mathematicians can be surprised by the clever ideas of computer scientists, and computer scientists can make use of deep ideas from mathematics. When the two perspectives build on one another in fruitful ways, the result is pleasing.

The theory of multilinear maps is closely connected to the theory of indistinguishability obfuscation (iO). While it's tempting to want to prove that efficient indistinguishability obfuscation cannot exist, it's unlikely that we will see a proof of that soon, since an unconditional impossibility result for iO would imply that $P \neq NP$.

3.3   Cryptography that Will Survive Future Attacks

Mathematics is useful for generating new ideas for post-quantum cryptography, i.e., cryptography that will withstand attacks by quantum computers, in addition to being useful for analyzing the security of proposed systems. Below are some areas where I think it would be helpful if there were more mathematicians looking more deeply at these questions.

Lattice-based cryptography. Interesting open questions include the question of whether supposedly hard lattice problems are as hard in ideal lattices as they are in general lattices. We should be able to use more algebraic number theory to give deeper insights to help us better understand this problem.

Isogeny-based cryptography. While a sufficiently good quantum computer would break classical elliptic curve cryptography, an interesting new area of research is cryptography based on the presumed difficulty of finding (high degree) isogenies between isogenous elliptic curves. As with much of public key cryptography, this is an area where a little mathematics has gone a long way. More work is needed to understand the security of the proposed schemes.

3.4 Cryptanalysis

Mathematics is especially powerful for cryptanalysis. When the security of a cryptosystem is based on the presumed difficulty of some mathematics problem, then one good mathematical idea or algorithm might suffice to break the system. I worry that security of some systems might be based largely on the lack of awareness of the "hard problem" by the mathematicians who would be most capable of breaking it. The more mathematicians work in this area, the more confident we can be in the security of systems that rely on relatively new or unfamiliar "hard problems".

4 Working Well Together

Cryptology and computer security would benefit from continued and greater input of mathematical ideas. I think it would be good if more mathematicians become part of the cryptography community, and if more cryptographers become part of the mathematics community. I found it easy to assimilate into the cryptography community. The community was welcoming, and was willing to explain concepts and jargon. More difficult is for computer scientists without mathematics degrees to participate in math conferences. There is room for the math community to learn how to bring others in. Each community can learn from the other.

Different groups have different cultures with regard to territoriality, giving or withholding credit, transparency, speed of publication, and choices about where to publish (for example, journals versus conference proceedings). These choices are sometimes motivated by publication pressures coming from academia, or by patents or other intellectual property or financial concerns. These cultural differences might depend in part on whether you're a mathematician, theoretical or applied computer scientist, or engineer, and on whether you work in academia, industry, or government. The incentives in your workplace might encourage you to maintain secrecy or to publicize findings, to be generous with giving credit, deserved or otherwise, or to only give limited acknowledgement to the work of others. Such differences might make it hard for people from different workplace cultures to work together, and might lead to misunderstandings or conflict.

I'm not convinced that the research that gets done under tight deadlines and page limits, with short time windows for reviewers, is better than research done carefully and correctly, with all details filled in, that reviewers have time to fully check. The mathematics community has started to borrow the deadline and page limit culture from the computer science community, but I'm not convinced that this is a good way to publish papers or encourage correct and careful research.

NTRU and braid group cryptography can perhaps be seen as illustrative examples for how better contact between the mathematics and cryptography communities might have been helpful. The usefulness of NTRU might have been recognized sooner had the communities been closer. For braid group cryptography, a succession of proposals and breaks have led some cryptographers to dismiss anything braid-related. Someone pointed out to me that if one comes up with a good cryptosystem based on braids, in order to have credibility in the crypto community it might be best to suppress the word "braid". This raises the question of whether a succession of proposals and breaks is a bad thing. On the one hand, earlier contact and better communication between proposers and cryptanalysts might lead to fewer insecure proposals. On the other hand, too cosy a relationship between proposers and cryptanalysts might not be a good thing; adversarial or competitive relationships might lead to more secure cryptosystems.

People don't like to be told what to do. I worry that if I write in the imperative, some readers will be rubbed the wrong way. However, sound bites are easy to remember. I hope you will forgive me for writing in the imperative, and will understand the below advice not as commands, but as (hopefully helpful!) suggestions.

Behave professionally. Treat your colleagues respectfully, and behave professionally.

In the late 1980s I spent a year at one of IBM's research centers. Afterwards I would tell people that the main difference I noticed between IBM and academia was that at IBM, they knew the law and obeyed it. Many of the problems and conflicts that I have seen over the years could have been avoided had people simply remembered to behave professionally, legally, and ethically.

Whether you are an advisor to students, a journal editor, a reviewer of papers, a program committee member, a manager, a student, a colleague, a chair or dean, and whether or not your behavior is questioned, ask yourself: Am I behaving professionally? Am I acting ethically? Am I setting a good example for others? Is this the way I want others to treat me? Could I do better?

Mathematicians and computer scientists sometimes have different ideas about what constitutes professional and ethical behavior. When working across disciplines, one needs to navigate and negotiate the terms of the relationship.

Learn constructive ways to communicate. Good communication is important not only to help cryptographers and mathematicians work well together, or more generally to help communicate across cultures; it's also useful in all our interactions. I find that it's important to keep communication channels open. Cutting off communication can close doors.

Many misunderstandings come from mistakenly thinking that you can correctly read the minds of other people, and attributing bad motives to them.

If you want to know what someone is thinking or feeling, ask them. Moreover, don't assume that others are correctly reading your mind.

Avoid jargon. When communicating across fields, avoid jargon, and avoid abbreviations.

It's hard for mathematicians to attend talks by computer scientists because of the unfamiliar abbreviations. "Learning with errors" has the same number of syllables as "LWE," so when you give a talk, you might as well say the words.

It's hard for computer scientists to read technical papers written by mathematicians. I think it would be helpful if mathematicians wrote more survey talks, in less technical language, in order to explain their technical papers to people outside their specialities who might be able to make use of the results.

Listen. Listen, and learn from what others have to offer. Listen to different points of view.

Ask for advice. Listen to advice (solicited or otherwise) with an open mind; you don't have to follow it.

Be curious. Be curious, open-minded, and open to opportunities.

It's helpful to try to see things from the point of view of the other person. Ask questions.

For every experience, good or bad, ask yourself "What can I learn from this?"

I learned the phrase "Get curious, not furious" from the book *A New Map for Relationships: Creating True Love at Home and Peace on the Planet* by Dorothie Hellman and Martin Hellman. That book makes an eloquent case for curiosity, and for not getting angry.

Be kind. As Lewis Carroll wrote about Alice in *Alice's Adventures in Wonderland,* "She generally gave herself very good advice (though she very seldom followed it)." I'm much better at giving advice, than following my own advice. For most of the advice that I'm giving here, I'm still learning how to follow it, and not doing as well as I would like.

It took me a very long time to learn that being kind solves many problems, and prevents many problems. To be clear, being kind does not mean that you let other people get their way. Being kind can include enforcing boundaries, standing up for what's right, sticking up for others, and being kind to yourself.

Best Paper Awards

Optimal Broadcast Encryption from Pairings and LWE

Shweta Agrawal[1(✉)] and Shota Yamada[2(✉)]

[1] IIT Madras, Chennai, India
shweta.a@cse.iitm.ac.in
[2] National Institute of Advanced Industrial Science and Technology (AIST),
Tokyo, Japan
yamada-shota@aist.go.jp

Abstract. Boneh, Waters and Zhandry (CRYPTO 2014) used multilinear maps to provide a solution to the long-standing problem of public-key broadcast encryption (BE) where all parameters in the system are small. In this work, we improve their result by providing a solution that uses only *bilinear* maps and Learning With Errors (LWE). Our scheme is fully collusion-resistant against any number of colluders, and can be generalized to an identity-based broadcast system with short parameters. Thus, we reclaim the problem of optimal broadcast encryption from the land of "Obfustopia".

Our main technical contribution is a ciphertext policy attribute based encryption (CP-ABE) scheme which achieves special efficiency properties – its ciphertext size, secret key size, and public key size are all independent of the size of the circuits supported by the scheme. We show that this special CP-ABE scheme implies BE with optimal parameters; but it may also be of independent interest. Our constructions rely on a novel interplay of bilinear maps and LWE, and are proven secure in the generic group model.

1 Introduction

Broadcast Encryption (BE) [30] enables a sender to encrypt a message for a subset of users who are listening on a broadcast channel. In more detail, in a BE system, a sender can encrypt to any set S of its choice, and any user in S can decrypt the broadcast using its secret key. The system is said to be fully collusion resistant if no collection of users outside S can learn anything about the plaintext.

Introduced in a seminal work by Fiat and Naor [30], the primitive of broadcast encryption has received significant attention, with diverse constructions achieving different tradeoffs in the sizes of ciphertext, secret key and public parameters. Of particular importance is the size of the ciphertext overhead: namely, the size of the ciphertext beyond what is necessary for the description of the recipient set S and the symmetric encryption of the plaintext message. A BE scheme is said to have low overhead if the ciphertext overhead depends at most logarithmically

A. Canteaut and Y. Ishai (Eds.): EUROCRYPT 2020, LNCS 12105, pp. 13–43, 2020.
https://doi.org/10.1007/978-3-030-45721-1_2

on the number of users in the system (N, say). In this work, we focus on BE systems that are public key, have low ciphertext overhead and are fully collusion resistant.

The first work to satisfy the above desiderata was by Boneh, Gentry, and Waters [13], and was based on hardness assumptions on bilinear maps. This construction achieved optimal (constant) ciphertext overhead and short secret keys, but suffered from public parameter size which is linear in the number of users N. Follow-ups based on bilinear maps improved some aspects of this construction [8,28,29,33,37,45], but could not improve the public key size. Indeed, even relying on the existence of the powerful indistinguishability obfuscation [31], BE with short public key remained elusive (though it achieved other remarkable properties) [16].

This state of affairs was improved considerably by the work of Boneh, Waters and Zhandry [15] who provided the first construction of broadcast encryption, achieving optimal parameters including short public key, by relying on multilinear maps. This marked the first solution to a long standing open problem. However, the constructions suggested by [15] also have some limitations. In more detail, the [15] provide three broadcast encryption systems that use an $O(\log N)$ way multilinear map – this necessitates the degree of the map to be *polynomial* when N is exponential. More importantly, existing candidates of multilinear maps have been subject to many attacks [7,23–27,38,42] and their security is poorly understood. Thus, the question of broadcast encryption with optimal parameter size has so far, remained squarely in the land of "Obfustopia".

Our Results. In this work, we reclaim broadcast encryption from Obfustopia by providing a solution that uses only *bilinear* maps and Learning With Errors (LWE). Our scheme is public key, fully collusion-resistant against any number of colluders, and can be generalized to an identity-based broadcast system with short parameters. Along the way, we provide the first ciphertext policy attribute based encryption scheme whose ciphertext size, secret key size, and public key size are all independent of the size of the circuits supported by the scheme. This construction may be of independent interest. Our constructions rely on a novel interplay between bilinear maps and LWE and are proven secure in the generic group model.

1.1   Our Techniques

Recasting BE as CP-ABE: Our starting observation is that the question of broadcast encryption can be re-stated in terms of the notion of *ciphertext policy attribute based encryption* (CP-ABE). In a CP-ABE scheme, a ciphertext for a message m is labelled with a function (policy) f, and secret keys are labelled with public attributes $\mathbf{x}$ from the domain of f. Decryption succeeds to yield the hidden message m if and only if the attribute satisfies the policy, namely $f(\mathbf{x}) = 1$. To see BE as a special case of CP-ABE, note that the ciphertext may encode a circuit F_S that checks membership of a given user index in a set of recipients S, and the attributes $\mathbf{x}$ may encode user index in the set N.

Thus, a user i can use her CP-ABE secret key to test whether i is a member of the set S encoded in the ciphertext, and recover the message m if and only if this is true. Then, a natural approach to construct BE is to leverage CP-ABE schemes. However, unsurprisingly, constructions of CP-ABE achieving optimal parameters that suffice for BE, has been elusive.

From Pairings to LWE: All known constructions of BE from standard assumptions (i.e. without relying on the existence of multilinear maps or indistinguishability obfuscation) are based on various assumptions on bilinear groups. Since the question of optimal BE from pairings has met with little progress for over a decade, it is evidently meaningful to look at assumptions on other mathematical structures to seek a way forward. The most obvious candidate that presents itself is the versatile Learning With Errors (LWE) assumption, which has led to breakthroughs in similar primitives, notably in fully homomorphic encryption [17,18,20].

Let us then examine what is known from LWE in this context. The dual notion of key-policy ABE has met with fantastic success from LWE – the works of Gorbunov et al. [34] and Boneh et al. [12] show how to construct KP-ABE for all circuits (on the other hand, constructions based on pairings could only support the much weaker circuit class NC_1). KP-ABE is the same as CP-ABE with the roles of circuit and attributes swapped. Additionally, the KP-ABE construction of Boneh et al. [12], henceforth denoted as BGG^+, manages to encode the circuit very succinctly – in more detail, the size of the public and secret keys in the BGG^+ construction are independent of the circuit size and depend only on the depth of the circuit. Additionally, the size of the ciphertext is also independent of the circuit size and depends only on input length. Since the input length for the circuit F_S that checks membership in S is an encoding of a user index, it is of size $O(\log N)$. Moreover, it is easy to check that the depth of F_S is also $O(\log N)$. Therefore, if we have a CP-ABE with analogous efficiency, namely, so that the public key size, secret key size, and ciphertext size do not depend on the size but only input length and depth of the circuit, it follows that we can obtain BE with optimal parameters.

Constructing CP-ABE from LWE: Thus, it suffices to ask whether we can have a CP-ABE scheme, denoted by cpABE, with the desired efficiency. To leverage the succinctness of the circuit encoding of BGG^+, a naive idea is to set $cpABE.CT(F_S) = BGG^+.SK(F_S)$. Two immediate problems present themselves: (i) Where to embed the message m[1], and (ii) Computing $BGG^+.SK(F_S)$ requires the master secret but encryption is a public key algorithm.

To address these challenges, a first idea is to exploit the *decomposability* of BGG^+. In more detail, decomposability means that the ciphertext for attribute $\mathbf{x}$ and message m may be decomposed into $|\mathbf{x}| + 1$ encodings, one for each bit x_i of the attribute string and message m – these are tied together using common randomness used during their generation. Let us denote the encoding corresponding to bit x_i as ψ_{i,x_i}. Then, a natural idea is to let the encryptor sample a fresh instance of the BGG^+ scheme, generate $BGG^+.SK(F_S)$ and encrypt each

---

[1] This question is surprisingly non-trivial even in the symmetric key setting.

$\psi_{i,b}$ using a different public key encryption scheme, say with PKE key $\mathsf{PK}_{i,b}$. This yields a CP-ABE with the desired efficiency, inherited directly from the succinctness of the BGG^+ key and the decomposability of the BGG^+ ciphertext.

Constraining the Information Leaked (Or, Back to Pairings): However, this scheme is obviously not collusion resistant: a user with keys for $\mathbf{x}$ and $\bar{\mathbf{x}}$ can decrypt every ciphertext. To make the scheme collusion resistant, we would like to replace the naive use of public key encryption above into a more sophisticated scheme, which hides all but the output of the BGG^+ decryption algorithm. This description bears close resemblance to a functional encryption scheme for some restricted functionality, for which we turn to—pairings! In particular, we isolate the $\psi_{i,b}$ by randomizing and lifting them to the exponent of a bilinear group. The hope is that we may provide a secret key for some attribute $\mathbf{x}$ such that it only allows the appropriate ψ_{i,x_i} to be selected and combined so that only the output of the BGG^+ decryption is revealed, and that the randomization, which will be unique to every cpABE ciphertext and secret key pair, prevents collusion attacks.

Evaluation of NC_1 Circuit in the Exponent: Several questions arise. First, we discussed above that the circuit for checking membership in set S is in NC_1 – however, pairings are only capable of supporting at most quadratic operations. How then, do we hope to compute an NC_1 circuit in the exponent of a bilinear group? The answer lies in the specific structure of the BGG^+ evaluation algorithm, which, even for a circuit in P is *linear* in the encodings and the secret key, followed by a final *rounding* step to remove the noise. Indeed, the knowledgeable reader may observe that this very linearity of the BGG^+ evaluation procedure has been the cause of attacks in other contexts [1] – what is a "curse" there is a "blessing" here! However, the rounding step remains – this is in NC_1 and clearly cannot be performed in the exponent.

An approach is to perform the linear computation (which represents the circuit F_S) in the exponent, recover the output via discrete log, and then compute the rounding in the clear. Again, it is unclear this satisfies either correctness or security. For the former, note that recovering the encoded output from the exponent requires that the output be polynomially bounded. In this case, the output is the message bit plus some noise that resulted from the homomorphic evaluation. While the noise in this context may be superpolynomial in general, we can convert our NC_1 circuit into a branching program and leverage the asymmetric noise growth for BP evaluation of BGG^+ encodings to ensure that the noise is bounded by a polynomial [35].

The more worrisome issue is that of security. It is well known that the noise that results from homomorphic evaluation of encodings leaks the noise in the original encodings and is often a security threat –in fact, the savvy reader may have observed that this leakage is one of the main barriers in constructing iO from standard assumptions [2,6]. However, here we are rescued by the serendipitous fact that what we are trying to build here is a kind of attribute based encryption, not functional encryption! In more detail, the leakage caused by the noise is a security threat in the context of functional encryption, as formalized in [1, 2, 6] – this is because a decryptor who possesses some secret keys for a functional encryption scheme must still not be able to learn anything about the encrypted message beyond what the keys reveal. On the other hand, attribute based encryption is a much simpler "all or nothing" primitive – if the adversary possesses a single key that decrypts a ciphertext, there are no more secrets the scheme withholds from her. Hence, if the adversary has a key that lets her recover the value encoded in the exponent, the additional leakage created by the noise terms do not pose a security threat.

Preventing Mix and Match Attacks: To prevent collusions, we design the decryption algorithm so that the decryptor obtains a randomized version of the ciphertext components in the exponents as $g_T^{\delta \psi_{i,x_i}}$, where g_T is the target group, ψ_{i,x_i} are BGG$^+$ encodings as defined above and δ is user specific randomness. Since δ is user specific, the attacker cannot combine partial decryption results of multiple users, preventing mix and match attacks.

Hence, it suffices to restrict our attention to the single user case. Here, we must ensure that the adversary only gets components $\{g_T^{\delta \psi_{i,x_i}}\}_i$ corresponding to the particular key $\mathbf{x}$ issued to her, instead of all the components $\{g_T^{\delta \psi_{i,b}}\}_{i,b}$ for $b \in \{0, 1\}$. Furthermore, we must ensure that the attribute vector $\mathbf{x}$ is processed in the correct sequence – i.e., its bits are not permuted. To prevent these attacks, we bind each entry of the ciphertext and each bit of the secret key attribute $\mathbf{x}$ to the corresponding positions. This is possible by setting the master public key to be $\{g^{w_{i,b}}\}_{i,b}$ where $w_{i,b}$ are randomly chosen for each position i and $b \in \{0, 1\}$ and setting the secret key and ciphertext as $\{g_2^{\delta/w_{i,x_i}}\}_i$ and $\{g_1^{\psi_{i,b} w_{i,b}}\}_{i,b}$ respectively. We remark that we need to use asymmetric pairings to prevent ciphertext (respectively key) components from being paired between themselves to leak information. By tying element values to their positions, we ensure that pairing of the ciphertext and secret key components corresponding to different positions result in a term which looks like $g_T^{\delta \psi_{i,b} w_{i,b}/w_{i',b'}}$ for $(i, b) \neq (i', b')$. Now, we claim that a term of the form $g^{\delta w_{i,b}/w_{i',b'}}$ is useless to the attacker – to see this, note that in the generic group model, an attacker cannot obtain any information about a value encoded in the exponent unless she finds a non-trivial linear relation that contains that term. However, since the term $\delta w_{i,b}/w_{i',b'}$ appears only when we pair the ciphertext component with position (i, b) with the secret key component with position (i', b') and cannot appear anywhere else, it follows that it cannot appear as a term in a linear combination that results in 0 (except with negligible probability). Thus, by using $\{w_{i,b}\}_{i,b}$, we enforce that the computation follows the desired path.

Combining the above ideas, we obtain our final CP-ABE scheme. By setting the circuit class appropriately, this yields BE and even Identity Based BE (or IBBE). Please see Sect. 3 for the CP-ABE and Sect. 5 for the construction of BE and IBBE.

Security in the Generic Group Model: We prove security in the generic group model, which closely follows the intuition we explained so far. Specifically, we will show that the adversary cannot find any non-trivial linear relation among the partial decryption results of the ciphertext components. The main challenge in the security proof is that the partial decryption results obtained by using different secret keys are correlated – in more detail, they can contain terms $g_1^{\delta \psi_{i,0}}$ and $g_1^{\delta' \psi_{i,1}}$ where $\psi_{i,0}$ and $\psi_{i,1}$, if learned simultaneously, lead to a complete break of security. Simulating these in the standard model using the security of BGG^+ appears difficult.

To address the issue we first observe that the adversary cannot take a linear combination among partial decryption results obtained by two different secret keys in a meaningful way, since they are randomized by the user specific randomness introduced for preventing collusions. This implies that if the adversary manages to find a non-trivial linear relation among the partial decryption results, all the terms involved should be obtained from the same secret key. We also observe that until the point when the adversary finds the *first* non-trivial linear relation, the simulator can simulate the generic group oracles without knowing the corresponding encodings. This can be done by simply pretending that there is no non-trivial linear relation among the terms.

The above observations allow us to concentrate on the security proof for the single-key case without worrying about the partial decryption results by other keys. We can then conclude by using the security of the BGG^+ scheme. In more detail, an adversary who can find a non-trivial linear relation among the partial decryption results can be used to distinguish a BGG^+ ciphertexts from random ones, since the partial decryption result by a single key essentially corresponds to a BGG^+ ciphertext in exponent and it cannot find any non-trivial linear relation among the random ciphertext components as long as the modulus size is exponential.

1.2   Related Works

In an independent work (that predates ours), Brakerski and Vaikuntanathan [21] also construct broadcast encryption achieving optimal parameters. Their techniques as well as final result are very different from ours – while our work crucially uses pairings in conjunction with LWE, they rely entirely on LWE and new assumptions in the regime of lattices. Both works can be seen as following the broad approach of starting with a succinct single-key CP-ABE from LWE[2], and adding collusion resistance using pairings (ours) or new techniques in the lattice regime (theirs).

The techniques in our work are similar in spirit to a growing line of work that uses "the best of both" of pairings and LWE [2,6,36,39], but quite different in details. Closest to our work are techniques used to construct *key policy functional encryption* [2,6,39], which use FHE (based on LWE) for encrypted evaluation and pairings for performing FHE decryption in the exponent. While a major challenge in these constructions is the leakage caused by FHE decryption noise,

---

[2] The single key CP-ABE with succinct CT was also discovered by Boneh and Kim [14].

we sidestep this issue altogether because BE is an "all or nothing primitive" with no secrets from a legitimate key holder. On the other hand, we need new tricks to handle the functionality and security of a *ciphertext-policy* scheme – for instance, we need to use position-wise randomness on the exponent to prevent ciphertext and secret key components from being paired in illegitimate positions to leak information.

2   Preliminaries

In this section, we define some preliminaries that we require.

2.1   Attribute Based Encryption

Let $R = \{R_\lambda : A_\lambda \times B_\lambda \to \{0,1\}\}_\lambda$ be a relation where A_λ and B_λ denote "ciphertext attribute" and "key attribute" spaces. An attribute-based encryption (ABE) scheme for R is defined by the following PPT algorithms:

Setup(1^λ) → (mpk, msk): The setup algorithm takes as input the unary representation of the security parameter λ and outputs a master public key mpk and a master secret key msk.

Enc(mpk, X, μ) → ct: The encryption algorithm takes as input a master public key mpk, a ciphertext attribute $X \in A_\lambda$, and a message bit μ. It outputs a ciphertext ct.

KeyGen(mpk, msk, Y) → sk$_Y$: The key generation algorithm takes as input the master public key mpk, the master secret key msk, and a key attribute $Y \in B_\lambda$. It outputs a private key sk$_Y$.

Dec(mpk, ct, X, sk$_Y$, Y) → μ or $\bot$: We assume that the decryption algorithm is deterministic. The decryption algorithm takes as input the master public key mpk, a ciphertext ct, ciphertext attribute $X \in A_\lambda$, a private key sk$_Y$, and private key attribute $Y \in B_\lambda$. It outputs the message μ or $\bot$ which represents that the ciphertext is not in a valid form.

Definition 2.1 (Correctness). *An ABE scheme for relation family R is correct if for all $\lambda \in \mathbb{N}$, $X \in A_\lambda, Y \in B_\lambda$ such that $R(X,Y) = 1$, and for all messages $\mu \in \mathcal{M}$,*

$$\Pr\left[\begin{array}{l} (\text{mpk}, \text{msk}) \leftarrow \text{Setup}(1^\lambda),\ \text{sk}_Y \leftarrow \text{KeyGen}(\text{mpk}, \text{msk}, Y), \\ \text{ct} \leftarrow \text{Enc}(\text{mpk}, X, \mu) :\ \text{Dec}\left(\text{mpk}, \text{sk}_Y, Y, \text{ct}, X\right) \neq \mu \end{array}\right] = \text{negl}(\lambda)$$

where the probability is taken over the coins of Setup, KeyGen, *and* Enc.

Definition 2.2 (Ada-IND security for ABE). *For an ABE scheme* ABE = {Setup, Enc, KeyGen, Dec} *for a relation family $R = \{R_\lambda : A_\lambda \times B_\lambda \to \{0,1\}\}_\lambda$ and a message space $\{\mathcal{M}_\lambda\}_{\lambda \in \mathbb{N}}$ and an adversary* A, *let us define* Ada-IND *security game as follows.*

1. **Setup phase:** *On input* 1^λ, *the challenger samples* $(\mathsf{mpk}, \mathsf{msk}) \leftarrow \mathsf{Setup}(1^\lambda)$ *and gives* mpk *to* A.
2. **Query phase:** *During the game,* A *adaptively makes the following queries, in an arbitrary order.* A *can make unbounded many key queries, but can make only single challenge query.*
    (a) **Key Queries:** A *chooses an input* $Y \in B_\lambda$. *For each such query, the challenger replies with* $\mathsf{sk}_Y \leftarrow \mathsf{KeyGen}(\mathsf{mpk}, \mathsf{msk}, Y)$.
    (b) **Challenge Query:** *At some point,* A *submits a pair of equal length messages* $(\mu_0, \mu_1) \in (\mathcal{M})^2$ *and the target* $X^\star \in A_\lambda$ *to the challenger. The challenger samples a random bit* $b \leftarrow \{0, 1\}$ *and replies to* A *with* $\mathsf{ct} \leftarrow \mathsf{Enc}(\mathsf{mpk}, X^\star, \mu_b)$.
    We require that $R(X^\star, Y) = 0$ *holds for any* Y *such that* A *makes a key query for* Y *in order to avoid trivial attacks.*
3. **Output phase:** A *outputs a guess bit* b' *as the output of the experiment.*

We define the advantage $\mathsf{Adv}_{\mathsf{ABE},A}^{\mathsf{Ada\text{-}IND}}(1^\lambda)$ *of* A *in the above game as*

$$\mathsf{Adv}_{\mathsf{ABE},A}^{\mathsf{Ada\text{-}IND}}(1^\lambda) := \left| \Pr[\mathsf{Exp}_{\mathsf{ABE},A}(1^\lambda) = 1 | b = 0] - \Pr[\mathsf{Exp}_{\mathsf{ABE},A}(1^\lambda) = 1 | b = 1] \right|.$$

The ABE scheme ABE *is said to satisfy* Ada-IND *security (or simply adaptive security) if for any stateful PPT adversary* A, *there exists a negligible function* $\mathsf{negl}(\cdot)$ *such that* $\mathsf{Adv}_{\mathsf{ABE},A}^{\mathsf{Ada\text{-}IND}}(1^\lambda) \neq \mathsf{negl}(\lambda)$.

We can consider the following stronger version of the security where we require the ciphertext to be pseudorandom.

Definition 2.3 (Ada-INDr security for ABE). *We define* Ada-INDr *security game similarly to* Ada-IND *security game except that the adversary* A *chooses single message* μ *instead of* (μ_0, μ_1) *at the challenge phase and the challenger returns* $\mathsf{ct} \leftarrow \mathsf{Enc}(\mathsf{mpk}, X^\star, \mu)$ *if* $b = 0$ *and a random ciphertext* $\mathsf{ct} \leftarrow \mathcal{CT}$ *from a ciphertext space* $\mathcal{CT}$ *if* $b = 1$. *We define the advantage* $\mathsf{Adv}_{\mathsf{ABE},A}^{\mathsf{Ada\text{-}INDr}}(1^\lambda)$ *of the adversary* A *accordingly and say that the scheme satisfies* Ada-INDr *security if the quantity is negligible.*

We also consider (weaker) selective versions of the above notions, where A specifies its target $X^\star$ at the beginning of the game.

Definition 2.4 (Sel-IND security for ABE). *We define* Sel-IND *security game as* Ada-IND *security game with the exception that the adversary* A *has to choose the challenge ciphertext attribute* $X^\star$ *before the setup phase but key queries* $Y_1, Y_2, \ldots$ *and choice of* (μ_0, μ_1) *can still be adaptive. We define the advantage* $\mathsf{Adv}_{\mathsf{ABE},A}^{\mathsf{Sel\text{-}IND}}(1^\lambda)$ *of the adversary* A *accordingly and say that the scheme satisfies* Sel-INDr *security (or simply selective security) if the quantity is negligible.*

Definition 2.5 (Sel-INDr security for ABE). *We define* Sel-INDr *security game as* Ada-INDr *security game with the exception that the adversary* A *has to choose the challenge ciphertext attribute* $X^\star$ *before the setup phase but key queries* $Y_1, Y_2, \ldots$ *and choice of* μ *can still be adaptive. We define the advantage* $\mathsf{Adv}_{\mathsf{ABE},A}^{\mathsf{Sel\text{-}INDr}}(1^\lambda)$ *of the adversary* A *accordingly and say that the scheme satisfies* Sel-INDr *security if the quantity is negligible.*

In the following, we recall definitions of various ABEs by specifying the relation. We start with the standard notions of ciphertext-policy attribute-based encryption (CP-ABE) and key-policy attribute-based encryption (KP-ABE).

CP-ABE for circuits. We define CP-ABE for circuit class $\{\mathcal{C}_\lambda\}_\lambda$ by specifying the relation. Here, $\mathcal{C}_\lambda$ is a set of circuits with input length $\ell(\lambda)$ and binary output. We define $A_\lambda^{\mathsf{CP}} = \mathcal{C}_\lambda$ and $B_\lambda^{\mathsf{CP}} = \{0,1\}^\ell$. Furthermore, we define the relation R_λ^{CP} as $R_\lambda^{\mathsf{CP}}(C, \mathbf{x}) = \neg C(\mathbf{x})$.[3]

KP-ABE for circuits. To define KP-ABE for circuits, we simply swap key and ciphertext attributes in CP-ABE for circuits. More formally, to define KP-ABE for circuits, we define $A_\lambda^{\mathsf{KP}} = \{0,1\}^\ell$ and $B_\lambda^{\mathsf{KP}} = \mathcal{C}_\lambda$. We also define $R_\lambda^{\mathsf{KP}} : A_\lambda^{\mathsf{KP}} \times B_\lambda^{\mathsf{KP}} \to \{0,1\}$ as $R_\lambda^{\mathsf{KP}}(\mathbf{x}, C) = \neg C(\mathbf{x})$.

We can also capture identity-based broadcast encryption (IBBE) and broadcast encryption (BE) as special cases of ABE by specifying the relations.

IBBE. To define IBBE, we define $A_\lambda^{\mathsf{IBBE}} = \mathcal{ID}(\lambda)^{\leq t}$ and $B_\lambda^{\mathsf{IBBE}} = \mathcal{ID}(\lambda)$, where $\mathcal{ID}(\lambda)$ is the identity space and $\mathcal{ID}(\lambda)^{\leq t}$ denotes all subsets of $\mathcal{ID}(\lambda)$ with size at most t. We also define $R_\lambda^{\mathsf{IBBE}} : A_\lambda^{\mathsf{IBBE}} \times B_\lambda^{\mathsf{IBBE}} \to \{0,1\}$ as $R_\lambda^{\mathsf{IBBE}}(S, \mathsf{id}) = \begin{cases} 1 & \text{if } \mathsf{id} \in S \\ 0 & \text{if } \mathsf{id} \notin S \end{cases}$. For IBBE, we typically require that the ciphertext size should be $o(t) \cdot \mathrm{poly}(\lambda)$, since otherwise we have a trivial construction from IBE.

BE. To define BE, we define $A_\lambda^{\mathsf{BE}} = 2^{[N(\lambda)]}$ and $B_\lambda^{\mathsf{BE}} = [N(\lambda)]$, where $N(\lambda) = \mathrm{poly}(\lambda)$ is the number of users in the system and $2^{[N(\lambda)]}$ denotes all subsets of $[N]$. We also define $R_\lambda^{\mathsf{BE}} : A_\lambda^{\mathsf{BE}} \times B_\lambda^{\mathsf{BE}} \to \{0,1\}$ as $R_\lambda^{\mathsf{BE}}(S, i) = 1$ when $i \in S$ and $R_\lambda^{\mathsf{BE}}(S, i) = 0$ otherwise. For BE, we typically require that the ciphertext size should be $o(N) \cdot \mathrm{poly}(\lambda)$, since otherwise we have a trivial construction from plain public key encryption.

We also define dual versions of BE and IBBE where the ciphertext and secret key attributes are swapped.

Dual IBBE (DIBBE). To define DIBBE, we define $A_\lambda^{\mathsf{DIBBE}} = \mathcal{ID}(\lambda)$ and $B_\lambda^{\mathsf{DIBBE}} = \mathcal{ID}(\lambda)^{\leq t}$, where $\mathcal{ID}(\lambda)$ is the identity space. We define $R_\lambda^{\mathsf{DIBBE}} : A_\lambda^{\mathsf{DIBBE}} \times B_\lambda^{\mathsf{DIBBE}} \to \{0,1\}$ as $R_\lambda^{\mathsf{IBBE}}(\mathsf{id}, S) = 1$ if $\mathsf{id} \in S$ and $R_\lambda^{\mathsf{IBBE}}(\mathsf{id}, S) = 0$ otherwise.

Dual BE (DBE). To define DBE, we define $A_\lambda^{\mathsf{DBE}} = [N(\lambda)]$ and $B_\lambda^{\mathsf{DBE}} = 2^{[N(\lambda)]}$, where $N(\lambda) = \mathrm{poly}(\lambda)$ is the number of users in the system. We also define $R_\lambda^{\mathsf{DBE}} : A_\lambda^{\mathsf{DBE}} \times B_\lambda^{\mathsf{DBE}} \to \{0,1\}$ as $R_\lambda^{\mathsf{DBE}}(i, S) = 1$ when $i \in S$ and $R_\lambda^{\mathsf{DBE}}(i, S) = 0$ otherwise.

2.2   Lattice Preliminaries

Here, we recall some facts on lattices that are needed for the exposition of our construction. Throughout this section, n, m, and q are integers such that

---

[3] Here, we follow the standard convention in lattice-based cryptography where the decryption succeeds when $C(\mathbf{x}) = 0$ rather than $C(\mathbf{x}) = 1$.

$n = \text{poly}(\lambda)$ and $m \geq n\lceil \log q \rceil$. In the following, let $\mathsf{SampZ}(\gamma)$ be a sampling algorithm for the truncated discrete Gaussian distribution over $\mathbb{Z}$ with parameter $\gamma > 0$ whose support is restricted to $z \in \mathbb{Z}$ such that $|z| \leq \sqrt{n}\gamma$.

Learning with Errors. We the introduce then learning with errors (LWE) problem.

Definition 2.6 (The LWE Assumption). *Let $n = n(\lambda)$, $m = m(\lambda)$, and $q = q(\lambda) > 2$ be integers and $\chi = \chi(\lambda)$ be a distribution over $\mathbb{Z}_q$. We say that the $\mathsf{LWE}(n, m, q, \chi)$ hardness assumption holds if for any PPT adversary A we have*

$$|\Pr[\mathsf{A}(\mathbf{A}, \mathbf{s}^\top \mathbf{A} + \mathbf{x}^\top) \to 1] - \Pr[\mathsf{A}(\mathbf{A}, \mathbf{v}^\top) \to 1]| \leq \text{negl}(\lambda)$$

where the probability is taken over the choice of the random coins by the adversary A and $\mathbf{A} \leftarrow \mathbb{Z}_q^{n \times m}$, $\mathbf{s} \leftarrow \mathbb{Z}_q^n$, $\mathbf{x} \leftarrow \chi^m$, and $\mathbf{v} \leftarrow \mathbb{Z}_q^m$. We also say that $\mathsf{LWE}(n, m, q, \chi)$ problem is subexponentially hard if the above probability is bounded by $2^{-n^\epsilon} \cdot \text{negl}(\lambda)$ for some constant $0 < \epsilon < 1$ for all PPT A.

As shown by previous works [19,43], if we set $\chi = \mathsf{SampZ}(\gamma)$, the $\mathsf{LWE}(n, m, q, \chi)$ problem is as hard as solving worst case lattice problems such as gapSVP and SIVP with approximation factor $\text{poly}(n) \cdot (q/\gamma)$ for some $\text{poly}(n)$. Since the best known algorithms for 2^k-approximation of gapSVP and SIVP run in time $2^{\tilde{O}(n/k)}$, it follows that the above $\mathsf{LWE}(n, m, q, \chi)$ with noise-to-modulus ratio 2^{-n^ϵ} is likely to be (subexponentially) hard for some constant ϵ.

Trapdoors. Let us consider a matrix $\mathbf{A} \in \mathbb{Z}_q^{n \times m}$. For all $\mathbf{V} \in \mathbb{Z}_q^{n \times m'}$, we let $\mathbf{A}_\gamma^{-1}(\mathbf{V})$ be an output distribution of $\mathsf{SampZ}(\gamma)^{m \times m'}$ conditioned on $\mathbf{A} \cdot \mathbf{A}_\gamma^{-1}(\mathbf{V}) = \mathbf{V}$. A γ-trapdoor for $\mathbf{A}$ is a trapdoor that enables one to sample from the distribution $\mathbf{A}_\gamma^{-1}(\mathbf{V})$ in time $\text{poly}(n, m, m', \log q)$ for any $\mathbf{V}$. We slightly overload notation and denote a γ-trapdoor for $\mathbf{A}$ by $\mathbf{A}_\gamma^{-1}$. We also define the special gadget matrix $\mathbf{G} \in \mathbb{Z}_q^{n \times m}$ as the matrix obtained by padding $\mathbf{I}_n \otimes (1, 2, 4, 8, \ldots, 2^{\lceil \log q \rceil})$ with zero-columns. The following properties had been established in a long sequence of works [3,4,19,22,32,41].

Lemma 2.7 (Properties of Trapdoors). *Lattice trapdoors exhibit the following properties.*

1. *Given $\mathbf{A}_\tau^{-1}$, one can obtain $\mathbf{A}_{\tau'}^{-1}$ for any $\tau' \geq \tau$.*
2. *Given $\mathbf{A}_\tau^{-1}$, one can obtain $[\mathbf{A} \| \mathbf{B}]_\tau^{-1}$ and $[\mathbf{B} \| \mathbf{A}]_\tau^{-1}$ for any $\mathbf{B}$.*
3. *There exists an efficient procedure $\mathsf{TrapGen}(1^n, 1^m, q)$ that outputs $(\mathbf{A}, \mathbf{A}_{\tau_0}^{-1})$ where $\mathbf{A} \in \mathbb{Z}_q^{n \times m}$ for some $m = O(n \log q)$ and is 2^{-n}-close to uniform, where $\tau_0 = \omega(\sqrt{n \log q \log m})$.*

Lattice Evaluation. The following is an abstraction of the evaluation procedure in previous LWE based FHE and ABE schemes. We follow the presentation by Tsabary [47], but with different parameters.

Lemma 2.8 (Fully Homomorphic Computation [35]). *There exists a pair of deterministic algorithms* (EvalF, EvalFX) *with the following properties.*

- EvalF$(\mathbf{B}, F) \to \mathbf{H}_F$. *Here,* $\mathbf{B} \in \mathbb{Z}_q^{n \times m\ell}$ *and* $F : \{0,1\}^\ell \to \{0,1\}$ *is a circuit.*
- EvalFX$(F, \mathbf{x}, \mathbf{B}) \to \widehat{\mathbf{H}}_{F,\mathbf{x}}$. *Here,* $\mathbf{x} \in \{0,1\}^\ell$ *with* $x_1 = 1^4$ *and* $F : \{0,1\}^\ell \to \{0,1\}$ *is a circuit with depth* d. *We have* $[\mathbf{B} - \mathbf{x} \otimes \mathbf{G}]\widehat{\mathbf{H}}_{F,\mathbf{x}} = \mathbf{B}\mathbf{H}_F - F(\mathbf{x})\mathbf{G}$ mod q, *where we denote* $[x_1\mathbf{G}\| \cdots \|x_k\mathbf{G}]$ *by* $\mathbf{x} \otimes \mathbf{G}$. *Furthermore, we have* $\|\mathbf{H}_F\|_\infty \leq m \cdot 2^{O(d)}$, $\|\widehat{\mathbf{H}}_{F,\mathbf{x}}\|_\infty \leq m \cdot 2^{O(d)}$.
- *The running time of* (EvalF, EvalFX) *is bounded by* poly$(n, m, \log q, 2^d)$.

The above algorithms are taken from [35], which is a variant of similar algorithms proposed by Boneh et al. [12]. The algorithms in [12] work for any polynomial-sized circuit F, but $\|\mathbf{H}_F\|_\infty$ and $\|\mathbf{H}_{F,\mathbf{x}}\|_\infty$ become super-polynomial even if the depth of the circuit is shallow (i.e., logarithmic depth). On the other hand, the above algorithms run in polynomial time only when F is of logarithmic depth, but $\|\mathbf{H}_F\|_\infty$ and $\|\mathbf{H}_{F,\mathbf{x}}\|_\infty$ can be polynomially bounded. The latter property is crucial for our purpose.

2.3   KP-ABE Scheme by Boneh et al. [12]

We will use a variant of the KP-ABE scheme proposed by Boneh et al. [12] as a building block of our construction of CP-ABE. We call the scheme BGG$^+$ and provide the description of the scheme in the following. We focus on the case where the policies associated with secret keys are limited to circuits with logarithmic depth rather than arbitrary polynomially bounded depth, so that we can use the evaluation algorithm due to Gorbunov and Vinayagamurthy [35] (see Lemma 2.8). This allows us to bound the noise growth during the decryption by a polynomial factor, which is crucial for our application.

The scheme supports the circuit class $\mathcal{C}_{\ell(\lambda),d(\lambda)}$, which is a set of all circuits with input length $\ell(\lambda)$ and depth at most $d(\lambda)$ with arbitrary $\ell(\lambda) = \text{poly}(\lambda)$ and $d(\lambda) = O(\log \lambda)$.

Setup(1^λ): On input 1^λ, the setup algorithm defines the parameters $n = n(\lambda)$, $m = m(\lambda)$, noise distribution χ over $\mathbb{Z}$, τ_0, τ, and $B = B(\lambda)$ as specified later. It then proceeds as follows.
   1. Sample $(\mathbf{A}, \mathbf{A}_{\tau_0}^{-1}) \leftarrow$ TrapGen$(1^n, 1^m, q)$ such that $\mathbf{A} \in \mathbb{Z}_q^{n \times m}$.
   2. Sample random matrix $\mathbf{B} = (\mathbf{B}_1, \ldots, \mathbf{B}_\ell) \leftarrow (\mathbb{Z}_q^{n \times m})^\ell$ and a random vector $\mathbf{u} \leftarrow \mathbb{Z}_q^n$.
   3. Output the master public key mpk $= (\mathbf{A}, \mathbf{B}, \mathbf{u})$ and the master secret key msk $= \mathbf{A}_{\tau_0}^{-1}$.
KeyGen(mpk, msk, F): The key generation algorithm takes as input the master public key mpk, the master secret key msk, and a circuit $F \in \mathcal{F}_\lambda$ and proceeds as follows.
   1. Compute $\mathbf{H}_F =$ EvalF$(\mathbf{B}, F)$ and $\mathbf{B}_F = \mathbf{B}\mathbf{H}_F$.

---

[4]   This condition may be necessary for the lemma to hold for arbitrary F.

2. Compute $[\mathbf{A}\|\mathbf{B}_F]_\tau^{-1}$ from $\mathbf{A}_{\tau_0}^{-1}$ and sample $\mathbf{r} \in \mathbb{Z}^{2m}$ as $\mathbf{r} \leftarrow [\mathbf{A}\|\mathbf{B}_F]_\tau^{-1}(\mathbf{u})$.

3. Output the secret key $\mathsf{sk}_F := \mathbf{r}$.

$\mathsf{Enc}(\mathsf{mpk}, \mathbf{x}, \mu)$: The encryption algorithm takes as input the master public key mpk, an attribute $\mathbf{x} \in \{0,1\}^\ell$ with $x_1 = 1$,[5] and a message $\mu \in \{0,1\}$ and proceeds as follows.

1. Sample $\mathbf{s} \leftarrow \mathbb{Z}_q^n$, $e_1 \leftarrow \chi$, $\mathbf{e}_2 \leftarrow \chi^m$, and $\mathbf{S}_{i,b} \leftarrow \{-1,1\}^{m \times m}$ for $i \in [\ell]$ and $b \in \{0,1\}$. Then, set $\mathbf{e}_{i,b} := \mathbf{S}_{i,b}^\top \mathbf{e}_2$ for $i \in [\ell]$ and $b \in \{0,1\}$.

2. Compute

$$\psi_1 := \mathbf{s}^\top \mathbf{u} + e_1 + \mu\lceil q/2 \rceil \in \mathbb{Z}_q, \quad \psi_2^\top := \mathbf{s}^\top \mathbf{A} + \mathbf{e}_2^\top \in \mathbb{Z}_q^m,$$

$$\psi_{i,b}^\top := \mathbf{s}^\top (\mathbf{B} - x_i \mathbf{G}) + \mathbf{e}_{i,b}^\top \in \mathbb{Z}_q^m \quad \text{for all } i \in [\ell] \text{ and } b \in \{0,1\}.$$

3. Output the ciphertext $\mathsf{ct}_\mathbf{x} := (\psi_1, \psi_2, \{\psi_{i,x_i}\}_{i \in [\ell]})$, where x_i is the i-th bit of $\mathbf{x}$.

$\mathsf{Dec}(\mathsf{mpk}, \mathsf{sk}_\mathbf{x}, \mathbf{x}, F, \mathsf{ct}_F)$: The decryption algorithm takes as input the master public key mpk, a secret key sk_F for a circuit F, and a ciphertext $\mathsf{ct}_\mathbf{x}$ for an attribute $\mathbf{x}$ and proceeds as follows.

1. Parse $\mathsf{ct}_\mathbf{x} \rightarrow (\psi_1 \in \mathbb{Z}_q, \psi_2 \in \mathbb{Z}_q^m, \{\psi_{i,x_i} \in \mathbb{Z}_q^m\}_{i \in [\ell]})$, and $\mathsf{sk}_F \in \mathbb{Z}^{2m}$. If any of the component is not in the corresponding domain or $F(\mathbf{x}) = 1$, output $\bot$.

2. Concatenate $\{\psi_{i,x_i}\}_{i \in [\ell]}$ to form $\psi_3^\top = (\psi_{1,x_1}^\top, \ldots, \psi_{\ell,x_\ell}^\top)$.

3. Compute $\psi' := \psi_1 - [\psi_2^\top \| \psi_3^\top] \mathbf{r}$.

4. Output 0 if $\psi' \in [-B, B]$ and 1 if $[-B + \lceil q/2 \rceil, B + \lceil q/2 \rceil]$.

Remark 2.9. We note that the encryption algorithm above computes redundant components $\{\psi_{i,\neg x_i}\}_{i \in [\ell]}$ in the second step, which are discarded in the third step. However, due to this redundancy, the scheme has the following special structure that will be useful for us. Namely, the first and the second steps of the encryption algorithm can be executed without knowing $\mathbf{x}$. Only the third step of the encryption algorithm needs the information of $\mathbf{x}$, where it chooses $\{\psi_{i,x_i}\}_{i \in [\ell]}$ from $\{\psi_{i,b}\}_{i \in [\ell], b \in \{0,1\}}$ depending on each bit of $\mathbf{x}$ and then output the former terms along with ψ_1 and ψ_2. Looking ahead, our construction of CP-ABE in Sect. 3 crucially relies on this special structure. There, the encryption algorithm, who takes as input a circuit C that specifies the policy and does not know the corresponding input $\mathbf{x}$, executes the first two steps of the above encryption algorithm. This is possible since these two steps do not need the knowledge of $\mathbf{x}$.

Parameters and Security. We choose the parameters for the scheme as follows:

$$m = n^{1.1} \log q, \qquad q = 2^{\Theta(\lambda)}, \qquad \chi = \mathsf{SampZ}(3\sqrt{n}),$$

$$\tau_0 = n \log q \log m, \qquad \tau = m^{3.1}\ell \cdot 2^{O(d)} \qquad B = n^2 m^2 \tau \cdot 2^{O(d)}.$$

---

[5] This restriction is required to apply Lemma 2.8. We can remove the condition by increasing the dimension of $\mathbf{x}$ by 1 and considering function F that ignores the first bit.

The parameter n will be chosen depending on whether we need Sel-INDr security or Ada-INDr security for the scheme. If it suffices to have Sel-INDr security, we set $n = \lambda^c$ for some constant $c > 1$. If we need Ada-INDr security, we have to enlarge the parameter to be $n = (\ell\lambda)^c$ in order to compensate for the security loss caused by the complexity leveraging.

We remark that if we were to use the above ABE scheme stand-alone, we would have been able to set q polynomially bounded as in [35]. The reason why we set q exponentially large is that we combine the scheme with bilinear maps of order q to lift the ciphertext components to the exponent so that they are "hidden" in some sense (See Sect. 4). In order to use the security of the bilinear map, we set the group order q to be exponentially large.

The following theorem summarizes the security and efficiency properties of the construction. There are two parameter settings depending on whether we assume subexponential hardness of LWE or not.

Theorem 2.10 (Adapted from [12,35]). *Assuming hardness of* LWE$(n, m,$ $q, \chi)$ *with* $\chi = \mathsf{SampZ}(3\sqrt{n})$ *and* $q = O(2^{n^{1/\epsilon}})$ *for some constant* $\epsilon > 1$, *the above scheme satisfies* Sel-INDr *security. Assuming* subexponential *hardness of* LWE(n, m, q, χ) *with the same parameters, the above scheme satisfies* Ada-INDr *security with respect to the ciphertext space* $\mathcal{CT} := \mathbb{Z}_q^{m(\ell+1)+1}$

2.4 Bilinear Map Preliminaries

Here, we introduce our notation for bilinear maps and the bilinear generic group model following Baltico et al. [9], who specializes the framework by Barthe [10] for defining generic k-linear groups to the bilinear group settings. The definition closely follows that of Maurer [40], which is equivalent to the alternative formulation by Shoup [46].

Notation on Bilinear Maps. A bilinear group generator takes as input 1^λ and outputs a group description $\mathbb{G} = (q, \mathbb{G}_1, \mathbb{G}_2, \mathbb{G}_T, e, g_1, g_2)$, where q is a prime of $\Theta(\lambda)$ bits, $\mathbb{G}_1$, $\mathbb{G}_2$, and $\mathbb{G}_T$ are cyclic groups of order q, $e : \mathbb{G}_1 \times \mathbb{G}_2 \to \mathbb{G}_T$ is a non-degenerate bilinear map, and g_1 and g_2 are generators of $\mathbb{G}_1$ and $\mathbb{G}_2$, respectively. We require that the group operations in $\mathbb{G}_1$, $\mathbb{G}_2$, and $\mathbb{G}_T$ as well as the bilinear map e can be efficiently computed. We employ the implicit representation of group elements: for a matrix $\mathbf{A}$ over $\mathbb{Z}_q$, we define $[\mathbf{A}]_1 := g_1^{\mathbf{A}}$, $[\mathbf{A}]_2 := g_2^{\mathbf{A}}$, $[\mathbf{A}]_T := g_T^{\mathbf{A}}$, where exponentiation is carried out component-wise.

We also use the following less standard notations. For vectors $\mathbf{w} = (w_1, \ldots, w_\ell)^\top \in \mathbb{Z}_q^\ell$ and $\mathbf{v} = (w_1, \ldots, w_\ell)^\top \in \mathbb{Z}_q^\ell$ of the same length, $\mathbf{w} \odot \mathbf{v}$ denotes the vector that is obtained by component-wise multiplications. Namely, $\mathbf{v} \odot \mathbf{w} = (v_1 w_1, \ldots, v_\ell w_\ell)^\top$. When $\mathbf{w} \in (\mathbb{Z}_q^*)^\ell$, $\mathbf{v} \oslash \mathbf{w}$ denotes the vector $\mathbf{v} \oslash \mathbf{w} = (v_1/w_1, \ldots, v_\ell/w_\ell)^\top$. It is easy to verify that for vectors $\mathbf{c}, \mathbf{d} \in \mathbb{Z}_q^\ell$

and $\mathbf{w} \in (\mathbb{Z}_q^*)^\ell$, we have $(\mathbf{c} \odot \mathbf{w}) \odot (\mathbf{d} \oslash \mathbf{w}) = \mathbf{c} \odot \mathbf{d}$. For group elements $[\mathbf{v}]_1 \in \mathbb{G}_1^\ell$ and $[\mathbf{w}]_1 \in \mathbb{G}_2^\ell$, $[\mathbf{v}]_1 \odot [\mathbf{w}]_2$ denotes $([v_1 w_1]_T, \ldots, [v_\ell w_\ell]_T)^\top$, which is efficiently computable from $[\mathbf{v}]_1$ and $[\mathbf{w}]_2$ using the bilinear map e.

Generic Bilinear Group Model. Let $\mathbb{G} = (q, \mathbb{G}_1, \mathbb{G}_2, \mathbb{G}_T, e, g_1, g_2)$ be a bilinear group setting, L_1, L_2, and L_T be lists of group elements in $\mathbb{G}_1$, $\mathbb{G}_2$, and $\mathbb{G}_T$ respectively, and let $\mathcal{D}$ be a distribution over L_1, L_2, and L_T. The generic group model for a bilinear group setting $\mathbb{G}$ and a distribution $\mathcal{D}$ is described in Fig. 1. In this model, the challenger first initializes the lists L_1, L_2, and L_T by sampling the group elements according to $\mathcal{D}$, and the adversary receives handles for the elements in the lists. For $s \in \{1, 2, T\}$, $L_s[h]$ denotes the h-th element in the list L_s. The handle to this element is simply the pair (s, h). An adversary running in the generic bilinear group model can apply group operations and bilinear maps to the elements in the lists. To do this, the adversary has to call the appropriate oracle specifying handles for the input elements. The challenger computes the result of a query, stores it in the corresponding list, and returns to the adversary its (newly created) handle. Handles are not unique (i.e., the same group element may appear more than once in a list under different handles).

We remark that we slightly simplify the definition of the generic group model by Baltico et al. [9]. Whereas they allow the adversary to access the equality test oracle, which is given two handles (s, h_1) and (s, h_2) and returns 1 if $L_s[h_1] = L_s[h_2]$ and 0 otherwise for all $s \in \{1, 2, T\}$, we replace this oracle with the zero-test oracle, which is given a handle (s, h) and returns 1 if $L_s[h] = 0$ and 0 otherwise only for the case of $s = T$. We claim that even with this modification, the model is equivalent to the original one. This is because we can perform the equality test for (s, h_1) and (s, h_2) using our restricted oracles as follows. Let us first consider the case of $s = T$. In this case, we can get the handle (T, h') corresponding to $L_T[h_1] - L_T[h_2]$ by calling neg_T and add_T. We then make a zero-test query for (T, h'). Clearly, we get 1 if $L_s[h_1] = L_s[h_2]$ and 0 otherwise. We next consider the case of $s \in \{1, 2\}$. This case can be reduced to the case of $s = T$ by lifting the group elements corresponding to h_1 and h_2 to the group elements in $\mathbb{G}_T$ by taking bilinear maps with an arbitrary non-unit group element in $\mathbb{G}_{3-s}$, which is possible by calling map_e.

Symbolic Group Model. The symbolic group model for a bilinear group setting $\mathbb{G}$ and a distribution $\mathcal{D}_P$ gives to the adversary the same interface as the corresponding generic group model, except that internally the challenger stores lists of element in the field $\mathbb{Z}_p(X_1, \ldots, X_n)$ instead of lists of group elements. The oracles add_s, neg_s, map, and zt computes addition, negation, multiplication, and equality in the field. In our work, we will use the subring $\mathbb{Z}_p[X_1, \ldots, X_n, 1/X_1, \ldots, 1/X_n]$ of the entire field $\mathbb{Z}_p(X_1, \ldots, X_n)$. Note that any element f in $\mathbb{Z}_p[X_1, \ldots, X_n, 1/X_1, \ldots, 1/X_n]$ can be represented as $f(X_1, \ldots, X_n) = \sum_{(c_1, \ldots, c_n) \in \mathbb{Z}^n} a_{c_1, \ldots, c_n} X_1^{c_1} \cdots X_n^{c_n}$ using $\{a_{c_1, \ldots, c_n} \in \mathbb{Z}_p\}_{(c_1, \ldots, c_n) \in \mathbb{Z}^n}$, where we have $a_{c_1, \ldots, c_n} = 0$ for all but finite $(c_1, \ldots, c_n) \in \mathbb{Z}^n$. Note that this expression is unique.

State: Lists L_1, L_2, L_T over $\mathbb{G}_1$, $\mathbb{G}_2$, $\mathbb{G}_T$ respectively.

Initializations: Lists L_1, L_2, L_T sampled according to distribution $\mathcal{D}$.

Oracles: The oracles provide black-box access to the group operations, the bilinear map, and equalities.

- For all $s \in \{1, 2, T\}$: $\mathsf{add}_s(h_1, h_2)$ appends $L_s[h_1] + L_s[h_2]$ to L_s and returns its handle $(s, |L_s|)$.
- For all $s \in \{1, 2, T\}$: $\mathsf{neg}_s(h_1, h_2)$ appends $-L_s[h_1]$ to L_s and returns its handle $(s, |L_s|)$.
- $\mathsf{map}_e(h_1, h_2)$ appends $e(L_1[h_1], L_2[h_2])$ to L_T and returns its handle $(T, |L_T|)$.
- $\mathsf{zt}_T(h)$ returns 1 if $L_T[h] = 0$ and 0 otherwise.

All oracles return $\perp$ when given invalid indices.

Fig. 1. Generic group model for bilinear group setting $\mathbb{G} = (q, \mathbb{G}_1, \mathbb{G}_2, \mathbb{G}_T, e, g_1, g_2)$ and distribution $\mathcal{D}$.

3   Our Construction of CP-ABE

Here, we describe our new construction of CP-ABE scheme. Our construction can deal with any circuit class $\mathcal{F} = \{\mathcal{F}_\lambda\}_\lambda$ that is subclass of $\{\mathcal{C}_{\ell(\lambda), d(\lambda)}\}_\lambda$ with arbitrary $\ell(\lambda) \leq \mathrm{poly}(\lambda)$ and $d(\lambda) = O(\log \lambda)$, where $\mathcal{C}_{\ell(\lambda), d(\lambda)}$ is a set of circuits with input length $\ell(\lambda)$ and depth at most $d(\lambda)$. As we will see in Sect. 5, we can obtain new constructions of BE, IBBE, CP-ABE by setting the circuit class $\mathcal{F}$ appropriately. In order to get the scheme, we use the KP-ABE scheme BGG^+ for the circuit class $\mathcal{F} = \{\mathcal{F}_\lambda\}_\lambda$ that is described in Sect. 2.3 as an ingredient. Our construction below can be seen as a conversion from an ABE scheme to another ABE scheme with dual predicate.

$\mathsf{Setup}(1^\lambda)$: On input 1^λ, the setup algorithm defines the parameters $n = n(\lambda)$, $m = m(\lambda)$, noise distribution χ over $\mathbb{Z}$, τ_0, τ, and $B = B(\lambda)$ as specified in Sect. 2.3. It samples a group description $\mathbb{G} = (q, \mathbb{G}_1, \mathbb{G}_2, \mathbb{G}_T, e, [1]_1, [1]_2)$. It then sets $L := (2\ell + 1)m + 2$ and proceeds as follows.

1. Sample $\mathbf{w} \leftarrow (\mathbb{Z}_q^*)^L$ and compute $[\mathbf{w}]_1$.
2. Output $\mathsf{mpk} = ([1]_1, [1]_2, [\mathbf{w}]_1)$ and $\mathsf{msk} = \mathbf{w}$.

$\mathsf{KeyGen}(\mathsf{mpk}, \mathsf{msk}, \mathbf{x})$: The key generation algorithm takes as input the master public key mpk, the master secret key msk, and an attribute $\mathbf{x} \in \{0, 1\}^\ell$ with $x_1 = 1$ and proceeds as follows.

1. Let $\mathbf{1} := (1, \ldots, 1)^\top \in \mathbb{Z}_q^m$ and $\mathbf{0} := (0, \ldots, 0)^\top \in \mathbb{Z}_q^m$. Set

$$\phi_0 = 1 \in \mathbb{Z}_q, \quad \phi_1 = 1 \in \mathbb{Z}_q, \quad \phi_2 := \mathbf{1} \in \mathbb{Z}_q^m,$$

$$\phi_{i,b} := \begin{cases} \mathbf{1} \in \mathbb{Z}_q^m & \text{if } b = x_i \\ \mathbf{0} \in \mathbb{Z}_q^m & \text{if } b \neq x_i \end{cases} \quad \text{for } i \in [\ell] \text{ and } b \in \{0, 1\}. \qquad (3.1)$$

2. Vectorize $(\phi_0, \phi_1, \phi_2, \{\phi_{i,b}\}_{i,b})$ to form a vector $\mathbf{d} \in \mathbb{Z}_q^L$ by concatenating each entry of the vectors in a predetermined order.

3. Sample $\delta \leftarrow \mathbb{Z}_q^*$.

4. Compute $[\delta \mathbf{d} \oslash \mathbf{w}]_2 \in \mathbb{G}_2^L$ from $\mathsf{msk} = \mathbf{w}$ in msk.

5. Output $\mathsf{sk}_{\mathbf{x}} = [\delta \mathbf{d} \oslash \mathbf{w}]_2$.

$\mathsf{Enc}(\mathsf{mpk}, F, \mu)$: The encryption algorithm takes as input the master public key mpk, the circuit F, and a message $\mu \in \{0, 1\}$ and proceeds as follows.

1. Sample fresh BGG^+ scheme:

   (a) Sample $(\mathbf{A}, \mathbf{A}_{\tau_0}^{-1}) \leftarrow \mathsf{TrapGen}(1^n, 1^m, q)$ such that $\mathbf{A} \in \mathbb{Z}_q^{n \times m}$.

   (b) Sample random matrix $\mathbf{B} = (\mathbf{B}_1, \dots, \mathbf{B}_\ell) \leftarrow (\mathbb{Z}_q^{n \times m})^\ell$ and a random vector $\mathbf{u} \leftarrow \mathbb{Z}_q^n$.

2. Compute BGG^+ function key for circuit F:

   (a) Compute $\mathbf{H}_F = \mathsf{EvalF}(\mathbf{B}, F)$ and $\mathbf{B}_F = \mathbf{B}\mathbf{H}_F$.

   (b) Compute $[\mathbf{A}\|\mathbf{B}_F]_\tau^{-1}$ from $\mathbf{A}_{\tau_0}^{-1}$ and sample $\mathbf{r} \in \mathbb{Z}^{2m}$ as $\mathbf{r} \leftarrow [\mathbf{A}\|\mathbf{B}_F]_\tau^{-1}(\mathbf{u})$.

3. Compute BGG^+ ciphertext for all possible inputs:

   (a) Sample $\mathbf{s} \leftarrow \mathbb{Z}_q^n$, $e_1 \leftarrow \chi$, $\mathbf{e}_2 \leftarrow \chi^m$, and $\mathbf{S}_{i,b} \leftarrow \{-1, 1\}^{m \times m}$ for $i \in [\ell]$ and $b \in \{0, 1\}$. Then, set $\mathbf{e}_{i,b} := \mathbf{S}_{i,b}^\top \mathbf{e}_2$ for $i \in [\ell]$ and $b \in \{0, 1\}$.

   (b) Compute

$$\psi_0 := 1 \in \mathbb{Z}_q, \quad \psi_1 := \mathbf{s}^\top \mathbf{u} + e_1 + \mu \lceil q/2 \rceil \in \mathbb{Z}_q,$$

$$\psi_2^\top := \mathbf{s}^\top \mathbf{A} + \mathbf{e}_2^\top \in \mathbb{Z}_q^m,$$

$$\psi_{i,b}^\top := \mathbf{s}^\top (\mathbf{B}_i - b\mathbf{G}) + \mathbf{e}_{i,b}^\top \in \mathbb{Z}_q^m \quad \text{for } i \in [\ell] \text{ and } b \in \{0, 1\}. \quad (3.2)$$

4. Encode BGG^+ ciphertexts in exponent of bilinear group:

   (a) Vectorize $(\psi_0, \psi_1, \psi_2, \{\psi_{i,b}\}_{i,b})$ to form a vector $\mathbf{c} \in \mathbb{Z}_q^L$ by concatenating each entry of the vectors in a predetermined order (that aligns with the one used in the key generation algorithm).

   (b) Sample $\gamma \leftarrow \mathbb{Z}_q^*$.

   (c) Compute $[\gamma \mathbf{c} \odot \mathbf{w}]_1 \in \mathbb{G}_2^L$ from γ, $\mathbf{c}$, and $[\mathbf{w}]_1$ in mpk.

5. Output $\mathsf{ct}_F = (\mathsf{ct}_0 = (\mathbf{A}, \mathbf{B}), \mathsf{ct}_1 = [\gamma \mathbf{c} \odot \mathbf{w}]_1, \mathsf{ct}_2 = \mathbf{r})$.

$\mathsf{Dec}(\mathsf{mpk}, \mathsf{sk}_{\mathbf{x}}, \mathbf{x}, F, \mathsf{ct}_F)$: The decryption algorithm takes as input the master public key mpk, the secret key $\mathsf{sk}_{\mathbf{x}}$ for an attribute $\mathbf{x}$, and the ciphertext ct_F for a circuit F and proceeds as follows.

1. Parse $\mathsf{ct}_F \to (\mathsf{ct}_0 = (\mathbf{A} \in \mathbb{Z}_q^{n \times m}, \mathbf{B} \in \mathbb{Z}_q^{n \times m\ell}), \mathsf{ct}_1 \in \mathbb{G}_1^L, \mathsf{ct}_2 \in \mathbb{Z}^{2m})$ and $\mathsf{sk}_{\mathbf{x}} \in \mathbb{G}_2^L$. If any of the component is not in the corresponding domain or $F(\mathbf{x}) = 1$, output $\bot$.

2. Unmask BGG^+ ciphertexts corresponding to $\mathbf{x}$ by using secret key: Compute $[\mathbf{v}]_T := \mathsf{ct}_1 \odot \mathsf{sk}_{\mathbf{x}}$ and de-vectorize $[\mathbf{v}]_T$ to obtain

$$[v_0]_T \in \mathbb{G}_T, \quad [v_1]_T \in \mathbb{G}_T, \quad [\mathbf{v}_2]_T \in \mathbb{G}_T^m, \quad [\mathbf{v}_{i,b}]_T \in \mathbb{G}_T^m, \quad \text{for } i \in [\ell], b \in \{0, 1\}.$$

3. Evaluate circuit F on BGG^+ ciphertexts in the exponent: Compute $\widehat{\mathbf{H}}_{F,\mathbf{x}} = \mathsf{EvalF}(F, \mathbf{x}, \mathbf{B})$.

4. Perform BGG^+ decryption in the exponent:

   Form $[\mathbf{v}_{\mathbf{x}}^\top]_T = [\mathbf{v}_{1,x_1}^\top, \ldots, \mathbf{v}_{\ell,x_\ell}^\top]_T$ and $\mathsf{ct}_2^\top = (\mathbf{r}_1^\top \in \mathbb{Z}_q^m, \mathbf{r}_2^\top \in \mathbb{Z}_q^m)$. Then compute

   $$[v']_T := [v_1 - (\mathbf{v}_2^\top \mathbf{r}_1 + \mathbf{v}_{\mathbf{x}}^\top \widehat{\mathbf{H}}_{F,\mathbf{x}} \mathbf{r}_2)]_T$$

   from $[v_1]_T$, $[\mathbf{v}_2]_T$, $[\mathbf{v}_{\mathbf{x}}]_T$, $\mathbf{r}_1$, $\mathbf{r}_2$, and $\widehat{\mathbf{H}}_{F,\mathbf{x}}$.

5. Recover exponent via brute force if $F(\mathbf{x}) = 0$:

   Find $\eta \in [-B, B] \cup [-B + \lceil q/2 \rceil, B + \lceil q/2 \rceil]$ such that $[v_0]_T^\eta = [v']_T$ by brute-force search. If there is no such η, output $\bot$. To speed up the operation, one can employ the baby-step giant-step algorithm.

6. Output 0 if $\eta \in [-B, B]$ and 1 if $[-B + \lceil q/2 \rceil, B + \lceil q/2 \rceil]$.

Correctness. To see correctness of the scheme, we first observe that we have $\mathsf{ct}_1 \odot \mathsf{sk}_{\mathbf{x}} = [\gamma \delta \cdot \mathbf{c} \odot \mathbf{d}]_T$ and thus

$$v_0 = \gamma \delta, \quad v_1 = \gamma \delta \left(\mathbf{s}^\top \mathbf{u} + e_1 + \mu \lceil q/2 \rceil \right), \quad \mathbf{v}_2^\top = \gamma \delta \left(\mathbf{s}^\top \mathbf{A} + \mathbf{e}_2^\top \right),$$

$$\mathbf{v}_{i,b}^\top = \begin{cases} \gamma \delta \left(\mathbf{s}^\top (\mathbf{B}_i - x_i \mathbf{G}) + \mathbf{e}_{i,x_i}^\top \right) & \text{if } b = x_i \\ \mathbf{0} & \text{if } b = 1 - x_i \end{cases}.$$

From the above, we have $\mathbf{v}_{\mathbf{x}}^\top = \mathbf{s}^\top (\mathbf{B} - \mathbf{x} \otimes \mathbf{G}) + \mathbf{e}_{\mathbf{x}}^\top$ for $\mathbf{e}_{\mathbf{x}}^\top := (\mathbf{e}_{1,x_1}^\top, \cdots, \mathbf{e}_{\ell,x_\ell}^\top)$. We then have

$$\mathbf{v}_2^\top \mathbf{r}_1 + \mathbf{v}_{\mathbf{x}}^\top \widehat{\mathbf{H}}_{F,\mathbf{x}} \mathbf{r}_2 = \gamma \delta \left(\mathbf{s}^\top \mathbf{A} + \mathbf{e}_2^\top \right) \mathbf{r}_1 + \gamma \delta \left(\mathbf{s}^\top (\mathbf{B} - \mathbf{x} \otimes \mathbf{G}) + \mathbf{e}_{\mathbf{x}}^\top \right) \widehat{\mathbf{H}}_{F,\mathbf{x}} \mathbf{r}_2$$

$$= \gamma \delta \left(\mathbf{s}^\top (\mathbf{A}\mathbf{r}_1 + \mathbf{B}_F \mathbf{r}_2) + \mathbf{e}_2^\top \mathbf{r}_1 + \mathbf{e}_{\mathbf{x}}^\top \widehat{\mathbf{H}}_{F,\mathbf{x}} \mathbf{r}_2 \right)$$

$$= \gamma \delta \left(\mathbf{s}^\top \mathbf{u} + \mathbf{e}_2^\top \mathbf{r}_1 + \mathbf{e}_{\mathbf{x}}^\top \widehat{\mathbf{H}}_{F,\mathbf{x}} \mathbf{r}_2 \right)$$

where the second equation follows from $(\mathbf{B} - \mathbf{x} \otimes \mathbf{G})\widehat{\mathbf{H}}_{F,\mathbf{x}} = \mathbf{B}_F$ and the third equation follows form $[\mathbf{A} \| \mathbf{B}_F]\mathbf{r} = \mathbf{u}$. This implies

$$v' = \gamma \delta \left(\mu \lceil q/2 \rceil + e_1 - \mathbf{e}_2^\top \mathbf{r}_1 - \mathbf{e}_{\mathbf{x}}^\top \widehat{\mathbf{H}}_{F,\mathbf{x}} \mathbf{r}_2 \right).$$

Recall that we set $\chi = \mathsf{SampZ}(3\sqrt{n})$. By the definition of SampZ, we have $\|e_1\|_\infty \leq 3n$ and $\|\mathbf{e}_2\|_\infty < 3n$. Furthermore, we have $\|\mathbf{e}_{i,b}\|_\infty = \|\mathbf{S}_{i,b}^\top \mathbf{e}_2\|_\infty \leq 3mn$ for $i \in [\ell]$ and $b \in \{0, 1\}$, $\|\mathbf{r}\|_\infty \leq \sqrt{n}\tau$, and $\|\widehat{\mathbf{H}}_{F,\mathbf{x}}\|_\infty \leq m \cdot 2^{O(d)}$, where the last inequality follows from Lemma 2.8. Thus, we have

$$\|e_1 - \mathbf{e}_2^\top \mathbf{r}_1 - \mathbf{e}_{\mathbf{x}}^\top \widehat{\mathbf{H}}_{F,\mathbf{x}} \mathbf{r}_2\|_\infty \leq O(n^{1.5} m^2 \tau \cdot 2^{O(d)}) \leq B$$

by our choice of B. The correctness therefore follows. Note that since $B = \mathrm{poly}(n, \ell) \cdot 2^{O(d)} = \mathrm{poly}(\lambda)$, the decryption algorithm runs in polynomial time.

Efficiency of the Scheme. Here, we evaluate the efficiency of the above scheme. In particular, we measure the sizes of the parameters. The master public key of the scheme consists of $L + 2$ group elements. Since $L = O(m\ell)$, we have that the master public key can be represented by a binary string of length $\ell \cdot \text{poly}(\lambda)$. Next, we observe that a secret key in the scheme consists of L group elements, which can be represented by a binary string of length $\ell \cdot \text{poly}(\lambda)$. Finally, a ciphertext in the scheme consists of $O(nm)$ elements of $\mathbb{Z}_q$ and L group elements. The former elements are represented by a binary string of length $\text{poly}(\lambda)$ if we only need Sel-INDr security for the underlying KP-ABE scheme. If we need Ada-INDr security, the length of the binary string is $\text{poly}(\ell, \lambda)$. Therefore, the length of the whole ciphertext is $\ell \cdot \text{poly}(\lambda)$ if we only need Sel-INDr security for the underlying KP-ABE scheme and $\text{poly}(\ell, \lambda)$ if we need Ada-INDr security. In any case, the sizes of all parameters in the system are independent of the size of the circuits being supported by the scheme, which is a notable feature of the scheme.

4   Security Proof for Our CP-ABE

This section is devoted to prove the following theorem that asserts the security of our CP-ABE scheme in Sect. 3.

Theorem 4.1. *Our CP-ABE scheme for function class $\mathcal{F}$ satisfies* Ada-IND *security in the generic group model assuming that the KP-ABE* BGG$^+$ *for function class $\mathcal{F}$ satisfies* Ada-INDr *security.*

Overview of the Proof. Before going to the formal proof, we give its overview. The proof is done by considering a sequence of games and consists of two parts. In the first part of the proof, which is captured by a series of game hops from **Game$_0$** through **Game$_5$** defined below, we prove that it is pointless for the adversary to take pairing products between unmatching positions of the ciphertext and secret key components and then take linear combinations among them. Therefore, the only possible strategy for the adversary is to take linear combination among "partial decryption results" obtained by taking pairing products between matching positions of the ciphertext and secret key components and infer information of the message being encrypted. In the second step of the proof, which is captured by the game hop from **Game$_5$** to **Game$_6$**, we show that this type of attack does not work either. To do so, we further consider a sequence of subgames from **Game$_{5.0}$** through **Game$_{5.8}$**. We first prove that taking linear combinations among partial decryption results from different secret keys is useless. This is the key step that excludes the collusion attack and is captured by the game hop from **Game$_{5.3}$** to **Game$_{5.4}$**. At this point, the only strategy for the adversary is to take linear combination among partial decryption result obtained by single secret key. Finally, in the step from **Game$_{5.7}$** to **Game$_{5.8}$**, we use the security of the BGG$^+$ ABE to conclude that this strategy does not work either. To invoke the security of BGG$^+$ ABE, we use the fact that the partial decryption result obtained by secret key for x forms randomized version of BGG$^+$ ABE ciphertext for attribute x in the exponent.

Proof. To prove the theorem, we fix a PPT adversary A that makes at most $Q_{\mathsf{kq}}(\lambda)$ key queries and $Q_{\mathsf{zt}}(\lambda)$ zero-test queries during the game. Furthermore, we assume that A always chooses $(\mu_0, \mu_1) = (0, 1)$ as its target message at the challenge phase. This can be assumed without loss of generality since our scheme is a single-bit scheme. In order to prove the security, we consider following sequence of games. Let us denote the event that A outputs correct guess for b at the end of $\mathbf{Game_x}$ as $\mathsf{E_x}$.

Game$_0$: This is the real game in the generic group model. To fix the notation and for the sake of concreteness, we briefly describe the game here. Without loss of generality, we assume that the challenger simulates the generic group oracle for A. At the beginning of the game, the challenger picks $\mathbf{w} \leftarrow (\mathbb{Z}_q^*)^L$ and sets the master public key $\mathsf{mpk} = ([1]_1, [1]_2, [\mathbf{w}]_1)$ and the master secret key $\mathsf{msk} = \mathbf{w}$. Then, it gives handles to the group elements in mpk to A. To respond to the j-th key query $\mathbf{x}^{(j)}$ made by A, the challenger samples $\delta_j \leftarrow \mathbb{Z}_q^*$, sets $\mathbf{d}^{(j)} \in \mathbb{Z}_q^L$ as specified in the key generation algorithm, and sets $\mathsf{sk}^{(j)} = [\delta_j \mathbf{d}^{(j)} \oslash \mathbf{w}]_2$. It then gives the handles corresponding to the group elements in $\mathsf{sk}^{(j)}$ to A. To answer the challenge query for a circuit F, the challenger first picks the message $b \leftarrow \{0, 1\}$ to be encrypted, chooses $\gamma \leftarrow \mathbb{Z}_q^*$, computes $\mathbf{A}, \mathbf{B}, \mathbf{r}, \mathbf{c}$ as specified in the encryption algorithm (where b is encrypted), and forms the challenge ciphertext as $\mathsf{ct}_F = (\mathsf{ct}_0 = (\mathbf{A}, \mathbf{B}), \mathsf{ct}_1 = [\gamma \mathbf{c} \odot \mathbf{w}]_1, \mathsf{ct}_2 = \mathbf{r})$. It then returns $\mathsf{ct}_0 = (\mathbf{A}, \mathbf{B})$, handles to $\mathsf{ct}_1 = [\gamma \mathbf{c} \odot \mathbf{w}]_1$, and ct_2 to A. By definition, the advantage of A against the scheme is $\left| \Pr[\mathsf{E}_0] - \frac{1}{2} \right|$.

Game$_1$: This game is the same as the previous game except that the challenger samples $\mathbf{w} = (w_1, \ldots, w_L)^\top, \delta_1, \ldots, \delta_{Q_{\mathsf{kq}}}, \mathbf{A}, \mathbf{B}, \mathbf{u}, \gamma, b$, and $\mathbf{c} = (c_1, \ldots, c_L)^\top$ at the beginning of the game. Note that $\mathbf{c}$ is sampled from the distribution that is only dependent on the bit b being encrypted, and is *independent* of the circuit F that is specified by A later in the game. Therefore, this game is well-defined. As we prove in Lemma 4.2, we have $\Pr[\mathsf{E}_0] = \Pr[\mathsf{E}_1]$.

Game$_2$: In this game, we (partially) switch to the symbolic group model and replace $\{w_i\}_{i \in [L]}, \{\delta_j\}_{j \in [Q_{\mathsf{kq}}]}, \gamma$, and $\{c_i\}_{i \in [L]}$ in $\mathbb{Z}_q$ with the formal variables $\{W_i\}_{i \in [L]}, \{\Delta_j\}_{j \in [Q_{\mathsf{kq}}]}, \Gamma$, and $\{C_i\}_{i \in [L]}$ respectively. As a result, all handles given to A refer to elements in the ring

$$\mathbb{T} := \mathbb{Z}_q[W_1, \ldots, W_L, 1/W_1, \ldots, 1/W_L, \Delta_1, \ldots, \Delta_{Q_{\mathsf{kq}}}, \Gamma, C_1, \ldots, C_L],$$

where $\{1/W_i\}_i$ are needed to represent the components in the secret keys. However, when the challenger answers the zero-test queries, it substitutes the formal variables with corresponding elements in $\mathbb{Z}_q$. Namely, in this game, the challenger picks $\{w_i\}_i, \{\delta_j\}_j, \gamma$, and $\{c_i\}_i$ at the beginning of the game as specified in the previous game and when A makes a zero-test query for a handle corresponding to $f(W_1, \ldots, W_L, \Delta_1, \ldots, \Delta_{Q_{\mathsf{kq}}}, \Gamma, C_1, \ldots, C_L) \in \mathbb{T}$, the challenger returns 1 if

$$f(w_1, \ldots, w_L, \delta_1, \ldots, \delta_{Q_{\mathsf{kq}}}, \gamma, c_1, \ldots, c_L) = 0$$

holds over $\mathbb{Z}_q$ and 0 otherwise. As we prove in Lemma 4.3, we have $\Pr[\mathsf{E}_1] = \Pr[\mathsf{E}_2]$.

Here, we list all the components in $\mathbb{T}$ for which corresponding handles are given to A in **Game$_2$** as either handles to the group elements in mpk, the challenge ciphertext, or secret keys:

$$S_1 := \left\{1, \ W_i, \ \{C_i \Gamma W_i\}_{i \in [L]}\right\}, \quad S_2 := \left\{1, \ \{d_i^{(j)} \Delta_j / W_i\}_{i \in [L], j \in [Q_{\mathsf{kq}}]}\right\}$$

where $d_i^{(j)} \in \{0, 1\}$ is the i-th entry of $\mathbf{d}^{(j)}$. Note that S_1 and S_2 correspond to handles for elements in $\mathbb{G}_1$ and $\mathbb{G}_2$, respectively. We then define S_T as $S_T := \{X \cdot Y : X \in S_1, Y \in S_2, X \cdot Y \neq 0\}$. If we explicitly write down S_T, we have $S_T = S_{T,1} \cup S_{T,2}$ where

$$S_{T,1} := \begin{cases} 1, & \\ W_i, \ C_i \Gamma W_i, & \text{for } i \in [L], \\ \Delta_j, & \text{for } j \in [Q_{\mathsf{kq}}], \\ \Delta_j / W_i, & \text{for } i \in [L], j \in [Q_{\mathsf{kq}}] \text{ such that } d_i^{(j)} = 1, \\ \Delta_j W_{i'} / W_i, & \text{for } i, i' \in [L], j \in [Q_{\mathsf{kq}}] \text{ such that } i \neq i' \text{ and } d_i^{(j)} = 1 \\ C_{i'} \Gamma \Delta_j W_{i'} / W_i & \text{for } i, i' \in [L], j \in [Q_{\mathsf{kq}}] \text{ such that } i \neq i' \text{ and } d_i^{(j)} = 1 \end{cases}$$

and $S_{T,2} = \{C_i \Gamma \Delta_j \text{ for } i \in [L], j \in [Q_{\mathsf{kq}}] \text{ such that } d_i^{(j)} = 1\}$. Here, $S_{T,2}$ consists of terms that are obtained by taking product between matching positions of the ciphertext and secret keys, whereas $S_{T,1}$ consists of terms that are obtained by taking product between unmatching positions of the ciphertext and secret keys or between master public key and the ciphertext or secret keys. Note that any handle submitted to the zero-test oracle by A during the game refers to an element f in $\mathbb{T}$ that can be represented as

$$f(W_1, \ldots, W_L, \Delta_1, \ldots, \Delta_{Q_{\mathsf{kq}}}, \Gamma, C_1, \ldots, C_L) = \sum_{Z \in S_T} a_Z Z \qquad (4.1)$$

where the coefficients $\{a_Z \in \mathbb{Z}_q\}_{Z \in S_T}$ can be efficiently computed. Furthermore, $\{a_Z \in \mathbb{Z}_q\}_{Z \in S_T}$ satisfying the above equation is unique since all monomials in S_T are distinct.

Game$_3$: In this game, we change the game so that $\{W_i\}_{i \in [L]}, \{\Delta_j\}_{j \in [Q_{\mathsf{kq}}]}, \Gamma$ are treated as formal variables rather than elements in $\mathbb{Z}_q$ even when answering zero-test queries. Namely, the challenger no longer samples $\{w_i\}_{i \in [L]}, \{\delta_j\}_{j \in [Q_{\mathsf{kq}}]}$, and γ at the beginning of the game and when A makes a zero-test query for a handle corresponding to $f(W_1, \ldots, W_L, \Delta_1, \ldots, \Delta_{Q_{\mathsf{kq}}}, \Gamma, C_1, \ldots, C_L) \in \mathbb{T}$, the challenger returns 1 if

$$f(W_1, \ldots, W_L, \Delta_1, \ldots, \Delta_{Q_{\mathsf{kq}}}, \Gamma, c_1, \ldots, c_L) = 0 \qquad (4.2)$$

holds over $\mathbb{T}$ and 0 otherwise, where $\{c_i\}_{i \in [L]}$ are sampled at the beginning of the game as specified in the previous game. As we prove in Lemma 4.4, we have $|\Pr[\mathsf{E}_2] - \Pr[\mathsf{E}_3]| \leq Q_{\mathsf{zt}}(L+3)^2/q$.

Game$_4$: This game is the same as the previous game except that the challenger aborts the game and enforces the adversary to output a random bit when there exists $i \in [L]$ such that $c_i = 0$, where $\mathbf{c} = (c_1, \ldots, c_L)^\top$ is sampled as in the previous game. As we prove in Lemma 4.5, we have $|\Pr[\mathsf{E}_3] - \Pr[\mathsf{E}_4]| \leq L/q$.

Game$_5$: In this game, we further change the way zero-test queries are answered. In particular, when A makes a zero-test query for a handle corresponding to $f \in \mathbb{T}$ that can be represented as

$$f(W_1, \ldots, W_L, \Delta_1, \ldots, \Delta_{Q_{kq}}, \Gamma, C_1, \ldots, C_L) = \sum_{Z \in S_{T,1}} a_Z Z + \sum_{Z \in S_{T,2}} a_Z Z,$$
$$(4.3)$$

the challenger returns 0 if there exists $Z \in S_{T,1}$ such that $a_Z \neq 0$. Otherwise, the challenger answers the query as in the previous game. As we prove in Lemma 4.6, we have $\Pr[\mathsf{E}_4] = \Pr[\mathsf{E}_5]$.

Game$_6$: In this game, we change the game so that zero-test queries are performed over the ring $\mathbb{T}$. Namely, when A makes a zero-test query for a handle corresponding to $f \in \mathbb{T}$ the challenger returns 0 if $f \neq 0$ over $\mathbb{T}$. Equivalently, the challenger returns 0 if there exists $Z \in S_T$ such that $a_Z = 0$ when A makes a zero-test query for a handle corresponding to $f \in \mathbb{T}$ that is represented as Eq. (4.1). Note that $(c_1, \ldots, c_L)$ is not used in this game and the challenger does not have to sample it any more. As we prove in Lemma 4.7, there exists a PPT adversary B such that $|\Pr[\mathsf{E}_5] - \Pr[\mathsf{E}_6]| \leq Q_{kq} Q_{zt} \cdot (\mathsf{Adv}_{\mathsf{BGG}^+,\mathsf{B}}^{\mathsf{Ada\text{-}INDr}}(1^\lambda) + 1/q)$.

We can see that the adversary cannot obtain any information about the encrypted message b in **Game$_6$** since the challenge ciphertext is replaced by formal variables $(C_1, \ldots, C_L)$ that does not contain any information of b and the answers to the zero test queries do not depend on b neither. Therefore, we have $\Pr[\mathsf{E}_6] = 1/2$. Thus, there exists a PPT adversary B against Ada-INDr security of BGG^+ such that

$$\left| \Pr[\mathsf{E}_0] - \frac{1}{2} \right| \leq Q_{kq} Q_{zt} \cdot \left(\mathsf{Adv}_{\mathsf{BGG}^+,\mathsf{B}}^{\mathsf{Ada\text{-}INDr}}(1^\lambda) + \frac{1}{q} \right) + \frac{Q_{zt}(L+3)^2 + L}{q}.$$

In particular, assuming BGG^+ satisfies Ada-INDr security, the above quantity is negligible as desired.

To finish the proof of Theorem 4.1, it remains to prove Lemmas 4.2, 4.3, 4.4, 4.5, 4.6, and 4.7 in the following.

Lemma 4.2 (Game$_0$ $\equiv$ Game$_1$). *We have* $\Pr[\mathsf{E}_0] = \Pr[\mathsf{E}_1]$.

Proof. Since this is only a conceptual change, the lemma immediately follows.

Lemma 4.3 (Game$_1$ $\equiv$ Game$_2$). *We have* $\Pr[\mathsf{E}_1] = \Pr[\mathsf{E}_2]$.

Proof. Since zero-test queries in **Game$_2$** are answered by using $\{w_i\}_i$, $\{\delta_j\}_j$, γ, and $\{c_i\}_i$ that are sampled from exactly the same distribution as that in **Game$_1$**, the view of A in **Game$_2$** is not altered from that in **Game$_1$**. The lemma therefore follows.

Lemma 4.4 (Game$_2$ $\approx_s$ Game$_3$). *We have* $|\Pr[E_2] - \Pr[E_3]| \leq Q_{zt}(L+3)^2/q$.

Proof. Let us observe that **Game$_2$** and **Game$_3$** differ only when A submits a handle corresponding to a polynomial $f(W_1, \ldots, W_L, \Delta_1, \ldots, \Delta_{Q_{kq}}, \Gamma, C_1, \ldots, C_L) \in \mathbb{T}$ satisfying $f(w_1, \ldots, w_L, \delta_1, \ldots, \delta_{Q_{kq}}, \gamma, c_1, \ldots, c_L) = 0$ and $f(W_1, \ldots, W_L, \Delta_1, \ldots, \Delta_{Q_{kq}}, \Gamma, c_1, \ldots, c_L) \neq 0$ to the zero-test oracle. Let F denote the event. It suffices to bound the probability of F occurring in **Game$_2$**. To do so, let us fix an element f in $\mathbb{T}$ and $c_1, \ldots, c_L$ in $\mathbb{Z}_q$. We then define a polynomial $g(W_1, \ldots, W_L, \Delta_1, \ldots, \Delta_{Q_{kq}}, \Gamma) \in \mathbb{Z}_q[W_1, \ldots, W_L, \Delta_1, \ldots, \Delta_{Q_{kq}}, \Gamma]$ as

$$g(W_1, \ldots, W_L, \Delta_1, \ldots, \Delta_{Q_{kq}}, \Gamma)$$
$$:= \left(\prod_{i \in [L]} W_i \right) \cdot f(W_1, \ldots, W_L, \Delta_1, \ldots, \Delta_{Q_{kq}}, \Gamma, c_1, \ldots, c_L).$$

Note that in the above, the term $(\prod_i W_i)$ is introduced in order to clear the denominators that possibly appear in f and to make sure that g is in the ring $\mathbb{Z}_q[W_1, \ldots, W_L, \Delta_1, \ldots, \Delta_{Q_{kq}}, \Gamma]$ rather than in $\mathbb{T}$. We observe that F occurs if and only if $g(w_1, \ldots, w_L, \delta_1, \ldots, \delta_{Q_{kq}}, \gamma) = 0$ and $g(W_1, \ldots, W_L, \Delta_1, \ldots, \Delta_{Q_{kq}}, \Gamma) \neq 0$ since we have $w_i \neq 0$ for all $i \in [L]$. We can bound this probability by $(L+3)^2/q$ using Schwartz-Zippel lemma since g is a polynomial in $\mathbb{Z}_q[W_1, \ldots, W_L, \Delta_1, \ldots, \Delta_{Q_{kq}}, \Gamma]$ with degree at most $L+3$. (Recall that f can be represented as a linear combination of the terms in S_T.) Since A makes at most Q_{zt} zero-test queries, the lemma follows by the union bound.

Lemma 4.5 (Game$_3$ $\approx_s$ Game$_4$). *We have* $|\Pr[E_3] - \Pr[E_4]| \leq L/q$.

Proof. We observe that each entry of $\mathbf{c} = (c_1, \ldots, c_L)$ is either fixed to be 1 or distributed uniformly at random over $\mathbb{Z}_q$. Therefore, by the union bound, the probability that there is $i \in [L]$ such that $c_i = 0$ can be bounded by L/q. The lemma therefore follows.

Lemma 4.6 (Game$_4$ $\equiv$ Game$_5$). *We have* $\Pr[E_4] = \Pr[E_5]$.

Proof. We observe that **Game$_4$** and **Game$_5$** differ only when A makes a zero-test query for a handle corresponding to $f \in \mathbb{T}$ that satisfies Eq. (4.2) and there exists $Z \in S_{T,1}$ such that $a_Z \neq 0$ when we express f as Eq. (4.3). We claim that such f does not exist and two games are actually equivalent. For the sake of contradiction, assume that such f exists. Then Eq. (4.2) implies

$$\sum_{Z \in S_{T,1}} a_Z Z(c_1, \ldots, c_L) + \sum_{Z \in S_{T,2}} a_Z Z(c_1, \ldots, c_L) = 0,$$

where $Z(c_1, \ldots, c_L)$ denotes $Z(W_1, \ldots, W_L, \Delta_1, \ldots, \Delta_{Q_{kq}}, \Gamma, c_1, \ldots, c_L) \in \mathbb{T}$ in the above. We can see that $\sum_{Z \in S_{T,1}} a_Z Z(c_1, \ldots, c_L) = 0$ holds since we have

$$\left\{ \sum_{Z \in S_{T,1}} a'_Z Z(c_1, \ldots, c_L) : a'_Z \in \mathbb{Z}_q \right\} \cap \left\{ \sum_{Z \in S_{T,2}} a''_Z Z(c_1, \ldots, c_L) : a''_Z \in \mathbb{Z}_q \right\} = \{0\},$$

which follows from the fact that monomials in $S_{T,1}$ and $S_{T,2}$ are distinct even if we substitute $\{C_i\}_i$ in $S_{T,1}$ and $S_{T,2}$ with $\{c_i\}_i$ and ignore the difference between the coefficients of the monomials. Furthermore, $\sum_{Z \in S_{T,1}} a_Z Z(c_1, \ldots, c_L) = 0$ implies $a_Z = 0$ for all $Z \in S_{T,1}$, which follows from $\mathbf{c} \in (\mathbb{Z}_q^*)^L$ and from the fact that all monomials in $S_{T,1}$ are distinct even if we substitute $\{C_i\}_i$ with $\{c_i\}_i$ and ignore the difference between the coefficients of the monomials. However, this contradicts the assumption that there exists $Z \in S_{T,1}$ such that $a_Z \neq 0$. This completes the proof of the lemma.

Lemma 4.7 (Game$_5$ $\approx_c$ Game$_6$). *There exists a PPT adversary* B *such that*
$$|\Pr[\mathsf{E}_5] - \Pr[\mathsf{E}_6]| \leq Q_{\mathsf{kq}} Q_{\mathsf{zt}} \cdot \left(\mathsf{Adv}_{\mathsf{BGG}^+,\mathsf{B}}^{\mathsf{Ada\text{-}INDr}}(1^\lambda) + 1/q \right).$$

Proof. We first observe that **Game$_5$** and **Game$_6$** differ only when A makes a zero-test query for a handle corresponding to $f \in \mathbb{T}$ that can be represented as

$$f(W_1, \ldots, W_L, \Delta_1, \ldots, \Delta_{Q_{\mathsf{kq}}}, \Gamma, C_1, \ldots, C_L) = \sum_{Z \in S_{T,2}} a_Z Z \qquad (4.4)$$

and satisfies $f \neq 0$ over $\mathbb{T}$ and Eq. (4.2). We call such a query *bad*. In the following, we prove that the probability that A makes a bad query in **Game$_5$** is negligible. To do so, we consider following sequence of games. We define F_x as the event that A makes a bad query in **Game$_{5.\mathsf{x}}$** and the challenger does not abort.

Game$_{5.0}$: This game is the same as **Game$_5$**. By definition, the probability that A makes a bad query in **Game$_5$** is $\Pr[\mathsf{F}_0]$.

Game$_{5.1}$: In this game, we change the previous game so that the challenger picks a random guess k^* for the first bad query as $k^* \leftarrow [Q_{\mathsf{zt}}]$ at the beginning of the game. Furthermore, we change the game so that the challenger aborts if the k^*-th zero-test query is not the first bad query. Since k^* is chosen uniformly at random and independent from the view of A, the guess is correct with probability $1/Q_{\mathsf{zt}}$ conditioned on F_0. Therefore, we have $\Pr[\mathsf{F}_1] = \Pr[\mathsf{F}_0]/Q_{\mathsf{zt}}$.

Game$_{5.2}$: This game is the same as the previous game except that the challenger aborts the game immediately after A makes the k^*-th zero-test query. Since whether F_1 occurs or not is irrelevant to how the game proceeds after the k^*-th zero-test query is made by A, we clearly have $\Pr[\mathsf{F}_2] = \Pr[\mathsf{F}_1]$.

Game$_{5.3}$: In this game, we change the game so that the challenger answers the first $k^* - 1$ zero-test queries by performing zero tests over $\mathbb{T}$. Furthermore, we change the game so that the sampling of $\mathbf{c}$ is deferred until the k^*-th zero-test query is made by A. We first observe that the game is well-defined since $\mathbf{c}$ is used only for the k^*-th zero-test query. Furthermore, since the first $k^* - 1$ zero-test queries that refer to $f \in \mathbb{T}$ such that $f \neq 0$ are answered by 0 whenever F_2 happens, we have $\Pr[\mathsf{F}_3] \geq \Pr[\mathsf{F}_2]$.

Game$_{5.4}$: To define the game, we first define the set $S_{T,2,j}$:= $\{C_i \Gamma \Delta_j\}_{i \in [L]}$ s.t. $d_i^{(j)} = 1$. By definition, we have $S_{T,2} = \cup_{j \in [Q_{kq}]} S_{T,2,j}$. Using this notation, any $f \in \mathbb{T}$ referred by a bad query can be represented as

$$f(W_1, \ldots, W_L, \Delta_1, \ldots, \Delta_{Q_{kq}}, \Gamma, C_1, \ldots, C_L) = \sum_{j \in [Q_{kq}]} \sum_{Z \in S_{T,2,j}} a_Z Z. \quad (4.5)$$

In this game, we change the game so that the challenger aborts the game if the bad query made by A refers to f such that there *does not* exist $j \in [Q_{kq}]$ satisfying

$$\sum_{Z \in S_{T,2,j}} a_Z Z \neq 0 \quad \text{and} \quad \sum_{Z \in S_{T,2,j}} a_Z Z(c_1, \ldots, c_L) = 0, \quad (4.6)$$

where $Z(c_1, \ldots, c_L)$ denotes $Z(W_1, \ldots, W_L, \Delta_1, \ldots, \Delta_{Q_{kq}}, \Gamma, c_1, \ldots, c_L) \in \mathbb{T}$ above. We claim that this actually cannot happen. To see this, we first observe that since we have $f \neq 0$ for a bad query, there exists $j \in [Q_{kq}]$ satisfying $\sum_{Z \in S_{T,2,j}} a_Z Z \neq 0$. Furthermore, we have

$$\sum_{Z \in S_{T,2,j}} a_Z Z(c_1, \ldots, c_L) = -\sum_{j' \neq j} \sum_{Z \in S_{T,2,j'}} a_Z Z(c_1, \ldots, c_L)$$

from Eq. (4.2). However, the above is impossible unless the left hand side equals to 0 since any monomial in $S_{T,2,j}$ never appears in $S_{T,2,j'}$ for $j' \neq j$ even if we replace $\{C_i\}_i$ with $\{c_i\}_i$ and ignore the difference between the coefficients of the monomials. Therefore, the change made in this game is only conceptual and we have $\Pr[F_4] = \Pr[F_3]$.

Game$_{5.5}$: In this game, we change the previous game so that the challenger picks $j^* \leftarrow [Q_{kq}]$ uniformly at random at the beginning of the game. Furthermore, we add the abort condition that the challenger aborts if Eq. (4.6) does not hold with respect to $j = j^*$ for f that is referred by the k^*-th zero-test query. Since there exists $j' \in [Q_{kq}]$ that satisfies Eq. (4.6) as long as F_4 occurs and j^* is chosen uniformly at random and independent from the view of A, we have $\Pr[F_5] \geq \Pr[F_4]/Q_{kq}$.

Game$_{5.6}$: In this game, we further change the game so that the challenger aborts the game if the j^*-th key query has not been made yet at the point when the k^*-th zero-test query is made. We claim that conditioned on F_5 happens, the challenger never aborts. To see this, we observe that if the j^*-th key query has not been made then terms that contain Δ_{j^*} has not been given to A and there is no way to make a zero-test query for f such that $\sum_{Z \in S_{T,2,j^*}} a_Z Z \neq 0$, since all terms in $S_{T,2,j^*}$ are multiples of Δ_{j^*}. We therefore have $\Pr[F_6] = \Pr[F_5]$.

Game$_{5.7}$: In this game, we further change the game so that the challenger samples c_i only for $i \in [L]$ such that $d_i^{(j^*)} = 1$, where j^* is chosen at the beginning of the game as in **Game$_{5.5}$**. The game is still well-defined since the only place in the game where we need the information of $\mathbf{c}$ is when checking Eq. (4.6) and we only need $\{c_i\}_{i \in [L]}$ s.t. $d_i^{(j^*)} = 1$ there. (Recall that we have

$S_{T,2,j} = \{C_i \Gamma \Delta_j\}_{i \in [L] \text{ s.t. } d_i^{(j)}=1}$.) Clearly, this does not change the view of A. We therefore have $\Pr[\mathsf{F}_7] = \Pr[\mathsf{F}_6]$.

From Eqs. (3.1) and (3.2), we can see that $\{c_i\}_{i \in [L] \text{ s.t. } d_i^{(j^*)}=1}$ consists of the following components:

$$\psi_0 = 1, \quad \psi_1 := \mathbf{s}^\top \mathbf{u} + e_1 + \mu\lceil q/2 \rceil, \quad \psi_2^\top := \mathbf{s}^\top \mathbf{A} + \mathbf{e}_2^\top,$$
$$\psi_{i,x_i^{(j^*)}}^\top := \mathbf{s}^\top (\mathbf{B}_i - x_i^{(j^*)} \mathbf{G}) + \mathbf{e}_{i,x_i^{(j^*)}}^\top \quad \text{for } i \in [\ell],$$

where $x_i^{(j^*)}$ is the i-th entry of $\mathbf{x}^{(j^*)}$.

Game$_{5.8}$: In this game, we further change the game so that the challenger samples

$$\psi_0 := 1 \in \mathbb{Z}_q, \quad \psi_1 \leftarrow \mathbb{Z}_q, \quad \psi_2 \leftarrow \mathbb{Z}_q^m, \quad \psi_{i,b} \leftarrow \mathbb{Z}_q^m \quad \text{for } i \in [\ell] \text{ and } b \in \{0,1\}$$

and sets $\{c_i\}_{i \in [L] \text{ s.t. } d_i^{(j^*)}=1}$ from the above components.[6] As we prove in Lemma 4.8, there exists a PPT adversary B such that $\mathsf{Adv}_{\mathsf{BGG}^+,\mathsf{B}}^{\mathsf{Ada\text{-}INDr}}(1^\lambda) \geq |\Pr[\mathsf{F}_7] - \Pr[\mathsf{F}_8]|$.

As we will prove in Lemma 4.9, we have $\Pr[\mathsf{F}_8] \leq 1/q$. This allows us to bound $\Pr[\mathsf{F}_0]$ as $\Pr[\mathsf{F}_0] \leq Q_{\mathsf{kq}} Q_{\mathsf{zt}} \cdot (\mathsf{Adv}_{\mathsf{BGG}^+,\mathsf{B}}^{\mathsf{Ada\text{-}INDr}}(1^\lambda) + 1/q)$, where B is a PPT adversary. This completes the proof of Lemma 4.7.

It remains to prove Lemmas 4.8 and 4.9 in the following.

Lemma 4.8 (Game$_{5.7} \approx_c$ Game$_{5.8}$). *There exists a PPT adversary* B *such that* $\mathsf{Adv}_{\mathsf{BGG}^+,\mathsf{B}}^{\mathsf{Ada\text{-}INDr}}(1^\lambda) \geq |\Pr[\mathsf{F}_7] - \Pr[\mathsf{F}_8]|$.

Proof. We show that if A can distinguish **Game$_{5.7}$** from **Game$_{5.8}$**, we can build another adversary B against Ada-INDr security of BGG$^+$. The adversary B acts as the challenger and simulates the game for A. Looking ahead, setup phase and key queries are trivial to handle since they do not need any parameter of BGG$^+$. The only steps we need care are the simulation of the challenge phase and the k^*-th zero-test query, where B needs to interact with its challenger in order to handle them. We describe how B proceeds in the following.

Setup phase. At the beginning of the game, B is given 1^λ and the master public key of BGG$^+$ $(\mathbf{A}, \mathbf{B}, \mathbf{u})$. It then gives the handles to $1, W_1, \ldots, W_L$ corresponding to $\mathbb{G}_1$ and the handle to 1 corresponding to $\mathbb{G}_2$ to A. These handles correspond to the master public key. B also samples $j^* \leftarrow [Q_{\mathsf{kq}}]$, $k^* \leftarrow [Q_{\mathsf{zt}}]$, and $b \leftarrow \{0,1\}$ and keeps them secret.

Key Queries. Given the j-th secret key query for $\mathbf{x}^{(j)}$ made by A, B proceeds as follows. B first forms $\mathbf{d}^{(j)} \in \mathbb{Z}_q^L$ as specified in the key generation algorithm and returns the handles corresponding to $(d_1^{(j)} \Delta_j/W_1, \ldots, d_L^{(j)} \Delta_j/W_L)$ in $\mathbb{G}_2$ to A.

---

[6] Note that until this step, we have not changed the distribution of $\{c_i\}_{i \in [L]}$ except that we stop sampling c_i for i such that $d_i^{(j^*)} = 1$ in **Game$_{5.7}$**.

Challenge Query. When A makes the challenge query for a circuit F, B makes a *secret key query* for F to its challenger and is given $\mathbf{r}$ sampled as $\mathbf{r} \leftarrow [\mathbf{A} \| \mathbf{B}_F]_\tau^{-1}(\mathbf{u})$. B then sets $\mathsf{ct}_0 = (\mathbf{A}, \mathbf{B})$, $\mathsf{ct}_2 := \mathbf{r}$, and ct_1 as the handles corresponding to the formal variables $(C_1, \ldots, C_L)$ and gives $\mathsf{ct} = (\mathsf{ct}_0, \mathsf{ct}_1, \mathsf{ct}_2)$ to A as the challenge ciphertext.

Generic Group Queries. B honestly handles the queries for the generic group oracle corresponding to addition, negation, and multiplication (bilinear map) made by A by keeping track of the underlying encodings in $\mathbb{T}$ associated with the handles. For the k-th zero-test query that refers to an element f in $\mathbb{T}$, B returns 1 if $f = 0$ over $\mathbb{T}$ and 0 otherwise if $k < k^*$. If $k = k^*$, B first checks whether the j^*-th key query has already been made and aborts otherwise, as specified in **Game$_{5.6}$**. It then makes the challenge query for the attribute $\mathbf{x}^{(j^*)}$, where $\mathbf{x}^{(j^*)}$ is the attribute for which A has made the j^*-th key query, and the message b to its challenger. Then B obtains its challenge ciphertext $(\psi_1, \psi_2, \{\psi_{i,x_i^{(j^*)}}\}_{i \in [\ell]})$. It then sets $\psi_0 = 1$ and forms $\{c_i\}_{i \in [L]}$ s.t. $d_i^{(j^*)} = 1$ by vectorizing the terms appropriately. Finally, it checks whether Eq. (4.6) holds or not using $\{c_i\}_{i \in [L]}$ s.t. $d_i^{(j^*)} = 1$ as specified in **Game$_{5.7}$** and outputs 1 if it holds and 0 otherwise.

Analysis. It is easy to see that B simulates **Game$_{5.7}$** if the challenge ciphertext for B is the real one and **Game$_{5.8}$** if it is chosen uniformly at random from the ciphertext space. Therefore, it can be seen that B outputs 1 with probability $\Pr[\mathsf{F}_7]$ if the challenge bit for B is 0 and $\Pr[\mathsf{F}_8]$ otherwise. Therefore, B's advantage against BGG$^+$ is $|\Pr[\mathsf{F}_7] - \Pr[\mathsf{F}_8]|$. This completes the proof of the lemma.

Lemma 4.9. *We have* $\Pr[\mathsf{F}_8] = 1/q$.

Proof. We observe that F_8 occurs only when A makes a zero-test query that refers to a handle $f \neq 0$ that can be represented as Eq. (4.4) and satisfies Eq. (4.6) with respect to j^* where $\{c_i\}_{i \in [L]}$ s.t. $d_i^{(j^*)} = 1$ are chosen as **Game$_{5.8}$**. However, Eq. (4.6) can happen only with probability at most $1/q$ since f is represented as a linear combination of $\{C_i \Gamma \Delta_j\}_{i,j}$ and all entries of $\{c_i\}_{i \in [L]}$ s.t. $d_i^{(j^*)} = 1$ are chosen uniformly at random except for the entry that is fixed to be 1. $\qquad\blacksquare$

5 Implications to CP-ABE, BE, and IBBE

In this section, we show that by setting the circuit class supported by our CP-ABE scheme in Sect. 3 appropriately, we can obtain various new schemes with different security and efficiency tradeoffs. In particular, we obtain new CP-ABE, BE, and IBBE schemes from the LWE assumption in the bilinear generic group model. Our CP-ABE scheme achieves the notable efficiency property that the sizes of all the parameters in the system do not depend on the size of the circuits supported by the scheme. Similarly, our BE (resp., IBBE) schemes achieve optimal parameter size, in the sense that the sizes of all parameters in the system are bounded by a fixed polynomial that is independent from the number of users (resp., upper bound on the number of recipients). These efficiency properties have never been achieved without using indistinguishability obfuscation or multilinear maps.

5.1   New CP-ABE Scheme

By setting $\mathcal{F}_{CP} := \{\mathcal{C}_{\ell(\lambda),d(\lambda)}\}_\lambda$ in the construction in Sect. 3, we obtain a CP-ABE scheme that can deal with the set of circuits whose input length and depth are $\ell(\lambda)$ and $d(\lambda)$, respectively. In order to prove Ada-IND security for the resulting scheme, we need to be able to prove Ada-INDr security for the KP-ABE scheme BGG$^+$ for the same circuit class as stated in Theorem 4.1. This is possible by assuming subexponential hardness of LWE as we see in Theorem 2.10. The notable feature of the resulting scheme is that the sizes of the master public key, ciphertexts, and secret keys are independent from the size of the circuits supported by the scheme. The sizes of these parameters are only dependant on the input length and the depth of the circuits.

Summarizing the above discussion, we get the following theorem.

Theorem 5.1. *Assuming the subexponential hardness of LWE, we have a CP-ABE scheme for circuit class $\mathcal{C}_{\ell,d}$ for arbitrary $\ell = \mathrm{poly}(\lambda)$ and $d = O(\log \lambda)$ that satisfies Ada-IND security in the bilinear generic group model. The sizes of the master public key, ciphertexts, and secret keys are bounded by $\mathrm{poly}(\lambda, \ell, d)$.*

We note that in all previous CP-ABE scheme (e.g., [11,44,48]) for NC_1, either the ciphertext or secret key size depends on the circuit size supported by the scheme.

5.2   New BE Scheme with Optimal Parameter Size

Here, we show that we can obtain a BE scheme with optimal parameter size by setting the circuit class $\mathcal{F}$ supported by the CP-ABE scheme in Sect. 3 appropriately.

Obtaining DBE from KP-ABE. In order to get the BE scheme, we first observe that we can implement a DBE scheme by a KP-ABE scheme for the following circuit class $\mathcal{F}_{BE}$ defined as $\mathcal{F}_{BE} = \left\{ F_S : \{0,1\}^{\lceil \log N \rceil} \to \{0,1\} \right\}_{S \subseteq [N]}$

where $F_S(i) = \begin{cases} 1 & \text{if } i \in S \\ 0 & \text{if } i \notin S \end{cases}$. Here, we identify a user index $i \in [N]$ and elements

in S with binary strings in $\{0,1\}^{\lceil \log N \rceil}$ by a natural bijection map between $\{0,1\}^{\lceil \log N \rceil}$ and $[2^{\lceil \log N \rceil}] \supseteq [N]$. Since the depth of F_S affects the efficiency of the DBE scheme, we want F_S to be as shallow as possible. For this purpose, we compute F_S by first computing $b_j := (i \overset{?}{=} j)$ for all $j \in S$ *in parallel* and then computing $\vee_{j \in S} b_j$. The first step can be implemented with depth $O(\log \log N)$ and the second step with $O(\log N)$. This allows us to implement F_S with depth $O(\log |S|) \le O(\log N)$. By the definition of F_S, one can see that this KP-ABE scheme implements the functionality of DBE.

Plugging the DBE into Our Construction in Sect. 3. We then instantiate the KP-ABE for the circuit class $\mathcal{F}_{\mathsf{BE}}$ with BGG^+ and plug this scheme into our CP-ABE construction in Sect. 3. Since the ciphertext and key attributes of the CP-ABE scheme are swapped from the underlying KP-ABE scheme, we obtain a BE scheme as a result. This instantiation is possible since the depth of the circuits is bounded by $O(\log N) \leq O(\log \lambda)$ and we can take the upper bound on the depth $d(\lambda)$ to be larger than this. The sizes of the master public key, ciphertexts, and secret keys in the resulting BE scheme are bounded by $\mathrm{poly}(\log N, \lambda) = \mathrm{poly}(\lambda)$, which is independent of the number of users, since the depth and input length of the circuits in $\mathcal{F}_{\mathsf{BE}}$ is bounded by $O(\log N)$. Note that we crucially rely on the efficiency property of our CP-ABE scheme that the sizes of all parameters in the system are independent of the size of the circuits being supported, where the latter can be as large as $O(N)$ for $\mathcal{F}_{\mathsf{BE}}$.

Security of the Resulting BE Scheme. In order for the resulting BE scheme to have Ada-IND security, we need the underlying KP-ABE scheme BGG^+ to have Ada-INDr security as stated in Theorem 4.1. In the general case where the input length for the circuits is of $\mathrm{poly}(\lambda)$, we need to assume subexponential hardness of LWE to prove Ada-INDr security for BGG^+ as we see in Theorem 2.10. However, since we restrict the circuit class for BGG^+ to be $\mathcal{F}_{\mathsf{BE}}$ here, we can avoid assuming subexponential hardness of LWE and base the security of our scheme on polynomial hardness of LWE. To see this, we first recall that for proving Sel-INDr security for BGG^+, polynomial hardness of LWE is enough (Theorem 2.10). We then observe that in the special case of DBE, Sel-INDr and Ada-INDr are actually equivalent, since one can guess the target attribute $i^\star \in [N]$ chosen by the adversary in the security game with only polynomial security loss.

Summarizing the above discussion, we get the following theorem.

Theorem 5.2. *Assuming the LWE assumption, we have a BE scheme that satisfies* Ada-IND *security in the bilinear generic group model. The sizes of the master public key, ciphertexts, and secret keys are bounded by a fixed polynomial* $\mathrm{poly}(\lambda)$ *that is independent of* N.

In the full version of our paper [5], we show that we can obtain an IBBE scheme with optimal parameter size by setting the circuit class $\mathcal{F}$ supported by the CP-ABE scheme in Sect. 3 appropriately.

Acknowledgement. We thank anonymous reviewers for helpful comments. Shota Yamada is supported by JST CREST Grant Number JPMJCR19F6 and JSPS KAKENHI Grant Number 16K16068.

References

1. Agrawal, S.: Stronger security for reusable garbled circuits, general definitions and attacks. In: Katz, J., Shacham, H. (eds.) CRYPTO 2017. LNCS, vol. 10401, pp. 3–35. Springer, Cham (2017). https://doi.org/10.1007/978-3-319-63688-7_1

2. Agrawal, S.: Indistinguishability obfuscation without multilinear maps: new methods for bootstrapping and instantiation. In: Ishai, Y., Rijmen, V. (eds.) EUROCRYPT 2019. LNCS, vol. 11476, pp. 191–225. Springer, Cham (2019). https://doi.org/10.1007/978-3-030-17653-2_7

3. Agrawal, S., Boneh, D., Boyen, X.: Efficient lattice (H)IBE in the standard model. In: Gilbert, H. (ed.) EUROCRYPT 2010. LNCS, vol. 6110, pp. 553–572. Springer, Heidelberg (2010). https://doi.org/10.1007/978-3-642-13190-5_28

4. Agrawal, S., Boneh, D., Boyen, X.: Lattice basis delegation in fixed dimension and shorter-ciphertext hierarchical IBE. In: Rabin, T. (ed.) CRYPTO 2010. LNCS, vol. 6223, pp. 98–115. Springer, Heidelberg (2010). https://doi.org/10.1007/978-3-642-14623-7_6

5. Agrawal, S., Yamada, S.: Optimal broadcast encryption from pairings and LWE. Eprint 2020/228

6. Ananth, P., Jain, A., Lin, H., Matt, C., Sahai, A.: Indistinguishability obfuscation without multilinear maps: IO from LWE, bilinear maps, and weak pseudorandomness. In: Crypto (2019)

7. Apon, D., Döttling, N., Garg, S., Mukherjee, P.: Cryptanalysis of indistinguishability obfuscations of circuits over GGH13. Eprint 2016 (2016)

8. Attrapadung, N., Libert, B.: Functional encryption for inner product: achieving constant-size ciphertexts with adaptive security or support for negation. In: Nguyen, P.Q., Pointcheval, D. (eds.) PKC 2010. LNCS, vol. 6056, pp. 384–402. Springer, Heidelberg (2010). https://doi.org/10.1007/978-3-642-13013-7_23

9. Baltico, C.E.Z., Catalano, D., Fiore, D., Gay, R.: Practical functional encryption for quadratic functions with applications to predicate encryption. In: Katz, J., Shacham, H. (eds.) CRYPTO 2017. LNCS, vol. 10401, pp. 67–98. Springer, Cham (2017). https://doi.org/10.1007/978-3-319-63688-7_3

10. Barthe, G., Fagerholm, E., Fiore, D., Mitchell, J., Scedrov, A., Schmidt, B.: Automated analysis of cryptographic assumptions in generic group models. In: Garay, J.A., Gennaro, R. (eds.) CRYPTO 2014. LNCS, vol. 8616, pp. 95–112. Springer, Heidelberg (2014). https://doi.org/10.1007/978-3-662-44371-2_6

11. Bethencourt, J., Sahai, A., Waters, B.: Ciphertext-policy attribute-based encryption. In: IEEE Symposium on Security and Privacy, pp. 321–334 (2007)

12. Boneh, D., et al.: Fully key-homomorphic encryption, arithmetic circuit ABE and compact garbled circuits. In: Nguyen, P.Q., Oswald, E. (eds.) EUROCRYPT 2014. LNCS, vol. 8441, pp. 533–556. Springer, Heidelberg (2014). https://doi.org/10.1007/978-3-642-55220-5_30

13. Boneh, D., Gentry, C., Waters, B.: Collusion resistant broadcast encryption with short ciphertexts and private keys. In: Shoup, V. (ed.) CRYPTO 2005. LNCS, vol. 3621, pp. 258–275. Springer, Heidelberg (2005). https://doi.org/10.1007/11535218_16

14. Boneh, D., Kim, S.: Single key CP-ABE. Personal Communication (2016)

15. Boneh, D., Waters, B., Zhandry, M.: Low overhead broadcast encryption from multilinear maps. In: Garay, J.A., Gennaro, R. (eds.) CRYPTO 2014. LNCS, vol. 8616, pp. 206–223. Springer, Heidelberg (2014). https://doi.org/10.1007/978-3-662-44371-2_12

16. Boneh, D., Zhandry, M.: Multiparty key exchange, efficient traitor tracing, and more from indistinguishability obfuscation. Algorithmica 79(4), 1233–1285 (2016). https://doi.org/10.1007/s00453-016-0242-8

17. Brakerski, Z.: Fully homomorphic encryption without modulus switching from classical GapSVP. In: Safavi-Naini, R., Canetti, R. (eds.) CRYPTO 2012. LNCS, vol. 7417, pp. 868–886. Springer, Heidelberg (2012). https://doi.org/10.1007/978-3-642-32009-5_50

18. Brakerski, Z., Gentry, C., Vaikuntanathan, V.: (Leveled) fully homomorphic encryption without bootstrapping. In: ITCS, pp. 309–325 (2012)

19. Brakerski, Z., Langlois, A., Peikert, C., Regev, O., Stehlé, D.: Classical hardness of learning with errors. In: Proceedings of the Forty-Fifth Annual ACM Symposium on Theory of Computing, STOC 2013. ACM (2013)

20. Brakerski, Z., Vaikuntanathan, V.: Efficient fully homomorphic encryption from (standard) LWE. In: FOCS (2011)

21. Brakerski, Z., Vaikuntanathan, V.: Lattice-inspired broadcast encryption and succinct ciphertext policy ABE. Personal communication (2020)

22. Cash, D., Hofheinz, D., Kiltz, E., Peikert, C.: Bonsai trees, or how to delegate a lattice basis. In: Gilbert, H. (ed.) EUROCRYPT 2010. LNCS, vol. 6110, pp. 523–552. Springer, Heidelberg (2010). https://doi.org/10.1007/978-3-642-13190-5_27

23. Cheon, J.H., Fouque, P.-A., Lee, C., Minaud, B., Ryu, H.: Cryptanalysis of the new CLT multilinear map over the integers. Eprint 2016/135

24. Cheon, J.H., Han, K., Lee, C., Ryu, H., Stehlé, D.: Cryptanalysis of the multilinear map over the integers. In: Oswald, E., Fischlin, M. (eds.) EUROCRYPT 2015. LNCS, vol. 9056, pp. 3–12. Springer, Heidelberg (2015). https://doi.org/10.1007/978-3-662-46800-5_1

25. Cheon, J.H., Jeong, J., Lee, C.: An algorithm for NTRU problems and cryptanalysis of the GGH multilinear map without a low level encoding of zero. Eprint 2016/139

26. Coron, J.-S., et al.: Zeroizing without low-level zeroes: new MMAP attacks and their limitations. In: Gennaro, R., Robshaw, M. (eds.) CRYPTO 2015. LNCS, vol. 9215, pp. 247–266. Springer, Heidelberg (2015). https://doi.org/10.1007/978-3-662-47989-6_12

27. Coron, J.-S., Lee, M.S., Lepoint, T., Tibouchi, M.: Zeroizing attacks on indistinguishability obfuscation over CLT13. In: Fehr, S. (ed.) PKC 2017. LNCS, vol. 10174, pp. 41–58. Springer, Heidelberg (2017). https://doi.org/10.1007/978-3-662-54365-8_3

28. Delerablée, C.: Identity-based broadcast encryption with constant size ciphertexts and private keys. In: Kurosawa, K. (ed.) ASIACRYPT 2007. LNCS, vol. 4833, pp. 200–215. Springer, Heidelberg (2007). https://doi.org/10.1007/978-3-540-76900-2_12

29. Delerablée, C., Paillier, P., Pointcheval, D.: Fully collusion secure dynamic broadcast encryption with constant-size ciphertexts or decryption keys. In: Takagi, T., Okamoto, T., Okamoto, E., Okamoto, T. (eds.) Pairing 2007. LNCS, vol. 4575, pp. 39–59. Springer, Heidelberg (2007). https://doi.org/10.1007/978-3-540-73489-5_4

30. Fiat, A., Naor, M.: Broadcast encryption. In: Stinson, D.R. (ed.) CRYPTO 1993. LNCS, vol. 773, pp. 480–491. Springer, Heidelberg (1994). https://doi.org/10.1007/3-540-48329-2_40

31. Garg, S., Gentry, C., Halevi, S., Raykova, M., Sahai, A., Waters, B.: Candidate indistinguishability obfuscation and functional encryption for all circuits. In: FOCS (2013). http://eprint.iacr.org/

32. Gentry, C., Peikert, C., Vaikuntanathan, V.: Trapdoors for hard lattices and new cryptographic constructions. In: STOC, pp. 197–206 (2008)

33. Gentry, C., Waters, B.: Adaptive security in broadcast encryption systems (with short ciphertexts). In: Joux, A. (ed.) EUROCRYPT 2009. LNCS, vol. 5479, pp. 171–188. Springer, Heidelberg (2009). https://doi.org/10.1007/978-3-642-01001-9_10

34. Gorbunov, S., Vaikuntanathan, V., Wee, H.: Attribute based encryption for circuits. In: STOC (2013)

35. Gorbunov, S., Vinayagamurthy, D.: Riding on asymmetry: efficient abe for branching programs. In: Iwata, T., Cheon, J.H. (eds.) ASIACRYPT 2015. LNCS, vol. 9452, pp. 550–574. Springer, Heidelberg (2015). https://doi.org/10.1007/978-3-662-48797-6_23

36. Goyal, R., Quach, W., Waters, B., Wichs, D.: Broadcast and trace with N^ε ciphertext size from standard assumptions. In: Boldyreva, A., Micciancio, D. (eds.) CRYPTO 2019. LNCS, vol. 11694, pp. 826–855. Springer, Cham (2019). https://doi.org/10.1007/978-3-030-26954-8_27. https://eprint.iacr.org/2019/636

37. He, K., Weng, J., Liu, J.-N., Liu, J.K., Liu, W., Deng, R.H.: Anonymous identity-based broadcast encryption with chosen-ciphertext security. In: Proceedings of the 11th ACM on Asia Conference on Computer and Communications Security, ASIA CCS 2016 (2016)

38. Hu, Y., Jia, H.: Cryptanalysis of GGH map. Cryptology ePrint Archive: Report 2015/301 (2015)

39. Jain, A., Lin, H., Sahai, A.: Simplifying constructions and assumptions for $i\mathcal{O}$. Cryptology ePrint Archive, Report 2019/1252 (2019). https://eprint.iacr.org/2019/1252

40. Maurer, U.: Abstract models of computation in cryptography In: Smart, N.P. (ed.) Cryptography and Coding 2005. LNCS, vol. 3796, pp. 1–12. Springer, Heidelberg (2005). https://doi.org/10.1007/11586821_1

41. Micciancio, D., Peikert, C.: Trapdoors for lattices: simpler, tighter, faster, smaller. In: Pointcheval, D., Johansson, T. (eds.) EUROCRYPT 2012. LNCS, vol. 7237, pp. 700–718. Springer, Heidelberg (2012). https://doi.org/10.1007/978-3-642-29011-4_41

42. Miles, E., Sahai, A., Zhandry, M.: Annihilation attacks for multilinear maps: cryptanalysis of indistinguishability obfuscation over GGH13. In: Robshaw, M., Katz, J. (eds.) CRYPTO 2016. LNCS, vol. 9815, pp. 629–658. Springer, Heidelberg (2016). https://doi.org/10.1007/978-3-662-53008-5_22

43. Regev, O.: On lattices, learning with errors, random linear codes, and cryptography. J. ACM **56**(6), 84–93 (2009). Extended abstract in STOC 2005

44. Rouselakis, Y., Waters, B.: Practical constructions and new proof methods for large universe attribute-based encryption. In: ACM-CCS, pp. 463–474 (2013)

45. Sakai, R., Furukawa, J.: Identity-based broadcast encryption. IACR Cryptology ePrint Archive (2007)

46. Shoup, V.: Lower bounds for discrete logarithms and related problems. In: Fumy, W. (ed.) EUROCRYPT 1997. LNCS, vol. 1233, pp. 256–266. Springer, Heidelberg (1997). https://doi.org/10.1007/3-540-69053-0_18

47. Tsabary, R.: Fully secure attribute-based encryption for t-CNF from LWE. In: Boldyreva, A., Micciancio, D. (eds.) CRYPTO 2019. LNCS, vol. 11692, pp. 62–85. Springer, Cham (2019). https://doi.org/10.1007/978-3-030-26948-7_3

48. Waters, B.: Ciphertext-policy attribute-based encryption: an expressive, efficient, and provably secure realization. In: Catalano, D., Fazio, N., Gennaro, R., Nicolosi, A. (eds.) PKC 2011. LNCS, vol. 6571, pp. 53–70. Springer, Heidelberg (2011). https://doi.org/10.1007/978-3-642-19379-8_4

Private Information Retrieval
with Sublinear Online Time

Henry Corrigan-Gibbs[1,2,3]([✉]) and Dmitry Kogan[1]([✉])

[1] Stanford University, Stanford, CA, USA
dkogan@cs.stanford.edu
[2] EFPL, Lausanne, Switzerland
[3] MIT CSAIL, Cambridge, MA, USA
henrycg@csail.mit.edu

Abstract. We present the first protocols for private information retrieval that allow fast (sublinear-time) database lookups without increasing the server-side storage requirements. To achieve these efficiency goals, our protocols work in an offline/online model. In an *offline* phase, which takes place before the client has decided which database bit it wants to read, the client fetches a short string from the servers. In a subsequent *online* phase, the client can privately retrieve its desired bit of the database by making a second query to the servers. By pushing the bulk of the server-side computation into the offline phase (which is independent of the client's query), our protocols allow the online phase to complete very quickly—in time sublinear in the size of the database. Our protocols can provide statistical security in the two-server setting and computational security in the single-server setting. Finally, we prove that, in this model, our protocols are optimal in terms of the trade-off they achieve between communication and running time.

1 Introduction

A private information retrieval protocol [CGKS95, CGKS98] takes place between a client, holding an index $i \in [n]$, and a database server, holding a string $x = x_1 x_2 \cdots x_n \in \{0,1\}^n$. The protocol allows the client to fetch its desired bit $x_i \in \{0,1\}$ from the database while hiding the client's index i from the server, and using total communication that is sublinear in the database size n. A beautiful line of work, starting with that of Chor, Goldreich, Kushilevitz, and Sudan [CGKS95], constructs private information retrieval (PIR) protocols with extremely small communication complexity, either when the client can access multiple non-colluding servers holding replicas of the database [Amb97, CG97, BI01, BIKR02, Yek08, Efr12, DG16] or under computational assumptions [KO97, CMS99, KO00, GR05, OS07].

The full version of this paper is available at https://eprint.iacr.org/2019/1075.

A. Canteaut and Y. Ishai (Eds.): EUROCRYPT 2020, LNCS 12105, pp. 44–75, 2020.
https://doi.org/10.1007/978-3-030-45721-1_3

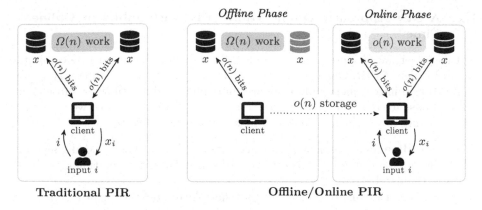

Fig. 1. A comparison of traditional two-server PIR (left) and offline/online PIR with sublinear online time (right). The servers store replicas of a database $x \in \{0,1\}^n$.

PIR is a fundamental privacy-preserving primitive: it has applications to private messaging [SCM05, AS16, ACLS18], certificate transparency [LG15], private media browsing [GCM+16], online anonymity [MOT+11, KLDF16], privacy-preserving ad targeting [Jue01], and more. In spite of the promise of PIR and the great advances in PIR protocols, there have been essentially no large-scale deployments of PIR technology to date. A primary reason is that while modern PIR protocols have very small *communication* requirements—as small as polylogarithmic in the database size—the *computational* burden they put on the server is still prohibitively expensive.

In particular, in all existing PIR schemes, the work at the servers grows linearly with the database size. That is, the servers essentially take a linear scan over the entire database to respond to each query. Beimel et al. [BIM04] proved that this limitation is in fact inherent: even in the multi-server setting, every secure PIR scheme on an n-bit database must incur $\Omega(n)$ total server-side work. (If the servers probe fewer than n database bits on average in responding to a client's query, then it is likely that the client is reading one of the probed bits.)

This $\Omega(n)$ server-side cost is the major bottleneck for PIR schemes *in theory*, since all other costs in today's PIR protocols (communication, client time, etc.) are sublinear, or even polylogarithmic, in the database size. This $\Omega(n)$ server-side cost is also the major bottleneck for PIR schemes *in practice*, as evidenced by the many heroic efforts to reduce the server-side computational cost in built PIR systems [LG15, AS16, GCM+16, TDG16, ACLS18].

In Sect. 1.4, we survey the known approaches to reducing the server-side computation in PIR-like schemes. All of these methods increase the storage requirements at the servers and the methods based on standard assumptions (i.e., not requiring obfuscation) increase the required server storage by potentially large polynomial factors. These increased storage costs present new barriers to deployment.

1.1   A New Approach: Offline/Online PIR with Sublinear Online Time

In this paper, we propose a new approach for reducing the server-side computational burden of PIR. Our idea is to push the (necessary) linear-time server-side computation into a query-independent offline phase, which allows a subsequent online phase to complete in sublinear time (Fig. 1). More precisely, we construct PIR schemes in which the client and servers interact in two phases:

- In an **offline** phase, which takes place *before* the client has decided which bit of the database it wants to retrieve, the client fetches a one-time-use "hint" from the database servers.
- In a subsequent **online** phase, which takes place *after* the client has decided which bit of the database it wants to retrieve, the client sends a query to the database servers. Given the servers' answers to this query, along with the hint prefetched earlier, the client can recover its database bit of interest.

Prior work has developed PIR offline/online schemes [DIO01, BIM04, BLW17, PPY18]. In this paper, we construct the first offline/online PIR schemes that simultaneously:

1. run in online time *sublinear* in the database size, and
2. do not increase the storage requirements at the servers.

(See Sect. 1.4 and Table 1 for a comparison to prior work.) Furthermore, our schemes are based on very simple assumptions—one-way functions in the two-server setting and linearly homomorphic encryption in the single-server setting—and are concretely efficient. The remaining performance bottleneck of our schemes is that one of the servers must perform an amount of *offline* computation in that is *linear* in the database size.

Our schemes advance the state of the art in PIR by enabling two new usage models:

1. **Do the heavy computation in advance.** Our schemes shift the heavy server-side computation out of the critical path of the client's request. For example, we envision deployments of our PIR schemes in which the client and server execute the offline phase overnight, while the user is asleep and when computation is relatively inexpensive. In the morning, when the user wakes up and wants to, say, privately fetch an article from Wikipedia, she can run the online phase to get her article in sublinear time.

   The idea of moving expensive cryptographic work into an input-independent offline phase has seen tremendous success in the setting of multiparty computation [BDOZ11, DPSZ12]. Our schemes achieve the same goal for PIR.
2. **Process a series of queries in sublinear amortized *total* time.** Often, a user wants to make a series of adaptive queries to the same database (e.g., as one does when jumping from one Wikipedia article to the next). In this setting, our two-server PIR scheme allows the client to reuse a single hint, fetched in the offline phase, to make *arbitrarily many* adaptive online queries

to the database. By reusing the hint, the amortized *total* server-side cost of each query—including both the costs of the offline and online phases—falls to sublinear in the database size. As far as we know, ours is the first PIR scheme that achieves sublinear amortized total time for adaptive queries without dramatically increasing the client or servers' storage requirements.

1.2   Our Results

We give the following results for offline/online private information retrieval with sublinear online time:

Two-server PIR. We give a two server offline/online scheme with sublinear online time. Specifically, for a database consisting of n bits, the offline phase requires the client to interact with one server, which performs $\widetilde{O}(n)$ offline computation. (The notation $\widetilde{O}(\cdot)$ hides arbitrary polylogarithmic factors. In this section, we also elide fixed polynomials in the security parameter.) In the online phase, the client interacts with the second server, which answers the client's query in time $\widetilde{O}(\sqrt{n})$. We give a scheme with statistical security that has total communication $\widetilde{O}(\sqrt{n})$. Assuming that one-way functions exist, the online communication cost falls to $O(\log n)$.

Two-server PIR with sublinear amortized *total* time. We extend our two-server scheme to allow the client to reuse a *single* offline-phase interaction to make a series of polynomially many adaptive online-phase queries. With this scheme, the online cost of each query is still $\widetilde{O}(\sqrt{n})$, but after q online queries, the average *total* computational cost—including the offline-phase computation—falls to $\widetilde{O}(n/q + \sqrt{n})$, or sublinear in the database size.

Single-server PIR. We show how to combine a linearly homomorphic encryption scheme and a standard single-server PIR scheme to obtain a single-server offline/online PIR scheme with sublinear online time. The resulting scheme uses $\widetilde{O}(n^{2/3})$ total communication and the server runs in online time $\widetilde{O}(n^{2/3})$. Furthermore, neither the client nor the server performs any public-key cryptographic operations in the online phase. Under the stronger assumption that fully homomorphic encryption exists, we obtain a single-server scheme with communication and online time $\widetilde{O}(\sqrt{n})$. One drawback is that, unlike its two-server counterpart, our single-server scheme supports only a single online query after each offline interaction, and thus we do not achieve sublinear amortized *total* time. The main benefit of shifting the heavy server-side computation to the offline phase remains.

A lower bound. Finally, we prove a lower bound for offline/online PIR schemes in which the servers store the database in unencoded form and keep no additional state. Specifically, we show that any scheme of this form, that uses C bits of communication in the offline phase, and that probes T bits of the database in the online phase, must satisfy $C \cdot T \geq \widetilde{\Omega}(n)$. This shows that in this model, as far as communication and online server time are concerned, our two-server scheme and the FHE-based single-server scheme are optimal, up to logarithmic factors.

1.3   Limitations

The primary drawback of our new PIR protocols is that they use more total communication than standard PIR schemes do. Today's PIR schemes (with *linear* online server-side time) can achieve polylogarithmic communication in the computational setting [CMS99, GR05, IP07, BGI16, DGI+19] and subpolynomial communication ($n^{O(\sqrt{\log \log n/ \log n})}$) in the two-server information-theoretic setting [DG16]. In contrast, our schemes with sublinear online time have communication $\widetilde{\Omega}_\lambda(\sqrt{n})$. While we show that it is possible to reduce the *online-phase* communication in the computational setting, our lower bound (Theorem 23) implies that any offline/online PIR scheme with online time $\widetilde{O}(\sqrt{n})$—such as ours—must have $\widetilde{\Omega}(\sqrt{n})$ *total* communication. This limitation is therefore inherent to PIR schemes that have sublinear online server time and in which the servers store the database in unmodified form.

In many settings, we expect that the $\sqrt{n}$ communication cost will be acceptable. Indeed, a number of built systems using PIR [GDL+14, GCM+16, AMBFK16, ACLS18] already suffice with $\sqrt{n}$ communication complexity, since server-side computational cost is the limiting factor. If $\sqrt{n}$ communication is still too high, we show in Corollary 18 that it is possible to amortize the $\sqrt{n}$ offline communication cost of our two-server scheme over polynomially many online reads, each of which requires only *logarithmic* communication. So, our results are still relevant to communication-sensitive settings, when having low amortized complexity is sufficient.

1.4   Related Work

Beimel, Ishai, and Malkin [BIM04] proved that the servers in any secure PIR scheme must collectively probe all n bits of the database (on average) to respond to a client's query. We survey the existing strategies for eliminating this key performance bottleneck.

Store the database in encoded form. One ingenious way to circumvent the $\Omega(n)$-server-time lower bound is to have the servers store the database in encoded form. Beimel et al. [BIM04] introduced the notion of *PIR with preprocessing*, in which the servers perform a *one-time* preprocessing of the database $x \in \{0, 1\}^n$ and store the database in encoded form $E(x) \in \{0, 1\}^N$, where E is a public encoding function and $N \gg n$. In the two-server setting, their PIR schemes with preprocessing achieve $n^{1/2+\epsilon}$ total communication and $n^{1/2+\epsilon}$ server-side time, for any $\epsilon > 0$. The downside of this approach is that the server-side encoding can be quite large. For example, to achieve $n^{0.6}$ server-side time and communication using their two-server scheme requires the server to store an encoded database of size $N = n^{3.2}$. Even for modest database sizes (e.g., $n \approx 2^{20}$), the encoded database would be much too large to materialize in practice (many petabytes). While it would be fascinating to construct improved schemes for two-server PIR with preprocessing—perhaps with encoding size $N = 10n$ and online time and communication $n^{1/3}$—this goal appears far out of reach.

Table 1. A comparison of PIR schemes when cast into the offline/online model, on database size n, in which each client makes q adaptive online queries, and in which m clients execute the offline phase before the first client executes the online phase.

- The offline and online costs are *per-query* costs. Thus, if a scheme has a offline phase of server cost n, which can be reused over q online queries, we write its per-query offline cost as n/q.
- If a scheme has a *one-time* offline phase that can be reused for an unbounded number of clients and queries (as in [BIM04, BIPW17]), we view the scheme as having zero offline cost.
- The extra storage cost is the number of bits, in addition to the database, that client and server must hold between the offline and online phases.

All columns omit poly(λ) factors, for security parameter λ, and also low-order polylog(n) factors. Here, $\epsilon > 0$ is an arbitrarily small constant and c refers to some constant in $\mathbb{N}$.

		Offline			Online			Extra storage	
		Time		Comm.	Time		Comm.		
	Assumption	Client	Server		Client	Server		Client	Server
Two-server									
[DG16]	None	0	0	0	$n^{o(1)}$	n	$n^{o(1)}$	0	0
[BGI16]	OWF	0	0	0	$\log n$	n	$\log n$	0	0
[BLW17]*	LWE	$\log n$	n	$\log n$	$\log n$	n	$\log n$	$\log n$	0
[BIM04]	None	0	0	0	$n^{0.9}$ $n^{0.6}$ $n^{0.55}$	$n^{0.9}$ $n^{0.6}$ $n^{0.55}$	$n^{0.9}$ $n^{0.6}$ $n^{0.55}$	0	$n^{1.27}$ $n^{3.2}$ $n^{37.7}$
[PR93]	None	n	n	n	$\log n$	n	n	0	0
[DIO01]†	OWF	0	n	0	$\log n$	$\log n$	$\log n$	0	mn
Thm. 11	None	$n^{1/2}$	n	$n^{1/2}$	$n^{1/2}$	$n^{1/2}$	$n^{1/2}$	$n^{1/2}$	0
Thm. 14	OWF	$n^{1/2}$	n	$n^{1/2}$	$n^{1/2}$	$n^{1/2}$	$\log n$	$n^{1/2}$	0
Thm. 17	OWF	$\frac{n^{1/2}}{q}$	n/q	$\frac{n^{1/2}}{q}$	$n^{1/2}$	$n^{1/2}$	$n^{1/2}$	$n^{1/2}$	0
Single-server									
[KO97]	Lin. hom. enc.	0	0	0	n^ϵ	n	n^ϵ	0	0
[CMS99]	ϕ-hiding	0	0	0	$\log^c n$	n	$\log^c n$	0	0
[Lip05]	DCR	0	0	0	$\log^c n$	n	$\log^2 n$	0	0
[Lip09]‡	Lin. hom. enc.	0	0	0	$\log n$	n	$\log n$	0	n
[PPY18]‡	Any PIR	n/q	n/q	n/q	n	n	n	$n^{1/2}$	0
[BIPW17]	OLDC	n/q	n/q	n/q	n^ϵ	n^ϵ	n^ϵ	c	mn
[CHR17]	OLDC	n/q	n/q	n/q	n^ϵ	n^ϵ	n^ϵ	c	mn
[BIPW17]§	OLDC+**VBB Obf.**	0	0	0	n^ϵ	n^ϵ	n^ϵ	0	n
Thm. 20	Lin. hom. enc.	$n^{2/3}$	n	$n^{2/3}$	$n^{2/3}$	$n^{2/3}$	$n^{1/3}$	$n^{2/3}$	0
Thm. 22	FHE	$n^{1/2}$	n	$n^{1/2}$	$n^{1/2}$	$n^{1/2}$	$n^{1/2}$	$n^{1/2}$	0
Lower bound (For any $1 \leq \beta \leq n$.)									
[BIM04]		–	n/β	–	–	–	–	–	β
Thm. 23		–	–	n/β	–	β	–	–	0¶

* Based on constrained PRFs, which initially required multilinear maps, but later constructed from standard assumptions [BKM17, CC17, BTVW17].

† A scheme combining ideas from [DIO01, BIM04, BGI16] can acheive these parameters [Ish19].

‡ Requires only a sublinear number of public-key operations.

§ Requires that a trustworthy party encodes the database using secret randomness.

¶ Our lower bound holds only for PIR schemes that store the database in its native form.

The schemes of Beimel et al. apply only to the multi-server setting. Two recent works [BIPW17, CHR17] study *doubly efficient PIR*, which are in some sense single-server PIR-with-preprocessing schemes. In the *designated-client* model of doubly efficient PIR, the client encodes the database using a long-term secret key (hidden from the server) and stores the encoded database on the server. Under a new cryptographic assumption, the client can subsequently privately query this encoded database many times, and the server can answer the query in time sublinear in the database size. In the *public-key* analogue of doubly efficient PIR, a server that stores a single database encoding enables multiple mutually distrusting clients to query the database using a short public key. Boyle et al. [BIPW17] construct a public-key doubly efficient PIR scheme with sublinear query time, under a new cryptographic assumption and in a model with virtual black-box obfuscation.

Hamlin et al. [HOWW18] introduce a notion of *private anonymous data access* ("PANDA") schemes, in which many clients can access an encoded database such that (1) as in standard PIR schemes, the server does not learn which bits of the database a client is reading and (2) the server can respond to a client's request in time sublinear—even polylogarithmic—in the database size. Unlike in doubly efficient PIR schemes, the server in PANDA may store mutable state. Hamlin et al. give an instantiation of a PANDA scheme from fully homomorphic encryption [Gen09]. A limitation of the existing PANDA schemes is that they require the server storage and time to grow with the number of malicious clients interacting with the system. In our setting, in which the number of malicious clients could be unbounded, the storage and online server time of a PANDA scheme would also be unbounded.

The general framework of PIR with preprocessing is extremely promising, since preprocessing schemes can plausibly allow both *polylogarithmic* total communication and total work—which is impossible in the offline/online setting. That said, these preprocessing schemes necessarily increase the storage costs at the servers, by large polynomial factors in many cases. The single-server preprocessing schemes additionally rely on relatively heavy cryptographic assumptions. In contrast, in our schemes, the servers store the database x in *unencoded* form and keep no additional state. The trade-off is that, in our schemes, the client and servers must run the linear-server-time offline phase *once per client* (Sect. 4) or *once per query* (Sects. 3 and 5).

Use *linear* additional storage *per query*. Beimel, Ishai, and Malkin [BIM04, Section 7.2], building on earlier work of Di Crescenzo, Ishai, and Ostrovsky [DIO98, DIO01], give an alternative way to reduce the server-side online time in PIR. In their model, the client submits a request to the servers in an offline phase. The servers use this request to generate a one-time-use n-bit encoding of the n-bit database, which the servers store. In a subsequent online phase, the client can privately query the servers for a database bit and the servers use their precomputed encoding to respond in sublinear online time. The total communication and online server-side work in these schemes can be as low as polylog(n) [Ish19]. However, the server-side storage costs can be large: for *each client*, the servers must store n additional bits until that client makes its online query. If m clients concurrently access the database, the storage requirements at the servers increase to mn bits. (In contrast, the schemes in our work require no extra server-side storage.)

Use *linear* online time. Another line of work reduces the server-side computational burden of PIR protocols by working in the offline/online model we consider. To our knowledge, all prior protocols in the offline/online model require *linear online time* at the servers.

Boneh, Lewi, and Wu [BLW17] show that "privately constrained PRFs" imply a two-server online/offline scheme in which only one of the servers needs to be active in the online phase. The scheme has polylogarithmic communication complexity, yet the online server's work is *linear* in the database size. Subsequent work [BKM17, CC17, BTVW17] constructs such PRFs from standard lattice assumptions.

Towards reducing the server's computation time in PIR protocols, Patel, Persiano, and Yeo [PPY18] introduce the notion of *private stateful information retrieval*. They give single-server schemes in which, after an offline phase, the client can privately retrieve a bit from the database while requiring the server to only perform a number of online public-key operations sublinear in the database size, along with a linear number of symmetric-key operations. The offline phase of their protocol requires the client to download a linear number of bits in the offline phase and the server must perform a linear number of total operations in the online phase. Their schemes do allow amortizing the linear-communication offline phase over multiple subsequent queries, although the online time is always linear. In contrast, our protocols have total communication and online time *sublinear* in the database size, even for a single query.

Demmler, Herzberg, and Schneider [DHS14] give a scheme which reduces the computational burden of each server by means of sharding the database. The combined work of all servers in their scheme is still linear.

Marginally sublinear online time. The original PIR paper [CGKS95] points out that a three-party communication protocol of Pudlák and Rödl [PR93, Theorem 3.5] yields a two-server PIR protocol. (See also the subsequent journal version [PRS97].) In particular, on an n-bit database, that protocol has total communication $\alpha(n) = O(n\frac{\log\log n}{\log n})$, or just slightly sublinear. Closer inspection of this protocol reveals that one of the two servers can additionally be made to run in *sublinear time* $\alpha(n)$, and thus this early scheme can be cast as an offline/online PIR scheme with just slightly sublinear offline communication. As far as we know, no prior work has drawn attention to this fact.

Lipmaa [Lip09] constructs a computational single-server PIR protocol with preprocessing. In its offline phase, the server encodes the database as a branching program with $(n + o(n))/\log n$ nodes, and stores the branching program, using $n + n/\operatorname{polylog}(n)$ bits. In the online phase, the server homomorphically evaluates the branching program, using a protocol of Ishai and Paskin [IP07], which requires $O(n/\log n)$ public key operations, or slightly sublinear in the database size. (The homomorphic ciphertexts must be no shorter than the security parameter $\lambda = \omega(\log n)$, and so, strictly speaking, the number of bit operations in the online phase is still linear. However, the running time is dominated by the public key operations.)

The complexity of these two protocols is much larger than ours but we still find it interesting to see such radically different ways to construct two-server PIR with sublinear online time.

Amortize work. It is also possible to improve the computational efficiency of PIR by having each PIR server jointly process a batch of queries. If a server can process a batch of Q queries to an n-bit database at $o(Qn)$ cost, processing queries in a batch yields sublinear amortized time per query at the server. This general strategy is fruitful both when the batched queries originate from the same client [IKOS04, Hen16, ACLS18] and from different clients [BIM04, IKOS06, LG15].

Our multi-query scheme of Sect. 4 similarly allows the client to amortize the server's linear-time offline computation over many queries—as in batch PIR. The difference is that our multi-query scheme allows the client to make its queries *adaptively* (one at a time), while batch-PIR schemes require the client to make all queries in a batch *non-adaptively* (all at once).

Relax the security property. One final approach to reducing the online server time in PIR is to aim for a weaker security property than standard cryptographic PIR schemes do. Toledo, Danezis, and Goldberg give PIR schemes with a differential-privacy-style notion of security and show that when some leakage of the client's query to the server is allowed, the servers can run in sublinear online time [TDG16].

1.5 Technical Overview

To illustrate our techniques, we start by presenting a simplified version of our two-server offline/online PIR scheme with statistical security. The online phase of this protocol runs in time $o(n)$, and the protocol's total communication is $o(n)$.

A toy protocol. Two servers hold a replica of the database $x \in \{0,1\}^n$. The two phases of the protocol proceed as follows:

Offline phase. This phase takes place before the client has decided which bit it wants to read from the database.

- The client divides the database indices $\{1, \ldots, n\}$ at random into $\sqrt{n}$ disjoint sets $(S_1, \ldots, S_{\sqrt{n}})$, each of size $\sqrt{n}$, and sends these sets to the first server. (Sending these sets explicitly would take $\Omega(n \log n)$ communication, which is too much. We explain later how to reduce the communication in this step.)
- The first server receives the sets $(S_1, \ldots, S_{\sqrt{n}})$ from the client. For each such set S_j, it computes the parity of the database bits indexed by the set. That is, for $j \in \{1, \ldots, \sqrt{n}\}$, the server computes the parity $h_j \leftarrow \sum_{i \in S_j} x_i \bmod 2$. The server sends these parity bits $(h_1, \ldots, h_{\sqrt{n}})$ to the client.
- The client stores the sets $(S_1, \ldots, S_{\sqrt{n}})$ and the parity bits $(h_1, \ldots, h_{\sqrt{n}})$.

Online phase. This phase begins once the client has decided on the index $i \in [n]$ of the bit it wants to read from the database.

- The client finds the set S_j that contains its desired index i. The client then removes a single item i^* from the set S_j, which it chooses as follows:
  - With probability $1 - (\sqrt{n} - 1)/n$ the client chooses $i^* \leftarrow i$.
  - With the remaining probability, the client chooses i^* randomly from the set of all other elements in S_j.
  The client then sends the set $S' \leftarrow S_j \setminus \{i^*\}$ to the second server.
- Upon receiving the set S' from the client, the second server computes and sends back to the client the parity of the database bits indexed by the set: $a \leftarrow \sum_{i \in S'} x_i \mod 2$. Computing the answer requires the second server to probe at most $|S'| = O(\sqrt{n})$ bits of the database, which allows the server to run in only $\widetilde{O}(\sqrt{n})$ time.
- Finally, when the client receives the answer from the second server, it recovers the value of the database bit x_{i^*} by computing $x_{i^*} \leftarrow h_j - a \mod 2$. Crucially, since the client has chosen i^* with a bias towards i, it recovers the value x_i of its bit of interest with high probability $1 - O(1/\sqrt{n})$. (By iterating the scheme λ times in parallel, the client can drive the failure probability down to at most $2^{-\lambda}$.)

With a bit of work, it is possible to show that the set S' that the client sends to the second server is a uniformly random subset of $[n]$ of size $\sqrt{n} - 1$. Thus, the values that both servers see are distributed independently of the index i that the client is trying to read.

The resulting scheme already achieves the main goal of interest: in the online phase, the server can respond to the client's query in time $O(\sqrt{n})$. However, the toy scheme also has two major shortcomings:

1. The communication in the *offline* phase is *super-linear*: sending the sets $(S_1, \ldots, S_{\sqrt{n}})$ to the first server requires $\Omega(n \log n)$ bits.
2. The scheme requires $\Theta(n \log n)$ bits of client storage between the offline phase and the online phase.

We can address both of these challenges at once by partially derandomizing the client. In the revised scheme, in the offline phase, the client chooses a *single* set $S \subseteq [n]$ of size $\sqrt{n}$. The client also sends to the server $\sqrt{n}$ random "shifts" $\Delta = \{\delta_1, \delta_2, \ldots, \delta_{\sqrt{n}}\} \in [n]$. The client and server then use S and Δ to construct a collection of $\sqrt{n}$ sets $(S_1, \ldots, S_{\sqrt{n}})$ by setting, for every $j \in \{1, \ldots, \sqrt{n}\}$, $S_j \leftarrow \{i + \delta_j \mid i \in S\}$. The client and the server then run the rest of the toy protocol using this collection of sets. This modification increases the failure probability, since there is now some chance that the client's desired index i will not be in any of the sets $(S_1, \ldots, S_{\sqrt{n}})$. Even so, the client and servers can repeat the protocol $O(\log n)$ times in parallel to drive down the failure probability.

This modifications reduces both the communication complexity of the offline phase and the amount of client storage and time to $\widetilde{O}(\sqrt{n})$. With some work, we can also argue that this modification preserves security.

Improvements to the toy scheme. While the above patched two-server scheme achieves all of our efficiency goals, it leaves a few things to be desired:

- *Reducing online communication with puncturable pseudorandom sets.* In the protocol sketched above, the communication in the online phase is $\Theta(\sqrt{n})$. Under the assumptions that one-way functions exist, we can reduce the online-phase communication to $\text{poly}(\lambda, \log n)$, for security parameter λ.

  To do so, we introduce a new tool, which we call a *puncturable pseudorandom set* (Sect. 2). Essentially, a puncturable pseudorandom set allows the client in the toy scheme above to send the server a compressed representation of the random set S, in the form of a short key k. Furthermore, the set key is "puncturable," in that for any $i^* \in S$, the client can produce a punctured set key k_{i^*} that is a compressed representation of $S \setminus \{i^*\}$. Crucially, the punctured key k_{i^*} also hides the identity of the removed element i^*.

  We construct a puncturable pseudorandom set from puncturable PRFs [BW13,KPTZ13,BGI14,SW14] (Theorem 3), which have simple constructions from pseudorandom generators. The keys in our construction have size $O(\lambda \log n)$ for sets of size $O(\sqrt{n})$ over a universe of size n and security parameter λ. Plugging this puncturable pseudorandom set construction into the toy scheme above reduces the communication complexity of the online phase to the length of a single punctured set key, plus the single bit answer, for $O(\lambda \log n)$ bits total.

- *Refreshing the client's state.* The client in the toy scheme can only use the results of the (computationally expensive) offline phase to read a *single* bit from the database. The following modification to the toy scheme allows the client to "refresh" the bits it downloads in the offline phase, so that it can reuse these bits for many online queries (Sect. 4).

  After the client makes a query for index $i \in [n]$ using set S_j, the client discards that set from its state. Now the client must somehow "refresh" its local state. Our observation is that the set S_j is a random size-$\sqrt{n}$ subset of $[n]$, conditioned on $i \in S_j$. The client refreshes its state by asking the first server for the parity of a random size-$(\sqrt{n} - 1)$ subset S' of $[n]$. Since the client already knows the value of x_i, it can compute and store the parity of the database bits in the set $S' \cup \{i\}$. (Ensuring that this refreshing process maintains security requires handling some technicalities.)

  Although this construction requires the client to use *independent* random sets $(S_1, \ldots, S_{\sqrt{n}})$, using puncturable pseudorandom sets the client can send to the offline server all of them using only $\tilde{O}(\sqrt{n})$ bits of communication.

- *From two servers to one.* Converting the two-server offline/online PIR scheme to a single-server one is conceptually simple. Say that in the offline phase of the two-server scheme, the client sends a query q to the first server and receives an answer a. To convert it into a single-server scheme, we have the client send an encryption $E(q)$ of its offline query to the server, and we have the server homomorphically compute and send back the encrypted answer $E(a)$. Since the server learns nothing about the offline query q, the online phase can proceed exactly as in the two-server scheme.

  With fully homomorphic encryption [Gen09], this transformation is straightforward and maintains the communication complexity of the original two-server scheme. We show in Theorem 20 that it is possible to execute these steps using the much lighter-weight tools of linearly homomorphic encryption and single-server PIR, with slightly worse communication efficiency and online time: $\widetilde{O}(n^{2/3}) \cdot \mathrm{poly}(\lambda)$, for security parameter λ.

- *Proving optimality.* Finally, we prove a lower bound on the offline communication and online time using a classic lower bound of Yao [Yao90]. In particular, we show (the full version of this work) that any offline/online PIR scheme with small offline communication and online time, and in which the servers store the database in unmodified form, implies a good solution to "Yao's Box Problem." We then apply a preexisting time/space lower bound against algorithms for Yao's Box Problem to complete the lower bound (Theorem 23).

1.6 Notation

We use $\mathbb{N}$ to denote the set of positive integers. For an integer $n \in \mathbb{N}$, $[n]$ denotes the set $\{1, 2, \ldots, n\}$ and 1^n denotes the all-ones binary string of length n. For $n \in \mathbb{N}$ and $s \in [n]$, an s-subset of $[n]$ is a subset of size exactly s, and $\binom{[n]}{s}$ denotes the set of all s-subsets of $[n]$. Logarithms are taken to the base 2. We ignore integrality concerns and treat expressions like $\sqrt{n}$, $\log n$, and m/n as integers.

The expression $\mathrm{poly}(\cdot)$ refers to a fixed (unspecified) polynomial in its parameter. The notation $\widetilde{O}(\cdot)$ hides arbitrary polylogarithmic factors, i.e., $f(n) = \widetilde{O}(g(n))$ if $f(n) = O(g(n)) \cdot \mathrm{poly}(\log n)$. The notation $O_\lambda(\cdot)$ hides arbitrary polynomial factors in (the security parameter) λ, i.e., $f(n, \lambda) = O_\lambda(g(n))$ if $f(n, \lambda) = O(g(n)) \cdot \mathrm{poly}(\lambda)$.

For a finite set S, the notation $x \xleftarrow{\mathrm{R}} S$ refers to choosing x independently and uniformly at random from the set S. For a distribution $\mathcal{D}$ over a set S, the notation $x \xleftarrow{\mathrm{R}} \mathcal{D}$ refers to choosing $x \in S$ according to distribution $\mathcal{D}$. For $p \in [0, 1]$, the notation $b \xleftarrow{\mathrm{R}} \mathrm{Bernoulli}(p)$ refers to choosing the bit b to be '1' with probability p and '0' with probability $1 - p$.

We use the RAM model of computation with the size of the word logarithmic in the input length and linear in the security parameter. To avoid dependence on the specifics of the computational model, we usually specify running times up to polylogarithmic factors. Throughout this text, an efficient algorithm is a probabilistic polynomial time algorithm. Furthermore, we allow all adversaries to be non-uniform. (Though this is not fundamental, and, with appropriate modifications in the security games, the results hold also in the uniform setting.)

We say that a pseudorandom generator (PRG) or pseudorandom permutation (PRP) is ϵ-secure if no efficient adversary can distinguish the PRG or PRP from random with advantage better than $\epsilon(\lambda)$, on security parameter λ.

2 Puncturable Pseudorandom Sets

In this section, we introduce a new cryptographic primitive called *puncturable pseudorandom sets* and give few natural constructions. Puncturable pseudorandom sets are a key component of our PIR schemes.

A puncturable pseudorandom set is very closely related to a puncturable pseudorandom function ("puncturable PRF") [BW13,KPTZ13,BGI14,SW14, HKW15]. To explain the difference by analogy: a PRF key is a compressed representation of a function $f : [n] \rightarrow [n]$, and a PRF key punctured at point $x^* \in [n]$ allows its holder to evaluate f at every point in $[n]$ except at the punctured point x^*. The punctured key should reveal nothing about the value of $f(x^*)$ to its holder. (The formal standard definition appears in the full version of this work.)

Analogously, the key for a *puncturable pseudorandom set* is a compressed representation of a pseudorandom set $S \subseteq [n]$. The set key punctured at element $x^* \in S$ allows its holder to recover all elements of S except the punctured element x^*. The punctured set key reveals nothing about x^* to its holder, apart from that fact that x^* is not one of the remaining elements in S.

2.1   Definitions

Let $s : \mathbb{N} \rightarrow \mathbb{N}$ be a function such that $s(n) \leq n$. A *puncturable pseudorandom set* with set size s consists of a key space $\mathcal{K}$, a punctured-key space $\mathcal{K}_\mathsf{p}$, and a triple of algorithms:

- $\mathsf{Gen}(1^\lambda, n) \rightarrow \mathsf{sk}$, a randomized algorithm that takes as input the security parameter $\lambda \in \mathbb{N}$, expressed in unary, and a universe size $n \in \mathbb{N}$, expressed in binary, and outputs a set key $\mathsf{sk} \in \mathcal{K}$,
- $\mathsf{Punc}(\mathsf{sk}, i) \rightarrow \mathsf{sk_p}$, a deterministic algorithm that takes in a key $\mathsf{sk} \in \mathcal{K}$ and an element $i \in [n]$, and outputs a punctured set key $\mathsf{sk_p} \in \mathcal{K}_\mathsf{p}$, and
- $\mathsf{Eval}(\mathsf{sk}) \rightarrow S$, a deterministic algorithm that takes in a key $\mathsf{sk} \in \mathcal{K} \cup \mathcal{K}_\mathsf{p}$ and outputs a description of a set $S \subseteq [n]$, written as $|S|$ strings of $\log n$ bits in length each.

A puncturable pseudorandom set must satisfy the following notions of *efficiency*, *correctness* and *security*.

Efficiency. For every security parameter $\lambda \in \mathbb{N}$ and universe size $n \in \mathbb{N}$, the routines Gen, Punc, and Eval run in time $s(n) \cdot \mathrm{poly}(\lambda, \log n)$, where $s(n)$ is the set size.

Correctness. For every $\lambda, n \in \mathbb{N}$, if one samples $\mathsf{sk} \leftarrow \mathsf{Gen}(1^\lambda, n)$ and computes $S \leftarrow \mathsf{Eval}(\mathsf{sk})$, it holds, with probability 1 over the randomness of Gen, that

1. $S \in \binom{[n]}{s(n)}$, where $\binom{[n]}{s(n)}$ denotes the set of all size-$s(n)$ subsets of $[n]$, and
2. for all $i \in S$, $\mathsf{Eval}(\mathsf{Punc}(\mathsf{sk}, i)) = S \setminus \{i\}$.

Security. Let Ψ be a puncturable pseudorandom set with set size $s \colon \mathbb{N} \rightarrow \mathbb{N}$. Let $W_{\lambda,n}$ be the event that adversary $\mathcal{A}$ wins in Game 1 with respect to Ψ, with security parameter λ and universe size n. Then we define $\mathcal{A}$'s guessing advantage as:

$$\mathsf{PSAdv}[\mathcal{A}, \Psi](\lambda, n) := \Pr[W_{\lambda,n}] - \frac{1}{n - s(n) + 1}. \tag{1}$$

A puncturable pseudorandom set Ψ is *computationally secure* if for every $\lambda \in \mathbb{N}$, every polynomially bounded $n = n(\lambda)$, and every non-uniform polynomial-time adversary $\mathcal{A}$, we have that $\mathsf{PSAdv}[\mathcal{A}, \Psi](\lambda, n) \leq \mathrm{negl}(\lambda)$. The puncturable pseudorandom set is ϵ-secure if that advantage is smaller than $\epsilon(\lambda, n)$. We say that Ψ is *perfectly secure* if for every $\lambda, n \in \mathbb{N}$ and for every (computationally unbounded) adversary $\mathcal{A}$, we have that $\mathsf{PSAdv}[\mathcal{A}, \Psi](\lambda, n) = 0$.

Game 1 (Puncturable pseudorandom set security). For $\lambda, n \in \mathbb{N}$, and a puncturable pseudorandom set $\Psi = (\mathsf{Gen}, \mathsf{Punc}, \mathsf{Eval})$, we define the following game, played between a challenger and an adversary:

- The challenger executes the following steps:
  - $\mathsf{sk} \leftarrow \mathsf{Gen}(1^\lambda, n)$
  - $S \leftarrow \mathsf{Eval}(\mathsf{sk})$
  - $x^* \xleftarrow{\mathrm{R}} S$
  - $\mathsf{sk_p} \leftarrow \mathsf{Punc}(\mathsf{sk}, x^*)$

  and sends 1^λ and $\mathsf{sk_p}$ to the adversary.
- The adversary outputs an integer $x' \in [n]$.

We say that the adversary "wins" if $x^* = x'$.

In the full version of this work, we show that this security property implies that the output of Eval on a random key is a pseudorandom set in $\binom{[n]}{s(n)}$.

Throughout this work, we often refer to puncturable pseudorandom sets as *puncturable pseudorandom sets* for brevity.

2.2 Constructions

Fact 2 (Perfectly secure puncturable pseudorandom set with linear-sized keys). *For any function $s : \mathbb{N} \to \mathbb{N}$ with $s(n) \leq n$, there is a perfectly secure puncturable pseudorandom set with set size s. Moreover, for universe size n, the set keys and punctured keys are both of length $(s(n) + O(1)) \log n$ bits.*

Proof. The set key is the description of a set $S \xleftarrow{\mathrm{R}} \binom{[n]}{s}$—written as s numbers, each of $\log n$ bits in length, along with a description of the universe size n. A punctured key is just this set of elements with the punctured element removed. $\square$

Theorem 3 (puncturable pseudorandom set with short keys from puncturable PRFs). *Suppose there exists an $\epsilon_{\mathcal{F}}$-secure puncturable PRF (we give the formal definition in the full version of this work) that, on security parameter λ and input-space size n, has keys of length $\kappa(\lambda, n)$ bits and punctured keys of length $\kappa_p(\lambda, n)$ bits. Then, there exists an ϵ-secure puncturable pseudorandom set with set size $\Theta(\sqrt{n})$ that, on security parameter λ and universe size n, has*

- *set keys of length $\kappa(\lambda, n) + O(\log n)$ bits and*
- *punctured keys of length $\kappa_p(\lambda, n) + O(\log n)$ bits, and*
- $\epsilon(\lambda, n) = \text{poly}(\lambda, n) \cdot (\epsilon_{\mathcal{F}} + 2^{-\lambda})$.

A puncturable pseudorandom set that proves the theorem appears in Construction 4. We prove security and correctness of the construction in the full version of this work.

Remark 4. The Gen routine in Construction 4 fails with negligible probability, and therefore, as presented, the construction has imperfect correctness. We can achieve perfect correctness by having the Eval and Punc routines treat sk = $\perp$ as some fixed set (e.g., the set $[s]$). Our security analysis accounts for this.

Construction 4 (Puncturable pseudorandom set from puncturable PRF).
Given a puncturable PRF $\mathcal{F} = (\text{PRFGen}, \text{PRFPunc}, \text{PRFEval})$, we construct a puncturable pseudorandom set $\Psi_{\mathcal{F}} = (\text{Gen}, \text{Punc}, \text{Eval})$ with set size $s(n) := \sqrt{n}/2$.

$\Psi_{\mathcal{F}}.\text{Gen}(1^\lambda, n) \to \text{sk}$

- Repeat at most λ times:
  - Sample k $\leftarrow$ PRFGen($1^\lambda, n$).
  - Compute $S \leftarrow \{\text{PRFEval}(k, 1), \text{PRFEval}(k, 2), \ldots, \text{PRFEval}(k, s(n))\}$.
  - If $|S| = s(n)$, halt and output sk $\leftarrow (n, k)$. output $\perp$.
- After running λ iterations of the loop unsuccessfully, output $\perp$.

$\Psi_{\mathcal{F}}.\text{Punc}(\text{sk}, i) \to \text{sk}_p$

- Parse the secret key as a pair (n, k).
- Find the least integer ℓ such that PRFEval(k, ℓ) = i.
  If no such ℓ exists, output $\perp$.
- Compute $k_p \leftarrow \text{PRFPunc}(k, \ell)$ and output $\text{sk}_p \leftarrow (n, k_p)$.

$\Psi_{\mathcal{F}}.\text{Eval}(\text{sk}) \to S$

- Parse the secret key as a pair (n, k).
- Output the set $S \leftarrow \{\text{PRFEval}(k, 1), \text{PRFEval}(k, 2), \ldots, \text{PRFEval}(k, s(n))\}$.
- (If k is punctured at some value, skip this value when computing S.)

Instantiating Theorem 3 with the puncturable PRF [BW13, KPTZ13, BGI14] based on the tree-based PRF of Goldreich, Goldwasser, and Micali [GGM86] leads to a very efficient puncturable pseudorandom set construction from pseudorandom generators. In the full version of this work, we prove the following:

Corollary 6. *Assuming that pseudorandom generators (PRGs) exist, there exists a secure puncturable pseudorandom set with set size $\Theta(\sqrt{n})$.*

In particular, for every ϵ_G-secure length-doubling PRG G, there exists an ϵ-secure puncturable pseudorandom set Ψ_G with set size $\sqrt{n/2}$, that has, for every security parameter $\lambda \in \mathbb{N}$ and universe size n,

- *set keys of $\lambda + O(\log n)$ bits in length,*
- *punctured keys of $O(\lambda \log n)$ bits in length, and*
- *$\epsilon(\lambda, n) \leq \text{poly}(\lambda, n) \cdot (\epsilon_G(\lambda) + 2^{-\lambda})$.*

A puncturable pseudorandom set with fast membership testing from PRPs. We say that a puncturable pseudorandom set Ψ on universe size n has a *fast membership test* if there exists an algorithm InSet that takes as input a set key sk and an element $i \in [n]$, runs in time $\text{poly}(\lambda, \log n)$, and outputs "1" if $i \in \Psi.\text{Eval}(\text{sk})$ and "0" otherwise. Crucially, the running time of the fast membership test must grow only with $\log n$, rather than linearly with the set size $s(n)$. The following is a construction of such a puncturable pseudorandom set. The proof appears in the full version of this work.

Theorem 7. *Suppose there exists an ϵ_P-secure pseudorandom permutation that, on security parameter λ and input-space size n, has keys of length $\kappa(\lambda, n)$ bits. Then, there exists an ϵ-secure puncturable pseudorandom set for any set size $s : \mathbb{N} \to \mathbb{N}$ that, on security parameter λ and universe size n, has*

- *set keys of length $\kappa(\lambda, n)$ bits,*
- *punctured keys of length $s \cdot O(\log n)$ bits,*
- *$\epsilon \leq \text{poly}(\lambda, n) \cdot \epsilon_P$, and*
- *a fast membership test.*

2.3 Shifting Puncturable Pseudorandom Sets

When using puncturable pseudorandom sets in this paper, we will want to equip them with two additional functionalities.

1. GenWith$(1^\lambda, n, i) \to$ sk is an algorithm that takes in $n \in \mathbb{N}$ and $i \in [n]$, and outputs a uniformly random puncturable pseudorandom set key sk for a $s(n)$-subset of $[n]$, subject to the constraint that $i \in \text{Eval}(\text{sk})$.
2. Shift$(\text{sk}, \delta) \to \text{sk}'$ is an algorithm that takes in a set key sk $\in \mathcal{K}$ and an integer $\delta \in [n]$, and outputs a set key sk$'$ such that $\text{Eval}(\text{sk}') = \{i + \delta \mid i \in \text{Eval}(\text{sk})\}$. (The addition $i + \delta$ is done modulo n, and we identify $0 \in \mathbb{Z}_n$ with $n \in [n]$.)

In the full version of this work, we show how to extend any puncturable pseudorandom set to efficiently support both these functionalities by including a shift $\Delta \in [n]$ with every key and interpreting every element i in the base set as $(i + \Delta) \mod n$ in the encompassing set. This transformation only increases the size of the puncturable set keys by an additive $O(\log n)$ term. Therefore, we subsequently assume without a loss of generality that every puncturable set is equipped with GenWith and Shift.

3   Two-Server PIR with Sublinear Online Time

We now formally define two-server offline/online PIR and construct such schemes that achieve sublinear online time and provide either statistical or computational security.

3.1   Definition

Informally, a two-server offline/online PIR scheme is a protocol between a client, an offline server, and an online server. Both servers have access to a database $x \in \{0, 1\}^n$. The PIR protocol proceeds in five steps:

1. First, the client uses the Setup algorithm to generate its own *client key* ck, along with a hint request q_h. The client sends the hint request q_h to the offline server. Crucially, the client can run the Setup algorithm *before* it has decided which bit of the database it wants to read.
2. The offline server feeds the hint request q_h and the database $x \in \{0, 1\}^n$ into the Hint algorithm, which generates a hint h that the offline server returns to the client.
3. Once the client has decided on the index $i \in [n]$ of the bit it wants to read from the database, it feeds its key ck and index i into the Query algorithm, which produces a query q. The client sends this query to the online server.
4. The online server feeds the client's query q into the Answer algorithm that is further given access to the database. (The focus is on schemes in which the Answer algorithm probes $o(n)$ bits of the database and run in time $o(n)$.) The online server then returns the answer a to the client.
5. The client feeds the hint h and the answer a into algorithm Reconstruct, which outputs the i-th bit of the database.

A *secure* offline/online PIR scheme should guarantee that neither server independently learns anything (in either a statistical or computational sense) about the client's private index i.

Definition 8 (Offline/online PIR). An offline/online PIR scheme is a tuple $\Pi = (\mathsf{Setup}, \mathsf{Hint}, \mathsf{Query}, \mathsf{Answer}, \mathsf{Reconstruct})$ of five efficient algorithms:

- $\mathsf{Setup}(1^\lambda, n) \to (\mathsf{ck}, q_h)$, a randomized algorithm that takes in security parameter λ and database length n and outputs a client key ck and a hint request q_h.
- $\mathsf{Hint}(x, q_h) \to h$, a deterministic algorithm that takes in a database $x \in \{0, 1\}^n$ and a hint request q_h and outputs a hint h,
- $\mathsf{Query}(\mathsf{ck}, i) \to q$, a randomized algorithm that takes in the client's key ck and an index $i \in [n]$, and outputs a query q,
- $\mathsf{Answer}^x(q) \to a$, a deterministic algorithm that takes as input a query q and gets access to an oracle that:
  - takes as input an index $j \in [n]$, and
  - returns the j-th bit of the database $x_j \in \{0, 1\}$,

outputs an answer string a, and

- Reconstruct$(h, a) \rightarrow x_i$, a deterministic algorithm that takes as a hint h and an answer a, and outputs a bit x_i.

Furthermore, the scheme Π must satisfy the following properties:

Correctness. For every $\lambda, n \in \mathbb{N}$, $x \in \{0, 1\}^n$, and $i \in [n]$, we require that

$$\Pr \left[\text{Reconstruct}(h, a) = x_i : \begin{array}{c} (\text{ck}, q_h) \leftarrow \text{Setup}(1^\lambda, n) \\ h \leftarrow \text{Hint}(x, q_h) \\ q \leftarrow \text{Query}(\text{ck}, i) \\ a \leftarrow \text{Answer}^x(q) \end{array} \right] = 1, \tag{2}$$

where the probability is taken over any randomness used by the algorithms.

Security. For $\lambda, n \in \mathbb{N}$, and $i, j \in [n]$, define the distribution

$$D_{\lambda, n, i} := \left\{ q : \begin{array}{c} (\text{ck}, q_h) \leftarrow \text{Setup}(1^\lambda, n) \\ q \leftarrow \text{Query}(\text{ck}, i) \end{array} \right\}, \tag{3}$$

and for an adversary $\mathcal{A}$, define the adversary's advantage as

$$\text{PIRadv}[\mathcal{A}, \Pi](\lambda, n) := \max_{i, j \in [n]} \left\{ \Pr\left[\mathcal{A}(1^\lambda, D_{\lambda, n, i}) = 1\right] - \Pr\left[\mathcal{A}(1^\lambda, D_{\lambda, n, j}) = 1\right] \right\}.$$

Scheme Π is *computationally secure* if for every polynomially bounded function $n(\lambda)$ and every efficient adversary $\mathcal{A}$, the quantity $\text{PIRadv}[\mathcal{A}, \Pi](\lambda, n(\lambda))$ is a negligible function of λ. In particular, we say it is ϵ-secure if this advantage is at most $\epsilon(\lambda, n)$. The scheme is *statistically secure* if the same holds true even for computationally unbounded adversaries.

Remark 9 (Online running time). In Definition 8, the online server's answer algorithm Answer gets oracle access to the bits of the database x. We do so to emphasize that, for all of the PIR schemes described in this paper, the online server runs in time *sublinear* in the database size n, and can thus reply to the client's query after probing only $o(n)$ bits of the database. In practice, the online server could implement each oracle call using a lookup to the database in $\widetilde{O}(1)$ time, in a reasonable model of computation (e.g., the RAM model).

Remark 10 (Information-theoretic PIR as offline/online PIR). It turns out that *any* two-server PIR scheme with perfect information-theoretic security can be cast as an offline/online PIR scheme. To see why: in a two-server perfectly secure PIR, the distribution over query strings that the client sends to each server is independent of the database bit that the client wants to read. (If not, the scheme cannot possibly be perfectly secure.) Thus, the client can query one of the two servers server before it knows which database bit it wants to read.

However, in all existing two-server perfectly secure PIR schemes, *both* servers run in time $\Omega(n)$ on databases of size n. Therefore, viewing any standard two-server PIR scheme as an offline/online scheme yields a two-server offline/online PIR scheme in which the online running time is $\Omega(n)$. In contrast, we construct offline/online PIR schemes in which the online server runs in time $o(n)$.

3.2   New Constructions

The following theorem, which we prove at the end of this subsection, captures our main result on two-server offline/online PIR. It shows that it is possible to simultaneously achieve sublinear total communication and sublinear online time:

Theorem 11 (Two-server statistically secure offline/online PIR). *There exists a statistically secure two-server offline/online PIR scheme, such that on every n-bit database and every security parameter $\lambda \in \mathbb{N}$:*

- *the offline phase uses $O(\lambda\sqrt{n}\log^2 n)$ bits of communication,*
- *the offline server runs in time $\tilde{O}_\lambda(n)$,*
- *the online phase uses $O(\lambda\sqrt{n}\log n)$ bits of communication,*
- *the online server runs in time $\tilde{O}_\lambda(\sqrt{n})$, and*
- *the client uses time and memory $\tilde{O}_\lambda(\sqrt{n})$.*

Moreover, the security advantage of any adversary is at most $\text{poly}(\lambda, n) \cdot 2^{-\lambda}$.

Remark 12 (Concrete efficiency). For simplicity, we give the running times of the routines in our schemes up to $\text{poly}(\lambda, \log n)$-factors. It is possible to make these hidden factors as small as $O(\lambda \log n)$.

Remark 13 (Trading communication for online time). By adjusting the parameters of the construction, it is possible to generalize Theorem 11 to give a two-server offline/online PIR scheme in which, for any function $C: \mathbb{N} \to \mathbb{N}$ with $C(n) \leq n/2$, the offline phases uses $C(n)$ bits of communication, and the online server runs in time $\tilde{O}(n/C(n))$. This adjustment requires the client and preprocessing server to have access to a sequence of common random bits, or, in the computational setting, assuming the existence of pseudorandom generators.

In the full version of this work we discuss additional issues such as support of databases with longer rows, further reducing the client's online time via a connection to the 3-SUM problem, and implications of Theorem 11 for random self-reductions.

The following theorem, which we prove at the end of this subsection, shows that, if we settle for only computational—rather than statistical—security, we can decrease the online communication cost of the PIR scheme of Theorem 11 from $O_\lambda(\sqrt{n}\log n)$ to $O_\lambda(\log n)$ without degrading any other efficiency metrics. It also allows us to slightly decrease the offline communication cost.

Theorem 14 (Two-server computational offline/online PIR). *Assuming the existence of pseudorandom generators, there exists a two-server offline/online PIR scheme Ψ that satisfies the efficiency criteria of Theorem 11, except that*

- *the communication cost of the offline phase decreases to $O(\lambda\sqrt{n}\log n)$,*
- *the communication cost of the online phase decreases to $O(\lambda^2\log n)$, and*
- *if the underlying PRG is ϵ_G-secure, the PIR scheme is ϵ-secure for $\epsilon(\lambda, n) = \text{poly}(\lambda, n) \cdot (\epsilon_G(\lambda, n) + 2^{-\lambda})$.*

The main building block we use to construct two-server PIR schemes with low communication complexity and low online server time is puncturable pseudorandom sets with small keys. We give the construction in the next subsection, and prove the following lemma about the construction in the full version of this work.

Lemma 15. *Let $s\colon \mathbb{N} \to \mathbb{N}$ be any function such that $s(n) \leq n/2$. Let Ψ be an ϵ_Ψ-secure puncturable pseudorandom set with set size s, key size κ, and punctured key size κ_p. Then there exists a two-server ϵ-secure offline/online PIR scheme Π_Ψ, such that on security parameter λ and every n-bit database, in the offline phase:*

- *the client sends $\lambda\kappa + (\lambda n/s(n))\log^2 n$ bits to the server,*
- *the offline server runs in time $n \cdot \text{poly}(\lambda, \log n)$,*
- *the offline server's answer is $O((\lambda n/s(n))\log n)$ bits in length.*

In the online phase:

- *the client sends $\lambda\kappa_p$ bits to the server,*
- *the online server runs in time $s(n)\ \text{poly}(\lambda, \log n)$, and*
- *the online server's answer consists of λ bits.*

Furthermore,

- *the client runs in time $(s(n) + n/s(n)) \cdot \text{poly}(\lambda, \log n)$ and stores $O(\lambda\kappa + (\lambda n/s(n))\log^2 n)$ bits between the offline and online phases, and*
- *the advantage $\epsilon(\lambda, n) \leq \text{poly}(\lambda, n) \cdot (\epsilon_\Psi(\lambda, n) + 2^{-\lambda})$.*

Theorem 11 follows by instantiating Lemma 15 with the information-theoretic puncturable pseudorandom set construction of Fact 2, which has keys and puncturable keys of length at most $(s + O(1))\log n$, and by setting $s = \sqrt{n}$.

Theorem 14 follows by instantiating Lemma 15 with the puncturable pseudorandom set of Corollary 6, which has keys of length $O(\lambda)$ and punctured keys of length $O(\lambda\log n)$, and setting $s = \sqrt{n}$. Additionally we reduce the offline communication from $O(\lambda\sqrt{n}\log^2 n)$ to $O(\lambda\sqrt{n}\log n)$ by replacing the random shifts used in Construction 16 with pseudorandom ones, generated from one seed of length λ.

Construction 16 (Two-server PIR with sublinear online time). The construction is parametrized by set size $s : \mathbb{N} \to \mathbb{N}$ and uses a puncturable pseudorandom set $\Psi = (\mathsf{Gen}, \mathsf{Punc}, \mathsf{Eval})$ with key space $\mathcal{K}$, punctured-key space $\mathcal{K}_\mathsf{p}$, and set size s, extended by routines $(\mathsf{Shift}, \mathsf{GenWith})$. The final scheme is obtained by running λ instances of this scheme in parallel. Throughout, let $m := (n/s(n)) \log n$.

Offline phase

$\underline{\mathsf{Setup}(1^\lambda, n) \to \mathsf{ck}, q_h}$
$\mathsf{sk} \leftarrow \mathsf{Gen}(1^\lambda, n)$
sample $\delta_1, \ldots, \delta_m \xleftarrow{\text{R}} [n]$
$\mathsf{ck} \leftarrow (\mathsf{sk}, \delta_1, \ldots, \delta_m)$
output ck and $q_h \leftarrow \mathsf{sk}$

$\underline{\mathsf{Hint}(q_h, x \in \{0,1\}^n) \to h \in \{0,1\}^m}$
parse q_h as $\mathsf{sk} \in \mathcal{K}$ and $\delta \in [n]^m$
for $j = 1, \ldots, m$ do:
$\quad S_j \leftarrow \mathsf{Eval}(\mathsf{Shift}(\mathsf{sk}, \delta_j))$
$\quad h_j \leftarrow \sum_{i \in S_j} x_i \bmod 2$
output $h \leftarrow (h_1, \ldots, h_m)$

Online phase

$\underline{\mathsf{Query}(\mathsf{ck}, i \in [n]) \to q \in \mathcal{K}_\mathsf{p}}$
parse ck as $\mathsf{sk} \in \mathcal{K}$ and $\delta \in [n]^m$
sample a bit $b \xleftarrow{\text{R}} \mathsf{Bernoulli}(\frac{s-1}{n})$
find a $j \in [m]$ s.t. $i - \delta_j \in \mathsf{Eval}(\mathsf{sk})$
if such a $j \in [m]$ exists:
$\quad \mathsf{sk}_q \leftarrow \mathsf{Shift}(\mathsf{sk}, \delta_j)$
otherwise:
$\quad j \leftarrow \perp$
$\quad i' \xleftarrow{\text{R}} \mathsf{Eval}(\mathsf{sk})$
$\quad \mathsf{sk}_q \leftarrow \mathsf{Shift}(\mathsf{sk}, i - i')$
if $b = 0$: $\quad i_\mathsf{punc} \leftarrow i$
else: $\qquad i_\mathsf{punc} \xleftarrow{\text{R}} \mathsf{Eval}(\mathsf{sk}_q) \setminus \{i\}$
output $q \leftarrow \mathsf{Punc}(\mathsf{sk}_q, i_\mathsf{punc})$

$\underline{\mathsf{Answer}^x(q \in \mathcal{K}_\mathsf{p}) \to a \in \{0,1\}}$
$S \leftarrow \mathsf{Eval}(q)$
return $a \leftarrow \sum_{i \in S} x_i \bmod 2$

$\underline{\mathsf{Reconstruct}(h \in \{0,1\}^m, a \in \{0,1\}) \to x_i}$
let j and b be as in $\mathsf{Query}^\dagger$
if $j = \perp$ or $b = 0$ then output $\perp$
output $x_i \leftarrow h_j - a \bmod 2$

† For simplicity, we avoid passing j and b explicitly from Query to $\mathsf{Reconstruct}$.

3.3 Construction of PIR from Puncturable Pseudorandom Sets

We first present an overview of the construction. The formal specification appears in the full version of this work, and the full analysis appears there as well.

The PIR scheme makes use of a puncturable pseudorandom set $\Psi = (\mathsf{Gen}, \mathsf{Punc}, \mathsf{Eval})$ with set size $s(n)$ extended by routines $(\mathsf{Shift}, \mathsf{GenWith})$. We denote $s := s(n)$ and assume without loss of generality that $s \geq \log n$, as otherwise, a scheme in which the offline server sends the entire database to the client trivially satisfies the lemma. We also define $m := (n/s) \log n$. The PIR scheme operates in two phases, in each of which the client interacts with one of the two servers:

Offline phase

1. The client samples a random set key $\mathsf{sk} \leftarrow \mathsf{Gen}(1^\lambda, n)$ for universe size n and set of size s. It also samples m random shifts $\delta_1, \ldots, \delta_m \in [n]$. The client sends the set key and the shifts to the offline server.

2. Upon receiving the set key sk and the random shifts $\delta_1, \ldots, \delta_m$ from the client, the offline server expands the set key to get the set $S \leftarrow \mathsf{Eval}(\mathsf{sk}) \subseteq [n]$. Each shift $\delta_j \in [n]$ defines a "shifted" set $S_j \leftarrow \{x + \delta_j \bmod n \mid x \in S\}$ (when adding elements in $[n]$, we identify it with $\mathbb{Z}_n$).

   For each shift δ_j, the offline server computes the parity of the bits pointed by the shifted set S_j, i.e., sets $h_j := \sum_{i \in S_j} x_i \bmod 2$. These bits constitute the hint $h = (h_1, \ldots, h_m) \in \{0,1\}^m$, which the server sends to the client.

Online phase. The client takes as input an index $i_{\mathsf{pir}} \in [n]$ of the database it wants to query. The client has its set key sk and the shifts vector δ from the offline phase and the hint $h \in \{0,1\}^m$ from the offline server.

1. The client expands the set key sk into the set $S \leftarrow \mathsf{Eval}(\mathsf{sk})$. It then searches for a value $j \in [m]$ such that $i_{\mathsf{pir}} + \delta_j \in S$. (The client can execute this search in $O(m + n)$ time using a hash table.)
   - If such a shift δ_j exists, the client computes the corresponding shifted set key $\mathsf{sk}_q \leftarrow \mathsf{Shift}(\mathsf{sk}, \delta_j)$, so that i_{pir} falls into the set $\mathsf{Eval}(\mathsf{sk}_q)$.
   - If such an index does not exist, the client samples an element $i \xleftarrow{\mathsf{R}} S$ and computes the shifted set $\mathsf{sk}_q \leftarrow \mathsf{Shift}(\mathsf{sk}, i_{\mathsf{pir}} - i')$.

   Either way, we refer to the chosen set key as sk_q and it holds $i_{\mathsf{pir}} \in \mathsf{Eval}(\mathsf{sk}_q)$.
2. The client samples a bit $b \xleftarrow{\mathsf{R}} \mathsf{Bernoulli}((s-1)/n)$ and then chooses an element i_{punc} at which to puncture its set key sk_q.

   If $b = 0$, the client punctures the key sk_q at the point: $i_{\mathsf{punc}} \leftarrow i_{\mathsf{pir}}$.
   - If $b = 1$, the client punctures the key sk_q at a random point: $i_{\mathsf{punc}} \xleftarrow{\mathsf{R}} \mathsf{Eval}(\mathsf{sk}_q) \setminus \{i_{\mathsf{pir}}\}$.

   The client sends the punctured key $q \xleftarrow{\mathsf{R}} \mathsf{Punc}(\mathsf{sk}_q, i_{\mathsf{punc}})$ to the online server. (In the proof, we show that this punctured key computationally hides the index i_{pir} of the bit that the client wants to fetch from the database.)
3. The online server computes the punctured set $S^* \leftarrow \mathsf{Eval}(q) \subseteq [n]$ and views this set as $s - 1$ pointers to bits in the database $x \in \{0,1\}^n$. The online server computes the parity of these $s - 1$ bits: $a \leftarrow \sum_{i \in S^*} x_i \bmod 2$. The online server then returns this parity to the client. Notice that the online server only needs to probe $s - 1$ bits of the database and can run in time $s \cdot \mathsf{poly}(\lambda, \log n)$.
4. If, in Step 2, the client's random bit $b = 0$, the client can recover the bit at position i_{pir} in the database from the hint h and the answer a by computing $(h - a) \bmod 2 = \sum_{i \in S} x_i - \sum_{S^*} x_i = \sum_{i \in S} x_i - \sum_{S \setminus i_{\mathsf{pir}}} x_i = x_{i_{\mathsf{pir}}}$.

Note that the scheme fails if either $i_{\mathsf{punc}} \neq i_{\mathsf{pir}}$ or $i_{\mathsf{pir}} \notin \cup_{j \in [m]} S_j$. The probability of the former is $(s-1)/n$ and, by setting $m \approx n \log n / s$, we can drive down the probability of the latter to be approximately $1/n$. By running $O(\lambda)$ instances of the scheme in parallel, using independent randomness for each instance, we can drive the overall failure probability to be negligible in λ.

It is now possible to transform the PIR scheme into one with perfect correctness, at the expense of a negligible security loss. To do so, if the client detects an error (which happens with only a negligible probability), it simply reads its desired bit from the database using a non-private lookup. (Achieving perfect correctness *and* security is also possible, at the cost of having an offline phase that runs in *expected* polynomial time.)

4   Two-Server PIR with Sublinear Amortized Time

One shortcoming of the PIR scheme of the previous section is that every execution of its offline phase supports only one subsequent query. To perform each additional query, the client and the server must rerun the offline phase. Therefore, although the online query-processing time is sublinear, the overall cost of each query, including that of the offline phase, remains linear.

We now extend the scheme of the previous section such that a single execution of the offline phase enables the client to subsequently query the database *polynomially many times*, without ever having to rerun the offline phase. The extended scheme is nearly as efficient as the basic, single-query scheme. The only loss in efficiency is the online communication, which increases to $\widetilde{O}(n^{1/2})$. We stress that the client can choose the retrieved indices adaptively, and so our scheme does *not* rely on jointly processing a batch of queries.

Our security definition, given in the full version of this work, accounts for an *active* (fully malicious) adversary that controls either of the two servers, and can adaptively choose the database indices that the client queries. Here, we give our main result:

Theorem 17 (Two-server multi-query offline/online PIR). *Assuming the existence of pseudorandom permutations, there exists a two-server multi-query offline/online PIR scheme, such that on every n-bit database and every security parameter $\lambda \in \mathbb{N}$, in the offline phase:*

- *the offline server runs in time $\widetilde{O}_\lambda(n)$,*
- *the total communication is $O(\lambda\sqrt{n}\log n)$ bits,*

and in the online phase:

- *the online server runs in time $\widetilde{O}_\lambda(\sqrt{n})$,*
- *the total communication is $O(\lambda\sqrt{n}\log n)$ bits, and*
- *if the underlying PRP is ϵ_P-secure, the PIR scheme is ϵ-secure for $\epsilon(\lambda, n) \leq$* $\text{poly}(\lambda, n) \cdot (\epsilon_P(\lambda, n) + 2^{-\lambda})$.

Furthermore, the client uses offline time, storage, and online time $\widetilde{O}_\lambda(n^{1/2})$.

In the full version of this work, we give the construction that fully specifies the scheme that proves Theorem 17. The full analysis appears in the full version of this work, where we also prove the following corollary:

Corollary 18 (Reducing communication). *Assuming the existence of pseudorandom generators, there exists a scheme as in Theorem 17, albeit*

- *the client offline time increases to $\widetilde{O}_\lambda(n)$,*
- *the client storage and online time increases to $\widetilde{O}_\lambda(n^{5/6})$, and*
- *the total online communication decreases to $O(\lambda^2 \log n)$.*

Remark 19. As in Sect. 3, it is possible to achieve statistical security, by replacing the computationally secure puncturable pseudorandom set in the proof of Theorem 17, with a perfectly secure one and applying a standard "balancing" technique [CGKS95, Section 4.3] to get a scheme with online work and communication $\widetilde{O}_\lambda(n^{2/3})$.

4.1   Sketch of the Construction

We sketch the construction here, but refer to In the full version of this work for the details.

Our starting point is the single-query scheme of Sect. 3. There, the hint consists of a list of $m = \sqrt{n} \log n$ random sets $S_1, \ldots, S_m \subseteq [n]$, each of size roughly $\sqrt{n}$, represented by m puncturable pseudorandom set keys, along with the parity of the database bits in each set. In the online phase, to read the ith database bit, the client finds a set $S_j \in \{S_1, \ldots, S_m\}$ such that $i \in S_j$ and with good probability sends to the right server the set $S' = S_j \setminus \{i\}$. Once the client has used the set S_j to make a query, the client cannot use S_j again. If the client used S_j to query for another index i', the right server would, with good probability, see $S_j \setminus \{i\}$ and $S_j \setminus \{i'\}$. Taking the difference of these sets would reveal the secret indices $\{i, i'\}$ to the right server, breaking security.

The key to supporting multiple queries with only one execution of the offline phase is to have the client "refresh" its hint every time it queries the database. We refer to the two servers as "left" and "right". The left server provides the hint to the client in the offline phase, and later helps the client to refresh that hint after each subsequent read operation. The right server answers the queries that allow the client to reconstruct the database bits it is attempting to read (as in our constructions of Sect. 3).

The online-phase interaction with the right server proceeds exactly as in the single-query scheme: the client sends a punctured set to the right server and recovers the bit x_i. However, the client in the multi-query scheme must somehow replace the set S_j (and the corresponding parity bit) with a fresh random set S_{new}. To make this work, we must answer two questions: (i) How does the client sample the set S_{new}? and (ii) How does the client fetch the corresponding parity bit $\sum_{i \in S_{\mathsf{new}}} x_i \bmod ??$

First, for correctness and privacy to hold for future queries, the client must sample the replacement set S_{new} in a way that preserves the joint distribution of the sets $S_1, \ldots, S_m$. Notice that sampling a fresh random set S_{new} of the proper size will *not* work, since it distorts the joint distribution of the sets. In particular, replacing a set S_j that contains i with a fresh random set causes the expected number of sets in $S_1, \ldots, S_m$ containing i to decrease. What *does* work is to have the client sample a fresh random set S_{new} subject to the constraint that it contains the index i that the client just read. This is possible since, as described in Sect. 2.3, punctured sets support biased sampling.

Second, the client needs to construct the correct parity bit $h_{\mathsf{new}} = \sum_{i \in S_{\mathsf{new}}} x_i \bmod 2$ for the new set S_{new}. The client obtains the new parity bit by (1) puncturing the set S_{new} at element i and (2) querying the left server on the punctured set. The left server then replies with the parity of the bits in the punctured set $S_{\mathsf{new}} \setminus \{i\}$. At this point the client can recover the parity of the new set S_{new} by adding the reply from the left server and the value x_i, which it reconstructs, as in the single-query case, using the reply from the right server.

The final complication is that, as in Sect. 5, in order for the punctured set to look random, the client occasionally needs to send to the servers a set punctured at the retrieved index i. In this case, the read operation fails. When this happens, the client sends a punctured version of the new set S_{new} to both servers, the client leaves its hint state unchanged, and the read operations fails.

As in Sect. 5, by running λ instances of the scheme in parallel we can drive the overall failure probability to be negligible in λ. We can then trade the failure probability for a negligible security loss and get a perfectly correct scheme.

5   Single-Server PIR with Sublinear Online Time

In this section, we introduce *single-server* offline/online PIR. The syntax and correctness properties of a single-server offline/online PIR scheme, formally defined in the full version of this work, are exactly as in Definition 8. The key difference is that, in the single-server setting, the client interacts with the *same* server in both the offline phase and the online phase. Still the server should learn nothing about the database index the client wants to retrieve.

Unlike in the two-server setting, where we can achieve statistical security, in the single-server setting, we must rely on computational assumptions [CGKS95]. Since non-trivial single-server PIR implies oblivious transfer [DMO00], our assumptions must imply public-key cryptography.

Our single-server schemes shift all of the expensive work of responding to the client's PIR query—the linear-time scan over the database and the public-key operations—into the offline phase. The server can then respond to the client's query in the online phase much more quickly, with

- *no* public-key cryptographic operations and
- server time *sublinear* in the size of the database.

Our main construction (Theorem 20) achieves $\widetilde{O}_\lambda(n^{2/3})$ communication and online time and $\widetilde{O}_\lambda(n)$ server computational time in the offline phase, using linearly homomorphic encryption and standard single-server PIR. We also sketch an asymptotically superior construction (Theorem 22) that achieves $\widetilde{O}_\lambda(n^{1/2})$ communication and online time, at the cost of using fully homomorphic encryption [Gen09]. Our lower bound of Sect. 6 proves the optimality of this latter scheme, up to log factors, with respect to the trade-off between offline communication and online time, given the restriction that the server must store the database in unencoded from and use no extra storage.

A drawback of our single-server PIR schemes is that they have polynomial communication $\Omega(n^{1/2})$, which is higher than the polylog(n) communication of state-of-the-art standard single-server PIR schemes [CMS99]. That said, in some applications, the benefits of sublinear online time and no public-key cryptography in the online phase may outweigh the costs.

The main result of this section is:

Theorem 20 (Single-server offline/online PIR). *Suppose there exist:*

- *a linearly homomorphic encryption scheme (as defined in the full version of this work) with ciphertext space $\mathbb{G}$ and*

– *single-server PIR with communication cost* $\mathrm{poly}(\lambda, \log n)$ *and server computation time* $\widetilde{O}_\lambda(n)$ *(for every database size* n *and security parameter* $\lambda \in \mathbb{N}$ *).*

Then, there exists a single-server offline/online PIR scheme, that makes black-box use of the group $\mathbb{G}$*, such that for every security parameter* $\lambda \in \mathbb{N}$ *and* n-*bit database, it uses*

– *in the offline phase:* $\widetilde{O}_\lambda(n^{2/3})$ *bits of communication and* $\widetilde{O}_\lambda(n)$ *operations in* $\mathbb{G}$*, and*
– *in the online phase:* $\widetilde{O}_\lambda(n^{1/3})$ *bits of communication,* $\widetilde{O}_\lambda(n^{2/3})$ *time, and no operations in* $\mathbb{G}$*.*

Moreover, the client uses time and memory $\widetilde{O}_\lambda(n^{2/3})$*.*

We prove Theorem 20 in the full version of this work.

Remark 21 (A much simpler scheme). In the full version of this work, we give a very simple—and likely easy-to-implement—single-server offline/online scheme that requires only linearly homomorphic encryption and has $O(\sqrt{n})$ total communication, online time, and client storage. The scheme uses no public-key cryptographic operations in the online phase, and its simplicity makes it potentially attractive for practical applications. The downside is that its online phase requires a *linear* number of bit operations (but no public-key operations).

Patel, Persiano, and Yeo [PPY18] give an offline/online scheme with linear communication and linear online server time (but a sublinear number of online public-key operations) while this simple scheme has sublinear communication and no public-key operations in the online phase. In contrast, the client in their scheme can use a single offline phase for many online operations, while our single-server scheme requires an offline phase before each online query.

Improving efficiency with higher-order homomorphisms

If we use a homomorphic encryption scheme that supports degree-two [BGN05] or higher-degree homomorphic computation, we can build offline/online PIR schemes that provide even better communication efficiency. For example, given a fully homomorphic encryption scheme [Gen09] (FHE), we can use the idea of Theorem 20 with the two-server PIR scheme of Construction 16 to obtain:

Theorem 22 (Informal). *Assume fully homomorphic encryption exists. Then, for all security parameters* $\lambda \in \mathbb{N}$*, there is a single-server offline/online PIR scheme on* n-*bit databases that uses* $\widetilde{O}_\lambda(\sqrt{n})$ *bits of communication and* $\widetilde{O}_\lambda(\sqrt{n})$ *server-side time in the online phase.*

The observation is that, in the two-server setting (Construction 16), the client only sends the server a PRG seed. By using FHE, the client in the single-server setting could send the server an encryption of that seed, and the server could homomorphically evaluate the offline server's algorithm on the encrypted seed. The online phase remains the same. In the full version of this work, we discuss possible routes towards obtaining a similarly efficient scheme under weaker assumptions.

6   Lower Bound for PIR with Sublinear Online Time

In this section, we prove that the offline/online PIR schemes we construct in Sect. 3 achieve the optimal trade-off, up to log factors, between

- the number of bits C that the client downloads in the offline phase and
- the running time T of the server in the online phase.

Specifically, we show that any offline/online PIR scheme, in which the servers store the database in its unmodified form and use no additional storage, and that succeeds with constant probability on a database of size n, must have $(C + 1)(T + 1) = \widetilde{\Omega}(n)$.

The fact that we are able to obtain a polynomial lower bound on the communication complexity of offline/online PIR schemes may be somewhat surprising, as it has been notoriously difficult to obtain communication lower bounds for standard two-server PIR, in which the servers' running time is unbounded. In particular, in the information-theoretic setting, the best communication lower bound for two-server PIR stands at $C \geq (5 - o(1)) \cdot \log_2 n$ bits. In contrast, for two-server PIR schemes in which one of the servers is restricted to run in time $T \leq \sqrt{n}$, we obtain a polynomial communication lower bound of $C \geq \widetilde{\Omega}(\sqrt{n})$.

Our lower bound holds even against offline/online PIR schemes that provide only *computational security*, as well as against *single-server* offline/online PIR schemes. Our PIR schemes of Section 3 achieve this bound, up to logarithmic factors, as does the single-server scheme of Theorem 22.

Theorem 23. *Consider a computationally secure offline/online PIR scheme such that, on security parameter $\lambda \in \mathbb{N}$ and database size $n \in \mathbb{N}$,*

- *the client downloads C bits in the offline phase,*
- *the online server stores the database in its original form and probes T bits of the database in the course of processing the client's query, and*
- *the client recovers its desired bit with probability at least ϵ, over the choice of its randomness.*

Then, for polynomially bounded $n = n(\lambda)$, it holds that

$$\epsilon \leq 1/2 + \widetilde{O}\left(T/n + \sqrt{C(T+1)/n}\right) + \mathrm{negl}(\lambda),$$

and in particular for $\epsilon \geq 1/2 + \Omega(1)$ and large enough λ it holds that

$$(C + 1) \cdot (T + 1) \geq \widetilde{\Omega}(n).$$

We prove Theorem 23 by showing that an offline/online PIR scheme implies a solution for a computational task called "Yao's Box Problem." Using a preexisting lower bound for the Box Problem immediately gives a communication-time lower bound on offline/online PIR schemes. The details appear in the full version of this work.

Remark 24. The lower bound of Theorem 23 does not preclude schemes that achieve better communication and lower bound by virtue of having the servers store some form of encoding of the database. We discuss schemes of this form [DIO01,BIM04] in Sect. 1.4. In particular, constructing PIR schemes with preprocessing [BIM04] that beat the above lower bound (in terms of their communication and online time) seems like an interesting open problem.

7   Open Questions

This work leaves open a number of questions:

- Is it possible to construct offline/online PIR schemes in which the client runs in total time $o(n)$, stores $o(n)$ bits, and has online running time polylog(n)?
- Does Theorem 22 follow from an assumption weaker than FHE?
- Can we construct a multi-query scheme (Sect. 4) with only one server?
- In the full version of this work, we show how to view our PIR construction via a new abstraction that we call *sparse distributed point functions* ("sparse DPFs"), inspired by the standard notion of DPFs [GI14]. Are there even simpler constructions of sparse DPFs than the ones implied by our PIR schemes?

Acknowledgements. We gratefully acknowledge Dan Boneh for his advice on technical questions and for supporting our work on this project from the beginning. We thank Yuval Ishai for answering our questions about PIR, Sam Kim and David Wu for feedback on early versions of this work, and Helger Lipmaa for kindly pointing us to related work. Finally, we would like to thank the anonymous Eurocrypt reviewers for their many constructive comments. This work was supported by CISPA, DARPA, NSF, ONR, and the Simons Foundation.

References

[ACLS18] Angel, S., Chen, H., Laine, K., Setty, S.T.V.: PIR with compressed queries and amortized query processing. In: S&P (2018)

[Amb97] Ambainis, A.: Upper bound on the communication complexity of private information retrieval. In: Degano, P., Gorrieri, R., Marchetti-Spaccamela, A. (eds.) ICALP 1997. LNCS, vol. 1256, pp. 401–407. Springer, Heidelberg (1997). https://doi.org/10.1007/3-540-63165-8_196

[AMBFK16] Aguilar-Melchor, C., Barrier, J., Fousse, L., Killijian, M.-O.: XPIR: private information retrieval for everyone. In: PETS 2016, no. 2, pp. 155–174 (2016)

[AS16] Angel, S., Setty, S.: Unobservable communication over fully untrusted infrastructure. In: SOSP 2016 (2016)

[BDOZ11] Bendlin, R., Damgård, I., Orlandi, C., Zakarias, S.: Semi-homomorphic encryption and multiparty computation. In: Paterson, K.G. (ed.) EURO-CRYPT 2011. LNCS, vol. 6632, pp. 169–188. Springer, Heidelberg (2011). https://doi.org/10.1007/978-3-642-20465-4_11

[BGI14] Boyle, E., Goldwasser, S., Ivan, I.: Functional signatures and pseudo-random functions. In: Krawczyk, H. (ed.) PKC 2014. LNCS, vol. 8383, pp. 501–519. Springer, Heidelberg (2014). https://doi.org/10.1007/978-3-642-54631-0_29

[BGI16] Boyle, E., Gilboa, N., Ishai, Y.: Function secret sharing: improvements and extensions. In: CCS 2016 (2016)

[BGN05] Boneh, D., Goh, E.-J., Nissim, K.: Evaluating 2-DNF formulas on cipher-texts. In: Kilian, J. (ed.) TCC 2005. LNCS, vol. 3378, pp. 325–341. Springer, Heidelberg (2005). https://doi.org/10.1007/978-3-540-30576-7_18

[BI01] Beimel, A., Ishai, Y.: Information-theoretic private information retrieval: a unified construction. In: Orejas, F., Spirakis, P.G., van Leeuwen, J. (eds.) ICALP 2001. LNCS, vol. 2076, pp. 912–926. Springer, Heidelberg (2001). https://doi.org/10.1007/3-540-48224-5_74

[BIKR02] Beimel, A., Ishai, Y., Kushilevitz, E., Raymond, J.: Breaking the $O(n^{1/(2k-1)})$ barrier for information-theoretic private information retrieval. In: FOCS 2002 (2002)

[BIM04] Beimel, A., Ishai, Y., Malkin, T.: Reducing the servers' computation in private information retrieval: PIR with preprocessing. J. Cryptol. **17**(2), 125–151 (2004)

[BIPW17] Boyle, E., Ishai, Y., Pass, R., Wootters, M.: Can we access a database both locally and privately? In: Kalai, Y., Reyzin, L. (eds.) TCC 2017. LNCS, vol. 10678, pp. 662–693. Springer, Cham (2017). https://doi.org/10.1007/978-3-319-70503-3_22

[BKM17] Boneh, D., Kim, S., Montgomery, H.: Private puncturable PRFs from standard lattice assumptions. In: Coron, J.-S., Nielsen, J.B. (eds.) EURO-CRYPT 2017. LNCS, vol. 10210, pp. 415–445. Springer, Cham (2017). https://doi.org/10.1007/978-3-319-56620-7_15

[BLW17] Boneh, D., Lewi, K., Wu, D.J.: Constraining pseudorandom functions privately. In: Fehr, S. (ed.) PKC 2017. LNCS, vol. 10175, pp. 494–524. Springer, Heidelberg (2017). https://doi.org/10.1007/978-3-662-54388-7_17

[BTVW17] Brakerski, Z., Tsabary, R., Vaikuntanathan, V., Wee, H.: Private con-strained PRFs (and more) from LWE. In: Kalai, Y., Reyzin, L. (eds.) TCC 2017. LNCS, vol. 10677, pp. 264–302. Springer, Cham (2017). https://doi.org/10.1007/978-3-319-70500-2_10

[BW13] Boneh, D., Waters, B.: Constrained pseudorandom functions and their applications. In: Sako, K., Sarkar, P. (eds.) ASIACRYPT 2013. LNCS, vol. 8270, pp. 280–300. Springer, Heidelberg (2013). https://doi.org/10.1007/978-3-642-42045-0_15

[CC17] Canetti, R., Chen, Y.: Constraint-hiding constrained PRFs for NC^1 from LWE. In: Coron, J.-S., Nielsen, J.B. (eds.) EUROCRYPT 2017. LNCS, vol. 10210, pp. 446–476. Springer, Cham (2017). https://doi.org/10.1007/978-3-319-56620-7_16

[CG97] Chor, B., Gilboa, N.: Computationally private information retrieval. In: STOC 1997 (1997)

[CGKS95] Chor, B., Goldreich, O., Kushilevitz, E., Sudan, M.: Private information retrieval. In: FOCS 1995 (1995)

[CGKS98] Chor, B., Goldreich, O., Kushilevitz, E., Sudan, M.: Private information retrieval. J. ACM **45**(6), 965–982 (1998)

[CHR17] Canetti, R., Holmgren, J., Richelson, S.: Towards doubly efficient private information retrieval. In: Kalai, Y., Reyzin, L. (eds.) TCC 2017. LNCS, vol. 10678, pp. 694–726. Springer, Cham (2017). https://doi.org/10.1007/978-3-319-70503-3_23

[CMS99] Cachin, C., Micali, S., Stadler, M.: Computationally private information retrieval with polylogarithmic communication. In: Stern, J. (ed.) EURO-CRYPT 1999. LNCS, vol. 1592, pp. 402–414. Springer, Heidelberg (1999). https://doi.org/10.1007/3-540-48910-X_28

[DG16] Dvir, Z., Gopi, S.: 2-server PIR with subpolynomial communication. J. ACM **63**(4), 39:1–39:15 (2016)

[DGI+19] Döttling, N., Garg, S., Ishai, Y., Malavolta, G., Mour, T., Ostrovsky, R.: Trapdoor hash functions and their applications. In: Boldyreva, A., Micciancio, D. (eds.) CRYPTO 2019. LNCS, vol. 11694, pp. 3–32. Springer, Cham (2019). https://doi.org/10.1007/978-3-030-26954-8_1

[DHS14] Demmler, D., Herzberg, A., Schneider, T.: RAID-PIR: practical multi-server PIR. In: CCSW 2014 (2014)

[DIO98] Di Crescenzo, G., Ishai, Y., Ostrovsky, R.: Universal service-providers for database private information retrieval. In: PODC (1998)

[DIO01] Di Crescenzo, G., Ishai, Y., Ostrovsky, R.: Universal service-providers for private information retrieval. J. Cryptol. **14**(1), 37–74 (2001)

[DMO00] Di Crescenzo, G., Malkin, T., Ostrovsky, R.: Single database private information retrieval implies oblivious transfer. In: Preneel, B. (ed.) EURO-CRYPT 2000. LNCS, vol. 1807, pp. 122–138. Springer, Heidelberg (2000). https://doi.org/10.1007/3-540-45539_6_10

[DPSZ12] Damgård, I., Pastro, V., Smart, N., Zakarias, S.: Multiparty computation from somewhat homomorphic encryption. In: Safavi-Naini, R., Canetti, R. (eds.) CRYPTO 2012. LNCS, vol. 7417, pp. 643–662. Springer, Heidelberg (2012). https://doi.org/10.1007/978-3-642-32009-5_38

[Efr12] Efremenko, K.: 3-query locally decodable codes of subexponential length. SIAM J. Comput. **41**(6), 1694–1703 (2012)

[GCM+16] Gupta, T., Crooks, N., Mulhern, W., Setty, S., Alvisi, L., Walfish, M.: Scalable and private media consumption with Popcorn. In: NSDI 2016 (2016)

[GDL+14] Goldberg, I., Devet, C., Lueks, W., Yang, A., Hendry, P., Henry, R.: Percy++, version 1.0 (2014). http://percy.sourceforge.net/

[Gen09] Gentry, C.: A fully homomorphic encryption scheme. Ph.D. thesis, Stanford University (2009)

[GGM86] Goldreich, O., Goldwasser, S., Micali, S.: How to construct random functions. J. ACM **33**(4), 792–807 (1986)

[GI14] Gilboa, N., Ishai, Y.: Distributed point functions and their applications. In: Nguyen, P.Q., Oswald, E. (eds.) EUROCRYPT 2014. LNCS, vol. 8441, pp. 640–658. Springer, Heidelberg (2014). https://doi.org/10.1007/978-3-642-55220-5_35

[GR05] Gentry, C., Ramzan, Z.: Single-database private information retrieval with constant communication rate. In: Caires, L., Italiano, G.F., Monteiro, L., Palamidessi, C., Yung, M. (eds.) ICALP 2005. LNCS, vol. 3580, pp. 803–815. Springer, Heidelberg (2005). https://doi.org/10.1007/11523468_65

[Hen16] Henry, R.: Polynomial batch codes for efficient IT-PIR. In: PoPETs 2016, no. 4, pp. 202–218 (2016)

[HKW15] Hohenberger, S., Koppula, V., Waters, B.: Adaptively secure puncturable pseudorandom functions in the standard model. In: Iwata, T., Cheon, J.H. (eds.) ASIACRYPT 2015. LNCS, vol. 9452, pp. 79–102. Springer, Heidelberg (2015). https://doi.org/10.1007/978-3-662-48797-6_4

[HOWW18] Hamlin, A., Ostrovsky, R., Weiss, M., Wichs, D.: Private anonymous data access. Cryptology ePrint Archive, Report 2018/363 (2018)

[IKOS04] Ishai, Y., Kushilevitz, E., Ostrovsky, R., Sahai, A.: Batch codes and their applications. In: STOC 2004 (2004)

[IKOS06] Ishai, Y., Kushilevitz, E., Ostrovsky, R., Sahai, A.: Cryptography from anonymity. In: FOCS 2006 (2006)

[IP07] Ishai, Y., Paskin, A.: Evaluating branching programs on encrypted data. In: Vadhan, S.P. (ed.) TCC 2007. LNCS, vol. 4392, pp. 575–594. Springer, Heidelberg (2007). https://doi.org/10.1007/978-3-540-70936-7_31

[Ish19] Ishai, Y.: Private communication (2019)

[Jue01] Juels, A.: Targeted advertising... and privacy too. In: Naccache, D. (ed.) CT-RSA 2001. LNCS, vol. 2020, pp. 408–424. Springer, Heidelberg (2001). https://doi.org/10.1007/3-540-45353-9_30

[KLDF16] Kwon, A., Lazar, D., Devadas, S., Ford, B.: Riffle: efficient communication system with strong anonymity. In: PoPETs 2016, no. 2, pp. 115–134 (2016)

[KO97] Kushilevitz, E., Ostrovsky, R.: Replication is not needed: single database, computationally-private information retrieval. In: FOCS 1997 (1997)

[KO00] Kushilevitz, E., Ostrovsky, R.: One-way trapdoor permutations are sufficient for non-trivial single-server private information retrieval. In: Preneel, B. (ed.) EUROCRYPT 2000. LNCS, vol. 1807, pp. 104–121. Springer, Heidelberg (2000). https://doi.org/10.1007/3-540-45539-6_9

[KPTZ13] Kiayias, A., Papadopoulos, S., Triandopoulos, N., Zacharias, T.: Delegatable pseudorandom functions and applications. In: CCS 2013 (2013)

[LG15] Lueks, W., Goldberg, I.: Sublinear scaling for multi-client private information retrieval. In: Böhme, R., Okamoto, T. (eds.) FC 2015. LNCS, vol. 8975, pp. 168–186. Springer, Heidelberg (2015). https://doi.org/10.1007/978-3-662-47854-7_10

[Lip05] Lipmaa, H.: An oblivious transfer protocol with log-squared communication. In: Zhou, J., Lopez, J., Deng, R.H., Bao, F. (eds.) ISC 2005. LNCS, vol. 3650, pp. 314–328. Springer, Heidelberg (2005). https://doi.org/10.1007/11556992_23

[Lip09] Lipmaa, H.: First CPIR protocol with data-dependent computation. In: Lee, D., Hong, S. (eds.) ICISC 2009. LNCS, vol. 5984, pp. 193–210. Springer, Heidelberg (2010). https://doi.org/10.1007/978-3-642-14423-3_14

[MOT+11] Mittal, P., Olumofin, F.G., Troncoso, C., Borisov, N., Goldberg, I.: PIR-Tor: scalable anonymous communication using private information retrieval. In: USENIX Security 2011 (2011)

[OS07] Ostrovsky, R., Skeith, W.E.: A survey of single-database private information retrieval: techniques and applications. In: Okamoto, T., Wang, X. (eds.) PKC 2007. LNCS, vol. 4450, pp. 393–411. Springer, Heidelberg (2007). https://doi.org/10.1007/978-3-540-71677-8_26

[PPY18] Patel, S., Persiano, G., Yeo, K.: Private stateful information retrieval. In: CCS 2018 (2018)

[PR93] Pudlák, P., Rödl, V.: Modified ranks of tensors and the size of circuits. In: STOC 1993 (1993)

[PRS97] Pudlák, P., Rödl, V., Sgall, J.: Boolean circuits, tensor ranks, and communication complexity. SIAM J. Comput. **26**(3), 605–633 (1997)

[SCM05] Sassaman, L., Cohen, B., Mathewson, N.: The Pynchon Gate: a secure method of pseudonymous mail retrieval. In: WPES 2005 (2005)

[SW14] Sahai, A., Waters, B.: How to use indistinguishability obfuscation: deniable encryption, and more. In: STOC 2014 (2014)

[TDG16] Toledo, R.R., Danezis, G., Goldberg, I.: Lower-cost ϵ-private information retrieval. In: PoPETs 2016, no. 4, pp. 184–201 (2016)

[Yao90] Yao, A.C.-C.: Coherent functions and program checkers. In: STOC 1990 (1990)

[Yek08] Yekhanin, S.: Towards 3-query locally decodable codes of subexponential length. J. ACM **55**(1), 1:1–1:16 (2008)

Obfuscation and Functional Encryption

Candidate iO from Homomorphic Encryption Schemes

Zvika Brakerski[1](✉), Nico Döttling[2], Sanjam Garg[3], and Giulio Malavolta[3,4](✉)

[1] Weizmann Institute of Science, Rehovot, Israel
zvika.brakerski@weizmann.ac.il
[2] CISPA Helmoltz Center for Information Security, Saarbrücken, Germany
[3] UC Berkeley, Berkeley, USA
giulio.malavolta@hotmail.it
[4] Carnegie Mellon University, Pittsburgh, USA

Abstract. We propose a new approach to construct general-purpose indistinguishability obfuscation (iO). Our construction is obtained via a new intermediate primitive that we call *split fully-homomorphic encryption* (split FHE), which we show to be sufficient for constructing iO. Specifically, split FHE is FHE where decryption takes the following two-step syntactic form: (i) A *secret* decryption step uses the secret key and produces a *hint* which is (asymptotically) shorter than the length of the encrypted message, and (ii) a *public* decryption step that only requires the ciphertext and the previously generated hint (and not the entire secret key), and recovers the encrypted message. In terms of security, the hints for a set of ciphertexts should not allow one to violate semantic security for any other ciphertexts.

Next, we show a *generic candidate* construction of split FHE based on three building blocks: (i) A standard FHE scheme with linear decrypt-and-multiply (which can be instantiated with essentially all LWE-based constructions), (ii) a linearly homomorphic encryption scheme with short decryption hints (such as the Damgård-Jurik encryption scheme, based on the DCR problem), and (iii) a cryptographic hash function (which can be based on a variety of standard assumptions). Our approach is *heuristic* in the sense that our construction is not provably secure and makes implicit assumptions about the interplay between these underlying primitives. We show evidence that this construction is secure by providing an argument in an appropriately defined oracle model.

The full version of this paper is available at https://eprint.iacr.org/2020/394.

Z. Brakerski—Supported by the Israel Science Foundation (Grant No. 468/14), Binational Science Foundation (Grants No. 2016726, 2014276) and European Union Horizon 2020 Research and Innovation Program via ERC Project REACT (Grant 756482) and via Project PROMETHEUS (Grant 780701).

S. Garg—Supported in part from AFOSR Award FA9550-19-1-0200, AFOSR YIP Award, NSF CNS Award 1936826, DARPA and SPAWAR under contract N66001-15-C-4065, a Hellman Award and research grants by the Okawa Foundation, Visa Inc., and Center for Long-Term Cybersecurity (CLTC, UC Berkeley). The views expressed are those of the authors and do not reflect the official policy or position of the funding agencies.

G. Malavolta—Part of the work done while at the Simons Institute for the Theory of Computing.

A. Canteaut and Y. Ishai (Eds.): EUROCRYPT 2020, LNCS 12105, pp. 79–109, 2020.
https://doi.org/10.1007/978-3-030-45721-1_4

We view our construction as a big departure from the state-of-the-art constructions, and it is in fact quite simple.

1   Introduction

The goal of program obfuscation is to transform an arbitrary circuit C into an unintelligible but functionally equivalent circuit $\tilde{C}$. The notion of program obfuscation was first studied by Hada [39] and Barak et al. [10]. However, these works showed that natural notions of obfuscation are impossible to realize for general functionalities. Specifically, Barak et al. [10] defined a very natural notion of security for program obfuscation called virtual black-box (VBB) security, which requires that an obfuscated program does not revel anything beyond what could be learned from just the input-output behavior of the original program. In the same work, they showed that this notion of program obfuscation is impossible to achieve for arbitrary circuits.

In light of this impossibility result, much of the work on obfuscation focused on realizing obfuscation for special functionalities. However, this changed with the work of Garg et al. [28] that proposed the first candidate indistinguishability obfuscation (iO) construction based on multilinear maps [26]. Furthermore, Garg et al. [28] showed powerful applications of iO to tasks such as functional encryption. Loosely speaking, iO requires that the obfuscations of two circuits C_0 and C_1 that have identical input output behavior are computationally indistinguishable. Subsequently, significant work on using program obfuscation (e.g., [16,27,55]) has shown that most cryptographic applications of interest can be realized using iO (and one-way functions), or that iO is virtually *crypto-complete*.

Given its importance, significant effort has been poured into realizing secure obfuscation candidates. The first approach to obfuscation relied on using new candidate constructions of multilinear maps [22,26,33], an algebraic object that significantly expands the structure available for cryptographic construction. Unfortunately, all multilinear map construction so far have relied on ad-hoc and new computational intractability assumptions. Furthermore, attacks [21,40] on the multilinear map candidates and attacks [20,51] on several of the multilinear map based iO constructions [9,18,28] were later found. In light of these attacks, follow up works (e.g., [31]) offered constructions that defended against these attacks by giving constructions in the so-called weak multilinear map model [51]. Several of these weak multilinear map model based iO constructions are still conjectured to be secure, however, the *break-and-repair* cycle of their development has left cryptographers wary, and rightly so.

Around the time when attacks on multilinear map candidates were at an all time high, cryptographers started exploring new approaches to iO without using multilinear maps (or reducing their usage). Toward this goal, Bitansky and Vaikunthanathan [15] and Ananth and Jain [4] showed that iO could be realized assuming just functional encryption. In another approach, instead of trying to remove multilinear maps completely, Lin [42] and Lin and Vaikuntanathan [47] attempted to reduce their usage, i.e., they proposed iO constructions using only constant degree multilinear maps. With the goal of ultimately basing iO constructions on standard assumptions on bilinear maps, cryptographers started developing new ideas for realizing iO candidates from smaller constant degree multilinear maps [5,43]. Recently, Lin and Tessaro [45] described a candidate iO construction from degree-L multilinear maps for any $L \geq 2$ and additionally assuming PRGs with certain special locality properties. Unfortunately, it was shown the needed PRGs for the case of $L = 2$ are insecure (in fact it was proved that they cannot exist) [8,48]. Thus, still leaving a gap between bilinear maps and iO constructions which could now be based on trilinear maps [46]. Very recent works [1,3,41] (and cryptanalysis [12]), develop new ideas to resolve these problems and realize constructions based on bilinear maps. However, these bilinear map based constructions, which are still conjectured to be secure, additionally rely on certain pseudorandom objects with novel security properties. Finally, we note that all the other (perhaps less popular) approaches to iO (e.g., [35]) also start from new computational hardness assumptions.

Given the prior work, it is plausible that new sources of hardness are necessary for realizing iO candidates. Thus, this break-and-repair cycle would be necessary as we understand the underlying new assumptions better. In fact, there is some evidence that iO constructions based on simpler primitives [29,30] are hard to realize. Making progress on this dilemma is the focus of this work.

1.1 Our Results

We propose a new approach to construct general-purpose indistinguishability obfuscation. Our approach is *heuristic* but *without* using any new sources of computational hardness. In other words, our constructions use well-studied cryptographic primitives in a generic way to realize obfuscation, while still being heuristic in the sense that our constructions are not provably secure and make implicit assumptions about the interplay of the underlying primitives. The primitives we use can themselves be securely realized based on standard assumptions, namely the hardness of the learning with errors (LWE) and the decisional composite residues (DCR) problem. At a high level, our heuristics are similar in flavor to (i) the random oracle heuristic that is often used in cryptographic constructions [13] and (ii) the circular security heuristic that has been widely used in the construction of fully-homomorphic encryption schemes (FHE) [32].

Split-FHE. The starting point of our work is the fact that iO can *provably* be based on *split FHE*, a new primitive that we introduce in this work. A split FHE is an FHE scheme that allows for certain special properties of the decryption algorithm. Specifically, we consider FHE schemes for which the decryption algorithm can be split into two subroutines:

- $\rho \leftarrow \mathsf{PDec}(\mathsf{sk}, c)$: A *private* procedure that takes the FHE secret key and a ciphertext as input and produces a decryption hint ρ, of size much smaller than the message encrypted in c.
- $m \leftarrow \mathsf{Rec}(\rho, c)$: A *public* procedure that takes as input the decryption hint ρ (generated by PDec) and the ciphertext c and recovers the full plaintext.

The security for a split FHE scheme requires that, for all pairs of messages (m_0, m_1) and all circuits C such that $C(m_0) = C(m_1)$, the encryption of m_0 is computationally indistinguishable from the encryption of m_1, even given the decryption hint for the ciphertext evaluated on C.

We show that split FHE alone suffices to construct exponentially-efficient iO [44], which in turn allows us to build fully-fledged iO. Concretely, we prove the following theorem.

Theorem 1 (Informal). *Assuming sub-exponentially hard LWE and the existence of sub-exponentially secure split FHE, then there exists indistinguishability obfuscation for all circuits.*

A Generic Candidate. Next, we show a *generic candidate* construction of split FHE based on three building blocks: (i) a standard FHE scheme with linear decrypt-and-multiply (which can be instantiated with essentially all LWE-based constructions), (ii) a linearly homomorphic encryption scheme with short decryption hints (such as the Damgård-Jurik encryption scheme [23], based on the DCR problem), and (iii) a cryptographic hash functions. The security of the scheme can be based on a new conjecture on the interplay of these primitives, which we view as a natural strengthening of circular security. In this sense, it is aligned with Gentry's heuristic step in the FHE bootstrapping theorem [32]. Additionally, our use of the cryptographic hash function has similarities to the other heuristic uses of hash functions, e.g., in the Fiat-Shamir transformation [25].

We expect that there will exist instantiations of the underlying primitives (though contrived) for which this construction is insecure. For example, if the underlying schemes are not circular secure to begin with, then the resulting split FHE would also be insecure. However, for natural instantiations of these primitives, security can be conjectured.

Evidence of Security. In order to build confidence in our construction, we show evidence that the above-mentioned conjecture on the interplay between the security holds in an appropriate oracle model, inspired by the random oracle model. Thus, pushing all the heuristic aspects of the construction to an oracle. In fact, we show that security can be proved in this oracle model.

An alternate way to think of this result is that we construct split FHE based on a obfuscation for a specific program (representing the oracle), for which we can offer a relatively simple and natural heuristic implementation.

Conceptual Simplicity. Another positive feature of our construction is its conceptual simplicity, which makes it much easier to analyze and thus have confidence in. Finally, we remark that our construction is a big departure from the previously-mentioned multilinear maps based and local PRG based iO constructions and will be accessible to readers without first understanding prior iO constructions.

1.2 Technical Overview

In the following we give an informal overview of the techniques we develop in this work and we refer the reader to the technical sections for more precise statements.

Chimeric FHE. Our starting point is the hybrid FHE scheme recently introduced by Brakerski et al. [17], which we recall in the following. The objective of their work is to build an FHE scheme with best possible rate (in an asymptotic sense) by leveraging the fact that most LWE-based FHE scheme admit an efficient *linear noisy decryption*. Specifically, given an FHE ciphertext c and an LWE secret key $(s_1, \ldots, s_n)$ one can rewrite the decryption operation as a linear function $L_c(\cdot)$ such that

$$L_c(s_1, \ldots, s_n) = \mathsf{ECC}(m) + e$$

where e is a B-bounded noise term and ECC is some encoding of the plaintext (in their scheme m is packed in the high-order bits so that it does not interfere with the noise term). The idea then is to encrypt the secret key $(s_1, \ldots, s_n)$ under a (high-rate) linearly homomorphic encryption (LHE) scheme, which allows one to compress evaluated FHE ciphertext by computing $L_c(\cdot)$ homomorphically.

One interesting property of this approach is that it is completely parametric in the choice of the schemes, as long as they satisfy some simple structural requirements: More concretely, one can use *any* LHE scheme as long as its plaintext domain matches the LWE modulus of the FHE scheme. As an example, one can set the LHE to be the Damgård-Jurik encryption scheme [23,52], which we briefly recall in the following. The public key of the scheme consists of a large composite $N = pq$ and an integer ζ, and the encryption algorithm a message m computes

$$c = r^{N^\zeta} \cdot (1 + N)^m \mod N^{\zeta+1}$$

for some uniform $r \leftarrow_\$ \mathbb{Z}_N$. Note that the corresponding plaintext space is $\mathbb{Z}_{N^\zeta}$ and therefore the rate of the scheme approaches 1 as ζ grows. Furthermore, we observe that the scheme has one additional property that we refer to as *split decryption*. A scheme has split decryption if the decryption algorithm can be divided into a private and a public subroutine:

- The *private* procedure takes as input a ciphertext c and the secret key $\phi(N)$ and computes a *decryption hint*

$$\rho = c^{N^{-\zeta}} \mod N$$

  using the extended Euclidean algorithm. It is crucial to observe that $\rho \in \mathbb{Z}_N$ is potentially much smaller than the plaintext m.
- The *public* procedure takes as input a ciphertext c and the decryption hint ρ and recovers the plaintext by computing

$$(1 + N)^m = c/\rho^{N^\zeta} \mod N^{\zeta+1}$$

  and decoding m in polynomial time using the binomial theorem.

In a nutshell, the subgroup homomorphism allows one to compute a compressed version of the randomness, which can be then publicly stretched and used to unmask the plaintext. This means that m can be fully recovered by communicating a small hint of size fixed and, in particular, independent of $|m|$. As we are going to discuss later, this property is going to be our main leverage to build general-purpose obfuscation.

Temporarily glossing over the security implications, we point out that the hybrid scheme of Brakerski et al. [17] already suffices to construct an FHE scheme with split decryption (in short, split FHE): Simply instantiate the LHE scheme with Damgård-Jurik and convert evaluated FHE ciphertexts before decryption using the algorithm described above.

Security for Split FHE. We now delve into the desired security property for a split FHE scheme. On a high level, we would like to ensure that the decryption hint does not reveal any additional information, beyond the plaintext of the corresponding ciphertext. It is instructive to observe that if we do not insist on this property, then every FHE scheme has a trivial split decryption procedure which simply outputs the secret key. We formalize this intuition as an indistinguishability definition that, roughly speaking, demands that for all plaintext pairs (m_0, m_1) and every set of circuits $(C_1, \ldots, C_\beta)$ such that $C_i(m_0) = C_i(m_1)$, then the encryption of m_0 and m_1 are computationally indistinguishable, even given the decryption hints ρ_i of the evaluated ciphertexts. The condition $C_i(m_0) = C_i(m_1)$ rules out trivial attacks where the distinguisher just checks the output of the evaluation. Here $\beta = \beta(\lambda)$ is an arbitrary (but a priori bounded) polynomial in the security parameter.

Unfortunately, our candidate as described above falls short in satisfying this security notion: The central problem is that our split decryption procedure reveals the complete plaintext encoded in the Damgård-Jurik ciphertext. This means that the distinguisher learns arbitrarily many relations of the form

$$L_{c_i}(s_1, \ldots, s_n) = \mathsf{ECC}(C_i(m_b)) + e_i$$

where c_i is the evaluated ciphertext and L_{c_i} is a publicly known linear function. Collecting a large enough sample allows the distinguisher to recompute the FHE secret key $(s_1, \ldots, s_n)$ via, e.g., Gaussian elimination. A standard approach to obviate this problem is to smudge the noise e_i with some mask r_i uniformly sampled from an exponentially larger domain. Thus, a natural solution would be to compute a randomizing ciphertext $d_i = \mathsf{DJ.Enc}(\mathsf{pk_{DJ}}, r_i)$ and output the decryption hint for

$$c_i \cdot d_i = \mathsf{DJ.Enc}(\mathsf{pk_{DJ}}, \mathsf{ECC}(C_i(m_b)) + e_i + r_i) \approx \mathsf{DJ.Enc}(\mathsf{pk_{DJ}}, \mathsf{ECC}(C_i(m_b)) + r_i)$$

where r_i is sampled from a domain exponentially larger than the noise bound B but small enough to allow one to decode $\mathsf{ECC}(C_i(m_b))$. While it is possible to show that this approach indeed satisfies the security notion outlined above, it introduces an overhead in the size of the hint, which now consists of the pair (ρ_i, d_i). Note that we cannot allow the distinguisher to recompute d_i locally as it is crucial that r_i remains hidden, so we have no other choice but append it to the decryption hint. However the decryption hint is now of size $O(|c_i|)$, which does not satisfy our compactness requirement and makes our efforts purposeless (one can just set the decryption hint to be $C_i(m_b)$ and achieve better efficiency).

Although we appear to have encountered a roadblock, a closer look reveals that we still gained something from this approach: The ciphertext d_i encodes a (somewhat small) random value and in particular is completely independent from c_i. Furthermore, the decryption hint of $c_i \cdot d_i$ can be computed using the secret key alone. Assume for the moment that we had access to an oracle $\mathcal{O}$ that outputs uniform Damgård-Jurik encryption of bounded random values, then our idea is to delegate the sampling of d_i to $\mathcal{O}$. This allows us to bypass the main obstacle: We do not need to include d_i in the decryption hint as it can be recomputed by querying $\mathcal{O}$. One can think of this approach as a more structured version of the Fiat-Shamir transform [25], which allows us to state the following theorem.

Theorem 2 (Informal). *Assuming the hardness of LWE and DCR, then there exists a split FHE scheme in the $\mathcal{O}$-hybrid model.*

Looking ahead to our end goal, another interpretation of this theorem is as a universality result: Assuming the hardness of LWE and DCR, we can bootstrap an obfuscator for a specific circuit (i.e., the one that samples a uniform Damgård-Jurik encryption of a bounded random value) to an obfuscator for all circuits.

Instantiating the Oracle. The most compelling question which arises from our main theorem is whether there exist plausible instantiations for the oracle $\mathcal{O}$. A first (flawed) attempt is to devise an oblivious sampling procedure for Damgård-Jurik ciphertext using a random oracle: Note that Damgård-Jurik ciphertexts live in a dense domain $\mathbb{Z}_{N^{\varsigma}+1}$ and indeed sampling a random integer $c_i \leftarrow_\$ \mathbb{Z}_{N^{\varsigma}+1}$ maps to a well-formed ciphertext with all but negligible probability. However, since c_i is uniform in the ciphertext domain, then so is the underlying plaintext $r_i \in \mathbb{Z}_{N^{\varsigma}}$. This makes c_i unusable for our purposes since we require r_i to be bounded by some value $\tilde{q}$, which is exponentially smaller than N^{ς}. If we were to sample r_i this way, then it would completely mask the term $\mathsf{ECC}(C_i(m_b))$, thus making the plaintext impossible to decode.

Ideally, we would like to restrict the oblivious sampling to ciphertexts encrypting $\tilde{q}$-bounded messages. Unfortunately, we are not aware of the existence of any such algorithm. Instead, our idea is to still sample c_i uniformly over the complete ciphertext domain and remove the high-order bits of r_i *homomorphically*: This can be done by including an FHE encryption of the Damgård-Jurik secret key, then homomorphically evaluating the circuit that decrypts c_i and computes $-\lfloor r_i/\tilde{q} \rfloor \cdot \tilde{q}$. The evaluated ciphertext is then converted again to the Damgård-Jurik domain using the linear noisy decryption of the FHE scheme. At this point, one can obtain a well-formed encryption of a $\tilde{q}$-bounded value by computing

$$\mathsf{DJ.Enc}(\mathsf{pk}_{\mathsf{DJ}}, -\lfloor r_i/\tilde{q}\rfloor \cdot \tilde{q} + e) \cdot c_i = \mathsf{DJ.Enc}(\mathsf{pk}_{\mathsf{DJ}}, -\lfloor r_i/\tilde{q}\rfloor \cdot \tilde{q} + e + r_i)$$
$$= \mathsf{DJ.Enc}(\mathsf{pk}_{\mathsf{DJ}}, (r_i \mod \tilde{q}) + e)$$

where the term $(r_i \mod \tilde{q}) + e$ is $\tilde{q}$-bounded with all but negligible probability by setting $\tilde{q} \gg B$. While this approach brings us tantalizingly close to a provably secure scheme, a careful analysis highlights two lingering conjectures.

(1) *Circular Security:* Adding and FHE encryption of the Damgård-Jurik secret key introduces a circular dependency in the security of the two schemes (recall that our construction already encodes a Damgård-Jurik encryption of the FHE secret key). While circular security falls outside of the realm of provable statements, it is widely accepted as a mild assumption and it is known to be achieved by most natural encryption schemes [11]. We stress that circular security is also inherent in the the bootstrapping theorem of Gentry [32], the only known method to construct fully (as opposed to levelled) homomorphic encryption from LWE.

(2) *Correlations:* While the homomorphically evaluated circuit essentially ignores the low-order bits of r_i, the corresponding decryption noise e might still depend on $(r_i \mod \tilde{q})$ in some intricate way. This might introduce some correlation and bias the distribution of the term $(r_i \mod \tilde{q}) + e$ with respect to a uniform $u \leftarrow_{\$} \mathbb{Z}_{\tilde{q}}$. However, the noise function is typically highly non-linear and therefore appears to be difficult to exploit. We also point out that the distinguisher has no control over the choice of e, which exclusively depends on an honest execution of the homomorphic evaluation algorithm. We therefore conjecture that the distribution of $(r_i \mod \tilde{q}) + e$ is computationally indistinguishable from u.

In light of the above insights, we put forward the conjecture that the proposed algorithm already gives us a secure implementation of the oracle $\mathcal{O}$. We view this as a natural strengthening of Gentry's heuristic for the bootstrapping theorem, which is justified by our more ambitious objective. As the conjecture pertains to standard cryptographic material (FHE and Damgård-Jurik encryption) we believe that any further insight on its veracity would substantially improve our understanding on these important and well-studied building blocks.

Finally, we mention that many heuristics can be used to weaken the correlation between the decryption noise e and the low-order bits $(r_i \mod \tilde{q})$, such as repeated applications of FHE bootstrapping [24]. We also propose a different heuristic approach to remove correlations based on binary extractors and we refer the reader to the technical sections for further details.

From Split FHE to iO. What is left to be shown is that split FHE does indeed suffice to construct program obfuscation. With this goal in mind, we recall a surprising result by Lin et al. [44] which states that, under the assumption that the LWE problem is sub-exponentially hard, iO for all circuits is implied by an obfuscator for circuits with logarithmic-size inputs with non-trivial efficiency. Here non-trivial efficiency means that the size of the obfuscated circuit $\tilde{C}$ with input domain $\{0,1\}^\eta$ is at most $\mathsf{poly}(\lambda, |C|) \cdot 2^{\eta \cdot (1-\varepsilon)}$, for some constant $\epsilon > 0$. This means that it suffices to show that split FHE implies the existence of an obfuscator (for circuits with polynomial-size input domain) with non-trivial efficiency.

The transformation is deceptively simple (and similar to [14]): The obfuscator computes a split FHE encryption of the circuit C and partitions the input domains in $2^{\eta/2}$ disjoint sets $(P_1, \ldots, P_{2^{\eta/2}})$ of equal size. Then, for each partition P_i, the algorithm homomorphically evaluates the universal circuit that evaluates C on all inputs in P_i and returns the concatenation of all outputs. Finally it returns the decryption hint ρ_i corresponding to the evaluated ciphertext. The obfuscated circuit consists of the public-key of the split FHE scheme, the encryption of C, and all of the decryption hints $(\rho_1, \ldots, \rho_{2^{\eta/2}})$. Note that the obfuscated circuit can be evaluated efficiently: On input x, let P_x be the partition that contains x, then the evaluator recomputes the homomorphic evaluation (which is a deterministic operation) of C on P_x and recovers the output using the decryption hint ρ_x. As for non-trivial efficiency, since the size of each decryption hint is that of a fixed polynomial mp, the total size of the obfuscated circuit is bounded by $\mathsf{poly}(\lambda, |C|) \cdot 2^{\eta/2}$, as desired.

Other Applications. To demonstrate that the scope of our split FHE scheme goes beyond program obfuscation, we outline two additional applications. In both cases we only rely on the hardness of the LWE and DCR problem, i.e., we do not need to introduce any new conjecture.

Two-Party Computation with Pre-Processing. We obtain a (semi-honest) two-party computation scheme for any circuit $C : \{0,1\}^\ell \to \{0,1\}^k$ with an input- and circuit-independent pre-processing where the communication complexity of the pre-processing phase is $\mathsf{poly}(\lambda, k)$, whereas the communication complexity of the online phase is $\mathsf{poly}(\lambda) + \ell$. This improves over garbled circuit-based approaches that require a pre-processing at least linear in $|C|$. The protocol works as follows: In the pre-processing phase Alice and Bob exchange their (independently sampled) public-keys for a split FHE scheme and Alice computes a randomizing ciphertext (in the scheme defined above this corresponds to a Damgård-Jurik encryption of a bounded random value), which is sent to Bob. In the online phase, Alice and Bob exchange their inputs encrypted under their own public keys (to achieve best-possible rate this can be done using hybrid encryption) and homomorphically compute the multi-key evaluation of f over both inputs. Note that multi-key evaluation is generically possible for the case of two parties by nesting the two split FHE evaluations. Then Alice consumes the randomizing ciphertext computed in the pre-processing and sends a partial decryption of the evaluated ciphertext in the form of a decryption hint. Bob can then locally complete the partial decryption using its own secret key and recover the output.

Rate-1 Reusable Garbled Circuits. The work of Goldwasser et al. [37] showed, assuming the hardness of the LWE problem, how to construct reusable garbled circuits where the size of the input encodings is $\mathsf{poly}(\lambda, d, \ell \cdot k)$, where $C : \{0,1\}^\ell \to \{0,1\}^k$ and d is the depth of C. Additionally assuming the hardness of the DCR problem, we can bring down the complexity to $\mathsf{poly}(\lambda, d, \ell) + k$. This is done by using their scheme to garble the circuit that computes C homomorphically over the input encrypted under a split FHE scheme an returns the decryption hint of the evaluated ciphertext. This effectively removes the dependency of the underlying reusable garbled circuit on the output size k. However, we also need to include in the input encoding a randomizing Damgård-Jurik ciphertext, which reintroduces an additive overhead in k.

1.3 Related Work

In the following we discuss more in depth the relation of our approach when compared with recent candidate constructions of iO from lattices and bilinear maps [1,3,41]. Very informally, this line of works leverages weak pseudorandom generators (PRG) to mask the noise of the LWE decryption. However, the output domain of such a PRG is only polynomially large: This is because of the usage of bilinear groups, where the plaintext space is polynomially bounded (decryption requires one to solve a discrete logarithm). This is especially problematic because statistical/computational indistinguishability cannot hold in this regime of parameters. To circumvent this problem, all papers in this line of work assume a strict bound on the distinguisher's success probability (e.g., 0.99) and then rely on amplification techniques. This however requires one to construct a weak PRG where the advantage of any PPT distinguisher is non-negligible but at the same time bounded by < 0.99.

On the other hand, we rely on the Damgård-Jurik encryption scheme, where the message domain is exponential. This allows us to sample the smudging factor from a distribution that is exponentially larger than the noise bound, which is necessary in order to argue about statistical indistinguishability. Thus in our settings, conjecturing that the advantage of the distinguisher is negligible is, at least in principle, plausible.

2 Preliminaries

We denote by $\lambda \in \mathbb{N}$ the security parameter. We say that a function $\mathsf{negl}(\cdot)$ is negligible if it vanishes faster than any polynomial. Given a set S, we denote by $s \leftarrow_\$ S$ the uniform sampling from S. We say that an algorithm is PPT if it can be implemented by a probabilistic machine running in time $\mathsf{poly}(\lambda)$. We abbreviate the set $\{1, \ldots, n\}$ as $[n]$. We recall the smudging lemma [6,7].

Lemma 1 (Smudging). *Let $B_1 = B_1(\lambda)$ and $B_2 = B_2(\lambda)$ be positive integers and let $e_1 \in [B_1]$ be a fixed integer. Let $e_2 \leftarrow_\$ [B_2]$ chosen uniformly at random. Then the distribution of e_2 is statistically indistinguishable from that of $e_2 + e_1$ as long as $B_1/B_2 = \mathsf{negl}(\lambda)$.*

2.1 Indistinguishability Obfuscation

We recall the notion of indistinguishability obfuscation (iO) from [28].

Definition 1 (Indistinguishability Obfuscation). *A PPT machine* iO *is an indistinguishability obfuscator for a circuit class* $\{\mathcal{C}_\lambda\}_{\lambda \in \mathbb{N}}$ *if the following conditions are satisfied:*

(Functionality) For all $\lambda \in \mathbb{N}$*, all circuit* $C \in \mathcal{C}_\lambda$*, all inputs* x *it holds that*

$$\Pr\left[\tilde{C}(x) = C(x)\Big|\tilde{C} \leftarrow \mathsf{iO}(C)\right] = 1.$$

(Indistinguishability) For all polynomial-size distinguishers $\mathcal{D}$ *there exists a negligible function* $\mathsf{negl}(\cdot)$ *such that for all* $\lambda \in \mathbb{N}$*, all pairs of circuit* $(C_0, C_1) \in \mathcal{C}_\lambda$ *such that* $|C_0| = |C_1|$ *and* $C_0(x) = C_1(x)$ *on all inputs* x*, it holds that*

$$|\Pr\left[1 = \mathcal{D}(\mathsf{iO}(C_0))\right] - \Pr\left[1 = \mathcal{D}(\mathsf{iO}(C_1))\right]| = \mathsf{negl}(\lambda).$$

2.2 Learning with Errors

We recall the (decisional) learning with errors (LWE) problem as introduced by Regev [54].

Definition 2 (Learning with Errors). *The LWE problem is parametrized by a modulus* q*, positive integers* n, m *and an error distribution* χ*. The LWE problem is hard if for all polynomial-size distinguishers* $\mathcal{D}$ *there exists a negligible function* $\mathsf{negl}(\cdot)$ *such that for all* $\lambda \in \mathbb{N}$ *it holds that*

$$\left|\Pr\left[1 = \mathcal{D}(\mathbf{A}, \boldsymbol{s}^\top \cdot \mathbf{A} + \boldsymbol{e})\right] - \Pr\left[1 = \mathcal{D}(\mathbf{A}, \boldsymbol{u})\right]\right| = \mathsf{negl}(\lambda).$$

where $\mathbf{A}$ *is chosen uniformly from* $\mathbb{Z}_q^{n \times m}$*,* $\boldsymbol{s}$ *is chosen uniformly from* $\mathbb{Z}_q^n$*,* $\boldsymbol{u}$ *is chosen uniformly from* $\mathbb{Z}_q^m$ *and* $\boldsymbol{e}$ *is chosen from* χ^m*.*

As shown in [53,54], for *any* sufficiently large modulus q the LWE problem where χ is a discrete Gaussian distribution with parameter $\sigma = \alpha q \geq 2\sqrt{n}$ (i.e. the distribution over $\mathbb{Z}$ where the probability of x is proportional to $e^{-\pi(|x|/\sigma)^2}$), is at least as hard as approximating the shortest independent vector problem (SIVP) to within a factor of $\gamma = \tilde{O}(n/\alpha)$ in *worst case* dimension n lattices. We refer to $\alpha = \sigma/q$ as the *modulus-to-noise* ratio, and by the above this quantity controls the hardness of the LWE instantiation. Hereby, LWE with polynomial α is (presumably) harder than LWE with super-polynomial or sub-exponential α. We can truncate the discrete Gaussian distribution χ to $\sigma \cdot \omega(\sqrt{\log(\lambda)})$ while only introducing a negligible error. Consequently, we omit the actual distribution χ but only use the fact that it can be bounded by a (small) value B.

3   Homomorphic Encryption

We recall the definition of homomorphic encryption in the following.

Definition 3 (Homomorphic Encryption). *A homomorphic encryption scheme consists of the following efficient algorithms.*

KeyGen(1^λ): *On input the security parameter 1^λ, the key generation algorithm returns a key pair* (sk, pk).

Enc(pk, m): *On input a public key* pk *and a message m, the encryption algorithm returns a ciphertext c.*

Eval(pk, C, ($c_1, \ldots, c_\ell$)): *On input the public key* pk, *an ℓ-inputs circuit C, and a vector of ciphertexts $(c_1, \ldots, c_\ell)$, the evaluation algorithm returns an evaluated ciphertext c.*

Dec(sk, c): *On input the secret key* sk *and a ciphertext c, the decryption algorithm returns a message m.*

We say that a scheme is fully-homomorphic (FHE) if it is homomorphic for all (unbounded) polynomial-size circuits. If the maximum size of the circuit that can be evaluated is bounded in the public parameters, then we call such a scheme a levelled FHE. We also consider a restricted class of homomorphism that supports linear functions and we refer to such a scheme as linearly-homomorphic encryption (LHE). We characterize correctness of a single evaluation, which suffices for our purposes. This can be extended to the more general notion of multi-hop correctness [34] if the condition specified below is required to hold for arbitrary compositions of circuits.

Definition 4 (Correctness). *A homomorphic encryption scheme* (KeyGen, Enc, Eval, Dec) *is correct if for all $\lambda \in \mathbb{N}$, all ℓ-inputs circuits C, all inputs $(m_1, \ldots, m_\ell)$, all* (sk, pk) *in the support of* KeyGen(1^λ), *and all c_i in the support of* Enc(pk, m_i) *it holds that*

$$\Pr\left[\mathsf{Dec}(\mathsf{sk}, \mathsf{Eval}(\mathsf{pk}, C, (c_1, \ldots, c_\ell))) = C(m_1, \ldots, m_\ell)\right] = 1.$$

We require a scheme to be compact in the sense that the size of the ciphertext should not grow with the size of the evaluated circuit.

Definition 5 (Compactness). *A homomorphic encryption scheme* (KeyGen, Enc, Eval, Dec) *is compact if there exists a polynomial* poly($\cdot$) *such that for all $\lambda \in \mathbb{N}$, all ℓ-inputs circuits C in the supported family, all inputs $(m_1, \ldots, m_\ell)$, all* (sk, pk) *in the support of* KeyGen(1^λ), *and all c_i in the support of* Enc(pk, m_i) *it holds that*

$$|\mathsf{Eval}(\mathsf{pk}, C, (c_1, \ldots, c_\ell))| = \mathsf{poly}(\lambda) \cdot |C(m_1, \ldots, m_\ell)|.$$

We define a weak notion of security (implied by the standard semantic security [38]) which is going to be more convenient to work with.

Definition 6 (Semantic Security). *A homomorphic encryption scheme* (KeyGen, Enc, Eval, Dec) *is semantically secure if for all polynomial-size distinguishers $\mathcal{D}$ there exists a negligible function* negl$(\cdot)$ *such that for all $\lambda \in \mathbb{N}$, all pairs of message (m_0, m_1), it holds that*

$$|\Pr\left[1 = \mathcal{D}(\mathsf{pk}, \mathsf{Enc}(\mathsf{pk}, m_0))\right] - \Pr\left[1 = \mathcal{D}(\mathsf{pk}, \mathsf{Enc}(\mathsf{pk}, m_1))\right]| = \mathsf{negl}(\lambda)$$

where $(\mathsf{sk}, \mathsf{pk}) \leftarrow \mathsf{KeyGen}(1^\lambda)$.

3.1 Linear Decrypt-and-Multiply

We consider schemes with a fine-grained correctness property. Specifically, we require that the decryption consists of the application of a linear function in the secret key, followed by some publicly computable function. Furthermore, we require that such a procedure allows us to specify an arbitrary constant ω that is multiplied to the resulting plaintext. We refer to such schemes as linear decrypt-and-multiply schemes. This property was introduced in an oral presentation by Micciancio [50] and recently formalized by Brakerski et al. [17]. We stress that all major candidate FHE constructions satisfy (or can be adapted to) such a constraint, e.g., [2,19,36]. We recall the definition in the following.

Definition 7 (Decrypt-and-Multiply). *We call a homomorphic encryption scheme* (KeyGen, Enc, Eval, Dec) *a decrypt-and-multiply scheme, if there exists bounds $B = B(\lambda)$ and $Q = Q(\lambda)$ and an algorithm* Dec&Mult *such that the following holds. For every $q \geq Q$, all $(\mathsf{sk}, \mathsf{pk})$ in the support of* KeyGen$(1^\lambda, q)$, *every ℓ-inputs circuit C, all inputs $(m_1, \ldots, m_\ell)$, all c_i in the support of* Enc(pk, m_i) *and every $\omega \in \mathbb{Z}_q$ that*

$$\mathsf{Dec\&Mult}(\mathsf{sk}, \mathsf{Eval}(\mathsf{pk}, C, (c_1, \ldots, c_\ell)), \omega) = \omega \cdot C(m_1, \ldots, m_\ell) + e \mod q$$

where Dec&Mult *is a linear function in* sk *over $\mathbb{Z}_q$ and $|e| \leq B$ with all but negligible probability.*

In our construction, we will need some additional structure for the modulus q. Fortunately, most LWE-based FHE schemes can be instantiated with an arbitrary q that does not depend on any secret input but only on the security parameter. Moreover, LWE-based FHE schemes can be instantiated with any (sufficiently large) modulus q without affecting the worst-case hardness of the underlying LWE problem [53]. In an abuse of notation, we often write KeyGen$(1^\lambda; q)$ to fix the modulus q in the key generation algorithm. In favor of a simpler analysis, we assume that e is always non-negative. Note that this is without loss of generality as it can be always guaranteed by adding B to the result of Dec&Mult and setting a slightly looser bound $B = 2B$.

3.2 Split Decryption

We define the notion of homomorphic encryption with split decryption, which is going to be central in our work. Loosely speaking, a scheme has split decryption if the decryption algorithm consists of two subroutines: A private algorithm (that depends on the secret key) that on input a ciphertext c computes a *small* hint ρ, and a publicly computable algorithm that takes as input ρ and c and returns the corresponding plaintext. We henceforth refer to such schemes as *split* homomorphic encryption. We introduce the syntax in the following.

Definition 8 (Split Decryption). *A homomorphic encryption scheme* (KeyGen, Enc, Eval, Dec) *has split decryption if the decryption algorithm* Dec *consist of the following two subroutines.*

PDec(sk, c): *On input the secret key* sk *and a ciphertext* c, *the partial decryption algorithm returns a decryption hint* ρ.
Rec(ρ, c): *On input the hint* ρ *and a ciphertext* c, *the recovery algorithm returns a message* m.

The notion of correctness is extended canonically.

Definition 9 (Split Correctness). *A homomorphic encryption scheme with split decryption* (KeyGen, Enc, Eval, PDec, Rec) *is correct if for all* $\lambda \in \mathbb{N}$, *all* ℓ-*inputs circuits* C *in the supported family, all inputs* $(m_1, \ldots, m_\ell)$, *all* (sk, pk) *in the support of* KeyGen(1^λ), *and all* c_i *in the support of* Enc(pk, m_i) *it holds that*

$$\Pr\left[\text{Rec}(\text{PDec}(\text{sk}, c), c) = C(m_1, \ldots, m_\ell)\right] = 1$$

where $c = $ Eval(pk, C, $(c_1, \ldots, c_\ell)$).

Beyond the standard compactness for homomorphic encryption, a scheme with split decryption must satisfy the additional property that the size of the decryption hint ρ is independent (or, more generally, sublinear) of the size of the message. Furthermore, the size of the public key and of a fresh encryption of a message m should depend polynomially in the security parameter and otherwise be linear in the size of the output. These are the properties that make split decryption non-trivial and that are going to be our main leverage to bootstrap this primitive into more powerful machinery. We formally characterize these requirements below.

Definition 10 (Split Compactness). *A homomorphic encryption scheme with split decryption* (KeyGen, Enc, Eval, PDec, Rec) *is compact if there exists a polynomial* poly($\cdot$) *and such that for all* $\lambda \in \mathbb{N}$, *all* ℓ-*inputs circuits* C *in the supported family, all inputs* $(m_1, \ldots, m_\ell)$, *all* (sk, pk) *in the support of* KeyGen(1^λ), *and all* c_i *in the support of* Enc(pk, m_i) *it holds that*

- $|\text{pk}| \leq \text{poly}(\lambda) \cdot |C(m_1, \ldots, m_\ell)|$,
- $|c_i| \leq \text{poly}(\lambda, |m_i|) \cdot |C(m_1, \ldots, m_\ell)|$, *and*
- $|\rho| \leq \text{poly}(\lambda)$

where $\rho = $ PDec(sk, Eval(pk, C, $(c_1, \ldots, c_\ell)$)).

Finally the notion of semantic security for split schemes requires that the decryption hint ρ for a certain ciphertext does not reveal any information beyond the corresponding plaintext. Note that we define a very weak notion where the above must hold only for a bounded number of ciphertexts, and the inputs are fixed prior to the public parameters of the scheme.

Definition 11 (Split Security). *A homomorphic encryption scheme with split decryption* (KeyGen, Enc, Eval, PDec, Rec) *is secure if for all polynomial-size distinguishers $\mathcal{D}$ there exists a negligible function* negl$(\cdot)$ *such that for all $\lambda \in \mathbb{N}$, all polynomials $\beta = \beta(\lambda)$, all pairs of messages (m_0, m_1), all vectors of circuits $(C_1, \ldots, C_\beta)$ such that, for all $i \in [\beta]$, $C_i(m_0) = C_i(m_1)$ it holds that*

$$\left| \Pr\left[1 = \mathcal{D}(\mathsf{pk}, c_0, \rho_{(1,0)}, \ldots, \rho_{(\beta,0)})\right] - \Pr\left[1 = \mathcal{D}(\mathsf{pk}, c_1, \rho_{(1,1)}, \ldots, \rho_{(\beta,1)})\right] \right|$$
$$= \mathsf{negl}(\lambda)$$

where $(\mathsf{sk}, \mathsf{pk}) \leftarrow \mathsf{KeyGen}(1^\lambda)$, *for all $b \in \{0,1\}$ define $c_b \leftarrow \mathsf{Enc}(\mathsf{pk}, m_b)$ and, for all $i \in [\beta]$ and all $b \in \{0,1\}$, define $\rho_{(i,b)} \leftarrow \mathsf{PDec}(\mathsf{sk}, \mathsf{Eval}(\mathsf{pk}, C_i, c_b))$.*

3.3 Damgård-Jurik Encryption

In the following we recall a variant of the Damgård-Jurik encryption linearly homomorphic encryption scheme [23]. We present a variant of the scheme that satisfies the notion of split correctness, which is going to be instrumental for our purposes. The scheme is parametrized by a non-negative integer ζ that we assume is given as input to all algorithms.

DJ.KeyGen(1^λ): On input the security parameter 1^λ, sample a uniform Blum integer $N = pq$, where p and q are λ-bits primes. Set $\mathsf{pk} = (N, \zeta)$ and $\mathsf{sk} = \varphi(N)$.

DJ.Enc(pk, m). On input a message $m \in \mathbb{Z}_{N^\zeta}$, sample a random $r \leftarrow \mathbb{Z}_N$ and compute
$$c = r^{N^\zeta} \cdot (1+N)^m \mod N^{\zeta+1}.$$

DJ.Eval$(\mathsf{pk}, f, (c_1, \ldots, c_\ell))$: On input a vector of ciphertexts $(c_1, \ldots, c_\ell)$ and a linear function $f = (\alpha_1, \ldots, \alpha_\ell) \in \mathbb{Z}_{N^\zeta}^\ell$, compute

$$c = \prod_{i=1}^{\ell} c_i^{\alpha_1} \mod N^{\zeta+1}.$$

DJ.PDec(sk, c): On input a ciphertext c, set $s = c \mod N$. Then compute $N^{-\zeta}$ such that $N^\zeta \cdot N^{-\zeta} = 1 \mod \varphi(N)$ using the extended Euclidean algorithm. Return
$$\rho = s^{N^{-\zeta}} \mod N.$$

DJ.Rec(ρ, c): On input a hint ρ and a ciphertext c, compute

$$(1+N)^m = c/\rho^{N^\zeta} \mod N^{\zeta+1}$$

and recover m using the polynomial-time algorithm described in [23].

It is well known that the scheme satisfies (standard) semantic security assuming the intractability of the decisional composite residuosity (DCR) problem, as defined in [52]. To prove correctness, we are going to use the fact that

$$x^{N^\varsigma} \mod N^{\varsigma+1} = (x \mod N)^{N^\varsigma} \mod N^{\varsigma+1} \tag{1}$$

for all non-negative integers (x, ς). We refer the reader to [49] for a proof of this equality. Recall that $c = r^{N^\varsigma} \cdot (1+N)^m$ and that

$$\rho = (c \mod N)^{N^{-\varsigma}} \mod N$$

$$= \left(r^{N^\varsigma} \cdot (1+N)^m \mod N \right)^{N^{-\varsigma}} \mod N$$

$$= \left(r^{N^\varsigma} \mod N \right)^{N^{-\varsigma}} \mod N.$$

Therefore we have that

$$\rho^{N^\varsigma} \mod N^{\varsigma+1} = \left(\left(r^{N^\varsigma} \mod N \right)^{N^{-\varsigma}} \mod N \right)^{N^\varsigma} \mod N^{\varsigma+1}$$

$$= \left(r^{N^\varsigma} \mod N \right)^{N^{-\varsigma} \cdot N^\varsigma} \mod N^{\varsigma+1}$$

$$= r^{N^\varsigma} \mod N^{\varsigma+1}$$

by an application of Eq. (1). Taking the inverse on both sides of the equation above we obtain

$$c/\rho^{N^\varsigma} \mod N^{\varsigma+1} = c/r^{N^\varsigma} \mod N^{\varsigma+1}$$

$$= r^{N^\varsigma} \cdot (1+N)^m / r^{N^\varsigma} \mod N^{\varsigma+1}$$

$$= (1+N)^m \mod N^{\varsigma+1}$$

as desired for correctness. Although such a scheme does not immediately give us a *secure* split LHE, we highlight a few salient properties that we are going to leverage in our main constructions.

Small Hints: The scheme satisfies a weakened notion of split compactness where the decryption hint is much smaller than the message space. The hint $\rho \in \mathbb{Z}_N$ consists of $\lceil \log(N) \rceil$ bits and in particular is independent of the size of the message space $\mathbb{Z}_{N^\varsigma}$, as the integer ς can be set to be arbitrarily large (within the range of polynomials in λ).

Simulatable Hints: Given a ciphertext c and a plaintext value m, one can efficiently compute a ciphertext $\tilde{c}$ such that the homomorphic sum of c and $\tilde{c}$ results in a uniform encryption of m and the corresponding decryption hint can be computed given only the random coins used to generate $\tilde{c}$. Concretely, let

$$\tilde{c} = \frac{r^{N^\varsigma} \cdot (1+N)^m}{c} \mod N^{\varsigma+1}$$

for some $r \leftarrow_\$ \mathbb{Z}_N$, then $\rho = r$.

Dense Ciphertexts: Sampling a random integer in $\mathbb{Z}_{N^{\zeta+1}}$ gives a well-formed ciphertext with all but negligible probability. This is because the group order $\varphi(N) \cdot N^\zeta$ is close to $N^{\zeta+1}$, i.e., $\frac{\varphi(N) \cdot N^\zeta}{N^{\zeta+1}} = \frac{\varphi(N)}{N} = 1 - \mathsf{negl}(\lambda)$.

4   Split Fully-Homomorphic Encryption

In the following we present our instantiation of FHE with split decryption. We first present a scheme from standard assumptions which assumes the existence of (a structured version of) a random oracle, then we propose plausible candidates for such an oracle.

4.1   Construction in the Presence of an Oracle

Before we delve into the details of our construction we give a definition of the oracle function that we consider. The oracle is parametrized by a pair of public keys for an FHE and an LHE scheme $(\mathsf{pk_{FHE}}, \mathsf{pk_{LHE}})$ and two integers $(q, \tilde{q})$. On input a bitstring $x \in \{0,1\}^*$, the oracle returns a uniform LHE encryption of a random value in $\mathbb{Z}_q$ and an FHE encryption of the same value rounded to the closest divisor of $\tilde{q}$. The oracle is deterministic and it is accessible by all parties, thus on input the same x, the oracle will always output the same pair of ciphertexts. The interface is formally defined in the following.

$\mathcal{O}_{(\mathsf{pk_{FHE}}, \mathsf{pk_{LHE}}, q, \tilde{q})}(x)$: On input a string $x \in \{0,1\}^*$ return two uniformly distributed ciphertexts

$$\mathsf{LHE.Enc}(\mathsf{pk_{LHE}}, m) \text{ and } \mathsf{FHE.Enc}(\mathsf{pk_{FHE}}, - \lfloor m/\tilde{q} \rfloor \cdot \tilde{q})$$

where $m \leftarrow_\$ \mathbb{Z}_{\tilde{q}}$.

It is useful to observe that the oracle output, along with an LHE encryption of the FHE secret key, gives us a uniformly distributed LHE encryption of a uniform value in $\mathbb{Z}_{\tilde{q}}$. This is because we can leverage the decrypt-and-multiply algorithm Dec&Mult of the FHE scheme (matching the FHE domain with the LHE paintext space appropriately) to compute $\mathsf{LHE.Enc}(\mathsf{pk_{LHE}}, - \lfloor m/\tilde{q} \rfloor \cdot \tilde{q} + noise)$, where *noise* is the decryption noise of the FHE scheme. Homomorphically summing up this term with the first output of the oracle we obtain

$$\mathsf{LHE.Enc}(\mathsf{pk_{LHE}}, m - \lfloor m/\tilde{q} \rfloor \cdot \tilde{q} + noise) = \mathsf{LHE.Enc}(\mathsf{pk_{LHE}}, (m \mod \tilde{q}) + noise)$$
$$\approx_s \mathsf{LHE.Enc}(\mathsf{pk_{LHE}}, (m \mod \tilde{q}))$$

for an appropriate choice of $\tilde{q}$, i.e., we obtain an ciphertext which is statistically indistinguishable from an LHE encryption of a uniform element of $\mathbb{Z}_{\tilde{q}}$.

Description. We are now in the position of giving formal description of our scheme. We assume the existence of the following primitives:

- A fully-homomorphic encryption scheme FHE = (FHE.KeyGen, FHE.Enc, FHE.Eval, FHE.Dec) with linear decrypt-and-multiply and with noise bound B.
- A linearly homomorphic encryption LHE = (LHE.KeyGen, LHE.Enc, LHE.Eval, LHE.PDec, LHE.Rec) with small and simulatable decryption hints (e.g., the Damgård-Jurik encryption scheme as described in Sect. 3.3).

If the underlying FHE scheme is levelled then so is going to be the resulting split FHE. Conversely, if the FHE scheme supports the evaluation of unbounded circuits, then so does the resulting split FHE construction. The scheme is formally described in the following.

KeyGen(1^λ): On input the security parameter 1^λ, sample a key pair $(\mathsf{sk}_{\mathsf{LHE}}, \mathsf{pk}_{\mathsf{LHE}}) \leftarrow$ LHE.KeyGen(1^λ). Let $\mathbb{Z}_q$ be the plaintext space defined by LHE, then sample $(\mathsf{sk}_{\mathsf{FHE}}, \mathsf{pk}_{\mathsf{FHE}}) \leftarrow$ FHE.KeyGen($1^\lambda; q$). Let $\mathsf{sk}_{\mathsf{FHE}} = (s_1, \ldots, s_n) \in \mathbb{Z}_q^n$, then return

$$\mathsf{sk} = \mathsf{sk}_{\mathsf{LHE}} \quad \text{and} \quad \mathsf{pk} = \left(\mathsf{pk}_{\mathsf{FHE}}, \mathsf{pk}_{\mathsf{LHE}}, c_{(\mathsf{LHE},1)}, \ldots, c_{(\mathsf{LHE},n)}\right)$$

where, for all $i \in [n]$, we define $c_{(\mathsf{LHE},i)} \leftarrow$ LHE.Enc($\mathsf{pk}_{\mathsf{LHE}}, s_i$).

Enc(pk, m): On input a message m return

$$c \leftarrow \mathsf{FHE.Enc}(\mathsf{pk}_{\mathsf{FHE}}, m).$$

Eval($\mathsf{pk}, f, (c_1, \ldots, c_\ell)$): On input a circuit C with ℓ bits of input and k bits of output and a vector of ciphertexts $(c_1, \ldots, c_\ell)$, let, for all $j \in [k]$, C_j be the circuit that returns the j-th bit of the output of C, then compute

$$d_j \leftarrow \mathsf{FHE.Eval}(\mathsf{pk}_{\mathsf{FHE}}, C_j, (c_1, \ldots, c_\ell)).$$

Define the following linear function over $\mathbb{Z}_q$:

$$g(x_1, \ldots, x_n) = \sum_{j=1}^{k} \mathsf{Dec\&Mult}\left((x_1, \ldots, x_n), d_j, 2^{\lceil \log(\tilde{q}+(k+1)B)\rceil + j}\right).$$

Compute $d \leftarrow$ LHE.Eval($\mathsf{pk}_{\mathsf{LHE}}, g, (c_{(\mathsf{LHE},1)}, \ldots, c_{(\mathsf{LHE},n)})$), then query $(a, \tilde{a}) \leftarrow \mathcal{O}_{(\mathsf{pk}_{\mathsf{FHE}}, \mathsf{pk}_{\mathsf{LHE}}, q, \tilde{q})}(d)$ and define the following linear function over $\mathbb{Z}_q$:

$$\tilde{g}(x_1, \ldots, x_n, x_{n+1}, x_{n+2}) = \mathsf{Dec\&Mult}\left((x_1, \ldots, x_n), \tilde{a}, 1\right) + x_{n+1} + x_{n+2}.$$

Return

$$c \leftarrow \mathsf{LHE.Eval}(\mathsf{pk}_{\mathsf{LHE}}, \tilde{g}, (c_{(\mathsf{LHE},1)}, \ldots, c_{(\mathsf{LHE},n)}, d, a)).$$

PDec(sk, c): On input an evaluated ciphertext c return

$$\rho \leftarrow \mathsf{LHE.PDec}(\mathsf{sk}_{\mathsf{LHE}}, c).$$

Rec(ρ, c): On input an evaluated ciphertext c, compute

$$\tilde{m} \leftarrow \mathsf{LHE.Rec}(\rho, c)$$

and return the binary representation of $\tilde{m}$ without its $\lceil \log(\tilde{q} + (k+1)B) \rceil$ least significant bits.

Analysis. We formally analyze our scheme in the following. During the analysis, we set the parameters on demand and we show afterwards that our choices lead to a satisfiable set of constraints for which the underlying computational problems are still conjectured to be hard. The following theorem establishes correctness.

Theorem 3 (Split Correctness). *Let* $q \geq 2^k + 2^{\lceil \log(\tilde{q} + (k+1)B) \rceil}$. *Let* FHE *be a correct fully-homomorphic encryption scheme with linear decrypt-and-multiply and let* LHE *be a split correct linearly homomorphic encryption scheme. Then the scheme as described above satisfies split correctness.*

Proof. Let us rewrite

$$\tilde{m} = \mathsf{LHE.Rec}(\rho, c) = \mathsf{LHE.Rec}(\mathsf{LHE.PDec}(\mathsf{sk}_{\mathsf{LHE}}, c), c)$$

where $c = \mathsf{LHE.Eval}(\mathsf{pk}_{\mathsf{LHE}}, g, (c_{(\mathsf{LHE},1)}, \ldots, c_{(\mathsf{LHE},n)}, d, a))$ We first expand the d term as

$$
\begin{aligned}
d &= \mathsf{LHE.Eval}(\mathsf{pk}_{\mathsf{LHE}}, g, (c_{(\mathsf{LHE},1)}, \ldots, c_{(\mathsf{LHE},n)})) \\
&= \mathsf{LHE.Eval}(\mathsf{pk}_{\mathsf{LHE}}, g, (\mathsf{LHE.Enc}(\mathsf{pk}_{\mathsf{LHE}}, s_1), \ldots, \mathsf{LHE.Enc}(\mathsf{pk}_{\mathsf{LHE}}, s_n))) \\
&= \mathsf{LHE.Enc}\left(\mathsf{pk}_{\mathsf{LHE}}, \sum_{j=1}^{k} \mathsf{Dec\&Mult}\left((s_1, \ldots, s_n), d_j, 2^{\lceil \log(\tilde{q} + (k+1)B) \rceil + j} \right) \right)
\end{aligned}
$$

by the correctness of the LHE scheme, where

$$d_j = \mathsf{FHE.Eval}(\mathsf{pk}_{\mathsf{FHE}}, C_j, (c_1, \ldots, c_\ell))$$

and $c_i = \mathsf{FHE.Enc}(\mathsf{pk}_{\mathsf{FHE}}, m_i)$. Thus by the decrypt-and-multiply correctness of the FHE scheme we can rewrite

$$d = \text{LHE.Enc}\left(\text{pk}_{\text{LHE}}, \sum_{j=1}^{k} 2^{\lceil \log(\tilde{q}+(k+1)B) \rceil + j} \cdot C_j(m_1, \ldots, m_\ell) + e_j\right)$$

$$= \text{LHE.Enc}\left(\text{pk}_{\text{LHE}}, \sum_{j=1}^{k} 2^{\lceil \log(\tilde{q}+(k+1)B) \rceil + j} \cdot C_j(m_1, \ldots, m_\ell) + \underbrace{\sum_{j=1}^{k} e_j}_{\tilde{e}}\right).$$

For the a variable we have that $a = \text{LHE.Enc}(\text{pk}_{\text{LHE}}, r)$, for some uniform $r \leftarrow_\$ \mathbb{Z}_q$, by definition of the oracle $\mathcal{O}_{(\text{pk}_{\text{FHE}}, \text{pk}_{\text{LHE}}, q, \tilde{q})}$. Recall that

$$\tilde{g}(x_1, \ldots, x_n, x_{n+1}, x_{n+2}) = \text{Dec\&Mult}\left((x_1, \ldots, x_n), \tilde{a}, 1\right) + x_{n+1} + x_{n+2}.$$

where $\tilde{a} = \text{FHE.Enc}(\text{pk}_{\text{FHE}}, -\lfloor r/\tilde{q} \rfloor \cdot \tilde{q})$. Thus $c = \text{LHE.Enc}(\text{pk}_{\text{LHE}}, \tilde{m})$ where

$$\tilde{m} = \text{Dec\&Mult}\left((s_1, \ldots, s_n), \tilde{a}, 1\right) + \sum_{j=1}^{k} 2^{\lceil \log(\tilde{q}+(k+1)B) \rceil + j} \cdot C_j(m_1, \ldots, m_\ell) + \tilde{e} + r$$

$$= -\lfloor r/\tilde{q} \rfloor \cdot \tilde{q} + e + \sum_{j=1}^{k} 2^{\lceil \log(\tilde{q}+(k+1)B) \rceil + j} \cdot C_j(m_1, \ldots, m_\ell) + \tilde{e} + r$$

$$= \sum_{j=1}^{k} 2^{\lceil \log(\tilde{q}+(k+1)B) \rceil + j} \cdot C_j(m_1, \ldots, m_\ell) + \tilde{e} + e + \underbrace{(r \mod \tilde{q})}_{\tilde{r}}$$

by the correctness of the FHE scheme. Note that the sum $\tilde{e} + e$ is bounded from above by $(k+1) \cdot B$, whereas the term $\tilde{r}$ is trivially bounded from above by $\tilde{q}$. This implies that the output of the circuit is encoded in the higher order bits of $\tilde{m}$ with probability 1, for a large enough q.

We then argue about the split security of the scheme. We remark that we analyze security in the presence of an oracle and we refer the reader to Sect. 4.2 for concrete instantiations.

Theorem 4 (Split Security). *Let $\tilde{q} \geq 2^\lambda \cdot (k+1) \cdot B$ and let $q \geq 2^\lambda \cdot \tilde{q}$. Let* FHE *be a semantically secure fully-homomorphic encryption scheme and let* LHE *be a semantically secure linearly homomorphic encryption scheme with simulatable decryption hints. Then the scheme as described above satisfies split security in the $\mathcal{O}_{(\text{pk}_{\text{FHE}}, \text{pk}_{\text{LHE}}, q, \tilde{q})}$-hybrid model.*

Proof. Let $(m_0, m_1, C_1, \ldots, C_\beta)$ be the inputs specified by the adversary at the beginning of the experiments. Consider the following series of hybrids.

Hybrid $\mathcal{H}_0$: Is defined as the original experiment. Denote the distribution induced by the random coins of the challenger by

$$(\text{pk}, c = \text{FHE.Enc}(\text{pk}_{\text{FHE}}, m_b), \rho_1, \ldots, \rho_\beta)$$

where

$$\mathsf{pk} = (\mathsf{pk_{FHE}}, \mathsf{pk_{LHE}}, \mathsf{LHE.Enc}(\mathsf{pk_{LHE}}, s_1), \ldots, \mathsf{LHE.Enc}(\mathsf{pk_{LHE}}, s_n))$$

and ρ_i is computed as $\mathsf{PDec}(\mathsf{sk}, \mathsf{Eval}(\mathsf{pk}, C_i, c))$.

Hybrids $\mathcal{H}_1 \ldots \mathcal{H}_\beta$: Let $d^{(i)}$ be the variable d defined during the execution of $\mathsf{Eval}(\mathsf{pk}, C_i, c)$. The i-th hybrid $\mathcal{H}_i$ is defined to be identical to $\mathcal{H}_{i-1}$, except that the oracle $\mathcal{O}_{(\mathsf{pk_{FHE}}, \mathsf{pk_{LHE}}, q, \tilde{q})}$ on input $d^{(i)}$ is programmed to output some a (along with a well-formed $\tilde{a}$) such that the resulting c is of the form

$$c = \mathsf{LHE.Enc}\left(\mathsf{pk_{LHE}}, \mathsf{ECC}(C_i(m_b)) + \tilde{e} + e + r - \lfloor r/\tilde{q} \rfloor \cdot \tilde{q}\right)$$

where ECC is the high-order bits encoding defined in the evaluation algorithm, $\tilde{e} + e$ is the sum of the decryption noises of the ciphertexts $(d^{(1)}, \ldots, d^{(k)}, \tilde{a})$, as defined in the evaluation algorithm, and $r \leftarrow_{\$} \mathbb{Z}_q$. Then $\tilde{\rho}_i$ is defined to be the decryption hint of c computed using the random coins of a.

First observe that $\tilde{e} + e$ is efficiently computable given the secret key of the FHE scheme and therefore $\tilde{\rho}_i$ is also computable in polynomial time. It is important to observe that the distribution of c is identical to the previous hybrid and the difference lies only in the way $\tilde{\rho}_i$ is computed. Since the LHE scheme has simulatable hints, it follows that the distribution of $\mathcal{H}_i$ is identical to that of $\mathcal{H}_{i-1}$ and the change described here is only syntactical. That is,

$$(\mathsf{pk}, \mathsf{FHE.Enc}(\mathsf{pk_{FHE}}, m_b), \tilde{\rho}_1, \ldots, \tilde{\rho}_{i-1}, \rho_i, \rho_{i+1}, \ldots, \rho_\beta)$$
$$= (\mathsf{pk}, \mathsf{FHE.Enc}(\mathsf{pk_{FHE}}, m_b), \tilde{\rho}_1, \ldots, \tilde{\rho}_{i-1}, \tilde{\rho}_i, \rho_{i+1}, \ldots, \rho_\beta).$$

Hybrids $\mathcal{H}_{\beta+1} \ldots \mathcal{H}_{2\beta}$: The $(\beta+i)$-th hybrid differs from the previous one in the sense that a is programmed such that

$$c = \mathsf{LHE.Enc}\left(\mathsf{pk_{LHE}}, \mathsf{ECC}(C_i(m_b)) + \tilde{e} + e + \lfloor r/\tilde{q} \rfloor \cdot \tilde{q} + \tilde{r} - \lfloor r/\tilde{q} \rfloor \cdot \tilde{q}\right)$$
$$= \mathsf{LHE.Enc}\left(\mathsf{pk_{LHE}}, \mathsf{ECC}(C_i(m_b)) + \tilde{e} + e + \tilde{r}\right)$$

where $\tilde{r} \leftarrow_{\$} \mathbb{Z}_{\tilde{q}}$. Note that the distributions induced by the two hybrids differ only in case where $r \in R$, where $R = \{q - (q \mod \tilde{q}), \ldots, q\}$. Since $\tilde{q}/q \leq 2^{-\lambda}$ we have that the two distributions are statistically close.

Hybrids $\mathcal{H}_{2\beta+1} \ldots \mathcal{H}_{3\beta}$: The $(\beta+i)$-th hybrid is defined to be identical to the previous ones except that a is programmed such that

$$c = \mathsf{LHE.Enc}\left(\mathsf{pk_{LHE}}, \mathsf{ECC}(C_i(m_b)) + \tilde{r}\right).$$

I.e., the noise term $\tilde{e}$ is omitted from the computation. Thus the only difference with respect to the previous hybrid is whether the noise term $\tilde{e} + e$ is included in the ciphertext or not. Since $\tilde{e} + e$ is bounded from above by $(k+1) \cdot B$ and $\tilde{q} \geq 2^\lambda \cdot (k+1) \cdot B$, by Lemma 1 the distribution induced by this hybrid is statistically indistinguishable from that of the previous one.

Hybrids $\mathcal{H}_{3\beta+1} \ldots \mathcal{H}_{3\beta+n}$: The $(3\beta + i)$-th hybrid is defined as the previous one, except that the ciphertext $c_{(\mathsf{LHE},i)}$ in the public parameters is computed as the encryption of 0. Note that the secret key of the LHE scheme is no longer used in the computation of $(\tilde{\rho}_1, \ldots, \tilde{\rho}_\beta)$ and therefore indistinguishability follows from an invocation of the semantic security of the LHE scheme. Specifically, the following distributions are computationally indistinguishable

$$\begin{pmatrix} \mathsf{LHE.Enc}(\mathsf{pk}_{\mathsf{LHE}}, 0), \ldots, \mathsf{LHE.Enc}(\mathsf{pk}_{\mathsf{LHE}}, 0), \mathsf{LHE.Enc}(\mathsf{pk}_{\mathsf{LHE}}, s_i), \\ \mathsf{LHE.Enc}(\mathsf{pk}_{\mathsf{LHE}}, s_{i+1}), \ldots, \mathsf{LHE.Enc}(\mathsf{pk}_{\mathsf{LHE}}, s_n) \end{pmatrix}$$
$$\approx_c \begin{pmatrix} \mathsf{LHE.Enc}(\mathsf{pk}_{\mathsf{LHE}}, 0), \ldots, \mathsf{LHE.Enc}(\mathsf{pk}_{\mathsf{LHE}}, 0), \mathsf{LHE.Enc}(\mathsf{pk}_{\mathsf{LHE}}, 0), \\ \mathsf{LHE.Enc}(\mathsf{pk}_{\mathsf{LHE}}, s_{i+1}), \ldots, \mathsf{LHE.Enc}(\mathsf{pk}_{\mathsf{LHE}}, s_n) \end{pmatrix}.$$

Hybrid $\mathcal{H}_{3\beta+n}^{(b)}$: We define the hybrid $\mathcal{H}_{3\beta+n}^{(b)}$ as $\mathcal{H}_{3\beta+n}$ with the challenger bit fixed to b. Note that the distribution induced by these hybrids is

$$(\mathsf{pk}, c = \mathsf{FHE.Enc}(\mathsf{pk}_{\mathsf{FHE}}, m_b), \tilde{\rho}_1, \ldots, \tilde{\rho}_\beta)$$

where

$$\mathsf{pk} = (\mathsf{pk}_{\mathsf{FHE}}, \mathsf{pk}_{\mathsf{LHE}}, \mathsf{LHE.Enc}(\mathsf{pk}_{\mathsf{LHE}}, 0), \ldots, \mathsf{LHE.Enc}(\mathsf{pk}_{\mathsf{LHE}}, 0)).$$

Observe that the secret key of the FHE scheme is no longer encoded in the public parameters and is not needed to compute $(\tilde{\rho}_1, \ldots, \tilde{\rho}_\beta)$ either. It follows that any advantage that the adversary has in distinguishing $\mathcal{H}_{3\beta+n}^{(0)}$ from $\mathcal{H}_{3\beta+n}^{(1)}$ cannot be greater than the advantage in distinguishing $\mathsf{FHE.Enc}(\mathsf{pk}_{\mathsf{FHE}}, m_0)$ from $\mathsf{FHE.Enc}(\mathsf{pk}_{\mathsf{FHE}}, m_1)$. Thus, computational indistinguishability follows from an invocation of the semantic security of the FHE scheme. This concludes our proof.

Parameters. When instantiating the LHE scheme with the Damgård-Jurik encryption scheme (as described in Sect. 3.3) and the FHE scheme with any LWE-based scheme with linear decrypt-and-multiply (e.g., the scheme proposed in [36]) we obtain a split FHE which satisfies the notion of split compactness: The hint ρ is of size $N = \mathsf{poly}(\lambda)$ and in particular is arbitrarily smaller than the size of the plaintext space $q = N^\varsigma$. For essentially any choice of the LWE-based FHE scheme with modulus q, the size of the public key and fresh ciphertexts depends polynomially in λ and linearly in $\log(q) = \log(N^\varsigma)$, which gives us the desired bound. The analysis above sets the following additional constraints:

- $q \geq 2^k + 2^{\lceil \log(\tilde{q}+(k+1)B) \rceil}$,
- $q \geq 2^\lambda \cdot \tilde{q}$, and
- $\tilde{q} \geq 2^\lambda \cdot (k+1) \cdot B$

which are always satisfied for $q = N^\varsigma$, by setting the integer ς to be large enough. Note that this choice of parameters fixes the modulus of the FHE with linear decrypt-and-multiply to $\mathbb{Z}_{N^\varsigma}$, which is super-polynomially larger than the noise bound B. Finally, the LWE parameter n is free and can be set to any value for which the corresponding problem (with super-polynomial modulus-to-noise ratio) is conjectured to be hard.

4.2   Instantiating the Oracle

To complete the description of our scheme, we discuss a few candidate instantiations for the oracle $\mathcal{O}_{(\mathsf{pk_{FHE}},\mathsf{pk_{LHE}},q,\tilde{q})}$. We require the underlying LHE scheme to have a dense ciphertext domain (which is the case for the Damgård-Jurik encryption scheme). Both of our proposal introduce new circularity assumptions between the FHE and the LHE schemes.

An alternate way to think of the oracle in Theorem 4 is to see it as an obfuscation for a special program, which is sufficient for realizing split FHE. The candidate constructions that we provide below can be seen as a very natural and simple obfuscation of this special program.

A Simple Candidate. Let $\mathfrak{C}$ be the ciphertext domain of LHE. Our first instantiation hardwires an FHE encryption of the LHE secret key $c_{\mathsf{FHE}} \leftarrow \mathsf{FHE.Enc}(\mathsf{pk_{FHE}}, \mathsf{sk_{LHE}})$. We fix the random coins of the algorithm (whenever needed) by drawing them from the evaluation of a cryptographic hash function Hash over the input. The intuition for our candidate is very simple: The LHE ciphertext is obliviously sampled without the knowledge of the underlying plaintext (which is the reason why we need dense ciphertexts) whereas the FHE term is computed by evaluating the decryption circuit homomorphically and rounding the resulting message to the closest multiple of $\tilde{q}$.

$\mathcal{O}_{(\mathsf{pk_{FHE}},\mathsf{pk_{LHE}},q,\tilde{q})}(x)$: On input a string $x \in \{0,1\}^*$ sample $y \leftarrow_\$ \mathfrak{C}$, using $\mathsf{Hash}(x)$ as the random coins, then compute

$$\tilde{y} \leftarrow \mathsf{FHE.Eval}\left(\mathsf{pk_{FHE}}, -\lfloor \mathsf{LHE.Dec}(\cdot, y)/\tilde{q} \rfloor \cdot \tilde{q}, c_{\mathsf{FHE}}\right)$$

and return $(y, \tilde{y})$.

Observe that y is an element in the ciphertext domain of LHE and it is of the form $y = \mathsf{LHE.Enc}(\mathsf{pk_{LHE}}, m)$, for some $m \in \mathbb{Z}_q$, since LHE has a dense ciphertext domain. Furthermore, by the correctness of the FHE and the LHE scheme, we have that

$$
\begin{aligned}
\tilde{y} &= \mathsf{FHE.Eval}\left(\mathsf{pk_{FHE}}, -\lfloor \mathsf{LHE.Dec}(\cdot, y)/\tilde{q} \rfloor \cdot \tilde{q}, c_{\mathsf{FHE}}\right) \\
&= \mathsf{FHE.Eval}\left(\mathsf{pk_{FHE}}, -\lfloor \mathsf{LHE.Dec}(\cdot, y)/\tilde{q} \rfloor \cdot \tilde{q}, \mathsf{FHE.Enc}(\mathsf{pk_{FHE}}, \mathsf{sk_{LHE}})\right) \\
&= \mathsf{FHE.Enc}\left(\mathsf{pk_{FHE}}, -\lfloor \mathsf{LHE.Dec}(\mathsf{sk_{LHE}}, y)/\tilde{q} \rfloor \cdot \tilde{q}\right) \\
&= \mathsf{FHE.Enc}\left(\mathsf{pk_{FHE}}, -\lfloor m/\tilde{q} \rfloor \cdot \tilde{q}\right).
\end{aligned}
$$

It follows that the pair $(y, \tilde{y})$ is syntactically well formed. However, a closer look to the oracle instantiation reveals two lingering assumptions.

(1) *Circular Security:* The addition of $c_{\mathsf{FHE}} = \mathsf{FHE.Enc}(\mathsf{pk_{FHE}}, \mathsf{sk_{LHE}})$ introduces a circular dependency in the security of the LHE and FHE schemes (recall that our split FHE construction includes in the public key an encryption of $\mathsf{sk_{FHE}}$ under $\mathsf{pk_{LHE}}$). Circular security is however widely considered to be a very mild assumption and currently is the only known approach to construct plain (as opposed to levelled) FHE from LWE via the bootstrapping theorem [32].

(2) *Correlations:* Although $\tilde{y}$ is an FHE encryption of the correct value, it is not necessarily uniformly distributed, conditioned on y. In particular the randomness of $\tilde{y}$ may depend in some intricate way on the low-order bits of m. For the specific case of LWE-based schemes, the *noise* term might carry some information about $m \bmod \tilde{q}$, which could introduce some harmful correlation. However, the noise function is typically highly non-linear and therefore appears to be difficult to exploit. We also stress that we only consider honest executions of the FHE.Eval algorithm.

While (1) can be regarded as a standard assumption, we view (2) as a natural conjecture which we believe holds true for any natural/known candidate instantiation of the FHE and LHE schemes. In light of these considerations, we conjecture that the implementation as describe above already leads to a secure split FHE scheme.

Towards Removing Correlations. A natural approach towards removing the correlation of the LHE and FHE ciphertexts is that of ciphertext sanitization [24]: One could expect that repeatedly bootstrapping the FHE ciphertext would decorrelate the noise from the companion LHE ciphertext. Unfortunately our settings are different than those typically considered in the literature, in the sense that the santiziation procedure must be carried out by the distinguisher and therefore cannot use private random coins. Although it appears hard to formally analyze the effectiveness of these methods in our settings, we expect that these techniques might (at least heuristically) help to obliterate harmful correlations. In this work we take a different route and we suggest a simple heuristic method to prevent correlations. In a nutshell, the idea is to sample a set of random plaintexts and define the random string as the sum of a uniformly sampled subset S of these plaintext. The key observation is that subset sum is a linear operation and therefore can be performed directly in the LHE scheme, which implies that the *leakage* of the FHE scheme cannot depend on S. As for the previous construction, our instantiation contains and a ciphertext $c_{\mathsf{FHE}} = \mathsf{FHE.Enc}(\mathsf{pk}_{\mathsf{FHE}}, \mathsf{sk}_{\mathsf{LHE}})$. The scheme is parametrized by some $\sigma \in \mathsf{poly}(\lambda)$, which defines the size of the set S. In the following description we present the algorithm as randomized, although this simplification can be easily bypassed with standard techniques (e.g., computing the random coins using a cryptographic hash $\mathsf{Hash}(x)$).

$\mathcal{O}_{(\mathsf{pk}_{\mathsf{FHE}}, \mathsf{pk}_{\mathsf{LHE}}, q, \tilde{q})}(x)$: On input a string $x \in \{0,1\}^*$ sample a random set $S \leftarrow_{\$} \{0,1\}^\sigma$.

Then, for all $i \in [\sigma]$, do the following:
- If $S_i = 1$, sample a uniform $y_i \leftarrow_{\$} \mathcal{C}$.
- If $S_i = 0$, sample a uniform encryption $y_i \leftarrow_{\$} \mathsf{LHE.Enc}(\mathsf{pk}_{\mathsf{LHE}}, m_i)$, for a random known m_i.

Then compute

$$\tilde{y} \leftarrow \mathsf{FHE.Eval}\left(\mathsf{pk}_{\mathsf{FHE}}, -\sum_{i=1}^{\sigma} \lfloor \mathsf{LHE.Dec}(\cdot, y_i)/\tilde{q} \rceil \cdot \tilde{q}, c_{\mathsf{FHE}}\right).$$

Let f be the following linear function

$$f(x_1, \ldots, x_{|S|}) = \sum_{i \in S} x_i + \sum_{i \notin S} \lfloor m_i/\tilde{q} \rfloor \cdot \tilde{q}$$

then compute $y \leftarrow \mathsf{LHE.Eval}\left(\mathsf{pk}_{\mathsf{LHE}}, f, \{y_i\}_{i \in S}\right)$ and return $(y, \tilde{y})$.

To see why the implementation is syntactically correct, observe that

$$\tilde{y} = \mathsf{FHE.Eval}\left(\mathsf{pk}_{\mathsf{FHE}}, -\sum_{i=1}^{\sigma} \lfloor \mathsf{LHE.Dec}(\cdot, y_i)/\tilde{q} \rfloor \cdot \tilde{q}, c_{\mathsf{FHE}}\right)$$

$$= \mathsf{FHE.Enc}\left(\mathsf{pk}_{\mathsf{FHE}}, -\sum_{i=1}^{\sigma} \lfloor \mathsf{LHE.Dec}(\mathsf{sk}_{\mathsf{LHE}}, y_i)/\tilde{q} \rfloor \cdot \tilde{q}\right)$$

$$= \mathsf{FHE.Enc}\left(\mathsf{pk}_{\mathsf{FHE}}, -\sum_{i=1}^{\sigma} \lfloor m_i/\tilde{q} \rfloor \cdot \tilde{q}\right)$$

by the evaluation correctness of the FHE scheme. Invoking to the correctness of the LHE scheme we have that

$$y = \mathsf{LHE.Eval}\left(\mathsf{pk}_{\mathsf{LHE}}, f, \{y_i\}_{i \in S}\right)$$

$$= \mathsf{LHE.Eval}\left(\mathsf{pk}_{\mathsf{LHE}}, f, \{\mathsf{LHE.Enc}(\mathsf{pk}_{\mathsf{LHE}}, m_i)\}_{i \in S}\right)$$

$$= \mathsf{LHE.Enc}\left(\mathsf{pk}_{\mathsf{LHE}}, \sum_{i \in S} m_i + \sum_{i \notin S} \lfloor m_i/\tilde{q} \rfloor \cdot \tilde{q}\right)$$

$$= \mathsf{LHE.Enc}\left(\mathsf{pk}_{\mathsf{LHE}}, \underbrace{\sum_{i \in S} (m_i \mod \tilde{q})}_{\tilde{m}} + \sum_{i=1}^{\sigma} \lfloor m_i/\tilde{q} \rfloor \cdot \tilde{q}\right)$$

which is exactly what we want, except that $\tilde{m}$ is slightly larger than $\tilde{q}$, by a factor of at most σ. This can still be used in our main construction by adjusting the error correcting code accordingly. The intuition why we believe that this variant is secure is that the leakage in the FHE randomness cannot depend on the set S, since the distributions of all y_i are statistically close (recall that LHE has dense ciphertexts). Thus, S (which is chosen uniformly) resembles the behavior of a binary extractor on $(m_i \mod \tilde{q})$. Nevertheless, proving a formal statement remains an interesting open question.

5   Split Fully-Homomorphic Encryption $\implies$ Obfuscation

In order to construct fully-fledged iO from split FHE, we rely on a theorem from Lin et al. [44], which we recall in the following. Roughly speaking, the theorem states that, under the assumption that the LWE problem is sub-exponentially hard, it suffices to consider circuits with a polynomial-size input domain and obfuscators that output obfuscated circuits of size slightly sublinear in size of the truth table of the circuit.

Theorem 5 ([44]). *Assuming sub-exponentially hard LWE, if there exists a sub-exponentially secure indistinguishability obfuscator for $\mathsf{P}^{\log}/\mathsf{poly}$ with non-trivial efficiency, then there exists an indistinguishability obfuscator for P/poly with sub-exponential security.*

Here $\mathsf{P}^{\log}/\mathsf{poly}$ denotes the class of polynomial-size circuits with inputs of length $\eta = O(\log(\lambda))$ and by non-trivial efficiency we mean that the size of the obfuscated circuit is bounded by $\mathsf{poly}(\lambda, |C|) \cdot 2^{\eta \cdot (1-\varepsilon)}$, for some constant $\varepsilon > 0$. Note that the above theorem poses no restriction on the runtime of the obfuscator, which can be as large as $\mathsf{poly}(\lambda, |C|) \cdot 2^{\eta}$.

In the following we show how to construct an obfuscator for $\mathsf{P}^{\log}/\mathsf{poly}$ with non-trivial efficiency. We assume only the existence of a (levelled) split FHE scheme $\mathsf{sFHE} = (\mathsf{KeyGen}, \mathsf{Enc}, \mathsf{Eval}, \mathsf{PDec}, \mathsf{Rec})$.

$\mathsf{iO}(C)$: On input the description of a circuit C, sample a fresh key pair $(\mathsf{sk}, \mathsf{pk}) \leftarrow \mathsf{KeyGen}(1^\lambda)$ and compute $c \leftarrow \mathsf{Enc}(\mathsf{pk}, C)$. For all $i \in \left[2^{\eta/2}\right]$ define the universal circuit $\mathfrak{U}_i$ as

$$\mathfrak{U}_i(C) = C\left((i-1) \cdot 2^{\eta/2}\right) \| \ldots \| C\left(i \cdot 2^{\eta/2} - 1\right).$$

Then compute $c_i \leftarrow \mathsf{Eval}(\mathsf{pk}, \mathfrak{U}_i, c)$ and $\rho_i \leftarrow \mathsf{PDec}(\mathsf{sk}, c_i)$. The obfuscated circuit is defined to be $(\mathsf{pk}, c, \rho_1, \ldots, \rho_{2^{\eta/2}})$.

First we discuss how to evaluate an obfuscated circuit: On input some $x \in \{0,1\}^\eta$, parse it as an integer and round it to the nearest multiple of $2^{\eta/2}$ (let such integer be $\bar{x}$) such that $\bar{x} \leq x$. Then compute $c_{\bar{x}} \leftarrow \mathsf{Eval}(\mathsf{pk}, \mathfrak{U}_{\bar{x}}, c)$ and $m \leftarrow \mathsf{Rec}(\rho_{\bar{x}}, c_{\bar{x}})$. Read the output as the $(x - \bar{x})$-th bit of m.

Analysis. Note that the runtime of the obfuscator is dominated by $2^{\eta/2}$ evaluations of the split FHE ciphertext, where each subroutine homomorphically evaluates the circuit C $2^{\eta/2}$-many times. Thus the total runtime of the obfuscator is in the order of $\mathsf{poly}(\lambda, |C|) \cdot 2^{\eta}$. We now argue that our obfuscator has non trivial efficiency in terms of output size. We analyze the size of each component of the obfuscated circuit:

- By the compactness of the split FHE scheme, the public key pk grows linearly with the size of the output domain, i.e., $2^{\eta/2}$, and polynomially in the security parameter.
- The ciphertext c grows linearly with the size of the encrypted message and therefore, by the compactness of the split FHE scheme, bounded by $\mathsf{poly}(\lambda, |C|) \cdot 2^{\eta/2}$.
- Each decryption hint ρ_i is of size $\mathsf{poly}(\lambda)$, since the underlying split FHE is compact. As an obfuscated circuit consists of $2^{\eta/2}$-many decryption hints, the size of the vector $(\rho_1, \ldots, \rho_{2^{\eta/2}})$ is $\mathsf{poly}(\lambda) \cdot 2^{\eta/2}$.

It follows that the total size of the obfuscated circuit is bounded from above by $\mathsf{poly}(\lambda, |C|) \cdot 2^{n/2}$. What is left to be shown is that our obfuscator satisfies the notion of indistinguishability obfuscation.

Theorem 6 (Indistinguishability Obfuscation). *Let* sFHE *be a sub-exponentially secure levelled split FHE scheme. Then the scheme as described above is a sub-exponentially secure indistinguishability obfuscator.*

Proof. By the perfect correctness of the split FHE scheme it follows that the obfuscated circuit is functionally equivalent to the plain circuit. Indistinguishability follows immediately from the split security of sFHE: If the split FHE is secure against a distinguisher running in sub-exponential time, then so is iO.

References

1. Agrawal, S.: Indistinguishability obfuscation without multilinear maps: new methods for bootstrapping and instantiation. In: Ishai, Y., Rijmen, V. (eds.) EUROCRYPT 2019, Part I. LNCS, vol. 11476, pp. 191–225. Springer, Cham (2019). https://doi.org/10.1007/978-3-030-17653-2_7

2. Alperin-Sheriff, J., Peikert, C.: Faster bootstrapping with polynomial error. In: Garay, J.A., Gennaro, R. (eds.) CRYPTO 2014, Part I. LNCS, vol. 8616, pp. 297–314. Springer, Heidelberg (2014). https://doi.org/10.1007/978-3-662-44371-2_17

3. Ananth, P., Jain, A., Lin, H., Matt, C., Sahai, A.: Indistinguishability obfuscation without multilinear maps: new paradigms via low degree weak pseudorandomness and security amplification. In: Boldyreva, A., Micciancio, D. (eds.) CRYPTO 2019, Part III. LNCS, vol. 11694, pp. 284–332. Springer, Cham (2019). https://doi.org/10.1007/978-3-030-26954-8_10

4. Ananth, P., Jain, A.: Indistinguishability obfuscation from compact functional encryption. In: Gennaro, R., Robshaw, M. (eds.) CRYPTO 2015, Part I. LNCS, vol. 9215, pp. 308–326. Springer, Heidelberg (2015). https://doi.org/10.1007/978-3-662-47989-6_15

5. Ananth, P., Sahai, A.: Projective arithmetic functional encryption and indistinguishability obfuscation from degree-5 multilinear maps. In: Coron, J.-S., Nielsen, J.B. (eds.) EUROCRYPT 2017, Part I. LNCS, vol. 10210, pp. 152–181. Springer, Cham (2017). https://doi.org/10.1007/978-3-319-56620-7_6

6. Applebaum, B., Ishai, Y., Kushilevitz, E.: How to garble arithmetic circuits. In: Ostrovsky, R. (ed.) 52nd FOCS, pp. 120–129. IEEE Computer Society Press, October 2011

7. Asharov, G., Jain, A., López-Alt, A., Tromer, E., Vaikuntanathan, V., Wichs, D.: Multiparty computation with low communication, computation and interaction via threshold FHE. In: Pointcheval, D., Johansson, T. (eds.) EUROCRYPT 2012. LNCS, vol. 7237, pp. 483–501. Springer, Heidelberg (2012). https://doi.org/10.1007/978-3-642-29011-4_29

8. Barak, B., Brakerski, Z., Komargodski, I., Kothari, P.K.: Limits on low-degree pseudorandom generators (or: sum-of-squares meets program obfuscation). Cryptology ePrint Archive, Report 2017/312 (2017). http://eprint.iacr.org/2017/312

9. Barak, B., Garg, S., Kalai, Y.T., Paneth, O., Sahai, A.: Protecting obfuscation against algebraic attacks. In: Nguyen, P.Q., Oswald, E. (eds.) EUROCRYPT 2014. LNCS, vol. 8441, pp. 221–238. Springer, Heidelberg (2014). https://doi.org/10.1007/978-3-642-55220-5_13

10. Barak, B., et al.: On the (im)possibility of obfuscating programs. In: Kilian, J. (ed.) CRYPTO 2001. LNCS, vol. 2139, pp. 1–18. Springer, Heidelberg (2001). https://doi.org/10.1007/3-540-44647-8_1

11. Barak, B., Haitner, I., Hofheinz, D., Ishai, Y.: Bounded key-dependent message security. In: Gilbert, H. (ed.) EUROCRYPT 2010. LNCS, vol. 6110, pp. 423–444. Springer, Heidelberg (2010). https://doi.org/10.1007/978-3-642-13190-5_22

12. Barak, B., Hopkins, S.B., Jain, A., Kothari, P., Sahai, A.: Sum-of-squares meets program obfuscation, revisited. In: Ishai, Y., Rijmen, V. (eds.) EUROCRYPT 2019, Part I. LNCS, vol. 11476, pp. 226–250. Springer, Cham (2019). https://doi.org/10.1007/978-3-030-17653-2_8

13. Bellare, M., Rogaway, P.: Random oracles are practical: a paradigm for designing efficient protocols. In: Denning, D.E., Pyle, R., Ganesan, R., Sandhu, R.S., Ashby, V. (eds.) ACM CCS 1993, pp. 62–73. ACM Press, November 1993

14. Bitansky, N., Nishimaki, R., Passelègue, A., Wichs, D.: From cryptomania to obfustopia through secret-key functional encryption. In: Hirt, M., Smith, A. (eds.) TCC 2016, Part II. LNCS, vol. 9986, pp. 391–418. Springer, Heidelberg (2016). https://doi.org/10.1007/978-3-662-53644-5_15

15. Bitansky, N., Vaikuntanathan, V.: Indistinguishability obfuscation from functional encryption. In: Guruswami, V. (ed.) 56th FOCS, pp. 171–190. IEEE Computer Society Press, October 2015

16. Boneh, D., Zhandry, M.: Multiparty key exchange, efficient traitor tracing, and more from indistinguishability obfuscation. In: Garay, J.A., Gennaro, R. (eds.) CRYPTO 2014, Part I. LNCS, vol. 8616, pp. 480–499. Springer, Heidelberg (2014). https://doi.org/10.1007/978-3-662-44371-2_27

17. Brakerski, Z., Döttling, N., Garg, S., Malavolta, G.: Leveraging linear decryption: rate-1 fully-homomorphic encryption and time-lock puzzles. Cryptology ePrint Archive, Report 2019/720 (2019)

18. Brakerski, Z., Rothblum, G.N.: Virtual black-box obfuscation for all circuits via generic graded encoding. In: Lindell, Y. (ed.) TCC 2014. LNCS, vol. 8349, pp. 1–25. Springer, Heidelberg (2014). https://doi.org/10.1007/978-3-642-54242-8_1

19. Brakerski, Z., Vaikuntanathan, V.: Lattice-based FHE as secure as PKE. In: Naor, M. (ed.) ITCS 2014, pp. 1–12. ACM, January 2014

20. Chen, Y., Gentry, C., Halevi, S.: Cryptanalyses of candidate branching program obfuscators. In: Coron, J.-S., Nielsen, J.B. (eds.) EUROCRYPT 2017, Part III. LNCS, vol. 10212, pp. 278–307. Springer, Cham (2017). https://doi.org/10.1007/978-3-319-56617-7_10

21. Cheon, J.H., Han, K., Lee, C., Ryu, H., Stehlé, D.: Cryptanalysis of the multilinear map over the integers. In: Oswald, E., Fischlin, M. (eds.) EUROCRYPT 2015, Part I. LNCS, vol. 9056, pp. 3–12. Springer, Heidelberg (2015). https://doi.org/10.1007/978-3-662-46800-5_1

22. Coron, J.-S., Lepoint, T., Tibouchi, M.: Practical multilinear maps over the integers. In: Canetti, R., Garay, J.A. (eds.) CRYPTO 2013, Part I. LNCS, vol. 8042, pp. 476–493. Springer, Heidelberg (2013). https://doi.org/10.1007/978-3-642-40041-4_26

23. Damgård, I., Jurik, M.: A generalisation, a simpli.cation and some applications of Paillier's probabilistic public-key system. In: Kim, K. (ed.) PKC 2001. LNCS, vol. 1992, pp. 119–136. Springer, Heidelberg (2001). https://doi.org/10.1007/3-540-44586-2_9

24. Ducas, L., Stehlé, D.: Sanitization of FHE ciphertexts. In: Fischlin, M., Coron, J.-S. (eds.) EUROCRYPT 2016, Part I. LNCS, vol. 9665, pp. 294–310. Springer, Heidelberg (2016). https://doi.org/10.1007/978-3-662-49890-3_12

25. Fiat, A., Shamir, A.: How to prove yourself: practical solutions to identification and signature problems. In: Odlyzko, A.M. (ed.) CRYPTO 1986. LNCS, vol. 263, pp. 186–194. Springer, Heidelberg (1987). https://doi.org/10.1007/3-540-47721-7_12

26. Garg, S., Gentry, C., Halevi, S.: Candidate multilinear maps from ideal lattices. In: Johansson, T., Nguyen, P.Q. (eds.) EUROCRYPT 2013. LNCS, vol. 7881, pp. 1–17. Springer, Heidelberg (2013). https://doi.org/10.1007/978-3-642-38348-9_1

27. Garg, S., Gentry, C., Halevi, S., Raykova, M.: Two-round secure MPC from indistinguishability obfuscation. In: Lindell, Y. (ed.) TCC 2014. LNCS, vol. 8349, pp. 74–94. Springer, Heidelberg (2014). https://doi.org/10.1007/978-3-642-54242-8_4

28. Garg, S., Gentry, C., Halevi, S., Raykova, M., Sahai, A., Waters, B.: Candidate indistinguishability obfuscation and functional encryption for all circuits. In: 54th FOCS, pp. 40–49. IEEE Computer Society Press, October 2013

29. Garg, S., Mahmoody, M., Mohammed, A.: Lower bounds on obfuscation from all-or-nothing encryption primitives. In: Katz, J., Shacham, H. (eds.) CRYPTO 2017, Part I. LNCS, vol. 10401, pp. 661–695. Springer, Cham (2017). https://doi.org/10.1007/978-3-319-63688-7_22

30. Garg, S., Mahmoody, M., Mohammed, A.: When does functional encryption imply obfuscation? In: Kalai, Y., Reyzin, L. (eds.) TCC 2017, Part I. LNCS, vol. 10677, pp. 82–115. Springer, Cham (2017). https://doi.org/10.1007/978-3-319-70500-2_4

31. Garg, S., Miles, E., Mukherjee, P., Sahai, A., Srinivasan, A., Zhandry, M.: Secure obfuscation in a weak multilinear map model. In: Hirt, M., Smith, A. (eds.) TCC 2016, Part II. LNCS, vol. 9986, pp. 241–268. Springer, Heidelberg (2016). https://doi.org/10.1007/978-3-662-53644-5_10

32. Gentry, C.: Fully homomorphic encryption using ideal lattices. In: Mitzenmacher, M. (ed.) 41st ACM STOC, pp. 169–178. ACM Press, May/June 2009

33. Gentry, C., Gorbunov, S., Halevi, S.: Graph-induced multilinear maps from lattices. In: Dodis, Y., Nielsen, J.B. (eds.) TCC 2015, Part II. LNCS, vol. 9015, pp. 498–527. Springer, Heidelberg (2015). https://doi.org/10.1007/978-3-662-46497-7_20

34. Gentry, C., Halevi, S., Vaikuntanathan, V.: i-Hop homomorphic encryption and rerandomizable Yao circuits. In: Rabin, T. (ed.) CRYPTO 2010. LNCS, vol. 6223, pp. 155–172. Springer, Heidelberg (2010). https://doi.org/10.1007/978-3-642-14623-7_9

35. Gentry, C., Jutla, C.S., Kane, D.: Obfuscation using tensor products. Cryptology ePrint Archive, Report 2018/756 (2018)

36. Gentry, C., Sahai, A., Waters, B.: Homomorphic encryption from learning with errors: conceptually-simpler, asymptotically-faster, attribute-based. In: Canetti, R., Garay, J.A. (eds.) CRYPTO 2013, Part I. LNCS, vol. 8042, pp. 75–92. Springer, Heidelberg (2013). https://doi.org/10.1007/978-3-642-40041-4_5

37. Goldwasser, S., Kalai, Y.T., Popa, R.A., Vaikuntanathan, V., Zeldovich, N.: Reusable garbled circuits and succinct functional encryption. In: Boneh, D., Roughgarden, T., Feigenbaum, J. (eds.) 45th ACM STOC, pp. 555–564. ACM Press, June 2013

38. Goldwasser, S., Micali, S.: Probabilistic encryption and how to play mental poker keeping secret all partial information. In: 14th ACM STOC, pp. 365–377. ACM Press, May 1982

39. Hada, S.: Zero-knowledge and code obfuscation. In: Okamoto, T. (ed.) ASIACRYPT 2000. LNCS, vol. 1976, pp. 443–457. Springer, Heidelberg (2000). https://doi.org/10.1007/3-540-44448-3_34

40. Hu, Y., Jia, H.: Cryptanalysis of GGH map. In: Fischlin, M., Coron, J.-S. (eds.) EUROCRYPT 2016, Part I. LNCS, vol. 9665, pp. 537–565. Springer, Heidelberg (2016). https://doi.org/10.1007/978-3-662-49890-3_21

41. Jain, A., Lin, H., Matt, C., Sahai, A.: How to leverage hardness of constant-degree expanding polynomials over $\mathbb{R}$ to build $i\mathcal{O}$. In: Ishai, Y., Rijmen, V. (eds.) EUROCRYPT 2019, Part I. LNCS, vol. 11476, pp. 251–281. Springer, Cham (2019). https://doi.org/10.1007/978-3-030-17653-2_9

42. Lin, H.: Indistinguishability obfuscation from constant-degree graded encoding schemes. In: Fischlin, M., Coron, J.-S. (eds.) EUROCRYPT 2016, Part I. LNCS, vol. 9665, pp. 28–57. Springer, Heidelberg (2016). https://doi.org/10.1007/978-3-662-49890-3_2

43. Lin, H.: Indistinguishability obfuscation from SXDH on 5-linear maps and locality-5 PRGs. In: Katz, J., Shacham, H. (eds.) CRYPTO 2017, Part I. LNCS, vol. 10401, pp. 599–629. Springer, Cham (2017). https://doi.org/10.1007/978-3-319-63688-7_20

44. Lin, H., Pass, R., Seth, K., Telang, S.: Indistinguishability obfuscation with nontrivial efficiency. In: Cheng, C.-M., Chung, K.-M., Persiano, G., Yang, B.-Y. (eds.) PKC 2016, Part II. LNCS, vol. 9615, pp. 447–462. Springer, Heidelberg (2016). https://doi.org/10.1007/978-3-662-49387-8_17

45. Lin, H., Tessaro, S.: Indistinguishability obfuscation from bilinear maps and block-wise local PRGs. Cryptology ePrint Archive, Report 2017/250, Version 20170320:142653 (2017)

46. Lin, H., Tessaro, S.: Indistinguishability obfuscation from trilinear maps and block-wise local PRGs. In: Katz, J., Shacham, H. (eds.) CRYPTO 2017, Part I. LNCS, vol. 10401, pp. 630–660. Springer, Cham (2017). https://doi.org/10.1007/978-3-319-63688-7_21

47. Lin, H., Vaikuntanathan, V.: Indistinguishability obfuscation from DDH-like assumptions on constant-degree graded encodings. In: Dinur, I. (ed.) 57th FOCS, pp. 11–20. IEEE Computer Society Press, October 2016

48. Lombardi, A., Vaikuntanathan, V.: Limits on the locality of pseudorandom generators and applications to indistinguishability obfuscation. In: Kalai, Y., Reyzin, L. (eds.) TCC 2017, Part I. LNCS, vol. 10677, pp. 119–137. Springer, Cham (2017). https://doi.org/10.1007/978-3-319-70500-2_5

49. Malavolta, G., Thyagarajan, S.A.K.: Homomorphic time-lock puzzles and applications. In: Boldyreva, A., Micciancio, D. (eds.) CRYPTO 2019, Part I. LNCS, vol. 11692, pp. 620–649. Springer, Cham (2019). https://doi.org/10.1007/978-3-030-26948-7_22

50. Micciancio, D.: From linear functions to fully homomorphic encryption. Technical report (2019). https://bacrypto.github.io/presentations/2018.11.30-Micciancio-FHE.pdf

51. Miles, E., Sahai, A., Zhandry, M.: Annihilation attacks for multilinear maps: cryptanalysis of indistinguishability obfuscation over GGH13. In: Robshaw, M., Katz, J. (eds.) CRYPTO 2016, Part II. LNCS, vol. 9815, pp. 629–658. Springer, Heidelberg (2016). https://doi.org/10.1007/978-3-662-53008-5_22

52. Paillier, P.: Public-key cryptosystems based on composite degree residuosity classes. In: Stern, J. (ed.) EUROCRYPT 1999. LNCS, vol. 1592, pp. 223–238. Springer, Heidelberg (1999). https://doi.org/10.1007/3-540-48910-X_16
53. Peikert, C., Regev, O., Stephens-Davidowitz, N.: Pseudorandomness of ring-LWE for any ring and modulus. In: Hatami, H., McKenzie, P., King, V. (eds.) 49th ACM STOC, pp. 461–473. ACM Press, June 2017
54. Regev, O.: On lattices, learning with errors, random linear codes, and cryptography. In: Gabow, H.N., Fagin, R. (eds.) 37th ACM STOC, pp. 84–93. ACM Press, May 2005
55. Sahai, A., Waters, B.: How to use indistinguishability obfuscation: deniable encryption, and more. In: Shmoys, D.B. (eds.) 46th ACM STOC, pp. 475–484. ACM Press, May/June 2014

Indistinguishability Obfuscation Without Maps: Attacks and Fixes for Noisy Linear FE

Shweta Agrawal[1](✉) and Alice Pellet-Mary[2](✉)

[1] IIT Madras, Chennai, India
shweta.a@gmail.com
[2] imec-COSIC, KU Leuven, Leuven, Belgium
alice.pelletmary@kuleuven.be

Abstract. Candidates of *Indistinguishability Obfuscation* (iO) can be categorized as "direct" or "bootstrapping based". Direct constructions rely on high degree multilinear maps [28,29] and provide heuristic guarantees, while bootstrapping based constructions [2,7,33,36,38,39] rely, in the best case, on *bilinear* maps as well as new variants of the Learning With Errors (LWE) assumption and pseudorandom generators. Recent times have seen exciting progress in the construction of indistinguishability obfuscation (iO) from bilinear maps (along with other assumptions) [2,7,33,38].

As a notable exception, a recent work by Agrawal [2] provided a construction for iO without using *any* maps. This work identified a new primitive, called *Noisy Linear Functional Encryption* (NLinFE) that provably suffices for iO and gave a direct construction of NLinFE from new assumptions on lattices. While a preliminary cryptanalysis for the new assumptions was provided in the original work, the author admitted the necessity of performing significantly more cryptanalysis before faith could be placed in the security of the scheme. Moreover, the author did not suggest concrete parameters for the construction.

In this work, we fill this gap by undertaking the task of thorough cryptanalytic study of NLinFE. We design two attacks that let the adversary completely break the security of the scheme. Our attacks are completely new and unrelated to attacks that were hitherto used to break other candidates of iO. To achieve this, we develop new cryptanalytic techniques which (we hope) will inform future designs of the primitive of NLinFE.

From the knowledge gained by our cryptanalytic study, we suggest modifications to the scheme. We provide a new scheme which overcomes the vulnerabilities identified before. We also provide a thorough analysis of all the security aspects of this scheme and argue why plausible attacks do not work. We additionally provide concrete parameters with which the scheme may be instantiated. We believe the security of NLinFE stands on significantly firmer footing as a result of this work.

© International Association for Cryptologic Research 2020
A. Canteaut and Y. Ishai (Eds.): EUROCRYPT 2020, LNCS 12105, pp. 110–140, 2020.
https://doi.org/10.1007/978-3-030-45721-1_5

1 Introduction

Indistinguishability Obfuscation (iO) is one of the most sought-after primitives in modern cryptography. While introduced in a work by Barak et al. in 2001 [11], the first candidate construction for this primitive was only provided in 2013 [29]. In this breakthrough work, the authors not only gave the first candidate for iO but also demonstrated its power by using it to construct the first full fledged functional encryption (FE) scheme. This work led to a deluge of ever more powerful applications of iO, ranging from classic to fantastic [13,15,18,19, 34,35,37,45]. Few years later, iO is widely acknowledged to be (almost) "crypto complete". We refer the reader to [36] for a detailed discussion.

However, constructions of iO have been far from perfect. The so called "first generation" constructions relied on the existence of *multilinear maps* of polynomial degree [9,29,30,47], "second generation" relied on multilinear maps of constant degree [36,38,39], and in a sequence of exciting recent works, "third generation" candidates rely only on multilinear maps of degree 2 (i.e. bilinear maps) along with assumptions on the complexity of certain special types of pseudorandom generators and new variants of the Learning With Errors (LWE) assumption [2,7,33]. It is well known that degree 2 maps can be instantiated on elliptic curve groups, so this brings us closer to realizing iO from believable assumptions than ever before.

iO Without maps: All the above constructions rely on multilinear maps of degree ≥ 2. While there exist candidates for multilinear maps of degree ≥ 3, they have been subject to many attacks [8,20,22–27,27,32,43,44] and their security is poorly understood. On the other hand, bilinear maps are well understood and considered safe to use (at least in the pre-quantum world). Recent works [2,7,33] have come tantalizingly close to basing iO on bilinear maps while minimizing the additional assumptions required. There is hope that these efforts will converge to a candidate whose security we may trust.

While realizing iO from degree 2 maps (along with other plausible assumptions) is a very worthy goal, it is nevertheless only one approach to take. Any cryptographic primitive, especially one of such central importance, deserves to be studied from different perspectives and based on diverse mathematical assumptions. Two works (that we are aware of) attempt to construct iO without using *any* maps – one by Gentry, Jutla and Keane [31] and another by Agrawal [2]. The work by Gentry et al. [31] constructs obfuscation schemes for matrix product branching programs that are purely algebraic and employ matrix groups and tensor algebra over a finite field. They prove security of their construction against a restricted class of attacks. On the other hand, the work of Agrawal formalizes a "minimal" (as per current knowledge) primitive called "Noisy Linear Functional Encryption" (NLinFE) which is showed to imply iO and provides a direct construction for this using new assumptions on NTRU lattices, which are quite different from assumptions used so far for building multilinear maps or iO.

Comparison with other approaches. The instantiation of iO via Agrawal's direct construction of NLinFE (henceforth referred to simply as NLinFE) has both advantages and disadvantages compared to other cutting-edge constructions. For instance, [31] has the advantage that it constructs full fledged iO directly, while NLinFE has the advantage that untested assumptions are used to construct a much *simpler* primitive. Next, consider constructions that use bilinear maps [2,7,33]. On the positive side, NLinFE has potential to be quantum secure, which evidently is not a property that bilinear map based constructions can hope to achieve. Additionally, the NLinFE supports outputs of *super-polynomial* size, while bilinear map based constructions can support only polynomially sized outputs. In particular, this leads to the latter constructions relying on a complicated and inefficient (albeit cool) "security amplification" step in order to be useful for iO. Moreover, there is a qualitative advantage to Agrawal's direct construction: while bilinear map based constructions use clever methods to compute a PRG output *exactly*, the direct construction of NLinFE relaxes correctness and settles for computing the PRG output only *approximately* – this allows for the usage of encodings that are not powerful enough for exact computation.

On the other hand, Agrawal's encodings are new, while assumptions over bilinear maps have stood the test of time (in the pre-quantum world). While bilinear map based constructions must also make new, non-standard assumptions, these constructions come with a clean proof from the non-standard assumptions. Meanwhile, Agrawal's NLinFE came with a proof in a very weak security game that only permits the adversary to request a *single* ciphertext, and that too from a non-standard assumption. Moreover, the author did not suggest concrete parameters for the construction, and admitted the necessity of substantially more cryptanalysis before faith could be placed in these new assumptions.

Our results. In this work, we undertake the task of thorough cryptanalytic study of Agrawal's NLinFE scheme. We design two attacks that let the adversary completely break the security of the scheme. To achieve this, we develop new cryptanalytic techniques which (we hope) will inform future designs of the primitive of NLinFE.

As mentioned above, Agrawal proved the security of her NLinFE in a weak security game where the attacker is only permitted to request a single ciphertext. Our first attack shows that this is not a co-incidence: an attacker given access to many ciphertexts can manipulate them to recover a (nonlinear) equation in secret terms, which, with some effort, can be solved to recover the secret elements. We emphasize that this attack is very different in nature from the annihilation attacks [43] studied in the context of breaking other constructions of iO. We refer to this attack as the *multiple ciphertext attack*. To demonstrate our attack, we formalize an assumption implicitly made by [2], and design an attack that breaks this assumption – this in turn implies an attack on the scheme. We implement this attack and provide the code as supplementary material with this work.

Our second attack, which we call the *rank attack* exploits a seemingly harmless property of the output of decryption in NLinFE. Recall that the primitive of NLinFE enables an encryptor to compute a ciphertext $CT(\mathbf{z})$, a key generator to compute a secret key $SK(\mathbf{v})$ and the decryptor, given $CT(\mathbf{z})$ and $SK(\mathbf{v})$ to recover $\langle \mathbf{z}, \mathbf{v} \rangle + \mathsf{Nse}$, where Nse must satisfy some weak pseudorandomness properties.

A detail that is important here is that for NLinFE to be useful for iO, the term Nse above must be a linear combination of noise terms, each multiplied with a different (public) modulus. In more detail, the noise term Nse output by NLinFE has the structure $\sum_i p_i \mu_i$ where p_i for $i \in [0, D-2]$ are a sequence of increasing moduli and μ_i are unstructured noise terms. Moreover, for decryption to succeed, these moduli must be public.

The NLinFE construction takes great care to ensure that the noise terms computed via NLinFE are high degree polynomials in values that are spread out over the entire ring, and argues (convincingly, in our opinion) that these may not be exploited easily. However, while some of the μ_i in the above equation are indeed "strong" and difficult to exploit, we observe that some of them are not. Moreover, since the moduli p_i are public, the μ_i can be "separated" into different "levels" according to the factor p_i. Hence, it is necessary that the noise at *each* "level" be "strong", but NLinFE fails to enforce this. Therefore, while there exist strong terms in some levels, the existence of a weak noise term in even one other level enables us to isolate them and use them to construct a matrix, whose rank reveals whether the message bit is 0 or 1.

From the knowledge gained by our cryptanalytic study, we suggest fixes to the scheme. The first attack can be overcome by disabling meaningful manipulation between different encodings. We achieve this by making the encodings non-commutative. The second attack can be overcome by ensuring that the noise terms for all levels are equally strong. We then provide a new scheme which overcomes the vulnerabilities described above. We also provide a thorough analysis of all the security aspects of this scheme and argue why plausible attacks do not work. We additionally provide concrete parameters with which the scheme may be instantiated.

Comparison with other attacks on iO. While Agrawal's NLinFE construction is quite different from previous iO constructions needing fresh cryptanalysis, there are still some high-level similarities between the rank attack we propose and previous attacks on candidate obfuscators [20,21,23,26]. In more detail, these attacks also combine public elements in a clever way to obtain a matrix, and computing the eigenvalues or the rank of this matrix then enables an attacker to break the scheme. We note however that while the main idea of the attack is the same (we compute a matrix and its rank leaks some secret information), the way we obtain the matrix is completely different from [20,21,26].

1.1   Our Techniques

We proceed to describe our techniques. We begin by defining the primitive of noisy linear functional encryption.

Noisy linear functional encryption. Noisy linear functional encryption (NLinFE) is a generalization of linear functional encryption (LinFE) [1,3]. Recall that in linear FE, the encryptor provides a $CT_{\mathbf{z}}$ which encodes vector $\mathbf{z} \in R^n$, the key generator provides a secret key $\mathsf{SK_v}$ which encodes vector $\mathbf{v} \in R^n$ and the decryptor combines them to recover $\langle \mathbf{z}, \mathbf{v} \rangle$. NLinFE is similar to linear FE, except that the function value is recovered only up to some bounded additive noise term, and indistinguishability holds even if the challenge messages evaluated on any function key are only "approximately" and not exactly equal. The functionality of NLinFE is as follows: given a ciphertext $\mathsf{CT_z}$ and a secret key $\mathsf{SK_v}$, the decryptor recovers $\langle \mathbf{z},\ \mathbf{v} \rangle + \mathsf{noise_{z,v}}$ where $\mathsf{noise_{z,v}}$ is specific to the message and function being evaluated.

It is well known that functional encryption (FE) for the function class $\mathsf{NC_1}$ which achieves *sublinear*[1] ciphertext is sufficient to imply iO [6,16]. Agrawal [2] additionally showed the following "bootstrapping" theorem.

Theorem 1.1 ([2]) *(Informal). There exists an* FE *scheme for the circuit class* $\mathsf{NC_1}$ *with sublinear ciphertext size and satisfying indistinguishability based security, assuming:*

- *A noisy linear FE scheme* NLinFE *with sublinear ciphertext size satisfying indistinguishability based security and supporting superpolynomially large outputs.*
- *The Learning with Errors (*LWE*) Assumption.*
- *A pseudorandom generator (*PRG*) computable in* $\mathsf{NC_0}$.

Since the last two assumptions are widely believed, it suffices to construct an NLinFE scheme to construct the all-powerful iO.

The NLinFE *Construction.* Agrawal provided a direct construction of NLinFE which supports superpolynomially large outputs, based on new assumptions that are based on the Ring Learning With Errors (RLWE) and NTRU assumptions (we refer the reader to Sect. 2 for a refresher on RLWE and NTRU).

The starting point of Agrawal's NLinFE scheme is the LinFE scheme of [3], which is based on LWE (or RLWE). NLinFE inherits the encodings and secret key structure of LinFE verbatim to compute inner products, and develops new techniques to compute the desired noise. Since the noise must be computed using a high degree polynomial for security [10,40], the work of [2] designs new encodings that are amenable to multiplication as follows.

Let $R = \mathbb{Z}[x]/\langle x^n + 1 \rangle$ and $R_{p_1} = R/(p_1 \cdot R)$, $R_{p_2} = R/(p_2 \cdot R)$ for some primes $p_1 < p_2$. Then, for $i \in \{1, \ldots, w\}$, sample f_{1i}, f_{2i} and g_1, g_2 from a discrete Gaussian over ring R. Set

$$h_{1i} = \frac{f_{1i}}{g_1}, \quad h_{2j} = \frac{f_{2j}}{g_2} \in R_{p_2} \ \forall \ i, j \in [w]$$

Thus, [2] assumes that the samples $\{h_{1i}, h_{2j}\}$ for $i, j \in [w]$ are indistinguishable from random, even though multiple samples share the same denominator.

Additionally, [2] assumes that RLWE with small secrets remains secure if the noise terms live in some secret ideal. The motivation for choosing such structured

---

[1] Here "sublinear" refers to the property that the ciphertext size is sublinear in the number of keys requested by the FE adversary.

secrets is that they can be multiplied with well chosen NTRU terms such as the $\{h_{1i}, h_{2j}\}$ above, to cancel the denominator and obtain a small element which can be absorbed in noise.

In more detail, for $i \in [w]$, let $\widehat{\mathcal{D}}(\Lambda_2), \widehat{\mathcal{D}}(\Lambda_1)$ be discrete Gaussian distributions over lattices Λ_2 and Λ_1 respectively. Then, sample

$$e_{1i} \leftarrow \widehat{\mathcal{D}}(\Lambda_2), \quad \text{where } \Lambda_2 \triangleq g_2 \cdot R. \text{ Let } \quad e_{1i} = g_2 \cdot \xi_{1i} \in \text{small},$$

$$e_{2i} \leftarrow \widehat{\mathcal{D}}(\Lambda_1), \quad \text{where } \Lambda_1 \triangleq g_1 \cdot R. \text{ Let } \quad e_{2i} = g_1 \cdot \xi_{2i} \in \text{small},$$

Here, small is used to collect terms whose norms may be bounded away from the modulus. Note that for $i, j \in [w]$, it holds that:

$$h_{1i} \cdot e_{2j} = f_{1i} \cdot \xi_{2j}, \quad h_{2j} \cdot e_{1i} = f_{2j} \cdot \xi_{1i} \in \text{small}$$

Now, sample small secrets t_1, t_2 and for $i \in [w]$, compute

$$d_{1i} = h_{1i} \cdot t_1 + p_1 \cdot e_{1i} \in R_{p_2}$$

$$d_{2i} = h_{2i} \cdot t_2 + p_1 \cdot e_{2i} \in R_{p_2}$$

Then, note that the products $d_{1i} \cdot d_{2j}$ do not suffer from large cross terms for any $i, j \in [w]$. As discussed above, due to the fact that the error of one sample is chosen to "cancel out" the large denominator in the other sample, the product yields a well behaved RLWE sample whose label is a product of the original labels. In more detail,

$$d_{1i} \cdot d_{2j} = \left(h_{1i} \cdot h_{2j}\right) \cdot (t_2\, t_2) + p_1 \cdot \text{noise}$$

where $\text{noise} = p_1 \cdot \left(f_{1i} \cdot \xi_{2j} \cdot t_1 + f_{2j} \cdot \xi_{1i} \cdot t_2 + p_1 \cdot g_1 \cdot g_2 \cdot \xi_{1i} \cdot \xi_{2j}\right) \in \text{small}$

The encoding $d_{1i} \cdot d_{2j}$ can be seen an RLWE encoding under a public label – this enables the noise term $p_1 \cdot \text{noise}$ above to be added to the inner product computed by LinFE, yielding the desired NLinFE. The actual construction [2] does several more tricks to ensure that the noise term is high entropy and spread across the ring – we refer the reader to Sect. 3 for details.

Exploiting Correlated Noise across Multiple Ciphertexts. As discussed above, Agrawal [2] provided a proof of security for the NLinFE construction (under a non-standard assumption) in a very weak security model where the adversary is only allowed to request a single ciphertext. In this work, we show that the construction is in fact insecure if the adversary has access to multiple ciphertexts. To do so, we first formally define a variant of the RLWE problem, which we call the RLWE problem with correlated noise. The distribution of the elements in this problem are similar to the one obtained by the encryption procedure of the NLinFE described above. We then show that this problem can be solved in polynomial time by an attacker, which in turn translates to an attack on Agrawal's NLinFE construction.

The key vulnerability exploited by the attack is that the noise terms across multiple ciphertexts are correlated. In more detail, we saw above that $d_{1i} = h_{1i} \cdot t_1 + p_1 \cdot e_{1i}$ where e_{1i} lives in the ideal $g_2 \cdot R$. Now, consider the corresponding element in another ciphertext: $d'_{1i} = h_{1i} \cdot t'_1 + p_1 \cdot e'_{1i}$ where e'_{1i} is also in the ideal $g_2 \cdot R$. The key observation we make is that the noise e_{1i} does not only annihilate the requisite large terms in the encodings of its own ciphertext namely $\{d_{2i}\}$ – it also annihilates large terms in the encodings of other ciphertexts, namely $\{d'_{2i}\}$.

This allows us to perform mix and match attacks, *despite* the fact that each encoding is randomized with fresh randomness. Consider the large terms in the following two products:

$$d_{1i} d'_{2j} = (h_{1i} h_{2j}) \cdot (t_1 t'_2) + p_1 \cdot \text{small}$$
$$d_{2j} d'_{1i} = (h_{2j} h_{1i}) \cdot (t_2 t'_1) + p_1 \cdot \text{small}$$

We see above that the labels $h_{1i} h_{2j}$ can be computed in two different ways (but the secrets are different). In a symmetric manner, if we consider other indices i' and j' for the ciphertext elements above, we can obtain

$$d_{1i} d_{2j} = (h_{1i} h_{2j}) \cdot (t_1 t_2) + p_1 \cdot \text{small}$$
$$d_{2j'} d_{1i'} = (h_{2j'} h_{1i'}) \cdot (t_2 t_1) + p_1 \cdot \text{small}.$$

Now, the secret is the same but the labels are changing. By playing on these symmetries, we can combine the products above (and the symmetric ones) so that all large terms are canceled and we are left with only small terms.

Intrinsically, what happens here is that in an element $d_{1i} = h_{1i} \cdot t_1 + p_1 \cdot e_{1i}$, we can change the h_{1i} and t_1 elements independently (the secret t_1 changes with the ciphertext and the label h_{1i} changes with the index of the element in the ciphertext). By varying these two elements independently, one can obtain 2×2 encodings (for 2 different choices of h_{1i} and 2 different choices of t_1), and consider the 2×2 matrix associated. More formally, let us write

$$d_{1i} = h_{1i} \cdot t_1 + p_1 \cdot e_{1i}, \qquad d_{1i'} = h_{1i'} \cdot t_1 + p_1 \cdot e_{1i'}$$
$$d'_{1i} = h_{1i} \cdot t'_1 + p_1 \cdot e'_{1i}, \qquad d'_{1i'} = h_{1i'} \cdot t'_1 + p_1 \cdot e'_{1i'}$$

these encodings. We consider the matrix

$$\begin{pmatrix} d_{1i} & d_{1i'} \\ d'_{1i} & d'_{1i'} \end{pmatrix} = \begin{pmatrix} t_1 \\ t'_1 \end{pmatrix} \cdot (h_{1i} \ h_{1i'}) + p_1 \cdot \begin{pmatrix} e_{1i} & e_{1i'} \\ e'_{1i} & e'_{1i'} \end{pmatrix}.$$

This matrix is the sum of a matrix of rank 1 with large coefficients plus a full rank matrix with small coefficients that are multiples of g_2. These properties ensure that its determinant will be of the form $g_2/g_1 \cdot \text{small}$. By doing the same thing with the encodings d_{2i}, we can also create an element of the form $g_1/g_2 \cdot \text{small}$. By multiplying these two elements, we finally obtain a linear combination of the encodings which is small. We can then distinguish whether the encodings are random or are RLWE with correlated noise elements. For more details, please see Sect. 4.

Unravelling the structure of the Noise. Our second attack, the so called "rank attack" exploits the fact that for the NLinFE noise to be useful for bootstrapping, it needs to be linear combination of noise terms, each of which is multiple of a fixed and public modulus p_i, for $i \in [0, D - 2]$. As discussed above, the noise terms that are multiples of distinct p_i may be separated from each other and attacked individually. In these piece-wise noise terms, we first isolate the noise term that encodes the message, which is 0 or m (say). Thus, our isolated noise term is of the form Nse or Nse $+ m$ depending on the challenge. Here, Nse is a complicated high degree multivariate polynomial, but we will find a way to learn the challenge bit *without* solving high degree polynomial equations.

To do so, we examine the noise term more carefully. As mentioned above, this term is a high degree, multivariate polynomial which looks difficult to analyze. However, we observe that each variable in this polynomial may be categorized into one of three "colours" – blue if it is fixed across all ciphertexts and secret keys, red if it is dependent only on the secret key and black if it is dependent only on the ciphertext. Next, we observe that if the challenge is 0, then the above polynomial may be expressed as a sum of scalar products, where in every scalar product one vector depends only on the secret key and the other one depends only on the cipher text. Concatenating all these vectors, one obtains a term $\langle a, b \rangle$, where a depends only on the secret key and b depends only on the ciphertext (and they are both secret). The dimension of a and b is the sum of the dimension of all the vectors involved in the sum above, let us denote this dimension by N.

Assume that we can make $N + 1$ requests for secret keys and ciphertexts. Now, in NLinFE, the message m itself depends on *both* the secret key and the ciphertext[2] – we denote by m_{ij} the message corresponding to the i-th secret key and the j-th ciphertext, and note that m_{ij} is known to the NLinFE adversary. We write $\hat{c}_{i,j} = \langle a_i, b_j \rangle + (0 \text{ or } m_{ij})$ the noise term obtained when computing decryption with the i-th secret key and the j-th ciphertext. Define $\mathbf{C}$ and $\mathbf{M}$ the $N \times N$ matrices $(c_{i,j})_{i,j}$ and $(m_{ij})_{i,j}$ respectively. Similarly, let A be the matrix whose rows are the a_i and $\mathbf{B}$ be the matrix whose columns are the b_j.

Then, depending on the challenge, we claim that $\mathbf{C}$ or $\mathbf{C} - \mathbf{M}$ is of rank at most N. To see this, note that we have $\mathbf{C} = \mathbf{A} \cdot \mathbf{B} + (0 \text{ or } M)$, where $\mathbf{A}$ has dimension $(N + 1) \times N$ and $\mathbf{B}$ has dimension $N \times (N + 1)$, so that $\mathbf{A} \cdot \mathbf{B}$ has rank at most N. On the other hand, the other matrix is of the form $\mathbf{A} \cdot \mathbf{B} \pm M$, which has full rank with good probability. We finish the attack by arguing that the adversary is indeed allowed to make $N + 1$ requests for secret keys and ciphertexts. Thus, by computing the rank of $\mathbf{C}$ and $\mathbf{C} - \mathbf{M}$, we can learn the challenge bit. For details, please see Sect. 5.

Fixing the construction. In light of the attacks described above, we propose a variant of Agrawal's NLinFE construction [2], designed to resist these attacks.

---

[2] This is created by the bootstrapping step. Intuitively m_{ij} is itself a noise term, which depends on both SK and CT, and we seek to "flood" this term using NLinFE. Please see [2] for more details.

Recall that for the multi-ciphertexts attack, we used the commutativity of the elements to ensure that, when multiplying elements in a certain way, the labels and secrets were the same. Hence, we prevent this attack by replacing the product of scalars $h_{1i} \cdot t_1$ in the encodings by an inner product $\langle \mathbf{h}_{1i}, \mathbf{t}_1 \rangle$, where the elements h_{1i} and t_1 have been replaced by vectors of dimension κ (the security parameter). This fix does not completely prevent the multi-ciphertexts attack, but the generalization of this attack to this non commutative setting requires a very large modulus, and is therefore not applicable to the range of parameters required for correctness.

To fix the rank attack, we first observe that we do not need to construct directly an NLinFE scheme with structured noise. Indeed, assume first that we have an NLinFE scheme with arbitrary noise, and we would like to have a noise term which is a multiple of p_0. Then, when we want to encode a vector $\mathbf{z}$, we simply encode $\mathbf{z}/p_0$ with our NLinFE with arbitrary noise. By decrypting the message, one would then recover $1/p_0 \cdot \langle \mathbf{z}, \mathbf{v} \rangle + \mathsf{noise}$, and by multiplying this by p_0, we obtain $\langle \mathbf{z}, \mathbf{v} \rangle + p_0 \cdot \mathsf{noise}$, with the desired noise shape. More generally, if we want a noise term which is a sum of multiples of p_i's, we could use an additive secret sharing of $\mathbf{z}$, i.e., compute random vectors $\mathbf{z}_i$ such that $\sum_i \mathbf{z}_i = \mathbf{z}$, and then encode $\mathbf{z}_i/p_i$ with the NLinFE scheme with arbitrary noise. By decrypting every ciphertexts, one could then recover $1/p_i \cdot \langle \mathbf{z}_i, \mathbf{v} \rangle + \mathsf{noise}$ for all i's, and by scaling and summing them, one will have a noise term of the desired shape.

Once we have made this observation that an NLinFE scheme with arbitrary noise is sufficient for our purpose, we can prevent the rank attack by removing the moduli p_i from Agrawal's construction. This means that the noise term we obtain at the end cannot be split anymore into smaller noise terms by looking at the "levels" created by the moduli. We now only have one big noise term, which contains noise terms of high degree and so seems hard to exploit. For technical reasons, we in fact have to keep one modulus, but the general intuition is the same as the one given here. For more details, please see Sect. 6.

2   Preliminaries

2.1   Noisy Linear Functional Encryption (NLinFE)

Let R be a ring, instantiated either as the ring of integers $\mathbb{Z}$ or the ring of polynomials $\mathbb{Z}[x]/f(x)$ where $f(x) = x^n + 1$ for n a power of 2. We let $R_{p_i} = R/p_i R$ for some prime p_i, $i \in [0, d]$ for some constant d. Let $B_1, B_2 \in \mathbb{R}^+$ be bounding values, where $\frac{B_2}{B_1} = \mathsf{superpoly}(\kappa)$. Let $N > 0$ be an integer (N will be the maximal number of key queries that an attacker is allowed to make). We define the symmetric key variant below.

Definition 2.1. *A (B_1, B_2, N)-noisy linear functional encryption scheme* FE *is a tuple* FE $=$ (FE.Setup, FE.Keygen, FE.Enc, FE.Dec) *of four probabilistic polynomial-time algorithms with the following specifications:*

- FE.Setup$(1^\kappa, R^\ell_{p_{d-1}})$ *takes as input the security parameter κ and the space of message and function vectors $R^\ell_{p_{d-1}}$ and outputs the public key and the master secret key pair* (PK, MSK).

- FE.Keygen(MSK, $\mathbf{v}$) *takes as input the master secret key* MSK *and a vector* $\mathbf{v} \in R_{p_{d-1}}^{\ell}$ *and outputs the secret key* SK$_{\mathbf{v}}$.
- FE.Enc(MSK, $\mathbf{z}$) *takes as input the public key* PK *and a message* $\mathbf{z} \in R_{p_{d-1}}^{\ell}$ *and outputs the ciphertext* CT$_{\mathbf{z}}$.
- FE.Dec(SK$_{\mathbf{v}}$, CT$_{\mathbf{z}}$) *takes as input the secret key of a user* SK$_{\mathbf{v}}$ *and the cipher-text* CT$_{\mathbf{z}}$, *and outputs* $y \in R_{p_{d-1}} \cup \{\bot\}$.

Definition 2.2 (Approximate Correctness). *A noisy linear functional encryption scheme* FE *is correct if for all* $\mathbf{v}, \mathbf{z} \in R_{p_{d-1}}^{\ell}$,

$$\Pr\left[\begin{array}{l} (\mathsf{PK}, \mathsf{MSK}) \leftarrow \mathsf{FE.Setup}(1^{\kappa}); \\ \mathsf{FE.Dec}\big(\mathsf{FE.Keygen}(\mathsf{MSK}, \mathbf{v}), \mathsf{FE.Enc}(\mathsf{MSK}, \mathbf{z})\big) = \langle \mathbf{v}, \mathbf{z} \rangle + \mathsf{noise_{fld}} \end{array}\right] = 1 - \mathsf{negl}(\kappa)$$

where $\mathsf{noise_{fld}} \in R$ *with* $\|\mathsf{noise_{fld}}\| \leq B_2$ *and the probability is taken over the coins of* FE.Setup, FE.Keygen, *and* FE.Enc.

Security. Next, we define the notion of Noisy-IND security and admissible adversary.

Definition 2.3 (Noisy-IND Security Game). *We define the security game between the challenger and adversary as follows:*

1. **Public Key:** *Challenger returns* PK *to the adversary.*
2. **Pre-Challenge Queries:** Adv *may adaptively request keys for any functions* $\mathbf{v}_i \in R_{p_{d-1}}^{\ell}$. *In response,* Adv *is given the corresponding keys* SK($\mathbf{v}_i$).
3. **Challenge Ciphertexts:** Adv *outputs the challenge message pairs* $(\mathbf{z}_0^i, \mathbf{z}_1^i) \in R_{p_{d-1}}^{\ell} \times R_{p_{d-1}}^{\ell}$ *for* $i \in [Q]$, *where* Q *is some polynomial, to the challenger. The challenger chooses a random bit* b, *and returns the ciphertexts* $\{\mathsf{CT}(\mathbf{z}_b^i)\}_{i \in [Q]}$.
4. **Post-Challenge Queries:** Adv *may request additional keys for functions of its choice and is given the corresponding keys.* Adv *may also output additional challenge message pairs which are handled as above.*
5. **Guess.** Adv *outputs a bit* b', *and succeeds if* $b' = b$.

The advantage of Adv *is the absolute value of the difference between the adversary's success probability and* 1/2.

Definition 2.4 (Admissible Adversary). *We say an adversary is admissible if it makes at most* N *key requests and if for any pair of challenge messages* $\mathbf{z}_0, \mathbf{z}_1 \in R_{p_{d-1}}^{\ell}$ *and any queried key* $\mathbf{v}_i \in R_{p_{d-1}}^{\ell}$, *it holds that* $|\langle \mathbf{v}_i, \mathbf{z}_0 - \mathbf{z}_1 \rangle| \leq B_1$.

Structure of Noise. The bootstrapping step in [2] requires that

$$|\langle \mathbf{v}_i, \mathbf{z}_0 - \mathbf{z}_1 \rangle| = \sum_{i=0}^{d-2} p_i \cdot \mathsf{noise_{ch,i}}$$

for some noise terms $\mathsf{noise_{ch,i}}$. Hence the flooding noise $\mathsf{noise_{fld}}$ that is added by the NLinFE must also be structured as $\sum_{i=0}^{d-2} p_i \cdot \mathsf{noise_{fld,i}}$.

Definition 2.5 (Noisy-IND security). *A* (B_1, B_2, N) *noisy linear FE scheme* NLinFE *is* Noisy-IND *secure if for all admissible probabilistic polynomial-time adversaries* Adv, *the advantage of* Adv *in the* Noisy-IND *security game is negligible in the security parameter* κ.

The works of [2,6,14,16] show that as long as the size of the ciphertext is sublinear in N, a $(B_1, B_2, N) - \mathsf{NLinFE}$ scheme implies indistinguishability obfuscation.

2.2   Sampling and Trapdoors

Ajtai [4] showed how to sample a random lattice along with a trapdoor that permits sampling short vectors from that lattice. Recent years have seen significant progress in refining and extending this result [5,42,46].

Let $R = \mathbb{Z}[x]/(f)$ where $f = x^n + 1$ and n is a power of 2. Let $R_q \triangleq R/qR$ where q is a large prime satisfying $q = 1 \mod 2n$. For $r \in R$, we use $\|r\|$ to refer to the Euclidean norm of r's coefficient vector.

We will make use of the following algorithms from [42]:

1. $\mathsf{TrapGen}(n, m, q)$: The $\mathsf{TrapGen}$ algorithm takes as input the dimension of the ring n, a sufficiently large integer $m = O(n \log q)$ and the modulus size q and outputs a vector $\mathbf{w} \in R_q^m$ such that the distribution of $\mathbf{w}$ is negligibly far from uniform, along with a "trapdoor" $\mathbf{T_w} \in R^{m \times m}$ for the lattice $\Lambda_q^\perp(\mathbf{w}) = \{\mathbf{x} : \langle \mathbf{w}, \mathbf{x} \rangle = 0 \mod q\}$.
2. $\mathsf{SamplePre}(\mathbf{w}, \mathbf{T_w}, a, \sigma)$: The $\mathsf{SamplePre}$ algorithm takes as input a vector $\mathbf{w} \in R_q^m$ along with a trapdoor $\mathbf{T_w}$ and a syndrome $a \in R_q$ and a sufficiently large $\sigma = O(\sqrt{n \log q})$ and outputs a vector $\mathbf{e}$ from a distribution within negligible distance to $\mathcal{D}_{\Lambda_q^a(\mathbf{w}), \sigma \cdot \omega(\sqrt{\log n})}$ where $\Lambda_q^a(\mathbf{w}) = \{\mathbf{x} : \langle \mathbf{w}, \mathbf{x} \rangle = a \mod q\}$.

2.3   Random Matrices over $\mathbf{Z}_q$

Lemma 2.6. *Let* q *be a prime integer and* $\mathbf{A}$ *be sampled uniformly in* $(\mathbf{Z}/(q\mathbf{Z}))^{m \times m}$. *Then*

$$\mathbf{P}\left(\det(\mathbf{A}) \in (\mathbf{Z}/(q\mathbf{Z}))^\times\right) = \prod_{i=1}^m \left(1 - \frac{1}{q^i}\right) \geq \frac{4\ln(2)}{q}.$$

Proof. The first equality is obtained by counting the number of invertible $m \times m$ matrices in $\mathbf{Z}/(q\mathbf{Z})$. For the lower bound, we observe that $1 - 1/q^i \geq 1/2$ for all $1 \leq i \leq m$. By concavity of the logarithm function, this implies that $\log(1 - 1/q^i) \geq -2/q^i$ for all $i \geq 1$ (recall that the logarithm is taken in base 2). We then have

$$\log \prod_{i=1}^m \left(1 - \frac{1}{q^i}\right) = \sum_{i=1}^m \log\left(1 - \frac{1}{q^i}\right) \geq \sum_{i=1}^m \frac{-2}{q^i} \geq \frac{-2}{q} \cdot \frac{1}{1 - 1/q} \geq \frac{-4}{q}.$$

Taking the exponential we obtain that $\mathbf{P}\left(\det(\mathbf{A}) \in (\mathbf{Z}/(q\mathbf{Z}))^\times\right) \geq 2^{-4/q} \geq 1 - \frac{4\ln(2)}{q}$ as desired. $\square$

Lemma 2.7 (Corollary 2.2 of [17]). *Let q be a prime integer and A be sampled uniformly in $(\mathbf{Z}/(q\mathbf{Z}))^{m \times m}$. For any $x \in (\mathbf{Z}/(q\mathbf{Z}))^{\times}$, we have*

$$\mathbf{P}\left(\det(\mathbf{A}) = x \mid \det(A) \in (\mathbf{Z}/(q\mathbf{Z}))^{\times}\right) = \frac{1}{|(\mathbf{Z}/(q\mathbf{Z}))^{\times}|} = \frac{1}{q-1}.$$

In other words, $\det(A)$ is uniform in $(\mathbf{Z}/(q\mathbf{Z}))^{\times}$ when conditioned on being invertible.

Corollary 2.2 of [17] even gives explicit values for the probability $\mathbf{P}(\det(\mathbf{A}) = x)$ for any x. Here, we only use the fact that these values are the same whenever the gcd of x and q is constant (in our case, the gcd is always 1 because x is invertible). Observe also that Corollary 2.2 of [17] is stated for a prime power q, and can be extended to any modulus q by Chinese reminder theorem (but we only use it here in the case of a prime modulus q).

3   Agrawal's Construction of Noisy Linear FE

We begin by recapping the construction of NLinFE by Agrawal [2]. The construction uses two prime moduli p_1 and p_2 with $p_1 \ll p_2$. The message and function vectors will be chosen from R_{p_1} while the public key and ciphertext are from R_{p_2}. The construction will make use of the fact that elements in R_{p_1} as well as elements sampled from a discrete Gaussian distribution denoted by $\mathcal{D}$, are small in R_{p_2}.

NLinFE.Setup($1^{\kappa}, 1^w$): On input a security parameter κ, a parameter w denoting the length of the function and message vectors, do the following:

1. Sample prime moduli $p_0 < p_1 < p_2$ and standard deviation σ for discrete Gaussian distributions $\mathcal{D}, \hat{\mathcal{D}}$ and $\hat{\mathcal{D}}'$ according to the parameter specification of [2].
2. Sample $\mathbf{w} \leftarrow R_{p_2}^m$ with a trapdoor $\mathbf{T_w}$ using the algorithm TrapGen as defined in Sect. 2.2.
3. Sample $\mathbf{E} \in \mathcal{D}^{m \times w}$ and set $\mathbf{a} = \mathbf{E}^{\mathsf{T}}\mathbf{w} \in R_{p_2}^w$.
4. For $i \in \{1, \ldots, r\}$, $\ell \in \{1, \ldots, k\}$, sample $f_{1i}^{\ell}, f_{2i}^{\ell} \leftarrow \mathcal{D}$ and $g_1^{\ell}, g_2^{\ell} \leftarrow \mathcal{D}$. If g_1^{ℓ}, g_2^{ℓ} are not invertible over R_{p_2}, resample. Set

$$h_{1i}^{\ell} = \frac{f_{1i}^{\ell}}{g_1^{\ell}}, \quad h_{2i}^{\ell} = \frac{f_{2i}^{\ell}}{g_2^{\ell}} \in R_{p_2}$$

5. Sample a PRF seed, denoted as seed.

Output

$$\mathsf{MSK} = \left(\mathbf{w}, \mathbf{T_w}, \mathbf{a}, \mathbf{E}, \left\{ f_{1i}^{\ell}, f_{2i}^{\ell} \right\}_{i \in [r], \ell \in [k]}, \left\{ g_1^{\ell}, g_2^{\ell} \right\}_{\ell \in [k]} \right\}, \mathsf{seed} \right)$$

NLinFE.Enc(MSK, $\mathbf{z}$): On input public key MSK, a message vector $\mathbf{z} \in R_{p_1}^w$, do:

1. **Construct Message Encodings.** Sample $\boldsymbol{\nu} \leftarrow \mathcal{D}^m, \boldsymbol{\eta} \leftarrow \mathcal{D}^w$ and $t_1, t_2 \leftarrow \mathcal{D}$. Set $s = t_1 \cdot t_2$. Compute:

$$\mathbf{c} = \mathbf{w} \cdot s + p_1 \cdot \boldsymbol{\nu} \in R_{p_2}^m, \quad \mathbf{b} = \mathbf{a} \cdot s + p_1 \cdot \boldsymbol{\eta} + \mathbf{z} \in R_{p_2}^w$$

2. **Sample Structured Noise.** To compute encodings of noise, do the following:
   (a) Define lattices:
   $$\Lambda_1^\ell \triangleq g_1^\ell \cdot R, \quad \Lambda_2^\ell \triangleq g_2^\ell \cdot R$$
   (b) Sample noise terms from the above lattices as:

   $$e_{1i}^\ell \leftarrow \widehat{\mathcal{D}}(\Lambda_2^\ell), \tilde{e}_{1i}^\ell \leftarrow \widehat{\mathcal{D}}'(\Lambda_2^\ell), \quad e_{2i}^\ell \leftarrow \widehat{\mathcal{D}}(\Lambda_1^\ell), \tilde{e}_{2i}^\ell \leftarrow \widehat{\mathcal{D}}'(\Lambda_1^\ell) \quad \forall i \in [r], \ell \in [k]$$

   Here $\widehat{\mathcal{D}}(\Lambda_1^\ell), \widehat{\mathcal{D}}'(\Lambda_1^\ell)$ are discrete Gaussian distributions on Λ_1^ℓ and $\widehat{\mathcal{D}}(\Lambda_2^\ell), \widehat{\mathcal{D}}'(\Lambda_2^\ell)$ are discrete Gaussian distributions on Λ_2^ℓ.
3. **Compute Encodings of Noise.**
   (a) Let
   $$d_{1i}^\ell = h_{1i}^\ell \cdot t_1 + p_1 \cdot \tilde{e}_{1i}^\ell + p_0 \cdot e_{1i}^\ell \in R_{p_2} \quad \forall i \in [r], \ell \in [k].$$

   Here, $p_1 \cdot \tilde{e}_{1i}^\ell$ behaves as noise and $p_0 \cdot e_{1i}^\ell$ behaves as the message. Let $\mathbf{d}_1^\ell = (d_{1i}^\ell)$.
   (b) Similarly, let

   $$d_{2i}^\ell = h_{2i}^\ell \cdot t_2 + p_1 \cdot \tilde{e}_{2i}^\ell + p_0 \cdot e_{2i}^\ell \in R_{p_2} \quad \forall i \in [r], \ell \in [k].$$

   Here, $p_1 \cdot \tilde{e}_{2i}^\ell$ behaves as noise and $p_0 \cdot e_{2i}^\ell$ behaves as the message. Let $\mathbf{d}_2^\ell = (d_{2i}^\ell)$.
4. **Output Ciphertext.** Output message encodings $(\mathbf{c}, \mathbf{b})$ and noise encodings $(\mathbf{d}_1^\ell, \mathbf{d}_2^\ell)$ for $\ell \in [k]$.

NLinFE.KeyGen(MSK, $\mathbf{v}, \mathbf{v}^\times$): On input the master secret key MSK, a NLinFE function vector $\mathbf{v} \in R_{p_1}^w$ and its corresponding noise polynomial (represented here as a quadratic polynomial) $\mathbf{v}^\times \in R_{p_1}^L$, where $L = |1 \leq j \leq i \leq r|$, do the following.

1. **Sampling Basis Preimage vectors.**
   (a) Sample short $\mathbf{e}_{ij} \in R^m$ using SamplePre (please see Sect. 2.2) with randomness PRF(seed, ij) such that

   $$\langle \mathbf{w}, \mathbf{e}_{ij} \rangle = h_{ij}, \text{ where } h_{ij} \triangleq \sum_{\ell \in [k]} h_{1i}^\ell h_{2j}^\ell + p_0 \cdot \Delta_{ij} + p_1 \cdot \tilde{\Delta}_{ij}$$

   Above $\Delta_{ij}, \tilde{\Delta}_{ij} \leftarrow \mathcal{D} \in R$ for $1 \leq j \leq i \leq r$.

   $$\text{Let } \mathbf{E}^\times = (\mathbf{e}_{ij}) \in R^{m \times L}, \quad \mathbf{h}^\times = (h_{ij}) \in R_{p_2}^L$$

   where $L = |1 \leq j \leq i \leq r|$.

2. **Combining Basis Preimages to Functional Preimage.** Define

$$\mathbf{k_v} = \mathbf{E} \cdot \mathbf{v} + \mathbf{E}^\times \cdot \mathbf{v}^\times \quad \in R^m \tag{3.1}$$

3. Output $(\mathbf{k_v}, \mathbf{v})$.

NLinFE.Dec($\mathsf{CT_z}, \mathsf{SK_v}$): On input a ciphertext $\mathsf{CT_z} = (\ \mathbf{c}, \mathbf{b}, \{\mathbf{d}_1^\ell, \mathbf{d}_2^\ell\}_{\ell \in [k]}\ )$ and a secret key $\mathbf{k_v}$ for function $\mathbf{v}$, do the following

1. Compute encoding of noise term on the fly as:

$$\mathbf{d}^\times \triangleq (\sum_{\ell \in [k]} \mathbf{d}_1^\ell \otimes \mathbf{d}_2^\ell) \in R_{p_2}^L$$

2. Compute functional ciphertext as:

$$b_\mathbf{v} = \mathbf{v}^\mathsf{T}\mathbf{b} + (\mathbf{v}^\times)^\mathsf{T}\mathbf{d}^\times \in R_{p_2}$$

3. Compute $b_\mathbf{v} - \mathbf{k_v}^\mathsf{T}\mathbf{c} \mod p_1$ and output it.

Remark on the parameters. In the above scheme, one should think of B_1 as being poly(κ), $B_2 = \mathsf{superpoly}(\kappa) \cdot B_1$ and $N = (kr \log(p_2))^{1+\varepsilon}$ for some $\varepsilon > 0$.

4   Multi-ciphertext Attack on Agrawal's NLinFE

Agrawal [2] provided a proof of security for her construction (under a non-standard assumption) in a weak security game where the adversary may only request a single ciphertext. In this section, we show that her construction is in fact insecure if the adversary has access to multiple ciphertexts.

The problem appearing in Agrawal's NLinFE construction is a variant of the RLWE problem, where the random elements in RLWE samples are chosen from some NTRU-like distribution, are kept secret, and the noise terms are correlated to these elements. In this section, we first formally define a variant of the RLWE problem, which we call the RLWE problem with correlated noise. The distribution of the elements in this problem are similar to the one obtained by the encryption procedure of the NLinFE described above. We then show that this problem can be solved in polynomial time by an attacker, hence resulting in an attack on Agrawal's NLinFE construction.

Definition 4.1 (*RLWE with correlated noise*). *Let R be some ring isomorphic to $\mathbf{Z}^n$ (for instance $R = \mathbf{Z}[X]/(X^n + 1)$ for n a power of two, and the isomorphism is the coefficient embedding). We define the RLWE problem with correlated noise as follows. Let m, k, q, σ, σ' be some parameters (q will be the modulus, m the number of samples and σ and σ' are small compared to q). We let $\mathcal{D}_\sigma$ be the discrete Gaussian distribution over R with parameter σ and $U(R_q)$ be the uniform distribution over R_q. Sample*

- $g_1, g_2 \leftarrow \mathcal{D}_\sigma$
- $f_{1i}, f_{2i} \leftarrow \mathcal{D}_\sigma$ for all $1 \leq i \leq k$
- $t_1[j], t_2[j] \leftarrow \mathcal{D}_\sigma$ for all $1 \leq j \leq m$
- $e_{1i}[j], e_{2i}[j] \leftarrow \mathcal{D}_{\sigma'}$ for all $1 \leq i \leq k$ and $1 \leq j \leq m$
- $u_{1i}[j], u_{2i}[j] \leftarrow U(R_q)$ for all $1 \leq i \leq k$ and $1 \leq j \leq m$.

The RLWE problem with correlated noise is to distinguish between

$$\left(\frac{f_{1i}}{g_1} t_1[j] + e_{1i}[j] \cdot g_2 \bmod q, \frac{f_{2i}}{g_2} t_2[j] + e_{2i}[j] \cdot g_1 \bmod q \right)_{i,j}$$

and

$$(u_{1i}[j], u_{2i}[j])_{i,j}.$$

Remark 4.2. This RLWE problem with correlated noise differs from the classical RLWE problem in 4 different ways:

- Instead of being uniform, the elements a are of the form $\frac{f_i}{g} \bmod q$ with f_i and g small modulo q,
- There are multiple secrets $t_1[j]$ and $t_2[j]$,
- The elements $\frac{f_i}{g}$ are secret,
- The noise is correlated with the elements $\frac{f_i}{g}$ (instead of following a small Gaussian distribution).

We observe that if we obtain m ciphertexts from the NLinFE construction described above, and if we only keep in each ciphertext the part corresponding to $\ell = 1$, then the elements obtained follow the RLWE distribution with correlated noise. The notation $[j]$ refers to the j-th ciphertext, and we dropped the index ℓ since we are only considering $\ell = 1$.

The next lemma explains how we can solve the RLWE problem with correlated noise in polynomial time, using 4 pairs of elements (obtained by varying i and j).

Lemma 4.3. *Assume $k, m \geq 2$ and that the modulus q is a prime integer congruent to 1 modulo $2n$. Let $(b_{1i}[j], b_{2i}[j])_{1 \leq i,j \leq 2}$ be obtained from either the RLWE distribution with correlated noise or the uniform distribution over R_q. Let us define*

$$b := (b_{1,1}[1] \cdot b_{2,1}[1] \cdot b_{1,2}[2] \cdot b_{2,2}[2] + b_{1,1}[2] \cdot b_{2,1}[2] \cdot b_{1,2}[1] \cdot b_{2,2}[1]$$
$$- b_{1,1}[2] \cdot b_{2,1}[1] \cdot b_{1,2}[1] \cdot b_{2,2}[2] - b_{1,1}[1] \cdot b_{2,1}[2] \cdot b_{1,2}[2] \cdot b_{2,2}[1]) \bmod q.$$

If the $b_{\beta i}[j]$ come from the uniform distribution, then $\|b\|_\infty \geq q/4$ with high probability (over the random choice of the $(b_{1i}[j], b_{2i}[j])_{1 \leq i,j \leq 2}$). Otherwise, $\|b\|_\infty$ is small compared to q.

Proof. Let us first consider the case where the $b_{\beta i}[j]$ are uniform modulo q and independent. Observe that b can be written as the determinant of a product of two matrices

$$\mathbf{M}_1 = \begin{pmatrix} b_{1,1}[1] & b_{1,1}[2] \\ b_{1,2}[1] & b_{1,2}[2] \end{pmatrix} \text{ and } \mathbf{M}_2 = \begin{pmatrix} b_{2,1}[1] & b_{2,1}[2] \\ b_{2,2}[1] & b_{2,2}[2] \end{pmatrix}.$$

These two matrices are uniform over R_q. Because $q \equiv 1 \bmod 2n$, we have that $x^n + 1 = \prod_i (x - \alpha_i) \bmod q$ and so $R_q \simeq \mathbf{Z}_q[x]/(x - \alpha_1) \times \cdots \times \mathbf{Z}_q[x]/(x - \alpha_1) \simeq (\mathbf{Z}_q)^n$. By Chinese reminder theorem, all the matrices $\mathbf{M}_b \bmod (x - \alpha_i)$ are uniform and independent matrices in $\mathbf{Z}_q$. Now, by Chinese reminder theorem and Lemma 2.6, we have that

$$\mathbf{P}(\det(\mathbf{M}_1) \notin R_q^\times) = \mathbf{P}(\exists i, \det(\mathbf{M}_1 \bmod (x - \alpha_i)) \notin \mathbf{Z}_q^\times) \leq O\left(\frac{n}{q}\right).$$

Because $n \ll q$, this implies that $\mathbf{M}_1$ and $\mathbf{M}_2$ are invertible with high probability. Recall from Lemma 2.7 that, when conditioned on being invertible, the determinant of $\mathbf{M}_1$ and $\mathbf{M}_2$ are uniformly distributed over the invertible elements of R_q. Hence, we conclude that with high probability, the product $\det(\mathbf{M}_1) \cdot \det(\mathbf{M}_2)$ is uniform in $R_q^\times$ and so is likely to have infinity norm larger than $q/4$.

Let us now assume that the $b_{\beta i}[j]$ come from the RLWE distribution with correlated noise. Then, we have

$$
\begin{aligned}
b = &\left(\frac{f_{1,1}}{g_1} t_1[1] + e_{1,1}[1] \cdot g_2\right)\left(\frac{f_{2,1}}{g_2} t_2[1] + e_{2,1}[1] \cdot g_1\right)\left(\frac{f_{1,2}}{g_1} t_1[2] + e_{1,2}[2] \cdot g_2\right)\left(\frac{f_{2,2}}{g_2} t_2[2] + e_{2,2}[2] \cdot g_1\right) \\
+ &\left(\frac{f_{1,1}}{g_1} t_1[2] + e_{1,1}[2] \cdot g_2\right)\left(\frac{f_{2,1}}{g_2} t_2[2] + e_{2,1}[2] \cdot g_1\right)\left(\frac{f_{1,2}}{g_1} t_1[1] + e_{1,2}[1] \cdot g_2\right)\left(\frac{f_{2,2}}{g_2} t_2[1] + e_{2,2}[1] \cdot g_1\right) \\
- &\left(\frac{f_{1,1}}{g_1} t_1[2] + e_{1,1}[2] \cdot g_2\right)\left(\frac{f_{2,1}}{g_2} t_2[1] + e_{2,1}[1] \cdot g_1\right)\left(\frac{f_{1,2}}{g_1} t_1[1] + e_{1,2}[1] \cdot g_2\right)\left(\frac{f_{2,2}}{g_2} t_2[2] + e_{2,2}[2] \cdot g_1\right) \\
- &\left(\frac{f_{1,1}}{g_1} t_1[1] + e_{1,1}[1] \cdot g_2\right)\left(\frac{f_{2,1}}{g_2} t_2[2] + e_{2,1}[2] \cdot g_1\right)\left(\frac{f_{1,2}}{g_1} t_1[2] + e_{1,2}[2] \cdot g_2\right)\left(\frac{f_{2,2}}{g_2} t_2[1] + e_{2,2}[1] \cdot g_1\right),
\end{aligned}
$$

where the computations are performed modulo q. Observe that in the products and sums above, all the elements are small. The only things that can be large are the division modulo q by g_1 and g_2. We are going to show that if we develop the products above, then all the terms containing divisions by g_1 or g_2 are annihilated. So b will be a polynomial of degree 4 of small elements (with no denominator) and hence it will be small compared to q.

Let us consider the first line of the equation above

$$\left(\frac{f_{1,1}}{g_1} t_1[1] + e_{1,1}[1] \cdot g_2\right) \cdot \left(\frac{f_{2,1}}{g_2} t_2[1] + e_{2,1}[1] \cdot g_1\right) \cdot \left(\frac{f_{1,2}}{g_1} t_1[2] + e_{1,2}[2] \cdot g_2\right) \cdot \left(\frac{f_{2,2}}{g_2} t_2[2] + e_{2,2}[2] \cdot g_1\right).$$

When we develop this product, we are going to produce terms with denominators of degree 0, 1, 2, 3 and 4 in the g_β. Observe that the third line is the same as the first line, where we have exchanged $t_1[1]$ and $t_1[2]$ and the corresponding noises. So every term of the first line containing $\frac{f_{1,1}}{g_1} t_1[1] \cdot \frac{f_{1,2}}{g_1} t_1[2]$ will be the same as the analogue term in the third line, and so will be annihilated. Similarly, the fourth line is the same as the first line, where we have exchanged $t_2[1]$ and $t_2[2]$ and the corresponding noises. So every term of the first line containing $\frac{f_{2,1}}{g_2} t_2[1] \cdot \frac{f_{2,2}}{g_2} t_2[2]$ will be the same as the analogue term in the fourth line, and so will be annihilated. Using this remark, we argue below that all the terms with denominators in the first line are annihilated.

- The term of degree 4 contains $\frac{f_{1,1}}{g_1}t_1[1] \cdot \frac{f_{1,2}}{g_1}t_1[2]$ and so is annihilated by the third line.
- The terms of degree 3 have to contain 3 denominators out of the 4. So they contain either $\frac{f_{1,1}}{g_1}t_1[1] \cdot \frac{f_{1,2}}{g_1}t_1[2]$ or $\frac{f_{2,1}}{g_2}t_2[1] \cdot \frac{f_{2,2}}{g_2}t_2[2]$. In both cases, they are annihilated.
- The terms of degree 2 containing either $\frac{f_{1,1}}{g_1}t_1[1] \cdot \frac{f_{1,2}}{g_1}t_1[2]$ or $\frac{f_{2,1}}{g_2}t_2[1] \cdot \frac{f_{2,2}}{g_2}t_2[2]$ are annihilated. It remains the terms of degree 2 whose denominator is g_1g_2. But these terms are multiplied by a noise which is a multiple of g_1 and another noise which is a multiple of g_2. Hence the denominator is annihilated and these terms are just polynomials in the small elements.
- The terms of degree 1 have denominator g_1 or g_2. But they are multiplied by noises that are multiples of g_1 and g_2. Hence the denominator is annihilated and these terms are polynomials in the small elements.

To conclude, all the terms are either eliminated thanks to the symmetries, or the denominators are removed by multiplication by g_1 and g_2. Similarly, we can show that this holds for all the four lines. The sage code for the above attack is provided as supplementary material with the paper. So b is a polynomial of constant degree in the g_β, $f_{\beta i}$, $t_\beta[j]$ and $e_{\beta i}[j]$, which are all much smaller than q. Hence, b is also much smaller than q.

Concluding the attack. To conclude the attack on Agrawal's NLinFE scheme, let us now explain how the distinguishing attack described above can be used to recover the secret elements of the RLWE with correlated noise instance. We have seen in Lemma 4.3 that, from four instances of RLWE with correlated noise, one can compute a quantity b which is significantly smaller than the modulus q. This means that one can recover b over the ring R, without reduction modulo q. Let us consider such an element b, obtained from the four RLWE with correlated noise instances $(b_{1i}[j], b_{2i}[j])$, $(b_{1i'}[j], b_{2i'}[j])$, $(b_{1i}[j'], b_{2i}[j'])$, $(b_{1i'}[j'], b_{2i'}[j'])$ (for simplicity, the lemma above is stated with $i, j = 1$ and $i', j' = 2$, but it can be generalized to any choice of (i, j, i', j'), with $i \neq i'$ and $j \neq j'$). Computing b as in Lemma 4.3, we obtain a polynomial over R of degree 8 in 16 variables (the g_β, the $t[j]$'s, the $f_{\beta,i}$ and the $e_{\beta,i}[j]$). More generally, if we consider all the equations one can create by computing b as above for i, j, i', j' varying in $\{1, \cdots, \ell\}$, with $i \neq i'$ and $j \neq j'$, then one can obtain $\ell^2(\ell - 1)^2$ equations of degree 8 in $2 + 3\ell + 2\ell^2$ variables. Choosing $\ell = 3$ provides 36 equations in 29 variables, hence one may hope that this system has a unique solution, and that solving it would reveal the values of the secret parameters.

Recall that solving a system of polynomial equations is hard in general, but the hardness increases with the number of variables. Hence, if the number of variable is constant (here equal to 29), solving a polynomial system of equations should be easy. One way to solve such a system is by computing a Gröbner basis of the ideal generated by the multivariate polynomials. This can be done in the worst case in time doubly exponential in the number of variables (see for instance [12, 41]), which is constant in our case, as we have a constant number of variables.[3] Once we have a Gröbner basis corresponding to our system of equations, we can solve it by computing the roots of a constant number of univariate polynomials over K. Since we know that the solution of our system is in R^{29}, it is sufficient to compute the roots of the polynomials over K with precision $1/2$, and then round them to the nearest integer element. Solving these univariate polynomial equations can hence be done in polynomial time (in the size of the output).

Alternatively, to avoid numerical issues, we could choose a large prime number p, which we know is larger than all the noise terms arising in the equations, and then solve the system in $R/(pR)$. Hopefully, the system is still overdetermined modulo p, and so has a unique solution which corresponds to the solution over R. Thanks to the fact that p is larger than the noise terms, recovering them modulo p reveals them exactly, so we can recover the solution over R from the one over $R/(pR)$. This approach can also be done in time doubly exponential in the number of variables, and polynomial in the degree of K and in $\log(p)$.

To conclude, the elements b enables us to recover equations of degree 8 in a constant number of variables, which can then be solved efficiently. This means that we can recover the secret elements g_β, $t[j]$, $f_{\beta,i}$ and $e_{\beta,i}[j]$ of the RLWE with correlated noise instances in polynomial time (given sufficiently many instances).

5   Rank Attack on Agrawal's NLinFE

In this section, we present a novel "rank attack" against the NLinFE scheme. The attack exploits the property that the NLinFE scheme must compute a noise term with special structure: in detail, the noise term must be expressible as a linear combination of noise terms which are multiples of moduli p_i for $i \in [0, D-2]$. The moduli p_i in this case are *public* – this enables the attacker to recover noise terms at different "levels", namely, corresponding to different moduli. The attack exploits the fact that while the noise terms corresponding to some moduli are highly non-linear and difficult to exploit, those corresponding to some others are in fact linear and may be exploited by carefully arranging them into a matrix and computing its rank. We provide details below.

5.1   Exploiting the Noise Obtained After Decrypting a Message

Let us first explicit the noise obtained after decryption. When computing $b_v - k_v^\mathsf{T} c$ for a valid ciphertext and secret key, one obtain something much smaller than p_2, which can hence be recovered exactly. This noise is the following

---

[3] In all this discussion, we are interested in the theoretical complexity. In practice, solving an arbitrary overdetermined system with 29 variables could take a lot of time, but this time would not increase with the security parameter κ, hence, it is constant for our purposes.

$b_{\mathbf{v}} - \mathbf{k}_{\mathbf{v}}^{\mathsf{T}} \mathbf{c}$

$= \mathbf{v}^T \mathbf{z} + p_1 \mathbf{v}^T \boldsymbol{\eta} - p_0 (\mathbf{v}^{\times})^T \boldsymbol{\Delta} \cdot s - p_1 (\mathbf{v}^{\times})^T \widetilde{\boldsymbol{\Delta}} \cdot s - p_1 (\mathbf{v}^T \mathbf{E} + (\mathbf{v}^{\times})^T \mathbf{E}^{\times}) \boldsymbol{\nu}$

$\quad + \sum_{\ell,i,j} v_{ij}^{\times} \Big[p_1 \cdot \Big(p_1 \cdot (g_2^{\ell} \cdot \tilde{\xi}_{1i}^{\ell} \cdot g_1^{\ell} \cdot \tilde{\xi}_{2j}^{\ell}) + p_0 \cdot (g_2^{\ell} \cdot \tilde{\xi}_{1i}^{\ell} \cdot g_1^{\ell} \cdot \xi_{2j}^{\ell} + g_2^{\ell} \cdot \xi_{1i}^{\ell} \cdot g_1^{\ell} \cdot \tilde{\xi}_{2j}^{\ell})$

$\quad + (f_{1i}^{\ell} \cdot t_1 \cdot \tilde{\xi}_{2j}^{\ell} + f_{2j}^{\ell} \cdot t_2 \cdot \tilde{\xi}_{1i}^{\ell}) \Big) + p_0 \cdot \Big(p_0 \cdot (g_2^{\ell} \cdot \xi_{1i}^{\ell} \cdot g_1^{\ell} \cdot \xi_{2j}^{\ell}) + (f_{1i}^{\ell} \cdot t_1 \cdot \xi_{2j}^{\ell} + f_{2j}^{\ell} \cdot t_2 \cdot \xi_{1i}^{\ell}) \Big) \Big],$

where $\boldsymbol{\Delta}$ and $\widetilde{\boldsymbol{\Delta}}$ are vectors of dimension L whose elements are respectively the Δ_{ij} and $\widetilde{\Delta}_{ij}$. This noise term is quite complicated, but since it involves multiples of p_1 and p_0, one can distinguish the noise terms that are multiples of p_0, p_0^2, p_1, p_1^2 and $p_0 p_1$. Here, we assume that the noise terms that are multiplied to the p_i's are small enough so that the different multiples do not overlap. While this should be true for correctness that p_1 is much larger than the multiples of p_0 appearing in the term above, this might not be true for instance when splitting the multiple of p_0 from the multiple of p_0^2 (one could for instance think of $p_0 = 4$). As we should see below however, this will not be a problem for our attack. To see this, let us write $p_0 \cdot \mathsf{small}_1 + p_0^2 \cdot \mathsf{small}_2 + p_1 \cdot \mathsf{small}_3$ the noise term above. As we have said, for correctness, it should hold that, when reducing this term modulo p_1, we obtain $p_0 \cdot \mathsf{small}_1 + p_0^2 \cdot \mathsf{small}_2$ over R. Now, dividing by p_0 and reducing the obtained term modulo p_0, we recover $\mathsf{small}_1 \bmod p_0$. In the rank attack below, we exploit the noise term small_1, which we might know only modulo p_0 (and not over R). However, all we do on this noise terms is linear algebra, and does not depend on the ring in which we are considering the elements. Hence, we could as well perform the attack in R_{p_0} if we recovered only $\mathsf{small}_1 \bmod p_0$.

Recall also that in the distinguishing game, the adversary chooses two messages $\mathbf{z}_0$ and $\mathbf{z}_1$ with the constraint that $\mathbf{v}^T \mathbf{z}_0 = \mathbf{v}^T \mathbf{z}_1 + p_0 \cdot \mu$ for any vector $\mathbf{v}$ for which she has a secret key (with a small μ). She then gets back the encryption of one of the two messages and wants to know which one was encoded. In other words, if $\mathbf{z}$ is the encrypted message, the adversary knows that $\mathbf{v}^T \mathbf{z} = x$ or $x + p_0 \cdot \mu$ for some known values of x and μ (with $p_0 \cdot \mu$ smaller than some bound B_1), and wants to distinguish between these two cases. We can then assume that the adversary removes x from the noise term, and is left with either 0 or $p_0 \cdot \mu$. The adversary can then obtain the following noise terms

$$\sum_{\ell} \left(\sum_{i,j} v_{ij}^{\times} \cdot \tilde{\xi}_{1i}^{\ell} \tilde{\xi}_{2j}^{\ell} \right) g_2^{\ell} g_1^{\ell} \tag{5.1}$$

$$\sum_{\ell} \left(\sum_{i,j} v_{ij}^{\times} \cdot \xi_{1i}^{\ell} \xi_{2j}^{\ell} \right) g_2^{\ell} g_1^{\ell} \tag{5.2}$$

$$\sum_{\ell} \left(\sum_{i,j} v_{ij}^{\times} \cdot (\tilde{\xi}_{1i}^{\ell} \xi_{2j}^{\ell} + \tilde{\xi}_{1i}^{\ell} \xi_{2j}^{\ell}) \right) g_2^{\ell} g_1^{\ell} \tag{5.3}$$

$$\sum_{i,j,\ell} v_{ij}^{\times} \cdot \left(f_{1i}^{\ell} \cdot t_1 \cdot \xi_{2j}^{\ell} + f_{2j}^{\ell} \cdot t_2 \cdot \xi_{1i}^{\ell} \right) \ + \ (\mathbf{v}^{\times})^T \mathbf{\Delta} \cdot s + (0 \text{ or } \mu) \qquad (5.4)$$

$$\sum_{i,j,\ell} v_{ij}^{\times} \cdot \left(f_{1i}^{\ell} \cdot t_1 \cdot \tilde{\xi}_{2j}^{\ell} + f_{2j}^{\ell} \cdot t_2 \cdot \tilde{\xi}_{1i}^{\ell} \right) \ + \ (\mathbf{v}^{\times})^T \tilde{\mathbf{\Delta}} \cdot s + \mathbf{v}^T \boldsymbol{\eta} + (\mathbf{v}^T \mathbf{E} + (\mathbf{v}^{\times})^T \mathbf{E}^{\times}) \boldsymbol{\nu}$$

$$(5.5)$$

In the noise terms above, the blue elements are secret and are fixed for all ciphertexts and secret keys, the red elements are known and depend only on the secret key, the black elements are secret and depend only on the ciphertexts and the brown element is the challenge. The value μ of the challenge can be chosen by the adversary, and the adversary has to decide, given the above noise terms, whether (5.4) contains 0 or μ. Recall also that the vector $\mathbf{v}$ can be chosen by the adversary whereas the vector $\mathbf{v}^{\times}$ is chosen by the challenger as the polynomial that computes a PRG. The blue and red elements above can be modified independently, by considering another secret key or another ciphertext.

5.2   Rank Attack to Distinguish Bit

The rank attack focuses on the noise term (5.4). As this noise term contains the challenge, it suffices to distinguish between a noise term with 0 or a noise term with μ to break the NLinFE construction. Let us rewrite the equation in a more convenient way.

$$\sum_{i,j,\ell} v_{ij}^{\times} \cdot \left(f_{1i}^{\ell} \cdot t_1 \cdot \xi_{2j}^{\ell} + f_{2j}^{\ell} \cdot t_2 \cdot \xi_{1i}^{\ell} \right) \ + \ (\mathbf{v}^{\times})^T \mathbf{\Delta} \cdot s + (0 \text{ or } \mu)$$

$$= \sum_{\ell} \left(\sum_{j} \left(\sum_{i} v_{ij}^{\times} \cdot f_{1i}^{\ell} \right) \cdot \xi_{2j}^{\ell} \cdot t_1 \right) + \sum_{\ell} \left(\sum_{j} \left(\sum_{i} v_{ij}^{\times} \cdot f_{2i}^{\ell} \right) \cdot \xi_{1j}^{\ell} \cdot t_1 \right)$$

$$+ \ ((\mathbf{v}^{\times})^T \mathbf{\Delta}) \cdot s + (0 \text{ or } \mu).$$

Recall that in the equations above, the blue terms are fixed, the red terms depend only on the secret key and the black terms depend only on the ciphertext. Hence, one can observe that if the challenge is 0, then the equation above is a sum of products, where in every product one term depends only on the secret key and the other one depends only on the ciphertext. Concatenating all these elements into two vectors, one obtains (5.4) $= \langle a, b \rangle$, where a depends only on the secret key and b depends only on the ciphertext (and they are both secret).

The dimension of a and b is the number of terms in the sum above. In our case, this dimension is $2rk+1$. To see this, note that $\ell \in [k]$ and $j \in [r]$, and that we are summing over ℓ and j so we obtain a sum of kr scalars. Hence, this term may be expressed as one big inner product of two vectors of dimension $2rk + 1$.

Assume that we can make $N := 2rk + 2$ requests for secret keys and ciphertexts, and let us write $c_{i,j} = \langle a_i, b_j \rangle + (0 \text{ or } \mu_{ij})$ the noise term obtained when evaluating the NLinFE scheme with the i-th secret key and the j-th ciphertext.

Recall that the values μ_{ij} are chosen by the adversary. Define $\mathbf{C}$ and $\mathbf{M}$ the $N \times N$ matrices $(c_{i,j})_{i,j}$ and $(\mu_{ij})_{i,j}$ respectively.

Then, depending on the challenge, we claim that $\mathbf{C}$ or $\mathbf{C} - \mathbf{M}$ is of rank at most $N - 1$. To see this, note that we have $\mathbf{C} = \mathbf{A} \cdot \mathbf{B} + (0 \text{ or } M)$, where $\mathbf{A}$ has dimension $N \times N - 1$ and $\mathbf{B}$ has dimension $N - 1 \times N$, so that $\mathbf{A} \cdot \mathbf{B}$ has rank at most $N - 1$. On the other hand, the other matrix is of the form $\mathbf{A} \cdot \mathbf{B} \pm M$, which has full rank with good probability (even if M has only rank 1, the sum of a matrix of rank $N - 1$ and a matrix of rank 1 is likely to have rank N if the two matrices are independent, which is the case here).[4] Hence, computing the determinant of the matrix $\mathbf{C}$ allows to determine what was the challenge, and to break the security of the NLinFE scheme.

The case of degree >2. In the general case, if the degree of the NLinFE scheme is d instead of 2, then the same reasoning applies. The only difference is that the vectors $\mathbf{a}$ and $\mathbf{b}$ will have dimension $d \cdot k \cdot r + 1$, so one needs to be able to make $N := d \cdot k \cdot r + 2$ key and ciphertext queries for the attack. More precisely, in degree d, the term (5.4) becomes

$$(5.4) = \sum_{\delta=1}^{d} \sum_{\ell=1}^{k} \sum_{1 \leq i_1, \cdots, i_d \leq r} v_{i_1, \cdots, i_d}^{\times} \left(\prod_{j \neq \delta} f_{j,i_j}^{\ell} \cdot t_j \right) \xi_{\delta, i_\delta}^{\ell} + (\mathbf{v}^{\times})^T \boldsymbol{\Delta} \cdot s + (0 \text{ or } \mu)$$

$$= \sum_{\delta=1}^{d} \sum_{\ell=1}^{k} \sum_{1 \leq i_1, \cdots, i_d \leq r} v_{i_1, \cdots, i_d}^{\times} \left(\prod_{j \neq \delta} f_{j,i_j}^{\ell} \prod_{j \neq \delta} t_j \right) \xi_{\delta, i_\delta}^{\ell} + (\mathbf{v}^{\times})^T \boldsymbol{\Delta} \cdot s + (0 \text{ or } \mu)$$

$$= \sum_{\delta=1}^{d} \sum_{\ell=1}^{k} \sum_{1 \leq i_1, \cdots, i_d \leq r} v_{i_1, \cdots, i_d}^{\times} \left(\prod_{j \neq \delta} f_{j,i_j}^{\ell} \prod_{j \neq \delta} t_j \right) \xi_{\delta, i_\delta}^{\ell} + (\mathbf{v}^{\times})^T \boldsymbol{\Delta} \cdot s + (0 \text{ or } \mu)$$

$$= \sum_{\delta=1}^{d} \sum_{\ell=1}^{k} \sum_{i_\delta=1}^{r} \left(\sum_{1 \leq i_j \leq r, j \neq \delta} v_{i_1, \cdots, i_d}^{\times} \cdot \prod_{j \neq \delta} f_{j,i_j}^{\ell} \cdot \xi_{\delta, i_\delta}^{\ell} \cdot \prod_{j \neq \delta} t_j \right) + (\mathbf{v}^{\times})^T \boldsymbol{\Delta} \cdot s + (0 \text{ or } \mu).$$

For the first term, we are now summing dkr elements, and each one corresponds to the product of two scalars. Hence, the left term can be written as one inner product of two vectors of dimension $d \cdot k \cdot r$, with one vector depending only on the secret key and one depending only on the ciphertext. The analysis of the term $(\mathbf{v}^{\times})^T \boldsymbol{\Delta} \cdot s$ is the same as before. To conclude, taking $N = d \cdot k \cdot r + 2$ and performing the same attack as above enables us to distinguish whether the challenge is 0 or μ.

---

[4] Observe that even if the μ_{ij} are somehow chosen by the adversary, they cannot be chosen arbitrarily. Indeed, μ_{ij} is the scalar product between the vector corresponding to the i-th secret key, with the difference of the two messages of the j-th pair of challenge messages. Hence, the matrix M has rank at most w, where w is the size of these vectors. However, as said above, it is sufficient to have M of rank at least 1 for the attack to go through, and this can be ensured by the attacker (it simply needs to take $M \neq 0$).

We thus obtain the bound $N := d \cdot k \cdot r + 2$ on the number of key requests that can be performed by the attacker. Since $k, r = \text{poly}(\kappa)$, the adversary can obtain this number of keys to conduct the above attack.

6   Modifying Construction to Fix Attacks

In this section, we describe an approach to fix the above two attacks (which we will refer to as "the multiple ciphertext attack" and as the "rank attack" respectively).

Intuitively, the reason for the multiple ciphertext attack to work is commutativity: we mix and match the LWE labels and secrets across multiple ciphertexts to compute the large term in two different ways. An over-simplification is that if two ciphertexts CT_1 and CT_2 have LWE secrets s and t respectively, and a and b are labels, then CT_1 contains encodings with large terms as and bs and CT_2 contains encodings with large terms at and bt. But now, $(as) \cdot (bt) = (bs) \cdot (at)$, which implies that we can multiply encodings from different ciphertexts in two different ways to get the same large term, which may then be removed by subtraction. While the attack developed in Sect. 4 is more elaborate, the intuition remains the same as in the simplification discussed here.

The reason the the rank attack on the other hand is the presence of the moduli p_0 and p_1, which allow to separate the noise terms, and obtain one noise term which is only linear in the freshly chosen error elements.

Fixing the multiple ciphertext attack. As shown by the above discussion, the chief vulnerability exploited by the attack is commutativity of polynomials. However, if we replace scalar product by inner product, we get that the first ciphertext contains the terms $\langle \mathbf{a}, \mathbf{s} \rangle$ and $\langle \mathbf{b}, \mathbf{s} \rangle$ and the second ciphertext contains the terms $\langle \mathbf{a}, \mathbf{t} \rangle$ and $\langle \mathbf{b}, \mathbf{t} \rangle$. Attempting to launch the above attack shows that:

$$\langle \mathbf{a}, \mathbf{s} \rangle \cdot \langle \mathbf{b}, \mathbf{t} \rangle \neq \langle \mathbf{b}, \mathbf{s} \rangle \cdot \langle \mathbf{a}, \mathbf{t} \rangle$$

This prevents the mix and match attacks of the kind discussed in Sect. 4 since each large term now uniquely corresponds to a single product of encodings and may not be generated in two different ways. As explained in the full version, the multiple ciphertext attack can still be generalized to this setting, but the modulus q will need to be exponential in the dimension of the vectors for the attack to work, and so we can prevent the attack by choosing the dimension to be larger than $\log q$.

Fixing the rank attack. In order to fix the rank attack, we propose to remove the modulus p_0 from the encodings, i.e., consider encodings of the form $d_{1i}^\ell = \langle \mathbf{h}_{1i}^\ell, \mathbf{t}_1 \rangle + p_1 \cdot e_{1i}^\ell + \tilde{e}_{1i}^\ell$. This way, it will be harder to split the noise term at the end (we will only have three "levels" 1, p_1 and p_1^2 instead of 5 before), and we will show that the noise terms obtained this way seem hard to exploit now. One may want to also remove the modulus p_1 from the construction, and only consider one noise term, but as we should see in the construction, the modulus

p_1 is needed for correctness (not only for the shape of the output noise), and so cannot be removed easily.

Recall that the modulus p_0 were present because we wanted to flood a noise term of the form $\mathsf{noise}_0 \cdot p_0$ (the modulus p_1 is used because the messages are living in R_{p_1}). In more generality, in the bootstrapping procedure used in [2] to construct iO, we will want to flood a noise term of the form $\mathsf{noise}_0 \cdot p_0 + \cdots + \mathsf{noise}_{D-2} \cdot p_{D-2}$ for some integer D related to the degree of the FE scheme we want to construct. We will also want the message space of the NLinFE scheme to be $R_{p_{D-1}}$ and the ciphertext space to be R_{p_D}, with $p_0 < p_1 < \cdots < p_D$ for prime numbers p_i. We also want for the bootsrapping procedure that the noise output by the NLinFE scheme be of the form $\mathsf{noise}'_0 \cdot p_0 + \cdots + \mathsf{noise}'_{D-2} \cdot p_{D-2}$, so that when we add this noise to the original noise, we still have a linear combination of the p_i's, with $i \leq D - 2$.

From arbitrary flooding noise to structured flooding noise. When we remove the moduli from Agrawal's construction as discussed above, we obtain an NLinFE scheme where the flooding noise term is arbitrary in R, and so not of the desired shape $\mathsf{noise}'_0 \cdot p_0 + \cdots + \mathsf{noise}'_{D-2} \cdot p_{D-2}$. We can however use this NLinFE scheme to construct a new NLinFE' scheme, with a flooding noise term of the desired shape. Intuitively, the idea is to use an additive secret sharing of the messages $\mathbf{z} = \mathbf{z}_0 + \cdots + \mathbf{z}_{D-2}$, and then encode $\mathbf{z}_0/p_0, \cdots, \mathbf{z}_{D-2}/p_{D-2}$ using the NLinFE scheme without moduli. To recover the scalar product $\langle \mathbf{v}, \mathbf{z} \rangle$, one then compute $p_0 \cdot \langle \mathbf{v}, \mathbf{z}_0/p_0 \rangle + \cdots + p_{D-2} \cdot \langle \mathbf{v}, \mathbf{z}_{D-2}/p_{D-2} \rangle$, and so the noise term will have the desired shape.

More precisely, the NLinFE' scheme proceeds as follows

NLinFE'.Setup($1^\kappa, 1^w$): Run NLinFE.Setup($1^\kappa, 1^w$) $D - 1$ times to obtain $D - 1$ master secret keys MSK_i and output $(\mathsf{MSK}_0, \cdots, \mathsf{MSK}_{D-2})$.

NLinFE'.Enc($(\mathsf{MSK}_0, \cdots, \mathsf{MSK}_{D-2}), \mathbf{z}$): where $\mathbf{z} \in R_{p_{D-1}}^w$.
1. Sample $(\mathbf{z}_0, \cdots, \mathbf{z}_{D-3})$ uniformly at random in $R_{p_{D-1}}$ and define $\mathbf{z}_{D-2}$ such that $\sum_{i=0}^{D-2} \mathbf{z}_i = \mathbf{z}$.
2. For i in $\{0, \cdots, D - 2\}$, compute $\mathsf{CT}_i = \mathsf{NLinFE.Enc}(\mathsf{MSK}_i, \mathbf{z}_i/p_i)$. Here, the division by p_i is performed modulo p_{D-1}, and is possible because p_i is coprime with p_{D-1} for all $i \leq D - 2$.
   Output $\mathsf{CT}_{\mathbf{z}} = (\mathsf{CT}_0, \cdots, \mathsf{CT}_{D-2})$.
NLinFE'.KeyGen($\mathsf{MSK}, \mathbf{v}, \mathbf{v}^\times$): output

$$\mathsf{SK}_{\mathbf{v}} = (\mathsf{NLinFE.KeyGen}(\mathsf{MSK}_0, \mathbf{v}, \mathbf{v}^\times), \cdots, \mathsf{NLinFE.KeyGen}(\mathsf{MSK}_{D-2}, \mathbf{v}, \mathbf{v}^\times)).$$

NLinFE'.Dec($\mathsf{CT}_{\mathbf{z}}, \mathsf{SK}_{\mathbf{v}}$): where $\mathbf{z} \in R_{p_{D-1}}^w$.
1. Parse $\mathsf{CT}_{\mathbf{z}}$ as $\mathsf{CT}_{\mathbf{z}} = (\mathsf{CT}_0, \cdots, \mathsf{CT}_{D-2})$ and $\mathsf{SK}_{\mathbf{v}}$ as $\mathsf{SK}_{\mathbf{v}} = (\mathsf{SK}_1, \cdots, \mathsf{SK}_{D-2})$.
2. Compute $y_i = \mathsf{NLinFE.Dec}(\mathsf{CT}_i, \mathsf{SK}_i) \in R_{p_{D-1}}$ for $0 \leq i \leq D - 2$.
   Output $\sum_{i=0}^{D-2} p_i y_i \bmod p_{D-1}$.

For correctness, observe that in the NLinFE' decryption algorithm, we have $y_i = \langle \mathbf{z}_i/p_i, \mathbf{v} \rangle + \mathsf{noise}_i$ by correctness of NLinFE (if the ciphertexts and secret keys are valid). So the output is indeed of the form $\langle \mathbf{z}, \mathbf{v} \rangle + \sum_i \mathsf{noise}_i \cdot p_i$: we have $\langle \mathbf{z}, \mathbf{v} \rangle$ plus a noise term of the desired shape.

We conclude that, for the bootstrapping procedure of [2], it is sufficient to construct an NLinFE scheme, with message space $R_{p_{D-1}}$, ciphertext space R_{p_D} and arbitrary flooding noise. The new NLinFE construction we propose below satisfies these conditions.

6.1   The New NLinFE Construction

Below, we present a modified variant of the NLinFE construction of [2], designed to avoid the multiple ciphertext attack and the rank attack, as discussed above.

NLinFE.Setup($1^\kappa, 1^w$): On input a security parameter κ, a parameter w denoting the length of the function and message vectors, do the following:

1. Sample $\mathbf{W} \leftarrow R_{p_D}^{m \times \kappa^2}$ with a trapdoor $\mathbf{T}$ using the algorithm TrapGen.
2. Sample $\mathbf{E} \in \mathcal{D}^{m \times w}$ and set $\mathbf{A} = \mathbf{E}^\mathsf{T} \mathbf{W} \in R_{p_D}^{w \times \kappa^2}$ (recall that $\mathcal{D}$ is a discrete Gaussian distribution over R of parameter σ).
3. For $i \in \{1, \dots, r\}$, $\ell \in \{1, \dots, k\}$, sample $\mathbf{f}_{1i}^\ell, \mathbf{f}_{2i}^\ell \leftarrow \mathcal{D}^\kappa$ and $g_1^\ell, g_2^\ell \leftarrow \mathcal{D}$. If g_1^ℓ, g_2^ℓ are not invertible over R_{p_D}, resample. Set

$$\mathbf{h}_{1i}^\ell = \frac{\mathbf{f}_{1i}^\ell}{g_1^\ell}, \quad \mathbf{h}_{2i}^\ell = \frac{\mathbf{f}_{2i}^\ell}{g_2^\ell} \in R_{p_D}^\kappa$$

4. Sample a PRF seed, denoted as seed.

Output

$$\mathsf{MSK} = \left(\mathbf{W}, \mathbf{T}, \mathbf{A}, \mathbf{E}, \{\mathbf{f}_{1i}^\ell, \mathbf{f}_{2i}^\ell\}_{i \in [r], \ell \in [k]}, \{g_1^\ell, g_2^\ell\}_{\ell \in [k]}\}, \mathsf{seed} \right)$$

NLinFE.Enc($\mathsf{MSK}, \mathbf{z}$): On input public key MSK, a message vector $\mathbf{z} \in R_{p_{D-1}}^w$, do:

1. Sample $\mathbf{t}_1, \mathbf{t}_2 \leftarrow \mathcal{D}^\kappa$. Set $\mathbf{s} = \mathbf{t}_1 \otimes \mathbf{t}_2 \in R^{\kappa^2}$.
2. **Construct Message Encodings.** Sample $\boldsymbol{\nu} \leftarrow \mathcal{D}^m$, $\boldsymbol{\eta} \leftarrow \mathcal{D}^w$ and compute:

$$\mathbf{c} = \mathbf{W}\mathbf{s} + p_{D-1} \cdot \boldsymbol{\nu} \in R_{p_D}^m, \quad \mathbf{b} = \mathbf{A}\mathbf{s} + p_{D-1} \cdot \boldsymbol{\eta} + \mathbf{z} \in R_{p_D}^w,$$

where $\mathbf{z} \in R_{p_{D-1}}^w$ is seen as a vector of R with coefficients in $(-\frac{p_{D-1}}{2}, \frac{p_{D-1}}{2}]$ and then reduced modulo p_D.
3. **Sample Structured Noise.** To compute encodings of noise, do the following:
   (a) Define lattices:

$$\Lambda_1^\ell \triangleq g_1^\ell \cdot R, \quad \Lambda_2^\ell \triangleq g_2^\ell \cdot R$$

   (b) Sample noise terms from the above lattices as:

$$e_{1i}^\ell \leftarrow \widehat{\mathcal{D}}(\Lambda_2^\ell), \tilde{e}_{1i}^\ell \leftarrow \widehat{\mathcal{D}}(\Lambda_2^\ell), \quad e_{2i}^\ell \leftarrow \widehat{\mathcal{D}}(\Lambda_1^\ell), \tilde{e}_{2i}^\ell \leftarrow \widehat{\mathcal{D}}(\Lambda_1^\ell) \quad \forall i \in [r], \ell \in [k].$$

   Here $\widehat{\mathcal{D}}(\Lambda_1^\ell)$ is a discrete Gaussian distribution on Λ_1^ℓ and $\widehat{\mathcal{D}}(\Lambda_2^\ell)$ is a discrete Gaussian distributions on Λ_2^ℓ, both of parameter σ.

4. **Compute Encodings of Noise.**
   (a) Let

$$d^\ell_{1i} = \langle \mathbf{h}^\ell_{1i}, \mathbf{t}_1 \rangle + p_{D-1} \cdot e^\ell_{1i} + \tilde{e}^\ell_{1i} \in R_{p_D} \quad \forall i \in [r], \ell \in [k].$$

Let $\mathbf{d}^\ell_1 = (d^\ell_{1i})$.
   (b) Similarly, let

$$d^\ell_{2i} = \langle \mathbf{h}^\ell_{2i}, \mathbf{t}_2 \rangle + p_{D-1} \cdot e^\ell_{2i} + \tilde{e}^\ell_{2i} \in R_{p_2} \quad \forall i \in [r], \ell \in [k].$$

Let $\mathbf{d}^\ell_2 = (d^\ell_{2i})$.
5. **Output Ciphertext.** Output message encodings $(\mathbf{c}, \mathbf{b})$ and noise encodings $(\mathbf{d}^\ell_1, \mathbf{d}^\ell_2)$ for $\ell \in [k]$.

NLinFE.KeyGen(MSK, $\mathbf{v}, \mathbf{v}^\times$): On input the master secret key MSK, NLinFE function vectors $\mathbf{v} \in R^w_{p_{D-1}}$ and $\mathbf{v}^\times \in R^L$ with coefficients small compared to p_{D-1}, do the following.

1. **Sampling Basis Preimage vectors.**
   (a) Sample short $\mathbf{e}_{ij} \in R^m$ using SamplePre with randomness PRF(seed, ij) such that

$$\mathbf{W}^\mathsf{T} \mathbf{e}_{ij} = \mathbf{h}_{ij}, \text{ where } \mathbf{h}_{ij} \triangleq \sum_{\ell \in [k]} \mathbf{h}^\ell_{1i} \otimes \mathbf{h}^\ell_{2j} + p_{D-1} \mathbf{\Delta}_{ij} + \tilde{\mathbf{\Delta}}_{ij}.$$

Above $\mathbf{\Delta}_{ij}, \tilde{\mathbf{\Delta}}_{ij} \leftarrow \mathcal{D}^{\kappa^2} \in R^{\kappa^2}$ for $1 \leq j \leq i \leq r$.

$$\text{Let } \mathbf{E}^\times = (\mathbf{e}_{ij}) \in R^{m \times L}$$

where $L = |1 \leq j \leq i \leq r|$.
2. **Combining Basis Preimages to Functional Preimage.** Define

$$\mathbf{k_v} = \mathbf{E} \cdot \mathbf{v} + \mathbf{E}^\times \cdot \mathbf{v}^\times \quad \in R^m \tag{5.6}$$

3. Output $(\mathbf{k_v}, \mathbf{v}, \mathbf{v}^\times)$.

NLinFE.Dec($\mathsf{CT_z}, \mathsf{SK_v}$): On input a ciphertext $\mathsf{CT_z} = \big(\mathbf{c}, \mathbf{b}, \{\mathbf{d}^\ell_1, \mathbf{d}^\ell_2\}_{\ell \in [k]} \big)$ and a secret key $\mathbf{k_v}$ for function $\mathbf{v}$, do the following

1. Compute encoding of noise term on the fly as:

$$\mathbf{d}^\times \triangleq \big(\sum_{\ell \in [k]} \mathbf{d}^\ell_1 \otimes \mathbf{d}^\ell_2 \big) \in R^L_{p_D}$$

2. Compute functional ciphertext as:

$$b_\mathbf{v} = \mathbf{v}^\mathsf{T} \mathbf{b} + (\mathbf{v}^\times)^\mathsf{T} \mathbf{d}^\times \in R_{p_D}$$

3. Compute $(b_\mathbf{v} - \mathbf{k}^\mathsf{T}_\mathbf{v} \mathbf{c} \bmod p_D) \bmod p_{D-1}$ and output it.

Correctness. In this section, we establish that the above scheme is correct. To simplify the analysis, we let small_{D-1} denote any term which is small compared to p_{D-1} and small_D be any term which is small compared to p_D. We also assume that summing polynomially many small_i terms or multiplying a constant number of them results in an element which is still a small_i (for $i = D - 1$ or D). We also assume that the parameters are set so that σ is small compared to p_{D-1} and that p_{D-1} is small compared to p_D.

Let us do the analysis by walking through the steps performed by the decrypt algorithm:

1. We compute an encoding of a correlated noise term on the fly as described in Fig. 1.

Computing Encoding of Correlated Noise Term for the new construction

We compute $d_{1i}^\ell \cdot d_{2j}^\ell$. Recall that

$$d_{1i}^\ell = \langle \mathbf{h}_{1i}^\ell, \mathbf{t}_1 \rangle + p_{D-1} \cdot e_{1i}^\ell + \tilde{e}_{1i}^\ell \in R_{p_D}$$

$$d_{2j}^\ell = \langle \mathbf{h}_{2j}^\ell, \mathbf{t}_2 \rangle + p_{D-1} \cdot e_{2i}^\ell + \tilde{e}_{2i}^\ell \in R_{p_D}$$

Recall also that $e_{1i}^\ell, \tilde{e}_{1i}^\ell$ are sampled from lattice Λ_2^ℓ and $e_{2i}^\ell, \tilde{e}_{2i}^\ell$ are sampled from lattice Λ_1^ℓ.

$$\text{Let} \quad e_{1i}^\ell = g_2^\ell \cdot \xi_{1i}^\ell, \quad \tilde{e}_{1i}^\ell = g_2^\ell \cdot \tilde{\xi}_{1i}^\ell,$$
$$\text{and} \quad e_{2i}^\ell = g_1^\ell \cdot \xi_{2i}^\ell, \quad \tilde{e}_{2i}^\ell = g_1^\ell \cdot \tilde{\xi}_{2i}^\ell$$

Now, we may compute:

$$d_{1i}^\ell \cdot d_{2j}^\ell = \left(\langle \mathbf{h}_{1i}^\ell, \mathbf{t}_1 \rangle + p_{D-1} \cdot e_{1j}^\ell + \tilde{e}_{1j}^\ell \right) \cdot \left(\langle \mathbf{h}_{2j}^\ell, \mathbf{t}_2 \rangle + p_{D-1} \cdot e_{2j}^\ell + \tilde{e}_{2j}^\ell \right)$$

$$= \langle \underbrace{\mathbf{h}_{1i}^\ell \otimes \mathbf{h}_{2j}^\ell, \ (\mathbf{t}_1 \otimes \mathbf{t}_2)}_{\mathbf{s}} \rangle + p_{D-1} \cdot \Big(\underbrace{p_{D-1} \cdot (g_2^\ell \cdot \xi_{1i}^\ell \cdot g_1^\ell \cdot \xi_{2j}^\ell)}_{\mathsf{small}_D}$$

$$+ \underbrace{(g_2^\ell \cdot \tilde{\xi}_{1i}^\ell \cdot g_1^\ell \cdot \xi_{2j}^\ell + g_2^\ell \cdot \xi_{1i}^\ell \cdot g_1^\ell \cdot \tilde{\xi}_{2j}^\ell)}_{\mathsf{small}_{D-1}} + \underbrace{(\langle \mathbf{f}_{1i}^\ell, \mathbf{t}_1 \rangle \cdot \xi_{2j}^\ell + \langle \mathbf{f}_{2j}^\ell, \mathbf{t}_2 \rangle \cdot \xi_{1i}^\ell)}_{\mathsf{small}_{D-1}} \Big)$$

$$+ \underbrace{\left((g_2^\ell \cdot \tilde{\xi}_{1i}^\ell \cdot g_1^\ell \cdot \tilde{\xi}_{2j}^\ell) + (\langle \mathbf{f}_{1i}^\ell, \mathbf{t}_1 \rangle \cdot \tilde{\xi}_{2j}^\ell + \langle \mathbf{f}_{2j}^\ell, \mathbf{t}_2 \rangle \cdot \tilde{\xi}_{1i}^\ell) \right)}_{\mathsf{small}_{D-1}}$$

(recall that small_i is a term that is small compared to p_i for $i = D - 1$ or D).

$$\text{Thus,} \quad \sum_{\ell \in [k]} d_{1i}^\ell \cdot d_{2j}^\ell = \langle \big(\sum_{\ell \in [k]} \mathbf{h}_{1i}^\ell \otimes \mathbf{h}_{2j}^\ell \big), \mathbf{s} \rangle + p_{D-1} \cdot \mathsf{small}_D + \mathsf{small}_{D-1}. \qquad (6.2)$$

Fig. 1. Computing encoding of noise term as polynomial of encodings in the new construction of Sect. 6.

2. The decryption equation is:

$$b_{\mathbf{v}} - \mathbf{k}_{\mathbf{v}}^{\mathsf{T}}\mathbf{c} = (\mathbf{v}^{\mathsf{T}}\mathbf{b} + (\mathbf{v}^{\times})^{\mathsf{T}}\mathbf{d}^{\times}) - \mathbf{k}_{\mathbf{v}}^{\mathsf{T}}\mathbf{c}$$

3. Recall that $\mathbf{b} = \mathbf{A} \cdot \mathbf{s} + p_{D-1} \cdot \boldsymbol{\eta} + \mathbf{z} \in R_{p_D}^w$. Hence,

$$\mathbf{v}^{\mathsf{T}}\mathbf{b} = \mathbf{v}^{\mathsf{T}}\mathbf{A} \cdot \mathbf{s} + p_{D-1} \cdot \mathsf{small}_D + \mathbf{v}^{\mathsf{T}}\mathbf{z}$$

4. Let $\mathbf{H}_{ij}^{\times} = \left(\sum_{\ell \in [k]} \mathbf{h}_{1i}^{\ell} \otimes \mathbf{h}_{2j}^{\ell} \right)$ be the $(i,j)^{th}$ row of $\mathbf{H}^{\times} \in R_{p_D}^{L \times \kappa^2}$. Since

$$\mathbf{d}^{\times} = \mathbf{H}^{\times}\mathbf{s} + p_{D-1} \cdot \mathsf{small}_D + \mathsf{small}_{D-1}$$

and $\mathbf{v}^{\times} \in R^L$ is small compared to p_{D-1}, we have

$$(\mathbf{v}^{\times})^{\mathsf{T}}\mathbf{d}^{\times} = (\mathbf{v}^{\times})^{\mathsf{T}}\mathbf{H}^{\times}\mathbf{s} + p_{D-1} \cdot \mathsf{small}_D + \mathsf{small}_{D-1}$$

Hence we have

$$\mathbf{v}^{\mathsf{T}}\mathbf{b} + (\mathbf{v}^{\times})^{\mathsf{T}}\mathbf{d}^{\times} = \left(\mathbf{v}^{\mathsf{T}}\mathbf{A} + (\mathbf{v}^{\times})^{\mathsf{T}}\mathbf{H}^{\times}\right)\mathbf{s} + p_{D-1} \cdot \mathsf{small}_D + \mathsf{small}_{D-1} + \mathbf{v}^{\mathsf{T}}\mathbf{z}$$

5. Next, note that

$$\mathbf{k}_{\mathbf{v}}^{\mathsf{T}}\mathbf{W} = \mathbf{v}^{\mathsf{T}}\mathbf{A} + (\mathbf{v}^{\times})^{\mathsf{T}}\mathbf{H}^{\times} + p_{D-1} \cdot \mathsf{small}_{D-1} + \mathsf{small}_{D-1} \triangleq \mathbf{a}_{\mathbf{v}} \in R_{p_D}^{1 \times \kappa^2}$$

6. Recall that $\mathbf{c} = \mathbf{W} \cdot \mathbf{s} + p_{D-1} \cdot \boldsymbol{\nu}$ hence,

$$\begin{aligned} \mathbf{k}_{\mathbf{v}}^{\mathsf{T}}\mathbf{c} &= \mathbf{a}_{\mathbf{v}}^{\mathsf{T}}\mathbf{s} + p_{D-1} \cdot \langle \boldsymbol{\nu}, \mathbf{k}_{\mathbf{v}} \rangle \\ &= \left(\mathbf{v}^{\mathsf{T}}\mathbf{A} + (\mathbf{v}^{\times})^{\mathsf{T}}\mathbf{H}^{\times}\right)\mathbf{s} + \mathsf{small}_{D-1} + p_{D-1} \cdot \mathsf{small}_D \end{aligned}$$

7. Hence, $b_{\mathbf{v}} - \mathbf{k}_{\mathbf{v}}^{\mathsf{T}}\mathbf{c} = \mathbf{v}^{\mathsf{T}}\mathbf{z} + \mathsf{small}_{D-1} + p_{D-1} \cdot \mathsf{small}_D$. The right hand side of this equation is smaller than p_D by assumption (if the parameters are carefully chosen), hence, by computing $b_{\mathbf{v}} - \mathbf{k}_{\mathbf{v}}^{\mathsf{T}}\mathbf{c}$ in R_{p_D}, we recover $\mathbf{v}^{\mathsf{T}}\mathbf{z} + \mathsf{small}_{D-1} + p_{D-1} \cdot \mathsf{small}_D$ over R. Now, reducing this term modulo p_{D-1} leads to $\mathbf{v}^{\mathsf{T}}\mathbf{z} + \mathsf{small}_{D-1} \bmod p_1$, where small_{D-1} is small compared to p_{D-1}.

On the degree of the noise term. As was already observed in Agrawal's original construction [2], the construction above is described with a noise term of degree $d = 2$, but it could easily be generalized to any constant degree d. In the case of a general degree d, we would have d-tuples of encodings $(d_{1i}^{\ell}, \cdots, d_{di}^{\ell})$, where the noise in d_{ai}^{ℓ} is a multiple of $\prod_{b \neq a} g_b^{\ell}$. Then, when computing $\mathbf{d}^{\times}$, one would consider all possible products $d_{1i_1}^{\ell} \cdots d_{d,i_d}^{\ell}$ and obtain a noise term of degree d. Please see the full version for details. For simplicity, we described above the variant with $d = 2$, but we show in the full version that for security we need $d \geq 3$.

7   Setting the Parameters

We provide in the full version a discussion on the security of the new NLinFE scheme described above. In particular, we generalize the attacks presented in Sects. 4 and 5 and argue that our new scheme is not vulnerable to them. Below, we provide an instantiation of the parameters of the scheme which we believe is secure, even against a quantum computer (see the full version for more details). Recall that the parameter N is the maximal number of key requests that an attacker is allowed to performed and that this parameter should be superlinearly larger than the ciphertext size for the NLinFE scheme to imply iO. In our construction, the ciphertext size is $(rk + m + w)\log(p_D)$. One can check that the choices of parameters proposed below ensure that this size is bounded by $N^{1-\varepsilon}$ for some $\varepsilon > 0$, hence the construction implies iO.

- κ is the security parameter and $B_1 = \mathrm{poly}(\kappa)$ is given as input
- $d = 3$
- $k = \kappa^3$ and $r = \kappa$
- $\sigma = 2^\kappa \cdot B_1$
- $p_{D-1} = \sigma^{2d}$ and $p_D = \sigma^{6d}$
- $m = \kappa^d \cdot \log p_D$
- w is arbitrary up to κ^{d+1}
- $N = \kappa^{d+2.5}$.

Acknowledgments. This work was supported in part by CyberSecurity Research Flanders with reference number VR20192203 and by the Research Council KU Leuven grant C14/18/067 on Cryptanalysis of post-quantum cryptography.

References

1. Abdalla, M., Bourse, F., De Caro, A., Pointcheval, D.: Simple functional encryption schemes for inner products. In: Katz, J. (ed.) PKC 2015. LNCS, vol. 9020, pp. 733–751. Springer, Heidelberg (2015). https://doi.org/10.1007/978-3-662-46447-2_33
2. Agrawal, S.: Indistinguishability obfuscation without multilinear maps: new methods for bootstrapping and instantiation. In: Ishai, Y., Rijmen, V. (eds.) EURO-CRYPT 2019, Part I. LNCS, vol. 11476, pp. 191–225. Springer, Cham (2019). https://doi.org/10.1007/978-3-030-17653-2_7
3. Agrawal, S., Libert, B., Stehle, D.: Fully secure functional encryption for linear functions from standard assumptions, and applications. In: Crypto (2016)
4. Ajtai, M.: Generating hard instances of the short basis problem. In: Wiedermann, J., van Emde Boas, P., Nielsen, M. (eds.) ICALP 1999. LNCS, vol. 1644, pp. 1–9. Springer, Heidelberg (1999). https://doi.org/10.1007/3-540-48523-6_1
5. Alwen, J., Peikert, C.: Generating shorter bases for hard random lattices. In: STACS, pp. 75–86 (2009)

6. Ananth, P., Jain, A.: Indistinguishability obfuscation from compact functional encryption. In: Gennaro, R., Robshaw, M. (eds.) CRYPTO 2015, Part I. LNCS, vol. 9215, pp. 308–326. Springer, Heidelberg (2015). https://doi.org/10.1007/978-3-662-47989-6_15

7. Ananth, P., Jain, A., Lin, H., Matt, C., Sahai, A.: Indistinguishability obfuscation without multilinear maps: new paradigms via low degree weak pseudorandomness and security amplification. In: Boldyreva, A., Micciancio, D. (eds.) CRYPTO 2019, Part III. LNCS, vol. 11694, pp. 284–332. Springer, Cham (2019). https://doi.org/10.1007/978-3-030-26954-8_10

8. Apon, D., Döttling, N., Garg, S., Mukherjee, P.: Cryptanalysis of indistinguishability obfuscations of circuits over GGH13. Eprint 2016 (2016)

9. Applebaum, B., Brakerski, Z.: Obfuscating circuits via composite-order graded encoding. In: Dodis, Y., Nielsen, J.B. (eds.) TCC 2015, Part II. LNCS, vol. 9015, pp. 528–556. Springer, Heidelberg (2015). https://doi.org/10.1007/978-3-662-46497-7_21

10. Barak, B., Brakerski, Z., Komargodski, I., Kothari, P.K.: Limits on low-degree pseudorandom generators (or: sum-of-squares meets program obfuscation). In: Nielsen, J.B., Rijmen, V. (eds.) EUROCRYPT 2018, Part II. LNCS, vol. 10821, pp. 649–679. Springer, Cham (2018). https://doi.org/10.1007/978-3-319-78375-8_21

11. Barak, B., et al.: On the (im)possibility of obfuscating programs. In: Kilian, J. (ed.) CRYPTO 2001. LNCS, vol. 2139, pp. 1–18. Springer, Heidelberg (2001). https://doi.org/10.1007/3-540-44647-8_1

12. Bardet, M., Faugère, J.-C., Salvy, B.: On the complexity of the F5 Gröbner basis algorithm. J. Symb. Comput. **70**, 49–70 (2015)

13. Bitansky, N., Garg, S., Lin, H., Pass, R., Telang, S.: Succinct randomized encodings and their applications. In: STOC, pp. 439–448 (2015)

14. Bitansky, N., Nishimaki, R., Passelègue, A., Wichs, D.: From cryptomania to obfustopia through secret-key functional encryption. In: TCC, pp. 391–418 (2016)

15. Bitansky, N., Paneth, O., Wichs, D.: Perfect structure on the edge of chaos. In: Kushilevitz, E., Malkin, T. (eds.) TCC 2016. LNCS, vol. 9562, pp. 474–502. Springer, Heidelberg (2016). https://doi.org/10.1007/978-3-662-49096-9_20

16. Bitansky, N., Vaikuntanathan, V.: Indistinguishability obfuscation from functional encryption. In: FOCS 2015, p. 163 (2015)

17. Brent, R.P., McKay, B.D.: Determinants and ranks of random matrices over ZM. Discret. Math. **66**(1–2), 35–49 (1987)

18. Canetti, R., Holmgren, J., Jain, A., Vaikuntanathan, V.: Succinct garbling and indistinguishability obfuscation for RAM programs. In: STOC, pp. 429–437 (2015)

19. Canetti, R., Lin, H., Tessaro, S., Vaikuntanathan, V.: Obfuscation of probabilistic circuits and applications. In: Dodis, Y., Nielsen, J.B. (eds.) TCC 2015, Part II. LNCS, vol. 9015, pp. 468–497. Springer, Heidelberg (2015). https://doi.org/10.1007/978-3-662-46497-7_19

20. Chen, Y., Gentry, C., Halevi, S.: Cryptanalyses of candidate branching program obfuscators. In: Coron, J.-S., Nielsen, J.B. (eds.) EUROCRYPT 2017, Part III. LNCS, vol. 10212, pp. 278–307. Springer, Cham (2017). https://doi.org/10.1007/978-3-319-56617-7_10

21. Chen, Y., Vaikuntanathan, V., Wee, H.: GGH15 beyond permutation branching programs: proofs, attacks, and candidates. In: Shacham, H., Boldyreva, A. (eds.) CRYPTO 2018, Part II. LNCS, vol. 10992, pp. 577–607. Springer, Cham (2018). https://doi.org/10.1007/978-3-319-96881-0_20

22. Cheon, J.H., Cho, W., Hhan, M., Kim, J., Lee, C.: Statistical zeroizing attack: cryptanalysis of candidates of BP obfuscation over GGH15 multilinear map. In: Boldyreva, A., Micciancio, D. (eds.) CRYPTO 2019, Part III. LNCS, vol. 11694, pp. 253–283. Springer, Cham (2019). https://doi.org/10.1007/978-3-030-26954-8_9
23. Cheon, J.H., Han, K., Lee, C., Ryu, H., Stehlé, D.: Cryptanalysis of the multilinear map over the integers. In: Oswald, E., Fischlin, M. (eds.) EUROCRYPT 2015, Part I. LNCS, vol. 9056, pp. 3–12. Springer, Heidelberg (2015). https://doi.org/10.1007/978-3-662-46800-5_1
24. Cheon, J.H., Hhan, M., Kim, J., Lee, C.: Cryptanalyses of branching program obfuscations over GGH13 multilinear map from the NTRU problem. In: Shacham, H., Boldyreva, A. (eds.) CRYPTO 2018, Part III. LNCS, vol. 10993, pp. 184–210. Springer, Cham (2018). https://doi.org/10.1007/978-3-319-96878-0_7
25. Coron, J.-S., et al.: Zeroizing without low-level zeroes: new MMAP attacks and their limitations. In: Gennaro, R., Robshaw, M. (eds.) CRYPTO 2015, Part I. LNCS, vol. 9215, pp. 247–266. Springer, Heidelberg (2015). https://doi.org/10.1007/978-3-662-47989-6_12
26. Coron, J.-S., Lee, M.S., Lepoint, T., Tibouchi, M.: Zeroizing attacks on indistinguishability obfuscation over CLT13. Eprint 2016 (2016)
27. Ducas, L., Pellet-Mary, A.: On the statistical leak of the GGH13 multilinear map and some variants. In: Peyrin, T., Galbraith, S. (eds.) ASIACRYPT 2018, Part I. LNCS, vol. 11272, pp. 465–493. Springer, Cham (2018). https://doi.org/10.1007/978-3-030-03326-2_16
28. Garg, S., Gentry, C., Halevi, S.: Candidate multilinear maps from ideal lattices. In: Johansson, T., Nguyen, P.Q. (eds.) EUROCRYPT 2013. LNCS, vol. 7881, pp. 1–17. Springer, Heidelberg (2013). https://doi.org/10.1007/978-3-642-38348-9_1
29. Garg, S., Gentry, C., Halevi, S., Raykova, M., Sahai, A., Waters, B.: Candidate indistinguishability obfuscation and functional encryption for all circuits. In: FOCS (2013). http://eprint.iacr.org/
30. Garg, S., Miles, E., Mukherjee, P., Sahai, A., Srinivasan, A., Zhandry, M.: Secure obfuscation in a weak multilinear map model. In: Hirt, M., Smith, A. (eds.) TCC 2016, Part II. LNCS, vol. 9986, pp. 241–268. Springer, Heidelberg (2016). https://doi.org/10.1007/978-3-662-53644-5_10
31. Gentry, C., Jutla, C.S., Kane, D.: Obfuscation using tensor products (2018)
32. Hu, Y., Jia, H.: Cryptanalysis of GGH map. In: Fischlin, M., Coron, J.-S. (eds.) EUROCRYPT 2016, Part I. LNCS, vol. 9665, pp. 537–565. Springer, Heidelberg (2016). https://doi.org/10.1007/978-3-662-49890-3_21
33. Jain, A., Lin, H., Matt, C., Sahai, A.: How to leverage hardness of constant-degree expanding polynomials over $\mathbb{R}$ to build iO. In: Ishai, Y., Rijmen, V. (eds.) EUROCRYPT 2019, Part I. LNCS, vol. 11476, pp. 251–281. Springer, Cham (2019). https://doi.org/10.1007/978-3-030-17653-2_9
34. Komargodski, I., Moran, T., Naor, M., Pass, R., Rosen, A., Yogev, E.: One-way functions and (im)perfect obfuscation. In: FOCS (2014)
35. Koppula, V., Lewko, A.B., Waters, B.: Indistinguishability obfuscation for turing machines with unbounded memory. In: STOC, pp. 419–428 (2015)
36. Lin, H.: Indistinguishability obfuscation from SXDH on 5-linear maps and locality-5 PRGs. In: Katz, J., Shacham, H. (eds.) CRYPTO 2017, Part I. LNCS, vol. 10401, pp. 599–629. Springer, Cham (2017). https://doi.org/10.1007/978-3-319-63688-7_20

37. Lin, H., Pass, R., Seth, K., Telang, S.: Output-compressing randomized encodings and applications. In: Kushilevitz, E., Malkin, T. (eds.) TCC 2016, Part I. LNCS, vol. 9562, pp. 96–124. Springer, Heidelberg (2016). https://doi.org/10.1007/978-3-662-49096-9_5

38. Lin, H., Tessaro, S.: Indistinguishability obfuscation from trilinear maps and block-wise local PRGs. In: Katz, J., Shacham, H. (eds.) CRYPTO 2017, Part I. LNCS, vol. 10401, pp. 630–660. Springer, Cham (2017). https://doi.org/10.1007/978-3-319-63688-7_21

39. Lin, H., Vaikuntanathan, V.: Indistinguishability obfuscation from DDH-like assumptions on constant-degree graded encodings. In: FOCS (2016)

40. Lombardi, A., Vaikuntanathan, V.: On the non-existence of blockwise 2-local PRGs with applications to indistinguishability obfuscation. IACR Cryptology ePrint Archive (2017). http://eprint.iacr.org/2017/301

41. Mayr, E.W.: Some complexity results for polynomial ideals. J. Complex. **13**(3), 303–325 (1997)

42. Micciancio, D., Peikert, C.: Trapdoors for lattices: simpler, tighter, faster, smaller. In: Pointcheval, D., Johansson, T. (eds.) EUROCRYPT 2012. LNCS, vol. 7237, pp. 700–718. Springer, Heidelberg (2012). https://doi.org/10.1007/978-3-642-29011-4_41

43. Miles, E., Sahai, A., Zhandry, M.: Annihilation attacks for multilinear maps: crypt-analysis of indistinguishability obfuscation over GGH13. In: Robshaw, M., Katz, J. (eds.) CRYPTO 2016, Part II. LNCS, vol. 9815, pp. 629–658. Springer, Heidelberg (2016). https://doi.org/10.1007/978-3-662-53008-5_22

44. Pellet-Mary, A.: Quantum attacks against indistinguishablility obfuscators proved secure in the weak multilinear map model. In: Shacham, H., Boldyreva, A. (eds.) CRYPTO 2018, Part III. LNCS, vol. 10993, pp. 153–183. Springer, Cham (2018). https://doi.org/10.1007/978-3-319-96878-0_6

45. Sahai, A., Waters, B.: How to use indistinguishability obfuscation: deniable encryption, and more. In: STOC (2014)

46. Stehlé, D., Steinfeld, R., Tanaka, K., Xagawa, K.: Efficient public key encryption based on ideal lattices. In: Matsui, M. (ed.) ASIACRYPT 2009. LNCS, vol. 5912, pp. 617–635. Springer, Heidelberg (2009). https://doi.org/10.1007/978-3-642-10366-7_36

47. Zimmerman, J.: How to obfuscate programs directly. In: Oswald, E., Fischlin, M. (eds.) EUROCRYPT 2015, Part II. LNCS, vol. 9057, pp. 439–467. Springer, Heidelberg (2015). https://doi.org/10.1007/978-3-662-46803-6_15

Combiners for Functional Encryption, Unconditionally

Aayush Jain$^{(\boxtimes)}$, Nathan Manohar$^{(\boxtimes)}$, and Amit Sahai

UCLA, Los Angeles, CA, USA
aayushjainiitd@gmail.com, nmanohar@cs.ucla.edu

Abstract. Functional encryption (FE) combiners allow one to combine many candidates for a functional encryption scheme, possibly based on different computational assumptions, into another functional encryption candidate with the guarantee that the resulting candidate is secure as long as at least one of the original candidates is secure. The fundamental question in this area is whether FE combiners exist. There have been a series of works Ananth et al. (CRYPTO '16), Ananth-Jain-Sahai (EURO-CRYPT '17), Ananth et al. (TCC '19) on constructing FE combiners from various assumptions.

We give the first *unconditional* construction of combiners for functional encryption, resolving this question completely. Our construction immediately implies an unconditional universal functional encryption scheme, an FE scheme that is secure if such an FE scheme exists. Previously such results either relied on algebraic assumptions or required subexponential security assumptions.

1 Introduction

In cryptography, many interesting cryptographic primitives rely on computational assumptions. Over the years, many assumptions have been proposed such as factoring, quadratic residuosity, decisional Diffie-Hellman, learning with errors, and many more. However, despite years of research, the security of these assumptions is still not firmly established. Indeed, we do not even know how to prove $\mathbf{P} \neq \mathbf{NP}$; our understanding of algebraic hardness is even more speculative. Moreover, we also do not have a strong understanding of how different cryptographic assumptions compare against each other. For instance, it is not known whether decisional Diffie-Hellman is a weaker or a stronger assumption than learning with errors. This inability to adequately compare different cryptographic assumptions induces the following problematic situation: suppose we have a cryptographic primitive (say, public key encryption) with many candidate constructions based on a variety of assumptions, and we want to pick the most secure candidate to use. Unfortunately, due to our limited knowledge of how these assumptions compare against each other, we cannot determine which candidate is the most secure one.

© International Association for Cryptologic Research 2020
A. Canteaut and Y. Ishai (Eds.): EUROCRYPT 2020, LNCS 12105, pp. 141–168, 2020.
https://doi.org/10.1007/978-3-030-45721-1_6

Unconditional Cryptographic Combiners. Cryptographic combiners were introduced to handle the above issue. Given many candidates of a cryptographic primitive, possibly based on different assumptions, a cryptographic combiner takes these candidates and produces another candidate for the same primitive with the guarantee that this new candidate is secure as long as at least *one* of the original candidates is secure. For example, a combiner for public key encryption can be used to transform two candidates, one based on decisional Diffie-Hellman and the other on learning with errors, into a new public-key encryption candidate that is secure provided *either* decisional Diffie-Hellman *or* learning with errors is secure. Thus, this new public-key encryption candidate relies on a strictly weaker assumption than the original two candidate constructions and allows us to hedge our bets on the security of the two original assumptions.

Furthermore, even if an underlying primitive, such as public-key encryption, requires an unproven hardness assumption, the security of a *combiner* for that primitive can be unconditional. Therefore, cryptographic combiners stand out in the world of cryptography in the sense that they are one of the few useful cryptographic objects that do not inherently require reliance on hardness assumptions. And indeed, combiners for fundamental primitives like one-way functions, public-key encryption, and oblivious transfer are known to exist unconditionally [28,38,39,42].

Obtaining unconditional combiners is particularly important because the entire purpose of constructing combiners is to make cryptographic constructions *future-proof* in case assumptions break down. In this work, we study combiners for *functional encryption*, an area where studying combiners is particularly important and where, prior to our work, only conditional constructions were known [2,5,6] (and in fact, these previous results required either algebraic or sub-exponentially strong assumptions). We obtain the first unconditional combiner for functional encryption. Furthermore, we do so by providing a general compiler, significantly simplifying previous work in this area. Along the way, we define and provide constructions of input-local MPC protocols, input-local garbling schemes, and combiner-friendly homomorphic secret sharing schemes, primitives that may be of independent interest.

Combiners for Functional Encryption. Functional encryption (FE), introduced by [52] and first formalized by [19,51], is one of the core primitives in the area of computing on encrypted data. This notion allows an authority to generate and distribute constrained keys associated with functions $f_1, \ldots, f_q$, called *functional keys*, which can be used to learn the values $f_1(x), \ldots, f_q(x)$ given an encryption of x. Intuitively, the security notion states that the functional keys associated with $f_1, \ldots, f_q$ and an encryption of x reveal nothing beyond the values $f_1(x), \ldots, f_q(x)$.

Function encryption has opened the floodgates to important cryptographic applications that have long remained elusive. These applications include, but are not limited to, multi-party non-interactive key exchange [34], universal samplers [34], reusable garbled circuits [36], verifiable random functions [10,13,37], and adaptive garbling [40]. FE has also helped improve our understanding of important theoretical questions, such as the hardness of Nash equilibrium [33,34].

One of the most important applications of FE is its implication to indistinguishability obfuscation (iO for short), which is considered the holy grail of cryptography [8,15]. In fact, if we are willing to tolerate subexponential security loss, then even secret-key FE is enough to imply iO [14,43,44].

Over the past few years, many constructions of functional encryption have been proposed [1,4,7,9,29,30,45–49] and studying what assumptions suffice for constructing general-purpose FE remains a very important and active area of investigation. Recent cryptanalytic attacks [11,12,23–26,41,49] on FE schemes further highlight the importance of careful study. Given these results, we should hope to minimize the trust we place on any individual FE candidate.

The notion of a functional encryption combiner achieves this purpose. Informally speaking, a functional encryption combiner allows for combining many functional encryption candidates in such a way that the resulting FE candidate is secure as long as at least *one* of the initial FE candidates is secure. In other words, a functional encryption combiner says that it suffices to place trust collectively on multiple FE candidates, instead of placing trust on any specific FE candidate. Furthermore, FE combiners are an important area of study for the following reasons:

- Most importantly, it gives a mechanism to hedge our bets and distribute our trust over multiple constructions. This has been highlighted above.
- Often, constructions of FE combiners give rise to constructions of robust FE combiners generically [2,6]. Any robust FE combiner gives us a universal construction of FE, which is an explicit FE scheme that is secure as long as there exists a secure functional encryption scheme.
- Studying FE combiners helps improve our understanding of the nature of assumptions we need to build FE.
- They give rise to theoretically important results in other branches of cryptography, such as round-optimal low-communication MPC [2].
- Constructions of robust FE combiners have encouraged research on understanding correctness amplification for FE, iO [6,16], and other fundamental cryptographic primitives [17].
- Finally, due to connections to security amplification, techniques used to build FE combiners are useful to give better constructions of FE. In particular, the work of [7] used techniques developed from the study of FE combiners to provide a generic security amplification of FE, which proved pivotal in giving the first construction of FE that does not rely on multilinear maps and makes use of simply stated, instance-independent assumptions.

There have been a series of works in this area. The starting point was the work of two concurrent papers [5,27], both appearing at CRYPTO, that studied the related question of obfuscation combiners. This was followed up by the work of [6], which gave a construction of FE combiners (and universal FE) assuming the existence of a subexponentially secure FE algorithm. They also gave a construction of a robust FE combiner assuming LWE. Then [2] gave construction of a robust FE combiner (and universal obfuscation) relying on the algebraic assumption of the existence of constant degree randomizing polynomials (which are known to exist assuming number-theoretic assumptions such as LWE, DDH, and quadratic residuosity). However, until now, the ultimate question in this area, of whether FE combiners exist without making any additional assumptions, has remained open.

1.1 Our Contributions

In this paper, we consider the following questions.

What is the minimal assumption necessary to construct FE combiners and universal FE?

In particular,

Is it possible to construct FE combiners and universal FE unconditionally?

We resolve the above question in the affirmative and prove the following.

Theorem 1 (Informal). *There exists an unconditionally secure FE combiner for* P/poly.

It turns out that our construction of an FE combiner also gives rise to a robust FE combiner using the results of [2,6].

Corollary 1 (Informal). *There exists an unconditionally secure robust FE combiner for* P/poly.

As any robust FE combiner gives a universal FE scheme [5,6], we obtain the following additional result.

Corollary 2 (Informal). *There exists an unconditional construction of a universal FE scheme for* P/poly.

We note that, as was the case in previous constructions, our construction of a universal FE scheme is parameterized by the maximum run-time of any of the algorithms of the secure FE scheme.

1.2 Technical Overview

Our starting point is the observation that FE combiners are related to the notion of secure multi-party computation and function secret sharing (also known as homomorphic secret sharing [18,20–22,50]). Suppose for a function f, it was possible to give out function shares $f_1, \ldots, f_n$ such that for any input x, we can n-out-of-n secret share x into shares $x_1, \ldots, x_n$ and recover $f(x)$ given $f_1(x_1), \ldots, f_n(x_n)$. Then, we would be able to build an FE combiner in the following manner. Given an input x, the encryptor would n-out-of-n secret share x and encrypt the ith share x_i under the ith FE candidate FE_i (depicted in Fig. 1). To generate a function key for a function f, FE_i would generate a function key for function share f_i. Using these ciphertexts and function keys, it would be possible to recover $f_i(x_i)$, from which it would be possible to recover $f(x)$.

Security would follow from the fact that since at least one FE candidate is secure, one of the input shares remains hidden, hiding the input. This overall approach was used in [2,6] to construct FE combiners from LWE. In this work, we would like to minimize the assumptions needed to construct an FE combiner, and, unfortunately, we do not know how to construct such a function sharing scheme for polynomial-sized circuits from one-way functions. Note that since FE implies one-way functions, any FE combiner can assume the existence of one-way functions since the individual one-way function candidates arising from each FE candidate can be trivially combined by independent concatenation (direct product) of the candidate one-way functions.

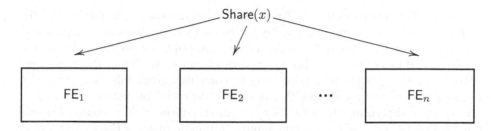

Fig. 1. A pictorial overview of splitting x amongst n FE candidates.

Our first step towards constructing an FE combiner unconditionally is that we observe that it is easy to build an FE combiner for a *constant* number of FE candidates by simply nesting the candidates. For example, if we had 2 FE candidates, FE_1 and FE_2, we could combine these two candidates by simply having encryption encrypt first under FE_1 and then encrypt the resulting ciphertext under FE_2. To generate a secret key for a function f, we would generate a function key $SK_{f,1}$ for f under FE_1 and then generate a function key $SK_{f,2}$ for the function that runs $FE_1.Dec(SK_{f,1}, \cdot)$ under FE_2. The function key $SK_{f,2}$ would then be the function key for f under the combined FE scheme. Using nestings of candidates, we can replace our original FE candidates with these new nested candidates. For example, if we use 2-nestings, we can consider all possible 2-nestings $FE_{i,j}$ for $i, j \in [n]$ as our new set of FE candidates. Observe now that we have replaced our original n FE candidates with n^2 "new" FE candidates. At first glance, this appears to not have helped much. However, note that previously, we needed to consider function sharing schemes that were secure against up to $n-1$ corruptions. When using nested candidates, it follows that if FE_{i^*} was originally secure, then $FE_{i,j}$ with at least one of $i, j = i^*$ is also secure. We show how to leverage this new corruption pattern of the candidates in the following manner (Fig. 2).

Suppose we had a "special" MPC protocol Φ where every bit in the transcript of an execution of Φ can be computed by a function on the inputs (and random coins) of a *constant* number of parties (say 2). Furthermore, the output of Φ can be determined solely from the transcript and Φ is secure against a semi-honest

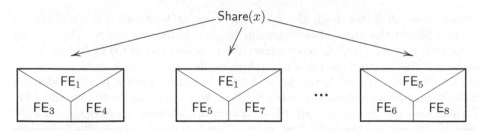

Fig. 2. A pictorial overview of 3-nested FE candidates (the required level of nesting in our construction). If FE_5 is secure, then $FE_{1,5,7}$ and $FE_{5,6,8}$ are secure.

adversary that corrupts up to $n-1$ parties. If Φ has the above properties, then the transcript of an execution of Φ can be determined via an alternate computation. Instead of running Φ normally to obtain the transcript, we can instead compute jointly on all pairs of parties' inputs (and randomness) to obtain the transcript. That is, if a bit τ_α in the transcript τ can be computed given only the inputs (and randomness) of parties P_i and P_j (we say it "depends" on parties P_i and P_j), then we can determine the value of τ_α in an execution of Φ by computing this function on (x_i, r_i) and (x_j, r_j) (the inputs and randomness of these two parties) rather than executing the protocol in the normal fashion. Proceeding in the same manner for every bit in the transcript, we can obtain the same exact transcript that we would have by executing the protocol normally, but we are able to do so by only evaluating functions on two parties' inputs (and randomness).

This observation leads us to the following approach for constructing an FE combiner. To encrypt an input x, additively secret share x into n shares $(x_1, \ldots, x_n)$ and encrypt each pair of shares (x_i, x_j) under $FE_{i,j}$. To generate a function key for a function f, consider the MPC protocol that computes $f(x_1 \oplus \ldots \oplus x_n)$. Then, for every bit τ_α in the transcript of such a protocol, if τ_α "depends" on parties P_i, P_j, we would generate a function key under $FE_{i,j}$ for the circuit C_{τ_α} that computes τ_α given x_i, x_j.

This approach immediately runs into the following problem. The MPC protocol is randomized, whereas the function keys in an FE scheme are for *deterministic* functions. Moreover, an FE ciphertext needs to be compatible with many function keys. Fortunately, these problems can easily be solved by having the encryptor also generate a PRF key K_i for each party P_i. The encryptor now encrypts (x_i, x_j, K_i, K_j) under FE candidate $FE_{i,j}$ and uses K_i and some fixed tag tag_f embedded in the function key for f to generate the randomness of P_i in the evaluation of the MPC protocol. Now, by using the function keys for the C_{τ_α}'s, it is possible for the decryptor to recover all the bits in the transcript of an execution of the protocol and, therefore, recover $f(x)$. Security would follow from the fact that if candidate FE_{i^*} is secure, then x_{i^*} and K_{i^*} remain hidden, and we can use the security of the MPC protocol to simulate the view of party P_{i^*}.

If such an MPC protocol as described above could be found, the above would suffice for constructing an FE combiner. However, the goal of this work is to construct an FE combiner *unconditionally* and so we would like to only assume the existence of one-way functions. However, semi-honest MPC secure against up to $n-1$ corruptions requires oblivious transfer (OT), which we do not want to assume. To deal with this, we adapt our MPC idea to settings with correlated randomness, such as the OT-hybrid model.

A first attempt at adapting this idea to protocols in the OT-hybrid model is the following. Suppose that we have a "special" MPC protocol Φ where every bit in the transcript of an execution of Φ can be computed by a function on the inputs (and random coins/correlated randomness) of a *constant* number of parties (say 2). Furthermore, the output of Φ can be determined solely from the transcript and Φ is secure against a semi-honest adversary that corrupts up to $n-1$ parties in the OT-hybrid model.

The first challenge is to instantiate the OT oracle. This can be done by having shared PRF keys $K_{i,j}$ between all pairs of parties P_i and P_j. Then $K_{i,j}$ will be used to generate correlated randomness between P_i and P_j. We can generate all the correlated randomness prior to the protocol execution and include it as part of the input to a party P_i. This allows us to generate correlated randomness, but we still run into a second issue. Since a party P_i has correlated randomness between itself and all other parties, its input now depends on all other parties! So, it appears that constant nestings of FE candidates will no longer suffice.

Fortunately, this second issue can be mitigated by a more refined condition on the "special" MPC protocol Φ. Let $(r_{i,j}, r_{j,i})$ denote the correlated randomness pair between parties P_i and P_j, where $r_{i,j}$ and $r_{j,i}$ are given to P_i and P_j, respectively. Instead of having the functions that compute bits of the transcript of Φ take as input the entire correlated randomness string $\{r_{i,j}\}_{j\neq i\in[n]}$ held by a party P_i, we instead allow it to take single components $r_{i,j}$ as input. If the function takes as input $r_{i,j}$, then *both* parties P_i and P_j are counted in the number of parties that the function depends on. More formally, the condition on the "special" MPC protocol Φ becomes the following. Let (x_i, r_i) denote the input and randomness of a party P_i and let $r_{i,j}$ denote the correlated randomness between parties P_i and P_j held by P_i. Every bit τ_α in the transcript τ of an execution of Φ can be computed by some deterministic function f_α on input

$$((x_i)_{i\in\mathcal{S}_\alpha}, (r_i)_{i\in\mathcal{S}_\alpha}, (r_{i,j})_{i,j\in\mathcal{S}_\alpha}),$$

where $|\mathcal{S}_\alpha| \leq t$ for some constant t. We call such an MPC protocol a t-input-local MPC protocol and define this formally in Sect. 4.

To summarize, if we had a t-input-local MPC protocol for some constant t, then we would be able to construct an FE combiner unconditionally using the ideas detailed above. However, it is unclear how to construct such an MPC protocol, and, unfortunately, no protocol in the literature for all polynomial-sized circuits in the OT-hybrid model satisfies all our required properties. However, the 2-round semi-honest MPC protocol of Garg-Srinivasan [35] transformed to operate in the OT-hybrid model [31] comes close. At a high level, this is because they compile an MPC protocol into a series of garbled circuits, where each garbled circuit is computed by a single party. However, there are several bottlenecks that make their protocol initially incompatible with our schema. One observation is that the protocol of [31,35] contains a pre-processing phase that causes the initial state (effectively input) of each party to be dependent on all other parties. This might seem like a major issue since messages dependent only on a single parties' state can now depend on all parties. Yet, a careful analysis shows that while individual messages sent by a party might "depend" on all parties in the protocol, each bit sent by a party still depends on only a constant number of parties.

The real issue is that in the protocol of [31,35], parties send garbled circuits of circuits whose descriptions depend on all parties. Thus, the resulting garbled circuit may depend on all parties. However, we observe that the way these circuits depend on all parties is very specific. The circuits garbled are keyed circuits of the form $C[v]$, where v is some hardcoded value. C itself is public and does not depend on any party. And while v depends on all parties, each bit of v only depends on a *constant* number of parties! To obtain an input-local MPC protocol, we construct a garbling scheme that has the property that garbling circuits of the form $C[v]$ described above results in a garbled circuit where each bit of the garbled circuit only depends on a constant number of parties. We call such a garbling scheme an input-local garbling scheme. By instantiating the protocol of [31,35] with this input-local garbling scheme, we are able to arrive at an input-local MPC protocol.

Combiner-Friendly Homomorphic Secret Sharing (CFHSS). In the sketch of our plan for constructing an FE combiner provided above, we wanted to generate function keys for various circuits with respect to nested FE candidates. As an intermediate tool, we introduce the notion of a combiner-friendly homomorphic secret sharing (CFHSS) scheme. Such an abstraction almost immediately gives rise to an FE combiner, but will be useful in simplifying the presentation of the construction.

Informally, a CFHSS scheme consists of input encoding and function encoding algorithms. The input encoding algorithm runs on an input x and outputs input shares $s_{i,j,k}$ for $i,j,k \in [n]$ (we define CFHSS schemes for triples of indices, since we will require 3-nestings of FE candidates in our construction). The function encoding algorithm runs on a circuit C and outputs function shares $C_{i,j,k}$ for $i,j,k \in [n]$. Then, the decoding algorithm takes as input the evaluation of all shares $C_{i,j,k}(s_{i,j,k})$ and recovers $C(x)$. Informally, the security notion of a CFHSS scheme says that if the shares corresponding to some index i^* remain hidden, then the input is hidden to a computationally bounded adversary and only the evaluation $C(x)$ is revealed.

In order to build an FE combiner from a CFHSS scheme, we will encrypt the share $s_{i,j,k}$ using the nested FE candidate corresponding to indices i,j,k. To provide a function key for a circuit C, we will issue function keys for the circuit $C_{i,j,k}$ with respect to the nested candidate corresponding to indices i,j,k. This allows the decryptor to compute $C_{i,j,k}(s_{i,j,k})$ for all $i,j,k \in [n]$, which by the properties of our CFHSS scheme, is sufficient to determine $C(x)$. Note that in order to argue security, we will have to rely on the Trojan method [3].

Organization. We begin by defining functional encryption, secure multi-party computation, and garbling schemes in Sect. 2. Then, in Sect. 3, we define the notion of a functional encryption combiner. In Sect. 4, we define the notion of an input-local MPC protocol and then show how to construct such a protocol. This is done by constructing a specific garbling scheme that, when used to instantiate the garbling scheme used in the protocol of [31,35], results in an input-local MPC protocol. In Sect. 5, we introduce and define the notion of a combiner-friendly homomorphic secret sharing (CFHSS) scheme and construct such a scheme using an input-local MPC protocol. In Sect. 6, we construct an FE combiner from a CFHSS scheme. Finally, in Sect. 7, we observe that our unconditional FE combiner implies a universal FE scheme.

2 Preliminaries

We denote the security parameter by λ. For an integer $n \in \mathbb{N}$, we use $[n]$ to denote the set $\{1, 2, \ldots, n\}$. We use $\mathcal{D}_0 \cong_c \mathcal{D}_1$ to denote that two distributions $\mathcal{D}_0, \mathcal{D}_1$ are computationally indistinguishable. We use $\mathsf{negl}(\lambda)$ to denote a function that is negligible in λ. We use $y \leftarrow \mathcal{A}$ to denote that y is the output of a randomized algorithm $\mathcal{A}$, where the randomness of $\mathcal{A}$ is sampled from the uniform distribution. We write $\mathcal{A}(x; r)$ to denote the output of $\mathcal{A}$ when ran on input x with randomness r. We use PPT as an abbreviation for probabilistic polynomial time.

2.1 Functional Encryption

We define the notion of a (secret key) functional encryption candidate and a (secret key) functional encryption scheme. A functional encryption candidate is associated with the correctness requirement, while a secure functional encryption scheme is associated with both correctness and security.

Syntax of a Functional Encryption Candidate/Scheme. A functional encryption (FE) candidate/scheme FE for a class of circuits $\mathcal{C} = \{\mathcal{C}_\lambda\}_{\lambda \in \mathbb{N}}$ consists of four polynomial time algorithms (Setup, Enc, KeyGen, Dec) defined as follows. Let $\mathcal{X}_\lambda$ be the input space of the circuit class $\mathcal{C}_\lambda$ and let $\mathcal{Y}_\lambda$ be the output space of $\mathcal{C}_\lambda$. We refer to $\mathcal{X}_\lambda$ and $\mathcal{Y}_\lambda$ as the input and output space of the candidate/scheme, respectively.

- **Setup**, MSK $\leftarrow$ FE.Setup(1^λ): It takes as input the security parameter λ and outputs the master secret key MSK.
- **Encryption**, CT $\leftarrow$ FE.Enc(MSK, m): It takes as input the master secret key MSK and a message $m \in \mathcal{X}_\lambda$ and outputs CT, an encryption of m.
- **Key Generation**, SK$_C \leftarrow$ FE.KeyGen (MSK, C): It takes as input the master secret key MSK and a circuit $C \in \mathcal{C}_\lambda$ and outputs a function key SK$_C$.
- **Decryption**, $y \leftarrow$ FE.Dec (SK$_C$, CT): It takes as input a function secret key SK$_C$, a ciphertext CT and outputs a value $y \in \mathcal{Y}_\lambda$.

Throughout this work, we will only be concerned with *uniform* algorithms. That is, (Setup, Enc, KeyGen, Dec) can be represented as Turing machines (or equivalently uniform circuits).

We describe the properties associated with the above candidate.

Correctness

Definition 1 (Correctness). *A functional encryption candidate* FE $=$ (Setup, KeyGen, Enc, Dec) *is said to be correct if it satisfies the following property: for every* $C : \mathcal{X}_\lambda \to \mathcal{Y}_\lambda \in \mathcal{C}_\lambda, m \in \mathcal{X}_\lambda$ *it holds that:*

$$\Pr \left[\begin{array}{c} \mathsf{MSK} \leftarrow \mathsf{FE.Setup}(1^\lambda) \\ \mathsf{CT} \leftarrow \mathsf{FE.Enc}(\mathsf{MSK}, m) \\ \mathsf{SK}_C \leftarrow \mathsf{FE.KeyGen}(\mathsf{MSK}, C) \\ C(m) \leftarrow \mathsf{FE.Dec}(\mathsf{SK}_C, \mathsf{CT}) \end{array} \right] \geq 1 - \mathsf{negl}(\lambda),$$

where the probability is taken over the coins of the algorithms.

IND-Security. We recall indistinguishability-based selective security for FE. This security notion is modeled as a game between a challenger Chal and an adversary $\mathcal{A}$ where the adversary can request functional keys and ciphertexts from Chal. Specifically, $\mathcal{A}$ can submit function queries C and Chal responds with the corresponding functional keys. $\mathcal{A}$ can also submit message queries of the form (x_0, x_1) and receives an encryption of messages x_b for some bit $b \in \{0, 1\}$. The adversary $\mathcal{A}$ wins the game if she can guess b with probability significantly more than $1/2$ and if for all function queries C and message queries (x_0, x_1), $C(x_0) = C(x_1)$. That is to say, any function evaluation that is computable by $\mathcal{A}$ gives the same value regardless of b. It is required that the adversary must declare the challenge messages at the beginning of the game.

Definition 2 (IND-secure FE). *A secret-key FE scheme* FE *for a class of circuits* $\mathcal{C} = \{\mathcal{C}_\lambda\}_{\lambda \in [\mathbb{N}]}$ *and message space* $\mathcal{X} = \{\mathcal{X}_\lambda\}_{\lambda \in [\mathbb{N}]}$ *is selectively secure if for any PPT adversary* $\mathcal{A}$, *there exists a negligible function* $\mu(\cdot)$ *such that for all sufficiently large* $\lambda \in \mathbb{N}$, *the advantage of* $\mathcal{A}$ *is*

$$\mathsf{Adv}_{\mathcal{A}}^{\mathsf{FE}} = \left| \Pr[\mathsf{Expt}_{\mathcal{A}}^{\mathsf{FE}}(1^\lambda, 0) = 1] - \Pr[\mathsf{Expt}_{\mathcal{A}}^{\mathsf{FE}}(1^\lambda, 1) = 1] \right| \leq \mu(\lambda),$$

where for each $b \in \{0, 1\}$ *and* $\lambda \in \mathbb{N}$, *the experiment* $\mathsf{Expt}_{\mathcal{A}}^{\mathsf{FE}}(1^\lambda, b)$ *is defined below:*

1. **Challenge message queries:** $\mathcal{A}$ *submits message queries,*

$$\left\{ (x_0^i, x_1^i) \right\}$$

   with $x_0^i, x_1^i \in \mathcal{X}_\lambda$ *to the challenger* Chal.
2. Chal *computes* $\mathsf{MSK} \leftarrow \mathsf{FE.Setup}(1^\lambda)$ *and then computes* $\mathsf{CT}_i \leftarrow \mathsf{FE.Enc}(\mathsf{MSK}, x_b^i)$ *for all* i. *The challenger* Chal *then sends* $\{\mathsf{CT}_i\}$ *to the adversary* $\mathcal{A}$.

3. **Function queries**: *The following is repeated an at most polynomial number of times: $\mathcal{A}$ submits a function query $C \in \mathcal{C}_\lambda$ to* Chal. *The challenger* Chal *computes* $\mathsf{SK}_C \leftarrow \mathsf{FE.KeyGen}(\mathsf{MSK}, C)$ *and sends it to $\mathcal{A}$.*
4. *If there exists a function query C and challenge message queries (x_0^i, x_1^i) such that $C(x_0^i) \neq C(x_1^i)$, then the output of the experiment is set to $\bot$. Otherwise, the output of the experiment is set to b', where b' is the output of $\mathcal{A}$.*

Adaptive Security. The above security notion is referred to as selective security in the literature. One can consider a stronger notion of security, called *adaptive security*, where the adversary can interleave the challenge messages and the function queries in any arbitrary order. Analogous to Definition 2, we can define an adaptively secure FE scheme. In this paper, we only deal with selectively secure FE schemes. However, the security of these schemes can be upgraded to adaptive with no additional cost [3].

Collusions. We can parameterize the FE candidate by the number of function secret key queries that the adversary can make in the security experiment. If the adversary can only submit an a priori upper bounded q secret key queries, we say that the scheme is q-key secure. We say that the functional encryption scheme is unbounded-key secure if the adversary can make an unbounded (polynomial) number of function secret key queries. In this work, we will allow the adversary to make an arbitrary polynomial number of function secret key queries.

FE Candidates vs. FE Schemes. As defined above, an FE scheme must satisfy *both* correctness and security, while an FE candidate is simply the set of algorithms. Unless otherwise specified, we will be dealing with FE candidates that satisfy correctness. We will only refer to FE constructions as FE schemes if it is known that the construction satisfies both correctness and security.

2.2   Secure Multi-party Computation

The syntax and security definitions for secure multi-party computation can be found in the full version. In this work, we will deal with protocols that follow a certain structure, introduced in [31,35], called conforming protocols. The full syntactic definition of conforming protocols can be found in the full version.

2.3   Garbling Schemes

The definition of garbling schemes can be found in the full version.

2.4   Correlated Randomness Model

In the correlated randomness model, two parties P_i and P_j are given correlated strings $r_{i,j}$ and $r_{j,i}$, respectively. If we set $r_{i,j} = (k_0, k_1)$ for two strings k_0, k_1

and $r_{j,i} = (b, k_b)$ for a random bit b and the string k_b, then these two parties can now perform a 2-round information-theoretically secure OT, where P_i is the sender and P_j is the receiver. In the first round, the receiver sends $v = b \oplus c$, where c is the receiver's choice bit. Then, the sender responds with $(y_0, y_1) = (m_0 \oplus k_v, m_1 \oplus k_{1 \oplus v})$. The receiver can then determine m_c by computing $y_c \oplus k_b$.

In this work, we will often say that parties generate correlated randomness necessary to perform a certain number of OTs. By this, we simply mean that the parties repeat the above procedure once for each necessary OT (with the appropriate party as sender/receiver) and use the above 2-round information-theoretically secure OT protocol for each necessary OT.

3   FE Combiners: Definition

In this section, we give a formal definition of an FE combiner. Intuitively, an FE combiner FEComb takes n FE candidates, $\mathsf{FE}_1, \ldots, \mathsf{FE}_n$ and compiles them into a new FE candidate with the property that FEComb is a secure FE scheme provided that at least one of the n FE candidates is a secure FE scheme.

Syntax of a Functional Encryption Combiner. A functional encryption combiner FEComb for a class of circuits $\mathcal{C} = \{\mathcal{C}_\lambda\}_{\lambda \in \mathbb{N}}$ consists of four polynomial time algorithms (Setup, Enc, KeyGen, Dec) defined as follows. Let $\mathcal{X}_\lambda$ be the input space of the circuit class $\mathcal{C}_\lambda$ and let $\mathcal{Y}_\lambda$ be the output space of $\mathcal{C}_\lambda$. We refer to $\mathcal{X}_\lambda$ and $\mathcal{Y}_\lambda$ as the input and output space of the combiner, respectively. Furthermore, let $\mathsf{FE}_1, \ldots, \mathsf{FE}_n$ denote the descriptions of n FE candidates.

- **Setup,** $\mathsf{FEComb.Setup}(1^\lambda, \{\mathsf{FE}_i\}_{i \in [n]})$: It takes as input the security parameter λ and the descriptions of n FE candidates $\{\mathsf{FE}_i\}_{i \in [n]}$ and outputs the master secret key MSK.
- **Encryption,** $\mathsf{FEComb.Enc}(\mathsf{MSK}, \{\mathsf{FE}_i\}_{i \in [n]}, m)$: It takes as input the master secret key MSK, the descriptions of n FE candidates $\{\mathsf{FE}_i\}_{i \in [n]}$, and a message $m \in \mathcal{X}_\lambda$ and outputs CT, an encryption of m.
- **Key Generation,** $\mathsf{FEComb.Keygen}(\mathsf{MSK}, \{\mathsf{FE}_i\}_{i \in [n]}, C)$: It takes as input the master secret key MSK, the descriptions of n FE candidates $\{\mathsf{FE}_i\}_{i \in [n]}$, and a circuit $C \in \mathcal{C}_\lambda$ and outputs a function key SK_C.
- **Decryption,** $\mathsf{FEComb.Dec}(\{\mathsf{FE}_i\}_{i \in [n]}, \mathsf{SK}_C, \mathsf{CT})$: It is a deterministic algorithm that takes as input the descriptions of n FE candidates $\{\mathsf{FE}_i\}_{i \in [n]}$, a function secret key SK_C, and a ciphertext CT and outputs a value $y \in \mathcal{Y}_\lambda$.

Remark 1. In the formal definition above, we have included $\{\mathsf{FE}_i\}_{i \in [n]}$, the descriptions of the FE candidates, as input to all the algorithms of FEComb. For notational simplicity, we will often forgo these inputs and assume that they are implicit.

We now define the properties associated with an FE combiner. The three properties are correctness, polynomial slowdown, and security. Correctness is analogous to that of an FE candidate, provided that the n input FE candidates are all valid FE candidates. Polynomial slowdown says that the running times of all the algorithms of FEComb are polynomial in λ and n. Finally, security intuitively says that if at least one of the FE candidates is also secure, then FEComb is a secure FE scheme. We provide the formal definitions below.

Correctness

Definition 3 (Correctness). *Suppose* $\{FE_i\}_{i \in [n]}$ *are correct FE candidates. We say that an FE combiner is correct if for every circuit* $C : \mathcal{X}_\lambda \to \mathcal{Y}_\lambda \in \mathcal{C}_\lambda$, *and message* $m \in \mathcal{X}_\lambda$ *it holds that:*

$$
\Pr \left[
\begin{array}{l}
\mathsf{MSK} \leftarrow \mathsf{FEComb.Setup}(1^\lambda, \{FE_i\}_{i \in [n]}) \\
\mathsf{CT} \leftarrow \mathsf{FEComb.Enc}(\mathsf{MSK}, \{FE_i\}_{i \in [n]}, m) \\
\mathsf{SK}_C \leftarrow \mathsf{FEComb.Keygen}(\mathsf{MSK}, \{FE_i\}_{i \in [n]}, C) \\
C(m) \leftarrow \mathsf{FEComb.Dec}(\{FE_i\}_{i \in [n]}, \mathsf{SK}_C, \mathsf{CT})
\end{array}
\right] \geq 1 - \mathsf{negl}(\lambda),
$$

where the probability is taken over the coins of the algorithms and $\mathsf{negl}(\lambda)$ *is a negligible function in* λ.

Polynomial Slowdown

Definition 4 (Polynomial Slowdown) *An FE combiner* FEComb *satisfies polynomial slowdown if on all inputs, the running times of* FEComb.Setup, FEComb.Enc, FEComb.Keygen, *and* FEComb.Dec *are at most* $\mathsf{poly}(\lambda, n)$, *where n is the number of FE candidates that are being combined.*

IND-Security

Definition 5 (IND-Secure FE Combiner). *An FE combiner* FEComb *is selectively secure if for any set* $\{FE_i\}_{i \in [n]}$ *of correct FE candidates, it satisfies Definition 2, where the descriptions of* $\{FE_i\}_{i \in [n]}$ *are public and implicit in all invocations of the algorithms of* FEComb, *if at least one of the FE candidates* $FE_1, \ldots, FE_n$ *also satisfies Definition 2.*

Note that *Definition 2* is the IND-security definition for FE.

Robust FE Combiners and Universal FE

Remark 2. We also define the notion of a robust FE combiner. An FE combiner FEComb is robust if it is an FE combiner that satisfies the three properties (correctness, polynomial slowdown, and security) associated with an FE combiner when given any set of FE candidates $\{FE_i\}_{i \in [n]}$, provided that one is a correct and secure FE candidate. No restriction is placed on the other FE candidates. In particular, they need not satisfy correctness at all.

Robust FE combiners can be used to build a universal functional encryption scheme defined below.

Definition 6 (*T*-Universal Functional Encryption). *We say that an explicit Turing machine* $\Pi_{\text{univ}} = (\Pi_{\text{univ}}.\text{Setup}, \Pi_{\text{univ}}.\text{Enc}, \Pi_{\text{univ}}.\text{KeyGen}, \Pi_{\text{univ}}.\text{Dec})$ *is a universal functional encryption scheme parametrized by* T *if* Π_{univ} *is a correct and secure FE scheme assuming the existence a correct and secure FE scheme with runtime* $< T$.

4   Input-Local MPC Protocols

As discussed in Sect. 1.2, if we had a "special" MPC protocol, where every bit of the transcript is computable by a deterministic function on a *constant* number of parties' inputs and randomness, and the output of the protocol can be computed solely from the transcript, we could use such a protocol to construct an FE combiner. Here, we formally define such a protocol and call it an *input-local* MPC protocol. Since our goal is to construct FE combiners unconditionally, we do not want to assume the existence of OT, so we will define our input-local MPC protocol in the correlated-randomness model.

4.1   Input-Local Protocol Specification

Let Φ be an MPC protocol for n parties $P_1, \ldots, P_n$ with inputs $x_1, \ldots, x_n$ in the correlated randomness model. We can view Φ as a deterministic MPC protocol, where the input of a party P_i is $(x_i, r_i, (r_{i,j})_{j \neq i})$, where r_i is the randomness used by P_i and $(r_{i,j}, r_{j,i})$ for $i \neq j$ is the correlated randomness tuple used between parties P_i and P_j. Φ is called t-input-local if the following holds:

- **Input-Local Transcript:** Let τ be a transcript of an execution of Φ. Every bit τ_α of τ can be written as a deterministic function of the inputs, randomness, and correlated randomness dependent on at most t parties. That is, there exists a deterministic function f_α such that

$$\tau_\alpha = f_\alpha\left((x_i)_{i \in \mathcal{S}_\alpha}, (r_i)_{i \in \mathcal{S}_\alpha}, (r_{i,j})_{i,j \in \mathcal{S}_\alpha}\right),$$

  where $|\mathcal{S}_\alpha| \leq t$. If $i \in \mathcal{S}_\alpha$, then τ_α depends on party P_i.

- **Publicly Recoverable Output:** Given a transcript τ of an execution of Φ, there exists a function Eval such that the output of the protocol Φ for all parties is given by
$$y = \text{Eval}(\tau).$$

- **Security:** Φ is simulation secure against $n-1$ semi-honest corruptions, assuming the existence of one-way functions.

No MPC protocol in the literature for all polynomial-sized circuits in the correlated randomness model satisfies the specification of a t-input-local MPC protocol for a constant t. However, the protocols of [31, 35] come "close", and we show that with a simple transformation, the protocol of [31, 35] can be made t-input-local.

[31, 35] show the following.

Theorem 2 ([31,32,35]). *Assuming one-way functions, for any circuit C, there exists a 2-round MPC protocol in the correlated randomness model that is secure against semi-honest adversaries that can corrupt up to $n - 1$ parties.*

The MPC protocol satisfying Theorem 2 is the MPC protocol of [35] modified to operate in the correlated randomness model. In [31], they additionally modify the protocol of [35] in other ways, since the focus of [31] is on achieving information-theoretic security for smaller circuit classes and better efficiency. However, one can simply modify the protocol of [35] to operate in the correlated randomness model without making the additional modifications present in [31], a fact which we confirmed with the authors [32].

The MPC protocol of Theorem 2 is not input-local, but can be made input-local via a simple modification. At a high level, the reason that the above protocol is not input-local is because parties P_i, as part of the protocol, send garbled circuits of circuits $C[v]$ that have values v hardcoded in them that depend on $(r_{i,j})_{j \neq i}$, the correlated randomness between P_i and all other parties. As a result, these garbled circuits depend on all parties, and thus, the protocol is not input-local for a constant t. Fortunately, this issue is easily fixable by instantiating the garbling scheme used by the protocol in a specific manner. We consider the garbling scheme for keyed circuits that garbles $C[v]$ by applying Yao's garbling scheme to the universal circuit U, where $U(C, v, x) = C[v](x)$. The garbled circuit of this new scheme consists of $\hat{U}$, the Yao garbling of U, along with input labels corresponding to C and v. The input labels of this new scheme are the input labels corresponding to x. Observe now that $\hat{U}$ and the input labels for C are clearly input-local, since they only depend on the party P_i that is garbling. Furthermore, since every bit of v only depends on a constant number of parties, each input label for each bit of v also depends on a constant number of parties, giving us an input-local protocol.

Formally, consider the following garbling scheme.

Definition 7 (Input-Local Garbling Scheme). *Let* $\mathsf{GC} = (\mathsf{GrbC}, \mathsf{EvalGC})$ *denote the standard Yao garbling scheme [53] for poly-sized circuits. Let $\mathcal{C}$ be a class of keyed circuits with keyspace $\mathcal{V}$. Let the description length of any $C \in \mathcal{C}$ be ℓ_1 and of any $v \in \mathcal{V}$ be ℓ_2. Let the input length of any circuit $C \in \mathcal{C}$ be ℓ_3. Let $\ell = \ell_1 + \ell_2 + \ell_3$. Let C_i, v_i denote the ith bit of the description of C, v, respectively. Let $\mathsf{GC}' = (\mathsf{GrbC}', \mathsf{EvalGC}')$ be a garbling scheme for the class of keyed circuits $\mathcal{C}$ defined as follows:*

- **Garbled Circuit Generation,** $\mathsf{GrbC}'(1^\lambda, C[v])$: *Let U be the universal circuit that, on input (C, v, x) with $|C| = \ell_1$, $|v| = \ell_2$, and $|x| = \ell_3$, computes $C[v](x)$. Compute $(\hat{U}, (\mathbf{k}_1, \ldots, \mathbf{k}_\ell)) \leftarrow \mathsf{GrbC}(1^\lambda, U)$. Output*

$$((\hat{U}, k_1^{C_1}, \ldots, k_{\ell_1}^{C_{\ell_1}}, k_{\ell_1+1}^{v_1}, \ldots, k_{\ell_1+\ell_2}^{v_{\ell_2}}), (\mathbf{k}_{\ell_1+\ell_2+1}, \ldots, \mathbf{k}_\ell)).$$

- **Evaluation,** $\mathsf{EvalGC}'(\widehat{C[v]}, (k_1^{x_1}, \ldots, k_{\ell_3}^{x_{\ell_3}}))$: *Parse $\widehat{C[v]}$ as $(\hat{U}, (k_1, k_2, \ldots, k_{\ell_1+\ell_2}))$. Run*

$$\mathsf{EvalGC}(\hat{U}, (k_1, \ldots, k_{\ell_1+\ell_2}, k_1^{x_1}, \ldots, k_{\ell_3}^{x_{\ell_3}}))$$

and output the result.

Correctness of the above garbling scheme follows immediately from the correctness of Yao's garbling scheme and the definition of U. In particular, for every keyed circuit $C[v]$, for any $x \in \{0,1\}^{\ell_3}$, EvalGC' runs EvalGC on $\hat{U}$ with input labels corresponding to (C, v, x), giving $U(C, v, x) = C[v](x)$ as desired.

Theorem 3. *The garbling scheme of Definition 7 is secure.*

Proof. Let SimGC be the simulator for Yao's garbling scheme. The simulator SimGC' operates as follows. Run

$$(\hat{U}, (k_1, \ldots, k_\ell)) \leftarrow \mathsf{SimGC}(1^\lambda, \phi(U), C[v](x))$$

and output

$$((\hat{U}, k_1, \ldots, k_{\ell_1 + \ell_2}), (k_{\ell_1 + \ell_2 + 1}, \ldots, k_\ell)).$$

Suppose there exists an adversary $\mathcal{A}$ that can distinguish the output of SimGC' from the real execution. Then, consider the adversary $\mathcal{A}'$ that breaks the security of Yao's garbling scheme by simply querying its challenger on the pair $(U, (C, v, x))$, rearranging the components of its received challenge to match the output of SimGC', and running $\mathcal{A}$. $\mathcal{A}'$ outputs the result of $\mathcal{A}$. $\mathcal{A}'$ simulates the role of $\mathcal{A}$'s challenger exactly and, therefore, must win with nonnegligible advantage, a contradiction. $\square$

Armed with the above garbling scheme, we are able to obtain an input-local MPC protocol. By taking the MPC protocol of Theorem 2 and instantiating the underlying garbling scheme with the one from Definition 7, we arrive at the following result.

Theorem 4. *Assuming one-way functions, there exists a 3-input-local MPC protocol for any poly-sized circuit C.*

Proof. The proof is included in the full version.

5   Combiner-Friendly Homomorphic Secret Sharing Schemes

As an intermediate step in our construction of an FE combiner, we define and construct what we call a combiner-friendly homomorphic secret sharing scheme (CFHSS). Informally, a CFHSS scheme consists of input encoding and function encoding algorithms. The input encoding algorithm runs on an input x and outputs input shares $s_{i,j,k}$ for $i, j, k \in [n]$. The function encoding algorithm runs on a circuit C and outputs function shares $C_{i,j,k}$ for $i, j, k \in [n]$. Then, the decoding algorithm takes as input the evaluation of all shares $C_{i,j,k}(s_{i,j,k})$ and recovers $C(x)$. Looking ahead, our CFHSS scheme has several properties that will be useful in constructing an FE combiner. Recall that the high-level idea of our construction was to view each FE candidate as a party P_i in an MPC protocol. In our construction of a CFHSS scheme, each input and function share depends on only the state of a constant number of parties. In particular, share $s_{i,j,k}$ will depend only on the state of parties P_i, P_j, and P_k. Informally, the security notion of a CFHSS scheme says that if the shares corresponding to some index i^* remain hidden, then the input is hidden to a computationally bounded adversary and only the evaluation $C(x)$ is revealed.

5.1 Definition

Definition 8. *A combiner-friendly homomorphic secret sharing scheme,* CFHSS = (InpEncode, FuncEncode, Decode), *for a class of circuits* $\mathcal{C} = \{\mathcal{C}_\lambda\}_{\lambda \in \mathbb{N}}$ *with input space* $\mathcal{X}_\lambda$ *and output space* $\mathcal{Y}_\lambda$ *supporting* $n \in \mathbb{N}$ *candidates consists of the following polynomial time algorithms:*

- **Input Encoding,** InpEncode($1^\lambda, 1^n, x$): *It takes as input the security parameter* λ, *the number of candidates* n, *and an input* $x \in \mathcal{X}_\lambda$ *and outputs a set of input shares* $\{s_{i,j,k}\}_{i,j,k \in [n]}$.
- **Function Encoding,** FuncEncode($1^\lambda, 1^n, C$): *It is an algorithm that takes as input the security parameter* λ, *the number of candidates* n, *and a circuit* $C \in \mathcal{C}$ *and outputs a set of function shares* $\{C_{i,j,k}\}_{i,j,k \in [n]}$.
- **Decoding,** Decode($\{C_{i,j,k}(s_{i,j,k})\}_{i,j,k \in [n]}$): *It takes as input a set of evaluations of function shares on their respective input shares and outputs a value* $y \in \mathcal{Y}_\lambda \cup \{\bot\}$.

A combiner-friendly homomorphic secret sharing scheme, CFHSS, *is required to satisfy the following properties:*

- **Correctness***: For every* $\lambda \in \mathbb{N}$, *circuit* $C \in \mathcal{C}_\lambda$, *and input* $x \in \mathcal{X}_\lambda$, *it holds that:*

$$\Pr \left[\begin{array}{l} \{s_{i,j,k}\}_{i,j,k \in [n]} \leftarrow \mathsf{InpEncode}(1^\lambda, 1^n, x) \\ \{C_{i,j,k}\}_{i,j,k \in [n]} \leftarrow \mathsf{FuncEncode}(1^\lambda, 1^n, C) \\ C(x) \leftarrow \mathsf{Decode}(\{C_{i,j,k}(s_{i,j,k})\}_{i,j,k \in [n]}) \end{array} \right] \geq 1 - \mathsf{negl}(\lambda),$$

where the probability is taken over the coins of the algorithms and $\mathsf{negl}(\lambda)$ *is a negligible function in* λ.

- **Security***:*

Definition 9 (IND-secure CFHSS). *A combiner-friendly homomorphic secret sharing scheme* CFHSS *for a class of circuits* $\mathcal{C} = \{\mathcal{C}_\lambda\}_{\lambda \in [\mathbb{N}]}$ *and input space* $\mathcal{X} = \{\mathcal{X}_\lambda\}_{\lambda \in [\mathbb{N}]}$ *is selectively secure if for any PPT adversary* $\mathcal{A}$, *there exists a negligible function* $\mu(\cdot)$ *such that for all sufficiently large* $\lambda \in \mathbb{N}$, *the advantage of* $\mathcal{A}$ *is*

$$\mathsf{Adv}_\mathcal{A}^{\mathsf{CFHSS}} = \left| \Pr[\mathsf{Expt}_\mathcal{A}^{\mathsf{CFHSS}}(1^\lambda, 1^n, 0) = 1] - \Pr[\mathsf{Expt}_\mathcal{A}^{\mathsf{CFHSS}}(1^\lambda, 1^n, 1) = 1] \right| \leq \mu(\lambda),$$

where for each $b \in \{0,1\}$ *and* $\lambda \in \mathbb{N}$ *and* $n \in \mathbb{N}$, *the experiment* $\mathsf{Expt}_\mathcal{A}^{\mathsf{CFHSS}}(1^\lambda, 1^n, b)$ *is defined below:*

1. **Secure share:** $\mathcal{A}$ *submits an index* $i^* \in [n]$ *that it will not learn the input shares for.*

2. **Challenge input queries**: $\mathcal{A}$ submits input queries,

$$\left(x_0^\ell, x_1^\ell\right)_{\ell \in [L]}$$

   with $x_0^\ell, x_1^\ell \in \mathcal{X}_\lambda$ to the challenger Chal, where $L = \mathsf{poly}(\lambda)$ is chosen by $\mathcal{A}$.
3. For all ℓ, Chal computes $\{s_{i,j,k}^\ell\}_{i,j,k \in [n]} \leftarrow \mathsf{InpEncode}(1^\lambda, 1^n, x_b^\ell)$. For all ℓ, the challenger Chal then sends $\{s_{i,j,k}^\ell\}_{i,j,k \in [n] \setminus \{i^*\}}$, the input shares that do not correspond to i^*, to the adversary $\mathcal{A}$.
4. **Function queries**: The following is repeated an at most polynomial number of times: $\mathcal{A}$ submits a function query $C \in \mathcal{C}_\lambda$ to Chal. The challenger Chal computes function shares $\{C_{i,j,k}\}_{i,j,k \in [n]} \leftarrow \mathsf{FuncEncode}(1^\lambda, 1^n, C)$ and sends them to $\mathcal{A}$ along with all evaluations $\{C_{i,j,k}(s_{i,j,k}^\ell)\}_{i,j,k \in [n]}$ for all $\ell \in [L]$.
5. If there exists a function query C and challenge message queries (x_0^ℓ, x_1^ℓ) such that $C(x_0^\ell) \neq C(x_1^\ell)$, then the output of the experiment is set to $\bot$. Otherwise, the output of the experiment is set to b', where b' is the output of $\mathcal{A}$.

5.2   Construction

Using 3-input-local MPC protocols $\{\Phi_C\}$ for a circuit class $\mathcal{C}$ and a PRF, we will construct a combiner-friendly homomorphic secret sharing scheme for $\mathcal{C}$. For a circuit $C \in \mathcal{C}$ and number of parties n, we say that Φ_C is an MPC protocol for C on n parties if it computes the function $C(x_1 \oplus \ldots \oplus x_n)$ on inputs $x_1, \ldots, x_n$.
    Formally, we show the following.

Theorem 5. Given 3-input-local MPC protocols $\{\Phi_C\}$ for a circuit class $\mathcal{C}$ and assuming one-way functions, there exists a combiner-friendly homomorphic secret sharing scheme for $\mathcal{C}$ for $n = \mathsf{poly}(\lambda)$ candidates.

Using Theorem 4 to instantiate the 3-input-local MPC protocols, we immediately arrive at the following.

Theorem 6. Assuming one-way functions, there exists a combiner-friendly homomorphic secret sharing scheme for $\mathsf{P/poly}$ for $n = \mathsf{poly}(\lambda)$ candidates.

Notation:

– Let PRF be a pseudorandom function with λ-bit keys that takes λ-bit inputs and outputs in $\{0,1\}^*$. PRF will be used to generate the randomness needed for various randomized algorithms. As the length of randomness needed varies by use case (but is always polynomial in length), we don't specify the output length of PRF here and the output length needed will be clear from context. It is easy to build our required pseudorandom function from one with a fixed length output. Let PRF' be a pseudorandom function that maps $\{0,1\}^{2\lambda}$-bit inputs to a single output bit in $\{0,1\}$. Then, to evaluate $\mathsf{PRF}(K, x)$ to an appropriate output length ℓ, we would simply compute the output bit by bit by evaluating $\mathsf{PRF}'(K, x||1), \mathsf{PRF}'(K, x||2), \ldots, \mathsf{PRF}'(K, x||\ell)$. When we write $(r_1, r_2, r_3) := \mathsf{PRF}(K, x)$, we mean that we generate the randomness needed for three different algorithms using this PRF, where the length of each r_i depends on the amount of randomness needed by the algorithm. This can be done in the same manner, by computing r_i bit by bit by evaluating $\mathsf{PRF}'(K, x||i||1), \mathsf{PRF}'(K, x||i||2), \ldots$ etc.

- For a 3-input-local protocol Φ for a circuit $C \in \mathcal{C}$, we use the same syntax as in Sect. 4 to refer to the various components and algorithms associated with this protocol. We implicitly assume that the description of the 3-input-local protocol Φ for C is included in the descriptions of the function shares for C.

- Let $\mathsf{Corr}(1^\lambda, 1^\ell, i, j) \to (r_{i,j}, r_{j,i})$ be the function that on input the security parameter λ, a length parameter ℓ, and indices $i \neq j \in [n]$ outputs correlated random strings $r_{i,j}$ and $r_{j,i}$ each in $\{0,1\}^\ell$. We will assume that $i < j$ and if not, we implicitly assume that the indices are swapped when evaluating the algorithm. Looking ahead, ℓ is set as the the length of the correlated randomness required between two parties in the execution of the 3-input-local protocol. For simplicity, we will omit the parameter ℓ in the description below when it is clear from the context. We note that Corr can be implemented by generating random OT-correlations.

- In the construction, for simplicity, we will denote input and function shares for the tuple of indices (i, i, i) by s_i and C_i, respectively. Similarly, we will denote the input and function shares for the tuple of indices (i, j, i) with $i \neq j$ by $s_{i,j}$ and $C_{i,j}$, respectively. We will denote input and function shares for the tuple of indices (i, j, k) with $i \neq j \neq k$ by $s_{i,j,k}$ and $C_{i,j,k}$ respectively. All other input and function shares are set to $\bot$.

Overview: We provided a sketch of our construction in Sect. 1.2. Here, we provide more details to assist in the understanding of our construction. The input encoding algorithm will take an input x, n-out-of-n secret share it into shares $x_1, \ldots, x_n$, sample PRF keys K_i for $i \in [n]$ and shared PRF keys K_{ij} for $i < j \in [n]$. Shares of the form s_i will be (x_i, K_i), shares of the form $s_{i,j}$ will be $(x_i, x_j, K_i, K_j, K_{ij})$, and shares of the form $s_{i,j,k}$ will be $(x_i, x_j, x_k, K_i, K_j, K_k, K_{ij}, K_{ik}, K_{jk})$. These will serve as the inputs to the function shares $\{C_{i,j,k}\}_{i,j,k \in [n]}$. Intuitively, a share $s_{i,j,k}$ (or $s_{i,j}$ or s_i) contains all the input shares and PRF keys that correspond to the indices i, j, k (or i, j or i).

The description of function shares of the form C_i, $C_{i,j}$, and $C_{i,j,k}$ is given in Fig. 3, Fig. 4, and Fig. 5, respectively. The purpose of C_i, $C_{i,j}$, and $C_{i,j,k}$ is to simply output input-local bits in the transcript of Φ_C dependent on either only P_i, the two parties P_i and P_j, or the three parties P_i, P_j, P_k, respectively.

Given evaluations of all the function shares, decoding operates by using the evaluations to obtain a transcript τ of an execution of Φ_C and then running the evaluation procedure of Φ_C.

Construction: We now provide the formal construction.

- **Input Encoding, $\mathsf{InpEncode}(1^\lambda, 1^n, x)$:**
  - XOR secret share x uniformly at random across n shares such that $x_1 \oplus \ldots \oplus x_n = x$.

- For $i \leq j \in [n]$, sample distinct PRF keys K_{ij}. For $i > j \in [n]$, set $K_{ij} = K_{ji}$. Set $K_i = K_{ii}$.
- For $i \in [n]$, set $s_i = (x_i, K_i)$.
- For $i, j \in [n]$ with $i < j$, set $s_{i,j} = (x_i, x_j, K_i, K_j, K_{ij})$.
- For $i, j, k \in [n]$ with $i < j < k$, set $s_{i,j,k} = (x_i, x_j, x_k, K_i, K_j, K_k, K_{ij}, K_{ik}, K_{jk})$.
- Set all other shares to $\perp$.
- Output all shares $\{s_{i,j,k}\}_{i,j,k \in [n]}$.

- **Function Encoding,** $\mathsf{FuncEncode}(1^\lambda, 1^n, C)$: Let Φ denote the 3-input-local MPC protocol for C on n parties. For every bit τ_α in τ, a transcript of Φ, let $\mathcal{S}_\alpha$ denote the set of parties that τ_α depends on and f_α be the function that computes τ_α with respect to these parties' inputs and randomness (see Sect. 4).
  - Sample tag $\mathsf{tag}_{\mathsf{rand}}$ from $\{0,1\}^\lambda$, uniformly at random.
  - For $i \in [n]$, function share C_i is given by circuit C_i in Fig. 3.
  - For $i, j \in [n]$ with $i < j$, function share $C_{i,j}$ is given by circuit $C_{i,j}$ in Fig. 4.
  - For $i, j, k \in [n]$ with $i < j < k$, function share $C_{i,j,k}$ is given by circuit $C_{i,j,k}$ in Fig. 5.
  - Set all other function shares to $\perp$ and output $\{C_{i,j,k}\}_{i,j,k \in [n]}$.

- **Decoding,** $\mathsf{Decode}(\{C_{i,j,k}(s_{i,j,k})\}_{i,j,k \in [n]})$: It does the following:
  - Rearrange all input-local bits τ_α output by the function shares to obtain τ, the transcript of an execution of Φ.
  - Run $\mathsf{Eval}(\tau)$ to obtain the output y.

Correctness: Correctness follows from the correctness of the underlying set of 3-input-local MPC protocols $\{\phi_C\}$. In particular, for any circuit $C \in \mathcal{C}_\lambda$ and input $x \in \mathcal{X}_\lambda$, we note that the Decode algorithm obtains τ, the transcript of an execution of ϕ_C. Therefore, by running Eval on τ, Decode obtains

$$y = C(x_1 \oplus \ldots \oplus x_n) = C(x)$$

as desired.

$$C_i$$

Input: Input x_i and PRF key K_i.
Hardwired: Index i, tag $\mathsf{tag}_{\mathsf{rand}}$ in $\{0,1\}^\lambda$.
- Compute $r_i := \mathsf{PRF}(K_i, \mathsf{tag}_{\mathsf{rand}})$.
- For every input-local bit τ_α in a transcript τ of Φ with $\mathcal{S}_\alpha = \{i\}$, compute $\tau_\alpha := f_\alpha(x_i, r_i)$.
- Output $(\tau_\alpha)_{\tau_\alpha \text{ input-local with } \mathcal{S}_\alpha = \{i\}}$.

Fig. 3. Description of function share C_i.

$$C_{i,j}$$

Input: Inputs x_i, x_j and PRF keys K_i, K_j, K_{ij}.
Hardwired: Indices i, j, tag $\mathsf{tag_{rand}}$ in $\{0, 1\}^\lambda$.

- For $u \in \{i, j\}$, compute $r_u := \mathsf{PRF}(K_u, \mathsf{tag_{rand}})$.
- Compute $r_{ij}^{\mathsf{Corr}} := \mathsf{PRF}(K_{ij}, \mathsf{tag_{rand}})$.
- Compute $(r_{i,j}, r_{j,i}) := \mathsf{Corr}(1^\lambda, i, j; r_{ij}^{\mathsf{Corr}})$.
- For every bit input-local bit τ_α in a transcript τ of Φ with $\mathcal{S}_\alpha = \{i, j\}$, compute

$$\tau_\alpha := f_\alpha((x_u)_{u \in \mathcal{S}_\alpha}, (r_u)_{u \in \mathcal{S}_\alpha}, (r_{u,v})_{u,v \in \mathcal{S}_\alpha}).$$

- Output $(\tau_\alpha)_{\tau_\alpha \text{ input-local with } \mathcal{S}_\alpha = \{i,j\}}$.

Fig. 4. Description of function share $C_{i,j}$.

Security: The security proof can be found in the full version.

6   Construction of an FE Combiner from a CFHSS Scheme

In this section, we show how to use a CFHSS scheme and one-way functions to construct an FE combiner. Instantiating the CFHSS scheme with the construction in Sect. 5 and the one-way function with the concatenation of the one-way function candidates implied by our FE candidates (as described in Sect. 1.2), we arrive at the following result.

Theorem 7. *There exists an unconditionally secure unbounded-key FE combiner for $n = \mathsf{poly}(\lambda)$ FE candidates for $\mathsf{P/poly}$.*

In the rest of this section, we show Theorem 7.

6.1   d-Nested FE

A tool used in our construction is d-nested FE (for $d = 3$). d-nested FE is a new FE candidate that can be created easily from d FE candidates by simply encrypting in sequence using the d FE candidates. Intuitively, this new FE candidate will be secure as long as one of the d candidates is secure since an adversary should be unable to break the encryption of the secure candidate. d-nested FE can be viewed as an FE combiner that can only handle a constant number of FE candidates since the runtime of its algorithms may depend exponentially on d. The construction and proof of d-nested FE can be found in the full version.

$$C_{i,j,k}$$

Input: Inputs x_i, x_j, x_k and PRF keys $K_i, K_j, K_k, K_{ij}, K_{ik}, K_{jk}$.
Hardwired: Indices i, j, k, tag $\mathsf{tag}_{\mathsf{rand}}$ in $\{0,1\}^\lambda$.

- For $u \in \{i, j, k\}$, compute $r_u := \mathsf{PRF}(K_u, \mathsf{tag}_{\mathsf{rand}})$.
- Compute $r_{ij}^{\mathsf{Corr}} := \mathsf{PRF}(K_{ij}, \mathsf{tag}_{\mathsf{rand}})$, $r_{ik}^{\mathsf{Corr}} := \mathsf{PRF}(K_{ik}, \mathsf{tag}_{\mathsf{rand}})$, and $r_{jk}^{\mathsf{Corr}} := \mathsf{PRF}(K_{jk}, \mathsf{tag}_{\mathsf{rand}})$.
- Compute $(r_{i,j}, r_{j,i}) := \mathsf{Corr}(1^\lambda, i, j; r_{ij}^{\mathsf{Corr}})$, $(r_{i,k}, r_{k,i}) := \mathsf{Corr}(1^\lambda, i, k; r_{ik}^{\mathsf{Corr}})$, and $(r_{j,k}, r_{k,j}) := \mathsf{Corr}(1^\lambda, j, k; r_{jk}^{\mathsf{Corr}})$.
- For every bit input-local bit τ_α in a transcript τ of Φ with $\mathcal{S}_\alpha = \{i, j, k\}$, compute
$$\tau_\alpha := f_\alpha((x_u)_{u \in \mathcal{S}_\alpha}, (r_u)_{u \in \mathcal{S}_\alpha}, (r_{u,v})_{u,v \in \mathcal{S}_\alpha}).$$
- Output $(\tau_\alpha)_{\tau_\alpha \text{ input-local with } \mathcal{S}_\alpha = \{i,j,k\}}$.

Fig. 5. Description of circuit $C_{i,j,k}$.

6.2 Construction

We now formally describe the construction. First, we provide some notation that will be used throughout the construction.

Notation:

- Let $\mathsf{FE}_1, \ldots, \mathsf{FE}_n$ denote n FE candidates. In the following construction, we assume that the descriptions $\{\mathsf{FE}_i\}_{i \in [n]}$ are implicit in all the algorithms of FEComb.
- Let FE_{ijk} denote the 3-nested FE candidate derived by nesting FE_i, FE_j, and FE_k.
- Let $\mathsf{CFHSS} = (\mathsf{InpEncode}, \mathsf{FuncEncode}, \mathsf{Decode})$ be a combiner-friendly homomorphic secret sharing scheme. Let ℓ_{output} denote the length of the outputs obtained from the evaluation of function shares on input shares.
- Let E be any λ-bit CPA-secure secret-key encryption scheme with message space $\{0,1\}^{\ell_{\mathsf{output}}}$.
- Let $\ell_x = \ell_x(\lambda)$ denote the length of the messages and let $\ell_{\mathsf{E}} = \ell_{\mathsf{E}}(\lambda)$ denote the length of the encryption key for the scheme E.

Construction:

- $\mathsf{FEComb.Setup}(1^\lambda)$: On input the security parameter, it runs $\mathsf{FE}_{ijk}.\mathsf{Setup}(1^\lambda)$ for $i, j, k \in [n]$ and $\mathsf{E.SK} \leftarrow \mathsf{E.Setup}(1^\lambda)$. It outputs $\mathsf{MSK} = (\{\mathsf{MSK}_{ijk}\}_{i,j,k \in [n]}, \mathsf{E.SK})$.
- $\mathsf{FEComb.Enc}(\mathsf{MSK}, x \in \{0,1\}^{\ell_x})$: It executes the following steps.

- First, encode x into n^3 shares by running CFHSS.InpEncode($1^\lambda, 1^n, x$) to compute $\{s_{i,j,k}\}_{i,j,k\in[n]}$. Then, for all $i, j, k \in [n]$, compute

$$\mathsf{CT}_{ijk} = \mathsf{FE}_{ij}.\mathsf{Enc}\left(\mathsf{MSK}_{ijk}, (s_{i,j,k}, 0^{\ell_\mathsf{E}}, 0)\right).$$

- Output $\mathsf{CT} = \{\mathsf{CT}_{ijk}\}_{i,j,k\in[n]}$.
- FEComb.KeyGen(MSK, C): It executes the following steps.
  - For all $i, j, k \in [n]$, it computes $c_{i,j,k} \leftarrow \mathsf{E}.\mathsf{Enc}(\mathsf{E}.\mathsf{SK}, 0^{\ell_\mathsf{output}})$, where ℓ_output is the length of evaluations of function shares on input shares of CFHSS.
  - It computes $\{C_{i,j,k}\}_{i,j,k\in[n]} \leftarrow \mathsf{CFHSS}.\mathsf{FuncEncode}(1^\lambda, 1^n, C)$.
  - For all $i, j, k \in [n]$, it computes $\mathsf{SK}_{H_{i,j,k}} \leftarrow \mathsf{FE}_{ijk}.\mathsf{KeyGen}(\mathsf{MSK}_{ijk}, H_{i,j,k})$, where circuit $H_{i,j,k}$ is described in Fig. 6.
  - It outputs $\mathsf{SK}_C = (\{\mathsf{SK}_{H_{i,j,k}}\}_{i,j,k\in[n]})$.

$$H_{i,j,k}$$

Input: Input share $s_{i,j,k}$, a string $t \in \{0,1\}^{\ell_\mathsf{E}}$, and a bit b
Hardwired: Ciphertext $c_{i,j,k}$, circuit $C_{i,j,k}$

* If $b \neq 0$, output $\mathsf{E}.\mathsf{Dec}(t, c_{i,j,k})$.

* Otherwise, output $C_{i,j,k}(s_{i,j,k})$.

Fig. 6. Description of the evaluation circuit.

- FEComb.Dec($\mathsf{SK}_C, \mathsf{CT}$): Parse SK_C as $(\{\mathsf{SK}_{H_{i,j,k}}\}_{i,j,k\in[n]})$ and CT as $\{\mathsf{CT}_{ijk}\}_{i,j,k\in[n]}$. For all $i, j, k \in [n]$, compute $y_{i,j,k} = \mathsf{FE}_{ijk}.\mathsf{Dec}(\mathsf{SK}_{H_{i,j,k}}, \mathsf{CT}_{ijk})$.
Run CFHSS.Decode($\{y_{i,j,k}\}_{i,j,k\in[n]}$) and output the result.

Correctness: Correctness follows from the correctness of CFHSS and the fact that all correct encryptions are encryptions of messages of the form $(s_{i,j,k}, 0^{\ell_\mathsf{E}}, 0)$. In particular, for all $i, j, k \in [n]$, $H_{i,j,k}(s_{i,j,k}, 0^{\ell_\mathsf{E}}, 0) = C_{i,j,k}(s_{i,j,k})$ and then CFHSS.Decode($\{C_{i,j,k}(s_{i,j,k})\}_{i,j,k\in[n]}$) = $C(x)$ by the correctness of CFHSS.

Polynomial Slowdown: The fact that all the algorithms of FEComb run in time poly(λ, n) is immediate from the efficiency of the FE candidates, CFHSS, and E and the fact that there are $n^3 = \mathsf{poly}(n)$ different tuples (i, j, k) for $i, j, k \in [n]$.

6.3   Security Proof

The security proof can be found in the full version.

7   Robust FE Combiners and Universal FE

We can consider a stronger notion of an FE combiner called a *robust* FE combiner. A robust FE combiner is an FE combiner that satisfies correctness and security provided that at least one FE candidate, FE_i, satisfies both correctness and security. No restrictions are placed on the other FE candidates. In particular, they may satisfy neither correctness nor security. We note that the FE combiner constructed in Sect. 6 is not robust. However, [2] showed how to unconditionally transform an FE combiner into a robust FE combiner.

Theorem 8 ([2]). *If there exists an FE combiner, then there exists a robust FE combiner.*

Combining Theorem 8 with Theorem 7, we obtain the following corollary.

Corollary 3. *There exists an unconditionally secure unbounded-key robust FE combiner for $n = \mathsf{poly}(\lambda)$ FE candidates for P/poly.*

Universal Functional Encryption: Robust FE combiners are closely related to the notion of universal functional encryption. Universal functional encryption is a construction of functional encryption satisfying the following simple guarantee. If there exists a Turing Machine with running time bounded by some $T(n) = \mathsf{poly}(n)$ that implements a correct and secure FE scheme, then the universal functional encryption construction is itself a correct and secure FE scheme. Using the existence of a robust FE combiner (Corollary 3) and the results of [2,5], we obtain the following corollary.

Corollary 4. *There exists a universal unbounded-key functional encryption scheme for P/poly.*

Acknowledgements. We thank Saikrishna Badrinarayanan for helpful discussions and the anonymous EUROCRYPT reviewers for useful feedback regarding this work. The authors were supported in part by a DARPA/ARL SAFEWARE award, NSF Frontier Award 1413955, NSF grants 1619348, 1228984, 1136174, and 1065276, BSF grant 2012378, a Xerox Faculty Research Award, a Google Faculty Research Award, an equipment grant from Intel, and an Okawa Foundation Research Grant. Aayush Jain was also supported by a Google PhD Fellowship (2018) in the area of Privacy and Security. This material is based upon work supported by the Defense Advanced Research Projects Agency through the ARL under Contract W911NF-15-C-0205. The views expressed are those of the authors and do not reflect the official policy or position of the Department of Defense, the National Science Foundation, the U.S. Government, or Google.

References

1. Agrawal, S.: Indistinguishability obfuscation without multilinear maps: new methods for bootstrapping and instantiation. In: Ishai, Y., Rijmen, V. (eds.) EUROCRYPT 2019. LNCS, vol. 11476, pp. 191–225. Springer, Cham (2019). https://doi.org/10.1007/978-3-030-17653-2_7

2. Ananth, P., Badrinarayanan, S., Jain, A., Manohar, N., Sahai, A.: From FE combiners to secure MPC and back. In: Hofheinz, D., Rosen, A. (eds.) TCC 2019. LNCS, vol. 11891, pp. 199–228. Springer, Cham (2019). https://doi.org/10.1007/978-3-030-36030-6_9

3. Ananth, P., Brakerski, Z., Segev, G., Vaikuntanathan, V.: From selective to adaptive security in functional encryption. In: Gennaro, R., Robshaw, M. (eds.) CRYPTO 2015. LNCS, vol. 9216, pp. 657–677. Springer, Heidelberg (2015). https://doi.org/10.1007/978-3-662-48000-7_32

4. Ananth, P., Jain, A., Lin, H., Matt, C., Sahai, A.: Indistinguishability obfuscation without multilinear maps: new paradigms via low degree weak pseudorandomness and security amplification. In: Boldyreva, A., Micciancio, D. (eds.) CRYPTO 2019. LNCS, vol. 11694, pp. 284–332. Springer, Cham (2019). https://doi.org/10.1007/978-3-030-26954-8_10

5. Ananth, P., Jain, A., Naor, M., Sahai, A., Yogev, E.: Universal constructions and robust combiners for indistinguishability obfuscation and witness encryption. In: Robshaw, M., Katz, J. (eds.) CRYPTO 2016. LNCS, vol. 9815, pp. 491–520. Springer, Heidelberg (2016). https://doi.org/10.1007/978-3-662-53008-5_17

6. Ananth, P., Jain, A., Sahai, A.: Robust transforming combiners from indistinguishability obfuscation to functional encryption. In: Coron, J.-S., Nielsen, J.B. (eds.) EUROCRYPT 2017. LNCS, vol. 10210, pp. 91–121. Springer, Cham (2017). https://doi.org/10.1007/978-3-319-56620-7_4

7. Ananth, P., Jain, A., Sahai, A.: Indistinguishability obfuscation without multilinear maps: iO from LWE, bilinear maps, and weak pseudorandomness. IACR Cryptology ePrint Archive 2018, 615 (2018)

8. Ananth, P., Jain, A.: Indistinguishability obfuscation from compact functional encryption. In: Gennaro, R., Robshaw, M. (eds.) CRYPTO 2015. LNCS, vol. 9215, pp. 308–326. Springer, Heidelberg (2015). https://doi.org/10.1007/978-3-662-47989-6_15

9. Ananth, P., Sahai, A.: Projective arithmetic functional encryption and indistinguishability obfuscation from degree-5 multilinear maps. In: Coron, J.-S., Nielsen, J.B. (eds.) EUROCRYPT 2017. LNCS, vol. 10210, pp. 152–181. Springer, Cham (2017). https://doi.org/10.1007/978-3-319-56620-7_6

10. Badrinarayanan, S., Goyal, V., Jain, A., Sahai, A.: A note on VRFs from verifiable functional encryption. IACR Cryptology ePrint Archive 2017, 51 (2017)

11. Barak, B., Brakerski, Z., Komargodski, I., Kothari, P.K.: Limits on low-degree pseudorandom generators (or: sum-of-squares meets program obfuscation). In: Nielsen, J.B., Rijmen, V. (eds.) EUROCRYPT 2018. LNCS, vol. 10821, pp. 649–679. Springer, Cham (2018). https://doi.org/10.1007/978-3-319-78375-8_21

12. Barak, B., Hopkins, S.B., Jain, A., Kothari, P., Sahai, A.: Sum-of-squares meets program obfuscation, revisited. In: Ishai, Y., Rijmen, V. (eds.) EUROCRYPT 2019. LNCS, vol. 11476, pp. 226–250. Springer, Cham (2019). https://doi.org/10.1007/978-3-030-17653-2_8

13. Bitansky, N.: Verifiable random functions from non-interactive witness-indistinguishable proofs. In: Kalai, Y., Reyzin, L. (eds.) TCC 2017. LNCS, vol. 10678, pp. 567–594. Springer, Cham (2017). https://doi.org/10.1007/978-3-319-70503-3_19

14. Bitansky, N., Nishimaki, R., Passelègue, A., Wichs, D.: From cryptomania to obfustopia through secret-key functional encryption. In: Hirt, M., Smith, A. (eds.) TCC 2016, Part II. LNCS, vol. 9986, pp. 391–418. Springer, Heidelberg (2016). https://doi.org/10.1007/978-3-662-53644-5_15

15. Bitansky, N., Vaikuntanathan, V.: Indistinguishability obfuscation from functional encryption. In: FOCS (2015)
16. Bitansky, N., Vaikuntanathan, V.: Indistinguishability obfuscation: from approximate to exact. In: Kushilevitz, E., Malkin, T. (eds.) TCC 2016. LNCS, vol. 9562, pp. 67–95. Springer, Heidelberg (2016). https://doi.org/10.1007/978-3-662-49096-9_4
17. Bitansky, N., Vaikuntanathan, V.: A note on perfect correctness by derandomization. In: Coron, J.-S., Nielsen, J.B. (eds.) EUROCRYPT 2017. LNCS, vol. 10211, pp. 592–606. Springer, Cham (2017). https://doi.org/10.1007/978-3-319-56614-6_20
18. Boneh, D., et al.: Threshold cryptosystems from threshold fully homomorphic encryption. In: Shacham, H., Boldyreva, A. (eds.) CRYPTO 2018. LNCS, vol. 10991, pp. 565–596. Springer, Cham (2018). https://doi.org/10.1007/978-3-319-96884-1_19
19. Boneh, D., Sahai, A., Waters, B.: Functional encryption: definitions and challenges. In: Ishai, Y. (ed.) TCC 2011. LNCS, vol. 6597, pp. 253–273. Springer, Heidelberg (2011). https://doi.org/10.1007/978-3-642-19571-6_16
20. Boyle, E., Gilboa, N., Ishai, Y.: Function secret sharing. In: Oswald, E., Fischlin, M. (eds.) EUROCRYPT 2015. LNCS, vol. 9057, pp. 337–367. Springer, Heidelberg (2015). https://doi.org/10.1007/978-3-662-46803-6_12
21. Boyle, E., Gilboa, N., Ishai, Y.: Breaking the circuit size barrier for secure computation under DDH. In: Robshaw, M., Katz, J. (eds.) CRYPTO 2016. LNCS, vol. 9814, pp. 509–539. Springer, Heidelberg (2016). https://doi.org/10.1007/978-3-662-53018-4_19
22. Boyle, E., Gilboa, N., Ishai, Y.: Function secret sharing: improvements and extensions. In: CCS, pp. 1292–1303 (2016)
23. Cheon, J.H., Han, K., Lee, C., Ryu, H., Stehlé, D.: Cryptanalysis of the multilinear map over the integers. In: Oswald, E., Fischlin, M. (eds.) EUROCRYPT 2015. LNCS, vol. 9056, pp. 3–12. Springer, Heidelberg (2015). https://doi.org/10.1007/978-3-662-46800-5_1
24. Cheon, J.H., Jeong, J., Lee, C.: An algorithm for CSPR problems and cryptanalysis of the GGH multilinear map without an encoding of zero. In: ANTS (2016)
25. Coron, J.-S., et al.: Zeroizing without low-level zeroes: new MMAP attacks and their limitations. In: Gennaro, R., Robshaw, M. (eds.) CRYPTO 2015. LNCS, vol. 9215, pp. 247–266. Springer, Heidelberg (2015). https://doi.org/10.1007/978-3-662-47989-6_12
26. Coron, J.-S., Lee, M.S., Lepoint, T., Tibouchi, M.: Cryptanalysis of GGH15 multilinear maps. In: Robshaw, M., Katz, J. (eds.) CRYPTO 2016. LNCS, vol. 9815, pp. 607–628. Springer, Heidelberg (2016). https://doi.org/10.1007/978-3-662-53008-5_21
27. Fischlin, M., Herzberg, A., Bin-Noon, H., Shulman, H.: Obfuscation combiners. In: Robshaw, M., Katz, J. (eds.) CRYPTO 2016. LNCS, vol. 9815, pp. 521–550. Springer, Heidelberg (2016). https://doi.org/10.1007/978-3-662-53008-5_18
28. Fischlin, M., Lehmann, A.: Security-amplifying combiners for collision-resistant hash functions. In: Menezes, A. (ed.) CRYPTO 2007. LNCS, vol. 4622, pp. 224–243. Springer, Heidelberg (2007). https://doi.org/10.1007/978-3-540-74143-5_13
29. Garg, S., Gentry, C., Halevi, S., Raykova, M., Sahai, A., Waters, B.: Candidate indistinguishability obfuscation and functional encryption for all circuits. In: FOCS (2013)
30. Garg, S., Gentry, C., Halevi, S., Zhandry, M.: Fully secure functional encryption without obfuscation. IACR Cryptology ePrint Archive 2014, 666 (2014)

31. Garg, S., Ishai, Y., Srinivasan, A.: Two-round MPC: information-theoretic and black-box. In: Beimel, A., Dziembowski, S. (eds.) TCC 2018. LNCS, vol. 11239, pp. 123–151. Springer, Cham (2018). https://doi.org/10.1007/978-3-030-03807-6_5
32. Garg, S., Ishai, Y., Srinivasan, A.: Personal communication (2019)
33. Garg, S., Pandey, O., Srinivasan, A.: Revisiting the cryptographic hardness of finding a nash equilibrium. In: Robshaw, M., Katz, J. (eds.) CRYPTO 2016. LNCS, vol. 9815, pp. 579–604. Springer, Heidelberg (2016). https://doi.org/10.1007/978-3-662-53008-5_20
34. Garg, S., Pandey, O., Srinivasan, A., Zhandry, M.: Breaking the sub-exponential barrier in obfustopia. In: Coron, J.-S., Nielsen, J.B. (eds.) EUROCRYPT 2017. LNCS, vol. 10212, pp. 156–181. Springer, Cham (2017). https://doi.org/10.1007/978-3-319-56617-7_6
35. Garg, S., Srinivasan, A.: Two-round multiparty secure computation from minimal assumptions. In: Nielsen, J.B., Rijmen, V. (eds.) EUROCRYPT 2018. LNCS, vol. 10821, pp. 468–499. Springer, Cham (2018). https://doi.org/10.1007/978-3-319-78375-8_16
36. Goldwasser, S., Kalai, Y.T., Popa, R.A., Vaikuntanathan, V., Zeldovich, N.: Reusable garbled circuits and succinct functional encryption. In: STOC (2013)
37. Goyal, R., Hohenberger, S., Koppula, V., Waters, B.: A generic approach to constructing and proving verifiable random functions. In: Kalai, Y., Reyzin, L. (eds.) TCC 2017. LNCS, vol. 10678, pp. 537–566. Springer, Cham (2017). https://doi.org/10.1007/978-3-319-70503-3_18
38. Harnik, D., Ishai, Y., Kushilevitz, E., Nielsen, J.B.: OT-combiners via secure computation. In: Canetti, R. (ed.) TCC 2008. LNCS, vol. 4948, pp. 393–411. Springer, Heidelberg (2008). https://doi.org/10.1007/978-3-540-78524-8_22
39. Harnik, D., Kilian, J., Naor, M., Reingold, O., Rosen, A.: On robust combiners for oblivious transfer and other primitives. In: Cramer, R. (ed.) EUROCRYPT 2005. LNCS, vol. 3494, pp. 96–113. Springer, Heidelberg (2005). https://doi.org/10.1007/11426639_6
40. Hemenway, B., Jafargholi, Z., Ostrovsky, R., Scafuro, A., Wichs, D.: Adaptively secure garbled circuits from one-way functions. In: Robshaw, M., Katz, J. (eds.) CRYPTO 2016. LNCS, vol. 9816, pp. 149–178. Springer, Heidelberg (2016). https://doi.org/10.1007/978-3-662-53015-3_6
41. Hu, Y., Jia, H.: Cryptanalysis of GGH map. In: Fischlin, M., Coron, J.-S. (eds.) EUROCRYPT 2016. LNCS, vol. 9665, pp. 537–565. Springer, Heidelberg (2016). https://doi.org/10.1007/978-3-662-49890-3_21
42. Ishai, Y., Prabhakaran, M., Sahai, A.: Founding cryptography on oblivious transfer – efficiently. In: Wagner, D. (ed.) CRYPTO 2008. LNCS, vol. 5157, pp. 572–591. Springer, Heidelberg (2008). https://doi.org/10.1007/978-3-540-85174-5_32
43. Kitagawa, F., Nishimaki, R., Tanaka, K.: Obfustopia built on secret-key functional encryption. In: Nielsen, J.B., Rijmen, V. (eds.) EUROCRYPT 2018. LNCS, vol. 10821, pp. 603–648. Springer, Cham (2018). https://doi.org/10.1007/978-3-319-78375-8_20
44. Komargodski, I., Segev, G.: From minicrypt to obfustopia via private-key functional encryption. In: Coron, J.-S., Nielsen, J.B. (eds.) EUROCRYPT 2017. LNCS, vol. 10210, pp. 122–151. Springer, Cham (2017). https://doi.org/10.1007/978-3-319-56620-7_5
45. Lin, H.: Indistinguishability obfuscation from constant-degree graded encoding schemes. In: Fischlin, M., Coron, J.-S. (eds.) EUROCRYPT 2016. LNCS, vol. 9665, pp. 28–57. Springer, Heidelberg (2016). https://doi.org/10.1007/978-3-662-49890-3_2

46. Lin, H.: Indistinguishability obfuscation from SXDH on 5-linear maps and locality-5 PRGs. In: Katz, J., Shacham, H. (eds.) CRYPTO 2017. LNCS, vol. 10401, pp. 599–629. Springer, Cham (2017). https://doi.org/10.1007/978-3-319-63688-7_20

47. Lin, H., Matt, C.: Pseudo flawed-smudging generators and their application to indistinguishability obfuscation. IACR Cryptology ePrint Archive 2018, 646 (2018)

48. Lin, H., Tessaro, S.: Indistinguishability obfuscation from trilinear maps and block-wise local PRGs. In: Katz, J., Shacham, H. (eds.) CRYPTO 2017. LNCS, vol. 10401, pp. 630–660. Springer, Cham (2017). https://doi.org/10.1007/978-3-319-63688-7_21

49. Lin, H., Vaikuntanathan, V.: Indistinguishability obfuscation from DDH-like assumptions on constant-degree graded encodings. In: FOCS (2016)

50. Mukherjee, P., Wichs, D.: Two round multiparty computation via multi-key FHE. In: Fischlin, M., Coron, J.-S. (eds.) EUROCRYPT 2016. LNCS, vol. 9666, pp. 735–763. Springer, Heidelberg (2016). https://doi.org/10.1007/978-3-662-49896-5_26

51. O'Neill, A.: Definitional issues in functional encryption. IACR Cryptology ePrint Archive 2010, 556 (2010)

52. Sahai, A., Waters, B.: Fuzzy identity-based encryption. In: Cramer, R. (ed.) EURO-CRYPT 2005. LNCS, vol. 3494, pp. 457–473. Springer, Heidelberg (2005). https://doi.org/10.1007/11426639_27

53. Yao, A.C.C.: How to generate and exchange secrets (extended abstract). In: FOCS, pp. 162–167 (1986)

Impossibility Results for Lattice-Based Functional Encryption Schemes

Akın Ünal[✉]

ETH Zurich, Zürich, Switzerland
auenal@inf.ethz.ch

Abstract. Functional Encryption denotes a form of encryption where a master secret key-holder can control which functions a user can evaluate on encrypted data. Learning With Errors (LWE) (Regev, STOC'05) is known to be a useful cryptographic hardness assumption which implies strong primitives such as, for example, fully homomorphic encryption (Brakerski-Vaikuntanathan, FOCS'11) and lockable obfuscation (Goyal et al., Wichs et al., FOCS'17). Despite its stre ngth, however, there is just a limited number of functional encryption schemes which can be based on LWE. In fact, there are functional encryption schemes which can be achieved by using pairings but for which no secure instantiations from lattice-based assumptions are known: function-hiding inner product encryption (Lin, Baltico et al., CRYPTO'17) and compact quadratic functional encryption (Abdalla et al., CRYPTO'18). This raises the question whether there are some mathematical barriers which hinder us from realizing function-hiding and compact functional encryption schemes from lattice-based assumptions as LWE.

To study this problem, we prove an impossibility result for function-hiding functional encryption schemes which meet some algebraic restrictions at ciphertext encryption and decryption. Those restrictions are met by a lot of attribute-based, identity-based and functional encryption schemes whose security stems from LWE. Therefore, we see our results as important indications why it is hard to construct new functional encryption schemes from LWE and which mathematical restrictions have to be overcome to construct secure lattice-based functional encryption schemes for new functionalities.

Keywords: Functional encryption · Function-hiding · Impossibility · LWE · Lattice-based · Online/offline

1 Introduction

Functional Encryption (FE) schemes are special encryption schemes in which the holder of a master secret key can issue secret keys for specific functions to

A. Ünal—The author is supported by ERC Project 724307 'PREP-CRYPTO'. Work done while the author was working at Karlsruhe Institute of Technology.

© International Association for Cryptologic Research 2020
A. Canteaut and Y. Ishai (Eds.): EUROCRYPT 2020, LNCS 12105, pp. 169–199, 2020.
https://doi.org/10.1007/978-3-030-45721-1_7

users. By knowing a secret key for a function f and a ciphertext for a message x, an adversary shall learn nothing more of x than $f(x)$. FE schemes have proven to be extremely versatile. Not only does their notion generalize other forms of encryption like Attribute-Based (ABE) or Identity-Based Encryption (IBE), but also do we know that compact single-key FE and linearly compact FE for cubic polynomials together with plausible assumptions imply indistinguishability obfuscation [10,14,29].

Function-Hiding Functional Encryption (FHFE) schemes are an even stronger subclass of FE where we demand that an adversary – given a secret key for a function f and a ciphertext for a message x – learns nothing about f *and* x except of $f(x)$; i.e., the secret keys now hide the functions they are supposed to evaluate.

We know that FE schemes *with a bounded number of secret keys*, an adversary may learn, are already achievable from minimal assumptions [11]. However, if we try to achieve security for an unbounded number of secret keys, then we are left with (function-hiding) inner-product encryption, linearly compact quadratic FE and FE schemes for constant-degree polynomials which are yielded by relinearizing. Of course, there are special cases of FE like attribute-based and identity-based encryption schemes. In those schemes, a ciphertext is accompanied with a non-hidden attribute or identity and decryption is successful iff the attribute/identity matches the policy of the secret key. However, the main focus in this work are FE schemes, since we are interested in schemes which perform various computations on hidden inputs. We stress here that for linearly compact quadratic FE and function-hiding inner-product FE there are just pairing-based constructions known so far [3,12,13,21,28].

Learning With Errors (LWE) [30] is a well-established hardness assumption. It states that it is hard to solve a system of linear equations over a modulus q, if the solution has sufficient entropy, the coefficients of the equations are chosen uniformly random from $\mathbb{Z}_q$ and one column of the presented system has been perturbed by a small noise-vector whose entries are sampled from a suitable error-distribution. Because of its strong homomorphic properties, there are fully homomorphic encryption schemes and lockable obfuscation schemes whose security can be proven solely under LWE [17,24,32]. Up to now, it is not possible to construct those schemes from other standard assumptions. Intuitively, one would assume that its homomorphic properties imply a lot of different FE schemes. But as we have stressed, the most complex already existing FE schemes cannot be replicated by lattice-based constructions. In fact, inner product encryption is the only FE scheme whose security can be based on LWE (again, putting ABE and IBE aside). Because of the aforementioned amply homomorphic properties of LWE, this is very surprising and leads us to the following question:

What hinders us from constructing function-hiding inner-product encryption schemes whose security can be proven solely from the learning with errors assumption?

We show that there are two properties, both very common under LWE-based FE schemes, which make it impossible for a function-hiding inner-product encryption scheme to be secure. The first property lies in the decryption algorithms of LWE-based encryption schemes: If we take a close look at the pairing-based schemes, we see that decryption is always complex, for it involves computing discrete logarithms of the target group of the pairing. On the other hand, a lot of LWE-based IBE and FE schemes have simple decryption algorithms [2,4,6,7,16,19]. In most cases, for moduli $q > p > 1$, a secret key sk in such a scheme usually determines a multivariate polynomial $g_{sk}(Y_1, \ldots, Y_s)$ of constant total degree, while the ciphertext is a vector $ct \in \mathbb{Z}_q^s$. At decryption, the polynomial is evaluated at the ciphertext which yields a value $g_{sk}(ct) \in \mathbb{Z}_q$; this value will be *rounded to the nearest number of* $\mathbb{Z}_p$, i.e., it will be divided by $\lfloor q/p \rfloor$ and then rounded to the nearest integer in $\{0, \ldots, p-1\}$. In full detail, this means

$$\mathsf{Dec}(\mathsf{sk}, \mathsf{ct}) = \left\lceil \frac{g_{sk}(ct)}{\lfloor q/p \rfloor} \right\rfloor.$$

We believe that this property already suffices to render a FHFE scheme insecure. Therefore, we state here the following conjecture:

Conjecture 1. Let $\mathsf{FE} = (\mathsf{Setup}, \mathsf{KeyGen}, \mathsf{Enc}, \mathsf{Dec})$ be a correct private-key functional encryption scheme for computing inner-products of vectors in $\mathbb{Z}_p^n$. If there is a constant $d' \in \mathbb{N}$ and a polynomial s in the security parameter, s.t.

- each ciphertext ct sampled by Enc is a vector in $\mathbb{Z}_q^s$,
- each secret key sk sampled by KeyGen is a multivariate polynomial in $\mathbb{Z}_q[Y_1, \ldots, Y_s]$ of total degree $\leq d'$
- and the decryption algorithm works by

$$\mathsf{Dec}(\mathsf{sk}, \mathsf{ct}) = \left\lceil \frac{\mathsf{sk}(ct)}{\lfloor q/p \rfloor} \right\rfloor,$$

then FE cannot be function-hiding secure for an unbounded number of secret keys.

We leave it as an open question to prove or refute Conjecture 1. Instead, we prove in this work a weaker version of the above statement. If we are to take a closer look at the aforementioned IBE and FE schemes and some ABE schemes [15,23], we can distinguish an additional property which seems to be common for some LWE-based schemes. They tend to have very *algebraic* encryption algorithms. Take, for example, a closer look at ciphertext encryption in the LWE-based inner-product encryption schemes of Agrawal et al. [7]. For an input vector $x \in \{0, \ldots, p-1\}^l$ and two publicly known matrices $A \in \mathbb{Z}_q^{m \times n}, U \in \mathbb{Z}_q^{l \times n}$, ciphertexts are generated by sampling a uniformly random vector $s \leftarrow \mathbb{Z}_q^n$, two gaussian noise vectors $e_0 \leftarrow \mathcal{D}_{\mathbb{Z}^m, \alpha q}, e_1 \leftarrow \mathcal{D}_{\mathbb{Z}^l, \alpha q}$ and outputting $\mathsf{ct} = (As + e_0, Us + e_1 + b \cdot x)$ where b is either $\lfloor q/K \rfloor$ or p^{k-1}. Note that we can distinguish two parts in this encryption algorithm: a very complex *offline* part, where $m + l$ multivariate degree-1 polynomials $g_1(X), \ldots, g_m(X), h_1(X), \ldots, h_l(X)$ are sampled by only knowing the public key (A, U, p, q, K) and without looking at the input x:

$$g_i(X_1, \ldots, X_l) = \langle a_i \mid s \rangle + e_{0,i},$$
$$h_i(X_1, \ldots, X_l) = \langle u_i \mid s \rangle + e_{1,i} + \lfloor q/K \rfloor \cdot X_i.$$

And, a simple *online* part which just consists of inserting x in the polynomials sampled before and outputting the ciphertext $\mathsf{ct} = (g_1(x), \ldots, g_m(x), h_1(x), \ldots, h_l(x))$. This distinction in a complex offline and a simple online part can be seen in the other aforementioned schemes, too. Therefore, we extract it as an additional characteristic of some LWE-based schemes and make it more precise in the following:

We say Enc is an encryption algorithm of *depth* d over $\mathbb{Z}_q$, if there is a ppt algorithm $\mathsf{Enc}_{\mathrm{offline}}$, s.t. we have for each master secret key msk and input $x \in \mathbb{Z}_p^n$:

$$\mathsf{Enc}(\mathsf{msk}, x) = \{$$
$$(r_1, \ldots, r_s) \leftarrow \mathsf{Enc}_{\mathrm{offline}}(\mathsf{msk}) \tag{1}$$
$$\mathsf{return}\ (r_1(x), \ldots, r_s(x)) \tag{2}$$
$$\}$$

where we demand that each r_i is a multivariate polynomial in $\mathbb{Z}_q[X_1, \ldots, X_n]$ of total degree $\leq d$. We will call line (1) the *offline* part and line (2) the *online* part of Enc. Indeed, with this additional property we can prove an FHFE scheme to be insecure.

1.1 Contribution

For moduli $q = q(\lambda) > p = p(\lambda)$ such that q is prime, $\frac{q}{p}$ is polynomially bounded and p is not bounded by a constant, we prove the following:

Theorem 1 (Informal Main Theorem). *Assume that the prerequisites of Conjecture 1 hold and that additionally* Enc *is of* depth d *over* $\mathbb{Z}_q$ *for some constant* $d \in \mathbb{N}$.

Then, FE *cannot be function-hiding secure for an unbounded number of secret keys.*

To be more precise, we give a bound of the maximum number of secret keys which can be issued to an adversary before he can break FE (Corollary 4). On a very high level, our proof idea is to use the algebraic structure of the composition $\mathsf{Dec} \circ \mathsf{Enc}$. By doing so, we show that the decryption noises are generated in a very algebraic way, are small and contain information about the encrypted ciphertexts. Therefore, we can prove Theorem 1 by analysing them.

As an additional result, we show that private-key encryption schemes where the encryption algorithms are of constant depth and the ciphertext vectors are short enough cannot be secure (Theorem 5 and Corollary 3). This result does not depend on the decryption algorithms of the private-key encryption schemes.

Generality of Our Results. We note here that there are a lot of LWE-based ABE schemes whose decryption algorithms are too complex to be subsumed by the equation $\mathsf{Dec}(\mathsf{sk}, \mathsf{ct}) = \lceil \mathsf{sk}(\mathsf{ct}) / \lfloor q/p \rfloor \rfloor$. This is because they allow policy-predicates which cannot be computed by constant-depth circuits. Since the policy-predicate needs to be computed at decryption, their decryption algorithms must be at least as complicated as the most complex policy-predicate they allow.

However, the aforementioned ABE schemes in [15, 23] have decryption algorithms that become simple enough to fit the equation $\mathsf{Dec}(\mathsf{sk}, \mathsf{ct}) = \lceil g_{\mathsf{sk}}(\mathsf{ct})/\lfloor q/p \rfloor \rfloor$, if we restrict the policy-circuits in those schemes to be of constant depth and if attributes and policy match at decryption.

Two-Input Quadratic Functional Encryption. We can derive from Theorem 1 an impossibility result for 2-input quadratic FE schemes. A 2-input quadratic FE scheme evaluates functions with two distinguished inputs and has a left and a right encryption algorithm. To decrypt a value $f(x, y)$, one needs a secret key for f, a left ciphertext for x and a right ciphertext for y. Since such a scheme contains a secret key for the quadratic function $f(x, y) = \langle x \mid y \rangle$, it can emulate a function-hiding inner-product encryption scheme, even if it is only single-key secure.

Corollary 1. *Let* $2\,\mathsf{FE} = (\mathsf{Setup}, \mathsf{KeyGen}, \mathsf{Enc}^R, \mathsf{Enc}^L, \mathsf{Dec})$ *be a correct private-key 2-input functional encryption scheme for quadratic functions* $f : \mathbb{Z}_p^n \times \mathbb{Z}_p^n \to \mathbb{Z}_p$. *If there are* $s \in \mathsf{poly}(\lambda)$ *and a constant* $d' \in \mathbb{N}$, *s.t.*

- *Enc^L is of constant depth d over $\mathbb{Z}_q$,*
- *each ciphertext ct^L sampled by Enc^L is a vector in $\mathbb{Z}_q^s$,*
- *each pair of a secret key sk and a right ciphertext ct^R determines a multivariate polynomial $g_{\mathsf{sk},\mathsf{ct}^R} \in \mathbb{Z}_q[X_1, \ldots, X_s]$ of total degree $\leq d'$ s.t. the decryption algorithm works by*

$$\mathsf{Dec}(\mathsf{sk}, \mathsf{ct}^L, \mathsf{ct}^R) = \left\lceil \frac{g_{\mathsf{sk},\mathsf{ct}^R}(\mathsf{ct})}{\lfloor q/p \rfloor} \right\rceil,$$

then $2\,\mathsf{FE}$ cannot be single-key secure.

1.2 Interpretation and Open Problems

To prove Theorem 1, we assume that the exterior modulus q of the FHFE scheme FE is prime. Furthermore, we need that the fraction q/p is bounded by a polynomial in the security parameter λ and that the interior modulus p is for almost all λ greater than some constant which depends on the depth of FE. Note that q/p is usually a bound for the error noise used in LWE-based schemes. Since LWE is assumed to be hard, even if its modulus q is a prime and the deviation of its error noise is bounded by a polynomial in λ, we do not think that those requirements are big restrictions for our results.

We see the results in this paper as a useful argument in understanding the difficulties in constructing LWE-based function-hiding functional encryption schemes. An even more useful argument would be to close the gap and prove Conjecture 1. Because of Theorem 1, to prove our conjecture, it now suffices to transform a function-hiding inner-product encryption scheme which is correct and secure and fulfils the requirements of the conjecture to one that fulfils the requirements of Theorem 1. In other words, it suffices to take an FHFE scheme which already decrypts in an LWE-like manner and simplify its encryption algorithm to one of constant depth which stays secure and correct.

Another way to extend the results here is to prove Theorem 1 for encryption algorithms where, in the online part, one first computes a bit-decomposition $G^{-1}(x)$ of an input vector x and then applies the polynomials sampled in the offline part to $G^{-1}(x)$. A lot of the techniques here would not be suitable for this task; indeed, one would need to develop more advanced techniques to show this.

1.3   Related Work

The idea of decomposing encryption algorithms into simple online and complex offline parts has already been studied with the purpose of finding FE schemes with practical usages (we cite [8,26] as examples). However, to the best of our knowledge, this is the first work where the online/offline structure of encryption has been used to prove an impossibility result.

Ananth and Vaikuntanathan showed that FE for P/poly with a bounded number of secret keys can already be achieved from minimal assumptions, i.e. public-key encryption in the asymmetric setting and one-way functions in the symmetric setting [11]. The ciphertexts in their schemes are growing linearly with the number of secret keys which can be handed out to an adversary. It is presumably hard to improve their result, since we know that a bounded FE scheme with sufficiently compact ciphertexts would already imply indistinguishability obfuscation [10,14].

As mentioned, it is hard to construct FE schemes for stronger functionalities. In recent years, researchers circumvented this problem and looked at novel FE schemes with additional properties: Abdalla, Chotard and other researchers constructed multi-input and decentralized multi-client inner-product encryption schemes [1,3,5,20]. Those are inner-product encryption schemes where a function has multiple inputs and to decrypt one needs a secret key and multiple suitable ciphertexts. In the decentralized schemes, one gets rid of the master secret key holder. Jain et al. introduced the notion of 3-restricted FE [9,27], which can be understood as cubic FE where a ciphertext just hides two out of three factors.

1.4   Technical Overview

To prove Theorem 1, we need to show the existence of a selective adversary who wins the function-hiding IND-CPA game against the function-hiding inner-product encryption scheme FE. In this game, the adversary submits an unbounded number of inputs x_i^0 and functions f_j^0 for world 0 and an unbounded number of inputs x_i^1 and functions f_j^1 for world 1. Then, the challenger draws a random bit $b \leftarrow \{0,1\}$ and sends the corresponding ciphertexts and secret keys of world b to the adversary. The adversary wins, if he guesses b correctly and if the submitted inputs and functions would not tell him trivially in which world he lives, i.e., if we have for all i and j

$$f_j^0(x_i^0) = f_j^1(x_i^1).$$

We do not directly construct an adversary to break FE. Instead, we show how an adversary can reduce the problem of breaking FE to the problem of breaking other encryption schemes with additional properties. To do so, we apply multiple transformations to FE. Eventually, we end with a private-key encryption scheme whose ciphertexts are short integer vectors and whose encryption algorithm is of constant depth. Then, we construct a simple adversary who can break such encryption schemes.

To make our argument go through, we need the transformations to preserve the security and correctness of the transformed schemes. It is easy to see that security is preserved, since we ensure that all changes to FE can be computed by an adversary while he plays the above security game against FE. On the other hand, we can not always guarantee that our transformations preserve correctness. In fact, one transformation step applied to FE changes it in such a way that decryption succeeds only in a non-negligible number of cases. Furthermore, it is important that at each time we have an encryption algorithm of constant depth. This means, each transformation step either changes the encryption algorithm without changing its depth or at most changes its depth to another constant value.

Our proof consists of three major steps:

(1) We first change FE s.t. all ciphertexts have short entries relative to the modulus q. To do this, the adversary queries a lot of secret keys for the zero function and learns, by doing so, the structure of the space of secret keys. Then, he can exchange a ciphertext with a vector of decryption noises. Those noises have to be short, because otherwise they would make a correct decryption impossible. On the other hand, however, we show that those noises contain enough information about the original ciphertext to make decryption possible in a non-negligible number of cases. Therefore, we can assume FE to have short ciphertexts.

Then, we use a straightforward transformation to convert FE to a private-key encryption scheme SKE_q whose ciphertexts are short relative to q and whose encryption algorithm is of constant depth over $\mathbb{Z}_q$.

(2) Since the encryption algorithm of SKE_q is of constant depth, SKE_q encrypts a number x by sampling some polynomials, evaluating those polynomials at x and reducing the result modulo q. To analyse the ciphertexts of SKE_q, we need to get rid of the arithmetic overflows in the online part of its encryption algorithm. We observe that, if $r(X)$ is a polynomial with small coefficients, then, for some small x values, $r(x)$ does not change when we reduce it modulo q. Furthermore, we know the ciphertexts of SKE_q to be short relative to q. By using this fact, we can apply simple changes to the encryption algorithm of SKE_q to ensure that the polynomials sampled by its offline algorithm have very small coefficients. By doing so, we can change SKE_q to a private-key encryption scheme SKE of constant depth whose ciphertext vectors are sufficiently short and where no arithmetic overflows do occur in the online part of its encryption algorithm.

(3) In SKE, a message x gets encrypted by sampling random integer polynomials $r_1, \ldots, r_m$ of constant degree and computing $(r_1(x), \ldots, r_m(x))$ as ciphertext without any arithmetic overflows. Intuitively, such a scheme should not

be secure and, indeed, we show that such a scheme can only be secure, if its ciphertexts do not contain any information about the encrypted messages. But this makes decryption impossible. Since we showed that a correct and secure FHFE scheme FE can be transformed into a secure private-key encryption scheme whose ciphertexts contain a non-negligible amount of information, it follows that FE could not be secure and correct in the first place.

We now take a closer look at the techniques used in each step.

Replacing Ciphertexts with Decryption Noise. We describe here how to make the ciphertexts of FE short. For simplicity, let us assume that we have already relinearized ciphertexts and secret keys, i.e. decryption works by

$$\mathsf{Dec}(\mathsf{sk}, \mathsf{ct}) = \left\lceil \frac{\langle \mathsf{sk} \mid \mathsf{ct} \rangle}{\lfloor q/p \rfloor} \right\rfloor .$$

Query a lot of secret keys $v_1, \ldots, v_m \leftarrow \mathsf{KeyGen}(\mathsf{msk}, 0)$ for the zero-function and draw a ciphertext ct_x for an arbitrary input $x \in \mathbb{Z}_p^n$. Each v_i must decrypt ct_x to zero, since this is the value of the zero-function applied to x. Because of decryption correctness of FE, we can therefore assume that we have for each v_i

$$|\langle v_i \mid \mathsf{ct}_x \rangle| \leq \left\lfloor \frac{q}{p} \right\rfloor .$$

Otherwise, $\langle v_i \mid \mathsf{ct}_x \rangle / \lfloor q/p \rfloor$ would not round to zero. We can now exchange ct_x with the following new ciphertext for x:

$$\mathsf{ct}'_x = (\langle v_1 \mid \mathsf{ct}_x \rangle, \ldots, \langle v_m \mid \mathsf{ct}_x \rangle).$$

This ciphertext just consists of noise values which are generated when decrypting ct_x with secret keys for the zero-function. Therefore, each entry of ct'_x is bounded by $\lfloor q/p \rfloor$. The question remains, how much information about x is left in ct'_x and if it is even possible to recover $f(x)$ from ct'_x and sk_f. We show that in a non-negligible number of cases a successful decryption is still possible. That is because of the function-hiding property of FE which vaguely implies that a secret key for f has to lie in $\mathsf{span}_{\mathbb{Z}_q}\{v_1, \ldots, v_m\}$ with non-negligible probability.

Getting Rid of Arithmetic Overflows. The key observation in step (2) is that, if we evaluate a polynomial of degree d with small coefficients at a small input, reducing the result modulo q will not change its value. However, the polynomials $r_1(X), \ldots, r_m(X)$ sampled in the offline part of the encryption algorithm of SKE_q do not necessarily have small coefficients. We only know them to have small output values. We prove that there is a constant c, s.t. each $c \cdot r_i$ has sufficiently small coefficients modulo q. The existence of c can be shown by using a *quasi-inverse*[1] of the Vandermonde matrix V for the tuple $(0, 1, \ldots, d)$, that is an integer matrix whose product with V equals a scaled identity matrix.

---

[1] Calling such matrices quasi-inverses is ambiguous. However, we will stick to this notion, since we lack better names.

By simply multiplying ciphertexts of SKE_q with c, we can make them behave like they were outputted from an encryption algorithm of constant depth where no arithmetic overflows do occur in its online part. Therefore, we can transform SKE_q into SKE.

Quasi-inverses of Vandermonde have been recently used by Esgin et al. to extract witnesses out of many polynomial relations [22]. However, in this work, we use a different quasi-inverse than them, which yields better bounds for our results.

Statistically Distinguishing Random Polynomials. We describe here, how our adversary breaks SKE in step (3). It suffices to look at the j-th coordinate of a ciphertext of SKE. At input x, the j-th coordinate is computed by sampling a random polynomial $r_j(X)$ of constant degree d in the offline part and evaluating it at x. Our adversary works by guessing one $x \neq 0$ and comparing $\mathbb{E}[r_j(x)^2]$ and $\mathbb{E}[r_j(0)^2]$. We show, if for each x the means $\mathbb{E}[r_j(x)^2]$ and $\mathbb{E}[r_j(0)^2]$ do not differ by a non-negligible amount, then $r_j(X)$ is of degree at most $d-1$ with overwhelming probability. By inductively using hybrids, one can see that $r_j(X)$ must be of degree 0, i.e. constant, with overwhelming probability. But, if $r_j(X)$ is constant, the value $r_j(x)$ does not carry any information about x. Therefore, if the ciphertexts of SKE contain a non-negligible amount of information about the encrypted messages, it follows that there must be some j and $x \neq 0$ s.t. our adversary can successfully distinguish $\mathbb{E}[r_j(x)^2]$ and $\mathbb{E}[r_j(0)^2]$ and, therefore, successfully distinguish ciphertexts for 0 from ciphertexts for x.

1.5   Organization of This Work

We first introduce some preliminaries in Sect. 2 and some important definitions and concepts in Sect. 3. Then, in Sect. 4, we give an adversary who breaks private-key encryption schemes of constant depth which do not make use of arithmetic overflows. In Sect. 5, we then derive an impossibility result for private-key encryption schemes of constant depth with short ciphertexts over $\mathbb{Z}_q$ by transforming them to schemes we broke in the preceding section. Finally, in Sect. 6, we show the impossibility of LWE-like FHFE schemes with simple online/offline encryption by transforming them to schemes of the preceding section.

Due to lack of space, we have ot omit the proofs of some lemmas. The reader can find those proofs in the full version of this paper [31].

2   Preliminaries

For $n \in \mathbb{N} = \{1, 2, 3, \ldots\}$, set $[n] := \{1, \ldots, n\}$. We define two sets of functions:

$$\mathsf{poly}(\lambda) := \{p : \mathbb{N} \to \mathbb{N} \mid \exists c, d \in \mathbb{N} \, \forall \lambda \in \mathbb{N} : \, \lambda^c + d \geq p(\lambda) \geq 1\},$$
$$\mathsf{negl}(\lambda) := \{\varepsilon : \mathbb{N} \to \mathbb{R} \mid \forall c \in \mathbb{N} : \, \lim_{\lambda \to \infty} \lambda^c \varepsilon(\lambda) = 0\}.$$

For functions $f, g : \mathbb{N} \to \mathbb{R}$, we write $f(\lambda) \geq g(\lambda) - \mathsf{negl}(\lambda)$, if there is an $\varepsilon \in \mathsf{negl}(\lambda)$ s.t. we have $f(\lambda) \geq g(\lambda) - \varepsilon(\lambda)$ for all λ.

For $x \in \mathbb{R}$, we define the following roundings: $\lfloor x \rfloor := \max\{z \in \mathbb{Z} \mid z \leq x\}$, $\lceil x \rceil := \min\{z \in \mathbb{Z} \mid z \geq x\}$ and $\lceil x \rfloor := \max\{z \in \mathbb{Z} \mid 2 \cdot |x - z| \leq 1\}$. For two discrete distributions $\mathcal{D}_1, \mathcal{D}_2$ over a set X we define the **statistical distance** of $(\mathcal{D}_1, \mathcal{D}_2)$ by $\Delta(\mathcal{D}_1, \mathcal{D}_2) := \frac{1}{2}\sum_{x \in X} |\mathcal{D}_1(x) - \mathcal{D}_2(x)|$.

2.1 Statistical Preliminaries

Theorem 2 (Hoeffding's Inequality). *Let $n \in \mathbb{N}$ and $B, t \geq 0$. For n independent random variables $X_1, \ldots, X_n$ with $|X_i| \leq B$, we have*

$$\Pr\left[\left|\frac{X_1 + \ldots + X_n}{n} - \mathbb{E}\left[\frac{X_1 + \ldots + X_n}{n}\right]\right| \geq 2Bt\right] \leq 2e^{-2nt^2}.$$

Corollary 2. *Let $\mathcal{D}$ be a memoryless source that outputs real numbers which are bounded by $B \geq 0$. Let $r \in \mathbb{N}$ and set $n = 2r^3$. Let μ be the mean of $\mathcal{D}$ and let E_n be the random variable which is sampled by n-fold querying $\mathcal{D}$, summing its outputs and dividing this sum by n. Then, we have*

$$\Pr\left[|E_n - \mu| \leq \frac{B}{r}\right] \geq 1 - 2e^{-r}.$$

2.2 Algebraic Preliminaries

Theorem 3. *Let $f(X) = \sum_{i=0}^{d} a_i X^i$ be a polynomial of degree d over $\mathbb{R}$. Then*

$$d! \cdot a_d = \sum_{k=0}^{d} (-1)^{d-k} \binom{d}{k} f(k).$$

This theorem can be proven by using discrete derivatives. For example, a proof can be deduced by trick 2 of [25], Section 5.3. Alternatively, the reader can find a full proof in [31].

Now, let $q \in \mathbb{N}$ be a modulus.

Definition 1. *For $a \in \mathbb{Z}$, we define the **absolute value modulo** q by*

$$|a \bmod q| := \min_{z \in q\mathbb{Z}} |a + z| \in \left\{0, \ldots, \left\lfloor \frac{q}{2} \right\rfloor\right\}.$$

Lemma 1.(a) *For $a \in \mathbb{Z}$, we have $|a \bmod q| = 0 \Leftrightarrow a \in q\mathbb{Z}$.*
(b) For $a_1, \ldots, a_n \in \mathbb{Z}$, we have $|\sum_{i=1}^{n} a_i \bmod q| \leq \sum_{i=1}^{n} |a_i \bmod q|$.
(c) For $a, z \in \mathbb{Z}$, we have $|z \cdot a \bmod q| \leq |z| \cdot |a \bmod q|$.

2.3 Learning Theory-Preliminaries

In this subsection, we study the problem of learning vector subspaces. Let $\mathbb{F}$ be an arbitrary field.

Lemma 2. *Let $s \in \mathbb{N}_0 = \{0, 1, 2, \ldots\}$ and let $\mathcal{D}$ be a discrete distribution over $\mathbb{F}^s$. For $m \in \mathbb{N}$, we have*

$$\Pr_{v_1, \ldots, v_m \leftarrow \mathcal{D}} [v_m \in \mathrm{span}_{\mathbb{F}} \{v_1, \ldots, v_{m-1}\}] \geq 1 - \frac{s}{m}.$$

Proof. Let $m > s$ and fix $v_1, \ldots, v_m \in \mathrm{supp}(\mathcal{D})$. Denote by S^m the group of permutations of the set $[m]$ and by $T \subset S^m$ the subgroup of order m which is generated by the cyclic rotation $(123\ldots m)$. For $\tau \in T$ set $V_\tau := \mathrm{span}_{\mathbb{F}} \{v_{\tau(1)}, \ldots, v_{\tau(m-1)}\}$. Since each v_i is an s-dimensional vector, we have

$$m - s \leq \# \{j \in [m] \mid v_j \in \mathrm{span}_{\mathbb{F}} \{v_i \mid i \in [m] \setminus \{j\}\}\} = \# \{\tau \in T \mid v_{\tau(m)} \in V_\tau\}.$$

Therefore, for each fixed choice $v_1, \ldots, v_m \in \mathrm{supp}(\mathcal{D})$ we have

$$\Pr_{\tau \leftarrow T} [v_{\tau(m)} \in V_\tau] \geq \frac{m - s}{m}.$$

Since the vectors $v_1, \ldots, v_m$ are identically and independently distributed, we furthermore have

$$\Pr_{v_1, \ldots, v_m \leftarrow \mathcal{D}} [v_m \in \mathrm{span}_{\mathbb{F}} \{v_1, \ldots, v_{m-1}\}] = \Pr_{\substack{v_1, \ldots, v_m \leftarrow \mathcal{D} \\ \tau \leftarrow T}} [v_{\tau(m)} \in V_\tau].$$

Combining both things, we get

$$\Pr_{v_1, \ldots, v_m \leftarrow \mathcal{D}} [v_m \in \mathrm{span}_{\mathbb{F}} \{v_1, \ldots, v_{m-1}\}] = \Pr_{\substack{v_1, \ldots, v_m \leftarrow \mathcal{D} \\ \tau \leftarrow T}} [v_{\tau(m)} \in V_\tau]$$

$$= \sum_{v_1, \ldots, v_m \in \mathrm{supp}(\mathcal{D})} \Pr_{\tau \leftarrow T} [v_{\tau(m)} \in V_\tau] \cdot \Pr_{w_1, \ldots, w_m \leftarrow \mathcal{D}} [\forall i : w_i = v_i]$$

$$\geq \sum_{v_1, \ldots, v_m \in \mathrm{supp}(\mathcal{D})} \frac{m - s}{m} \cdot \Pr_{w_1, \ldots, w_m \leftarrow \mathcal{D}} [\forall i : w_i = v_i] = \frac{m - s}{m}. \qquad \square$$

Theorem 4. *Let $s \in \mathbb{N}_0$ and let $\mathcal{D}$ be a discrete distribution over $\mathbb{F}^s$. Then, there exists an algorithm which makes s queries to $\mathcal{D}$ and $O(s^3)$-fold use of the four basic arithmetic operations in $\mathbb{F}$ to compute a number $k \leq s$, a matrix $B \in \mathbb{F}^{s \times k}$ which consists of k samples of $\mathcal{D}$ and a second matrix $B^+ \in \mathbb{F}^{k \times s}$ s.t. with $V := B \cdot \mathbb{F}^k$*

(a) we have $B^+ \cdot B = 1_{k \times k}$,
(b) $B \cdot B^+$ is the identity on V, i.e., for all $v \in V$, we have $B \cdot B^+ \cdot v = v$,
(c) a certain proportion of the samples of $\mathcal{D}$ lies in V, i.e. $\Pr_{v \leftarrow \mathcal{D}} [v \in V] \geq \frac{1}{s}$.

3   Definitions

In this section, we give basic definitions and state elementary lemmas for this work.

3.1   Functional Encryption

Throughout this work, let λ denote the security parameter. Let $(F_\lambda)_\lambda$ be a family of function descriptions with a family of domains $(X_\lambda)_\lambda$ and codomains $(Y_\lambda)_\lambda$. We tacitly assume in the following that the size of each $f \in F_\lambda, x \in X_\lambda$ and $y \in Y_\lambda$ is bounded by a polynomial in λ, that we can efficiently sample uniformly random elements of those families and that there is a deterministic polytime evaluation algorithm which on input $(f, x) \in F_\lambda \times X_\lambda$ outputs the correct value $y \in Y_\lambda$. We denote the output of this algorithm by $f(x)$.

Definition 2. *A **functional encryption scheme** FE = (Setup, KeyGen, Enc, Dec) for the family $(F_\lambda)_\lambda$ is a quadruple of four ppt algorithms where*

> $Setup(1^\lambda)$ *on input 1^λ generates a master secret key msk,*
> $KeyGen(msk, f)$ *on input msk and a function $f \in F_\lambda$ generates a secret key sk_f,*
> $Enc(msk, x)$ *on input msk and an input value $x \in X_\lambda$ generates a ciphertext ct_x,*
> $Dec(sk_f, ct_x)$ *on input a secret key sk_f and a ciphertext ct_x outputs a value $y \in Y_\lambda$.*

*We call **FE correct**, if we have for each* samplable[2] *$(f_\lambda)_\lambda \in (F_\lambda)_\lambda$ an $\varepsilon \in negl(\lambda)$, s.t. it holds for all $(x_\lambda)_\lambda \in (X_\lambda)_\lambda$*

$$\Pr \left[Dec\left(sk_f, ct_x\right) = f_\lambda(x_\lambda) \;\middle|\; \begin{array}{l} msk \leftarrow Setup(1^\lambda), \\ sk_f \leftarrow KeyGen(msk, f_\lambda), \\ ct_x \leftarrow Enc(msk, x_\lambda) \end{array} \right] \geq 1 - \varepsilon(\lambda).$$

*We call **FE better than guessing** (by $\frac{1}{r}$), if there exists a polynomial $r \in poly(\lambda)$ s.t. we have for each $(x_\lambda)_\lambda \in (X_\lambda)_\lambda$ and each samplable $(f_\lambda)_\lambda \in (F_\lambda)_\lambda$*

$$\Pr \left[Dec\left(sk_f, ct_x\right) = f_\lambda(x_\lambda) \;\middle|\; \begin{array}{l} msk \leftarrow Setup(1^\lambda) \\ sk_f \leftarrow KeyGen(msk, f_\lambda), \\ ct_x \leftarrow Enc(msk, x_\lambda) \end{array} \right] \geq \frac{1}{r(\lambda)} + \frac{1}{\#Y_\lambda} - negl(\lambda).$$

*We call **FE useless**, if we have for each polynomial $r \in poly(\lambda)$*

$$\Pr_{msk \leftarrow Setup(1^\lambda)} \left[\forall x, y \in X_\lambda : \; \Delta\left(Enc(msk, x), Enc(msk, y)\right) < \frac{1}{r(\lambda)} \right] \geq 1 - negl(\lambda).$$

---

[2] By being **samplable**, we mean here that there is a uniform deterministic poly-time algorithm which on input 1^λ outputs f_λ.

While being correct is a common requirement for encryption schemes, being useless implies that a successful decryption is almost impossible, since the ciphertexts contain nearly no information. Being better than guessing, however, implies that in some cases the ciphertexts and secret keys contain enough information for a successful decryption. Now, one would assume that a scheme cannot be useless and better than guessing at the same time and, indeed, we have the following lemma:

Lemma 3. *Let $\#Y_\lambda \geq 2$ for all λ and let $(F_\lambda)_\lambda$ contain a samplable $(f_\lambda)_\lambda$ s.t. each f_λ is surjective. Then, we have:*

(a) If FE is correct, it is better than guessing.
(b) If FE is useless, it is not better than guessing.

3.2   Encryption Algorithms

Now, let R be a ring with an associated valuation $|\cdot|_R : R \to \mathbb{N}_0$. In this work, we always assume $R = \mathbb{Z}$ or $R = \mathbb{Z}_q$ for a prime $q = q(\lambda)$. In the first case $|\cdot|_\mathbb{Z} = |\cdot|$ is the archimedean absolute value. In the latter case $|\cdot|_{\mathbb{Z}_q} = |\cdot \bmod q|$ is the absolute value modulo q we defined in Definition 1.

Furthermore, let $X_\lambda = \{0, \ldots, N\}^n$ now consist of n-dimensional vectors for a polynomial $n = n(\lambda) \in \mathsf{poly}(\lambda)$ and some $N = N(\lambda)$.

Definition 3. *We say the scheme FE or rather its encryption algorithm Enc is of **length** s over R, if the output of Enc is always an element of R^s. Furthermore, we say in this case that Enc is of*

*(a) **width** B, if the infinity-norm of almost all ciphertexts is bounded by B. I.e., there is an $\varepsilon \in \mathsf{negl}(\lambda)$, s.t. we have for each $(x_\lambda)_\lambda \in (X_\lambda)_\lambda$*

$$\Pr_{\mathsf{msk} \leftarrow \mathsf{Setup}(1^\lambda)} [\, \exists i \in [s] : |c_i|_R > B \mid c \leftarrow \mathsf{Enc}(\mathsf{msk}, x_\lambda)] \leq \varepsilon(\lambda),$$

*(b) **depth** d, if Enc consists of two parts: an **offline part** – a ppt algorithm $\mathsf{Enc}_{\mathsf{offline}}$ which on input msk generates s polynomials over $R[X_1, \ldots, X_n]$ of total degree $\leq d$ – and an **online part** which generates a ciphertext by evaluating the polynomials sampled by $\mathsf{Enc}_{\mathsf{offline}}$ at the input x. I.e., Enc works as follows*

$$
\begin{array}{l}
\underline{\mathsf{Enc}(\mathsf{msk}, x):} \\
(p_1, \ldots, p_s) \leftarrow \mathsf{Enc}_{\mathsf{offline}}(\mathsf{msk}) \\
ct_x := (p_1(x), \ldots, p_s(x)) \\
\underline{\mathsf{return}\ ct_x}
\end{array}
$$

where we demand that each p_i is a polynomial of total degree $\leq d$ over R.

3.3   Security Notions

In this work, we study the notion of *selective* and *function-hiding* IND-CPA security where the adversary is allowed to submit a priori multiple challenge inputs (x_i^0, x_i^1) and a bounded number of challenge functions (f_j^0, f_j^1). To be feasible, the adversary must ensure that the output values $f_j^b(x_i^b)$ do not already tell him, if he lives in world 0 or world 1, i.e. he must ensure $f_j^0(x_i^0) = f_j^1(x_i^1)$. The challenger will send the adversary the ciphertexts and secret keys for one random bit $b \leftarrow \{0, 1\}$. To win, the adversary has to guess the bit b.

Definition 4. *Let* FE $=$ (Setup, KeyGen, Enc, Dec) *be a functional encryption scheme for the family* $(F_\lambda)_\lambda$ *and let* $m \in$ poly(λ). *We say that* FE *is **selectively** m-**bounded function-hiding IND-CPA secure** (m-**fh-IND-CPA secure**), if each ppt adversary* $\mathcal{A}$ *has a negligible advantage in winning the following game:*

Step 1: The adversary $\mathcal{A}$ *submits two lists*[3] *of possible inputs* $(x_i^0)_{i=1}^n, (x_i^1)_{i=1}^n$
    and two lists of possible functions $(f_j^0)_{j=1}^m, (f_j^1)_{j=1}^m$ *to the challenger* $\mathcal{C}$.
Step 2: The challenger $\mathcal{C}$ *generates a master secret key* msk $\leftarrow$ Setup(1^λ) *and*
    draws a secret bit $b \leftarrow \{0, 1\}$. *Then,* $\mathcal{C}$ *computes* $\mathsf{ct}_{x_i^b} :=$ Enc(msk, x_i^b) *for each*
    $i = 1, \dots, n$, $\mathsf{sk}_{f_j^b} :=$ KeyGen(msk, f_j^b) *for each* $j = 1, \dots, m$ *and sends the*
    lists $(\mathsf{ct}_{x_i^b})_{i=1}^n$ *and* $(\mathsf{sk}_{f_j^b})_{j=1}^m$ *to* $\mathcal{A}$.
Step 3: The adversary $\mathcal{A}$ *guesses* b.

The adversary wins the above game, if he guesses b *correctly, and, if we have* $f_j^0(x_i^0) = f_j^1(x_i^1)$ *for all* $i = 1, \dots, n$ *and* $j = 1, \dots, m$. *The **advantage** of* $\mathcal{A}$ *is defined by*

$$\mathsf{Adv}(\mathcal{A}) := 2\Pr[\mathcal{A} \text{ wins}] - 1 = \Pr[\mathcal{A} \text{ wins} \mid b = 0] + \Pr[\mathcal{A} \text{ wins} \mid b = 1] - 1.$$

We call FE *selectively **unbounded function-hiding IND-CPA secure** (**fh-IND-CPA secure**), if* FE *is* m-fh-IND-CPA *secure for each polynomial* $m \in$ poly(λ), *and we call* FE *selectively **IND-CPA secure** (**IND-CPA secure**), if* FE *is* 0-fh-IND-CPA *secure.*

3.4   Private-Key Encryption

We define private-key encryption schemes as a special case of functional encryption schemes:

Definition 5. *A **private-key encryption scheme** is a functional encryption scheme* SKE $=$ (Setup, KeyGen, Enc, Dec) *for a function family* $(F_\lambda)_\lambda$ *where each* F_λ *only contains the identity function* Id $: X_\lambda \to X_\lambda$.

---

[3] The size n is determined by the descryiption of $\mathcal{A}$ and bounded by $\mathcal{A}$'s running time. n may be zero, which means that $\mathcal{A}$ is always sending two empty lists of inputs.

When discussing private-key encryption schemes we sometimes omit KeyGen from the header of the scheme and write Dec(msk, $\cdot$) instead of Dec(KeyGen(msk, Id), $\cdot$). Note that we call SKE IND-CPA secure, if it is selectively 0-bounded function-hiding IND-CPA secure in the sense of Definition 4. This differs from the usual security notion in literature, where the adversary is usually allowed to submit only one pair of challenge messages and can inquire ciphertexts adaptively. However, by using a hybrid argument, one can show that the security loss which occurs by allowing multiple challenge messages is polynomially bounded. If we consider message spaces of superpoly size, then we can construct private-key encryption schemes which are selectively, but not adaptively, secure. Therefore, the security notion for SKE we use here is weaker than the usual one in literature.

3.5   Transformations

Definition 6. *Let* FE $=$ (Setup, KeyGen, Enc, Dec), FE$'$ $=$ (Setup$'$, KeyGen$'$, Enc$'$, Dec$'$) *be two functional encryption schemes for the same functionality. We say that* FE *is **virtually** FE$'$, if* Setup $=$ Setup$'$, KeyGen $=$ KeyGen$'$, Dec $=$ Dec$'$ *and there is an* $\varepsilon \in$ negl(λ), *s.t. for all sequences* $(x_\lambda)_\lambda \in (X_\lambda)_\lambda$ *the statistical distance between the following two distributions is bounded from above by* ε:

$$\left\{ (msk, ct_x) \mid msk \leftarrow Setup(1^\lambda), ct_x \leftarrow Enc(msk, x_\lambda) \right\},$$
$$\left\{ (msk, ct'_x) \mid msk \leftarrow Setup(1^\lambda), ct'_x \leftarrow Enc'(msk, x_\lambda) \right\}.$$

Now, let FE *be a functional encryption scheme for functions* (F_λ) *with inputs* (X_λ) *and let* FE *be one for functions* (F'_λ) *with inputs* (X'_λ). *We say there is an **adversarial transformation** from* FE *to* FE$'$, *if there are ppt algorithms* T_{ct}, T_{sk}, T_F, T_X *s.t. we have the following equalities of distributions for all* $x' \in X'_\lambda$, $f' \in F'_\lambda$, $msk \in supp(Setup)$:

$$Setup'(1^\lambda) = Setup(1^\lambda),$$
$$Enc'(msk, x') = T_{ct}(Enc(msk, T_X(x'))),$$
$$KeyGen'(msk, f') = T_{sk}(KeyGen(msk, T_F(f'))).$$

If $(F_\lambda) = (F'_\lambda)$, *then we always assume* $T_F = \mathrm{Id}_{F_\lambda}$ *and* $T_X = \mathrm{Id}_{X_\lambda}$.

Let $k \in \mathbb{N}$ *be constant and let* $(FE^i)_{i=1}^k$ *be a sequence of functional encryption schemes. We say there is a **virtual adversarial transformation** from* FE^1 *to* FE^k, *if, for each* $i = 1, \ldots, k-1$, FE^i *is virtually* FE^{i+1} *or there is an adversarial transformation from* FE^i *to* FE^{i+1}.

We can now observe the following facts:

Lemma 4.(a) *If* FE *is virtually* FE$'$, *then* FE *is m-fh-IND-CPA secure, correct, better than guessing resp. useless iff* FE$'$ *is so.*
(b) *If* FE *is m-fh-IND-CPA secure and there is an adversarial transformation from* FE *to* FE$'$, *then* FE$'$ *is m-fh-IND-CPA secure.*

At some points, we want to ensure that an encryption algorithm Enc of width B never outputs a ciphertext whose largest entry is not bounded by B. We can ensure such a behaviour by replacing each ciphertext of Enc which is too big with the zero vector. It is clear that this change just has a statistically negligible impact on a scheme. One can even ensure that by doing so we do not harm the depth of Enc:

Lemma 5. *For $n = 1$, let FE be of length s, width B and depth d over R. If d is constant and B is polynomial, then FE is virtually a scheme $FE' = (Setup', KeyGen', Enc', Dec')$ of length s and depth d over R where we have $Enc'(msk', x) \in \{-B, \ldots, B\}^s$ for all λ, $x \in X_\lambda$ and $msk' \in supp(Setup'(1^\lambda))$.*

4   Online/Offline Encryption Without Overflows

In this section, we show that private-key encryption schemes of polynomial width that are better than guessing cannot be IND-CPA secure, if their encryption algorithms have a very simple online part in which no arithmetical overflows do occur.

Theorem 5. *Let $d \in \mathbb{N}$ be constant, $N \geq 2d$ and let SKE be a private-key encryption scheme of depth d and width $B \in poly(\lambda)$ with message space $X_\lambda = \{0, \ldots, N\}$ over $\mathbb{Z}$.*
If SKE is selectively IND-CPA secure, then SKE is useless.

Proof (Theorem 5 Part 1). Let SKE be an IND-CPA secure scheme of length s, depth d and width B over $\mathbb{Z}$ for messages $X_\lambda = \{0, \ldots, N\}$. If we define $SKE' = (Setup', Enc', Dec')$ like in Lemma 5, then SKE is virtually SKE'. In particular, SKE' is of the same length and depth and is secure and useless iff SKE is so. Furthermore, SKE' is now strictly of width B, i.e., it never outputs a ciphertext outside of $\{-B, \ldots, B\}^s$. It now suffices to prove that SKE' is useless. ∎

To prove Theorem 5, we define an adversary which we will show to have a non-negligible advantage against SKE', if SKE' is not useless.

Definition 7. *Let $r \in poly(\lambda)$, $N \geq 2d$ and $s \geq 1$. Set $m = 2r^3$.*
We define the following selective adversary $\mathcal{A}$ which plays the IND-CPA security-game in Definition 4 with the scheme SKE':

Step 1: The adversary $\mathcal{A}$ draws $y \leftarrow [2d]$ and then, for $b = 0, 1$, submits the following two lists of $3m$ messages each:

$$x_i^b = \begin{cases} 0, & \text{if } i \in \{1, \ldots, m\}, \\ b \cdot y, & \text{if } i \in \{m+1, \ldots, 2m\}, \\ y, & \text{if } i \in \{2m+1, \ldots, 3m\}. \end{cases}$$

He submits two empty lists of possible functions.

Step 2: The adversary $\mathcal{A}$ receives a list of ciphertexts $(\mathsf{ct}'_{x_i^b})_{i=1}^{3m}$. Let $\mathsf{ct}'_{x_i^b,j}$ denote the j-th entry of $\mathsf{ct}'_{x_i^b}$. For $k = 0, 1, 2$ and $j = 1, \ldots, s$ he computes the arithmetical means

$$c_{k,j} := \frac{1}{m} \sum_{i=1+km}^{(k+1)m} (\mathsf{ct}'_{x_i^b,j})^2$$

Step 3: If there is a j s.t. $|c_{2,j} - c_{1,j}| > 2\frac{B}{r}$, the adversary outputs 0. Otherwise, if there is a j s.t. $|c_{0,j} - c_{1,j}| > 2\frac{B}{r}$, he outputs 1. If none of the above requirements should be met, then the adversary outputs a random bit $b' \leftarrow \{0,1\}$.

The following lemma shows in which cases $\mathcal{A}$ has a non-negligible advantage.

Lemma 6. *Let $r \in \mathsf{poly}(\lambda)$ s.t. $r \geq \lambda$. For a fixed msk', set $CT'_y = \mathsf{Enc}'(\mathsf{msk}', y)$. The adversary in Definition 7 has a non-negligible advantage in the selective IND-CPA game against SKE', if the following probability is non-negligible*

$$\Pr_{\mathsf{msk}' \leftarrow \mathsf{Setup}'(1^\lambda)} \left[\exists j \in [s], y^* \in [2d] : \left| \mathbb{E}\left[(CT'_{y^*,j})^2 \right] - \mathbb{E}\left[(CT'_{0,j})^2 \right] \right| > 4\frac{B}{r} \right].$$

Proof. Fix for this proof a master secret key $\mathsf{msk}' \in \mathsf{supp}(\mathsf{Setup}'(1^\lambda))$ and denote by CT'^2_y the distribution of drawing $\mathsf{ct}'_y \leftarrow \mathsf{Enc}'(\mathsf{msk}', y)$ and squaring all its entries. In step 2, $\mathcal{A}$ approximates the means of $CT'^2_0, CT'^2_{b \cdot y}$ and CT'^2_y. By Bounded we denote the event that for each $k = 0, 1, 2$ the distance between c_k and its mean is at most B/r, i.e. the event Bounded holds iff

$$\max\left(\left\| c_0 - \mathbb{E}\left[CT'^2_0 \right] \right\|_\infty, \left\| c_1 - \mathbb{E}\left[CT'^2_{b \cdot y} \right] \right\|_\infty, \left\| c_2 - \mathbb{E}\left[CT'^2_y \right] \right\|_\infty \right) \leq \frac{B}{r}.$$

Since Enc' always outputs values bounded by B, we have, according to Corollary 2, that the probability that event Bounded will occur is at least $(1 - 2e^{-r})^{3s} \geq 1 - 6se^{-r}$. Therefore, for each fixed msk', it follows

$$\Pr[\mathcal{A} \text{ fails} \mid b = 0] \leq \Pr\left[\|c_0 - c_1\|_\infty > 2\frac{B}{r} \right] + \frac{1}{2}$$

$$\leq \Pr[\neg\mathsf{Bounded}] + \frac{1}{2} \leq 6se^{-r} + \frac{1}{2}.$$

Similarly, for each fixed $\mathsf{msk}' \in \mathsf{supp}(\mathsf{Setup}'(1^\lambda))$, we get $\Pr[\mathcal{A} \text{ fails} \mid b = 1] \leq 6se^{-r} + \frac{1}{2}$.

Now, assume additionally for msk' that the following event Seperated does hold

$$\mathsf{Seperated} : \quad \exists y^* \in [2d] : \quad \left\| \mathbb{E}\left[CT'^2_0 \right] - \mathbb{E}\left[CT'^2_{y^*} \right] \right\|_\infty > 4\frac{B}{r}.$$

Let y denote the value drawn by $\mathcal{A}$ in step 1. If Seperated holds for msk', then

$$\Pr\left[\mathcal{A} \text{ wins} \mid b = 0, y = y^*\right]$$

$$\geq \Pr\left[\|c_2 - c_1\|_\infty > 2\frac{B}{r} \,\middle|\, b = 0, y = y^*\right]$$

$$\geq \Pr[\mathsf{Bounded}] \cdot \Pr\left[\|c_2 - c_1\|_\infty > 2\frac{B}{r} \,\middle|\, \mathsf{Bounded}, b = 0, y = y^*\right]$$

$$\geq (1 - 6se^{-r}) \cdot 1 = 1 - 6se^{-r}.$$

Similarly, we get $\Pr\left[\mathcal{A} \text{ wins} \mid b = 1, y = y^*\right] \geq 1 - 6se^{-r}$. Therefore, for $\mathsf{msk}' \leftarrow \mathsf{Setup}'(1^\lambda)$, we get now

$$\Pr\left[\mathcal{A} \text{ wins} \mid \mathsf{Seperated}\right]$$

$$= \frac{1}{2d}\left(\Pr\left[\mathcal{A} \text{ wins} \mid \mathsf{Seperated}, y = y^*\right] + \frac{2d-1}{2d} \Pr\left[\mathcal{A} \text{ wins} \mid \mathsf{Seperated}, y \neq y^*\right]\right)$$

$$\geq \frac{1}{2d}(1 - 6se^{-r}) + \frac{2d-1}{2d}\left(\frac{1}{2} - 6se^{-r}\right) \geq \frac{1}{4d} + \frac{1}{2} - 6se^{-r}.$$

Now, if we set $\varepsilon := \Pr\left[\mathsf{Seperated}\right]$, we have

$$\Pr\left[\mathcal{A} \text{ wins}\right] = \varepsilon \cdot \Pr\left[\mathcal{A} \text{ wins} \mid \mathsf{Seperated}\right] + (1 - \varepsilon) \cdot \Pr\left[\mathcal{A} \text{ wins} \mid \neg\mathsf{Seperated}\right]$$

$$\geq \varepsilon\left(\frac{1}{4d} + \frac{1}{2} - 6se^{-r}\right) + (1 - \varepsilon)\left(\frac{1}{2} - 6se^{-r}\right) = \varepsilon\frac{1}{4d} + \frac{1}{2} + 6se^{-r}.$$

Since our lemma requires ε to be non-negligible and $r \geq \lambda$, it follows that $\mathcal{A}$ has a non-negligible advantage. □

To conclude the proof of Theorem 5, we need to show that the prerequisites of Lemma 6 do occur, if SKE' is not useless. In fact, we show a purely mathematical statement in the following which implies the uselessness of SKE', if the prerequisites of Lemma 6 are not met. Our statement says that for a distribution of polynomials the means of the squared outputs of the polynomials for $x = 0, \ldots, 2d$ need to be widespread, because, otherwise, it is very unlikely for the sampled polynomials to be non-constant. If the polynomials sampled by $\mathsf{Enc}'_{\mathsf{offline}}(\mathsf{msk}')$ are with overwhelming probability constant, then, of course, the sampled ciphertexts do not carry any information about the encrypted input x.

Lemma 7. *Let $\mathcal{D}$ be a distribution over integer polynomials of degree $d > 0$. If there is a function $\varepsilon = \varepsilon(\lambda)$ s.t. for all $x \in \{1, \ldots, 2d\}$ we have*

$$\left|\mathop{\mathbb{E}}_{p \leftarrow \mathcal{D}}\left[p(x)^2 - p(0)^2\right]\right| \leq \varepsilon,$$

then it follows

$$\mathop{\Pr}_{p \leftarrow \mathcal{D}}\left[\deg p \leq d - 1\right] \geq 1 - 2\varepsilon.$$

Proof. For $p \leftarrow \mathcal{D}$, we set $f(X) := p(X)^2 - p(0)^2$. Then, f is a random integer polynomial of degree $2d$. If we have $p(X) = \sum_{i=0}^{d} a_i X^i$, then the leading coefficient of f is a_d^2. Now, by Theorem 3, it follows

$$(2d)! \cdot a_d^2 = \sum_{i=0}^{2d} (-1)^{2d-i} \binom{2d}{i} f(i).$$

Hence

$$\mathop{\mathbb{E}}_{p \leftarrow \mathcal{D}} [a_d^2] = \frac{1}{(2d)!} \left| \sum_{i=0}^{2d} (-1)^{2d-i} \binom{2d}{i} \mathop{\mathbb{E}}_{p \leftarrow \mathcal{D}} [f(i)] \right|$$

$$\leq \frac{1}{(2d)!} \sum_{i=0}^{2d} \binom{2d}{i} \left| \mathop{\mathbb{E}}_{p \leftarrow \mathcal{D}} [f(i)] \right| \leq \frac{1}{(2d)!} \sum_{i=0}^{2d} \binom{2d}{i} \cdot \varepsilon = \frac{2^{2d}}{(2d)!} \varepsilon \leq 2\varepsilon.$$

If we draw $p(X) = \sum_{i=0}^{d} a_i X^i \leftarrow \mathcal{D}$, it follows

$$\Pr [\deg p = d] = \sum_{i \in \mathbb{Z} \setminus \{0\}} \Pr [a_d = i] \leq \sum_{i \in \mathbb{Z} \setminus \{0\}} i^2 \cdot \Pr [a_d = i] = \mathop{\mathbb{E}}_{p \leftarrow \mathcal{D}} [a_d^2] \leq 2\varepsilon. \quad \square$$

Lemma 7 already implies that the offline algorithm of an IND-CPA secure encryption scheme of depth d and polynomial width will – with overwhelming probability – sample polynomials of degree $d - 1$. In the following theorem, we generalize this observation for arbitrary degrees $d - k$.

Theorem 6. *Let $\mathcal{D}$ be a distribution over integer polynomials of degree d. If there are functions $\varepsilon = \varepsilon(\lambda)$ and $B = B(\lambda)$ s.t. for all $x \in \{1, \ldots, 2d\}$ and $p \in \mathsf{supp}(\mathcal{D})$ we have*

$$\left| p(x)^2 - p(0)^2 \right| \leq B^2 \qquad and \qquad \left| \mathop{\mathbb{E}}_{p \leftarrow \mathcal{D}} [p(x)^2 - p(0)^2] \right| \leq \frac{1}{2} \varepsilon,$$

then we have for all $k = 0, \ldots, d$

$$\mathop{\Pr}_{p \leftarrow \mathcal{D}} [\deg p \leq d - k] \geq 1 - (2 + 2B^2)^k \varepsilon.$$

Theorem 6 is proven by using induction over k where the base case and the induction step both follow by Lemma 7. Since its proof is very technical, we omit it here. We can now finish the proof of Theorem 5.

Proof (Theorem 5 Part 2). Let $\mathcal{A}$ be the adversary in Definition 7. For $\mathcal{A}$ to have negligible advantage against SKE', according to Lemma 6, it is necessary to have for all $r = 4r'B \in \mathsf{poly}(\lambda)$

$$\Pr \left[\forall j \in [s], y \in [2d] : \left| \mathbb{E} \left[(\mathsf{CT}'_{y,j})^2 \right] - \mathbb{E} \left[(\mathsf{CT}'_{0,j})^2 \right] \right| \leq \frac{1}{r'} \right] \geq 1 - \mathsf{negl}(\lambda)$$

where we take the probability over $\mathsf{msk}' \leftarrow \mathsf{Setup}'(1^\lambda)$. But now, by Theorem 6, we have for each $r \in (2 + 2B^2)^d \cdot \mathsf{poly}(\lambda)$

$$\Pr\left[\forall j \in [s] : \Pr_{(p_1,\ldots,p_s) \leftarrow \mathsf{Enc}'_{\mathrm{offline}}} [\deg p_j = 0] \geq 1 - (2 + 2B^2)^d \frac{1}{r}\right] \geq 1 - \mathsf{negl}(\lambda).$$

Therefore, the uselessness of SKE' and, in particular, the uselessness of SKE follow.   □

5   Online/Offline Encryption with Short Ciphertexts

In Sect. 4, we showed that encryption schemes of constant depth and polynomial width without arithmetic overflows cannot be secure. In this section, we show the same result for encryption schemes of constant depth and polynomial width which may make use of arithmetic overflows but have short ciphertexts. We do so by transforming such schemes to encryption schemes without arithmetic overflows. I.e., if the ciphertexts are of short width, we can transform their encryption algorithm to one of constant depth over $\mathbb{Z}$ by using a simple multiplication trick. As before, throughout this section, let λ denote the security parameter and let $B = B(\lambda), d = d(\lambda)$ and $N = N(\lambda)$ be arbitrary variables depending on λ. Let $s \in \mathsf{poly}(\lambda)$. Additionally, introduce a modulus variable $q = q(\lambda)$. We prove in this section the following theorem:

Theorem 7. *Let q be a prime, $N \geq d+1$ and let SKE_q be a private-key encryption scheme of depth d and width B over $\mathbb{Z}_q$ for messages $X_\lambda = \{0,\ldots,N\}$ s.t.*

$$2(d + 1)^2 \cdot (d!)^3 \cdot d^d \cdot N^d \cdot B \leq q - 1.$$

If SKE_q is selectively IND-CPA secure, then there exists a virtual adversarial transformation to an encryption scheme SKE of depth d and width $(d!)^2 B$ over $\mathbb{Z}$ for messages $X_\lambda = \{0,\ldots,N\}$ which preserves selective IND-CPA security and – in both directions – correctness, being better than guessing and uselessness.

Theorems 7 and 5 imply together the following impossibility result:

Corollary 3. *Let q be a prime and let SKE_q be a private-key encryption scheme of depth d and width B for messages $x = 0,\ldots,N$ over $\mathbb{Z}_q$ s.t. $N \geq 2d$ and*

$$2(d + 1)^2 \cdot (d!)^3 \cdot d^d \cdot N^d \cdot B \leq q - 1.$$

If SKE_q is selectively IND-CPA secure, $B \in \mathsf{poly}(\lambda)$ and $d \in \mathbb{N}$ constant, then SKE_q is useless.

Proof. Because of Theorem 7, there is an IND-CPA secure private-key encryption scheme SKE over $\mathbb{Z}$ of polynomial width $(d!)^2 B$ and constant depth $d \in \mathbb{N}$ for messages $X_\lambda = \{0,\ldots,N\}$ which is useless iff SKE_q is useless. Since $N \geq 2d$, SKE is useless according to Theorem 5.   □

To prove Theorem 7, let $q > 2$ be a prime and define a map $\iota : \mathbb{Z}_q \to \{-\frac{q-1}{2}, \ldots, 0, \ldots, \frac{q-1}{2}\} \subset \mathbb{Z}$ by setting for all $a \in \mathbb{Z}_q$

$$\iota(a \bmod q) := a + zq \quad \text{for } z \in \mathbb{Z} \text{ s.t. } |a + zq| = |a \bmod q|.$$

Then, ι preserves absolute values and we have

$$\iota(a \bmod q) \bmod q = a \bmod q.$$

One first idea for proving Theorem 7 could be to just apply ι component-wise to each ciphertext, i.e. treat each ciphertext modulo q as it would be an integer vector. Technically, we would replace Enc by $\iota \circ \mathsf{Enc}$. While $\iota \circ \mathsf{Enc}$ would be indeed of length s and width B over $\mathbb{Z}$, it is not clear, if it would be of depth d over $\mathbb{Z}$. To make this precise, for $p \in \mathbb{Z}_q[X]$, we denote by $I(p \bmod q)$ the coefficient-wise application of ι, i.e.

$$I\left(\sum_{i=0}^{d} a_i X^i \bmod q\right) := \sum_{i=0}^{d} \iota(a_i \bmod q) X^i.$$

Then, we have the equation $I(p \bmod q) \bmod q = p \bmod q$ again. Now, for $\iota \circ \mathsf{Enc}$ to be of depth d over $\mathbb{Z}$, we would need a suitable offline algorithm. We could, for example, take $I \circ \mathsf{Enc}_{\text{offline}}$ as candidate. If p is a polynomial over $\mathbb{Z}_q$ sampled by $\mathsf{Enc}_{\text{offline}}$, we would then need the following kind of equality for all $x \in X_\lambda$

$$\iota(p(x) \bmod q) = I(p \bmod q)(x). \tag{3}$$

While Eq. (3) holds for polynomials p with small coefficients, it does not hold in general. Therefore, we need to apply minor changes to the polynomials sampled by $\mathsf{Enc}_{\text{offline}}$ as we will see later. To this end, consider the Vandermonde matrix for the tuple $(0, 1, \ldots, d)$

$$V := ((i-1)^{j-1})_{i,j=1,\ldots,d+1} = \begin{pmatrix} 1 & 0 & 0 & \ldots & 0 \\ 1 & 1 & 1 & \ldots & 1 \\ 1 & 2 & 4 & \ldots & 2^d \\ \vdots & & & & \vdots \\ 1 & d & d^2 & \ldots & d^d \end{pmatrix} \in \mathbb{Z}^{(d+1) \times (d+1)}.$$

We can deduce the coefficients of a polynomial by applying V^{-1} to its output values. However, V^{-1} has very large entries modulo q, therefore we use the following integer *quasi-inverse* W with bounded entries.

Lemma 8. *There exists an integer matrix $W \in \mathbb{Z}^{(d+1) \times (d+1)}$ whose entries are bounded by $(d!)^3 d^d$, s.t. $V \cdot W = W \cdot V = (d!)^2 \cdot \mathrm{Id}_{(d+1) \times (d+1)}$.*

Lemma 9. *Let $q > 2$ be a prime, set $c = (d!)^2$ and let $p \in \mathbb{Z}_q[X]$ be a polynomial of degree d. Furthermore, let $N \geq d+1$. If we have for all $x = 0, \ldots, d$*

$$|p(x) \bmod q| \leq \frac{q-1}{2(d+1)^2 \cdot (d!)^3 \cdot d^d \cdot N^d},$$

then we have for all $x = 0, \ldots, N$

$$I(c \cdot p \bmod q)(x) = \iota(c \cdot p(x) \bmod q).$$

Proof. It is clear that we have for any integer polynomial p and any $x \in \mathbb{Z}$

$$I(c \cdot p \bmod q)(x) \bmod q = c \cdot p(x) \bmod q = \iota(c \cdot p(x) \bmod q) \bmod q.$$

Therefore, in our case, it suffices to show that the absolute value of $I(c \cdot p \bmod q)(x)$ is bounded by $\frac{q-1}{2}$, since $\iota(c \cdot p(x) \bmod q)$ is a value of $\{-\frac{q-1}{2}, \ldots, \frac{q-1}{2}\}$ which differs from $I(c \cdot p \bmod q)(x)$ only by a value in $q\mathbb{Z}$.

Let $p(X) = \sum_{i=0}^{d} a_i X^i \in \mathbb{Z}_q[X]$ and set $a = (a_0, \ldots, a_d) \in \mathbb{Z}_q^{d+1}$ to be the column vector of $p's$ coefficients. Then, we have

$$V \cdot a \bmod q = \begin{pmatrix} 1 & 0 & 0 & \ldots & 0 \\ 1 & 1 & 1 & \ldots & 1 \\ 1 & 2 & 4 & \ldots & 2^d \\ \vdots & & & & \vdots \\ 1 & d & d^2 & \ldots & d^d \end{pmatrix} \cdot \begin{pmatrix} a_0 \\ a_1 \\ a_2 \\ \vdots \\ a_d \end{pmatrix} \bmod q = \begin{pmatrix} p(0) \\ p(1) \\ p(2) \\ \vdots \\ p(d) \end{pmatrix} \bmod q.$$

Let $W = (w_{i,j})_{i,j} \in \mathbb{Z}^{(d+1) \times (d+1)}$ be the quasi-inverse of V from Lemma 8. Since $WVa = ca \bmod q$, we have for each a_i

$$c \cdot a_i \bmod q = \sum_{i=0}^{d} w_{i,j} p(j) \bmod q.$$

In particular, we have now

$$|c \cdot a_i \bmod q| = \left| \sum_{i=0}^{d} w_{i,j} p(j) \bmod q \right| \leq \sum_{i=0}^{d} |w_{i,j}| \cdot |p(j) \bmod q|.$$

Set

$$B := \max_{x=0,\ldots d} |p(x) \bmod q| \leq \frac{q-1}{2(d+1)^2 \cdot (d!)^3 \cdot d^d \cdot N^d}.$$

Since each $|w_{i,j}|$ is bounded by $(d!)^3 d^d$ and each $|p(j) \bmod q|$ is bounded by B, we get

$$|c \cdot a_i \bmod q| \leq \sum_{i=0}^{d} |w_{i,j}| \cdot |p(j) \bmod q| \leq \sum_{i=0}^{d} (d!)^3 d^d B = (d+1)(d!)^3 d^d B.$$

Therefore, we have for all $x = 0, \ldots, N$

$$|I(c \cdot p \bmod q)(x)|$$

$$= \left| \sum_{i=0}^{d} \iota \left(c \cdot a_i \bmod q \right) x^i \right| \leq \sum_{i=0}^{d} \left| \iota \left(c \cdot a_i \bmod q \right) x^i \right|$$

$$\leq \sum_{i=0}^{d} \left| \iota \left(c \cdot a_i \bmod q \right) \right| \cdot |x^i| \leq \sum_{i=0}^{d} (d+1)(d!)^3 d^d B \cdot |x|^i$$

$$\leq (d+1)(d!)^3 d^d B \cdot \left(\sum_{i=0}^{d} N^i \right) \leq (d+1)(d!)^3 d^d B \cdot (d+1) N^d \leq \frac{q-1}{2}.$$

Ergo, the claim follows. $\square$

Proof (Theorem 7). Because of Lemma 5, we can – by using the same argument we used in the first part of the proof of Theorem 5 – w.l.o.g. assume that the encryption algorithm of $\mathsf{SKE}_q = (\mathsf{Setup}_q, \mathsf{Enc}_q, \mathsf{Dec}_q)$ never outputs a ciphertext whose entries modulo q are not bounded by B. Set

$$c := (d!)^2 \in \mathbb{Z}, \quad h := c^{-1} \bmod q \in \mathbb{Z}_q$$

and define a scheme $\mathsf{SKE} = (\mathsf{Setup}, \mathsf{Enc}, \mathsf{Dec})$ over $\mathbb{Z}$ by applying the following adversarial transformation to SKE_q:

$$\mathsf{Setup}(1^\lambda) := \mathsf{Setup}_q(1^\lambda),$$

$$\mathsf{Enc}(\mathsf{msk}, x) := \iota(c \cdot \mathsf{Enc}_q(\mathsf{msk}, x) \bmod q),$$

$$\mathsf{Dec}(\mathsf{msk}, \mathsf{ct}) := \mathsf{Dec}_q(\mathsf{msk}, (h \cdot \mathsf{ct} \bmod q)).$$

It is clear that SKE_q is correct, better than guessing (resp. useless) iff SKE is correct, better than guessing (resp. useless), since we have

$$(h \cdot (\iota(c \cdot \mathsf{ct} \bmod q)) \bmod q) = (h \cdot (c \cdot \mathsf{ct}) \bmod q) = \mathsf{ct} \bmod q.$$

Since SKE_q is IND-CPA secure and the above transformations are adversarial, SKE is IND-CPA secure.

It remains to show that Enc is an encryption algorithm of depth d and width cB over $\mathbb{Z}$. Now, for each $(\mathsf{ct}_1, \ldots, \mathsf{ct}_s) \leftarrow \mathsf{Enc}_q(\mathsf{msk}, x)$, we have

$$|\iota(c \cdot \mathsf{ct}_j \bmod q)| = |c \cdot \mathsf{ct}_j \bmod q| \leq c \cdot |\mathsf{ct}_j \bmod q| \leq cB,$$

therefore Enc is of width cB over $\mathbb{Z}$. To show that Enc is of depth d we have to give a feasible offline algorithm $\mathsf{Enc}_{\mathsf{offline}}$ for $\mathsf{Enc} = \iota(c \cdot \mathsf{Enc}_q)$. This is done by setting

$$\mathsf{Enc}_{\mathsf{offline}}(\mathsf{msk}) := I(c \cdot \mathsf{Enc}_{\mathsf{offline},q}(\mathsf{msk}) \bmod q).$$

Let $x \in \{0, \ldots, N\}$. If we fix the randomness r of $\mathsf{Enc}(\mathsf{msk}, x, r)$ and set $(p_1, \ldots, p_s) = \mathsf{Enc}_{\mathsf{offline},q}(\mathsf{msk}, r)$ and $(p'_1, \ldots, p'_s) = \mathsf{Enc}_{\mathsf{offline}}(\mathsf{msk}, r)$, then

$$\mathsf{Enc}(\mathsf{msk}, x, r) = \iota(c \cdot \mathsf{Enc}_q(\mathsf{msk}, x, r) \bmod q)$$

$$= (\iota(c \cdot p_1(x) \bmod q), \ldots, \iota(c \cdot p_s(x) \bmod q))$$

$$\overset{(*)}{=} (I(c \cdot p_1 \bmod q)(x), \ldots, I(c \cdot p_s \bmod q)(x)) = (p'_1(x), \ldots, p'_s(x)),$$

where eq. $(*)$ follows from Lemma 9. Therefore, $\mathsf{Enc}(\mathsf{msk}, x)$ is of depth d. $\square$

6   Lattice-Based Function-Hiding Functional Encryption

In this section, let $n(\lambda) \geq 1$ be a polynomial in λ and let $q(\lambda) > p(\lambda) \geq N(\lambda) \geq 1$. Further, let $X_\lambda = \{0, \ldots, p\}^n$, $Y_\lambda = \{0, \ldots, p\}$ and let $(F_\lambda)_\lambda$ be a function family which contains (besides other functions) the zero-function $0 \in F_\lambda$ – which maps each $x \in X_\lambda$ to zero – and the projection $\pi_1 \in F_\lambda$ – which maps each $x \in X_\lambda$ to its first coordinate.

Let $\mathsf{FE} = (\mathsf{Setup}, \mathsf{KeyGen}, \mathsf{Enc}, \mathsf{Dec})$ be a functional encryption scheme for $(F_\lambda)_\lambda$ of depth d_1 and length s over $\mathbb{Z}_q$ and let $d_2 \in \mathbb{N}$ be a constant s.t. each secret key $\mathsf{sk} \in \mathsf{supp}(\mathsf{KeyGen})$ is a polynomial in $\mathbb{Z}_q[X_1, \ldots, X_s]$ of total degree $\leq d_2$ with

$$\mathsf{Dec}(\mathsf{sk}, \mathsf{ct}) = \lceil \mathsf{sk}(\mathsf{ct}) / \lfloor q/p \rfloor \rfloor .$$

Finally, set $m = \binom{s+d_2}{d_2}$. We prove in this section the following theorem:

Theorem 8. *If q is a prime and FE is selectively $(m+1)$-bounded function-hiding IND-CPA secure and correct, then there exists an adversarial transformation from FE to a private-key encryption scheme of depth $d := d_1 \cdot d_2$, width $\lfloor q/p \rfloor$ and length m over $\mathbb{Z}_q$ for messages $x = 0, \ldots, N$ which is selectively IND-CPA secure and better than guessing.*

Corollary 4 (Impossibility Result). *Assume that q is a prime, d_1 is constant and $\frac{q}{p}$ is bounded by a polynomial in λ and that for almost all $\lambda \in \mathbb{N}$ we have*

$$p(\lambda) \geq (d+1)^2 \cdot 2^{d+1} \cdot (d!)^3 \cdot d^{2d}.$$

Then, FE cannot be both selectively $(m+1)$-bounded function-hiding IND-CPA secure and correct.

Proof. Assume that FE is both and set $N = 2d$. Because of Theorem 8, we can transform FE to a private-key encryption scheme over $\mathbb{Z}_q$ with depth d and width $B := \lfloor q/p \rfloor$ for messages $X'_\lambda = \{0, \ldots, 2d\}$ which is IND-CPA secure and better than guessing. Then, we have

$$B = \left\lfloor \frac{q}{p} \right\rfloor \leq \frac{q-1}{p} \leq \frac{q-1}{2(d+1)^2 \cdot (d!)^3 \cdot d^d \cdot (2d)^d}.$$

Now, according to Corollary 3, this encryption scheme must be useless and therefore cannot be better than guessing. In particular, FE cannot be correct. $\square$

We prove Theorem 8 by applying adversially three transformations to FE. First, we relinearize the ciphertexts and secret keys s.t. decryption becomes evaluating a scalar product, dividing by $\lfloor q/p \rfloor$ and rounding down. Second, we draw m secret keys $v_1, \ldots, v_m \leftarrow \mathsf{KeyGen}'(\mathsf{msk}, 0)$ for the zero-function and replace a ciphertext ct' with a vector of decryption noises $\langle \mathsf{ct}' \mid v_i \rangle$. Because of decryption correctness, each noise value must be small; therefore, we get a new ciphertext of small width. By using sufficiently many secret keys, we can ensure that the new ciphertext contains enough information s.t. the probability of a correct decryption becomes high enough. We will not always be able to decrypt correctly, but we show that we are still better than guessing by $\frac{1}{m}$. In fact, this is implied by Lemma 10 which states that a secret key of a non-zero function must sufficiently resemble a secret key of the zero-function. As a last step, we convert the current FE scheme into a private-key encryption scheme for messages $x \in \{0, \ldots, N\}$ which is better than guessing and of small width over $\mathbb{Z}_q$. Since all transformations can be applied by an adversary, the scheme stays IND-CPA secure (however, we lose some security in the second transformation step, since we have to ask for m secret keys). If we started with a FE scheme of constant depth, then the final scheme will also be of constant depth.

Proof (Theorem 8 Step 1). As a first step, we relinearize the ciphertexts and secret keys of FE. Note that each polynomial $\mathsf{sk} \in \mathbb{Z}_q[X_1, \ldots, X_s]$ of total degree $\leq d_2$ can be written as a vector of its coefficients. This yields a linear transformation

$$\Phi : \{\mathsf{sk} \in \mathbb{Z}_q[X_1, \ldots, X_s] \mid \deg \mathsf{sk} \leq d_2\} \longrightarrow \mathbb{Z}_q^{\binom{s+d_2}{d_2}}.$$

On the other hand, there is a polynomial map $\Phi^+ : \mathbb{Z}_q^s \longrightarrow \mathbb{Z}_q^m$ of degree d_2 which maps each vector to a vector of different products of its entries s.t. we have for all $\mathsf{sk} \in \mathbb{Z}_q[X_1, \ldots, X_s]$ of total degree $\leq d_2$ and all $\mathsf{ct} \in \mathbb{Z}_q^s$

$$\mathsf{sk}(\mathsf{ct}) = \langle \Phi(\mathsf{sk}) \mid \Phi^+(\mathsf{ct}) \rangle. \tag{4}$$

Now, we define a new scheme $\mathsf{FE}' = (\mathsf{Setup}', \mathsf{KeyGen}', \mathsf{Enc}', \mathsf{Dec}')$ by setting

$$\mathsf{Setup}'(1^\lambda) := \mathsf{Setup}(1^\lambda), \qquad \mathsf{KeyGen}'(\mathsf{msk}', f) := \Phi(\mathsf{KeyGen}(\mathsf{msk}', f)),$$
$$\mathsf{Enc}'(\mathsf{msk}', x) := \Phi^+(\mathsf{Enc}(\mathsf{msk}', x)), \qquad \mathsf{Dec}'(\mathsf{sk}', \mathsf{ct}') := \lceil \langle \mathsf{sk}' \mid \mathsf{ct}' \rangle / \lfloor q/p \rfloor \rfloor.$$

Applying Φ and Φ^+ together forms an adversarial transformation, therefore FE' is $(m+1)$-fh-IND-CPA secure. Because of Eq. (4), FE' is correct. Further, Enc' is of depth $d := d_1 \cdot d_2$ and its outputs are vectors of length $m = \binom{s+d_2}{d_2}$.   ∎

Lemma 10. *For each sampleable $(f_\lambda)_\lambda \in (F_\lambda)_\lambda$ there is an $\varepsilon \in \mathsf{negl}(\lambda)$ s.t.*

$$\Pr \left[\mathsf{sk}'_f \in \mathsf{span}_{\mathbb{Z}_q}\{v_1, \ldots, v_m\} \middle| \begin{array}{l} \mathsf{msk}' \leftarrow \mathsf{Setup}'(1^\lambda) \\ v_1, \ldots, v_m \leftarrow \mathsf{KeyGen}'(\mathsf{msk}, 0) \\ \mathsf{sk}'_f \leftarrow \mathsf{KeyGen}'(\mathsf{msk}', f_\lambda) \end{array} \right] \geq \frac{1}{m+1} - \varepsilon(\lambda).$$

Proof. Lemma 2 states

$$P_1 := \Pr \left[\mathsf{sk}'_0 \in \mathsf{span}_{\mathbb{Z}_q}\{v_1, \ldots, v_m\} \middle| \begin{array}{l} \mathsf{msk}' \leftarrow \mathsf{Setup}'(1^\lambda) \\ v_1, \ldots, v_m \leftarrow \mathsf{KeyGen}'(\mathsf{msk}', 0) \\ \mathsf{sk}'_0 \leftarrow \mathsf{KeyGen}'(\mathsf{msk}', 0) \end{array} \right] \geq 1 - \frac{1}{m+1}.$$

Consider an adversary $\mathcal{A}$ who plays the IND-CPA game from Definition 4 against FE' and works as follows:

Step 1: For $b = 0, 1$ and $i = 1, \ldots, m+1$, the adversary sets

$$g_i^b := \begin{cases} 0, & \text{if } i \leq m \text{ or } b = 0, \\ f_\lambda, & \text{if } i = m+1 \text{ and } b = 1. \end{cases}$$

and submits two empty lists of possible inputs and two lists of possible functions $(g_i^0)_{i=1}^{m+1}, (g_i^1)_{i=1}^{m+1}$.

Step 2: After receiving $(\mathsf{sk}'_{g_i^b})_{i=1}^{m+1}$, $\mathcal{A}$ computes $V := \mathsf{span}_{\mathbb{Z}_q} \left\{ \mathsf{sk}'_{g_1^b}, \ldots, \mathsf{sk}'_{g_m^b} \right\}$.

Step 3: The adversary outputs 0, if $\mathsf{sk}'_{g_{m+1}^b} \in V$, and 1 otherwise.

If we set

$$P_2 := \Pr \left[\mathsf{sk}'_f \in \mathsf{span}_{\mathbb{Z}_q} \{v_1, \ldots, v_m\} \,\middle|\, \begin{array}{l} \mathsf{msk}' \leftarrow \mathsf{Setup}'(1^\lambda), \\ v_1, \ldots, v_{m-1} \leftarrow \mathsf{KeyGen}'(\mathsf{msk}', 0), \\ \mathsf{sk}'_f \leftarrow \mathsf{KeyGen}'(\mathsf{msk}', f_\lambda) \end{array} \right],$$

then we can compute the advantage of $\mathcal{A}$ by

$$\varepsilon := \Pr[\mathcal{A} \text{ wins} \mid b = 0] + \Pr[\mathcal{A} \text{ wins} \mid b = 1] - 1 = P_1 + (1 - P_2) - 1 = P_1 - P_2.$$

ε is negligible, since FE' is $(m+1)$-fh-IND-CPA secure. Therefore

$$P_2 = P_1 - \varepsilon(\lambda) \geq \frac{1}{m+1} - \varepsilon(\lambda). \qquad \square$$

Proof (Theorem 8 Step 2). Let $\mathsf{FE}' = (\mathsf{Setup}', \mathsf{KeyGen}', \mathsf{Enc}', \mathsf{Dec}')$ be a correct and $(m+1)$-fh-IND-CPA secure functional encryption scheme where Enc' is of depth d and length m over $\mathbb{Z}_q$. Let furthermore Dec' be computed by

$$\mathsf{Dec}'(\mathsf{sk}', \mathsf{ct}') = \lceil \langle \mathsf{sk}' \mid \mathsf{ct}' \rangle / \lfloor q/p \rfloor \rceil.$$

We now adversarially transform FE' to a functional encryption scheme FE'' for the same functionality which is 1-fh-IND-CPA secure, better than guessing and whose encryption algorithm has depth d, width $\lfloor q/p \rfloor$ and length m over $\mathbb{Z}_q$.

In the IND-CPA game against FE', our adversary first queries m secret keys $v_1, \ldots, v_m \leftarrow \mathsf{KeyGen}'(\mathsf{msk}', 0)$ for the zero function and then makes use of the algorithm $\mathcal{B}$ described in Theorem 4 to compute $V, A, A^+ \leftarrow \mathcal{B}(v_1, \ldots, v_m)$ s.t. $V = \mathsf{span}_{\mathbb{Z}_q} \{v_1, \ldots, v_m\}$ and $A \in \mathbb{Z}_q^{m \times k}, A^+ \in \mathbb{Z}_q^{k \times m}$ are matrices with

$$V = A \cdot \mathbb{Z}_q^k \quad \text{and} \quad A \cdot A^+ v = v \text{ for all } v \in V.$$

After our adversary queried m secret keys, FE' remains 1-fh-IND-CPA secure. However, by doing so, the adversary gained the additional data V, A, A^+ with which he can transform FE' to $\mathsf{FE}'' = (\mathsf{Setup}'', \mathsf{KeyGen}'', \mathsf{Enc}'', \mathsf{Dec}'')$ by setting:

$$\mathsf{Setup}''(1^\lambda) := \mathsf{Setup}'(1^\lambda) \qquad \mathsf{Enc}''(\mathsf{msk}'', x) := A^T \cdot \mathsf{Enc}'(\mathsf{msk}'', x)$$

$\underline{\mathsf{KeyGen}''(\mathsf{msk}'', f):}$
$\mathsf{sk}'_f \leftarrow \mathsf{KeyGen}'(\mathsf{msk}', f)$
if $\mathsf{sk}'_f \in V$
$\quad \mathsf{sk}''_f := A^+ \cdot \mathsf{sk}'_f$
else
$\quad \mathsf{sk}''_f := \bot$
return sk''_f

$\underline{\mathsf{Dec}''(\mathsf{sk}'', \mathsf{ct}''):}$
if $\mathsf{sk}'' = \bot$
$\quad y \leftarrow \{0, \ldots, p\}$
else
$\quad y \leftarrow \mathsf{Dec}'(\mathsf{sk}'', \mathsf{ct}'')$
return y

FE'' has the following properties:

Security: The above changes can be applied by an adversary while he plays the IND-CPA game from Definition 4. Therefore, FE'' is 1-fh-IND-CPA secure, since our adversary has to query m secret keys for the zero function which does not leak any information about encrypted messages.

Depth and Length: Since the transformation of the encryption algorithm is done by multiplication with the matrix $A^T \in \mathbb{Z}_q^{k \times m}$, the depth of the encryption algorithm does not change. Furthermore, Enc'' is of length[4] $k \leq m$ over $\mathbb{Z}_q$.

Width: We have to show that Enc'' is of width $\lfloor q/p \rfloor$. To this end, let $(x_\lambda)_\lambda \in (X_\lambda)_\lambda$, draw $\mathsf{msk}'' \leftarrow \mathsf{Setup}''(1^\lambda)$, $\mathsf{ct}'' \leftarrow \mathsf{Enc}''(\mathsf{msk}'', x_\lambda)$ and fix a component ct''_i of $\mathsf{ct}'' = (\mathsf{ct}''_1, \ldots, \mathsf{ct}''_k) \in \mathbb{Z}_q^k$. Note that the columns of the matrix $A = (v_{j_1} | \ldots | v_{j_k})$ are some of the vectors $v_1, \ldots, v_m \leftarrow \mathsf{KeyGen}'(\mathsf{msk}', 0)$ according to Theorem 4. Since $\mathsf{ct}'' = A^T \mathsf{ct}'$ for some $\mathsf{ct}' \leftarrow \mathsf{Enc}'(\mathsf{msk}', x_\lambda)$, there is, because of the correctness of FE', an $\varepsilon_0 \in \mathsf{negl}(\lambda)$ s.t. for all $(x_\lambda)_\lambda \in (X_\lambda)_\lambda$

$$\Pr\left[|\mathsf{ct}''_i| \leq \left\lfloor \frac{q}{p} \right\rfloor\right] = \Pr\left[|v_{j_i}^T \cdot \mathsf{ct}'| \leq \left\lfloor \frac{q}{p} \right\rfloor\right] \geq \Pr\left[\left[\frac{v_{j_i}^T \cdot \mathsf{ct}'}{\lfloor q/p \rfloor}\right] = 0\right]$$

$$= \Pr\left[\mathsf{Dec}'(v_{j_i}, \mathsf{ct}') = 0 \,\middle|\, \begin{array}{l} \mathsf{msk}' \leftarrow \mathsf{Setup}'(1^\lambda) \\ v_{j_i} \leftarrow \mathsf{KeyGen}'(\mathsf{msk}', 0), \\ \mathsf{ct}' \leftarrow \mathsf{Enc}'(\mathsf{msk}', x) \end{array}\right] \geq 1 - \varepsilon(\lambda)$$

where in the first three terms we take the randomness over the computation of msk'' and ct''. Therefore, Enc'' is of width $\lfloor q/p \rfloor$.

Better than Guessing: It remains to show that FE'' is better than guessing. Fix $(x_\lambda)_\lambda \in (X_\lambda)_\lambda$ and a samplable $(f_\lambda)_\lambda \in (F_\lambda)_\lambda$ and draw $\mathsf{msk}'' \leftarrow \mathsf{Setup}''(1^\lambda)$,

---

[4] Note that k is not fixed but rather a random variable. However, this is not a problem, since we can always pad the output of Enc'' to be of length m over $\mathbb{Z}_q$.

$sk_f'' \leftarrow KeyGen''(msk'', f_\lambda)$, $ct_x'' \leftarrow Enc''(msk'', x_\lambda)$. Then, we have

$$\Pr\left[Dec''(sk_f'', ct_x'') = f(x)\right]$$
$$= \Pr\left[Dec''(sk_f'', ct_x'') = f(x) \mid sk_f'' = \bot\right] \cdot \Pr\left[sk_f'' = \bot\right]$$
$$+ \Pr\left[Dec''(sk_f'', ct_x'') = f(x) \mid sk_f'' \neq \bot\right] \cdot \Pr\left[sk_f'' \neq \bot\right]$$
$$= \frac{1}{p+1} \cdot \Pr\left[sk_f'' = \bot\right] + \Pr\left[Dec''(sk_f'', ct_x'') = f(x) \mid sk_f'' \neq \bot\right] \cdot \Pr\left[sk_f'' \neq \bot\right].$$

Now, we have $sk_f'' \neq \bot$ iff $sk_f' \in V$. Because of Lemma 10, the probability for this is at least $\frac{1}{m+1} - \varepsilon_1$ for some $\varepsilon_1 \in negl(\lambda)$. If $sk_f' \in V$, we have

$$Dec''(sk_f'', ct_x'') = Dec'(sk_f'', ct_x'') = \left\lceil \frac{\langle sk_f'' \mid ct_x'' \rangle}{\lfloor q/p \rfloor} \right\rfloor = \left\lceil \frac{\langle A^+ sk_f' \mid A^T ct_x' \rangle}{\lfloor q/p \rfloor} \right\rfloor$$
$$= \left\lceil \frac{\langle AA^+ sk_f' \mid ct_x' \rangle}{\lfloor q/p \rfloor} \right\rfloor = Dec'(sk_f', ct_x').$$

The last term equals $f_\lambda(x_\lambda)$ with probability at least $1 - \varepsilon_2$ for some $\varepsilon_2 \in negl(\lambda)$. Now, let λ be big enough s.t. $1 - \varepsilon_2(\lambda) \geq \frac{1}{p(\lambda)+1}$, then

$$\Pr\left[Dec''(sk_f'', ct_x'') = f(x)\right]$$
$$= \frac{1}{p+1} \cdot \Pr\left[sk_f'' = \bot\right] + \Pr\left[Dec''(sk_f'', ct_x'') = f(x) \mid sk_f'' \neq \bot\right] \cdot \Pr\left[sk_f'' \neq \bot\right]$$
$$\geq \frac{1}{p+1} \cdot \left(1 - \Pr\left[sk_f'' \neq \bot\right]\right) + (1 - \varepsilon_2) \cdot \Pr\left[sk_f'' \neq \bot\right]$$
$$= \frac{1}{p+1} + \Pr\left[sk_f'' \neq \bot\right]\left(1 - \varepsilon_2 - \frac{1}{p+1}\right)$$
$$\geq \frac{1}{p+1} + \left(\frac{1}{m+1} - \varepsilon_1\right)\left(1 - \varepsilon_2 - \frac{1}{p+1}\right)$$
$$\geq \frac{1}{p+1} + \frac{p}{(m+1)(p+1)} - negl(\lambda). \tag{5}$$

Therefore, FE'' is better than guessing by $\frac{p}{(m+1)(p+1)}$. ∎

Since $(F_\lambda)_\lambda$ contains the projection onto the first coordinate, there is a straightforward way to adversarially transform FE'' to a private encryption scheme over $\mathbb{Z}_q$ with width $\lfloor q/p \rfloor$ and depth d which is better than guessing and selectively IND-CPA secure. For this purpose set $\widetilde{X}_\lambda = \{0, \ldots, N(\lambda)\}$.

Proof (Theorem 8 Step 3). Let $FE'' = (Setup'', KeyGen'', Enc'', Dec'')$ be the functional encryption scheme of the preceding step. Then, FE'' is 1-fh-IND-CPA secure, better than guessing and of depth d and width $B := \lfloor q/p \rfloor$ over $\mathbb{Z}_q$. Additionally, FE'' has the special property that for all samplable $(f_\lambda)_\lambda$ there is an $\varepsilon \in \mathsf{negl}(\lambda)$, s.t. we have for all $(x_\lambda)_\lambda$

$$\Pr_{\mathsf{msk}'' \leftarrow \mathsf{Setup}''(1^\lambda)} \left[\mathsf{Dec}''(\mathsf{sk}''_f, \mathsf{ct}''_x) = f_\lambda(x_\lambda) \, \middle| \, \begin{array}{l} \mathsf{sk}''_f \leftarrow \mathsf{KeyGen}''(\mathsf{msk}'', f_\lambda) \\ \mathsf{ct}''_x \leftarrow \mathsf{Enc}''(\mathsf{msk}'', x_\lambda) \\ \mathsf{sk}''_f \neq \bot \end{array} \right] \geq 1 - \varepsilon(\lambda).$$

We adversarially transform FE'' to a private-key encryption scheme $\mathsf{SKE}''' = (\mathsf{Setup}''', \mathsf{Enc}''', \mathsf{KeyGen}''', \mathsf{Dec}''')$ of depth d and width B over $\mathbb{Z}_q$ for the message space $\widetilde{X}_\lambda$ which is IND-CPA secure and better than guessing. For this end set:

$$\mathsf{Setup}'''(1^\lambda) := \mathsf{Setup}''(1^\lambda)$$
$$\mathsf{Enc}'''(\mathsf{msk}''', x) := \mathsf{Enc}''(\mathsf{msk}''', (x, 0\ldots, 0))$$
$$\mathsf{KeyGen}'''(\mathsf{msk}''', \mathsf{Id}_{\widetilde{X}_\lambda}) := \mathsf{KeyGen}''(\mathsf{msk}''', \pi_1)$$

$$\underline{\mathsf{Dec}'''(\mathsf{sk}''', \mathsf{ct}''') :}$$
$$\text{if } \mathsf{sk}''' = \bot$$
$$\quad y \leftarrow \{0, \ldots, N\}$$
$$\text{else}$$
$$\quad y \leftarrow \mathsf{Dec}''(\mathsf{sk}''', \mathsf{ct}''')$$
$$\underline{\text{return } y}$$

Note that this adversarial transformation is the only one in this work, where we have two functional encryption schemes for different functionalities. Now, SKE''' is IND-CPA secure, because FE'' is 1-fh-IND-CPA secure (in fact, FE'' being 0-fh-IND-CPA secure would already suffice). Enc''' is of depth d and width B over $\mathbb{Z}_q$, since Enc'' is so. The computations marked by the number (5) in the preceding transformation step show – mutatis mutandis – that SKE''' is better than guessing by $\frac{N}{(m+1)\cdot(N+1)}$. $\qquad\square$

Acknowledgements. I would like to thank my doctoral supervisor Dennis Hofheinz and my former colleagues Geoffroy Couteau, Valerie Fetzer, Michael Klooß and Sven Maier for helpful comments and advices on how to improve this text. Further, I would like to thank the reviewers and everyone who listened to the talk preceding this work for their questions and suggestions.

References

1. Abdalla, M., Benhamouda, F., Kohlweiss, M., Waldner, H.: Decentralizing inner-product functional encryption. In: Lin, D., Sako, K. (eds.) PKC 2019, Part II. LNCS, vol. 11443, pp. 128–157. Springer, Heidelberg (2019). https://doi.org/10.1007/978-3-030-17259-6_5
2. Abdalla, M., Bourse, F., De Caro, A., Pointcheval, D.: Simple functional encryption schemes for inner products. In: Katz, J. (ed.) PKC 2015. LNCS, vol. 9020, pp. 733–751. Springer, Heidelberg (2015). https://doi.org/10.1007/978-3-662-46447-2_33
3. Abdalla, M., Catalano, D., Fiore, D., Gay, R., Ursu, B.: Multi-input functional encryption for inner products: function-hiding realizations and constructions without pairings. In: Shacham, H., Boldyreva, A. (eds.) CRYPTO 2018, Part I. LNCS, vol. 10991, pp. 597–627. Springer, Heidelberg (2018). https://doi.org/10.1007/978-3-319-96884-1_20

4. Agrawal, S., Boneh, D., Boyen, X.: Efficient lattice (H)IBE in the standard model. In: Gilbert, H. (ed.) EUROCRYPT 2010. LNCS, vol. 6110, pp. 553–572. Springer, Heidelberg (2010). https://doi.org/10.1007/978-3-642-13190-5_28

5. Agrawal, S., Clear, M., Frieder, O., Garg, S., O'Neill, A., Thaler, J.: Ad hoc multi-input functional encryption. Cryptology ePrint Archive, Report 2019/356 (2019). https://eprint.iacr.org/2019/356

6. Agrawal, S., Freeman, D.M., Vaikuntanathan, V.: Functional encryption for inner product predicates from learning with errors. In: Lee, D.H., Wang, X. (eds.) ASIACRYPT 2011. LNCS, vol. 7073, pp. 21–40. Springer, Heidelberg (2011). https://doi.org/10.1007/978-3-642-25385-0_2

7. Agrawal, S., Libert, B., Stehlé, D.: Fully secure functional encryption for inner products, from standard assumptions. In: Robshaw, M., Katz, J. (eds.) CRYPTO 2016, Part III. LNCS, vol. 9816, pp. 333–362. Springer, Heidelberg (2016). https://doi.org/10.1007/978-3-662-53015-3_12

8. Agrawal, S., Rosen, A.: Functional encryption for bounded collusions, revisited. In: Kalai, Y., Reyzin, L. (eds.) TCC 2017, Part I. LNCS, vol. 10677, pp. 173–205. Springer, Heidelberg (2017). https://doi.org/10.1007/978-3-319-70500-2_7

9. Ananth, P., Jain, A., Sahai, A.: Indistinguishability obfuscation without multilinear maps: iO from LWE, bilinear maps, and weak pseudorandomness. Cryptology ePrint Archive, Report 2018/615 (2018). https://eprint.iacr.org/2018/615

10. Ananth, P., Jain, A.: Indistinguishability obfuscation from compact functional encryption. In: Gennaro, R., Robshaw, M.J.B. (eds.) CRYPTO 2015, Part I. LNCS, vol. 9215, pp. 308–326. Springer, Heidelberg (2015). https://doi.org/10.1007/978-3-662-47989-6_15

11. Ananth, P., Vaikuntanathan, V.: Optimal bounded-collusion secure functional encryption. Cryptology ePrint Archive, Report 2019/314 (2019). https://eprint.iacr.org/2019/314

12. Baltico, C.E.Z., Catalano, D., Fiore, D., Gay, R.: Practical functional encryption for quadratic functions with applications to predicate encryption. In: Katz, J., Shacham, H. (eds.) CRYPTO 2017, Part I. LNCS, vol. 10401, pp. 67–98. Springer, Heidelberg (2017). https://doi.org/10.1007/978-3-319-63688-7_3

13. Bishop, A., Jain, A., Kowalczyk, L.: Function-hiding inner product encryption. In: Iwata, T., Cheon, J.H. (eds.) ASIACRYPT 2015, Part I. LNCS, vol. 9452, pp. 470–491. Springer, Heidelberg (2015). https://doi.org/10.1007/978-3-662-48797-6_20

14. Bitansky, N., Vaikuntanathan, V.: Indistinguishability obfuscation from functional encryption. In: Guruswami, V. (ed.) 56th FOCS, pp. 171–190. IEEE Computer Society Press, October 2015. https://doi.org/10.1109/FOCS.2015.20

15. Boneh, D., et al.: Fully key-homomorphic encryption, arithmetic circuit ABE and compact garbled circuits. In: Nguyen, P.Q., Oswald, E. (eds.) EUROCRYPT 2014. LNCS, vol. 8441, pp. 533–556. Springer, Heidelberg (2014). https://doi.org/10.1007/978-3-642-55220-5_30

16. Boneh, D., Raghunathan, A., Segev, G.: Function-private identity-based encryption: hiding the function in functional encryption. In: Canetti, R., Garay, J.A. (eds.) CRYPTO 2013, Part II. LNCS, vol. 8043, pp. 461–478. Springer, Heidelberg (2013). https://doi.org/10.1007/978-3-642-40084-1_26

17. Brakerski, Z., Gentry, C., Vaikuntanathan, V.: (Leveled) fully homomorphic encryption without bootstrapping. In: Goldwasser, S. (ed.) ITCS 2012, pp. 309–325. ACM, January 2012. https://doi.org/10.1145/2090236.2090262

18. Brakerski, Z., Vaikuntanathan, V.: Efficient fully homomorphic encryption from (standard) LWE. In: Ostrovsky, R. (ed.) 52nd FOCS, pp. 97–106. IEEE Computer Society Press, October 2011. https://doi.org/10.1109/FOCS.2011.12
19. Cash, D., Hofheinz, D., Kiltz, E., Peikert, C.: Bonsai trees, or how to delegate a lattice basis. In: Gilbert, H. (ed.) EUROCRYPT 2010. LNCS, vol. 6110, pp. 523–552. Springer, Heidelberg (2010). https://doi.org/10.1007/978-3-642-13190-5_27
20. Chotard, J., Dufour Sans, E., Gay, R., Phan, D.H., Pointcheval, D.: Decentralized multi-client functional encryption for inner product. In: Peyrin, T., Galbraith, S. (eds.) ASIACRYPT 2018, Part II. LNCS, vol. 11273, pp. 703–732. Springer, Heidelberg (2018). https://doi.org/10.1007/978-3-030-03329-3_24
21. Datta, P., Dutta, R., Mukhopadhyay, S.: Functional encryption for inner product with full function privacy. In: Cheng, C.M., Chung, K.M., Persiano, G., Yang, B.Y. (eds.) PKC 2016, Part I. LNCS, vol. 9614, pp. 164–195. Springer, Heidelberg (2016). https://doi.org/10.1007/978-3-662-49384-7_7
22. Esgin, M.F., Steinfeld, R., Liu, J.K., Liu, D.: Lattice-based zero-knowledge proofs: new techniques for shorter and faster constructions and applications. In: Boldyreva, A., Micciancio, D. (eds.) CRYPTO 2019, Part I. LNCS, vol. 11692, pp. 115–146. Springer, Heidelberg (2019). https://doi.org/10.1007/978-3-030-26948-7_5
23. Gorbunov, S., Vaikuntanathan, V., Wee, H.: Attribute-based encryption for circuits. In: Boneh, D., Roughgarden, T., Feigenbaum, J. (eds.) 45th ACM STOC, pp. 545–554. ACM Press, June 2013. https://doi.org/10.1145/2488608.2488677
24. Goyal, R., Koppula, V., Waters, B.: Lockable obfuscation. In: Umans, C. (ed.) 58th FOCS, pp. 612–621. IEEE Computer Society Press, October 2017. https://doi.org/10.1109/FOCS.2017.62
25. Graham, R.L., Knuth, D.E., Patashnik, O.: Concrete Mathematics: A Foundation for Computer Science, 2nd edn. Addison-Wesley Longman Publishing Co., Inc., Boston (1994)
26. Hohenberger, S., Waters, B.: Online/offline attribute-based encryption. In: Krawczyk, H. (ed.) PKC 2014. LNCS, vol. 8383, pp. 293–310. Springer, Heidelberg (2014). https://doi.org/10.1007/978-3-642-54631-0_17
27. Jain, A., Lin, H., Matt, C., Sahai, A.: How to leverage hardness of constant-degree expanding polynomials over $\mathbb{R}$ to build $i\mathcal{O}$. In: Ishai, Y., Rijmen, V. (eds.) EUROCRYPT 2019, Part I. LNCS, vol. 11476, pp. 251–281. Springer, Cham (2019). https://doi.org/10.1007/978-3-030-17653-2_9
28. Lin, H.: Indistinguishability obfuscation from SXDH on 5-linear maps and locality-5 PRGs. In: Katz, J., Shacham, H. (eds.) CRYPTO 2017, Part I. LNCS, vol. 10401, pp. 599–629. Springer, Cham (2017). https://doi.org/10.1007/978-3-319-63688-7_20
29. Lin, H., Tessaro, S.: Indistinguishability obfuscation from trilinear maps and block-wise local PRGs. In: Katz, J., Shacham, H. (eds.) CRYPTO 2017, Part I. LNCS, vol. 10401, pp. 630–660. Springer, Heidelberg (2017). https://doi.org/10.1007/978-3-319-63688-7_21
30. Regev, O.: On lattices, learning with errors, random linear codes, and cryptography. In: Gabow, H.N., Fagin, R. (eds.) 37th ACM STOC, pp. 84–93. ACM Press, May 2005. https://doi.org/10.1145/1060590.1060603
31. Ünal, A.: Impossibility results for lattice-based functional encryption schemes. Cryptology ePrint Archive, Report 2020/163 (2020). https://eprint.iacr.org/2020/163
32. Wichs, D., Zirdelis, G.: Obfuscating compute-and-compare programs under LWE. In: Umans, C. (ed.) 58th FOCS, pp. 600–611. IEEE Computer Society Press, October 2017. https://doi.org/10.1109/FOCS.2017.61

Symmetric Cryptanalysis

Mind the Composition: Birthday Bound Attacks on EWCDMD and SoKAC21

Mridul Nandi$^{(\boxtimes)}$

Indian Statistical Institute, Kolkata, India
mridul.nandi@gmail.com

Abstract. In an early version of CRYPTO'17, Mennink and Neves proposed EWCDMD, a dual of EWCDM, and showed n-bit security, where n is the block size of the underlying block cipher. In CRYPTO'19, Chen et al. proposed permutation based design SoKAC21 and showed $2n/3$-bit security, where n is the input size of the underlying permutation. In this paper we show birthday bound attacks on EWCDMD and SoKAC21, invalidating their security claims. Both attacks exploit an inherent composition nature present in the constructions. Motivated by the above two attacks exploiting the composition nature, we consider some generic relevant composition based constructions of ideal primitives (possibly in the ideal permutation and random oracle model) and present birthday bound distinguishers for them. In particular, we demonstrate a birthday bound distinguisher against (1) a secret random permutation followed by a public random function and (2) composition of two secret random functions. Our distinguishers for SoKAC21 and EWCDMD are direct consequences of (1) and (2) respectively.

Keywords: PRF · Birthday bound · SoKAC21 · EWCDMD

1 Introduction

Motivated from DES block cipher design, Luby and Rackoff [LR88] formally analyzed a paradigm of constructing a pseudorandom permutation (PRP) from a pseudorandom function (PRF). However, the opposite trend is more popular due to wide availability of block ciphers (modeled to be pseudorandom permutations). So pseudorandom functions are traditionally built upon block ciphers. A straightforward application of the classical PRP-PRF switch [Sho04] gives security up to the birthday bound. However, in view of lightweight block ciphers [BPP+17,BKL+07] this bound may not be suitable. For example, a birthday bound secure PRF construction based on DES (64-bit block cipher) may be broken in approximately 2^{32} bits of data. In fact, Bhargavan and Leurent [BL16] performed practical attacks on TLS and OpenVPN when a 64-bit block cipher is used. To resist such attacks, several beyond birthday bound secure constructions have been proposed. This includes popular constructions such as sum of permutations (or SoP in short) [HWKS98,Pat08,DHT17,BN18b], truncation of

© International Association for Cryptologic Research 2020
A. Canteaut and Y. Ishai (Eds.): EUROCRYPT 2020, LNCS 12105, pp. 203–220, 2020.
https://doi.org/10.1007/978-3-030-45721-1_8

permutation [HWKS98,BN18a], EDM type constructions [CS16,CS18], Sum-ECBC [Yas10], Pmac_Plus [Yas11], 3Kf9 [ZWSW12], DbHtS [DDNP18] and 1kPmac_Plus [DDN+17a].

Apart from block cipher, the recent trend of using ideal (unkeyed) permutation has also motivated several pseudorandom functions from ideal permutation. Sponge-based PRF [BDPVA11b,CDH+12,BDPVA11a,ADMVA15] and Farfalle [BDH+17] are two such examples of PRF from ideal permutations. Recently, Chen et al. in Crypto 2019 [CLM19] considered permutation versions of SoP and EDM-dual. Depending on the choice of the keys and the permutation, some of the constructions provide birthday bound security, while some achieve beyond the birthday bound. They have also claimed tight security by showing some matching attacks.

1.1 Some Beyond Birthday Bound Constructions

Most of the constructions mentioned above are sequential in nature. Some of these constructions can be viewed as composition of two simpler constructions. For a permutation π, we denote $\pi(x) \oplus x$ as $\pi^{\oplus}(x)$ (this is known as Davies-Meyer function which has been used to define hash functions in case of public permutation). Let π_1 and π_2 be two independent keyed random permutations over $\{0,1\}^n$.

EDM and Its Dual. For a message $m \in \{0,1\}^n$, we define

$$\mathsf{EDM}(m) = \pi_2(\pi_1^{\oplus}(m)) \tag{1}$$

In other words, EDM (encrypted Davies-Meyer) is a composition function $\pi_2 \circ \pi_1^{\oplus}$. Here π_1 and π_2 are two independently keyed block ciphers (or random permutations). Dual version of EDM (denoted as EDMD) is defined as the composition in the other direction:

$$\mathsf{EDMD}(m) = \pi_1^{\oplus}(\pi_2(m)).$$

In [CS16,CS18] it has been proved that EDM is PRF secure up to $2^{2n/3}$ queries (i.e. $2n/3$-bit secure). Later in Crypto 2017 [DHT17], security of EDM is shown to be at least $3n/4$-bit using χ^2-method. Independently, Mennink and Neves in [MN17] proved that EDM and EDMD have n-bit PRF security using the generalized version of Patarin's mirror theory [Pat08]. However, the proofs of mirror theory are extremely sketchy and contain several unverified gaps.

EWCDM and Its Dual. The previous constructions can only process n-bit message. With the help of universal hash $\mathscr{H}$, one can extend the message space, using the Wegman Carter paradigm [WC81]. We now recall the construction EWCDM [CS16] and its dual version EWCDMD [MN17] (see Fig. 1). For a nonce (which should be fresh for every execution of MAC) $\nu \in \{0,1\}^n$ and a message $m \in \mathscr{M}$, we define

$$\mathsf{EWCDM}(\nu, m) = \pi_2(\pi_1^{\oplus}(\nu) \oplus \mathscr{H}(m)) \tag{2}$$

$$\mathsf{EWCDMD}(\nu, m) = \pi_2^{\oplus}(\pi_1(\nu) \oplus \mathscr{H}(m)) \tag{3}$$

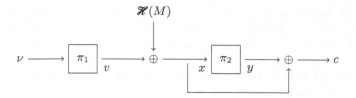

$$\mathscr{H}(M)$$

Fig. 1. EWCDMD: Wegman-Carter followed by Davies-Meyer.

In [CS16], Cogliati and Seurin proved $2n/3$-bit PRF (pseudorandom function) and MAC (message authentication) security for EWCDM in a nonce respecting model.

SoKAC21. So far we have considered constructions based on secret keyed primitives. Very recently, Chen et al. in CRYPTO 2019 [CLM19] proposed a pseudorandom function, called SoKAC21 (see Fig. 2), based on ideal public permutations. It is designed for small message space and claimed to be achieving beyond birthday bound security. For an n-bit message m, and two ideal permutations $\pi_1^{\text{pub}}, \pi_2^{\text{pub}}$, and an n-bit secret key K, we define

$$\text{SoKAC21}(K, m) = \pi_2^{\text{pub}}\big(\pi_1^{\text{pub}}(m \oplus K) \oplus K\big) \oplus \pi_1^{\text{pub}}(m \oplus K) \oplus K \qquad (4)$$

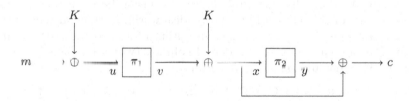

Fig. 2. SoKAC21 - Sum of Key Alternating Cipher with a single key.

This construction can be viewed as a composition of Even Mansour followed by Davies-Meyer. We note that an equivalent view (due to which it is named sum of key alternating cipher) of the above construction is $\pi_2(v \oplus K) \oplus \pi_1(m \oplus K) \oplus K$ where $v = \pi_1(m \oplus K)$.

1.2 Composition Constructions and Our Contribution

All the constructions mentioned in the previous subsection can be viewed as composition of ideal primitives or some functions derived from ideal primitives.

PUBLIC AND SECRET IDEAL PRIMITIVES. Let $\gamma \leftarrow_\$ \text{Func}(n)$ and $\pi \leftarrow_\$ \text{Perm}(n)$ denote n-bit random function and random permutation respectively. A random function or permutation is called *public* if adversary has direct access to these primitives or their inverses whenever exist, in addition with concerned constructions based on these primitives. In this case we call the adversarial model ideal function or ideal permutation model. We denote the public random function and permutation as γ^{pub} and π^{pub} respectively.

When the ideal primitives are secret (i.e. cannot accessed directly by an adversary), we denote them as γ^{sec} and π^{sec}. Note that secret primitives appears when a keyed function (e.g. a keyed compression function) or a keyed permutation (e.g., a block cipher) is replaced by the ideal counterpart through hybrid argument.

We use subscript notation to denote independent copies of the primitives. For example, π_1, π_2 are two independent random permutations (either secret or public which would be understood from the superscript notation).

Our Contribution. In this paper, we first analyze the PRF or PRP constructions $g \circ f$ where

$$f, \ g \in \{\gamma^{\mathsf{pub}}, \gamma^{\mathsf{sec}}, \pi^{\mathsf{sec}}\}.$$

Due to a trivial reason[1] we exclude π^{pub}. Moreover, we must assume that at least one of the functions is secret. In this paper, we show birthday bound PRF attack on (1) $\gamma_2^{\mathsf{sec}} \circ \gamma_1^{\mathsf{sec}}$ and (2) $\gamma^{\mathsf{pub}} \circ \pi^{\mathsf{sec}}$. The idea behind the attacks for these constructions are simple. For $\gamma_2^{\mathsf{sec}} \circ \gamma_1^{\mathsf{sec}}$ we expect more collisions than perfect random function. In other words, we have higher probability of realizing collision on $\gamma_2^{\mathsf{sec}} \circ \gamma_1^{\mathsf{sec}}$ than that of γ^{sec}. For the second construction, we observe the outputs of public function γ^{pub} and outputs of $\gamma^{\mathsf{pub}} \circ \pi^{\mathsf{sec}}$ (or γ^{sec} in case of ideal oracle). We show that the probability of collision between these two lists is higher in case of the real world than the ideal world. In the real construction, collision can happen in two ways – (1) an output of π^{sec} collides with an input of public function call γ^{pub}, (2) accidental collision (which happens in the final outputs without having collision among inputs).

BIRTHDAY ATTACK ON EWCDMD. We exploit the attack idea of $\gamma_2^{\mathsf{sec}} \circ \gamma_1^{\mathsf{sec}}$ to describe a PRF attack against EWCDMD in query complexity $2^{n/2}$. In an early version of CRYPTO 2017[2], Mennink and Neves [MN17] showed almost n-bit PRF security for EWCDMD. So our result invalidates the initial claim of the construction.

The main idea of the attack is simple. EWCDMD can be viewed as a composition of two keyed *non-injective functions* (and so it follows birthday paradox), namely $\pi_2^{\oplus}$ and a function f mapping (ν, m) to $\pi_1(\nu) \oplus \mathscr{H}(m)$. Thus, we expect that the collision probability of the composition $\pi_2^{\oplus} \circ f$ is almost double of the collision probability for the random function. So, by observing a collision we can

---

[1] Note that if the outer function g is π^{pub} or the inner function f is π^{pub} then the composition is essentially reduced to a single primitive. An adversary can always uncover π^{pub} by making calls to π^{pub} and $(\pi^{\mathsf{pub}})^{-1}$.

[2] The early version can be accessed on ePrint 2017/473 posted on 28-May-2017. This paper was initially accepted in CRYPTO 2017. Later, after finding the flaw in the analysis, authors removed this analysis from the final proceeding.

distinguish EWCDMD from a random function. Note that EWCDM is a composition of a permutation and a non-injective keyed function. Hence our observation is not applicable to it.

BIRTHDAY ATTACK ON SoKAC21. Similarly, we exploit the attack idea of $\gamma^{\mathsf{pub}} \circ \pi^{\mathsf{sec}}$ to have birthday bound PRF attack on SoKAC21. In this construction we have $\pi_2^{\oplus}$ instead of public random function. However, with a careful analysis (and using the recent result on sum of permutation) we can have birthday attack on SoKAC21. This again violates the beyond birthday security claimed in [CLM19].

2   Preliminaries

Notation. For $n \in \mathbb{N}$, $[n]$ denotes the set $\{1, 2, \ldots, n\}$. For $n, k \in \mathbb{N}$, such that $n \geq k$, we define the falling factorial $(n)_k := n!/(n-k)! = n(n-1) \cdots (n-k+1)$. For $a \in \mathbb{N}$, an a-tuple $(x_1, x_2, \ldots, x_a)$ and also a multi-set $\{x_1, \ldots, x_a\}$ is simply denoted as x^a (this should be clear from the context). For any set $\mathcal{X}$, $(\mathcal{X})_a$ denotes the set of all x^a so that $x_1, \ldots, x_a$ are distinct. We call all those x^a element-wise distinct. Note, $|(\mathcal{X})_q| = (|\mathcal{X}|)_q$.

The set of all functions from $\mathcal{X}$ to $\mathcal{Y}$ is denoted as $\mathsf{Func}(\mathcal{X}, \mathcal{Y})$ and the set of all permutations over $\mathcal{X}$ is denoted as $\mathsf{Perm}(\mathcal{X})$. We use shorthand notations $\mathsf{Perm}(n)$ (or $\mathsf{Func}(n)$) to denote the set of all permutations (or functions respectively) from $\{0, 1\}^n$ to itself.

For a finite set $\mathcal{X}$, $\mathsf{X} \leftarrow_{\$} \mathcal{X}$ denotes the uniform and random sampling of X from $\mathcal{X}$. We write $\mathsf{X}_1, \ldots, \mathsf{X}_a \leftarrow_{\$} \mathcal{D}$ when X_i's are chosen uniformly and independently from the set $\mathcal{D}$. In other words, $\mathsf{X}_1, \ldots, \mathsf{X}_a$ is a random with replacement sample. We write $\mathsf{X}_1, \ldots, \mathsf{X}_a \leftarrow_{\mathsf{wor}} \mathcal{D}$ when X_i's are chosen randomly from $\mathcal{D}$ in without replacement manner. More precisely, for all element-wise distinct $x^a \in (\mathcal{D})_a$,

$$\Pr(\mathsf{X}_1 = x_1, \ldots, \mathsf{X}_a = x_a) = \frac{1}{(|\mathcal{D}|)_a}.$$

2.1   Statistical Distance

Let X, Y be two random variables over a sample space $\mathcal{S}$. Then the statistical distance between X and Y is defined as

$$\mathsf{D}(\mathsf{X}, \mathsf{Y}) := \frac{1}{2} \sum_{a \in \mathcal{S}} |\Pr(\mathsf{X} = a) - \Pr(\mathsf{Y} = a)|.$$

An equivalent definition of statistical distance is the following:

$$\mathsf{D}(\mathsf{X}, \mathsf{Y}) = \max_{E \subseteq \mathcal{S}} |\Pr(\mathsf{X} \in E) - \Pr(\mathsf{Y} \in E)|.$$

To see why it is an equivalent definition, we first note that the maximization holds for $E_1 = \{a \in \mathcal{S} : \Pr(\mathsf{X} = a) > \Pr(\mathsf{Y} = a)\}$. From the definition of E_1, we can write the sum $\sum_{a \in \mathcal{S}} |\Pr(\mathsf{X} = a) - \Pr(\mathsf{Y} = a)|$ (after splitting over E_1 and E_1^c) as

$$\sum_{a \in E_1} (\Pr(\mathsf{X} = a) - \Pr(\mathsf{Y} = a)) + \sum_{a \in E_1^c} \Pr(\mathsf{Y} = a) - \Pr(\mathsf{X} = a)$$

$$= \Pr(\mathsf{X} \in E_1) - \Pr(\mathsf{Y} \in E_1) + \Pr(\mathsf{Y} \in E_1^c) - \Pr(\mathsf{X} \in E_1^c)$$

$$= 2(\Pr(\mathsf{X} \in E_1) - \Pr(\mathsf{Y} \in E_1)).$$

Thus we have established the equivalence.

Lemma 1 (replacement lemma). *Let* X, Y *be two random variables over a sample space* $\mathcal{S}$ *and* Z *be independent with* X *and* Y *sampled from* $\mathcal{T}$. *Let* $E \subseteq \mathcal{S} \times \mathcal{T}$ *then*

$$|Pr((\mathsf{X}, \mathsf{Z}) \in E) - Pr((\mathsf{Y}, \mathsf{Z}) \in E)| \leq \mathsf{D}(\mathsf{X}, \mathsf{Y}). \tag{5}$$

Proof. For every z, let $E_z = \{s \in \mathcal{S} : (s, z) \in E\}$. Then by independence, we have

1. $p_1 := \Pr((\mathsf{X}, \mathsf{Z}) \in E) = \sum_z \Pr(\mathsf{Z} = z) \cdot \Pr(\mathsf{X} \in E_z)$ and similarly,
2. $p_2 := \Pr((\mathsf{Y}, \mathsf{Z}) \in E) = \sum_z \Pr(\mathsf{Z} = z) \cdot \Pr(\mathsf{Y} \in E_z)$.

Hence,

$$|p_1 - p_2| = |\sum_z \Pr(\mathsf{Z} = z) \cdot \Pr(\mathsf{X} \in E_z) - \sum_z \Pr(\mathsf{Z} = z) \cdot \Pr(\mathsf{Y} \in E_z)|$$

$$\leq \sum_z \Pr(\mathsf{Z} = z) \cdot |\Pr(\mathsf{X} \in E_z) - \Pr(\mathsf{Y} \in E_z)|$$

$$\leq \sum_z \Pr(\mathsf{Z} = z) \cdot \mathsf{D}(\mathsf{X}, \mathsf{Y})$$

$$= \mathsf{D}(\mathsf{X}, \mathsf{Y})$$

2.2   Sum of Without Replacement Samples

Let $\mathcal{D}$ be a set of size N. In [DHT17] it has been proved that sum of two independent without replacement sample almost behaves like one with replacement sample. More precisely, let $\mathsf{X}_1, \ldots, \mathsf{X}_a \leftarrow_{\mathrm{wor}} \mathcal{D}$, $\mathsf{Y}_1, \ldots, \mathsf{Y}_a \leftarrow_{\mathrm{wor}} \mathcal{D}$, $\mathsf{Z}_1, \ldots, \mathsf{Z}_a \leftarrow_\$ \mathcal{D}$ and X^a, Y^a are independent. Define $\mathsf{W}_i = \mathsf{X}_i \oplus \mathsf{Y}_i$ for all $i \in [a]$. Then, in [DHT17] it is shown[3] that

$$\mathsf{D}(\mathsf{Z}^a, \mathsf{W}^a) \leq \frac{4a}{N}. \tag{6}$$

Due to Lemma 1, we can simply replace sum of random without replacement sample involved in an event by the random sample at the cost of probability $4a/N$. We use this idea of replacement while we analyze SoKAC21 construction.

---

[3] The original bound is $\frac{1.5a}{N} + \frac{3\sqrt{a}}{N}$ which is less than the bound we consider here for all $a \geq 3$. For $a = 2$, one can easily establish the bound.

2.3   Security Definitions

RANDOM FUNCTION AND RANDOM PERMUTATION. $\gamma \leftarrow_\$ \mathsf{Func}(\mathcal{X}, \mathcal{Y})$ is said to be the random function from the set $\mathcal{X}$ to $\mathcal{Y}$. Similarly, $\pi \leftarrow_\$ \mathsf{Perm}(\mathcal{Y})$ is said to be the random permutation over the set $\mathcal{Y}$. In this paper we mostly use the set $\mathcal{X} = \mathcal{Y} = \{0,1\}^n$.

KEYED FUNCTION AND PERMUTATION. A keyed function with key space $\mathcal{K}$, domain $\mathcal{X}$ and range $\mathcal{Y}$ is a function $\mathsf{F} : \mathcal{K} \times \mathcal{X} \to \mathcal{Y}$ and we denote $\mathsf{F}(K, X)$ by $\mathsf{F}_K(X)$. Similarly, a keyed permutation with key space $\mathcal{K}$ and domain $\mathcal{X}$ is a mapping $\mathsf{E} : \mathcal{K} \times \mathcal{X} \to \mathcal{X}$ such that for all key $K \in \mathcal{K}$, $X \mapsto \mathsf{E}(K, X)$ is a permutation over $\mathcal{X}$ and we denote $\mathsf{E}_K(X)$ for $\mathsf{E}(K, X)$.

PRF. Given an oracle algorithm A with oracle access to a function from $\mathcal{X}$ to $\mathcal{Y}$, making at most q queries, running time at most t and outputting a single bit, we define the prf-advantage of A against the family of keyed functions F as

$$\mathbf{Adv}_\mathsf{F}^{\mathrm{PRF}}(\mathsf{A}) := |\Pr(K \leftarrow_\$ \mathcal{K} : \mathsf{A}^{\mathsf{F}_K} = 1) - \Pr(\gamma \leftarrow_\$ \mathsf{Func}(\mathcal{X}, \mathcal{Y}) : \mathsf{A}^\gamma = 1)|.$$

PRP. Given an oracle algorithm A with oracle access to a permutation of $\mathcal{X}$, making at most q queries, running time at most t and outputting a single bit, we define the prp-advantage of A against the family of keyed permutations E as

$$\mathbf{Adv}_\mathsf{E}^{\mathrm{PRP}}(\mathsf{A}) := |\Pr(K \leftarrow_\$ \mathcal{K} : \mathsf{A}^{\mathsf{E}_K} = 1) - \Pr(\pi \leftarrow_\$ \mathsf{Perm}(\mathcal{X}) : \mathsf{A}^\pi = 1)|.$$

PRF AND PRP IN IDEAL MODEL. Some keyed constructions uses ideal public primitive such as a random function and a random permutation. Let $P_1, \ldots, P_r$ be such all primitives used for a keyed construction $\mathsf{F}_K := \mathsf{F}_K^{P_1, \ldots, P_r}$. Let $P_i^\pm$ denotes both P_i and its inverse P_i^{-1}. We define PRF and PRP-advantage in the public primitive model as follows.

$$\mathbf{Adv}_\mathsf{F}^{\mathrm{PRF}}(\mathsf{A}) := |\Pr(\mathsf{A}^{\mathsf{F}_K, P_1^\pm, \ldots, P_r^\pm} = 1) - \Pr(\mathsf{A}^{\gamma, P_1^\pm, \ldots, P_r^\pm} = 1)|.$$

In the above two probabilities, $K, \gamma, P_1, \ldots, P_r$ are all independently drawn. Similarly, we define PRP-advantage in public model as

$$\mathbf{Adv}_\mathsf{F}^{\mathrm{PRP}}(\mathsf{A}) := |\Pr(\mathsf{A}^{\mathsf{F}_K, P_1^\pm, \ldots, P_r^\pm} = 1) - \Pr(\mathsf{A}^{\pi, P_1^\pm, \ldots, P_r^\pm} = 1)|.$$

ALMOST XOR UNIVERSAL HASH FUNCTION. A keyed hash function $\mathcal{H}_K : \mathcal{D} \to \mathcal{R}$ is called ϵ-AXU (almost xor universal) if $\Pr(\mathcal{H}_K(m) \oplus \mathcal{H}_K(m') = \delta) \leq \epsilon$ for all $m \neq m'$ and for all δ. Here the probability is computed under randomness of the key chosen uniformly from the key space.

3   Collision Probability

Let $\mathscr{D}$ be a set of size N. We quickly recall collision probability for a uniform random sample $X_1, \ldots, X_a \leftarrow_\$ \mathscr{D}$. For any positive integers $a \leq N$, we write $\mathsf{dp}_N(a) := \frac{(N)_a}{N^a}$ and $\mathsf{cp}_N(a) := 1 - \mathsf{dp}_N(a)$. When N is understood from the context, we skip the notation N. If a is very small compared to N (i.e. $a/N \approx 0$), a precise estimation of $\mathsf{dp}_N(a)$ is $e^{-a(a-1)/2N}$. This follows from the approximation $1 - \epsilon \approx e^{-\epsilon}$ for very small positive ϵ. In fact the error term $|e^{-\epsilon} - (1 - \epsilon)|$ is in the order $O(\epsilon^2)$.

Given a list $\mathscr{L}$ of elements $x_1, \ldots, x_a$, we write $\mathsf{Dist}(\mathscr{L})$ if x_i's are distinct. Otherwise, we write $\mathsf{Coll}(\mathscr{L})$.

Lemma 2 (collision probability). *Let $\mathscr{D}$ be a set of size N. Let $X_1, \ldots, X_a \leftarrow_\$ \mathscr{D}$ and let $\mathscr{L}$ denote the list containing X_i's, $1 \leq i \leq a$. Then,*

1. $Pr(\mathsf{Dist}(\mathscr{L})) = \mathsf{dp}_N(a)$.
2. $Pr(\mathsf{Coll}(\mathscr{L})) = \mathsf{cp}_N(a) \leq a^2/2N$.

We skip the proof as it is straightforward conclusion from the definition. The second statement follows from the union bound.

Now we compute probability for having a collision between two lists. We say that there is a collision between two lists, denoted as $\mathsf{LColl}(\mathscr{L}_1, \mathscr{L}_2)$ if the lists are not disjoint.

Lemma 3 (list-collision probability for without replacement sample). *Let $X_1, \ldots, X_p \leftarrow_{wor} \mathscr{D}$ and $Y_1, \ldots, Y_q \leftarrow_{wor} \mathscr{D}$ such that X^p and Y^q arc independent. Then,*

$$Pr(\mathsf{LColl}(X^p, Y^q)) = 1 - \frac{(N - p)_q}{(N)_q}$$

Proof. We compute the complement event, i.e., X^p and Y^q are disjoint. The conditional probability of the complement event conditioning on $X^p = x^p$ is $\frac{(N-p)_q}{(N)_q}$. This can be easily seen as the number of choices of Y^q is exactly $(N-p)_q$. As the conditional probability is independent of choice of x^p, the unconditional probability is also same as $\frac{(N-p)_q}{(N)_q}$. This completes the proof.   □

We denote the probability $1 - \frac{(N-p)_q}{(N)_q}$ as $\mathsf{lcp}_N^{wor}(p, q)$ (or simply $\mathsf{lcp}^{wor}(p, q)$ whenever N is understood from the context).

When $\mathscr{L}_1 := X^p$ and $\mathscr{L}_2 := Y^q$, where $X_1, \ldots, X_p, Y_1, \ldots, Y_q \leftarrow_\$ \mathscr{D}$, we denote the list-collision probability $Pr(\mathsf{LColl}(\mathscr{L}_1, \mathscr{L}_2))$ as $\mathsf{lcp}_N^\$(p, q)$ (or simply $\mathsf{lcp}^\$(p, q)$ whenever N is understood from the context). Here $\mathscr{D}$ is a set of size N.

Lemma 4 (list-collision probability for random samples). *For all positive integers p, q, we have*

$$|\mathsf{lcp}_N^\$(p, q) - 1 + \left(1 - \frac{q}{N}\right)^p| \leq 2\mathsf{cp}_N(p). \tag{7}$$

(When p is small compared to $\sqrt{N}$, the collision probability $\mathsf{cp}_N(p)$ is almost zero and in that case, the above result says that $1 - \left(1 - \frac{p}{N}\right)^q$ is a very good approximation of $\mathsf{lcp}_N^\$(p, q)$.)

Proof. Let $X_1, \ldots, X_p, Y_1, \ldots, Y_q \leftarrow_{\$} \mathscr{D}$ and E denote the event $\mathsf{Dist}(X^p)$. So $\Pr(E) = \mathsf{dp}_N(p)$. Fix any distinct x^p. Then, the list collision $\mathsf{LColl}(x^p, Y^q)$ holds with probability $1 - (1 - \frac{p}{N})^q$. Now,

$$\Pr(\mathsf{LColl}(X^p, Y^q)) = \Pr(\mathsf{LColl}(X^p, Y^q) \wedge E) + \Pr(\mathsf{LColl}(X^p, Y^q) \wedge E^c)$$

$$= \sum_{x^p \in (\mathscr{D})_p} \Pr(\mathsf{LColl}(x^p, Y^q) \wedge X^p = x^p) + \Pr(\mathsf{LColl}(X^p, Y^q) \wedge E^c)$$

$$= (1 - (1 - \frac{p}{N})^q) \times \sum_{x^p \in (\mathscr{D})_p} \Pr(X^p = x^p) + \Pr(\mathsf{LColl}(X^p, Y^q) \wedge E^c)$$

$$= (1 - (1 - \frac{p}{N})^q) \times \Pr(E) + \Pr(\mathsf{LColl}(X^p, Y^q) \wedge E^c)$$

$$= (1 - (1 - \frac{p}{N})^q) \times (1 - \Pr(E^c)) + \Pr(\mathsf{LColl}(X^p, Y^q) \wedge E^c)$$

Note that in our notation, $\Pr(\mathsf{LColl}(X^p, Y^q)) = \mathsf{lcp}_N^{\$}(p, q)$. Hence,

$$|\mathsf{lcp}_N^{\$}(p, q) - 1 + (1 - \frac{q}{N})^p| = |(1 - (1 - \frac{p}{N})^q) \times \Pr(E^c) + \Pr(\mathsf{LColl}(X^p, Y^q) \wedge E^c)|$$

$$\leq 2 \cdot \Pr(E^c).$$

The lemma follows from the definition that $\Pr(E^c) = \mathsf{cp}_N(p)$.   □

4   Birthday Attack on Composition of Ideal Primitives

In this section, we analyze compositions of ideal primitives. We recall that $\gamma \leftarrow_{\$} \mathsf{Func}(n)$ and $\pi \leftarrow_{\$} \mathsf{Perm}(n)$ denote n-bit random function and random permutation respectively. We follow the notations described in Sect. 1.2. Here $\equiv$ is used to mean two systems equivalent (i.e. the probabilistic behavior of interaction for any adversary would be same for both).

1. It is easy to verify that $\pi^{\mathsf{sec}} \circ \gamma^{\mathsf{sec}} \equiv \gamma^{\mathsf{sec}} \circ \pi^{\mathsf{sec}} \equiv \gamma$ and $\pi_1^{\mathsf{sec}} \circ \pi_2^{\mathsf{sec}} \equiv \pi$. In [MS15] $\pi^{\mathsf{sec}} \circ \pi^{\mathsf{sec}}$ (iterated random permutation) has been analyzed and it almost behaves as π^{sec} with a maximum distinguishing advantage $O(q/2^n)$ where q is the number of queries. Authors of [MS15, Nan15] have actually analyzed a more general construction $\pi^{\mathsf{sec}} \circ \cdots \circ \pi^{\mathsf{sec}}$ (applied r times).

2. In [BDD+17], $\gamma^{\mathsf{sec}} \circ \gamma^{\mathsf{sec}}$ (iterated random function) has also been analyzed. This is equivalent to γ^{sec} with a maximum distinguishing advantage $O(q^2/2^n)$. Authors of [BDD+17] actually analyzed more general construction $\gamma^{\mathsf{sec}} \circ \cdots \circ \gamma^{\mathsf{sec}}$ (applied r times). The main idea behind the distinguishing attack is that the collision probability of an iterated random function is more probable than that of a random function.

   Using a similar argument, we can show that $\gamma_2^{\mathsf{sec}} \circ \gamma_1^{\mathsf{sec}}$ can be distinguished from γ^{sec} by making $2^{n/2}$ queries. Let $x_1, \ldots, x_q$ be q queries and let $y_1, \ldots, y_q$ be the responses. In case of the real world, $y_i = \gamma_2^{\mathsf{sec}}(z_i)$ where $z_i = \gamma_1^{\mathsf{sec}}(x_i)$. Let $\mu := \mathsf{cp}_{2^n}(q)$. Now,

$$\Pr(\mathsf{Coll}(y^q)) = \Pr(\mathsf{Coll}(z^q)) + \Pr(\mathsf{Coll}(y^q) \mid \mathsf{Dist}(z^q)) \times \Pr(\mathsf{Dist}(z^q))$$

$$= \mu + \mu(1 - \mu)$$

Let $\mathscr{A}$ return 1 if it observes a collision among outputs. Thus, the distinguishing advantage of the adversary is at least $\mu(1 - \mu)$. When $q = 2^{n/2}$, $\mathsf{cp}(q) \approx 1 - \frac{1}{\sqrt{e}}$ and hence advantage is $\frac{1}{\sqrt{e}} \times (1 - \frac{1}{\sqrt{e}})$ which is at least 0.2. One can also choose q (which should be again $O(2^{n/2})$) such that $\mu \approx 1/2$ and hence the advantage would be about 0.25.

Same attack can be applied to $\gamma^{\mathsf{sec}} \circ \gamma^{\mathsf{pub}}$ and $\gamma^{\mathsf{pub}} \circ \gamma^{\mathsf{sec}}$ as if the adversary does not take an advantage of accessing the public random function γ^{pub}.

3. Let us consider the construction $\pi^{\mathsf{sec}} \circ \gamma^{\mathsf{pub}}$. An adversary $\mathscr{A}$ first finds a collision pair (m, m') of γ^{pub} by making $2^{n/2}$ queries to it. Then, $\pi^{\mathsf{sec}} \circ \gamma^{\mathsf{pub}}(m) = \pi^{\mathsf{sec}} \circ \gamma^{\mathsf{pub}}(m')$. Clearly, in the ideal world, $\gamma(m) = \gamma(m')$ holds with probability 2^{-n}. So $\mathscr{A}$ is a PRF-distinguisher against $\pi^{\mathsf{sec}} \circ \gamma^{\mathsf{pub}}$ making about $2^{n/2}$ queries to the public random function. The same attack is also applied to $\gamma^{\mathsf{sec}} \circ \gamma^{\mathsf{pub}}$.

4. Although $\gamma^{\mathsf{sec}} \circ \pi^{\mathsf{sec}}$ is equivalent to a random function, we have the following birthday bound complexity PRF-attack on $\gamma^{\mathsf{pub}} \circ \pi^{\mathsf{sec}}$ (replacing the outer layer of secret random function by public random function). Here we exploit the public access of γ^{pub} (since otherwise it is equivalent to a random function) (Fig. 3).

PRF Distinguisher $\mathscr{A}^{\mathcal{O}, \gamma^{\mathsf{pub}}}$

1: $x_1, \ldots, x_p \xleftarrow{\mathsf{wor}} \{0, 1\}^n$

2: **queries** $x_1, \ldots, x_p$ **to** γ^{pub}

3: $y_i = \gamma^{\mathsf{pub}}(x_i), i \in [p]$ **be the responses**

4: **for** $i \in [q], i$ **is queried to** $\mathcal{O}$

5: **let** $c_i = \mathcal{O}(i), i \in [q]$ **be the responses**

6: **if** $\exists i, j, y_i = c_j$

7: **return** 1

8: **else**

9: **return** 0

Fig. 3. Distinguisher for composition construction $\gamma^{\mathsf{pub}} \circ \pi^{\mathsf{sec}}$.

Let E denote the event that there are i, j such that $y_i = c_j$.

IDEAL WORLD: In the ideal world we have $c_1, \ldots, c_q, y_1, \ldots, y_p \xleftarrow{\$} \{0, 1\}^n$. So

$$\Pr(E) = \mathsf{lcp}^{\$}(p, q) = \mu \text{ (say).}$$

REAL WORLD: In the real world, let $z_i = \pi^{\mathsf{sec}}(i)$. So $c_i = \gamma^{\mathsf{pub}}(z_i)$. Thus, $z_1, \ldots, z_q \xleftarrow{\mathsf{wor}} \{0, 1\}^n$ independent of x^p. Now, we write the event E as the disjoint union (denoted as $\sqcup$)

$$\mathsf{LColl}(z^q, x^p) \sqcup \left(\neg \mathsf{LColl}(z^q, x^p) \wedge \mathsf{LColl}(c^q, y^p) \right).$$

Given that z^q is distinct from x^p, we have $c_1, \ldots, c_q, y_1, \ldots, y_p \xleftarrow{\$} \{0,1\}^n$. Now, $\Pr(\mathsf{LColl}(z^q, x^p)) = \mathsf{lcp}^{wor}(p, q) := \mu_1$ (say). Then,

$$\Pr(E) = \mu_1 + (1 - \mu_1)\mu.$$

So, the distinguishing advantage of our adversary is $\mu_1(1 - \mu)$. By Lemma 3 and Lemma 4, the distinguishing advantage is at least

$$(1 - \frac{(2^n - p)_q}{(2^n)_q}) \times ((1 - \frac{p}{2^n})^q - 2\mathsf{cp}_{2^n}(q)). \tag{8}$$

Further, we have

$$\frac{(2^n - p)_q}{(2^n)_q} = \prod_{i=0}^{q-1} (1 - \frac{p}{2^n - i})$$

$$\leq (1 - \frac{p}{2^n})^q$$

$$\leq 1 - \frac{pq}{2^n} + \frac{pq^2}{2^{2n+1}}.$$

The last inequality follows from the following fact:

$$(1 - x)^q \leq 1 - \binom{q}{1} x + \binom{q}{2} x^2, \quad 0 \leq x \leq 1.$$

We also have $(1 - \frac{p}{2^n})^q \geq 1 - \frac{pq}{2^n}$. By substituting the above inequalities in Eq. 8, the distinguishing advantage is at least

$$(1 - \frac{pq}{2^n} - \frac{q^2}{2^n}) \times \frac{pq}{2^n} \times (1 - \frac{q}{2^{n+1}}).$$

Now if we choose $p = q = \sqrt{2^n/3}$ then the advantage is at least $\frac{1}{9}(1 - \frac{1}{3 \times 2^{n/2}})$. This value is almost $1/9$ for a reasonably large n.

5 Birthday Attack on SoKAC21

In the previous section we have shown the basic attacks on composition of ideal primitives. A similar idea can be used for composition of constructions which are not ideal. However, a more dedicated analysis of advantage computation is required. In this section we show a birthday attack on a recent proposal SoKAC21. In the following section we show birthday attack of Dual EWCDM.

We first recall the definition of SoKAC21 (see Fig. 2 and Eq. 4 for details). It uses two public n-bit random permutations π_1^{pub} and π_2^{pub}. Given an n-bit key K, an n-bit input m, we define SoKAC21 output as

$$F_K(m) := \pi_2^{\mathsf{pub}}(x) \oplus x, \quad \text{where } x = \pi_1^{\mathsf{pub}}(m \oplus K) \oplus K.$$

Our attack does not exploit public queries to π_1^{pub} and hence $\pi_1^{\mathsf{pub}}(m \oplus K) \oplus K$ behaves identically to a secret random permutation $\pi^{\mathsf{sec}}(m)$. Let $\mathsf{DM}(x) := \pi_2^{\mathsf{pub}}(x) \oplus x$ (Davies-Meyer construction based on a public random permutation). So SoKAC21 is actually the composition $\mathsf{DM} \circ \pi^{\mathsf{sec}}$. However, DM is not perfect random function. But if we choose the inputs of DM in a without replacement manner, the output of DM can be viewed as the sum of two WOR samples and hence it is very close to uniform distribution. We use this principle along with the attack strategy as described in the previous section for the composition construction $\gamma^{\mathsf{pub}} \circ \pi^{\mathsf{sec}}$. We simply write π^{pub} instead of π_2^{pub} and π^{sec} instead of the Even-Mansour construction on π_1^{pub} (Fig. 4).

PRF Distinguisher $\mathscr{A}^{\mathscr{O}, \pi^{\mathsf{pub}}}$

1: $\quad x_1, \ldots, x_p \xleftarrow{\mathsf{wor}} \{0,1\}^n$

2: $\quad$ queries $x_1, \ldots, x_p$ to π^{pub}

3: $\quad x_i' = \pi^{\mathsf{pub}}(x_i), i \in [p]$ be the responses

4: $\quad$ let $y_i = x_i' \oplus x_i$

5: $\quad$ for $i \in [q], i$ is queried to $\mathscr{O}$

6: $\quad$ let $c_i = \mathscr{O}(i), i \in [q]$ be the responses

7: $\quad$ if $\exists i, j, y_i = c_j$ return 1

8: $\quad$ else   return 0

Fig. 4. Distinguisher for SoKAC21 which can be viewed as the composition construction $\mathsf{DM} \circ \pi^{\mathsf{sec}}$.

We define the event $E := \mathsf{LColl}(c^q, y^p)$ (i.e. there exists i, j such that $y_i = c_j$).

IDEAL WORLD: In the ideal world $c_1, \ldots, c_q \xleftarrow{\$} \{0,1\}^n$. Moreover, y_i is defined as sum of two without replacement sample. By Eq. 6, y_i's are close to a with replacement sample $y_1', \ldots, y_p'$ with the statistical distance at most $4p/2^n$. Moreover y_i''s are independent of c^q. Let $\mu := \mathsf{Pr}(\mathsf{LColl}(c^q, (y')^p)) = \mathsf{lcp}^{\$}(p, q)$. So by using Lemma 1,

$$\mathsf{Pr}(E) = \mathsf{Pr}(\mathsf{LColl}(c^q, y^p)) \leq \mathsf{lcp}^{\$}(p, q) + 4p/2^n.$$

REAL WORLD: In the real world, let $z_i = \pi^{\mathsf{sec}}(i)$. So $c_i = \pi^{\mathsf{pub}}(z_i) \oplus z_i$ for all i and $z_1, \ldots, z_q \xleftarrow{\mathsf{wor}} \{0,1\}^n$ independent of x^p. Now, the event E can be written as a disjoint union $E_1 \sqcup E_2$ where

1. E_1 is $\mathsf{LColl}(z^q, x^p)$ and
2. E_2 is $\neg\mathsf{LColl}(z^q, x^p) \wedge \mathsf{LColl}(c^q, y^p)$.

Let $\mathsf{Pr}(E_1) = \mathsf{lcp}^{wor}(p, q) = \mu_1$ (say).

Now, we compute the probability of the event E_2 which is same as $E_1^c \wedge$ LColl(c^q, y^p). Given that z^q is distinct from x^p (i.e. E_1^c holds) we have

$$z_1, \ldots, z_q, x_1, \ldots, x_p \leftarrow_{\text{wor}} \{0,1\}^n.$$

As $c_i = \text{DM}(z_i)$ and $y_i = \text{DM}(x_i)$, c_i's and y_i's are almost uniformly distributed. More precisely, for $c'_1, \ldots, c'_q, y'_1, \ldots, y'_p \leftarrow_{\$} \{0,1\}^n$,

$$\text{D}((c^q, y^p); ((c')^q, (y')^p)) \leq 4(p+q)/2^n.$$

So by Lemma 1, $\Pr(E_2) \geq (1 - \mu_1) \times (\mu - 4(p+q)/2^n)$ where $\mu = \text{lcp}^{\$}(p,q)$. Now,

$$\Pr(E) = \Pr(E_1) + \Pr(E_2)$$
$$\geq \mu_1 + (1 - \mu_1)(\mu - \frac{4(p+q)}{2^n}).$$

So, subtracting the probability $\Pr(E)$ of the real world from that of the ideal world, the distinguishing advantage is at least

$$\mu_1(1 - \mu) - \frac{8p + 4q}{2^n}.$$

We have already shown that $\mu_1(1-\mu)$ is at least $\frac{1}{9} - \frac{1}{27 \cdot 2^{n/2}}$ when $p = q = \sqrt{2^n/3}$ (see the last paragraph of our analysis on $\gamma^{\text{pub}} \circ \pi^{\text{sec}}$). Hence the advantage is at least $\frac{1}{9} - \frac{1}{2^{n/2-1}}$.

6 Birthday Attack on Dual-EWCDM

In this section we provide details of a nonce respecting distinguishing attack on EWCDMD. For better understanding we consider a specific hash function $\mathcal{H}(m) = K \cdot m$ where K is a nonzero random key chosen uniformly from $\{0,1\}^n \setminus \{0\}$ and $m \in \mathcal{M} := \{0,1\}^n$. Here $K \cdot m$ means the field multiplication with respect to a fixed primitive polynomial. Clearly, $\mathcal{H}$ is $\frac{1}{2^n-1}$ AXU hash. Moreover it is injective hash. In other words, for distinct messages $m_1, \ldots, m_q$, $\mathcal{H}(m_1), \ldots, \mathcal{H}(m_q)$ are distinct.

Distinguishing Attack. $\mathcal{A}$ choses $(\nu_1, m_1), \ldots, (\nu_q, m_q) \in \{0,1\}^n \times \mathcal{M}$ where all ν_i's are distinct and all m_i's are distinct. Suppose $T_1, \ldots, T_q$ are all responses. $\mathcal{A}$ returns 1 if there is a collision among T_i values, otherwise returns zero.

When $\mathcal{A}$ is interacting with a random function, $\Pr[\mathcal{A} \to 1] \leq q(q-1)/2^{n+1}$ (by using the union bound). Now we provide lower bound of $\Pr[\mathcal{A} \to 1]$ while $\mathcal{A}$ is interacting with EWCDMD in which π_1, π_2 are two independent random permutations and $\mathcal{H}$ is the above hash function whose key is chosen independently. To obtain a lower bound we first prove the following lemma. Let $N = 2^n$.

Lemma 5. *Let $x_1, \ldots, x_q \in \{0,1\}^n$ be q distinct values. Let π be a random permutation. Then, for all distinct $\nu_1, \ldots, \nu_q$, let C denote the event that there is a collision among values of $\pi(\nu_i) \oplus x_i$, $1 \le i \le q$. Then,*

$$\alpha(1 - \beta) \le Pr[C] \le \alpha$$

where $\alpha = \frac{q(q-1)}{2(N-1)}$ and $\beta = \frac{(q-2)(q+1)}{4(N-3)}$. In particular, for distinct x_i's, there is a collision among $\pi(x_i) \oplus x_i$ values has probability at least $\alpha(1 - \beta)$.

Proof. Let $E_{i,j}$ denote the event that $\pi(\nu_i) \oplus \pi(\nu_j) = x_i \oplus x_j$. So for all $i \ne j$, $Pr[E_{i,j}] = 1/(N-1)$. Let $C = \cup_{i \ne j} E_{i,j}$ denote the collision event. By using union bound we can easily upper bound

$$Pr[C] \le \alpha := \frac{q(q-1)}{2(N-1)}.$$

Now, we show the lower bound. For this, we apply Boole's inequality and we obtain lower bound of collision probability as

$$Pr[C] \ge \alpha - \sum Pr[E_{i,j} \cap E_{k,l}]$$

where the sum is taken over all possible choices of $\{\{i,j\}, \{k,l\}\}$, and the number of such choices is at most $\binom{q(q-1)/2}{2} = q(q-1)(q+1)(q-2)/8$. Note that for each such choice i, j, k, l,

$$Pr[E_{i,j} \cap E_{k,l}] \le \frac{1}{(N-1)(N-3)}.$$

Hence,

$$Pr[C] \ge \alpha - \frac{q(q-1)(q+1)(q-2)}{8(N-1)(N-3)} \tag{9}$$

$$= \alpha(1 - \frac{(q-2)(q+1)}{4(N-3)}) = \alpha(1 - \beta). \tag{10}$$

This completes the proof. $\square$

Advantage Computation. Using the above Lemma we now show that the probability that $\mathscr{A}$ returns 1 while interacting with EWCDMD is significant when $q = O(2^{n/2})$.

Let C_1 denote the event that there is a collision among the values $z_i := \pi_1(\nu_i) \oplus \mathscr{H}(m_i)$. We can apply our lemma as $\mathscr{H}(m_i)$'s are distinct due to our choice of the hash function. Thus, $Pr[C_1] \ge \alpha(1-\beta)$. Moreover, $Pr[\neg C_1] \ge (1-\alpha)$. Given $\neg C_1$, T values are outputs of Davies-Meyer based on random permutation π_2 for distinct inputs. So by using previous lemma,

$$Pr(\text{collision in } T \text{ values} \mid \neg C_1) \ge \alpha(1 - \beta).$$

Hence,

$$\begin{aligned}
\Pr(\mathscr{A} \to 1) &\geq \Pr(C_1) + \Pr(\text{collision in T values} \mid \neg C_1) \times \Pr[\neg C_1] \\
&\geq \alpha(1 - \beta) + (1 - \alpha) \times \Pr(\text{collision in T values} \mid \neg C_1) \\
&\geq \alpha(1 - \beta) + \alpha(1 - \alpha)(1 - \beta) \\
&= (2\alpha - \alpha^2)(1 - \beta) \geq 2\alpha - 2\alpha\beta - \alpha^2.
\end{aligned}$$

Thus, the advantage of the adversary is at least $\alpha - 2\alpha\beta - \alpha^2$. It is easy to see that when $2q^2 \geq N$, we have $1 - 2\beta - \alpha \leq 1/2$ and hence the advantage is at least $\alpha/2 = q(q-1)/4(N-1)$.

Remark 1. We would like to note that the distinguishing advantages of both constructions can be made closer to one if we repeat the whole process independently $O(n)$ times.

6.1   Issues in the Previous Proofs

Now we briefly describe what were the issues in the proofs of [CLM19, MN17]. Both proofs used H-technique and hence it is broadly divided into two parts: bounding probability of bad events and finding good lower bound for realizing any fixed good transcript in the real world. The flaws in their proof lie on the good transcript analysis.

Suppose π_1 and π_2 are two random permutations. In the both proofs, good transcript analysis deals to compute the probability distribution of sum of the two random permutations. More precisely, for fixed $\lambda_1, x_1, y_1, \ldots x_q, y_q, \lambda_q \in \{0,1\}^n$, we want to provide a lower bound of the event $\pi_1(x_i) \oplus \pi_2(y_i) = \lambda_i$ for all i. This is also known as mirror theory and have been studied in several papers [Pat10, Pat13, DDN+17a, DDNY19, DDNY18]. A desired lower bounds are known if the equality patterns of x_i and y_i's satisfy certain conditions. In the proofs of [CLM19, MN17], equality pattern of y_i's depend on the values of $\pi_1(x_i)$ for all i. So, clearly, we cannot use the mirror theory based lower bound. This is the main flaw of the proofs.

7   Concluding Discussion

We have demonstrated a distinguishing attack on EWCDMD. We would like to note that this attack does not work for EDM, EWCDM and EDMD as we can not write them as a composition of two non-injective functions. We also demonstrate a birthday attack on SoKAC21. Our attack also does not work if we mask the final output by a key (which is another variant of sum of key alternating ciphers). However, at the same time, we do not know how to prove its beyond birthday security.

7.1   Some Open Problems

Followings are some of open problems on which cryptography community could have interest.

1. We would like to note that our attack against EWCDMD is a PRF attack and it is not easy to extend to a forging attack in a nonce respecting situation. Thus, proving MAC security would be an interesting research problem.
2. One can consider the following dual variant:

$$\pi_2(\pi_1(\nu) \oplus \mathscr{H}(m)) \oplus \pi_1(\nu). \tag{11}$$

   This is very close to the sum of permutations. However, the presence of $\mathscr{H}(m)$ makes it very difficult to prove (without using Patarin's claim or conjecture on the interpolation probability of sum of random permutations). Moreover, it can not be expressed as a composition function with n-bit outputs. Hence it is a potential dual candidate of EWCDM.
3. Another possibility is to use three independent random permutations. As mentioned in [CS16], we can consider

$$\pi_3(\pi_1(\nu) \oplus \pi_2(\nu) \oplus \mathscr{H}(m)).$$

   This will give 2^n security in nonce respecting model assuming that the sum of permutations would give n-bit PRF security. However, we don't know the trade-off between the number of allowed repetition of nonce and the security bound.
4. Proving beyond birthday security (or demonstrating birthday attacks) of some other variants of SoKAC21 would be an interesting open problem.

Acknowledgment. This work is supported by the project "Study and Analysis of IoT Security" under Government of India at R. C. Bose Centre for Cryptology and Security, Indian Statistical Institute, Kolkata.

References

[ADMVA15] Andreeva, E., Daemen, J., Mennink, B., Van Assche, G.: Security of keyed sponge constructions using a modular proof approach. In: Leander, G. (ed.) FSE 2015. LNCS, vol. 9054, pp. 364–384. Springer, Heidelberg (2015). https://doi.org/10.1007/978-3-662-48116-5_18

[BDD+17] Bhaumik, R., Datta, N., Dutta, A., Mouha, N., Nandi, M.: The iterated random function problem. In: Takagi, T., Peyrin, T. (eds.) ASIACRYPT 2017. LNCS, vol. 10625, pp. 667–697. Springer, Cham (2017). https://doi.org/10.1007/978-3-319-70697-9_23

[BDH+17] Bertoni, G., Daemen, J., Hoffert, S., Peeters, M., Van Assche, G., Van Keer, R.: Farfalle: parallel permutation-based cryptography. IACR Trans. Symmetric Cryptol. **2017**, 1–38 (2017)

[BDPVA11a] Bertoni, G., Daemen, J., Peeters, M., Van Assche, G.: Duplexing the sponge: single-pass authenticated encryption and other applications. In: Miri, A., Vaudenay, S. (eds.) SAC 2011. LNCS, vol. 7118, pp. 320–337. Springer, Heidelberg (2012). https://doi.org/10.1007/978-3-642-28496-0_19

[BDPVA11b] Bertoni, G., Daemen, J., Peeters, M., Van Assche, G.: On the security of the keyed sponge construction. In: Symmetric Key Encryption Workshop, vol. 2011 (2011)

[BKL+07] Bogdanov, A., et al.: PRESENT: an ultra-lightweight block cipher. In: Paillier, P., Verbauwhede, I. (eds.) CHES 2007. LNCS, vol. 4727, pp. 450–466. Springer, Heidelberg (2007). https://doi.org/10.1007/978-3-540-74735-2_31

[BL16] Bhargavan, K., Leurent, G.: On the practical (in-) security of 64-bit block ciphers: collision attacks on HTTP over TLS and OpenVPN. In: Proceedings of the 2016 ACM SIGSAC Conference on Computer and Communications Security, pp. 456–467. ACM (2016)

[BN18a] Bhattacharya, S., Nandi, M.: A note on the chi-square method: a tool for proving cryptographic security. Cryptogr. Commun. 10(5), 935–957 (2018). https://doi.org/10.1007/s12095-017-0276-z

[BN18b] Bhattacharya, S., Nandi, M.: Revisiting variable output length XOR pseudorandom function. IACR Trans. Symmetric Cryptol. 2018(1), 314–335 (2018)

[BPP+17] Banik, S., Pandey, S.K., Peyrin, T., Sasaki, Y., Sim, S.M., Todo, Y.: GIFT: a small present. In: Fischer, W., Homma, N. (eds.) CHES 2017. LNCS, vol. 10529, pp. 321–345. Springer, Cham (2017). https://doi.org/10.1007/978-3-319-66787-4_16

[CDH+12] Chang, D., Dworkin, M., Hong, S., Kelsey, J., Nandi, M.: A keyed sponge construction with pseudorandomness in the standard model. In: The Third SHA-3 Candidate Conference, March 2012, vol. 3, p. 7 (2012)

[CLM19] Chen, Y.L., Lambooij, E., Mennink, B.: How to build pseudorandom functions from public random permutations. In: Boldyreva, A., Micciancio, D. (eds.) CRYPTO 2019. LNCS, vol. 11692, pp. 266–293. Springer, Cham (2019). https://doi.org/10.1007/978-3-030-26948-7_10

[CS16] Cogliati, B., Seurin, Y.: EWCDM: an efficient, beyond-birthday secure, nonce-misuse resistant MAC. In: Robshaw, M., Katz, J. (eds.) CRYPTO 2016. LNCS, vol. 9814, pp. 121–149. Springer, Heidelberg (2016). https://doi.org/10.1007/978-3-662-53018-4_5

[CS18] Cogliati, B., Seurin, Y.: Analysis of the single-permutation encrypted Davies-Meyer construction. Des. Codes Cryptogr. 86(12), 2703–2723 (2018). https://doi.org/10.1007/s10623-018-0470-9

[DDN+17a] Datta, N., Dutta, A., Nandi, M., Paul, G., Zhang, L.: Single key variant of PMAC_Plus. IACR Trans. Symmetric Cryptol. 2017(4), 268–305 (2017)

[DDNP18] Datta, N., Dutta, A., Nandi, M., Paul, G.: Double-block hash-then-sum: a paradigm for constructing BBB secure PRF. IACR Trans. Symmetric Cryptol. 2018, 36–92 (2018)

[DDNY18] Datta, N., Dutta, A., Nandi, M., Yasuda, K.: Encrypt or decrypt? To make a single-key beyond birthday secure nonce-based MAC. In: Shacham, H., Boldyreva, A. (eds.) CRYPTO 2018. LNCS, vol. 10991, pp. 631–661. Springer, Cham (2018). https://doi.org/10.1007/978-3-319-96884-1_21

[DDNY19] Datta, N., Dutta, A., Nandi, M., Yasuda, K.: DWCDM+: a BBB secure nonce based MAC. Adv. Math. Comm. **13**(4), 705–732 (2019)

[DHT17] Dai, W., Hoang, V.T., Tessaro, S.: Information-theoretic indistinguishability via the chi-squared method. In: Katz, J., Shacham, H. (eds.) CRYPTO 2017. LNCS, vol. 10403, pp. 497–523. Springer, Cham (2017). https://doi.org/10.1007/978-3-319-63697-9_17

[HWKS98] Hall, C., Wagner, D., Kelsey, J., Schneier, B.: Building PRFs from PRPs. In: Krawczyk, H. (ed.) CRYPTO 1998. LNCS, vol. 1462, pp. 370–389. Springer, Heidelberg (1998). https://doi.org/10.1007/BFb0055742

[LR88] Luby, M., Rackoff, C.: How to construct pseudorandom permutations from pseudorandom functions. SIAM J. Comput. **17**(2), 373–386 (1988)

[MN17] Mennink, B., Neves, S.: Encrypted Davies-Meyer and its dual: towards optimal security using mirror theory. In: Katz, J., Shacham, H. (eds.) CRYPTO 2017. LNCS, vol. 10403, pp. 556–583. Springer, Cham (2017). https://doi.org/10.1007/978-3-319-63697-9_19

[MS15] Minaud, B., Seurin, Y.: The iterated random permutation problem with applications to cascade encryption. In: Gennaro, R., Robshaw, M. (eds.) CRYPTO 2015. LNCS, vol. 9215, pp. 351–367. Springer, Heidelberg (2015). https://doi.org/10.1007/978-3-662-47989-6_17

[Nan15] Nandi, M.: A simple proof of a distinguishing bound of iterated uniform random permutation. IACR Cryptol. ePrint Arch. **2015**, 579 (2015)

[Pat08] Patarin, J.: A proof of security in $O(2^n)$ for the XOR of two random permutations. In: Safavi-Naini, R. (ed.) ICITS 2008. LNCS, vol. 5155, pp. 232–248. Springer, Heidelberg (2008). https://doi.org/10.1007/978-3-540-85093-9_22

[Pat10] Patarin, J.: Introduction to mirror theory: analysis of systems of linear equalities and linear non equalities for cryptography. IACR Cryptol. ePrint Arch. **2010**, 287 (2010)

[Pat13] Patarin, J.: Security in $o(2^n)$ for the XOR of two random permutations - proof with the standard H technique. IACR Cryptol. ePrint Arch. **2013**, 368 (2013)

[Sho04] Shoup, V.: Sequences of games: a tool for taming complexity in security proofs. IACR Cryptol. ePrint Arch. **2004**, 332 (2004)

[WC81] Wegman, M.N., Carter, L.: New hash functions and their use in authentication and set equality. J. Comput. Syst. Sci. **22**(3), 265–279 (1981)

[Yas10] Yasuda, K.: The sum of CBC MACs is a secure PRF. In: Pieprzyk, J. (ed.) CT-RSA 2010. LNCS, vol. 5985, pp. 366–381. Springer, Heidelberg (2010). https://doi.org/10.1007/978-3-642-11925-5_25

[Yas11] Yasuda, K.: A new variant of PMAC: beyond the birthday bound. In: Rogaway, P. (ed.) CRYPTO 2011. LNCS, vol. 6841, pp. 596–609. Springer, Heidelberg (2011). https://doi.org/10.1007/978-3-642-22792-9_34

[ZWSW12] Zhang, L., Wu, W., Sui, H., Wang, P.: 3kf9: enhancing 3GPP-MAC beyond the birthday bound. In: Wang, X., Sako, K. (eds.) ASIACRYPT 2012. LNCS, vol. 7658, pp. 296–312. Springer, Heidelberg (2012). https://doi.org/10.1007/978-3-642-34961-4_19

Improving Key-Recovery in Linear Attacks: Application to 28-Round PRESENT

Antonio Flórez-Gutiérrez[⊠] and María Naya-Plasencia[⊠]

Inria, Paris, France
{antonio.florez_gutierrez,maria.naya_plasencia}@inria.fr

Abstract. Linear cryptanalysis is one of the most important tools in use for the security evaluation of symmetric primitives. Many improvements and refinements have been published since its introduction, and many applications on different ciphers have been found. Among these upgrades, Collard et al. proposed in 2007 an acceleration of the key-recovery part of Algorithm 2 for last-round attacks based on the FFT.

In this paper we present a generalized, matrix-based version of the previous algorithm which easily allows us to take into consideration an arbitrary number of key-recovery rounds. We also provide efficient variants that exploit the key-schedule relations and that can be combined with multiple linear attacks.

Using our algorithms we provide some new cryptanalysis on PRESENT, including, to the best of our knowledge, the first attack on 28 rounds.

Keywords: Linear cryptanalysis · FFT · Walsh Transform · Algorithm 2 · Key-recovery algorithm · PRESENT

1 Introduction

The foundation of the trust we have on symmetric primitives is based on the amount of cryptanalysis these primitives have received. The distance between the highest number of rounds that can be attacked and the full version is what determines the security margin of a cipher. For this quantity to have a meaning, the best reduced-round attacks within each known family of attacks should be accurately determined. In order to facilitate the application of known cryptanalysis families to new ciphers, generalizing the corresponding algorithms is an important task as it allows to: (1) accurately and semi-automatically determine the security margin, (2) find errors or suboptimal parts from previous attacks and (3) find new improvement ideas thanks to the clearer understanding of the attack. Several such examples exist, including impossible differential attacks [13,14], invariant attacks [5], and meet-in-the-middle attacks [15], to cite a few.

Linear cryptanalysis was introduced by Matsui in 1993 [31], and is one of the main symmetric cryptanalysis families. These statistical attacks, which in their

© International Association for Cryptologic Research 2020
A. Canteaut and Y. Ishai (Eds.): EUROCRYPT 2020, LNCS 12105, pp. 221–249, 2020.
https://doi.org/10.1007/978-3-030-45721-1_9

most basic version exploit linear correlations between some bits of the plaintext, key and ciphertext, have benefited from many improvements and refinements over the years. For example, the introduction of linear hulls in [36] deepened the understanding of the underlying principles of linear attacks. There has also been a progressive development of techniques which exploit several linear approximations at the same time. In particular, multiple linear attacks were proposed in [7], and multidimensional attacks in [25,26]. Also important is the construction of statistical models which effectively predict the parameters of these attacks - in this respect, we highlight works such as [9,12,21,38].

In [31] Matsui proposed the partial key-recovery attack known as Algorithm 2 in the form of a last round-attack. The time complexity of this algorithm was greatly improved by the results from Collard et al. [18] using the FFT (Fast Fourier Transform). Despite the focus of many publications on improved ways of searching for linear distinguishers and estimating their capacity, little has been done regarding improvements of the key-recovery part, and the result from [18] and its application to some last-round multidimensional attacks in [35] are, to the best of our knowledge, the main known contributions in this direction.

Matsui introduced linear cryptanalysis for an attack on DES [34]. Linear cryptanalysis is a powerful tool that provides the best known attacks (like [12] or [24]) on several popular ciphers, such as PRESENT [11], NOEKEON [20], some variants of Simon [4] and most recently TRIFLE-BC [22].

In particular, the lightweight block cipher PRESENT [11], proposed in 2007 and made an ISO standard in 2012, is a popular cipher that has been the target of around 30 reduced-round cryptanalysis efforts, and some of the most successful are linear attacks. Out of its 31 total rounds, Ohkuma found a weak-key linear attack on 24 in [37]. Collard et al. found a statistical saturation attack on up to 26 rounds in 2009 [17]. Nakahara et al. proposed another 26-round linear attack in [33], and Cho described a multidimensional attack with a larger success probability in 2010 [16]. It wasn't until 2015 that 27 rounds were reached by Zheng et al. in [41]. A different 27-round attack was given by Bogdanov et al. in [12], but no attack on 28 rounds has been proposed.

Motivation of our work. The contrast between the amount of results devoted to the construction of effective linear distinguishers and the results regarding the key-recovery algorithms seemed quite surprising to us. In particular, the nice algorithm provided in [18] considers the simplified version in which only the final round is inverted and the only key to guess is directly xored to the ciphertext (though an application for a first and last round key-recovery attack is also sketched). In [35] a variant for multidimensional attacks with a fixed input mask is proposed. Many linear attacks and analysis don't consider this final round acceleration, for example in [8], or [33]. In [16], the author says *"The computational complexity may be further reduced by applying Fast Fourier Transform at the cost of the increased memory complexity"* without developing any further. In [27], the authors state *"It is not clear if the trick proposed by Collard, et al. [18] can be used in multiple dimensions"*. Of the ones that do, some only apply it as a black box in the simplified last-round case, like in [3], in [19], or in [2] where the authors state that *"...we note that when the key addition layer is composed of XOR, we can optimize the parity evaluations by applying the algorithm of* [18]". Others assume that the same formulas directly apply in the multiple-round case [6,23,29,30], and a few mention technical extended versions of the algorithm in dedicated cryptanalysis, for example [12,41], but a generalized algorithm for an arbitrary number of rounds in the key-recovery part has never been described in full.

It seems clear from the existing literature that the correct use of the key-recovery speed-up is not the norm, and its application is far from trivial. Furthermore, the treatment of the key-schedule relations has not been discussed either. A generalized FFT-based key-recovery algorithm would allow to build more efficient linear attacks easily. Taking into account the key-schedule relations and the scenario of multiple linear cryptanalysis in this algorithm also seem to be important tasks that should be considered.

Our main results. We have been able to provide an efficient generalized key-recovery algorithm with an associated time complexity formula. The algorithm is given in a matricial form (as opposed to the vectorial form of previous descriptions) as we believe it to be easier to understand and facilitate optimization in some cases, such as multiple linear attacks. When considering a linear attack with M approximations on a key-alternating cipher using N plaintext-ciphertext pairs with key-recovery on l_{ext} bits of the first and last subkey and l_{in} bits of the rest, the time complexity with our algorithm is

$$\mathcal{O}\left(N\right) + \mathcal{O}\left(Ml_{ext}2^{l_{ext}+l_{in}}\right).$$

In addition, we propose two methods which efficiently exploit the dependence relationships between the keybits that need to be guessed. The first reduces the second term to $\mathcal{O}\left(M2^{l_{ext}+l_{in}}\right)$, if some of the bits of the external keys can be deduced from the internal keys. The second allows to reduce the time complexity of this part to $\mathcal{O}\left(M2^{l_{tot}}\right)$ (where l_{tot} is the strict amount of information bits about the key which are necessary to deduce all the key-recovery bits) in some multiple linear attacks.

In our results on PRESENT we consider new multiple linear attacks which are only possible thanks to our algorithms, the best of which reach 28 rounds of the cipher for the first time. The expected time complexity was evaluated using the statistical model from [9]. In order to validate these predictions, we have implemented reduced-round versions of the attacks and found that the experimental results closely resemble the theoretical model.

Organization of the paper. Section 2 presents the preliminaries and notations that will be used throughout the paper, as well as the essential ideas of linear cryptanalysis, the 2007 FFT algorithm and PRESENT. In Sect. 3 we introduce our new generalized and efficient key-recovery algorithm and its variants. Section 4 describes the application to PRESENT and our new attacks, including discussions of the design of our linear distinguishers and key-recovery algorithms, as well as a comparison with previous attacks and the results of our experimental simulations. The conclusions of this paper are extracted in Sect. 5.

2   Preliminaries

We now cover some preliminaries and notations needed for the other sections of the paper. We briefly describe Matsui's Algorithm 2, which is the basis of linear key-recovery attacks. We also provide a short description of the ideas behind linear hulls and multiple linear cryptanalysis, as they are essential to our attacks on PRESENT. The statistical model that was used to compute the parameters of these attacks is also summarised. Next, we present the FFT-based algorithm which allows the speed-up of the key-recovery phase and was proposed in [18]. Finally we outline the specification of the PRESENT block cipher.

In the following, we will consider a block cipher E of length n and key length κ. Given a plaintext x and a key K, we denote the associated ciphertext by $y = E_K(x) = E(x, K)$, so that $E^{-1}(y, K) = E_K^{-1}(y) = x$. In particular we will consider key-alternating ciphers consisting of r rounds, each one being the composition of a round permutation F and the bitwise addition of a round subkey K_i which is derived from the master key K with a key schedule. We also consider that the first round is preceded by the addition of a whitening key K_0.

2.1   Matsui's Algorithm 2

Matsui's last round attack in [31] separates the last round of the cipher, $E_K(x) = (F \circ E'_K)(x) \oplus K_r$ as represented in Fig. 1, and supposes the attacker knows a correlated linear approximation $\alpha \cdot x \oplus \beta \cdot \hat{y} \oplus \gamma(K)$ of E'_K (where $\cdot$ denotes the dot product). The vectors α and β are the input and output masks, while γ determines the key mask. The correlation of the approximation is

$$c(\alpha, \beta, \gamma) = Pr_{x,K}(\alpha \cdot x \oplus \beta \cdot F^{-1}(E_K(x) \oplus K_r) \oplus \gamma(K) = 0) \\ - Pr_{x,K}(\alpha \cdot x \oplus \beta \cdot F^{-1}(E_K(x) \oplus K_r) \oplus \gamma(K) = 1). \tag{1}$$

Matsui also proved that (under statistical independence assumptions) the correlation of the addition of several approximations is the product of their correlations (piling-up lemma). This allows to construct approximations of a cipher by chaining approximations of each individual round.

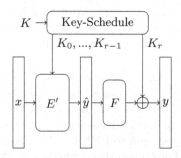

Fig. 1. Attack on last round of a cipher.

Algorithm 1: Naïve Matsui's Algorithm 2

Input: A set $\mathcal{D} = \{(x, y = E_K(x))\}$ of N plaintext-ciphertext pairs.
Output: A probable guess for k.
$\mathbf{T} \leftarrow \underline{\mathbf{0}}$;
forall $(x, y) \in \mathcal{D}$ **do**   // Compute $T_k = \#\{(x,y) : \alpha \cdot x \oplus f(y|_\chi \oplus k) = 0\}$
    for $k \leftarrow 0$ **to** $2^{|k|} - 1$ **do**
       | **if** $\alpha \cdot x \oplus f(y|_\chi \oplus k) = 0$ **then** $T_k \leftarrow T_k + 1$;
    end
end
return $argmax_k(|T_k - N/2|)$;   // Find the T_k most different to $N/2$

We suppose that computing $\beta \cdot F^{-1}(y \oplus K_r)$ from y only requires guessing $|k| < |K_r| = n$ bits of K_r, which are selected by the mask χ (so that $k = K_r|_\chi$). Here $x|_\chi$ will denote the vector of length $HW(\chi)$ whose components are the coordinates of x corresponding to non-zero entries of χ, and $|x|$ just denotes the length of the vector x. We can substitute the term associated to the partial decryption of the last round for a map $f : \mathbb{F}_2^{|k|} \longrightarrow \mathbb{F}_2$:

$$f(y|_\chi \oplus K_r|_\chi) = \beta \cdot F^{-1}(y \oplus K_r) \text{ for all } y \in \mathbb{F}_2^n, K_r \in \mathbb{F}_2^n \qquad (2)$$

Given a collection $\mathcal{D}$ of N plaintext-ciphertext pairs, the partial subkey k can be retrieved with Matsui's Algorithm 2, which relies on the assumption that for any wrong guess of the last round subkey, the linear approximation will have value 0 with probability $1/2$. Matsui proved that the probability of success is reasonable when $N = \mathcal{O}\left(1/c(\alpha, \beta, \gamma)^2\right)$ pairs are available.

The complexity of the algorithm is $N2^{|k|}$ one-round decryptions and $2^{|k|}$ memory registers of up to $\log N$ bits to compute the counters T_k, with an additional $2^{\kappa - |k|}$ full encryptions if the rest of the key is searched for exhaustively.

In [32], Matsui noted that since the only information required about each (x, y) pair are the values of $\alpha \cdot x$ and $y|_\chi$, it is possible to first count the number of occurrences of each $(\alpha \cdot x, y|_\chi)$ in the data (*distillation phase*) and then compute the T_k using these counters (*analysis phase*). With this technique the attack takes N parity evaluations and $2^{2|k|}$ one-round decryptions, which reduces the complexity to $\mathcal{O}(N) + \mathcal{O}\left(2^{2|k|}\right)$ when $2^{|k|} < N$, which is often the case.

Algorithm 2 can also be used with an approximation over even less rounds of the cipher by skipping several rounds at the beginning and/or the end. The limitation is that the number $|k|$ of involved subkey bits and the time complexity increase with the number of key-recovery rounds.

2.2 Linear Hulls

The original version of linear cryptanalysis by Matsui assumes that, given an input mask α and an output mask β, then there exists at most one key mask which leads to a biased approximation (in modern language, there is a dominant linear trail). This is often not the case, and there can exist many different sets of round subkey masks $(\gamma_0, \ldots, \gamma_r)$ or linear trails which contribute to the linear approximation. Furthermore, when this happens, then the probability of success of Matsui's Algorithm 2 is dependant on the key K. Nyberg introduced the idea of the linear hull of an approximation in [36], as well as its linear potential:

$$ELP(\alpha, \beta) = \mathrm{Exp}_K(c(\alpha, \beta)^2) = \sum_{\gamma_0, \ldots, \gamma_r} c(\alpha, \beta, (\gamma_0, \ldots, \gamma_r))^2 \qquad (3)$$

An Algorithm 2 attack using the approximation given by the masks α, β roughly requires $N = \mathcal{O}(1/ELP(\alpha, \beta))$ plaintext-ciphertext pairs to succeed, although the specific success probability depends on the key K.

There are several algorithms which permit the estimation of the ELP of a linear approximation. In our attacks on PRESENT we used the sparse correlation matrix method in a similar manner to [1].

2.3 Multiple and Multidimensional Linear Attacks

Linear cryptanalysis can also be extended by using more than one linear approximation. The first approach to allow the use of any set of linear approximations was introduced by Biryukov et al. in [7], and is commonly referred to as *multiple linear cryptanalysis*.

We will now describe a multiple version of Matsui's Algorithm 2. Let ν_i be M linear approximations of E'_K with masks α_i, β_i. We suppose that $\beta_i \cdot F^{-1}(y \oplus K_r)$ can be replaced by $f_i(y|_\chi \oplus k)$ for each approximation. For each guess of k, the attacker computes the empirical correlations

$$\begin{aligned} q_k^i = \ &\# \left\{ (x, y) \in \mathcal{D} : \alpha_i \cdot x \oplus f_i(y|_\chi \oplus k) = 0 \right\} \\ &- \# \left\{ (x, y) \in \mathcal{D} : \alpha_i \cdot x \oplus f_i(y|_\chi \oplus k) = 1 \right\} \end{aligned} \qquad (4)$$

which are then aggregated into the multiple linear cryptanalysis statistic

$$Q_k = \frac{1}{N} \sum_{i=1}^{M} \left(q_k^i \right)^2 \qquad (5)$$

The guess with the largest associated value of Q_k is probably correct. Under the assumption that all the linear approximations are statistically independent, the data complexity is inversely proportional to the capacity C of the set of approximations. If $c_i(K)$ is the correlation of the i-th approximation for the key K, then the capacity for the key K and the overall capacity are defined as

$$C(K) = \sum_{i=1}^{M} (c_i(K))^2, \quad C = \mathrm{Exp}_K(C(K)) = \sum_{i=1}^{M} ELP(\alpha_i, \beta_i) \qquad (6)$$

Hermelin et al. proposed multidimensional linear cryptanalysis in [25] and [26]. It uses linear approximations whose input and output masks constitute linear subspaces of $\mathbb{F}_2^n$, so that the estimation of the probability of success takes into account the joint distribution of all these approximations and doesn't require the assumption of statistical independence.

2.4   Statistical Models for the Probability of Success

An issue that has also been studied is the probabilistic behaviour of linear approximations and how it can be used to better estimate the data complexity of a linear attack. In an attack based on Matsui's Algorithm 2, it is possible to keep more than one key candidate, which increases the probability of success. Selçuk introduced the notion of advantage [38] in order to measure the effectiveness of this type of attack. An attack that ranks the partial key guesses k according to a statistic X_k achieves an *advantage* of a bits if the right key ranks among the best $2^{|k|-a}$ key candidates. Given a desired advantage a, the probability of success is the probability that the actual advantage surpasses a.

Supposing that the key-ranking statistic X_k has the cumulative distribution function F_R for the right key guess and F_W for any wrong guess, then the success probability of the associated statistical attack for a given desired advantage a is

$$P_S = 1 - F_R\left(F_W^{-1}(1 - 2^{-a})\right) \tag{7}$$

For multiple and multidimensional linear cryptanalysis, Blondeau et al. have provided estimations of the distributions of the test statistics in [9]. These estimations can also be found in the Appendix C.

Another approach to estimating the probability of success was recently introduced by Bogdanov et al. in [12] with the name multivariate profiling. Its main advantage is the fact that it allows to use any set of linear approximations without supposing the statistical independence of the variables. In this case the estimate for the joint distribution of the correlation of the approximations is obtained by drawing a large enough sample of random keys, and computing the individual correlation contribution of each trail (in a large enough set of highly biased trails) for each of the random keys.

2.5   Last-Round Key-Recovery with FFT/FWT

We now describe the FFT-accelerated version of Algorithm 2 presented in [18], which applies to the construction from Fig. 1 and will be the starting point of our work in Sect. 3.

There are $2^{|k|}$ possibilities for the partial subkey guess, and we recall that χ is the mask which extracts these relevant bits, so $k = K_r|_\chi$. Let $f(y|_\chi \oplus k) = \beta \cdot F^{-1}(y \oplus K_r)$ denote the term of the approximation associated to the partial last round decryption. The attacker wants to compute the vector $\mathbf{q} \in \mathbb{Z}^{2^m}$ of experimental correlations whose entries are

$$q_k = \#\left\{(x,y) \in \mathcal{D} : \alpha \cdot x \oplus f(y|_\chi \oplus k) = 0\right\} \\ - \#\left\{(x,y) \in \mathcal{D} : \alpha \cdot x \oplus f(y|_\chi \oplus k) = 1\right\} \tag{8}$$

with the aim of extracting the key candidate(s) with the largest $|q_k|$ (as $q_k = 2T_k - N$). Each experimental correlation can be rewritten as a sum

$$q_k = \sum_{(x,y)\in\mathcal{D}} (-1)^{\alpha \cdot x \oplus f(y|_\chi \oplus k)} = \sum_{j=0}^{2^{|k|}-1} (-1)^{f(j\oplus k)} \sum_{\substack{(x,y)\in\mathcal{D} \\ y|_\chi = j}} (-1)^{\alpha \cdot x} \tag{9}$$

where j represents the relevant $|k|$ bits of the ciphertext. This suggests that the attack should begin by computing the integer vector $\mathbf{a} \in \mathbb{Z}^{2^{|k|}}$ with coordinates

$$a_j = \sum_{\substack{(x,y) \in \mathcal{D} \\ y|_x = j}} (-1)^{\alpha \cdot x} \tag{10}$$

This constitutes the distillation phase of the algorithm of [18]. We can also define the matrix $C \in \mathbb{Z}^{2^{|k|} \times 2^{|k|}}$ with entries

$$c_{jk} = (-1)^{f(j \oplus k)} \tag{11}$$

The vector $\mathbf{q} = (q_0, \ldots, q_{2^{|k|}-1})$ can thus be calculated as the product

$$\mathbf{q}^T = \mathbf{a}^T C \tag{12}$$

However, the time complexity of constructing C and computing the matrix-vector product is still $O\left(2^{2|k|}\right)$. The product can be computed in a much more efficient manner by making use of the following result:

Proposition 1. *Let* $f : \mathbb{F}_2^m \longrightarrow \mathbb{F}_2$ *be a boolean function. We consider a matrix of 1s and* -1*s* $C \in \mathbb{Z}^{2^m \times 2^m}$ *whose entries are of the form*

$$c_{ij} = (-1)^{f(i \oplus j)}, \quad 0 \leq i, j \leq 2^m - 1 \tag{13}$$

This matrix diagonalizes as

$$2^m C = H_{2^m} \Delta H_{2^m} \tag{14}$$

where H_{2^m} *is the Hadamard-Sylvester matrix of size* 2^m *whose entries are* $h_{ij} = (-1)^{i \cdot j}$*, and* $\Delta = \mathrm{diag}(\boldsymbol{\lambda})$*,* $\boldsymbol{\lambda} \in \mathbb{Z}^{2^m}$ *is a diagonal matrix. The eigenvalue vector* $\boldsymbol{\lambda}$ *is the matrix-vector product* $H_{2^m} C_{\cdot 1}$*, where* $C_{\cdot 1}$ *denotes the first column of* C*.*

The matrix-vector product $\mathbf{a}^T C$ can then be further decomposed into:

$$2^{|k|} \mathbf{q}^T = \mathbf{a}^T H_{2^{|k|}} \mathrm{diag}(H_{2^{|k|}} C_{\cdot 1}) H_{2^{|k|}} \tag{15}$$

The decomposition of C justifies Algorithm 2, which reduces computing $\mathbf{q}$ to three products of the form $H_{2^{|k|}} \mathbf{v}$, which can in turn be evaluated efficiently with the Fast Walsh Transform (sometimes called Fast Walsh-Hadamard Transform or simply FWT or FWHT) with $|k|2^{|k|}$ additions/substractions (see the appendix for more details). We denote by ρ_D the cost of checking a plaintext-ciphertext pair in the distillation phase, by ρ_f the cost of evaluating $f(j)$, by ρ_A, ρ_M, ρ_C the cost of adding, multiplying and comparing two n-bit integers, by ρ_E the cost of one encryption and by a the advantage of the attack.

Proposition 2. *The previous algorithm has time complexity*

$$\underbrace{\rho_D N}_{\substack{distillation \\ phase}} + \underbrace{3\rho_A |k| 2^{|k|} + (\rho_f + \rho_M + \rho_C) 2^{|k|}}_{analysis\ phase} + \underbrace{\rho_E 2^{\kappa-a}}_{\substack{search \\ phase}} \tag{16}$$

The memory requirement is $2 \cdot 2^{|k|} \cdot (n + |k|)$ *bits.*

Algorithm 2: The algorithm of [18] (without the final phase)

Input: A collection $\mathcal{D} = \{(x, y = E_K(x))\}$ of N plaintext-ciphertext pairs (possibly on-the-fly).

Output: The experimental correlations q_k (multiplied by $2^{|k|}$).

```
// DISTILLATION PHASE
```
$a \leftarrow 0$;

forall $(x, y) \in \mathcal{D}$ **do**

   | **if** $\alpha \cdot x = 0$ **then** $a_{y|_x} \leftarrow a_{y|_x} + 1$ **else** $a_{y|_x} \leftarrow a_{y|_x} - 1$;

end

```
// ANALYSIS PHASE
```

for $j \leftarrow 0$ **to** $2^{|k|} - 1$ **do** $\lambda_j \leftarrow f(j)$;   `// First column of` C

$\boldsymbol{\lambda} \leftarrow \mathrm{FWT}(\boldsymbol{\lambda})$;   `// Eigenvalues of` C

$\mathbf{a} \leftarrow \mathrm{FWT}(\mathbf{a})$;   `// Apply the FWT to a`

for $j \leftarrow 0$ **to** $2^{|k|} - 1$ **do** $a_j \leftarrow a_j \cdot \lambda_j$;   `// Multiply a by` λ

$\mathbf{q} \leftarrow \mathrm{FWT}(\mathbf{a})$;   `// Apply the FWT to a`

return q;

2.6 The Lightweight Block Cipher PRESENT

PRESENT is a key-alternating block cipher which takes a 64-bit plaintext $x = x_{63} \ldots x_0$ and an 80-bit (or 128-bit) key $K = \kappa_{79} \ldots \kappa_0$ (or $K = \kappa_{127} \ldots \kappa_0$) and returns a 64-bit ciphertext $y = y_{63} \ldots y_0$. The encryption is performed by iteratively applying a round transformation to the state $b = b_{63} \ldots b_0 = w_{15} \| \ldots \| w_0$, where each of the w_i represents a 4-bit nibble, $w_i = b_{4i+3} b_{4i+2} b_{4i+1} b_{4i}$.

Both variants of PRESENT consist of 31 rounds, plus the addition of a whitening key at the output. Each round is the composition of three transformations:

- **addRoundKey:** Given the round key $K_i = \kappa_{63}^i \ldots \kappa_0^i$, $0 \leq i \leq 31$ and the state b, the round key is XORed bitwise to the state.
- **sBoxLayer:** A fixed 4-bit S-box $S : \mathbb{F}_2^4 \longrightarrow \mathbb{F}_2^4$ is applied to each nibble w_i of the state. The S-box S is given as a lookup table (in hexadecimal notation):

x	0	1	2	3	4	5	6	7	8	9	A	B	C	D	E	F
$S(x)$	C	5	6	B	9	0	A	D	3	E	F	8	4	7	1	2

- **pLayer:** A fixed bitwise permutation P is applied to the state b.

$$
\begin{aligned}
P : \{0, \ldots 63\} &\longrightarrow \{0, \ldots, 63\} \\
j \neq 63 &\longmapsto 16j \bmod 63 \\
63 &\longmapsto 63
\end{aligned} \tag{17}
$$

Key-schedule. It is the only difference between the 80 and the 128-bit variants, both algorithms can be found in Appendix A.

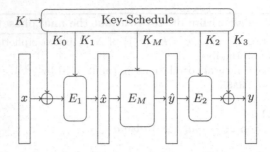

Fig. 2. The general description of the cipher.

3 Efficient Key-Recovery for Algorithm 2

In this section we will present our generalized efficient key-recovery algorithm inspired from the one in [18], described in Sect. 2.5.

We were surprised to see that after the publication of [18], many new linear attack publications did not use the algorithm to speed up the key-recovery part (see for instance [8,16,33]), or they just used it without getting into the details as a black box (see [2,3]). A few publications implicitly used extensions of the technique, such as [12,41], always in the context of a dedicated attack.

Here we propose a generalized version of the algorithm for an arbitrary number of rounds which encompasses these contributions and permits a finer analysis of the time complexity. We also propose two variants of the algorithm which efficiently exploit the key-schedule relations between keybits as well as the multiple approximation setting, which are interesting scenarios requiring consideration.

We believe that the new algorithm and its variants will simplify the evaluation of the time complexity of an attack given a suitable linear distinguisher, which would in turn help designers assess the security margin of a block cipher.

3.1 The Extended Algorithm

Consider a block cipher E of block size n and key size κ which can be decomposed as in Fig. 2. The ciphers E_1 and E_2 represent the first and last few rounds. They take some *inner keys* K_1 and K_2. The first and last round will be the *outer keys* K_0 and K_3. We suppose that the inner cipher E_M has a linear approximation

$$\nu : \ \alpha \cdot \hat{x} \oplus \beta \cdot \hat{y}.$$

As before, we assume that the values of $\alpha \cdot E_1(x \oplus K_0, K_1)$ (resp. $\beta \cdot E_2^{-1}(y \oplus K_3, K_2)$) can be obtained from a part of x (resp. y) by guessing some bits of the keys K_0 and K_1 (resp. K_3 and K_2). We will denote the necessary part of the plaintext by i (resp. ciphertext, j), while the guessed parts of the subkeys will be denoted by k_0, k_1 (resp. k_3, k_2). We can consider masks $\chi_0, \chi_1, \chi_2, \chi_3$, so that

$$i = x|_{\chi_0}, \ k_0 = K_0|_{\chi_0}, \ k_1 = K_1|_{\chi_1}, \ k_2 = K_2|_{\chi_2}, \ j = y|_{\chi_3}, \ k_3 = K_3|_{\chi_3} \quad (18)$$

Let $f_1 : \mathbb{F}_2^{|k_0|} \times \mathbb{F}_2^{|k_1|} \longrightarrow \mathbb{F}_2$ and $f_2 : \mathbb{F}_2^{|k_3|} \times \mathbb{F}_2^{|k_2|} \longrightarrow \mathbb{F}_2$ be maps for which

$$f_1\left(x|_{\chi_0} \oplus K_0|_{\chi_0}, K_1|_{\chi_1}\right) = \alpha \cdot E_1\left(x \oplus K_0, K_1\right) \text{ for all } x, K_0, K_1 \quad (19)$$

$$f_2\left(y|_{\chi_3} \oplus K_3|_{\chi_3}, K_2|_{\chi_2}\right) = \beta \cdot E_2^{-1}\left(y \oplus K_3, K_2\right) \text{ for all } y, K_3, K_2 \quad (20)$$

The attacker has a set $\mathcal{D}$ of N pairs $(x, y = E(x, K))$ for some fixed key K. They need to compute, for each possible guess of the subkeys:

$$q(k_0, k_1, k_2, k_3) = \# \{(x, y) \in \mathcal{D} : f_1(i \oplus k_0, k_1) \oplus f_2(j \oplus k_3, k_2) = 0\}$$
$$- \# \{(x, y) \in \mathcal{D} : f_1(i \oplus k_0, k_1) \oplus f_2(j \oplus k_3, k_2) = 1\} \quad (21)$$

The attack begins with the distillation phase, in which a matrix $A \in \mathbb{Z}^{2^{|k_0|} \times 2^{|k_3|}}$ is constructed from the data. Its entries are

$$a_{ij} = \# \{(x, y) \in \mathcal{D} : \ x|_{\chi_0} = i, \ y|_{\chi_3} = j\}. \quad (22)$$

We can rewrite the experimental correlation for any key guess as the sum

$$q(k_0, k_1, k_2, k_3) = \sum_{i=0}^{2^{|k_0|}-1} \sum_{j=0}^{2^{|k_3|}-1} a_{ij}(-1)^{f_1(i \oplus k_0, k_1)}(-1)^{f_2(j \oplus k_3, k_2)} \quad (23)$$

Let us now consider that the values of k_1 and k_2 are fixed. The associated experimental correlations form a matrix $Q^{k_1, k_2} \in \mathbb{Z}^{2^{|k_0|} \times 2^{|k_3|}}$ with entries

$$q_{k_0, k_3}^{k_1, k_2} = q(k_0, k_1, k_2, k_3) \quad (24)$$

We can see that $Q^{k_1, k_2} = B^{k_1} A C^{k_2}$, where $B^{k_1} \in \mathbb{Z}^{2^{|k_0|} \times 2^{|k_0|}}$ and $C^{k_2} \in \mathbb{Z}^{2^{|k_3|} \times 2^{|k_3|}}$, and the elements of these matrices are defined as

$$b_{k_0, i}^{k_1} = (-1)^{f_1(i \oplus k_0, k_1)}, \quad c_{j, k_3}^{k_2} = (-1)^{f_2(j \oplus k_3, k_2)} \quad (25)$$

The matrices B^{k_1}, C^{k_2} adhere to the structure described in Proposition 1, and the Fast Walsh Transform can be used to multiply vector by them.

$$2^{|k_0|} B^{k_1} = H_{2^{|k_0|}} \text{diag}\left(\boldsymbol{\lambda}_1^{k_1}\right) H_{2^{|k_0|}}, \text{ where } \boldsymbol{\lambda}_1^{k_1} = H_{2^{|k_0|}} B_{\cdot 1}^{k_1} \quad (26)$$

$$2^{|k_3|} C^{k_2} = H_{2^{|k_3|}} \text{diag}\left(\boldsymbol{\lambda}_2^{k_2}\right) H_{2^{|k_3|}}, \text{ where } \boldsymbol{\lambda}_2^{k_2} = H_{2^{|k_3|}} C_{\cdot 1}^{k_2} \quad (27)$$

The matrices $Q^{k_1 k_2}$ can therefore be calculated as

$$2^{|k_0|+|k_3|} Q^{k_1 k_2} = H_{2^{|k_0|}} \text{diag}\left(\boldsymbol{\lambda}_1^{k_1}\right) H_{2^{|k_0|}} A H_{2^{|k_3|}} \text{diag}\left(\boldsymbol{\lambda}_2^{k_2}\right) H_{2^{|k_3|}} \quad (28)$$

As a result, the attack can be performed efficiently using Algorithm 3 as follows:

1. **Distillation phase:** Construct the matrix A by looking at each plaintext-ciphertext pair (x, y), finding the associated values of $i = x|_{\chi_0}$ and $j = y|_{\chi_3}$ and incrementing the corresponding a_{ij} by one.

Algorithm 3: General FFT algorithm (without the final phase)

Input: A collection $\mathcal{D} = \{(x, y = E_K(x))\}$ of N plaintext-ciphertext pairs.
Output: The experimental correlations $Q^{k_1,k_2}_{k_0,k_3}$.

// DISTILLATION PHASE
$A \leftarrow 0$;
forall $(x, y) \in \mathcal{D}$ **do** $a_{x|_{X_0}, y|_{X_3}} \leftarrow a_{x|_{X_0}, y|_{X_3}} + 1$;
// ANALYSIS PHASE
for $i \leftarrow 0$ **to** $2^{|k_0|} - 1$ **do** $A_{i\cdot} \leftarrow \mathrm{FWT}(A_{i\cdot})$;   // FWT on rows
for $j \leftarrow 0$ **to** $2^{|k_3|} - 1$ **do** $A_{\cdot j} \leftarrow \mathrm{FWT}(A_{\cdot j})$;   // FWT on columns
for $k_1 \leftarrow 0$ **to** $2^{|k_1|} - 1$; $i \leftarrow 0$ **to** $2^{|k_0|} - 1$ **do** $(\lambda_1^{k_1})_i \leftarrow f_1(i, k_1)$;   // $B^{k_1}_{\cdot 1}$
for $k_2 \leftarrow 0$ **to** $2^{|k_2|} - 1$; $j \leftarrow 0$ **to** $2^{|k_3|} - 1$ **do** $(\lambda_2^{k_2})_j \leftarrow f_2(j, k_2)$;   // $C^{k_2}_{\cdot 1}$
for $k_1 \leftarrow 0$ **to** $2^{|k_1|} - 1$ **do** $\lambda_1^{k_1} \leftarrow \mathrm{FWT}(\lambda_1^{k_1})$;   // Compute $\lambda_1^{k_1}$
for $k_2 \leftarrow 0$ **to** $2^{|k_2|} - 1$ **do** $\lambda_2^{k_2} \leftarrow \mathrm{FWT}(\lambda_2^{k_2})$;   // Compute $\lambda_2^{k_2}$
for $k_1 \leftarrow 0$ **to** $2^{|k_1|} - 1$; $k_2 \leftarrow 0$ **to** $2^{|k_2|} - 1$ **do**   // Compute $Q^{k_1,k_2}_{k_0,k_3}$
$\quad$ **for** $k_0 \leftarrow 0$ **to** $2^{|k_0|} - 1$; $k_3 \leftarrow 0$ **to** $2^{|k_3|} - 1$ **do**
$\quad\quad Q^{k_1,k_2}_{k_0 k_3} \leftarrow A_{k_0 k_3} \cdot (\lambda_1^{k_1})_{k_0} \cdot (\lambda_2^{k_2})_{k_3}$;
$\quad$ **for** $k_0 \leftarrow 0$ **to** $2^{|k_0|} - 1$ **do** $Q^{k_1,k_2}_{k_0\cdot} \leftarrow \mathrm{FWT}(Q^{k_1,k_2}_{k_0\cdot})$;
$\quad$ **for** $k_3 \leftarrow 0$ **to** $2^{|k_3|} - 1$ **do** $Q^{k_1,k_2}_{\cdot k_3} \leftarrow \mathrm{FWT}(Q^{k_1,k_2}_{\cdot k_3})$;
end
return $\{Q^{k_1,k_2}\}_{k_1,k_2}$;

---

2. **Analysis phase:** Compute all the experimental correlations $q(k_0, k_1, k_2, k_3)$:
   (a) Apply the FWT on all rows and columns of A to obtain a matrix $\widehat{A}$.
   (b) Construct the eigenvalue vectors $\lambda_1^{k_1}$ and $\lambda_2^{k_2}$ for all k_1, k_2 by calculating the first column of B^{k_1} or C^{k_2} and then applying the FWT.
   (c) Compute Q^{k_1,k_2} for all the values of k_1 and k_2:
      i. Copy $\widehat{A}$ and multiply each column by $\lambda_1^{k_1}$ and each row by $\lambda_2^{k_2}$ elementwise.
      ii. Apply the FWT on all the rows and columns to obtain Q^{k_1,k_2}.
   (d) Select the subkey guesses with the largest values of $|q(k_0, k_1, k_2, k_3)|$.
3. **Search phase.**

The time complexity of the distillation phase is $\rho_D N$ binary operations, where ρ_D is the cost of checking one pair. The distilled data occupies $2^{|k_0|+|k_3|}$ memory registers of up to n bits. The cost of applying the initial FWTs of step 2(a) is $\rho_A (|k_0| + |k_3|) 2^{|k_0|+|k_3|}$ (ρ_A/ρ_M is the cost of addition/multiplication) with no additional memory. The eigenvalue vectors can be precomputed with cost

$$\rho_{f_1} 2^{|k_0|+|k_1|} + \rho_{f_2} 2^{|k_2|+|k_3|} + \rho_A \left(|k_0| 2^{|k_0|+|k_1|} + |k_3| 2^{|k_2|+|k_3|} \right) \qquad (29)$$

where ρ_{f_1} and ρ_{f_2} are the costs of evaluating f_1 and f_2. These vectors are stored in $2^{|k_0|+|k_1|} + 2^{|k_2|+|k_3|}$ registers of $\max\{|k_0|, |k_3|\}$ bits. The cost of step 2(c) is

$$2\rho_M 2^{|k_0|+|k_1|+|k_2|+|k_3|} + \rho_A (|k_0| + |k_3|) 2^{|k_0|+|k_1|+|k_2|+|k_3|} \qquad (30)$$

This computation requires $2^{|k_0|+|k_3|}$ working registers of up to $n+|k_0|+|k_3|$ bits. If the experimental correlations need to be stored in full (for example if the FFT algorithm is used as a part of a multiple linear attack), then $2^{|k_0|+|k_1|+|k_2|+|k_3|}$ memory registers of n bits are required (we can divide by $2^{|k_0|+|k_3|}$).

It's interesting to compare the computational costs $\rho_D, \rho_{f_1}, \rho_{f_2}, \rho_A$ and ρ_M with the cost of a block cipher encryption ρ_E. In general, ρ_D, ρ_{f_1} and ρ_{f_2} should be negligible, as they are much simpler operations. For most cases ρ_A and ρ_M should be comparable to or smaller to the cost of an encryption, though this depends on the implementations of the cipher and the operations.

The adaptability of this algorithm to multiple and multidimensional linear attacks should also be considered. The distillation phase only needs to be performed once, which means our approach generalises the results of [35]. If there is no structure to the set of approximations, then the time cost of the analysis phase is multiplied by the number of approximations M. Additionally, the cost of computing the statistic Q_k from the correlations of each approximation is

$$M(\rho_M + \rho_A)2^{|k_0|+|k_1|+|k_2|+|k_3|} \tag{31}$$

If there are several approximations which share the same input mask α but differ in their output masks (or the other way around), then it is possible to reuse some partial results such as $B^{k_1}\widehat{A}$, which only need to be computed once. This can lead to a further reduction in time complexity.

3.2   Exploiting the Key Schedule of the Cipher

So far, we have assumed that the attacker must guess k_0, k_1, k_2 and k_3 independently. However, the key schedule of a cipher often induces dependence relationships between these four subkeys. These relationships can be easily exploited in the implementation of Matsui's Algorithm 2 without FFT, but it is not obvious how they can be used in accelerated attacks. We will now consider two strategies.

Walsh Transform Pruning

The first approach consists of applying the FWT algorithm but only computing the outputs which correspond to possible values of the subkeys, as suggested in [41]. To this end, we have studied pruned Walsh Transform algorithms, which efficiently compute a subset of outputs of the classical "full" transform. We have found a particularly useful pruned algorithm, which is detailed in Appendix B:

Proposition 3. *The components of the Walsh Transform of a vector of length 2^m which have n fixed bits in their position can be computed with complexity*

$$2^m + (m - n - 1)2^{m-n} \tag{32}$$

We have designed a modified analysis phase which considers the bits of k_0 which can be deduced from (k_1, k_2) and the bits of k_3 which can be deduced from (k_0, k_1, k_2). The roles of k_0 and k_3 can be easily exchanged if necessary.

1. Compute $H_{2^{k_0}}AH_{2^{k_3}}$ as normal.
2. Only compute the products $\mathrm{diag}(\lambda_1^{k_1})H_{2^{k_0}}AH_{2^{k_3}}\mathrm{diag}(\lambda_2^{k_2})$ for the values of (k_1, k_2) which are possible according to the key schedule.
3. For each pair (k_1, k_2), consider only the possible values of k_0 and prune the associated (column) Walsh Transforms accordingly.
4. For each of the rows of the resulting matrix, consider the possible values of k_3 and prune the associated Walsh Transform to these positions.

If (k_1, k_2) can only take $2^{|k_1|+|k_2|-l_{12}}$ different values, l_0 bits of k_0 can be deduced from (k_1, k_2) and l_3 bits of k_3 can be deduced from (k_0, k_1, k_2) then the complexity of the "pruned" analysis phase is

$$
\begin{aligned}
\rho_A(|k_0| + |k_3|)2^{|k_0|+|k_3|} &+ 2\rho_M 2^{|k_0|+|k_1|+|k_2|+|k_3|-l_{12}} \\
&+ \rho_A 2^{|k_1|+|k_2|+|k_3|-l_{12}}\left(2^{|k_0|} + (|k_0| - l_0 - 1)2^{|k_0|-l_0}\right) \\
&+ \rho_A 2^{|k_0|-l_0+|k_1|+|k_2|-l_{12}}\left(2^{|k_3|} + (|k_3| - l_3 - 1)2^{|k_3|-l_3}\right)
\end{aligned}
\tag{33}
$$

As l_0 and l_3 increase with respect to $|k_0|$ and $|k_3|$, the complexity approaches

$$
\rho_A(|k_0| + |k_3|)2^{|k_0|+|k_3|} + 2\left(\rho_M + \rho_A\right)2^{|k_0|+|k_1|+|k_2|+|k_3|-l_{12}}
\tag{34}
$$

This variant of the attack algorithm requires $2^{|k_0|+|k_3|}$ memory registers to hold the counters from the distillation phase, $2^{|k_0|+|k_1|} + 2^{|k_2|+|k_3|}$ registers for the eigenvalue vectors and $2^{|k_0|+|k_1|+|k_2|+|k_3|-l_{12}-l_0-l_3}$ registers to hold the experimental correlations, if they need to be stored in full.

Since applying Walsh Transform on all the rows and columns of a matrix is equivalent to performing the Walsh Transform on a vectorization of the matrix, it should be possible to prune this unique transform to the possible values of (k_0, k_3) associated to the current (k_1, k_2). In particular, it would be interesting to consider more complex relationships between these bits.

Multiple Linear Cryptanalysis

The previous approach has limited results if $2^{|k_0|+|k_3|}$ is already too large. In the case of multiple linear cryptanalysis, it is possible to reduce the complexity further by performing the algorithm separately for each linear approximation and then combining the information to obtain Q_k, as done in [41] and [12].

Let $\nu_i : \alpha_i \cdot \hat{x} \oplus \beta_i \cdot \hat{y}$, $i = 1, \ldots, M$ be a linear approximations of the inner cipher E_M. Multiple linear cryptanalysis requires the attacker to compute

$$
Q(k_0, k_1, k_2, k_3) = \frac{1}{N}\sum_{i=1}^{M}\left(q^i(k_0, k_1, k_2, k_3)\right)^2
\tag{35}
$$

In order to calculate one particular $\mathbf{q}^i$ some subkey bits might be unnecessary: some part of the subkey might be necessary for one approximation but not for a different one. Let us suppose that $q^i(k_0, k_1, k_2, k_3)$ can be calculated as $\hat{q}^i(k_0^i, k_1^i, k_2^i, k_3^i)$ (where $k_0^i = k_0|_{\chi_0^i}$ is a part of k_0, and so on), and that (k_0, k_1, k_2, k_3) can be deduced from a part k_T of the master key K. We will also suppose that the sets of masks (χ_0^i, χ_3^i) and $(\chi_0^i, \chi_1^i, \chi_2^i, \chi_3^i)$ take M_1 and M_2 different values over the set of M approximations, respectively. In this situation, the attacker can perform the following modified attack:

1. In the distillation phase, construct M_1 tables: for each plaintext-ciphertext mask pair (X_0, X_3), the table $A_{(X_0,X_3)}$ of size $2^{HW(\chi_0^i)} \times 2^{HW(\chi_3^i)}$.
2. For each approximation ν_i, compute a table of length $2^{|k_0^i|+|k_1^i|+|k_2^i|+|k_3^i|}$ containing all the possible values of $q^i(k_0^i, k_1^i, k_2^i, k_3^i)$ by using the FFT algorithm on the appropriate table from the distillation phase, $A_{(\chi_0^i,\chi_3^i)}$.
3. Merge the M tables from the previous step into M_2 "condensed" tables by adding the square correlations of approximations corresponding to the same choice of subkey bits, that is, one table for each possible value of (X_0, X_1, X_2, X_3). The associated condensed table contains the coefficients:

$$\sum_{\substack{(\chi_0^i,\chi_1^i,\chi_2^i,\chi_3^i) \\ =(X_0,X_1,X_2,X_3)}} \left(q^i(k_0^i, k_1^i, k_2^i, k_3^i)\right)^2 \quad \text{for all} \quad (k_0^i, k_1^i, k_2^i, k_3^i) \qquad (36)$$

4. For each possible guess of the partial master key k_T, use the key schedule to compute the associated values of $k_0^i, k_1^i, k_2^i, k_3^i$. Use the tables from the previous step to compute $Q(k_0, k_1, k_2, k_3)$.

Note that the individual calls to the FFT linear cryptanalysis algorithm can also be pruned in order to combine both key schedule exploitation approaches, and that steps 2 and 3 can be mixed in order to reduce the memory requirement.

The cost of the distillation phase is now $M_1 \rho_D N$. If ρ_{KS} denotes the cost of computing (k_0, k_1, k_2, k_3) from k_T, then the cost of the analysis phase is

$$\sum_{i=1}^{M} \left(2\rho_M 2^{|k_0^i|+|k_1^i|+|k_2^i|+|k_3^i|} + \rho_A(|k_0^i| + |k_3^i|)\left(2^{|k_0^i|+|k_1^i|+|k_2^i|+|k_3^i|} + 2^{|k_0^i|+|k_3^i|}\right)\right)$$

$$+ \sum_{i=1}^{M} \left(\rho_M 2^{|k_0^i|+|k_1^i|+|k_2^i|+|k_3^i|} + \rho_A 2^{|k_0^i|+|k_1^i|+|k_2^i|+|k_3^i|}\right) + (M_2\rho_A + \rho_{KS})2^{|k_T|}$$

$$(37)$$

The algorithm requires $\sum_{(X_0,X_3)} 2^{HW(X_0)+HW(X_3)}$ memory positions for the distillation counters and $\sum_{(X_0,X_1,X_2,X_3)} 2^{HW(X_0)+HW(X_1)+HW(X_2)+HW(X_3)}$ positions for the M_2 condensed correlation tables.

This algorithm can produce large gains in the case of multiple linear cryptanalysis (especially when the $|k_.^i|$ are significantly smaller than the $|k_.|$), but its success is more limited in multidimensional attacks, as there is always a linear approximation for which the $|k^i|$ are maximal.

Example implementation. We have implemented our key-recovery algorithm on a toy version of PRESENT with the aim of illustrating how all these different techniques can be used. The C code can be found at:

https://project.inria.fr/quasymodo/results/codes/.

4   Application to PRESENT

In order to showcase the potential of our key-recovery techniques, in this section we describe some new attacks on reduced-round variants of the block cipher PRESENT, which surpass the best previously known attacks (that were also linear), specifically [12,16,41]. Our results include new attacks on 26 and 27-round PRESENT which improve the parameters of the aforementioned attacks, as well as (to the best of our knowledge) the first attacks on 28-round PRESENT.

4.1   Linear Distinguishers for PRESENT

Previous linear attacks on PRESENT [12,16,33,37,41] have used the fact that the S-box has eight linear approximations with correlation 2^{-3} and whose input and output masks have Hamming weight 1. These approximations lead to many linear trails with one active S-box in each round, which form linear hulls with high potential and masks of weight 1. Our attacks make use of three different sets of approximations with masks of weight 1 or 2, which were found as follows.

We begin by computing the correlation of all approximations of one round of PRESENT which: (1) only have up to two active S-boxes and (2) only require up to two active S-boxes in the previous and the next rounds. There are 2800 input and output masks which verify these bounds on the number of active S-boxes, so a 2800 × 2800 correlation matrix was constructed. Then, the element-wise square of this matrix can be elevated to the number of rounds r to obtain an approximation of the ELP of all the linear approximations whose input and output masks are in this family. A similar approach is detailed in [1].

The analysis of the resulting matrices showed that the linear approximations of PRESENT with the largest ELP only have one active S-box in the first and the last rounds. Table 1 contains a classification (according to the ELP) of approximations with one active S-box in the first and the last round, and masks of Hamming weight 1 or 2. From these approximations, we have selected three different sets as linear distinguishers, considering both their linear capacity as well as the number of keybits involved in a two-round key-recovery.

Set I, with 128 approximations, has the lowest capacity, but only uses masks of Hamming weight 1 and has a cheaper key-recovery than the others. Set III has 448 approximations and the largest capacity but requires guessing a lot of bits in the key-recovery, as it has approximations with both masks of Hamming weight 2. Set II is an intermediate where masks of Hamming weight 2 are only used in the input. The capacity for these three sets can be found in Table 2. We have also estimated the advantage that is obtained by these sets of approximations using the statistical model that can be found in [9] and Appendix C.

Table 1. An empirical classification of linear approximations of PRESENT with input and output masks of Hamming weight 1 or 2 according to their ELP. Indicated are the active S-box of the first and last rounds, as well as the input and output masks of said S-boxes. Our three sets of approximations are indicated as I:*, II:o and III:†.

Group	Input Mask	Input S-Box	Output Mask	Output S-Box	Qty.	ELP $r=22$	ELP $r=23$	ELP $r=24$
A	$A_o^\dagger$	$5_o^\dagger, 6_o^\dagger, 9_o^\dagger, 10_o^\dagger$	$2_o^\dagger, 8_o^\dagger, 3^\dagger, 9^\dagger$	$5_o^\dagger, 7_o^\dagger, 13_o^\dagger, 15_o^\dagger$	64	$2^{-59.9}$	$2^{-62.5}$	$2^{-65.1}$
B	$C_o^\dagger$	$5_o^\dagger, 6_o^\dagger, 9_o^\dagger, 10_o^\dagger$	$2_o^\dagger, 8_o^\dagger, 3^\dagger, 9^\dagger$	$5_o^\dagger, 7_o^\dagger, 13_o^\dagger, 15_o^\dagger$	64	$2^{-60.4}$	$2^{-63.0}$	$2^{-65.6}$
C1	$A^\dagger$	$5_o^\dagger, 6_o^\dagger, 9_o^\dagger, 10_o^\dagger$	$2_o^\dagger, 8_o^\dagger, 3^\dagger, 9^\dagger$	$6_o^\dagger, 9, 11, 14^\dagger$	64			
C2	A	$5, 6, 9, 10$	$4, 5$	$5, 7, 13, 15$	32	$2^{-60.6}$	$2^{-63.2}$	$2^{-65.8}$
C3	$A_o^\dagger$	$7^\dagger, 11^\dagger, 13_o^\dagger, 14_o^\dagger$	$2_o^\dagger, 8_o^\dagger, 3^\dagger, 9^\dagger$	$5_o^\dagger, 7_o^\dagger, 13_o^\dagger, 15_o^\dagger$	64			
D	$^*2_o^\dagger, ^*4_o^\dagger, 3, 5$	$^*5_o^\dagger, ^*6_o^\dagger, ^*9_o^\dagger, ^*10_o^\dagger$	$^*2_o^\dagger, ^*8_o^\dagger, 3^\dagger, 9^\dagger$	$^*5_o^\dagger, ^*7_o^\dagger, ^*13_o^\dagger, ^*15_o^\dagger$	256	$2^{-60.8}$	$2^{-63.4}$	$2^{-66.0}$
E1	$C_o^\dagger$	$5_o^\dagger, 6_o^\dagger, 9_o^\dagger, 10_o^\dagger$	$2_o^\dagger, 8_o^\dagger, 3^\dagger, 9^\dagger$	$6_o^\dagger, 9, 11, 14^\dagger$	64			
E2	C	$5, 6, 9, 10$	$4, 5$	$5, 7, 13, 15$	32	$2^{-61.1}$	$2^{-63.7}$	$2^{-66.3}$
E3	$C_o^\dagger$	$7^\dagger, 11^\dagger, 13_o^\dagger, 14_o^\dagger$	$2_o^\dagger, 8_o^\dagger, 3^\dagger, 9^\dagger$	$5_o^\dagger, 7_o^\dagger, 13_o^\dagger, 15_o^\dagger$	64			
F1	A	$5, 6, 9, 10$	$2, 8, 3, 9$	10	16			
F2	A	$5, 6, 9, 10$	$4, 5$	$6, 9, 11, 14$	32			
F3	A	$5, 6, 9, 10$	$6, C$	$5, 7, 13, 15$	32	$2^{-61.3}$	$2^{-63.9}$	$2^{-66.5}$
F4	A_o	$7, 11, 13_o, 14_o$	$2_o, 8_o, 3, 9$	$6_o, 9, 11, 14_o$	64			
F5	A	$7, 11, 13, 14$	$4, 5$	$5, 7, 13, 15$	32			
F6	A	15	$2, 8, 3, 9$	$5, 7, 13, 15$	16			
G1	$^*2_o, ^*4_o, 3, 5$	$^*5_o, ^*6_o, ^*9_o, ^*10_o$	$^*2_o, ^*8_o, 3, 0$	$^*6_o, 9, 11, ^*14_o$	256			
G2	$2, 4, 3, 5$	$5, 6, 9, 10$	$4, 5$	$5, 7, 13, 15$	128	$2^{-61.5}$	$2^{-64.1}$	$2^{-66.7}$
G3	$8_o, 9$	$5_o, 6_o, 9_o, 10_o$	$2_o, 8_o, 3, 9$	$5_o, 7_o, 13_o, 15_o$	64			
G4	$^*2_o, ^*4_o, 3, 5$	$7, 11, ^*13_o, ^*14_o$	$^*2_o, ^*8_o, 3, 9$	$^*5_o, ^*7_o, ^*13_o, ^*15_o$	256			

Table 2. The capacities of our three sets of approximations.

	# Approx.	Capacity $(r=22)$	Capacity $(r=23)$	Capacity $(r=24)$
I (*)	128	$2^{-54.11}$	$2^{-56.71}$	$2^{-59.31}$
II (o)	296	$2^{-52.60}$	$2^{-55.20}$	$2^{-57.80}$
III (†)	448	$2^{-51.78}$	$2^{-54.38}$	$2^{-56.98}$

These approximations are not statistically independent (as they are not even linearly independent). One possible solution would be the application of multidimensional linear cryptanalysis. However, this would consider all the linear combinations of the approximations, and the benefits of the masks of low Hamming weight would be lost. Instead, we use the multiple linear cryptanalysis statistic, and we have estimated the probability of success under the assumption that the approximations are statistically independent. In order to justify the validity of the resulting estimations, we provide experimental results which conform to the theoretical predictions for a reduced number of rounds. Another possible approach would be the multivariate profiling technique of [12].

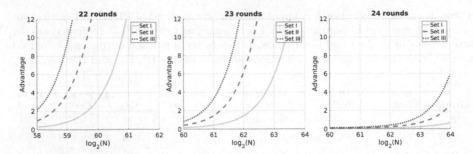

Fig. 3. Advantage obtained by each of our sets of approximations for 22, 23 and 24 rounds of PRESENT with 0.95 probability in a distinct known plaintext scenario.

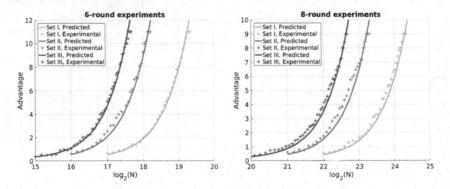

Fig. 4. Experimental advantage for attacks on 10 (resp. 12) rounds of PRESENT (using the linear distinguishers over 6 (resp. 8) rounds, with key-recovery on the first two and last two rounds). The statistic Q_k of the right key was compared against a random sample of 2^{12} (resp. 2^{10}) keys. The position of the right-key statistic among these provides an estimation of the advantage of up to 12 (resp. 10) bits. This was repeated for 20 different random right keys and 20 different random data samples for each value of N, providing a sample of 400 values of the advantage. The 5th percentile was used as an estimation of the advantage that's achieved with probability 0.95.

Figures 3 and 4 contain our advantage predictions for the 22, 23 and 24 round distinguishers as well as experiments for 6 and 8 rounds.

4.2   Improved Key-Recovery Attacks on 26 and 27-Round PRESENT

The first attack on PRESENT that we propose is based on set I of linear approximations. Since this set is only effective on up to 23 internal rounds and the attack will perform a key-recovery on the first two and last two rounds, the attack is effective on up to 27 rounds. In order to describe of these attacks more easily, we make use of the following properties of the bit permutation:

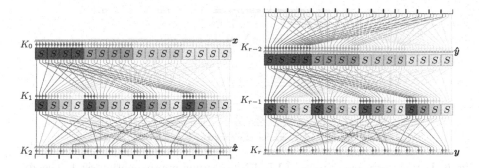

Fig. 5. The four groups of bits for the key-recovery on the first and last rounds.

Proposition 4 (Key-recovery on PRESENT). *Let $\hat{x}$ be the state at the beginning of the second round of PRESENT. Given two fixed values of i, j between 0 and 3, the four bits $\hat{x}_{48+4i+j}, \hat{x}_{32+4i+j}, \hat{x}_{16+4i+j}$ and $\hat{x}_{4i+j}$ can be obtained from the 16 bits of the plaintext $x_{16j+15} \ldots x_{16j}$, as well as the 16 bits of the first round subkey $\kappa^0_{16j+15} \ldots \kappa^0_{16j}$ and the 4 bits of the second round subkey $\kappa^1_{16i+4j+3} \kappa^1_{16i+4j+2} \kappa^1_{16i+4j+1} \kappa^1_{16i+4j}$.*

Let $\tilde{y}$ be the state before the application of sBoxLayer in the $(r-1)$-th round of PRESENT. Given two fixed values of i, j between 0 and 3, the four bits $\tilde{y}_{P(16j+12+i)}, \tilde{y}_{P(16j+8+i)}, \tilde{y}_{P(16j+4+i)}$ and $\tilde{y}_{P(16j+i)}$ can be obtained from the 16 bits of the ciphertext $y_{60+i}, y_{56+i}, \ldots, y_{4+i}, y_i$, as well as the 16 bits of the last round subkey $\kappa^r_{60+i}, \kappa^r_{56+i}, \ldots, \kappa^r_{4+i}, \kappa^r_i$ and the 4 bits of the previous round subkey $\kappa^{r-1}_{48+4i+j} \kappa^{r-1}_{32+4i+j} \kappa^{r-1}_{16+4i+j} \kappa^{r-1}_{4i+j}$.

With the help of the previous proposition, we can mount key-recovery attacks on up to 27-round PRESENT-80 by extending approximation set 1 with two rounds of key-recovery at both the top and bottom of the cipher using our multiple linear cryptanalysis key-recovery algorithm. The parameters of the time complexity formula can be computed using Proposition 4, and the details on the key schedule for 26 and 27 rounds can be found in Figs. 6 and 7. In particular

$$M_1 = 4, \ M_2 = 16, \ |k_0| = |k_3| = 32, \ |k_1| = |k_2| = 12$$
$$|k_0^i| = |k_3^i| = 16, \ |k_1^i| = |k_2^i| = 4 \text{ for all } i \tag{38}$$
$$|k_T| = 61 \text{ for 26 rounds}, \ |k_T| = 68 \text{ for 27 rounds}$$

A simple lower bound on the cost of a PRESENT encryption ρ_E is $2 \cdot 64 \cdot r + 64$ binary operations (since each round requires at the very least adding the round subkey and writing each output bit for sBoxLayer). For 26 rounds, this is 3392 binary operations. On the other hand, $\rho_A \simeq 128$, $\rho_M \simeq 3 \cdot 64^{\log_2(3)} \simeq 2143$. This means that the time complexity of the analysis phase should be lower than 2^{65} full encryptions for 26 rounds and 2^{72} full encryptions for 27 rounds. The search phase time complexity depends on the available data and can

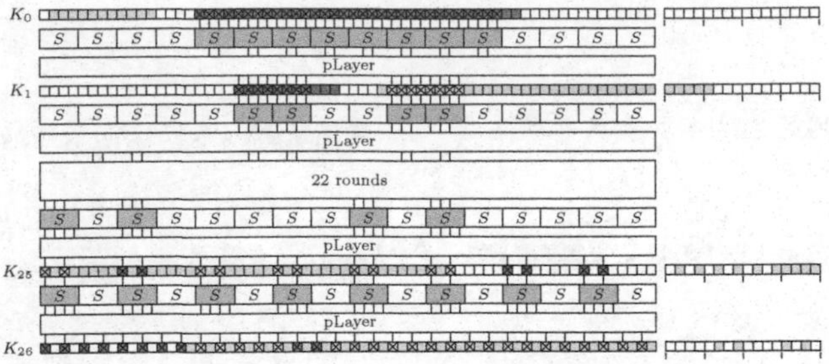

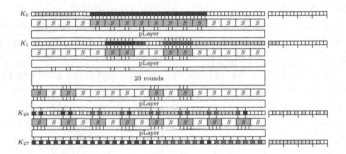

Fig. 6. Key-recovery on 26-round PRESENT-80 using approximation set I. The key-schedule effect is also represented in the figure. In total there are 96 bits of the subkeys which need to be guessed, which have been indicated by a cross. However, they can all be deduced from the $|k_T| = 61$ bits of key which have been highlighted in (dark) red. From these bits of key, all the bits in (light) green can be extracted, which includes all the necessary bits for the attack. (Color figure online)

Fig. 7. Key-recovery on 27-round PRESENT-80 using approximation set I.

be estimated thanks to the graphs in Fig. 3. The complexities of both attacks are given in Table 3. These attacks can be easily extended to the 128-bit key variant.

4.3 Key-Recovery Attacks on 28-Round PRESENT

Sets II and III can be extended by two rounds of key-recovery at both sides to construct attacks on up to 28-round PRESENT. As set III has a larger capacity but requires an expensive key-recovery, we found that set II is best suited to attack PRESENT-80 and set III gives better results on PRESENT-128.

The parameters for an attack using approximation set II on PRESENT-80, with the key-schedule analysis represented in Fig. 8 are:

$$M_1 = 8, \ M_2 = 32, \ |k_0| = 48, \ |k_1| = 24, \ |k_2| = 16, \ |k_3| = 32$$
$$|k_0^i| \leq 32, \ |k_1^i| \leq 8, \ |k_2^i| = 4, \ |k_3^i| = 16 \text{ for all } i, \ |k_T| = 73 \tag{39}$$

This attack requires use of the Pruned Walsh Transform. There are 160 approximations for which the input and output masks have weight 1. For each of

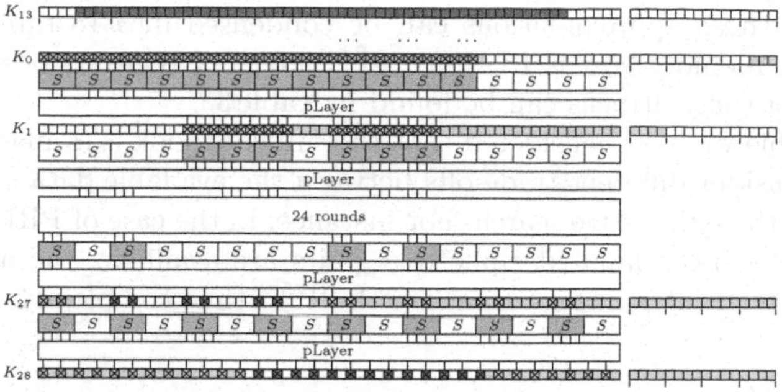

Fig. 8. Key-recovery on 28-round PRESENT-80 using approximation set II.

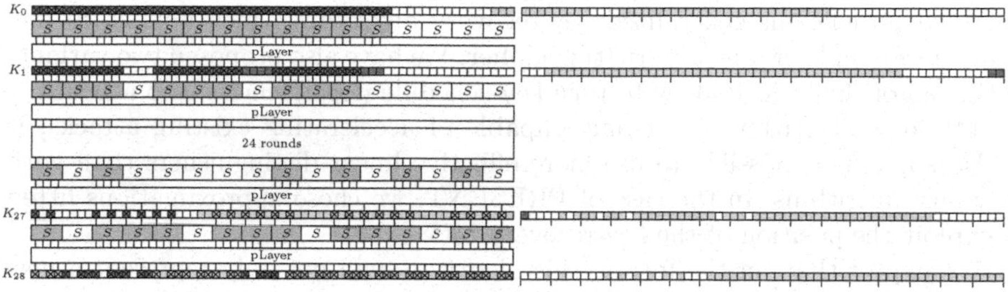

Fig. 9. Key-recovery on 28-round PRESENT-128 using approximation set III.

these approximations, computing the 2^{40} experimental correlations has cost $(16 + 16) \cdot 2^{16+4+4+16} = 2^{45}$ operations. For the remaining approximations, the cost should be $(32 + 16)2^{32+8+4+16} = 2^{65.58}$. However, all these approximations have an input S-box mask A or C. A look at the key-recovery diagrams shows that at least 5 bits of k_0^i can be deduced from k_1^i. By pruning the Walsh Transforms corresponding to the matrices B^{k_1}, the cost is reduced from 2^{37} to $2^{32.9}$ each. It also means that the memory requirement for each approximation is reduced by a factor of 2^5. After this first pruning, the transforms associated with the last two rounds (or the matrices C^{k_2}) can be pruned by fixing the bits of k_3 which can be deduced from k_0 and k_1, reducing the complexity of each transform to 2^{16}. This allows to keep the time complexity of the analysis phase below 2^{77} full PRESENT encryptions, and reduces the memory cost to 2^{51} registers.

For an attack using approximation set III on PRESENT-128, with the key-recovery part represented in Fig. 9 we have:

$$M_1 = 16, \ M_2 = 96, \ |k_0| = 48, \ |k_1| = 36, \ |k_2| = 36, \ |k_3| = 48$$
$$|k_0^i| \le 32, \ |k_1^i| \le 8, \ |k_2^i| \le 8, \ |k_3^i| \le 32 \text{ for all } i, \ |k_T| = 114 \tag{40}$$

This means that the time complexity of the analysis phase of the attack should be smaller than 2^{121}. The memory is mainly devoted to the condensed correlation tables corresponding to the largest value of $|k_0^i| + |k_1^i| + |k_2^i| + |k_3^i|$, that is, for approximations which require 80 bits of subkey to be guessed. Since the correlation of these approximations can be condensed into 18 tables, we conclude that the memory cost is $18 \cdot 2^{80} \simeq 2^{84.6}$ memory registers of 80 bits. The complexities of these attacks can be found in Table 3.

For the table we have considered that the full codebook is available, but it is possible to consider different trade-offs between the available data and the time complexity of the exhaustive search. For instance, in the case of PRESENT-128, if $N = 2^{63.5}$ distinct plaintext-ciphertext pairs are available, the advantage is 2.8 bits. This translates into an attack with $2^{125.2}$ time complexity.

5   Conclusion

New general and efficient key-recovery algorithm. First and foremost, we have provided an efficient generalized key-recovery algorithm which applies to any number of rounds of a key-alternating cipher. We have also proposed two variants of this algorithm which allow to take key-schedule dependencies into account.

The new algorithm is not only capable of accelerating existing attacks, it is also sometimes possible to use more effective linear distinguishers than with previous algorithms. In the case of PRESENT, we chose approximations fitted to exploit the position of the key-recovery bits.

We expect that, in the future, this algorithm will not only represent a new cryptanalysis tool, but will also allow to easily and accurately evaluate the security margin of new primitives with respect to linear attacks.

Table 3. Comparison of linear attacks on PRESENT. DKP: Distinct known plaintexts.

#Rounds	Key size	#KR rounds	#Approx.	Capacity	Data		Time	Memory	Success prob.	Source
	80	2	2295 (MD)	$2^{-55.38}$	$2^{64.0}$	KP	$2^{72.0}$	$2^{32.0}$	0.95	[16]
	80	2	2295 (MD)	$2^{-55.38}$	$2^{63.8}$	KP	$2^{72.0}$	$2^{32.0}$	0.51	[9,16] †
26	80	4	135	$2^{-55.47}$	$2^{63.0}$	KP	$2^{68.6}$	$2^{48.0}$	0.95	[12] *
	80	4	128	$2^{-54.11}$	$2^{61.1}$	KP	$2^{68.2}$	$2^{44.0}$	0.95	Set I
	80	4	128	$2^{-54.11}$	$2^{60.8}$	KP	$2^{71.8}$	$2^{44.0}$	0.95	Set I
	80	4	405 (MD)	$2^{-55.33}$	$2^{64.0}$	KP	$2^{74.0}$	$2^{67.0}$	0.95	[41] ‡
27	80	4	135	$2^{-58.06}$	$2^{63.8}$	DKP	$2^{77.3}$	$2^{48.0}$	0.95	[12] *
	80	4	128	$2^{-56.71}$	$2^{63.4}$	DKP	$2^{72.0}$	$2^{44.0}$	0.95	Set I
28	80	4	296	$2^{-57.80}$	$2^{64.0}$	DKP	$2^{77.4}$	$2^{51.0}$	0.95	Set II
	128	4	448	$2^{-56.98}$	$2^{64.0}$	DKP	2^{122}	$2^{84.6}$	0.95	Set III

†: [9] reevaluated the success probability of [16] with a more recent statistical model.
‡: [41] effectively uses one fourth of the data, as well as an older statistical model.
*: The capacities differ from those of [12] ($2^{-55.01}$ and $2^{-56.38}$ for 26 and 27 rounds) due to the different methods for its estimation. Furthermore, here we consider just the signal component, while [12] also includes noise (second term in Eq. 46).

Best attacks on PRESENT. Thanks to our algorithms, we have been able to provide the best known attacks on reduced round PRESENT, which in particular reach 28 rounds, while the best previous ones only reached up to 27. We believe it would be very hard to extend this attack further without any new ideas, and PRESENT still seems secure with 3 (instead of 4) rounds of security margin.

Open problems

– It would be interesting to implement semi-automatic tools to find the key-recovery complexity for a given set of approximations. Or, even further, one which finds an optimal set of approximations in terms of linear capacity *and* cost of key-recovery. The first seems feasible, but the second seems harder. It would be very interesting to find some results in this direction.
– Better linear attacks on other primitives, like NOEKEON, TRIFLE-BC, Simon,...
– Future applications to other cryptanalysis families: in [10] an equivalent to the algorithm from [18] was applied to zero-correlation attacks, and in [39] the same was done regarding integral attacks. It might be possible to extend and generalize these algorithms as we did with linear key-recovery.

Acknowledgements. This project has received funding from the European Research Council (ERC) under the European Union's Horizon 2020 research and innovation programme (grant agreement no. 714294 - acronym QUASYModo).

A   Key-Schedule of PRESENT

Algorithm 4: Key-schedule of PRESENT-80

Input: A master key K of 80 bits, a number of rounds r.
Output: $r + 1$ round subkeys K_i of 64 bits.
$\kappa_{63}^0 \ldots \kappa_0^0 \longleftarrow \kappa_{79} \ldots \kappa_{16}$;   // Extract first round subkey
for $i \leftarrow 1$ **to** r **do**

  $\kappa_{79} \ldots \kappa_0 \longleftarrow \kappa_{18} \ldots \kappa_{19}$;   // Rotate 19 bits to the right
  $\kappa_{79}\kappa_{78}\kappa_{77}\kappa_{76} \longleftarrow S(\kappa_{79}\kappa_{78}\kappa_{77}\kappa_{76})$;   // S on leftmost nibble
  $\kappa_{19}\kappa_{18}\kappa_{17}\kappa_{16}\kappa_{15} \longleftarrow \kappa_{19}\kappa_{18}\kappa_{17}\kappa_{16}\kappa_{15} \oplus i$;   // Add round counter
  $\kappa_{63}^i \ldots \kappa_0^i \longleftarrow \kappa_{79} \ldots \kappa_{16}$;   // Extract round subkey

end
return $\{K_i\}_{i=0}^r$;

Algorithm 5: Key-schedule of PRESENT-128

Input: A master key K of 128 bits, a number of rounds r.
Output: $r + 1$ round subkeys K_i of 64 bits.
$\kappa_{63}^0 \ldots \kappa_0^0 \longleftarrow \kappa_{127} \ldots \kappa_{64};$ `// Extract the first round subkey`
for $i \leftarrow 1$ **to** r **do**
   | $\kappa_{127} \ldots \kappa_0 \longleftarrow \kappa_{66} \ldots \kappa_{67};$ `// Rotate 61 bits to the left`
   | $\kappa_{127}\kappa_{126}\kappa_{125}\kappa_{124} \longleftarrow S(\kappa_{127}\kappa_{126}\kappa_{125}\kappa_{124});$
   | $\kappa_{123}\kappa_{122}\kappa_{121}\kappa_{120} \longleftarrow S(\kappa_{123}\kappa_{122}\kappa_{121}\kappa_{120});$ `// S on 2 nibbles`
   | $\kappa_{66}\kappa_{65}\kappa_{64}\kappa_{63}\kappa_{62} \longleftarrow \kappa_{66}\kappa_{65}\kappa_{64}\kappa_{63}\kappa_{62} \oplus i;$ `// Add round counter`
   | $\kappa_{63}^i \ldots \kappa_0^i \longleftarrow \kappa_{127} \ldots \kappa_{64};$ `// Extract i-th round subkey`
end
return $\{K_i\}_{i=0}^r;$

B   The (Pruned) Fast Walsh Transform

This appendix discusses the Fast Walsh Transform and how its pruned version can be computed efficiently in some cases. Other results on the Walsh-Hadamard matrices are covered by [40], while our pruning approach to the Walsh Transform is inspired by the treatment of the Fast Fourier Transform that was done in [28].

Definition 1. *The recursively-defined matrices*

$$H_1 = (1), \quad H_2 = \begin{pmatrix} 1 & 1 \\ 1 & -1 \end{pmatrix}, \quad H_{2^m} = \left((-1)^{i \cdot j} \right)_{0 \le i,j < 2^m} = H_2 \otimes H_{2^{m-1}} \in \mathbb{Z}^{2^m \times 2^m} \tag{41}$$

(where $\cdot$ denotes the inner product of binary vectors) are called Hadamard-Sylvester matrices. Given a vector $\boldsymbol{x} \in \mathbb{Z}^{2^m}$, we define its Walsh or Walsh-Hadamard Transform as the product $\mathcal{W}(\boldsymbol{x}) = H_{2^m}\boldsymbol{x}$:

$$\mathcal{W}(\boldsymbol{x})_i = \sum_{j=0}^{2^m-1} (-1)^{i \cdot j} x_j \tag{42}$$

If the absolute values of the coordinates of $\boldsymbol{x}$ are bound by the constant M, then the coordinates of its Walsh Transform are bound by $2^m M$.

The Walsh Transform of a vector can be computed efficiently using the result:

Proposition 5. *Given any $\pi \in S_m$, the matrix H_{2^m} can be decomposed as:*

$$H_{2^m} = \prod_{k=1}^m \left(I_{2^{m-\pi(k)+1}} \otimes H_2 \otimes I_{2^{\pi(k)}} \right) \tag{43}$$

Proof. This matrix equality is derived from the mixed product property:

$$H_{2^m} = \bigotimes_{k=1}^m H_2 = \bigotimes_{k=1}^m \left(I_2^{m-\pi(k)+1} H_2 I_2^{\pi(k)} \right) = \prod_{k=1}^m \left(I_{2^{m-\pi(k)+1}} \otimes H_2 \otimes I_{2^{\pi(k)}} \right)$$

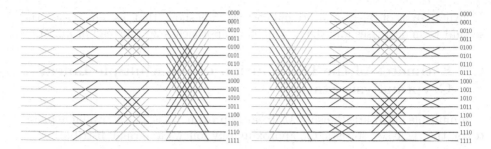

Fig. 10. Two different ways of computing the Pruned Walsh Transform of size $2^4 = 16$ when the leftmost bit of the output coordinates is set to zero and the second rightmost bit is set to one. The algorithm on the left requires 36 integer operations while the one on the right only requires 20.

The product of a vector by the matrix $H_{2^m}^k = I_{2^{m-k+1}} \otimes H_2 \otimes I_{2^k}$ can be computed with 2^m operations. This is represented graphically by 2^{m-1} "butterflies" (a denomination is borrowed from the literature on the FFT) which apply the matrix H_2 on pairs of coordinates.

The Walsh Transform of any vector is thus computable with $m2^m$ additions/substractions. Since we can choose any permutation of the indices k, there are $m!$ different ways of doing this. There are two examples in Fig. 10.

A *pruned* Fast Walsh Transform is any algorithm which aims to efficiently compute a subset of coordinates of $\mathcal{W}(\mathbf{x})$. Here we will consider the strict case in which n binary digits of the output indices are fixed. An approach to pruning the Fast Walsh Transform is working back from the desired outputs and only performing the operations which are strictly necessary. Since the number of required operations depends on the ordering of the matrices of the transform, we want to know which is the optimal ordering.

Proposition 6. *The Pruned Walsh Transform of a vector of length 2^m with n fixed output index bits can be computed with the following number of operations:*

$$2^m + (m - n - 1)2^{m-n} \tag{44}$$

Proof. The number of operations in each stage increases from the last stage of the transform to the first. This suggests that the last stages should be those which require the same number of inputs as they do outputs. There are $m - n$ such stages: those corresponding to the matrices $H_{2^m}^k$ where k is one of the bits whose values are *not* fixed. This is true because the output y_{i2^k+j} must be computed iff so must $y_{i2^k+2^{k-1}+j}$. These stages have a cost $(m-n)2^{m-n}$.

The other n stages, which should be performed at the beginning, successively double the number of operations from 2^{m-n} to 2^m. This means that the total cost of the optimized pruned FWT is

$$(m-n)2^{m-n} + \sum_{i=m-n+1}^{m} 2^{i-1} = (m-n)2^{m-n} + 2^m - 2^{m-n} = 2^m + (m-n-1)2^{m-n}.$$

An analysis of the computational cost formula shows that, as n increases, the second term decreases and the cost quickly approaches 2^m (instead of $m2^m$).

C   Estimates of the Distribution of the Multiple Linear Cryptanalysis Statistic

In a multiple linear attack using M linear approximations and N available plain-texts, the right-key statistic Q_k approximately follows a normal distribution:

$Q_k \sim \mathcal{N}(\mu_R, \sigma_R)$, where

$$\begin{cases} \mu_R = Exp_{D,K}(Q_k) = BM + NExp_K\left(C(K)\right) \\ \sigma_R^2 = Var_{D,K}(Q_k) = 2B^2M + 4BNExp_K\left(C(K)\right) + N^2Var_K\left(C(K)\right) \end{cases}$$

$$B = \begin{cases} 1 & \text{if repeated plaintexts are allowed} \\ \frac{2^n - N}{2^n - 1} & \text{for distinct known plaintexts} \end{cases}$$

$$\tag{45}$$

The moments of $C(K)$ can be estimated using a set $\mathcal{S}$ of significant linear trails:

$$Exp_K\left(C(K)\right) \simeq \sum_{i=1}^{M} \sum_{\gamma \in \mathcal{S}} \left(c(\alpha_i, \beta_i, \gamma)\right)^2 + M2^{-n} \tag{46}$$

$$Var_K\left(C(K)\right) \simeq 2\sum_{i=1}^{M} \left(\sum_{\gamma \in \mathcal{S}} \left(c(\alpha_i, \beta_i, \gamma)\right)^2 + 2^{-n}\right)^2 \tag{47}$$

Meanwhile, if the key guess $\tilde{k} \neq k$ is different from the right one, a multiple of the wrong key statistic follows a χ^2 distribution with M degrees of freedom:

$$\frac{1}{B + N2^{-n}}Q_{\tilde{k}} \sim \chi_M^2, \text{ so } \begin{cases} \mu_W = Exp_{D,K}(Q_{\tilde{k}}) = BM + NM2^{-n} \\ \sigma_W^2 = Var_{D,K}(Q_{\tilde{k}}) = 2M(B + N2^{-n})^2 \end{cases} \tag{48}$$

References

1. Abdelraheem, M.A.: Estimating the probabilities of low-weight differential and linear approximations on PRESENT-like ciphers. In: Kwon, T., Lee, M.-K., Kwon, D. (eds.) ICISC 2012. LNCS, vol. 7839, pp. 368–382. Springer, Heidelberg (2013). https://doi.org/10.1007/978-3-642-37682-5_26
2. Bar-On, A., Dinur, I., Dunkelman, O., Lallemand, V., Keller, N., Tsaban, B.: Cryptanalysis of SP networks with partial non-linear layers. In: Oswald, E., Fischlin, M. (eds.) EUROCRYPT 2015, Part I. LNCS, vol. 9056, pp. 315–342. Springer, Heidelberg (2015). https://doi.org/10.1007/978-3-662-46800-5_13
3. Bay, A., Huang, J., Vaudenay, S.: Improved linear cryptanalysis of reduced-round MIBS. In: Yoshida, M., Mouri, K. (eds.) IWSEC 2014. LNCS, vol. 8639, pp. 204–220. Springer, Cham (2014). https://doi.org/10.1007/978-3-319-09843-2_16
4. Beaulieu, R., Shors, D., Smith, J., Treatman-Clark, S., Weeks, B., Wingers, L.: The SIMON and SPECK lightweight block ciphers. In: Proceedings of the 52nd Annual Design Automation Conference, San Francisco, CA, USA, 7–11 June 2015, pp. 175:1–175:6. ACM (2015)

5. Beyne, T.: Block cipher invariants as eigenvectors of correlation matrices. In: Peyrin, T., Galbraith, S. (eds.) ASIACRYPT 2018, Part I. LNCS, vol. 11272, pp. 3–31. Springer, Cham (2018). https://doi.org/10.1007/978-3-030-03326-2_1

6. Biham, E., Perle, S.: Conditional linear cryptanalysis - cryptanalysis of DES with less than 242 complexity. IACR Trans. Symmetric Cryptol. 2018(3), 215–264 (2018). https://doi.org/10.13154/tosc.v2018.i3.215-264

7. Biryukov, A., De Cannière, C., Quisquater, M.: On multiple linear approximations. In: Franklin, M. (ed.) CRYPTO 2004. LNCS, vol. 3152, pp. 1–22. Springer, Heidelberg (2004). https://doi.org/10.1007/978-3-540-28628-8_1

8. Blondeau, C., Nyberg, K.: New links between differential and linear cryptanalysis. In: Johansson, T., Nguyen, P.Q. (eds.) EUROCRYPT 2013. LNCS, vol. 7881, pp. 388–404. Springer, Heidelberg (2013). https://doi.org/10.1007/978-3-642-38348-9_24

9. Blondeau, C., Nyberg, K.: Improved parameter estimates for correlation and capacity deviates in linear cryptanalysis. IACR Trans. Symmetric Cryptol. 2016(2), 162–191 (2016). https://doi.org/10.13154/tosc.v2016.i2.162-191

10. Bogdanov, A., Geng, H., Wang, M., Wen, L., Collard, B.: Zero-correlation linear cryptanalysis with FFT and improved attacks on ISO standards Camellia and CLEFIA. In: Lange, T., Lauter, K., Lisoněk, P. (eds.) SAC 2013. LNCS, vol. 8282, pp. 306–323. Springer, Heidelberg (2014). https://doi.org/10.1007/978-3-662-43414-7_16

11. Bogdanov, A., et al.: PRESENT: an ultra-lightweight block cipher. In: Paillier, P., Verbauwhede, I. (eds.) CHES 2007. LNCS, vol. 4727, pp. 450–466. Springer, Heidelberg (2007). https://doi.org/10.1007/978-3-540-74735-2_31

12. Bogdanov, A., Tischhauser, E., Vejre, P.S.: Multivariate profiling of hulls for linear cryptanalysis. IACR Trans. Symmetric Cryptol. 2018(1), 101–125 (2018). https://doi.org/10.13154/tosc.v2018.i1.101-125

13. Boura, C., Lallemand, V., Naya-Plasencia, M., Suder, V.: Making the impossible possible. J. Cryptol. 31(1), 101–133 (2018). https://doi.org/10.1007/s00145-016-9251-7

14. Boura, C., Naya-Plasencia, M., Suder, V.: Scrutinizing and improving impossible differential attacks: applications to CLEFIA, Camellia, LBlock and SIMON. In: Sarkar, P., Iwata, T. (eds.) ASIACRYPT 2014, Part I. LNCS, vol. 8873, pp. 179–199. Springer, Heidelberg (2014). https://doi.org/10.1007/978-3-662-45611-8_10

15. Canteaut, A., Naya-Plasencia, M., Vayssière, B.: Sieve-in-the-middle: improved MITM attacks. In: Canetti, R., Garay, J.A. (eds.) CRYPTO 2013, Part I. LNCS, vol. 8042, pp. 222–240. Springer, Heidelberg (2013). https://doi.org/10.1007/978-3-642-40041-4_13

16. Cho, J.Y.: Linear cryptanalysis of reduced-round PRESENT. In: Pieprzyk, J. (ed.) CT-RSA 2010. LNCS, vol. 5985, pp. 302–317. Springer, Heidelberg (2010). https://doi.org/10.1007/978-3-642-11925-5_21

17. Collard, B., Standaert, F.: A statistical saturation attack against the block cipher PRESENT. In: Fischlin, M. (ed.) CT-RSA 2009. LNCS, vol. 5473, pp. 195–210. Springer, Heidelberg (2009). https://doi.org/10.1007/978-3-642-00862-7_13

18. Collard, B., Standaert, F., Quisquater, J.: Improving the time complexity of Matsui's linear cryptanalysis. In: Nam, K.-H., Rhee, G. (eds.) ICISC 2007. LNCS, vol. 4817, pp. 77–88. Springer, Heidelberg (2007). https://doi.org/10.1007/978-3-540-76788-6_7

19. Collard, B., Standaert, F., Quisquater, J.: Experiments on the multiple linear cryptanalysis of reduced round serpent. In: Nyberg, K. (ed.) FSE 2008. LNCS, vol. 5086, pp. 382–397. Springer, Heidelberg (2008). https://doi.org/10.1007/978-3-540-71039-4_24

20. Daemen, J., Peeters, M., Assche, G.V., Rijmen, V.: Nessie proposal: the block cipher Noekeon. Nessie submission (2000). http://gro.noekeon.org/

21. Daemen, J., Rijmen, V.: Probability distributions of correlation and differentials in block ciphers. J. Math. Cryptol. 1(3), 221–242 (2007). https://doi.org/10.1515/JMC.2007.011

22. Datta, N., Ghoshal, A., Mukhopadhyay, D., Patranabis, S., Picek, S., Sadhukhan, R.: TRIFLE. Candidates to the NIST Lightweight competition (2019). https://csrc.nist.gov/projects/lightweight-cryptography/round-1-candidates

23. Etrog, J., Robshaw, M.J.B.: The cryptanalysis of reduced-round SMS4. In: Avanzi, R.M., Keliher, L., Sica, F. (eds.) SAC 2008. LNCS, vol. 5381, pp. 51–65. Springer, Heidelberg (2009). https://doi.org/10.1007/978-3-642-04159-4_4

24. Florez-Gutierrez, A.: Cryptanalysis of TRIFLE-BC. Official comment to the NIST-LWC forum (2019). https://csrc.nist.gov/CSRC/media/Projects/Lightweight-Cryptography/documents/round-1/official-comments/TRIFLE-official-comment.pdf

25. Hermelin, M., Cho, J.Y., Nyberg, K.: Multidimensional linear cryptanalysis of reduced round serpent. In: Mu, Y., Susilo, W., Seberry, J. (eds.) ACISP 2008. LNCS, vol. 5107, pp. 203–215. Springer, Heidelberg (2008). https://doi.org/10.1007/978-3-540-70500-0_15

26. Hermelin, M., Cho, J.Y., Nyberg, K.: Multidimensional extension of Matsui's algorithm 2. In: Dunkelman, O. (ed.) FSE 2009. LNCS, vol. 5665, pp. 209–227. Springer, Heidelberg (2009). https://doi.org/10.1007/978-3-642-03317-9_13

27. Hermelin, M., Nyberg, K.: Linear cryptanalysis using multiple linear approximations. Cryptology ePrint Archive, Report 2011/093 (2011). https://eprint.iacr.org/2011/093

28. Hu, Z., Wan, H.: A novel generic fast fourier transform pruning technique and complexity analysis. IEEE Trans. Signal Process. 53(1), 274–282 (2005). https://doi.org/10.1109/TSP.2004.838925

29. Kim, T.H., Kim, J., Hong, S., Sung, J.: Linear and differential cryptanalysis of reduced SMS4 block cipher. IACR Cryptology ePrint Archive 2008, 281 (2008). http://eprint.iacr.org/2008/281

30. Liu, M., Chen, J.: Improved linear attacks on the Chinese block cipher standard. J. Comput. Sci. Technol. 29(6), 1123–1133 (2014). https://doi.org/10.1007/s11390-014-1495-9

31. Matsui, M.: Linear cryptanalysis method for DES cipher. In: Helleseth, T. (ed.) EUROCRYPT 1993. LNCS, vol. 765, pp. 386–397. Springer, Heidelberg (1994). https://doi.org/10.1007/3-540-48285-7_33

32. Matsui, M.: The first experimental cryptanalysis of the data encryption standard. In: Desmedt, Y.G. (ed.) CRYPTO 1994. LNCS, vol. 839, pp. 1–11. Springer, Heidelberg (1994). https://doi.org/10.1007/3-540-48658-5_1

33. Nakahara, J.J., Sepehrdad, P., Zhang, B., Wang, M.: Linear (Hull) and algebraic cryptanalysis of the block cipher PRESENT. In: Garay, J.A., Miyaji, A., Otsuka, A. (eds.) CANS 2009. LNCS, vol. 5888, pp. 58–75. Springer, Heidelberg (2009). https://doi.org/10.1007/978-3-642-10433-6_5

34. National Institute of Standards and Technology (ed.): "FIPS-46: DataEncryption Standard (DES)" revised as FIPS 46-1:1988, FIPS 46-2:1993, FIPS46-3:1999 (1979). http://csrc.nist.gov/publications/fips/fips46-3/fips46-3.pdf

35. Nguyen, P.H., Wu, H., Wang, H.: Improving the Algorithm 2 in multidimensional linear cryptanalysis. In: Parampalli, U., Hawkes, P. (eds.) ACISP 2011. LNCS, vol. 6812, pp. 61–74. Springer, Heidelberg (2011). https://doi.org/10.1007/978-3-642-22497-3_5

36. Nyberg, K.: Linear approximation of block ciphers. In: De Santis, A. (ed.) EURO-CRYPT 1994. LNCS, vol. 950, pp. 439–444. Springer, Heidelberg (1995). https://doi.org/10.1007/BFb0053460

37. Ohkuma, K.: Weak keys of reduced-round PRESENT for linear cryptanalysis. In: Jacobson, M.J., Rijmen, V., Safavi-Naini, R. (eds.) SAC 2009. LNCS, vol. 5867, pp. 249–265. Springer, Heidelberg (2009). https://doi.org/10.1007/978-3-642-05445-7_16

38. Selçuk, A.A.: On probability of success in linear and differential cryptanalysis. J. Cryptol. 21(1), 131–147 (2008). https://doi.org/10.1007/s00145-007-9013-7

39. Todo, Y., Aoki, K.: FFT key recovery for integral attack. In: Gritzalis, D., Kiayias, A., Askoxylakis, I. (eds.) CANS 2014. LNCS, vol. 8813, pp. 64–81. Springer, Cham (2014). https://doi.org/10.1007/978-3-319-12280-9_5

40. Yarlagadda, R.K., Hershey, J.E.: Hadamard Matrix Analysis and Synthesis - With Applications to Communications and Signal/Image Processing. The Springer International Series in Engineering and Computer Science, vol. 383. Springer, Heidelberg (1997). https://doi.org/10.1007/978-1-4615-6313-6

41. Zheng, L., Zhang, S.: FFT-based multidimensional linear attack on PRESENT using the 2-bit-fixed characteristic. Secur. Commun. Netw. 8(18), 3535–3545 (2015). https://doi.org/10.1002/sec.1278

New Slide Attacks on Almost Self-similar Ciphers

Orr Dunkelman[1]([⊠])(iD), Nathan Keller[2]([⊠]), Noam Lasry[2], and Adi Shamir[3]

[1] Computer Science Department, University of Haifa, Haifa, Israel
orrd@cs.haifa.ac.il
[2] Department of Mathematics, Bar-Ilan University, Ramat-Gan, Israel
nkeller@math.biu.ac.il, noam.lasry@gmail.com
[3] Faculty of Mathematics and Computer Science, Weizmann Institute of Science,
Rehovot, Israel
adi.shamir@weizmann.ac.il

Abstract. The slide attack is a powerful cryptanalytic tool which can break iterated block ciphers with a complexity that does not depend on their number of rounds. However, it requires complete self similarity in the sense that all the rounds must be identical. While this can be the case in Feistel structures, this rarely happens in SP networks since the last round must end with an additional post-whitening subkey. In addition, in many SP networks the final round has additional asymmetries – for example, in AES the last round omits the MixColumns operation. Such asymmetry in the last round can make it difficult to utilize most of the advanced tools which were developed for slide attacks, such as deriving from one slid pair additional slid pairs by repeatedly re-encrypting their ciphertexts. Consequently, almost all the successful applications of slide attacks against real cryptosystems (e.g., FF3, GOST, SHACAL-1) had targeted Feistel structures rather than SP networks.

In this paper we overcome this "last round problem" by developing four new types of slide attacks. We demonstrate their power by applying them to many types of AES-like structures (with and without linear mixing in the last round, with known or secret S-boxes, with periodicity of 1, 2 and 3 in their subkeys, etc). In most of these cases, the time complexity of our attack is close to $2^{n/2}$, the smallest possible complexity for most slide attacks. Our new slide attacks have several unique properties: The first uses *slid sets* in which each plaintext from the first set forms a slid pair with some plaintext from the second set, but without knowing the exact correspondence. The second makes it possible to create from several slid pairs an exponential number of new slid pairs which form a hypercube spanned by the given pairs. The third has the unusual property that it is always successful, and the fourth can use known messages instead of chosen messages, with only slightly higher time complexity.

1 Introduction

Most modern block ciphers are constructed as a cascade of r keyed components, called rounds. Each round by itself can be cryptographically weak, but as r

© International Association for Cryptologic Research 2020
A. Canteaut and Y. Ishai (Eds.): EUROCRYPT 2020, LNCS 12105, pp. 250–279, 2020.
https://doi.org/10.1007/978-3-030-45721-1_10

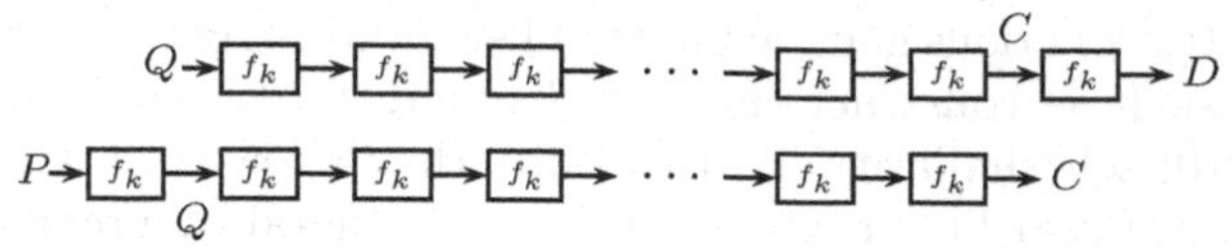

Fig. 1. A slid pair

increases, the scheme becomes resistant against almost all the standard crypt-analytic attacks (e.g., differential cryptanalysis [8], linear cryptanalysis [28]). However, there is one type of attack called a *slide attack* (introduced in 1999 by Biryukov and Wagner [9][1]) which can handle an arbitrarily large number of rounds with the same complexity.

The original slide attack targets ciphers that are a cascade of r *identical* rounds, i.e.,

$$E_k = f_k^r = f_k \circ f_k \circ \cdots \circ f_k,$$

and tries to find a *slid pair* of plaintexts (P, Q) such that $Q = f_k(P)$, as demonstrated in Fig. 1. Due to the structure of E_k, the corresponding ciphertexts $C = E_k(P), D = E_k(Q)$ must satisfy $D = f_k(C)$. Hence, if a slid pair (P, Q) is given, the adversary can use the simplicity of f_k to solve the system of equations to recover k:

$$\begin{cases} Q = f_k(P), \\ D = f_k(C), \end{cases} \tag{1}$$

The adversary can start from any collection of $O(2^{n/2})$ plaintexts along with their ciphertexts, and consider their $O(2^n)$ pairs. One of them is likely to be a slid pair, but the adversary does not know which one it is. By trying to solve the system of Equation (1) for all the pairs, she gets a simple slide attack whose data complexity is $O(2^{n/2})$ known plaintexts, memory complexity is $O(2^{n/2})$ (which is used to store the data), and time complexity is $O(t \cdot 2^n)$ (where t is the time required for solving the system (1)).

1.1 Applicability of Slide Attacks to Modern Ciphers

The original slide attack can be used only when f_k is so simple that it can be broken efficiently using only two known input/output pairs. Subsequent papers (e.g., [4,10,14,16,18]) developed advanced variants of the slide attack that allow attacking self-similar constructions in which f_k is rather complex. A central observation used in many of these variants is that if (P, Q) is a slid pair, then $(E_k(P), E_k(Q))$ is also a slid pair, and thus the adversary can create from a single slid pair arbitrarily many additional *friend pairs* by repeatedly encrypting P and Q in an adaptively chosen message attack. These advanced variants made

---

[1] The slide attack is related to several previous techniques, e.g., the attack of Grossman and Tucherman on Feistel ciphers [24] and Biham's related-key attack [6]. Sometimes, differential, linear, or subspace invariant attacks [27] may also succeed independently of the number of rounds, when the underlying property is "strong" enough.

it possible to attack various generic forms of Feistel constructions with a periodic key schedule, such as constructions with 1-round [9], 2-round [9], 3-round [4] and 4-round [10] self similarity. Furthermore, they allowed obtaining practical attacks on several real life cryptosystems – most notably, breaking the block cipher Keeloq [1] and the 128-bit key variant of the block cipher GOST [4], and attacking several hash functions [20].

While the advanced slide attacks extended the applicability of the technique, the basic requirement that all the round functions must be exactly the same has remained. As a result, it seemed that slide attacks can be thwarted completely by inserting into the encryption process round constants that break the full symmetry between the rounds. This countermeasure has become standard and is applied in most modern block ciphers.

However, it turned out that round constants are not an ultimate solution, as in many cases improper choice of the constants or interrelation between the round constants and other components of the cipher, can be used to mount a slide attack despite the countermeasure.

A recent example is the format preserving encryption scheme FF3 [11]. This scheme was selected as a US standard by NIST in 2016, but had to be revised in 2017 due to a devastating slide attack by Durak and Vaudenay [17]. This happened even though the slide attack is well known, leading the designers of the cryptosystem to use the standard countermeasure of using different round constants to avoid them. Yet another example is the block cipher SHACAL-1 that was broken by Biham et al. [7] using a slide attack, although it used round constants. It thus turns out that while adding round constants may be a useful countermeasure, it is far from being a universal countermeasure, and slide attacks remain highly relevant in practice.

1.2 Slide Attacks on SP Networks

Most of the previously known slide attacks, including the attacks on FF3, GOST, Lilliput-AE and SHACAL1 described above, apply to Feistel constructions. The other major type of a block cipher, the Substitution-Permutation (SP) Network, cannot be directly attacked by a slide attack since its last round is always different from the other rounds.

Consider, for example, an AES-like structure in which each round consists of XORing a subkey (which we denote by K), applying a parallel layer of S-boxes (denoted by S), and linearly mixing their outputs (denoted by A). Assume in addition that two subkeys are used in the cyclic order $(k_1, k_2, k_1, k_2, \ldots)$. Simply composing these round functions makes no sense since the last layers of S-boxes and linear mapping are known and can thus be stripped off. Any sensible design must thus add to the last round a final post-whitening subkey, such as k_1, before outputting the ciphertext. This makes the last round different from the other rounds, and we cannot simply complete the construction into a self similar structure by applying to it $A \circ S \circ K \circ A \circ S$ since we do not know the subkey k_2 used in K. A similar situation arises when the S-boxes are secret or when the last round operation A (before the post-whitening key) differs from previous rounds.

Any such asymmetry suffices in order to destroy the crucial property that if two plaintexts (P, Q) are a slid pair then so are their ciphertexts $(E_k(P), E_k(Q))$, upon which many advanced slide attacks rely. In fact, the only advanced slide attack on SP networks published so far, by Bar-On et al. [4, Sect. 2.2, 2.3] on an AES-like cipher with a 2-round or 3-round self-similarity, applies only under a non-standard additional assumption on the structure of the cipher.[2]

1.3   Our Settings

In this paper we overcome the *last round problem* by developing new slide attacks that can be applied to SP-networks with an arbitrarily large number of rounds in which the last round is different from the previous rounds. To be concrete, we consider ciphers that can be viewed as a cascade

$$K \circ A \circ S \circ K \circ A \circ S \circ \ldots K \circ A \circ S \circ K,$$

where K denotes the XORing of a secret subkey, S is a non-linear operation (S-box) applied in parallel to sub-blocks of size s of the state, and A is an affine operation. We call this structure KSA, and say that it has an ℓ-round self-similarity if the subkeys have the periodic structure $k_1, k_2, \ldots, k_\ell, k_1, k_2, \ldots, k_\ell, \ldots$. We denote such a structure by ℓ-KSA.

We note that extremely simple key schedules, and in particular periodic key-schedules with a short period, are widely used in modern lightweight block ciphers, for the sake of saving place on the hardware taken by the key schedule mechanism. Examples include LED-64 [25], Zorro [19], PRINTcipher [26], CGEN [29] and MIDORI128 [3] (which have identical subkeys), LED-128 [25], CRAFT [5] and MIDORI64 [3] (which have period 2), and many others.

Of course, designers of most modern block ciphers protect the ciphers against slide attacks by adding round constants in order to destroy the self-similarity. However, as was mentioned above, this countermeasure is not always sufficient. In addition, some lightweight cryptosystems have a large number of simple rounds, and XOR'ing a different randomly generated constant to each round greatly increases the amount of memory required to implement the scheme, which is very undesirable in many IoT applications. Consequently, designers of such cryptosystems may be tempted to use other forms of asymmetry into their designs, such as using a different last round, but as we show in this paper, such a simple countermeasure can be defeated by new variants of slide attacks.

We study two types of KSA constructions: The first is ℓ-KSAf, composed of a sequence of rounds of the form $A \circ S \circ K$ with an ℓ-periodic key, augmented by a final key whitening – which is the structure of many modern SP networks. The second type is ℓ-KSAt, which differs from ℓ-KSAf by omission of the affine operation A in the last round. Such a change is performed in some block ciphers for implementation reasons—most notably, in the AES.

---

[2] The additional assumption (that was not mentioned in [4]) is that either the final key whitening step is omitted, or the number of rounds is *odd* (for 2-round self similarity) or of the form $3\ell + 2$ (for 3-round self-similarity).

We usually assume that the operations S, A are not key-dependent (like in AES). However, interestingly, some of our new attacks apply with only a small complexity overhead when S is key-dependent (like in the AES variant with a secret S-box studied in [21,23,30,31]). We denote the block size by n and the S-box size by s, and state our results in terms of the parameters n, s.

1.4   Our Contributions

We present four entirely new types of slide attacks, which solve the last round problem in four different ways:

Slid sets. In this attack, we attach to each candidate slid pair (P, Q) a pair of *sets* $\mathcal{T}_P = \{P_1, P_2, \ldots, P_d\}$ and $\mathcal{T}_Q = \{Q_1, Q_2, \ldots, Q_d\}$ such that for each i there exists j for which (P_i, Q_j) is a slid pair. That is, the set $\mathcal{T}_P$ is transformed into the set $\mathcal{T}_Q$, while we do not know what is the counterpart of each specific value in $\mathcal{T}_P$. Of course, this technique requires entirely different ways to solve the equation system (1), and we provide such techniques as well.

Hypercube of slid pairs. This technique first uses differential properties of the cipher to attach to each candidate slid pair (P, Q) a pair of d-tuples $\mathcal{T}_P = (P_1, P_2, \ldots, P_d)$ and $\mathcal{T}_Q = (Q_1, Q_2, \ldots, Q_d)$ such that with some unexpectedly high probability, each (P_i, Q_i) is a slid pair. Then, it uses a 'mixing' construction reminiscent of the recently proposed *mixture* attack [22] to leverage the d-tuples into 2^d-tuples of slid pairs. Roughly speaking, if the slid pairs are placed at d vertices of a d-dimensional hypercube, the technique allows us to attach to them $2^d - d$ additional slid pairs which are placed at all other vertices of the cube.

Suggestive plaintext structures. This attack uses two plaintext structures $\mathcal{T}_P$ and $\mathcal{T}_Q$, designed in such a way that the mere knowledge that some $P \in \mathcal{T}_P$ has a slid counterpart $Q \in \mathcal{T}_Q$ reveals significant key information, which is used in the solution of the equation system (1). An interesting feature of this attack is that while its data complexity is $3 \cdot 2^{n/2}$, which is only slightly more than the $2^{n/2}$ complexity of standard slide attacks, it has 100% success probability. Note that the success probability of standard slide attacks is about 63%; it can be increased by using more data, but cannot get to 100% success unless the data complexity is made extremely large.

Substitution slide. This attack is aimed at truncated ℓ-KSA constructions, in which in the equation system (1), the second equation is much more complex than the first one. We use substitution into the (easier) first equation in order to remove the key dependence from the (harder) second equation and transform it into an even more complex equation which depends only on plaintexts and ciphertexts and not on the key. This attack type applies even in the more restrictive (and more realistic, of course) known plaintext model.

1.5   Our Results

Here are a few concrete results that can be obtained with our new slide attacks (the full summary can be found in Table 1):

Table 1. Summary of our new results

Cipher	Technique	Complexity (general)		AES-like	
		Data/Memory	Time	Data/Memory	Time
Known S-Boxes					
1-KSAf	Slide [4]	$2^{n/2}$ (KP)	$2^{n/2}$	2^{64} (KP)	2^{64}
2-KSAf	Slide [4]*	$s \cdot 2^{s+n/2}$ (ACPC)	$s \cdot 2^{s+n/2}$	2^{69}	2^{69}
3-KSAfi[†]	Slide [4]**	$2^{(m+n)/2}$ (ACPC)	$2^{(m+n)/2}$	2^{81}	2^{81}
1-KSAt	Suggestive str. (Sect. 5)	$3 \cdot 2^{n/2}$ (CP)	$4 \cdot 2^{n/2}$	$2^{65.6}$ (CP)	2^{66}
1-KSAt	Sub. slide (Sect. 6)	$2^{n/2}$ (KP)	$2^{3n/4}$	2^{64} (KP)	2^{96}
2-KSAf	Slid sets (Sect. 3)	$2^{(n+s)/2+1}$ (CP)	$2^{(n+s)/2+1}$	2^{69} (CP)	2^{69}
2-KSAf	Slide + Key Guessing (FV)	$(n/s)2^{n/2}$ (CP)	$2^{n/2+s}$	2^{68} (CP)	2^{72}
2-KSAf	Slide + Pt/Ct Coll. (FV)*	See Full Version for full details		$2^{82‡}$ (KP)	2^{82}
2-KSAtpi[†]	Slid sets (FV)	$2^{(n+m)/2+1}$ (CP)	$\max\{2^{(n+m)/2+1}, 2^{2m}\}$	2^{78} (CP)	2^{78}
3-KSAfi[†]	Slid sets (FV)	$2^{(n+m)/2+1}$ (CP)	$\max\{2^{(n+m)/2+1}, 2^{2m}\}$	2^{81} (CP)	2^{81}
Secret S-Boxes					
1-KSAf	Slid sets (Sect. 3)	$1.17\sqrt{s}2^{(n+s)/2}$ (CP)	$1.17\sqrt{s}2^{(n+s)/2}$	$2^{70.3}$ (CP)	$2^{70.3}$
1-KSAf	Hypercube (Sect. 4)	$\sqrt{s}2^{n/2+s(s+3)/4+1}$ (CP)	$\sqrt{s}2^{n/2+s(s+3)/4+1}$	2^{88} (CP)	2^{88}

The exact definition of all variants is given in Sect. 2.1
KP – Known Plaintext; CP – Chosen Plaintext; ACPC – Adaptive Chosen Plaintext and Ciphertext
FV—Full version of the paper
For AES-like $n = 128$, $s = 8$
[†] – this version has incomplete diffusion layer, m denotes the "word" size of the linear operation.
[‡] – the memory complexity of this attack is 2^{47}.
* – this attack works for an odd number of rounds.
** – this attack works when the number of rounds is 1 mod 3.

1. Using the *suggestive plaintext structures* technique, we can break 1-KSAt (e.g. a variant of AES with identical round subkeys and with no MixColumns operation in the last round) with data and time complexity of $2^{n/2}$ (2^{64} in the special case of AES). In [4], Bar-On et al. presented an attack with the same complexity, but only on 1-KSAf, or equivalently, AES in which the MixColumns operation in the last round is not omitted.
2. Using *substitution slide*, we can break 1-KSAt with complexity of $2^{(n+4s)/2}$ known plaintexts and time (2^{80} in the special case of AES).
3. Using *slid sets*, we can break 2-KSAt (e.g., a variant of AES with 2-periodic round subkeys and with no MixColumns operation in the last round) with data and time complexity of $2^{(n+3s)/2}$ (2^{76} in the specific case of AES).

Organization of the Paper

In Sect. 2 we present the setting and notations used throughout the paper, as well as some preliminary steps that are routinely performed in all our attacks. In addition, we present the previous attack by Bar-On et al. [4] on 1-KSA. In Sect. 3 we present the *slid sets* technique and use it for attacking several constructions (e.g., 2-KSAf and 1-KSA with secret S-boxes). Section 4 presents the new *hypercube of slid pairs* technique and presents an attack on 1-KSA with secret S-boxes. The *suggestive plaintext structures* technique is presented in Sect. 5. We introduce the *substitution slide* in Sect. 6. Several of our attacks are presented in the full version. Finally, Sect. 7 concludes the paper.

2   Preliminaries

In this section we present the setting and notations that are used throughout the paper, and describe the slide attack of Bar-On et al. [4] on SPNs with a 1-round self similarity, which provides a simple example of the attack frameworks that we use in this paper.

2.1   Setting and Notations

While the attacks presented in the paper target many different constructions and use different techniques, they are all presented using a uniform setting and set of notations. All these notations are given and explained in this section.

The general structure of the ciphers we study. Throughout the paper, we consider a block cipher $E : \{0,1\}^n \times \{0,1\}^\kappa \rightarrow \{0,1\}^n$, which transforms an n-bit plaintext P into an n-bit ciphertext C, using a κ-bit key k. For the sake of simplicity, we assume that $\kappa = n$, but the results can be easily adapted for other values of κ. We assume that the cipher is iterative, that is, consists of a composition of r simpler functions, called rounds. All the attacks we present are applicable with the same complexity to an arbitrarily large number of rounds.[3]

We assume that the first $r-1$ rounds of the cipher have the standard general structure of an SPN, that is,

$$(A \circ S \circ K)^{r-1} = A \circ S \circ K \circ A \circ S \circ \ldots K \circ A \circ S \circ K,$$

where K denotes key addition, S denotes a non-linear operation (S-box) applied in parallel to words of s bits into which the state is partitioned, and A denotes an affine operation. As the cipher essentially consists of repetitions of the sequence of operations $A \circ S \circ K$, we name it KSA.

The structure of the last round. Regarding the last round, we study two types of constructions:

- *Full last round* constructions, in which a single key addition operation is appended at the end of the last round. That is,

  Full r-round KSA $= (K \circ A \circ S \circ K) \circ (A \circ S \circ K)^{r-1} = K \circ (A \circ S \circ K)^r.$

  This structure is exemplified in Fig. 2.
- *Truncated last round* constructions, in which a key addition is appended at the end of the last round, and in addition, the last round affine transformation A is omitted. That is,

  Truncated r-round KSA $= (K \circ S \circ K) \circ (A \circ S \circ K)^{r-1}.$

---

[3] The attacks presented in the full version (Slide and Key Guessing, and Slide and plaintext/ciphertext collision) depend on the residue of r modulo the period of the subkey sequence, but not on the number of repetitions. All other attacks are independent of the number of rounds.

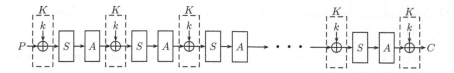

Fig. 2. The structure of 1-KSAf

The first type corresponds to a generic SPN construction, while the second type corresponds to an AES-like construction, as removal of the last round affine operation is adopted in the AES design.[4]

The structure of the operations K, S, A. In addition to the last round, the constructions we study differ in the assumptions on the operations K, S, A:

- *Key addition:* We shall always assume that the operation K in round i denotes XOR with an n-bit round subkey k_i, where the sequence of subkeys $k_1, k_2, k_3, \ldots$ is periodic. We study the variants 1-KSA, 2-KSA, and 3-KSA, in which the length of the period is 1, 2, and 3, respectively. We assume that all subkeys are derived from the n-bit secret key K using some "sufficiently complex" function; hence, we never exploit relations between distinct subkeys, and at the same time, we aim for attacks of complexities lower than 2^n, as otherwise, the attack is slower than exhaustive key search. (We note that such an assumption on the key schedule algorithm is made in many papers analyzing the security of generic constructions; see, e.g., [2]).
- *The S-box layer S:* We shall always assume that the operation S consists of partition of the state into s-bit words and parallel application of the same function $S : \{0,1\}^s \to \{0,1\}^s$ to the blocks. We study two types of constructions: the standard type in which the S-box S is publicly known (like in AES), and the secret S-box type in which S is derived from the secret key using a complex function, and thus, is unknown to the adversary (like in the variants of AES studied in [21,23,30,31]). In both types of constructions, we do not exploit the specific structure of the S-box.
- *The affine layer A:* We consider two variants of the operation A. In the *complete diffusion* variant, A applies a publicly known affine transformation to the entire state (i.e., the state is viewed as an n-bit vector v, and is transformed into $A'v + w$, where A' is an n-by-n binary matrix, $w \in \{0,1\}^n$, and the operations are performed over Z_2). In the *incomplete diffusion* variant, the state is partitioned into several parts (e.g., 4 parts in the case of AES), and the same affine transformation A is applied to each of them in parallel.

---

[4] We note that in AES, only part of the last round affine layer is omitted. Namely, the MixColumns operation is omitted, while the ShiftRows operation is left unchanged. While maintaining the ShiftRows operation affects the complexity of some attacks that exploit the key schedule (just like the omission of MixColumns, see [15]), it has no effect on our attacks. Hence, for the sake of this paper, the design of the last round of AES is equivalent to removing the entire affine layer.

In this variant, we introduce an additional parameter, m, to denote the size of each part (e.g., 32 bits in AES).

Summary of types of constructions. To summarize, the constructions we consider are defined by four parameters:

1. The length of the key period (1, 2, or 3);
2. Type of the last round – *full* (only a key addition appended) or *truncated* (key addition appended and affine operation removed);
3. Type of the substitution layer S – *public* S-box or *secret* S-box derived from the secret key;
4. Type of the affine layer – *complete diffusion* (i.e., A acts on the entire state) or *incomplete diffusion* (i.e., A acts on several parts of the state in parallel).

Notation of types of constructions. The notation we use for the constructions reflects all four parameters: the number at the beginning is the length of the key period, then the letter 'f' or 't' says whether the last round is full or truncated, then the letter 'p' or 's' denotes whether the S-box is public or secret, and finally, the letter 'c' or 'i' denotes whether the diffusion is complete or incomplete. If some parameter is not included (e.g., neither 'p' nor 's' appear), this means that the attack applies to both types described by that parameter.

For example, 2-KSAfpi denotes KSA with a 2-round key period, full last round, public S layer and incomplete diffusion. Similarly, 1-KSAtc denotes KSA with a 1-round key period, truncated last round, and complete diffusion, where the omission of 'p' and 's' means that the corresponding attack works for both public and secret S-boxes.

Notation of data sets and slid pairs. In all the attacks proposed in this paper, the data consists of two sets of plaintexts/ciphertext pairs. All the plaintext/ciphertext pairs (P_i, C_i) are split such that T_P contains the plaintexts $P_i, i = 1, 2, \ldots, d$ and T_C contains the ciphertexts $C_i, i = 1, 2, \ldots, d$. Similarly, the plaintext/ciphertext pairs (Q_j, D_j) are split between T_Q that contains[5] $Q_j, j = 1, 2, \ldots, d'$ and T_D that contains $D_j, j = 1, 2, \ldots, d'$.

If the considered variant is ℓ-KSA, then a pair (P_i, Q_j) of plaintexts is called a *slid pair* if $(A \circ S \circ K)^\ell (P_i) = Q_j$. If the cipher was completely self-similar like in standard slide attacks, this would guarantee that the corresponding pair of ciphertexts (C_i, D_j) satisfies $(A \circ S \circ K)^\ell (C_i) = D_j$. In our case, the relation depends on whether the considered ℓ-KSA construction is full or truncated. If (P_i, Q_j) is a slid pair, we call Q_j *the slid counterpart* of P_i.

In some of our attacks, in order to save data complexity we use the same plaintext set T both as T_P and as T_C. In such cases, we use both notations T_P and T_Q for T, and in each candidate slid pair, we denote the 'left' element by $P_i \in T_P$ and the 'right' element by $Q_j \in T_Q$. In this context, it is worth noting that the pairs (X, Y) and (Y, X) are distinct candidates for a slid pair, since the equations $(A \circ S \circ K)^\ell (X) = Y$ and $(A \circ S \circ K)^\ell (Y) = X$ are not equivalent.

---

[5] In most of the slide attacks $d = d'$. However, this is not a mandatory requirement by the attack.

Modification of the plaintexts and the ciphertexts. In all our attacks, we consider a pair of plaintexts (P_i, Q_j) for which we want to decide whether it is a slid pair or not, and study the relation between P_i and Q_j, and the relation between the corresponding ciphertexts C_i and D_j. In order to simplify these relations, we would like to "remove" unkeyed operations that can be computed in advance for all plaintexts/ciphertexts in the data set. There are two types of operations we can remove: the first is operations that can be precomputed directly, and the second is operations that can be precomputed after interchanging the order of the operations K and A.

Let us exemplify this modification process on a concrete example. In 1-KSAp, for each slid pair (P_i, Q_j), we have

$$Q_j = A \circ S \circ K(P_i),$$

or equivalently, $S^{-1} \circ A^{-1}(Q_j) = K(P_i)$. The left hand side $S^{-1} \circ A^{-1}(Q_j)$ can be computed in advance for any plaintext Q_j. We thus replace each $Q_j \in \mathcal{T}_Q$ by $Q'_j = S^{-1} \circ A^{-1}(Q_j)$, and work with the simplified equation

$$Q'_j = K(P_i).$$

Furthermore, the corresponding ciphertexts, (C_i, D_j), satisfy

$$D_j = K \circ A \circ S(C_i),$$

(or equivalently, $A^{-1} \circ K^{-1}(D_j) = S(C_i)$). The right hand side $S(C_i)$ can be computed in advance for any ciphertext C_i. As for the left hand side, note that by distributivity, for every invertible binary matrix A' and binary vectors x, w, k the following holds: $(A'x + w) + k = A'(x + (A')^{-1}k) + w$. Hence, we can always interchange the order of the operations A, K, at the expense of replacing the subkey k in the operation K with $(A')^{-1}k$, where A' is the matrix used in the operation A. Thus, we have $A^{-1} \circ K^{-1}(D_j) = (K')^{-1} \circ A^{-1}(D_j)$, where K' denotes addition of the key $A'k$. The value $D'_j = A^{-1}(D_j)$ can be computed an advance for any ciphertext D_j. Thus, we replace each $C_i \in \mathcal{T}_C$ with $C'_i = S(C_i)$ and each $D_j \in \mathcal{T}_D$ with $D'_j = A^{-1}(D_j)$, and work with the simplified equation

$$D'_j = K'(C'_i).$$

Notations for modified plaintexts and ciphertexts. We perform such a change routinely, whenever there is an unkeyed operation that can be performed in advance (including cases where one has to interchange the order of the operations K, A). We use the notation $\bar{P}_i, \bar{C}_i$ to say that such a modification was performed to P_i, C_i (respectively), and the notation $\tilde{Q}_j, \tilde{D}_j$ to say that such a modification was performed to Q_j, D_j (respectively). Note that the exact modification differs between different variants of KSA.

We denote the sets of modified values that correspond to $\mathcal{T}_P, \mathcal{T}_C, \mathcal{T}_Q$, and $\mathcal{T}_D$ by $\bar{\mathcal{T}}_P, \bar{\mathcal{T}}_C, \tilde{\mathcal{T}}_Q$, and $\tilde{\mathcal{T}}_D$, respectively. We abuse notation and call the pair $(\bar{P}_i, \tilde{Q}_j)$ a *slid pair* whenever the corresponding pair (P_i, Q_j) is a real slid pair.

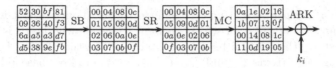

Fig. 3. An AES round

2.2   AES Notations

As the best-known prototype of the constructions we consider is AES, we shall present all our attacks in the special case of an AES-like construction with a periodic key schedule, and then we will briefly explain how do these attacks apply for generic ℓ-KSA constructions. Hence, for the sake of convenience, we briefly recall the structure of AES.

The structure of AES. The Advanced Encryption Standard (AES) [13] is an SPN that supports key sizes of 128, 192, and 256 bits. A 128-bit plaintext is treated as a byte matrix of size 4×4, where each byte represents a value in $GF(2^8)$. An AES round, depicted in Fig. 3, applies four operations to the state matrix:

- SubBytes (SB)—applying the same 8-bit to 8-bit invertible S-box 16 times in parallel on each byte of the state,
- ShiftRows (SR)—cyclically shifting the i'th row by i bytes to the left,
- MixColumns (MC)—multiplication of each column by a constant 4×4 matrix over the field $GF(2^8)$, and
- AddRoundKey (ARK)—XORing the state with a 128-bit subkey.

Before the first round, an additional AddRoundKey operation takes place. Thus, we "redefine" an AES round as starting with an AddRoundKey operation, with the last round AddRoundKey operation serving as a post-whitening key. In the last round of AES, the MixColumns operation is omitted. The number of rounds depends on the key size, ranging between 10 and 14.

Notations for the variants of AES we study. Since we use AES-like constructions as a prototype of general KSA constructions, their types and notations are similar to the types of KSA constructions discussed above. Namely, in all variants we consider, the key schedule is replaced by a periodic key schedule, with a period of 1, 2, or 3. Following [4], we denote by ℓK-AES a variant with period ℓ in the key schedule. We call the variant *truncated* if in its last round, the MixColumns operation is removed (like in original AES), and otherwise, we call the variant *full*.[6] We say that the S-box is *public* if it is publicly known (like in AES), and say that it is *secret* if it is key-dependent (like in the variants of

---

[6] We note that in [4], the notation ℓK-AES was used for a variant with a MixColumns operation in the last round (unlike AES), and the variant with no MixColumns in the last round was not considered.

AES studied in [21,23,30,31]). The diffusion of the affine layer in AES (namely, $MC \circ SR$) is inherently incomplete, and so we use ℓK-AES as a prototype only for KSA constructions with *incomplete diffusion*; constructions with complete diffusion are treated separately.

Like for general KSA constructions, the notation we use for AES-like constructions reflects the three relevant parameters: the number at the beginning is the length of the key period, then the letter 'f' or 't' says whether the last round is full or truncated, and then the letter 'p' or 's' denotes whether the S-box is public or secret. If some parameter is not included (e.g., neither 'p' nor 's' appear), this means that the attack applies to both types described by that parameter. (Note that the letters 'c' or 'i' are irrelevant in the case of AES as explained above, and so are always omitted). For example, 3K-AEStts denotes a variant of AES with a 3-round key period, no MixColumns operation in the last round, and secret S-boxes.

Notations for intermediate values in AES. We denote the bytes of the state matrix of AES by $0, 1, 2, \ldots, 15$, in the order described in Fig. 3, and denote the value of the i'th byte of a state x by x_i. When several bytes $i_1, \ldots, i_\ell$ are considered simultaneously, they are denoted $x_{\{i_1,\ldots,i_\ell\}}$. The columns are numbered $0, 1, 2, 3$; the j'th column of the state x is denoted by $x_{\mathrm{Col}(j)}$, and if several columns are considered simultaneously, we denote them by $x_{\mathrm{Col}(j_1,\ldots,j_\ell)}$. Sometimes we are interested in 'shifted' columns, i.e., the result of the application of ShiftRows to a set of columns. This is denoted by $x_{SR(\mathrm{Col}(j_1,\ldots,j_\ell))}$. Similarly, a set of 'inverse shifted' columns (i.e., the result of the application of SR^{-1} to a set of columns) is denoted by $x_{SR^{-1}(\mathrm{Col}(j_1,\ldots,j_\ell))}$.

2.3 The Attack of [4] on 1-KSAf

Bar-On et al. [4] considered 1-KSAf, that is, $E = K \circ (A \circ S \circ K)^r$ where all operations K use the same key k. They showed that this variant can be broken with probability of about 63%, given $2^{n/2}$ known plaintexts, and roughly the same amount of time and memory.

The idea behind the attack is simple. Assume that (P_i, Q_j) is a slid pair, i.e., that $A \circ S \circ K(P_i) = Q_j$. Denoting $\tilde{Q}_j = S^{-1} \circ A^{-1}(Q_j)$, we have

$$P_i \oplus \tilde{Q}_j = k. \tag{2}$$

On the other hand, by the structure of E, the corresponding ciphertexts (C_i, D_j) must satisfy $D_j = K \circ A \circ S(C_i)$. Thus, denoting $\bar{C}_i = A \circ S(C_i)$, we have

$$D_j \oplus \bar{C}_i = k. \tag{3}$$

Combining (2) and (3), we get

$$P_i \oplus \bar{C}_i = \tilde{Q}_j \oplus D_j. \tag{4}$$

This relation allows one to mount the attack described in Algorithm 1. Note that the data used in the attack consists of a single set $\mathcal{T}$ of $2^{n/2}$ known plaintexts.

Algorithm 1. A Slide Attack on 1-KSAf [4]

Initialize an empty hash table T.
Ask for the encryption of a set T of $2^{n/2}$ known plaintexts.
for each plaintext/ciphertext pair (P_i, C_i), where $P_i \in T$ **do**
    Compute the value $\bar{C}_i = A \circ S(C_i)$,
    Compute the value $P_i \oplus \bar{C}_i$,
    Store in T the value $(P_i \oplus \bar{C}_i, P_i)$.
for each plaintext/ciphertext pair (Q_j, D_j), where $Q_j \in T$ **do**
    Compute the value $\tilde{Q}_j = S^{-1} \circ A^{-1}(Q_j)$,
    Compute the value $\tilde{Q}_j \oplus D_j$,
    if $\tilde{Q}_j \oplus D_j$ is the first coordinate of an entry $(P_i \oplus \bar{C}_i, P_i) \in T$ **then**
        Test the key candidate $k = P_i \oplus \tilde{Q}_j$ by trial encryption.

As was described above, this single set is treated both as T_P and as T_Q, and when we consider a candidate slid pair composed of two elements of T, we denote it by (P_i, Q_j) and denote the corresponding ciphertexts by C_i, D_j.

As the data set contains $2^{n/2} \cdot (2^{n/2} - 1) \approx 2^n$ pairs, the probability that the data set contains a slid pair, i.e., a pair that satisfies $Q_j = A \circ S \circ K(P_i)$, is about $1 - (1 - 2^{-n})^{2^n} \approx 1 - 1/e \approx 0.63$. Each slid pair leads to a collision in the table which suggests the right key candidate. On the other hand, for a random pair (P_i, Q_j), the probability that $P_i \oplus \bar{C}_i = \tilde{Q}_j \oplus D_j$ is 2^{-n}, and thus, only a single collision in the table is expected (though the actual number follows a Poisson distribution with a mean of 1). Thus, the right key can be found easily by going over all collisions in the table and checking the values of k they suggest. The data complexity of the attack is $2^{n/2}$ known plaintexts, its time and memory complexities are about $2^{n/2}$ operations, and its success probability is about 63%.

In addition to the attack described above, Bar-On et al. presented a memoryless variant of the attack, based on classical cycle detection algorithms. The attack requires $2^{n/2}$ adaptively chosen plaintexts, $2^{n/2}$ time, and a negligible amount of memory.

3 The Slid Sets Attack

In this section we present a new cryptanalytic technique, the *slid sets attack*, and use it to attack 2-KSAfp with complexity $O(2^{(n+s)/2})$ and 1-KSAs with complexity $O(\sqrt{s} \cdot 2^{(n+s)/2})$. In particular, our attack allows us to break an AES-like cipher with secret S-boxes and the same round keys with complexity of $2^{70.3}$ – only slightly higher than 2^{64}, which is a natural lower bound for the complexity of a slide attack on a 128-bit cipher.

The key idea behind the slide sets technique is to consider pairs of plaintext sets $U = \{P_i\}_{i=1,\dots,d}$ and $V = \{Q_j\}_{j=1,\dots,d}$, such that if for some (i_0, j_0), (P_{i_0}, Q_{j_0}) is a slid pair, then the entire set V is the *slid counterpart* of the entire set U, in the sense that for any $P_i \in U$, there exists $1 \le j \le d$ such that the slid counterpart of P_i is Q_j. Interestingly, we will not be able to know (until the very end of the attack) which Q_j is the counterpart of a specific P_i. This attack paradigm stands in contrast with all previously known slide attacks which treated either single slid pairs or slid tuples $(P_1, \ldots, P_d), (Q_1, \ldots, Q_d)$ in which each Q_i is the slid counterpart of P_i.

We begin with presenting the attack in the special case of 2-KSAf, where its application is the simplest one. Then we show the more complex attack on 1-KSAs. Even more complex attacks on 2-KSAtpi and on 3-KSAfpi are given in full version.

3.1   Slid Sets Attack on 2-KSAf

The setting. For the sake of helping readability, we present the attack in the special case of 2K-AESfp (i.e., an AES-like cipher with 2-round periodic subkeys, publicly known S-boxes, and with a MixColumns operation in the last round). We assume that the number of rounds is *even*; it will be apparent from the attack that it applies to the 'odd' case without change (as the only difference it the last round's key). First, we would like to simplify the problem.

Assume that (P_i, Q_j) is a slid pair. This means that

$$Q_j = MC \circ SR \circ SB \circ ARK_2 \circ MC \circ SR \circ SB \circ ARK_1(P_i),$$

where ARK_ℓ denotes key addition with the subkey k_ℓ. As was described in Sect. 2.1, we can peel off unkeyed operations by denoting $\tilde{Q}_j = SR^{-1} \circ MC^{-1} \circ SB^{-1} \circ SR^{-1} \circ MC^{-1}(Q_j)$, and obtain

$$\tilde{Q}_j = ARK_2' \circ SB \circ ARK_1(P_i), \tag{5}$$

where ARK_2' denotes the addition of the subkey $MC^{-1} \circ SR^{-1}(k_2)$. By the basic slide property, the relation between the corresponding ciphertexts (C_i, D_j) is similar to the relation between the plaintexts (but of course, is not the same, due to the last round asymmetry). Namely, we have

$$D_j = ARK_1 \circ MC \circ SR \circ SB \circ ARK_2 \circ MC \circ SR \circ SB(C_i).$$

Like with the plaintexts, this relation can be simplified to

$$\tilde{D}_j = ARK_1' \circ SB \circ ARK_2(\bar{C}_i), \tag{6}$$

where $\bar{C}_i = MC \circ SR \circ SB(C_i)$, $\tilde{D}_j = MC^{-1} \circ SR^{-1}(D_j)$, and ARK_1' denotes the addition of the subkey $MC^{-1} \circ SR^{-1}(k_1)$ The important gain from obtaining the simplified equations is that now the transformation from P_i to $\tilde{Q}_j$ consists of application of 16 independent functions on the bytes of the state, and the same goes for the transition from $\bar{C}_i$ to $\tilde{D}_j$. This plays a significant role in the attack.

Construction of candidate slid sets. The idea behind this step is as follows. Let $(P_i, Q_j), (P_{i'}, Q_{j'})$ be slid pairs, and let $\tilde{Q}_j, \tilde{Q}_{j'}$ be computed from $Q_j, Q_{j'}$, as defined above. The fact that the transformation from P_i to $\tilde{Q}_j$ consists of application of 16 independent functions on the bytes of the state, implies that if $P_{i'}$ differs from P_i only in a single byte, then $\tilde{Q}_{j'}$ differs from $\tilde{Q}_j$ only in a single byte as well.

We observe that this property can be generalized from pairs to sets, as follows. Consider two sets $U = \{P_i\}$, $\tilde{V} = \{\tilde{Q}_j\}$ which form Λ-sets (see [12]) with respect to byte 0 of the state, i.e., each of them is a set of 256 values that are equal in all S-boxes but S-box 0, and attains all possible values in S-box 0. (Of course, the same can be performed with another byte instead of byte 0.) Let $V = \{Q_j\}$ be the plaintext set obtained from $\tilde{V}$ by setting $Q_j = MC \circ SR \circ SB \circ MC \circ SR(\tilde{Q}_j)$ for each $\tilde{Q}_j \in \tilde{V}_j$. By the above property, if the slid counterpart of some $P_i \in U$ is $Q_j \in V$, then any $P_{i'} \in U$ has a slid counterpart $Q_{j'}$ in V. We call two sets of plaintexts U, V that satisfy this property (namely, that each element of U has a slid counterpart in V and vice versa) *slid sets*.

The same process can be performed in the converse direction: Each candidate slid pair (P_i, Q_j) suggests a pair of *slid sets* (U, V), by defining U to be a Λ-set that contains P_i, defining $\tilde{V}$ to be a Λ-set that contains $\tilde{Q}_j$, and computing V from $\tilde{V}$ as described above. (Of course, we have to make sure that the permuted byte in the Λ-set is the same byte.) Importantly, we do not know which element in V is the slid counterpart of a given element of U; we only know that this counterpart exists in V, if indeed the original pair (P_i, Q_j) is a slid pair.

The attack is based on collecting sufficiently many pairs of sets (U, V), such that with a high probability the data contains a pair of slid sets. Then, the question is how to find the slid sets among them.

Identifying the slid sets. Let (U, V) be a candidate pair of slid sets. Let $W = \{C_i\}$ be the set of ciphertexts corresponding to the plaintexts of U, and let $X = \{D_j\}$ be the set of ciphertexts corresponding to the plaintexts of V. Define the sets $\bar{W}$ and $\tilde{X}$ by setting $\bar{C}_i = MC \circ SR \circ SB(C_i)$ for any $C_i \in W$ and $\tilde{D}_j = MC^{-1} \circ SR^{-1}(D_j)$ for any $D_j \in X$. If (U, V) are slid sets, then for each $\bar{C}_i \in \bar{W}$, there exists $\tilde{D}_j \in \bar{W}$ such that Eq. (6) holds for the pair $(\bar{C}_i, \tilde{D}_j)$. However, we have to check many combinations of U and V, and even if we know that (U, V) are slid sets, we do not know which Q_j corresponds to which P_i.

Luckily, the relation (6) consists of applying 16 independent functions on the bytes of the state. This implies that in each byte separately, for each pair $C_{i_1}, C_{i_2} \in W$, the equality $\bar{C}_{i_1} = \bar{C}_{i_2}$ holds if and only if the equality $\tilde{D}_{j_1} = \tilde{D}_{j_2}$ holds for some $D_{j_1}, D_{j_2} \in X'$ (though, we still do not know for which values!). Consequently, the statistic: "how many values are attained q times in byte ℓ" is preserved between the sets $\bar{W}$ and $\tilde{X}$, for any byte ℓ and any multiplicity!

This can be used for obtaining a significant amount of filtering, in the following way. We pick sufficiently many Λ-sets U^l (all with the same permuted byte), and for each corresponding $\bar{W}^l$, for each byte ℓ, we compute the sequence of multiplicities (i.e., the sequence which records: how many values are not obtained, how many are obtained once, etc.), defined formally by

$$a_q^\ell = \Big| \{v \in \{0, 1, \ldots, 255\} : |\{\bar{C}_i \in \bar{W}^l : (\bar{C}_i)_\ell = v\}| = q\} \Big|,$$

and store the sequence-of-sequences $(a_q^\ell)_{\ell=0,1,\ldots,15,q=0,1,\ldots}$ in a hash table. Then, we pick sufficiently many Λ-sets $\tilde{V}^l$, and for each corresponding V^l, we look at the ciphertext structure X^l corresponding to V^l. For each corresponding $\tilde{X}^l$, we compute the sequence $\{b_q^\ell\}_{\ell=0,1,\ldots,15,q=0,1,\ldots}$ defined by

$$b_q^\ell = \left| \left\{ v \in \{0,1,\ldots,255\} : \left| \left\{ \tilde{D}_j \in \tilde{X}^l : (\tilde{D}_j)_\ell = v \right\} \right| = q \right\} \right|,$$

and check for a match in the table. If (U^i, V^j) are slid sets, a match must occur.

We now analyze the probability that two unrelated sets match, i.e., we calculate an upper bound on the probability that two non-slid sets have the same sequences. For this analysis, we can safely assume that each of the sets induce a sequence generated by picking 256 random values selected from $\{0,1,\ldots,255\}$. If the two vectors have for each multiplicity the same number of elements, then the sequences collide, i.e., if the number of elements not appearing in both sets is different, then the sequences do collide. We can thus define the multiplicity vector for each set—how many elements appear zero times, once, twice, etc.

The actual distribution of the multiplicity vector is a multinomial one. As we are interested in an upper bound on the collision probability of two such multiplicity vectors, we offer a lower bound on the entropy of these vectors. To do so, we consider the number of values that do not appear. While we expect about $256/e$ such elements, the exact number of values not appearing follows a binomial distribution for 256 experiments, each with success probability of $1/e$. The entropy of this binomial distribution is $\frac{1}{2}\log_2(2\pi \cdot e \cdot 256 \cdot \frac{1}{e} \cdot (1 - \frac{1}{e})) \approx 4.99$ bits. The same is true also w.r.t. the number of entries which appear once.

Thus, each byte of the sequence carries at least 9.98 bits of information, or in total for the entire state more than 159 bits of information. This is more than enough to detect all correct pairs of slid sets (U^i, V^j) with an overwhelming probability. We verified experimentally that this statistic contains at least 8 bits of information in each byte (and thus, at least 128 bits of information in total), assuming random and uniform distribution of the ciphertexts.

Retrieving the key from a pair of slid sets. Given a pair of slid sets (U^i, V^j), and the corresponding sets of values $(\bar{W}^i, \tilde{X}^j)$ we can easily and efficiently find the round keys k_2 and $k_1' = MC^{-1}(k_1)$. The attack is based on Eq. (6), which consists of 16 independent byte equations of the form $(\tilde{D}_j)_\ell = (ARK_1' \circ SB \circ ARK_2(\bar{C}_i))_\ell$, as was mentioned above. In each byte ℓ, we know from W the multiplicity of each value entering this byte (e.g., input value 0 appears once in $\bar{W}^i$ in this byte position). Note that the statistic we use here is more refined than the statistic we used above: we do not only ask how many values are obtained q times, but rather which are the values that are obtained q times.

We now guess the value of byte ℓ of k_2 and of k_1', and so, we can compute the value $(ARK_1' \circ SB \circ ARK_2(\bar{C}_i))_\ell$ for each $C_i \in W$. We compute this value for every $\bar{C}_i \in \bar{W}$, and check whether the multiplicities of the obtained values conform to their multiplicities in $\tilde{X}^j$. If there is no match, we discard the guess of $(k_2)_\ell(k_1')_\ell$.

This procedure offers a very strong filtering, and so with overwhelming probability, in each byte only a single candidate for k_2 and k_1' remains.

We note that this attack algorithm does not rely on the actual order of keys used in the last two rounds. Thus, even though we presented the attack for the case of even number of rounds, it can be applied in exactly the same way to an odd number of rounds (where Eq. (6) is replaced by $\tilde{D}_j = ARK_2' \circ SB \circ ARK_1(\bar{C}_i)$) and we obtain a single candidate for k_1 and k_2').

The attack algorithm. As shown in Algorithm 2, we consider two structures $\mathcal{T}_P, \mathcal{T}_Q$ of 2^{68} chosen plaintexts each. The structure $\mathcal{T}_P$ consists of 2^{60} Λ-sets, all with the first byte permuted and the rest fixed. Similarly, $\mathcal{T}_Q$ is chosen such that $\tilde{\mathcal{T}}_Q$ contains 2^{60} Λ-sets, all with the first byte permuted and the rest fixed. We then compute for each Λ-set in $\mathcal{T}_P$ its a_q^ℓ statistics and for each Λ-set in $\mathcal{T}_Q$ its b_q^ℓ statistics, and look for collisions between the statistics. Once such a collision is found (i.e., a pair of slid sets is identified), we apply the key recovery algorithm.

The data complexity of the attack is 2^{69} chosen plaintexts, the memory complexity is 2^{69} and the time complexity is 2^{69} as well. The success probability is the probability that the data contains a pair of slid sets. As the probability of each set pair of sets $U^i \in \mathcal{T}_P$ and $V^j \in \mathcal{T}_Q$ to be slid is 2^{-120} (since a match in 15 bytes is needed), the probability of containing pair of slid sets is $1 - (1 - 2^{-120})^{2^{120}} \approx 0.63$, which is the success rate of the attack.

Attacking 2-KSAfp. The same attack applies to any variant of 2-KSAfp, either with complete or incomplete diffusion. The data, memory and time complexities are $2^{(n+s)/2+1} = O(2^{(n+s)/2})$.

3.2 Slid Sets Attack on 1-KSAs

In this section we show that a modification of the above attack can be used to break 1-KSA in which the operation S is key-dependent – i.e., consists of a parallel application of n/s key-dependent permutations on s-bit words. The complexity of the attack is only slightly higher than the complexity of the attack described above – namely, data, memory, and time complexity of $2\sqrt{s\log 2} 2^{(n+s)/2} = O(\sqrt{s}2^{(n+s)/2})$ (i.e., a factor of $\sqrt{s\log 2}$ with respect to the attack of Sect. 3.1).

The setting. For the sake of helping readability, we first present the attack in the special case of 1K-AESf with a key-dependent S-box. A related variant (1-KSAfs) was studied in a number of papers, e.g., [21,23,30,31]. First, we would like to simplify the problem.

Assume that (P_i, Q_j) is a slid pair. This means that

$$Q_j = MC \circ SR \circ SB \circ ARK(P_i),$$

where ARK denotes key addition with the subkey k. We can peel off the unkeyed operations MC, SR by denoting $\tilde{Q}_j = SR^{-1} \circ MC^{-1}(Q_j)$, and obtain

$$\tilde{Q}_j = SB \circ ARK(P_i). \tag{7}$$

Algorithm 2. A slide attack on 2K-AESfp using slid sets

Ask for the encryption of two structures T_P, T_Q, each of size 2^{68}, defined above.

Initialize an empty hash table T.

for all Λ-sets $U^i \in T_P$ **do**

 Let the ciphertexts corresponding to the plaintexts U^i be W^i, and consider the corresponding set $\bar{W}^i$,

 Compute the sequence-of-sequences $(a_q^\ell)_{\ell=0,1,\ldots,15, q=0,1,\ldots}$, and store it in T, along with the index i.

for all $V^j \in T_Q$ **do**

 Let the ciphertexts of corresponding to the plaintexts of V^j be X^j.

 Compute from X^j the corresponding $\tilde{X}^j$.

 Compute the sequence-of-sequences $(b_q^\ell)_{\ell=0,1,\ldots,15, q=0,1,\ldots}$, and check for a matching sequence in T.

 if a match exists **then**

  Assume that (U^i, V^j) are slid sets, and consider the corresponding sets $(\bar{W}^i, \tilde{X}^j)$.

  for all bytes $\ell \in \{0, \ldots, 15\}$ **do**

   for all guesses of byte $k_{2,\ell}$ and $k'_{1,\ell}$ **do**

    Partially encrypt all $(\bar{C}_i)_\ell \in W^i$ and obtain a set of values $\{t_1, t_2, \ldots t_{256}\}$.

    if the set $\{t_1, t_2, \ldots t_{256}\}$ matches the set $\{\tilde{D}_{j,\ell} : \tilde{D}_j \in \tilde{X}\}$ **then**

     Output "the subkey values in byte ℓ are $k_{2,\ell}$ and $k'_{1,\ell}$".

By the slide property, the corresponding ciphertexts (C_i, D_j) satisfy

$$D_j = ARK \circ MC \circ SR \circ SB(C_i).$$

We can simplify this relation by interchanging the operations ARK and MC, at the expense of replacing the subkey k with $SR^{-1} \circ MC^{-1}(k)$, and then peeling off MC and SR as well. We obtain

$$\tilde{D}_j = ARK' \circ SB(C_i). \tag{8}$$

Detection of slid sets. Equations (7) and (8) show that the transformation from P_i to $\tilde{Q}_j$ consists of application of 16 independent functions on the bytes of the state, and the same goes for the transition from C_i to $\tilde{D}_j$. Hence, we can use the same algorithm for detecting slid sets in as the previous attack (i.e., using the sequences a_q^ℓ and b_q^ℓ that count multiplicities of values).

Deducing slid pairs from slid sets. The remaining goal is to retrieve the subkey k and the key-dependent S-box S given a few pairs of slid sets (U^i, V^j). (As we shall see, a single pair of slid sets does not contain enough information for determining the S-box uniquely). The simple algorithm for this step described above cannot be applied here since the S-box S is unknown. Instead, we make use of a refined statistic that allows us deducing the slid counterpart $Q_j \in V$ of each $P_i \in U$. Namely, while in Sect. 3.1 we used the multiplicities of values in

---

Algorithm 3. Retrieving slid pairs from slid sets, for 1K-AESfs

---

Initialize a list L of candidate slid pairs.
for Each $C_i \in W$ **do**
    Compute the sequence $(c_\ell^i)_{\ell=0,1,\ldots,15}$, and store in a hash table, along with P_i.
for Each $\tilde{D}_j \in \tilde{X}$ **do**
    Compute the sequence $(d_\ell^j)_{\ell=0,1,\ldots,15}$, and check for a match in the table,
    for Each match in the hash table **do**
        Add the corresponding pair (P_i, Q_j) to L.

---

each byte separately, here we use the sequence of multiplicities of a value in all bytes simultaneously.

As in Sect. 3.1, we denote by W, X the sets of ciphertexts that correspond to the plaintext sets U, V, respectively. Furthermore, we denote by $\tilde{X}$ the set obtained from X by setting $\tilde{D}_j = SR^{-1} \circ MC^{-1}(D_j)$, for any $D_j \in X$.

For each $C_i \in W$, and for each byte $0 \leq \ell \leq 15$, we count the number of other elements $C_{i'} \in W$ such that $(C_i)_\ell = (C_{i'})_\ell$. That is, we construct the 16-element sequence $\{c_\ell^i\}_{\ell=0,1,\ldots,15}$, where

$$c_\ell^i = |\{C_{i'} \in W : (i' \neq i) \wedge ((C_i)_\ell = (C_{i'})_\ell)\}|.$$

Similarly, for each $\tilde{D}_j \in \tilde{X}$, and for each byte $0 \leq \ell \leq 15$, we construct the 16-element sequence $\{d_\ell^j\}_{\ell=0,1,\ldots,15}$, where

$$d_\ell^j = |\{\tilde{D}_{j'} \in \tilde{X} : (j' \neq j) \wedge ((\tilde{D}_{j'})_\ell = (\tilde{D}_j)_\ell)\}|.$$

We observe that the statistic represented by the sequences $\{c_\ell^i\}$ and $\{d_\ell^j\}$ is preserved by slid pairs. That is, if Q_j is the slid counterpart of P_i, then the corresponding sequences $\{c_\ell^i\}, \{d_\ell^j\}$ must be equal! Indeed, if for some i' we have $(C_i)_\ell = (C_{i'})_\ell$, then the equality $(\tilde{D}_j)_\ell = (\tilde{D}_{j'})_\ell$ must hold for $\tilde{D}_j$, where $Q_{j'}$ is the slid counterpart of $P_{i'}$. Therefore, we can retrieve the right slid pairs (P_i, Q_j) by the simple procedure described in Algorithm 3.

We experimentally checked and found that the statistic $(c_\ell^i)_{\ell=0,1,\ldots,15}$ contains about 27 bits of information, assuming random and uniform distribution of the ciphertexts. This means that the probability of a random pair (P_i, Q_j) to yield a match in the table is 2^{-27}. As the plaintext sets (U, V) contain only 2^{16} pairs (P_i, Q_j), with a high probability only the right slid pairs match in the table.

Hence, the above algorithm, whose complexity is about 2^{16} operations, finds the slid counterpart $Q_j \in V$ of each $P_i \in U$.

Retrieving the secret material, given several pairs of slid sets. By Eq. (8) (applied in each byte separately), each slid pair (P_i, Q_j) provides us with an input/output pair for the function $f_\ell(x) = k_\ell' \oplus SB(x)$, where k_ℓ' denotes the ℓ's byte of $k' = SR^{-1} \circ MC^{-1}(k)$. Hence, each pair of slid sets provides us with 256 input/output pairs for each function f_ℓ. However, these input/output pairs are not distinct. A reasonable assumption is that the values $(C_i)_\ell$ (where C_i ranges over elements of W)

are distributed uniformly at random in $\{0, 1, \ldots, 255\}$. Hence, by the *coupon collector's* problem, we need $256 \cdot \log 256$ input/output pairs in order to recover f_ℓ completely with a high probability. Therefore, about $\log 256 \approx 6$ pairs of slid sets are sufficient for recovering all functions f_ℓ.

Once the function $ARK' \circ SB$ is recovered, the key k can be recovered instantly, by picking some (already queried) ciphertext C and partially decrypting it using the knowledge of the functions $ARK' \circ SB, SR, MC$. The entire decryption process can be simulated, except for the initial ARK operation. Hence, we obtain the value $P \oplus k$, where P is the plaintext that corresponds to C. As P is known, k can be retrieved.

The complexity of the attack. The attack presented above contains two steps, in addition to the steps of the attack described in Sect. 3.1. The first is a step that recovers slid pairs from pairs of slid sets. As described above, the complexity of this step is 2^{16}, which is negligible with respect to other steps of the attack. The second step is recovering the function $ARK' \circ SB$. Its complexity is also negligible, but it requires 6 pairs of slid sets, instead of a single pair in the attack of Sect. 3.1. This increases the data complexity of the attack by a factor of $\sqrt{6}$, and increases the data and time complexity of the attack accordingly.

Therefore, the data, memory and time complexity of the attack on 1K-AES with a secret S-box and a MixColumns operation in the last round, is about $2^{70.3}$, and its success probability is about 63%.

Attacking 1-KSAs. The same attack applies to any variant of 1-KSAfs. The only difference is that the number of required pairs of slid sets is $s \log 2 = \log(2^s)$ (instead of $\log 256$ in 1K-AES). Hence, the data, memory, and time complexity of the attack is $2\sqrt{s \log 2} \cdot 2^{(n+s)/2}$.

Furthermore, the attack applies with the same complexity also to any variant of 1-KSAts. Indeed, the difference between 1-KSAfs and 1-KSAts is in the relation between C_i and D_j, which becomes

$$D_j = ARK \circ SR \circ SB \circ ARK \circ MC \circ ARK(C_i).$$

By replacing ARK with linear operations, we can simplify this equation into

$$\tilde{D}_j = ARK' \circ SB \circ ARK''(\bar{C}_i), \tag{9}$$

where $\tilde{D}_j = SR^{-1}(D_j)$, $\bar{C}_i = MC(C_i)$, ARK' denotes addition with $SR^{-1}(k)$ and ARK'' denotes addition with $MC(k) \oplus k$. Equation (9) has exactly the same structure as Eq. (8), and hence, the attack described above applies, with the same complexity, to 1-KSAts.

4   Slide Attack Using a Hypercube of Slid Pairs

In this section we present a new technique which we call a *hypercube of slid pairs*, and use it to attack 1-KSAts (*with a secret S-box*) with data, memory, and time complexity of $\sqrt{s}2^{(n+s(s/2+1)+s/2)/2+1}$ (in the special case of 1K-AESt: 2^{88}). For sake of concreteness, we demonstrate the attack on 1K-AES.

The idea behind the attack. The attack consists of two steps. First we detect a slid pair, and then we use it to recover the key used in the ARK operation and in the secret S-box. In order to detect a slid pair, we want to attach to each candidate slid pair many "friend pairs", such that if the candidate is indeed a slid pair, then all the friend pairs are slid pairs as well.

To be specific, we consider 1K-AES with a secret S-box. Consider a slid pair (P_i, Q_j). As was shown in Sect. 3.2, the relation between P_i and Q_j can be simplified into the equation $\tilde{Q}_j = SB \circ ARK(P_i)$, where $\tilde{Q}_j = SR^{-1} \circ MC^{-1}(Q_j)$. Furthermore, it was shown that if $(P_i, Q_j), (P_{i'}, Q_{j'})$ are slid pairs, $\tilde{Q}_j, \tilde{Q}_{j'}$ are computed from $Q_j, Q_{j'}$, and if $P_{i'}$ differs from P_i only in a single byte, then $\tilde{Q}_{j'}$ differs from $\tilde{Q}_j$ only in a single byte as well.

It follows that if we take a, a' be two vectors that are non-zero only in byte 0 (where they assume arbitrary values), then with probability 2^{-8}, $(P_i \oplus a, \tilde{Q}_j \oplus a')$ also corresponds to a slid pair.

In the same way, we take values b, c, d, e which are non-zero only in byte $1, 2, 3, 4$, respectively. Then we define b', c', d', e' similarly to the definition of a', and obtain the pairs $(P_i \oplus b, \tilde{Q}_j \oplus b'), \ldots, (P_i \oplus e, \tilde{Q}_j \oplus e')$, such that each of them is a slid pair with probability 2^{-8}. Thus, we may attach to the pair (P_i, Q_j) five friend pairs, such that if (P_i, Q_j) is a slid pair, then each of its friend pairs is a slid pair with probability 2^{-8}.

Constructing a hypercube of slid pairs. We are ready to present the construction of the *hypercube of slid pairs*. Assume that all five pairs $(P_i \oplus a, \tilde{Q}_j \oplus a'), \ldots, (P_i \oplus e, \tilde{Q}_j \oplus e')$ correspond to slid pairs. We observe that this implies that for any quintet $\alpha = (\alpha_1, \alpha_2, \alpha_3, \alpha_4, \alpha_5) \in \{0,1\}^5$, the pair

$$(P_i \oplus \alpha_1 a \oplus \alpha_2 b \oplus \alpha_3 c \oplus \alpha_4 d \oplus \alpha_5 e, \tilde{Q}_j \oplus \alpha_1 a' \oplus \alpha_2 b' \oplus \alpha_3 c' \oplus \alpha_4 d' \oplus \alpha_5 e')$$

is a slid pair as well. Indeed, in each of the 16 functions applied in parallel, the two values of the new slid pair are equal either to the values of $(P_i, \tilde{Q}_j)$ or to the values of one of its 5 "friends" which we assumed to be slid pairs as well. (For example, in byte 0 the values are equal either to those of $(P_i, \tilde{Q}_j)$ or to those of $(P_i \oplus a, \tilde{Q}_j \oplus a')$.) We denote the new pair by $(P_{i,\alpha}, \tilde{Q}_{j,\alpha})$.

This allows us to leverage 5 friend pairs into $2^5 - 1$ friend pairs (or more generally, t friend pairs into $2^t - 1$ friend pairs). As the friend pairs we construct correspond to the vertices of the hypercube $\{0,1\}^t$, we call this method of constructing a *hypercube of slid pairs*. We note that this construction idea is motivated by the *mixture differential* attack presented by Grassi [22]. Hence, so far we have attached to the pair (P_i, Q_j) 31 friend pairs, such that if (P_i, Q_j) is a slid pair, then with probability 2^{-40}, all the friend pairs are slid pairs as well.

Using the hypercube of slid pairs in the attack. Consider the ciphertexts (C_i, D_j) that correspond to a slid pair (P_i, Q_j). As was shown in Sect. 3.2, the relation between C_i and D_j can be simplified into the equation

$$\tilde{D}_j = ARK' \circ SB(C_i).$$

As both the transformation from P_i to $\tilde{Q}_j$ and the transformation from C_i to $\tilde{D}_j$ consist of application of 16 independent functions on the bytes of the state, it follows that if for some $\alpha, \alpha' \in \{0,1\}^5$ and for some byte $\ell \in \{0, 1, \ldots, 15\}$, we have $(C_{i,\alpha})_\ell = (C_{i,\alpha'})_\ell$, then we must have $(D_{j,\alpha})_\ell = (D_{j,\alpha'})_\ell$ as well. Note that the same property was exploited in the attack of Sect. 3.2. In our attack, the size of the structure is smaller, which restricts the amount of information that can be collected. On the other hand, we know that the slid counterpart of each $P_{i,\alpha}$ is $Q_{i,\alpha}$, and this turns out to be sufficient for detecting the slid pairs.

Indeed, the expected number of such collisions is $2^{-8} \cdot \binom{32}{2} \cdot 16 = 31$. We denote each such collision by the triple (α, α', ℓ), and store the list of all collisions in a lexicographic order. The exhaustive list of all locations of collisions contains more than 256 bits of information, and thus, the probability that two lists of triples that do not originate from a slid pair are equal, is negligible. Hence, equality of two lists implies a slid pair (with overwhelming probability).

Recovering the secret S-box. Once a slid pair (P_i, Q_j), along with 31 friend pairs, are detected, they provide us with 32 input/output values to the function $ARK \circ SB$. As was shown in Sect. 3.2, about $256 \log 256 \approx 1420$ input/output values are needed in order to recover the S-box, and thus, we have to take a sufficiently large data set so that it will contain at least 45 slid pairs. Namely, we take two structures T_P, T_Q of 2^{87} plaintexts each. The structures contain 2^{174} pairs. As the probability that a pair and all its friend pairs are slid pairs is $2^{-128} \cdot 2^{-40} = 2^{-168}$, the expected number of slid hypercubes is 64, and so, with a high probability the number of slid pairs is sufficient for recovering $ARK \circ SB$. Once this operation is recovered, all the operations in the cipher except for the final ARK operation are known, and thus, the key k can be immediately retrieved. The resulting attack algorithm is given in Algorithm 4.

We note that the plaintext structures can be chosen in such a way that constructing the friend pairs does not require increasing the data complexity. Indeed, we can choose each of the structures $T_P, \tilde{T}_Q$ as a union of 2^{47} sub-structures of size 2^{40}, where in each sub-structure, all plaintexts attain some equal value in bytes $5, 6, \ldots, 15$ and all possible values in bytes $0, 1, \ldots, 4$. This guarantees that for any a, b, c, d, e, α and for any $P_i \in T_P$, the value $P_i \oplus \alpha_1 a \oplus \alpha_2 b \oplus \alpha_3 c \oplus \alpha_4 d \oplus \alpha_5 e$ also belongs to T_P, and the same for $\tilde{T}_Q$.

As was explained above, the algorithm requires 2^{88} chosen plaintexts, memory and time, and succeeds with a high probability. The same attack applies to any variant of 1-KSAts (possibly with a complete diffusion). First, in the detection of a hypercube of slid pairs of dimension t (given s-bit S-boxes in n-bit cipher) we get from each candidate hypercube $2^{-s} \cdot \binom{2^t}{2} \cdot n/s$ values in the list. As each such value suggests about s bits of entropy (i.e., a total of $2^{-s} \cdot \binom{2^t}{2} \cdot n$ bits), and as we have at most 2^{2n} sets of slid pairs, we require that $2^{-s} \cdot \binom{2^t}{2} \cdot n \approx 2n$. In other words, one needs to set $2^{2t-s-1} \cdot n = 2n$, i.e., $t = \lceil s/2 \rceil$. Now, if T_P and T_Q have D plaintexts each, we expect $D^2 \cdot 2^{-n} \cdot 2^{-ts}$ hypercubes of slid pairs, each suggesting 2^t slid pairs. As we need about $\log 2^s \cdot 2^s \approx 0.7 \cdot s \cdot 2^s$ slid

---

Algorithm 4. A Slide Attack on 1K-AES with a Secret S-box using Hypercube of Slid Pairs

---

Ask for the encryption of two structures $\mathcal{T}_P, \mathcal{T}_Q$, each of 2^{87} chosen plaintexts, constructed as defined above..

Initialize an empty list L (intended to store the detected slid pairs).

for each plaintext/ciphertext pair $(P_i, C_i) \in \mathcal{T}_P$ **do**
  Compute the 31 friend pairs $(P_{i,\alpha}, C_{i,\alpha})$ and the corresponding values $\tilde{D}_{i,\alpha}$,
  Find all collisions of the form $(\bar{C}_{i,\alpha})_l = (\tilde{C}_{i,\alpha'})_l$,
  Store in a hash table the sequence of triples (α, α', l) that represent all collisions, arranged in lexicographic order, along with the value P_i used to create them.

for Each plaintext/ciphertext pair (Q_j, D_j) **do**
  Compute the 31 'friend values' $\bar{Q}_{j,\alpha}$ and the corresponding pairs $(Q_{j,\alpha}, D_{j,\alpha})$,
  Find all collisions of the form $(D_{j,\alpha})_l = (D_{j,\alpha'})_l$,
  Compute the sequence of triples (α, α', l) that represent all collisions and check for a match in the hash table.

for Each collision in the table **do**
  Add the corresponding pair (P_i, Q_j) and its 31 friends to L.

for Each slid pair $(P_i, Q_j) \in L$ **do**
  Use the relation between P_i and $\bar{Q}_j$ to detect an input/output pair of $SB \circ ARK$ for each byte, until the entire function is detected.

Once $SB \circ ARK$ in all bytes is detected, find the final key whitening operation ARK using a single trial encryption.

---

pairs, we need $D = \sqrt{s} \cdot 2^{(n+s(s/2+1)+s/2)/2}$, or a total of data, memory, and time complexities of $\sqrt{s} 2^{(n+s(s/2+1)+s/2)/2+1}$.

We note that the complexity of the 'hypercube of slides' attack on 1-KSAts is inferior to the complexity of the 'slid sets' attack of Sect. 3.2. However, this attack may be advantageous in specific instances of 1-KSAts, e.g., when the operation S admits differential characteristics with a non-negligible probability.

5   Slide Attack Using Suggestive Plaintext Structures

In this section we present a new technique which we call *suggestive plaintext structures*, and use it to attack 1-KSAt (and in particular, 1K-AES) with data, memory of $3 \cdot 2^{n/2}$ and time complexity of $4 \cdot 2^{n/2}$. Interestingly, unlike most other slide attacks, this attack's success rate is guaranteed at 100%.

The idea behind the attack is using two tailor-made plaintext structures $\mathcal{T}_P = \{P_i\}_{i=1,\dots,2^{n/2}}$ and $\mathcal{T}_Q = \{Q_j\}_{j=1,\dots,2^{n/2}}$, such that the mere knowledge that some P_i has a slid counterpart in the structure $\{Q_j\}$ (even without the knowledge of which Q_j exactly is the counterpart) yields some key information that can be used in the attack.

To be specific, we consider 1K-AES. Let $\mathcal{T}_P = \{P_i\}$ be a structure of 2^{64} plaintexts that assume the constant value 0 in $\mathrm{Col}(2,3)$, and assume all 2^{64} possible values in $\mathrm{Col}(0,1)$. We let $\mathcal{T}_Q = \{Q_j\}$ be a structure of 2^{64} plaintexts such that the plaintexts of the corresponding structure $\tilde{\mathcal{T}}_Q = \{\tilde{Q}_j\}$ (where for each j, $\tilde{Q}_j = SB^{-1} \circ SR^{-1} \circ MC^{-1}(Q_j)$) assume the constant value 0 in $\mathrm{Col}(0,1)$, and assume all 2^{64} possible values in $\mathrm{Col}(2,3)$.

The main observations behind the attack. Observe that (P_i, Q_j) is a slid pair if and only if the corresponding pair $(P_i, \tilde{Q}_j)$ satisfies $P_i \oplus \tilde{Q}_j = k$. We use two conclusions of this observation:

1. *Friend pairs for free.* If $(P_i, \tilde{Q}_j)$ is a slid pair, then for any a, $(P_i \oplus a, \tilde{Q}_j \oplus a)$ is a slid pair as well.

   This allows attaching to each candidate slid pair a friend pair, thus enhancing the filtering condition on the ciphertext side. However, in our case, we have $\tilde{Q}_j \oplus a \in \tilde{T}_Q$ only if $a_{\mathrm{Col}(0,1)} = 0$. In such a case, $P_i \oplus a \notin T_P$, unless $a = 0$ (which means that the new pair is identical to the initial one).

   To overcome this problem, we add to the data set another structure $T_R = \{R_i\}$ of 2^{64} plaintexts that assume the constant value 0 in $\mathrm{Col}(2)$ and the constant value 1 in $\mathrm{Col}(3)$, and assume all 2^{64} possible values in $\mathrm{Col}(0,1)$. Then, we can attach to each $P_i \in T_P$ a friend $R_i = P_i \oplus (0,0,0,1) \in T_R$, such that for each $Q_j \in T_Q$, the pair $(P_i, \tilde{Q}_j)$ is a slid pair if and only if $(R_i, \tilde{Q}_j \oplus (0,0,0,1))$ is a slid pair as well. We denote the ciphertext that corresponds to the plaintext R_i by F_i. Furthermore, we denote the element of $\tilde{T}_Q$ that corresponds to $\tilde{Q}_j \oplus (0,0,0,1) \in \tilde{T}_Q$ by Q'_j, and denote the corresponding ciphertext by D'_j.

2. *Key information for free.* Since all $\tilde{Q}_j \in \tilde{T}_Q$ satisfies $(\tilde{Q}_j)_{\mathrm{Col}(0,1)} = 0$, it follows that for any $P_i \in T_P$, we may have $P_i \oplus \tilde{Q}_j = k$ only if $(P_i)_{\mathrm{Col}(0,1)} = k_{\mathrm{Col}(0,1)}$. Therefore, when we consider some $P_i \in T_P$ as a candidate for being part of a slid pair (with counterpart from T_Q), we immediately obtain a candidate value for the two initial columns of the key k.

   Of course, the adversary does not know whether some $P_i \in T_P$ has a slid counterpart in T_Q, and so does not obtain the key information directly. However, this key information can be used indirectly to check the validity of many slid pair candidates simultaneously, as shown below.

We note that the latter observation also explains why the attack succeeds deterministically. By the choice of the structure T_P, its elements assume all possible values in $\mathrm{Col}(0,1)$. In particular, for the right secret key k, there exists $P_i \in T_P$ such that $(P_i)_{\mathrm{Col}(0,1)} = k_{\mathrm{Col}(0,1)}$. For that plaintext P_i, we have $(P_i \oplus k)_{\mathrm{Col}(0,1)} = 0$. However, the structure $\tilde{T}_Q$ contains all 2^{64} values whose first two columns are equal to 0. Hence, $\tilde{Q}_j := P_i \oplus k \in \tilde{T}_Q$, and so, $(P_i, \tilde{Q}_j)$ is a slid pair. Hence, the data set is *guaranteed* to contain a slid pair.

Exploiting the key information. Assume that (P_i, Q_j) is a slid pair. Then, due to the omission of MixColumns from the last round of AES, the corresponding ciphertexts satisfy the relation

$$D_j = ARK \circ SR \circ SB \circ ARK \circ MC \circ ARK(C_i). \tag{10}$$

Similarly, since $(R_i, \tilde{Q}_j \oplus (0,0,0,1))$ is a slid pair (by property (1) above), the corresponding ciphertexts F_i, D'_j, satisfy

$$D'_j = ARK \circ SR \circ SB \circ ARK \circ MC \circ ARK(F_i). \tag{11}$$

Algorithm 5. A Slide Attack on 1K-AES

Ask for the encryption of three structures T_P, T_Q, T_R, each of 2^{64} plaintexts, as described in the text.

Initialize an empty hash table T.

for each plaintext/ciphertext pair $(Q_j, D_j) \in T_Q$ **do**

    Compute the value $\tilde{Q}_j = SB^{-1} \circ SR^{-1} \circ MC^{-1}(Q_j)$,

    Compute the value $Q'_j = MC \circ SR \circ SB(\tilde{Q}_j \oplus (0,0,0,1))$,

    Denote the corresponding ciphertext by D'_j.

    Store in T the pairs $((D_j \oplus D'_j)_{SR(\mathrm{Col}(0,1))}, Q_j)$.

for each plaintext/ciphertext pair $(P_i, C_i) \in T_P$ **do**

    Set $k_{\mathrm{Col}(0,1)} = (P_i)_{\mathrm{Col}(0,1)}$,

    Compute shifted columns $SR(\mathrm{Col}(0,1))$ of the value $SR \circ SB \circ ARK \circ MC \circ ARK(C_i) \oplus SR \circ SB \circ ARK \circ MC \circ ARK(R_i)$,

    if the computed value is the first coordinate of an entry $(((D_j \oplus D'_j)_{SR(\mathrm{Col}(0,1))}, Q_j)$ **then**

        Test the key candidate $k = P_i \oplus \tilde{Q}_j$ by trial encryption.

Now, assume that some specific $P_i \in T_P$ has a slid counterpart in T_Q. By property (2) above, this implies $k_{\mathrm{Col}(0,1)} = (P_i)_{\mathrm{Col}(0,1)}$. This allows us to compute $\mathrm{Col}(0,1)$ of $ARK \circ MC \circ ARK(C_i)$ (since we know $k_{\mathrm{Col}(0,1)}$), and consequently, also shifted columns $SR(\mathrm{Col}(0,1))$ of the state $SR \circ SB \circ ARK \circ MC \circ ARK(C_i)$. In a similar way, we can compute the value of shifted columns $SR(\mathrm{Col}(0,1))$ of the state $SR \circ SB \circ ARK \circ MC \circ ARK(F_i)$. Hence, we can compute the value of shifted columns $SR(\mathrm{Col}(0,1))$ of

$$SR \circ SB \circ ARK \circ MC \circ ARK(C_i) \oplus SR \circ SB \circ ARK \circ MC \circ ARK(F_i)$$
$$= ARK \circ SR \circ SB \circ ARK \circ MC \circ ARK(C_i) \oplus$$
$$ARK \circ SR \circ SB \circ ARK \circ MC \circ ARK(F_i).$$

By Eqs. (10), (11), this value is equal to $(D_j \oplus D'_j)_{SR(\mathrm{Col}(0,1))}$. This gives us a 64-bit filtering condition that can be checked for all j's simultaneously, by searching for a collision in a precomputed hash table. This results in the attack algorithm given in Algorithm 5.

Since the match checked in the hash table is a 64-bit filtering condition, in expectation a single value of j is suggested for each value of i. As each match yields a suggestion for the entire key, any random match is almost surely discarded using a single additional encryption operation. (The probability that some wrong guess survives is as low as 2^{-64}, and so, can be neglected.) On the other hand, as explained above, the data set must contain a slid pair (P_i, Q_j), and this slid pair suggests the correct value of the secret key.

Therefore, the attack requires data complexity of $3 \cdot 2^{64}$ chosen plaintexts, memory complexity of $3 \cdot 2^{64}$, time complexity of $4 \cdot 2^{64}$ encryptions, and succeeds with probability 100%.

The attack applies, with exactly the same complexity, to any variant of 1-KSAt with *incomplete diffusion*. Indeed, the only place where the exact structure of AES was used in the attack is the ability to compute 64 bits of the value $ARK \circ MC \circ ARK(C_i)$, given $k_{\mathrm{Col}(0,1)}$. The adversary has this ability (or equivalent ability with some other part of the state) as long as the operation A is applied to blocks of size at most half of the state. This is indeed the case in any variant of 1-KSAt with incomplete diffusion. Therefore, we obtain an attack with data complexity of $3 \cdot 2^{n/2}$ chosen plaintexts, memory complexity of $3 \cdot 2^{n/2}$, time complexity of $4 \cdot 2^{n/2}$ encryptions, and success probability of 100%.

For 1-KSAt with complete diffusion, the above attack does not apply, and we are not aware of any attack with complexity close to $2^{n/2}$ on this variant.

6   Substitution Slide Attack

We now present a new technique which we call *substitution slide*, and use it to attack 1-KSAt (and in particular, 1K-AES) using only $2^{n/2}$ *known plaintexts*, $2^{n/2}$ memory and about $2^{3n/4}$ time. Unlike the attack presented in Sect. 5, this attack applies also for 1-KSAt with complete diffusion.

The idea behind the attack. As before, we present the attack on 1K-AES for sake of simplicity. Consider a structure $\mathcal{T}_P$ of 2^{64} *known* plaintexts, and let $\tilde{T}$ be the structure obtained by[7] setting $\tilde{P}_i = SB^{-1} \circ SR^{-1} \circ MC^{-1}(P_i)$ for any $P_i \in \mathcal{T}_P$. As was explained in Sect. 5, if (P_i, P_j) is a slid pair, then we have:

$$\begin{cases} P_i \oplus \tilde{P}_j = k, \\ C_j = ARK \circ SR \circ SB \circ ARK \circ MC \circ ARK(C_i). \end{cases}$$

The basic observation we use in this attack is that the (simpler) first equation can be substituted into the (complex) second equation, in order to get rid of key dependence.

Specifically, the second equation can be rewritten as

$$SB^{-1} \circ SR^{-1} \circ ARK(C_j) = ARK \circ MC \circ ARK(C_i). \tag{12}$$

The right hand side of this equation can be written as

$$ARK \circ MC \circ ARK(C_i) = k \oplus MC(C_i \oplus k) = MC(k) \oplus k \oplus MC(C_i),$$

Now, we can get rid of the key dependence by *substituting* the value of k from the first equation above. We have

$$MC(k) \oplus k \oplus M \cdot C_i = MC(P_i \oplus \tilde{P}_j) \oplus P_i \oplus \tilde{P}_j \oplus MC(C_i).$$

Hence, Eq. (12) can be rewritten as

$$SB^{-1} \circ SR^{-1} \circ ARK(C_j) \oplus MC(\tilde{P}_j) \oplus \tilde{P}_j = MC(P_i) \oplus P_i \oplus MC(C_i). \tag{13}$$

---

[7] We alert the reader that in this section we use (P_i, P_j) to denote a slid pair (rather than (P_i, Q_j)). This was done to emphasize that P_i and P_j, both, are part of a set of known plaintexts.

Algorithm 6. A Known Plaintext Slide Attack on 1K-AES

Ask for 2^{64} known plaintexts/ciphertext pairs (P_i, C_i).
Initialize an empty hash table T.
for each plaintext/ciphertext pair (P_i, C_i) **do**
  Compute the value $\mathcal{P}_i = MC(P_i) \oplus P_i \oplus MC(C_i)$,
  Store in T the triples $((\mathcal{P}_i)_{\mathrm{Col}(0)}, (P_i)_{SR(\mathrm{Col}(0))}, (P_i)_{SR(\mathrm{Col}(1,2,3))})$, indexed by the first two coordinates.
for each guess of $k_{SR(\mathrm{Col}(0))}$ **do**
  for each plaintext/ciphertext pair (P_j, C_j) **do**
    Compute Column 0 of the value $\mathcal{Q} = SB^{-1} \circ SR^{-1} \circ ARK(C_j) \oplus MC(P_j) \oplus P_j$,
    Check for entries in the hash table whose first two coordinates match the pair $((\mathcal{Q}_j)_{\mathrm{Col}(0)}, (\tilde{P}_j \oplus k)_{SR(\mathrm{Col}(0))})$.

    for Each match found in the table **do**
      Test the key candidate $k = P_i \oplus \tilde{P}_j$.

Equation (13) is almost what we need. The right hand side depends only on (P_i, C_i) and thus can be computed in advance for all values of i and stored in a hash table. The left hand side depends on (P_j, C_j); however, it depends also on the secret key, and thus, we cannot just evaluate it for all j and check for a match in the table.

In order to evaluate ℓ bytes of the left hand side, we have to guess ℓ bytes of the key k. However, this does not really provide filtering, as the amount of filtering we obtain is equal to the amount of key material we have to guess. Instead, we appeal again to the first equation, and note that it also provides ℓ bytes of filtering, once ℓ bytes of k are guessed. Therefore, we obtain 2ℓ bytes of filtering, at the expense of guessing ℓ key bytes.

The attack algorithm. Choosing $\ell = 4$, this allows mounting the attack described in Algorithm 6.

Since the match checked in the hash table is a 64-bit filtering condition, on expectation a single value of i is suggested for each value of j. As each match yields a suggestion for the entire key, any random match is almost surely discarded using a single additional encryption operation. (The probability that at least one wrong candidate pair is not discarded is as low as 2^{-32}, and thus, can be neglected). On the other hand, the data set contains a slid pair with probability $1 - (1 - 2^{-128})^{2^{128}} \approx 0.63$, and for the correct guess of $k_{SR(\mathrm{Col}(0))}$, each slid pair suggests the correct value of the secret key.

Therefore, the attack requires data complexity of 2^{64} known plaintexts, memory complexity of 2^{64}, and time complexity of 2^{96} encryptions, and succeeds with probability of about 63%.

The attack applies to any variant of 1-KSAt in which the transformations S, A are publicly known, including variants with *complete diffusion*. Indeed, the exact structure of AES (or more generally, the incomplete diffusion of the MixColumns transformation) are not used in the attack at all. Therefore, we obtain an attack with data complexity of $2^{n/2}$ known plaintexts, memory complexity of $2^{n/2}$, time complexity of $2^{3n/4}$ encryptions, and succeeds probability of about 63%.

We note that the time complexity can be somewhat reduced by choosing another value of ℓ and using two plaintext structures of different sizes. For example, in the case of AES, the time complexity can be reduced to 2^{88}, by guessing 5 key bytes (instead of 4), taking two different structures of plaintexts – $\mathcal{T}_P$ of size 2^{84} and $\mathcal{T}_Q$ of size 2^{44}, and searching for slid pairs of the form (P_i, Q_j) where $P_i \in \mathcal{T}_P$ and $Q_j \in \mathcal{T}_Q$. However, this leads to a significant increase in the data and memory complexities (in the case of AES we described – to 2^{84}), and thus, this tradeoff does not seem profitable.

7 Summary and Conclusions

In this paper we studied slide attacks on *almost self similar* constructions, in which the symmetry is broken by the last round. As a study case, we concentrated on SP networks, in which such a symmetry break is inherent due to the final key whitening step, and especially, on AES-type constructions. We devised four new techniques: slid sets, hypercube of slid pairs, suggestive plaintext structures and substitution slides. We used the new techniques to attack various general SPN schemes—of different key periods, with different structures of the last round, with known or secret S boxes, and with full or an incomplete diffusion.

Open problems left for further work include:

– Use the techniques proposed in the paper to attack other general SPN constructions.
– Find other types of slide attacks on almost self similar constructions.
– Find (lightweight) block ciphers, with periodic key schedule, susceptible to these attacks.

Acknowledgements. The research was partially supported by European Research Council under the ERC starting grant agreement n. 757731 (LightCrypt) and by the BIU Center for Research in Applied Cryptography and Cyber Security in conjunction with the Israel National Cyber Bureau in the Prime Minister's Office. Orr Dunkelman was supported in part by the Israel Ministry of Science and Technology, the Center for Cyber, Law, and Policy in conjunction with the Israel National Cyber Bureau in the Prime Minister's Office and by the Israeli Science Foundation through grants No. 880/18 and 3380/19.

References

1. Aerts, W., et al.: A practical attack on KeeLoq. J. Cryptol. **25**(1), 136–157 (2012)
2. Andreeva, E., Bogdanov, A., Dodis, Y., Mennink, B., Steinberger, J.P.: On the indifferentiability of key-alternating ciphers. In: Canetti, R., Garay, J.A. (eds.) CRYPTO 2013. LNCS, vol. 8042, pp. 531–550. Springer, Heidelberg (2013). https://doi.org/10.1007/978-3-642-40041-4_29

3. Banik, S., et al.: Midori: a block cipher for low energy. In: Iwata, T., Cheon, J.H. (eds.) ASIACRYPT 2015. LNCS, vol. 9453, pp. 411–436. Springer, Heidelberg (2015). https://doi.org/10.1007/978-3-662-48800-3_17

4. Bar-On, A., Biham, E., Dunkelman, O., Keller, N.: Efficient slide attacks. J. Cryptol. **31**(3), 641–670 (2017). https://doi.org/10.1007/s00145-017-9266-8

5. Beierle, C., Leander, G., Moradi, A., Rasoolzadeh, S.: CRAFT: lightweight tweakable block cipher with efficient protection against DFA attacks. IACR Trans. Symmetric Cryptol. **2019**(1), 5–45 (2019)

6. Biham, E.: New types of cryptanalytic attacks using related keys. J. Cryptology **7**(4), 229–246 (1994)

7. Biham, E., Dunkelman, O., Keller, N.: A simple related-key attack on the full SHACAL-1. In: Abe, M. (ed.) CT-RSA 2007. LNCS, vol. 4377, pp. 20–30. Springer, Heidelberg (2006). https://doi.org/10.1007/11967668_2

8. Biham, E., Shamir, A.: Differential Cryptanalysis of the Data Encryption Standard. Springer, Heidelberg (1993)

9. Biryukov, A., Wagner, D.: Slide attacks. In: Knudsen, L. (ed.) FSE 1999. LNCS, vol. 1636, pp. 245–259. Springer, Heidelberg (1999). https://doi.org/10.1007/3-540-48519-8_18

10. Biryukov, A., Wagner, D.: Advanced slide attacks. In: Preneel, B. (ed.) EUROCRYPT 2000. LNCS, vol. 1807, pp. 589–606. Springer, Heidelberg (2000). https://doi.org/10.1007/3-540-45539-6_41

11. Brier, E., Peyrin, T., Stern, J.: BPS: a format-preserving encryption proposal (2010). http://csrc.nist.gov/groups/ST/toolkit/BCM/documents/proposedmodes/bps/bps-spec.pdf

12. Daemen, J., Knudsen, L., Rijmen, V.: The block cipher Square. In: Biham, E. (ed.) FSE 1997. LNCS, vol. 1267, pp. 149–165. Springer, Heidelberg (1997). https://doi.org/10.1007/BFb0052343

13. Daemen, J., Rijmen, V.: The Design of Rijndael: AES - The Advanced Encryption Standard. Information Security and Cryptography. Springer, Heidelberg (2002). https://doi.org/10.1007/978-3-662-04722-4

14. Dinur, I., Dunkelman, O., Keller, N., Shamir, A.: Reflections on slide with a twist attacks. Des. Codes Crypt. **77**(2–3), 633–651 (2015)

15. Dunkelman, O., Keller, N.: The effects of the omission of last round's MixColumns on AES. Inf. Process. Lett. **110**(8–9), 304–308 (2010)

16. Dunkelman, O., Keller, N., Shamir, A.: Slidex attacks on the Even-Mansour encryption scheme. J. Cryptol. **28**(1), 1–28 (2015)

17. Durak, F.B., Vaudenay, S.: Breaking the FF3 format-preserving encryption standard over small domains. In: Katz, J., Shacham, H. (eds.) CRYPTO 2017. LNCS, vol. 10402, pp. 679–707. Springer, Cham (2017). https://doi.org/10.1007/978-3-319-63715-0_23

18. Furuya, S.: Slide attacks with a known-plaintext cryptanalysis. In: Kim, K. (ed.) ICISC 2001. LNCS, vol. 2288, pp. 214–225. Springer, Heidelberg (2002). https://doi.org/10.1007/3-540-45861-1_17

19. Gérard, B., Grosso, V., Naya-Plasencia, M., Standaert, F.-X.: Block ciphers that are easier to mask: how far can we go? In: Bertoni, G., Coron, J.-S. (eds.) CHES 2013. LNCS, vol. 8086, pp. 383–399. Springer, Heidelberg (2013). https://doi.org/10.1007/978-3-642-40349-1_22

20. Gorski, M., Lucks, S., Peyrin, T.: Slide attacks on a class of hash functions. In: Pieprzyk, J. (ed.) ASIACRYPT 2008. LNCS, vol. 5350, pp. 143–160. Springer, Heidelberg (2008). https://doi.org/10.1007/978-3-540-89255-7_10

21. Grassi, L.: MixColumns properties and attacks on (round-reduced) AES with a single secret S-Box. In: Smart, N.P. (ed.) CT-RSA 2018. LNCS, vol. 10808, pp. 243–263. Springer, Cham (2018). https://doi.org/10.1007/978-3-319-76953-0_13

22. Grassi, L.: Mixture differential cryptanalysis: a new approach to distinguishers and attacks on round-reduced AES. IACR Trans. Symmetric Cryptol. **2018**(2), 133–160 (2018)

23. Grassi, L., Rechberger, C., Rønjom, S.: Subspace trail cryptanalysis and its applications to AES. IACR Trans. Symmetric Cryptol. **2016**(2), 192–225 (2016)

24. Grossman, E.K., Tucherman, B.: Analysis of a weakened Feistel-like cipher. In: Proceedings of International Conference on Communications 1978, pp. 46.3.1–46.3.5 (1978)

25. Guo, J., Peyrin, T., Poschmann, A., Robshaw, M.: The LED block cipher. In: Preneel, B., Takagi, T. (eds.) CHES 2011. LNCS, vol. 6917, pp. 326–341. Springer, Heidelberg (2011). https://doi.org/10.1007/978-3-642-23951-9_22

26. Knudsen, L., Leander, G., Poschmann, A., Robshaw, M.J.B.: PRINTCIPHER: a block cipher for IC-printing. In: Mangard, S., Standaert, F.-X. (eds.) CHES 2010. LNCS, vol. 6225, pp. 16–32. Springer, Heidelberg (2010). https://doi.org/10.1007/978-3-642-15031-9_2

27. Leander, G., Abdelraheem, M.A., AlKhzaimi, H., Zenner, E.: A cryptanalysis of PRINTCIPHER: the invariant subspace attack. In: Rogaway, P. (ed.) CRYPTO 2011. LNCS, vol. 6841, pp. 206–221. Springer, Heidelberg (2011). https://doi.org/10.1007/978-3-642-22792-9_12

28. Matsui, M.: Linear cryptanalysis method for DES cipher. In: Helleseth, T. (ed.) EUROCRYPT 1993. LNCS, vol. 765, pp. 386–397. Springer, Heidelberg (1994). https://doi.org/10.1007/3-540-48285-7_33

29. Robshaw, M.J.B.: Searching for compact algorithms: CGEN. In: Nguyen, P.Q. (ed.) VIETCRYPT 2006. LNCS, vol. 4341, pp. 37–49. Springer, Heidelberg (2006). https://doi.org/10.1007/11958239_3

30. Sun, B., Liu, M., Guo, J., Qu, L., Rijmen, V.: New Insights on AES-like SPN ciphers. In: Robshaw, M., Katz, J. (eds.) CRYPTO 2016. LNCS, vol. 9814, pp. 605–624. Springer, Heidelberg (2016). https://doi.org/10.1007/978-3-662-53018-4_22

31. Tiessen, T., Knudsen, L.R., Kölbl, S., Lauridsen, M.M.: Security of the AES with a secret S-box. In: Leander, G. (ed.) FSE 2015. LNCS, vol. 9054, pp. 175–189. Springer, Heidelberg (2015). https://doi.org/10.1007/978-3-662-48116-5_9

The Retracing Boomerang Attack

Orr Dunkelman[1]([✉]) [ID], Nathan Keller[2]([✉]), Eyal Ronen[3,4], and Adi Shamir[5]

[1] Computer Science Department, University of Haifa, Haifa, Israel
orrd@cs.haifa.ac.il
[2] Department of Mathematics, Bar-Ilan University, Ramat Gan, Israel
nkeller@math.biu.ac.il
[3] School of Computer Science, Tel Aviv University, Tel Aviv, Israel
er@eyalro.net
[4] COSIC, KU Leuven, Heverlee, Belgium
[5] Faculty of Mathematics and Computer Science, Weizmann Institute of Science,
Rehovot, Israel
adi.shamir@weizmann.ac.il

Abstract. Boomerang attacks are extensions of differential attacks, that make it possible to combine two unrelated differential properties of the first and second part of a cryptosystem with probabilities p and q into a new differential-like property of the whole cryptosystem with probability p^2q^2 (since each one of the properties has to be satisfied twice). In this paper we describe a new version of boomerang attacks which uses the counterintuitive idea of throwing out most of the data in order to force equalities between certain values on the ciphertext side. In certain cases, this creates a correlation between the four probabilistic events, which increases the probability of the combined property to p^2q and increases the signal to noise ratio of the resultant distinguisher. We call this variant a *retracing boomerang attack* since we make sure that the boomerang we throw follows the same path on its forward and backward directions. To demonstrate the power of the new technique, we apply it to the case of 5-round AES. This version of AES was repeatedly attacked by a large variety of techniques, but for twenty years its complexity had remained stuck at 2^{32}. At Crypto'18 it was finally reduced to 2^{24} (for full key recovery), and with our new technique we can further reduce the complexity of full key recovery to the surprisingly low value of $2^{16.5}$ (i.e., only 90,000 encryption/decryption operations are required for a full key recovery on half the rounds of AES).

In addition to improving previous attacks, our new technique unveils a hidden relationship between boomerang attacks and two other cryptanalytic techniques, the yoyo game and the recently introduced mixture differentials.

1 Introduction

Differential attacks, which were introduced by Biham and Shamir [9] in 1990, use the evolution of differences between pairs of encryptions in order to construct

Electronic supplementary material The online version of this chapter (https://doi.org/10.1007/978-3-030-45721-1_11) contains supplementary material, which is available to authorized users.

© International Association for Cryptologic Research 2020
A. Canteaut and Y. Ishai (Eds.): EUROCRYPT 2020, LNCS 12105, pp. 280–309, 2020.
https://doi.org/10.1007/978-3-030-45721-1_11

high probability distinguishers. They can concatenate two short differential properties with probabilities p and q into a longer property with probability pq, but only when the output difference of the first property is equal to the input difference of the second property. To overcome this restriction, Wagner [34] introduced in 1999 the idea of the boomerang attack, which "throws" two plaintexts through the encryption process, and then watches the two resultant ciphertexts (with some modifications) return back through the decryption process. This made it possible to concatenate two arbitrary differential properties whose probabilities are p and q into a longer property whose probability is p^2q^2, since it requires that four probabilistic events will simultaneously happen. This seems to be inferior to plain vanilla differential attacks, but in many cases we can find two short unrelated differential properties with much higher probabilities p and q, which more than compensates for their quadratic occurrence in p^2q^2. A typical example of the successful application of a boomerang attack is the best known related-key attack on the full versions of AES-192 and AES-256, presented by Biryukov and Khovratovich [11]. Consequently, boomerang attacks have become an essential part of the toolkit of any cryptanalyst, and many variants of this technique had been developed over the last 20 years.

In this paper we develop a new variant of the boomerang attack. We call it a *retracing boomerang attack*, since the boomerang we throw through the encryption not only returns to the plaintext side, but also follows closely related paths on its forward and backward journey. In certain cases, this makes it possible to increase the probability of the combined differential property to p^2q, since an event that happened once with probability q will reoccur a second time with probability 1. This idea had already been used by Biryukov and Khovratovich [11] in 2009 to get an extra free round in the middle of the encryption, but we use it in a different way which yields better attacks on several AES variants.

The main AES variant we consider in this paper is the 5-round version of AES. This variant had been repeatedly attacked in many papers by a large variety of techniques over the last 20 years, but all the published key recovery attacks had a complexity of 2^{32} or higher. It was only in 2018 that this record had been broken, when [2] showed how to recover the full secret key[1] for this variant with a complexity of 2^{24}. In this paper we use our new retracing boomerang attack to break the record again, reducing the complexity to $2^{16.5}$, albeit in the stronger attack model of adaptive chosen plaintext and ciphertext. This attack was fully verified experimentally.

Another AES variant we successfully attack is the 5-round version of AES in which the S-box and the linear mixing operations are secret key-dependent components of the same general structure as in AES. The best currently known key-recovery attack on this variant, presented by Tiessen et al. [32] in 2015, had data and time complexity of 2^{40}. In this paper we show how to use our new techniques in order to reduce this complexity to just 2^{26}. A comparison of our

---

[1] Besides the full key recovery attack, the authors of [2] present an attack with complexity of $2^{21.5}$ that recovers 24 bits of the secret key. Since our attack recovers the full secret key, we compare it with the full key recovery attack of [2].

new attacks on 5-round AES and on 5-round AES with a secret S-box with previous attacks[2] is presented in Table 1.

Apart of allowing us to obtain better results in cryptanalysis of specific AES variants, our new technique unveils a hidden relation between the boomerang attack and the *yoyo tricks with AES*, introduced recently by Rønjom et al. [30]. While the 'yoyo tricks' differ significantly from classical boomerang attacks, we show that they fit naturally into the retracing boomerang framework. In a similar way, we show that *mixture differentials*, introduced recently by Grassi [22], is closely related to a retracing type of the rectangle attack [6,26] (which is the chosen plaintext version of the boomerang attack). In the case of mixture differentials, the relation between the attacks is even more surprising, and may unveil additional interesting features of the mixture differential technique.

This paper is organized as follows. In Sect. 2 we present the previous related work and introduce our notations. We introduce the retracing boomerang attack in Sect. 3. We apply our new attack to 5-round AES and to 5-round AES with a secret S-box in Sects. 4 and 5, respectively. In Sect. 6 we present the retracing rectangle attack and show a relation between the mixture differential technique and the rectangle technique. We summarize the paper in Sect. 7.

2   Background and Previous Work

The retracing boomerang attack is related to a number of other variants of the boomerang attack, as well as to several other previously known techniques. In this section we briefly present the techniques that are most relevant to our results, while the other techniques are presented in the full version of the paper.

2.1   The Boomerang Attack

As the boomerang attack builds upon differential cryptanalysis, a short introduction to the latter is due.

Differential cryptanalysis. Introduced by Biham and Shamir [9] in 1990, differential cryptanalysis is a statistical attack on block ciphers that studies the development of differences between two encrypted plaintexts through the encryption process. Assume that we are given an iterative block cipher $E :$ $\{0,1\}^n \times \{0,1\}^k \rightarrow \{0,1\}^n$ that consists of m (similar) rounds, and denote the intermediate value at the beginning of the i'th round in the encryption processes of the plaintexts P and P' by X_i and X'_i, respectively. An r-round *differential characteristic* with probability p of a cipher is a property of the form $\Pr[X_{i+r} \oplus X'_{i+r} = \Omega_O | X_i \oplus X'_i = \Omega_I] = p$, denoted in short $\Omega_I \xrightarrow{p} \Omega_O$.

---

[2] We note that [4,15,21,24,25,31] attacked an intermediate variant, in which only the S-box is key-dependent, while MixColumns is the same one as in AES. The best currently known attack on this variant, obtained by Bardeh and Rønjom [4], has complexity of 2^{32}. Obviously, our attack applies to this variant as well.

Table 1. Attacks on 5-round AES (full key recovery)

Attack	Data (Chosen plaintexts)	Memory (128-bit blocks)	Time (encryptions)
	5-Round AES		
Square [29]	2^{11}	small	2^{45}
Partial Sum [33]	2^8	small	2^{40}
Improved Square [20]	2^{33}	small	2^{35}
Imp. Diff. [7]	$2^{33.5}$	2^{38}	2^{35}
Mixture Diff. [22]	2^{32}	2^{32}	2^{34}
Yoyo [30]	$2^{11.3}$ ACC	small	2^{31}
Mixture Diff. [2]	2^{24} †	$2^{21.5}$	2^{24} †
Our Attack (Sect. 4)	2^9 ACC	2^9	2^{23}
Our Attack (Sect. 4)	2^{15} ACC	2^9	$2^{16.5}$
	5-Round AES with Secret S-boxes		
Integral [31]	2^{128}	small	2^{128}
Integral [25]	2^{96}	2^8	2^{96}
Imp. Diff. [24]	2^{102}	2^8	2^{102}
Imp. Diff. [21]	$2^{76.4}$	2^8	$2^{76.4}$
Mult.-of-n. [21]	$2^{53.3}$	2^{16}	$2^{53.3}$
Square‡ [32]	2^{40}	2^{36}	2^{40}
Yoyo [4]	2^{32} ACC	small	2^{31}
Our Attack‡ (Sect. 5)	$2^{17.5}$ ACC	2^{17}	2^{29}
Our Attack† (Sect. 5)	$2^{25.8}$ ACC	2^{17}	$2^{25.8}$

†—the data and time complexity for partial key recovery is $2^{21.5}$
‡—the attack applies also when the linear transformation is key-dependent
ACC—Adaptive Chosen Plaintexts and Ciphertexts

Differential cryptanalysis shows that if there exists a differential characteristic for most of the rounds of the cipher that holds with a non-negligible probability, then the cipher can be broken faster than exhaustive search by an attack that requires $O(1/p)$ chosen plaintexts. Differential cryptanalysis was used to mount the first attack faster than exhaustive search on the full DES [28], as well as on many other block ciphers.

The boomerang attack. Introduced by Wagner [34], the boomerang attack was one of the first techniques to show that non-existence of 'long' high-probability differentials is not sufficient to guarantee security with respect to differential-type attacks. Suppose that the cipher E can be decomposed as $E = E_1 \circ E_0$, such that for E_0, there exists a differential characteristic $\alpha \xrightarrow{p} \beta$, and for E_1, there exists a differential characteristic $\gamma \xrightarrow{q} \delta$, depicted in Fig. 1, where $pq \gg 2^{-n/2}$. Then one can distinguish E from a random permutation, using Algorithm 1 presented below.

Algorithm 1. The Boomerang Attack Algorithm

1: Initialize a counter $ctr \leftarrow 0$.
2: Generate $(pq)^{-2}$ unique plaintext pairs (P_1, P_2) with input difference α.
3: **for all** pairs (P_1, P_2) **do**
4:       Ask for the encryption of (P_1, P_2) to (C_1, C_2).
5:       Compute $C_3 = C_1 \oplus \delta$ and $C_4 = C_2 \oplus \delta$.   ▷ δ-shift
6:       Ask for the decryption of (C_3, C_4) to (P_3, P_4).
7:       **if** $P_3 \oplus P_4 = \alpha$ **then**
8:             Increment ctr
9: **if** $ctr \geq 1$ **then**
10:       **return:** This is the cipher E.
11: **else**
12:       **return:** This is a random permutation.

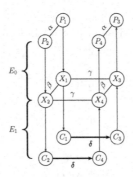

Fig. 1. The boomerang attack

The theoretical analysis of the algorithm is as follows. Denote the intermediate values after the partial encryption by E_0 of the plaintext P_j by X_j, for $1 \leq j \leq 4$. Let (P_1, P_2) by a plaintext pair such that $P_1 \oplus P_2 = \alpha$. By the differential characteristic of E_0, we have

$$X_1 \oplus X_2 = \beta, \tag{1}$$

with probability p. On the other side, as the ciphertexts satisfy $C_1 \oplus C_3 = C_2 \oplus C_4 = \delta$, by the differential characteristic of E_1 we have

$$(X_1 \oplus X_3 = \gamma) \wedge (X_2 \oplus X_4 = \gamma), \tag{2}$$

with probability q^2. (We recall that the differential characteristic $\gamma \xrightarrow{q} \delta$ for E_1 is identical to the differential characteristic $\delta \xrightarrow{q} \gamma$ for E_1^{-1}, in the sense that both count the same set of input/output pairs for E_1.) If both Eq. (1) and (2) hold, then we have

$$X_3 \oplus X_4 = (X_3 \oplus X_1) \oplus (X_1 \oplus X_2) \oplus (X_2 \oplus X_4) = \gamma \oplus \beta \oplus \gamma = \beta. \tag{3}$$

Therefore, by the differential characteristic of E_0, we have $P_3 \oplus P_4 = \alpha$, with probability p. Hence, assuming (somewhat non-carefully, as discussed in [27]) that all these events are independent, we have

$$\Pr[P_3 \oplus P_4 = \alpha | P_1 \oplus P_2 = \alpha] = p^2 q^2. \tag{4}$$

As we take $1/(pq)^2$ pairs (P_1, P_2), then with a high probability $(= 1 - e^{-1} \approx 63\%)$,[3] for at least one of them we obtain $P_3 \oplus P_4 = \alpha$, and hence, the algorithm outputs 'the cipher E'. On the other hand, for a random permutation we have $\Pr[P_3 \oplus P_4 = \alpha] = 2^{-n}$, and hence, the expected number of pairs (P_1, P_2) for which $P_3 \oplus P_4 = \alpha$ holds is $2^{-n} \cdot (pq)^{-2} \ll 1$ (as we assumed $pq \gg 2^{-n/2}$). Thus, with an overwhelming probability, the algorithm outputs 'random permutation'.

Therefore, the above algorithm indeed allows distinguishing E from a random permutation, using in total $4(pq)^{-2}$ adaptively chosen plaintexts and ciphertexts (in the sequel: ACPC).

2.2   The S-Box Switch

In [11], Biryukov and Khovratovich showed that in certain cases, the boomerang attack can be improved significantly by 'bypassing for free' some operations in the middle of the cipher. One of those cases, called *S-box switch*, is particularly relevant to our results. Assume that $E = F_1 \circ E_0$, where the last operation in E_0 is a layer S of S-boxes applied in parallel (which is the usual scenario in SP networks, like the AES). That is, S divides the state ρ into $\rho = (\rho_1, \rho_2, \ldots, \rho_t)$ and transforms it to $S(\rho) = (f_1(\rho_1) || f_2(\rho_2) || \ldots || f_t(\rho_t))$, for t independent (keyed) functions f_j. Suppose that the differential characteristics in E_0, E_1 are such that in both β and γ, the difference in the part of the intermediate state X that corresponds to the output of some f_j is Δ. In other words, denoting this part of the intermediate state X by X_j, if both characteristics hold then we have

$$(X_1)_j \oplus (X_2)_j = (X_1)_j \oplus (X_3)_j = (X_2)_j \oplus (X_4)_j = \Delta.$$

In such a case, we have $(X_1)_j = (X_4)_j$ and $(X_2)_j = (X_3)_j$, and hence, if the differential characteristic in the function $(f_j)^{-1}$ holds for the pair (X_1, X_2) then it must hold for the pair (X_3, X_4). Thus, the overall probability of the boomerang distinguisher is increased by a factor of $(q')^{-1}$, where q' is the probability of the differential characteristic in f_j.

This 'switch', along with other 'switches in the middle', was a key ingredient in the attack of [11] on the full AES-192 and AES-256. Later on, some of these switches were generalized in the Sandwich attack of [19] for the case of a probabilistic transition in the middle layer and used to attack KASUMI, the cipher of 3G cellular networks. Recently, a more complete and rigorous analysis of the transition between E_0 and E_1 was suggested, using the Boomerang Connectivity Table [14] that covers these and related ideas. These developments are described in more detail in the full version of the paper.

---

[3] The success probability of the attack can be increased by slightly enlarging the data complexity. If we start with $c/(pq)^2$ pairs, then the success probability is $1 - e^{-c}$.

2.3 The Yoyo Game and Mixture Differentials

In addition to the classical boomerang attack, two more techniques – the yoyo game and mixture differentials – are closely related to our attacks. We describe them very briefly below, but in more detail in the sequel. Our new type of boomerang attacks allows us to unveil a close relation of these two techniques to the boomerang and rectangle techniques, respectively.

The yoyo game. The yoyo technique was introduced by Biham et al. [5] in 1998. Like the boomerang attack, the yoyo game is based on encrypting a pair of plaintexts (P_1, P_2), modifying the corresponding ciphertexts (C_1, C_2) into (C_3, C_4), and decrypting them. However, while the boomerang distinguisher just checks whether the resulting plaintexts (P_3, P_4) satisfy some property, in the yoyo game the process continues: (P_3, P_4) are modified into (P_5, P_6) which are encrypted into (C_5, C_6), those in turn are modified into (C_7, C_8) which are decrypted into (P_7, P_8), etc. The process satisfies the property that all *pairs of intermediate values* $(X_{2\ell+1}, X_{2\ell+2})$ at some specific point of the encryption process satisfy some property (e.g., zero difference in some part of the state). Since for a random permutation, the probability that such a property is satisfied by a sequence of pairs $(X_{2\ell+1}, X_{2\ell+2})$ is extremely low, this property can theoretically be used for distinguishing the cipher from a random permutation. Practically, exploiting this property is not so easy, as the adversary does not see the intermediate values $(X_{2\ell+1}, X_{2\ell+2})$. Nevertheless, Biham et al. showed that in some specific cases, such a distinguishing is possible and even allows for key recovery [5].

Biham et al. [5] applied the yoyo technique to a 16-round variant of the block cipher Skipjack. Biryukov et al. [12] applied it to attack generic 5-round Feistel constructions, and Rønjom et al. [30] used it to attack reduced-round AES with at most 5 rounds. As the attack of Rønjom et al. [30] is a central ingredient in our attacks on 5-round AES, it is presented in detail in Sect. 4.

Mixture differentials. The mixture differential technique was presented by Grassi [22]. The technique works in the following setting. Assume that the cipher E can be decomposed as $E = E_1 \circ E_0$, where E_0 can be considered as a concatenation of several permutations, i.e., $P = (\rho_1, \rho_2, \ldots, \rho_t)$ and $E_0(P) = f_1(\rho_1) \| f_2(\rho_2) \| \ldots \| f_t(\rho_t))$, for t independent functions f_j. A well known example of such E_0 is 1.5 rounds of AES, that can be treated as four parallel super S-boxes (see [16]).

Definition 1. *Given a plaintext pair (P^1, P^2), where $P^1 = (\rho_1^1, \ldots, \rho_t^1)$ and $P^2 = (\rho_1^2, \ldots, \rho_t^2)$ we say that (P^3, P^4), where $P^3 = (\rho_1^3, \ldots, \rho_t^3)$ and $P^4 = (\rho_1^4, \ldots, \rho_t^4)$ is a mixture counterpart of (P^1, P^2) if for each $1 \le j \le t$, the quartet $(\rho_j^1, \rho_j^2, \rho_j^3, \rho_j^4)$ consists of two pairs of equal values or of four equal values. The quartet (P^1, P^2, P^3, P^4) is called a mixture.*

The main observation behind the mixture differential technique is that if (P^1, P^2, P^3, P^4) is a mixture then the XOR of the corresponding intermediate values (X^1, X^2, X^3, X^4) is zero. Indeed, for each j, as $(\rho_j^1, \rho_j^2, \rho_j^3, \rho_j^4)$ consists of two pairs of equal values, then the same holds for $(f_j(\rho_j^1), f_j(\rho_j^2), f_j(\rho_j^3), f_j(\rho_j^4))$ as well. In particular, $f_j(\rho_j^1) \oplus f_j(\rho_j^2) \oplus f_j(\rho_j^3) \oplus f_j(\rho_j^4)) = 0$. As a result, if we have $X^1 \oplus X^3 = \gamma$, then $X^2 \oplus X^4 = \gamma$ holds as well. Now, if there exists a differential characteristic $\gamma \xrightarrow{q} \delta$ for E_1, then with probability q^2, the corresponding ciphertexts satisfy $C^1 \oplus C^3 = C^2 \oplus C^4 = \delta$.

Grassi [22,23] applied the technique to mount several attacks on AES with up to 6 rounds. The 5-round attack of Grassi was recently improved in [2] into an attack with overall complexity of 2^{24} for full key-recovery (or $2^{21.5}$ for recovering 24 bits of the secret key), that is significantly faster than all other known attacks on 5-round AES.

3   The Retracing Boomerang Attack

Our new *retracing boomerang* framework contains two attack types – a *shifting* type and a *mixing* type. In this section we present these two types and discuss their advantages over the standard boomerang attack and their relation to previous works. In the following sections and in the appendix we present applications of the new techniques, along with a few variants and extensions.

3.1   The Shifting Retracing Attack

Assumptions. Suppose that the block cipher E can be decomposed as $E = E_{12} \circ E_{11} \circ E_0$, where E_{12} consists of dividing the state into two parts (a left part of b bits and a right part of $n - b$ bits) and applying to them the functions E_{12}^L, E_{12}^R, respectively. Furthermore, suppose that for E_0, there exists a differential characteristic $\alpha \xrightarrow{p} \beta$, for E_{11}, there exists a differential characteristic $\gamma \xrightarrow{q_1} (\mu_L, \mu_R)$, for E_{12}^L, there exists a differential characteristic $\mu_L \xrightarrow{q_2^L} \delta_L$, and for E_{12}^R, there exists a differential characteristic $\mu_R \xrightarrow{q_2^R} \delta_R$ (see Fig. 2).[4]

In other words, we make the same assumptions as in the boomerang attack, with the additional assumption that E_1 can be further decomposed into two sub-ciphers, and that the second sub-cipher has a specific structure. While this additional assumption may look very restrictive, it applies for a wide class of block ciphers. For example, if E is a SASAS construction [13], then E_{12} can be taken to be the last S layer; a specific such example is AES [29], where E_{12} can be taken to be the last 1.5 rounds.

The attack procedure and its analysis. Assuming that $pq_1 q_2^L q_2^R \gg 2^{-n/2}$, the standard boomerang attack can be used to distinguish E from a random permutation, with data complexity of $4(pq_1 q_2^L q_2^R)^{-2}$.

The basic idea of the retracing boomerang attack is to add an artificial $(b-1)$-bit filtering in the middle of the attack procedure. Namely, after encrypting

---

[4] A variant of the attack that is applicable when the top part of the cipher can be further decomposed into two sub-ciphers, is presented in the full version of the paper.

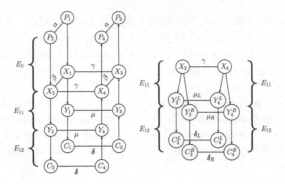

Fig. 2. The retracing boomerang framework

(P_1, P_2) into (C_1, C_2), we first check whether

$$C_1^L \oplus C_2^L = 0 \text{ or } \delta_L. \tag{5}$$

Only if there is equality, we continue with the boomerang process. Otherwise, we simply discard the pair (P_1, P_2). See Fig. 3 for the process.

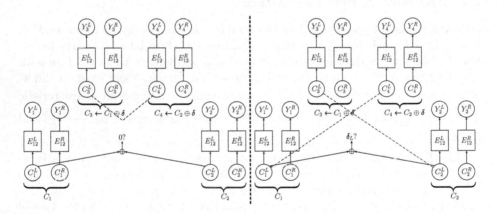

Fig. 3. A shifted quartet (dashed line means equality)

This is a surprising move, as the discarded pair may actually be a *right pair* with respect to the differential characteristic $\alpha \to \beta$ (i.e., a pair that satisfies the characteristic). Hence, a natural question arises: *What do we gain from this filtering?*

Note that for any value of δ_L, if Eq. (5) holds then the two unordered pairs (C_1^L, C_3^L) and (C_2^L, C_4^L) are identical. Hence, if one of these pairs satisfies the differential characteristic $\delta_L \xrightarrow{q_2^L} \mu_L$, then the other one *must* satisfy it as well. As a result, the probability of the boomerang distinguisher *among the examined pairs* is increased by a factor of $(q_2^L)^{-1}$ from $(pq_1 q_2^L q_2^R)^2$ to $(pq_1 q_2^R)^2 q_2^L$.

Advantages of the new technique. At first glance, our new variant of the boomerang attack seems completely odd and useless. Note that as the block size of E_{12}^L is b bits, then any possible differential characteristic of E_{12}^L has probability of at least 2^{-b+1}, and so, the overall probability of the boomerang distinguisher is increased by a factor of at most 2^{b-1}. On the other hand, our filtering leaves only 2^{-b+1} of the pairs, so we either gain nothing (if $q_2^L = 2^{-b+1}$) or even lose (otherwise)!

It turns out that there are several advantages to this approach:

1. Improving the signal to noise ratio. Recall that the ordinary boomerang attack applies if $pq_1 q_2^L q_2^R \gg 2^{-n/2}$, as otherwise, the probability that $P_3 \oplus P_4 = \alpha$ holds for E is not larger than the respective probability for a random permutation. In the retracing boomerang attack, the probability that $P_3 \oplus P_4 = \alpha$ holds *among the examined pairs* is increased by a factor of $(q_2^L)^{-1}$, while the probability for a random permutation remains unchanged. As a result, the attack can succeed in cases where the ordinary boomerang attack fails due to insufficient filtering.

Furthermore, the adversary can use the increased gap between the probabilities of the checked event for E and for a random permutation to replace the differential characteristic $\beta \xrightarrow{p} \alpha$ used for the pair (X_3, X_4) in the backward direction with a truncated differential characteristic. $\beta \xrightarrow{p'} \alpha'$ of a higher probability p' in which α' specifies the difference in only some part of the bits, while still having a larger probability of the event $P_3 \oplus P_4 = \alpha'$ for E than for a random permutation. An example of this advantage is demonstrated in the attack on 5-round AES presented in the full version of the paper.

2. Reducing the data complexity. The new attack saves data complexity on the decryption side. Indeed, as decryption is performed only to the pairs that satisfy the filtering condition, the number of decryptions is reduced by a factor of 2^{b-1}. While usually, the effect of this reduction is not significant as then the encryptions dominate the overall complexity, there are cases in which more queries are made on the decryption side, and in such cases, the data complexity may be reduced significantly. This advantage (like the previous one) is demonstrated in the attack on 5-round AES in the full version of the paper.

3. Reducing the time complexity. The smaller number of pairs on the decryption side may affect also the time complexity of the attack. This effect is not significant when the attack complexity is dominated by encryption/decryption of the data. However, in many cases (e.g., where a round is added before the distinguisher and the adversary has to guess some key material in the added round and check whether the condition $P_3 \oplus P_4 = \alpha$ holds), the complexity of the attack is dominated by analysis of the pairs (P_3, P_4). In such cases, the time complexity may be reduced by a factor of $(q_2^L)^{-1}$, as the number of pairs (P_3, P_4) is reduced by this ratio.

Relation to previous works. Our new technique uses several ideas that already appeared in previous works in different contexts. Those include:

- *Discarding part of the data before the analysis.* The counter-intuitive idea of neglecting part of the data appears in various previous works, e.g., in the context of time-memory tradeoff attacks on stream ciphers [18], and in the context of conditional linear attacks on DES [8].
- *Increasing the probability of the boomerang attack by exploiting dependency between differentials.* As we mentioned above, several previous works on the boomerang attack used dependency between differentials, and in particular, situations in which the four inputs to some function in the encryption process are composed of two pairs of equal values, to increase the probability of the boomerang distinguisher (see, e.g., [10,11,14,19]). The closest to our attack is the *S-box switch* of Biryukov and Khovratovich [11] described in Sect. 2. In all these attacks, the gain is obtained *in the transition between the two sub-ciphers* E_0, E_1. In contrast, the retracing boomerang exploits dependency between the two differentials in the same sub-cipher (by forcing dependency via the artificial filtering).
- *Increasing the probability of the boomerang attack by exploiting representation of a sub-cipher as two (or more) functions applied in parallel.* Such a probability increase was obtained by Biryukov and Khovratovich [11] in the *ladder switch* technique, which exploits a subdivision into multiple functions (e.g., a layer of S-boxes) along with dependency between differentials, to increase the probability of the transition between the two sub-ciphers.
- *Using quartets of the form* (x, x, y, y) *to force dependency.* This idea was recently used by Grassi in [22, Theorem 4], in the context of the mixture differential attack described in Sect. 2.

3.2　The Mixing Retracing Attack

The attack setting. Recall that the shifting retracing boomerang attack increases the probability of the boomerang distinguisher by forcing equality between the unordered pairs (C_1^L, C_2^L) and (C_3^L, C_4^L) that enter $(E_{12}^L)^{-1}$. Such an equality can be forced in an alternative way, without inserting an artificial filtering.

Instead of working with the same shift δ for all ciphertexts, one may shift each ciphertext pair (C_1, C_2) by $(C_1^L \oplus C_2^L, 0)$, thus obtaining the ciphertexts

$$C_3 = (C_3^L, C_3^R) = (C_1^L \oplus (C_1^L \oplus C_2^L), C_1^R \oplus 0) = (C_2^L, C_1^R),$$

and (similarly) $C_4 = (C_1^L, C_2^R)$, see Fig. 4. In such a case, the unordered pairs (C_1^L, C_3^L) and (C_2^L, C_4^L) are equal, and hence, we gain a factor of $(q_2^L)^{-1}$, like in the shifting retracing attack. Furthermore, in the right part we have $C_1^R = C_3^R$

and $C_2^R = C_4^R$, and thus, we gain also a factor of $(q_2^R)^{-2}$ (as both characteristics in E_{12}^R hold trivially with probability 1). This results in a total gain of $(q_2^L)^{-1}(q_2^R)^{-2}$.

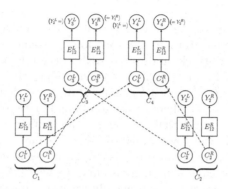

Fig. 4. A mixture quartet of ciphertexts (a dashed line means equality)

Relation to 'yoyo tricks with AES'. Interestingly, in the special case of the AES, the mixing described here is exactly the core step of the yoyo attack of Rønjom et al. [30] (presented in detail in Sect. 4). Hence, this type of retracing boomerang is not entirely novel, but rather generalizes and presents a new viewpoint on the yoyo attack of Rønjom et al.

Comparison between the two types of retracing boomerang. At first glance, it seems that the mixing retracing attack is clearly better than the shifting retracing attack presented above. Indeed, it obtains an even larger gain in the probability of the distinguisher, while not discarding ciphertext pairs! However, there are several advantages of the shifting variant that make it more beneficiary in various scenarios:

- *Using structures.* A central technique for extending the basic boomerang attack is adding a round at the top of the distinguisher, using structures. This technique can be combined with the shifting retracing technique, as follows. First, the adversary performs the ordinary boomerang attack with structures (i.e., encrypts structures of plaintexts, shifts all ciphertexts by δ and decrypts the resulting ciphertexts), and then she checks the artificial filtering together with the condition on P_3, P_4, since both can be checked simultaneously using a hash table. As a result, the data complexity remains the same as in the ordinary boomerang attack (with structures!), while the retracing boomerang leads to an improvement in the signal to noise ratio, which can be translated to a reduction in the data complexity, as described above.

For mixing retracing, such a combination is impossible, since each ciphertext pair (C_1, C_2) has to be modified by its own shift $(C_1^L \oplus C_2^L, 0)$, and so, one cannot shift entire structures as a single block. Therefore, the reduction of data complexity by using structures cannot be obtained.

A similar advantage of the shifting variant is the ability to combine it with extension of the boomerang attack by adding a round at the bottom, as we demonstrate in our attack on 6-round AES in the full version of the paper.

– *Combination with E_{11}.* In the mixing variant, since the output difference for $(E_{12}^L)^{-1}$ (namely, $(C_1)^L \oplus (C_2)^L$), is arbitrary and changes between different pairs, in most cases there is no good combination between differential characteristics of $(E_{12}^L)^{-1}$ that can be used and differential characteristics of $(E_{11})^{-1}$. Indeed, in the yoyo attack of [30] on 5-round AES, this part of the attack succeeds simply because E_{11} is empty. It seems that while the mixing retracing technique can be applied also in cases where E_{11} is non-linear (and, in particular, non-empty), it will usually (or even almost always) be inferior to the shifting retracing boomerang in such cases.

– *Construction of 'friend pairs'.* An important ingredient in many boomerang attacks is 'friend pairs', which are pairs that are attached to given pairs in such a way that if some pair satisfies a desired property then all its 'friend pairs' satisfy the same property as well (such pairs are used in most attacks in this paper). While both types of the retracing boomerang attack allow constructing several 'friend pairs' for each pair, the number of pairs in the shifting variant is significantly larger, which makes it advantageous in some cases.

The names of the attacks. The shifting type of the retracing boomerang is named this way since it preserves the δ-shift of the original boomerang attack, and uses the filtering to enhance the probability of the original boomerang process. The mixing type is named this way since it replaces the δ-shift by a mixing procedure, like the one used in mixture differentials [22].

4 Retracing Boomerang Attack on 5-Round AES

Our first application of the retracing boomerang framework is an improved attack on 5-round AES, which allows recovering the full secret key with data complexity of 2^{15}, time complexity of $2^{16.5}$, and memory complexity of 2^9. The attack was fully implemented experimentally. Since our attack is based on central components of the yoyo attack of Rønjom et al. [30] on 5-round AES (which can be seen as a mixing retracing boomerang attack, as was shown in Sect. 3.2), we begin this section with describing the structure of the AES and presenting the attack of [30]. Then we present our attack, its analysis, and its experimental verification.

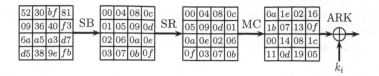

Fig. 5. An AES round

4.1 Brief Description of the AES and Notations

The Advanced Encryption Standard (AES) [29] is a substitution-permutation (SP) network which has 128-bit plaintexts and 128, 192, or 256-bit keys. Since the descriptions of all attacks we present in this paper are independent of the key schedule, we do not differentiate between these variants.

The 128-bit internal state of AES is treated as a byte matrix of size 4×4, where each byte represents a value in $GF(2^8)$. An AES round (described in Fig. 5) applies four operations to this state matrix:

- SubBytes (SB)—applying the same 8-bit to 8-bit invertible S-box 16 times in parallel on each byte of the state,
- ShiftRows (SR)—cyclically shifting the i'th row by i bytes to the left,
- MixColumns (MC)—multiplication of each column by a constant 4×4 matrix over the field $GF(2^8)$, and
- AddRoundKey (ARK)—XORing the state with a 128-bit subkey.

An additional AddRoundKey operation is applied before the first round, and in the last round the MixColumns operation is omitted. The number of rounds is between 10 and 14, depending on the key length. We omit the key schedule, as it does not affect the description of our attacks.

The bytes of each state of AES are numbered $0, 1, \ldots, 15$, where for $0 \leq i, j \leq 3$, the j'th byte in the i'th row is numbered $i + 4j$ (see the state after SB in Fig. 5). We always consider 5-round AES, where the MixColumns operation in the last round in omitted. The rounds are numbered $0, 1, 2, 3, 4$. The subkeys are numbered $k_{-1}, k_0, \ldots, k_4$, where k_{-1} is the secret key XORed to the plaintext at the beginning of the encryption process. We denote by W, Z, and X the intermediate states before the MixColumns operation of round 0, at the input to round 1 and before the MixColumns operation of round 2, respectively. The j'th byte of a state or a key X_i is denoted by $X_{i,j}$ or by $(X_i)_j$. When several bytes $j_1, \ldots, j_\ell$ are considered simultaneously, they are denoted by $X_{i,\{j_1,\ldots,j_\ell\}}$ or by $(X_i)_{\{j_1,\ldots,j_\ell\}}$.

The term 'ℓ'th shifted column' (resp. 'ℓ'th inverse shifted column') refers to the result of application of SR (resp., SR^{-1}) to the ℓ'th column. For example, the 0'th shifted column consists of bytes $0, 7, 10, 13$, and the 0'th inverse shifted columns consists of bytes $0, 5, 10, 15$. We also denote by $SR(j)$ (resp., $SR^{-1}(j)$) the byte position to which byte j is transformed by SR (resp., SR^{-1}).

When considering differences between the encryption processes of a pair of plaintexts, we say that a component (e.g., byte or column) at some stage of the encryption process is *active* if the difference in that component is non-zero. Otherwise, we call the component *passive*. Finally, we say that some values $x_1, x_2, \ldots, x_m$ 'sum up to zero' if $x_1 \oplus x_2 \oplus \ldots \oplus x_m = 0$.

4.2   The Yoyo Attack of Rønjom et al. on 5-Round AES

The idea behind the attack. The attack decomposes 5-round AES as $E = E_{12} \circ E_{11} \circ E_0$, where E_0 consists of the first 2.5 rounds, E_{11} is the MC operation of round 2, and E_{12} consists of rounds 3 and 4. For E_0 in the forward direction, the adversary uses a truncated differential characteristic whose input difference is zero in three inverse shifted columns, and whose output difference is zero in a single shifted column. The probability of the characteristic is $4 \cdot 2^{-8} = 2^{-6}$, since it holds if and only if the output difference of the active column in round 0 is zero in at least one byte. For E_{12} in the backward direction, recall that 1.5 rounds of AES can be represented as four 32-bit to 32-bit super S-boxes applied in parallel (see [16]). For each ciphertext pair (C_1, C_2), the adversary modifies it into one of its mixture counterparts (see Definition 1) with respect to the division into super S-boxes, calls the new ciphertext pair (C_3, C_4), and asks for its decryption. Due to the mixture construction, the four outputs of each super S-box are composed of two pairs of equal values, and hence, the four corresponding inputs to the super S-boxes sum up to 0. As MC is a linear operation, this implies that $X_1 \oplus X_2 \oplus X_3 \oplus X_4 = 0$. Therefore, with probability 2^{-6}, the difference $X_3 \oplus X_4$ equals zero in a shifted column. This, in turn, implies that the difference $Z_3 \oplus Z_4$ equals zero in an inverse shifted column (i.e., one of the four quartets of bytes: $(0, 5, 10, 15), (1, 4, 11, 14), (2, 5, 8, 15), (3, 6, 9, 12)$).

At this point, the adversary would like to attack bytes $0, 5, 10, 15$ of the subkey k_{-1}, using the fact that in one of the bytes of the first column, we have $Z_3 \oplus Z_4 = 0$. However, this information provides only an 8-bit filtering, while 32 subkey bits are involved. In order to improve the filtering, the authors of [30] construct 'friend pairs' of the pair (Z_3, Z_4), such that if we have $Z_3 \oplus Z_4 = 0$ in byte ℓ, then the same holds for all friend pairs. The resulting attack algorithm (of [30]) is given in Algorithm 2.

Analysis of the attack. The data complexity of the attack is about 2^9, since for each of 2^6 pairs (P_1, P_2), the adversary decrypts four ciphertext pairs (C_3^j, C_4^j). The time and memory complexities are dominated by the attack on k_{-1} in Step 7. In a naive application, this attack requires about 2^{32} operations for each pair (P_1, P_2) and each value of $\ell \in \{0, 1, 2, 3\}$, and thus, the overall time complexity of the attack is about $2^{32} \cdot 2^6 \cdot 4 = 2^{40}$. The authors of [30] managed to improve the overall complexity to 2^{31}, using a careful analysis of round 0, including exploitation of the specific matrix used in MC. We do not present this part of the attack, as it can be replaced by a simpler and stronger tool, as we describe below. To summarize, the data complexity of the attack is 2^9 adaptively chosen plaintexts and ciphertexts, the memory complexity is 2^9 and the time complexity is 2^{31} encryptions.

Algorithm 2. Rønjom et al.'s Yoyo Attack on 5-Round AES

1: Ask for the encryption of 2^6 pairs (P_1, P_2) of chosen plaintexts that have non-zero difference only in bytes 0,5,10,15.

2: **for all** corresponding ciphertext pairs (C_1, C_2) **do**

3:     Define four modified ciphertext pairs (C_3^j, C_4^j) $(j = 1, 2, 3, 4)$ to be mixture counterparts of the pair (C_1, C_2).

4:     Ask for the decryption of the ciphertext pairs and consider the pairs of intermediate values after round 0, (Z_3^j, Z_4^j).

5:     **for all** $\ell \in \{0, 1, 2, 3\}$ **do**

6:         Assume that all four pairs (Z_3^j, Z_4^j) and the pair (Z_1, Z_2) have zero difference in byte ℓ.

7:         Use the assumption to extract bytes $0, 5, 10, 15$ of k_{-1}.

8:         **if** a contradiction is reached **then**

9:             Increment ℓ

10:             **if** $\ell > 3$ **then**

11:                 Discard the pair

12:         **else**

13:             Use the fact that $Z_3^j \oplus Z_4^j = 0$ in the entire ℓ'th inverse shifted column to attack the three remaining columns of round 0 (sequentially) and thus to deduce the rest of k_{-1}.

4.3 A Simple Improvement of the Yoyo Attack on 5-Round AES

A simple improvement of the attack of Rønjom et al. is to use a meet-in-the-middle (MITM) procedure to attack bytes $0, 5, 10, 15$ of k_{-1} in Step 7.

Denote the intermediate value in byte m before the MC operation of round 0 in the encryption of a plaintext P by W_m. W.l.o.g. we consider the case $\ell = 0$, and recall that by the structure of AES, byte 0 in the input to round 1 satisfies

$$Z_0 = 02_x \cdot W_0 \oplus 03_x \cdot W_1 \oplus 01_x \cdot W_2 \oplus 01_x \cdot W_3. \tag{6}$$

In the MITM procedure, the adversary guesses bytes $0, 5$ of k_{-1}, computes the value

$$02_x \cdot (W_3^j)_0 \oplus 03_x \cdot (W_3^j)_1 \oplus 02_x \cdot (W_4^j)_0 \oplus 03_x \cdot (W_4^j)_1 \tag{7}$$

for $j = 1, 2, 3$, and stores the concatenation of these values (i.e., a 24-bit value) in a sorted table. Then she guesses bytes $10, 15$ of k_{-1}, computes the value

$$01_x \cdot (W_3^j)_2 \oplus 01_x \cdot (W_3^j)_3 \oplus 01_x \cdot (W_4^j)_2 \oplus 01_x \cdot (W_4^j)_3 \tag{8}$$

for $j = 1, 2, 3$, and checks for a match in the table (which is, of course, equivalent to the condition $(Z_3^j)_0 = (Z_4^j)_0$ for $j = 1, 2, 3$). As this condition is a 24-bit filtering, about $2^{32} \cdot 2^{-24} = 2^8$ suggestions for bytes $0, 5, 10, 15$ of k_{-1} remain, and those can be checked using the conditions $(Z_3^4)_0 = (Z_4^4)_0$ and $(Z_1)_0 = (Z_2)_0$.

The data complexity of the attack remains 2^9. The time complexity is reduced to $2^6 \cdot 4 \cdot 2^{16} = 2^{24}$ operations, where each operation is roughly equivalent to a computation of one AES round in a single column for 6 plaintexts, or a total of less than 2^{23} encryptions.

It seems that the use of MITM increases the memory complexity of the attack to about 2^{16}. However, one can maintain the memory at 2^9 using the *dissection* technique [17] (see, e.g., [2] for similar applications of dissection). Therefore, the time complexity of the attack is reduced to 2^{23} encryptions, while the data and memory complexities remain unchanged at 2^9.

4.4   An Attack on 5-Round AES with Overall Complexity of $2^{16.5}$

We now show how one can reduce the time complexity of the attack described above to $2^{16.5}$, at the expense of increasing the data complexity to about 2^{15}.

The idea behind the attack is to enhance the MITM procedure, such that on each of the two sides, the number of possible key values is reduced to 2^8 (instead of 2^{16}). The reduction is obtained using two methods:

Constructing an extra equation by a specific choice of plaintexts. In order to reduce the number of possible values of $k_{-1,\{0,5\}}$, we choose plaintext pairs with non-zero difference only in bytes $0, 5$. For such pairs, the condition $(Z_1)_0 = (Z_2)_0$ simplifies into

$$02_x \cdot (W_1)_0 \oplus 03_x \cdot (W_1)_1 \oplus 02_x \cdot (W_2)_0 \oplus 03_x \cdot (W_2)_1, \tag{9}$$

as bytes $2, 3$ of W cancel out. This equation depends only on the plaintexts and on bytes $0, 5$ of k_{-1}, and since it is an 8-bit filtering, it leaves only 2^8 possible values of $k_{-1,\{0,5\}}$. In order to detect these 2^8 candidates efficiently, we make our choice of plaintexts even more specific.

We choose only pairs of plaintexts (P_1, P_2) that satisfy $(P_1)_5 \oplus (P_2)_5 = 01_x$. In addition, as a precomputation phase we compute the row of the Difference Distribution Table (DDT) of the AES S-box that corresponds to input difference 01_x and store it in memory, where each output difference is stored along with the value(s) that lead to it.[5]

As a result, for each pair (P_1, P_2) and for each guess of $k_{-1,0}$, we can use Eq. (9) to compute the output difference of the SB operation in byte 5. As the input difference is fixed to be 01_x, we can use the precomputed row of the DDT to find the inputs to that SB operation by a single table lookup, and hence, to retrieve instantly the possible value(s) of $k_{-1,5}$ that correspond to the guessed value of $k_{-1,0}$.

This process allows us to compute the 2^8 possible values of $k_{-1,\{0,5\}}$ in about 2^8 simple operations for each pair.

Eliminating a key byte from the equation by using multiple 'friend pairs'. In order to reduce the number of possible values of $k_{-1,\{10,15\}}$, we attach to each plaintext pair (P_1, P_2) multiple 'friend pairs', such that if (P_1, P_2) satisfies the differential characteristic of E_0, then all friend pairs satisfy the same characteristic as well.

---

[5] Constructing this row takes 2^9 simple operations, and storing it takes much less than 2^9 128-bit cells of memory.

We perform the boomerang process for all friend pairs together with the original pairs, obtaining many pairs (P_3^j, P_4^j). We choose one such pair for which we have

$$(P_3^j)_{10} \oplus (P_4^j)_{10} = 0 \qquad \text{or} \qquad (P_3^j)_{15} \oplus (P_4^j)_{15} = 0. \qquad (10)$$

Assume w.l.o.g. that the equality holds in byte 10. We perform the MITM procedure presented above with *the single pair* (P_3^j, P_4^j). Note that the first step provided us with 2^8 possible values for $k_{-1,\{0,5\}}$. Hence, in the MITM attack there are only 2^8 possible values for the expression (7). On the other hand, by the choice of the pair, there is zero difference in byte 2 before the MC operation, and thus, the subkey byte $k_{-1,10}$ cancels out from the expression (8). As a result, this expression depends on a single key byte, and thus, has only 2^8 possible values, just like Eq. (7). Thus, the MITM procedure requires about 2^9 simple operations and (as the data provides an 8-bit filtering) leaves 2^8 suggestions for subkey bytes $k_{-1,\{0,5,15\}}$. Finally, we can take any other couple of 'friend pairs' and recover the unique value of $k_{-1,\{0,5,10,15\}}$ by another MITM procedure in which one side computes the contribution of bytes $0, 1, 3$ to Eq. (9) (applied for the difference $(Z_3)_0 \oplus (Z_4)_0$) and the other side computes the contribution of byte 2, as on each side there are about 2^8 possible values.

Therefore, the complexity of the MITM attack on $k_{-1,\{0,5,10,15\}}$ is reduced to about 2^8 operations for each pair (P_1, P_2) and each value of ℓ, or a total of about 2^{16} operations. As for the data complexity, in order to have a friend pair that satisfies Eq. (10) with a high probability, we have to take about 2^7 friend pairs for each of the 2^6 pairs (P_1, P_2). Hence, the total data complexity is increased to about 2^{15}. A more precise analysis is given below.

Attack algorithm. The algorithm of our improved attack on 5-round AES is as follows.

1. **Precomputation:** Compute the row of the DDT of the AES S-box that corresponds to input difference 01_x, along with the actual values.
2. **Online phase:** Take 64 pairs (P_1, P_2) of plaintexts such that in each pair, we have $(P_1)_5 = 00_x$ and $(P_2)_5 = 01_x$, in byte 0 the values (P_1, P_2) are distinct, and in all other bytes, the values (P_1, P_2) are equal.
3. To each plaintext pair (P_1, P_2), attach 2^7 'friend pairs' (P_1^j, P_2^j), such that for each j we have $(P_1^j \oplus P_2^j) = P_1 \oplus P_2$, and $(P_1^j)_{\{0,5,10,15\}} = (P_1)_{\{0,5,10,15\}}$.
4. Do the following for each plaintext pair (P_1, P_2), and for each $\ell \in \{0, 1, 2, 3\}$: [we present the operations for $\ell = 0$, the other cases are similar.]
   (a) For each guess of byte $k_{-1,0}$, partially encrypt (P_1, P_2) through the SB operation in byte 0 of round 0 to find its output difference. Then, assuming that the pair (P_1, P_2) satisfies the characteristic of E_0 with $\ell = 0$ (i.e., that $(Z_1)_0 = (Z_2)_0$), use Eq. (9) to find the output difference of the SB operation in byte 5 of round 0. Then use the precomputed DDT to deduce the actual inputs to that SB operation, and deduce from them the value of subkey byte $k_{-1,5}$. Store in a table the 2^8 possible values $k_{-1,\{0,5\}}$.
   (b) Ask for the encryption of (P_1, P_2) and of its 2^7 'friend pairs' (P_1^j, P_2^j). For each ciphertext pair (C_1, C_2) or (C_1^j, C_2^j) we obtain, replace it by

one of its mixture counterparts, which we denote by (C_3, C_4) or (C_3^j, C_4^j) (respectively), and ask for its decryption. Denote the resulting plaintext pairs by (P_3, P_4) and (P_3^j, P_4^j).

(c) Find a value j for which the pair (P_3^j, P_4^j) satisfies Eq. (10). [In the following steps we assume w.l.o.g. that the condition yields equality in byte 10. If the equality is in byte 15, the steps should be modified accordingly.]

(d) Perform a MITM attack on Column 0 of round 0, using the plaintext pair (P_3^j, P_4^j). Specifically, use the 2^8 possible values for $k_{-1,\{0,5\}}$ computed in Step 4(a) to obtain 2^8 possible values for (7) and store them in a table. Then, for each guess of subkey byte $k_{-1,15}$, compute (8) and check in the table for a collision. Each collision provides us with a possible value of $k_{-1,\{0,5,15\}}$.

(e) Perform a MITM attack on Column 0 of round 0, using two other plaintext pairs $(P_3^{j'}, P_4^{j'})$. Specifically, use the 2^8 possible values for $k_{-1,\{0,5,15\}}$ computed in the previous step to obtain the contribution of bytes $0, 1, 3$ to Eq. (6) (applied for the difference $(Z_3)_0 \oplus (Z_4)_0$, for both pairs) and store it in a table. Then, for each guess of subkey byte $k_{-1,10}$, compute the contribution of byte 2 to Eq. (6) and check in the table for a collision. (Each collision provides us with a possible value of $k_{-1,\{0,5,10,15\}}$, along with a filtering for wrong pairs.) If a contradiction is reached, move to the next value of ℓ; if contradiction is reached for all values of ℓ, discard the pair (P_1, P_2) and move to the next pair.

5. Using a pair (P_1, P_2) for which no contradiction occurred in Step 4 and its 'friend pairs', perform MITM attacks on Columns $1, 2$, and 3 of round 0 (sequentially), exploiting the fact that $Z_3 \oplus Z_4$ equals zero in the ℓ'th inverse shifted column (e.g., for $\ell = 0$ this column consists of bytes $0, 5, 10, 15$), to recover the rest of the subkey k_{-1}.

Attack analysis. The attack succeeds if the data contains a pair that satisfies the truncated differential characteristic of E_0 (i.e., leads to a zero difference in at least one byte in the active column in round 0), and in addition, for one of the 'friend pairs' of that pair, the corresponding plaintext pair (P_3^j, P_4^j) has zero difference in either byte 10 or 15. With 64 plaintext pairs and 128 'friend pairs' for each pair, each of these events occurs with probability of about $1 - e^{-1} \approx 0.63$, and hence, under standard randomness assumptions, the success probability of the attack is about $0.63^2 \approx 0.4$. This probability can be increased significantly by increasing the number of pairs we start with and the number of their 'friend pairs'. For example, with 128 plaintext pairs and 128 friend pairs for each of them, the expected success probability is $(1 - e^{-2})(1 - e^{-1}) \approx 0.54$.

We note that the success probability can be increased further by exploiting other ways to cancel terms in Eq. (8). For example, if for some j, j', the unordered pairs $\{(P_3^j)_{10}, (P_4^j)_{10}\}$ and $\{(P_3^{j'})_{10}, (P_4^{j'},)_{10}\}$ are equal, then we can use the XOR of Eq. (8) for both pairs to cancel out the effect of subkey byte $k_{-1,10}$ on the equation. This allows us to apply the efficient MITM attack described above also in cases where no 'friend pair' of (P_1, P_2) satisfies Eq. (10), thus increasing the success probability of the attack. Our analysis shows that under standard randomness assumptions, for the same amount of 64 initial pairs and 128 'friend pairs' for each pair considered above, this improvement increases the success probability of the attack from 0.4 to about 0.5.

The data complexity of the attack, for the success probability 0.4 computed above, is $2 \cdot 2^6 \cdot 2^7 = 2^{14}$ chosen plaintexts and 2^{14} adaptively chosen ciphertexts. We note that the amount of chosen plaintexts can be reduced by considering two structures of 8 plaintexts each (where in the first structure we have $(P_1)_5 = 00_x$ and $(P_1)_0$ assumes 8 different values, and in the second structure we have $(P_2)_5 = 01_x$ and $(P_2)_0$ assumes 8 different values) and taking the 64 pairs (P_1, P_2) composed of one plaintext in each structure. (In such a case, the 'friend pairs' are also taken in structures obtained by XORing the same value to all elements in the two initial structures.) This reduces the data complexity to slightly more than 2^{14} adaptively chosen plaintexts and ciphertexts (as the number of encrypted plaintexts is negligible with respect to the number of decrypted ciphertexts). On the other hand, this slightly reduces the success probability of the attack, due to dependencies between the examined pairs (P_1, P_2), as demonstrated in the next subsection. To conclude, with data complexity of 2^{15} adaptively chosen plaintexts and ciphertexts we obtain success probability of more than 50%.

The memory complexity of the attack is no more than 2^9 128-bit memory cells, like in the yoyo attack of Rønjom et al. [30].

As for the time complexity, it is dominated by several steps that consist of about 2^{16} simple operations each. The comparison of these operations to AES encryptions is problematic, and hence, we adopt a common strategy of counting the number of S-box applications and dividing it by 80, which is the number of S-boxes in 5-round AES. The number we obtain (divided by 2^{16}), in addition to the $2^{14} + 2^{11}$ full encryptions of Step 4(b), is: negligible for Steps 1 and 4(c), 2 for Step 4(a), 6 for Step 4(d), 8 for Step 4(e), and $24 \cdot 3 = 72$ for Step 5. Hence, the total complexity is less than $2^{16.5}$ full encryptions.

We conclude that our 5-round attack requires 2^{15} adaptively chosen plaintexts and ciphertexts, 2^9 memory and $2^{16.5}$ time, and recovers the full secret key with success probability of more than 50%.

4.5   Experimental Verification

To verify the success probability of our attack computed above, we implemented two variants of the 5-round attack. The first variant uses up to 128 *independent* plaintext pairs. The second variant uses two structures, one of 8 plaintexts and another of 16 plaintexts, to create a total of 128 plaintext pairs. For each pair (P_1, P_2), we generated 128 friend pairs. We ran the attack on 500 different randomly generated keys. For each success of the attack, we saved the number of pairs we had to try before finding the key. Then we extracted from this data the success probability of the attack, as a function of the amount of available data. Figure 6 shows this success probability, as a function of the number of plaintext pairs, up to a maximum of 128 pairs.

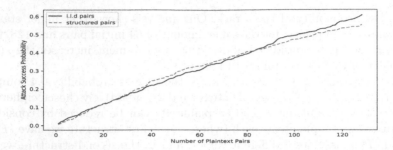

Fig. 6. Attack success probability

It can be seen that the success probability is slightly lower than the probability predicted by the above analysis. In particular, for 64 initial pairs, the success probability is slightly higher than 0.3 (rather than the predicted 0.4). We conjecture that the deviation from the theoretical estimate occurs due to dependency issues, but leave this small discrepancy for further research. Anyway, for data complexity of 2^{15}, the experimental success probability is well above 50%.

The source code used in the experiments, along with the raw data, is included as a supplementary material, and will be made public together with the online version of the paper.

5   Improved Attack on 5-Round AES with a Secret S-Box

In [32], Tiessen et al. initiated the study of *AES with a secret S-box*, namely a variant of AES in which the SB operation is replaced by a key-dependent S-box. They showed that 5 rounds of the new variant can be broken with complexity of 2^{40} and 6 rounds can be broken with complexity of 2^{90}, using variants of the Square attack on AES [29]. In the last four years, six more papers analyzed 5-round variants of AES with a secret S-box: in [15, 25, 31] using the Square attack, in [24, 25] using impossible differentials, in [21] using impossible differentials and the multiple-of-n property, and in [4] using the yoyo technique. The best currently known result was obtained by Bardeh and Rønjom [4] – data complexity of 2^{32} adaptively chosen plaintexts and ciphertexts and time complexity of 2^{31} operations (in addition to generating the data).

In this section we use the retracing boomerang technique to devise an attack on 5-round AES with a secret S-box with a complexity of $2^{25.8}$ in the adaptively chosen plaintext and ciphertext model. Like the attacks of [4, 21, 24, 25, 31], our attack recovers the secret key, without fully recovering the secret S-box. (Actually, we recover the S-box up to an invertible affine transformation in $(GF(2))^8$; as our attack is of a differential nature, it cannot distinguish between secret S-boxes that differ by such transformation.) On the other hand, it applies even against a stronger variant in which MC is also replaced by a key-dependent MDS transformation (see [16]) applied on each column. Among the previous attacks, only the Square attack of Tiessen et al. [32] applies to this variant and can break it with complexity of 2^{40}.

Our attack uses the same retracing boomerang framework as our attack on 5-round AES. Namely, we start with plaintext pairs (P_1, P_2) with difference only in bytes $0, 5, 10, 15$, and for each such pair, we modify the corresponding ciphertext pair (C_1, C_2) into one of its mixture counterparts, which we denote by (C_3, C_4), and ask for its decryption. We know that with probability 2^{-6}, the corresponding pair (Z_3, Z_4) of intermediate values at the input of round 1 has zero difference in an inverse shifted column (e.g., in bytes $0, 5, 10, 15$). (Note that this part does not use the specific structure of SB or of MC, and hence, can be applied also to a variant of AES with key-dependent SB and MC operations). Our goal now is to use this knowledge to attack round 0, as the attack we used for 5-round AES heavily relies on the fact that the S-box is known to the adversary.

Partial recovery of the secret S-box. To attack round 0, we use the strategy proposed in the structural attack of Biryukov and Shamir on SASAS [13], that was already used against AES with a secret S-box in [32], albeit inside the framework of the Square attack. Assume w.l.o.g. that the retracing boomerang predicts zero difference in byte 0 of the state Z, i.e., yields the equation $(Z_3)_0 \oplus (Z_4)_0 = 0$. (In the actual attack, if the procedure with byte 0 leads to a contradiction, the adversary has to perform it again with bytes $1, 2, 3$.) By Eq. (6), we can rewrite this equation as

$$
\begin{aligned}
0 = (Z_3)_0 \oplus (Z_4)_0 = {} & 02_x \cdot ((W_3)_0 \oplus (W_4)_0) \oplus 03_x \cdot ((W_3)_1 \oplus (W_4)_1) \\
& \oplus 01_x \cdot ((W_3)_2 \oplus (W_4)_2) \oplus 01_x \cdot ((W_3)_3 \oplus (W_4)_3).
\end{aligned}
\tag{11}
$$

Note that each of the values $(W_3)_j$ has the form $\mathrm{SB}(P_3 \oplus k_{-1,j'})$, where for $j = 0, 1, 2, 3$, $j' = \mathrm{SR}^{-1}(j)$ takes the value $0, 5, 10, 15$, respectively. Therefore, if we define $4 \cdot 256 = 1024$ variables $x_{m,j} = \mathrm{SB}(m \oplus k_{-1,j'})$ (for $m = 0, 1, \ldots, 255$ and $j' = 0, 1, 2, 3$), then each plaintext pair (P_1, P_2) for which the corresponding intermediate values (Z_3, Z_4) satisfy

$$
(Z_3)_0 \oplus (Z_4)_0 = 0,
\tag{12}
$$

provides us with a linear equation in the variables $\{x_{m,j}\}$.

In order to recover the variables $\{x_{m,j}\}$ by solving a system of linear equations, we need many pairs (Z_3, Z_4) that satisfy Eq. (12) simultaneously. We obtain these pairs by attaching about 2^{10} 'friend pairs' to each original pair (P_1, P_2), like we did in the attack on 5-round AES in Sect. 4. Hence, we start with 2^6 pairs (P_1, P_2), and for each pair and about 2^{10} friend pairs we perform the mixing retracing boomerang process and use each of the pairs to obtain a linear equation in the variables $\{x_{m,j}\}$. (This part of the attack has to be repeated for $\ell = 0, 1, 2, 3$, as each value of ℓ leads to different equations. The equations presented above correspond to $\ell = 0$.) Then, we recover as many as we can of the variables $\{x_{m,j}\}$ by solving a system of linear equations. We take a bit more than 2^{10} friend pairs for each pair in order to obtain extra filtering, which allows us to efficiently discard pairs (P_1, P_2) that do not satisfy the boomerang property.

As was shown in [32], the equations do not allow determining the variables $\{x_{m,j}\}$ (and thus, the secret S-box) completely. Indeed, as our basic Eq. (11) represents differences and not actual values, it is invariant under composition of the secret S-box with an invertible linear transformation over $(GF(2))^8$. Thus, the best we can obtain at this stage is four functions S_0, S_1, S_2, S_3, such that

$$S_j(x) = L_0(\mathrm{SB}(x \oplus k_{-1,j'})),$$

for some unknown invertible linear transformation L_0. In addition, by repeating the attack for three other columns in round 0 (using the fact that for a pair (P_1, P_2) that satisfies the boomerang property, an entire inverse shifted column of $Z_3 \oplus Z_4$ equals zero), we obtain the S-boxes $S_j(x)$ for all $j \in \{0, 1, \ldots, 15\}$, albeit with multiplication by a different matrix L_t in all the S-boxes of (inverse shifted) Column(t).

Recovering the secret key. While this information does not recover the S-box completely, it does allow us to recover the secret key k_{-1}, up to 256 possible values. This is done in two steps.

First, for each $j' \in \{1, 2, 3\}$ we can easily recover $\bar{k}_{j'} = k_{-1,0} \oplus k_{-1,j'}$ in time 2^8, as $\bar{k}_{j'}$ is the unique value of c such that $S_j(x) = S_0(x \oplus c)$ for all x. In a similar way, we can recover each inverse shifted column of k_{-1} up to 256 possible values (e.g., to find the values $k_{-1,1} \oplus k_{-1,s}$ for $s \in \{6, 11, 12\}$ by attacking Column 3). This already reduces the number of possible values of k_{-1} to 2^{32}.

Second, we find the differences $k_{-1,0} \oplus k_{-1,j}$ for $j = 1, 2, 3$ by taking several quartets of values (x_1, x_2, x_3, x_4) such that $S_0(x_1) \oplus S_0(x_2) \oplus S_0(x_3) \oplus S_0(x_4) = 0$ and finding the unique value of c_j such that

$$S_j(c_j \oplus x_1) \oplus S_j(c_j \oplus x_2) \oplus S_j(c_j \oplus x_3) \oplus S_j(c_j \oplus x_4) = 0.$$

(The quartets are used to eliminate the effect of the difference between the linear transformations L_0 and L_j in the definitions of S_0 and S_j.) Thus, in about 2^{12} operations we recover the entire secret key k_{-1}, up to the value of a single byte $k_{-1,0}$. Assuming that the secret S-boxes are determined by the secret key, the attack can be completed by exhaustive search over the 2^8 remaining key possibilities. The resulting attack algorithm is given in Algorithm 3.

Attack analysis. The data complexity of the attack is $2^6 \cdot 2 \cdot 2^{10} = 2^{17}$ chosen plaintexts and 2^{17} adaptively chosen ciphertexts. Like in the attack on 5-round AES presented in Sect. 4, we can reduce the required amount of chosen plaintexts to about 2^{14} using structures, and so the overall data complexity is less than $2^{17.5}$ adaptively chosen plaintexts and ciphertexts.

The time complexity is dominated by solving a system of 1034 equations in 1024 variables in Step 10, that has to be performed for each of the 2^6 pairs (P_1, P_2) and for $\ell = 0, 1, 2, 3$. Using the Four Russians Algorithm ([1]; see [3] for the motivation for choosing it), each solution of the system takes about $(2^{10})^3 / \log(2^{10}) \approx 2^{27}$ simple operations, that are equivalent to about $2^{27}/80 \approx 2^{21}$ encryptions. Hence, the time complexity of the attack is 2^{29}. (Note that the

---

Algorithm 3. Attack on 5-Round AES with Secret S-Box and MixColumns

---

1: Ask for the encryption of 2^6 pairs (P_1, P_2) of chosen plaintexts that have non-zero difference only in bytes 0,5,10,15.
2: **for all** Plaintext pairs (P_1, P_2) **do**
3:     Generate $2^{10} + 10$ 'friend pairs' (P_1^j, P_2^j), such that for each j: $(P_1^j \oplus P_2^j) = P_1 \oplus P_2$, and $(P_1^j)_{\{0,5,10,15\}} = (P_1)_{\{0,5,10,15\}}$.
4:     Ask for the encryption of all 'friend pairs' (P_1^j, P_2^j)
5: **for all** pairs (P_1, P_2) and for each $\ell \in \{0, 1, 2, 3\}$ **do**   ▷ We present the case of $\ell = 0$, the other cases are similar.
6:     **for all** $m \in \{0, 1, \ldots, 255\}$ and $j \in \{0, 1, 2, 3\}$ **do**
7:         Define $x_{m,j} = SB(m \oplus k_{-1, SR^{-1}(j)})$
8:     Assume that Eq. (11) is satisfied for all Z_3^j, Z_4^j of the 'friend pairs' (P_1^j, P_2^j)
9:     Obtain the corresponding linear system of equations in $x_{m,j}$
10:    Solve the system of 1034 linear equations in 1024 variables
11:    **if** a contradiction is reached **then**
12:        Increment ℓ
13:        **if** $\ell > 3$ **then**
14:            Discard the pair
15:    **else**
16:        The solution yields four functions $S_j(x) = L_0(SB(x \oplus k_{-1, SR^{-1}(j)}))$, for some unknown invertible linear transformation L_0.
17:        Repeat the attack on the other three columns with (P_1, P_2) to obtain $S_j(x)$ for $j = 4, 5, \ldots, 15$.
18: Find the rest of the secret key by exhaustive key search (assuming the secret S-box depends on the master 128-bit key k_{-1})

---

solution of a system of equations in Step 17 is much cheaper, as it has to be performed only for a single pair (P_1, P_2).)

The memory complexity is dominated by the memory required for solving the system of equations, which is less than 2^{17} 128-bit blocks. (There is no need to store the plaintext/ciphertext pairs, as they can be analyzed 'on the fly'.)

We conclude that the data complexity of the attack is $2^{17.5}$ adaptively chosen plaintexts and ciphertexts, the time complexity is 2^{29} encryptions, and the memory complexity is 2^{17} 128-bit blocks.

Improving the overall complexity by applying a distinguisher before the attack. Note that in the attack, we have to apply the equation-solving step 2^8 times, since we do not know which pair (P_1, P_2) and which value of ℓ satisfies the boomerang property. Hence, if we can obtain this information in some other way, this will speedup the attack considerably.

A possible way to find a pair that satisfies the boomerang condition is to apply the yoyo distinguishing attack on 5-round AES of Rønjom et al. [30], which does not depend on knowledge of the S-box, and thus, can be applied in the secret S-box setting. (Note however that this attack depends on the MDS property of MC (see [16]). Hence, unlike the attack described above which applies when MC is replaced by an arbitrary invertible linear transformation, this attack applies only if the transformation is assumed to satisfy the MDS property.) The attack of [30] requires $2^{25.8}$ adaptively chosen plaintexts and ciphertexts, and in addition to distinguishing 5-round AES from a random permutation, it finds a pair (P_1, P_2) with non-zero difference only in bytes $0, 5, 10, 15$, such that the corresponding intermediate values (Z_1, Z_2) have non-zero difference in only two bytes. This pair satisfies our boomerang property, and thus, can be used (along with 1034 friend pairs) in the attack described above. This reduces the complexity of each equation-solving step to 2^{21}, and thus, the overall complexity of the attack is dominated by the complexity of Rønjom et al.'s attack. We conclude that this variant of the attack has data and time complexities of $2^{25.8}$ and memory complexity of 2^{17}.

6   The Retracing Rectangle Attack – Connection to Mixture Differentials

In this section we present the *retracing rectangle* attack, which is the retracing variant of the rectangle attack [6]. First we recall the amplified boomerang (a.k.a. rectangle) attack, then we present and analyze the new retracing rectangle attack, and then we use our new framework to expose a relation of the recently introduced *mixture differential* attack [22] to the rectangle attack.

6.1   The Amplified Boomerang (a.k.a. Rectangle) Attack

An apparent drawback of the boomerang attack is the need to use adaptively chosen plaintexts and ciphertexts – a very strong ability for the attacker. In [26], Kelsey et al. presented the amplified boomerang attack, which imitates the procedure of the boomerang attack using only chosen plaintexts. In the attack, the adversary considers *pairs of pairs* of plaintexts $((P_1, P_2), (P_3, P_4))$ such that $P_1 \oplus P_2 = P_3 \oplus P_4 = \alpha$, and for each of them, she checks whether the corresponding quartet of ciphertexts $((C_1, C_2), (C_3, C_4))$ satisfies $C_1 \oplus C_3 = C_2 \oplus C_4 = \delta$. For the analysis of the attack, we refer the reader to [26].

Kelsey et al. applied the amplified boomerang attack to the AES' candidates MARS and SERPENT. In a subsequent work, Biham et al. [6] presented several enhancements of the attack, and gave it the name rectangle attack, which is the currently more commonly-used name.

6.2   The Retracing Rectangle Attack

The transformation from the retracing boomerang attack to the retracing rectangle attack is similar to the transformation from the (classical) boomerang attack to the rectangle attack.

The attack setting. We assume that E can be decomposed as $E = E_1 \circ E_{02} \circ E_{01}$, where E_{01} consists of dividing the state into two parts (a left part of b bits and a right part of $n - b$ bits) and applying to them the functions E_{01}^L, E_{01}^R. Furthermore, we suppose that for E_{01}^L, there exists a differential characteristic $\alpha_L \xrightarrow{p_1^L} \mu_L$, for E_{01}^R, there exists a differential characteristic $\alpha_R \xrightarrow{p_1^R} \mu_R$, for E_{02}, there exists a differential characteristic $\mu \xrightarrow{p_2} \beta$, and for E_1, there exists a differential characteristic $\gamma \xrightarrow{q} \delta$ (see Fig. 7).

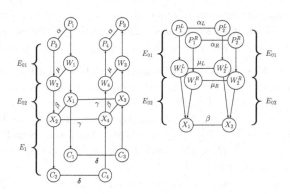

Fig. 7. The retracing rectangle setting

Assuming that $p_1^R p_1^L p_2 q \gg 2^{-n/2}$, the rectangle attack can be used to distinguish E from a random permutation, with data complexity of $O((p_1^R p_1^L p_2 q)^{-1} \cdot 2^{n/2})$ chosen plaintexts. Recall that in the standard rectangle attack, we consider quartets of plaintexts $((\Gamma_1, \Gamma_2), (\Gamma_3, \Gamma_4))$ such that $P_1 \oplus P_2 = P_3 \oplus P_4 = \alpha$, and check whether the corresponding quartets of ciphertexts $((C_1, C_2), (C_3, C_4))$ satisfy $C_1 \oplus C_3 = C_2 \oplus C_4 = \delta$. In the retracing rectangle attack, we consider only quartets of plaintexts that satisfy

$$(P_1 \oplus P_2 = \alpha) \wedge (P_3 \oplus P_4 = \alpha) \wedge ((P_1)^L \oplus (P_3)^L = 0 \text{ or } \alpha^L). \qquad (13)$$

As a result, the two unordered pairs (P_1^L, P_2^L) and (P_3^L, P_4^L) are identical, and hence, if one of them satisfies the differential characteristic of E_{10}^L, then so does the other. Thus, the probability of the rectangle distinguisher is improved by a factor of $(p_1^L)^{-1}$.

Advantages. Unlike the shifting retracing boomerang attack, here we obtain an improvement in the probability of the distinguisher without a need to discard some part of the data. (This holds since the adversary can choose the plaintexts as she wishes, and in particular, can force the additional restriction $(P_1^L \oplus P_3^L = 0 \text{ or } \alpha^L)$ 'for free'.) In addition, the signal to noise ratio is improved, like in the retracing boomerang attack.

It should however be noted that in most applications of the rectangle attack, the adversary starts with structures S of pairs with input difference α, such that each pair-of-pairs within the same structure satisfies the initial condition of the rectangle distinguisher. Then, for each structure, the adversary uses a hash table to check all these $\binom{|S|}{2}$ quartets in time $|S|$. In the retracing rectangle attack, one has to either give up the structures and work with each pair-of-pairs that satisfies Eq. (13) separately, or else perform the ordinary rectangle attack and then check the additional condition ($P_1^L \oplus P_3^L = 0$ or α^L) simultaneously with the condition $C_1 \oplus C_3 = C_2 \oplus C_4 = \delta$ (which can be done using a hash table). In either case, the overall data complexity of the attack is not reduced, compared to the rectangle attack with structures, and thus, improvement of the signal to noise ratio is the main advantage of the retracing rectangle technique.

A mixing variant – relation to mixture differentials. Like in the mixing retracing boomerang attack, the adversary can force equality between the unordered pairs $(P_1^L, P_2^L), (P_3^L, P_4^L)$ by choosing $P_3 = (P_2^L, P_1^R)$ and $P_4 = (P_1^L, P_2^R)$, or in other words, by taking the pair (P_3, P_4) to be the *mixture counterpart* of the pair (P_1, P_2). As this choice also forces equality between the pairs (P_1^R, P_2^R) and (P_3^R, P_4^R), the probability of the rectangle distinguisher is increased by a factor of $(p_1^L p_1^R)^{-1}$.

Interestingly, it turns out that the core step of the *mixture differential* attack of Grassi [22] on 5-round AES fits into the mixture retracing rectangle attack framework.

Specifically, the core of [22]'s result is a chosen plaintext distinguishing attack on a 3.5-round variant of AES. In this attack, 3.5-round AES is decomposed as $E_1 \circ E_{02} \circ E_{01}$, where E_{01} consists of the first 1.5 rounds, E_{02} consists of a single MC layer, and E_1 is composed of the last 1.5 rounds. The attack uses quartets of plaintexts (P_1, P_2, P_3, P_4) constructed by a mixing procedure, as described in Definition 1, and considers the corresponding quartets (X_1, X_2, X_3, X_4) and (Y_1, Y_2, Y_3, Y_4) of intermediate values after E_{01} and E_{02}, respectively. The representation of 1.5-round AES as four Super-S-boxes applied in parallel [16] allows deducing that $X_1 \oplus X_2 \oplus X_3 \oplus X_4 = 0$ holds with probability 1. As E_{02} is linear, the same holds for Y_1, Y_2, Y_3, Y_4. Finally, the attack uses a truncated differential characteristic of E_1 with probability 1 that starts with difference 0 in an inverse shifted column (e.g., bytes $0, 5, 10, 15$) and ends with difference 0 in a shifted column (e.g., bytes $0, 7, 10, 13$). (This characteristic also follows from the Super-S-boxes representation of 1.5-round AES.) If the pair (Y_1, Y_3) satisfies the input difference of this characteristic – an event that occurs with probability of 2^{-32} – then (Y_2, Y_4) satisfies the input difference as well, and then we know for sure that both (C_1, C_3) and (C_2, C_4) have zero difference in bytes $0, 7, 10, 13$. This provides a 64-bit filtering, that is exploited in [22] to obtain a key recovery attack on 5-round AES.

While this may not be apparent at a first glance, this attack is indeed a variant of the mixing retracing rectangle attack described above. The choice of plaintext quartets is exactly the same, and so is the treatment of E_1 (taking note that the differential characteristics used in a boomerang/rectangle attack may be truncated, as mentioned above). The only seeming difference is E_0, where instead of considering a specific differential characteristic we only make sure that the four outputs sum up to zero. However, this is actually the same as using all possible differential characteristics simultaneously, as is commonly done in boomerang/rectangle attacks.

7   Summary and Open Problems

In this paper we introduced a new version of boomerang attacks called a retracing boomerang attack, and used it to significantly improve the best known key recovery attacks on 5 rounds of AES (both in its standard form and when the S-box and the linear transformation are secret key-dependent components). The most interesting problems left open in this paper are:

- Find additional applications of the new technique.
- Find other types of correlations which can further increase the probability of the combined differential property.
- Create a "grand unified theory" of boomerang-like attacks which will explore their hidden relationships and treat them rigorously.

Acknowledgements. The authors thank the anonymous referees and Senyang Huang for their proposals and suggestions for improving the manuscript.

The research was supported in part by the European Research Council under the ERC starting grant agreement n. 757731 (LightCrypt), by the BIU Center for Research in Applied Cryptography and Cyber Security, by the Israel Ministry of Science and Technology, the Center for Cyber, Law, and Policy, by the Israel National Cyber Bureau in the Prime Minister's Office, and by the Israeli Science Foundation through grants No. 3380/19, No. 880/18 and No. 1523/14.

The first author is a member of the Center for Cyber, Law, and Policy at the university of Haifa. The second author is a member of the BIU Center for Research in Applied Cryptography and Cyber Security. The third author is a member of CPIIS.

References

1. Arlazarov, V., Dinic, E., Kronrod, A.M., Faradžev, I.: On economical construction of the transitive closure of a directed graph. Dokl. Akad. Nauk SSSR **194**(11), 1201–1290 (1970)
2. Bar-On, A., Dunkelman, O., Keller, N., Ronen, E., Shamir, A.: Improved key recovery attacks on reduced-round AES with practical data and memory complexities. In: Shacham, H., Boldyreva, A. (eds.) CRYPTO 2018. LNCS, vol. 10992, pp. 185–212. Springer, Cham (2018). https://doi.org/10.1007/978-3-319-96881-0_7
3. Bard, G.V.: Achieving a log(n) speed up for boolean matrix operations and calculating the complexity of the dense linear algebra step of algebraic stream cipher attacks and of integer factorization methods. IACR Cryptology ePrint Archive, 2006:163 (2006)
4. Bardeh, N.G., Rønjom, S.: Practical attacks on reduced-round AES. In: Buchmann, J., Nitaj, A., Rachidi, T. (eds.) AFRICACRYPT 2019. LNCS, vol. 11627, pp. 297–310. Springer, Cham (2019). https://doi.org/10.1007/978-3-030-23696-0_15

5. Biham, E., Biryukov, A., Dunkelman, O., Richardson, E., Shamir, A.: Initial observations on Skipjack: cryptanalysis of Skipjack-3XOR. In: Tavares, S., Meijer, H. (eds.) SAC 1998. LNCS, vol. 1556, pp. 362–375. Springer, Heidelberg (1999). https://doi.org/10.1007/3-540-48892-8_27
6. Biham, E., Dunkelman, O., Keller, N.: The rectangle attack — rectangling the Serpent. In: Pfitzmann, B. (ed.) EUROCRYPT 2001. LNCS, vol. 2045, pp. 340–357. Springer, Heidelberg (2001). https://doi.org/10.1007/3-540-44987-6_21
7. Biham, E., Keller, N.: Cryptanalysis of Reduced Variants of Rijndael (1999). Unpublished manuscript
8. Biham, E., Perle, S.: Conditional linear cryptanalysis - cryptanalysis of DES with less than 2^{42} complexity. IACR Trans. Symmetric Cryptol. **2018**(3), 215–264 (2018)
9. Biham, E., Shamir, A.: Differential cryptanalysis of DES-like cryptosystems. J. Cryptol. **4**(1), 3–72 (1991). https://doi.org/10.1007/BF00630563
10. Biryukov, A., De Cannière, C., Dellkrantz, G.: Cryptanalysis of SAFER++. In: Boneh, D. (ed.) CRYPTO 2003. LNCS, vol. 2729, pp. 195–211. Springer, Heidelberg (2003). https://doi.org/10.1007/978-3-540-45146-4_12
11. Biryukov, A., Khovratovich, D.: Related-key cryptanalysis of the full AES-192 and AES-256. In: Matsui, M. (ed.) ASIACRYPT 2009. LNCS, vol. 5912, pp. 1–18. Springer, Heidelberg (2009). https://doi.org/10.1007/978-3-642-10366-7_1
12. Biryukov, A., Leurent, G., Perrin, L.: Cryptanalysis of Feistel networks with secret round functions. In: Dunkelman, O., Keliher, L. (eds.) SAC 2015. LNCS, vol. 9566, pp. 102–121. Springer, Cham (2016). https://doi.org/10.1007/978-3-319-31301-6_6
13. Biryukov, A., Shamir, A.: Structural cryptanalysis of SASAS. J. Cryptol. **23**(4), 505–518 (2010). https://doi.org/10.1007/s00145-010-9062-1
14. Cid, C., Huang, T., Peyrin, T., Sasaki, Y., Song, L.: Boomerang connectivity table: a new cryptanalysis tool. In: Nielsen, J.B., Rijmen, V. (eds.) EUROCRYPT 2018. LNCS, vol. 10821, pp. 683–714. Springer, Cham (2018). https://doi.org/10.1007/978-3-319-78375-8_22
15. Cui, T., Chen, H., Mesnager, S., Sun, L., Wang, M.: Statistical integral distinguisher with multi-structure and its application on AES-like ciphers. Cryptogr. Commun. **10**(5), 755–776 (2018). https://doi.org/10.1007/s12095-018-0286-5
16. Daemen, J., Rijmen, V.: The Design of Rijndael: AES - The Advanced Encryption Standard. Information Security and Cryptography. Springer, Heidelberg (2002). https://doi.org/10.1007/978-3-662-04722-4
17. Dinur, I., Dunkelman, O., Keller, N., Shamir, A.: Efficient dissection of composite problems, with applications to cryptanalysis, knapsacks, and combinatorial search problems. In: Safavi-Naini, R., Canetti, R. (eds.) CRYPTO 2012. LNCS, vol. 7417, pp. 719–740. Springer, Heidelberg (2012). https://doi.org/10.1007/978-3-642-32009-5_42
18. Dunkelman, O., Keller, N.: Treatment of the initial value in time-memory-data tradeoff attacks on stream ciphers. Inf. Process. Lett. **107**(5), 133–137 (2008)
19. Dunkelman, O., Keller, N., Shamir, A.: A practical-time related-key attack on the KASUMI cryptosystem used in GSM and 3G telephony. J. Cryptol. **27**(4), 824–849 (2013). https://doi.org/10.1007/s00145-013-9154-9
20. Ferguson, N., et al.: Improved cryptanalysis of Rijndael. In: Goos, G., Hartmanis, J., van Leeuwen, J., Schneier, B. (eds.) FSE 2000. LNCS, vol. 1978, pp. 213–230. Springer, Heidelberg (2001). https://doi.org/10.1007/3-540-44706-7_15
21. Grassi, L.: MixColumns properties and attacks on (round-reduced) AES with a single secret S-box. In: Smart, N.P. (ed.) CT-RSA 2018. LNCS, vol. 10808, pp. 243–263. Springer, Cham (2018). https://doi.org/10.1007/978-3-319-76953-0_13

22. Grassi, L.: Mixture differential cryptanalysis: a new approach to distinguishers and attacks on round-reduced AES. IACR Trans. Symmetric Cryptol. **2018**(2), 133–160 (2018)

23. Grassi, L.: Probabilistic mixture differential cryptanalysis on round-reduced AES. In: Paterson, K.G., Stebila, D. (eds.) SAC 2019. LNCS, vol. 11959, pp. 53–84. Springer, Cham (2020). https://doi.org/10.1007/978-3-030-38471-5_3

24. Grassi, L., Rechberger, C., Rønjom, S.: Subspace trail cryptanalysis and its applications to AES. IACR Trans. Symmetric Cryptol. **2016**(2), 192–225 (2016)

25. Hu, K., Cui, T., Gao, C., Wang, M.: Towards key-dependent integral and impossible differential distinguishers on 5-round AES. In: Cid, C., Jacobson Jr., M. (eds.) SAC 2018. LNCS, vol. 11349, pp. 139–162. Springer, Cham (2019). https://doi.org/10.1007/978-3-030-10970-7_7

26. Kelsey, J., Kohno, T., Schneier, B.: Amplified boomerang attacks against reduced-round MARS and Serpent. In: Goos, G., Hartmanis, J., van Leeuwen, J., Schneier, B. (eds.) FSE 2000. LNCS, vol. 1978, pp. 75–93. Springer, Heidelberg (2001). https://doi.org/10.1007/3-540-44706-7_6

27. Murphy, S.: The return of the cryptographic boomerang. IEEE Trans. Inf. Theory **57**(4), 2517–2521 (2011)

28. US National Bureau of Standards: Data Encryption Standard, Federal Information Processing Standards publications no. 46 (1977)

29. US National Institute of Standards and Technology: Advanced Encryption Standard, Federal Information Processing Standards publications no. 197 (2001)

30. Rønjom, S., Bardeh, N.G., Helleseth, T.: Yoyo tricks with AES. In: Takagi, T., Peyrin, T. (eds.) ASIACRYPT 2017. LNCS, vol. 10624, pp. 217–243. Springer, Cham (2017). https://doi.org/10.1007/978-3-319-70694-8_8

31. Sun, B., Liu, M., Guo, J., Qu, L., Rijmen, V.: New insights on AES-like SPN ciphers. In: Robshaw, M., Katz, J. (eds.) CRYPTO 2016. LNCS, vol. 9814, pp. 605–624. Springer, Heidelberg (2016). https://doi.org/10.1007/978-3-662-53018-4_22

32. Tiessen, T., Knudsen, L.R., Kölbl, S., Lauridsen, M.M.: Security of the AES with a secret S-box. In: Leander, G. (ed.) FSE 2015. LNCS, vol. 9054, pp. 175–189. Springer, Heidelberg (2015). https://doi.org/10.1007/978-3-662-48116-5_9

33. Tunstall, M.: Improved "Partial Sums"-based square attack on AES. In: SECRYPT 2012, pp. 25–34 (2012)

34. Wagner, D.: The boomerang attack. In: Knudsen, L. (ed.) FSE 1999. LNCS, vol. 1636, pp. 156–170. Springer, Heidelberg (1999). https://doi.org/10.1007/3-540-48519-8_12

Randomness Extraction

Extracting Randomness from Extractor-Dependent Sources

Yevgeniy Dodis[1], Vinod Vaikuntanathan[2(✉)], and Daniel Wichs[3,4(✉)]

[1] NYU, New York, USA
[2] MIT, Cambridge, USA
vinod.nathan@gmail.com
[3] Northeastern University, Boston, USA
danwichs@gmail.com
[4] NTT Research Inc., East Palo Altos, USA

Abstract. We revisit the well-studied problem of extracting nearly uniform randomness from an arbitrary source of sufficient min-entropy. Strong seeded extractors solve this problem by relying on a public random seed, which is unknown to the source. Here, we consider a setting where the seed is reused over time and *the source may depend on prior calls to the extractor with the same seed*. Can we still extract nearly uniform randomness?

In more detail, we assume the seed is chosen randomly, but the source can make arbitrary oracle queries to the extractor with the given seed before outputting a sample. We require that the sample has entropy and differs from any of the previously queried values. The extracted output should look uniform even to a distinguisher that gets the seed. We consider two variants of the problem, depending on whether the source only outputs the sample, or whether it can also output some correlated public *auxiliary information* that preserves the sample's entropy. Our results are:

Without Auxiliary Information: We show that every *pseudo-random function* (PRF) with a sufficiently high security level is a good extractor in this setting, even if the distinguisher is computationally unbounded. We further show that the source necessarily needs to be computationally bounded and that such extractors imply one-way functions.

With Auxiliary Information: We construct secure extractors in this setting, as long as both the source and the distinguisher are computationally bounded. We give several constructions based on different intermediate primitives, yielding instantiations based on the DDH, DLIN, LWE or DCR assumptions. On the negative side, we show that one cannot prove security against computationally unbounded distinguishers in this setting under any standard assumption via a black-box reduction. Furthermore, even when restricting to computationally bounded distinguishers, we show that there exist PRFs that are insecure as extractors in this setting and that a large class of constructions cannot be proven secure via a black-box reduction from standard assumptions.

1 Introduction

EXTRACTING RANDOMNESS. Randomness is an important ingredient in many algorithmic tasks, and is especially crucial in cryptography. Indeed, much of

© International Association for Cryptologic Research 2020
A. Canteaut and Y. Ishai (Eds.): EUROCRYPT 2020, LNCS 12105, pp. 313–342, 2020.
https://doi.org/10.1007/978-3-030-45721-1_12

cryptography relies on the assumption that parties can sample uniformly random bits. However, most natural sources of randomness are imperfect and not uniformly random. This motivates the study of *randomness extraction*, whose goal is to extract (nearly) uniform randomness from imperfect sources.

Ideally, we would have a deterministic function Ext that converts an imperfect source of randomness X into a (nearly) uniformly random output $\text{Ext}(X)$. Furthermore, such an extractor should work for all sources of randomness X having a sufficiently large amount of (min-)entropy. Unfortunately, this is easily seen to be impossible, even if we only want to output 1 bit [CG85]: for every extractor function Ext, there is a source X that has almost full min-entropy yet the output of $\text{Ext}(X)$ is completely fixed.

There have been two broad lines of work to get around this. The first line of work designs extractors for restricted types of sources X that satisfy additional requirements beyond just having entropy (see e.g., [von51, CGH+85, Blu86, LLS89, CG85, TV00, BST03, BIW04, CZ16]). While this is an important research direction, we often know very little about natural sources of randomness and they may fail to satisfy the imposed requirements. The second line of work considers *(strong) seeded* extractors [NZ93, NZ96], where the extractor is given a public uniformly random seed S, which is independent of the source X, and we require that the extracted output $\text{Ext}(X; S)$ is close to uniform even given the seed S.

EXTRACTOR-DEPENDENT SOURCES. In this work, we consider a seeded extractor and envision a scenario where a single uniformly random seed S is chosen once and then is reused over time by many different users and/or applications to extract randomness from various "natural" sources of entropy. For example, the seed S could be a part of a system *random number generator* (RNG) that extracts randomness from physical sources of entropy, such as the timing of interrupts etc. If the sources are truly independent of the seed S, then standard (strong) seeded extractors suffice to guarantee that the extracted outputs are nearly uniform. However, since the seed S is continuously reused, past outputs of the extractor will make their way back into "nature" and may affect the sources in the future. For example, interrupts may depend on processes that themselves rely on previous outputs of the extractor. Furthermore, since we cannot assume that all users/applications use the extractor securely, we have to allow for the possibility that some of the prior calls to the extractor were made on arbitrary samples that may not have any entropy. Unfortunately, if the source can depends on prior calls to the extractor with the same seed S, we violate the condition that the source is independent of the seed and can no longer rely on the security of standard seeded extractors. We emphasize that, although the seed S is public, the sources are *not* fully adversarial and *not* arbitrarily dependent on S. (A restriction of this sort is of course necessary to circumvent the obvious impossibility result.) Instead, we assume that the sources can only depend on prior calls to the extractor with the given seed S, but are otherwise independent of S. We call such sources "extractor-dependent". Can we design *extractors for extractor-dependent sources (ED-Extractors)* that manage to extract nearly uniform randomness in this setting?

DEFINING THE PROBLEM. We now specify the problem in more detail. Our goal is to design a seeded extractor EDExt that extracts randomness from extractor-dependent sources. We consider a setting where a seed S is chosen uniformly at random. A *source* $\mathcal{S}^{\mathsf{EDExt}(\cdot, S)}$ gets oracle access to the extractor with the seed S and outputs a sample X along with some public auxiliary information AUX. We say that such a source $\mathcal{S}$ is a *legal* extractor-dependent source of entropy α if two conditions hold: (1) the (conditional min-entropy) of X given S, AUX is at least α, and (2) the source never queries the oracle on the value X that it outputs. An α-ED-Extractor needs to ensure that for all legal extractor-dependent sources of entropy α, the output $\mathsf{EDExt}(X, S)$ is indistinguishable from uniform, even given the seed S and the auxiliary information AUX.

DISCUSSION ON THE LEGALITY CONDITIONS. We motivate the reason behind the two legality conditions imposed by the definition.

Firstly, just like for standard (seeded) extractors, we need to assume that X has a sufficient level of entropy even conditioned on AUX in order to extract randomness from it. In our case, the source also has access to the oracle $\mathsf{EDExt}(\cdot, S)$ with a random seed S, but we want the entropy to come from the internal randomness of the source rather than from the seed S since the latter is public and known to the distinguisher. Therefore, it is natural to also condition on S.

The second condition is clearly necessary: without it we could define a source that queries the oracle on random values and outputs the first such value on which the extracted output starts with a 0. Such a source would have almost full entropy, yet the extracted output would be easily distinguishable from uniform. Moreover, this condition is also reasonable when modeling our intended scenario since the sample should have entropy even given all the prior extractor calls that influenced nature, and therefore it should differ from all of them.

In particular, the two legality conditions include the following simpler subclass of sources, which already intuitively captures our intended scenario. Consider sources $\mathcal{S} = (\mathcal{S}_1, \mathcal{S}_2)$ that consists of two components. The first component $\mathcal{S}_1^{\mathsf{EDExt}(\cdot, S)}$ makes arbitrary oracle calls to the extractor and models the influence that these calls have on nature; it outputs some value state. The second component $\mathcal{S}_2(\mathsf{state})$ then outputs X, AUX without making any further oracle queries and captures the entropic process that produces the sample. The only condition we impose is that, for every possible fixed value of state, the entropy of X conditioned on AUX when they are sampled according to $\mathcal{S}_2(\mathsf{state})$ should be at least α. If α is large enough then $\mathcal{S}$ satisfies both of the previous legality conditions. In particular, $\mathcal{S}_1$ could not have queried the oracle on X since the entropy of X comes only from the random coins of $\mathcal{S}_2$ that are unknown to $\mathcal{S}_1$.

DISCUSSION ON AUXILIARY INFO. Our default definition allows the source to output some public auxiliary info AUX that can be correlated with the sample X as long as it preserves its (average conditional min-)entropy. It is natural that some such information may be public (e.g., the source X denotes the timing of interrupts, but the adversary can learn some auxiliary info AUX denoting the high-order bits of such timings by interacting with the system). We also consider a weaker setting *without auxiliary info*, where we don't have AUX. In the case of standard seeded extractors, it turns out that there is not much difference between a setting with auxiliary info and without [DORS08]. However, as we will see, there is a significant difference between the two settings when it comes to ED-Extractors.

PRIOR WORK. The work of Coretti et al. [CDKT19] initiates the study of extracting from extractor-dependent sources in the special case where the extractor is a *random oracle*. While their definition is specifically tailored to the random-oracle model, our definition can be seen as the natural extension of it to the standard model. In particular, they consider the setting where $\mathcal{O}(\cdot) = \mathsf{EDExt}(\cdot, S)$ is a truly random function. They show that this is an α-ED-Extractor for any super-logarithmic entropy α, as long as the source only makes polynomially many queries, but even if the distinguisher is computationally unbounded and can see the entire truth table of the oracle. This gives us heuristic evidence that a "good" cryptographic hash function is an ED-Extractor in the standard model even against computationally unbounded distinguishers (as long as the source is computationally bounded). The main open question is therefore whether we can construct ED-Extractors under standard computational assumptions.

1.1 Our Results

We give positive and negative results for ED-Extractors with and without auxiliary info.

WITHOUT AUXILIARY INFO. On the positive side, we show that any pseudorandom function (PRF) with a sufficiently high security level is a good ED-Extractor without auxiliary info. In particular, assuming the existence of subexponentially secure one-way functions, there exist α-ED-Extractors with any output size m for entropy $\alpha = m + \omega(\log \lambda)$, where λ is the security parameter. Furthermore, such extractors achieve security even against computationally unbounded distinguishers, as long as the source runs in polynomial time. If we only want security against polynomial-time distinguishers, we can allow the output size to grow to an arbitrary polynomial m while only requiring entropy $\alpha = \lambda^{\Omega(1)}$.

On the negative side, we show that ED-Extractors imply one-way functions and therefore cannot be constructed unconditionally. This holds even without auxiliary info, even if we require that the source has almost full entropy, and even if the extractor outputs only 1 bit. Furthermore, we show that such ED-Extractors cannot exist for computationally unbounded sources.

WITH AUXILIARY INFO. We construct ED-Extractors in the setting with auxiliary info under standard assumptions. In particular, we give three constructions.

– The first construction relies on (adaptively secure) *constrained PRFs* [BGI14, KPTZ13,BW13] for NC1 constraints. These can be instantiated under the sub-exponential security of either the *learning with errors (LWE)* [BV15] or the *Decisional Diffie-Hellman Inversion (DDHI)* assumption in arbitrary prime-order groups (without requiring pairings) [AMN+18].[1]

- The second construction relies on *shift-hiding shiftable functions* [PS18], which can be seen as a type of constraint-hiding constrained PRFs, and can be instantiated under LWE without requiring sub-exponential security.
- The third construction relies on lossy functions and can be instantiated under any of: decisional Diffie-Hellman (DDH), decisional-linear (DLIN), LWE, or decisional composite residuosity (DCR) assumptions.

In all cases, we prove security against polynomial-time sources and distinguishers. Our α-ED-Extractors can have arbitrarily large polynomial input size n and output size m, and require entropy $\alpha = \lambda^{\Omega(1)}$.

Note that, in the setting without auxiliary info, we achieved security even against computationally unbounded distinguishers. Furthermore, the random-oracle based result of [CDKT19] heuristically suggests that good cryptographic hash functions achieve security against computationally unbounded distinguishers even in the auxiliary info setting. However, our constructions in the auxiliary info setting from standard assumptions only achieve security against polynomial-time distinguishers. Unfortunately, we show that this is inherent. In particular, we show that in the auxiliary info setting, one cannot prove the security of any ED-Extractor against computationally unbounded distinguishers under any standard assumption via a black-box reduction.

Furthermore, our instantiations in the auxiliary info setting rely on "crypto-mania" assumptions (known to imply public-key encryption) rather than one-way functions, and we ask whether this is necessary. While we do not resolve this question, we give some evidence that the two settings necessitate substantially different constructions. Firstly, one may be tempted to conjecture that every PRF is also a good ED-Extractor even in the auxiliary info setting. We show that this is not the case: there exist PRFs that are insecure as ED-Extractors in the auxiliary info setting even for very high levels/rates of entropy α. Moreover, we show that a large class of natural PRFs (e.g., the Naor-Reingold PRF) cannot be proven to be secure ED-Extractors in the setting of auxiliary info via a black-box reduction from any standard assumption.

1.2 Our Techniques

ED-EXTRACTORS WITHOUT AUXILIARY INFO FROM PRFS. Our first result shows that every PRF is already a good ED-Extractor in the setting without auxiliary info. In particular, the seed of the extractor is the PRF key and the extractor just evaluates the PRF on the sample X. The main difficulty in proving ED-Extractor security is that the distinguisher gets the seed of the ED-Extractor, but PRF security only holds if the key is never revealed. Our insight

---

[1] The DDHI assumption in a cyclic group $\mathbb{G}$ of order q with generator g states that, given any polynomially many values of the form $(g, g^a, g^{a^2}, \ldots, g^{a^L})$ where $a \leftarrow \mathbb{Z}_q$, the value $g^{1/a}$ is computationally indistinguishable from uniform.

is to design a reduction that never calls the distinguisher – indeed, this allows us to prove security even for computationally unbounded distinguishers.

Let's start with the case where the PRF/Extractor only outputs 1 bit. If the extracted output is statistically far from uniform given the seed, it means that it is biased towards either 0 or 1, but the direction of the bias is unknown and may be different for each seed. Consider running the source S twice with independent randomness, while giving it oracle access to the PRF/Extractor with the same random key/seed. Let X_0, X_1 be the samples that the two runs output respectively. Then the PRF/Extractor evaluations on those samples are more likely to agree than disagree, since they are biased in the same direction. But the legality conditions ensure that X_0, X_1 were never queried during either of the two runs and are different from each other (since each run cannot query its own output and the output of the other run should have enough entropy to be unpredictable). So, given oracle access to the PRF, we can use the source S to find two values X_0, X_1 that we haven't yet queried, but if we then proceed to query the PRF on them, the outputs are noticeably more likely to agree than disagree. This cannot be the case given oracle access to a random function, and therefore allows us to distinguish the two and break PRF security. The analysis extends to a larger output size m, but the advantage of the reduction shrinks by a factor of 2^{-m}. Therefore, we need very secure PRFs that cannot be distinguished from random functions with advantage better than $\mathsf{negl}(\lambda)2^{-m}$, which requires sub-exponential security assumptions.

Note that the above argument completely breaks down in the setting with auxiliary info. The problem is that now the direction of the bias can be different for each choice of the key/seed *and* the auxiliary info. But the two independent runs of the source S are unlikely to produce the same auxiliary info and hence we cannot argue that the bias would go in the same direction. Indeed, we show that there are PRFs that are completely insecure as ED-Extractors in the setting with auxiliary info.

ED-EXTRACTORS IMPLY ONE-WAY FUNCTIONS. We show that ED-Extractors cannot exist if the source is allowed to be computationally unbounded. This holds even in the setting without auxiliary info, even if we only consider polynomial-time distinguishers, even if we require that the source has almost full entropy, and even if the extractor outputs only 1 bit. The high level idea is that a computationally unbounded source S with oracle access to the function $\mathsf{EDExt}(\cdot, S)$ can learn the function sufficiently well to predict its output on a random value with high probability. It can then sample a random X subject to predicting that $\mathsf{EDExt}(X, S) = 0$, without querying the extractor on X. This is a legal source with almost full entropy, yet the extractor output is highly biased towards 0. We extend the above argument to showing that such extractors imply one-way functions.

ED-EXTRACTORS WITH AUXILIARY INFO FROM CONSTRAINED PRFS. We construct ED-Extractors in the setting with auxiliary info, using constrained pseudorandom functions (C-PRF). A C-PRF allows us to constrain a PRF key

k on some constraint function C to yield a constrained key, denoted $k\{C\}$. The constrained key allows us to evaluate the PRF on all points x such that $C(x) = 0$. However, given the constrained key $k\{C\}$, the PRF outputs at all points x for which $C(x) = 1$ look random. We need to rely on *adaptively secure* constrained PRFs, where the adversary can choose the constraint C after seeing some PRF outputs.

Our construction of ED-Extractors uses a constrained PRF and a standard (seeded) randomness extractors Ext. The seed of the ED-Extractor is a constrained PRF key $k\{C_{S,U}\}$, with the constraint $C_{S,U}(X)$ that outputs 1 (i.e., prevents evaluation) on all points X such that $\mathsf{Ext}(X; S) = U$, where S, U are chosen randomly. We choose the output size of the extractor to be $\ell = \omega(\log \lambda)$ and therefore the key is constrained on a negligible fraction of points. On input X, the ED-Extractor checks if $C_{S,U}(X) = 1$, in which case it outputs some fixed dummy value, and otherwise it uses the seed $k\{C_{S,U}\}$ to evaluate the PRF on X.

To argue ED-Extractor security, we consider a source $\mathcal{S}^{\mathsf{EDExt}(\cdot, k\{C_{S,U}\})}$ that gets oracle access to the ED-Extractor with a random seed $k\{C_{S,U}\}$ and outputs X, AUX. A distinguisher $\mathcal{D}$ then gets the seed $k\{C_{S,U}\}$ together with AUX and the extracted output $R = \mathsf{EDExt}(X, k\{C_{S,U}\})$. We first argue that this is statistically indistinguishable from giving the source $\mathcal{S}$ oracle access to the unconstrained PRF and setting R to be the output of the PRF with the unconstrained key on X (since the probability that any of the queries of $\mathcal{S}$ or its output lie in the constrained set is negligible). Now, instead of giving the distinguisher $\mathcal{D}$ the constrained key $k\{C_{S,U}\}$ where U is uniform, we give it the key $k\{C_{S,\mathsf{Ext}(X;S)}\}$ which is constrained on X. This is statistically indistinguishable since X has entropy even conditioned on AUX and is sampled independently of S; therefore $\mathsf{Ext}(X; S)$ is close to uniform even given AUX. But now we can switch R from the output of the PRF on X to uniform, and this is computationally indistinguishable even given the constrained PRF key $k\{C_{S,\mathsf{Ext}(X;S)}\}$ since it is constrained on X (and we know that the source didn't query the oracle on X). This shows that the extracted output is indistinguishable form uniform even given the ED-Extractor seed and the auxiliary info. (The above proof outline conveys the intuition but is slightly oversimplified and ignores some subtleties; see the full proof for details).

Since standard extractors can be evaluated in NC1, we only need constrained PRFs for NC1 circuits. Fortunately, we have such constructions from the LWE and DDHI assumptions [BV15, AMN+18]. However, they only achieve selective security, where the constrained circuit needs to be chosen ahead of time before any PRF outputs are given out, while we need adaptive security. We can get this via standard complexity leveraging at the cost of having to assume the sub-exponential security of the LWE and DDHI assumptions.

ADDITIONAL CONSTRUCTIONS (IN THE FULL VERSION). We give two alternate constructions of ED-Extractors in the setting with auxiliary info. The first uses *shift-hiding shiftable functions* [PS18], which can be instantiated from standard LWE, without needing complexity leveraging. The construction and proof of security differ substantially from the one above. The second one uses *lossy functions*, which are essentially equivalent to lossy trapdoor functions (LTDFs) [PW08] without requiring a trapdoor. The construction can be instantiated from several different assumptions (DDH,DLIN,LWE,DCR). Both constructions are omitted from this proceedings version due to lack of space; please see the full version [DVW19].

NOT ALL PRFS ARE ED-EXTRACTORS WITH AUX INFO. We construct PRFs, which fail to be good extractors in the setting of auxiliary info. For example, consider a PRF which first hashes the input x into a small digest using a collision-resistant hash function and then applies another PRF on the output. Consider a source that chooses a random x and sets the auxiliary info to be the hash of x. Since the hash is small, this does not reduce the entropy of x by much. However, if the distinguisher is given the PRF key (which is the ED-Extractor seed) and the auxiliary info, it can compute the PRF on x and therefore easily distinguish it from uniform. In this example, the auxiliary info reduces the entropy of x by some small super-logarithmic amount. We give an even more dramatic example of this type using fully-homomorphic encryption (FHE) where the auxiliary info reduces the entropy of x by only 1 bit.

BLACK-BOX SEPARATION RESULTS. Lastly, we give two black-box separation results showing that, in the auxiliary info setting, one cannot prove security (via a black-box reduction under a standard assumption) against computationally unbounded distinguishers or for certain natural classes of constructions. Our results rely on the framework of [Wic13] and rely on the fact that the ED-Extractor definition is expressed as a two-stage game where the attacker consists of two components (the source and the distinguisher) that cannot communicate. This allows us to give black-box separations showing that, in certain cases, we cannot prove security under any standard assumption which is in the form of a single-stage game between a challenger and a single stateful adversary.

1.3 Additional Related Work

RNGS. Our scenario is partially motivated by the problem of extracting randomness from physical sources as part of a system Random Number Generator (RNG). We note that extracting randomness is only one component of a good RNG; see e.g., [BH05, DPR+13, DSSW14, GT16, Hut16, CDKT19] for works that formally deal with the broader problem of RNG design.

UNIVERSAL COMPUTATIONAL EXTRACTORS (UCE). The notion of universal computational extractors (UCE) [BHK13, ST17] was originally proposed as a way of capturing "random-oracle like" security properties of hash functions via a standard-model definition. While the format of the UCE definition is also given in terms of an extraction game with a source and a distinguisher, there are major differences between the UCE definition and that of ED-Extractors, both in terms of their syntactic structure, but also more conceptually in terms of what they aim to capture. The key such difference is that the notion of legal source is defined in the "ideal model", and permits sources which only have *computational* unpredictability in the "real" model (say, conditioned on the auxiliary information).[2] In contrast, this work only aimed to capture a smaller class of sources that have entropy even in the "real model", but could depend of the previous extractor output.

Unfortunately, it is known that even the weakest form of UCE security cannot be achieved under standard assumptions (via black-box reductions; this indirectly follows from [Wic13]), while our work shows that ED-Extractors can. It remains an interesting open problem whether ED-Extractors can be used in place of UCEs to get any broader cryptographic applications beyond the immediate ones of extracting randomness.

LOW-COMPLEXITY SAMPLERS. Introduced by Trevisan and Vadhan [TV00] and later extended by [KRVZ11], these seedless extractors assume that the entropy source producing input X is unable to run the extractor even once. In contrast, our sampler can be much slower than the extractor, but we use a seed and give the sampler oracle access to the extractor, before releasing the seed to the distinguisher.

SEED-DEPENDENT CONDENSERS. This approach, formalized by Dodis, Ristenpart and Vadhan [DRV12], relaxes the security guarantees of the randomness extractor to only ensure that the output of the condenser is almost full entropy, but not necessarily close to uniform. In this sense it is weaker than ED-Extractors. However, the sampler is given the actual seed, which is stronger than our setting. Interestingly, the availability of auxiliary information also played a crucial role in the constructions of seed-dependent condensers from standard assumptions.

2   Preliminaries

When X is a distribution, or a random variable following this distribution, we let $x \leftarrow X$ denote the process of sampling x according to the distribution X. If X is a set, we let $x \leftarrow X$ denote sampling x uniformly at random from X.

Let X, Y be random variables with supports S_X, S_Y, respectively. We define their *statistical difference* as

$$\mathsf{SD}(X, Y) = \frac{1}{2} \sum_{u \in S_X \cup S_Y} |\Pr[X = u] - \Pr[Y = u]|.$$

The *min-entropy* of a random variable X is $H_\infty(X) = -\log(\max_x \Pr[X = x])$. Following Dodis et al. [DORS08], we define the (average) conditional min-entropy of X given Y as: $H_\infty(X|Y) = -\log\left(\mathbb{E}_{y \leftarrow Y}\left[2^{-H_\infty(X|Y=y)}\right]\right)$. Note that $H_\infty(X|Y) = k$ iff the optimal strategy for guessing X given Y succeeds with probability 2^{-k}.

---

[2] Somewhat confusingly, this is true even for so called "UCEs for statistically unpredictable sources".

Lemma 1. *For any random variables X, Y where Y is supported over a set of size T we have $H_\infty(X|Y) \leq H_\infty(X) - \log T$.*

Definition 1 ((Strong, Average-Case) Seeded Extractor [NZ96]). *We say that an efficient function* Ext $: \{0,1\}^n \times \{0,1\}^d \to \{0,1\}^\ell$ *is an (α, ε)-extractor if for all random variables (X, Z) such that X is supported over $\{0,1\}^n$ and $H_\infty(X|Z) \geq \alpha$ we have* $\mathsf{SD}((Z, S, \mathsf{Ext}(X; S)), (Z, S, U_\ell)) \leq \varepsilon$ *where S, U_ℓ are uniformly random and independent bit-strings of length d, ℓ respectively.*

Theorem 1 ([ILL89]). *There exist (α, ε)-extractors with input length n and output length ℓ as long as $\alpha \geq \ell + 2\log(1/\varepsilon)$.*

Definition 2 ((Strong, Average-Case) Two-Source Extractor [CG88]). *We say that an efficient function* 2Ext $: \{0,1\}^n \times \{0,1\}^n \to \{0,1\}^m$ *is an (e_1, e_2, δ)-strong 2-source extractor if for all random variables (X_1, X_2, Z) such that X_1, X_2 are independent conditioned on Z and $H_\infty(X_1|Z) \geq e_1$, $H_\infty(X_2|Z) \geq e_2$ we have* $\mathsf{SD}((Z, X_2, 2\mathsf{Ext}(X_1; X_2)), (Z, X_2, U_m)) \leq \delta$ *where U_m is a uniformly string of length m.*

Theorem 2 ([Raz05]). *For any polynomial input length $n = \mathrm{poly}(\lambda)$, any $e_1 = \lambda^{\Omega(1)}$ and any $e_2 = (1/2 + \Omega(1))n$, there exist (e_1, e_2, δ)-extractor with input length n, output length $m = \lambda^{\Omega(1)}$ and error $\delta = 2^{-\lambda^{\Omega(1)}}$.*

Definition 3. *The collision probability of a random variable A is defined as* $\mathsf{Col}(A) = \Pr[a = a' : a \leftarrow A, a' \leftarrow A]$. *The conditional collision probability of A given B is defined as* $\mathsf{Col}(A|B) = \Pr[a = a' : b \leftarrow B, a \leftarrow (A|B = b), a' \leftarrow (A|B = b)]$.

Claim 1 (Statistical Distance vs Collision Probability [IZ89]). *Let A be a random variable supported over $\{0,1\}^m$ such that $\mathsf{SD}(A, U_m) \geq \varepsilon$, where U_m is uniform over $\{0,1\}^m$. Then $\mathsf{Col}(A) \geq \frac{1}{2^m}(1 + 4\varepsilon^2)$.*

Furthermore, let A, B be correlated random variables, where A is supported over $\{0,1\}^m$ and

$$\mathsf{SD}((A, B), (U_m, B)) \geq \varepsilon.$$

Then $\mathsf{Col}(A|B) \geq \frac{1}{2^m}(1 + 4\varepsilon^2)$.

Learning with Errors. The (n, m, q, χ) LWE assumption states that $(A, sA + e)$ is computationally indistinguishable from (A, u) where $A \leftarrow \mathbb{Z}_q^{n \times m}$, $s \leftarrow \mathbb{Z}_q^n$, $e \leftarrow \chi^m$ and $u \leftarrow \mathbb{Z}_q^m$. Throughout this work, the LWE assumption (without qualification), refers to assuming that there exists some $n = \mathrm{poly}(\lambda)$, some $q \geq 2^{\lambda^{\Omega(1)}}$ and some distribution χ over $\mathbb{Z}$ which is $\mathrm{poly}(\lambda)$ bounded such that the (n, m, q, χ) assumption holds for all $m = \mathrm{poly}(\lambda)$. This is implied by the hardness of worst-case lattice problems with sub-exponential approximation factors.

Definition 4 (Pseudorandom Function (PRF) [GGM84]). *A polynomial-time function $F : \{0,1\}^\ell \times \{0,1\}^n \to \{0,1\}^m$ with key length $\ell = \ell(\lambda)$, input* *length $n = n(\lambda)$ and output length $m = m(\lambda)$ is a PRF if for any polynomial-time attacker $\mathcal{A}$ there exists some negligible function $\mu(\lambda) = \mathrm{negl}(\lambda)$ such that*

$$| \; \Pr[\mathcal{A}^{F(k,\cdot)}(1^\lambda) = 1] - \Pr[\mathcal{A}^{\mathcal{O}(\cdot)}(1^\lambda) = 1] \; | \le \mu(\lambda).$$

where we choose $k \leftarrow \{0,1\}^\ell$ and $\mathcal{O} : \{0,1\}^n \to \{0,1\}^m$ is a uniformly random function. We say that the PRF has security level $\sigma = \sigma(\lambda)$ if $\mu(\lambda) \le 1/\sigma(\lambda)$.

Definition 5 (Constrained PRFs (CPRF)) [BGI14, KPTZ13, BW13]). *A CPRF for a class of constraints $\mathcal{C} = \{\mathcal{C}_\lambda\}$ consists of two polynomial-time algorithms $(F, \mathsf{Constrain})$ where:*

- *$y = F(k, x)$ is a deterministic polynomial-time function that takes as input a key k (either constrained or unconstrained) and a value $x \in \{0,1\}^n$ and outputs $y \in \{0,1\}^m$ for some polynomial length parameters $n = n(\lambda), m = m(\lambda)$ in the security parameter λ.*
- *$k\{C\} \leftarrow \mathsf{Constrain}(k, C)$ takes as input a key $k \in \{0,1\}^\lambda$ and a constraint $C : \{0,1\}^n \to \{0,1\}$ with $C \in \mathcal{C}_\lambda$. It outputs a constrained key, denoted $k\{C\}$.*

We require that the scheme satisfies a correctness and a security property defined below:

Correctness: *We require that no adversary can find an input which is not constrained, yet the constrained key disagrees with the original key. More concretely, consider the following game between a stateful adversary $\mathcal{A}$ and a challenger:*
  - *The adversary $\mathcal{A}(1^\lambda)$ chooses $C \in \mathcal{C}_\lambda$.*
  - *The challenger chooses $k \in \{0,1\}^\lambda$ and $k\{C\} \leftarrow \mathsf{Constrain}(k, C)$.*
  - *The adversary $\mathcal{A}^{F(k,\cdot)}(k\{C\})$ gets the constrained key $k\{C\}$ and oracle access to $F(k, \cdot)$. It outputs a value $x \in \{0,1\}^n$.*

  We require that, in the context of the above experiment, we have $\Pr[C(x) = 0 \wedge F(k, x) \ne F(k\{C\}, x)] \le \mathrm{negl}(\lambda)$.

(Adaptive) Security: *Consider the following distinguishing game between an adversary $\mathcal{A}$ and a challenger:*
  - *Challenger chooses $k \leftarrow \{0,1\}^\lambda$ and a bit $b \leftarrow \{0,1\}$.*
  - *Adversary $\mathcal{A}^{F(k,\cdot)}(1^\lambda)$ gets oracle access to $F(k, \cdot)$ and outputs a constraint $C \in \mathcal{C}_\lambda$ and a values x such that $C(x) = 1$ and x was never queries to the oracle.*
  - *If $b = 0$, the challenger sets $r = F(k, x)$ and else it chooses $r \leftarrow \{0,1\}^m$. The challenger also computes $k\{C\} \leftarrow \mathsf{Constrain}(k, C)$.*
  - *The adversary $\mathcal{A}$ is given $k\{C\}$ and r. It outputs a bit b'.*

  We require that for all polynomial-time adversaries $\mathcal{A}$, we have $| \Pr[b = b'] - \frac{1}{2}| = \mathrm{negl}(\lambda)$.

We also consider several variants of the definition. Firstly, we define the notion of no-constrained-evaluation security, where we restrict the adversary to never querying the oracle $F(k, \cdot)$ on a point x for which $C(x) = 1$. Secondly, we *consider selective security where the adversary chooses $C \in \mathcal{C}_\lambda$ at the beginning of the game before getting oracle access to $F(k, c)$). Lastly, we consider no-evaluation security where the adversary does not get oracle access to $F(k, \cdot)$ at all.*

Note that, via a simple guessing argument where we guess the adversary's choice of C, selective security with a sufficiently high security level $\sigma(\lambda) = |\mathcal{C}_\lambda|\omega(\log \lambda)$ implies adaptive security. Furthermore by the same argument, no-evaluation security (which is inherently selective) with a sufficiently high security level $\sigma(\lambda) = |\mathcal{C}_\lambda|\omega(\log \lambda)$ implies no-constrained-evaluation security. This is because, if we guess the adversary's choice of C ahead of time and gets $k\{C\}$, we can answer queries on unconstrained points using $k\{C\}$ rather than calling the PRF oracle.

3   Defining ED-Extractors

In this section, we give a formal definition of extractors for extractor-dependent sources (ED-Extractors) and provide some discussion on the various aspects of the definition.

Definition 6 (Extractor-Dependent   Extraction). *An extractor for α-entropy extractor-dependent sources (α-ED-Extractor) consists of two polynomial-time algorithms $(\mathsf{SeedGen}, \mathsf{EDExt})$ with the following syntax:*

- *seed $\leftarrow \mathsf{SeedGen}(1^\lambda)$ is a randomized algorithm that generates seed.*
- *$\mathsf{EDExt}(x, \mathsf{seed})$ is a deterministic algorithm that takes a sample $x \in \{0,1\}^n$, together with seed and outputs a value $y \in \{0,1\}^m$ for some polynomial length parameters $n = n(\lambda), m = m(\lambda)$.*

Consider an adversarial source/distinguisher pair $(\mathcal{S}, \mathcal{D})$ and define the following extraction experiment $\mathsf{EDGame}^{\mathcal{S},\mathcal{D}}(1^\lambda)$:

- *Sample a random bit $b \leftarrow \{0,1\}$ and a random seed $\leftarrow \mathsf{SeedGen}(1^\lambda)$.*
- *Run $(x, \mathsf{aux}) \leftarrow \mathcal{S}^{\mathsf{EDExt}(\cdot, \mathsf{seed})}(1^\lambda)$.*
- *If $b = 0$ set $r = \mathsf{EDExt}(x, \mathsf{seed})$ else if $b = 1$ set $r \leftarrow \{0,1\}^m$.*
- *Let $b' = \mathcal{D}(1^\lambda, \mathsf{seed}, \mathsf{aux}, r)$.*

We say that $\mathcal{S}$ is an α-legal extractor-dependent source if the following conditions hold:

1. *The probability that $\mathcal{S}$ queries its oracle on the value x that it outputs is negligible.*
2. *$H_\infty(X|\mathsf{AUX}, \mathsf{SEED}) \geq \alpha(\lambda)$, where $X, \mathsf{SEED}, \mathsf{AUX}$ denotes the joint distribution of the values $x, \mathsf{seed}, \mathsf{aux}$ in the above experiment.*

An α-ED-Extractor is secure if for all α-legal polynomial-time sources $\mathcal{S}$ and all polynomial-time distinguishers $\mathcal{D}$, the above experiment satisfies

$$\left| \Pr[b = b'] - \frac{1}{2} \right| = \mathsf{negl}(\lambda).$$

We can also define a weaker notion without auxiliary info *by restricting* aux *to be empty. We can also strengthen security to* computationally unbounded sources or distinguishers *by removing the restriction that the source or the distinguisher runs in polynomial time.*

Remark on the Legality Conditions. As we discussed in the introduction, the legality conditions above may not seem entirely intuitive on first look. For example, it may be unclear why we prohibit the source from querying the extractor on the value it outputs. Another undesirable aspect of definition is that the legality conditions are construction-dependent: in other words, a source may be legal for some constructions of the ED-Extractor but illegal for others since the entropy of the output may depend on the oracle queries. Ideally, the legality of the source could be checked independently of the construction. For these reasons, we can also consider an alternate, weaker, definition, which may be more intuitively compelling and does not suffer from the above issue. We say that source $\mathcal{S}$ is α-*super-legal* if:

- It can be written as $\mathcal{S} = (\mathcal{S}_1, \mathcal{S}_2)$ where $\mathcal{S}_1^{\mathsf{EDExt}(\cdot, \mathsf{seed})}(1^\lambda)$ gets oracle access to the extractor and outputs some value $\mathsf{state} \in \{0,1\}^{p(\lambda)}$ for some polynomial p, and $\mathcal{S}_2(\mathsf{state})$ outputs x, aux without getting any further access to the extractor.
- For all choices of $\mathsf{state} \in \{0,1\}^{p(\lambda)}$ it holds that $H_\infty(X|\mathsf{AUX}) \geq \alpha(\lambda)$, where (X, AUX) are random variables for the output of $\mathcal{S}_2(\mathsf{state})$.

Note that "super-legality" is only a condition of $\mathcal{S}_2$ which does not have oracle access to the extractor, and is therefore construction-independent.

We claim that for any $\alpha(\lambda) = \omega(\log \lambda)$, every α-super-legal source $\mathcal{S}$ is also α-legal. Firstly, if $\mathcal{S}_1$ only makes polynomially many queries and has a non-negligible probability of querying the oracle on the value x that $\mathcal{S}_2$ outputs then there must be some value of state for which we can predict the value x that $\mathcal{S}_2(\mathsf{state})$ outputs with non-negligible probability. But this contradicts $H_\infty(X) \geq H_\infty(X|\mathsf{AUX}) \geq \omega(\log \lambda)$. Therefore $\mathcal{S}$ satisfies the first legality condition. Secondly, let STATE be a random variable for the value $\mathsf{state} \leftarrow \mathcal{S}_1^{\mathsf{EDExt}(\cdot, \mathsf{seed})}(1^\lambda)$. Then SEED is independent of (X, AUX) if we condition on STATE. Therefore, $H_\infty(X|\mathsf{AUX}, \mathsf{SEED}) \geq H_\infty(X|\mathsf{AUX}, \mathsf{STATE}) \geq \min_{\mathsf{state}} H_\infty(X_{\mathsf{state}}|\mathsf{AUX}_{\mathsf{state}}) \geq \alpha(\lambda)$ where $X_{\mathsf{state}}, \mathsf{AUX}_{\mathsf{state}}$ is the conditional distribution of X, AUX conditioned on $\mathsf{STATE} = \mathsf{state}$, which is just the distribution of the outputs of $\mathcal{S}_2(\mathsf{state})$. Therefore $\mathcal{S}$ satisfies the second legality condition.

As discussed in the introduction, the super-legality condition can also be interpreted very intuitively: we think of $\mathcal{S}_1$ as capturing all of the influence that prior extractor call can have on nature and $\mathcal{S}_2$ as modeling the entropic process that's responsible for generating x, aux. We chose to use "legality" rather than "super-legality" in our default definition since it makes the definition stronger and thus gives stronger positive results. We mention that (by simple inspection) all of our negative results also hold for the weaker definition using super-legality.

Remark about Conditioning on the Seed. Our legality condition in the formal definition requires that the entropy $H_\infty(X|\text{AUX}, \text{SEED}) \geq \alpha(\lambda)$, where we condition on SEED. Note that we could remove this conditioning and have an alternate, stronger, definition where we only require $H_\infty(X|\text{AUX}) \geq \alpha(\lambda)$. We observe that, assuming one-way functions, any α-ED-Extractor according to our definition can be converted into an $(\alpha' = \alpha + \lambda^\varepsilon)$-ED-Extractor according to the stronger definition for any constant $\varepsilon > 0$. The idea is that we can modify the SeedGen algorithm to only use λ^ε random bits by expanding them out using a PRG to get as many pseudorandom bits as needed by the original algorithm. By the security of the PRG, this change cannot harm ED-Extractor security. But now SEED comes from a domain of size only 2^{λ^ε} and therefore $H_\infty(X|\text{AUX}, \text{SEED}) \geq H_\infty(X|\text{AUX}) - \lambda^\varepsilon \geq \alpha' - \lambda^\varepsilon \geq \alpha$. Hence the new construction is an α'-ED-Extractor according to the stronger definition. The takeaway is that (as long as we're only considering polynomial-time distinguishers) it does not make much difference whether or not we condition on the seed in the definition.

Remark on Output Size. Note that if we have an α-ED-Extractor with output size $m = \lambda^\varepsilon$ for some constant $\varepsilon > 0$ then, assuming one-way functions, we can also construct an α-ED-Extractor for arbitrarily large output size $m = \lambda^c$ for any constant c just by using a pseudorandom generator (PRG) to expand the output. This holds as long as we're only considering polynomial-time distinguishers.

4   Security Without Auxiliary Info

4.1   Construction from Any PRF

We first show that every pseudorandom function (PRF) with a sufficiently high level of security is a good ED-Extractor in the setting without auxiliary info.

Theorem 3. *Let $F(\cdot, \cdot) : \{0,1\}^\ell \times \{0,1\}^n \to \{0,1\}^m$ be a pseudorandom function (PRF) with key-length $\ell = \ell(\lambda)$, input length $n = n(\lambda)$ and output length $m = m(\lambda)$, having security level $\sigma(\lambda) = 2^{m(\lambda)}\omega(\log \lambda)$. Define (SeedGen, EDExt) where SeedGen(1^λ) outputs seed $\leftarrow \{0,1\}^{\ell(\lambda)}$ and EDExt(x, seed) = F(seed, x). Then (SeedGen, EDExt) is an α-ED Extractor without auxiliary info for any $\alpha \geq m + \omega(\log \lambda)$. Furthermore, it has security for unbounded distinguishers.*

Proof. Assume that $(\mathcal{S}, \mathcal{D})$ is some α-legal source and distinguisher pair with advantage $\varepsilon = \varepsilon(\lambda)$ in the ED-Extractor security game. Assume that $\mathcal{S}$ runs in polynomial time, but $\mathcal{D}$ can be unbounded. We define a polynomial-time adversary $\mathcal{A}$ that has $(\varepsilon^2 - \text{negl}(\lambda))/2^m$ advantage in the PRF game. In particular, $\mathcal{A}^{\mathcal{O}(\cdot)}$ is given access to an oracle $\mathcal{O}$ and runs $\mathcal{S}^{\mathcal{O}(\cdot)}$ twice with independent randomness to derive two values x, x'. Then $\mathcal{A}^{\mathcal{O}(\cdot)}$ computes $r = \mathcal{O}(x), r' = \mathcal{O}(x')$. If $r = r'$, it outputs 1 else 0.

Firstly, consider the experiment where we sample $k \leftarrow \{0,1\}^\ell, x \leftarrow \mathcal{S}^{F(k,\cdot)}$, $r = F(k, x)$ and let K, R be the random variables for the values k, r respectively.

Then the statistical distance $\mathsf{SD}(((K,R),(K,U_m)) \geq \varepsilon$ since $\mathcal{D}$ distinguishes the two distributions with probability ε. Therefore, by Claim 1, we have $\mathsf{Col}(R|K) \geq \frac{1}{2^m}(1 + 4\varepsilon^2)$ where Col denotes the collision probability (Definition 3). It's easy to see that, by the definition of $\mathcal{A}$, we have $\Pr[\mathcal{A}^{F(k,\cdot)} = 1 \ : \ k \leftarrow \{0,1\}^\ell] = \mathsf{Col}(R|K) \geq \frac{1}{2^m}(1 + 4\varepsilon^2)$.

Secondly, consider the experiment where we sample $k \leftarrow \{0,1\}^\ell$ and then sample $x \leftarrow \mathcal{S}^{F(k,\cdot)}, x' \leftarrow \mathcal{S}^{F(k,\cdot)}$ by running $\mathcal{S}$ twice with independent randomness and let K, X, X' be the random variables for the value k, x, x' in the experiment. Since $\mathcal{S}$ is an α-legal source we know that:

- The probability that $\mathcal{S}$ queried the oracle on x during the first run or on x' during the second run is negligible.
- Since $H_\infty(X|K) = H_\infty(X'|K) \geq \alpha \geq m + \omega(\log \lambda)$, the probability that either (1) $\mathcal{S}$ queried the oracle on x' during the first run or (2) $\mathcal{S}$ queried the oracle on x during the second run or (3) $x = x'$ is bounded by $\mathsf{negl}(\lambda)/2^m$.

To summarize, in the above experiment, if we define the "bad event' that $x = x'$ or that the oracle is queried on one of x, x' during the course of the experiment, then the probability of the bad event is at most $\mathsf{negl}(\lambda)/2^m$. Now, consider the modified experiment where we sample $x \leftarrow \mathcal{S}^{U(\cdot)}, x' \leftarrow \mathcal{S}^{U(\cdot)}$ and U is a truly random function. By $\sigma(\lambda)$ security of the PRF, the probability of the bad even occuring in the modified experiment is still be bounded by $\mathsf{negl}(\lambda)/2^m$. If the bad event does not occur, then $r = U(x), r' = U(x')$ are random and independent values and therefore $\Pr[r = r'] = \frac{1}{2^m}$. This shows that $\Pr[\mathcal{A}^{U(\cdot)} = 1] \leq (1 + \mathsf{negl}(\lambda))2^m$.

This shows that the advantage of $\mathcal{A}$ in the PRF security game is $(4\varepsilon^2(\lambda) - \mathsf{negl}(\lambda))/2^m$ which must be $\leq 1/\sigma(\lambda) \leq \mathsf{negl}(\lambda)/2^m$, by the $\sigma(\lambda)$ security of the PRF. Therefore $\varepsilon(\lambda) = \mathsf{negl}(\lambda)$, which concludes the proof of the ED-Extractor security.

Corollary 1. *Assuming the existence of sub-exponentially secure one-way functions, for any polynomial input size $n = n(\lambda)$ the following holds:*

- *For any polynomial output size $m = m(\lambda)$, there exists an α-ED Extractor in the setting without auxiliary info and with security for unbounded distinguishers as long as $\alpha \geq m + \omega(\log \lambda)$.*
- *For any constant $\varepsilon > 0$ and any polynomial output size $m = m(\lambda)$, there exists an α-ED Extractor in the setting without auxiliary info and security for polynomial-time distinguishers as long as $\alpha \geq \lambda^\varepsilon$.*

Proof. We note that sub-exponentially secure one-way functions imply the existence of PRFs with security level $2^{p(\lambda)}$ for any polynomial p (by making the key sufficiency large). Therefore the first part of the corollary follows directly from the preceding Theorem. The second part follows by using a pseudorandom generator (PRG) to expand the output-size of the ED-Extractor as discussed in the Remark on Output Size in Sect. 3.

4.2   Necessity of One-Way Functions

Theorem 4. *For any input length $n = n(\lambda)$, the existence of an $(\alpha = n-1)$-ED-Extractor, even without auxiliary info and even with output length $m = 1$, implies the existence of one-way functions. Furthermore, such extractors cannot be secure for computationally unbounded sources, even if we restrict to polynomial-time distinguishers.*

Proof. Let (SeedGen, EDExt) be an ED Extractor as in the theorem statement. Assume SeedGen(1^λ) uses at most $\ell = \ell(\lambda)$ bits of randomness and let $q = 7\ell + \lambda$. Define the function $f(r, x_1, \ldots, x_q) = (x_1, \ldots, x_q, y_1, \ldots, y_q)$, which takes as input a uniformly random $r \in \{0,1\}^\ell$ and $x_i \in \{0,1\}^n$ and computes seed $=$ SeedGen($1^\lambda; r$) and $y_i = $ EDExt(seed, x_i) for $i \in [q]$. Then we claim that f is a one-way function.

Assume by way of contradiction that a polynomial-size adversary $\mathcal{A}$ breaks the one-wayness of f with non-negligible probability. We define a source $\mathcal{S}^{\text{EDExt}(\text{seed},\cdot)}$ as follows:

1. Choose $x_1, \ldots, x_q$ uniformly at random form $\{0,1\}^n$. Query the oracle to learn $y_i = $ EDExt(seed, x_i) for each $i \in [q]$.
2. Run $\mathcal{A}(x_q, \ldots, x_q, y_1, \ldots, y_q)$ and get some value $(r', x'_1, \ldots, x'_q)$.
3. Test if $f(r', x_q, \ldots, x'_q) = (x_1, \ldots, x_q, y_1, \ldots, y_q)$. If not, output a uniformly random $x_0^* \leftarrow \{0,1\}^n$ and halt. Else continue.
4. Compute seed$'$ $=$ SeedGen($1^\lambda; r'$). Choose a random $x_1^* \leftarrow \{0,1\}^n$ and if EDExt(seed$'$, x_1^*) $= 0$ output x_1^* and halt. Else continue.
5. Choose a random $x_2^* \leftarrow \{0,1\}^n$ and output it.

We define a corresponding distinguisher $D(\text{seed}, r)$, which outputs r. We claim that the pair $(\mathcal{S}, \mathcal{D})$ breaks the $(\alpha = n - 1)$-ED-Extractor security.

Firstly, we claim that $\mathcal{S}$ is an $(\alpha = n - 1)$-legal source. It is easy to see that the probability of it outputting a value x that it previously queried is negligible since it outputs one of x_0^*, x_1^*, x_2^* each of which is individually uniformly random and independent of the prior queries. To analyze entropy, let us fix any choice of the values of seed, $x_1, \ldots, x_q$ and randomness of $\mathcal{A}$ and let X be the random variable for the output of $\mathcal{S}$ in the above experiment. We argue that, even for any choice of the fixed values, it holds that $H_\infty(X) \geq n - 1$, which proves the claim. The fixed values determine whether the test in line 3 passes or fails. If it fails, then X is uniformly random and so $H_\infty(X) = n$. If it passes, then let us define the variable V which is 0 if x is output in line 4 and 1 if it is output in line 5. Let us define the value $P_0 = |\{x : \text{EDExt}(x, \text{seed}) = 0\}|$. Then we have

$$\max_x \Pr[X = x] = \max_x \left(\Pr[X = x|V = 0]\Pr[V = 0] + \Pr[X = x|V = 1]\Pr[V = 1]\right)$$

$$\leq \frac{1}{P_0} \cdot \frac{P_0}{2^n} + \frac{1}{2^n}\left(1 - \frac{1}{P_0}\right)$$

$$\leq 2^{-(n-1)}$$

and therefore $H_\infty(X) \geq n - 1$.

Next, we analyze the success probability of the pair $(\mathcal{S}, \mathcal{D})$ in the ED-Extractor security game. If the challenger chooses the challenge bit $b = 1$ then, since r is uniformly random, we have $\Pr[b' = 1] = \frac{1}{2}$. On the other hand, let's analyze the security game when the challenge chooses the bit $b = 0$. Assume that the adversary $\mathcal{A}$ breaks the security of the one-way function f with some non-negligible probability $\varepsilon = \varepsilon(\lambda)$. Then $\varepsilon(\lambda) \geq 1/p(\lambda)$ for some polynomial p and for infinitely many values of λ. We define several events in the context of the ED-Extractor security game with the particular sampler defined above:

FAIR: Let's call a seed *biased* if $\Pr_{x \leftarrow \{0,1\}^n}[\mathsf{EDExt}(\mathsf{seed}, x) = 0] \leq \frac{1}{2} - \delta$ where we set $\delta := \frac{1}{20p}$. Let's define the event FAIR to occur if the seed is not biased. Since we assumed that the ED-Extractor is secure, it must be the case that probability that a random seed is biased is negligible (otherwise the sampler that outputs a random x and the distinguisher that tests if the seed is biased and if so outputs r else outputs random would break security). Therefore, $\Pr[\mathsf{FAIR}] = 1 - \mathsf{negl}(\lambda)$.

INV: Let this be the event that the test in line 3 of the execution of $\mathcal{S}$ succeeds, meaning that $\mathcal{A}$ succeeded to invert correctly. By definition $\Pr[\mathsf{INV}] = \varepsilon$.

CLOSE: Let this be the event that for the value seed' computed in line 4, it holds that

$$\Pr_{x \leftarrow \{0,1\}^n}[\mathsf{EDExt}(x, \mathsf{seed}) = \mathsf{EDExt}(x, \mathsf{seed}')] \geq .9$$

where, if the process terminates before line 4, we define $\mathsf{seed}' = \mathsf{seed}$. If CLOSE does not occur, it means that there exists some seed' for which $\Pr_{x \leftarrow \{0,1\}^n}[\mathsf{EDExt}(x, \mathsf{seed}) = \mathsf{EDExt}(x, \mathsf{seed}')] < .9$ but for all $i \in [q]$ it holds that $\mathsf{EDExt}(x_i, \mathsf{seed}) = \mathsf{EDExt}(x_i, \mathsf{seed}')$. The probability of this happening for any fixed seed' is $.9^q \leq .9^{7\ell + \lambda} \leq 2^{-\ell}\mathsf{negl}(\lambda)$. By taking a union bound over all 2^ℓ values of seed' the probability that some such good' exists is negligible and therefore $\Pr[\mathsf{CLOSE}] \geq 1 - \mathsf{negl}(\lambda)$.

For simplicity, we also define the event $\mathsf{IFC} = \mathsf{INV} \wedge \mathsf{FAIR} \wedge \mathsf{CLOSE}$. When $b = 0$ we therefore have:

$$\begin{aligned}
\Pr[b' = 0] &\geq \Pr[b' = 0 \wedge \mathsf{INV}] + \Pr[b' = 0 \wedge \neg\mathsf{INV}] \\
&\geq \Pr[b' = 0 \wedge \mathsf{INV} \wedge \mathsf{FAIR} \wedge \mathsf{CLOSE}] + \Pr[b' = 0 \wedge \neg\mathsf{INV} \wedge \mathsf{FAIR}] \\
&\geq \Pr[b' = 0|\mathsf{IFC}](\Pr[\mathsf{INV}] - \Pr[\neg\mathsf{FAIR}] - \Pr[\neg\mathsf{CLOSE}]) \\
&\quad + \Pr[b' = 0|\neg\mathsf{INV} \wedge \mathsf{FAIR}](\Pr[\neg\mathsf{INV}] - \Pr[\neg\mathsf{FAIR}]) \\
&\geq \Pr[b' = 0|\mathsf{IFC}](\varepsilon - \mathsf{negl}(\lambda)) + \Pr[b' = 0|\neg\mathsf{INV} \wedge \mathsf{FAIR}](1 - \varepsilon - \mathsf{negl}(\lambda)) \\
&\geq \Pr[b' = 0|\mathsf{IFC}](\varepsilon - \mathsf{negl}(\lambda)) + \left(\frac{1}{2} - \delta\right)(1 - \varepsilon - \mathsf{negl}(\lambda))
\end{aligned}$$

To analyze $\Pr[b' = 0|\mathsf{IFC}]$ let us fix all randomness z of the experiment except for the choice of x_1^*, x_2^*, such that this fixing makes the event IFC occurs. Let IFC_z be the event that the randomness takes on this value. For any such choice, let E_1 be the event that $\mathsf{EDExt}(x_1^*, \mathsf{seed}) = 0$, let E_1' be the event that $\mathsf{EDExt}(x_1^*, \mathsf{seed}') = 0$, let A be the even that $\mathsf{EDExt}(x_1^*, \mathsf{seed}) = \mathsf{EDExt}(x_1^*, \mathsf{seed}')$ and let E_2 be the event that $\mathsf{EDExt}(\mathsf{seed}, x_2^*) = 0$, where the randomness is only over the choice of x_1^*, x_2^*. Since we conditioned on CLOSE we have $\Pr[A] \geq .9$. Since we conditioned on FAIR we have $\Pr[E_1] \geq (1/2 - \delta), \Pr[E_2] \geq (1/2 - \delta)$. Therefore, for any such choice of randomness z we have:

$$
\begin{aligned}
\Pr[b' = 0 | \mathsf{IFC}_z] &= \Pr[E_1 \wedge E_1'] + \Pr[E_2 \wedge \neg E_1'] \\
&= \Pr[A \wedge E_1'] + \Pr[E_2] \left(1 - \Pr[E_1']\right) \\
&\geq \Pr[E_1'] - \Pr[\neg A] + \left(\frac{1}{2} - \delta\right)\left(1 - \Pr[E_1']\right) \\
&\geq \frac{1}{2} - \delta - .1 + \frac{1}{2}\Pr[E_1'] \\
&\geq \frac{1}{2} - \delta - .1 + \frac{1}{2}(\Pr[E_1] - \Pr[\neg A]) \\
&\geq \frac{1}{2} - \delta - .1 + \frac{1}{2}(\frac{1}{2} - \delta - .1) \\
&\geq .6 - \frac{3}{2}\delta
\end{aligned}
$$

which also implies that $\Pr[b' = 0 | \mathsf{IFC}] \geq .6 - \frac{3}{2}\delta$. Combining, we have:

$$
\begin{aligned}
\Pr[b' = 0] &\geq \left(.6 - \frac{3}{2}\delta\right)(\varepsilon - \mathsf{negl}(\lambda)) + \left(\frac{1}{2} - \delta\right)(1 - \varepsilon - \mathsf{negl}(\lambda)) \\
&\geq \frac{1}{2} - \delta + \varepsilon(.1 - \delta/2) - \mathsf{negl}(\lambda) \\
&\geq \frac{1}{2} + \varepsilon/10 - (3/2)\delta - \mathsf{negl}(\lambda) \\
&\geq \frac{1}{2} + \frac{1}{10p(\lambda)} - \frac{3}{40p(\lambda)} - \mathsf{negl}(\lambda) \\
&\geq \frac{1}{2} + \frac{1}{40p(\lambda)} - \mathsf{negl}(\lambda)
\end{aligned}
$$

for infinitely many values of λ. Therefore $\Pr[b' = b] - \frac{1}{2}$ is non-negligible, which leads to a contradiction and hence f must be one-way.

For the second part of the theorem, note that we showed how to convert an inverter for f into a source $\mathcal{S}$ together with an efficient distinguisher $\mathcal{D}$ that break ED-Extractor security. Since an inefficient inverter for f always exists, it means that there exists an inefficient source $\mathcal{S}$ and an efficient distinguisher $\mathcal{D}$ that break the security of the ED-Extractor.

5   Security with Auxiliary Info

5.1   Construction via Constrained PRFs

We now show how to construct an ED-Extractor in the setting with auxiliary info, using constrained PRFs (Definition 5) and standard seeded extractors (Definition 1).

Construction. Let $\mathsf{Ext} : \{0,1\}^n \times \{0,1\}^d \to \{0,1\}^\ell$ be an (α', ε)-seeded extractor for some lengths $n = n(\lambda), d = d(\lambda), \ell = \ell(\lambda)$ and some $\alpha' = \alpha'(\lambda), \varepsilon = \varepsilon(\lambda)$. Further let Ext also be a universal hash function. Let $(F, \mathsf{Constrain})$ be a constrained PRF with input length n and output length $m = m(\lambda)$ for the class of constraints $\mathcal{C} = \{C_{s,u}\}_{s \in \{0,1\}^d, u \in \{0,1\}^\ell}$ where $C_{s,u}(x) = 1$ iff $\mathsf{Ext}(x; s) = u$. We construct an ED-Extractor $(\mathsf{SeedGen}, \mathsf{EDExt})$ as follows:

- $\mathsf{SeedGen}(1^\lambda)$: Choose a random $k \leftarrow \{0,1\}^\lambda$. Choose a random $s \leftarrow \{0,1\}^d$, $u \leftarrow \{0,1\}^\ell$ and let $C_{s,u} \in \mathcal{C}$ be the corresponding constraint. Let $k\{C_{s,u}\} \leftarrow \mathsf{Constrain}(k, C_{s,u})$. Output $\mathsf{seed} = k\{C_{s,u}\}$.
- $\mathsf{EDExt}(x, \mathsf{seed})$: Output $F(k\{C_{s,u}\}, x)$.

Note that F always outputs some value, even if x is in the constrained set. Without loss of generality, we can assume that the constrained key $k\{C_{s,u}\}$ reveals s, u in the clear and that, $F(k\{C_{s,u}\}, x)$ outputs 0^m whenever $C_{s,u}(x) = 1$.

Theorem 5. *Assuming the constrained PRF has no-constrained-evaluation security, the construction above is an α-entropy secure ED-Extractor for $\alpha = \alpha' + m$, as long as the parameters satisfy $\ell(\lambda) = \omega(\log \lambda)$, and $\varepsilon(\lambda) = \mathrm{negl}(\lambda)$.*

Proof. Our proof of security follows by a sequence of hybrid games:

Hybrid 0: This is the game $\mathsf{EDGame}^{\mathcal{S}, \mathcal{D}}(1^\lambda)$ with a source $\mathcal{S}$ and a distinguisher $\mathcal{D}$ as in Definition 6. The game proceeds as follows:

- Sample a random bit $b \leftarrow \{0,1\}$ and a random $\mathsf{seed} \leftarrow \mathsf{SeedGen}(1^\lambda)$. The latter consists of sampling $k \leftarrow \{0,1\}^\lambda, s \leftarrow \{0,1\}^d, u \leftarrow \{0,1\}^\ell$, $k\{C_{s,u}\} \leftarrow \mathsf{Constrain}(k, C_{s,u})$ and setting $\mathsf{seed} = k\{C_{s,u}\}$.
- Run $(x, \mathsf{aux}) \leftarrow \mathcal{S}^{\mathsf{EDExt}(\cdot, \mathsf{seed})}(1^\lambda)$.
- If $b = 0$ set $r = \mathsf{EDExt}(x, \mathsf{seed})$ else if $b = 1$ set $r \leftarrow \{0,1\}^m$.
- Let $b' = \mathcal{D}(1^\lambda, \mathsf{seed}, \mathsf{aux}, r)$.

Hybrid 1: In this game, instead of giving the source $\mathcal{S}^{\mathsf{EDExt}(\cdot; \mathsf{seed})}$ access to the oracle $\mathsf{EDExt}(\cdot, \mathsf{seed}) = F(k\{C_{s,u}\}, \cdot)$, we replace it with the oracle $F(k, \cdot)$ using the unconstrained key k. Furthermore, if $b = 0$, instead of setting $r = \mathsf{EDExt}(x, \mathsf{seed}) = F(k\{C_{s,u}\}, x)$, we now set $r = F(k, x)$. In detail, the hybrid is defined as follows:

1. Sample a random bit $b \leftarrow \{0,1\}$ and a random $k \leftarrow \{0,1\}^\lambda$.
2. Run $(x, \mathsf{aux}) \leftarrow \mathcal{S}^{F(k, \cdot)}(1^\lambda)$.
3. If $b = 0$ set $r = F(k, x)$ else if $b = 1$ set $r \leftarrow \{0,1\}^m$. Choose $s \leftarrow \{0,1\}^d, u \leftarrow \{0,1\}^\ell$ and $\mathsf{seed} \leftarrow \mathsf{Constrain}(k, C_{s,u})$.
4. Let $b' = \mathcal{D}(1^\lambda, \mathsf{seed}, \mathsf{aux}, r)$.

Hybrids 0 and 1 are indistinguishable. The only time Hybrid 0 differs from Hybrid 1 is if in Hybrid 0 either: (A) some oracle query or the final output x produced by $\mathcal{S}$ satisfy $\mathsf{Ext}(x; s) = u$, or (B) some oracle query or the final output x produced by $\mathcal{S}$ satisfy $C_{s,u}(x) = 0 \wedge F(k, x) \neq F(k\{C_{s,u}\}, x)$. Since u is uniformly random, the probability of (A) happening when $\mathcal{S}$ makes q queries is at most $(q + 1)/2^{\ell}$ which is negligible. By the correctness of the constrained PRF, the probability of (B) happening is also negligible.

Hybrid 2: This is the same as Hybrid 1, except that we give the source access to an oracle $\mathsf{EDExt}(\cdot; \mathsf{seed}')$ where $\mathsf{seed}' = k\{C_{s',u'}\} \leftarrow \mathsf{Constrain}(k, C_{s',u'})$ is a constrained PRF key for random and independent values s', u'. In detail, the hybrid is defined as follows:

1. Sample a random bit $b \leftarrow \{0, 1\}$ and a random $k \leftarrow \{0, 1\}^{\lambda}$. Choose $s' \leftarrow \{0, 1\}^d, u' \leftarrow \{0, 1\}^{\ell}$ and $\mathsf{seed}' \leftarrow \mathsf{Constrain}(k, C_{s',u'})$.
2. Run $(x, \mathsf{aux}) \leftarrow \mathcal{S}^{\mathsf{EDExt}(\cdot, \mathsf{seed}')}(1^{\lambda})$.
3. If $b = 0$ set $r = F(k, x)$ else if $b = 1$ set $r \leftarrow \{0, 1\}^m$. Choose $s \leftarrow \{0, 1\}^d, u \leftarrow \{0, 1\}^{\ell}$ and $\mathsf{seed} \leftarrow \mathsf{Constrain}(k, C_{s,u})$.
4. Let $b' = \mathcal{D}(1^{\lambda}, \mathsf{seed}, \mathsf{aux}, r)$.

Hybrids 1 and 2 are statistically close. The only time Hybrid 1 differs from Hybrid 2 is if in Hybrid 2 either: (A) some oracle query x_i produced by $\mathcal{S}$ satisfies $\mathsf{Ext}(x_i; s') = u'$, or (B) some oracle query x_i produced by $\mathcal{S}$ satisfy $C_{s',u'}(x) = 0 \wedge F(k, x) \neq F(k\{C_{s',u'}\}, x)$. Since u' is uniformly random, the probability of (A) happening when $\mathcal{S}$ makes q queries is at most $q/2^{\ell}$ which is negligible. By the correctness of the constrained PRF, the probability of (B) happening is also negligible.

Hybrid 3: This is the same as Hybrid 2, except that in step 3, instead of choosing $u \leftarrow \{0, 1\}^{\ell}$ we now set $u = \mathsf{Ext}(x; s)$. In detail, the hybrid is defined as follows:

1. Sample a random bit $b \leftarrow \{0, 1\}$ and a random $k \leftarrow \{0, 1\}^{\lambda}$. Choose $s' \leftarrow \{0, 1\}^d, u' \leftarrow \{0, 1\}^{\ell}$ and $\mathsf{seed}' \leftarrow \mathsf{Constrain}(k, C_{s',u'})$.
2. Run $(x, \mathsf{aux}) \leftarrow \mathcal{S}^{\mathsf{EDExt}(\cdot, \mathsf{seed}')}(1^{\lambda})$.
3. If $b = 0$ set $r = F(k, x)$ else if $b = 1$ set $r \leftarrow \{0, 1\}^m$. Choose $s \leftarrow \{0, 1\}^d$ $u = \mathsf{Ext}(x; s)$ and $\mathsf{seed} \leftarrow \mathsf{Constrain}(k, C_{s,u})$.
4. Let $b' = \mathcal{D}(1^{\lambda}, \mathsf{seed}, \mathsf{aux}, r)$.

Hybrids 2 and 3 are statistically close if Ext is an (α, ε)-extractor. To argue this, let us use capital letters to denote random variables for the corresponding values in the experiment. Firstly, note that the view of the source $\mathcal{S}$ in hybrid 2 is identically distributed to that of hybrid 0.[3] Therefore, we can rely on the legality to $\mathcal{S}$ (which is defined relative to the distribution of hybrid 0) to argue that $H_{\infty}(X | \mathsf{AUX}, \mathsf{SEED}') \geq \alpha$. By Lemma 1, we also have $H_{\infty}(X | \mathsf{AUX}, \mathsf{SEED}', R) \geq \alpha - m \geq \alpha'$. Lastly since K is independent of X when conditioned on SEED', R, we also have $H_{\infty}(X | \mathsf{AUX}, K, R) \geq \alpha'$. Therefore, by the security of the extractor, $U = \mathsf{Ext}(X; S)$ is statistically close to a uniformly random and independent U even given AUX, K, R, S. Lastly, since the view of $\mathcal{D}$ in hybrids 2 and 3 is a function of AUX, K, R, S, U where

---

[3] This was the reason for introducing hybrid 2 rather than directly going from 1 to 3.

$U = \mathsf{Ext}(X; S)$ in hybrid 3 and U is uniform/independent in hybrid 2, the two hybrids are statistically close.

Hybrid 4: This is the same as Hybrid 3, except that we switch back from giving $\mathcal{S}$ oracle access to $\mathsf{EDExt}(\cdot, \mathsf{seed}')$ to giving it access to the unconstrained PRF $F(k, \cdot)$. In detail, the hybrid is defined as follows:

1. Sample a random bit $b \leftarrow \{0, 1\}$ and a random $k \leftarrow \{0, 1\}^\lambda$.
2. Run $(x, \mathsf{aux}) \leftarrow \mathcal{S}^{F(k,\cdot)}(1^\lambda)$.
3. If $b = 0$ set $r = F(k, x)$ else if $b = 1$ set $r \leftarrow \{0, 1\}^m$. Choose $s \leftarrow \{0, 1\}^d$ $u = \mathsf{Ext}(x; s)$ and $\mathsf{seed} \leftarrow \mathsf{Constrain}(k, C_{s,u})$.
4. Let $b' = \mathcal{D}(1^\lambda, \mathsf{seed}, \mathsf{aux}, r)$.

Hybrids 3 and 4 are indistinguishable by the same argument as the indistinguishability of hybrid 1 and 2.

Advantage in Hybrid 4: We now claim that in Hybrid 4, the advantage $|\Pr[b = b'] - \frac{1}{2}|$ is negligible by the no-constrained-evaluation security of the constrained PRF. In particular, we define a reduction that runs $(x, \mathsf{aux}) \leftarrow \mathcal{S}^{F(k,\cdot)}(1^\lambda)$ by making queries to its PRF oracle. The reduction chooses $s \leftarrow \{0, 1\}^d$, sets $u = \mathsf{Ext}(x; s)$ and gives the constraint $C_{s,u}$ together with the value x to its challenger. Since $\mathcal{S}$ is a legal source, x was never queried by the oracle and, by the definition of the constraint, we have $C_{s,u}(x) = 1$. Secondly, since $\mathsf{Ext}(\cdot; s)$ is a universal hash function, the probability that of any of the previous queries x_i made by $\mathcal{S}$ satisfy $\mathsf{Ext}(x_i; s) = \mathsf{Ext}(x; s)$ is also negligible. Therefore, our reduction makes no constrained-evaluation queries to the PRF.

So, the reduction is a legal attacker in the no-constrained-evaluation security game of constrained PRF. The reduction receives a value r, which is either $F(k, x)$ or uniform, along with a constrained key $k\{C_{s,u}\}$. It sets $\mathsf{seed} = k\{C_{s,u}\}$ and outputs the bit $b' = \mathcal{D}(1^\lambda, \mathsf{seed}, \mathsf{aux}, r)$. The advantage of the reduction in the constrained PRF security game is exactly the same as that of the adversary in hybrid 3, and therefore the latter is negligible.

Since the advantage in hybrid 3 is negligible and hybrid 3 is indistinguishable from hybrid 0, the advantage in hybrid 0 must be negligible as well. This proves the theorem.

Corollary 2. *Under the sub-exponential security of either the LWE assumption or the DDHI assumption in an arbitrary prime-order group, there exists an ED-Extractor for α-entropy sources with auxiliary info, for any $\alpha = \lambda^{\Omega(1)}$ and with any polynomial input length n and output length m. Security holds against polynomial-time sources and distinguishers.*

Proof. The work of [BV15] construct selectively secure constrained PRFs for all circuits from LWE. We can then use complexity leveraging to get adaptive security by assuming sub-exponential LWE. The results of [AMN+18] constructs no-evaluation secure PRFs for NC1 from the DDHI assumption in arbitrary prime-order groups (the also construct selectively secure PRFs from the DDHI assumption in specific groups). We then use complexity leveraging to get no-constrained-evaluation security under sub-exponential DDHI, as discussed in the remarks after Definition 5.

We use an extractor with output length $\alpha/4$ which is secure for entropy $\alpha' = \alpha/2$ with $\varepsilon = 2^{-(\alpha/8)} = \mathrm{negl}(\lambda)$. We combine this with a constrained PRF with output length $m = \alpha/2$ which ensures $\alpha \geq \alpha' + m$. This gives us an ED-Extractor with output length $\alpha/2 = \lambda^{\Omega(1)}$. We can then use a PRG to then get arbitrarily large polynomial output size as discussed in the Remark on Output Size in Sect. 3.

5.2   Negative Results for ED Extractors with Auxiliary Info

Our constructions of ED-Extractors in the auxiliary info setting have several disadvantages compared to our construction in the setting without auxiliary info. Firstly, in the auxiliary info setting we needed complex constructions based on "cryptomania" assumptions (LWE and DDHI), whereas in the setting without auxiliary info, we showed that any sufficiently secure PRF is a good ED-Extractor. Secondly, in the auxiliary info setting we only achieved security for polynomial-time distinguishers while in the setting without auxiliary info we got security even for computationally unbounded distinguishers. In this section, we give some evidence that the two setting are substantially different and that we indeed need to work harder and cannot hope for as much in the setting with auxiliary info.

Not All PRFs Are ED-Extractors with Aux Info. Firstly, we show that *not* every PRF is a good ED-Extractor in the setting with auxiliary info. We give two variants of this result. The first is based on collision-resistant hash functions (CRHFs) and gives a PRF that is not an α-ED-Extractor for entropy $\alpha = n - \lambda^{\varepsilon}$. The second one is based on fully homomorphic encryption and gives a PRF that is not an α-ED Extractor even for entropy $\alpha = n - 1$. In both cases, the result holds even if the PRF/ED-Extractor only outputs 1 bit.

CRHF-based Construction. Let $F' : \{0,1\}^{\ell} \times \{0,1\}^{n'} \to \{0,1\}$ be a PRF with key-length $\ell = \ell(\lambda)$, input length $n' = n'(\lambda)$ and output length 1. Let $H : \{0,1\}^{d} \times \{0,1\}^{n} \to \{0,1\}^{n'}$ be a collision-resistant hash function (CRHF) with seed length $d = d(\lambda)$, input length $n = n(\lambda)$ and output length $n' = n'(\lambda)$. We define a PRF $F : \{0,1\}^{\ell+d} \times \{0,1\}^{n} \to \{0,1\}$ as follows. Parse the key $k = (k', s)$ with $k' \in \{0,1\}^{\ell}, s \in \{0,1\}^{d}$. Define $F(k,x)$:

- If $x \leq d$ output $s[x]$, where we interpret x as an integer in the range $[2^n]$ and $s[x]$ denotes the x'th bit of s.
- Else output $F(k', H(s, x))$.

It is easy to see that F is a PRF if F' is a PRF and H is a CRHF. On the other hand it is not an $\alpha = (n - n')$-ED-Extractor. In particular, consider the source that queries the oracle on values $1, \ldots, d$ to learn the CRHF seed s. It then chooses a random $x \leftarrow \{0,1\}^{n}$ and outputs $x, \mathsf{aux} = H(s, x)$. It is clearly an α legal source. Yet we can define a distinguisher D that gets $k = (k', s)$, aux, r and outputs 1 iff $r = F(k', \mathsf{aux})$. Then D always outputs 1 if r is the outputs of the

ED-Extractor on x but only outputs 1 with probability $1/2$ if r is truly random, giving it a non-negligible advantage of $1/2$. For parameters, we note that the existence of CRHFs implies the existence of a CRHF with arbitrary polynomial input size $n = n(\lambda)$ and output size λ^ε for any constant $\varepsilon > 0$. Therefore, we get a PRF with arbitrary polynomial input size $n = n(\lambda)$ and output size $m = 1$, which is not an α-ED-Extractor for $\alpha = n - \lambda^\varepsilon$.

Theorem 6. *Assuming the existence of collision-resistant hash functions, for every polynomial $n = n(\lambda)$ and every constant $\varepsilon > 0$ there exists a PRF with n-bit input and 1-bit output which is not a secure α-ED-Extractor with auxiliary input for $\alpha = n - \lambda^\varepsilon$.*

FHE-based Construction. Let $F' : \{0,1\}^\ell \times \{0,1\}^{n'} \to \{0,1\}$ be a PRF with key-length $\ell = \ell(\lambda)$, input length $n' = n'(\lambda)$ and output length 1. Let $(\mathsf{KeyGen}, \mathsf{Enc}, \mathsf{Dec}, \mathsf{Eval})$ be an FHE scheme capable of evaluating the PRF F'. Furthermore assume that the ciphertexts are pseudorandom and that the Eval procedure is statistically circuit private. Assume that the key-generation algorithm and the encryption algorithm each use at most $d = d(\lambda)$ bits of randomness, and that the encryption of an ℓ-bit message produces an ℓ'-bit ciphertext. Define the PRF $F : \{0,1\}^{\ell+2d} \times \{0,1\}^n \to \{0,1\}$ as follows. Parse the key $k = (k', s_1, s_2)$ with $k' \in \{0,1\}^\ell, s_1, s_2 \in \{0,1\}^d$. Define $F(k, x)$:

- Check if $x \le \ell'$(where we interpret x as an integer in the range $[2^n]$). If so let $(\mathsf{pk}, \mathsf{sk}) \leftarrow \mathsf{KeyGen}(1^\lambda; s_1)$, $\mathsf{ct} \leftarrow \mathsf{Enc}(\mathsf{pk}, k; s_2)$. Output the x'th bit of ct denoted by $\mathsf{ct}[x]$.
- Else output $F(k, x)$.

It is easy to see that F is a secure PRF: by the security of the FHE with pseudorandom ciphertexts, we can replace ct by a uniformly random value independent of k, and by the security of the PRF F' the above is then a good PRF. On the other hand it is not an $\alpha = (n-1)$-ED-Extractor. In particular, consider the source that queries the oracle on values $1, \ldots, \ell'$ to learn the the ciphertext ct. It then chooses a random $x \leftarrow \{0,1\}^n$ and outputs $x, \mathsf{aux} = \mathsf{Eval}(F'(\cdot, x), \mathsf{ct})$ so that aux is an FHE encryption of $F'(k, x)$. Since Eval is circuit private aux does not reveal anything about x beyond $F(k, x)$ and therefore is an $\alpha = n - 1$ legal source. Yet we can define a distinguisher D that gets $k = (k', s_1, s_2)$, aux, r and outputs 1 iff $\mathsf{Dec}(\mathsf{sk}, \mathsf{aux}) = r$ where $(\mathsf{pk}, \mathsf{sk}) \leftarrow \mathsf{KeyGen}(1^\lambda; s_1)$. Then D outputs 1 with probability 1) if r is the outputs of the ED-Extractor on x, but only outputs 1 with probability $1/2$ if r is truly random, giving it a non-negligible advantage of $1/2 - \mathsf{negl}(\lambda)$. Therefore, we get a PRF with arbitrary polynomial input size $n = n(\lambda)$ and output size $m = 1$, which is not an α-ED-Extractor for $\alpha = n - 1$.

Theorem 7. *Assuming the existence of Fully Homomorphic Encryption (FHE) with statistical circuit privacy and pseudorandom ciphertexts, for every polynomial $n = n(\lambda)$ there exists a PRF with n-bit input and 1-bit output which is not a secure α-ED-Extractor with auxiliary input for $\alpha = n - 1$.*

Black-Box Separations. We now show give two black-box separation results, showing that certain types of ED-Extractors cannot be proven secure via a black-box reduction from virtually any "standard" computational assumption (e.g.,including general assumptions such as the existence of one-way functions or public-key encryption, as well as specific assumptions such as DDH, LWE, RSA, etc., even if we assume (sub-)exponential security). In particular, we show two results of this type. Firstly, we show that one cannot prove the security of any ED-Extractor in the auxiliary info setting against computationally unbounded distinguishers (and polynomial-time sources) under such assumptions. This is contrast to the setting without auxiliary info, where we were able to do so. Secondly, we show that one cannot prove security in the auxiliary input setting (even for polynomial-time sources and distinguisher) of any ED-Extractor that has a certain type of *seed-committing* property: if you query the extractor EDExt on some polynomial set of values $x_1, \ldots, x_q$ then the output uniquely fixes a single possible seed that could have produced it. This is true for many natural constructions, such as the Naor-Reingold PRF or most block-cipher and hash-function based constructions. (But is crucially not true for our constructions based on constrained PRFs.) We view this as partial evidence that more complex constructions are necessary in the setting with auxiliary info.

Note that these results do not show that ED-Extractors with such properties cannot be constructed; in fact the work of Coretti et al. [CDKT19] in the random-oracle model can be interpreted as showing that "good" hash functions are heuristically likely to be good ED-Extractors in the auxiliary info setting with security even against computationally unbounded distinguishers, *and* they are also likely to be seed-committing. However, our results show that we cannot prove security under standard assumptions.

Our results are of the same flavor as the work of Wichs [Wic13]. They define the class of (single-stage) cryptographic game assumptions, which are modeled via a game between a challenger and a stateful adversary. They require that any polynomial-time (or sub-exponential time) attacker has at most a negligible (or inverse sub-exponential) success probability in winning the game. This captures essentially all standard assumptions used in cryptography. However, the security definition of ED-Extractors is *not* a single-stage game since it involves two separate entities (the source and the distinguisher) who cannot share state.

We use the "simulatable attacker" paradigm (also called a meta-reduction) to prove our black box separations. This paradigm is formalized in [Wic13] and we give a high-level overview. To prove a separation, we design a class of inefficient attackers $\mathcal{A}_h$ indexed by some h that break the security property but otherwise satisfy any structural/legality conditions (e.g., being multi-stage, entropy conditions etc.). However we also design an efficient simulator $\mathcal{A}'$ that may not satisfy such conditions, such that one cannot distinguish between black-box access to $\mathcal{A}_h$ for a random h versus $\mathcal{A}'$. Therefore if some reduction can break an assumption given black-box access to every $\mathcal{A}_h$ it would also be able to do so given access to $\mathcal{A}'$. If for any polynomial ℓ we can further show such a simulatable attack which is $2^{-\ell(\lambda)}$ indistinguishable, then we also rule out black-box reductions under sub-exponential or even exponential assumptions.

Unbounded Distinguishers. We first give a black-box reduction for ED-Extractors in the auxiliary info setting with security against unbounded distinguishers. Since the distinguisher can be computationally unbounded, a black-box reduction cannot call it. Therefore it suffices to construct a class of simulatable inefficient sources $\mathcal{A}_h$ that satisfy the legality conditions and ensure that for the output (x, aux) it holds that $\mathsf{seed}, \mathsf{aux}, \mathsf{EDExt}(x, \mathsf{seed})$, is statistically far from $\mathsf{seed}, \mathsf{aux}, u$ where u is uniform. Our a high level, the source $\mathcal{A}_h$ that we construct makes oracle queries and inefficiently learns the function $\mathsf{EDExt}(\cdot, \mathsf{seed})$ sufficiently well to predict $\mathsf{EDExt}(x, \mathsf{seed})$ for a random x with high accuracy without querying it. It chooses such random x and sets aux to be a "statistically binding commitment" of its prediction for $\mathsf{EDExt}(x, \mathsf{seed})$. This ensures that the distribution of $(\mathsf{seed}, \mathsf{aux}, \mathsf{EDExt}(x, \mathsf{seed}))$ is statistically far from $(\mathsf{seed}, \mathsf{aux}, uniform)$. The commitment is generated using an exponentially large random function h and can therefore be simultaneously statistically hiding and binding. Therefore this attack is simulatable by an efficient simulator that chooses a random x and outputs a commitment to a random value.

Theorem 8. *For any candidate ED-Extractor* (SeedGen, EDExt) *with* $n(\lambda)$-*bit input and 1 bit output and for any polynomial* $\ell = \ell(\lambda)$ *there exists a* $2^{-\ell(\lambda)}$-*simulatable attack against the* $\alpha = (n-1)$-*ED-Extractor security of the candidate in the setting with auxiliary info and unbounded distinguishers.*

In particular, if there is a black-box reduction showing this type of security for the candidate based on the security of some cryptographic game $\mathcal{G}$, *then* $\mathcal{G}$ *is not secure. If the reduction is based on the* $2^{\ell(\lambda)}$-*security of the game* $\mathcal{G}$ *then* $\mathcal{G}$ *is not* $2^{\ell(\lambda)}$ *secure.*

Proof. Assume that the length of $\mathsf{seed} \leftarrow \mathsf{SeedGen}(1^\lambda)$ is bounded by $|\mathsf{seed}| \leq p(\lambda)$ for some polynomial p. Let $q = q(\lambda) = 3p(\lambda) + \lambda$. Let H_λ be the set of all functions from $\{0,1\}^{\ell(\lambda)}$ to $\{0,1\}$. For any $h \in \mathsf{H}_\lambda$, consider the inefficient source $\mathcal{S}_{\lambda,h}$ that chooses $x_1, \ldots, x_q$ uniformly at random and queries its oracle on them, gets back $y_1, \ldots, y_q$, and finds the (lexicographically first) value seed' such that $\mathsf{EDExt}(x_i, \mathsf{seed}') = y_i$ for all $i \in [q]$. It chooses a random x, computes $z' = \mathsf{EDExt}(x, \mathsf{seed}')$ and sets $\mathsf{aux} = (r, h(r) \oplus z')$ where $r \leftarrow \{0,1\}^\ell$.

First we claim that for any $h \in \mathsf{H}_\lambda$, the above source $\mathcal{S}_{\lambda,h}$ breaks the security of the ED-Extractor with auxiliary info and an unbounded distinguisher. It's easy to see that $\mathcal{S}_{\lambda,h}$ is a legal source with entropy $n - 1$ since x is uniformly random and aux can reveal at most 1-bit of information z' about x. Secondly, we claim that if $\mathcal{S}_{\lambda,h}$ has oracle access to $\mathsf{EDExt}(\cdot, \mathsf{seed})$, then with overwhelming probability the value seed' that it finds must agree with seed on at least $3/4$ of all inputs. Otherwise there exists some seed' that agrees with seed on $< 3/4$ inputs yet agrees with it on $x_1, \ldots, x_q$ which occurs with probability at most $2^p(3/4)^q = \mathsf{negl}(\lambda)$. This also implies that if we let $z' = \mathsf{EDExt}(x, \mathsf{seed}'), z = \mathsf{EDExt}(x, \mathsf{seed})$ in the experiment, then $z' = z'$ with probability $3/4 - \mathsf{negl}(\lambda)$. But this shows that the distribution $(\text{seed}, \text{aux}, u = \text{EDExt}(\text{seed}, x))$ is statistically far from $(\text{seed}, \text{aux}, u \leftarrow \{0, 1\})$ since in the first case, if we let $\text{aux} = (r, v)$ then $h(r) \oplus v = u$ with probability at least $3/4 - \text{negl}(\lambda)$ while in the second case this happens with probability at most $1/2$.

Secondly, we claim that for a random $h \leftarrow \mathsf{H}_\lambda$, the above source $\mathcal{S}_{\lambda, h}$ can be simulated by an efficient $\mathcal{S}'_\lambda$ that runs in time $\text{poly}(\lambda)$. We define $\mathcal{S}'_\lambda$ which chooses $x_1, \ldots, x_q$ uniformly at random and queries its oracle on them, gets back $y_1, \ldots, y_q$, and outputs a uniformly random $(r, v) \leftarrow \{0, 1\}^\ell \times \{0, 1\}$.

The only way that $\mathcal{S}_{\lambda, h}$ for a random h can be distinguished from $\mathcal{S}'_\lambda$ using black-box access is if two different executions of $\mathcal{S}$ use the same randomness r. Given Q queries to $\mathcal{S}$, this happens with probability at most $\text{poly}(Q)2^\ell$.

Seed-Committing Extractors. We show that one cannot prove security in the auxiliary input setting (even for polynomial-time sources and distinguisher) of any ED-Extractor that has a certain type of *seed-committing* property.

Definition 7. *An ED-Extractor is* seed-committing *if there exist some polynomial* $q = q(\lambda)$ *and some inputs* $x_1, \ldots, x_q \in \{0, 1\}^{n(\lambda)}$ *such that for any* $\text{seed}, \text{seed}'$ *for which* $\text{EDExt}(x_i, \text{seed}) = \text{EDExt}(x_i, \text{seed}')$ *for all* $i \in [q]$ *it must hold that for all* x^* *we have* $\text{EDExt}(x^*, \text{seed}) = \text{EDExt}(x^*, \text{seed}')$.

For example, if we use the Naor-Reingold PRF [NR97] as an ED-Extractor then it is seed-committing. Moreover, we believe that ED-Extractor constructions using standard hash-functions and block-cipher will be seed-committing.

Theorem 9. *For any candidate seed-committing ED-Extractor* (SeedGen, EDExt) *with* $n(\lambda)$-bit input and $m(\lambda)$ bit output and for any polynomial $\ell = \ell(\lambda)$ *there exists a* $2^{-\ell(\lambda)}$-simulatable attack against the $\alpha = (n-1)$-ED-Extractor *security of the candidate in the setting with auxiliary info.*

In particular, if there is a black-box reduction showing this type of security for the candidate based on the security of some cryptographic game $\mathcal{G}$*, then* $\mathcal{G}$ *is not secure. If the reduction is based on the* $2^{\ell(\lambda)}$-security of the game $\mathcal{G}$ then $\mathcal{G}$ *is not* $2^{\ell(\lambda)}$ *secure.*

Proof. Let H_λ be the set of all pairs of functions $h_1 : \{0, 1\}^\ell \rightarrow \{0, 1\}^{q\ell+1}$, $h_2 : \{0, 1\}^{q\ell+1} \rightarrow \{0, 1\}^\ell$. First we define $(\text{Enc}_{h_1, h_2}, \text{Dec}_{h_1, h_2})$ to be an information-theoretic authenticated encryption scheme whose key is h_1, h_2. In particular, $\text{Enc}_{h_1, h_2}(m) = (r, h_1(r) \oplus m, h_2(r, h_1(r) \oplus m))$ where $r \leftarrow \{0, 1\}^\ell$ is uniformly random and $\text{Dec}_{h_1, h_2}(r, c, \sigma) = h_1(r) \oplus c$ if $h_2(r, c) = \sigma$ and $\perp$ otherwise.

For any $h = (h_1, h_2) \in \mathsf{H}_\lambda$, consider an inefficient source/distinguisher pair $\mathcal{A}_{\lambda, h} = (\mathcal{S}_{\lambda, h}, \mathcal{D}_{\lambda, h})$ defined as follow. The source $\mathcal{S}_{\text{sec}, h}$ chooses $x_1, \ldots, x_q$ as given by the seed-committing definition and queries its oracle on them, gets back $y_1, \ldots, y_q$, and finds the (lexicographically first) seed' such that $\text{EDExt}(x_i, \text{seed}') = y_i$ for all $i \in [q]$. It chooses a random x, computes z' to be the first bit of $\text{EDExt}(x, \text{seed}')$ and sets $\text{aux} \leftarrow \text{Enc}_h(y_1, \ldots, y_q, z')$. The distinguisher $\mathcal{D}_{\lambda, h}$ gets $(\text{seed}, \text{aux}, u)$, it computes z to be the first bit of u. It sets

$\mathsf{Dec}_h(\mathsf{aux}) = (y_1, \ldots, y_q, z')$. If $\mathsf{EDExt}(\mathsf{seed}, x_i) = y_i$ for all $i \in [q]$ and $z' = z$ it outputs 0 else 1.

It is easy to see that, for any h, the adversary $\mathcal{A}_{\lambda,h}$ is an $\alpha = (n-1)$-legal adversary and breaks ED-Extractor security with advantage $1/4$: If the challenge bit is $b = 0$, the distinguisher always outputs 0 and if the challenge bit is $b = 1$ the distinguisher only outputs 1 with probability $> 1/2$.

Secondly, for a random $h = (h_1, h_2)$ the adversary $\mathcal{A}_{\lambda,h}$ can be efficiently simulated by a stateful adversary $\mathcal{A}' = (\mathcal{S}', \mathcal{D}')$ that acts as both the source and the distinguisher but allows them to share state. On input $y_1, \ldots, y_q$ to $\mathcal{S}'$, it chooses a random x, aux and remembers the tuple $(\mathsf{aux}, y_1, \ldots, y_q, x)$. On input $(\mathsf{seed}, \mathsf{aux}, u)$ to $\mathcal{D}'$ it checks if it stores a tuple of the form $(\mathsf{aux}, y_1, \ldots, y_q, x)$. If it does store such a tuple and $\mathsf{EDExt}(\mathsf{seed}, x_i) = y_i$ for all $i \in [q]$ and u is equal to the first bit of $\mathsf{EDExt}(x, \mathsf{seed})$ it outputs 0 else 1.

To show that one cannot distinguish between black-box access to $\mathcal{A}$ vs $\mathcal{A}'$ we define an intermediate $\mathcal{A}^*$ which is inefficient but also stateful. In particular, $\mathcal{A}^* = (\mathcal{S}^*, \mathcal{D}^*)$ acts just like $\mathcal{A}$, but instead of encrypting, the source $\mathcal{S}$ sets aux to be uniformly random and stores the tuple $(\mathsf{aux}, y_1, \ldots, y_q, z')$ and instead of decrypting $\mathcal{D}^*$ retrieves the tuple indexed by aux to uses the corresponding $(y_1, \ldots, y_q, z')$.

Firstly, we claim that $\mathcal{A}$ and $\mathcal{A}^*$ are indistinguishable by any (comp. unbounded) distinguisher that makes Q queries with probability better than $\mathsf{poly}(Q) \cdot 2^{-\ell}$. This essentially follows by the authenticated-encryption security of the encryption scheme.

Secondly, we claim that $\mathcal{A}^*$ and $\mathcal{A}'$ are perfectly indistinguishable. The only difference between them is that $\mathcal{A}^*$ compares u against the first bit of $\mathsf{EDExt}(\mathsf{seed}', x)$ while $\mathcal{A}'$ compares it against $\mathsf{EDExt}(\mathsf{seed}, x)$. But since $\mathsf{seed}, \mathsf{seed}'$ agree on $x_1, \ldots, x_q$, the seed-committing property ensures that $\mathsf{EDExt}(\mathsf{seed}', x) = \mathsf{EDExt}(\mathsf{seed}, x)$.

Acknowledgements. YD was partially supported by gifts from VMware Labs, Facebook and Google, and NSF grants 1314568, 1619158, 1815546. VV was supported in part by NSF Grants CNS-1350619 and CNS-1414119, an NSF-BSF grant CNS-1718161, the Defense Advanced Research Projects Agency (DARPA) and the U.S. Army Research Office under contracts W911NF-15-C-0226 and W911NF-15-C-0236, an IBM-MIT grant and a Microsoft Trustworthy and Robust AI grant. DW was supported by NSF grants CNS-1314722, CNS-1413964, CNS-1750795 and the Alfred P. Sloan Research Fellowship.

References

[AMN+18] Attrapadung, N., Matsuda, T., Nishimaki, R., Yamada, S., Yamakawa, T.: Constrained PRFs for NC^1 in traditional groups. In: Shacham, H., Boldyreva, A. (eds.) CRYPTO 2018, Part II. LNCS, vol. 10992, pp. 543–574. Springer, Cham (2018). https://doi.org/10.1007/978-3-319-96881-0_19

[BGI14] Boyle, E., Goldwasser, S., Ivan, I.: Functional signatures and pseudorandom functions. In: Krawczyk, H. (ed.) PKC 2014. LNCS, vol. 8383, pp. 501–519. Springer, Heidelberg (2014). https://doi.org/10.1007/978-3-642-54631-0_29

[BH05] Barak, B., Halevi, S.: A model and architecture for pseudo-random generation with applications to /dev/random. In: Atluri, V., Meadows, C., Juels, A. (eds.) ACM CCS 2005: 12th Conference on Computer and Communications Security, pp. 203–212. ACM Press, November 2005

[BHK13] Bellare, M., Hoang, V.T., Keelveedhi, S.: Instantiating random oracles via UCEs. In: Canetti, R., Garay, J.A. (eds.) CRYPTO 2013, Part II. LNCS, vol. 8043, pp. 398–415. Springer, Heidelberg (2013). https://doi.org/10.1007/978-3-642-40084-1_23

[BIW04] Barak, B., Impagliazzo, R., Wigderson, A.: Extracting randomness using few independent sources. In: 45th Annual Symposium on Foundations of Computer Science, pp. 384–393. IEEE Computer Society Press, October 2004

[Blu86] Blum, M.: Independent unbiased coin flips from a correlated biased source-a finite state Markov chain. Combinatorica **6**(2), 97–108 (1986)

[BST03] Barak, B., Shaltiel, R., Tromer, E.: True random number generators secure in a changing environment. In: Walter, C.D., Koç, Ç.K., Paar, C. (eds.) CHES 2003. LNCS, vol. 2779, pp. 166–180. Springer, Heidelberg (2003). https://doi.org/10.1007/978-3-540-45238-6_14

[BV15] Brakerski, Z., Vaikuntanathan, V.: Constrained key-homomorphic PRFs from standard lattice assumptions. In: Dodis, Y., Nielsen, J.B. (eds.) TCC 2015, Part II. LNCS, vol. 9015, pp. 1–30. Springer, Heidelberg (2015). https://doi.org/10.1007/978-3-662-46497-7_1

[BW13] Boneh, D., Waters, B.: Constrained pseudorandom functions and their applications. In: Sako, K., Sarkar, P. (eds.) ASIACRYPT 2013, Part II. LNCS, vol. 8270, pp. 280–300. Springer, Heidelberg (2013). https://doi.org/10.1007/978-3-642-42045-0_15

[CDKT19] Coretti, S., Dodis, Y., Karthikeyan, H., Tessaro, S.: Seedless fruit is the sweetest: random number generation, revisited. In: Boldyreva, A., Micciancio, D. (eds.) CRYPTO 2019, Part I. LNCS, vol. 11692, pp. 205–234. Springer, Cham (2019). https://doi.org/10.1007/978-3-030-26948-7_8

[CG85] Chor, B., Goldreich, O.: Unbiased bits from sources of weak randomness and probabilistic communication complexity (extended abstract). In: 26th Annual Symposium on Foundations of Computer Science, pp. 429–442. IEEE Computer Society Press, October 1985

[CG88] Chor, B., Goldreich, O.: Unbiased bits from sources of weak randomness and probabilistic communication complexity. SIAM J. Comput. **17**(2), 230–261 (1988)

[CGH+85] Chor, B., Goldreich, O., Håstad, J., Friedman, J., Rudich, S., Smolensky, R.: The bit extraction problem of t-resilient functions (preliminary version). In: 26th Annual Symposium on Foundations of Computer Science, pp. 396–407. IEEE Computer Society Press, October 1985

[CZ16] Chattopadhyay, E., Zuckerman, D.: Explicit two-source extractors and resilient functions. In: Wichs, D., Mansour, Y. (eds.) 48th Annual ACM Symposium on Theory of Computing, pp. 670–683. ACM Press, June 2016

[DORS08] Dodis, Y., Ostrovsky, R., Reyzin, L., Smith, A.D.: Fuzzy extractors: how to generate strong keys from biometrics and other noisy data. SIAM J. Comput. **38**(1), 97–139 (2008)

[DPR+13] Dodis, Y., Pointcheval, D., Ruhault, S., Vergnaud, D., Wichs, D.: Security analysis of pseudo-random number generators with input: /dev/random is not robust. In: Sadeghi, A.-R., Gligor, V.D., Yung, M. (eds.) ACM CCS 2013: 20th Conference on Computer and Communications Security, pp. 647–658. ACM Press, November 2013

[DRV12] Dodis, Y., Ristenpart, T., Vadhan, S.: Randomness condensers for efficiently samplable, seed-dependent sources. In: Cramer, R. (ed.) TCC 2012. LNCS, vol. 7194, pp. 618–635. Springer, Heidelberg (2012). https://doi.org/10.1007/978-3-642-28914-9_35

[DSSW14] Dodis, Y., Shamir, A., Stephens-Davidowitz, N., Wichs, D.: How to eat your entropy and have it too – optimal recovery strategies for compromised RNGs. In: Garay, J.A., Gennaro, R. (eds.) CRYPTO 2014, Part II. LNCS, vol. 8617, pp. 37–54. Springer, Heidelberg (2014). https://doi.org/10.1007/978-3-662-44381-1_3

[DVW19] Dodis, Y., Vaikuntanathan, V., Wichs, D.: Extracting randomness from extractor-dependent sources. Cryptology ePrint Archive, Report 2019/1339 (2019). https://eprint.iacr.org/2019/1339

[GGM84] Goldreich, O., Goldwasser, S., Micali, S.: How to construct random functions (extended abstract). In: 25th Annual Symposium on Foundations of Computer Science, pp. 464–479. IEEE Computer Society Press, October 1984

[GT16] Gaži, P., Tessaro, S.: Provably robust sponge-based PRNGs and KDFs. In: Fischlin, M., Coron, J.-S. (eds.) EUROCRYPT 2016, Part I. LNCS, vol. 9665, pp. 87–116. Springer, Heidelberg (2016). https://doi.org/10.1007/978-3-662-49890-3_4

[Hut16] Hutchinson, D.: A robust and sponge-like PRNG with improved efficiency. Cryptology ePrint Archive, Report 2016/886 (2016). http://eprint.iacr.org/2016/886

[ILL89] Impagliazzo, R., Levin, L.A., Luby, M.: Pseudo-random generation from one-way functions (extended abstracts). In: Johnson, D.S. (ed.) Proceedings of the 21st Annual ACM Symposium on Theory of Computing, Seattle, Washington, USA, 14–17 May 1989, pp. 12–24. ACM (1989)

[IZ89] Impagliazzo, R., Zuckerman, D.: How to recycle random bits. In: 30th Annual Symposium on Foundations of Computer Science, pp. 248–253. IEEE Computer Society Press, October/November 1989

[KPTZ13] Kiayias, A., Papadopoulos, S., Triandopoulos, N., Zacharias, T.: Delegatable pseudorandom functions and applications. In: Sadeghi, A.-R., Gligor, V.D., Yung, M. (eds.) ACM CCS 2013: 20th Conference on Computer and Communications Security, pp. 669–684. ACM Press, November 2013

[KRVZ11] Kamp, J., Rao, A., Vadhan, S.P., Zuckerman, D.: Deterministic extractors for small-space sources. J. Comput. Syst. Sci. **77**(1), 191–220 (2011)

[LLS89] Lichtenstein, D., Linial, N., Saks, M.E.: Some extremal problems arising form discrete control processes. Combinatorica **9**(3), 269–287 (1989)

[NR97] Naor, M., Reingold, O.: Number-theoretic constructions of efficient pseudo-random functions. In: 38th Annual Symposium on Foundations of Computer Science, pp. 458–467. IEEE Computer Society Press, October 1997

[NZ93] Nisan, N., Zuckerman, D.: More deterministic simulation in logspace. In: 25th Annual ACM Symposium on Theory of Computing, pp. 235–244. ACM Press, May 1993

[NZ96] Nisan, N., Zuckerman, D.: Randomness is linear in space. J. Comput. Syst. Sci. **52**(1), 43–52 (1996)

[PS18] Peikert, C., Shiehian, S.: Privately constraining and programming PRFs, the LWE way. In: Abdalla, M., Dahab, R. (eds.) PKC 2018, Part II. LNCS, vol. 10770, pp. 675–701. Springer, Cham (2018). https://doi.org/10.1007/978-3-319-76581-5_23

[PW08] Peikert, C., Waters, B.: Lossy trapdoor functions and their applications. In: Ladner, R.E., Dwork, C. (eds.) 40th Annual ACM Symposium on Theory of Computing, pp. 187–196. ACM Press, May 2008

[Raz05] Raz, R.: Extractors with weak random seeds. In: Gabow, H.N., Fagin, R. (eds.) 37th Annual ACM Symposium on Theory of Computing, pp. 11–20. ACM Press, May 2005

[ST17] Soni, P., Tessaro, S.: Public-seed pseudorandom permutations. In: Coron, J.-S., Nielsen, J.B. (eds.) EUROCRYPT 2017, Part II. LNCS, vol. 10211, pp. 412–441. Springer, Cham (2017). https://doi.org/10.1007/978-3-319-56614-6_14

[TV00] Trevisan, L., Vadhan, S.P.: Extracting randomness from samplable distributions. In: 41st Annual Symposium on Foundations of Computer Science, pp. 32–42. IEEE Computer Society Press, November 2000

[von51] von Neumann, J.: Various techniques used in connection with random digits. In: Householder, A.S., Forsythe, G.E., Germond, H.H. (eds.) Monte Carlo Method. National Bureau of Standards Applied Mathematics Series, vol. 12, pp. 36–38. U.S. Government Printing Office, Washington, D.C. (1951)

[Wic13] Wichs, D.: Barriers in cryptography with weak, correlated and leaky sources. In: Kleinberg, R.D. (ed.) ITCS 2013: 4th Innovations in Theoretical Computer Science, pp. 111–126. Association for Computing Machinery, January 2013

How to Extract Useful Randomness from Unreliable Sources

Divesh Aggarwal[3]($\boxtimes$), Maciej Obremski[3]($\boxtimes$), João Ribeiro[2], Luisa Siniscalchi[1], and Ivan Visconti[4]

[1] Concordium Blockchain Research Center, Aarhus University, Aarhus, Denmark
lsiniscalchi@cs.au.dk
[2] Imperial College London, London, UK
j.lourenco-ribeiro17@imperial.ac.uk
[3] National University of Singapore, Singapore, Singapore
divesh@comp.nus.edu.sg, obremski.math@gmail.com
[4] University of Salerno, Fisciano, Italy
visconti@unisa.it

Abstract. For more than 30 years, cryptographers have been looking for public sources of uniform randomness in order to use them as a set-up to run appealing cryptographic protocols without relying on trusted third parties. Unfortunately, nowadays it is fair to assess that assuming the existence of physical phenomena producing public uniform randomness is far from reality.

It is known that uniform randomness cannot be extracted from a single weak source. A well-studied way to overcome this is to consider several independent weak sources. However, this means we must trust the various sampling processes of weak randomness from physical processes.

Motivated by the above state of affairs, this work considers a set-up where players can access multiple *potential* sources of weak randomness, several of which may be jointly corrupted by a computationally unbounded adversary. We introduce *SHELA* (Somewhere Honest Entropic Look Ahead) sources to model this situation.

We show that there is no hope of extracting uniform randomness from a *SHELA* source. Instead, we focus on the task of *Somewhere-Extraction* (i.e., outputting several candidate strings, some of which are uniformly distributed – yet we do not know which). We give explicit constructions of *Somewhere-Extractors* for *SHELA* sources with good parameters.

Then, we present applications of the above somewhere-extractor where the public uniform randomness can be replaced by the output of such extraction from corruptible sources, greatly outperforming trivial solutions. The output of somewhere-extraction is also useful in other settings, such as a suitable source of random coins for many randomized algorithms.

In another front, we comprehensively study the problem of *Somewhere-Extraction* from a *weak* source, resulting in a series of bounds. Our bounds highlight the fact that, in most regimes of parameters (including those relevant for applications), *SHELA* sources significantly outperform *weak* sources of comparable parameters both when it comes to the process of *Somewhere-Extraction*, and in the task of amplification

A. Canteaut and Y. Ishai (Eds.): EUROCRYPT 2020, LNCS 12105, pp. 343–372, 2020.
https://doi.org/10.1007/978-3-030-45721-1_13

of success probability in randomized algorithms. Moreover, the low quality of somewhere-extraction from weak sources excludes its use in various efficient applications.

1 Introduction

Perfect (i.e., uniform) public randomness is an extremely valuable resource in computer science, and in cryptography in particular. For example, it can be used to create a Common Reference String (CRS) drawn from an uniform distribution, which is a widely used set-up for cryptographic protocols. However, the randomness that we can obtain from physical phenomena (such as solar radiation, temperature readings, and electricity fluctuations) is far from perfect (in particular when public randomness sources are taken into account). Such phenomena belong to the family of *weak* randomness sources [20]. These are sources that carry some min-entropy, but are still very far from uniformly distributed. As a result, in most applications a so-called randomness extractor must be applied to the weak sources in order to extract (close to) uniformly distributed bits. A basic result about randomness extraction dictates that deterministic extraction from one weak source is not possible. Nevertheless, deterministic extraction *is* possible if one has access to at least two independent weak sources.

Sampling from several independent physical weak sources presents serious security issues. For example, if different phenomena are being publicly measured (to ensure some kind of independence), then different instrumentation and potentially different entities must be involved in the sampling process. Not only that, but sampling may also be compromised by instrument failures. Going back to our CRS example, if we want to generate CRS from such sources, then we are assuming that every instrument and entity that took part in sampling the weak sources is trusted. This is not a desirable situation, and indeed it was previously noticed that generating a uniformly distributed CRS from such weak sources is complicated [15]. A natural question follows: *Which forms of common public set-up can we achieve (or, more generally, what kind of randomness can we extract) if some of the sources are maliciously corrupted, but some of them remain honest?*

Intuitively, this scenario leads us to define a structured weak source in an adversarial setting where a sample from the source is divided into multiple sub-parts, that we call *blocks*. One may imagine that each block corresponds to a different sampling process as per the previous paragraph. In this setting there is an ordered sequence of samplings from the sub-sources and some of them are controlled by the adversary. More specifically, the adversary can decide the positions of the honest blocks since it can decide which sampling processes to corrupt. Honest blocks correspond to (correct) samples from independent weak sources (these sources are known to the adversary but are not controlled by the adversary). Given a sequence of blocks the sampling proceeds by obtaining blocks in chronological order. As a result, if the i-th block is to be corrupted, then the adversary is allowed to fix it to any value based on the (already determined) values from the first through $(i-1)$-th blocks.

We will call such source a "t-out-of-ℓ" Somewhere Honest Entropic Look-Ahead (SHELA) source, where ℓ indicates the total number of blocks, out of which t must be honest. We consider only the case $t \geq 2$, since the case $t = 1$ essentially reduces to the setting with a single weak source. Moreover, we assume without loss of generality[1] that each block has length n, and the honest blocks have min-entropy at least k for some decent parameter k. Observe that corrupted blocks are heavily correlated with previous honest blocks, and may even have zero min-entropy. Moreover, we allow the number of honest blocks t to be any function of ℓ, as long as $t \geq 2$.

There is a second real-world scenario that can be naturally modelled as a SHELA source. Some blockchains can be considered as sequences of blocks generated in chronological order, some of which contain high min-entropy strings. For instance, such strings could be the new wallet's identifier used to cash a reward when a new block is added to the chain, financial data containing some min-entropy [21], or a random nonce added for some security reasons. It is well-known [40,59] that in a sequence of blocks of the blockchain there will be a fraction ν of them added by honest players. Moreover, we could assume that when a new block is added to the blockchain by an honest player, such a block (sometimes) contains high min-entropy strings that are independent of the previous ones already in the blockchain (we notice that a similar assumption has already been used in [66]). Therefore, if we consider ℓ consecutive blocks and for each of them we consider the part of the block that, in case the block is honest, could contain an independent weak source with decent min-entropy, we obtain a public SHELA source[2].

1.1 Our Contributions

Our main goal in this paper is to study SHELA sources and what kind of applications their availability enables.

The first natural question that arises when encountering SHELA sources is the following: *Are we able to extract independent and (close to) uniformly distributed bits from it?* We will prove in this work that the answer to this question is negative. Given this, we shift our focus from standard randomness extraction, and instead we investigate the possibility of constructing a deterministic *somewhere-extractor* SomeExt for SHELA sources. Intuitively, the somewhere-extractor SomeExt takes as input a SHELA source and outputs a distribution that is close (in statistical distance) to a convex combination of so-called "T-out-of-L" Somewhere-Random (SR) sources. SR sources are composed of L blocks,

---

[1] Given blocks of different sizes, one can always fill out the shorter blocks with zeros, similarly given blocks of different min-entropy we can assume k to be the minimum of min-entropies of honest blocks.

[2] In this example we are assuming that when using a blockchain as a SHELA source, the adversary of the sampling procedure from a SHELA source has no control over the choices of the honest blocks posted permanently in the blockchain (i.e., the adversary does not decide which honest block is selected and remains permanently in the blockchain out of multiple candidates).

T of which (at fixed, unknown positions) are jointly independent and uniformly distributed. We call a convex combination of SR-sources a convSR-source for short.

It turns out that convSR sources are an extremely useful type of randomness. For example, armed with our somewhere-extractor, we show how to build non-interactive (and thus accepted by any receiver) commitments from one-way functions and non-interactive (and thus publicly verifiable) witness indistinguishable proofs from generic complexity assumptions[3] when both players (a sender and a receiver, or a prover and a verifier, respectively) have access to a public SHELA source. Remarkably, convSR-sources are also important intermediate objects used in the construction of multi-source and non-malleable extractors for weak sources (we discuss this in more detail later).

Parameters of the somewhere-extractor for SHELA sources. The computational complexity and security of our applications of convSR-sources will heavily depend on various parameters of the convSR-source: the number of total blocks L, the number of "good" (i.e., independent and uniformly distributed) blocks T, and the length m of each block. In turn, these depend on the parameters of the underlying SHELA source and the quality of the somewhere-extractor.

Ideally, we want our somewhere-extractor SomeExt to extract a convSR source with low error, small number of total blocks, and large block length from a SHELA source. More precisely, the error ε of SomeExt should satisfy $\varepsilon = 2^{-\Omega(n)}$, where n is the block length of the SHELA source, the total number L of blocks of the convSR source should be at most $O(\ell)$, where ℓ denotes the total number of blocks in the SHELA source, and the length m of each output block should satisfy $m = \Omega(n)$. We will comment later that these parameters ensure that the output of SomeExt can be used in our applications without compromising security, while ensuring that the efficiency and reliability of the application in question remain good enough.

Moreover, we do not want to assume that honest blocks in the SHELA source must have significant amounts of min-entropy for extraction to be successful. Instead, we aim to extract such high-quality convSR-sources from SHELA sources whose honest blocks have *arbitrary* constant min-entropy rate. In other words, we allow the min-entropy k of each honest n-bit block to satisfy $k = \delta n$ for an arbitrarily small constant $\delta > 0$.

A very first naive approach to designing a somewhere-extractor (that we will denote by NaiveSomeExt) is to apply a c-source extractor, for $c \geq 2$, to every subset of c blocks of a SHELA source. This immediately leads to a convSR-source. However, the total number of output blocks satisfies $L = \Theta(\ell^c)$ for $c \geq 2$, where ℓ denotes the total number of blocks of the SHELA source. This leads to a much worse efficiency blow-up for applications than what we aim to obtain, as detailed earlier. Another problem of the naive construction is that, if we wish to minimize the blowup of L with respect to ℓ by setting $c = 2$, we run into problems of

---

[3] We will show how to start from any public-coin 2-round WI proof system in the standard model which in turn means any non-interactive zero-knowledge proof system in the common random string model [34].

explicitness. In fact, known explicit constructions of 2-source extractors require sources with high min-entropy to achieve exponentially small error [12,18,46]. We also note that, besides leading to worse efficiency, using a c-source extractor for $c > 2$ requires assuming that there are at least $c > 2$ honest blocks in the SHELA source, which might not be reasonable in some scenarios.

In this work, we design a non-trivial somewhere-extractor SomeExt that achieves our ideal goals put forth above. We begin by looking at the setting where the min-entropy rate k/n of honest blocks in the SHELA source is a large enough constant. In this case, if $X \in \{0,1\}^{n \cdot \ell}$ is a t-out-of-ℓ SHELA source with honest block min-entropy $k = \delta n$, then SomeExt(X) is ε-close to a T-out-of-L convSR-source $Y \in \{0,1\}^{m \cdot L}$ with $T = t - 1$, $L = \ell - 1$, $\varepsilon = 2^{-\Omega(n)}$, and output block length $m = \Omega(n)$. The only thing missing is that, as previously discussed, we wish to extract with similar parameters from SHELA sources whose honest blocks have arbitrarily small constant min-entropy rate (i.e., $k = \delta n$ for arbitrarily small constant $\delta > 0$). Notably, using a modified construction, we are able to transfer these ideal parameters to the "arbitrary constant min-entropy rate" setting. The only difference is that now $L = O(\ell)$.

Somewhere-extraction of SHELA source vs. weak source. We have already established that we can deterministically extract high-quality convSR-sources from SHELA sources. However, an attentive reader might notice that deterministic somewhere extraction is also possible from *weak sources*. In fact, any strong seeded (k, ε)-extractor with seed length d yields a somewhere-extractor with error ε, $L = 2^d$ total output blocks, and $T = 1$ uniform blocks for weak sources with min-entropy at least k by considering a block for each possible fixing of the seed. This naive construction of a convSR-source is actually crucial in many constructions of multi-source extractors (we expand on this later in this section). However, it has strong limitations. In particular, even if we use an optimal strong seeded extractor, seed length lower bounds [61] imply that

$$L = \Omega\left(\frac{1}{\varepsilon^2}\right). \tag{1}$$

This means that if we require $\varepsilon = 2^{-\Omega(n)}$, then $L = 2^{\Omega(n)}$, which precludes any efficient cryptographic application of the resulting convSR-source.

Given the above shortcoming, one might wonder whether significantly better somewhere-extractors exist for weak sources. We dedicate part of our paper to the study of this problem. It turns out that the answer to this question is largely negative. In particular, a disperser-based lower bound shows that, similarly to the naive construction above, *every* somewhere-extractor for weak sources with error $\varepsilon = 2^{-\Omega(n)}$ and output block length $m = \Omega(n)$ must have $L = 2^{\Omega(n)}$ total output blocks.

In our work, we derive a set of lower bounds that complement each other and succeed in showing that somewhere-extractors for weak sources must perform significantly worse than the analogous objects for SHELA sources over various regimes of parameters. We are particularly interested in lower bounds on the total number of blocks of the output convSR-source, as this dictates the computational complexity blow-up suffered by a protocol when using this source. In the end, we put forth the conjecture that the above lower bound (1) actually holds for *every* somewhere-extractor (regardless of the output block length m), and we make some progress towards proving it.

Randomized algorithms and amplification of success probability using SHELA source vs. weak source. We remark that convSR-sources are well-suited for simulation of randomized algorithms whose outputs can be efficiently checked for correctness (e.g., searching for witnesses for the membership of some string in an NP language, or approximation algorithms for NP languages). In fact, one can simply run the algorithm using each block as its randomness. As a result, one obtains a few candidate solutions, and can efficiently check if at least one of them is correct. The success probability of the algorithm is thus amplified by the number of good (i.e., uniform) blocks.

It is well-known and easy to see that, in the procedure above, we do not need good blocks to be exactly uniformly distributed. Indeed, it is enough to rely on the weaker guarantee that good blocks are sufficiently close to uniform in statistical distance, say, $1/\mathrm{poly}(n)$-close, where n is some soundness parameter. We call this weaker family of sources *somewhere-amplifiable* (SA) sources, and denote the class of convex combinations of SA-sources as convSA-sources.

While weak sources can be used to efficiently produce convSA-sources, we show that this comes at a heavy price: Roughly speaking, if one wants to generate enough, and long enough, good blocks for appropriate and efficient success probability amplification, then the weak source needs to have very high min-entropy. Therefore, in many reasonable regimes of parameters, one is unable to extract suitable convSA-sources from weak sources, while one can extract high-quality convSR-sources (a stronger notion) from SHELA sources in those regimes. We refer to Sect. 6 for a more detailed discussion.

We conclude from the two discussions above that there is a fundamental separation between somewhere-extraction from SHELA and weak sources. Indeed, we are able to efficiently extract convSR-sources with much higher quality from a SHELA source than what we can obtain from a weak source.

Non-interactive witness indistinguishable proofs assuming public-coin ZAPs and relying on public SHELA sources. In a proof system, a prover proves to a verifier the veracity of some statement $x \in \mathcal{L}$ (where $\mathcal{L}$ is an NP-language). A soundness property guarantees that it is unlikely that an honest verifier accepts the proof of a false statement. When a proof system is non-interactive any verifier is able to check the validity of the proof. Non-interactive proofs are therefore publicly verifiable and they are very appealing since the prover computes the proof once, while still it can be useful in many different cases (i.e., with many different verifiers). Non-interactiveness is usually trivial since a prover could just send a witness proving membership in the language. The interesting case consists of offering some form of privacy for the secret (i.e., the witness) of the prover. We will in particular consider witness indistinguishability

[36] that requires that the proof hides which witness has been used by the prover out of multiple witnesses. A special category of interactive proof systems is called "public coin" and refers to the role of the verifier that sends random strings only as messages. When there is only one message played by the verifier then a 2-round witness indistinguishable proof system is referred as ZAP [34]. The round of the verifier can be recycled among any polynomial number of proofs givens by provers. Since public-coin ZAPs exist, a natural question is whether the verifier can just be replaced by a sample from a high min-entropy source, therefore obtaining a non-interactive WI proof under the same computational assumptions of ZAPs and relying on the existence of SHELA sources. The answer is unfortunately negative. Indeed, consider the ZAP of [34]. The message of the prover consists of computing some non-interactive zero-knowledge (NIZK) proofs in the common random string model. In general, NIZK proofs (e.g., [36]) are not sound when the common random string is replaced by the output of high min-entropy sources. In turn, when trying to make a generic public-coin ZAP relying on a high min-entropy source non-interactive, soundness could be lost. Moreover, the issue with soundness remains also in case of parallel repetition since for some high min-entropy sources an accepting proof of a false statement can be produced with probability 1.

On the positive side, equipped with our constructive results about obtaining a convSR-source from a SHELA source, we show that assuming a public SHELA source, non-interactive witness indistinguishable proofs exist by just using a parallel repetition of any public-coin ZAP[4].

Finally, we notice that Goyal and Goyal [41] construct a non-interactive zero-knowledge argument of knowledge relying on any proof-of-stake (PoS) blockchain. The construction of [41] requires the existence of non-interactive witness-indistinguishable proof systems. If the proof-of-stake blockchain can be used to implement a SHELA source (as discussed previously), then by plugging our non-interactive witness-indistinguishable proof system in the construction of [41] we obtain a non-interactive zero-knowledge argument of knowledge with improved complexity assumptions using specific PoS blockchains.

Non-interactive commitments from one-way functions and SHELA sources. In a commitment scheme, sender and receiver interact in a commitment phase so that the (even malicious) sender can later on show only one message consistent with such interaction, while the (even malicious) receiver has no specific advantage in detecting the message committed by the sender. The security property for the receiver is called "binding" while the security for the sender is called "hiding".

Non-interactive commitments guarantee that the sender has to work only once to produce a commitment of a message, while this commitment can be used to convince any receiver about the committed message. We focus on statistically

---

[4] Notice that we are considering generic weak sources and it is unknown whether such distributions can all be efficiently simulatable. Consequently we cannot obtain a non-interactive zero knowledge proof.

binding commitments where, except with negligible probability, there is a unique message that is consistent with the transcript of the commitment phase, regardless of the computational power of the (even malicious) sender. A commitment scheme is "public coin" if the receiver sends only random strings.

Public-coin statistically binding commitment schemes in two rounds exist under the minimal assumption of the existence of any one-way function [56]. A natural question is whether, given any public-coin 2-round commitment scheme from one-way functions, the receiver can just be replaced by a sample from a high min-entropy source, therefore obtaining a non-interactive commitment scheme relying on the existence of SHELA sources[5]. We show that the answer is in general negative, by providing a variation of the construction of [56] where the binding property breaks down when the first round is sampled from a specific SHELA source. Moreover, parallel repetitions do not help to obtain binding. The construction of [56] can become non-interactive using any SHELA source, however in this last case there is a price to pay in communication complexity since the size of the resulting non-interactive commitment scheme is equal to the size of the SHELA source X.

The real good news come from using our tool: a convSR-source extracted from a SHELA source (without adding any computational assumption). Indeed, in this case we can get a non-interactive statistically binding commitment scheme just by running a parallel repetition of any public-coin 2-round statistically binding commitment scheme. When applied to the scheme of [56], we can get better communication complexity compared to the previously described approach that consists of using a SHELA source directly. Indeed, consider a 2-round statistically binding commitment scheme where the first round of the receiver (in the commitment phase) consists of λ bits, and let us assume that in each high min-entropy honest block of a 2-out-of-ℓ SHELA there are k bits of min-entropy, where $k \gg \lambda$. If $Y = \mathsf{SomeExt}(X) \in \{0,1\}^{m \cdot L}$ for $L = \ell - 1$ and we set $m = \lambda$ (by truncation), then $|Y| = m \cdot L \ll n \cdot \ell = |X|$. Therefore, with the parameters discussed above, if we instantiate the scheme of [56] using X directly, the resulting non-interactive commitment scheme has significantly worse communication complexity than the one built from the convSR-source.

Additional contributions. In the full version of this work [1], we also consider somewhere-extraction from an *online* variant of SHELA sources.

1.2   Related Work

Applications of convSR-sources in pseudorandomness. We would like to point out that the convSR-sources are also very useful in a context different than those already presented. Indeed, convSR-sources are key intermediate objects in several constructions of multi-source and non-malleable randomness extractors for weak sources. A central approach in such constructions is to reduce the task of extracting a uniform string from independent weak sources to that of extracting

---

[5] We recall that obviously a SHELA source is also a high min-entropy source.

such a string from one or more independent convSR-sources potentially satisfying a few additional properties, sometimes coupled with additional independent weak sources or small uniform seeds.

The connection between multi-source extraction and convSR-sources has been known since they were first defined [67]. convSR-sources have also been used in early constructions of seeded extractors [55].

Barak et al. [2] and Raz [64] showed how to convert two independent weak sources into an convSR-source with few blocks. This reduction was then used directly to obtain 3- and 4-source extractors with constant error. Such an approach has also proved useful in the construction of dispersers [2,3].

To obtain extractors for a constant number of sources with lower error and min-entropy requirement $n^{\Omega(1)}$, Rao [63] transforms independent input sources into several independent *aligned* convSR-sources, i.e., there is at least one position at which all convSR-sources have a uniform block. If the number of blocks in each convSR-source is not too large, then an iterative procedure succeeds in extracting a uniform string from such independent aligned convSR-sources with small error. Li [48] also used a similar approach with aligned convSR-sources to obtain better 3-source extractors.

An important step in many recent constructions of 2- and 3-source extractors [7,18,50–53] consists in generating convSR-sources with many "good" blocks (i.e., blocks close to uniform) which additionally satisfy a notion of w-wise independence for an appropriate parameter w: Every set of w good blocks is also close to jointly uniformly distributed. convSR-sources are also used in other recent constructions of multi-source extractors [22,23].

The usefulness of convSR-sources extends to more recent notions of randomness extraction. In fact, convSR-sources have been used in the construction of seedless non-malleable extractors [17] for weak sources, which are closely connected to non-malleable codes.

The ubiquity of convSR-sources (generated from weak sources) in extractor constructions provides one more compelling reason for our study of lower bounds for deterministic somewhere-extraction from weak sources.

Finally, we should mention that, because of the close connection between convSR-sources and randomness extraction from general weak sources, several works other than those already mentioned have focused directly on designing randomness extractors for the restricted class of convSR-sources [29,31–33,73]. Such extractors are usually called *mergers*.

Deterministic randomness extraction from restricted classes of sources. Our work is also related to the fundamental and well-studied problem of deterministic randomness extraction. Given the impossibility of deterministic extraction from general weak sources, the following natural question arises: *Under which conditions is deterministic randomness extraction possible from imperfect sources of randomness?*

Several works (some even predating the definition of weak sources [20]) have studied this question from various perspectives. Some works have considered deterministic randomness extraction from streams of bits generated i.i.d.

with unknown bias [35,57], or according to a Markov chain [11]. In a parallel line of research, settings where some input bits may be (adversarially or not) fixed, while the remaining ones are random, have also been considered [8,19,24,27,39, 45,54,60,62,69]. Other classes of sources considered in the context of deterministic extraction include sources with efficient sampling procedures [25,68] or sampled in small space [44], sources defined over subspaces [13,14,26,38,49,51,62,72], sources determined by zero sets of polynomials [30,47], sources sampled by Turing machines [70] or small circuits [71], and sets of independent weak sources (already discussed in this section). Some works have constructed such extractors for subclasses of Santha-Vazirani sources [4,5], which are known not to admit deterministic extraction in general. We note that Bentov, Gabizon, and Zuckerman [9] studied deterministic randomness extraction from the blockchain of Bitcoin, which has some connections to our model. However, their focus is on standard deterministic extraction, instead of somewhere-extraction. They show that standard deterministic extraction is impossible against an adversary with an unbounded budget, and then study the same problem against a "budget-constrained" adversary.

Although we are not dealing with standard randomness extraction like most of the works above, we present a result of a similar flavor: The restricted (and practically motivated) class of SHELA sources allows for deterministic *somewhere*-extraction with much better parameters than the class of weak sources.

Randomness extraction from adversarial sources. Subsequently to the announcement of our work, the problem of extracting randomness from adversarial sources (of which SHELA sources are an example) has received significant attention.

Chattopadhyay, Goodman, Goyal, and Li [16] study randomness extraction from an adversarial source model similar to SHELA sources. However, there are important distinctions between the two models, which we discuss next. In both cases, a source can be divided into blocks, some of which are independently generated and contain appropriate min-entropy, while other blocks are adversarially controlled. However, in SHELA sources the adversarial block is allowed to depend arbitrarily on all previous blocks (but *not* on subsequent blocks), while in [16] is only allowed to depend on at most d other arbitrary blocks for a small "locality parameter" d. Deterministic randomness extraction turns out to be possible in the adversarial model from [16], while it is impossible in the SHELA model and we instead study deterministic *somewhere*-extraction and its applications. Based on this, the results in these two models are incomparable.

Dodis, Vaikuntanathan, and Wichs [28] study seeded randomness extraction from so-called *extractor-dependent* sources. This adversarial model differs significantly from SHELA sources. At a very high level, a source is sampled by an adversary that is first allowed to query the extractor on different inputs with the same seed, with the condition that the source contains enough min-entropy and other sensible constraints to make the problem non-trivial. Extractor-dependent sources aim to capture scenarios where a random seed may be re-used several times.

1.3   Technical Overview on Deterministic Somewhere-Extraction from SHELA and Weak Sources

Impossibility of deterministic extraction from SHELA sources. We show that if at most a γ-fraction of the ℓ blocks in a SHELA source are honest, where $\gamma \in [0,1)$ is an *arbitrary* constant, and ℓ is a large enough constant depending on γ, then deterministic randomness extraction is impossible from this class of SHELA sources. Notably, this impossibility result holds even if we allow the honest blocks to be *uniformly distributed*, instead of only requiring them to have enough min-entropy.

This result is obtained by reducing the problem of deterministic extraction from SHELA sources to the problem of deterministic extraction from so-called *resettable* sources, introduced in [9]. In the same work, the latter problem has been shown to be closely related to deterministic extraction from Santha-Vazirani (SV) sources [65], which is widely known to be an impossible task. For more details we refer to [1].

Constructions of somewhere-extractors for SHELA sources. Our constructions of somewhere-extractors for SHELA sources are mainly based on the following trick, which we illustrate for a SHELA source with three blocks B_1, B_2, B_3, two of which are honest. If we applied the naive somewhere-extractor previously discussed with a 2-source extractor, we would obtain a convSR-source with three rows. Recall that one of our main goals is to reduce the total number of blocks in the resulting convSR-source as much as possible due to efficiency concerns. With this in mind, instead of applying the naive somewhere-extractor, we can notice that there are two cases:

- B_3 is honest. Then, B_3 and (B_1, B_2) are two independent weak sources. This means we can extract randomness from the two sources (B_1, B_2) and B_3;
- B_3 is not honest. Then, B_1 and B_2 are honest, and hence are independent weak sources. In this case, we can extract randomness from the two sources B_1 and B_2.

For the sake of this example, let Ext_1 and Ext_2 be two-source extractors, and compute $\mathsf{Ext}_1((B_1, B_2), B_3)$ and $\mathsf{Ext}_2(B_1, B_2)$.[6] The key observation, stemming from the two cases above, is that we are guaranteed that at least one of the two outputs is close to uniformly distributed. As a result, we obtain a convSR-source with two rows instead of three.

As already mentioned, we design explicit somewhere-extractors in two main settings. Our first, simpler, somewhere-extractor can be applied whenever the underlying SHELA source has $t \geq 2$ honest n-bit blocks with min-entropy $k = (1-\gamma)n$ for a small enough constant $\gamma > 0$. The construction is a generalization of

---

[6] In reality, we are able to use strong seeded extractors (for which we know much better explicit constructions) in place of two-source extractors. This is due to the disproportion in the size of the sources. In fact, the size of one of the sources given to the extractor grows linearly with the total number of blocks.

the reasoning we presented for three blocks above. It proceeds by iteratively using a strong seeded extractor to extract randomness from ever-growing sequences of blocks (using another block as a seed). A bit more precisely, if $X \in \{0,1\}^{n \cdot \ell}$ is a SHELA source and $X = (B_1, B_2, \ldots, B_\ell)$, then for every $i = 2, 3, \ldots, \ell$ we consider

$$B_i' = \mathsf{Ext}_i((B_1, \ldots, B_{i-1}), B_i), \tag{2}$$

where $(B_1, \ldots, B_{i-1})$ acts as the input weak source, B_i acts as the seed, and Ext_i is an appropriate strong seeded extractor. Then, we set $\mathsf{SomeExt}(X) = (B_2', \ldots, B_\ell')$. The first problem we run into is that in usual applications of seeded extractors, the seed is uniformly distributed. This is not the case here, since, even if B_i is an honest block, it is only guaranteed to have min-entropy $(1 - \gamma)n$. However, it is not hard to show, using the strongness of the extractor, that using a source with high min-entropy as the seed is sufficient. Another issue we encounter is that we are reutilizing many SHELA blocks when computing output blocks via (2). This appears to be at odds with the requirement that good output blocks should be close (in statistical distance) to independent and uniformly distributed. A careful conditioning argument, again exploiting the strongness of the extractor, shows that independence and uniformity are actually attained with small error. In fact, whenever B_i is honest and there is an honest block in $(B_1, \ldots, B_{i-1})$, we succeed in generating (with small error) a new good block of the output convSR-source. Instantiating this construction with the nearly-optimal GUV strong seeded extractor [43] and assuming the SHELA source $X \in \{0,1\}^{n \cdot \ell}$ has t honest blocks, we output a distribution $Y \in \{0,1\}^{m \cdot L}$ that is $(t \cdot 2^{-\Omega(n)})$-close to a T-out-of-L convSR-source with $m = \Omega(n)$. Moreover, from the discussion above it follows that $L = \ell - 1$ and $T = t - 1$.

In the second setting, we consider deterministic somewhere-extractors for SHELA sources with honest blocks having *arbitrary* constant min-entropy rate k/n. In other words, we allow the min-entropy requirement k of honest blocks to satisfy $k = \delta n$ for arbitrarily small $\delta > 0$. Notably, in this significantly harder setting we are able to obtain essentially the same parameters as the somewhere-extractor for the high min-entropy setting detailed above. In fact, all parameters remain unchanged, except that now we cannot guarantee that $L = \ell - 1$, and instead have the (still highly desirable) relationship $L = O(\ell)$. The main barrier towards making the previous construction work in this setting is that if honest blocks do not have high min-entropy, they can no longer be used as seeds for strong seeded extractors. This issue is surpassed by using the somewhere-condenser for weak sources from [2,64]. Intuitively, a somewhere-condenser is to a randomness condenser as a deterministic somewhere-extractor is to an extractor. On input a weak source with low min-entropy, the somewhere-condenser $\mathsf{SomeCond}$ outputs (with small error) a constant number of (sufficiently long) blocks with the guarantee that at least one block has very high min-entropy rate. Because the focus is not on extraction of *perfect* randomness, somewhere-condensers for weak sources are allowed to have much better parameters than somewhere-extractors for the same class of sources. We modify the construction for honest blocks with high min-entropy above by adding a first step of somewhere-condensation for each block of the input SHELA source. We show that our somewhere-extractors designed for SHELA sources can also be applied to *online* SHELA sources as is to extract convSR-sources (for full definitions and discussion please see [1]).

Lower bounds for deterministic somewhere-extraction from weak sources. We consider the natural problem of understanding the performance of somewhere-extractors for weak sources, and derive a set of lower bounds which show that, particularly for parameters relevant to cryptographic applications, *every* somewhere-extractor (regardless of efficiency) for weak sources must have significantly worse parameters than the somewhere-extractors we obtain for the class of SHELA sources. As previously discussed, these negative results for weak sources are strong enough that they preclude the use of convSR-sources generated from weak sources in efficient cryptographic protocols.

Suppose $\mathsf{SomeExt} : \{0,1\}^{\tilde{n}} \to \{0,1\}^{m \cdot L}$ is a somewhere-extractor for $(\tilde{n}, k)$-sources[7]. We begin by noting that a simple reasoning analogous to the proof of impossibility of deterministic extraction from weak sources immediately shows that $L = \Omega(\tilde{n} - k)$. Our first non-trivial lower bound is obtained by relating a somewhere-extractor to a *disperser* (for weak sources). Roughly speaking, a disperser is a fundamental pseudorandom object that transforms a weak source and a short uniform seed into an output distribution that hits every appropriately large subset of the output space with non-zero probability. Optimal seed length lower bounds are known for dispersers [61]. We show that if $\mathsf{SomeExt} : \{0,1\}^{\tilde{n}} \to \{0,1\}^{m \cdot L}$ is a somewhere-extractor for $(\tilde{n}, k)$-sources with error ε, then the function $G : \{0,1\}^{\tilde{n}} \times [L] \to \{0,1\}^m$ given by

$$G(x, i) = \mathsf{SomeExt}(X)_i$$

is a disperser with seed length $\log L$ and error ε. This immediately leads to a lower bound on the number L of output blocks of $\mathsf{SomeExt}$ (excluding a minor technicality that does not affect the quality of the lower bound),

$$L = \Omega\left(\frac{\tilde{n} - k}{\max(\varepsilon, 2^{-m})}\right). \tag{3}$$

This means, as discussed in more detail in Sect. 5, weak sources behave exponentially worse than comparable SHELA sources for somewhere-extraction in the linear output block length regime.

Note that the two lower bounds in the previous paragraph do not give anything when $k \approx \tilde{n}$ and m is small. This naturally leads us to consider lower bounds for L in an extreme 1-bit block setting with $k = \tilde{n} - 1$ and $m = 1$. Although we do not obtain a lower bound for extraction of convSR-sources in this extreme regime, we are able to prove a non-trivial lower bound that scales with the error for the harder, but related, task of extracting an SR-source from a weak source (*not* a convex combination of SR-sources as before). Note that,

---

[7] The set of $(\tilde{n}, k)$-sources consists of all weak sources over $\{0,1\}^{\tilde{n}}$ with min-entropy at least k. We use $\tilde{n}$ to avoid confusion with the block length of SHELA sources.

in particular, the naive somewhere-extractor obtained by enumerating the seed of a strong extractor satisfies this property. To be precise, we show that in this setting we must have

$$L = \Omega\left(\log\left(\frac{1}{\max(\varepsilon, 2^{-k})}\right)\right). \tag{4}$$

The lower bound in (4) is obtained by an adaptive version of the basic argument for the impossibility of deterministic extraction from weak sources. Given a candidate function $F : \{0,1\}^{\tilde{n}} \to \{0,1\}^{L}$, our goal is to show the existence of a weak source $X^{\star}$ with enough min-entropy such that *every* bit $F(X^{\star})_i$ is sufficiently biased. We begin by setting $X_0^{\star}$ to be uniformly distributed over $\{0,1\}^{\tilde{n}}$, and analyze its performance w.r.t. F. If $F_i(X_0^{\star})$ is the first bit close to uniform, we remove an appropriate set of elements from the support of $X_0^{\star}$ to obtain $X_1^{\star}$ such that $F_i(X^{\star})$ biased enough. Then, we repeat the reasoning with the new source $X_1^{\star}$ and so on, until every bit is biased[8]. Then, L must be large enough to ensure the outcome $X^{\star}$ of this process has too small support (and hence does not satisfy the min-entropy requirement of F), which yields the lower bound.

With these bounds in mind, it is natural to consider whether arguments that yield lower bounds of this type on the seed length of extractors, more precisely the granularity argument of Nisan and Zuckerman [58, Theorem 3] and the techniques due to Radhakrishnan and Ta-Shma [61, Section 2.2], could be extended to the setting of somewhere-extraction. Unfortunately, such arguments crucially rely on the ability of picking a seed at random: There, one is only worried about showing that the bias is large enough *on average*, while we must show that the bias is large enough *for every choice of the seed*[9].

1.4   Technical Overview on Non-Interactive Proof Systems and Commitments from Public SHELA Sources

Non-interactive (publicly verifiable) witness indistinguishable proof system. We will now describe how to construct a non-interactive (and therefore publicly verifiable) Witness Indistinguishable (WI) proof system Π_{pv} from a public SHELA source X and starting with the existence of a public-coin ZAP Π. Π_{pv} works as follows: The prover of Π_{pv} receives X and runs the somewhere-extractor $\mathsf{SomeExt}$ on X to obtain $(R_1, \ldots, R_L)$. Then, the prover on input the witness w for the statement x computes a second-round π_i from Π using R_i for $i = 1, \ldots, L$. The verifier of Π_{pv}, having access to X, also computes $(R_1, \ldots, R_L) = \mathsf{SomeExt}(X)$, and accepts the proof only if all pairs (R_i, π_i) are accepting by the verifier of Π w.r.t. the statement x. Observe that WI of Π is preserved under parallel composition and holds even when the first round of Π is chosen by a malicious verifier. Therefore, Π_{pv} also enjoys the WI property. The

---

[8] When biasing the next coordinates, we have to be careful not to 'spoil' biases of previous coordinates. This results in the log factor in the bound.

[9] By *seed* we mean i in $F_i(X^{\star})$.

soundness of Π_{pv} is based on the observation that T blocks of $(R_1, \ldots, R_L)$ are negligibly close to a uniform distribution over $\{0,1\}^m$. Denote them by $R_{I_1}, \ldots, R_{I_T}$. Then, the soundness of Π ensures that a malicious prover could not cheat when the second round of Π is computed w.r.t. $R_{I_1}, \ldots, R_{I_T}$.

As a result, using known constructions of public-coin ZAPs, we are able to construct a non-interactive WI proof system from trapdoor permutations that requires as a set-up a SHELA source only. Notice that a SHELA source is a CRS that can be corrupted (in a natural, structured manner) by an unbounded adversary. Still, we assume that the adversarial verifier can run only in polynomial time to distinguish the witness, even though he does not have such restriction when affecting the sample from the public SHELA source. Previous constructions of non-interactive WI proof systems either require a common random string as set-up, or were based on specific number-theoretic hardness assumptions in bilinear groups [37, 42], or on indistinguishability obfuscation and one-way permutations [10].

From another point of view, one can see our result as a Non-Interactive (NI) WI proof system where the soundness and the WI property hold even when the set-up phase is partially generated by the adversary. We note that the work of [6] investigates if soundness and WI of a NIWI proof system hold even when the adversary takes complete control of the set-up phase. They achieve a positive result relying on some specific number-theoretic assumption in bilinear groups. Instead, our NIWI proof system can be instantiated from trapdoor permutations and the adversary has only a partial control over the set-up.

Notice that [15] studies cryptographic protocols with simulatable security by considering a simulatable CRS drawn from a high min-entropy distribution. In this work we do not assume that public sources of randomness are simulatable and we do not investigate simulatable security. Our CRS is not a generic min-entropy string but instead corresponds to a structured min-entropy source that is partially controlled by an unbounded adversary.

Given the above construction of a non-interactive WI proof system Π_{pv}, one could argue that a convSA-source suffices for constructing Π_{pv}. Recall that a convSA-source is a convex combination of T-out-of-L SA-sources, which consist of L blocks, T of which are independent and $\frac{1}{\text{poly}(n)}$-close to uniform in statistical distance, where n is some relevant security parameter. This is because the soundness of the protocol can be amplified by using the T "good" blocks, which correspond to independent parallel repetitions of the underlying protocol Π.

In order to adequately compare the performance of the protocol under convSA-extraction from weak sources and convSR-extraction from SHELA sources, we compare a t-out-of-ℓ SHELA source $X \in \{0,1\}^{n \cdot \ell}$ with honest blocks having linear min-entropy k' with an arbitrary weak $(\tilde{n} = n \cdot \ell, k = k' \cdot t)$-source $\tilde{X}$. We are able to show that convSR-sources extracted from X are much better suited for applications than convSA-sources generated from $\tilde{X}$ in two aspects:

1. **Efficiency:** The efficiency of Π_{pv} depends on L. It is not hard to see that every convSA-source extractor for weak sources $\tilde{X}$ must have $\Omega(\tilde{n}) = \Omega(n \cdot \ell)$ total output blocks (even if we only require constant error). On the other hand, we can extract convSR-sources from X with only $O(\ell)$ blocks.

2. **Security:** Let us assume that Π requires a first round of $m = \Omega(k')$ bits. Then, we show that every *efficient, low-error* convSA-source extractor for weak sources outputs at most $T = O(k/m) = O(k' \cdot t/m)$ *good* blocks of length m. As a result, if t is constant, it follows that such an extractor only outputs $T = O(1)$ good blocks. This is not enough to successfully amplify the soundness of the protocol. Finally, we note that if we build our Π_{pv} starting from a convSR-source extracted from a t-out-of-ℓ SHELA source with constant t, the analysis of soundness described in this subsection holds, and therefore Π_{pv} is sound.

Improving the efficiency of [66]. We note that the work of [66] constructs a publicly verifiable proof system from any blockchain under some assumptions on the min-entropy of honestly generated blocks. Notably, under the same assumptions the blockchain can be used to implement also a SHELA source. In [66], the authors construct a publicly verifiable proof system by applying the naive somewhere-extractor NaiveSomeExt (that we discussed earlier) to extract a convSR-source from the blockchain. Therefore our somewhere-extractor SomeExt (instead of NaiveSomeExt) could be used in their work to immediately improve the efficiency of their proof system. More details are provided in [1].

Non-interactive statistically binding commitments. We introduce now a construction of non-interactive statistically binding commitments from a public SHELA source relying on one-way functions. This is achieved by making use of any two-round public-coin commitment scheme Π_{com} from one-way functions.

First of all, we remark that one can not simply replace the first round of Π_{com} with a sample from a source with linear min-entropy (say, min-entropy $0.5n$). Indeed, start from Π_{com} and consider a scheme Π'_{com} where: (a) the random string played as first round of Π_{com} must be twice in length, and (b) the sender ignores the first half of the first round and continues as in Π_{com} using the second half. It is straightforward to see that Π'_{com} is a 2-round public-coin statistically binding commitment scheme from any one-way functions. If we replace the first round of Π'_{com} with the output of a high min-entropy source we might have that the entire min-entropy is in the first half of the first round and is therefore wasted completely. The malicious sender could therefore violate binding since it would end up running Π_{com} on input a first round with zero min-entropy! Obviously, in this case parallel repetition does not help.

We now proceed to describe how our scheme Π_{compv} works starting with any 2-round public-coin statistically binding commitment scheme (including the above Π'_{com}). Moreover, Π_{compv} can be run with efficient parameters because of the use of SomeExt.

Our commitment scheme Π_{compv} works as follows: First, the sender runs the somewhere-extractor SomeExt on the public SHELA source X, obtaining $\mathsf{SomeExt}(X) = (R_1, \ldots, R_L)$. Then, the sender on input the message m and R_i (used as the receiver's first round) computes a commitment com_i and the opening information dec_i using the sender of Π_{com}, for $i = 1, \ldots, L$. In the opening phase, the receiver on input $\mathsf{dec}_1, \ldots, \mathsf{dec}_L$ having access to X computes

$(R_1, \ldots, R_L) = \mathsf{SomeExt}(X)$, and outputs the message m only if it holds that for all $i = 1, \ldots, L$ the message committed in com_i is m. Hiding of our scheme holds from the observation that hiding is preserved under parallel composition and when the first round of Π_{com} is chosen by a malicious receiver. The binding of Π_{compv} is based on the observation that at least T blocks $R_{I_1}, \ldots, R_{I_T}$ are negligibly close to a uniform distribution over $\{0,1\}^m$. This implies that there are at least T commitments computed w.r.t. a good block R_{I_j} that is statistically close to a first round sent by a receiver of Π_{com}. Therefore, from the statistically binding of Π_{com} it follows that a malicious sender could not cheat when the commitment is computed w.r.t. $R_{I_1}, \ldots, R_{I_T}$.

1.5 Open Questions

We present some interesting directions for future research:

- Prove (or disprove) Conjecture 12.
- Given any SHELA or convSR source, we can define its *rate* as number of good[10] blocks divided by total number of blocks. Our constructions from Sect. 4 transform SHELA sources with rate t/ℓ into convSR-sources with rate $\frac{t-1}{\ell-1} \leq \frac{t}{\ell}$. We conjecture that the rate of the output convSR-source cannot be larger than t/ℓ.
- Find good bounds on the number of output blocks of convSA-source extractors for weak sources.

1.6 Organization of the Paper

We introduce relevant notation and definitions in Sect. 2. SHELA sources are defined in Sect. 3, and deterministic somewhere-extractors are presented in Sect. 4. Lower bounds for somewhere-extraction are studied in Sect. 5, and the limits of SA-source extraction are considered in Sect. 6. Detailed arguments, along with standard definitions and lemmas, have been deferred to the full version [1].

2 Preliminaries and Definitions

2.1 Notation

Sets are usually denoted by calligraphic letters such as $\mathcal{S}$ and $\mathcal{I}$. Random variables are usually denoted by uppercase letters such as X, Y, and Z. We may identify a random variable X with its distribution. The support of a distribution X is denoted by $\mathsf{supp}(X)$. We denote the uniform distribution over $\{0,1\}^m$ by U_m. We may write $X \sim Y$ to denote that X has the same distribution as Y. All logarithms $\log$ are taken to base 2. The Shannon entropy of a distribution X is denoted by $H(X)$, and we denote the binary entropy function by h. The notation $\mathsf{poly}(n)$ denotes an arbitrary polynomial in n. We denote a negligible function of a parameter n by $\mathsf{negl}(n)$.

---

[10] For a SHELA source, a good blocks correspond to honest blocks, while they correspond to jointly uniform blocks in convSR-sources.

2.2   Somewhere-Random Sources and Somewhere-Extractors

In this section, we define SR- and convSR-sources, along with the notion of a deterministic somewhere-extractor and a basic result.

Definition 1 (Somewhere-random source). *A distribution* $X = (X_1, \ldots, X_L)$ *over* $\{0,1\}^{m \cdot L}$ *is said to be a* (T, L, m)-*somewhere-random source, SR-source in short, if there exist indices* $i_1 < i_2 < \cdots < i_T$ *such that the tuple* $(X_{i_1}, X_{i_2}, \ldots, X_{i_T})$ *is uniformly distributed over* $\{0,1\}^{m \cdot T}$. *We denote the set of all* (T, L, m)-*somewhere-random sources by* $\mathsf{SR}_{T,L,m}$, *and the set of all convex combinations of sources in* $\mathsf{SR}_{T,L,m}$ *by* $\mathsf{convSR}_{T,L,m}$.

Definition 2 (Somewhere-extractor). *Given a set of sources* $\mathcal{F}$ *over* $\{0,1\}^{\tilde{n}}$, *a function* $\mathsf{SomeExt} : \{0,1\}^{\tilde{n}} \to \{0,1\}^{m \cdot L}$ *is said to be a* (T, L, ε)-*somewhere-extractor for* $\mathcal{F}$ *if for every* $X \in \mathcal{F}$ *there exists* $Y \in \mathsf{convSR}_{T,L,m}$ *such that*

$$\mathsf{SomeExt}(X) \approx_\varepsilon Y.$$

A simple construction shows that strong (k, ε)-extractors imply the existence of deterministic somewhere-extractors for the class of general (n, k)-sources with the same error ε.

Lemma 3. *Let* $\mathsf{Ext} : \{0,1\}^n \times \{0,1\}^d \to \{0,1\}^m$ *be a strong* (k, ε)-*extractor, and set* $\{0,1\}^d = \{s_1, s_2, \ldots, s_{2^d}\}$. *Given* $x \in \{0,1\}^n$, *define* $\mathsf{SomeExt}(x) : \{0,1\}^n \to \{0,1\}^{m \cdot 2^d}$ *as*

$$\mathsf{SomeExt}(x) = (\mathsf{Ext}(x, s_1), \mathsf{Ext}(x, s_2), \ldots, \mathsf{Ext}(x, s_{2^d})).$$

Then, $\mathsf{SomeExt}$ *is a* $(1, 2^d, \varepsilon)$-*somewhere-extractor for the class of* (n, k)-*sources.*

The construction from Lemma 3 actually guarantees that a very large fraction of blocks of $Y = \mathsf{SomeExt}(X)$ will be close to uniform over $\{0,1\}^m$, provided X is an (n, k)-source. However, there is no guarantee that any pair of blocks (Y_{i_1}, Y_{i_2}) will be close to uniformly distributed over $\{0,1\}^{2m}$, as we cannot ensure that such blocks are close to being independent. Therefore, we only know that Y is ε-close to a $(1, 2^d, m)$-somewhere-random source.

2.3   Somewhere-Condensers

In this section, we introduce somewhere-condensers and related notions.

Definition 4 (Somewhere-entropic source). *A distribution* $X = (X_1, \ldots, X_L)$ *over* $\{0,1\}^{m \cdot L}$ *is said to be a* (T, L, m, k)-*somewhere-entropic source if there exist indices* $i_1 < i_2 < \cdots < i_T$ *such that the random variables* $X_{i_1}, X_{i_2}, \ldots, X_{i_T}$ *are independently distributed and satisfy* $\mathbf{H}_\infty(X_{i_j}) \geq k$ *for all* j. *We denote the set of all* (T, L, n, k)-*somewhere-entropic sources by* $\mathsf{SE}_{T,L,n,k}$, *and the set of all convex combinations of sources in* $\mathsf{SE}_{T,L,n,k}$ *by* $\mathsf{convSE}_{T,L,n,k}$.

Definition 5 (Somewhere-condenser). *A function* SomeCond : $\{0,1\}^n \rightarrow \{0,1\}^{m\cdot\ell}$ *is said to be a* (k, k', L, ε)-*somewhere condenser if for every* (n, k)-*source X there exists $Y \in$* convSE$_{1,L,m,k'}$ *such that*

$$\text{SomeCond}(X) \approx_\varepsilon Y.$$

There exist explicit constructions of somewhere-condensers with a constant number of output blocks, linear output block length, and exponentially small error for arbitrarily low linear min-entropy.

Lemma 6 ([64]). *For all constants $\delta, \delta' > 0$ there exist constants $b, \beta, \rho > 0$ such that for large enough n there exists an explicit (k, k', b, ε)-somewhere condenser* SomeCond : $\{0,1\}^n \rightarrow \{0,1\}^{m\cdot b}$ *with $k = \delta n$, $m = \beta n$, $k' = (1 - \delta')m$, and $\varepsilon = 2^{-\rho m}$.*

Remark 1. The version of Lemma 6 presented in [64] is specialized for $\delta' = \delta$. However, inspection of [64, Lemmas 4.2 and 4.3] shows that the construction works for any constant $\delta' > 0$, as long as we allow the constants ℓ, β, ρ to depend simultaneously on δ and δ'. This observation is similar to the remark in [2] after Theorem 5.2.

3 SHELA Sources

In this section, we give a formal definition of Somewhere Honest Entropic Look Ahead (SHELA) sources, and present explicit constructions of somewhere-extractors with good parameters for this class of sources.

Definition 7 (SHELA source). *A distribution $X \in \{0,1\}^{n\cdot\ell}$ is said to be an (n, k, t, ℓ)-SHELA source if there exist random variables $1 \leq I_1 < I_2 < \cdots < I_t \leq \ell$ with arbitrary joint distribution, t independent (n, k)-sources $Z_1, Z_2, \ldots, Z_t$, and a (possibly randomized) adversary $\mathcal{A}$ such that X is generated as follows:*

1. *Sample $(i_1, i_2, \ldots, i_t) \leftarrow (I_1, I_2, \ldots, I_t)$;*
2. *For each $j \in [t]$, set $B_{i_j} \leftarrow Z_j$;*
3. *For each $i \in [\ell] \setminus \{i_1, \ldots, i_t\}$, $\mathcal{A}$ sets $B_i = \mathcal{A}(B_1, \ldots, B_{i-1}, i_1, \ldots, i_t)$;*
4. *Set $X = (B_1, B_2, \ldots, B_\ell)$.*

We denote the set of all such SHELA sources by SHELA$_{n,k,t,\ell}$.

A precise definition of online SHELA sources discussed in Sect. 1, along with associated notions and results on deterministic somewhere-extraction, can be found in [1].

4 Deterministic Somewhere-Extractors for SHELA Sources

In this section, we construct deterministic somewhere-extractors for regular SHELA sources.

4.1   Honest Blocks with High Min-Entropy

In this section, we consider the case where each honest block in a SHELA source has min-entropy $(1-\gamma)n$ for some sufficiently small constant $\beta > 0$. The following result states that an explicit somewhere-extractor with exponentially small error and linear output block length exists for such SHELA sources. Notably, it is also the case that if the number of honest input blocks is t and the total number of input blocks is ℓ, then the number of uniform output blocks is $T = t - 1$ and the number of total output blocks is $L = \ell - 1$.

Theorem 8. *There exists a small enough constant $\gamma > 0$ such that for n large enough and $2 \leq t \leq \ell \leq \text{poly}(n)$ there exists an explicit $(t-1, \ell-1, \varepsilon')$-somewhere extractor* $\textsf{SomeExt} : \{0,1\}^{n \cdot \ell} \to \{0,1\}^{m \cdot (\ell-1)}$ *for* $\textsf{SHELA}_{n,k',t,\ell}$ *with* $k' = (1-\gamma)n$, $m = \frac{(1-7\gamma)n}{3}$, *and* $\varepsilon' = 2(t-1) \cdot 2^{-\gamma n}$.

The construction we use to prove Theorem 8 makes use of the following objects: For $i \in \{2, \ldots, \ell\}$, let $\textsf{Ext}_i : \{0,1\}^{n \cdot (i-1)} \times \{0,1\}^n \to \{0,1\}^m$ be an average-case strong seeded (k, ε)-extractor with $k = 2k'/3$, $k' = (1-\gamma)n$, $m = \frac{(1-7\gamma)n}{3}$ and $\varepsilon = 2^{-2\gamma n}$ for a small enough constant $\gamma > 0$. These can be obtained by using the explicit GUV extractor [43] with appropriate parameters. The instantiation is detailed in [1]. We are now ready to describe our construction of the somewhere-extractor $\textsf{SomeExt} : \{0,1\}^{n \cdot \ell} \to \{0,1\}^{m \cdot (\ell-1)}$ for $X \in \textsf{SHELA}_{n,k,t,\ell}$. First, write $X = (B_1, B_2, \ldots, B_\ell)$. Then, the output $\textsf{SomeExt}(X)$ can be written as $\textsf{SomeExt}(X) = (B'_2, B'_3, \ldots, B'_\ell)$, where each B'_i is obtained as

$$B'_i = \textsf{Ext}_i((B_1, B_2, \ldots, B_{i-1}), B_i) \in \{0,1\}^m. \tag{5}$$

4.2   Honest Blocks with Low Linear Min-Entropy

In this section, we construct somewhere-extractors for SHELA sources that have honest blocks with min-entropy δn for some arbitrarily small constant $\delta > 0$. We show that there is an explicit somewhere-extractor for such SHELA sources with exponentially small error and linear output block length. Moreover, if the number of input honest and total blocks are t and ℓ, respectively, then the number of output uniform and total blocks are $T = t - 1$ and $L = O(\ell)$, respectively.

Theorem 9. *For every constant $\delta > 0$ there exist constants $a_1, a_2, a_3 > 0$ such that for n large enough and all $2 \leq t \leq \ell \leq \text{poly}(n)$ there exists an explicit (T, L, ε')-somewhere extractor* $\textsf{SomeExt} : \{0,1\}^{n \cdot \ell} \to \{0,1\}^{m \cdot L}$ *for* $\textsf{SHELA}_{n,k',t,\ell}$ *with $k' = \delta n$, $m = a_1 \cdot n$, $\varepsilon' = 2(t-1)2^{-a_2 \cdot n}$, $T = t - 1$, and $L = a_3 \cdot \ell$.*

We now turn to a precise description of our construction. Fix a constant $\delta \in (0,1)$ and consider the $(\delta n, (1-\gamma)n', b, 2^{-\rho n'})$-somewhere-condenser $\textsf{SomeCond} : \{0,1\}^n \to \{0,1\}^{b \cdot n'}$ from Lemma 6, where $\gamma > 0$ is a small constant to be determined, $n' \geq \beta n$, and b, β, and ρ depend only on δ and γ. For each $i = 2, \ldots, \ell$, consider also the average-case strong (k, ε)-extractor

$$\textsf{Ext}_i : \{0,1\}^{b \cdot n'(i-1)} \times \{0,1\}^{n'} \to \{0,1\}^m$$

with $\varepsilon = 2^{-2\gamma n'}$, $k = \frac{2(1-3\gamma)n'}{3}$, and $m = \frac{(1-3\gamma)n'}{3}$. These extractors can be instantiated using the strong GUV extractor [43] with appropriate parameters.

We are now ready to define $\mathsf{SomeExt}(X)$ for $X = (B_1, \ldots, B_\ell) \in \mathsf{SHELA}_{n,k',t,\ell}$. We write

$$\mathsf{SomeCond}(B_i) = (B_{i1}, \ldots, B_{ib}) \in \{0,1\}^{n' \cdot b}.$$

Then, we have

$$\mathsf{SomeExt}(X) = (B'_{ij})_{i \in [\ell], j \in [b]} \in \{0,1\}^{m \cdot L}$$

for B'_{ij} defined as

$$B'_{ij} = \mathsf{Ext}_i((B_{i'j'})_{i' < i, j' \in [b]}, B_{ij}) \in \{0,1\}^m. \tag{6}$$

5   Lower Bounds for Deterministic Somewhere-Extraction from Weak Sources

In this section, we study lower bounds for somewhere-extractors that work for the general class of weak $(\tilde{n}, k)$-sources (we use $\tilde{n}$ to avoid confusion with the block length n of a SHELA source). Here, we are mostly interested in lower bounds on the number of output blocks generated by such somewhere-extractors with respect to the length $\tilde{n}$ of a source, the length m of an output block, and the error ε of the somewhere-extractor.

The only known construction of a somewhere-extractor for general $(\tilde{n}, k)$-sources described in Lemma 3 requires 2^d blocks, where d is the seed length of the underlying strong extractor/non-malleable extractor. As stated in [1], it holds that $d \geq \log(\tilde{n} - k) + 2\log(1/\varepsilon) + O(1)$ for every extractor, and so the somewhere-random source output by the somewhere-extractor from Lemma 3 has

$$L = \Omega\left(\frac{\tilde{n} - k}{\varepsilon^2}\right)$$

blocks. We remark that a probabilistic argument with a random function yields somewhere-extraction with the same number of output blocks.

The discussion in the previous paragraph leads to the following natural questions: *Is it possible to do better than Lemma 3 for $(\tilde{n}, k)$-sources? In particular, is it possible to obtain a number of output blocks comparable to that obtained from SHELA sources?*

We present some results that aim to answer this question in several parameter regimes. The first result comes from the observation that the basic argument for impossibility of deterministic extraction yields a non-trivial lower bound on the number of output blocks whenever the min-entropy requirement k is not very large.

Theorem 10. *Suppose $F : \{0,1\}^{\tilde{n}} \to \{0,1\}^{m \cdot L}$ is a $(1, L, \varepsilon)$-somewhere extractor for $(\tilde{n}, k)$-sources with $\varepsilon \leq 1 - 2^{-c}$ for some $1 \leq c \leq m$ (i.e., ε is not trivial). Then, it holds that*

$$L \geq \frac{\tilde{n} - k}{c}.$$

The lower bound from Theorem 10 is already enough to yield a separation between somewhere-extraction of SHELA and comparable $(\tilde{n}, k)$-sources whenever the min-entropy requirement k is not extremely large. Consider a SHELA source with constant entropy rate and ℓ blocks, each of length $n = \tilde{n}/\ell$ (so that the total length of the source is $\tilde{n}$). The constructions from Theorems 8 and 9 applied to the SHELA source lead to convSR-sources with $L = O(\ell)$ blocks with small error and large output block length if honest blocks have some constant entropy rate. In particular, L *does not depend directly on the input block length* n. On the other hand, the lower bound from Theorem 10 forces that $L = \Omega(\tilde{n} - k) = \Omega(n \cdot \ell)$ for convSR-sources extracted from $(\tilde{n}, k)$-sources, even with error $\varepsilon = 1/2$ (assuming $k/\tilde{n}$ is constant).

The second result is a disperser-based lower bound on the number of output blocks L. This bound is considerably stronger than the one in Theorem 10 whenever the output block length m is not very small and the error ε is small.

Theorem 11. *Suppose $F : \{0,1\}^{\tilde{n}} \to \{0,1\}^{m \cdot L}$ is a $(1, L, \varepsilon)$-somewhere extractor for $(\tilde{n}, k)$-sources with $\varepsilon \leq 1/2$ and $L \leq \frac{(1 - \max(\varepsilon, 2^{-m}))2^m}{2}$. Then, it holds that*

$$L = \Omega\left(\frac{\tilde{n} - k}{\max(\varepsilon, 2^{-m})}\right).$$

Referring again to the comparison between SHELA and weak $(\tilde{n}, k)$-sources above, if we want to extract a 1-out-of-L convSR-source with block length $\Omega(n)$ from the weak source with error $2^{-\Omega(n)}$, as is possible for the relevant SHELA source, then Theorem 11 forces that $L = \tilde{n} \cdot 2^{\Omega(n)} = \ell \cdot n2^{\Omega(n)}$. On the other hand, the convSR-source we extract from the relevant t-out-of-ℓ SHELA source only has $O(\ell)$ blocks.

While Theorems 10 and 11 imply strong separation between SHELA and weak sources for any conceivable application, they do not yield useful lower bounds for some regimes of parameters. For example, in the easiest setting for somewhere-extraction, when the min-entropy requirement k is very large (say, $k = \tilde{n} - 1$) and the output block length is very small (say, $m = 1$), both theorems only give a trivial $\Omega(1)$ lower bound on L, *even when ε is exponentially small in* $\tilde{n}$. On the other hand, the number of output blocks in the somewhere-extractor obtained from Lemma 3 instantiated with an optimal strong extractor scales as $1/\varepsilon^2$ even when $k = \tilde{n} - 1$ and $m = 1$. We believe it is not possible to improve significantly on the basic construction from Lemma 3, and so we put forth the following conjecture.

Conjecture 12. *Suppose $F : \{0,1\}^{\tilde{n}} \to \{0,1\}^{m \cdot L}$ is a (T, L, ε)-somewhere extractor for $(\tilde{n}, k)$-sources. Then, there exists a constant $c > 0$ such that if $\varepsilon \leq c$, we have*

$$L = \Omega\left(\frac{\tilde{n} - k}{\varepsilon^2}\right). \tag{7}$$

We do not prove Conjecture 12 and leave it as an interesting open problem. Nevertheless, we prove a weaker lower bound on L in a similar spirit to (7) under a stronger property than somewhere-extraction, which is still satisfied by the construction from Lemma 3. This result can be regarded both as a first step towards a full proof of Conjecture 12, and a non-trivial lower bound on L (under this stronger property) that scales with ε and holds even when k is large and m is small. Before we state our result, we must first define the alternative notion of somewhere-extraction. Observe that the construction of F from Lemma 3 actually ensures that for every $(\tilde{n}, k)$-source X it holds that $F(X)$ is ε-close to an element of $\mathsf{SR}_{T,L,m}$, instead of only a convex combination of such elements. We call a function that satisfies this for all $(\tilde{n}, k)$-sources a *strong* (T, L, ε, k)-somewhere extractor.

We may think of a strong $(1, L, \varepsilon, k)$-somewhere-extractor $F : \{0,1\}^{\tilde{n}} \rightarrow \{0,1\}^L$ as a family of L functions $F_1, \ldots, F_L$ such that for every $(\tilde{n}, k)$-source X, there is F_i such that $F_i(X) \approx_\varepsilon U_1$. Therefore, in order to show such a function F is not a strong somewhere-extractor, we must show the existence of an $(\tilde{n}, k)$-source X that is "bad" for all F_i's, in the sense that $F_i(X) \not\approx_\varepsilon U_1$ for every i. As previously discussed, existing techniques used in proving lower bounds for extractors cannot be applied to obtain similar lower bounds for strong somewhere-extractors. We use a fundamentally different technique to prove the following lower bound on L for strong somewhere-extractors.

Theorem 13. *Suppose $F : \{0,1\}^{\tilde{n}} \rightarrow \{0,1\}^{m \cdot L}$ is a strong $(1, L, \varepsilon, k)$-somewhere extractor for $k \leq n - 1$. Then, there exists an absolute constant $c > 0$ such that if $\varepsilon < c$, we have*

$$L = \Omega\left(\log\left(\frac{1}{\max(\varepsilon, 2^{-k})} \right) \right). \tag{8}$$

6 Bounds for Somewhere-Amplifiable-Source Extraction from Weak Sources

The lower bounds obtained in Sect. 5 show that convSR-sources extracted from SHELA sources are much better (in terms of number of blocks with respect to desired extraction error) than convSR-sources extracted from weak sources. This has direct consequences in the time complexity blowup incurred when using convSR-sources in several applications, as discussed in Sect. 1. However, as discussed in that same section, it is possible in some scenarios to use a weaker object than convSR-sources, which we call *somewhere-amplifiable sources*, where the good independent blocks are not required to be exactly uniformly distributed. A precise definition follows.

Definition 14 (Somewhere-amplifiable source). *We say $Y = (Y_1, \ldots, Y_L)$ over $\{0,1\}^{m \cdot L}$ is a (T, L, ε)-somewhere-amplifiable source if there exist distinct indices $i_1, \ldots, i_T$ such that $Y_{i_1}, \ldots, Y_{i_T}$ are independent and $Y_{i_j} \approx_\varepsilon U_m$ for all $j = 1, \ldots, T$. The set of all such SA sources is denoted by $\mathsf{SA}_{T,L,\varepsilon}$, and the set of all convex combinations of sources in $\mathsf{SA}_{T,L,\varepsilon}$ is denoted by $\mathsf{convSA}_{T,L,\varepsilon}$.*

Since the error required from each good block in a convSA-source is not that small (in fact, it can even be constant), one may hope to transform weak sources into convSA-sources whose number of blocks is much closer to that of convSR-sources obtained from SHELA sources, and which have blocks long enough to be used in the applications already discussed in Sect. 1 and later in Sect. 7. To this end, we define *somewhere-amplifiable source extractors* (convSA-source extractors).

Definition 15 (Somewhere-amplifiable source extractor). *A function* SomeExt : $\{0,1\}^{\tilde{n}} \rightarrow \{0,1\}^{m \cdot L}$ *is said to be a* $(T, L, k, \varepsilon_1, \varepsilon_2)$*-somewhere-amplifiable extractor if for every* $(\tilde{n}, k)$*-source* X *there exists* $Y \in \text{convSA}_{T,L,\varepsilon_2}$ *such that*

$$\text{SomeExt}(X) \approx_{\varepsilon_1} Y.$$

We begin by noting that Theorem 10 also applies to convSA-source extractors for weak sources. This shows that every such extractor (even with constant error) must have $L = \Omega(\tilde{n} - k)$. As discussed in Sect. 1, this already provides an efficiency separation between convSA-source extraction from weak sources and convSR-source extraction from SHELA sources.

The main result we prove in this section is a different type of separation between convSA-source extraction from weak sources and convSR-source extraction from SHELA sources. Roughly speaking, we show that if we want to extract a convSA-source with many good blocks (necessary to obtain good final error) from an $(\tilde{n}, k)$-source, then either the resulting convSA-source has too many blocks to allow for efficient construction of the publicly verifiable protocols, or the length of each block is very small, and so they may not be usable in some protocols. This is discussed for the particular case of our publicly verifiable proof system in Sect. 1.4. A precise statement follows.

Theorem 16. *Suppose* $F : \{0,1\}^{\tilde{n}} \rightarrow \{0,1\}^{m \cdot L}$ *is a* $(T, L, k, \varepsilon_1, \varepsilon_2)$*-somewhere-amplifiable extractor for* $\varepsilon_1 = \text{negl}(\tilde{n})$*, and* $\varepsilon_2 \leq c_2$ *for some arbitrary constant* $c_2 \leq 1 - 2^{-m}$ *(so that* ε_1 *is useful for applications and* ε_2 *is non-trivial). Then, either the number of blocks* L *is superpolynomial in* $\tilde{n}$ *(and hence amplification is inefficient), or we have* $m = O(k/T)$.

Some comments are due about Theorem 16. First, Theorem 16 provides a strong separation between convSA-source extraction from weak sources and convSR-source extraction from SHELA sources, as already evidenced in Sect. 1.4. Consider a SHELA source with ℓ blocks of length n, $\ell = \text{poly}(n)$, $t = 2$ of which are honest with arbitrary linear min-entropy. Then, Theorem 9 shows we can efficiently extract (to within error $2^{-\Omega(\text{poly}(n))}$) a convSR-source with $\text{poly}(n)$ number of blocks each of length $\Omega(n)$ and at least one good block from the SHELA source. Such SHELA source can be compared with an arbitrary weak $(\tilde{n} = n \cdot \ell, k = O(n))$-source. In this case, Theorem 16 shows that if we want to obtain a T-out-of-L convSA-source with block length $\Omega(n)$ from the weak source, then T must be constant. This precludes many applications of the resulting convSA-source as discussed in Sect. 1. Finally, note that Theorem 16 also applies to the extraction of convSR-sources with several uniform blocks from weak sources.

7 Non-Interactive Protocols from Public SHELA Sources

7.1 CRS Generation Through a SHELA Sample

The definitions of proof systems and commitment schemes in the plain model and in the CRS model are standard and can be found in [1].

Such definitions assume the existence of an efficient CRS generation procedure $\mathcal{G}$ that, however, will instead be realized in our protocols through a sample from a public SHELA source. Our constructions will convert 2-round public-coin protocols into non-interactive protocols by using a SHELA source and the somewhere-extractor to replace the first round. Therefore, following the notation in the CRS model, when running $\mathcal{G}$ on input 1^m to generate a sufficiently long CRS, we assume that the CRS is generated through a sample $\sigma \leftarrow \mathsf{SHELA}_{n,k,t,\ell}$ from a SHELA source such that when running $\mathsf{SomeExt}(\sigma)$ and obtaining blocks $R_1, \ldots, R_L$ we have that the size of each R_i is equal to the size of the first round of the 2-round public-coin protocol. We recall that $\mathcal{G}$ is not supposed to be efficient and neither simulatable. Moreover, this procedure allows an unbounded adversary to partially control the sampling process. We obviously require that the output of $\mathcal{G}$ be available to all players. In our protocols, some adversaries are restricted to run in polynomial-time only, but still can affect the outcome of the SHELA sample without such restriction.

NON-INTERACTIVE WI PROOF SYSTEM $\varPi_{\mathsf{pv}} = (\mathcal{G}, \mathcal{P}_{\mathsf{pv}}, \mathcal{V}_{\mathsf{pv}})$

CRS GENERATION: $\mathcal{G}$ on input 1^m outputs $\sigma \leftarrow \mathsf{SHELA}_{n,k,t,\ell}$.
PROVER PROCEDURE: $\mathcal{P}_{\mathsf{pv}}$. Input: instance x, witness w s.t. $(x, w) \in \mathcal{R}$ and $\sigma \in \mathsf{SHELA}_{n,k,t,\ell}$.
  1. Run $\mathsf{SomeExt}(\sigma)$ obtaining $R_1, \ldots, R_L$.
  2. For $i = 1, \ldots, L$: Run $\pi_i \leftarrow \mathcal{P}(1^m, x, w, R_i)$.
  3. Set $\pi = (\pi_1, \ldots, \pi_L)$, output π.
VERIFIER PROCEDURE: $\mathcal{V}_{\mathsf{pv}}$. Input: instance x and $\sigma \in \mathsf{SHELA}_{n,k,t,\ell}$.
  1. Run $\mathsf{SomeExt}(\sigma)$ obtaining $R_1, \ldots, R_L$.
  2. If $\mathcal{V}(x, w, R_i, \pi_i) = 1 \ \forall i = 1, \ldots, L$ accept, otherwise reject.

Fig. 1. Non-interactive WI Proof System $\varPi_{\mathsf{pv}} = (\mathcal{G}, \mathcal{P}_{\mathsf{pv}}, \mathcal{V}_{\mathsf{pv}})$.

7.2 Non-Interactive WI Proof System $\varPi_{\mathsf{pv}}$

Here we present our construction of NIWI proof system from SHELA sources assuming public-coin ZAPs. In order to describe our proof system $\varPi_{\mathsf{pv}} = (\mathcal{G}, \mathcal{P}_{\mathsf{pv}}, \mathcal{V}_{\mathsf{pv}})$ for the NP-language $\mathcal{L}$, we will make use of the following tools:
(1) A somewhere extractor $\mathsf{SomeExt} : \{0,1\}^{n \cdot \ell} \to \{0,1\}^{m \cdot L}$ defined in Sect. 4[11].
(2) A 2-round public-coin WI proof system $\varPi = (\mathcal{P}, \mathcal{V})$. Our Non-Interactive WI proof system $\varPi_{\mathsf{pv}} = (\mathcal{G}, \mathcal{P}_{\mathsf{pv}}, \mathcal{V}_{\mathsf{pv}})$ with a CRS generated through a sample from a SHELA source is described in Fig. 1.

---

[11] With high min-entropy we set $L = \ell - 1$, while with low min-entropy we set $L = O(\ell)$.

Theorem 17. *Assuming the existence of public SHELA sources, if public-coin ZAPs exist, then Π_{pv} is a non-interactive proof system for all NP-languages.*

We stress that our protocol can be instantiated using doubly enhanced trapdoor permutations. The proof can be found in [1].

7.3   Non-Interactive Commitment Scheme Π_{pvcom}

Here we present our construction of non-interactive statistically binding commitment scheme from SHELA sources assuming 2-round public-coin statistically binding commitments. In order to describe our commitment scheme $\Pi_{\mathsf{pvcom}} = (\mathcal{G}, \mathcal{P}_{\mathsf{pvcom}}, \mathcal{V}_{\mathsf{pvcom}})$ for the message space M, we will make use of the following tools: (1) a somewhere extractor $\mathsf{SomeExt} : \{0,1\}^{n\cdot\ell} \to \{0,1\}^{m\cdot L}$ defined in Sect. 4[12]; (2) a 2-round public-coin statistically binding commitment scheme $\Pi_{\mathsf{com}} = (\mathcal{S}, \mathcal{R})$. Our Non-Interactive Commitment Scheme $\Pi_{\mathsf{pvcom}} = (\mathcal{G}, \mathcal{P}_{\mathsf{pvcom}}, \mathcal{V}_{\mathsf{pvcom}})$ using a public SHELA source is described in in Fig. 2.

NON-INTERACTIVE COMMITMENT SCHEME $\Pi_{\mathsf{pvcom}} = (\mathcal{G}, \mathcal{S}_{\mathsf{pvcom}}, \mathcal{R}_{\mathsf{pvcom}})$

CRS GENERATION: $\mathcal{G}$ on input 1^m outputs $\sigma \leftarrow \mathsf{SHELA}_{n,k,t,\ell}$.
SENDER PROCEDURE: $\mathcal{S}_{\mathsf{pvcom}}$. Input: message msg and $\sigma \in \mathsf{SHELA}_{n,k,t,\ell}$.
  1. Run $\mathsf{SomeExt}(\sigma)$ obtaining $R_1, \ldots R_L$.
  2. For $i = 1, \ldots, L$: Run $\mathsf{com}_i, \mathsf{dec}_i \leftarrow \mathcal{S}(1^m, \mathsf{msg}, R_i)$.
  3. Set $\mathsf{com} = (\mathsf{com}_1, \ldots, \mathsf{com}_L)$, $\mathsf{dec} = (\mathsf{dec}_1, \ldots, \mathsf{dec}_L)$ and output com.
RECEIVER PROCEDURE: $\mathcal{R}_{\mathsf{pvcom}}$. Input: commitment com, decommitment $\mathsf{dec}, \mathsf{msg}$ and $\sigma \in \mathsf{SHELA}_{n,k,t,\ell}$.
  1. Run $\mathsf{SomeExt}(\sigma)$ obtaining $R_1, \ldots, R_L$.
  2. If $\mathcal{R}(\mathsf{msg}, \mathsf{com}_i, R_i, \mathsf{dec}_i) = 1 \; \forall i = 1, \ldots, L$ outputs msg, otherwise reject.

Fig. 2. Non-interactive Commitment Scheme from OWFs $\Pi_{\mathsf{pvcom}} = (\mathcal{G}, \mathcal{S}_{\mathsf{pvcom}}, \mathcal{R}_{\mathsf{pvcom}})$.

Theorem 18. *Assuming the existence of public SHELA sources, if 2-round public-coin statistically binding commitment schemes exist then Π_{pvcom} is a non-interactive commitment scheme.*

We stress that our protocol can be instantiated through a black-box use of any one-way function.

Acknowledgments. DA and MO were funded by the Singapore Ministry of Education and the National Research Foundation under grant R-710-000-012-135. Part of this work was done while MO was visiting the University of Warsaw (visit supported by TEAM/2016-1/4 grant from the Foundation for Polish Science). Part of this work was done while JR was visiting the Centre for Quantum Technologies, National University of Singapore. Part of this work was done while LS was at the University of Salerno and visiting the Centre for Quantum Technologies, National University of Singapore. LS and IV were supported in part by the European Union's Horizon 2020 research and innovation programme under grant agreement No 780477 (project PRIViLEDGE) and in part by "GNCS - INdAM".

---

[12] We set L precisely as specified in the previous footnote.

References

1. Aggarwal, D., Obremski, M., Ribeiro, J., Siniscalchi, L., Visconti, I.: How to extract useful randomness from unreliable sources. Cryptology ePrint Archive, Report 2019/1156 (2019). https://eprint.iacr.org/2019/1156
2. Barak, B., Kindler, G., Shaltiel, R., Sudakov, B., Wigderson, A.: Simulating independence: new constructions of condensers, Ramsey graphs, dispersers, and extractors. J. ACM **57**(4) (2010). https://doi.org/10.1145/1734213.1734214
3. Barak, B., Rao, A., Shaltiel, R., Wigderson, A.: 2-source dispersers for $n^{o(1)}$ entropy, and Ramsey graphs beating the Frankl-Wilson construction. Ann. Math. **176**(3), 1483–1543 (2012)
4. Beigi, S., Bogdanov, A., Etesami, O., Guo, S.: Optimal deterministic extractors for generalized Santha-Vazirani sources. In: APPROX/RANDOM 2018. LIPIcs, vol. 116, pp. 30:1–30:15. Schloss Dagstuhl-Leibniz-Zentrum fuer Informatik, Dagstuhl (2018). https://doi.org/10.4230/LIPIcs.APPROX-RANDOM.2018.30
5. Beigi, S., Etesami, O., Gohari, A.: Deterministic randomness extraction from generalized and distributed Santha-Vazirani sources. SIAM J. Comput. **46**(1), 1–36 (2017). https://doi.org/10.1137/15M1027206
6. Bellare, M., Fuchsbauer, G., Scafuro, A.: NIZKs with an untrusted CRS: security in the face of parameter subversion. In: Cheon, J.H., Takagi, T. (eds.) ASIACRYPT 2016. LNCS, vol. 10032, pp. 777–804. Springer, Heidelberg (2016). https://doi.org/10.1007/978-3-662-53890-6_26
7. Ben-Aroya, A., Chattopadhyay, E., Doron, D., Li, X., Ta-Shma, A.: A new approach for constructing low-error, two-source extractors. In: CCC 2018, pp. 3:1–3:19. Schloss Dagstuhl-Leibniz-Zentrum fuer Informatik, Germany (2018)
8. Bennett, C.H., Brassard, G., Robert, J.-M.: How to reduce your enemy's information (extended abstract). In: Williams, H.C. (ed.) CRYPTO 1985. LNCS, vol. 218, pp. 468–476. Springer, Heidelberg (1986). https://doi.org/10.1007/3-540-39799-X_37
9. Bentov, I., Gabizon, A., Zuckerman, D.: Bitcoin beacon. arXiv e-prints arXiv:1605.04559, May 2016
10. Bitansky, N., Paneth, O.: Point obfuscation and 3-round zero-knowledge. In: Cramer, R. (ed.) TCC 2012. LNCS, vol. 7194, pp. 190–208. Springer, Heidelberg (2012). https://doi.org/10.1007/978-3-642-28914-9_11
11. Blum, M.: Independent unbiased coin flips from a correlated biased source—a finite state Markov chain. Combinatorica **6**(2), 97–108 (1986). https://doi.org/10.1007/BF02579167
12. Bourgain, J.: More on the sum-product phenomenon in prime fields and its applications. Int. J. Number Theory **01**(01), 1–32 (2005)
13. Bourgain, J.: On the construction of affine extractors. GAFA Geom. Funct. Anal. **17**(1), 33–57 (2007)
14. Bourgain, J., Dvir, Z., Leeman, E.: Affine extractors over large fields with exponential error. Comput. Complex. **25**(4), 921–931 (2016). https://doi.org/10.1007/s00037-015-0108-5
15. Canetti, R., Pass, R., Shelat, A.: Cryptography from sunspots: how to use an imperfect reference string. In: FOCS 2007, pp. 249–259, October 2007. https://doi.org/10.1109/FOCS.2007.70
16. Chattopadhyay, E., Goodman, J., Goyal, V., Li, X.: Extractors for adversarial sources via extremal hypergraphs. Cryptology ePrint Archive, Report 2019/1450 (2019, to appear in STOC 2020). https://eprint.iacr.org/2019/1450

17. Chattopadhyay, E., Goyal, V., Li, X.: Non-malleable extractors and codes, with their many tampered extensions. In: STOC 2016, pp. 285–298. ACM, New York (2016). https://doi.org/10.1145/2897518.2897547
18. Chattopadhyay, E., Zuckerman, D.: Explicit two-source extractors and resilient functions. Ann. Math. **189**(3), 653–705 (2019)
19. Chor, B., Goldreich, O., Hasted, J., Freidmann, J., Rudich, S., Smolensky, R.: The bit extraction problem or t-resilient functions. In: FOCS 1985, pp. 396–407, October 1985. https://doi.org/10.1109/SFCS.1985.55
20. Chor, B., Goldreich, O.: Unbiased bits from sources of weak randomness and probabilistic communication complexity. SIAM J. Comput. **17**(2), 230–261 (1988). https://doi.org/10.1137/0217015
21. Clark, J., Hengartner, U.: On the use of financial data as a random beacon. In: EVT/WOTE 2010, pp. 1–8. USENIX Association, Berkeley (2010)
22. Cohen, G., Schulman, L.J.: Extractors for near logarithmic min-entropy. In: FOCS 2016, pp. 178–187, October 2016. https://doi.org/10.1109/FOCS.2016.27
23. Cohen, G.: Local correlation breakers and applications to three-source extractors and mergers. SIAM J. Comput. **45**(4), 1297–1338 (2016). https://doi.org/10.1137/15M1029837
24. Cohen, G., Shinkar, I.: Zero-fixing extractors for sub-logarithmic entropy. In: Halldórsson, M.M., Iwama, K., Kobayashi, N., Speckmann, B. (eds.) ICALP 2015. LNCS, vol. 9134, pp. 343–354. Springer, Heidelberg (2015). https://doi.org/10.1007/978-3-662-47672-7_28
25. De, A., Watson, T.: Extractors and lower bounds for locally samplable sources. In: Goldberg, L.A., Jansen, K., Ravi, R., Rolim, J.D.P. (eds.) APPROX/RANDOM 2011. LNCS, vol. 6845, pp. 483–494. Springer, Heidelberg (2011). https://doi.org/10.1007/978-3-642-22935-0_41
26. DeVos, M., Gabizon, A.: Simple affine extractors using dimension expansion. In: CCC 2010, pp. 50–57. IEEE Computer Society, USA (2010). https://doi.org/10.1109/CCC.2010.14
27. Dodis, Y.: New imperfect random source with applications to coin-flipping. In: Orejas, F., Spirakis, P.G., van Leeuwen, J. (eds.) ICALP 2001. LNCS, vol. 2076, pp. 297–309. Springer, Heidelberg (2001). https://doi.org/10.1007/3-540-48224-5_25
28. Dodis, Y., Vaikuntanathan, V., Wichs, D.: Extracting randomness from extractor-dependent sources. Cryptology ePrint Archive, Report 2019/1339 (2019). https://eprint.iacr.org/2019/1339
29. Dvir, Z., Kopparty, S., Saraf, S., Sudan, M.: Extensions to the method of multiplicities, with applications to Kakeya sets and mergers. SIAM J. Comput. **42**(6), 2305–2328 (2013)
30. Dvir, Z., Gabizon, A., Wigderson, A.: Extractors and rank extractors for polynomial sources. Comput. Complex. **18**(1), 1–58 (2009). https://doi.org/10.1007/s00037-009-0258-4
31. Dvir, Z., Raz, R.: Analyzing linear mergers. Random Struct. Algorithms **32**(3), 334–345 (2008)
32. Dvir, Z., Shpilka, A.: An improved analysis of linear mergers. Comput. Complex. **16**(1), 34–59 (2007). https://doi.org/10.1007/s00037-007-0223-z
33. Dvir, Z., Wigderson, A.: Kakeya sets, new mergers, and old extractors. SIAM J. Comput. **40**(3), 778–792 (2011). https://doi.org/10.1137/090748731
34. Dwork, C., Naor, M.: Zaps and their applications. In: FOCS 2000, pp. 283–293, November 2000. https://doi.org/10.1109/SFCS.2000.892117
35. Elias, P.: The efficient construction of an unbiased random sequence. Ann. Math. Stat. **43**(3), 865–870 (1972)

36. Feige, U., Lapidot, D., Shamir, A.: Multiple noninteractive zero knowledge proofs under general assumptions. SIAM J. Comput. **29**(1), 1–28 (1999)
37. Fuchsbauer, G., Orrù, M.: Non-interactive zaps of knowledge. In: Preneel, B., Vercauteren, F. (eds.) ACNS 2018. LNCS, vol. 10892, pp. 44–62. Springer, Cham (2018). https://doi.org/10.1007/978-3-319-93387-0_3
38. Gabizon, A., Raz, R.: Deterministic extractors for affine sources over large fields. In: FOCS 2005, pp. 407–416, October 2005. https://doi.org/10.1109/SFCS.2005.31
39. Gabizon, A., Raz, R., Shaltiel, R.: Deterministic extractors for bit-fixing sources by obtaining an independent seed. SIAM J. Comput. **36**(4), 1072–1094 (2006)
40. Garay, J., Kiayias, A., Leonardos, N.: The bitcoin backbone protocol: analysis and applications. In: Oswald, E., Fischlin, M. (eds.) EUROCRYPT 2015. LNCS, vol. 9057, pp. 281–310. Springer, Heidelberg (2015). https://doi.org/10.1007/978-3-662-46803-6_10
41. Goyal, R., Goyal, V.: Overcoming cryptographic impossibility results using blockchains. In: Kalai, Y., Reyzin, L. (eds.) TCC 2017. LNCS, vol. 10677, pp. 529–561. Springer, Cham (2017). https://doi.org/10.1007/978-3-319-70500-2_18
42. Groth, J., Ostrovsky, R., Sahai, A.: Non-interactive zaps and new techniques for NIZK. In: Dwork, C. (ed.) CRYPTO 2006. LNCS, vol. 4117, pp. 97–111. Springer, Heidelberg (2006). https://doi.org/10.1007/11818175_6
43. Guruswami, V., Umans, C., Vadhan, S.: Unbalanced expanders and randomness extractors from Parvaresh-Vardy codes. J. ACM **56**(4), 20:1–20:34 (2009)
44. Kamp, J., Rao, A., Vadhan, S., Zuckerman, D.: Deterministic extractors for small-space sources. J. Comput. Syst. Sci. **77**(1), 191–220 (2011)
45. Kamp, J., Zuckerman, D.: Deterministic extractors for bit-fixing sources and exposure-resilient cryptography. SIAM J. Comput. **36**(5), 1231–1247 (2007)
46. Lewko, M.: An explicit two-source extractor with min-entropy rate near 4/9. Mathematika **65**(4), 950–957 (2019)
47. Li, F., Zuckerman, D.: Improved extractors for recognizable and algebraic sources. Electronic Colloquium on Computational Complexity (ECCC) 25, 110 (2018)
48. Li, X.: Improved constructions of three source extractors. In: CCC 2011, pp. 126–136, June 2011. https://doi.org/10.1109/CCC.2011.26
49. Li, X.: A new approach to affine extractors and dispersers. In: CCC 2011, pp. 137–147, June 2011. https://doi.org/10.1109/CCC.2011.27
50. Li, X.: Extractors for a constant number of independent sources with polylogarithmic min-entropy. In: FOCS 2013, pp. 100–109, October 2013. https://doi.org/10.1109/FOCS.2013.19
51. Li, X.: Improved two-source extractors, and affine extractors for polylogarithmic entropy. In: FOCS 2016, pp. 168–177, October 2016. https://doi.org/10.1109/FOCS.2016.26
52. Li, X.: New independent source extractors with exponential improvement. In: STOC 2013, pp. 783–792. ACM, New York, June 2013
53. Li, X.: Three-source extractors for polylogarithmic min-entropy. In: FOCS 2015, pp. 863–882, October 2015. https://doi.org/10.1109/FOCS.2015.58
54. Lichtenstein, D., Linial, N., Saks, M.: Some extremal problems arising from discrete control processes. Combinatorica **9**(3), 269–287 (1989). https://doi.org/10.1007/BF02125896
55. Lu, C.J., Reingold, O., Vadhan, S., Wigderson, A.: Extractors: optimal up to constant factors. In: STOC 2003, pp. 602–611. ACM, New York (2003)
56. Naor, M.: Bit commitment using pseudorandomness. J. Cryptol. **4**(2), 151–158 (1991). https://doi.org/10.1007/BF00196774

57. von Neumann, J.: Various techniques used in connection with random digits. In: Monte Carlo Method, National Bureau of Standards Applied Mathematics Series, vol. 12, chap. 13, pp. 36–38. US Government Printing Office, Washington, DC (1951)
58. Nisan, N., Zuckerman, D.: Randomness is linear in space. J. Comput. Syst. Sci. **52**(1), 43–52 (1996)
59. Pass, R., Seeman, L., Shelat, A.: Analysis of the blockchain protocol in asynchronous networks. In: Coron, J.-S., Nielsen, J.B. (eds.) EUROCRYPT 2017. LNCS, vol. 10211, pp. 643–673. Springer, Cham (2017). https://doi.org/10.1007/978-3-319-56614-6_22
60. Pudlak, P., Rodl, V.: Extractors for small zero-fixing sources. arXiv e-prints arXiv:1904.07949, April 2019
61. Radhakrishnan, J., Ta-Shma, A.: Bounds for dispersers, extractors, and depth-two superconcentrators. SIAM J. Discrete Math. **13**(1), 2–24 (2000)
62. Rao, A.: Extractors for low-weight affine sources. In: CCC 2009, pp. 95–101, July 2009. https://doi.org/10.1109/CCC.2009.36
63. Rao, A.: Extractors for a constant number of polynomially small min-entropy independent sources. SIAM J. Comput. **39**(1), 168–194 (2009)
64. Raz, R.: Extractors with weak random seeds. In: STOC 2005, pp. 11–20. ACM, New York (2005). https://doi.org/10.1145/1060590.1060593
65. Santha, M., Vazirani, U.V.: Generating quasi-random sequences from slightly-random sources. In: FOCS 1984, pp. 434–440, October 1984. https://doi.org/10.1109/SFCS.1984.715945
66. Scafuro, A., Siniscalchi, L., Visconti, I.: Publicly verifiable proofs from blockchains. In: Lin, D., Sako, K. (eds.) PKC 2019. LNCS, vol. 11442, pp. 374–401. Springer, Cham (2019). https://doi.org/10.1007/978-3-030-17253-4_13
67. Ta-Shma, A.: On extracting randomness from weak random sources (extended abstract). In: STOC 1996, pp. 276–285. ACM, New York (1996)
68. Trevisan, L., Vadhan, S.: Extracting randomness from samplable distributions. In: FOCS 2000, pp. 32–42. IEEE Computer Society, Washington, DC (2000)
69. Vazirani, U.V.: Towards a strong communication complexity theory or generating quasi-random sequences from two communicating slightly-random sources. In: STOC 1985, pp. 366–378. ACM, New York (1985)
70. Viola, E.: Extractors for turing-machine sources. In: Gupta, A., Jansen, K., Rolim, J., Servedio, R. (eds.) APPROX/RANDOM 2012. LNCS, vol. 7408, pp. 663–671. Springer, Heidelberg (2012). https://doi.org/10.1007/978-3-642-32512-0_56
71. Viola, E.: Extractors for circuit sources. SIAM J. Comput. **43**(2), 655–672 (2014)
72. Yehudayoff, A.: Affine extractors over prime fields. Combinatorica **31**(2), 245 (2011). https://doi.org/10.1007/s00493-011-2604-9
73. Zuckerman, D.: Linear degree extractors and the inapproximability of max clique and chromatic number. In: STOC 2006. pp. 681–690. ACM, New York, NY, USA (2006)

Low Error Efficient Computational Extractors in the CRS Model

Ankit Garg[1](✉), Yael Tauman Kalai[2](✉), and Dakshita Khurana[3]

[1] Microsoft Research India, Bangalore, India
garga@microsoft.com
[2] Microsoft Research New England, Cambridge, USA
yael@microsoft.com
[3] University of Illinois Urbana-Champaign, Champaign, IL, USA
dakshita@illinois.edu

Abstract. In recent years, there has been exciting progress on building two-source extractors for sources with low min-entropy. Unfortunately, all known explicit constructions of two-source extractors in the low entropy regime suffer from non-negligible error, and building such extractors with negligible error remains an open problem. We investigate this problem in the computational setting, and obtain the following results.

We construct an explicit 2-source extractor, and even an explicit non-malleable extractor, with negligible error, for sources with low min-entropy, under computational assumptions in the Common Random String (CRS) model. More specifically, we assume that a CRS is generated once and for all, and allow the min-entropy sources to depend on the CRS. We obtain our constructions by using the following transformations.

1. Building on the technique of [5], we show a general transformation for converting any computational 2-source extractor (in the CRS model) into a computational non-malleable extractor (in the CRS model), for sources with similar min-entropy.

   We emphasize that the resulting computational non-malleable extractor is resilient to *arbitrarily many* tampering attacks (a property that is impossible to achieve information theoretically). This may be of independent interest.

   This transformation uses cryptography, and relies on the sub-exponential hardness of the Decisional Diffie Hellman (DDH) assumption.

2. Next, using the blueprint of [1], we give a transformation converting our computational non-malleable extractor (in the CRS model) into a computational 2-source extractor for sources with low min-entropy (in the CRS model). Our 2-source extractor works for unbalanced sources: specifically, we require one of the sources to be larger than a specific polynomial in the other.

   This transformation does not incur any additional assumptions. Our analysis makes a novel use of the leakage lemma of Gentry and Wichs [18].

© International Association for Cryptologic Research 2020
A. Canteaut and Y. Ishai (Eds.): EUROCRYPT 2020, LNCS 12105, pp. 373–402, 2020.
https://doi.org/10.1007/978-3-030-45721-1_14

1   Introduction

Randomness is fundamental for cryptography. It is well known that even the most basic cryptographic primitives, such as semantically secure encryption, commitments and zero-knowledge proofs, require randomness. In fact, Dodis *et al.* [15] proved that these primitives require *perfect* randomness, and cannot be constructed using a weak source of randomness, not even one that has nearly full min-entropy.[1]

Unfortunately, in reality, perfect randomness is very hard to come by, and *secret* randomness is even harder. Indeed, several attacks on cryptographic systems rely on the fact that the randomness that was used in the implementation was imperfect. Very recently, this was demonstrated in the regime of cryptocurrencies by Breitner and Heninger [6], who computed hundreds of Bitcoin private keys by exploiting the fact that the randomness used to generate them was imperfect (other examples include [3,20]).

Randomness Extractors. These attacks give rise to a very natural question: Can we take weak sources of randomness and "boost" them into perfect random sources? This is the basic question that underlies the field of randomness extractors. Extractors are algorithms that extract perfect randomness from weak random sources. As eluded to above, one cannot hope to deterministically take only a single weak random source and generate perfect randomness from it.

Nevertheless, two common types of randomness extractors have been considered in the literature. The first is a *seeded extractor*, which uses a uniform seed to extract randomness from any (n, k) source, for k as small as $k = \mathsf{polylog}(n)$. This seed is typically very short, often of length $O(\log n)$. However, it is paramount that this seed is perfectly random, and independent of the source. In reality, unfortunately, even generating such short perfectly random strings may be challenging.

The second type of extractor is a 2-source extractor. A 2-source extractor takes as input two *independent* weak sources and outputs pure randomness. We stress that a 2-source extractor does not require perfect randomness at all! It only requires two independent sources with sufficiently large min-entropy. Such sources may be arguably easier to generate.

Until recently, we had an explicit construction of a 2-source extractor only in the high-entropy regime, i.e. assuming one of the sources has min-entropy $k \geq 0.499n$ [4,26]. Over the last three years, there has been remarkable and exciting progress [2,7–9,11–14,24], giving rise to 2-source extractors in the low-entropy regime, albeit with non-negligible error.

More formally, an $(n_1, n_2, k_1, k_2, \epsilon)$ 2-source extractor is a function $E{:}\{0,1\}^{n_1} \times \{0,1\}^{n_2} \rightarrow \{0,1\}^m$ such that for any independent sources X and Y, with min-entropy at least k_1 and k_2 respectively, $E(X, Y)$ is ϵ-close (in statistical distance) to

---

[1] A weak source is modeled as an (n, k)-source, which is a distribution that generates elements in $\{0,1\}^n$ with min-entropy k. A distribtion $X \subseteq \{0,1\}^n$ is said to have min-entropy k if for every $x \in \{0,1\}^n$, $\Pr[X = x] \leq 2^{-k}$.

the uniform distribution over $\{0,1\}^m$. The line of recent breakthroughs discussed above can support min-entropy as small as $O(\log(n)\log(\log(n)))$ in the balanced regime $n_1 = n_2 = n$. *However, in all the above constructions, the running time of the extractor is proportional to* $\mathrm{poly}(1/\epsilon)$*!*

This state-of-the-art is far from ideal for cryptographic applications, where typically the error is required to be negligible in the security parameter. Unfortunately, in the negligible error regime, the extractors mentioned above run in super-polynomial time. The question of whether one can obtain a 2-source extractor with negligible error, even for sources with min-entropy δn, for a small constant $\delta > 0$, is one of the most important open problems in the area of randomness extractors.

In this work, we explore this problem in the computational setting. We note that solving this problem, even in the computational setting, may facilitate generating useful randomness for many cryptographic applications.

1.1   Prior Work on Computational Extractors

There has been some prior work [22,23] on building computational extractors. However, these works rely on extremely strong computational assumptions. Loosely speaking, the assumption is (slightly stronger than) assuming the existence of an "optimally exponentially hard" one-way permutation $f : \{0,1\}^n \to \{0,1\}^n$, that is hard to invert even with probability $2^{-(1-\delta)n}$ (this gives extractors for sources with min-entropy roughly δn).

Intuitively, such a strong assumption seems to be necessary. This is the case since to prove security we need to construct a reduction that uses an adversary $\mathcal{A}$, that breaks the 2-source extractor, to break the underlying assumption. If this assumption is a standard one, then the challenge provided by the assumption comes from a specific distribution (often the uniform distribution). On the other hand, the adversary $\mathcal{A}$ may break the extractor w.r.t. *arbitrary* independent sources X and Y with sufficient min-entropy. It is completely unclear how one could possibly use $(X, Y, \mathcal{A})$ to break this challenge, since $\mathcal{A}$ only helps to distinguish the specific distribution $E(X,Y)$ from uniform (where E is the 2-source extractor). Since X and Y are *arbitrary* low min-entropy distributions, it is unclear how one could embed the challenge in X or Y, or in $E(X,Y)$.

1.2   Our Results

In this paper, we get around this barrier by resorting to the Common Random String (CRS) model.[2] As a result, under the sub-exponential hardness of DDH (which is a comparatively mild assumption), we obtain a computational 2-source extractor, and a computational non-malleable extractor, both with negligible error, for low min-entropy sources (in the CRS model).

---

[2] Jumping ahead, we note that in the proof we break the assumption by embedding the challenge in the CRS.

At first one may think that constructing such extractors in the CRS model is trivial since the CRS can be used a seed. However, as mentioned above, we emphasize that this is not the case, since the CRS is fixed once and for all, and the sources can depend on this CRS. Indeed, constructing an information theoretic 2-source extractor in the CRS model is an interesting open problem.

Secondly, one could ask why assuming the existence of a CRS is reasonable, since our starting point is the belief that fresh randomness is hard to generate, and thus in a sense assuming a CRS brings us back to square one. However, as emphasized above, this CRS is generated once and for all, and can be reused over and over again. Indeed, we believe that true randomness is hard, yet not impossible, to generate. Thus, reducing the need for true randomness to a single one-time need, is significant progress. Importantly, we emphasize that in cryptography, there are many natural applications where a CRS is assumed to exist, and in such applications this same CRS can be used to extract randomness from weak sources.

The computational CRS model. In our constructions, we assume that a CRS is (efficiently) generated once and for all. We consider any two weak sources X and Y. These sources *can each depend on the CRS,*[3] but are required to be independent from each other, and each have sufficient min-entropy, conditioned on the CRS. We require that X and Y are efficiently sampleable given the CRS. This is needed since we are in the computational setting, and in particular, security breaks down if the sources can be used to break our hardness assumption.

Our 2-source extractor. We define an (n_1, n_2, k_1, k_2) computational 2-source extractor (in the CRS model) as a function $E : \{0,1\}^{n_1} \times \{0,1\}^{n_2} \times \{0,1\}^c \rightarrow \{0,1\}^m$ such that for all sources (X, Y), which conditioned on the crs, are independent, are polynomially sampleable, and have min-entropy at least k_1, k_2 respectively, it holds that $(E(X, Y, \mathsf{crs}), Y, \mathsf{crs})$ is computationally indistinguishable from (U, Y, crs), namely, any polynomial size adversary cannot distinguish $(E(X, Y, \mathsf{crs}), Y, \mathsf{crs})$ from (U, Y, crs) with non-negligible advantage.[4]

We construct such a 2-source extractor (with unbalanced sources) assuming the sub-exponential security of DDH [5].

Theorem 1 (Informal). *Let $\lambda \in \mathbb{N}$ denote the security parameter and assume the sub-exponential hardness of DDH. For every constant $\epsilon > 0$, there exist constants $\delta > 0, c > 1$ such that there exists an explicit (n_1, n_2, k_1, k_2) computational 2-source extractor in the CRS model, with $n_1 = \Omega(\lambda), n_2 \leq \lambda^\delta$ and min-entropy $k_1 = n_1^\epsilon, k_2 = \log^c(\lambda)$.*

---

[3] In this way, the CRS is different from the seed of a seeded extractor, which must be completely independent of the source.

[4] Requiring the output of the extractor to be random even given the source Y is a standard requirement, and such an extractor is known as a *strong* extractor.

[5] The sub-exponential DDH assumption asserts that there exists a group G such that no sub-exponential time algorithm can distinguish between (g^a, g^b, g^{ab}) and (g^a, g^b, g^c), where g is a fixed generator of G, and where a, b, c are chosen randomly from $\mathbb{Z}_q$, where q denotes the order of G.

Our non-malleable extractor. We also construct a computational non-malleable extractor in the CRS model. A non-malleable extractor is a notion that was introduced by Dodis and Wichs [17]. This notion is motivated by cryptography, and was used to achieve *privacy amplification*, i.e., to "boost" a private weak key into a private uniform one.

Similar to standard extractors, one can consider non-malleable extractors both in the seeded setting and in 2-source setting. The seeded version is defined as follows: A strong (k, ϵ) t-non-malleable-extractor is a function $E : \{0,1\}^n \times \{0,1\}^d \to \{0,1\}^m$ s.t. for all functions $f_1, \ldots, f_t : \{0,1\}^d \to \{0,1\}^d$, that have no fixed points, it holds that

$$(Y, E(X,Y), E(X, f_1(Y)), \ldots, E(X, f_t(Y))) \equiv_\epsilon (Y, U, E(X, f_1(Y)), \ldots, E(X, f_t(Y)))$$

where X, Y, U are independent, X has min-entropy at least k, Y is distributed uniformly over $\{0,1\}^d$ and U is distributed uniformly over $\{0,1\}^m$. Non-malleable 2-source extractors are defined similarly to seeded ones, except that the requirement that Y is uniformly distributed is relaxed; i.e., it is only required to have sufficient min-entropy and be independent of X. In addition, both the sources can be tampered independently.

Clearly, in the information theoretic setting, such non-malleable extractors (both seeded and 2-sources ones) can exist only for a bounded t.

In this work we construct a computational analogue of a non-malleable extractor in the CRS model. As opposed to the information theoretic setting, where the number of tampering attacks t is a-priori bounded, in the computational setting we allow the adversary to tamper an *arbitrary* (polynomial) number of times (i.e., we do not fix an a priori bound t on the number of tampering functions). In fact, in addition to giving the adversary $Y, E(X,Y)$, we can even give the adversary access to an oracle that on input $Y' \neq Y$, outputs $E(X, Y')$.

We would like to note that the object we construct is somewhere in between a seeded and a 2-source non-malleable extractor. While the source Y need not be uniformly distributed, we only allow tampering with Y, and do not allow tampering with the other source.

More formally, we define an (n_1, n_2, k_1, k_2) computational non-malleable extractor (in the CRS model) as a function $E : \{0,1\}^{n_1} \times \{0,1\}^{n_2} \times \{0,1\}^c \to \{0,1\}^m$ such that for all sources X, Y that are polynomially sampleable, are independent, and have min-entropy at least k_1 and k_2 respectively, conditioned on the CRS, it holds that $(E(X, Y, \mathrm{CRS}), \mathrm{CRS}, Y)$ is computationally indistinguishable from (U, CRS, Y), even with respect to PPT adversaries that are given access to an oracle that on input $Y' \neq Y$ outputs $E(X, Y', \mathrm{CRS})$. Clearly, such adversaries can obtain $E(X, Y', \mathrm{CRS})$ for an arbitrary $t = \mathrm{poly}(n)$ number of different samples Y', that depend on Y and the CRS.

In this setting, we obtain the following two incomparable results, in the high and low min-entropy regimes respectively.

Theorem 2 (Informal). *Let $\lambda \in \mathbb{N}$ denote the security parameter and assume the sub-exponential security of DDH. For every constant $\epsilon > 0$, there exists a constant $c > 0$ such that there exists an explicit (n_1, n_2, k_1, k_2) computational non-malleable extractor resisting arbitrarily polynomial tamperings where:*

$$n_1 = \Omega(\lambda), \log^c \lambda \leq n_2, k_1 = n_1^\epsilon, k_2 = 0.51 n_2$$

Theorem 3 (Informal). *Let $\lambda \in \mathbb{N}$ denote the security parameter and assume the sub-exponential security of DDH. For every constant $\epsilon > 0$, there exist constants $\delta, c > 0$ such that there exists an explicit (n_1, n_2, k_1, k_2) computational non-malleable extractor resisting arbitrarily polynomial tamperings, where:*

$$n_1 = \Omega(\lambda), \log^c \lambda \leq n_2 \leq \lambda^\delta, k_1 = n_1^\epsilon, k_2 = \log^c n_2$$

We mention that in our formal theorems, under the sub-exponential hardness of DDH, we allow the sources to be sampled in super-polynomial time and the adversary to run in super-polynomial time. This will be used in Sect. 6 to convert a non-malleable extractor (in the high entropy regime) into a 2-source extractor (in the low entropy regime). We refer the reader to Sects. 5 and 6 for more details.

2   Our Techniques

We obtain our results in three steps.

1. We first construct a computational non-malleable extractor in the CRS model, for sources in the *high entropy* regime (i.e., assuming one of the sources has min entropy rate larger than 1/2). Our construction follows the blueprint of [5], who built leaky pseudo-entropy functions based on the sub-exponential hardness of DDH. When viewed differently, their construction can be framed as showing how to use cryptography to convert any (information theoretic) 2-source extractor (with negligible error) into a computational non-malleable extractor in the CRS model (for sources with roughly the same min-entropy as in the underlying 2-source extractor). Since we only have information theoretic 2-source extractors for sources in the high entropy regime, we obtain a computational non-malleable extractor (in the CRS model) for sources in the high entropy regime.

   Importantly, this extractor is non-malleable w.r.t. *arbitrarily many* tampering functions (a property that is impossible to achieve information theoretically). This contribution is mainly conceptual.

2. We then describe how this extractor can be used to obtain a computational 2-source extractor (in the CRS model) with negligible error for *low min-entropy* sources. This part contains the bulk of the technical difficulty of this work. Specifically, we follow the blueprint of [1], which shows how to convert any (information-theoretic) non-malleable extractor into a 2-source extractor (with negligible error for low min-entropy sources). However, this transformation assumes that the non-malleable extractor has a somewhat

optimal dependence between the seed length and the allowable number of tampering functions. Prior to our work, no explicit constructions of non-malleable extractors were known to satisfy this requirement.

Our computational non-malleable extractor does satisfy this requirement, and therefore we manage to use the [1] blueprint to construct the desired 2-source extractor. Nevertheless, there are multiple unique challenges that come up when trying to apply their transformation in the computational setting. One of our key ideas to overcome these challenges involves using the leakage lemma of Gentry and Wichs [18]. We elaborate on this in Sect. 2.2.

3. To achieve our final construction of a computational non-malleable extractor (in the CRS model) with negligible error for *low min-entropy* sources, we again use the blueprint from [5], however, this time we use our *computational* 2-source extractor as a building block. To argue security, we prove that the [5] transformation goes through even if we start with a *computational* 2-source extractor. As above, many technical challenges arise when considering the computational setting.

2.1 From 2-Source Extractors to Non-malleable Extractors

We begin with the observation that the construction of leaky psuedo-random functions from [5], can be framed more generally as a cryptographic reduction from (information theoretic) 2-source extractors to computational non-malleable extractors in the CRS model. Since we only know information theoretic 2-source extractors (with negligible error) in the high-entropy regime, we obtain a computational non-malleable extractor (in the CRS model) in the high entropy regime.

Moreover, we generalize the [5] blueprint, by showing that one can convert any *computational* 2-source extractor (in the CRS model) to a computational non-malleable extractor (in the CRS model). This introduces several technical difficulties which we elaborate on in Sect. 5. This generalization is needed to obtain our final result, of a computational non-malleable extractor (in the CRS model) for sources with low min-entropy (i.e., to achieve Item 3 in the overview above).

We next describe our interpretation of the [5] blueprint for converting any (information theoretic) 2-source extractor into a computational non-malleable one (in the CRS model):

Start with any 2-source extractor

$$2\mathsf{Ext} : \{0,1\}^{n_1} \times \{0,1\}^{n_2} \to \{0,1\}^m,$$

with negligible error (eg., [4,26]).

Assume the existence of the following two cryptographic primitives:

1. A collision resistant function family $\mathcal{H}$, where for each $h \in \mathcal{H}$,

$$h : \{0,1\}^{n_2} \to \{0,1\}^k,$$

where k is significantly smaller than the min-entropy of the second source of 2Ext.

A collision resistant hash family has the guarantee that given a random function $h \leftarrow \mathcal{H}$ it is hard to find two distinct elements $y_1, y_2 \in \{0,1\}^{n_2}$ such that $h(y_1) = h(y_2)$.

2. A family of lossy functions $\mathcal{F}$, where for each $f \in \mathcal{F}$,

$$f : \{0,1\}^{n_1} \to \{0,1\}^{n_1}.$$

A lossy function family consist of two types of functions: injective and lossy. Each lossy function loses most of the information about the input (i.e., the image size is very small). It is assumed that it is hard to distinguish between a random injective function and a random lossy function in the family.

We note that both these primitive can be constructed under the DDH assumption, which is a standard cryptographic assumption.[6]

We next show how these cryptographic primites can be used to convert 2Ext into a computational non-malleable 2-source extractor in the CRS model. We start by describing the CRS.

The CRS consists of a random function $h \leftarrow \mathcal{H}$ from the collision-resistant hash family, and consists of $2k$ random injective functions from the lossy function family $\mathcal{F}$, denoted by

$$f_{1,0}, f_{2,0}, \ldots, f_{k,0}$$
$$f_{1,1}, f_{2,1}, \ldots, f_{k,1}$$

The computational non-malleable extractor (in the CRS model) is defined by

$$\mathsf{cnm\text{-}Ext}(x, y, \mathsf{crs}) := 2\mathsf{Ext}(f_{\mathsf{crs}, h(y)}(x), y),$$

where

$$f_{\mathsf{crs}, s}(x) := f_{1, s_1} \circ \ldots \circ f_{k, s_k}(x)$$

In what follows, we recall the proof idea from [5]. To this end, consider any polynomial size adversary $\mathcal{A}$ that obtains either $(\mathsf{cnm\text{-}Ext}(x, y), y, \mathsf{crs})$ or (U, y, crs), together with an oracle $\mathcal{O}$ that has (x, y, crs) hardwired, and on input y' outputs $\perp$ if $y' = y$, and otherwise outputs nm-Ext(x, y', crs). By the collision resistance property of h, $\mathcal{A}$ queries the oracle on input y' s.t. $h(y') = h(y)$ only with negligible probability. Therefore, the oracle $\mathcal{O}$ can be replaced by a different oracle, that only hardwires $(\mathsf{crs}, h(y), x)$ and on input y' outputs $\perp$ if $h(y') = h(y)$, and otherwise outputs $\mathsf{cnm\text{-}Ext}(x, y')$.

A key observation is that access to this oracle can be simulated entirely given only $\mathsf{crs}, h(y)$ and $(Z_1, \ldots Z_k)$, where

$$Z_k = f_{k, 1-h(y)_k}(x)$$
$$Z_{k-1} = f_{k-1, 1-h(y)_{k-1}}(f_{k, h(y)_k}(x))$$
$$\vdots$$
$$Z_1 = f_{1, 1-h(y)_1}(f_{2, h(y)_2}(\ldots f_{k, h(y)_k}(x)))$$

---

[6] The DDH assumption asserts that there exists a group G such that (g^a, g^b, g^{ab}) is computationally indistinguishable from (g^a, g^b, g^c), where g is a fixed generator of G, and where a, b, c are chosen randomly from $\mathbb{Z}_q$, where q denotes the order of G.

Since the adversary $\mathcal{A}$ cannot distinguish between random injective functions and random lossy ones, we can change the CRS to ensure that functions $f_{1,h(y)_1}, \ldots, f_{k,h(y)_k}$ are injective, whereas the functions $f_{1,1-h(y)_1}, \ldots, f_{k,1-h(y)_k}$ are all lossy. By setting k (the size of the output of the hash) to be small enough, we can guarantee that Y has high min-entropy conditioned on $h(y)$ and $Z = (Z_1, \ldots, Z_k)$. In addition, by setting the image of the lossy functions to be small enough, we can guarantee that X also has high min-entropy conditioned on $h(y)$ and $Z = (Z_1, \ldots, Z_k)$. Moreover, it is easy to seet that X and Y remain independent conditioned on $h(Y)$ and Z. Thus, we can use the fact that 2Ext is a (strong) 2-source extractor, to argue that the output of our non-malleable extractor is close to uniform.

This was, of course, a very simplified overview. A careful reader may have observed a circularity in the intuition above: Recall that we sample the crs such that for $b = h(y)$, the functions $f_{1,b_1}, \ldots, f_{k,b_k}$ are injective, whereas $f_{1,1-b_1}, \ldots, f_{k,1-b_k}$ are lossy. Thus, the crs implicitly depends on y (via $b = h(y)$). This results in a circularity, because y is then sampled as a function of this crs, and hence may not satisfy that $b = h(y)$. The formal proof requires us to carefully deal with this (and other) dependency issues that arise when formalizing this intuition. In a nutshell, we overcome this circularity by strengthening our assumption to a sub-exponential one, namely we assume the sub-exponential hardness of DDH as opposed to the (more standard) polynomial hardness of DDH.

In addition, as mentioned above, we prove that this transformation goes through even if the underlying 2-source extractor is a *computational* one (in the CRS model). This introduces various other technical difficulties. We refer the reader to Sect. 5 for the details.

2.2   Our 2-Source Extractor

As mentioned earlier, we construct our computational 2-source extractor by following the blueprint of [1], which shows how to use a non-malleable seeded extractor to construct a 2-source extractor (in the low entropy regime). However, they need the non-malleable seeded extractor to have the property that the seed length is significantly smaller than $t \log(1/\epsilon)$, where t is the number of tampering functions that the non-malleable extractor is secure against, and where ϵ is the error.[7] Unfortunately, all known (information theoretic) non-malleable extractors require the seed length to be at least $t \log(1/\epsilon)$.

We note that in Sect. 2.1, we obtained computational non-malleable extractor (in the CRS model) for sources in the high-entropy regime (by using a 2-source extractor from [4,26] as a building block). This extractor, in particular, can be seen as a non-malleable *seeded* extractor. Importantly, it satisfies the requirements of [1], since in our construction the seed length is independent of t. Thus, one would expect that instantiating the [1] transformation with our computational non-malleable extractor (in the CRS model), would directly yield a

---

[7] The exact parameters are not relevant to this overview.

computational 2-source extractor (in the CRS model), with negligible error for low min-entropy sources. However, this turns out not to be the case.

The reason is that the analysis of [1] crucially requires the underlying non-malleable extractor to be secure against adversaries that run in *unbounded time*. Specifically, even given an efficient adversary that contradicts the security of the 2-source extractor, [1] obtain an *inefficient* adversary that contradicts the security of the underlying non-malleable extractor. Since our underlying non-malleable extractor is *computational*, it is not clear if this gets us anywhere. Moreover, dealing with sources that can depend on the CRS causes further technical problems. Nevertheless, we show that the construction of [1] can be instantiated with our computational non-malleable extractor in the CRS model, but with a substantially different (and more technically involved) analysis. In particular, in our analysis we make a novel use of the leakage lemma of Gentry and Wichs [18].

The blueprint of [1]. To better understand these technicalities, we begin by describing the transformation of [1]. Their transformation uses a disperser as a building block.

A (K, K') disperser is a function

$$\Gamma : \{0, 1\}^{n_2} \times [t] \to \{0, 1\}^d$$

such that for every subset A of $\{0, 1\}^{n_2}$ that is of size $\geq K$, it holds that the size of the set of neighbors of A under Γ is at least K'.

The [1]-transformation takes a seeded non-malleable extractor

$$\text{nm-Ext} : \{0, 1\}^{n_1} \times \{0, 1\}^d \to \{0, 1\}^m$$

and a disperser

$$\Gamma : \{0, 1\}^{n_2} \times [t] \to \{0, 1\}^d,$$

and constructs the following 2-source extractor $2\text{Ext} : \{0, 1\}^{n_1} \times \{0, 1\}^{n_2} \to \{0, 1\}^m$, defined by

$$2\text{Ext}(x_1, x_2) = \bigoplus_{y : \exists i \text{ s.t. } \Gamma(x_2, i) = y} \text{nm-Ext}(x_1, y)$$

In this work, we instantiate their transformation in the computational setting. In what follows, we first describe the key ideas in the proof from [1], and then we explain the technical difficulties that arise in the computational setting, and how we resolve them.

Fix any two independent sources X_1 and X_2 with "sufficient" min-entropy. One can argue that

$$(2\text{Ext}(X_1, X_2), X_2) \equiv (U, X_2)$$

as follows:

1. By the definition of an (information-theoretic) t-non-malleable extractor nm-Ext, for a random $y \in \{0,1\}^d$, for all $y'_1, \ldots, y'_t$ that are distinct from y, it holds that

$$(\text{nm-Ext}(X_1, y), \text{nm-Ext}(X_1, y'_1), \ldots, \text{nm-Ext}(X_1, y'_t)) \equiv$$
$$(U, \text{nm-Ext}(X_1, y'_1), \ldots, \text{nm-Ext}(X_1, y'_t)).$$

   We call a y that satisfies the above property, a good y. By a standard averaging argument one can argue that an overwhelming fraction of y's are good.

2. Fix any x_2 for which there exists an $i \in [t]$ such that $y = \Gamma(x_2, i)$ is good. This means that nm-Ext(X_1, y) is statistically close to uniform, even given nm-Ext$(X_1, \Gamma(x_2, j))$ for every $j \in [t]\backslash\{i\}$ such that $\Gamma(x_2, j) \neq y$, which in turn implies that the XOR of these (distinct) values is close to uniform, which implies that $2\text{Ext}(X_1, x_2)$ is close to uniform.

3. It thus suffice to show that for $x_2 \leftarrow X_2$, with overwhelming probability there exists an $i \in [t]$ such that $y = \Gamma(x_2, i)$ is good. This can be done by relying on the disperser. Specifically, consider the set of bad x_2's for which $y = \Gamma(x_2, i)$ is not good for all $i \in [t]$. Loosely speaking, if this set occurs with noticeable probability, then one can use the property of the disperser to argue that the support of $\Gamma(x_2, i)$ for $x_2 \in$ bad, $i \in [t]$ covers a large fraction of the y's, and by definition, none of these y's can be good, contradicting the fact that we argued above that an overwhelming fraction of y's must be good.

This completes the outline of the proof in [1].

The Computational Setting. The intuitive analysis above, while easy to formalize in the information theoretic setting, does not carry over to the computational setting, for various reasons.

1. First, it is not clear that a *computational non-malleable extractor* satisfies the first property of the [1] outline. Namely, it is not clear that for an overwhelming fraction of $y \in \{0,1\}^d$, it holds that for all $y'_1, \ldots y'_t$ distinct from y,

$$(\text{cnm-Ext}(X_1, y), \text{cnm-Ext}(X_1, y'_1), \ldots, \text{cnm-Ext}(X_1, y'_t)) \approx$$
$$(U, \text{cnm-Ext}(X_1, y'_1), \ldots, \text{cnm-Ext}(X_1, y'_t)),$$

   where $\approx$ denotes computational indistinguishability. This is because the computational advantage of an efficient adversary on different y's could cancel out.

2. More importantly, in the computational setting, we would have to construct an *efficient* reduction $\mathcal{R}$ that breaks the non-malleable extractor, given any adversary $\mathcal{A}$ that breaks the 2-source extractor.

$\mathcal{R}$ obtains input $(\alpha, \widehat{y})$, where $\widehat{y}$ is a random seed and where α is either chosen according to cnm-Ext$(X_1, \widehat{y})$ or is chosen uniformly at random. In addition, $\mathcal{R}$ obtains an oracle that outputs cnm-Ext(X_1, y') on input $y' \neq \widehat{y}$. The reduction $\mathcal{R}$ is required to *efficiently* distinguish between the case where $\alpha \leftarrow$ cnm-Ext$(X_1, \widehat{y})$ and the case where α is chosen uniformly at random.

In order to use $\mathcal{A}$, $\mathcal{R}$ needs to generate a challenge for $\mathcal{A}$ that corresponds either to the output of the 2-source extractor (if α was the output of cnm-Ext) or uniform (if α was uniform). $\mathcal{R}$ also needs to generate a corresponding x_2 for $\mathcal{A}$, that is sampled according to X_2. How can it generate these values? If $\mathcal{R}$ were allowed to be inefficient, then a simple strategy for $\mathcal{R}$ would be the following:

- Sample $\widehat{x}_2 \leftarrow X_2$ conditioned on the existence of $i \in [t]$ such that $\widehat{y} = \Gamma(\widehat{x}_2, i)$.
- Next, query the oracle on inputs $(y_1, \ldots y_t)$ where for every $i \in [t]$, $y_i = \Gamma(\widehat{x}_2, i)$. As a result, $\mathcal{R}$ obtains $z_i = $ cnm-Ext(x_1, y_i) for all $i \in [t] \backslash \widehat{i}$, and sets $z = \left(\bigoplus_{i \in [t]} z_i \right) \oplus \alpha$ (after removing duplicates).
- It is easy to see that $\widehat{x}_2$ is generated from the distribution X_2. Moreover, if α is the output of cnm-Ext, then z corresponds to 2Ext(x_1, x_2), and otherwise to uniform.
- At this point, if $\mathcal{A}$ distinguishes z from uniform, $\mathcal{R}$ can echo the output of $\mathcal{A}$ to distinguish α from uniform.

Unfortunately, this does not help us much, because the underlying non-malleable extractor is only guaranteed to be secure against *efficient* adversaries, whereas the adversary $\mathcal{R}$ that we just outlined, crucially needs to invert the disperser. It is not clear that one can build dispersers in our parameter setting that are efficiently invertible. Moreover, even if there was a way to invert the disperser, $\mathcal{R}$ would need to ensure that the inverse $\widehat{x}_2$ is sampled from the correct distribution, and it is unclear whether this can be done efficiently.

Our key ideas. Our first key idea is to get around this technicality by using the leakage lemma as follows: Since $\mathcal{R}$ on input $\widehat{y}$ cannot find $\widehat{x}_2$ efficiently, we will attempt to view $\widehat{x}_2$ as inefficiently computable *leakage* on $\widehat{y}$, and *simulate* $\widehat{x}_2$ using the following leakage lemma. Informally, this lemma says that any inefficiently computable function that outputs γ bits, can be simulated in time roughly $O(2^\gamma)$ relative to all efficient distinguishers.

Lemma 1 [10,18,21]. *Fix $d, \gamma \in \mathbb{N}$ and fix $\epsilon > 0$. Let $\mathcal{Y}$ be any distribution over $\{0,1\}^d$. Consider any randomized leakage function $\pi : \{0,1\}^d \rightarrow \{0,1\}^\gamma$. For every T, there exists a randomized function $\widehat{\pi}$ computable by a circuit of size* $\mathrm{poly}\left(2^\gamma \epsilon^{-1} T^{\log T} \right)$ *such that for every randomized distinguisher $\mathcal{D}$ that runs in time at most T,*

$$| \Pr[\mathcal{D}(\mathcal{Y}, \pi(\mathcal{Y})) = 1] - \Pr[\mathcal{D}(\mathcal{Y}, \widehat{\pi}(\mathcal{Y})) = 1] | \leq \epsilon$$

By Lemma 1, simulating $\widehat{x}_2$ given $\widehat{y}$ would take time roughly $O(2^{|\widehat{x}_2|})$.[8] While this simulator is clearly not as efficient as we would like, one can hope that things still work out if the underlying non-malleable extractor is secure against adversaries running in time $O(2^{|\widehat{x}_2|})$.

---

[8] Jumping ahead, this is the reason that we end up with a 2-source extractor for unbalanced sources (see Theorem 3).

However, any disperser (with our setting of parameter, where t is small) must be compressing, which means that $|\hat{x}_2| > |\hat{y}|$. Therefore, the simulator's running time would be more than $O(2^{|\hat{y}|})$. Howeover, $\hat{y}$ corresponds to the input of the non-malleable extractor, and recall that our non-malleable extractor applies a (compressing) collision-resistant hash function to its input y. Therefore, the non-malleable extractor is completely *insecure* against adversaries that run in time $O(2^{|\hat{y}|})$. This creates a circular dependency, and it may appear that this approach is doomed to fail. Nevertheless, we manage to apply the leakage lemma in a more sophisticated way. Recall that the adversary outlined above queries its oracle on $\{y_j\}_{j \in [t] \setminus \{i\}}$, where $y_j = \Gamma(\hat{x}_2, j)$ and where $\hat{x}_2 \leftarrow X_2$ such that $\hat{y} = \Gamma(\hat{x}_2, i)$. Importantly, we show that the elements in $\{y_j\}_{j \in [t]}$ form a hash collision only with negligible probability, assuming the sources for the 2-source extractor are somewhat efficiently sampleable. Otherwise, it would be possible to break the hash function in time proportional to that required to sample sources for the 2-source extractor.

Thus, in order to use the leakage lemma effectively, we prove a stronger form of security of our non-malleable extractor: we show that it is secure against adversaries that potentially run in time larger than the time against which the hash function is secure; as long as these adversaries do not query the oracle of the non-malleable extractor on hash collisions. By setting the parameters appropriately, this allows us to use the leakage lemma, and thus complete the argument outlined above. We therefore get a construction of a 2-source extractor, by relying on a non-malleable extractor that is secure against adversaries running in time $O(2^{|\hat{y}|})$, as long as they do not make hash collision queries.

Roadmap. The rest of this paper is organized as follows. In Sect. 3, we provide the relevant preliminaries. In Sect. 4, we provide our new definitions of computational 2-source extractors and non-malleable extractors in the CRS model.

In Sect. 5 we show how to convert a computational 2-source extractor (in the CRS model) into a computational non-malleable extractor (in the CRS model), with similar min-entropy guarantees. By applying this transformation to the information theoretic 2-source extractors of [4] or [26], we get a computational non-malleable extractor (in the CRS model) for sources in the high min-entropy regime.

In Sect. 6 we show how to convert our computatational non-malleable extractor (in the CRS model) into a computational 2-source extractor (in the CRS model) in the low entropy regime. Finally, we obtain a computational non-malleable extractor (in the CRS model) in the low entropy regime, by applying the transformation from Sect. 5 to the computational 2-source extractor that we constructed in Sect. 6.

3   Preliminaries

In this section, we discuss some preliminaries needed for the later sections. This includes facts about min-entropy, lossy functions, dispersers, and the leakage lemma that we rely on.

Definition 1. *A function* $\mu : \mathbb{N} \to \mathbb{N}$ *is said to be* negligible, *denoted by* $\mu = \text{neg}(\lambda)$, *if for every polynomial* $p : \mathbb{N} \to \mathbb{N}$ *there exists a constant* $c \in \mathbb{N}$ *such that for every* $\lambda > c$ *it holds that*

$$\mu(\lambda) \leq 1/p(\lambda).$$

For any function $T : \mathbb{N} \to \mathbb{N}$, *we say that* μ *is* negligible in T, *denoted by* $\mu(\lambda) = \text{neg}(T(\lambda))$ *if for every polynomial* $p : \mathbb{N} \to \mathbb{N}$ *there exists a constant* $c \in \mathbb{N}$ *such that for every* $\lambda > c$ *it holds that*

$$\mu(\lambda) \leq 1/p(T(\lambda)).$$

Definition 2. *Two distribution ensembles* $X = \{X_\lambda\}_{\lambda \in \mathbb{N}}$ *and* $Y = \{Y_\lambda\}_{\lambda \in \mathbb{N}}$ *are said to be* $T(\lambda)$-indistinguishable *if for every* $\text{poly}(T)$ *size circuit* $\mathcal{A}$,

$$\left| \Pr_{x \leftarrow X_\lambda} [\mathcal{A}(x) = 1] - \Pr_{y \leftarrow Y_\lambda} [\mathcal{A}(y) = 1] \right| = \text{neg}(T(\lambda))$$

Definition 3. *A distribution* X *over a domain* D *is said to have* min-entropy k, *denoted by* $H_\infty(X) = k$, *if for every* $z \in D$,

$$\Pr_{x \leftarrow X} [x = z] \leq 2^{-k}.$$

In this paper, we consider sources with average conditional min entropy, as defined in [16] (and also in the quantum information literature). This notion is less restrictive than worst case conditional min-entropy (and therefore this strengthens our results), and is sometimes more suitable for cryptographic applications.

Definition 4 [16]. *Let* X *and* Y *be two distributions. The average conditional min-entropy of* X *conditioned on* Y, *denoted by* $H_\infty(X|Y)$[9] *is*

$$H_\infty(X|Y) = -\log E_{y \leftarrow Y} \max_x \Pr[X = x | Y = y] = -\log(\mathbb{E}_{y \leftarrow Y}[2^{-H_\infty(X|Y=y)}])$$

Note that $2^{-H_\infty(X|Y)}$ *is the highest probability of guessing the value of the random variable* X *given the value of* Y.

We will rely on the following useful claims about average conditional min-entropy.

Claim [16]. Let X, Y and Z be three distributions, where 2^b is the number of elements in the support of Y. Then,

$$H_\infty(X|Y, Z) \geq H_\infty(X, Y|Z) - b$$

Claim. Let X, Y and Z be three distributions, then

$$H_\infty(X|Y) \geq H_\infty(X|Y, Z)$$

We defer the proof of this claim to the full version.

---

[9] This is often denoted by $\tilde{H}_\infty(X|Y)$ in the literature.

3.1   Collision Resistan Hash Functions

In this work we rely on the existence of a collision resistant function family. Our setting of parameters is slightly non-standard, since our input domain may differ from the security parameter.

Definition 5 ($T(\lambda)$-secure collision resistant hash functions). *Let* n, k : $\mathbb{N} \to \mathbb{N}$ *be functions of the security parameter, and let* $\mathcal{H} = \{\mathcal{H}_\lambda\}_{\lambda \in \mathbb{N}}$ *be a family of functions where for every* $\lambda \in \mathbb{N}$ *and every* $h \in \mathcal{H}_\lambda$,

$$h : \{0,1\}^{n(\lambda)} \to \{0,1\}^{k(\lambda)}.$$

This function family is said to be a $T(\lambda)$-*secure collision resistant hash family if for every* $\text{poly}(T(\lambda))$-*size adversary* $\mathcal{A}$ *there exists a negligible function* ν *such that for every* $\lambda \in \mathbb{N}$,

$$\Pr_{h \leftarrow \mathcal{H}_\lambda} [\mathcal{A}(h) = (x_1, x_2) \text{ s.t. } (x_1 \neq x_2) \wedge h(x_1) = h(x_2)] = \nu(T(\lambda)).$$

Theorem 4. *Assuming sub-exponential hardness of DDH, there exists a constant* $\delta > 0$ *such that for every pair of polynomials* $n, k : \mathbb{N} \to \mathbb{N}$ *such that* $\text{poly}(\lambda) \geq n(\lambda) > k(\lambda) \geq \Omega(\lambda)$ *and for* $T(\lambda) = 2^{\lambda^\delta}$, *there exists a* $T(\lambda)$-*secure collision resistant hash family* $\mathcal{H}_\lambda$, *where for every* $h \in \mathcal{H}_\lambda$, $h : \{0,1\}^{n(\lambda)} \to \{0,1\}^{k(\lambda)}$.

3.2   Lossy Functions

Lossy functions were defined by Peikert and Waters in [25]. Loosely speaking a lossy function family consists of functions of two types: lossy functions and injective ones. The lossy ones (information theoretically) lose most of the information about the input; i.e., the image is significantly smaller than the domain. The injective functions, on the other hand, are injective. It is required that it is (computationally) hard to distinguish between a random lossy function in the family and a random injective function in the family. In our setting, we will need a lossy function family where the range and the domain are of a similar size (or close to being a similar size). Intuitively, the reason is that we apply these functions to our min-entropy source, and if the functions produce output strings that are much longer than the input strings then we will lose in the min-entropy rate.

Definition 6 (Lossy functions). *A function family* $\mathcal{F} = \{\mathcal{F}_\lambda\}_{\lambda \in \mathbb{N}}$ *is a* (T, n, w)-*lossy function family if the following conditions hold:*

- *There are two probabilistic polynomial time seed generation algorithms* Gen_{inj} *and* Gen_{loss} *s.t. for any* $\text{poly}(T(\lambda))$-*size* $\mathcal{A}$, *it holds that*

$$\left| \Pr_{s \leftarrow \text{Gen}_{\text{inj}}(1^\lambda)} [\mathcal{A}(s) = 1] - \Pr_{s \leftarrow \text{Gen}_{\text{loss}}(1^\lambda)} [\mathcal{A}(s) = 1] \right| = \text{neg}(T(\lambda)).$$

- For every $\lambda \in \mathbb{N}$ and every $f \in \mathcal{F}_\lambda$, $f : \{0,1\}^{n(\lambda)} \to \{0,1\}^{n(\lambda)}$.
- For every $\lambda \in \mathbb{N}$ and every $s \in \text{Gen}_{\text{inj}}(1^\lambda)$, $f_s \in \mathcal{F}_\lambda$ is injective.
- For every $\lambda \in \mathbb{N}$ and every $s \in \text{Gen}_{\text{loss}}(1^\lambda)$, $f_s \in \mathcal{F}_\lambda$ is lossy i.e. its image size is at most $2^{n(\lambda)-w}$.
- There is a polynomial time algorithm Eval s.t. $\text{Eval}(s,x) = f_s(x)$ for every $\lambda \in \mathbb{N}$, every s in the support of $\text{Gen}_{\text{inj}}(1^\lambda) \cup \text{Gen}_{\text{loss}}(1^\lambda)$ and every $x \in \{0,1\}^{n(\lambda)}$.

Modifying the construction in [25] (to ensure that the input and output lengths of the functions are the same for every $n = \text{poly}(\lambda)$), [5] gave a construction of a (T, n, w)-lossy function family, for $w = n - n^\epsilon$ (where $\epsilon > 0$ can be any arbitrary small constant), and for every T assuming the DDH assumption holds against $\text{poly}(T)$-size adversaries.

In this work, we use the following lemma.

Lemma 2 [5,25]. *For any constant $\epsilon > 0$ there exists a constant $\delta > 0$ such that for every $\Omega(\lambda) \leq n(\lambda) \leq \text{poly}(\lambda)$ there exists a (T, n, w)-lossy function family, with $T(\lambda) = 2^{\lambda^\delta}$ and $w = n - n^\epsilon$, assuming the sub-exponential DDH assumption.*

3.3 Leakage Lemma

We make use of the following lemma, which shows that any inefficient leakage function can be simulated efficiently relative to a class of distinguishers.

Lemma 3 [10,18,21]. *Fix $d, \gamma \in \mathbb{N}$ and fix $\epsilon > 0$. Let $\mathcal{Y}$ be any distribution over $\{0,1\}^d$. Consider any randomized leakage function $\pi : \{0,1\}^d \to \{0,1\}^\gamma$.*

For every T, there exists a randomized function $\widehat{\pi}$ computable by a circuit of size $\text{poly}(2^\gamma \epsilon^{-1} T)$ such that for every randomized distinguisher $\mathcal{D}$ that runs in time at most T,

$$|\Pr[\mathcal{D}(\mathcal{Y}, \pi(\mathcal{Y})) = 1] - \Pr[\mathcal{D}(\mathcal{Y}, \widehat{\pi}(\mathcal{Y})) = 1]| \leq \epsilon$$

3.4 Dispersers

Definition 7. *A function $\Gamma : [N] \times [t] \to [D]$ is a (K, K') disperser if for every $A \subseteq [N]$ with $|A| \geq K$ it holds that $\left| \bigcup_{a \in A, i \in [t]} \{\Gamma(a, i)\} \right| \geq K'$.*

We will rely on dispersers which follow from the known constructions of seeded extractors (e.g. [19]).

Theorem 5 (e.g. [19]). *There exists a constant c such that the following holds. For every N, K, K', D such that $D \leq \sqrt{K}$ and $K' \leq D/2$, there exists an efficient (K, K')-disperser*

$$\Gamma : [N] \times [t] \to [D]$$

with degree

$$t = \log^c(N)$$

4 Computational Extractors: Definitions

In this section, we define extractors in the computational setting with a CRS. We define both a 2-source extractor and a non-malleable extractor in this setting.

In both definitions, we allow the min-entropy sources to depend on the CRS, but require that they are efficiently sampleable conditioned on the CRS (where the efficiency is specified by a parameter T). We also allow each source to partially leak, as long as the source has sufficient min-entropy conditioned on the CRS and the leakage.

At first, it may seem that there is no need to consider leakage explicitly, since one can incorporate the leakage as part of the definition of the min-entropy source; i.e., define the source w.r.t. a fixed leakage value. However, the resulting source may not be efficiently sampleable. For example, if the leakage on a source X is $h(X)$, where h is a collision resistant hash function, then sampling $x \leftarrow X$ conditioned on a given leakage value is computationally hard, due to the collision resistance property of h. Therefore, in the definitions below we consider leakage explicitely.

More specifically, for two sources X and Y we allow leakage on Y, which we will denote by L_{init}; and then allow leakage on X (that can also depend on L_{init}), which we will denote by L_{final}. Moreover, both L_{init} and L_{final} can depend on the CRS. We mention that a more general leakage model is one which allows first leakage on Y, then allows leakage on X (that may depend on the initial leakage), and then again allows leakage on Y (that may depend on all the leakage so far), etc. Unfortunately, we do not know how to obtain our results in this more general leakage model.

For technical reasons, we also allow one of the sources (the one which is given to the adversary in the clear, as part of the definition of a strong extractor) to be sampled together with auxiliary information AUX. This auxiliary information depends on the source and on the CRS. As in the leakage case, we need to consider this auxiliary information explicitly, since in our proofs we will use an auxiliary input which is hard to compute given the source and CRS (and therefore cannot generate it while ensuring the security of our underlying hardness assumption). Importantly, it is easy to generate this auxiliary information together with the source, jointly as a function of CRS. As opposed to the case of leakage, the source is not required to have min-entropy conditioned on AUX.

Definition 8 (T-Admissible Leaky (n_1, n_2, k_1, k_2) Source Distribution). *A T-admissible leaky (n_1, n_2, k_1, k_2) source distribution with respect to a CRS distribution $\{\text{CRS}_\lambda\}_{\lambda \in \mathbb{N}}$ consists of an ensemble of sources $X = \{X_\lambda\}_{\lambda \in \mathbb{N}}$, $Y = \{Y_\lambda\}_{\lambda \in \mathbb{N}}$, leakage $L = \{L_\lambda\}$ and auxiliary input $\text{AUX} = \{\text{AUX}_\lambda\}$, such that for every $\lambda \in \mathbb{N}$, the following holds:*

- *For every $\text{crs} \in \text{Supp}(\text{CRS}_\lambda)$, $\text{Supp}(X_\lambda|\text{crs}) \subseteq \{0,1\}^{n_1(\lambda)}$ and $\text{Supp}(Y_\lambda|\text{crs}) \subseteq \{0,1\}^{n_2(\lambda)}$.*
- *The leakage L_λ consists of two parts, L_{init} and L_{final}, such that for every $\text{crs} \in \text{Supp}(\text{CRS})$, $(Y, \text{AUX}, L_{\text{init}}|\text{crs})$ is sampleable in time $\text{poly}(T)$, and for every $\ell_{\text{init}} \in \text{Supp}(L_{\text{init}}|\text{crs})$, $(X, L_{\text{final}}|\text{crs}, \ell_{\text{init}})$ is sampleable in time $\text{poly}(T)$.*

- $H_\infty(X_\lambda|\mathrm{CRS}_\lambda, L_\lambda) \geq k_1$ and $H_\infty(Y_\lambda|\mathrm{CRS}_\lambda, L_\lambda) \geq k_2$.
- For every $\mathsf{crs} \in \mathrm{CRS}_\lambda$ and $\ell \in \mathsf{Supp}(L_\lambda|\mathsf{crs})$, the distributions $(X_\lambda|\mathsf{crs}, \ell)$ and $(Y_\lambda, \mathsf{AUX}_\lambda|\mathsf{crs}, \ell)$ are independent.[10]
- For every $\mathsf{aux} \in \mathsf{Supp}(\mathsf{AUX}_\lambda), |\mathsf{aux}| = O(\log T(\lambda))$.[11]

Definition 9 (Computational strong 2-source extractors in the CRS model). *For functions* $n_1 = n_1(\lambda)$, $n_2 = n_2(\lambda)$, $c = c(\lambda)$, *and* $m = m(\lambda)$, *a function ensemble* $2\mathsf{Ext} = \{2\mathsf{Ext}_\lambda\}_{\lambda \in \mathbb{N}}$, *where*

$$2\mathsf{Ext}_\lambda : \{0,1\}^{n_1(\lambda)} \times \{0,1\}^{n_2(\lambda)} \times \{0,1\}^{c(\lambda)} \to \{0,1\}^{m(\lambda)},$$

is said to be a (n_1, n_2, k_1, k_2) *strong* T-*computational 2-source extractor in the CRS model if there is an ensemble* $\{\mathrm{CRS}_\lambda\}_{\lambda \in \mathbb{N}}$ *where* $\mathrm{CRS}_\lambda \in \{0,1\}^{c(\lambda)}$, *such that the following holds:*

For every T-*admissible leaky* (n_1, n_2, k_1, k_2) *source distribution* (X, Y, L, AUX) *with respect to* CRS, *for every polynomial* p, *there exists a negligible function* $\nu(\cdot)$ *such that for every* λ *and every* $p(T(\lambda))$-*size adversary* $\mathcal{A}$,

$$\left| \Pr\left[\mathcal{A}\left(2\mathsf{Ext}_\lambda(x, y, \mathsf{crs}), y, \mathsf{crs}, \ell, \mathsf{aux}\right) = 1 \right] - \right.$$
$$\left. \Pr\left[\mathcal{A}\left(U, y, \mathsf{crs}, \ell, \mathsf{aux}\right) = 1 \right] \right| = \nu(T(\lambda)),$$

where the probabilities are over the randomness of sampling $(\mathsf{crs}, x, y, \ell, \mathsf{aux}) \leftarrow (\mathrm{CRS}_\lambda, X_\lambda, Y_\lambda, L_\lambda, \mathsf{AUX}_\lambda)$, *and over* U *which is uniformly distributed over* $\{0,1\}^{m(\lambda)}$ *independent of everything else.*

Definition 10 (Computational strong non-malleable extractors in the CRS model). *For functions* $n_1 = n_1(\lambda)$, $n_2 = n_2(\lambda)$, $c = c(\lambda)$, *and* $m = m(\lambda)$, *a function ensemble* $\mathsf{cnm\text{-}Ext} = (\mathsf{cnm\text{-}Ext}_\lambda)_{\lambda \in \mathbb{N}}$, *where*

$$\mathsf{cnm\text{-}Ext}_\lambda : \{0,1\}^{n_1(\lambda)} \times \{0,1\}^{n_2(\lambda)} \times \{0,1\}^{c(\lambda)} \to \{0,1\}^{m(\lambda)}$$

is said to be a (n_1, n_2, k_1, k_2) *strong* T-*computational non-malleable extractor in the CRS model if there is an ensemble* $\{\mathrm{CRS}_\lambda\}_{\lambda \in \mathbb{N}}$, *where* $\mathrm{CRS}_\lambda \in \{0,1\}^{c(\lambda)}$, *such that the following holds:*

For every T-*admissible leaky* (n_1, n_2, k_1, k_2) *source distribution* (X, Y, L, AUX) *with respect to* CRS, *for every polynomial* p, *there exists a negligible function* $\nu(\cdot)$ *such that for every* λ *and every* $p(T(\lambda))$-*size adversary* $\mathcal{A}$,

$$\left| \Pr\left[\mathcal{A}^{\mathcal{O}^y_{x, \mathsf{crs}}}\left(\mathsf{cnm\text{-}Ext}(x, y, \mathsf{crs}), y, \mathsf{crs}, \ell, \mathsf{aux}\right) = 1 \right] - \right.$$
$$\left. \Pr\left[\mathcal{A}^{\mathcal{O}^y_{x, \mathsf{crs}}}\left(U, y, \mathsf{crs}, \ell, \mathsf{aux}\right) = 1 \right] \right| = \nu(T(\lambda)),$$

---

[10] This condition follows from the way X and Y are sampled, and we add it only for the sake of being explicit.

[11] We restrict the length of aux to be at most $O(\log T(\lambda))$ for technical reasons.

where the oracle $\mathcal{O}^y_{x,crs}$ on input $y' \neq y$ outputs cnm-Ext(x, y, crs), and otherwise outputs $\perp$; and where the probabilities are over the randomness of sampling $(crs, x, y, \ell, aux) \leftarrow (CRS_\lambda, X_\lambda, Y_\lambda, L_\lambda, AUX_\lambda)$, and over U which is uniformly distributed over $\{0, 1\}^{m(\lambda)}$ independent of everything else.

We will occasionally need to impose a different requirement on the error distribution. In such cases we specify the error requirement explicitly. Specifically, we say that a (n_1, n_2, k_1, k_2) strong T-computational two source (or nonmalleable) extractor has error neg$(T'(\lambda))$ if it satisfies Definition 9 (or Definition 10), where the adversary's distinguishing advantage is required to be at most negligible in $T'(\lambda)$.

For our constructions, we will rely on the following theorem from [26] (simplified to our setting). This is a statistical 2-source extractor; i.e., one that considers sources that are sampled in unbounded time, and fools adversaries with unbounded running time.

Theorem 6 [26]. *There exists a (n_1, n_2, k_1, k_2) strong statistical 2-source extractor according to Definition 9 where $n_2 = \omega(\log n_1)$, $k_1 \geq \log n_1$, and $k_2 \geq \alpha n_2$ for any constant $\alpha > \frac{1}{2}$, and error $\exp^{-\Theta(\min\{k_1, k_2\})}$.*

5 Computational Strong Non-malleable Extractors in the CRS Model

In this section, we describe our construction of computational non-malleable extractors in the CRS model, and prove the following theorem.

Theorem 7. *Let $T, T', n_1, n_2, k_1, k_2, k_3, w : \mathbb{N} \to \mathbb{N}$ be functions of the security parameter, where $T \geq 2^{k_3}$ and such that the following primitives exist.*

- *A (n_1, n_2, k_1, k_2) strong T-computational 2-source extractor with in the CRS model, denoted by:*

$$2\text{Ext}_\lambda : \{0, 1\}^{n_1(\lambda)} \times \{0, 1\}^{n_2(\lambda)} \times \{0, 1\}^{c(\lambda)} \to \{0, 1\}^{m(\lambda)}$$

- *A (T, n_1, w)-lossy function family $\mathcal{F} = \{\mathcal{F}_\lambda\}_{\lambda \in \mathbb{N}}$, according to Definition 6, where $w = n_1 - n_1^\gamma$ for some constant $\gamma \in (0, 1)$.*
- *A T'-secure family of collision resistant hash functions $\mathcal{H} = \{\mathcal{H}_\lambda\}_{\lambda \in \mathbb{N}}$ with $h : \{0, 1\}^{n_2} \to \{0, 1\}^{k_3}$.*

Then there exists a (n_1, n_2, K_1, K_2) strong T'-computational non-malleable extractor, satisfying Definition 10 for $K_1 = k_1 + k_3(n_1 - w + 1) + 1, K_2 = k_2 + k_3 + 1$.

Before we describe the construction (Sect. 5.1), we point out that the guarantees of the non-malleable extractor from Theorem 7 are not sufficient to instantiate the compiler in Sect. 6. To this end, we prove (Sect. 5.2) that our nonmalleable extractor construction satisfies a stronger (yet more technical) property which turns out to be sufficient.

5.1   Construction

We begin by defining the CRS distribution.

Generating the common reference string (CRS). For a given security parameter $\lambda \in \mathbb{N}$, the common reference string is generated as follows.

1. Sample $\mathsf{crs}_{2\mathsf{Ext}}$ for the (n_1, n_2, k_1, k_2) strong T-computational 2-source extractor with respect to the security parameter 1^λ.
2. Sample $h \leftarrow \mathcal{H}_\lambda$.
3. Sample $b = (b_1, \ldots, b_{k_3}) \leftarrow \{0,1\}^{k_3}$.
4. Sample independently k_3 pairs of random injective functions from $\mathcal{F}_\lambda$,

$$f_{1,b_1}, f_{2,b_2}, \ldots, f_{k_3,b_{k_3}} \leftarrow \mathsf{Gen}_{\mathsf{inj}}(1^\lambda).$$

5. Sample independently k_3 pairs of random lossy functions from $\mathcal{F}_\lambda$,

$$f_{1,1-b_1}, f_{2,1-b_2}, \ldots, f_{k_3,b_1-k_3} \leftarrow \mathsf{Gen}_{\mathsf{loss}}(1^\lambda).$$

Output

$$\mathsf{crs} = \left(\mathsf{crs}_{2\mathsf{Ext}}, h, \begin{matrix} f_{1,0}, f_{2,0}, \ldots, f_{k_3,0} \\ f_{1,1}, f_{2,1}, \ldots, f_{k_3,1} \end{matrix} \right)$$

Our computational non-malleable extractor, $\mathsf{cnm\text{-}Ext} = \{\mathsf{cnm\text{-}Ext}_\lambda\}_{\lambda \in \mathbb{N}}$, is defined as follows: For any $\lambda \in \mathbb{N}$, denote by $c = c(\lambda) = |\mathsf{crs}|$, then

$$\mathsf{cnm\text{-}Ext}_\lambda : \{0,1\}^{n_1} \times \{0,1\}^{n_2} \times \{0,1\}^c \to \{0,1\}^m,$$

where $\forall (x, y, \mathsf{crs}) \in \{0,1\}^{n_1} \times \{0,1\}^{n_2} \times \{0,1\}^c$, $\mathsf{crs} = \left(\mathsf{crs}_{2\mathsf{Ext}}, h, \{f_{i,b}\}_{i \in [k_3], b \in \{0,1\}} \right)$

$$\mathsf{cnm\text{-}Ext}_\lambda(x, y, \mathsf{crs}) = 2\mathsf{Ext}_\lambda \left(f_{1,h(y)_1} \circ f_{2,h(y)_2} \circ \cdots \circ f_{k_3,h(y)_{k_3}}(x), y, \mathsf{crs}_{2\mathsf{Ext}} \right). \tag{1}$$

As mentioned above, Theorem 7 is insufficient for instantiating our compiler (in Sect. 6) which converts a non-mallealbe extractor into a 2-source extractor. Rather, we need the non-malleable extractor to have the following more general (and more complex) guarantee, which is tailored to our construction (in Sect. 5.1): If the underlying 2-source extractor 2Ext is T-secure (for $T \geq 2^{k_3}$) then the resulting non-malleable extractor is also T-secure with error $\mathsf{neg}(2^{k_3})$, assuming the adversary (i.e., distinguisher) does not query its oracle on y' such that $h(y) = h(y')$. We next formalize this guarantee, and begin by defining the notion of an $\mathcal{H}$-admissible adversary corresponding to our non-malleable extractor from Sect. 5.1.

Definition 11 ($\mathcal{H}$-Admissible Adversary). *We say that an adversary $\mathcal{A}$ is $\mathcal{H}$-admissible if on any input $(v, y, \mathsf{crs}, \ell, \mathsf{aux})$ (where v is either $\mathsf{cnm\text{-}Ext}(x, y, \mathsf{crs})$ or a uniformly random string), it does not query its oracle $\mathcal{O}^y_{x,\mathsf{crs}}$ with y' such that $h(y') = h(y)$, where h is the hash function in crs.*

Theorem 8. *Let $T, n_1, n_2, k_1, k_2, k_3, w : \mathbb{N} \to \mathbb{N}$ be functions of the security parameter, and let $\mathcal{H} = \{\mathcal{H}_\lambda\}_{\lambda \in \mathbb{N}}$ with $h : \{0,1\}^{n_2} \to \{0,1\}^{k_3}$ be a family of functions. Assume that $T \geq 2^{k_3}$ and the following primitives exist.*

- *A (n_1, n_2, k_1, k_2) strong T-computational 2-source extractor in the CRS model, denoted by:*

$$2\mathsf{Ext}_\lambda : \{0,1\}^{n_1(\lambda)} \times \{0,1\}^{n_2(\lambda)} \times \{0,1\}^{c(\lambda)} \to \{0,1\}^{m(\lambda)}$$

- *A (T, n_1, w)-lossy function family $\mathcal{F} = \{\mathcal{F}_\lambda\}_{\lambda \in \mathbb{N}}$, according to Definition 6, where $w = n_1 - n_1^\gamma$ for some constant $\gamma \in (0,1)$.*

Then the extractor constructed in Sect. 5.1 is a (n_1, n_2, K_1, K_2) strong T-computational non-malleable extractor with error $\mathrm{neg}(2^{k_3})$ against $\mathcal{H}$-admissible adversaries, for $K_1 = k_1 + k_3(n_1 - w + 1) + 1, K_2 = k_2 + k_3 + 1$.

Corollary 1 instantiates Theorem 8 with the 2-source extractor from Theorem 6; this corollary will be used in the next section.

Corollary 1. *Let $\mathcal{H} = \{\mathcal{H}_\lambda\}_{\lambda \in \mathbb{N}}$ with $h : \{0,1\}^{n_2} \to \{0,1\}^{k_3}$ be a family of functions. Assume the sub-exponential hardness of DDH, and fix any constant $\epsilon > 0$. Then there exists a constant $\delta > 0$ such that for any parameters (n_1, n_2, K_1, K_2) satisfying*

$$\Omega(\lambda) \leq n_1 \leq \mathrm{poly}(\lambda), \quad n_2 = \omega(\log n_1), \quad K_1 = n_1^\epsilon, \quad \text{and } K_2 = 0.51 n_2$$

there exists a (n_1, n_2, K_1, K_2) strong T-computational non-malleable extractor with error $\mathrm{neg}(2^{k_3})$ against $\mathcal{H}$-admissible adversaries (satisfying Definition 10) for $T(\lambda) = 2^{\lambda^\delta}$ and $k_3 \leq \min\{\lambda^\delta, n_1^{\epsilon/2}, n_2^{0.9}\}$.

Proof of Corollary 1. Fix a constant $\epsilon > 0$, and fix $n_1 = n_1(\lambda)$ and $n_2 = n_2(\lambda)$ as in the statement of Corollary 1. By Lemma 2, the sub-exponential hardness of DDH (together with the restrictions on n_1 and n_2) implies that there exists a constant $\delta > 0$ for which there exists a (T, n_1, w)-lossy function family $\mathcal{F} = \{\mathcal{F}_\lambda\}_{\lambda \in \mathbb{N}}$ where $T(\lambda) = 2^{\lambda^\delta}$ and w is such that $n_1 - w = n_1^{\epsilon/3}$.

By Theorem 6, for $n_2 = \omega(\log n_1)$, there exists a (n_1, n_2, k_1, k_2) strong statistical 2-source extractor for $k_1 = n_1^{\epsilon/3}$ and $k_2 = 0.501 n_2$ with error $\exp^{-\Theta(\min(k_1, k_2))} = \mathrm{neg}(2^{k_3})$. In particular, this extractor is a (n_1, n_2, k_1, k_2) strong T-computational 2-source extractor in the CRS model (where the CRS is empty).

Note that by our setting of parameters $T \geq 2^{k_3}$. Therefore, by Theorem 8, there exists a (n_1, n_2, K_1, K_2) strong T-computational non-malleable extractor with error $\mathrm{neg}(2^{k_3})$ against $\mathcal{H}$-admissible adversaries, where $K_1 = k_1 + k_3(n_1 - w + 1) + 1 \leq n_1^{\epsilon/3} + n_1^{\epsilon/2} \cdot n_1^{\epsilon/3} + 1 \leq n_1^\epsilon$ and $K_2 = k_2 + k_3 + 1 \leq 0.501 n_2 + n_2^{0.9} + 1 \leq 0.51 n_2$, as desired. □

5.2   Analysis

In this section, we prove Theorem 8; namely, we prove the T-security of the non-malleable extractor against $\mathcal{H}$-admissible adversaries. The proof of Theorem 7 follows from the observation that every adversary $\mathcal{A}$ that runs in time $\text{poly}(T')$ on input sources sampled in time $\text{poly}(T')$, cannot query the oracle on hash collisions, except with probability $\text{neg}(T')$, and thus is $\mathcal{H}$-admissible (except with probability $\text{neg}(T')$).

The proof proceeds in stages. First we replace the oracle $\mathcal{O}^y_{x,\text{crs}}$ with an oracle $\tilde{\mathcal{O}}^y_{x,\text{crs}}$ which refuses to answer when queried on a y' s.t. the hash values of y and y' match. Note that since our adversary is assumed to be $\mathcal{H}$-admissible, it cannot distinguish between these two oracles since it never makes such a query. Then we prove that if the adversary succeeds in distinguishing the output of the non-malleable extractor from random, then he can also distinguish even if we condition on the event that $h(y) = b$ (recall that $b \in \{0,1\}^{k_3}$ is used to determine which functions are lossy or injective in the crs). Finally, we design a distribution for the 2-source extractor and break it using the supposed adversary for the non-malleable extractor.

Proof (of Theorem 8). In this proof, we will sometimes suppress the dependence on λ in the notation for convenience.

Fix any T-admissible leaky (n_1, n_2, K_1, K_2) source distribution (X, Y, L, AUX) with respect to CRS. Suppose for the sake of contradiction, that there exists a polynomial p, and a $\text{poly}(T)$-size $\mathcal{H}$-admissible adversary $\mathcal{A}$, such that for infinitely many $\lambda \in \mathbb{N}$,

$$\Pr[\mathcal{A}^{\mathcal{O}^y_{x,\text{crs}}}(\text{cnm-Ext}(x, y, \text{crs}), y, \text{crs}, \ell, \text{aux}) = 1] -$$
$$\Pr[\mathcal{A}^{\mathcal{O}^y_{x,\text{crs}}}(U, y, \text{crs}, \ell, \text{aux}) = 1] \geq \frac{1}{p(2^{k_3})}, \tag{2}$$

where the probabilities are over $(\text{crs}, x, y, \ell, \text{aux}) \leftarrow (\text{CRS}, X, Y, L, \text{AUX})$ and over uniformly distribution $U \leftarrow \{0,1\}^m$.

For any $x \in \{0,1\}^{n_1}$ and $y \in \{0,1\}^{n_2}$, let

$$z_{k_3} = f_{k_3, 1-h(y)_{k_3}}(x)$$
$$z_{k_3-1} = f_{k_3-1, 1-h(y)_{k_3-1}}(f_{k_3, h(y)_{k_3}}(x))$$
$$\vdots$$
$$z_1 = f_{1, 1-h(y)_1}(f_{2, h(y)_2}(\ldots f_{k_3, h(y)_{k_3}}(x)))$$

Denote by $z_{x,h(y)} = (z_1, \ldots, z_{k_3})$.

Let $\tilde{\mathcal{O}}^y_{x,\text{crs}}$ (abusing notation we will call it just $\tilde{\mathcal{O}}$) be the oracle that on input $y' \in \{0,1\}^{n_2}$, if $h(y') \neq h(y)$ outputs

$$\mathcal{O}^y_{x,\text{crs}}(y') = \text{cnm-Ext}(x, y', \text{crs}) = 2\text{Ext}_\lambda(f_{1,h(y')_1} \circ \cdots \circ f_{k_3, h(y')_{k_3}}(x), y', \text{crs}_{2\text{Ext}}),$$

and otherwise outputs $\perp$. The key observation is that this oracle can be simulated efficiently given only $(h(y), z_{x,h(y)}, \text{crs})$, without any additional information about x or y. This will come in handy later.

Since $\mathcal{A}$ is $\mathcal{H}$-admissible, by definition, $\mathcal{A}$ does not generate a query $y' \neq y$ such that $h(y') = h(y)$, and therefore, the oracles are indistinguishable. This, together with Eq. (2), implies that for infinitely many $\lambda \in \mathbb{N}$,

$$\Pr[\mathcal{A}^{\tilde{\mathcal{O}}}(\text{cnm-Ext}(x, y, \text{crs}), y, \text{crs}, \ell, \text{aux}) = 1] -$$
$$\Pr[\mathcal{A}^{\tilde{\mathcal{O}}}(U, y, \text{crs}, \ell, \text{aux}) = 1] \geq \frac{1}{p(2^{k_3})} \tag{3}$$

where the probabilities are over $(\text{crs}, x, y, \ell, \text{aux}) \leftarrow (\text{CRS}, X, Y, L, \text{AUX})$ and over uniformly distribution $U \leftarrow \{0, 1\}^m$. Next, the T-security of the lossy function family, together with the assumption that $T \geq 2^{k_3}$, implies that for every $\text{poly}(T)$-size adversary $\mathcal{B}$ (recall $b \in \{0, 1\}^{k_3}$ is used to determine which functions are lossy or injective in the crs),

$$2^{-k_3} + \text{neg}(T) \geq \Pr[\mathcal{B}(\text{crs}) = b] \geq 2^{-k_3} - \text{neg}(T). \tag{4}$$

This, together with the fact that $(X, Y, L, \text{AUX}|\text{crs})$ can be sampled in time $\text{poly}(T)$, implies that

$$2^{-k_3} + \text{neg}(T) \geq \Pr[h(y) = b] \geq 2^{-k_3} - \text{neg}(T), \tag{5}$$

where the probability is over $\text{crs} \leftarrow \text{CRS}$, and over $(x, y, \ell, \text{aux}) \leftarrow (X, Y, L, \text{AUX}|\text{crs})$.

Claim. For infinitely many $\lambda \in \mathbb{N}$,

$$\Pr\left[\left(\mathcal{A}^{\tilde{\mathcal{O}}}(\text{cnm-Ext}(x, y, \text{crs}), y, \text{crs}, \ell, \text{aux}) = 1\right)\Big|(h(y) = b)\right]$$
$$- \Pr\left[\left(\mathcal{A}^{\tilde{\mathcal{O}}}(U, y, \text{crs}, \ell, \text{aux}) = 1\right)\Big|(h(y) = b)\right] \geq \frac{1}{4p(2^{k_3})} \tag{6}$$

The proof of this claim appears in the full version of our paper.

This Claim, together with Eq. (5), implies that for infinitely many $\lambda \in \mathbb{N}$:

$$\Pr\left[\left(\mathcal{A}^{\tilde{\mathcal{O}}}(\text{cnm-Ext}(x, y, \text{crs}), y, \text{crs}, \ell, \text{aux}) = 1\right) \wedge (h(y) = b)\right]$$
$$- \Pr\left[\left(\mathcal{A}^{\tilde{\mathcal{O}}}(U, y, \text{crs}, \ell, \text{aux}) = 1\right) \wedge (h(y) = b)\right]$$
$$= \Pr\left[\left(\mathcal{A}^{\tilde{\mathcal{O}}}(\text{cnm-Ext}(x, y, \text{crs}), y, \text{crs}, \ell, \text{aux}) = 1\right)\Big|(h(y) = b)\right] \cdot \Pr\left[h(y) = b\right]$$
$$- \Pr\left[\left(\mathcal{A}^{\tilde{\mathcal{O}}}(U, y, \text{crs}, \ell, \text{aux}) = 1\right)\Big|(h(y) = b)\right] \cdot \Pr\left[h(y) = b\right]$$
$$\geq \frac{1}{4p(2^{k_3})} \cdot (2^{-k_3} - \text{neg}(2^{k_3})) \geq \frac{1}{p''(2^{k_3})} \tag{7}$$

where the last inequality holds for some polynomial $p''(\cdot)$.

Next, substituting

$$\mathsf{cnm\text{-}Ext}(x, y, \mathsf{crs}) = 2\mathsf{Ext}(f_{1,h(y)_1} \circ f_{2,h(y)_2} \circ \cdots \circ f_{k_3,h(Y)_{k_3}}(x), y, \mathsf{crs_{2Ext}})$$

in Eq. (7), we conclude that for infinitely many $\lambda \in \mathbb{N}$,

$$\Pr\left[\left(\mathcal{A}^{\tilde{\mathcal{O}}}\left(2\mathsf{Ext}(f_{1,h(y)_1} \circ f_{2,h(y)_2} \circ \cdots \circ f_{k_3,h(y)_{k_3}}(x), y, \mathsf{crs_{2Ext}}), y, \mathsf{crs}, \ell, \mathsf{aux}\right) = 1\right)\right.$$
$$\left. \wedge \left(h(y) = b\right)\right] - \Pr\left[\left(\mathcal{A}^{\tilde{\mathcal{O}}}(U, y, \mathsf{crs}, \ell, \mathsf{aux}) = 1\right) \wedge \left(h(y) = b\right)\right] \geq \frac{1}{p''(2^{k_3})} \qquad (8)$$

We will now use the T-admissible leaky (n_1, n_2, K_1, K_2) source distribution (X, Y, L, AUX) for the non-malleable extractor, to define a new T-admissible leaky (n_1, n_2, k_1, k_2) source distribution $(X', Y', L', \mathsf{AUX'})$ for the underlying two-source extractor with CRS distribution $\mathsf{CRS_{2Ext}}$, where $k_1 = K_1 - k_3 \cdot (n_1 - w + 1) - 1$ and $k_2 = K_2 - k_3 - 1$. Then, we will prove that there exists an adversary $\mathcal{A}'$ that breaks the (n_1, n_2, k_1, k_2) strong T-computational 2-source extractor for $(X', Y', L', \mathsf{AUX'})$.

Define $(X', Y', L', \mathsf{AUX'}|\mathsf{crs_{2Ext}})$ as follows:

1. We first define $(Y', L'_{\mathsf{init}}, \mathsf{AUX'})|\mathsf{crs_{2Ext}})$:
   (a) Sample $b \leftarrow \{0, 1\}^{k_3}$.
   (b) Sample $f_h = \left(h, \dfrac{f_{1,0}, f_{2,0}, \ldots, f_{k_3,0}}{f_{1,1}, f_{2,1}, \ldots, f_{k_3,1}}\right)$ such that $\{f_{i,b_i}\}_{i \in [k_3]}$ are injective and the rest are lossy. Set $\mathsf{crs} = (\mathsf{crs_{2Ext}}, f_h)$.
   (c) Sample $(y, \ell_{\mathsf{init}}, \mathsf{aux}) \leftarrow (Y, L_{\mathsf{init}}, \mathsf{AUX}|\mathsf{crs})$.
   (d) Set $(y', \mathsf{aux'}) = (y, \mathsf{aux})$.
   (e) Set $\ell'_{\mathsf{init}} = (d, \ell_{\mathsf{init}}, f_h, b)$, where $d = 0$ if $h(y) \neq b$ and 1 otherwise.
2. We next define $(X', L'_{\mathsf{final}}|\mathsf{crs_{2Ext}}, \ell'_{\mathsf{init}})$:
   (a) Parse $\ell'_{\mathsf{init}} = (d, \ell_{\mathsf{init}}, f_h, b)$, and set $\mathsf{crs} = (\mathsf{crs_{2Ext}}, f_h)$.
   (b) Sample $(x, \ell_{\mathsf{final}}) \leftarrow (X, L_{\mathsf{final}}|\mathsf{crs}, \ell_{\mathsf{init}})$. Set $x' = f_{1,b_1} \circ f_{2,b_2} \circ \cdots \circ f_{k_3,b_{k_3}}(x)$ and $\ell'_{\mathsf{final}} = (\ell_{\mathsf{final}}, z_{x,b})$, where
   $$z_{x,b} = \{z_1, \ldots, z_{k_3}\} \text{ and for every } i \in [\ell], z_i := f_{i,1-b_i}(f_{i+1,b_{i+1}}(\ldots f_{k_3,b_{k_3}}(x))).$$

Claim. $(X', Y', L', \mathsf{AUX'})$ is a T-admissible leaky (n_1, n_2, k_1, k_2) source distribution with respect to $\mathsf{CRS_{2Ext}}$, where $k_1 = K_1 - k_3 \cdot (n_1 - w + 1) - 1$ and $k_2 = K_2 - k_3 - 1$.

The proof of this claim appears in the full version of our paper.

We next argue that Equation (8), together with the definition of the distribution $(X', Y', L', \mathsf{AUX'}|\mathsf{crs2Ext})$, implies that there exists a T-size adversary $\mathcal{A}'$, that simulates the adversary $\mathcal{A}$, as well as its oracle, such that for infinitely many $\lambda \in \mathbb{N}$,

$$\Pr[\mathcal{A}'(2\mathsf{Ext}(X', Y', \mathsf{crs_{2Ext}}), y', \mathsf{crs_{2Ext}}, \ell', \mathsf{aux'}) = 1] - \qquad (9)$$
$$\Pr[\mathcal{A}'(U, y', \mathsf{crs_{2Ext}}, \ell', \mathsf{aux'}) = 1] \geq 1/\mathsf{poly}(2^{k_3}).$$

The algorithm $\mathcal{A}'$ on input $(\alpha, y', \mathsf{crs_{2Ext}}, \ell', \mathsf{aux'})$ does the following:

1. Parse $\ell' = (\ell'_{\text{init}}, \ell'_{\text{final}})$ and further parse $\ell'_{\text{init}} = (d, \ell_{\text{init}}, f_h, h(y))$, $\ell'_{\text{final}} = (\ell_{\text{final}}, z_{x,h(y)})$. and obtain d from ℓ'_{init}.
2. If $d = 0$ then output $\perp$.
3. Else, set $\ell = (\ell_{\text{init}}, \ell_{\text{final}})$, and set $\text{crs} = (\text{crs}_{2\text{Ext}}, f_h)$.
4. Output $\mathcal{A}^{\tilde{\mathcal{O}}}(\alpha, y', \text{crs}, \ell, \text{aux}')$, where $\tilde{\mathcal{O}}$ is simulated using $(h(y), z_{x,h(y)}, \text{crs})$.

Equation (8) implies that indeed Eq. (9) holds, as desired. This contradicts the fact that 2Ext is a strong T-computational 2-source extractor for $(X', Y', L', \text{AUX}')$. This completes the proof of Theorem 8.

6 Computational Strong 2-Source Extractors in the CRS Model

In this section, we describe our compiler that converts a computational non-malleable extractor (in the CRS model) with negligible error for sources in the high entropy regime, into a computational 2-source extractor (in the CRS model) with negligible error for sources in the low entropy regime. This construction is essentially identical to that suggested by [1]. However, the analysis in the computational setting introduces many technical challenges which result from the existence of the CRS, and the necessity of building an efficient reduction. Due to these challenges, our compiler is not as general as the one in the information theoretic setting. In particular, in Theorem 9 below, we use as an ingredient a collision resistant hash family $\mathcal{H}$, and show how to convert a computational non-malleable extractor that is secure against $\mathcal{H}$-admissible adversaries (such as the one from Theorem 8) into a computational 2-source extractor.

Theorem 9. *Let $T, T', n_1, n_2, k_1, k_2, k_3, d : \mathbb{N} \to \mathbb{N}$ be functions of the security parameter, such that $T = (T')^{\omega(1)}, T = \lambda^{\Omega(1)}, n_2 = O(\log T), k_2 = \omega(\log T')$, and such that the following primitives exist.*

- *A family of T'-secure collision-resistant hash functions functions $\mathcal{H} = \{\mathcal{H}_\lambda\}_{\lambda \in \mathbb{N}}$ with $h : \{0,1\}^d \to \{0,1\}^{k_3}$*
- *A (n_1, d, k_1, d) strong T-computational non-malleable extractor against $\mathcal{H}$-admissible adversaries in the CRS model with error $\text{neg}(2^{k_3})$, where the CRS is generated by sampling $h \leftarrow \mathcal{H}$ and sampling $\text{crs}' \leftarrow \text{CRS}'$, where CRS' is a $\text{poly}(T)$-time sampleable distribution, and setting $\text{crs} = (h, \text{crs}')$. This non-mallealbe extractor is denoted by*

$$\text{cnm-Ext}_\lambda : \{0,1\}^{n_1} \times \{0,1\}^d \times \{0,1\}^c \to \{0,1\}^m$$

- *A $\left(\frac{2^{k_2}}{T' \log T'}, 2^{d-1}\right)$ disperser*

$$\Gamma : \{0,1\}^{n_2} \times [t] \to \{0,1\}^d$$

with degree $t = \text{poly}(\lambda)$ (according to Definition 7).

Then there exists a $(n_1, n_2, k_1, 2k_2)$ strong T'-computational 2-source extractor in the CRS model (according to Definition 9).

We defer the construction of the 2-source extractor from Theorem 9 to Sect. 6.1, and defer the analysis to Sect. 6.2. In what follows we present two corollaries. Corollary 2 instantiates Theorem 9 with the non-malleable extractor from Corollary 1.

Corollary 2. *Fix any constant $\epsilon > 0$. Then assuming the sub-exponential hardness of the DDH assumption, there exists a constant $\delta > 0$ such that for any constant $c \geq 1$ and any parameters n_1, n_2, k_1, k_2, T' satisfying*

$$\Omega(\lambda) \leq n_1 \leq \text{poly}(\lambda), \ \lambda^{O(1)} \leq n_2 \leq O(\lambda^\delta), \ k_1 = n_1^\epsilon, \ k_2 = \log^{c/\delta} n_2, \ T' = 2^{\log^c \lambda}$$

there exists a (n_1, n_2, k_1, k_2) strong T'-computational 2-source extractor in the CRS model (satisfying Definition 9).

Proof. Fix any constant $\epsilon > 0$. By Corollary 1, there exists a constant $\delta > 0$ for which there exists a (n_1, d, K_1, d) strong T-computational non-malleable extractor with error $\text{neg}(2^{k_3})$ in the CRS model against $\mathcal{H}$-admissible adversaries, for $\mathcal{H} : \{0, 1\}^d \to \{0, 1\}^{k_3}$, where $T = 2^{\lambda^\delta}$, $k_3 = \min\{n_1^{\epsilon/2}, d^{0.9}, \lambda^\delta\}$, and for any n_1, d, K_1 such that

$$\Omega(\lambda) \leq n_1 \leq \text{poly}(\lambda), \ d = \omega(\log n_1), K_1 = n_1^\epsilon$$

Moreover, this is the computational non-malleable extractor from Construction 5.1 where the crs is distributed as required in the theorem statement.

Next, fix any n_1 such that $\Omega(\lambda) \leq n_1 \leq \text{poly}(\lambda)$. By Theorem 5, there exists a polynomial $t = \text{poly}(\lambda)$ for which there exists a $\left(\frac{2^{k_2}}{T'^{(\log T')}}, 2^{d-1}\right)$ disperser

$$\Gamma : \{0, 1\}^{n_1} \times [t] \to \{0, 1\}^d$$

for any d, k_2, T' that satisfy

$$k_2 \geq 2d + \log^2 T'. \tag{10}$$

Fix any constant $c \geq 1$, let $k_2 = \log^{c/\delta} n_2$ and let $T' = 2^{\log^c \lambda}$. Set $d = k_2/4$. Note that Eq. (10) is satisfied by the definition of d and T'. Also,

$$k_3 = \min\{\lambda^\delta, n_1^{\epsilon/2}, d^{0.9}\} = \Omega((\log \lambda)^{0.9c/\delta}).$$

Therefore, assuming the sub-exponential hardness of DDH, and setting the security parameter in Theorem 4 to be $\kappa = k_3$, we conclude that there exists a constant δ' such that there exists a $2^{k_3^{\delta'}}$-secure collision resistant hash $\mathcal{H} : \{0, 1\}^d \to \{0, 1\}^{k_3}$. Assume without loss of generality that $\delta \leq 0.9\delta'$ (otherwise, reduce the size of δ). This implies that $T' \leq 2^{k_3^{\delta'}}$.

Theorem 9 implies that there exists a $(n_1, n_2, k_1, 2k_2)$ strong T'-computational 2-source extractor in the CRS model, as long as $n_2 = O(\log T) = O(\lambda^\delta)$, and as long as $k_2 = \omega(\log T')$ and in particular for $k_2 = \log^{c/\delta} n_2$.

By using the 2-source extractor obtained as a result of Corollary 2 to instantiate the non-malleable extractor in Theorem 7, we obtain the following corollary:

Corollary 3. *Fix any constant $\epsilon > 0$. Then, assuming the sub-exponential hardness of the DDH assumption, there exists a constant $\delta > 0$ for which there exists a (n_1, n_2, K_1, K_2) strong T'-computational non-malleable extractor satisfying Definition 10 whenever*

$$\Omega(\lambda) \leq n_1 \leq \text{poly}(\lambda), \ \lambda^{O(1)} \leq n_2 \leq O(\lambda^\delta), \ K_1 = n_1^\epsilon, \ K_2 = \log^{1/\delta^2} n_2, T' = \lambda.$$

Proof. Fix n_1, n_2 as in the statement of the corollary. Fix any constant $\epsilon > 0$. By Corollary 2, assuming the sub-exponential hardness of DDH, there exists a constant $\delta > 0$ such that for any constant $c \geq 1$, there exists a (n_1, n_2, k_1, k_2) strong T-computational 2-source extractor for k_1, k_2, T satisfying

$$k_1 = n_1^{\epsilon/3}, \ k_2 = \log^{c/\delta} n_2, \ T = 2^{\log^c \lambda}.$$

Furthermore, the sub-exponential hardness of DDH, together with the fact that $n_1 = \Omega(\lambda)$, implies that the following exist:

- A (T, n_1, w)-lossy function family $\mathcal{F} = \{\mathcal{F}_\lambda\}_{\lambda \in \mathbb{N}}$ where each $f \in \mathcal{F}_\lambda$ is of the form $f : \{0,1\}^{n_1} \to \{0,1\}^{n_1}$, where $T(\lambda) = 2^{\log^c \lambda}$ as above and w is such that $n_1 - w = n_1^{\epsilon/3}$. This follows from Lemma 2.
- A collision resistant hash family $\mathcal{H} = \{\mathcal{H}_\lambda\}_{\lambda \in \mathbb{N}}$, where each $h \in \mathcal{H}_\lambda$ is of the form $h : \{0,1\}^{n_2} \to \{0,1\}^{k_3}$ where $k_3 = \log^{1/\delta} \lambda$, that is secure against poly(λ)-size adversaries (this follows by setting the security parameter to be $\kappa = k_3$ in Theorem 4.[12])

Set $c \geq \frac{1}{\delta}$ which implies that $T \geq 2^{k_3}$. Therefore, by Theorem 7, there exists a (n_1, n_2, K_1, K_2) strong T'-computational non-malleable extractor for $T' = \lambda$ for $K_1 = k_1 + k_3(n_1 - w) + 1 \leq n_1^{\epsilon/3} + \log^{1/\delta} \lambda \cdot n_1^{\epsilon/3} + 1 < n_1^\epsilon$, and thus in particular for $K_1 = n_1^\epsilon$, and for $K_2 = k_2 + k_3 + 1 = \log^{c/\delta} n_2 + (\log \lambda)^{1/\delta} + 1$, and thus for $K_2 = \log^{c/\delta'} n_2$ for any constant $\delta' < \delta$. The corollary follows by reassigning δ to be δ'.

6.1 Construction

In what follows, we construct the 2-source extractor from Theorem 9. To this, end, fix any parameters $T, T', n_1, n_2, k_1, k_2, d$ according to Theorem 9. Fix any collision-resistant hash function $\mathcal{H}$ and a (n_1, d, k_1, d) strong T-computational non-malleable extractor against $\mathcal{H}$-admissible adversaries in the CRS model

$$\text{cnm-Ext} : \{0,1\}^{n_1} \times \{0,1\}^d \times \{0,1\}^c \to \{0,1\}^m$$

and any $\left(\frac{2^{k_2}}{T' \log T'}, 2^{d-1}\right)$ disperser

$$\Gamma : \{0,1\}^{n_2} \times [t] \to \{0,1\}^d.$$

---

[12] We assume that δ is small enough so that the hash function is 2^{κ^δ} secure.

Define a 2-source extractor

$$2\mathsf{Ext} : \{0,1\}^{n_1} \times \{0,1\}^{n_2} \times \{0,1\}^c \to \{0,1\}^m$$

by

$$2\mathsf{Ext}(x_1, x_2, \mathrm{crs}) = \bigoplus_{y:\ \exists i\ \mathrm{s.t.}\ \Gamma(x_2,i)=y} \mathsf{cnm\text{-}Ext}(x_1, y, \mathrm{crs})$$

6.2   Analysis

We prove the security of the 2-source extractor 2Ext described above in several steps. We start by assuming (for contradiction) that there exists an adversary running in time $\mathrm{poly}(T')$ that breaks the 2-source extractor 2Ext on a specific $(n_1, n_2, k_1, 2k_2)$ T'-admissible leaky source distribution. Using this adversary, we define an adversary that breaks the non-malleable extractor (on a distribution to be defined later). To this end, we define the sets BAD-rand and BAD-seed. These capture the places where the adversary breaks the non-malleable extractor. Next, we prove that these sets are large. Finally we define the distribution on which the adversary breaks the non-malleable extractor. This relies on the leakage lemma. The complete proof appears in the full version of our paper.

Acknowledgement. We thank Maciej Obremski and João Ribeiro for pointing out a subtle error in an initial draft of this work.

References

1. Ben-Aroya, A., Chattopadhyay, E., Doron, D., Li, X., Ta-Shma, A.: Low-error, two-source extractors assuming efficient non-malleable extractors. In: CCC (2017)
2. Ben-Aroya, A., Doron, D., Ta-Shma, A.: Explicit two-source extractors for near-logarithmic min-entropy. In: Electronic Colloquium on Computational Complexity (ECCC), vol. 23, p. 88 (2016)
3. Bernstein, D.J., et al.: Factoring RSA keys from certified smart cards: Coppersmith in the wild. In: Sako, K., Sarkar, P. (eds.) ASIACRYPT 2013. LNCS, vol. 8270, pp. 341–360. Springer, Heidelberg (2013). https://doi.org/10.1007/978-3-642-42045-0_18
4. Bourgain, J.: More on the sum-product phenomenon in prime fields and its applications. Int. J. Number Theory **1**, 1–32 (2005)
5. Braverman, M., Hassidim, A., Kalai, Y.T.: Leaky pseudo-entropy functions. In: Innovations in Computer Science (2011)
6. Breitner, J., Heninger, N.: Biased nonce sense: lattice attacks against weak ECDSA signatures in cryptocurrencies. Cryptology ePrint Archive, Report 2019/023 (2019). https://eprint.iacr.org/2019/023
7. Chattopadhyay, E., Goyal, V., Li, X.: Non-malleable extractors and codes, with their many tampered extensions. In: Proceedings of the Forty-Eighth Annual ACM Symposium on Theory of Computing, pp. 285–298. ACM (2016)
8. Chattopadhyay, E., Li, X.: Explicit non-malleable extractors, multi-source extractors, and almost optimal privacy amplification protocols. In: 2016 IEEE 57th Annual Symposium on Foundations of Computer Science (FOCS), pp. 158–167. IEEE (2016)

9. Chattopadhyay, E., Zuckerman, D.: Explicit two-source extractors and resilient functions. In: Proceedings of the Forty-Eighth Annual ACM Symposium on Theory of Computing, pp. 670–683. ACM (2016)
10. Chung, K., Lui, E., Pass, R.: From weak to strong zero-knowledge and applications. In: Dodis, Y., Nielsen, J.B. (eds.) TCC 2015. LNCS, vol. 9014, pp. 66–92. Springer, Heidelberg (2015). https://doi.org/10.1007/978-3-662-46494-6_4
11. Cohen, G.: Local correlation breakers and applications to three-source extractors and mergers. SIAM J. Comput. **45**(4), 1297–1338 (2016)
12. Cohen, G.: Making the most of advice: new correlation breakers and their applications. In: 2016 IEEE 57th Annual Symposium on Foundations of Computer Science (FOCS), pp. 188–196. IEEE (2016)
13. Cohen, G.: Non-malleable extractors-new tools and improved constructions. In: LIPIcs-Leibniz International Proceedings in Informatics, vol. 50. Schloss Dagstuhl-Leibniz-Zentrum fuer Informatik (2016)
14. Cohen, G.: Two-source extractors for quasi-logarithmic min-entropy and improved privacy amplification protocols. In: Electronic Colloquium on Computational Complexity (ECCC), vol. 23, p. 114 (2016)
15. Dodis, Y., Ong, S.J., Prabhakaran, M., Sahai, A.: On the (im)possibility of cryptography with imperfect randomness. In: Proceedings of the 45th Symposium on Foundations of Computer Science (FOCS 2004), Rome, Italy, 17–19 October 2004, pp. 196–205 (2004). https://doi.org/10.1109/FOCS.2004.44
16. Dodis, Y., Ostrovsky, R., Reyzin, L., Smith, A.D.: Fuzzy extractors: how to generate strong keys from biometrics and other noisy data. SIAM J. Comput. **38**(1), 97–139 (2008). https://doi.org/10.1137/060651380
17. Dodis, Y., Wichs, D.: Non-malleable extractors and symmetric key cryptography from weak secrets. In: Proceedings of the 41st Annual ACM Symposium on Theory of Computing, STOC 2009, Bethesda, MD, USA, 31 May–2 June 2009, pp. 601–610 (2009). https://doi.org/10.1145/1536414.1536496
18. Gentry, C., Wichs, D.: Separating succinct non-interactive arguments from all falsifiable assumptions. In: Fortnow, L., Vadhan, S.P. (eds.) Proceedings of the 43rd ACM Symposium on Theory of Computing, STOC 2011, San Jose, CA, USA, 6–8 June 2011, pp. 99–108. ACM (2011). https://doi.org/10.1145/1993636.1993651
19. Guruswami, V., Umans, C., Vadhan, S.: Unbalanced expanders and randomness extractors from Parvaresh-Vardy codes. J. ACM (JACM) **56**(4) (2009). Article No. 20
20. Heninger, N., Durumeric, Z., Wustrow, E., Halderman, J.A.: Mining your Ps and Qs: detection of widespread weak keys in network devices. In: Proceedings of the 21th USENIX Security Symposium, Bellevue, WA, USA, 8–10 August 2012, pp. 205–220 (2012). https://www.usenix.org/conference/usenixsecurity12/technical-sessions/presentation/heninger
21. Jetchev, D., Pietrzak, K.: How to fake auxiliary input. In: Lindell, Y. (ed.) TCC 2014. LNCS, vol. 8349, pp. 566–590. Springer, Heidelberg (2014). https://doi.org/10.1007/978-3-642-54242-8_24
22. Kalai, Y.T., Li, X., Rao, A.: 2-source extractors under computational assumptions and cryptography with defective randomness. In: 2009 50th Annual IEEE Symposium on Foundations of Computer Science, FOCS 2009, pp. 617–626. IEEE (2009)
23. Kalai, Y.T., Li, X., Rao, A., Zuckerman, D.: Network extractor protocols. In: 49th Annual IEEE Symposium on Foundations of Computer Science, FOCS 2008, Philadelphia, PA, USA, 25–28 October 2008, pp. 654–663 (2008). https://doi.org/10.1109/FOCS.2008.73

24. Li, X.: Improved non-malleable extractors, non-malleable codes and independent source extractors. In: Proceedings of the 49th Annual ACM SIGACT Symposium on Theory of Computing, pp. 1144–1156. ACM (2017)
25. Peikert, C., Waters, B.: Lossy trapdoor functions and their applications. In: STOC, pp. 187–196 (2008)
26. Raz, R.: Extractors with weak random seeds. In: STOC, pp. 11–20 (2005)

Symmetric Cryptography I

Tight Time-Space Lower Bounds
for Finding Multiple Collision Pairs
and Their Applications

Itai Dinur[(✉)]

Department of Computer Science, Ben-Gurion University, Beer Sheva, Israel
dinuri@cs.bgu.ac.il

Abstract. We consider a *collision search problem* (CSP), where given a parameter C, the goal is to find C collision pairs in a random function $f : [N] \rightarrow [N]$ (where $[N] = \{0, 1, \ldots, N - 1\}$) using S bits of memory. Algorithms for CSP have numerous cryptanalytic applications such as space-efficient attacks on double and triple encryption. The best known algorithm for CSP is *parallel collision search* (PCS) published by van Oorschot and Wiener, which achieves the time-space tradeoff $T^2 \cdot S = \tilde{O}(C^2 \cdot N)$.

In this paper, we prove that any algorithm for CSP satisfies $T^2 \cdot S = \tilde{\Omega}(C^2 \cdot N)$, hence the best known time-space tradeoff is optimal (up to poly-logarithmic factors in N). On the other hand, we give strong evidence that proving similar unconditional time-space tradeoff lower bounds on CSP applications (such as breaking double and triple encryption) may be very difficult, and would imply a breakthrough in complexity theory. Hence, we propose a new restricted model of computation and prove that under this model, the best known time-space tradeoff attack on double encryption is optimal.

Keywords: Collision search problem · Time-space tradeoff · R-way branching program · Provable security · Cryptanalysis · Parallel collision search · Double encryption

1 Introduction

A time-space tradeoff for a problem is a curve that quantifies the difficulty of solving it in terms of the required time complexity T and space complexity S (and perhaps additional problem-specific parameters). Such tradeoffs play a significant role in algorithmic research, as they provide a more realistic estimate of how difficult it is to solve a problem by considering the available space, as opposed to analysis that only considers the available computation power.

In this work we consider time-space tradeoffs for the *collision search problem* (CSP), where given a parameter C and oracle access to a random function $f : [N] \rightarrow [N]$, the goal is to find C distinct unordered colliding pairs $(i_1, i_2) \in [N]^2$ in f (i.e., $i_1 \neq i_2$, but $f(i_1) = f(i_2)$) using S bits of memory. We also

© International Association for Cryptologic Research 2020
A. Canteaut and Y. Ishai (Eds.): EUROCRYPT 2020, LNCS 12105, pp. 405–434, 2020.
https://doi.org/10.1007/978-3-030-45721-1_15

consider another variant of CSP, where given oracle access to two random and independent functions $f_1, f_2 : [N] \to [N]$ the goal is to find C distinct ordered colliding pairs between f_1 and f_2 (i.e., $(i_1, i_2) \in [N]^2$ such that $f_1(i_1) = f_2(i_2)$) using S bits of memory.

The best known algorithm for the collision search problem is *parallel collision search* (PCS) which was published by van Oorschot and Wiener [32] and has found numerous applications in cryptanalysis (such as space-efficient attacks on double and triple encryption and various dedicated meet-in-the-middle attacks). PCS obtains the time-space tradeoff $T^2 \cdot S = \tilde{O}(C^2 \cdot N)$ for both variants of CSP (where $\tilde{O}$ hides a poly-logarithmic factor in N).

Given the importance of PCS, it is natural to ask whether its time-space tradeoff is optimal. First, for $S \approx C$, the answer is clearly positive (ignoring poly-logarithmic factors). This follows by simple probabilistic analysis, as evaluating a random function on T inputs is unlikely to yield more than about T^2/N collisions (i.e., $C = \tilde{O}(T^2/N)$, or $T^2 \cdot S = \tilde{\Omega}(C^2 \cdot N)$). Therefore, the optimality of the tradeoff is not straightforward only when $S \ll C$, as in this range the limited amount of space comes into play.

1.1 Applications of the Collision Search Problem for $S \ll C$

The parameter regime $S \ll C$ for CSP may not seem very interesting at first sight, as it implies that the algorithm has to produce more collisions than it is able store in memory. However, in many CSP applications, we are only interested in a particular collision (referred to as the "golden collision" in [32]) and therefore do not need to store the collisions produced. Thus, the range of parameters where $S \ll C$ is, in fact, very important. Below, we demonstrate the relevance of CSP in case $S \ll C$ for the classical problem of breaking double encryption.

In the double encryption setting, the adversary obtains plaintext-ciphertext pairs (p_i, c_i) for $i \in \{1, 2, \ldots\}$, where $c_i = E2_{k_2}(E1_{k_1}(p_i))$ for block ciphers[1] $E1, E2 : [N] \to [N]$ and key $(k_1, k_2) \in [N]^2$. The adversary focuses on (p_1, c_1) and defines the functions $f_1, f_2 : [N] \to [N]$ as

$$f_1(k) = E1_k(p_1), \text{ and } f_2(k) = E2_k^{-1}(c_1).$$

Then, the adversary applies a collision search algorithm in order to obtain collisions between f_1 and f_2. Each output collision gives a candidate for the key pair (k_1, k_2), which is then verified against the remaining plaintext-ciphertext pairs. Note that there is no need to store a wrong key pair. Since f_1 and f_2 are expected to have N different colliding pairs, after obtaining about N collisions between them, the adversary recovers the correct key pair (or the "golden collision") with high probability.

Consequently, we can use an algorithm for the collision search problem with $C \approx N$ in order to break double encryption given an arbitrary value of S. Plugging $C = N$ into the PCS time-space tradeoff curve gives $T^2 \cdot S = \tilde{O}(N^3)$, which

---

[1] We assume for the sake of simplicity that the key and block sizes are equal.

is the currently best known time-space tradeoff for breaking double encryption for any value of S.

Besides breaking double encryption, there are numerous additional applications that are also based on finding a "golden collision" which gives a solution to the problem for appropriately defined functions f_1, f_2. A partial list of these applications includes breaking triple encryption [32], and more generally, breaking multiple encryption [17], solving the subset sum problem [16,17] and solving the generalized birthday problem [33]. Furthermore, in various (more specialized) settings one can reduce the task of breaking a concrete symmetric-key primitive to a meet-in-the-middle procedure which can then be reduced to an instance of the collision search problem with $S \ll C$.

1.2 Optimality of the Known Time-Space Tradeoff for the Collision Search Problem

The importance of CSP (in case $S \ll C$) motivates the question of whether the best known time-space tradeoff for it $T^2 \cdot S = \tilde{O}(C^2 \cdot N)$ can be improved. In this paper, we give a strong negative answer to this question. More specifically, we prove that any algorithm that outputs C distinct collisions in a random function $f : [N] \rightarrow [N]$ (or between two independent random functions) with probability at least N^{-2}, satisfies the time-space tradeoff $T^2 \cdot S = \tilde{\Omega}(C^2 \cdot N)$ (where $\tilde{\Omega}$ hides polylogarithmic factors in N). As an example, given space of $S = 10 \log N$ bits, our lower bound implies that finding $C = N/4$ collisions in f requires time complexity $T = \tilde{\Omega}(N^{3/2})$. On the other hand, prior to this work, even an algorithm with time complexity $T = N$ for the problem could not be ruled out.

An immediate consequence of this result is that the time-space tradeoffs for the cryptanalytic applications mentioned in Sect. 1.1 cannot be improved by a more efficient collision search procedure (as long as the underlying functions to which collision search is applied are modeled as random functions).

In order to obtain our bound, we use the R-way branching program model of computation, which is a standard non-uniform model for analyzing time-space tradeoffs [11]. In this model, a general approach for proving time-space tradeoff lower bounds was introduced by Borodin and Cook [11]. Since its introduction, this technique has been used to prove time-space tradeoff lower bounds for several problems such as sorting [7,11], matrix multiplication and fast Fourier transform [36], and universal hashing [25].

We adapt the approach of [11] to the collision search problem, which seems to be its first application in the domain of cryptography. More specifically, we divide a branching program for CSP with running time T into L short time intervals of length T/L, and prove that in each such interval, the program cannot make a lot of *progress* towards outputting the desired number of C collisions. In particular, the probability that the program (starting its computation from any specific memory state) outputs C/L collisions in an interval is minuscule. Finally, a union bound over all possible memory states establishes the result. Our adaptation requires deeper insight about the collision search problem and a careful choice of parameters.

1.3   Time-Space Tradeoffs in Various Models of Computation

Given the optimality of best known time-space tradeoff for CSP, one may wonder whether we can prove the optimality of the best known tradeoffs for its applications (such as the ones mentioned in Sect. 1.1). Unfortunately, we give strong evidence that proving such a result may be very difficult and would overcome a variant of a long-standing barrier in complexity theory.

The property of the collision search problem that enables proving tight time-space tradeoff lower bounds for it, is that its output length is (about) C words. Since it is possible to find C collisions in f for a small value of C with negligible space and nearly-optimal time complexity (e.g., by Floyd's algorithm [24]), time-space tradeoffs for such parameters are already known to be tight. Hence, we may assume that the output length C is large (namely $C = N^\alpha$ for some $\alpha > 0$). In contrast, the output length in the above applications is very short (e.g., in breaking double encryption, the output is a short key). The challenge of proving strong time-space tradeoff lower bounds for such short-output problems with polynomial-time algorithms[2] is open since the study of such tradeoffs was introduced in 1966 by Cobham [15] (and it has been subject of extensive research [10]).[3] In particular, the technique for proving time-space lower bounds of [11] (that we adapt here to CSP) is inapplicable to short-output problems since it is not clear how to measure the progress of an algorithm towards solving such a problem.

While the barrier of proving time-space lower bounds for short-output problems seems very difficult to overcome, it only applies to general (unrestricted) models of computation. On the other hand, under more restricted computational models, very strong time-space lower bounds are known for various problems. One such restricted model is the streaming model. Here, the input is a stream of elements that can be read sequentially, but a (single-pass) streaming algorithm cannot access a previous element of the stream, unless it is stored in memory. The streaming model is subject to active research in general (see [2], and [30] for a recent result), and specifically in the area of cryptography (cf., [13,22,27]).

The pebbling model is another well-studied restricted model of computation in which strong time-space tradeoff lower bounds are known [29]. In this model, a pebbling game is played on a specific circuit realizing the function considered. The circuit is viewed as a directed acyclic graph (DAG) and the goal is to pebble each of the output nodes given a limited number of pebbles (which model words of memory). The main rule of the pebbling game is that a non-input node can be pebbled only if all its processors are pebbled. In the context of cryptography, the

---

[2] The input length of a problem with access to some function $f : [M] \rightarrow [N]$ is the number of bits required to represent the function, namely, $N \log M$. With this encoding, it is clear, for example, that breaking double encryption can be done in polynomial time in the input length.

[3] For general problems in NP, stronger time-space tradeoff lower bounds are known in the uniform setting for problems such as SAT (cf. [20]). However, as far as we know, these lower bounds are very loose and do not seem to be relevant to cryptography.

pebbling model has played a significant role in the design and analysis memory-hard functions [3, 4, 19].

We also mention comparison-based models where the algorithm does not have direct access to the internal representation of the elements of the input, but can only compare them in pairs. A well-known time-space lower bound in such models was obtained by Yao for the *element distinctness problem* [35], where the goal is to determine whether there exist two identical elements in an array of length N. While Yao's bound $T \cdot S = \Omega(N^{2-o(1)})$ for element distinctness is almost tight in comparison-based models, the algorithm of Beame et al. [8] showed how to beat this bound and obtained $T^2 \cdot S = O(N^3)$ by working outside the restricted model (i.e., exploiting the internal representations of the elements). Recently, Tessaro and Thiruvengadam showed bi-directional space-tight reductions between breaking double encryption and solving the element distinctness problem [31]. In fact, the algorithm of [8] is a variant of PCS which obtains a similar tradeoff for breaking double encryption.

Finally, a different restricted model of computation for proving time-space tradeoff lower bounds in the domain of cryptography was proposed in [6] by Barkan, Biham and Shamir. This work analyzed the problem of inverting a random function $f : [N] \to [N]$ with preprocessing, and proposed a model that generalizes the algorithms of Hellman [21] and Oechslin [28] for the problem. The main result of [6] was a proof that any algorithm in their model cannot substantially improve upon the known time-space tradeoffs for the function inversion problem.

1.4   The Post-filtering Model of Computation

Even though restricted computational models are natural choices for analyzing a variety of problems, none of the existing ones seems relevant to obtaining time-space lower bounds for the cryptanalytic problems described in Sect. 1.1. For example, the streaming model is inapplicable to cryptanalysis of double encryption, since the best known key-recovery attack requires only two plaintext-ciphertext pairs (and it does not make sense to restrict access to the block cipher itself). The pebbling model is irrelevant since it is not clear which circuit should be pebbled. Considering comparison-based models, one can apply Yao's bound for element distinctness to the problem of breaking double encryption (as implied by the result of Tessaro and Thiruvengadam [31]). However, PCS beats Yao's bound, which implies that the model is too restrictive for this specific problem. Finally, the precomputation setting analyzed in [6, 21, 28] is quite different from ours and the tools used in its analysis seem inapplicable in our context.

Nevertheless, we would still like to obtain some meaningful time-space lower bounds that apply to basic cryptanalytic problems. Hence, we put forward a new restricted model of computation, which we call the *post-filtering model*, where the algorithm obtains full access to a *part* of the input, while access to the remaining part is replaced with access to a *post-filtering oracle*.

The post-filtering model may seem to have little to do with space complexity, yet it allows proving time-space lower bounds. The reason for this is that in some problems the input can be partitioned such that given the first part, there are many equally-likely potential solutions. Consequently, an algorithm with full access to (only) the first part of the input has to produce many potential outputs to be post-filtered by the oracle. Thus, the model forces a reduction from a problem with a short output to a related problem with a long output, for which time-space tradeoff lower bounds are provable with existing techniques.

In the post-filtering model, we focus on double encryption, as it seems to be the most fundamental problem listed in Sect. 1.1. Indeed, it is the basis for many other more involved meet-in-the-middle type of attacks (such as breaking triple encryption and specialized attacks on concrete symmetric-key constructions). In our analysis, we give the adversary full access to (p_1, c_1) and the block ciphers $E1, E2$, while access to the remaining plaintext-ciphertext pairs is replaced with access to a post-filtering oracle that filters out wrong key guesses. We exploit the fact that there are many possible (k_1, k_2) pairs that are consistent with (p_1, c_1), and prove that any post-filtering attack on double encryption that succeeds with constant probability satisfies the time-space tradeoff curve $T^2 \cdot S = \tilde{\Omega}(N^3)$. This matches the performance of the best known attack that uses PCS.

Technically, we obtain this result based on the optimality of the tradeoff for CSP, but it is a conceptually stronger result, as the post-filtering model abstracts away the (lower-level) collision search problem. The optimality of the tradeoff for double encryption in the post-filtering model implies that if an improved algorithm exists, then it must deviate from the post-filtering model by simultaneously combining information from several plaintext-ciphertext pairs in a meaningful way. This can be viewed both as a barrier, but also as an opportunity for improvement.

We also mention that a different approach to obtaining meaningful results for short-output problems (despite the aforementioned barrier) is to use space-efficient reductions in order to prove relations among tradeoffs for these problems [5]. The recent work by Tessaro and Thiruvengadam [31] (that showed reductions between attacking double encryption and solving the element distinctness problem) is a relevant example of this approach. We note that it is possible to adapt the post-filtering model to the element distinctness problem, and obtain a similar bound to the one we obtain for double encryption.

1.5   Paper Organization

The rest of the paper is structured as follows. We describe preliminaries in Sect. 2. Then, we prove time-space tradeoff lower bounds for collision search in a single function and between two functions in Sect. 3 and Sect. 4, respectively. We discuss relevant barriers in complexity theory in Sect. 5 and prove a time-space tradeoff lower bound for double encryption in the post-filtering model in Sect. 6. Finally, we conclude the paper in Sect. 7.

2   Preliminaries

Let N be a natural number and denote $[N] = \{0, 1, \ldots, N - 1\}$. We use the standard $\tilde{O}$ and $\tilde{\Omega}$ notations that suppress poly-logarithmic factors in N.

Let X be a finite set. We write $x \xleftarrow{\$} X$ to indicate that x is a random variable sampled uniformly from X. We denote by $x \leftarrow \mathcal{D}$ a random variable x sampled according to the distribution $\mathcal{D}$.

We use a weak version of Stirling's approximation, which asserts that $n! > (n/e)^n$ for every positive integer n.

In this paper, we are interested in counting distinct collision pairs. A colliding pair in a function $f : [N] \to [N]$ is an unordered pair of indices $(i_1, i_2) \in [N]^2$ such that $i_1 \neq i_2$ and $f(i_1) = f(i_2)$. When considering two functions $f_1, f_2 : [N] \to [N]$, a colliding pair between f_1 and f_2 is an ordered pair $(i_1, i_2) \in [N]^2$ such that $f_1(i_1) = f_2(i_2)$. Two pairs (i_1, i_2) and (j_1, j_2) and *disjoint* if they do not share any index.

Let $f : [N] \to [N]$ be a function. For an integer $t \geq 2$, a t-way collision in f is an (unordered) set of t distinct indices $\{i_1, \ldots, i_t\}$ such that $f(i_1) = f(i_2) = \ldots = f(i_t)$. Note that a t-way collision in f contains $t(t-1)/2$ distinct colliding pairs, but can only be partitioned into $\lfloor t/2 \rfloor$ disjoint colliding pairs.

We may refer to a function $f : [N] \to [N]$ as a vector (or a string) in the space $[N]^N$, and visa versa. More specifically a string $x \in [N]^N$ represents a function $f_x : [N] \to [N]$ defined as $f_x(i) = x[i]$. In this paper, we will switch between these representations. For example, we define a collision in $x \in [N]^N$ as an unordered pair of indices $(i_1, i_2) \in [N]^2$ such that $i_1 \neq i_2$ and $x[i_1] = x[i_2]$.

2.1   The Collision Search Problem

Let N, C be positive integer parameters. Given random access to a function $f : [N] \to [N]$, the goal in the collision search problem $\mathrm{CSP}(C)$ is to output a multi-set of pairs $(i_1^{(j)}, i_2^{(j)}) \in [N]^2$ for $j \in \{1, 2, \ldots\}$ (at any order) such that each pair is colliding (i.e., $f(i_1^{(j)}) = f(i_2^{(j)})$ but $i_1^{(j)} \neq i_2^{(j)}$) and the multi-set contains at least C distinct (unordered) colliding pairs.

CSP can be extended to two functions $f_1, f_2 : [N] \to [N]$. Here, the goal is to output at least C distinct ordered colliding pairs between the functions.

We define CSP such that all distinct colliding pairs are accounted for, as most CSP applications (such as breaking double encryption) are interested in each such pair. Of course, if we under-count pairs induced by t-way collisions (e.g., by considering only disjoint pairs), we can obtain a (slightly) better lower bound.

In Appendix A we summarize the PCS algorithm that solves $\mathrm{CSP}(C)$ and obtains the time-space tradeoff $T^2 \cdot S = \tilde{O}(C^2 \cdot N)$.

2.2 R-Way Branching Programs

The model of R-way branching programs is a very general and powerful non-uniform model of computation, introduced in [11]. An R-way branching program is a directed acyclic graph in which each node represents a memory state of the program. At each node, a single input variable is queried and the program branches to the next state according to the value of this variable (possibly printing an output value along the way). Thus, a path in the graph of length T represents T time steps (input variable queries) of the program.

Let $R \geq 2$ be an integer. Formally, an R-way branching program $\mathcal{P}$ on an input vector consisting of N input variables $x = x[1], \ldots, x[N] \in [R]^N$ is a directed acyclic graph with a single source node, such that every non-sink node has out-degree R and is labeled with an index $i \in [N]$ corresponding to an input variable to be queried. Every edge is labeled with an element of $[R]$ (corresponding to the value of the queried variable) such that no edge (u, v) and (u, w) where $v \neq w$ share a label. Furthermore, every vertex v is associated with an instruction to print a (possibly empty) value $p(v)$.

The computation path of $\mathcal{P}$ on input x is the (unique) path $\pi = (v_0, v_1), (v_1, v_2), \ldots, (v_{\ell-1}, v_\ell)$ such that v_0 is the source node, v_ℓ is a sink node, and for all $i \in \{0, \ldots, \ell - 1\}$, if v_i is labeled j, then the label of (v_i, v_{i+1}) is equal to $x[j]$. We denote by $\mathcal{P}(x)$ the output of $\mathcal{P}$ on input x. It is defined as the concatenation of the values printed by the vertices along the computation path of $\mathcal{P}$ on input x, namely, $p(v_0)p(v_1)\ldots p(v_\ell)$.

The *height* of an R-way branching program $\mathcal{P}$ is the length of the longest path in its graph, and its *size* is its number of vertices. The *time complexity* of a branching program is defined as its length, while the *space* used by a branching program is defined as the log of its size. Note that the input and output are not counted towards the space used by the branching program, and time complexity is measured only in terms of the number of queries to the input variables.

An R-way branching program is called *levelled* if its nodes are assigned levels such that the source is in level 0 and the out-edges of each node at level k go only to nodes at level $k + 1$. It is shown in [12] that any branching program of size 2^S can be converted into an equivalent levelled branching program with the same length and size of at most 2^{2S}.

2.3   Our Model of Computation

We use the R-way branching program model in order to prove the time-space lower bound for collision search in Sect. 3. However, in Sects. 4 and 6 it will be more natural to consider algorithms rather than branching programs. Nevertheless, the model of computation that we use in these sections is equivalent to the branching program model. More specifically, we consider an algorithm $\mathcal{A}$ with access to input variables in $[R]$ (for a value of R depending on the problem). The algorithm has space of S bits, where the input and output do not count towards the space complexity. Each query of $\mathcal{A}$ to one of its input variables costs one time unit, but other operations (such as reading or writing to memory) are for free. This makes our computational model (and our lower bounds) very strong. Note that an algorithm $\mathcal{A}$ in our model is equivalent to an R-way branching program $\mathcal{P}$ with the same time and space complexities.

R-Way Branching Programs for Collision Search. We model the algorithm for CSP(C) as an N-way branching program $\mathcal{P}$ of height T and size 2^S. We assume that $\mathcal{P}$ is deterministic, but our lower bounds extend to randomized branching programs as well by Yao's minimax principle [34].

For convenience, we denote by $|\mathcal{P}(x)|$ the number of distinct colliding pairs (ignoring duplicates) output by $\mathcal{P}$ on input $x \in [N]^N$, which represents a function $f_x : [N] \rightarrow [N]$ defined as $f_x(i) = x[i]$. We define $|\mathcal{P}(x)| = -1$ if $\mathcal{P}(x)$ is erroneous, i.e., it outputs a pair which does not collide on x.

Input Representation. In the domain of complexity theory, if an algorithm $\mathcal{A}$ (or branching program $\mathcal{P}$) has random access to $x \in [N]^N$, then x is typically treated as an input, using the notation $\mathcal{A}(x)$ (or $\mathcal{P}(x)$). We use such notation in Sects. 3, 4 and 5. On the other hand, in cryptography, similar random access of an algorithm $\mathcal{A}$ to a function $f_x : [N] \rightarrow [N]$ is typically modeled by viewing $f = f_x$ as an oracle and using the notation $\mathcal{A}^f$. We use this notation in Sect. 6.

3   A Time-Space Tradeoff Lower Bound for Collision Search in a Function

In this section, we prove the following theorem

Theorem 1. *Let N, C, T, S be positive integer parameters such that $N > 8$, $S \geq 5(\log^2 N + \log N)$ and $C \leq N/4$. If an N-way branching program $\mathcal{P}$ for CSP(C) of height T and size 2^S satisfies*

$$\Pr_x[|\mathcal{P}(x)| \geq C] \geq N^{-2}, \text{ where } x \xleftarrow{\$} [N]^N, \text{ then}$$

$$T^2 \cdot S \geq \frac{1}{(6e \cdot \log N)^2} \cdot C^2 \cdot N.$$

Remark 1. If $S < 5(\log^2 N + \log N)$, we can apply the theorem with $S' = 5(\log^2 N + \log N)$. If $C > N/4$, we can apply the theorem with $C' = N/4$ (note that with high probability a random function only contains $O(N)$ collisions). In both cases the loss in the bound is small.

Remark 2. The theorem is formulated for deterministic algorithms (or branching programs). However, by Yao's minimax principle it also applies to randomized algorithms, which are viewed as distributions over deterministic algorithms. In this case, the probability is also taken over the randomness of the algorithm.

3.1   Overview of the Proof

The proof is an adaptation of the general approach of [11]. This adaptation requires additional insight which we summarize below.

We first prove that every shallow branching program of a small height T' outputs C' (distinct) collisions in a random input x with negligible probability, denoted here by $\epsilon = \epsilon(T', C')$ (for appropriate values of T' and C'). Note that this proof has nothing to do with space complexity.

Then, given a branching program $\mathcal{P}$ of size 2^S and height T, we level it to obtain a levelled branching program $\mathcal{P}'$, losing a factor of 2 in its space S. We then split $\mathcal{P}'$ into L layers (for a carefully chosen value of L), each of height at most $T' = T/L$. In order to produce C collisions, at least one such layer has to produce $C' = C/L$ collisions, namely, there exists a subprogram of $\mathcal{P}'$ (defined by its source node) of length T' in some layer that outputs C' collisions. Since $\mathcal{P}'$ contains 2^{2S} such subprograms, we take a union bound over all of them and conclude that the probability in which $\mathcal{P}'$ outputs C (distinct) collisions is upper bounded by $2^{2S} \cdot \epsilon$.

With T' queries to the input x, the expected number of encountered collisions is about $(T')^2/N$, and we would like to prove a strong concentration inequality which shows that it is extremely unlikely to encounter $C' = c \cdot (T')^2/N$ collisions for sufficiently small $c > 1$, thus obtaining a strong upper bound on ϵ. Indeed, in order to obtain a meaningful upper bound on the success probability of $\mathcal{P}'$, we need $\epsilon \ll 2^{-2S}$.

The above calculation justifies the relation between C' and T'. It remains to choose L such that we can indeed prove that $\epsilon \ll 2^{-2S}$ and obtain the desired bound $T^2 \cdot S = \tilde{\Omega}(C^2 \cdot N)$. Some calculation shows that for the sake of obtaining a tight bound, we need to choose L such that C' is a bit larger than the space $2S$. Intuitively, a choice of L such that C' is much larger than $2S$ will artificially allow the program to output too many collisions (much more than its space) in limited time and result in a loose bound. On the other hand, if we choose L for which C' is smaller than $2S$, $\mathcal{P}'$ will actually be able to output C' collisions with sufficiently high probability and we will not be able to obtain the required upper bound on ϵ such that $\epsilon \ll 2^{-2S}$.

Hence, the constraint $\epsilon \ll 2^{-2S}$ translates into $\epsilon = 2^{-\tilde{\Omega}(C')}$. In other words, we need to prove a concentration inequality that decays exponentially with the number of collisions per layer C'. Unfortunately, obtaining such a strong bound on ϵ is impossible in general. For example, suppose that $T' - N^{3/4}$, hence $C' \approx N^{1/2}$. Note that $C' \approx N^{1/2}$ distinct colliding pairs can be obtained via a t-way collision for $t \approx N^{1/4}$. The probability of obtaining such a t-way collision is at least

$$N^{-N^{1/4}} = 2^{-\log N \cdot N^{1/4}} \gg 2^{-N^{1/2}} \approx 2^{-C'}.$$

Fortunately, most functions do not contain such a large t-way collision (as proved in Lemma 1), and for these functions, we can prove the required bound on ϵ. Restricting our attention to such functions allows the proof to go through.

We note that the poly-logarithmic factors in Theorem 1 can be improved. In particular, a refined version of Lemma 1 (which would consider t-way collisions for various values of t, rather than merely $t = 3\log N$) would yield such an improvement. However, in this paper we opt for simplicity at the expense of low-level optimizations.

Finally, we also mention the related work by Chakrabarti and Chen [14] which analyzed time-space tradeoffs for the *memory game* with cards. This game is played with N distinct pairs of cards laid face-down, and the goal is to output all "colliding" pairs. Although the memory game resembles CSP (and the lower bound obtained in [14] is similar to ours), its analysis in [14] does not seem to apply to CSP. This is mainly due to t-way collisions for $t > 2$ which are possible in the collision search problem, but not in the memory game where the cards are composed of distinct pairs.

3.2 Bounding the Number of Collisions Output by Shallow Branching Programs

Lemma 1. *Let $t > 0$ be an integer. Then,*

$$\Pr_x[x \text{ contains a } t\text{-way collision}] \leq \frac{N}{t!},$$

where $x \xleftarrow{\$} [N]^N$. In particular, for $N > 8$,

$$\Pr_x[x \text{ contains a } 3\log N\text{-way collision}] \leq \frac{N}{(3\log N)!} \leq N \cdot \left(\frac{e}{3\log N}\right)^{3\log N} \leq N^{-3}.$$

Proof. Fix a set of t distinct indices in $[N]$, $\{i_1, \ldots, i_t\}$. We have

$$\Pr[x[i_1] = x[i_2] = \ldots = x[i_t]] = N^{-t+1}.$$

The number of such sets of indices is $\binom{N}{t} \leq \frac{N^t}{t!}$. Taking a union bound over all sets,

$$\Pr[x \text{ contains a } t\text{-way collision}] \leq \frac{N^t}{t!} \cdot N^{-t+1} = \frac{N}{t!}. \qquad \blacksquare$$

Lemma 2. *For all T', C' and $N > 8$, any N-way branching program $\mathcal{P}$ of height at most T' satisfies*

$$\Pr_x[|\mathcal{P}(x)| \geq C' \mid x \text{ does not have a } 3\log N\text{-way collision}] \leq$$

$$2 \cdot N^{3\log N} \cdot \left(\frac{3e \cdot \log N \cdot (T')^2}{C' \cdot N}\right)^{C'/6\log N}, \quad \text{where } x \xleftarrow{\$} [N]^N.$$

Proof. Denote by $\mathcal{E}$ the event that x does not have a $3\log N$-way collision. Suppose that x satisfies this condition and assume that C' distinct colliding index pairs are output by $\mathcal{P}(x)$. Assume that these pairs form k disjoint sets, where set i is of size t_i for $2 \leq t_i < 3\log N$, and gives a t_i-way collision. Since a t-way collision results in $t(t-1)/2$ distinct colliding pairs, we have $\sum_{i=1}^k t_i(t_i - 1)/2 \geq C'$. On the other hand, each set of size t_i can be partitioned into $\lfloor t_i/2 \rfloor$ disjoint colliding pairs. Altogether, the C' distinct colliding index pairs can be partitioned into

$$\sum_{i=1}^k \lfloor t_i/2 \rfloor \geq \sum_{i=1}^k (t_i - 1)/2 \geq \frac{1}{3\log N} \cdot \sum_{i=1}^k t_i(t_i - 1)/2 \geq \frac{C'}{3\log N}$$

disjoint colliding pairs.

Using the fact that $\Pr_x[\mathcal{E}] \geq N^{-3\log N}$, we obtain

$$\Pr_x[|\mathcal{P}(x)| \geq C' \mid \mathcal{E}] \leq$$

$$\Pr_x\left[\mathcal{P}(x) \text{ is correct and outputs } \frac{C'}{3\log N} \text{ disjoint colliding pairs} \mid \mathcal{E}\right] \leq$$

$$\Pr_x\left[\mathcal{P}(x) \text{ is correct and outputs } \frac{C'}{3\log N} \text{ disjoint colliding pairs}\right] / \Pr_x[\mathcal{E}] \leq$$

$$N^{3\log N} \cdot \Pr_x\left[\mathcal{P}(x) \text{ is correct and outputs } \frac{C'}{3\log N} \text{ disjoint colliding pairs}\right].$$

It remains to prove that

$$\Pr_x[\mathcal{P}(x) \text{ is correct and outputs } \frac{C'}{3\log N} \text{ disjoint colliding pairs}] \leq$$

$$2\left(\frac{3e \cdot \log N \cdot (T')^2}{C' \cdot N}\right)^{C'/6\log N}.$$

For $K = \frac{C'}{6\log N}$, denote by $\mathcal{E}_1$ the event that $\mathcal{P}(x)$ queries K disjoint colliding index pairs and by $\mathcal{E}_2$ the event that $\mathcal{P}(x)$ is correct and outputs K disjoint colliding index pairs such that in each one, at least one index is not queried. Note that if $\mathcal{P}(x)$ is correct and outputs $\frac{C'}{3\log N}$ disjoint colliding pairs, then either $\mathcal{E}_1$ or $\mathcal{E}_2$ occurs.

For a fixed set of disjoint K pairs of query indices, the probability that they all collide on a uniform input x is N^{-K}. The number of ways to select such K query index pairs from a set of T' index queries is

$$\binom{T'}{2K} \cdot \frac{(2K)!}{2^K \cdot K!} \leq \frac{(T')^{2K}}{2^K \cdot (K/e)^K} = \left(\frac{(T')^2}{2/e \cdot K}\right)^K.$$

Taking a union bound over all sets of K query index pairs, we conclude

$$\Pr[\mathcal{E}_1] \leq \left(\frac{(T')^2}{2/e \cdot K}\right)^K \cdot N^{-K}.$$

In addition,

$$\Pr[\mathcal{E}_2] = N^{-K}.$$

Finally,

$$\Pr_x[\mathcal{P}(x) \text{ is correct and outputs } \frac{C'}{3\log N} \text{ disjoint colliding pairs}] \leq$$

$$\Pr[\mathcal{E}_1] + \Pr[\mathcal{E}_2] \leq \left(\frac{(T')^2}{2/e \cdot K}\right)^K \cdot N^{-K} + N^{-K} \leq 2\left(\frac{3e \cdot \log N \cdot (T')^2}{C' \cdot N}\right)^{C'/6\log N},$$

as claimed.   ■

3.3   Proof of Theorem 1

Proof (of Theorem 1). Let $\mathcal{P}$ be a branching program of height T and size 2^S. We prove the contrapositive statement of the theorem by assuming

$$T^2 \cdot S < \frac{1}{(6e \cdot \log N)^2} \cdot C^2 \cdot N, \tag{1}$$

and showing that

$$\Pr_x[|\mathcal{P}(x)| < C] \geq 1 - N^{-2}.$$

Denote by $\mathcal{E}$ the event that x does not have a $3 \log N$-way collision. We lower bound the failure probability of $\mathcal{P}$ by

$$\Pr_x[|\mathcal{P}(x)| < C] \geq \Pr[\mathcal{E}] \cdot \Pr[|\mathcal{P}(x)| < C \mid \mathcal{E}] = (1 - \Pr[\neg\mathcal{E}]) \cdot \Pr[|\mathcal{P}(x)| < C \mid \mathcal{E}] \geq$$
$$\Pr[|\mathcal{P}(x)| < C \mid \mathcal{E}] - \Pr[\neg\mathcal{E}].$$

In the following, we prove based on Lemma 2 that

$$\Pr_x[|\mathcal{P}(x)| \geq C \mid \mathcal{E}] \leq N^{-3}. \tag{2}$$

Therefore, combining (2) with Lemma 1,

$$\Pr_x[|\mathcal{P}(x)| < C] \geq \Pr[|\mathcal{P}(x)| < C \mid \mathcal{E}] - \Pr[\neg\mathcal{E}] \geq 1 - N^{-3} - N^{-3} \geq 1 - N^{-2},$$

as required.

It remains to prove (2). We first level the branching program to obtain a levelled branching problem $\mathcal{P}'$ of length T and size at most 2^{2S}. Partition $\mathcal{P}'$ into $L = \frac{T}{\sqrt{S \cdot N}}$ layers, each of height at most $T' = T/L$. By an averaging argument, if $\mathcal{P}'$ outputs C distinct colliding pairs, then there exists a layer that outputs at least $C' = C/L$ distinct colliding pairs.[4] Hence, the probability that $\mathcal{P}'$ outputs at least C distinct colliding pairs is upper bounded by the probability that some layer outputs C' pairs. Since there are at most 2^{2S} subprograms (each defined by its source node) in $\mathcal{P}'$, by Lemma 2 and a union bound over all subprograms we obtain

$$\Pr_x[|\mathcal{P}'(x)| \geq C \mid \mathcal{E}] \leq$$

$$2^{2S} \cdot 2 \cdot N^{3 \log N} \cdot \left(\frac{3e \cdot \log N \cdot (T')^2}{C' \cdot N} \right)^{C'/6 \log N} =$$

$$2^{2S} \cdot 2 \cdot N^{3 \log N} \cdot \left(\frac{3e \cdot \log N \cdot (T/L)^2}{C/L \cdot N} \right)^{C'/6 \log N} =$$

$$2^{2S} \cdot 2 \cdot N^{3 \log N} \cdot \left(\frac{3e \cdot \log N \cdot T^2}{C \cdot L \cdot N} \right)^{C'/6 \log N} =$$

$$2^{2S} \cdot 2 \cdot N^{3 \log N} \cdot \left(\frac{3e \cdot \log N \cdot T \cdot \sqrt{S}}{C \cdot \sqrt{N}} \right)^{C'/6 \log N}.$$

---

[4] Note that $C' = C/L = \frac{C \cdot \sqrt{S \cdot N}}{T} \approx S$, as suggested in the overview at the beginning of Sect. 3.

If $\frac{3e \cdot \log N \cdot T \cdot \sqrt{S}}{C \cdot \sqrt{N}} > 1/2$, then $T^2 \cdot S > \frac{1}{(6e \cdot \log N)^2} \cdot C^2 \cdot N$, in contradiction to (1). Therefore,

$$2^{2S} \cdot 2 \cdot N^{3 \log N} \cdot \left(\frac{3e \cdot \log N \cdot T \cdot \sqrt{S}}{C \cdot \sqrt{N}} \right)^{C'/6 \log N} \leq$$

$$2^{2S} \cdot 2 \cdot N^{3 \log N} \cdot 2^{-C'/6 \log N} = 2^{2S+1+3 \log^2 N - \frac{1}{6 \log N} \cdot C \cdot \sqrt{S \cdot N}/T}.$$

According to (1),

$$\frac{1}{6 \log N} \cdot \frac{C \cdot \sqrt{N}}{T} \geq e \cdot \sqrt{S}.$$

Hence,

$$2^{2S+1+3 \log^2 N - \frac{1}{6 \log N} \cdot C \cdot \sqrt{S \cdot N}/T} \leq 2^{2S+1+3 \log^2 N - e \cdot S} = 2^{S(2-e)+1+3 \log^2 N} \leq N^{-3}$$

(since $S \geq 5(\log^2 N + \log N)$), concluding the proof. ∎

4 A Time-Space Tradeoff Lower Bound for Collision Search Between Two Functions

In this section, we analyze the problem of collision search between two independent and random functions. For convenience, we consider algorithms rather than branching programs, even though they are equivalent in the computational model we consider.

Theorem 2. *Let N, C, T, S be positive integer parameters such that $S \geq 5(\log^2 N + \log N)$, $C \leq N$ and $N > 4$. Let $\mathcal{A}$ be an algorithm that outputs C colliding pairs between two independent random functions $f_1, f_2 : [N] \to [N]$ with probability at least N^{-2}, using T queries to f_1 and f_2 and space of S bits. Then, $\mathcal{A}$ satisfies the time-space tradeoff lower bound*

$$T^2 \cdot S \geq \frac{1}{(24e \cdot \log N)^2} \cdot C^2 \cdot N.$$

We note that as Theorems 1 and 2 also applies to randomized algorithms.

It is possible to prove Theorem 2 by using the same technique that was used to prove Theorem 1 (in fact, this results in slightly better parameters). Instead, we give a simpler proof by a reduction from the problem of collision search in a single function, under the mild assumption that the output length of $\mathcal{A}$ (i.e., the total number of elements of $[N]$ that it outputs) is not larger than its number of queries T. This assumption is not needed in general.

Proof. We reduce the problem of outputting C collisions between two independent random functions $f_1, f_2 : [N] \to [N]$ from the problem of outputting $C' = C/2$ collisions in a single random function $f : [2N] \to [2N]$.

Let $\mathcal{A}$ be an algorithm for finding colliding pairs between two functions with domain and range $[N]$. Let $f : [2N] \rightarrow [2N]$ be a random function. We devise an algorithm $\mathcal{A}'$ that outputs $C' = C/2$ collisions in f as follows. Define $f_1, f_2 : [N] \rightarrow [N]$ as

$$f_1(i) = f(i) \bmod N, \text{ and}$$
$$f_2(i) = f(i + N) \bmod N.$$

It is easy to verify that f_1, f_2 are two independent random functions.

The algorithm $\mathcal{A}'$ runs $\mathcal{A}$ with parameter C, giving it access to f_1, f_2. For every pair (i_1, i_2) such that $f_1(i_1) = f_2(i_2)$ output by $\mathcal{A}$, algorithm $\mathcal{A}'$ checks whether $f(i_1) = f(i_2 + N)$, and if so, outputs the pair $(i_1, i_2 + N)$. Since we assume that the output length of $\mathcal{A}$ is not larger than its number of queries T, we have $T' \leq 2T$. Moreover, the space used by $\mathcal{A}'$ is essentially the same as that of $\mathcal{A}$ (in particular , $S' \leq 2S$).

We call a function $f : [2N] \rightarrow [2N]$ *bad* if $\mathcal{A}$ outputs at least C collisions on f_1, f_2 derived from f, but $\mathcal{A}'$ outputs less than $C/2$ collision on f. We call f *good*, if $\mathcal{A}$ outputs at least C collisions on f_1, f_2 derived from f, and $\mathcal{A}'$ outputs at least $C/2$ collision on f. We claim that the number of good functions is at least the number of bad functions. Indeed, let M be a mapping between functions $f : [2N] \rightarrow [2N]$ which maps f to $\hat{f} = M(f)$, defined as follows:

$$\hat{f}(i) = \begin{cases} f(i), & \text{for } i < N \\ f(i) - N, & \text{for } i \geq N \text{ and } f(i) \geq N \\ f(i) + N, & \text{for } i \geq N \text{ and } f(i) < N. \end{cases}$$

Note that $\mathcal{A}$ is run with the same input on f and $M(f)$, hence it produces the same output. Moreover, for every $(i_1, i_2) \in [N]^2$, if $f_1(i_1) = f_2(i_2)$ and $f(i_1) \neq f(i_2 + N)$ then $\hat{f}_1(i_1) = \hat{f}_2(i_2)$ and $\hat{f}(i_1) = \hat{f}(i_2 + N)$ (where $\hat{f} = M(f)$). Hence, every bad function is mapped by M to a good function. Finally, $M(M(f)) = f$, implying that M is a permutation on the space of functions, proving that the number of good functions is at least the number of bad functions.

Let X, X' be random variables for the number of distinct number of colliding pairs output by $\mathcal{A}, \mathcal{A}'$, respectively. We have shown that

$$\Pr[X' \geq C/2] \geq 1/2 \cdot \Pr[X \geq C], \text{ or } \Pr[X \geq C] \leq 2 \cdot \Pr[X' \geq C/2].$$

Applying Theorem 1 with $N' = 2N, C' = C/2, S' = 2S, T' = 2T$ concludes the proof. ∎

5   Time-Space Complexity Barriers and Their Cryptanalytic Variants

In this section, we argue that it may be very difficult to prove tight time-space lower bounds (i.e., analogs of Theorems 1 and 2) for cryptanalytic problems with short outputs, whose most efficient algorithms seem to require substantial space. The results of this section motivate the restricted post-filtering model of computation used in Sect. 6 to prove a time-space tradeoff lower bound for double encryption.

The *smallest fundamental complexity barrier* (as named in [10], and formulated as a challenge) is to find an explicit Boolean decision problem $h : \{0,1\}^n \to \{0,1\}$ in P for which $T \cdot S = O(n \log n)$ is not possible. Since its formulation, the original barrier has been overcome in [9] by Beame et al. which gave explicit examples of problems for which any algorithm for computing them with space of $S = n^{1-\epsilon}$ bits (where $\epsilon > 0$ is an arbitrarily small constant), requires time complexity of at least $T = \Omega(n\sqrt{\log n / \log \log n})$. This time-space tradeoff lower bound was proved for R-way branching programs.

Despite this breakthrough, its does not give any non-trivial lower bound on the space of an algorithm running in time (say) $T = n \log n$. Therefore, the complexity barrier was reformulated in [9] to proving a non-trivial time-space tradeoff lower bound when $T = n(\log n)^{\omega(1)}$.

In order to generalize this barrier to cryptanalytic problems, we consider problems with longer input variables and longer outputs (but still polylogarithmic in the input length). Consequently, we require that $T \cdot S = \Omega(n^{1+\epsilon})$ for some $\epsilon > 0$.

As a simple example, we consider the problem of finding a 3-way collision in a function, represented by an input $x \in [N]^N$. The goal in this problem is to find 3 distinct indices i_1, i_2, i_3 such that $x[i_1] = x[i_2] = x[i_3]$. Note that the output length is $3 \log N$ and is short (poly-logarithmic in the length of x which is $n = N \cdot \log N$). We can formulate the generalized barrier for this problem as proving that any algorithm requires $T \cdot S = \Omega(N^{1+\epsilon})$. However, in cryptography, we are typically interested in average-case, rather than worst-case problems. In particular, one is typically interested in finding collisions in random functions.

Consider the uniform distribution over $x \in [N]^N$ and a trivial algorithm that evaluates $T = O(N^{2/3})$ arbitrary input variables and looks for a 3-way collision among them. Simple probabilistic analysis shows that the algorithm succeeds with high probability. Such sub-linear algorithms demonstrate that we need to further generalize the challenge above to average-case problems. Below we formulate a challenge for finding a 3-way collision.

Challenge 1. *Prove that there exist $\epsilon > 0$ and $\delta > 0$ such that any algorithm that succeeds in finding a 3-way collision in a uniformly chosen $x \in [N]^N$ for all sufficiently large N with probability at least $3/4$ and $T = N^{2/3+\epsilon}$, satisfies $S \geq N^\delta$.*

The difficulty in overcoming Challenge 1 stems from the fact that currently known techniques are not able to prove space lower bounds (of the form $S \geq n^\delta$ for $\delta > 0$) for short-output problems with input size n that are solvable in time $\hat{T}$ whenever we allow $T = \hat{T} \cdot n^\epsilon$ for some $\epsilon > 0$. In contrast, for problems where the output size is $n^{\Omega(1)}$, such lower bounds are known. Thus, overcoming Challenge 1 would be a breakthrough and perhaps lead towards overcoming a similar barrier for decision problems.

We note that the best known time-space tradeoff algorithm for finding a 3-way collision was published by Joux and Lucks [23] and obtains $T \cdot S = \tilde{O}(N)$

for $T \geq N^{2/3}$. While we would like to prove that it is optimal, we cannot even overcome Challenge 1 which is generally much weaker (e.g., for the values $\delta = \epsilon = 0.01$).

Challenge 1 deals with the specific problem of finding a 3-way collision. Similar challenges can be formulated for other short-output cryptanalytic problems whose most time-efficient algorithm seems to require a large amount of space. The adaptation is performed by adjusting the distribution on inputs and the exponent $2/3$ according to the specific problem. For example, for the problem of breaking double encryption we would consider an exponent of 1. In the next section, we propose a restricted model of computation which allows to bypass the challenge for the specific case of breaking double encryption.

6   A Time-Space Tradeoff Lower Bound for Post-filtering Attacks on Double Encryption

Double encryption is one of the most fundamental constructions in symmetric-key cryptography. The classical meet-in-the-middle attack on the scheme (due to Merkle and Hellman [26]) gives the time-space tradeoff $T \cdot S = \tilde{O}(K^2)$ (where $(k_1, k_2) \in [K]^2$ is the key). This tradeoff was improved by van Oorschot and Wiener to $T^2 \cdot S = \tilde{O}(K^3)$ using the PCS algorithm [32]. In terms of lower bounds, the scheme is known to be secure up to $T = O(K)$ queries [1]. On the other hand, there are no known unconditional lower bounds that take into consideration space complexity for $S \ll T$. Indeed, in Sect. 5 we argued that proving such bounds may be very difficult.

In this section, we analyze the security of double encryption assuming that the space of the adversary is bounded. Our setting is similar to the one considered by Tessaro and Thiruvengadam in [31]. However, [31] reduced problem of breaking double encryption (i.e., distinguishing the scheme from a random permutation) to solving the element distinctness problem, and thus obtained a conditional result based on the current state-of-the-art for element distinctness algorithms. On the other hand, we obtain an unconditional security proof for a class of algorithms which is restricted, yet broad enough to capture the best known space-efficient attack algorithm (and its potential generalizations).

Let $E : [K] \times [N] \to [N]$ be a block cipher, which is a permutation on $[N]$ for each $k \in [K]$. The inverse block cipher is denoted by E^{-1}. Given block ciphers $E1, E2$, double encryption $DE : [K] \times [K] \times [N] \to [N]$ is defined as

$$DE_{k_1,k_2}(p) = E2_{k_2}(E1_{k_1}(p)),$$

for keys $(k_1, k_2) \in [K]^2$.

Let $BC_{K,N}$ be the set of all block ciphers with key space $[K]$ and block space $[N]$. Throughout this section, we assume for the sake of simplicity that $K = N$ and that $E1$ is independent of $E2$. It is not difficult to extend our results (with negligible loss in the bound) to the case of $K \neq N$ (as long as $K = O(N)$) and\or $E1 = E2$.

Recall from Sect. 1.1 that in the attack based on collision search, except for the main (p_1, c_1) plaintext-ciphertext pair, all other pairs are accessed only for post-filtering purposes. We now define a model which captures this attack and potentially additional post-filtering attacks on double-encryption (the model also captures the classical meet-in-the-middle attack [26]). Using this model, we prove that the time-space tradeoff obtained by the best know attack (which is based on PCS) is optimal for post-filtering algorithms.

We consider a post-filtering adversary $\mathcal{A}$ that attempts to distinguish between the real world (where ciphertexts are generated by a double encryption scheme) and an ideal world (where ciphertexts are generated at random). The adversary has access to the following functionalities:

1. Block ciphers $E1, E2 \in BC_{N,N}$ (chosen uniformly at random from the space of block ciphers), along with their inverses $E1^{-1}, E2^{-1}$.
2. In the real world, an arbitrary plaintext $p \in [N]$, along with $c = DE_{k_1, k_2}(p)$ for uniformly and independently chosen $(k_1, k_2) \in [N]^2$. In the ideal world, the adversary receives p and a uniformly chosen $c \in [N]$.
3. A post-filtering oracle $\mathcal{O} : [N]^2 \to \{0, 1\}$. In the real world, $\mathcal{O}_{(k_1, k_2)}(k_1', k_2') = 1$ if $(k_1', k_2') = (k_1, k_2)$ and $\mathcal{O}_{(k_1, k_2)}(k_1', k_2') = 0$ otherwise. In the ideal world, $\mathcal{O} = \mathcal{O}_\perp$ returns 0 on any input.

The access to the post-filtering oracle $\mathcal{O}$ is restricted, as it is only invoked on candidates (k_1', k_2') that satisfy $c = E2_{k_2'}(E1_{k_1'}(p))$. We thus assume that if $\mathcal{A}$ calls $\mathcal{O}$ with input (k_1', k_2') such that $c \neq E2_{k_2'}(E1_{k_1'}(p))$, the algorithm is terminated with failure.

The adversary issues T queries to $E1, E2$ and their inverses and has space of S bits. Finally, the adversary outputs a bit which represents a guess as to whether the interaction occurred in the real world, or in the ideal world.

Formally, we define the advantage of the adversary in the post-filtering double encryption (PFDE) game as

$$\text{Adv}(\mathcal{A})^{\text{PFDE}}_{DE[E1, E2]} =$$

$$|\Pr[E1, E2 \overset{\$}{\leftarrow} BC_{N,N}, (k_1, k_2) \overset{\$}{\leftarrow} [N]^2 :$$

$$\mathcal{A}^{E1, E1^{-1}, E2, E2^{-1}, \mathcal{O}_{(k_1, k_2)}}(p, c = DE_{k_1, k_2}(p)) = 1] -$$

$$\Pr[E1, E2 \overset{\$}{\leftarrow} BC_{N,N}, c \overset{\$}{\leftarrow} [N] : \mathcal{A}^{E1, E1^{-1}, E2, E2^{-1}, \mathcal{O}_\perp}(p, c) = 1]|.$$

The main result of this section is given by the theorem below.

Theorem 3. *Let N, S, T be parameters such that $N \geq 3000, S \geq 5(\log^2 N + \log N)$. Any adversary $\mathcal{A}$ with space of S bits that makes at most T queries to $E1, E2$ and $E1^{-1}, E2^{-1}$ satisfies*

$$\text{Adv}(\mathcal{A})^{\text{PFDE}}_{DE[E1, E2]} \leq \min\left(\frac{T^2}{N^2}, 288e \cdot \log N \cdot \frac{T\sqrt{S}}{N^{3/2}} + N^{-1/2}\right).$$

Hence, the advantage is $o(1)$ unless $T = \tilde{\Omega}\left(\frac{N^{3/2}}{S^{1/2}}\right)$, matching the best known attack.

6.1 Proof Overview

In order to prove Theorem 3, we first define the *restricted* post-filtering double-encryption game (RPFDE). The difference between this game and its unrestricted version above is that the adversary can only query $E1_k(p)$ and $E2_k^{-1}(c)$ for any choice of k, but cannot issue any other query. In Lemma 4, we show that despite the restriction on the adversary's queries in RPFSE, the distinguishing advantage remains the same as in PFSE. Hence it is sufficient to analyze RPFSE.

Next, we denote $f_1(k) = E1_k(p)$ and $f_2(k) = E2_k^{-1}(c)$, which syntactically transforms RPFSE to the notation used in Sect. 4 and allows to define the equivalent post-filtering collision search (PFCS) game. The goal is to show that in order to distinguish between the real and ideal worlds in PFCS (and RPFSE) with high probability, the adversary has to find $\Omega(N)$ collisions between f_1 and f_2 in the real world. Indeed, there are about N possible collisions between f_1 and f_2, but only one of them suggests the correct key and is accepted by the post-filtering oracle. Since the adversary is forced to find $\Omega(N)$ collisions, we can apply Theorem 2 to bound the success probability based on the adversary's time and space.

Applying Theorem 2 is not immediate since the assumption in this theorem is that f_1 and f_2 are independent, but in PFCS (and RPFSE) the functions are not independent, as they are known to collide for the correct choice of key. Hence, the application of Theorem 2 is made possible after an additional (hybrid argument) step that bounds the statistical distance between the dependent and independent distributions on (f_1, f_2).

Overall, the proof is somewhat more involved than one may expect. One reason for this is that we aim to prove security for parameter ranges of $T = \omega(N)$ (assuming $S = o(N)$), whereas standard security analysis of double encryption is only valid up to $T = N$. Consequently, some simple proof strategies that work up to $T = N$ are not good enough for our purposes.

Throughout the rest of this section, we denote $\alpha = \alpha(N) = 24e \log N$ (this expression appears in the time-space tradeoff formula of Theorem 2).

6.2 Restricted Post-filtering Double Encryption

As noted above, the difference between PFDE and its restricted version is that in RPFDE the adversary can only query $E1_k(p)$ and $E2_k^{-1}(c)$ for any choice of k, but cannot issue any other query. We denote the advantage of the adversary in the restricted game as $\mathrm{Adv}(\mathcal{A})_{DE[E1,E2]}^{\mathrm{RPFDE}}$.

Theorem 3 follows from the two lemmas below. The first lemma shows that the restricted game does not hurt the distinguishing advantage of the adversary. The second lemma upper bounds the distinguishing advantage in RPFDE and its proof is given in Sect. 6.3.

Lemma 3. *Let N, S, T be parameters. If there exists an adversary $\mathcal{A}$ with space of S bits that makes at most T queries to $E1, E2$ and $E1^{-1}, E2^{-1}$ in the PFDE* *game, then there exists an adversary $\mathcal{A}'$ in the RPFDE game with space S and time T such that*

$$\mathrm{Adv}(\mathcal{A}')^{\mathrm{RPFDE}}_{DE[E1,E2]} = \mathrm{Adv}(\mathcal{A})^{\mathrm{PFDE}}_{DE[E1,E2]}.$$

Lemma 4. *Let N, S, T be parameters such that $N \geq 3000, S \geq 5(\log^2 N + \log N)$. Then, any adversary $\mathcal{A}$ with space of S bits that makes at most T (restricted) queries to $E1$ and $E2^{-1}$ in the RPFDE game satisfies*

$$\mathrm{Adv}(\mathcal{A})^{\mathrm{RPFDE}}_{DE[E1,E2]} \leq \frac{12\alpha \cdot T\sqrt{S}}{N\sqrt{N}} + N^{-1/2}.$$

Proof (of Theorem 3). First, $\mathrm{Adv}(\mathcal{A})^{\mathrm{PFDE}}_{DE[E1,E2]} \leq \frac{T^2}{N^2}$ by [1], which provides a general distinguishing advantage bound for double encryption that obviously holds here as well.

Moreover, by Lemmas 3 and 4,

$$\mathrm{Adv}(\mathcal{A})^{\mathrm{PFDE}}_{DE[E1,E2]} = \mathrm{Adv}(\mathcal{A}')^{\mathrm{RPFDE}}_{DE[E1,E2]} \leq \frac{12\alpha \cdot T\sqrt{S}}{N\sqrt{N}} + N^{-1/2}.$$

∎

Proof (of Lemma 3). Given black-box access to adversary $\mathcal{A}$, we describe adversary $\mathcal{A}'$ that can only issue queries of the form $E1_k(p)$ and $E2_k^{-1}(c)$ for an arbitrary choice of k. In order to simulate answers to additional queries to $E1, E2, E1^{-1}$ and $E2^{-1}$, $\mathcal{A}'$ will utilize randomness that is independent of $E1, E2$ and used in order to construct block ciphers $E1', E2' : [N] \times [N] \to [N]$ that are chosen uniformly at random from $BC_{N,N}$, subject to the constraint that for each $k \in [N]$, $E1'_k(p) = E1_k(p)$ and $(E2'_k)^{-1}(c) = E2_k^{-1}(c)$.

The adversary $\mathcal{A}'$ runs $\mathcal{A}$ and answers every query to $E1$ or $E2$ (or their inverses) by issuing an identical query to $E1'$ or $E2'$ (or their inverses) and feeding the answer back to $\mathcal{A}$. Access to $\mathcal{O}$ remains identical. Finally, $\mathcal{A}'$ outputs the same value as $\mathcal{A}$.

We now describe how $E1', E2'$ are constructed. For each $k \in [N]$, the randomness of $\mathcal{A}'$ simply complements the constraint $E1'_k(p) = E1_k(p)$ to a random permutation (under this constraint), and similarly, complements the constraint $(E2'_k)^{-1}(c) = E2_k^{-1}(c)$ to a random permutation (under this constraint). Such randomness is independent of $E1, E2$, while a query to $E1', E2', (E1')^{-1}, (E2')^{-1}$ can be answered by querying $E1_k(p)$ (or $E2_k^{-1}(c)$) and the randomness.

It remains to analyze the complexity and advantage of $\mathcal{A}'$. We start by analyzing its advantage. First, note that for any k'_1, k'_2 such that $c = E2_{k'_2}(E1_{k'_1}(p))$, we have $c = E2'_{k'_2}(E1'_{k'_1}(p))$, hence the behaviour of $\mathcal{O}$ remains unchanged by the simulation (it is only invoked on legal inputs). Second, $\mathcal{A}'$ perfectly simulates the distribution of answers of $E1, E2, E1^{-1}, E2^{-1}$ in both the real and the ideal worlds. In other words, for every choice of $E1, E2$ in the real world, there is an equally likely choice of $E1' = E1, E2' = E2$ in the real world for which $\mathcal{A}'$ with access to $E1', E2'$ answers the same as $\mathcal{A}$ (and a similar statement holds in the ideal world). We conclude that $\text{Adv}(\mathcal{A}')_{DE[E1,E2]}^{\text{RPFDE}} = \text{Adv}(\mathcal{A})_{DE[E1,E2]}^{\text{PFDE}}$.

In terms of complexity, the block ciphers $E1', E2'$ are constructed such that every query to $E1', E2'$ (or their inverses) can be answered with at most one query to $E1_k(p)$ or $E2_k^{-1}(c)$ (for the same value of k). Since $\mathcal{A}$ makes at most T queries to $E1, E2, E1^{-1}, E2^{-1}$, then $\mathcal{A}'$ makes at most T such (restricted) queries. Furthermore, $\mathcal{A}'$ uses essentially the same space as $\mathcal{A}$ (in our model, the use of randomness is not counted towards the space nor the time complexity). ∎

Remark 3. In the proof of Lemma 3, it may be tempting to implement $E1', E2'$: $[N]^2 \to [N]$ as independent block ciphers, and to query them for each query of $\mathcal{A}$ which is not to $E1_k(p)$ or $E2_k^{-1}(c)$. The problem with this implementation is that the answers that $\mathcal{A}$ receives for queries to $E1, E2$ (and their inverses) may no longer form a permutation for each $k \in [N]$, as they may contain a collision in the plaintext-ciphertext space for each k (due to the inconsistency between $E1$ and $E1'$ and between $E2$ and $E2'$). A single collision per $k \in [N]$ may not be a concern when $\mathcal{A}$ issues only $T \ll N$ queries, but in our case $T = \omega(N)$ (for $S = o(N)$) is possible.

6.3 Post-filtering Collision Search

Towards proving Lemma 4, we first translate the cryptographic setting of double encryption to the more generic setting of Sect. 4 and relate these settings in Lemma 5 below. Lemma 4 then follows from Lemma 5 and Lemma 6 below (whose proof is given in Sect. 6.4) that bounds the adversary's advantage in the setting of Sect. 4.

Let $\mathcal{F} = \{f : [N] \to [N]\}$. We now define the post-filtering collision search (PFCS) game, where an algorithm $\mathcal{A}$ has access to functions $f_1, f_2 : [N] \to [N]$ and a post-filtering oracle $\mathcal{O} : [N]^2 \to \{0, 1\}$, initialized as follows:

1. In the real world, $(i_1, i_2) \in [N]^2$ is chosen uniformly at random. Then $f_1, f_2 :$ $[N] \to [N]$ are chosen uniformly at random, subject to the constraint that $f_1(i_1) = f_2(i_2)$. We denote this distribution on (f_1, f_2, i_1, i_2) by $\mathcal{D}_2$. We define $\mathcal{O}_{(i_1,i_2)}(i_1', i_2') = 1$ if $(i_1', i_2') = (i_1, i_2)$ and $\mathcal{O}_{(i_1,i_2)}(i_1', i_2') = 0$ otherwise.
2. In the ideal world, $f_1, f_2 : [N] \to [N]$ are chosen uniformly at random and $\mathcal{O}_\perp$ returns 0 on any input.

As previously, access to the post-filtering oracle $\mathcal{O}$ is restricted, and it is only invoked on candidates (i_1', i_2') that satisfy $f_1(i_1') = f_2(i_2')$ (otherwise $\mathcal{A}$ is terminated). We define the advantage of the algorithm in the post-filtering collision search game as

$$\text{Adv}(\mathcal{A})_{f_1,f_2}^{\text{PFCS}} =$$

$$|\Pr[(f_1, f_2, i_1, i_2) \leftarrow \mathcal{D}_2 : \mathcal{A}^{f_1,f_2,\mathcal{O}_{(i_1,i_2)}} = 1] - \Pr[f_1, f_2 \xleftarrow{\$} \mathcal{F} : \mathcal{A}^{f_1,f_2,\mathcal{O}_\perp} = 1]|.$$

The PFCS game is merely a syntactical transformation of the RPFDE game, hence the following lemma is straightforward.

Lemma 5. *Let* N, S, T *be parameters. If there exists an adversary* $\mathcal{A}$ *with space of* S *bits that makes at most* T *queries to* $g_1(k) = E1_k(p)$ *and* $g_2(k) = E2_k^{-1}(c)$ *in the RPFCS game, then there exists an algorithm* $\mathcal{A}'$ *in the PFCS game with space* S *that makes at most* T *queries to* f_1 *and* f_2 *such that*

$$\text{Adv}(\mathcal{A}')^{\text{PFCS}}_{f_1,f_2} = \text{Adv}(\mathcal{A})^{\text{RPFDE}}_{DE[E1,E2]}.$$

Proof. Denoting $g_1(k) = E1_k(p)$ and $g_2(k) = E2_k^{-1}(c)$ as in the theorem, (g_1, g_2, k_1, k_2) in the real world is distributed according to $\mathcal{D}_2$, while g_1, g_2 in the ideal world are uniform and independent functions. Hence, given black-box access to an adversary $\mathcal{A}$ for RPFCS, an algorithm $\mathcal{A}'$ in PFCS with the desired properties can be constructed in a straightforward manner. ∎

In the following, we will prove:

Lemma 6. *Let* N, T, S *be parameters such that* $N \geq 3000, S \geq 5(\log^2 N + \log N)$. *Then, any algorithm* $\mathcal{A}$ *for PFCS that queries* f_1 *and* f_2 *on* T *inputs and has space complexity of* S *bits satisfies*

$$\text{Adv}(\mathcal{A})^{\text{PFCS}}_{f_1,f_2} \leq \frac{12\alpha \cdot T\sqrt{S}}{N\sqrt{N}} + N^{-1/2}.$$

Based on this lemma, we can prove Lemma 4.

Proof (of Lemma 4). By Lemmas 5 and 6,

$$\text{Adv}(\mathcal{A})^{\text{RPFDE}}_{DE[E1,E2]} = \text{Adv}(\mathcal{A}')^{\text{PFCS}}_{f_1,f_2} \leq \frac{12\alpha \cdot T\sqrt{S}}{N\sqrt{N}} + N^{-1/2}. \quad ∎$$

6.4   Bounding the Advantage in Post-filtering Collision Search

It remains to prove Lemma 6. The proof is by a hybrid argument. We define *world 1* as an intermediate between the real and ideal worlds in PFCS. In world 1, algorithm $\mathcal{A}$ has access to f_1, f_2 and an oracle $\mathcal{O}$, initialized as follows:

1. The functions $f_1, f_2 : [N] \to [N]$ are chosen uniformly at random. Then, an index pair $(i_1, i_2) \in [N]^2$ is chosen uniformly at random from the collision set $\{(i'_1, i'_2) \mid f_1(i'_1) = f_2(i'_2)\}$ (if the collision set is empty, define $(i_1, i_2) = (0, 0)$). We denote this distribution on (f_1, f_2, i_1, i_2) by $\mathcal{D}_1$.
2. If the set $\{(i'_1, i'_2) \mid f_1(i'_1) = f_2(i'_2)\}$ is empty, then $\mathcal{O} = \mathcal{O}_\perp$ returns 0 on any input. If the collision set is non-empty, $\mathcal{O}_{(i_1,i_2)}(i'_1, i'_2) = 1$ if $(i'_1, i'_2) = (i_1, i_2)$ and $\mathcal{O}_{(i_1,i_2)}(i'_1, i'_2) = 0$ otherwise.

We define Game 1 as the problem of distinguishing the real world in PFCS from world 1, and Game 2 as the problem of distinguishing world 1 from the ideal world in PFCS. Correspondingly, we define

$$\text{Adv}(\mathcal{A})^{\text{G1}}_{f_1,f_2} =$$
$$|\Pr[(f_1, f_2, i_1, i_2) \leftarrow \mathcal{D}_2 : \mathcal{A}^{f_1, f_2, \mathcal{O}_{(i_1,i_2)}} = 1] -$$
$$\Pr[(f_1, f_2, i_1, i_2) \leftarrow \mathcal{D}_1 : \mathcal{A}^{f_1, f_2, \mathcal{O}_{(i_1,i_2)}} = 1]|,$$

and

$$\text{Adv}(\mathcal{A})^{\text{G2}}_{f_1, f_2} =$$

$$|\Pr[(f_1, f_2, i_1, i_2) \leftarrow \mathcal{D}_1 : \mathcal{A}^{f_1, f_2, \mathcal{O}_{(i_1, i_2)}} = 1] - \Pr[f_1, f_2 \xleftarrow{\$} \mathcal{F} : \mathcal{A}^{f_1, f_2, \mathcal{O}_\perp} = 1]|.$$

We will prove the following two lemmas.

Lemma 7. *Any algorithm $\mathcal{A}$ in Game 1 satisfies*

$$\text{Adv}(\mathcal{A})^{\text{G1}}_{f_1, f_2} \leq N^{-1/2} + 2e^{-N/120}.$$

Lemma 8. *Let N, T, S be parameters such that $N \geq 3000, S \geq 5(\log^2 N + \log N)$. Then, any algorithm $\mathcal{A}$ in Game 2 that makes T queries to f_1 and f_2 and has space of S bits satisfies*

$$\text{Adv}(\mathcal{A})^{\text{G2}}_{f_1, f_2} \leq \frac{10\alpha \cdot T\sqrt{S}}{N\sqrt{N}}.$$

Proof (of Lemma 6). By a hybrid argument,

$$\text{Adv}(\mathcal{A})^{\text{PFCS}}_{f_1, f_2} \leq \text{Adv}(\mathcal{A})^{\text{G1}}_{f_1, f_2} + \text{Adv}(\mathcal{A})^{\text{G2}}_{f_1, f_2} \leq$$

$$\frac{10\alpha \cdot T\sqrt{S}}{N\sqrt{N}} + N^{-1/2} + 2e^{-N/120} \leq \frac{12\alpha \cdot T\sqrt{S}}{N\sqrt{N}} + N^{-1/2},$$

where the penultimate inequality is due to Lemmas 7 and 8, and the final inequality follows since $\alpha = 24e \log N$ and $N \geq 3000$. ∎

It remains to prove Lemmas 7 and 8. The proof of these lemmas requires an auxiliary lemma whose proof is given in Appendix B. We denote $\text{Col}(f_1, f_2) = |\{(i_1, i_2) \mid f_1(i_1) = f_2(i_2)\}|$, i.e., the size of the collision set. Lemma 9 provides concentration inequalities for $\text{Col}(f_1, f_2)$, when f_1, f_2 are independent random functions (which is the case when they are chosen according to $\mathcal{D}_1$).

Lemma 9. *Let $c > 0$ be any constant and suppose that f_1, f_2 are selected independently and uniformly at random from $\mathcal{F}$. Then,*

$$\Pr_{f_1, f_2} [|\text{Col}(f_1, f_2) - N| \geq c \cdot N^{1/2}] \leq c^{-2}.$$

Moreover,

$$\Pr_{f_1, f_2} [\text{Col}(f_1, f_2) < N/8] \leq 4e^{-N/120}.$$

Remark 4. It is possible to prove concentration inequalities for $\text{Col}(f_1, f_2)$ which are sharper than the ones of Lemma 9. However, Lemma 9 is sufficient for our purposes and is relatively easy to prove.

Proof (of Lemma 7). We have

$$\mathrm{Adv}(\mathcal{A})^{\mathrm{G1}}_{f_1,f_2} \le SD(\mathcal{D}_1, \mathcal{D}_2),$$

where $SD(\mathcal{D}_1, \mathcal{D}_2)$ is the statistical distance between $\mathcal{D}_1$ and $\mathcal{D}_2$. Hence, it suffices to prove that

$$SD(\mathcal{D}_1, \mathcal{D}_2) \le N^{-1/2} + 2e^{-N/120}.$$

We denote by Λ the space

$$\{(f_1, f_2, i_1, i_2) \in \mathcal{F} \times \mathcal{F} \times [N] \times [N] \mid f_1(i_1) = f_2(i_2)\},$$

where $|\Lambda| = N^{2N+1}$. Recall that in order to sample according to $\mathcal{D}_2$, we first sample a uniform index pair (i_1, i_2) and then uniformly sample (f_1, f_2) under the restriction $f_1(i_1) = f_2(i_2)$. Hence, $\mathcal{D}_2$ is the uniform distribution over Λ, namely, for each $(f'_1, f'_2, i'_1, i'_2) \in \Lambda$,

$$\Pr_{(f_1,f_2,i_1,i_2)\leftarrow\mathcal{D}_2}[(f_1, f_2, i_1, i_2) = (f'_1, f'_2, i'_1, i'_2)] = 1/|\Lambda| = N^{-2N-1}.$$

On the other hand, in order to sample according to $\mathcal{D}_1$, we first sample (f_1, f_2) uniformly and then sample (i_1, i_2) from the collision set. Therefore, for each $(f'_1, f'_2, i'_1, i'_2) \in \Lambda$,

$$\Pr_{(f_1,f_2,i_1,i_2)\leftarrow\mathcal{D}_1}[(f_1, f_2, i_1, i_2) = (f'_1, f'_2, i'_1, i'_2)] =$$

$$\Pr[(f_1, f_2) = (f'_1, f'_2)] \cdot \Pr[(i_1, i_2) = (i'_1, i'_2) \mid (f_1, f_2) = (f'_1, f'_2)] =$$

$$N^{-2N} \cdot \frac{1}{Col(f'_1, f'_2)} = \frac{N}{Col(f'_1, f'_2) \cdot |\Lambda|},$$

whereas

$$\Pr_{(f_1,f_2,i_1,i_2)\leftarrow\mathcal{D}_1}[(f_1, f_2, i_1, i_2) \notin \Lambda] = \Pr[Col(f_1, f_2) = 0] \le 4e^{-N/120},$$

by the second part of Lemma 9. Hence, treating the distributions $\mathcal{D}_1, \mathcal{D}_2$ as vectors over $\mathcal{F} \times \mathcal{F} \times [N] \times [N]$,

$$SD(\mathcal{D}_1, \mathcal{D}_2) =$$

$$1/2 \cdot \sum_{(f_1,f_2,i_1,i_2)\in\Lambda} |\mathcal{D}_1(f_1, f_2, i_1, i_2) - \mathcal{D}_2(f_1, f_2, i_1, i_2)| +$$

$$1/2 \cdot \sum_{(f_1,f_2,i_1,i_2)\notin\Lambda} |\mathcal{D}_1(f_1, f_2, i_1, i_2) - \mathcal{D}_2(f_1, f_2, i_1, i_2)| \le$$

$$1/2 \cdot \sum_{(f_1,f_2,i_1,i_2)\in\Lambda} |\mathcal{D}_1(f_1, f_2, i_1, i_2) - \mathcal{D}_2(f_1, f_2, i_1, i_2)| + 2e^{-N/120}.$$

It remains to upper bound the first term above by $N^{-1/2}$. We have

$$1/2 \cdot \sum_{(f_1,f_2,i_1,i_2)\in\Lambda} |\mathcal{D}_1(f_1,f_2,i_1,i_2) - \mathcal{D}_2(f_1,f_2,i_1,i_2)| \le$$

$$1/2 \cdot \frac{1}{|\Lambda|} \cdot \sum_{(f_1,f_2,i_1,i_2)\in\Lambda} \left| \frac{N}{Col(f_1,f_2)} - 1 \right| =$$

$$1/2 \cdot \frac{1}{|\Lambda|} \cdot \sum_{(f_1,f_2)} \left(\sum_{\{(i_1,i_2)|f_1(i_1)=f_2(i_2)\}} \left| \frac{N}{Col(f_1,f_2)} - 1 \right| \right) =$$

$$1/2 \cdot \frac{1}{|\Lambda|} \cdot \sum_{(f_1,f_2)} Col(f_1,f_2) \cdot \left| \frac{N}{Col(f_1,f_2)} - 1 \right| =$$

$$1/2 \cdot \frac{1}{|\Lambda|} \cdot \sum_{(f_1,f_2)} |N - Col(f_1,f_2)| =$$

$$1/2 \cdot N^{-1} \cdot \mathrm{E}_{f_1,f_2}[|Col(f_1,f_2) - N|] =$$

$$1/2 \cdot N^{-1} \cdot \sum_{i=0}^{\infty} \Pr_{f_1,f_2}[|Col(f_1,f_2) - N| \ge i] =$$

$$1/2 \cdot N^{-1} \cdot \left(\sum_{i=0}^{N^{1/2}-1} \Pr_{f_1,f_2}[|Col(f_1,f_2) - N| \ge i] + \sum_{i=N^{1/2}}^{\infty} \Pr_{f_1,f_2}[|Col(f_1,f_2) - N| \ge i] \right) \le$$

$$1/2 \cdot N^{-1} \cdot \left(N^{1/2} + \sum_{i=N^{1/2}}^{\infty} \Pr_{f_1,f_2}\left[|Col(f_1,f_2) - N| \ge (i \cdot N^{-1/2}) \cdot N^{1/2}\right] \right) \le$$

$$1/2 \cdot N^{-1} \left(N^{1/2} + \sum_{i=N^{1/2}}^{\infty} (i \cdot N^{-1/2})^{-2} \right) = 1/2 \cdot \left(N^{-1/2} + \sum_{i=N^{1/2}}^{\infty} i^{-2} \right) \le N^{-1/2},$$

where the penultimate inequality is by the first part of Lemma 9. This completes the proof. ∎

Remark 5. In $\mathcal{D}_2$, the dependency of f_1 and f_2 is only due to the index pair (i_1,i_2). Such a dependency is unnoticeable to an algorithm $\mathcal{A}$ as long as it does not query both i_1 and i_2, which occurs with probability of at most $\frac{T^2}{N^2}$. Hence, if we were interested in bounding the advantage of $\mathcal{A}$ only up to $T = N$, we could easily replace the proof of Lemma 7 by a simpler proof. However, it is not clear how to obtain such a simple proof that gives a meaningful bound for $T = \omega(N)$ (when $S = o(N)$).

Proof (of Lemma 8). Denote by $\mathcal{E}$ the event that $\mathcal{O}$ is invoked with (i_1,i_2) (and answers 1) in world 1. Note that $\mathrm{Adv}(\mathcal{A})_{f_1,f_2}^{\mathrm{G2}} \le \Pr[\mathcal{E}]$, as conditioned on $\neg\mathcal{E}$ in world 1, both worlds are identical and the advantage is 0.

We focus on world 1. For $C \ge 0$, denote by $\mathcal{E}_C$ the event that $\mathcal{A}^{f_1,f_2,\mathcal{O}}$ calls the oracle $\mathcal{O}$ with at most C distinct pairs (i_1',i_2') such that $f_1(i_1') = f_2(i_2')$. According to the distribution $\mathcal{D}_1$, the probability that any pair (i_1',i_2') satisfies $(i_1',i_2') = (i_1,i_2)$ is $1/Col(f_1,f_2)$. Hence, for any positive value of $Col(f_1,f_2)$ and $0 \le C \le Col(f_1,f_2)$,

$$\Pr[\mathcal{E} \mid \mathcal{E}_C] \le \frac{C}{Col(f_1,f_2)}.$$

By the above inequality and the second part of Lemma 9,

$$\Pr[\mathcal{E} \mid \mathcal{E}_C] \leq$$

$$\Pr[\mathcal{E} \mid \mathcal{E}_C \wedge Col(f_1, f_2) \geq N/8] + \Pr[Col(f_1, f_2) < N/8] \leq \frac{8}{N} \cdot C + 4e^{-N/120}.$$

$$(3)$$

Define $\hat{C} = \frac{\alpha \cdot T\sqrt{S}}{\sqrt{N}}$. We have

$$\mathrm{Adv}(\mathcal{A})^{G2}_{f_1,f_2} \leq \Pr_{(f_1,f_2,i_1,i_2) \leftarrow \mathcal{D}_1} [\mathcal{E}] \leq \Pr\left[\mathcal{E} \mid \mathcal{E}_{\hat{C}}\right] + \Pr\left[\neg\mathcal{E}_{\hat{C}}\right] \leq$$

$$\frac{8}{N} \cdot \frac{\alpha \cdot T\sqrt{S}}{\sqrt{N}} + 4e^{-N/120} + N^{-2} \leq \frac{10\alpha \cdot T\sqrt{S}}{N\sqrt{N}},$$

where the penultimate inequality is by (3) and Theorem 2, and the final inequality follows since $\alpha = 24e \log N$ and $N \geq 3000$. ∎

7   Conclusions and Future Work

In this paper we proved that the well-known time-space tradeoff $T^2 \cdot S = \tilde{O}(C^2 \cdot N)$ for the collision search problem is optimal using the framework of Borodin and Cook. We further proved that the best known time-space tradeoff attack on double encryption is optimal among post-filtering algorithms.

In the future it would be interesting to find more problems in cryptography for which time-space tradeoff lower bounds can be proved by the method of Borodin and Cook. Another research direction is to extend the post-filtering model and prove time-space tradeoff lower bounds for additional (short-output) cryptanalytic problems under reasonable restrictions.

Acknowledgements. The author was supported by the Israeli Science Foundation through grant No. 573/16 and by the European Research Council under the ERC starting grant agreement No. 757731 (LightCrypt).

A   The Parallel Collision Search Algorithm [32]

In this section, we briefly summarize the PCS algorithm for computing C colliding pairs in a random function $f : [N] \rightarrow [N]$. For more details, refer to [32]. Given $\tilde{O}(S)$ bits of memory, PCS builds a chain structure containing S chains, where a chain starts at an arbitrary point $x_0 \in [N]$ and computed iteratively as $x_{i+1} = f(x_i)$. Each chain is terminated after about $\sqrt{N/S}$ evaluations, hence the structure contains a total of about $S \cdot \sqrt{N/S} = \sqrt{N \cdot S}$ distinct points. As the chains are of length $\sqrt{N/S}$, each chain collides with a different chain in the structure with constant probability according to the birthday paradox, since the number of relevant pairs of points is $\sqrt{N/S} \cdot \sqrt{N \cdot S} = N$. Therefore, the structure contains an expected number of about S colliding pairs.

The collisions can be recovered efficiently by defining a set of $\sqrt{N \cdot S}$ distinguished points according to an easily verifiable condition on the points $x_i \in [N]$. Each chain in the structure is terminated at a distinguished point (and hence its expected length is $N/\sqrt{N \cdot S} = \sqrt{N/S}$ as required). The PCS algorithm stores the distinguished points sorted in memory and collisions between chains are detected at their distinguished points. The actual collisions in f are recovered by recomputing the colliding chains.

In total, PCS finds $C = \Theta(S)$ distinct colliding pairs in f using space of $\tilde{O}(S)$ bits and time complexity $T = \tilde{O}(\sqrt{N \cdot S})$.

When $C > S$ collisions are required, the algorithm is repeated $O(C/S)$ times. In order to (heuristically) eliminate the dependency between the different executions, in repetition i we run PCS on the function $f_i = \pi_i \circ f$, where $\pi_i : [N] \to [N]$ is some simple permutation. Note that a collision in f_i gives a collision in f. Altogether, PCS finds C distinct colliding pairs in f using space of $\tilde{O}(S)$ bits and time complexity $T = \tilde{O}(C/S \cdot \sqrt{N \cdot S}) = \tilde{O}(C \cdot \sqrt{N/S})$, which gives the time-space tradeoff curve $T^2 \cdot S = \tilde{O}(C^2 \cdot N)$.

B   Proof of Lemma 9

Proof (of Lemma 9). We begin by proving the first part of the lemma. For every $(i_1, i_2) \subset [N]^2$ define an indicator random variable $C_{i_1 i_2}$ that is equal to 1 if $f_1(i_1) = f_2(i_2)$. We have

$$\mathrm{E}[C_{i_1 i_2}] = \mathrm{Pr}[C_{i_1 i_2} = 1] = N^{-1}, \text{ and}$$
$$\mathrm{Var}[C_{i_1 i_2}] = \mathrm{E}[(C_{i_1 i_2})^2] - (\mathrm{E}[C_{i_1 i_2}])^2 = N^{-1} - N^{-2} < N^{-1}.$$

Hence,

$$\mathrm{E}[Col(f_1, f_2)] = \mathrm{E}\left[\sum_{(i_1,i_2)\in[N]^2} C_{i_1 i_2}\right] = \sum_{(i_1,i_2)\in[N]^2} \mathrm{E}[C_{i_1 i_2}] = N^2 \cdot N^{-1} = N.$$

Since the random variables $\{C_{i_1 i_2}\}$ are pairwise independent,

$$\mathrm{Var}[Col(f_1, f_2)] = \mathrm{Var}\left[\sum_{(i_1,i_2)\in[N]^2} C_{i_1 i_2}\right] = \sum_{(i_1,i_2)\in[N]^2} \mathrm{Var}[C_{i_1 i_2}] < N^2 \cdot N^{-1} = N.$$

For a parameter $c > 0$, Chebyshev's inequality gives

$$\mathrm{Pr}\left[|Col(f_1, f_2) - \mathrm{E}[Col(f_1, f_2)]| \geq c \cdot \sqrt{\mathrm{Var}[Col(f_1, f_2)]}\right] \leq c^{-2}.$$

Therefore, we obtain

$$\mathrm{Pr}[|Col(f_1, f_2) - N| \geq c \cdot N^{1/2}] \leq c^{-2},$$

as required.

For the second part of the lemma, we view the process of sampling f_1 (and f_2) as a classical Balls-and-Bins problem, where we throw N balls into N bins uniformly at random, and ball i falls into bin $f_1(i)$. Denote by Z_1 the number of empty bins induced by f_1 (i.e., the number of points $x \in [N]$ with no preimage under f_1) and by Z_2 the number of empty bins induced by f_2. Hence, the number of non-empty bins (image points) induced by f_1 and f_2 are $N - Z_1$ and $N - Z_2$, respectively. The number of colliding pairs between f_1, f_2 is at least the size of the intersection of the non-empty bins, which is at least $(N - Z_1) + (N - Z_2) - N = N - Z_1 - Z_2$.

Hence, if $Col(f_1, f_2) < N/8$, then $N - Z_1 - Z_2 < N/8$, which implies that $Z_1 + Z_2 > 7N/8$. Therefore, either $Z_1 > 7N/16$, or $Z_2 > 7N/16$. By [18, p. 75], we have

$$\Pr[|Z_1 - \mathrm{E}[Z_1]| > t] \le 2e^{-2t^2/N},$$

and the same holds for Z_2.

The probability that any particular bin is empty is $(1 - N^{-1})^N \le 1/e$, hence $\mathrm{E}[Z_1] \le N/e$. Therefore,

$$\Pr[Z_1 > 7N/16] = \Pr[Z_1 - N/e > 7N/16 - N/e] \le \Pr[Z_1 - \mathrm{E}[Z_1] > N/15] \le$$
$$\Pr[|Z_1 - \mathrm{E}[Z_1]| > N/15] \le 2e^{-N/120}.$$

Finally,

$$\Pr[Col(f_1, f_2) < N/8] \le \Pr[Z_1 > 7N/16] + \Pr[Z_2 > 7N/16] \le 4e^{-N/120}.$$

■

References

1. Aiello, W., Bellare, M., Crescenzo, G.D., Venkatesan, R.: Security amplification by composition: the case of doubly-iterated, ideal ciphers. In: Krawczyk, H. (ed.) CRYPTO 1998. LNCS, vol. 1462, pp. 390–407. Springer, Heidelberg (1998). https://doi.org/10.1007/BFb0055743
2. Alon, N., Matias, Y., Szegedy, M.: The space complexity of approximating the frequency moments. J. Comput. Syst. Sci. **58**(1), 137–147 (1999)
3. Alwen, J., Chen, B., Pietrzak, K., Reyzin, L., Tessaro, S.: Scrypt is maximally memory-hard. In: Coron, J.-S., Nielsen, J.B. (eds.) EUROCRYPT 2017. LNCS, vol. 10212, pp. 33–62. Springer, Cham (2017). https://doi.org/10.1007/978-3-319-56617-7_2
4. Alwen, J., Serbinenko, V.: High parallel complexity graphs and memory-hard functions. In: Servedio, R.A., Rubinfeld, R. (eds.) Proceedings of the Forty-Seventh Annual ACM on Symposium on Theory of Computing, STOC 2015, Portland, OR, USA, 14–17 June 2015, pp. 595–603. ACM (2015)
5. Auerbach, B., Cash, D., Fersch, M., Kiltz, E.: Memory-tight reductions. In: Katz, J., Shacham, H. (eds.) CRYPTO 2017. LNCS, vol. 10401, pp. 101–132. Springer, Cham (2017). https://doi.org/10.1007/978-3-319-63688-7_4
6. Barkan, E., Biham, E., Shamir, A.: Rigorous bounds on cryptanalytic time/memory tradeoffs. In: Dwork, C. (ed.) CRYPTO 2006. LNCS, vol. 4117, pp. 1–21. Springer, Heidelberg (2006). https://doi.org/10.1007/11818175_1

7. Beame, P.: A general sequential time-space tradeoff for finding unique elements. SIAM J. Comput. **20**(2), 270–277 (1991)
8. Beame, P., Clifford, R., Machmouchi, W.: Element distinctness, frequency moments, and sliding windows. In: 54th Annual IEEE Symposium on Foundations of Computer Science, FOCS 2013, 26–29 October, 2013, Berkeley, CA, USA, pp. 290–299. IEEE Computer Society (2013)
9. Beame, P., Saks, M.E., Sun, X., Vee, E.: Time-space trade-off lower bounds for randomized computation of decision problems. J. ACM **50**(2), 154–195 (2003)
10. Borodin, A.: Time space tradeoffs (getting closer to the barrier?). In: Ng, K.W., Raghavan, P., Balasubramanian, N.V., Chin, F.Y.L. (eds.) ISAAC 1993. LNCS, vol. 762, pp. 209–220. Springer, Heidelberg (1993). https://doi.org/10.1007/3-540-57568-5_251
11. Borodin, A., Cook, S.A.: A Time-Space Tradeoff for Sorting on a General Sequential Model of Computation. SIAM J. Comput. **11**(2), 287–297 (1982)
12. Borodin, A., Fischer, M.J., Kirkpatrick, D.G., Lynch, N.A., Tompa, M.: A time-space tradeoff for sorting on non-oblivious machines. J. Comput. Syst. Sci. **22**(3), 351–364 (1981)
13. Cachin, C., Maurer, U.: Unconditional security against memory-bounded adversaries. In: Kaliski, B.S. (ed.) CRYPTO 1997. LNCS, vol. 1294, pp. 292–306. Springer, Heidelberg (1997). https://doi.org/10.1007/BFb0052243
14. Chakrabarti, A., Chen, Y.: Time-space tradeoffs for the memory game. CoRR, abs/1712.01330 (2017)
15. Cobham, A.: The recognition problem for the set of perfect squares. In: 7th Annual Symposium on Switching and Automata Theory, Berkeley, California, USA, 23–25 October 1966, pp. 78–87. IEEE Computer Society (1966)
16. Delaplace, C., Esser, A., May, A.: Improved low-memory subset sum and LPN algorithms via multiple collisions. IACR Cryptology ePrint Archive 2019, 804 (2019)
17. Dinur, I., Dunkelman, O., Keller, N., Shamir, A.: Efficient dissection of composite problems, with applications to cryptanalysis, knapsacks, and combinatorial search problems. In: Safavi-Naini, R., Canetti, R. (eds.) CRYPTO 2012. LNCS, vol. 7417, pp. 719–740. Springer, Heidelberg (2012). https://doi.org/10.1007/978-3-642-32009-5_42
18. Dubhashi, D.P., Panconesi, A.: Concentration of Measure for the Analysis of Randomized Algorithms. Cambridge University Press, Cambridge (2009)
19. Dwork, C., Naor, M., Wee, H.: Pebbling and proofs of work. In: Shoup, V. (ed.) CRYPTO 2005. LNCS, vol. 3621, pp. 37–54. Springer, Heidelberg (2005). https://doi.org/10.1007/11535218_3
20. Fortnow, L., Lipton, R.J., van Melkebeek, D., Viglas, A.: Time-space lower bounds for satisfiability. J. ACM **52**(6), 835–865 (2005)
21. Hellman, M.E.: A cryptanalytic time-memory trade-off. IEEE Trans. Inf. Theory **26**(4), 401–406 (1980)
22. Jaeger, J., Tessaro, S.: Tight time-memory trade-offs for symmetric encryption. In: Ishai, Y., Rijmen, V. (eds.) EUROCRYPT 2019. LNCS, vol. 11476, pp. 467–497. Springer, Cham (2019). https://doi.org/10.1007/978-3-030-17653-2_16
23. Joux, A., Lucks, S.: Improved generic algorithms for 3-collisions. In: Matsui, M. (ed.) ASIACRYPT 2009. LNCS, vol. 5912, pp. 347–363. Springer, Heidelberg (2009). https://doi.org/10.1007/978-3-642-10366-7_21
24. Knuth, D.E.: The Art of Computer Programming, Volume II: Seminumerical Algorithms. Addison-Wesley, Boston (1969)
25. Mansour, Y., Nisan, N., Tiwari, P.: The computational complexity of universal hashing. Theor. Comput. Sci. **107**(1), 121–133 (1993)

26. Merkle, R.C., Hellman, M.E.: On the security of multiple encryption. Commun. ACM **24**(7), 465–467 (1981)
27. Nisan, N.: Pseudorandom generators for space-bounded computation. Combinatorica **12**(4), 449–461 (1992). https://doi.org/10.1007/BF01305237
28. Oechslin, P.: Making a faster cryptanalytic time-memory trade-off. In: Boneh, D. (ed.) CRYPTO 2003. LNCS, vol. 2729, pp. 617–630. Springer, Heidelberg (2003). https://doi.org/10.1007/978-3-540-45146-4_36
29. Paul, W.J., Tarjan, R.E., Celoni, J.R.: Space bounds for a game on graphs. Math. Syst. Theory **10**, 239–251 (1977). https://doi.org/10.1007/BF01683275
30. Raz, R.: Fast learning requires good memory: a time-space lower bound for parity learning. J. ACM **66**(1), 3:1–3:18 (2019)
31. Tessaro, S., Thiruvengadam, A.: Provable time-memory trade-offs: symmetric cryptography against memory-bounded adversaries. In: Beimel, A., Dziembowski, S. (eds.) TCC 2018. LNCS, vol. 11239, pp. 3–32. Springer, Cham (2018). https://doi.org/10.1007/978-3-030-03807-6_1
32. van Oorschot, P.C., Wiener, M.J.: Parallel collision search with cryptanalytic applications. J. Cryptol. **12**(1), 1–28 (1999). https://doi.org/10.1007/PL00003816
33. Wagner, D.: A generalized birthday problem. In: Yung, M. (ed.) CRYPTO 2002. LNCS, vol. 2442, pp. 288–304. Springer, Heidelberg (2002). https://doi.org/10.1007/3-540-45708-9_19
34. Yao, A.C.: Probabilistic computations: toward a unified measure of complexity (extended abstract). In: 18th Annual Symposium on Foundations of Computer Science, Providence, Rhode Island, USA, 31 October–1 November, pp. 222–227. IEEE Computer Society (1977)
35. Yao, A.C.: Near-optimal time-space tradeoff for element distinctness. SIAM J. Comput. **23**(5), 966–975 (1994)
36. Yesha, Y.: Time-space tradeoffs for matrix multiplication and the discrete Fourier transform on any general sequential random-access computer. J. Comput. Syst. Sci. **29**(2), 183–197 (1984)

Tight Security Bounds for Double-Block Hash-then-Sum MACs

Seongkwang Kim$^{(\boxtimes)}$, Byeonghak Lee$^{(\boxtimes)}$, and Jooyoung Lee$^{(\boxtimes)}$

KAIST, Daejeon, Korea
{ksg0923,lbh0307,hicalf}@kaist.ac.kr

Abstract. In this work, we study the security of deterministic MAC constructions with a double-block internal state, captured by the *double-block hash-then-sum* (DbHtS) paradigm. Most DbHtS constructions, including PolyMAC, SUM-ECBC, PMAC-Plus, 3kf9 and LightMAC-Plus, have been proved to be pseudorandom up to $2^{\frac{2n}{3}}$ queries when they are instantiated with an n-bit block cipher, while the best known generic attacks require $2^{\frac{3n}{4}}$ queries.

We close this gap by proving the PRF-security of DbHtS constructions up to $2^{\frac{3n}{4}}$ queries (ignoring the maximum message length). The core of the security proof is to refine Mirror theory that systematically estimates the number of solutions to a system of equations and non-equations, and apply it to prove the security of the finalization function. Then we identify security requirements of the internal hash functions to ensure $3n/4$-bit security of the resulting constructions when combined with the finalization function.

Within this framework, we prove the security of DbHtS whose internal hash function is given as the concatenation of a universal hash function using two independent keys. This class of constructions include PolyMAC and SUM-ECBC. Moreover, we prove the security of PMAC-Plus, 3kf9 and LightMAC-Plus up to $2^{\frac{3n}{4}}$ queries.

Keywords: Message authentication codes · Beyond-birthday-bound security · Pseudorandom functions · Mirror theory

1 Introduction

MACs. A message authentication code (MAC) is typically built from a block cipher, e.g., CBC-MAC [3], PMAC [5], OMAC [10], LightMAC [13] or from a cryptographic hash function, e.g., HMAC [2]. At a high level, many of these constructions follow the well-established *UHF-then-PRF* design paradigm: a message is first mapped onto a short string through a universal hash function (UHF), and

J. Lee was supported by a National Research Foundation of Korea (NRF) grant funded by the Korean government (Ministry of Science and ICT), No. NRF-2017R1E1A1A03070248.

© International Association for Cryptologic Research 2020
A. Canteaut and Y. Ishai (Eds.): EUROCRYPT 2020, LNCS 12105, pp. 435–465, 2020.
https://doi.org/10.1007/978-3-030-45721-1_16

then encrypted through a fixed-input-length PRF to obtain a short tag. This method is simple, in particular, being deterministic and stateless, yet its security caps at the so-called birthday bound; any collision at the output of the UHF, which translates into a tag collision, is usually enough to break the security of the scheme. However, the birthday bound security might not be enough, in particular, when the MAC construction is instantiated with a lightweight block cipher such as PRESENT [6], LED [9], GIFT [1] operating on small blocks.

DOUBLE-BLOCK HASH-THEN-SUM. Many studies tried to tweak the UHF-then-PRF design in order to obtain beyond-birthday secure MACs, while they possess a similar structural design; the internal state of the hash function is doubled, the two n-bit hash values are encrypted by a block cipher using independent keys, and the outputs are xored to generate the final tag. Datta et al. [7] have dubbed this generic design principle the *double-block hash-then-sum* (DbHtS) paradigm. Within this unified framework, they revisited the security proof of existing DbHtS constructions, including PolyMAC (based on polynomial evaluation [4,8,17]), SUM-ECBC [18], PMAC-Plus [19], 3kf9 [20] and LightMAC-Plus [14], and confirmed that all the constructions are secure up to $2^{\frac{2n}{3}}$ queries (ignoring the maximum message length) when they are instantiated with an n-bit block cipher. Recently, Leurent et al. [12] proposed generic attacks on all these constructions using $2^{\frac{3n}{4}}$ (short message) queries, leaving a gap between the upper and lower bounds for the provable security of DbHtS constructions.

OUR RESULTS. The goal of this paper is to close this gap by proving the exact PRF-security of DbHtS constructions. In order to do this, we take a modular approach; the first step is to refine Mirror theory [15,16] that systematically estimates the number of solutions to a system of equations and non-equations in order to prove the security of the finalization function up to $2^{\frac{3n}{4}}$ queries. However, we cannot directly apply Mirror theory to the problem in a black box manner since it requires that $\xi_{max}^2 q \leq 2^n$ in its original form, where ξ_{max} and q denote the maximum component size and the number of equations, respectively. So we refine Mirror theory by distinguishing components of size two and larger ones, and make sharp estimation for components of size two, while we use the fact that the number of larger components is probabilistically small.

The next step is to identify security requirements of the internal hash functions to ensure $3n/4$-bit security of the entire constructions, combined with the finalization function. Existing security proofs limit the probability of having a trail of length 3 in the transcript graph when an adversary makes $2^{\frac{2n}{3}}$ queries, while our proof allows an adversary making $2^{\frac{3n}{4}}$ queries. So in this case, we need to limit the probability of having a trail of length 4 in the transcript graph; this is the most challenging part of the proof (e.g., Lemma 4 for the proof of PMAC-Plus) that needs a careful case analysis.

As a result, we prove the security of various DbHtS constructions including PolyMAC, SUM-ECBC, PMAC-Plus, 3kf9 and LightMAC-Plus up to $2^{\frac{3n}{4}}$ queries, ignoring the maximum message length. Table 1 compares our new bounds to the old ones given in [7]. For some constructions, one cannot simply ignore the influence of the maximum message length on the security bounds. As seen in

Fig. 1, our bound for PMAC-Plus is better than the old one when ℓ is relatively small (while our bound is worse for a larger ℓ). So our new bound should be seen as complementary to the old one. However, we also remark that our security proof does not use independent randomness of two masking keys Δ_0 and Δ_1; a single masking key is sufficient for our security proof. We would be able to remove the $\ell^2 q/2^n$ term from the security bound by a more complicated proof using the independent randomness of two masking keys.

Table 1. New security bounds for DbHtS MACs. The number of queries and the maximum message length (in blocks) are denoted q and ℓ, respectively. All the constructions (except PolyMAC) are based on an n-bit block cipher. LightMAC-Plus uses an additional parameter s, which is the size of the prefix for each block cipher call; one can assume $\ell = 2^s - 1$.

Construction	# Keys	Rate	Old bound	New bound
PolyMAC	4	−	$\ell^2 q^3/2^{2n}$	$\ell q^{\frac{4}{3}}/2^n$
SUM-ECBC	4	$\frac{1}{2}$	$\ell^2 q/2^n + q^3/2^{2n}$	$\ell^{o(1)} q^{\frac{4}{3}}/2^n + \ell^4 q^{\frac{4}{3}}/2^{2n}$
PMAC-Plus	3	1	$\ell q^3/2^{2n} + \ell^2 q^2/2^{2n}$	$\ell/2^{\frac{n}{2}} + \ell^{\frac{2}{3}} q^{\frac{4}{3}}/2^n + \ell^2 q/2^n$
3kf9	3	1	$\ell^4 q^3/2^{2n}$	$\ell^{\frac{4}{3}} q^{\frac{4}{3}}/2^n + \ell^2 q^2/2^{2n} + \ell^6 q^4/2^{3n}$
LightMAC-Plus	3	$\frac{n-s}{n}$	$q^3/2^{2n}$	$q^{\frac{4}{3}}/2^n$

2 Preliminaries

BASIC NOTATION. In all of the following, we fix a positive integer n, and denote $N = 2^n$. We denote 0^n (i.e., n-bit string of all zeros) by $\mathbf{0}$. The set $\{0,1\}^n$ is sometimes regarded as a set of integers $\{0, 1, \ldots, 2^n - 1\}$ by converting an n-bit string $a_{n-1} \cdots a_1 a_0 \in \{0,1\}^n$ to an integer $a_{n-1} 2^{n-1} + \cdots + a_1 2 + a_0$. We also identify $\{0,1\}^n$ with a finite field $\mathbf{GF}(2^n)$ with 2^n elements. For a positive integer q, we write $[q] = \{1, \ldots, q\}$.

Given a non-empty set $\mathcal{X}$, $x \leftarrow_\$ \mathcal{X}$ denotes that x is chosen uniformly at random from $\mathcal{X}$. The set of all functions from $\mathcal{X}$ to $\mathcal{Y}$ is denoted $\mathsf{Func}(\mathcal{X}, \mathcal{Y})$, and the set of all permutations of $\mathcal{X}$ is denoted $\mathsf{Perm}(\mathcal{X})$. The set of all permutations of $\{0,1\}^n$ is simply denoted $\mathsf{Perm}(n)$. The set of all sequences that consist of b pairwise distinct elements of $\mathcal{X}$ is denoted $\mathcal{X}^{*b}$. For integers $1 \leq b \leq a$, we will write $(a)_b = a(a-1) \cdots (a - b + 1)$ and $(a)_0 = 1$ by convention. If $|\mathcal{X}| = a$, then $(a)_b$ becomes the size of $\mathcal{X}^{*b}$.

When two sets $\mathcal{X}$ and $\mathcal{Y}$ are disjoint, their (disjoint) union is denoted $\mathcal{X} \sqcup \mathcal{Y}$. For a set $\mathcal{X} \subset \{0,1\}^n$ and $\lambda \in \{0,1\}^n$, we will write $\mathcal{X} \oplus \lambda = \{x \oplus \lambda : x \in \mathcal{X}\}$.

PRFs AND PRPs. Let $F : \mathcal{K} \times \mathcal{X} \to \mathcal{Y}$ be a keyed function with key space $\mathcal{K}$, domain $\mathcal{X}$, and range $\mathcal{Y}$, where $\mathcal{X}$ is a subset of $\{0,1\}^*$. We will denote $F_K(X)$ for

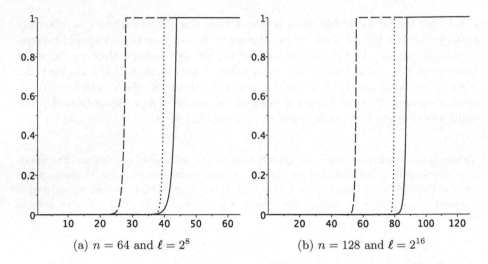

(a) $n = 64$ and $\ell = 2^8$ (b) $n = 128$ and $\ell = 2^{16}$

Fig. 1. Upper bounds on distinguishing advantage for PMAC-Plus. The solid and the dotted lines represent the new and the old bounds, respectively. The dashed line represents the security bound $\ell q^2/2^n$ for PMAC. The x-axis gives the log (base 2) of q, and the y-axis gives the security bounds.

$F(K, X)$. A (q, t, ℓ)-distinguisher against F is an algorithm $\mathcal{D}$ with oracle access to a function from $\mathcal{X}$ to $\mathcal{Y}$, making at most q oracle queries, each of length at most ℓ in blocks, running in time at most t, and outputting a single bit. The advantage of $\mathcal{D}$ in breaking the PRF-security of F, i.e., in distinguishing F from a uniformly randomly chosen function $R \leftarrow_\$ \mathsf{Func}(\mathcal{X}, \mathcal{Y})$, is defined as

$$\mathbf{Adv}_F^{\mathsf{prf}}(\mathcal{D}) = \left| \Pr\left[K \leftarrow_\$ \mathcal{K} : \mathcal{D}^{F_K} = 1 \right] - \Pr\left[R \leftarrow_\$ \mathsf{Func}(\mathcal{X}, \mathcal{Y}) : \mathcal{D}^R = 1 \right] \right|.$$

When $\mathcal{X} = \mathcal{Y}$ and $F(K, \cdot)$ is a permutation for each $K \in \mathcal{K}$, the PRP-security of F is defined as

$$\mathbf{Adv}_F^{\mathsf{prp}}(\mathcal{D}) = \left| \Pr\left[K \leftarrow_\$ \mathcal{K} : \mathcal{D}^{F_K} = 1 \right] - \Pr\left[R \leftarrow_\$ \mathsf{Perm}(\mathcal{X}, \mathcal{Y}) : \mathcal{D}^R = 1 \right] \right|.$$

For atk $\in \{\mathsf{prf}, \mathsf{prp}\}$, we define $\mathbf{Adv}_F^{\mathsf{atk}}(q, t, \ell)$ as the maximum of $\mathbf{Adv}_F^{\mathsf{atk}}(\mathcal{D})$ over all (q, t, ℓ)-distinguishers against F. We will consider PRP-security only for a block cipher whose input size is fixed (e.g., $\mathcal{X} = \{0, 1\}^n$); in this case, we will simply drop the parameter ℓ. On the other hand, when we consider information theoretic security, we will drop the parameter t.

ALMOST UNIVERSAL HASH FUNCTIONS. Let $\delta > 0$, and let $H : \mathcal{K}_h \times \mathcal{X} \to \mathcal{Y}$ be a keyed function for three non-empty sets $\mathcal{K}_h$, $\mathcal{X}$, and $\mathcal{Y}$. H is said to be δ-*almost universal* if for any distinct X and $X' \in \mathcal{X}$,

$$\Pr\left[K_h \leftarrow_\$ \mathcal{K}_h : H_{K_h}(X) = H_{K_h}(X') \right] \leq \delta.$$

DOUBLE-BLOCK HASH-THEN-SUM CONSTRUCTIONS. Let

$$H : \mathcal{K}_h \times \mathcal{M} \longrightarrow \{0,1\}^n \times \{0,1\}^n$$
$$(K_h, M) \longmapsto H_{K_h}(M)$$

be a keyed function. We will write the $2n$-bit function H as the concatenation of two n-bit functions F and G. So we have

$$H_{K_h}(M) = (F_{K_h}(M), G_{K_h}(M)) .$$

Given a block cipher

$$E : \mathcal{K} \times \{0,1\}^n \longrightarrow \{0,1\}^n$$
$$(K, X) \longmapsto E_K(X),$$

one can define the DbHtS construction based on H and E as follows.

$$\mathsf{DbHtS}[H, E] : (\mathcal{K}_h \times \mathcal{K}^2) \times \mathcal{M} \longrightarrow \{0,1\}^n$$
$$((K_h, K_1, K_2), M) \longmapsto E_{K_1}(F_{K_h}(M)) \oplus E_{K_2}(G_{K_h}(M)).$$

In a typical MAC based on an n-bit block cipher, the message space is given as the set of all binary strings, namely $\{0,1\}^*$, and a padding scheme

$$\mathsf{pad} : \{0,1\}^* \longrightarrow \bigcup_{i=1}^{\infty} (\{0,1\}^n)^i$$

is used, where pad is a public injective function. Since the padding scheme does not affect the PRF-security of its MAC, we will simply assume that

$$\mathcal{M} = \bigcup_{i=1}^{\ell} (\{0,1\}^n)^i ,$$

where ℓ denotes the maximum message length in blocks (after padding).

H-COEFFICIENT TECHNIQUE. Consider the DbHtS construction based on H and E using keys $K = (K_h, K_1, K_2)$. The first step of the security proof is to replace the keyed permutations E_{K_1} and E_{K_2} by independent random permutations; the resulting construction will be denoted $\mathsf{DbHtS}[H]$ instead of $\mathsf{DbHtS}[H, E]$.

Suppose that a distinguisher $\mathcal{D}$ adaptively makes q queries to the construction oracle, which is either $\mathsf{DbHtS}[H]_{K_h, \pi_1, \pi_2}$ for a random key $K_h \in \mathcal{K}_h$ and independent random permutations π_1 and π_2 (in the real world) or a truly random function R (in the ideal world), recording all the queries $(M_i, T_i)_{1 \le i \le q}$. So according to the instantiation, it would imply either $\mathsf{DbHtS}[H]_{K_h, \pi_1, \pi_2}(M_i) = T_i$ or $R(M_i) = T_i$.

At the end of the interaction, we will give K_h to $\mathcal{D}$ for free. In the ideal world, a dummy key K_h will be selected uniformly at random from $\mathcal{K}_h$, and given to $\mathcal{D}$. This will not degrade the adversarial distinguishing advantage since the distinguisher is free to ignore this additional information. We will call

$$\tau = (K_h, (M_1, T_1), \ldots, (M_q, T_q))$$

the *transcript* of the attack; it contains all the information that $\mathcal{D}$ has obtained at the end of the attack. We will assume that $\mathcal{D}$ is information theoretic, so we can further assume that $\mathcal{D}$ is deterministic without making any redundant query.

A transcript τ is called *attainable* if the probability to obtain this transcript in the ideal world is non-zero. Any key $K_h \in \mathcal{K}_h$ and any sequence $(T_1, \ldots, T_q) \in (\{0,1\}^n)^q$ uniquely determine an attainable transcript $\tau = (K_h, (M_i, T_i)_{1 \leq i \leq q})$ containing them, for some $(M_i) \in (\{0,1\}^n)^q$. We denote Γ the set of attainable transcripts. We also denote T_{re} (resp. T_{id}) the probability distribution of the transcript τ induced by the real world (resp. the ideal world). By extension, we use the same notation to denote a random variable distributed according to each distribution.

In order to upper bound the advantage of the distinguisher, we will partition the set of attainable transcripts Γ into a set of "good" transcripts Γ_{good} such that the probabilities to obtain some transcript $\tau \in \Gamma_{\mathrm{good}}$ are close in the real and in the ideal world, and a set Γ_{bad} of "bad" transcripts such that the probability to obtain any $\tau \in \Gamma_{\mathrm{bad}}$ is small in the ideal world, and use the following theorem.

Lemma 1. *Fix a distinguisher $\mathcal{D}$. Let $\Gamma = \Gamma_{\mathrm{good}} \sqcup \Gamma_{\mathrm{bad}}$ be a partition of the set of attainable transcripts. Assume that there exists ε_1 such that for any $\tau \in \Gamma_{\mathrm{good}}$,*

$$\frac{\Pr\left[\mathsf{T}_{\mathrm{re}} = \tau\right]}{\Pr\left[\mathsf{T}_{\mathrm{id}} = \tau\right]} \geq 1 - \varepsilon_1,$$

and that there exists ε_2 such that $\Pr[\mathsf{T}_{\mathrm{id}} \in \Gamma_{\mathrm{bad}}] \leq \varepsilon_2$. Then one has

$$\mathbf{Adv}^{\mathrm{prf}}_{\mathsf{DbHtS}[H]}(\mathcal{D}) \leq \varepsilon_1 + \varepsilon_2.$$

3   Mirror Theory

The goal of this section is to lower bound the number of solutions to a certain type of systems of equations and non-equations. We will represent a system of equations and non-equations by a simple graph containing no loops or multiple edges; each vertex denotes an n-bit unknown (for a fixed n), and each edge is labeled with an element in $\{0,1\}^n \cup \{\neq\}$, where $\neq$ is a special symbol meaning non-equality. Let $\mathcal{G} = (\mathcal{V}, \mathcal{E})$ be a graph and let $\overline{PQ} \in \mathcal{E}$ be an edge for $P, Q \in \mathcal{V}$. If this edge is labeled with $\lambda \in \{0,1\}^n$, then it means an equation $P \oplus Q = \lambda$, while if it is labeled with a special symbol $\neq$, then it means that P and Q are distinct. We will sometimes write $P \overset{\star}{-} Q$ when an edge $\overline{PQ}$ is labeled with $\star \in \{0,1\}^n \cup \{\neq\}$.

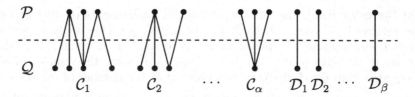

Fig. 2. A bipartite graph $\mathcal{G}^=$ with two parts $\mathcal{P}$ and $\mathcal{Q}$.

Let $\mathcal{G}^=$ denote the graph obtained by deleting all $\neq$-labeled edges from $\mathcal{G}$. For $\ell > 0$ and a trail[1]

$$\mathcal{L} : P_0 \overset{\lambda_1}{-} P_1 \overset{\lambda_2}{-} \cdots \overset{\lambda_\ell}{-} P_\ell$$

in $\mathcal{G}^=$, its label is defined as

$$\lambda(\mathcal{L}) \overset{\mathrm{def}}{=} \lambda_1 \oplus \lambda_2 \oplus \cdots \oplus \lambda_\ell.$$

In this work, we will focus on a graph $\mathcal{G} = (\mathcal{V}, \mathcal{E})$ with certain properties, as listed below.

1. $\mathcal{G}^=$ contains no isolated vertex; every vertex is incident with at least one edge.
2. The vertex set $\mathcal{V}$ is partitioned into two disjoint parts, denoted $\mathcal{P}$ and $\mathcal{Q}$; the edge set $\mathcal{E}$ contains $P \overset{\neq}{-} P'$ for any different $P, P' \in \mathcal{P}$, and $Q \overset{\neq}{-} Q'$ for any different $Q, Q' \in \mathcal{Q}$.
3. $\mathcal{G}^=$ contains no cycle.
4. $\lambda(\mathcal{L}) \neq \mathbf{0}$ for any trail $\mathcal{L}$ of even length in $\mathcal{G}^=$.

Any graph $\mathcal{G}$ satisfying the above properties will be called a *nice* graph. For a nice graph $\mathcal{G}$, $\mathcal{G}^=$ is a bipartite graph with no cycle, where every edge connects a vertex in $\mathcal{P}$ to one in $\mathcal{Q}$. So $\mathcal{G}^=$ is decomposed into its connected components, all of which are trees; let

$$\mathcal{G}^= = \mathcal{C}_1 \sqcup \mathcal{C}_2 \sqcup \cdots \sqcup \mathcal{C}_\alpha \sqcup \mathcal{D}_1 \sqcup \mathcal{D}_2 \sqcup \cdots \sqcup \mathcal{D}_\beta$$

for some α, $\beta \geq 0$, where $\mathcal{C}_i$ denotes a component of size greater than 2, and $\mathcal{D}_i$ denotes a component of size 2. We will also write $\mathcal{C} = \mathcal{C}_1 \sqcup \mathcal{C}_2 \sqcup \cdots \sqcup \mathcal{C}_\alpha$ and $\mathcal{D} = \mathcal{D}_1 \sqcup \mathcal{D}_2 \sqcup \cdots \sqcup \mathcal{D}_\beta$ (Fig. 2).

Any solution to $\mathcal{G}$ (identifying $\mathcal{G}$ with its corresponding system of equations and non-equations) should satisfy all the equations in $\mathcal{G}^=$, while all the variables in $\mathcal{P}$ (resp. $\mathcal{Q}$) should take on different values. We remark that if we assign any value to a vertex P, then the labeled edges determine the values of all the other vertices in the component containing P, where the assignment is unique since $\mathcal{G}^=$ contains no cycle, and the values in the same part are all distinct since $\lambda(\mathcal{L}) \neq \mathbf{0}$ for any trail $\mathcal{L}$ of even length.

---

[1] A trail is a walk in which all edges are distinct.

On the other hand, the number of possible assignments of distinct values to the vertices in $\mathcal{P}$ (resp. $\mathcal{Q}$) is $(N)_{|\mathcal{P}|}$ (resp. $(N)_{|\mathcal{Q}|}$). One might expect that when such an assignment is chosen uniformly at random, it would satisfy all the equations in $\mathcal{G}^=$ with probability $1/N^q$, where q denotes the number of edges (i.e., equations) in $\mathcal{G}^=$. Indeed, we can prove that the number of solutions to $\mathcal{G}$ is close to $\frac{(N)_{|\mathcal{P}|}(N)_{|\mathcal{Q}|}}{N^q}$ up to a certain error (that can be negligible according to the parameters).

Theorem 1. *Let $\mathcal{G}$ be a nice graph, and let q and q_c denote the number of edges of $\mathcal{G}^=$ and C, respectively. If $q < \frac{N}{8}$, then the number of solutions to $\mathcal{G}$, denoted $h(\mathcal{G})$, satisfies*

$$\frac{h(\mathcal{G})N^q}{(N)_{|\mathcal{P}|}(N)_{|\mathcal{Q}|}} \geq 1 - \frac{9q_c^2}{8N} - \frac{3q_c q^2}{2N^2} - \frac{q^2}{N^2} - \frac{9q_c^2 q}{8N^2} - \frac{8q^4}{3N^3}.$$

Proof. For $i = 1, \ldots, \alpha$, C_i is a bipartite graph, where one part consists of the vertices in $\mathcal{P}$ and the other vertices in $\mathcal{Q}$; the two parts are denoted $\mathcal{P}_i$ and $\mathcal{Q}_i$, respectively. Let $r_i = |\mathcal{P}_i|$ and $s_i = |\mathcal{Q}_i|$, let $d_i = r_i + s_i$.

Let $h_c(i)$ be the number of solutions to $C_1 \sqcup \cdots \sqcup C_i$. In order to find a relation between $h_c(i)$ and $h_c(i+1)$, we fix a solution to $C_1 \sqcup \cdots \sqcup C_i$. If we fix a vertex $P^* \in \mathcal{P}_{i+1}$ and assign any value to P^*, then the other unknowns are uniquely determined, since there is a unique trail from P^* to any other vertex in C_{i+1}. In order to satisfy the non-equations, it is sufficient that

$$P^* \notin \bigcup_{\substack{1 \leq j \leq i \\ P \in \mathcal{P}_{i+1}}} (\mathcal{P}_j \oplus \lambda_P) \cup \bigcup_{\substack{1 \leq j \leq i \\ Q \in \mathcal{Q}_{i+1}}} (\mathcal{Q}_j \oplus \lambda_Q),$$

where λ_X denotes the label of the unique trail from P^* to X if $X \neq P^*$ and $\lambda_{P^*} = \mathbf{0}$. The number of such choices is at least

$$N - (r_1 + \cdots + r_i)r_{i+1} - (s_1 + \cdots + s_i)s_{i+1}.$$

Then we have

$$h_c(\alpha) \geq N^\alpha \left(1 - \frac{r_1 r_2 + s_1 s_2}{N}\right) \cdots \left(1 - \frac{(r_1 + \cdots + r_{\alpha-1})r_\alpha + (s_1 + \cdots + s_{\alpha-1})s_\alpha}{N}\right)$$

$$\geq N^\alpha \left(1 - \frac{1}{N} \sum_{1 \leq i < j \leq \alpha} (r_i r_j + s_i s_j)\right)$$

$$\geq N^\alpha \left(1 - \frac{1}{2N} \left(\sum_{i=1}^\alpha d_i\right)^2\right)$$

$$\geq N^\alpha \left(1 - \frac{9q_c^2}{8N}\right) \tag{1}$$

since $h_c(1) = N$, $\sum_{i=1}^\alpha d_i = \alpha + q_c$ and $\alpha \leq q_c/2$.

For $i = 1, \ldots, \beta$, we will write

$$\mathcal{D}_i : P_i \overset{\lambda_i}{-} Q_i$$

where $P_i \in \mathcal{P}$ and $Q_i \in \mathcal{Q}$. Let $h_d(i)$ be the number of solutions to $\mathcal{C} \sqcup \mathcal{D}_1 \sqcup \cdots \sqcup \mathcal{D}_i$ for $i = 1, \ldots, \beta$. Note that $h_d(0) = h_c(\alpha)$ and $h_d(\beta) = h(\mathcal{G})$. In order to find a relation between $h_d(i)$ and $h_d(i+1)$, we fix a solution to $\mathcal{C} \sqcup \mathcal{D}_1 \sqcup \cdots \sqcup \mathcal{D}_i$. Then we can choose P_{i+1} from $\{0,1\}^n \setminus (\mathcal{X}_i \cup (\mathcal{Y}_i \oplus \lambda_{i+1}))$, where

$$\mathcal{X}_i \overset{\text{def}}{=} \bigsqcup_{1 \leq j \leq \alpha} \mathcal{P}_j \sqcup \{P_1, \ldots, P_i\},$$

$$\mathcal{Y}_i \overset{\text{def}}{=} \bigsqcup_{1 \leq j \leq \alpha} \mathcal{Q}_j \sqcup \{Q_1, \ldots, Q_i\}.$$

For $i = 0, \ldots, \beta - 1$, let

$$R_i = r_1 + \cdots + r_\alpha + i,$$
$$S_i = s_1 + \cdots + s_\alpha + i.$$

Then, since $|\mathcal{X}_i| = R_i$ and $|\mathcal{Y}_i| = S_i$, we have

$$h_d(i+1) = \sum_{\substack{\text{solutions to} \\ \mathcal{C} \sqcup \mathcal{D}_1 \sqcup \cdots \sqcup \mathcal{D}_i}} (N \quad |\mathcal{X}_i \cup (\mathcal{Y}_i \oplus \lambda_{i+1})|)$$

$$= \sum_{\substack{\text{solutions to} \\ \mathcal{C} \sqcup \mathcal{D}_1 \sqcup \cdots \sqcup \mathcal{D}_i}} (N - R_i - S_i + |\mathcal{X}_i \cap (\mathcal{Y}_i \oplus \lambda_{i+1})|)$$

$$= (N - R_i - S_i)h_d(i) + \sum_{\substack{\text{solutions to} \\ \mathcal{C} \sqcup \mathcal{D}_1 \sqcup \cdots \sqcup \mathcal{D}_i}} |\mathcal{X}_i \cap (\mathcal{Y}_i \oplus \lambda_{i+1})|. \quad (2)$$

For $X \in \mathcal{X}_i$ and $Y \in \mathcal{Y}_i$, let $h'(X, Y)$ denote the number of solutions to $\mathcal{C} \sqcup \mathcal{D}_1 \sqcup \cdots \sqcup \mathcal{D}_i$ such that $X \oplus Y = \lambda_{i+1}$. Then we have

$$\sum_{\substack{\text{solutions to} \\ \mathcal{C} \sqcup \mathcal{D}_1 \sqcup \cdots \sqcup \mathcal{D}_i}} |\mathcal{X}_i \cap (\mathcal{Y}_i \oplus \lambda_{i+1})| = \sum_{X \in \mathcal{X}_i, Y \in \mathcal{Y}_i} h'(X, Y)$$

$$\geq \sum_{\substack{X \in \{P_1, \ldots, P_i\} \\ Y \in \{Q_1, \ldots, Q_i\}}} h'(X, Y). \quad (3)$$

If $X = P_j$, $Y = Q_j$, and $\lambda_{i+1} = \lambda_j$ for some $j = 1, \ldots, i$, then the additional equation $X \oplus Y = \lambda_{i+1}$ is redundant, and hence $h'(X, Y) = h_d(i)$. Suppose that $X = P_j$ and $Y = Q_{j'}$ for distinct j and j', and $\lambda_{i+1} \notin \{\lambda_j, \lambda_{j'}\}$. In this case, and for $i \geq 2$, we have

$$h'(X, Y) \geq \frac{h_d(i)}{N} \left(1 - \frac{2(R_i + S_i)}{N}\right) \quad (4)$$

since

$$h'(X,Y) \geq (N - 2(R_i + S_i - 4)) h_d(i-2) \geq (N - 2(R_i + S_i)) h_d(i-2),$$
$$h_d(i-2)N^2 \geq h_d(i-2)(N - (R_i + S_i - 4))(N - (R_i + S_i - 2)) \geq h_d(i).$$

Let

$$G = |\{1 \leq j \leq i : \lambda_j = \lambda_{i+1}\}|,$$
$$H = |\{(j,j') \in [i]^{*2} : \lambda_j \neq \lambda_{i+1}, \lambda_{j'} \neq \lambda_{i+1}\}|.$$

Then we have

$$H \geq i(i-1) - 2iG. \tag{5}$$

By (3), (4), (5), and since $2i \leq 2q \leq N$, we have

$$\sum_{\substack{\text{solutions to} \\ \mathcal{C} \sqcup \mathcal{D}_1 \sqcup \cdots \sqcup \mathcal{D}_i}} |\mathcal{X}_i \cap (\mathcal{Y}_i \oplus \lambda_{i+1})| \geq \left(G + \frac{i(i-1) - 2iG}{N} \left(1 - \frac{2(R_i + S_i)}{N} \right) \right) h_d(i)$$

$$\geq \frac{i(i-1)}{N} \left(1 - \frac{2(R_i + S_i)}{N} \right) h_d(i),$$

and by (2),

$$h_d(i+1) \geq (N - R_i - S_i) h_d(i) + \frac{i(i-1)}{N} \left(1 - \frac{2(R_i + S_i)}{N} \right) h_d(i).$$

Since $\frac{R_i + S_i}{2} \leq q < \frac{N}{8}$ and $R_0 + S_0 = \alpha + q_c \leq \frac{3q_c}{2}$, we have

$$\frac{h_d(i+1)N}{h_d(i)(N - R_i)(N - S_i)} \geq \frac{N^2 - (R_i + S_i)N + (i^2 - i)\left(1 - \frac{2(R_i + S_i)}{N} \right)}{N^2 - (R_i + S_i)N + R_i S_i}$$

$$= 1 - \frac{R_i S_i - (i^2 - i)\left(1 - \frac{2(R_i + S_i)}{N} \right)}{N^2 - (R_i + S_i)N + R_i S_i}$$

$$\geq 1 - \frac{(R_0 + i)(S_0 + i) - (i^2 - i) + \frac{2(R_i + S_i)i^2}{N}}{N^2/2}$$

$$\geq 1 - \frac{2R_0 S_0}{N^2} - \frac{2(R_0 + S_0 + 1)i}{N^2} - \frac{4(R_i + S_i)i^2}{N^3}$$

$$\geq 1 - \frac{9q_c^2}{8N^2} - \frac{3q_c i + 2i}{N^2} - \frac{8qi^2}{N^3}. \tag{6}$$

Since $q = q_c + \beta$, $|\mathcal{P}| = R_0 + \beta$, $|\mathcal{Q}| = S_0 + \beta$ and $\alpha + q_c = R_0 + S_0$, and by (1) and (6), we have

$$
\frac{h(\mathcal{G})N^q}{(N)_{|\mathcal{P}|}(N)_{|\mathcal{Q}|}} = \frac{h(\mathcal{G})N^{q_c+\beta}}{(N)_{R_0}(N-R_0)_\beta(N)_{S_0}(N-S_0)_\beta}
$$

$$
= \frac{h_c(\alpha)N^{q_c}}{(N)_{R_0}(N)_{S_0}} \prod_{i=0}^{\beta-1} \left(\frac{h_d(i+1)N}{h_d(i)(N-R_i)(N-S_i)} \right)
$$

$$
\geq \frac{h_c(\alpha)}{N^\alpha} \prod_{i=0}^{\beta-1} \left(\frac{h_d(i+1)N}{h_d(i)(N-R_i)(N-S_i)} \right)
$$

$$
\geq \left(1 - \frac{9q_c^2}{8N} \right) \prod_{i=0}^{\beta-1} \left(1 - \frac{9q_c^2}{8N^2} - \frac{3q_c i + 2i}{N^2} - \frac{8qi^2}{N^3} \right)
$$

$$
\geq \left(1 - \frac{9q_c^2}{8N} \right) \left(1 - \sum_{i=0}^{\beta-1} \left(\frac{9q_c^2}{8N^2} + \frac{3q_c i + 2i}{N^2} + \frac{8qi^2}{N^3} \right) \right)
$$

$$
\geq \left(1 - \frac{9q_c^2}{8N} \right) \left(1 - \frac{9q_c^2 q}{8N^2} - \frac{3q_c q^2}{2N^2} - \frac{q^2}{N^2} - \frac{8q^4}{3N^3} \right)
$$

$$
\geq 1 - \frac{9q_c^2}{8N} - \frac{9q_c^2 q}{8N^2} - \frac{3q_c q^2}{2N^2} - \frac{q^2}{N^2} - \frac{8q^4}{3N^3}
$$

which completes the proof.   □

4   A Framework for Security Proof of DbHtS MACs

In this section, we consider DbHtS$[H, E]$ based on a $2n$-bit function H and an n-bit block cipher E. A message M is encrypted as

$$
E_{K_1}(F_{K_h}(M)) \oplus E_{K_2}(G_{K_h}(M))
$$

by keys K_h, K_1 and K_2, where we write $H_{K_h}(M) = (F_{K_h}(M), G_{K_h}(M))$ (see Sect. 2).

Up to the PRP-security of E, the keyed permutations E_{K_1} and E_{K_2} can be replaced by independent random permutations π_1 and π_2, in which case we simply write DbHtS$[H]$ instead of DbHtS$[H, E]$. The goal of this section is to establish a general framework for security proof of DbHtS$[H]$ using Theorem 1.

Graph Representation of Transcripts. At the end of the attack, the distinguisher $\mathcal{D}$ will be given K_h for free. Then, from the transcript

$$
\tau = (K_h, (M_i, T_i)_{1 \leq i \leq q}),
$$

$H_{K_h}(M_i) = (U_i, V_i)$ are fixed for $i = 1, \ldots, q$. The core of the security proof is to estimate the number of possible ways of fixing $\pi_1(U_i)$ and $\pi_2(V_i)$ in a way that

$\pi_1(U_i) \oplus \pi_2(V_i) = T_i$ for $i = 1, \ldots, q$. So $\{\pi_1(U_i)\}$ and $\{\pi_2(V_i)\}$ are identified with two sets of unknowns

$$P = \{P_1, \ldots, P_{q_1}\},$$
$$Q = \{Q_1, \ldots, Q_{q_2}\},$$

respectively, where $q_1, q_2 \leq q$, since there might be collisions between U_i's or between V_i's. Assuming that P and Q are disjoint, we connect P_j and $Q_{j'}$ with an edge of label T_i if $\pi_1(U_i) = P_j$ and $\pi_2(V_i) = Q_{j'}$ for some i. Any pair of vertices in the same set of either P or Q are connected by a $\neq$-labeled edge. In this way, we obtain a graph on $P \sqcup Q$, called the *transcript graph* of τ and denoted $\mathcal{G}_\tau$.

GOOD TRANSCRIPTS. Fix a parameter $\bar{q}_c$ (to be optimized later). A transcript $\tau = (K_h, (M_i, T_i)_{1 \leq i \leq q})$ is defined as *good* if

1. the transcript graph $\mathcal{G}_\tau$ is nice (as defined in Sect. 3);
2. the number of edges in $\mathcal{C}$ (i.e., edges in the components of size greater than two) is not greater than $\bar{q}_c$.

If a transcript τ is not good, then it will be called a *bad* transcript.

For a transcript graph $\mathcal{G}_\tau$, let $\mathcal{G}_\tau^=$ denote the graph obtained by deleting all $\neq$-labeled edges from $\mathcal{G}_\tau$. Then $\mathcal{G}_\tau^=$ is a bipartite graph with q edges. By definition, $\mathcal{G}_\tau^=$ has no isolated vertices. So in order to see if $\mathcal{G}_\tau$ is nice, it is sufficient to check out if

1. $\mathcal{G}_\tau^=$ has no cycle;
2. $\lambda(\mathcal{L}) \neq \mathbf{0}$ for any trail $\mathcal{L}$ of even length.

A FRAMEWORK FOR SECURITY PROOF. Once bad transcripts have been defined, we will show that

$$\Pr[\mathsf{T}_{\mathsf{id}} \in \Gamma_{\mathsf{bad}}] \leq \varepsilon_2$$

for a small $\varepsilon_2 > 0$. Next, we fix a good transcript τ. Obviously, we have

$$\Pr[\mathsf{T}_{\mathsf{id}} = \tau] = \frac{1}{|K_h| \cdot N^q}.$$

The probability of obtaining τ in the real world is computed over the randomness of π_1 and π_2. By Theorem 1 and since $q_c \leq \bar{q}_c$, the number of possible ways of fixing $\pi_1(U_i)$ and $\pi_2(V_i)$ (i.e., $h(\mathcal{G}_\tau)$) is lower bounded by

$$\frac{(N)_{|P|}(N)_{|Q|}}{N^q}(1 - \varepsilon_1)$$

where

$$\varepsilon_1 \overset{\text{def}}{=} \frac{9\bar{q}_c^2}{8N} + \frac{3\bar{q}_c q^2}{2N^2} + \frac{q^2}{N^2} + \frac{9\bar{q}_c^2 q}{8N^2} + \frac{8q^4}{3N^3}. \tag{7}$$

The probability that π_1 and π_2 realize each assignment is exactly $1/(N)_{|\mathcal{P}|}(N)_{|\mathcal{Q}|}$. So we have

$$\frac{\Pr\left[\mathsf{T}_{\mathrm{re}} = \tau\right]}{\Pr\left[\mathsf{T}_{\mathrm{id}} = \tau\right]} \geq 1 - \varepsilon_1,$$

and by Lemma 1,

$$\mathbf{Adv}^{\mathrm{prf}}_{\mathsf{DbHtS}[H]}(\mathcal{D}) \leq \varepsilon_1 + \varepsilon_2.$$

5   Concatenating Universal Hash Functions

In this section, we will prove the security of DbHtS when the underlying hash function H is defined as the concatenation of two copies of an almost universal hash function using independent keys.

Let $\delta > 0$, and let $F : \mathcal{K} \times \mathcal{M} \to \{0,1\}^n$ be a δ-almost universal hash function. We will consider DbHtS$[H]$, where

$$H : (\mathcal{K} \times \mathcal{K}) \times \mathcal{M} \longrightarrow \{0,1\}^n \times \{0,1\}^n$$
$$((K_1, K_2), M) \longmapsto (F_{K_1}(M), F_{K_2}(M)).$$

We fix the parameter $\bar{q}_c$, and define bad events as follows.

- $\mathsf{Bad}_1 \Leftrightarrow$ there is a pair of distinct queries (M_i, M_j) such that $F_{K_1}(M_i) = F_{K_1}(M_j)$ and $F_{K_2}(M_i) = F_{K_2}(M_j)$.
- $\mathsf{Bad}_2 \Leftrightarrow \mathsf{Bad}_{2a} \vee \mathsf{Bad}_{2b}$, where
  - $\mathsf{Bad}_{2a} \Leftrightarrow$ there is a quadruple of distinct queries $(M_{i_1}, M_{i_2}, M_{i_3}, M_{i_4})$ such that $F_{K_1}(M_{i_1}) = F_{K_1}(M_{i_2})$, $F_{K_2}(M_{i_2}) = F_{K_2}(M_{i_3})$, $F_{K_1}(M_{i_3}) = F_{K_1}(M_{i_4})$,
  - $\mathsf{Bad}_{2b} \Leftrightarrow$ there is a quadruple of distinct queries $(M_{i_1}, M_{i_2}, M_{i_3}, M_{i_4})$ such that $F_{K_2}(M_{i_1}) = F_{K_2}(M_{i_2})$, $F_{K_1}(M_{i_2}) = F_{K_1}(M_{i_3})$, $F_{K_2}(M_{i_3}) = F_{K_2}(M_{i_4})$.
- $\mathsf{Bad}_3 \Leftrightarrow$ there is a pair of distinct queries (M_i, M_j) such that $T_i \oplus T_j = \mathbf{0}$ and either $F_{K_1}(M_i) = F_{K_1}(M_j)$ or $F_{K_2}(M_i) = F_{K_2}(M_j)$.
- $\mathsf{Bad}_4 \Leftrightarrow \mathsf{Bad}_{4a} \vee \mathsf{Bad}_{4b}$, where
  - $\mathsf{Bad}_{4a} \Leftrightarrow$ the number of distinct queries (M_i, M_j) such that $F_{K_1}(M_i) = F_{K_1}(M_j)$ is greater than $\bar{q}_c/4$,
  - $\mathsf{Bad}_{4b} \Leftrightarrow$ the number of distinct queries (M_i, M_j) such that $F_{K_2}(M_i) = F_{K_2}(M_j)$ is greater than $\bar{q}_c/4$.

We observe that

1. $\mathcal{G}_\tau^=$ contains no cycle of length 2 without Bad_1;
2. $\mathcal{G}_\tau^=$ contains no trail of length 4 without Bad_2;
3. $\lambda(\mathcal{L}) \neq \mathbf{0}$ for any trail $\mathcal{L}$ of length 2 without Bad_3.

A distinct pair of "half-colliding" queries such that either $F_{K_1}(M_i) = F_{K_1}(M_j)$ or $F_{K_2}(M_i) = F_{K_2}(M_j)$ will add an edge to any component containing it, and make the size of the component greater than two; the number of edges in $\mathcal{C}$ cannot be twice as many as the number of half-collisions. So the number of edges in $\mathcal{C}$ is not greater than $\bar{q}_c$ without Bad_4. With this observation, we conclude that a transcript is good without any bad event above; namely,

$$\Pr[\mathsf{T}_{\mathrm{id}} \in \Gamma_{\mathsf{bad}}] \leq \Pr[\mathsf{Bad}_1 \vee \mathsf{Bad}_2 \vee \mathsf{Bad}_3 \vee \mathsf{Bad}_4].$$

We can upper bound the probability of each bad event as follows.

1. The probability that there exists a pair of distinct queries (M_i, M_j) such that $F_{K_1}(M_i) = F_{K_1}(M_j)$ and $F_{K_2}(M_i) = F_{K_2}(M_j)$ is upper bounded by $q^2 \delta^2$ since K_1 and K_2 are independent. Namely,

$$\Pr[\mathsf{Bad}_1] \leq q^2 \delta^2.$$

2. By the Markov inequality, we have

$$\Pr[\mathsf{Bad}_{4a}], \ \Pr[\mathsf{Bad}_{4b}] \leq \frac{4q^2 \delta}{\bar{q}_c}.$$

3. Given that the number of F_{K_1}-collisions is upper bounded by $\bar{q}_c/4$, the probability that there exist two F_{K_1}-colliding pairs (M_{i_1}, M_{i_2}) and (M_{i_3}, M_{i_4}) such that $F_{K_2}(M_{i_2}) = F_{K_2}(M_{i_3})$ is upper bounded by $\frac{\bar{q}_c^2 \delta}{16}$. Namely, we have

$$\Pr[\mathsf{Bad}_{2a} \mid \neg\mathsf{Bad}_{4a}] \leq \frac{\bar{q}_c^2 \delta}{16}.$$

Similarly, we have

$$\Pr[\mathsf{Bad}_{2b} \mid \neg\mathsf{Bad}_{4b}] \leq \frac{\bar{q}_c^2 \delta}{16}.$$

4. For each pair of distinct queries (M_i, M_j), the probability that $T_i \oplus T_j = \mathbf{0}$ is $1/N$, and the probability that either $F_{K_1}(M_i) = F_{K_1}(M_j)$ or $F_{K_2}(M_i) = F_{K_2}(M_j)$ is upper bounded by δ. Since the two events are independent and by the union bound, we have

$$\Pr[\mathsf{Bad}_3] \leq \frac{q^2 \delta}{N}.$$

All in all, we have

$$\begin{aligned}
\Pr[\mathsf{T}_{\mathrm{id}} \in \Gamma_{\mathsf{bad}}] &\leq \Pr[\mathsf{Bad}_1 \vee \mathsf{Bad}_2 \vee \mathsf{Bad}_3 \vee \mathsf{Bad}_4] \\
&\leq \Pr[\mathsf{Bad}_1] + \Pr[\mathsf{Bad}_3] + \Pr[\mathsf{Bad}_{4a}] + \Pr[\mathsf{Bad}_{2a} \mid \neg\mathsf{Bad}_{4a}] \\
&\quad + \Pr[\mathsf{Bad}_{4b}] + \Pr[\mathsf{Bad}_{2b} \mid \neg\mathsf{Bad}_{4b}] \\
&\leq q^2 \delta^2 + \frac{q^2 \delta}{N} + \frac{8q^2 \delta}{\bar{q}_c} + \frac{\bar{q}_c^2 \delta}{8}.
\end{aligned} \tag{8}$$

Combining (7) and (8), we have

$$\mathbf{Adv}^{\mathrm{prf}}_{\mathsf{DbHtS}[H]}(\mathcal{D}) \leq q^2\delta^2 + \frac{q^2\delta}{N} + \frac{8q^2\delta}{\bar{q}_c} + \frac{\bar{q}_c^2\delta}{8}$$
$$+ \frac{9\bar{q}_c^2}{8N} + \frac{3\bar{q}_c q^2}{2N^2} + \frac{q^2}{N^2} + \frac{9\bar{q}_c^2 q}{8N^2} + \frac{8q^4}{3N^3}$$

for any distinguisher $\mathcal{D}$ making q queries, and for any $\bar{q}_c > 0$. When $\bar{q}_c = 4q^{\frac{2}{3}}$ (by setting $8q^2\delta/\bar{q}_c = \bar{q}_c^2\delta/8$), we obtain the following theorem.

Theorem 2. *Let $\delta > 0$, and let $F : \mathcal{K} \times \mathcal{M} \to \{0,1\}^n$ be a δ-almost universal hash function. Let*

$$H : (\mathcal{K} \times \mathcal{K}) \times \mathcal{M} \longrightarrow \{0,1\}^n \times \{0,1\}^n$$
$$((K_1, K_2), M) \longmapsto (F_{K_1}(M), F_{K_2}(M)).$$

Then one has

$$\mathbf{Adv}^{\mathrm{prf}}_{\mathsf{DbHtS}[H]}(\mathcal{D}) \leq 4q^{\frac{4}{3}}\delta + q^2\delta^2 + \frac{q^2\delta}{N} + \frac{18q^{\frac{4}{3}}}{N}$$
$$+ \frac{6q^{\frac{8}{3}}}{N^2} + \frac{18q^{\frac{7}{3}}}{N^2} + \frac{q^2}{N^2} + \frac{8q^4}{3N^3}.$$

When $\delta \approx \frac{1}{N}$, $\mathsf{DbHtS}[H]$ becomes a PRF that is secure up to $2^{\frac{3n}{4}}$ queries.

5.1 Security of PolyMAC

An n-bit keyed function PolyHash is defined with key space $\mathcal{K} = \{0,1\}^n$, where $\{0,1\}^n$ is identified with a finite field $\mathbf{GF}(2^n)$ with 2^n elements. For a padded message $M = M[1]\|M[2]\|\cdots\|M[m]$ where $m \leq \ell$, and a key $K \in \mathcal{K}$, $\mathrm{PolyHash}_K(M)$ is defined using finite field addition and multiplication, denoted $\oplus$ and $\cdot$, respectively.

> **Function** $\mathrm{PolyHash}_K(M)$
> $Z[0] \leftarrow 0$
> **for** $\alpha \leftarrow 1$ **to** m **do**
> $\quad Z[\alpha] \leftarrow K \cdot (Z[\alpha - 1] \oplus M[\alpha])$
> **return** $Z[m]$

The PolyMAC MAC is defined as $\mathsf{DbHtS}[H]$, where

$$H : (\mathcal{K} \times \mathcal{K}) \times \mathcal{M} \longrightarrow \{0,1\}^n \times \{0,1\}^n$$
$$((K_1, K_2), M) \longmapsto (\mathrm{PolyHash}_{K_1}(M), \mathrm{PolyHash}_{K_2}(M)).$$

It is not hard to show that PolyHash is $\frac{\ell}{N}$-almost universal. Therefore, by Theorem 2, we obtain the following theorem.

Theorem 3. *When* PolyMAC *is based on a block cipher* E, *one has*

$$\mathbf{Adv}_{\mathsf{PolyMAC}}^{\mathsf{prf}}(q,t,\ell) \leq \frac{(4\ell + 18)q^{\frac{4}{3}}}{N} + \frac{6q^{\frac{8}{3}}}{N^2} + \frac{18q^{\frac{7}{3}}}{N^2} + \frac{(\ell^2 + \ell + 1)q^2}{N^2} + \frac{8q^4}{3N^3}$$
$$+ \ 2\mathbf{Adv}_E^{\mathsf{prp}}(q,t+t'),$$

where t' *is the time complexity necessary to compute* E *for* q *times.*

5.2 Security of SUM-ECBC

An n-bit hash function CBC is based an n-bit block cipher E using k-bit keys. For a padded message $M = M[1]\|M[2]\|\cdots\|M[m]$ where $m \leq \ell$, and a key $K \in \{0,1\}^k$, $\mathsf{CBC}_K(M)$ is defined as follows.

> **Function** $\mathsf{CBC}_K(M)$
> $\quad Z[0] \leftarrow 0$
> $\quad$**for** $\alpha \leftarrow 1$ to m **do**
> $\quad\quad Z[\alpha] \leftarrow E_K\left(Z[\alpha - 1] \oplus M[\alpha]\right)$
> $\quad$**return** $Z[m]$

The SUM-ECBC MAC is defined as DbHtS[H] (Fig. 3), where

$$H : (\{0,1\}^k \times \{0,1\}^k) \times \mathcal{M} \longrightarrow \{0,1\}^n \times \{0,1\}^n$$
$$((K_1, K_2), M) \longmapsto (\mathsf{CBC}_{K_1}(M), \mathsf{CBC}_{K_2}(M)).$$

For $m \leq \ell$, let $d(m)$ be the number of divisors of m and let $d'(\ell) = \max_{m \leq \ell} d(m)$. It is known that $d'(\ell) = \ell^{o(1)}$. In [11, Corollary 2], it has been proved that CBC is δ-almost universal when the underlying block cipher is replaced by a truly random permutation, where

$$\delta = \frac{d'(\ell)}{N - 2\ell} + \frac{16\ell^4}{N^2}.$$

Therefore, by Theorem 2, we obtain the following theorem.

Theorem 4. *Assume that* $\ell \leq N/4$. *When* SUM-ECBC *is based on a block cipher* E, *one has*

$$\mathbf{Adv}_{\mathsf{SUM\text{-}ECBC}}^{\mathsf{prf}}(q,t,\ell) \leq \frac{(8d'(\ell) + 18)q^{\frac{4}{3}}}{N} + \frac{6q^{\frac{8}{3}}}{N^2} + \frac{18q^{\frac{7}{3}}}{N^2} + \frac{(4d'(\ell)^2 + 2d'(\ell) + 1)q^2}{N^2}$$
$$+ \ \frac{64\ell^4 q^{\frac{4}{3}}}{N^2} + \frac{8q^4}{3N^3} + \frac{(64d'(\ell) + 16)\ell^4 q^2}{N^3} + \frac{256\ell^8 q^2}{N^4}$$
$$+ \ 4\mathbf{Adv}_E^{\mathsf{prp}}(\ell q, t+t'),$$

where t' *is the time complexity necessary to compute* E *for* ℓq *times.*

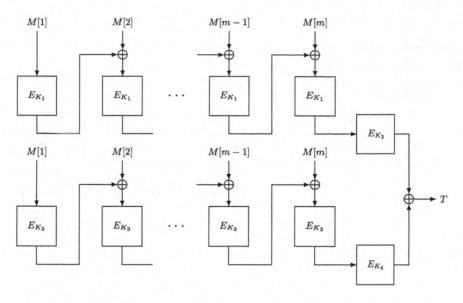

Fig. 3. SUM-ECBC based on a block cipher E using four keys K_i, $i = 1, 2, 3, 4$.

6   Security of **PMAC-Plus**

A $2n$-bit hash function PHash is based an n-bit block cipher E using k-bit keys. For a padded message $M = M[1] \| M[2] \| \cdots \| M[m]$ where $m \leq \ell$, and a key $K \in \{0,1\}^k$, $\mathsf{PHash}_K(M)$ is defined as follows.

> **Function** $\mathsf{PHash}_K(M)$
> $\Delta_0 \leftarrow E_K(0)$
> $\Delta_1 \leftarrow E_K(1)$
> **for** $\alpha \leftarrow 1$ **to** m **do**
> $\quad X[\alpha] \leftarrow M[\alpha] \oplus 2^\alpha \cdot \Delta_0 \oplus 2^{2\alpha} \cdot \Delta_1$
> $\quad Y[\alpha] \leftarrow E_K(X[\alpha])$
> $U \leftarrow Y[1] \oplus Y[2] \oplus \cdots \oplus Y[m]$
> $V \leftarrow Y[1] \oplus 2 \cdot Y[2] \oplus \cdots \oplus 2^{m-1} \cdot Y[m]$
> **return** (U, V)

The PMAC-Plus MAC is defined as DbHtS[PHash] (Fig. 4).

For simplicity of proof, we will replace keyed permutations E_{K_1}, E_{K_2}, E_{K_3} by independent random permutations π, π', π'', respectively, up to the PRP-security of E (to be captured by the term $3\mathbf{Adv}_E^{\mathsf{prp}}(\ell q, t + t')$ in Theorem 5). So we will focus on PHash based on a truly random permutation π, and upper bound the probability of bad transcripts (as defined in Sect. 4).[2]

---

[2] We will simply omit key $\pi \in \mathsf{Perm}(n)$ in PHash and its halves F and G.

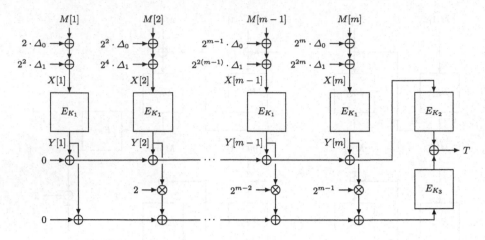

Fig. 4. PMAC-Plus based on a block cipher E using three keys K_1, K_2, K_3, where $\Delta_0 = E_{K_1}(0)$ and $\Delta_1 = E_{K_1}(1)$.

BAD EVENTS. Note that $\mathsf{PHash}(M) = (F(M), G(M))$ for any message M. We fix a parameter $\bar{q}_c$, and define bad events as follows.

- $\mathsf{Bad}_1 \Leftrightarrow$ there is a pair of distinct queries (M_i, M_j) such that $\mathsf{PHash}(M_i) = \mathsf{PHash}(M_j)$.
- $\mathsf{Bad}_2 \Leftrightarrow$ there is a quadruple of distinct queries $(M_{i_1}, M_{i_2}, M_{i_3}, M_{i_4})$ such that $F(M_{i_1}) = F(M_{i_2})$, $G(M_{i_2}) = G(M_{i_3})$, $F(M_{i_3}) = F(M_{i_4})$.
- $\mathsf{Bad}_3 \Leftrightarrow$ there is a quadruple of distinct queries $(M_{i_1}, M_{i_2}, M_{i_3}, M_{i_4})$ such that $G(M_{i_1}) = G(M_{i_2})$, $F(M_{i_2}) = F(M_{i_3})$, $G(M_{i_3}) = G(M_{i_4})$ and $T_{i_1} \oplus T_{i_2} \oplus T_{i_3} \oplus T_{i_4} = \mathbf{0}$.
- $\mathsf{Bad}_4 \Leftrightarrow$ there is a pair of distinct queries (M_i, M_j) such that $T_i \oplus T_j = \mathbf{0}$ and either $F(M_i) = F(M_j)$ or $G(M_i) = G(M_j)$.
- $\mathsf{Bad}_5 \Leftrightarrow \mathsf{Bad}_{5a} \vee \mathsf{Bad}_{5b}$, where
  - $\mathsf{Bad}_{5a} \Leftrightarrow$ the number of distinct queries (M_i, M_j) such that $F(M_i) = F(M_j)$ is greater than $\bar{q}_c/4$,
  - $\mathsf{Bad}_{5b} \Leftrightarrow$ the number of distinct queries (M_i, M_j) such that $G(M_i) = G(M_j)$ is greater than $\bar{q}_c/4$.

We distinguish two types of trails of length 4; a trail of type M consists of two F-collisions and one G-collision, while a trail of type W consists of two G-collisions and one F-collision. Then we observe that

1. $\mathcal{G}_\mathcal{T}^=$ contains no cycle of length 2 without Bad_1;
2. $\mathcal{G}_\mathcal{T}^=$ contains no trail of type M without Bad_2;
3. $\mathcal{G}_\mathcal{T}^=$ contains no trail of type W whose label is $\mathbf{0}$ without Bad_3;
4. $\mathcal{G}_\mathcal{T}^=$ contains no trail of length 2 whose label is $\mathbf{0}$ without Bad_4;
5. the number of edges in $\mathcal{C}$ is not greater than $\bar{q}_c$ without Bad_5.

Without Bad_2, $\mathcal{G}_{\mathcal{T}}^=$ contains neither a cycle of length 4 nor a trail of length 5. We also note that $\lambda(\mathcal{L}) \neq \mathbf{0}$ for any trail $\mathcal{L}$ of even length without Bad_2, Bad_3 and Bad_4. Therefore, we have

$$\Pr[\mathsf{T}_{\mathsf{id}} \in \Gamma_{\mathsf{bad}}] \leq \Pr[\mathsf{Bad}_1 \vee \mathsf{Bad}_2 \vee \mathsf{Bad}_3 \vee \mathsf{Bad}_4 \vee \mathsf{Bad}_5].$$

AUXILIARY EVENTS. For each $i = 1, \ldots, q$, the i-th message is denoted $M_i = M_i[1]\|\cdots\|M_i[m_i]$, where m_i is the length of M_i in blocks. For distinct $i, j \in [q]$, let

$$\mathsf{NEQ}_{i,j} \overset{\text{def}}{=} \{\alpha \in [\min\{m_i, m_j\}] : M_i[\alpha] \neq M_j[\alpha]\}$$
$$\sqcup \{\alpha : \min\{m_i, m_j\} < \alpha \leq \max\{m_i, m_j\}\}.$$

Since $M_i[\alpha] = M_j[\alpha]$ for any index $\alpha \notin \mathsf{NEQ}_{i,j}$, we can simply ignore such an index when we consider F- and G-collisions. We also note that $\mathsf{NEQ}_{i,j} \neq \emptyset$ if M_i and M_j are distinct.

Once $\Delta_0 = \pi(0)$ and $\Delta_1 = \pi(1)$ are fixed, we obtain $X_i = X_i[1]\|\cdots\|X_i[m_i]$, where $X_i[\alpha] = M_i[\alpha] \oplus 2^\alpha \cdot \Delta_0 \oplus 2^{2\alpha} \cdot \Delta_1$. Let

$$\mathcal{I}_{\mathsf{col}} \overset{\text{def}}{=} \{(i,j) \in [q]^{*2} : X_i[\alpha] = X_j[\beta] \text{ for some } \alpha, \beta \text{ such that } \alpha \neq \beta\},$$

$$\mathcal{I}'_{\mathsf{col}} \overset{\text{def}}{=} \{(i,j) \in [q]^{*2} : \min\{\mathsf{NEQ}_{i,j}\} \leq m_i \text{ and } X_i[\min\{\mathsf{NEQ}_{i,j}\}] = X_j[\beta] \text{ for some } \beta\}.$$

In order to analyze the probability of the bad events, we need to introduce certain auxiliary events as follows.

- $\mathsf{Aux}_1 \Leftrightarrow$ either $\pi(0) = 0$ or $\pi(1) = 0$;
- $\mathsf{Aux}_2 \Leftrightarrow X_i[\alpha] = X_i[\beta]$ for some $i \in [q]$ and two distinct indices α and β;
- $\mathsf{Aux}_3 \Leftrightarrow X_i[\alpha] \in \{0, 1, \pi^{-1}(0)\}$ for some $i \in [q]$ and $\alpha \in [m_i]$;
- $\mathsf{Aux}_4 \Leftrightarrow |\mathcal{I}_{\mathsf{col}}| > \hat{q}_c$;
- $\mathsf{Aux}_5 \Leftrightarrow |\mathcal{I}'_{\mathsf{col}}| > \bar{q}_c$.

Note that $\bar{q}_c$ has been introduced in Sect. 3, while $\hat{q}_c$ is a new one. Let $\mathsf{Aux} = \mathsf{Aux}_1 \vee \mathsf{Aux}_2 \vee \mathsf{Aux}_3 \vee \mathsf{Aux}_4 \vee \mathsf{Aux}_5$. It is not hard to see that if $\ell \leq N$, then

$$\Pr[\mathsf{Aux}_1 \vee \mathsf{Aux}_3] \leq \frac{3\ell q}{N-2} + \frac{2}{N}, \qquad \Pr[\mathsf{Aux}_2] \leq \frac{\ell^2 q}{2N},$$

$$\Pr[\mathsf{Aux}_4] \leq \frac{\ell^2 q^2}{\hat{q}_c N}, \qquad \Pr[\mathsf{Aux}_5] \leq \frac{\ell q^2}{\bar{q}_c N}$$

over the random choice of $\pi(0), \pi(1), \pi^{-1}(0)$. Simplifying the bounds, we have

$$\Pr[\mathsf{Aux}] \leq \frac{(\ell^2 + 8\ell)q}{2N} + \frac{\ell^2 q^2}{\hat{q}_c N} + \frac{\ell q^2}{\bar{q}_c N}. \qquad (9)$$

ALMOST UNIVERSALITY. The almost universality of each half of PHash will be used to upper bound the probability of Bad_4 and Bad_5.

Lemma 2. *Let* $\mathsf{PHash}(M) = (F(M), G(M))$ *for any message* M. *If* $\ell \leq N/4$, *then* F *and* G *are* δ-*almost universal, where*

$$\delta = \frac{8\ell}{N}.$$

We refer to [19] for the proof of Lemma 2.

CLASSIFYING X-VARIABLES. In order to upper bound the probability of Bad_1, Bad_2, Bad_3, we need to classify X-variables for each pair of messages, assuming that Aux has not occurred; let

$$\mathcal{X}_{i,j} = \mathcal{X}_{\bar{i},j} \sqcup \mathcal{X}_{i,\bar{j}} \sqcup \mathcal{X}_{\bar{i},\bar{j}}$$

where

$$\mathcal{X}_{\bar{i},j} \overset{\text{def}}{=} \{X_i[\alpha] : \alpha \in \mathsf{NEQ}_{i,j}\} \setminus \{X_j[\alpha] : \alpha \in \mathsf{NEQ}_{i,j}\},$$

$$\mathcal{X}_{i,\bar{j}} \overset{\text{def}}{=} \{X_j[\alpha] : \alpha \in \mathsf{NEQ}_{i,j}\} \setminus \{X_i[\alpha] : \alpha \in \mathsf{NEQ}_{i,j}\},$$

$$\mathcal{X}_{\bar{i},\bar{j}} \overset{\text{def}}{=} \{X_i[\alpha] : \alpha \in \mathsf{NEQ}_{i,j}\} \cap \{X_j[\alpha] : \alpha \in \mathsf{NEQ}_{i,j}\}.$$

We make the following observations.

1. If $X \in \mathcal{X}_{\bar{i},\bar{j}}$, then we have $X = X_i[\alpha] = X_j[\beta]$ for distinct indices α and β.
2. If $\mathcal{X}_{\bar{i},j} \cup \mathcal{X}_{i,\bar{j}} = \emptyset$, then $F(M_i) = F(M_j)$ (regardless of π); the probability that $\mathcal{X}_{\bar{i},j} \cup \mathcal{X}_{i,\bar{j}} = \emptyset$ is upper bounded by $\frac{\ell}{N-1}$ over the random choice of Δ_0 and Δ_1.
3. If $\mathcal{X}_{\bar{i},j} \cup \mathcal{X}_{i,\bar{j}}$ contains either one or two elements, then it is not possible that $F(M_i) = F(M_j)$.
4. The probability that $\mathcal{X}_{\bar{i},\bar{j}} \neq \emptyset$ is upper bounded by $\frac{\ell^2}{N-1}$ over the random choice of Δ_0 and Δ_1.

By relabeling, let

$$\mathcal{X}_{i,j} = \{X[1], \ldots, X[t]\},$$

$$\mathcal{Y}_{i,j} = \{Y[1], \ldots, Y[t]\},$$

where $t = |\mathcal{X}_{i,j}|$ and $Y[\alpha] = \pi(X[\alpha])$ for $\alpha = 1, \ldots, t$. We also partition the set of indices $\{1, \ldots, t\}$ into three subsets; $\{1, \ldots, t\} = I_{\bar{i},j} \sqcup I_{i,\bar{j}} \sqcup I_{\bar{i},\bar{j}}$, where

$$\alpha \in I_{\bar{i},j} \Leftrightarrow X[\alpha] \in \mathcal{X}_{\bar{i},j},$$

$$\alpha \in I_{i,\bar{j}} \Leftrightarrow X[\alpha] \in \mathcal{X}_{i,\bar{j}},$$

$$\alpha \in I_{\bar{i},\bar{j}} \Leftrightarrow X[\alpha] \in \mathcal{X}_{\bar{i},\bar{j}}.$$

Then we can represent F- and G-collisions by equations in $Y[\alpha]$ as follows.

$$F(M_i) = F(M_j) \Leftrightarrow A_1 \cdot Y[1] \oplus \cdots \oplus A_t \cdot Y[t] = 0, \tag{10}$$

$$G(M_i) = G(M_j) \Leftrightarrow B_1 \cdot Y[1] \oplus \cdots \oplus B_t \cdot Y[t] = 0. \tag{11}$$

where

1. $A_\alpha = 1$ if $\alpha \in I_{\bar{i},j} \cup I_{i,\bar{j}}$, and $A_\alpha = 0$ if $\alpha \in I_{\bar{i},\bar{j}}$;
2. $B_\alpha = 2^\beta$ for some β if $\alpha \in I_{\bar{i},j} \cup I_{i,\bar{j}}$, and $B_\alpha = 2^\beta \oplus 2^\gamma$ for distinct β and γ if $\alpha \in I_{\bar{i},\bar{j}}$.

Each unknown $Y[\alpha]$ can be seen as a random variable whose value is taken from a set of size $N - 3$, namely $\{0, 1\}^n \setminus \{0, \pi(0), \pi(1)\}$.

UPPER BOUNDING THE PROBABILITY OF BAD EVENTS. We are now ready to upper bound the probability of each bad event above.

Lemma 3. *Assume that $\ell \leq \frac{N}{8}$. Then, in the ideal world, one has*

$$\Pr[\mathsf{Bad}_1 \wedge \neg\mathsf{Aux}] \leq \frac{4\ell q^2}{N^2}.$$

Proof. We fix distinct $i, j \in [q]$, and distinguish the following two cases.

CASE 1: $\mathcal{X}_{\bar{i},j} \cup \mathcal{X}_{i,\bar{j}} = \emptyset$. This case happens with probability at most $\frac{\ell}{N-1}$ over the random choice of Δ_0 and Δ_1. Since all the coefficients B_α in (11) are nonzero, the probability that $G(M_i) = G(M_j)$ is upper bounded by $(N-3)_{t-1}/(N-3)_t$, which is not greater than $\frac{1}{N-2\ell-2}$ since $t \leq 2\ell$.

CASE 2: $\mathcal{X}_{\bar{i},j} \cup \mathcal{X}_{i,\bar{j}} \neq \emptyset$. It should be the case that $|\mathcal{X}_{\bar{i},j} \cup \mathcal{X}_{i,\bar{j}}| \geq 2$ since otherwise we have $F(M_i) \neq F(M_j)$. Consider Eqs. (10) and (11) (with the same pair of i and j). There are at least two indices $\alpha, \alpha' \in I_{\bar{i},j} \cup I_{i,\bar{j}}$, where $A_\alpha = A_{\alpha'} = 1$, $B_\alpha = 2^\beta$ and $B_{\alpha'} = 2^\gamma$ for distinct β and γ. So the system of equations has rank 2, and hence the equations are satisfied with probability at most $(N-3)_{t-2}/(N-3)_t$, which is not greater than $\frac{1}{(N-2\ell-1)(N-2\ell-2)}$.

Overall, we have $\Pr[\mathsf{Bad}_1 \wedge \neg\mathsf{Aux}] \leq \frac{4\ell q^2}{N^2}$ since $\ell \leq \frac{N}{8}$. $\qquad\square$

Lemma 4. *Assume that $\ell \leq \frac{N}{16}$. Then, in the ideal world, one has*

$$\Pr[\mathsf{Bad}_2 \wedge \neg\mathsf{Aux}] \leq \frac{2\bar{q}_c^2}{N} + \frac{4\hat{q}_c}{N} + \frac{2}{N} + \frac{2\sqrt{2}q^2}{N^{\frac{3}{2}}} + \frac{8\hat{q}_c q^2}{N^2} + \frac{96q^2}{N^2} + \frac{8q^4}{N^3}.$$

Proof. We partition the set $[q]^{*4}$ of quadruples into five subsets; $[q]^{*4} = \mathcal{J}_1 \sqcup \mathcal{J}_2 \sqcup \mathcal{J}_3 \sqcup \mathcal{J}_4 \sqcup \mathcal{J}_5$, where

$$\mathcal{J}_1 \stackrel{\text{def}}{=} \left\{ (i_1, i_2, i_3, i_4) \in [q]^{*4} : (i_2, i_3) \in \mathcal{I}_{\mathsf{col}} \right\},$$

$$\mathcal{J}_2 \stackrel{\text{def}}{=} \left\{ (i_1, i_2, i_3, i_4) \in [q]^{*4} : (i_2, i_3) \notin \mathcal{I}_{\mathsf{col}} \wedge (i_1, i_2) \in \mathcal{I}_{\mathsf{col}} \wedge (i_3, i_4) \in \mathcal{I}_{\mathsf{col}} \right\},$$

$$\mathcal{J}_3 \stackrel{\text{def}}{=} \left\{ (i_1, i_2, i_3, i_4) \in [q]^{*4} : (i_2, i_3) \notin \mathcal{I}_{\mathsf{col}} \wedge (i_1, i_2) \notin \mathcal{I}_{\mathsf{col}} \wedge (i_3, i_4) \in \mathcal{I}_{\mathsf{col}} \right\},$$

$$\mathcal{J}_4 \stackrel{\text{def}}{=} \left\{ (i_1, i_2, i_3, i_4) \in [q]^{*4} : (i_2, i_3) \notin \mathcal{I}_{\mathsf{col}} \wedge (i_1, i_2) \in \mathcal{I}_{\mathsf{col}} \wedge (i_3, i_4) \notin \mathcal{I}_{\mathsf{col}} \right\},$$

$$\mathcal{J}_5 \stackrel{\text{def}}{=} \left\{ (i_1, i_2, i_3, i_4) \in [q]^{*4} : (i_2, i_3) \notin \mathcal{I}_{\mathsf{col}} \wedge (i_1, i_2) \notin \mathcal{I}_{\mathsf{col}} \wedge (i_3, i_4) \notin \mathcal{I}_{\mathsf{col}} \right\}.$$

For $(i_1, i_2, i_3, i_4) \in [q]^{*4}$, let

$$\mathsf{Bad}_2^{i_1, i_2, i_3, i_4} \Leftrightarrow F(M_{i_1}) = F(M_{i_2}) \wedge G(M_{i_2}) = G(M_{i_3}) \wedge F(M_{i_3}) = F(M_{i_4}).$$

Then we have

$$\mathsf{Bad}_2 \Leftrightarrow \bigvee_{(i_1,i_2,i_3,i_4)\in[q]^{*4}} \mathsf{Bad}_2^{i_1,i_2,i_3,i_4},$$

and hence,

$$\Pr\left[\mathsf{Bad}_2 \wedge \neg\mathsf{Aux}\right] \le \mathsf{p}_1 + \mathsf{p}_2 + \mathsf{p}_3 + \mathsf{p}_4 + \mathsf{p}_5,$$

where

$$\mathsf{p}_j \stackrel{\mathrm{def}}{=} \Pr\left[\left(\bigvee_{(i_1,i_2,i_3,i_4)\in\mathcal{J}_j} \mathsf{Bad}_2^{i_1,i_2,i_3,i_4}\right) \wedge \neg\mathsf{Aux}\right]$$

for $j = 1, 2, 3, 4, 5$.

For a fixed quadruple (i_1, i_2, i_3, i_4), we can represent $\mathsf{Bad}_2^{i_1,i_2,i_3,i_4}$ by a system of three linear equations;

$$F(M_{i_1}) = F(M_{i_2}) \Leftrightarrow A_{1,1} \cdot Y[1] \oplus \cdots \oplus A_{1,t} \cdot Y[t] = 0,$$
$$G(M_{i_2}) = G(M_{i_3}) \Leftrightarrow A_{2,1} \cdot Y[1] \oplus \cdots \oplus A_{2,t} \cdot Y[t] = 0,$$
$$F(M_{i_3}) = F(M_{i_4}) \Leftrightarrow A_{3,1} \cdot Y[1] \oplus \cdots \oplus A_{3,t} \cdot Y[t] = 0$$

for some $A_{j,\alpha}$, where each column corresponds to a variable in

$$\mathcal{X}_{\bar{i_1},i_2} \cup \mathcal{X}_{i_1,\bar{i_2}} \cup \mathcal{X}_{i_2,i_3} \cup \mathcal{X}_{i_3,i_4} \cup \mathcal{X}_{i_3,\bar{i_4}},$$

so the number of columns, denoted t, is the size of this set. This system of equations can also be regarded as a $3 \times t$ matrix $(A_{j,\alpha})$. This matrix will sometimes be denoted $A^{(i_1,i_2,i_3,i_4)}$ to specify the corresponding quadruple. For $j = 1, 2, 3$, the j-th row of $(A_{j,\alpha})$ is denoted $A_j^{(i_1,i_2,i_3,i_4)}$, or simply A_j. We observe that the second row A_2 is always nonzero, namely, the G-collision is nontrivial.

UPPER BOUNDING p_1. We have

$$\left(\bigvee_{(i_1,i_2,i_3,i_4)\in\mathcal{J}_1} \mathsf{Bad}_2^{i_1,i_2,i_3,i_4}\right) \wedge \neg\mathsf{Aux} \Rightarrow \left(\bigvee_{(i_2,i_3)\in\mathcal{I}_{\mathsf{col}}} G(M_{i_2}) = G(M_{i_3})\right) \wedge \neg\mathsf{Aux}.$$

Since $|\mathcal{I}_{\mathsf{col}}| \le \hat{q}_c$ and the G-collision is nontrivial, the probability of the event on the right-hand side is upper bounded by $\hat{q}_c/(N - 2\ell - 2)$. So we have

$$\mathsf{p}_1 \le \frac{2\hat{q}_c}{N}. \tag{12}$$

UPPER BOUNDING p_2. We have

$$\left(\bigvee_{(i_1,i_2,i_3,i_4)\in\mathcal{J}_2} \mathsf{Bad}_2^{i_1,i_2,i_3,i_4}\right) \wedge \neg\mathsf{Aux} \Rightarrow \left(\bigvee_{(i_1,i_2)\in\mathcal{I}_{\mathsf{col}}\setminus\mathcal{I}'_{\mathsf{col}}} F(M_{i_1}) = F(M_{i_2})\right)$$

$$\wedge \left(\bigvee_{\substack{(i_1,i_2)\in\mathcal{I}'_{\mathsf{col}} \\ (i_3,i_4)\in\mathcal{I}'_{\mathsf{col}} \\ (i_2,i_3)\notin\mathcal{I}_{\mathsf{col}}}} G(M_{i_2}) = G(M_{i_3})\right) \wedge \neg\mathsf{Aux}$$

We see that

1. for any pair of messages in $\mathcal{I}_{\mathsf{col}} \setminus \mathcal{I}'_{\mathsf{col}}$, their F-collision is nontrivial;
2. for any pair of messages in $[q]^{*2} \setminus \mathcal{I}_{\mathsf{col}}$, their G-collision is nontrivial;
3. $|\mathcal{I}_{\mathsf{col}} \setminus \mathcal{I}'_{\mathsf{col}}| \leq \hat{q}_c$ and $|\mathcal{I}'_{\mathsf{col}}| \leq \bar{q}_c$.

Therefore we have

$$\mathsf{p}_2 \leq \frac{\hat{q}_c}{N - 2\ell - 2} + \frac{\bar{q}_c^2}{N - 2\ell - 2} \leq \frac{2\hat{q}_c}{N} + \frac{2\bar{q}_c^2}{N}. \tag{13}$$

UPPER BOUNDING p_3. Fix a quadruple $(i_1, i_2, i_3, i_4) \in \mathcal{J}_3$, and consider the corresponding matrix $A^{(i_1,i_2,i_3,i_4)} = (A_{j,\alpha})$. A_1 is a zero-one matrix, but nonzero since $(i_1, i_2) \notin \mathcal{I}_{\mathsf{col}}$, while A_2 contains at least two entries, say 2^β and 2^γ for distinct β and γ. This implies that A_2 cannot be a multiple of A_1, and hence $(A_{j,\alpha})$ has rank at least two. Therefore the probability that random variables $Y[1], \ldots, Y[t]$ satisfy the system of equations is upper bounded by $(N - 3)_{t-2}/(N - 3)_t$, which is $1/(N - t - 1)(N - t - 2)$. Since the number of quadruples $(i_1, i_2, i_3, i_4) \in [q]^{*4}$ such that $(i_2, i_3) \notin \mathcal{I}_{\mathsf{col}}$ is at most $\hat{q}_c q^2$ and since $t \leq 4\ell$, we have

$$\mathsf{p}_3 < \frac{\hat{q}_c q^2}{(N - 4\ell - 1)(N - 4\ell - 2)} \leq \frac{4\hat{q}_c q^2}{N^2}. \tag{14}$$

UPPER BOUNDING p_4. In a similar manner to the analysis of p_3, we obtain

$$\mathsf{p}_4 \leq \frac{\hat{q}_c q^2}{(N - 4\ell - 1)(N - 4\ell - 2)} \leq \frac{4\hat{q}_c q^2}{N^2}. \tag{15}$$

UPPER BOUNDING p_5. Fix a quadruple $(i_1, i_2, i_3, i_4) \in \mathcal{J}_5$, and consider the corresponding matrix $A^{(i_1,i_2,i_3,i_4)} = (A_{j,\alpha})$. We can assume that A_1 and A_3 contain at least three 1's, since otherwise we will not have two F-collisions for A_1 and A_3. Every entry of A_2 should be given as 2^α for some α (since $(i_2, i_3) \notin \mathcal{I}_{\mathsf{col}}$), and for each α, 2^α appears at most twice in the row. Furthermore, A_2 should contain at least two distinct entries, since otherwise we will not have the G-collision (with distinct nonzero Y-variables). So A_2 cannot be a multiple of A_1, and hence the rank of $(A_{j,\alpha})$ is at least two. In this case, we have two possibilities; one is that $A_1 = A_3$, and the other is that $A_2 = CA_1 \oplus DA_3$ for some nonzero constants C and D.

All in all, $\mathcal{J}_5$ can be represented by a union of three subsets; $\mathcal{J}_5 = \mathcal{J}_{5,1} \cup \mathcal{J}_{5,2} \cup \mathcal{J}_{5,3}$, where

$$\mathcal{J}_{5,1} \stackrel{\text{def}}{=} \left\{ (i_1, i_2, i_3, i_4) \in \mathcal{J}_5 : A^{(i_1,i_2,i_3,i_4)} \text{ has rank } 3 \right\},$$

$$\mathcal{J}_{5,2} \stackrel{\text{def}}{=} \left\{ (i_1, i_2, i_3, i_4) \in \mathcal{J}_5 : A_1^{(i_j)} = A_3^{(i_j)} \right\},$$

$$\mathcal{J}_{5,3} \stackrel{\text{def}}{=} \left\{ (i_1, i_2, i_3, i_4) \in \mathcal{J}_5 : A_2^{(i_j)} = CA_1^{(i_j)} \oplus DA_3^{(i_j)} \text{ for nonzero } C \text{ and } D \right\}.$$

For $(i_1, i_2, i_3, i_4) \in \mathcal{J}_{5,1}$, it is not hard to see that the probability of Y-variables satisfying the corresponding system of equations is upper bounded by $(N - 3)_{t-3}/(N-3)_t$, which is $1/(N-t)(N-t-1)(N-t-2)$. Since $t \leq 4\ell$, we have

$$\Pr\left[\left(\bigvee_{(i_1,i_2,i_3,i_4)\in\mathcal{J}_{5,1}} \mathsf{Bad}_2^{i_1,i_2,i_3,i_4}\right) \wedge \neg\mathsf{Aux}\right]$$

$$\leq \frac{q^4}{(N-4\ell)(N-4\ell-1)(N-4\ell-2)} \leq \frac{8q^4}{N^3}. \tag{16}$$

In order to upper bound the probability of $\mathsf{Bad}_2^{i_1,i_2,i_3,i_4}$ for $(i_1, i_2, i_3, i_4) \in \mathcal{J}_{5,2}$, we need to define an equivalence relation, denoted $\sim$, on $[q]^{*2} \setminus \mathcal{I}_{\mathsf{col}}$, where

$$(i_1, i_2) \sim (i_3, i_4) \Leftrightarrow \mathcal{X}_{\bar{i_1},i_2} \sqcup \mathcal{X}_{i_1,\bar{i_2}} = \mathcal{X}_{\bar{i_3},i_4} \sqcup \mathcal{X}_{i_3,\bar{i_4}}.$$

The relation $(i_1, i_2) \sim (i_3, i_4)$ implies that $A_1 = A_3$ for $A^{(i_1,i_2,i_3,i_4)}$. In other words, $F(M_{i_1}) = F(M_{i_2}) \Leftrightarrow F(M_{i_3}) = F(M_{i_4})$, namely, the two F-collisions are dependent on each other. We will assume that this relation partitions $[q]^{*2} \setminus \mathcal{I}_{\mathsf{col}}$ into r subsets, denoted $\mathcal{I}_1, \ldots, \mathcal{I}_r$, respectively. So we have

$$[q]^{*2} \setminus \mathcal{I}_{\mathsf{col}} = \mathcal{I}_1 \sqcup \cdots \sqcup \mathcal{I}_r.$$

For $j = 1, \ldots, r$, let

$$\mathsf{E}_j \Leftrightarrow F(M_{i_1}) = F(M_{i_2}) \text{ for every } (i_1, i_2) \in \mathcal{I}_j.$$

Then we have

$$\Pr[\mathsf{E}_j \wedge \neg\mathsf{Aux}] \leq \frac{1}{N - 2\ell - 2}.$$

Given $\neg\mathsf{Aux}$, we have

$$\left(\bigvee_{(i_1,i_2,i_3,i_4)\in\mathcal{J}_{5,2}} \mathsf{Bad}_2^{i_1,i_2,i_3,i_4}\right) \Rightarrow \left(\bigvee_{j\in[r]} \bigvee_{(i_1,i_2),(i_3,i_4)\in\mathcal{I}_j} \mathsf{Bad}_2^{i_1,i_2,i_3,i_4}\right).$$

For each $j = 1, \ldots, r$, we have

$$\Pr\left[\left(\bigvee_{(i_1,i_2),(i_3,i_4)\in\mathcal{I}_j} \mathsf{Bad}_2^{i_1,i_2,i_3,i_4}\right) \wedge \neg\mathsf{Aux}\right]$$

$$\leq \Pr[\mathsf{E}_j \wedge \neg\mathsf{Aux}] \cdot \Pr\left[\bigvee_{(i_1,i_2),(i_3,i_4)\in\mathcal{I}_j} G(M_{i_2}) = G(M_{i_3}) \,\middle|\, \mathsf{E}_j \wedge \neg\mathsf{Aux}\right]$$

$$\leq \frac{1}{N - 2\ell - 2} \cdot \min\left(\frac{|\mathcal{I}_j|^2}{N - 3\ell - 2}, 1\right)$$

since the first and the second rows of $A^{(i_1,i_2,i_3,i_4)}$ are always linearly independent. Overall, we have

$$
\Pr\left[\left(\bigvee_{(i_1,i_2,i_3,i_4)\in\mathcal{J}_{5,2}} \mathsf{Bad}_2^{i_1,i_2,i_3,i_4}\right) \wedge \neg\mathsf{Aux}\right] \leq \sum_{j=1}^{r} \frac{2}{N} \cdot \min\left(\frac{2|\mathcal{I}_j|^2}{N},1\right) \quad (17)
$$

where we use $\ell \leq N/16$. Subject to the condition $\sum_{j=1}^{r}|\mathcal{I}_j| = q^2$ (and with no restriction on r), $\sum_{j=1}^{r}\min\left(\frac{2|\mathcal{I}_j|^2}{N},1\right)$ is maximized when $r = \left\lfloor q^2/(\frac{N}{2})^{\frac{1}{2}}\right\rfloor + 1$, $|\mathcal{I}_j| = (\frac{N}{2})^{\frac{1}{2}}$ for $j = 1,\ldots,r-1$ and $|\mathcal{I}_r| = q^2 - (r-1)\left(\frac{N}{2}\right)^{\frac{1}{2}}$, in which case we have

$$
\sum_{j=1}^{r}\frac{2}{N}\cdot\min\left(\frac{2|\mathcal{I}_j|^2}{N},1\right) \leq \frac{2\sqrt{2}q^2}{N^{\frac{3}{2}}} + \frac{2}{N}. \quad (18)
$$

Finally, we focus on $A^{(i_1,i_2,i_3,i_4)}$ for $(i_1,i_2,i_3,i_4)\in\mathcal{J}_{5,3}$. We note that A_2 is represented by a linear combination of A_1 and A_3, where we can assume that

1. A_2 does not contain the same entry more than twice;
2. A_2 contains at least two different nonzero entries;
3. each of A_1 and A_3 contains at least three 1's.

Therefore the supports of A_1 and A_3 cannot intersect at more than two positions, nor be disjoint each other. So we should be able to find a 3×3 submatrix

$$
\begin{bmatrix} 1 & 1 & 0 \\ C & C\oplus D & D \\ 0 & 1 & 1 \end{bmatrix}
$$

where $C = 2^\alpha$ and $D = 2^\beta$ for distinct α and β. Furthermore, it should be the case that $2^\alpha \oplus 2^\beta = 2^\gamma$ for some γ since $(i_2,i_3)\notin\mathcal{I}_{\mathsf{col}}$. Since a linear combination of A_1 and A_3 generates at most three different nonzero values in A_2, we conclude that $\mathsf{NEQ}_{i_2,i_3} = \{\alpha,\beta,\gamma\}$.

Suppose that we begin with two messages M_{i_2} and M_{i_3} such that $|\mathsf{NEQ}_{i_2,i_3}| = 3$, and try to find M_{i_1} and M_{i_4} such that $(i_1,i_2,i_3,i_4)\in\mathcal{J}_{5,3}$. Let $\mathsf{NEQ}_{i_2,i_3} = \{\alpha,\beta,\gamma\}$, where $2^\alpha \oplus 2^\beta \oplus 2^\gamma = 0$ and $\alpha < \beta < \gamma$. Then A_2 is uniquely determined by M_{i_2} and M_{i_3}, and its nonzero elements are 2^α, 2^β, 2^γ, each of which appears once or twice in the row. Once we choose a pair of distinct coefficients $(C,D) \in \{2^\alpha,2^\beta,2^\gamma\}^{*2}$, we can fix A_1 and A_3 such that $CA_1 \oplus DA_3 = A_2$. For example, if every nonzero element appears exactly twice in A_2, and if $C = 2^\alpha$ and $D = 2^\beta$, then A will contain a 3×6 submatrix

$$
\begin{bmatrix} 1 & 0 & 1 & 1 & 0 & 1 \\ 2^\alpha & 2^\beta & 2^\gamma & 2^\alpha & 2^\beta & 2^\gamma \\ 0 & 1 & 1 & 0 & 1 & 1 \end{bmatrix}
$$

with all the other entries being zero. Since we have at most two possibilities for M_{i_1} (resp. M_{i_4}) yielding A_1 (resp. A_3), the number of possible ways of choosing

M_{i_1} and M_{i_4} is at most 24 (given M_{i_2} and M_{i_3}), and for each of such quadruples, the probability that the Y-variables satisfy the corresponding system of equations is upper bounded by $1/(N - 4\ell - 1)(N - 4\ell - 2)$. Therefore we have

$$\Pr\left[\left(\bigvee_{(i_1,i_2,i_3,i_4)\in\mathcal{J}_{5,3}} \mathsf{Bad}_2^{i_1,i_2,i_3,i_4}\right) \wedge \neg\mathsf{Aux}\right]$$
$$\leq \frac{24q^2}{(N - 4\ell - 1)(N - 4\ell - 2)} \leq \frac{96q^2}{N^2}. \quad (19)$$

By (16), (17), (18), (19), we have

$$\mathsf{p}_5 \leq \frac{2}{N} + \frac{2\sqrt{2}q^2}{N^{\frac{3}{2}}} + \frac{96q^2}{N^2} + \frac{8q^4}{N^3}. \quad (20)$$

The proof is now complete by (12), (13), (14), (15), (20).   □

Lemma 5. *Assume that* $\ell \leq \frac{N}{8}$. *Then, in the ideal world, one has*

$$\Pr[\mathsf{Bad}_3 \wedge \neg\mathsf{Aux}] \leq \frac{6\ell^2 q^4}{N^3}.$$

Proof. Fix a quadruple of distinct queries. For simplicity of notation and without loss of generality, we will consider (M_1, M_2, M_3, M_4). In the ideal world, the probability that $T_1 \oplus T_2 \oplus T_3 \oplus T_4 = 0$ is $\frac{1}{N}$.

Next, we will upper bound the probability that $F(M_1) = F(M_2)$ and $G(M_2) = G(M_3)$, focusing on the first three messages. We consider the following three cases.

CASE 1: $\mathcal{X}_{\bar{1},2} \cup \mathcal{X}_{1,\bar{2}} = \emptyset$. The analysis is similar to Case 1 in Lemma 3; the probability that $F(M_1) = F(M_2)$ and $G(M_2) = G(M_3)$ in this case is upper bounded by $\frac{\ell}{(N-1)(N-2\ell-2)}$.

CASE 2: $\mathcal{X}_{\bar{1},2} \cup \mathcal{X}_{1,\bar{2}} \neq \emptyset$ and $\mathcal{X}_{2,3} \neq \emptyset$. The probability that $\mathcal{X}_{2,3} \neq \emptyset$ (over the random choice of Δ_0 and Δ_1) is upper bounded by $\frac{\ell^2}{N-1}$. Once Δ_0 and Δ_1 are fixed, the probability that $F(M_1) = F(M_2)$ (over the random choice of π) is upper bounded by $\frac{1}{N-2\ell-2}$.

CASE 3: $\mathcal{X}_{\bar{1},2} \cup \mathcal{X}_{1,\bar{2}} \neq \emptyset$ and $\mathcal{X}_{2,3} = \emptyset$. It should be the case that $|\mathcal{X}_{\bar{1},2} \cup \mathcal{X}_{1,\bar{2}}| \geq 2$. The F- and G-collisions can be represented by a system of equations

$$A_{1,1} \cdot Y[1] \oplus \cdots \oplus A_{1,t} \cdot Y[t] = 0,$$
$$A_{2,1} \cdot Y[1] \oplus \cdots \oplus A_{2,t} \cdot Y[t] = 0,$$

for some $A_{j,\alpha}$, where $t = |\mathcal{X}_{\bar{1},2} \cup \mathcal{X}_{1,\bar{2}} \cup \mathcal{X}_{2,3}|$. We can also partition the set of indices $\{1, \ldots, t\}$ into two subsets; $\{1, \ldots, t\} = I_1 \sqcup I_2$, where

$$\alpha \in I_1 \Leftrightarrow X[\alpha] \in \mathcal{X}_{\bar{1},2} \cup \mathcal{X}_{1,\bar{2}},$$
$$\alpha \in I_2 \Leftrightarrow X[\alpha] \in \mathcal{X}_{2,3} \setminus (\mathcal{X}_{\bar{1},2} \cup \mathcal{X}_{1,\bar{2}}).$$

We note that $A_{1,\alpha} = 1$ for every $\alpha \in I_1$ and $A_{1,\alpha} = 0$ for every $\alpha \in I_2$. Furthermore, for every $\alpha \in I_2$, $A_{2,\alpha}$ is nonzero. So if I_2 is nonempty, then $(A_{i,\alpha})$ contains a 2×2 submatrix

$$\begin{bmatrix} 1 & 0 \\ * & 2^\beta \end{bmatrix}$$

for some β, and hence the system of equations has rank 2.

If I_2 is empty, then $\mathcal{X}_{\bar{2},3} \cup \mathcal{X}_{2,\bar{3}} \subset \mathcal{X}_{\bar{1},2} \sqcup \mathcal{X}_{1,\bar{2}}$. We also have $|\mathcal{X}_{\bar{2},3} \cup \mathcal{X}_{2,\bar{3}}| \geq 2$ since otherwise $G(M_2) \neq G(M_3)$. So we have two indices α, $\alpha' \in I_1$ such that $X[\alpha]$, $X[\alpha'] \in \mathcal{X}_{\bar{2},3} \cup \mathcal{X}_{2,\bar{3}}$. Since $A_{2,\alpha} = 2^\beta$ and $A_{2,\alpha'} = 2^\gamma$ for distinct β and γ, $(A_{i,\alpha})$ contains a 2×2 submatrix

$$\begin{bmatrix} 1 & 1 \\ 2^\beta & 2^\gamma \end{bmatrix}$$

for distinct β and γ, and hence the system of equations has rank 2. So in any case, the system of equations are satisfied with probability at most $\frac{1}{(N-2\ell-1)(N-2\ell-2)}$. Overall, we have $\Pr[\mathsf{Bad}_3 \wedge \neg\mathsf{Aux}] \leq \frac{6\ell^2 q^4}{N^3}$ since $\ell \leq \frac{N}{8}$. $\square$

The following two lemmas are easy to prove using the Markov inequality and the almost universality of F and G.

Lemma 6. *In the ideal world, one has*

$$\Pr[\mathsf{Bad}_4] \leq \frac{16\ell^2 q^2}{N^2}.$$

Lemma 7. *In the ideal world, one has*

$$\Pr[\mathsf{Bad}_5] \leq \frac{64\ell q^2}{\bar{q}_c N}.$$

By Lemma 3, 4, 5, 6, 7, and (9), we can upper bound the probability of Bad, and then combining it with (7) (setting $\hat{q}_c = \ell N^{\frac{1}{2}}/2\sqrt{2}$ and $\bar{q}_c = 2\ell^{\frac{1}{3}} q^{\frac{2}{3}}$), we obtain the following theorem.

Theorem 5. *Assume that $\ell \leq N/16$. When PMAC-Plus is based on a block cipher E, one has*

$$\mathbf{Adv}^{\mathrm{prf}}_{\mathsf{PMAC\text{-}Plus}}(q,t,\ell) \leq \frac{\sqrt{2}\ell}{N^{\frac{1}{2}}} + \frac{45\ell^{\frac{2}{3}} q^{\frac{4}{3}}}{N} + \frac{(\ell^2 + 8\ell)q}{2N} + \frac{2}{N} + \frac{(4\sqrt{2}\ell + 2\sqrt{2})q^2}{N^{\frac{3}{2}}}$$
$$+ \frac{3\ell^{\frac{1}{3}} q^{\frac{8}{3}}}{N^2} + \frac{9\ell^{\frac{2}{3}} q^{\frac{7}{3}}}{2N^2} + \frac{(16\ell^2 + 4\ell + 97)q^2}{N^2} + \frac{(18\ell^2 + 32)q^4}{3N^3}$$
$$+ 3\mathbf{Adv}^{\mathrm{prp}}_E(\ell q, t + t'),$$

where t' is the time complexity necessary to compute E for ℓq times.

Note that all the constant coefficients are loosely estimated in our bounds; most large coefficients appear since we replace $N - c\ell$ by $N/2$ for any small integer c.

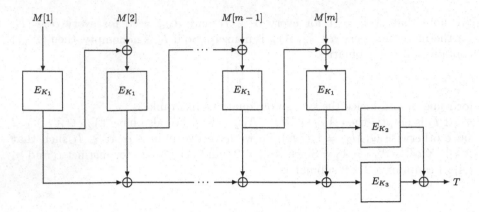

Fig. 5. 3kf9 based on a block cipher E using three keys K_1, K_2, K_3.

7   Security of **3kf9** and **LightMAC-Plus**

In this section, we provide upper bounds on the PRF-security of 3kf9 and LightMAC-Plus. Due to space constraints, the proof is deferred to the full version of this paper. We remark that the security proof of LightMAC-Plus is much simpler than PMAC-Plus; the structure of LightMAC-Plus is similar to PMAC-Plus, while domain separation by distinct prefixes removes most bad events in the proof.

7.1   Security of **3kf9**

A $2n$-bit hash function 3kf9Hash is based an n-bit block cipher E using k-bit keys. For a padded message $M = M[1]\|M[2]\|\cdots\|M[m]$ where $m \leq \ell$, and for a key $K \in \{0,1\}^k$, 3kf9Hash$_K(M)$ is defined as follows.

> **Function** 3kf9Hash$_K(M)$
>
> $Z[0] \leftarrow 0$
> **for** $\alpha \leftarrow 1$ to m **do**
> $Z[\alpha] \leftarrow E_K(Z[\alpha - 1] \oplus M[\alpha])$
> $U \leftarrow Z[m]$
> $V \leftarrow Z[1] \oplus Z[2] \oplus \cdots \oplus Z[m]$
> **return** (U, V)

The 3kf9 MAC is defined as DbHtS[3kf9Hash] (Fig. 5). We prove the security of 3kf9 as follows.

Theorem 6. *Assume that $\ell \leq N/8$. When* 3kf9 *is based on a block cipher E, one has*

$$\mathbf{Adv}^{\mathsf{prf}}_{\mathsf{3kf9}}(q, t, \ell) \leq \frac{18\ell^{\frac{4}{3}}q^{\frac{4}{3}}}{N} + \frac{2\ell^{\frac{2}{3}}q^{\frac{8}{3}}}{N^2} + \frac{2\ell^{\frac{4}{3}}q^{\frac{7}{3}}}{N^2} + \frac{11\ell^2 q^2}{N^2} + \frac{11\ell^6 q^4}{N^3}$$
$$+ 3\mathbf{Adv}^{\mathsf{prp}}_E(\ell q, t + t'),$$

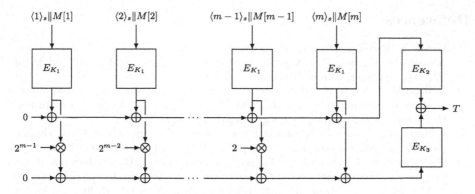

Fig. 6. LightMAC-Plus based on a block cipher E using three keys K_1, K_2, K_3.

where t' is the time complexity necessary to compute E for ℓq times.

7.2   Security of LightMAC-Plus

A $2n$-bit hash function LHash is based an n-bit block cipher E using k-bit keys. In this construction, a message is padded so that its length is a multiple of $n - s$, where s is a fixed parameter such that $0 < s < n$. So a padded message M can be broken into $(n - s)$-bit blocks; let

$$M = M[1]\|M[2]\|\cdots\|M[m],$$

where $m < 2^s$ and $M(\alpha)$ is $n - s$ bits for $\alpha = 1, \ldots, m$. Let $\langle\alpha\rangle_s$ denote the s-bit binary representation of integer α. Then for a key $K \in \{0,1\}^k$, $\text{LHash}_K(M)$ is defined as follows.

> **Function** $\text{LHash}_K(M)$
>
> **for** $\alpha \leftarrow 1$ to m **do**
> $\quad X[\alpha] \leftarrow \langle\alpha\rangle_s\|M[\alpha]$
> $\quad Y[\alpha] \leftarrow E_K(X[\alpha])$
> $U \leftarrow Y[1] \oplus Y[2] \oplus \cdots \oplus Y[m]$
> $V \leftarrow 2^{m-1} \cdot Y[1] \oplus 2^{m-2} \cdot Y[2] \oplus \cdots \oplus Y[m]$
> **return** (U, V)

The LightMAC-Plus MAC is defined as $\text{DbHtS}[\text{LHash}]$ (Fig. 6). We prove the security of LightMAC-Plus as follows.

Theorem 7. *Assume that $\ell \leq N/16$. When LightMAC-Plus is based on a block cipher E, one has*

$$\mathbf{Adv}^{\text{prf}}_{\text{LightMAC-Plus}}(q, t, \ell) \leq \frac{17q^{\frac{4}{3}}}{2N} + \frac{2}{N} + \frac{2\sqrt{2}q^2}{N^{\frac{3}{2}}} + \frac{3q^{\frac{8}{3}}}{N^2} + \frac{9q^{\frac{7}{3}}}{2N^2} + \frac{30q^2}{N^2} + \frac{44q^4}{3N^3}$$
$$+ 3\mathbf{Adv}^{\text{prp}}_E(\ell q, t + t'),$$

where t' is the time complexity necessary to compute E for ℓq times.

References

1. Banik, S., Pandey, S.K., Peyrin, T., Sasaki, Y., Sim, S.M., Todo, Y.: GIFT: a small present. In: Fischer, W., Homma, N. (eds.) CHES 2017. LNCS, vol. 10529, pp. 321–345. Springer, Cham (2017). https://doi.org/10.1007/978-3-319-66787-4_16
2. Bellare, M., Canetti, R., Krawczyk, H.: Keying hash functions for message authentication. In: Koblitz, N. (ed.) CRYPTO 1996. LNCS, vol. 1109, pp. 1–15. Springer, Heidelberg (1996). https://doi.org/10.1007/3-540-68697-5_1
3. Bellare, M., Kilian, J., Rogaway, P.: The security of the cipher block chaining message authentication code. J. Comput. Syst. Sci. **61**(3), 362–399 (2000)
4. Bierbrauer, J., Johansson, T., Kabatianskii, G., Smeets, B.: On families of hash functions via geometric codes and concatenation. In: Stinson, D.R. (ed.) CRYPTO 1993. LNCS, vol. 773, pp. 331–342. Springer, Heidelberg (1994). https://doi.org/10.1007/3-540-48329-2_28
5. Black, J., Rogaway, P.: A block-cipher mode of operation for parallelizable message authentication. In: Knudsen, L.R. (ed.) EUROCRYPT 2002. LNCS, vol. 2332, pp. 384–397. Springer, Heidelberg (2002). https://doi.org/10.1007/3-540-46035-7_25
6. Bogdanov, A., et al.: PRESENT: an ultra-lightweight block cipher. In: Paillier, P., Verbauwhede, I. (eds.) CHES 2007. LNCS, vol. 4727, pp. 450–466. Springer, Heidelberg (2007). https://doi.org/10.1007/978-3-540-74735-2_31
7. Datta, N., Dutta, A., Nandi, M., Paul, G.: Double-block hash-then-sum: a paradigm for constructing BBB secure PRF. IACR Trans. Symmetric Cryptol. **2018**(3), 36–92 (2018)
8. den Boer, B.: A simple and key-economical unconditional authentication scheme. J. Comput. Secur. **2**, 65–72 (1993)
9. Guo, J., Peyrin, T., Poschmann, A., Robshaw, M.: The LED block cipher. In: Preneel, B., Takagi, T. (eds.) CHES 2011. LNCS, vol. 6917, pp. 326–341. Springer, Heidelberg (2011). https://doi.org/10.1007/978-3-642-23951-9_22
10. Iwata, T., Kurosawa, K.: OMAC: one-key CBC MAC. In: Johansson, T. (ed.) FSE 2003. LNCS, vol. 2887, pp. 129–153. Springer, Heidelberg (2003). https://doi.org/10.1007/978-3-540-39887-5_11
11. Jha, A., Nandi, M.: Revisiting structure graphs: applications to CBC-MAC and EMAC. J. Math. Cryptol. **10**(3–4), 157–180 (2016)
12. Leurent, G., Nandi, M., Sibleyras, F.: Generic attacks against beyond-birthday-bound MACs. In: Shacham, H., Boldyreva, A. (eds.) CRYPTO 2018. LNCS, vol. 10991, pp. 306–336. Springer, Cham (2018). https://doi.org/10.1007/978-3-319-96884-1_11
13. Luykx, A., Preneel, B., Tischhauser, E., Yasuda, K.: A MAC mode for lightweight block ciphers. In: Peyrin, T. (ed.) FSE 2016. LNCS, vol. 9783, pp. 43–59. Springer, Heidelberg (2016). https://doi.org/10.1007/978-3-662-52993-5_3
14. Naito, Y.: Blockcipher-based MACs: beyond the birthday bound without message length. In: Takagi, T., Peyrin, T. (eds.) ASIACRYPT 2017. LNCS, vol. 10626, pp. 446–470. Springer, Cham (2017). https://doi.org/10.1007/978-3-319-70700-6_16
15. Patarin, J.: Introduction to mirror theory: analysis of systems of linear equalities and linear non equalities for cryptography. IACR Cryptology ePrint Archive, Report 2010/287 (2010). http://eprint.iacr.org/2010/287
16. Patarin, J.: Mirror theory and cryptography. IACR Cryptology ePrint Archive, Report 2016/702 (2016). http://eprint.iacr.org/2016/702
17. Taylor, R.: An integrity check value algorithm for stream ciphers. In: Stinson, D.R. (ed.) CRYPTO 1993. LNCS, vol. 773, pp. 40–48. Springer, Heidelberg (1994). https://doi.org/10.1007/3-540-48329-2_4

18. Yasuda, K.: The sum of CBC MACs is a secure PRF. In: Pieprzyk, J. (ed.) CT-RSA 2010. LNCS, vol. 5985, pp. 366–381. Springer, Heidelberg (2010). https://doi.org/10.1007/978-3-642-11925-5_25
19. Yasuda, K.: A new variant of PMAC: beyond the birthday bound. In: Rogaway, P. (ed.) CRYPTO 2011. LNCS, vol. 6841, pp. 596–609. Springer, Heidelberg (2011). https://doi.org/10.1007/978-3-642-22792-9_34
20. Zhang, L., Wu, W., Sui, H., Wang, P.: 3kf9: enhancing 3GPP-MAC beyond the birthday bound. In: Wang, X., Sako, K. (eds.) ASIACRYPT 2012. LNCS, vol. 7658, pp. 296–312. Springer, Heidelberg (2012). https://doi.org/10.1007/978-3-642-34961-4_19

Modeling for Three-Subset Division Property Without Unknown Subset
Improved Cube Attacks Against Trivium and Grain-128AEAD

Yonglin Hao[1]($\boxtimes$), Gregor Leander[2], Willi Meier[3], Yosuke Todo[4]($\boxtimes$),
and Qingju Wang[5]

[1] State Key Laboratory of Cryptology, P.O. Box 5159, Beijing 100878, China
haoyonglin@yeah.net
[2] Horst Görtz Institute for IT Security, Ruhr University Bochum, Bochum, Germany
gregor.leander@rub.de
[3] FHNW, Windisch, Switzerland
willimeier48@gmail.com
[4] NTT Secure Platform Laboratories, Tokyo 180-8585, Japan
yosuke.todo.xt@hco.ntt.co.jp
[5] SnT, University of Luxembourg, Esch-sur-Alzette, Luxembourg
qingju.wang@uni.lu

Abstract. A division property is a generic tool to search for integral distinguishers, and automatic tools such as MILP or SAT/SMT allow us to evaluate the propagation efficiently. In the application to stream ciphers, it enables us to estimate the security of cube attacks theoretically, and it leads to the best key-recovery attacks against well-known stream ciphers. However, it was reported that some of the key-recovery attacks based on the division property degenerate to distinguishing attacks due to the inaccuracy of the division property. Three-subset division property (without unknown subset) is a promising method to solve this inaccuracy problem, and a new algorithm using automatic tools for the three-subset division property was recently proposed at Asiacrypt2019. In this paper, we first show that this state-of-the-art algorithm is not always efficient and we cannot improve the existing key-recovery attacks. Then, we focus on the feature of the three-subset division property without unknown subset and propose another new efficient algorithm using automatic tools. Our algorithm is more efficient than existing algorithms, and it can improve existing key-recovery attacks. In the application to TRIVIUM, we show a 841-round key-recovery attack. We also show that a 855-round key-recovery attack, which was proposed at CRYPTO2018, has a critical flaw and does not work. As a result, our 841-round attack becomes the best key-recovery attack. In the application to Grain-128AEAD, we show that the known 184-round key-recovery attack degenerates to distinguishing attacks. Then, the distinguishing attacks are improved up to 189 rounds, and we also show the best key-recovery attack against 190 rounds.

Keywords: Stream ciphers · Cube attack · Division property ·
Three-subset division property · MILP · TRIVIUM · Grain-128AEAD

© International Association for Cryptologic Research 2020
A. Canteaut and Y. Ishai (Eds.): EUROCRYPT 2020, LNCS 12105, pp. 466–495, 2020.
https://doi.org/10.1007/978-3-030-45721-1_17

1   Introduction

Division Property. Integral cryptanalysis [1], a.k.a. Square attacks [2] or higher-order differential attacks [3], are one of the most powerful cryptanalysis techniques. Let C_I be the set of chosen plaintexts. The integral distinguisher for a cipher E_k is defined as the property $\bigoplus_{p \in C_I} E_k(p) = 0$ for any secret key k. Since the probability that such a zero-sum property holds is low for ideal ciphers, we can distinguish E_k from an ideal one.

The division property, as originated in [4], is the most accurate and generic tool to search for integral distinguishers. Ever since its proposal, it has been widely applied to many block ciphers ([5–8] etc.). For a set of texts $\mathbb{X} \subseteq \mathbb{F}_2^n$, its division property is defined by dividing a set of $\boldsymbol{u}$'s into two subsets: vectors $\boldsymbol{u} \in \mathbb{F}_2^n$ of the 1st subset satisfy $\bigoplus_{x \in \mathbb{X}} \boldsymbol{x}^{\boldsymbol{u}} = 0$ (referred as *0-subset* hereafter), and those of the 2nd subset make $\bigoplus_{x \in \mathbb{X}} \boldsymbol{x}^{\boldsymbol{u}}$ undetermined (referred as *unknown subset* hereafter). The initial division property is defined according to a set of chosen plaintexts, and those of the intermediate states are deduced round by round according to propagation rules. Finally, the division property for the set of corresponding ciphertexts is evaluated, and the integral distinguisher can be derived accordingly. The propagation of the division property was evaluated with the breadth-first search algorithm in [4,5,7], but it is computationally impractical for ciphers with large block size. Then, Xiang et al. introduced the useful concept called *division trail* and propose an MILP-based algorithm [9], enabling us to apply the division property to various ciphers ([10–12] etc.). Nowadays, the division property is often used not only for third party cryptanalysis but also for the design of new ciphers ([13,14] etc.).

Although the division property can find more accurate integral distinguishers than other methods, the accuracy is never perfect. As is pointed out by Todo and Morii [7], the practically verified 15-round integral distinguisher for Simon32 [15] cannot be proved with the conventional division property. To find more accurate distinguishers, the three-subset division property was proposed in [7]. A set of $\boldsymbol{u}$'s is divided into three subsets rather than two ones: the first one is the *0-subset*, another one is the *unknown subset*, and the third one is the subset satisfying $\bigoplus_{x \in \mathbb{X}} \boldsymbol{x}^{\boldsymbol{u}} = 1$ (referred as *1-subset* hereafter). The three-subset division property enables us to prove the 15-round integral distinguisher of Simon32 [7].

Despite of its successful combination of the MILP and the conventional division property, the MILP modeling technique does not work quite well with the three-subset version. Very recently, two methods were proposed to tackle this problem. The first method is a variant of the three-subset division property [16]. Although it sacrifices quite some accuracy of the three-subset division property, this method has MILP-model-friendly propagation rules and improves some integral distinguishers. The latter, proposed by Wang et al. [17], models the propagation for the three-subset division property accurately. Wang et al.'s idea is to combine the MILP with the original breadth-first search algorithm [7]. In their algorithm, each node on the breadth-first search algorithm is regarded as the starting point of division trails, and the MILP evaluates whether there is a feasible solution from every node. When there is no feasible solution, we can prune these nodes from the breadth-first search algorithm as redundant ones.

Cube Attack. The cube attack was proposed by Dinur and Shamir in [18]. For a cipher with public variables $v \in \mathbb{F}_2^m$ and secret variables $x \in \mathbb{F}_2^n$, the cipher can be regarded as a polynomial of v, x denoted as $f(x, v)$. A set of indices, referred as the *cube indices*, is selected as $I = \{i_1, i_2, \ldots, i_{|I|}\} \subset \{1, 2, \ldots, m\}$. Such an I determines a specific structure called *cube*, denoted as C_I, containing $2^{|I|}$ values where variables in $\{v_{i_1}, v_{i_2}, \ldots, v_{i_{|I|}}\}$ take all possible combinations of values and all remaining (key and non-cube IV) variables are static. Then the sum of f over all values of the cube C_I is

$$\bigoplus_{C_I} f(x, v) = \bigoplus_{C_I} (t_I \cdot p(x, v) + q(x, v)) = p(x, v),$$

where t_I denotes a monomial as $t_I = v_{i_1} \cdot v_{i_2} \cdots v_{i_{|I|}}$, and each term of $q(x, v)$ misses at least one variable from $\{v_{i_1}, v_{i_2}, \ldots, v_{i_{|I|}}\}$. Then, $p(x, v)$ is called the *superpoly* of the cube C_I. The cube attack consists of two steps. First, attackers recover the superpoly in the offline phase. Then, attackers query the cube to the encryption oracle, compute the summation, and get the value of the superpoly. The secret key can be recovered when the polynomial $p(x, v)$ is simple. Therefore, the superpoly recovery plays the critical role in the cube attack.

Previously, superpolies could only be recovered experimentally. Therefore, the size of cube indices $|I|$ had to be limited within practical reach. In [11], the division property was first introduced to cube attacks, and it enables us to identify the secret variables **NOT** involved in the superpoly efficiently. After removing such secret variables, the remaining variables are stored into the set J as the secret variables that might be involved. It enables the attackers to recover the truth table of the superpoly with a time complexity $2^{|I|+|J|}$. Then, Wang et al. improved it by introducing flag and term enumeration technique that can lower the complexities for the superpoly recoveries [12]. It is noticeable that neither [11] nor [12] recovers the superpoly directly, and it only guarantees the time complexity to recover the superpoly $p(x, v)$. They only identify the key variables (or monomials [12]) and make the assumption that such variables (monomials) might be involved in the superpoly. If such an assumption does not hold, the superpoly can be much simpler than estimated, or even in the extreme case: $p \equiv 0$ degenerates key-recovery attacks to distinguishing attacks. Such degeneration issues are reported in [19] and [17], where Wang et al.'s attack on 839-round Trivium in [12] cannot recover secret keys because $p \equiv 0$.

Motivation. Our work is motivated by the latest three-subset division property model with pruning technique [17]. In its application to the cube attack, they claim that the three-subset division property without unknown subset can recover the actual superpoly because it deterministically divides the set of $u \in \mathbb{F}_2^n$ into two subsets whose summations are either 0 or 1. We do not need to assume

Table 1. Summary of flaws or issues in some of the previous best key-recovery attacks

Cipher	# Rounds	Ref.	Note	Where discovered
TRIVIUM	839	[12]	Degeneration to distinguisher	[17,19]
TRIVIUM	855	[20]	Attack does not work because of a flaw in the degree estimation	This paper
Grain-128a	184	[12]	Degeneration to distinguisher	This paper

the accuracy of the division property, and the recovered superpolies are always accurate. In spite of such a powerful tool, it was used to degenerate the key-recovery attack against 839-round TRIVIUM in [12]. Such a degeneration from key-recovery to distinguisher implies unexpectedly simpler superpolies. Therefore, we can expect that the superpolies for 840-round TRIVIUM are also simpler than previous estimations, and the key-recovery attacks can be carried out to 840 or more rounds. Thus, we implemented and executed the algorithm based on the pruning technique, and we find that the algorithm is not always efficient: we cannot recover the superpoly of 840-round TRIVIUM in reasonable time. To recover the more complicated superpoly, a more efficient algorithm for the three-subset division property is required.

Our Contribution. We propose a new modeling method for the three-subset division property without unknown subset. Here, we first introduce a modified three-subset division property that is completely equivalent with the three-subset division property without unknown subset. While the original three-subset division property without unknown subset is defined by using the set $\mathbb{L}$, the modified one is defined by using the multiset $\bar{\mathbb{L}}$ instead of the set $\mathbb{L}$, and it is suited to modeling with MILP or SAT/SMT solvers. The previous algorithm focuses on the feasibility of the model, but our algorithm focuses on all feasible solutions that are enumerated by using the solver.

To demonstrate the efficiency of our new algorithm, we apply it to cube and cube-like attacks against TRIVIUM and Grain-128AEAD. We have two types of contributions. The first one is to show flaws or issues in some of the best previous key-recovery attacks, and these results are summarized in Table 1. The second one is the best key-recovery attacks against TRIVIUM and Grain-128AEAD, and these results are summarized in Table 2.

We first apply our algorithm to the superpoly recovery for 840-round TRIVIUM, which was impossible in the previous algorithm. As a result, we can recover the exact superpoly for not only 840-round TRIVIUM but also for 841-round TRIVIUM. Moreover, the recovered superpolies are simple balanced Boolean functions. In other words, we can recover 1-bit of information on the secret key against 840- and 841-round TRIVIUM, and exhaustive search with the recovered superpoly allows us to recover the entire secret key with the time complexity 2^{79}. Note that the recovered superpoly is accurate and there is no assumption like in the theoretical superpoly recoveries [11,12]. We next use our algorithm to

Table 2. Summary of our results

Cipher	# Rounds	Type of attacks	Time complexity
TRIVIUM	840	Key recovery	2^{79}
TRIVIUM	841	Key recovery	2^{79}
Grain-128AEAD	184, 185, 186, 187, 188, 189	Distinguisher	2^{96}
Grain-128AEAD	190	Key recovery	2^{123}

verify a new-type of cube attack [20] shown by Fu et al. In the new-type of cube attack, the part of secret key bits is first guessed, one bit of the intermediate state (denoted by P_1) is computed, and the sum of $(1 + P_1) \cdot z$ over the cube is evaluated, where z denotes the key stream bit. The authors claimed that the sum of $(1 + P_1) \cdot z$ can be simpler than the sum of z by choosing P_1 appropriately. As a result, they claimed that the algebraic degree of $(1 + P_1) \cdot z$ is at most 70. Unfortunately, this claim was based on their algorithm including some man-made work that is not written in the paper, and a cluster of 600–2400 cores is necessary to run their code. Thus, no one can verify their algorithm. Our algorithm is very simple, can run on a normal PC, and recovers the exact superpoly. As we recover the superpoly of $(1 + P_1) \cdot z$ over the cube, we find that the algebraic degree of $(1 + P_1) \cdot z$ is not bounded by 70, and there is a monomial whose degree is $75 + 26 = 101$. In other words, even if we guess the correct P_1, the sum of $(1 + P_1) \cdot z$ over the cube is not 0. It implies that we cannot attack 855-round TRIVIUM by using their method.

Another application is Grain-128AEAD, which was previously referred to as Grain-128a. Grain-128AEAD is one of the 2nd round candidates of the NIST LWC standardization process. And the specification is slightly revised from Grain-128a according to [21,22]. Assuming that the first pre-output key stream can be observed, there is no difference between Grain-128AEAD and Grain-128a in the context of the cube attack. As a result, we show that the key-recovery attack against 184-round Grain-128AEAD shown in [12] is a distinguisher rather than a key recovery. Moreover, we show that the distinguishing attack can be improved up to 189 rounds. From 190 rounds onwards, the superpoly involves some secret key bits, and it can be used in a key-recovery attack. However, since the recovered superpoly is highly biased toward 0, using one superpoly is not sufficient to recover any secret key bit. Therefore, we recover 15 different superpolies for 190-round Grain-128AEAD, and show an attack procedure to recover the secret key by using their superpolies. As a result, we can recover the secret key of 190-round Grain-128AEAD with 2^{123} time complexity.

2   Brief Introduction of Division Property

We first introduce some notations for bitvectors. For any bitvector $\boldsymbol{x} \in \mathbb{F}_2^m$, $x[i]$ denotes the ith bit of $\boldsymbol{x}$. Given two bitvectors $\boldsymbol{x} \in \mathbb{F}_2^m$ and $\boldsymbol{u} \in \mathbb{F}_2^m$, $\boldsymbol{x}^{\boldsymbol{u}} = \prod_{i=1}^m x[i]^{u[i]}$. Moreover, $\boldsymbol{x} \succeq \boldsymbol{u}$ denotes $x[i] \geq u[i]$ for all $i \in \{1, 2, \ldots, m\}$.

2.1 Conventional Division Property

The (conventional) division property was proposed at Eurocrypt 2015, and it is regarded as the generalization of the integral property.

Definition 1 ((Bit-based) division property). *Let* $\mathbb{X}$ *be a multiset whose elements take a value of* $\mathbb{F}_2^m$, *and* $\boldsymbol{k} \in \mathbb{F}_2^m$. *When the multiset* $\mathbb{X}$ *has the division property* $\mathcal{D}_{\mathbb{K}}^{1^m}$, *it fulfills the following conditions:*

$$\bigoplus_{x \in \mathbb{X}} \boldsymbol{x}^{\boldsymbol{u}} = \begin{cases} \text{unknown} & \text{if there are } \boldsymbol{k} \in \mathbb{K} \text{ s.t. } \boldsymbol{u} \succeq \boldsymbol{k}, \\ 0 & \text{otherwise.} \end{cases}$$

For example, when a multiset $\mathbb{X} \subset \mathbb{F}_2^4$ has the division property $\mathcal{D}_{\{1100,1010,0011\}}^{1^4}$, it guarantees that $\bigoplus_{x \in \mathbb{X}} \boldsymbol{x}^{\boldsymbol{u}} = 0$ for any $\boldsymbol{u} \in \{0000, 1000, 0100, 0010, 0001, 1001, 0110, 0101\}$.

2.2 Three-Subset Division Property

The set of u is divided into two subsets in the conventional division property, where one is the subset such that $\bigoplus_{x \in \mathbb{X}} \boldsymbol{x}^{\boldsymbol{u}}$ is unknown and the other is the subset such that the sum is 0. Three-subset division property was proposed in [7], where the number of divided subsets is extended from two to three.

Definition 2 (Three-subset division property). *Let* $\mathbb{X}$ *be a multiset whose elements take a value of* $\mathbb{F}_2^m$, *and* $\boldsymbol{k} \in \mathbb{F}_2^m$. *When the multiset* $\mathbb{X}$ *has the three-subset division property* $\mathcal{D}_{\mathbb{K},\mathbb{L}}^{1^m}$, *it fulfills the following conditions:*

$$\bigoplus_{x \in \mathbb{X}} \boldsymbol{x}^{\boldsymbol{u}} = \begin{cases} \text{unknown} & \text{if there are } \boldsymbol{k} \in \mathbb{K} \text{ s.t. } \boldsymbol{u} \succeq \boldsymbol{k}, \\ 1 & \text{else if there is } \boldsymbol{\ell} \in \mathbb{L} \text{ s.t. } \boldsymbol{u} = \boldsymbol{\ell}, \\ 0 & \text{otherwise.} \end{cases}$$

For example, when a multiset $\mathbb{X} \subset \mathbb{F}_2^4$ has the three-subset division property $\mathcal{D}_{\mathbb{K},\mathbb{L}}^{1^4}$, where $\mathbb{K} = \{1100, 1010, 0011\}$ and $\mathbb{L} = \{1000, 0010, 0110\}$, it guarantees that $\bigoplus_{x \in \mathbb{X}} \boldsymbol{x}^{\boldsymbol{u}}$ is 0 for any $\boldsymbol{u} \in \{0000, 0100, 0001, 1001, 0101\}$ and 1 for any $\boldsymbol{u} \in \{1000, 0010, 0110\}$.

2.3 Propagation Rules for Division Property

The propagation rule of the division property is shown for three basic operations: "copy," "and," and "xor" in [7].

Rule 1 (copy). *Let* F *be a copy function, where the input* $\boldsymbol{x} \in \mathbb{F}_2^m$ *and the output is calculated as* $(x[1], x[1], x[2], x[3], \ldots, x[m])$. *Let* $\mathbb{X}$ *and* $\mathbb{Y}$ *be the* input and output multisets, respectively. Assuming that $\mathbb{X}$ has $\mathcal{D}_{\mathbb{K},\mathbb{L}}^{1^m}$, $\mathbb{Y}$ has $\mathcal{D}_{\mathbb{K}',\mathbb{L}'}^{1^{m+1}}$, where $\mathbb{K}'$ and $\mathbb{L}'$ are computed as

$$\mathbb{K}' \leftarrow \begin{cases} (0,0,k[2],\ldots,k[m]), & \text{if } k[1]=0 \\ (1,0,k[2],\ldots,k[m]),(0,1,k[2],\ldots,k[m]), & \text{if } k[1]=1 \end{cases},$$

$$\mathbb{L}' \leftarrow \begin{cases} (0,0,\ell[2],\ldots,\ell[m]), & \text{if } \ell[1]=0 \\ (1,0,\ell[2],\ldots,\ell[m]),(0,1,\ell[2],\ldots,\ell[m]),(1,1,\ell[2],\ldots,\ell[m]) & \text{if } \ell[1]=1 \end{cases}.$$

from all $\mathbf{k} \in \mathbb{K}$ and all $\boldsymbol{\ell} \in \mathbb{L}$, respectively. Here, $\mathbb{K}' \leftarrow \mathbf{k}$ (resp. $\mathbb{L}' \leftarrow \boldsymbol{\ell}$) denotes that $\mathbf{k}$ (resp. $\boldsymbol{\ell}$) is inserted into $\mathbb{K}'$ (resp. $\mathbb{L}'$).

Rule 2 (and). Let F be a function compressed by an AND, where the input $\mathbf{x} \in \mathbb{F}_2^m$ and the output is calculated as $(x[1] \wedge x[2], x[3], \ldots, x[m])$. Let $\mathbb{X}$ and $\mathbb{Y}$ be the input and output multisets, respectively. Assuming that $\mathbb{X}$ has $\mathcal{D}_{\mathbb{K},\mathbb{L}}^{1^m}$, $\mathbb{Y}$ has $\mathcal{D}_{\mathbb{K}',\mathbb{L}'}^{1^{m-1}}$, where $\mathbb{K}'$ is computed from all $\mathbf{k} \in \mathbb{K}$ as

$$\mathbb{K}' \leftarrow \left(\left\lceil \frac{k[1]+k[2]}{2} \right\rceil, k[3], k[4], \ldots, k[m] \right).$$

Moreover, $\mathbb{L}'$ is computed from all $\boldsymbol{\ell} \in \mathbb{L}$ s.t. $(\ell_1, \ell_2) = (0,0)$ or $(1,1)$ as

$$\mathbb{L}' \leftarrow \left(\left\lceil \frac{\ell[1]+\ell[2]}{2} \right\rceil, \ell[3], \ell[4], \ldots, \ell[m] \right).$$

Rule 3 (xor). Let F be a function compressed by an XOR, where the input $\mathbf{x} \in \mathbb{F}_2^m$, and the output is calculated as $(x[1] \oplus x[2], x[3], \ldots, x[m])$. Let $\mathbb{X}$ and $\mathbb{Y}$ be the input and output multisets, respectively. Assuming that $\mathbb{X}$ has $\mathcal{D}_{\mathbb{K},\mathbb{L}}^{1^m}$, $\mathbb{Y}$ has $\mathcal{D}_{\mathbb{K}',\mathbb{L}'}^{1^{m-1}}$, where $\mathbb{K}'$ is computed from all $\mathbf{k} \in \mathbb{K}$ s.t. $(k[1], k[2]) = (0,0)$, $(1,0)$, or $(0,1)$ as

$$\mathbb{K}' \leftarrow (k[1]+k[2], k[3], k[4], \ldots, k[m]).$$

Moreover, $\mathbb{L}'$ is computed from all $\boldsymbol{\ell} \in \mathbb{L}$ s.t. $(\ell[1], \ell[2]) = (0,0)$, $(1,0)$, or $(0,1)$ as

$$\mathbb{L}' \stackrel{x}{\leftarrow} (\ell[1]+\ell[2], \ell[3], \ell[4], \ldots, \ell[m]).$$

Here, $\mathbb{L}' \stackrel{x}{\leftarrow} \boldsymbol{\ell}$ denotes that $\boldsymbol{\ell}$ is inserted if it is not included in $\mathbb{L}'$. If it is already included in $\mathbb{L}'$, $\boldsymbol{\ell}$ is removed from $\mathbb{L}'$. Hereinafter, we call this property the *cancellation property*.

Another important rule is that bitvectors in $\mathbb{L}$ influence $\mathbb{K}$. Assuming that a state has $\mathcal{D}_{\mathbb{K},\mathbb{L}}^{1^m}$, the secret key is XORed with the first bit in the state. Then, for all $\boldsymbol{\ell} \in \mathbb{L}$ satisfying $\ell[1] = 0$, a new bitvector $(1, \ell[2], \ldots, \ell[m])$ is generated and stored into $\mathbb{K}$. Hereinafter, we call this property the *unknown-producing property*.

2.4   Various Algorithms to Evaluate Propagation of Division Property and Three-Subset Division Property

Breadth-First Search Algorithm. Evaluating the propagation of the division property is not easy. The first few papers [4,5,7] use the so-called breadth-first search algorithm, where $\mathbb{K}_{i+1}$ (resp. $\mathbb{L}_{i+1}$) is computed from $\mathbb{K}_i$ (resp. $\mathbb{L}_i$) from $i = 0$ to $i = R - 1$ step by step to evaluate R-round ciphers. Each node in the depth level i corresponds to each bitvector in $\mathbb{K}_i$ and $\mathbb{L}_i$. When the block length is large, the sizes of $\mathbb{K}_i$ and $\mathbb{L}_i$ increase explosively. Therefore, we cannot manage all nodes, and the in breadth-first search algorithm becomes impractical.

MILP Modeling for Conventional Division Property. Xiang et al. showed that a mixed integer linear programming (MILP) can efficiently evaluate the propagation of the conventional division property [9]. First, they introduced the *division trail* as follows.

Definition 3 (Division Trail). *Let $\mathcal{D}_{\mathbb{K}_i}$ be the division property of the input for the ith round function. Let us consider the propagation of the division property $\{k\} \overset{\text{def}}{=} \mathbb{K}_0 \rightarrow \mathbb{K}_1 \rightarrow \mathbb{K}_2 \rightarrow \cdots \rightarrow \mathbb{K}_r$. Moreover, for any bitvector $k_{i+1}^* \in \mathbb{K}_{i+1}$, there must exist a bitvector $k_i^* \in \mathbb{K}_i$ such that k_i^* can propagate to k_{i+1}^* by the propagation rule of the division property. Furthermore, for $(k_0, k_1, \ldots, k_r) \in (\mathbb{K}_0 \times \mathbb{K}_1 \times \cdots \times \mathbb{K}_r)$ if k_i can propagate to k_{i+1} for all $i \in \{0, 1, \ldots, r - 1\}$, we call $(k_0 \rightarrow k_1 \rightarrow \cdots \rightarrow k_r)$ an r-round division trail.*

Let E_k be the target r-round iterated cipher. If we can prove that there is no division trail $k_0 \xrightarrow{E_k} e_i$, which is an unit vector whose ith element is 1, the ith bit of r-round ciphertexts is always balanced.

Using MILP we can efficiently solve this problem. Three fundamental operations, i.e., copy, xor, and and, can be modeled by using MILP. We generate an MILP model that covers all division trails, and the MILP solver evaluates the feasibility whether there are division trails from the input division property to the output one or not. If the solver guarantees that there is no division trail, we can prove that the target bit is balanced.

MILP Modeling for Variant Three-Subset Division Property. Unlike the conventional division property, evaluating the propagation of the three-subset division property is difficult. The main difficulty comes from the cancellation property in Rule 3 (xor) and the unknown-producing property. The cancellation property implies that just focusing on the single trail is not enough, and the unknown-producing property implies that we need to know $\mathbb{L}_i$ when the secret key is XORed.

Hu and Wang tackled this problem [16], and they built the so-called variant three-subset division property, where only the cancellation property is neglected from the original one. The accuracy of the variant three-subset division property is worse than the original three-subset division property because of this neglect. However, they showed that such a variant is still useful and it is at least more accurate than the conventional division property.

Pruning Technique for Three-Subset Division Property. The technique for the accurate modeling for three-subset division property was proposed by Wang et al. [17]. The new idea is the combination between the breadth-first search algorithm and an intelligent MILP-based pruning technique. The first step of their algorithm is the same as the breadth-first search algorithm. The pruning technique is applied to $\mathbb{K}_i$ and $\mathbb{L}_i$ for every i. For all $\ell \in \mathbb{L}_i$, we create an MILP model of the conventional division property for the $(R - i)$-round cipher, and evaluate the feasibility of the division trail from ℓ to the observed bit. Then, the bitvector ℓ can be removed from $\mathbb{L}_i$ if it is infeasible. We also apply the similar pruning technique to $\mathbb{K}_i$. As a result, this pruning technique allows the sizes of $\mathbb{K}_i$ and $\mathbb{L}_i$ to decrease dramatically, and the evaluation of the three-subset division property becomes possible.

They applied this new modeling technique to Simon, Simeck, PRESENT, RECTANGLE, LBlock, and TWINE. Moreover, they also applied this algorithm to the cube attack against Trivium. As a result, they showed that the 839-round key recovery attack proposed in [12] degenerates into a zero-sum distinguisher.

3 Cube Attack and Division Property

3.1 Cube Attack

The cube attack was proposed by Dinur and Shamir in [18]. A cipher is regarded as a public Boolean function whose input is divided into two parts: secret variables $\boldsymbol{x}$ and public ones $\boldsymbol{v}$. Then, the algebraic normal form of the Boolean function is represented as

$$f(\boldsymbol{x}, \boldsymbol{v}) = \bigoplus_{\boldsymbol{u} \in \mathbb{F}_2^{n+m}} a_{\boldsymbol{u}}^f (\boldsymbol{x} \| \boldsymbol{v})^{\boldsymbol{u}}.$$

For a set of indices $I = i_1, i_2, \ldots, i_{|I|} \subset \{1, 2, \ldots, m\}$, which is referred as cube indices, t_I denotes a monomial as $t_I = v_{i_1} \cdot v_{i_2} \cdots v_{i_{|I|}}$. The Boolean function $f(\boldsymbol{x}, \boldsymbol{v})$ can also be decomposed as

$$f(\boldsymbol{x}, \boldsymbol{v}) = t_I \cdot p(\boldsymbol{x}, \boldsymbol{v}) + q(\boldsymbol{x}, \boldsymbol{v}).$$

Let C_I, which is referred as a cube (defined by I), be a set of $2^{|I|}$ values where variables in $\{v_{i_1}, v_{i_2}, \ldots, v_{i_{|I|}}\}$ are taking all possible combinations of values, and all remaining variables are fixed to any value. The sum of f over all values of the cube C_I is

$$\bigoplus_{C_I} f(\boldsymbol{x}, \boldsymbol{v}) = \bigoplus_{C_I} t_I \cdot p(\boldsymbol{x}, \boldsymbol{v}) + \bigoplus_{C_I} q(\boldsymbol{x}, \boldsymbol{v}) = p(\boldsymbol{x}, \boldsymbol{v})$$

because $t_I = 1$ for only one case in C_I and each term in $q(\boldsymbol{x}, \boldsymbol{v})$ misses at least one variable from $\{v_{i_1}, v_{i_2}, \ldots, v_{i_{|I|}}\}$. Then, $p(\boldsymbol{x}, \boldsymbol{v})$ is called the superpoly of the cube C_I, and the goal of the cube attack is to recover the superpoly.

3.2 Division Property and Cube Attack

The division property is formally developed as the generalization of the integral property, and it has been initially used to evaluate the integral distinguisher. When the division property is applied to the cube attack [11], the authors showed the relationship between the division property and the algebraic normal form of public functions.

Lemma 1 ([11]). *Let $f(x)$ be a polynomial from $\mathbb{F}_2^n$ to $\mathbb{F}_2$ and $a_u^f \in \mathbb{F}_2$ $(u \in \mathbb{F}_2^n)$ be the ANF coefficients. Let k be an n-dimensional bitvector. Then, assuming that the initial division property $\mathcal{D}_{\{k\}}^{1^n}$ cannot propagate to $\mathcal{D}_1^1$ after evaluating the function f, a_u^f is always 0 for $u \succeq k$.*

Even if the function f is complicated and practically impossible to describe the algebraic normal form, the partial information can be recovered by using the division property. The division property based cube attack first evaluates secret variables that are not involved in the superpoly. Let $\bar{J}$ be the set of such secret variables, and the set $J := \{1, 2, \ldots, n\} \setminus \bar{J}$ denotes secret variables that could be involved in the superpoly. Then, we can recover the superpoly with the time complexity of $2^{|I|+|J|}$.

In the ANF of the superpoly recovered by the division property, if certain coefficients are 0, it is guaranteed that these coefficients are 0. However, if certain coefficients are 1, they cannot be guaranteed to be 1. Therefore, only using the division property does not allow us to recover the exact algebraic normal form. This limitation of the division property causes the so-called strong and weak assumptions in [11], i.e., they assume $a_u^f = 1$ when the division property $\mathcal{D}_u^{1^n}$ can propagate to $\mathcal{D}_1^1$. When these assumptions do not hold, the superpoly can be much simpler than estimated, and in the extreme case, the superpoly becomes a constant function. Then, the key recovery attack degenerates into the distinguishing attack. Such degeneration is reported in [19] and [17], where the key-recovery attack against 839-round TRIVIUM in [12] degenerates into the distinguishing attack.

3.3 Three-Subset Division Property and Cube Attack

The authors in [17] showed that these assumptions can be removed by using three-subset division property. Proposition 4 in [17] addresses this problem, but a more simple formula is enough for our application.

Lemma 2 (Simple case of [17]). *Let $f(x)$ be a polynomial from $\mathbb{F}_2^n$ to $\mathbb{F}_2$ and $a_u^f \in \mathbb{F}_2$ $(u \in \mathbb{F}_2^n)$ be the ANF coefficients. Let ℓ be an n-dimensional bitvector. Then, assuming that the initial division property $\mathcal{D}_{\phi, \{\ell\}}^{1^n}$ propagates to $\mathcal{D}_{\phi, 1}^1$ after evaluating the function f, $a_\ell^f = 1$.*

Note that we only consider the case that the function f is a public function. Then, since the function f is not key-dependent, the propagation for $\mathbb{K}$ and that for $\mathbb{L}$ are perfectly independent. In other words, we no longer consider the propagation for $\mathbb{K}$ because the initial division property is empty ϕ.

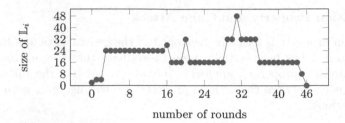

Fig. 1. Size of $\mathbb{L}_i$ after applying the pruning technique. Check if the superpoly involves $K[61]$ in the cube shown in [12].

4   Three-Subset Division Property w/o Unknown Subset

4.1   Motivation and Limitation of Pruning Technique

Our initial motivation is to verify the potential of the state-of-the-art modeling technique with the pruning technique [17]. They claimed that the exact superpoly can be recovered, but the application for the largest number of rounds was the degeneration from the key-recovery attack to a zero-sum distinguisher.[1] The natural question is why they did not show improved key-recovery attacks. Since such a degeneration implies unexpectedly simpler superpoly, we can expect that the cube described in [12] leads to a key-recovery attack for 840-round TRIVIUM. If we can recover the superpoly of such a cube, we can directly improve the key-recovery attack against Trivium. Therefore, we implemented their algorithm by ourselves and verified whether or not we can recover the actual superpoly of 840-round Trivium. As a result, in order to make the breadth-first search algorithm with pruning technique feasible, it requires an assumption that almost all elements in $\mathbb{L}_i$ must be pruned.

We first verify that the breadth-first search algorithm with pruning technique is feasible to prove that the 839-round cube attack shown in [12] cannot recover any secret key bit. In this attack, the number of cube bits is 78, where all IV bits except for $IV[34]$ and $IV[47]$ are active and these constant bits are fixed as $(IV[34], IV[47]) = (0, 1)$. Then, the conventional division property shows that a secret key bit $K[61]$ could be involved in the superpoly [12]. We now evaluate the same cube by using the three-subset division property. According to [17], the corresponding initial property $\mathbb{L}_0$ consists of sixteen 288-bit bitvectors, where 1 is assigned for cube bits and involved-key bit, any value is assigned for four constant-1 bits ($s_{93+47}, s_{286}, s_{287}, s_{288}$), and 0 is assigned for other bits. We applied the pruning technique to sixteen bitvectors, and only two bitvectors are remaining and the other fourteen bitvecotrs can be removed. We applied the

---

[1] They showed that the superpoly of 842-round TRIVIUM can be recovered with the complexity 2^{32}, but the unit of the complexity is the breadth-first search algorithm with pruning technique. Even one unit requires to solve many MILPs, and the complexity of the algorithm is not bounded. Therefore, unlike the previous theoretical cube attack [11,12], we cannot guarantee that it is faster than the exhaustive search.

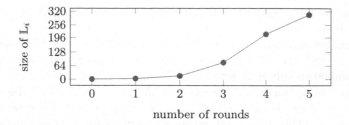

Fig. 2. Size of $\mathbb{L}_i$ after applying the pruning technique. Check if the superpoly for 840-round TRIVIUM has constant-1 term.

pruning technique in every round, and Fig. 1 summarizes the size of $\mathbb{L}_i$ for the ith round. The size of $\mathbb{L}_i$ is bounded by a reasonable range and all bitvectors are removed in 46 rounds. It implies that the actual superpoly does not involve $K[61]$.

We next try whether or not the breadth-first search algorithm with pruning technique is available to attack 840-round TRIVIUM. We use a cube similar to the one above, but non-cube bits $(IV[34], IV[47])$ are fixed to 0 in order for the superpoly to be more simplified. Before we recover all monomials in the superpoly, as the first step, we aim to identify if the superpoly has the constant-1 term. In other words, we evaluate whether or not 840-round TRIVIUM has a monomial $\prod_{i\in\{1,2,...,80\}\backslash\{34,47\}} s_{93+i}$. Figure 2 shows the increase of $\mathbb{L}_i$. The more the size of $\mathbb{L}_i$ increases, the more MILP instances we need to solve. We used Gurobi Optimizer on a server (Intel Xeon CPU E5-2699 v3, 18 cores, 128 GB RAM), and we spent almost two weeks to even draw Fig. 2, where only five rounds are evaluated. To recover the superpoly for 841-round TRIVIUM, we need to finish this algorithm and apply the same algorithm to all other monomials that could be involved. Therefore, we conclude that the breadth-first search algorithm with pruning technique cannot recover the superpoly for 841-round TRIVIUM in reasonable time. It is inefficient unless the size of $\mathbb{L}_i$ is bounded by reasonable size, e.g., 100, for all i.

4.2 Three-Subset Division Property Without Unknown Subset

The pruning technique is not always efficient to evaluate the cube attack, and we cannot improve the key-recovery attack against Trivium due to the explosive increase of $|\mathbb{L}_i|$. To address this problem, we need to develop a new modeling technique. Two properties, i.e., the unknown-producing property and the cancellation property, make it difficult to model the three-subset division property directly. Thus, we first explain how to overcome these properties.

Unknown-Producing Property. Due to the unknown-producing property, we need to evaluate the accurate $\mathbb{L}$ when the secret key is XORed. Otherwise, we cannot generate accurate bitvectors that are newly inserted to $\mathbb{K}$. Unfortunately, no efficient model is known to handle the accurate intermediate $\mathbb{L}$ by using automatic tools.

The simplest solution to address this property is the use of three-subset division property without unknown subset. Recall the definition of the division property. The unknown subset is defined as the set of $\boldsymbol{u}$ in which a parity $\bigoplus_{x \in X} \boldsymbol{x}^{\boldsymbol{u}}$ is unknown, where "unknown" means that the parity depends on the secret key. The unknown subset is used to evaluate the key-dependent function such as in block ciphers. On the other hand, when we evaluate the ANF coefficients of the public function, we do not need to use the unknown subset. At first glance, it looks like the application is restricted to public functions, but it does not matter in the application to the cube attack. Besides, if the key-schedule function is also included into the evaluated function, we can regard the block cipher as the public function.

Cancellation Property. Another property that we need to address is the cancellation property. Our idea to overcome this property is to count the number of solutions by using an MILP instead of evaluating the feasibility[2]. To understand our modeling, we introduce the following slightly modified definition. Note that this definition is equivalent to the definition of the three-subset division property without unknown subset. It is introduced only for ease of understanding of our modeling, and by itself does not yield new insight.

Definition 4 (Modified three-subset division property). *Let $\mathbb{X}$ be a multiset whose elements take a value of $\mathbb{F}_2^m$. Let $\tilde{\mathbb{L}}$ be also a **multiset** whose elements take a value of $\mathbb{F}_2^m$. When the multiset $\mathbb{X}$ has the modified three-subset division property (shortly $\mathcal{T}_{\tilde{\mathbb{L}}}^{1^m}$), it fulfils the following conditions:*

$$\bigoplus_{\boldsymbol{x} \in \mathbb{X}} \boldsymbol{x}^{\boldsymbol{u}} = \begin{cases} 1 & \text{if there are odd-number of } \boldsymbol{u}\text{'s in } \tilde{\mathbb{L}}, \\ 0 & \text{otherwise.} \end{cases}$$

Note that $\boldsymbol{x}^{\boldsymbol{u}} = \prod_{i=1}^m x[i]^{u[i]}$.

Instead of considering the cancellation property, we count the number of appearances in each bitvector in the multiset $\tilde{\mathbb{L}}$ and check its parity. Since we do not need to consider the cancellation property, the modeling for xor is simplified as follows:

Rule 3' (xor). Let F be a function compressed by an XOR, where the input $\boldsymbol{x} \in \mathbb{F}_2^m$, and the output is calculated as $(x[1] \oplus x[2], x[3], \ldots, x[m])$. Let $\mathbb{X}$ and $\mathbb{Y}$ be the input and output multisets, respectively. Assuming that $\mathbb{X}$ has $\mathcal{T}_{\tilde{\mathbb{L}}}^{1^m}$, $\mathbb{Y}$ has $\mathcal{T}_{\tilde{\mathbb{L}}'}^{1^{m-1}}$, where $\tilde{\mathbb{L}}'$ is computed from all $\boldsymbol{\ell} \in \mathbb{L}$ s.t. $(\ell[1], \ell[2]) = (0,0)$, $(1,0)$, or $(0,1)$ as

$$\tilde{\mathbb{L}}' \leftarrow (\ell[1] + \ell[2], \ell[3], \ell[4], \ldots, \ell[m]).$$

---

[2] The same idea was already described in [17] although the authors did not use the idea in their model.

Here, $\tilde{\mathbb{L}}$ and $\tilde{\mathbb{L}}'$ are multisets, and $\tilde{\mathbb{L}}' \leftarrow \ell$ allows the same ℓ is stored into $\tilde{\mathbb{L}}'$ several times.

We no longer use insertions with the cancellation property, and the produced bitvector is always inserted to a multiset. We introduce a *three-subset division trail*, which is similar to the division trail.

Definition 5 (Three-Subset Division Trail). *Let $\mathcal{T}_{\tilde{\mathbb{L}}_i}$ be the three-subset division property of the input for the ith round function. Let us consider the propagation of the three-subset division property $\{\ell\} \stackrel{\text{def}}{=} \tilde{\mathbb{L}}_0 \rightarrow \tilde{\mathbb{L}}_1 \rightarrow \tilde{\mathbb{L}}_2 \rightarrow \cdots \rightarrow \tilde{\mathbb{L}}_r$. Moreover, for any bitvector $\ell_{i+1}^* \in \tilde{\mathbb{L}}_{i+1}$, there must exist a bitvector $\ell_i^* \in \tilde{\mathbb{L}}_i$ such that ℓ_i^* can propagate to ℓ_{i+1}^* by the propagation rule of the modified three-subset division property. Furthermore, for $(\ell_0, \ell_1, \dots, \ell_r) \in (\tilde{\mathbb{L}}_0 \times \tilde{\mathbb{L}}_1 \times \cdots \times \tilde{\mathbb{L}}_r)$ if ℓ_i can propagate to ℓ_{i+1} for all $i \in \{0, 1, \dots, r-1\}$, we call $(\ell_0 \rightarrow \ell_1 \rightarrow \cdots \rightarrow \ell_r)$ an r-round three-subset division trail.*

The modified three-subset division property implies that we do not need to consider the cancellation property in every round. We just enumerate the number of three-subset division trails $\ell \stackrel{f}{\rightarrow} e_i$. When the number of trails is odd, the algebraic normal form of f contains x^ℓ. Otherwise, it does not contain x^ℓ.

In summary, removing the unknown subset allows us to skip recovering the accurate $\mathbb{L}$ when the secret key is XORed. Using multisets instead of sets allows us to handle the cancellation property by automatic tools such as MILP easily.

4.3 New Modeling Method

Unlike the pruning technique in [17], our method no longer uses the breadth-first search algorithm and it just uses an MILP model. The previous algorithm uses the MILP model for the conventional division property. On the other hand, we use the MILP model for the modified three-subset division property, and all feasible solutions are enumerated by using an off-the-shelf MILP solver[3].

Proposition 1 (MILP Model for copy). *Let* a $\xrightarrow{\text{copy}}$ (b_1, b_2) *be a three-subset division trail of* copy. *The following inequalities are sufficient to describe the propagation of the modified three-subset division property for* copy.

$$\begin{cases} \mathcal{M}.var \leftarrow a, b_1, b_2 \text{ as binary.} \\ \mathcal{M}.con \leftarrow b_1 + b_2 \geq a \\ \mathcal{M}.con \leftarrow a \geq b_1 \\ \mathcal{M}.con \leftarrow a \geq b_2 \end{cases}$$

---

[3] Our model is very similar to the model for variant three-subset division property proposed in [16], but there are two differences. First, we do not treat the unknown subset. Second, the goal of our model is to enumerate all feasible solutions, but the goal in [16] is to evaluate the feasibility of the model.

When the or operation is supported in the MILP solver, e.g., Gurobi optimizer supports the or operation, we can simply write $\mathcal{M}.con \leftarrow a = b_1 \vee b_2$. Unlike the conventional division property, we need to allow the following propagation $1 \xrightarrow{copy} (1,1)$. Otherwise, we miss any feasible solutions.

Proposition 2 (MILP Model for and). *Let* $(a_1, a_2, \ldots, a_m) \xrightarrow{and} b$ *be a three-subset division trail of* and. *The following inequalities are sufficient to describe the propagation of the modified three-subset division property for* and.

$$\begin{cases} \mathcal{M}.var \leftarrow a_1, a_2, \ldots, a_m, b \text{ as binary.} \\ \mathcal{M}.con \leftarrow b = a_i \text{ for all } i \in \{1, 2, \ldots, m\} \end{cases}$$

Some feasible propagation on the conventional division property becomes infeasible. For example, $(1, 1, 0) \xrightarrow{and} 1$ is feasible for the conventional division property, but it is not so in the modified three-subset division property.

Proposition 3 (MILP Model for xor). *Let* $(a_1, a_2, \ldots, a_m) \xrightarrow{xor} b$ *be a three-subset division trail of* xor. *The following inequalities are sufficient to describe the propagation of the modified three-subset division property for* xor.

$$\begin{cases} \mathcal{M}.var \leftarrow a_1, a_2, \ldots, a_m, b \text{ as binary.} \\ \mathcal{M}.con \leftarrow a_1 + a_2 + \cdots + a_m = b \end{cases}$$

Note that this is the same as the one for the conventional division property.

While the goal of the previous method is to find one feasible solution or to prove its infeasibility, the goal of our method is to enumerate all feasible solutions. Three Propositions are enough to represent any cipher, but such a straightforward model sometimes increases the number of feasible solutions explosively. A more clever model is sometimes required to avoid the explosive increase of feasible (but redundant) solutions, and we discuss this in Sect. 6 in detail.

4.4   Algorithm to Recover ANF Coefficients of Public Function

Let f be a public Boolean function whose input denotes an n-bit string $x = (x[1], x[2], \ldots, x[n])$, and let it consist of the iteration of simple public functions. Then, the algebraic normal form of f is represented as

$$f(x) = \bigoplus_{u \in \mathbb{F}_2^n} a_u^f x^u.$$

Our goal is to recover the value of a_u^f for some u. We first prepare an MILP model $\mathcal{M}$ that represents the modified three-subset division property of the function f. Algorithm 1 shows the algorithm to recover an ANF coefficient a_u^f. The initial modified three-subset division property is defined by u, and the number of feasible solutions is enumerated by using the MILP solver. Note that

---

Algorithm 1. Algorithm to recover an ANF coefficient a_u^f

1: **procedure** attackFramework($\mathcal{M}$, u)
2:     Let $\mathbf{x_i}$ be an MILP variable of $\mathcal{M}$ corresponding to the ith input of f.
3:     $\mathcal{M}.con \leftarrow \mathbf{x_i} = 1$ for all i s.t. $u[i] = 1$.
4:     $\mathcal{M}.con \leftarrow \mathbf{x_i} = 0$ for all i s.t. $u[i] = 0$.
5:     solve MILP model $\mathcal{M}$ and enumerate all feasible solutions
6:     **if** the number of solutions is odd **then**
7:         $a_u^f = 1$
8:     **else**
9:         $a_u^f = 0$
10:    **end if**
11: **end procedure**

Algorithm 2. Algorithm to recover the superpoly

1: **procedure** attackFramework($\mathcal{M}$, I, (C_0))
2:     Let $\mathbf{x_i}$ be an MILP variable of $\mathcal{M}$ corresponding to the ith secret variable.
3:     Let $\mathbf{v_i}$ be an MILP variable of $\mathcal{M}$ corresponding to the ith public variable.
4:     $\mathcal{M}.con \leftarrow \mathbf{v_i} = 1$ for all $i \in I$
5:     $\mathcal{M}.con \leftarrow \mathbf{v_i} = 0$ for all $i \in C_0$
6:     prepare a hash table J whose key is $(n + m)$-bit string and value is counter.
7:     solve MILP model $\mathcal{M}$ and enumerate all feasible solutions
8:     **for all feasible solutions do**
9:         get $\boldsymbol{u} = (\mathbf{x_1}, \mathbf{x_2}, \ldots, \mathbf{x_n}, \mathbf{v_1}, \mathbf{v_2}, \ldots, \mathbf{v_m})$ in every found solution
10:        increase $J[\boldsymbol{u}]$ by 1
11:    **end for**
12:    prepare a polynomial $p = 0$
13:    **for all** u whose $J[\boldsymbol{u}]$ is an odd number **do**
14:        $p = p + (\boldsymbol{x}\|\boldsymbol{v})^u$.
15:    **end for**
16:    **return** p/t_I
17: **end procedure**

---

the efficiency of Algorithm 1 depends on the number of feasible solutions. When there are too many solutions, it is practically impossible to enumerate all feasible solutions. In other words, the necessary condition that Algorithm 1 stops by reasonable time is that the number of feasible solutions is bounded by reasonable size, e.g., at most 2^{16}.

While Algorithm 1 is very simple, it is less efficient for the application to the cube attack because we need to recover all monomials in the superpoly. The number of monomials that Algorithm 1 can evaluate is only one. Therefore, we need to repeat Algorithm 1 many times while changing the input $\boldsymbol{u}$ until all monomials are recovered exactly. One of the advantages of our modeling method is that we can simply extend the algorithm to recover the superpoly, and the extended algorithm uses only one MILP model. Algorithm 2 shows the dedicated algorithm to recover the superpoly. Unlike Algorithm 1, the initial division property is not determined and only the part corresponding to the cube bits is fixed to 1. When we enumerate all feasible solutions under such constraints, all monomials that could be involved in the superpoly can be found as the feasible solutions. The third input C_0 is an option to declare that some public variables are fixed to 0. Specific attention should be paid to the situation that $C_0 = \phi$. In this case, Algorithm 2 gives the ANF of $p(\boldsymbol{x}, \boldsymbol{v})$ consisting of all secret and non-cube public variables. In other words, we do not need to specify the assignment of non-cube public variables in advance. This is an obvious advantage of our method over the existing breadth-first search algorithm with pruning technique. On the other hand, when the assignment of non-cube public variables is determined in advance, C_0 should be set because it decreases the number of three-subset division trails and increases the efficiency of the algorithm.

As far as we applied these algorithms to the cube attack against TRIVIUM or Grain-128AEAD, Algorithm 2 is not only simpler but also more efficient than the iteration of Algorithm 1. Unfortunately, we cannot say the explicit reason because it depends on the inside of MILP solvers. As one observation, many three-subset division trails with different initial division property share the same trail in the last several rounds. Therefore, we expect that their trails are efficiently enumerated in Algorithm 2. On the other hand, the iteration of Algorithm 1 needs to find the shared part of trails every time.

5   Improved Cube Attacks Against Trivium

5.1   Specification of Trivium and Its MILP Model

TRIVIUM [23] is an NLFSR-based stream cipher, and the internal state is represented by a 288-bit state $(s_1, s_2, \ldots, s_{288})$. The 80-bit secret key K is loaded to the first register, and the 80-bit initialization vector IV is loaded to the second register. The other state bits are set to 0 except the last three bits in the third register. Namely, the initial state bits are represented as

$$(s_1, s_2, \ldots, s_{93}) = (K[1], K[2], \ldots, K[80], 0, \ldots, 0),$$
$$(s_{94}, s_{95}, \ldots, s_{177}) = (IV[1], IV[2], \ldots, IV[80], 0, \ldots, 0),$$
$$(s_{178}, s_{279}, \ldots, s_{288}) = (0, 0, \ldots, 0, 1, 1, 1).$$

The pseudo code of the update function is given as follows.

$$t_1 \leftarrow s_{66} \oplus s_{93}, \qquad t_2 \leftarrow s_{162} \oplus s_{177}, \qquad t_3 \leftarrow s_{243} \oplus s_{288},$$
$$z \leftarrow t_1 \oplus t_2 \oplus t_3,$$
$$t_1 \leftarrow t_1 \oplus s_{91}s_{92} \oplus s_{171}, \quad t_2 \leftarrow t_2 \oplus s_{175}s_{176} \oplus s_{264}, \quad t_3 \leftarrow t_3 \oplus s_{286}s_{287} \oplus s_{69},$$

where z denotes the key stream. The state of the next round is computed as

$$(s_1, s_2, \ldots, s_{93}) \leftarrow (t_3, s_1, \ldots, s_{92}),$$
$$(s_{94}, s_{95}, \ldots, s_{177}) \leftarrow (t_1, s_{94}, \ldots, s_{176}),$$
$$(s_{178}, s_{279}, \ldots, s_{288}) \leftarrow (t_2, s_{178}, \ldots, s_{287}).$$

Algorithm 3. Model for modified three-subset division property for TRIVIUM

1: **procedure** TriviumCore($\mathcal{M}, x_1, \ldots, x_{288}, i_1, i_2, i_3, i_4, i_5$)
2:     $\mathcal{M}.var \leftarrow y_{i_1}, y_{i_2}, y_{i_3}, y_{i_4}, y_{i_5}, z_1, z_2, z_3, z_4, a$ as binary
3:     $\mathcal{M}.con \leftarrow x_{i_j} = y_{i_j} \vee z_j$ for all $j \in \{1, 2, 3, 4\}$
4:     $\mathcal{M}.con \leftarrow a = z_3$
5:     $\mathcal{M}.con \leftarrow a = z_4$
6:     $\mathcal{M}.con \leftarrow y_{i_5} = x_{i_5} + a + z_1 + z_2$
7:     **for all** $i \in \{1, 2, \ldots, 288\}$ w/o i_1, i_2, i_3, i_4, i_5 **do**
8:         $y_i = x_i$
9:     **end for**
10:    **return** $(\mathcal{M}, y_1, \ldots, y_{288})$
11: **end procedure**

1: **procedure** TriviumEval(round R)
2:     Prepare empty MILP Model $\mathcal{M}$
3:     $\mathcal{M}.var \leftarrow s_i^0$ for $i \in \{1, 2, \ldots, 288\}$
4:     **for** $i = 81$ to 93 and $i = 93 + 80$ to 285 **do**
5:         $\mathcal{M}.con \leftarrow s_i^0 = 0$
6:     **end for**
7:     **for** $r = 1$ to R **do**
8:         $(\mathcal{M}, x_1, \ldots, x_{288}) = $ TriviumCore$(\mathcal{M}, s_1^{r-1}, \ldots, s_{288}^{r-1}, 66, 171, 91, 92, 93)$
9:         $(\mathcal{M}, y_1, \ldots, y_{288}) = $ TriviumCore$(\mathcal{M}, x_1, \ldots, x_{288}, 162, 264, 175, 176, 177)$
10:        $(\mathcal{M}, z_1, \ldots, z_{288}) = $ TriviumCore$(\mathcal{M}, y_1, \ldots, y_{288}, 243, 69, 286, 287, 288)$
11:        $(s_1^r, \ldots, s_{288}^r) = (z_{288}, z_1, \ldots, z_{287})$
12:     **end for**
13:    **for all** $i \in \{1, 2, \ldots, 288\}$ w/o $66, 93, 162, 177, 243, 288$ **do**
14:        $\mathcal{M}.con \leftarrow s_i^R = 0$
15:    **end for**
16:    $\mathcal{M}.con \leftarrow (s_{66}^R + s_{93}^R + s_{162}^R + s_{177}^R + s_{243}^R + s_{288}^R) = 1$
17:    **return** $\mathcal{M}$
18: **end procedure**

In the initialization, the state is updated 1152 times without producing an output. After the initialization, one bit key stream is produced by every update function.

MILP Model. TriviumEval in Algorithm 3 generates a model $\mathcal{M}$ as the input of Algorithm 1 or 2, and all three-subset division trails are included as feasible solutions of this model $\mathcal{M}$. TriviumCore in Algorithm 3 generates MILP variables and constraints of the update function for each register.

5.2   Practical Verification

To verify our new algorithm, we select the same parameters as the one in the previous works [11, 12]. Example 1 takes parameters from [11] and set the empty set ϕ for C_0. Then, Algorithm 2 recovers the algebraic normal form of $p(\boldsymbol{x}, \boldsymbol{v})$ involving all key and non-cube IV bits.

Table 3. The monomial $(x\|v)^u/t_I$'s and their $J[u]$'s corresponding to Example 1

Parity	$J[u]$	$(x\|v)^u/t_I$	Parity	$J[u]$	$(x\|v)^u/t_I$
0	2	$x_{60}v_{22}$	1	1	v_9v_{20}
1	1	$x_{60}v_{19}v_{20}$	1	1	$v_6v_7v_8v_{20}$
1	1	$x_{60}v_{20}$	0	2	$v_{22}v_{72}$
1	1	$x_{60}v_6v_{20}$	1	1	v_7v_8
1	1	$x_{60}v_7$	1	1	$v_6v_9v_{20}$
1	1	$v_7v_8v_{19}v_{20}$	1	1	$v_{19}v_{20}v_{72}$
0	2	$v_7v_8v_{22}$	1	1	v_7v_9
1	1	$v_9v_{19}v_{20}$	1	1	$v_{20}v_{72}$
0	2	v_9v_{22}	1	1	$v_6v_{20}v_{72}$
1	1	$v_7v_8v_{20}$	1	1	v_7v_{72}

Example 1 (**Parameters from** [11]). We let $I = \{1, 11, 21, 31, 41, 51, 61, 71\}$ and evaluate z_{590}. We first run Algorithm 3 as $\mathcal{M} \leftarrow \texttt{TriviumEval}(590)$ and get the MILP model based three-subset division property. Then, we set $C_0 = \phi$ and acquire $p(x, v)$ by running Algorithm 2 as $p(x, v) \leftarrow \texttt{attackFramework}(I, \mathcal{M}, \phi)$. The monomial $(x\|v)^u/t_I$'s along with their $J[u]$'s are listed in Table 3. The ANF of $p(x, v)$ can therefore be determined as

$$p(x) = x_{60}(v_{19}v_{20} + v_{20} + v_6v_{20} + v_7)$$
$$+ (v_7v_8v_{19}v_{20} + v_9v_{19}v_{20} + v_7v_8v_{20} + v_9v_{20} + v_6v_7v_8v_{20} + v_7v_8$$
$$+ v_6v_9v_{20} + v_{19}v_{20}v_{72} + v_7v_9v_{20}v_{72} + v_6v_{20}v_{72} + v_7v_{72})$$

5.3   Cube Attacks Against 840-Round and 841-Round Trivium

To demonstrate that our modeling method is more efficient than the previous method, we applied it to TRIVIUM. For R-round TRIVIUM, the model $\mathcal{M}$ is generated as $\mathcal{M} \leftarrow \texttt{TriviumEval}(R)$ by calling Algorithm 3. Then, we set all non-cube IV bits to constant 0, i.e., for arbitrary cube I, the corresponding parameter C_0 is defined as the complement of I: $C_0 \leftarrow \{0, \ldots, 80\}\backslash I$. With such $\mathcal{M}$, I and C_0, the superpoly is defined as $p(x) \leftarrow \texttt{attackFramework}(\mathcal{M}, I, C_0)$ by calling Algorithm 2. As a result, we can successfully recover the superpoly of 840-round and 841-round TRIVIUM. In other words, we show key-recover attacks against 840- and 841-round TRIVIUM without any assumption. The detailed parameters of the two attacks are as follows:

Superpoly of 840-Round Trivium. We used the same cube as the one shown in Sect. 4.1, i.e., the cube indices are

$$I = \{1, 2, \ldots, 33, 35, 36, \ldots, 46, 48, 49, \ldots, 80\},$$

and $IV[34] = IV[47] = 0$. Note that the previous algorithm cannot recover the corresponding superpoly as we already showed in Sect. 4.1. As a result, 12,909 feasible three-subset division trails are enumerated, and $J[u]$ in Algorithm 2 is non zero for 228 different u's. Out of 228 u's, there are 67 u's whose $J[u]$ is an odd number. In other words, the superpoly is represented as the sum of 67 monomials, and the following

$$
\begin{aligned}
p(x) = {} & 1 + x_{80} + x_{79} + x_{79}x_{80} + x_{78}x_{79} + x_{76}x_{77} + x_{75}x_{76}x_{78} + x_{75}x_{76}x_{77} \\
& + x_{70} + x_{68} + x_{68}x_{80} + x_{68}x_{79}x_{80} + x_{68}x_{78}x_{79} + x_{68}x_{69} + x_{66}x_{67} \\
& + x_{66}x_{67}x_{80} + x_{66}x_{67}x_{79}x_{80} + x_{66}x_{67}x_{78}x_{79} + x_{65} + x_{64}x_{66} + x_{64}x_{65} \\
& + x_{63}x_{64} + x_{59}x_{63} + x_{54}x_{68} + x_{54}x_{66}x_{67} + x_{53}x_{68} + x_{53}x_{66}x_{67} + x_{52} \\
& + x_{52}x_{53} + x_{51}x_{77} + x_{51}x_{75}x_{76} + x_{51}x_{52} + x_{50}x_{78} + x_{50}x_{76}x_{77} + x_{50}x_{51} \\
& + x_{43} + x_{41} + x_{41}x_{80} + x_{41}x_{79}x_{80} + x_{41}x_{78}x_{79} + x_{41}x_{54} + x_{41}x_{53} + x_{39} \\
& + x_{39}x_{64} + x_{38} + x_{37}x_{38} + x_{35}x_{55} + x_{33}x_{34}x_{55} + x_{27} + x_{26} + x_{22}x_{66} \\
& + x_{22}x_{64}x_{65} + x_{22}x_{39} + x_{20}x_{21}x_{66} + x_{20}x_{21}x_{64}x_{65} + x_{20}x_{21}x_{39} + x_{12} \\
& + x_{8}x_{78} + x_{8}x_{77} + x_{8}x_{76}x_{77} + x_{8}x_{75}x_{76} + x_{8}x_{55} + x_{8}x_{51} + x_{8}x_{50} \\
& + x_{1}x_{35} + x_{1}x_{33}x_{34} + x_{1}x_{8}
\end{aligned}
$$

is the recovered superpoly, where $x = (x_1, x_2, \ldots, x_{80})$ denotes the secret key, i.e., $x_i = K[i]$. This superpoly is a balanced Boolean function because there is a monomial x_{12} that is independent of other monomials. Therefore, we can recover 1 bit of information by using 2^{78} data and time complexities. The dominant part of the whole key recovery attack is the exhaustive search after 1-bit key recovery, which is 2^{79} time complexity.

Superpoly of 841-Round Trivium. We next aim to recover the superpoly of 841-round TRIVIUM, but it has too many trails to enumerate all of them. Therefore, we heuristically change cube indices such that the number of trails is not large. As a result, the following cube is considered:

$$
I = \{1, 2, \ldots, 8, 10, 11, \ldots, 78, 80\},
$$

and $IV[9] = IV[79] = 0$. As a result, 30, 177 feasible three-subset division trails are enumerated, and $J[u]$ in Algorithm 2 is non zero for 216 different u's. Out of 216 u's, there are 53 u's whose $J[u]$ is an odd number. In other words, the superpoly $p(x)$ is represented as the sum of 53 monomials, and the following

$$
\begin{aligned}
p(x) = {} & x_{78} + x_{76} + x_{75}x_{76} + x_{74} + x_{74}x_{75} + x_{74}x_{75}x_{77} + x_{74}x_{75}x_{76} + x_{72}x_{73} \\
& + x_{68} + x_{67} + x_{63} + x_{61}x_{62} + x_{59} + x_{59}x_{72} + x_{59}x_{70}x_{71} + x_{59}x_{61} + x_{58} \\
& + x_{58}x_{80} + x_{58}x_{78}x_{79} + x_{58}x_{66} + x_{58}x_{59} + x_{53}x_{58} + x_{51}x_{74} + x_{51}x_{73} \\
& + x_{51}x_{72}x_{73} + x_{51}x_{71}x_{72} + x_{50}x_{76} + x_{50}x_{74}x_{75} + x_{49} + x_{49}x_{77} \\
& + x_{49}x_{75}x_{76} + x_{49}x_{50}x_{74} + x_{49}x_{50}x_{73} + x_{49}x_{50}x_{72}x_{73} + x_{49}x_{50}x_{71}x_{72} \\
& + x_{47} + x_{47}x_{51} + x_{47}x_{49}x_{50} + x_{46}x_{51} + x_{46}x_{49}x_{50} + x_{45}x_{59} + x_{36} + x_{32} \\
& + x_{30}x_{31} + x_{24} + x_{24}x_{74} + x_{24}x_{73} + x_{24}x_{72}x_{73} + x_{24}x_{71}x_{72} + x_{24}x_{47} \\
& + x_{24}x_{46} + x_{9} + x_{5}
\end{aligned}
$$

is the recovered superpoly. This superpoly is also a balanced Boolean function because there is a monomial x_5 that is independent of other monomials. Therefore, we can recover 1 bit of information by using 2^{78} data and time complexities. The dominant part of the whole key recovery attack is the exhaustive search after 1-bit key recovery, which is 2^{79} time complexity.

5.4   Verification of 855-Round Attack from CRYPTO2018 [20]

In CRYPTO2018, a new type of cube attacks was proposed, where a key recovery attack against 855-round TRIVIUM was shown. The authors claimed the following statement.

Statement 1 ([20]). *When $IV[31] = IV[49] = IV[61] = IV[75] = IV[76] = 0$, the degree of $(1 + s_{94}^{210})z_{855}$ is bounded by 70.*

Attackers first guess the part of a secret key involved in s_{94}^{210} and compute the sum of $(1 + s_{94}^{210})z_{855}$ over cubes whose dimension is larger than 70. When the correct key is guessed, the sum must be 0. In other words, if the sum is 1, we can discard the guessed key.

To prove Statement 1, the authors developed a new algorithm to evaluate the upper bound of the degree. However, their algorithm includes some man-made work that is not written in their paper, and a cluster of 600–2400 cores is necessary to run their code. As a result, no one can verify their algorithm and the correctness of Statement 1. The only supportive material is the practical example by using 721-round TRIVIUM[4]. Later, Hao et al. reviewed Statement 1 by using the conventional bit-based division property [24]. They showed that the sum of $(1 + s_{94}^{210})z_{855}$ over 75-dimensional cube could involve all 80 key bits with degree bound 27. According to this result, Hao et al. pointed out that Statement 1 unlikely holds. However, as we already pointed out, the conventional bit-based division property is not always accurate. Therefore, the correctness of Statement 1 becomes an open question.

In comparison with Fu et al.'s algorithm, our algorithm using three-subset division property has three advantages:

- Cheap implementation cost. Our task is to generate an MILP model, and the complicated part is solved by using off-the-shelf MILP solvers. Our verification code using Gurobi C++ API contains about 300 lines.
- Run on the normal PC. We do not need to prepare many clusters.
- Tight bound is proven. Our algorithm can recover the ANF coefficient $a_{\boldsymbol{u}}^f$ for some $\boldsymbol{u}$ accurately.

With such a method, we inspect Statement 1.

---

[4] In [20], the authors showed that the degree of $(1+s_{94}^{290})z_{721}$ is bounded by 32 when the correct s_{94}^{290} is guessed. However, Hao et al. pointed out that the degree is bounded by 32 even if we guess s_{94}^{290} with incorrect secret key, as a consequence we cannot distinguish the correct key from the wrong keys [24]. Response to this error, Fu et al. reproduced the practical example for 721-round TRIVIUM [25].

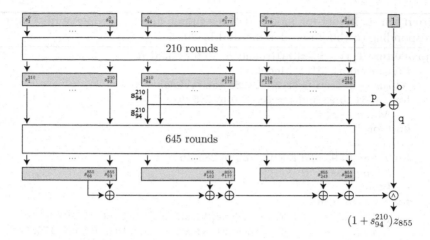

Fig. 3. Overview of new type of cube attack for 855-round Trivium

MILP Model to Verify 855-Round Attack. To verify Statement 1, we consider a circuit shown in Fig. 3 and generate the corresponding MILP model by calling Algorithm 4 as $\mathcal{M} \leftarrow \texttt{TriviumSecEval}(855, 210)$. Corresponding to the setting of [20], we set I as the largest possible cube, i.e., $I = \{1, \ldots, 80\} \setminus \{31, 49, 61, 75, 76\}$, and all non-cube IVs are set to 0, i.e., $C_0 = \{31, 49, 61, 75, 76\}$. Then, with such $\mathcal{M}, I, C_0$, we run Algorithm 2 as $p(\boldsymbol{x}) \leftarrow \texttt{attackFramework}(\mathcal{M}, I, C_0)$ to check whether $p(\boldsymbol{x})$ is constant 0. According to the result by Hao et al. by using the conventional bit-based division property, we first evaluated whether or not $p(\boldsymbol{x})$ has monomials whose degree is 27. Then, the number of appearance $J[\boldsymbol{u}]$ is non-zero for the following two 27-degree monomials

$$\prod_{i \in \{29,30,41,42,44,45,46,47,49,54,55,56,57,59,60,63,66,67,68,69,70,71,72,73,74,75,76\}} x_i,$$

$$\prod_{i \in \{29,30,41,42,43,44,45,46,47,49,54,55,56,57,59,60,63,66,67,69,70,71,72,73,74,75,76\}} x_i,$$

but $J[\boldsymbol{u}] = 2$ for the two monomials above. Therefore, these monomials do not appear in $p(\boldsymbol{x})$. We next evaluated whether or not $p(\boldsymbol{x})$ has monomials whose degree is 26. Since there are quite many candidates of $\boldsymbol{u}$ whose $J[\boldsymbol{u}]$ is non zero, we randomly picked one from these candidates and evaluated the number of trails. As a result, $J[\boldsymbol{u}] = 1$ in the following monomial

$$\prod_{i \in \{40,41,42,53,54,55,56,57,58,61,62,63,65,66,67,68,69,70,71,72,73,74,75,76,78,79\}} x_i.$$

Note that finding one $\boldsymbol{u}$ such that $J[\boldsymbol{u}]$ is an odd number is enough to disprove Statement 1.

Algorithm 4. Model for modified three-subset division property of TRIVIUM corresponding to the Fu et al.'s method in [20]

1: **procedure** TriviumSecEval(round R, sector round R')
2:     Prepare empty MILP Model $\mathcal{M}$
3:     $\mathcal{M}.var \leftarrow s_i^0$ for $i \in \{1, 2, \ldots, 288\}$ and $\mathcal{M}.var \leftarrow o$
4:     **for** $i = 81$ to 93 and $i = 93 + 80$ to 285 **do**
5:         $\mathcal{M}.con \leftarrow s_i^0 = 0$
6:     **end for**
7:     $\mathcal{M}.var \leftarrow o$
8:     **for** $i = 81$ to 93 and $i = 93 + 80$ to 285 **do**
9:         $\mathcal{M}.con \leftarrow s_i^0 = 0$
10:    **end for**
11:    **for** $r = 1$ to R **do**
12:        $(\mathcal{M}, x_1, \ldots, x_{288}) = \mathtt{TriviumCore}(\mathcal{M}, s_1^{r-1}, \ldots, s_{288}^{r-1}, 66, 171, 91, 92, 93)$
13:        $(\mathcal{M}, y_1, \ldots, y_{288}) = \mathtt{TriviumCore}(\mathcal{M}, x_1, \ldots, x_{288}, 162, 264, 175, 176, 177)$
14:        $(\mathcal{M}, z_1, \ldots, z_{288}) = \mathtt{TriviumCore}(\mathcal{M}, y_1, \ldots, y_{288}, 243, 69, 286, 287, 288)$
15:        $(s_1^r, \ldots, s_{288}^r) = (z_{288}, z_1, \ldots, z_{287})$
16:        **if** $r = R'$ **then**
17:            $\mathcal{M}.var \leftarrow \bar{s}_{94}^{R'}, p, q$
18:            $\mathcal{M}.con \leftarrow s_{94}^{R'} = \bar{s}_{94}^{R'} \bigvee p$
19:            $\mathcal{M}.con \leftarrow q = o + p$
20:            $s_{94}^{R'} = \bar{s}_{94}^{R'}$
21:        **end if**
22:    **end for**
23:    **for all** $i \in \{1, 2, \ldots, 288\}$ w/o $66, 93, 162, 177, 243, 288$ **do**
24:        $\mathcal{M}.con \leftarrow s_i^R = 0$
25:    **end for**
26:    $\mathcal{M}.con \leftarrow (s_{66}^R + s_{93}^R + s_{162}^R + s_{177}^R + s_{243}^R + s_{288}^R) = q$
27:    $\mathcal{M}.con \leftarrow q = 1$
28:    **return** $\mathcal{M}$
29: **end procedure**

---

6   Improved Cube Attacks Against Grain-128AEAD

6.1   Specification of Grain-128AEAD and Its MILP Model

Grain-128AEAD [26] is a member of Grain family and also one of the 2nd-round candidates of the NIST LWC standardization process. Grain-128AEAD inherits many specifications from Grain-128a, which was proposed in 2011 [27]. There are four differences between Grain-128AEAD and Grain-128a: (1) larger MACs, (2) no encryption-only mode, (3) initialization hardening, and (4) keystream limitation. These differences do not come only from the requirement for the NIST LWC standardization process but also from recent cryptanalysis result against Grain-128a [21, 22].

The internal state is represented by two 128-bit states, $(b_0, b_1, \ldots, b_{127})$ and $(s_0, s_1, \ldots, s_{127})$. The 128-bit key is loaded to the first register b, and the 96-bit initialization vector is loaded to the second register s. The other state bits are set to 1 except the least one bit in the second register. Namely, the initial state bits are represented as

$$(b_0, b_1, \ldots, b_{127}) = (K_1, K_2, \ldots, K_{128}),$$
$$(s_0, s_1, \ldots, s_{127}) = (IV_1, IV_2, \ldots, IV_{96}, 1, \ldots, 1, 0).$$

The pseudo code of the update function in the initialization is given as follows.

$$g \leftarrow b_0 + b_{26} + b_{56} + b_{91} + b_{96} + b_3 b_{67} + b_{11} b_{13} + b_{17} b_{18} + b_{27} b_{59}$$
$$+ b_{40} b_{48} + b_{61} b_{65} + b_{68} b_{84} + b_{88} b_{92} b_{93} b_{95} + b_{22} b_{24} b_{25} + b_{70} b_{78} b_{82}, \quad (1)$$
$$f \leftarrow s_0 + s_7 + s_{38} + s_{70} + s_{81} + s_{96}, \quad (2)$$
$$h \leftarrow b_{12} s_8 + s_{13} s_{20} + b_{95} s_{42} + s_{60} s_{79} + b_{12} b_{95} s_{94}, \quad (3)$$
$$z \leftarrow h + s_{93} + b_2 + b_{15} + b_{36} + b_{45} + b_{64} + b_{73} + b_{89}, \quad (4)$$
$$(b_0, b_1, \ldots, b_{127}) \leftarrow (b_1, \ldots, b_{127}, g + s_0 + z),$$
$$(s_0, s_1, \ldots, s_{127}) \leftarrow (s_1, \ldots, s_{127}, f + z).$$

In the initialization, the state is updated 256 times without producing an output. After the initialization, the update function is tweaked such that z is not fed to the state, and z is used as a pre-output key stream. Hereinafter, we assume that the first bit of the pre-output key stream can be observed. Note that there is no difference between Grain-128a and Grain-128AEAD under this assumption.

MILP Model. Grain128aEval in Algorithm 5 generates MILP model $\mathcal{M}$ as the input of Algorithm 1 and 2, and the model $\mathcal{M}$ can evaluate all three-subset division trails for Grain-128AEAD whose initialization rounds are reduced to R. funcZ generates MILP variables and constraints for Eq. (3) and Eq. (4), funcG generates MILP variables and constraints for Eq. (1), and funcF generates MILP variables and constraints for Eq. (2).

6.2   Verification of 184-Round Attack from [12]

In [12], the cube attack against 184-round Grain-128AEAD (Grain-128a) was shown. Here, the following cube indices

$$I = \{1, 2, \ldots, 46, 48, 49, \ldots, 96\},$$

where $IV[47] = 0$ are used.[5] The conventional bit-based division property with flag technique reveals that the algebraic degree of the corresponding superpoly is at most 14 and the number of monomials is at most $2^{14.61}$. It implies that the corresponding superpoly can be recovered with $2^{95+14.61}$ time complexity.

We run Algorithm 2 with the model generated by Algorithm 5. Surprisingly, the superpoly does not involve the secret key. There are 16,384 three-subset

---

[5] The first bit of IV is included in the cube index. When the target is Grain-128a, this attack requires queries to both authentication and encryption-only modes. Note that the first bit of IV can also be active in Grain-128AEAD.

Algorithm 5. Model for Grain-128AEAD

1: **procedure** Grain128aEval(round R)
2:    Prepare empty MILP Model $\mathcal{M}$
3:    $\mathcal{M}.var \leftarrow b_i^0$ for $i \in \{0, 1, \ldots, 127\}$ as binary
4:    $\mathcal{M}.var \leftarrow s_i^0$ for $i \in \{0, 1, \ldots, 127\}$ as binary
5:    $\mathcal{M}.con \leftarrow s_{127}^0 = 0$
6:    **for** $r = 1$ to R **do**
7:       $(\mathcal{M}, b_0', \ldots, b_{127}', s_0', \ldots, s_{127}', z^r) = \texttt{funcZ}(\mathcal{M}, b_0^{r-1}, \ldots, b_{127}^{r-1}, s_0^{r-1}, \ldots, s_{127}^{r-1})$
8:       $\mathcal{M}.var \leftarrow \mathbf{zg}, \mathbf{zf}$ as binary
9:       $\mathcal{M}.con \leftarrow z^r = \mathbf{zg} \vee \mathbf{zf}$
10:      $(\mathcal{M}, b_0'', \ldots, b_{127}'', g) = \texttt{funcG}(\mathcal{M}, b_0', \ldots, b_{127}')$
11:      $(\mathcal{M}, s_0'', \ldots, s_{127}'', f) = \texttt{funcF}(\mathcal{M}, s_0', \ldots, s_{127}')$
12:      **for** $i = 0$ to 126 **do**
13:         $b_i^r = b_{i+1}''$
14:         $s_i^r = s_{i+1}''$
15:      **end for**
16:      $\mathcal{M}.var \leftarrow b_{127}^r, s_{127}^r$ as binary
17:      $\mathcal{M}.con \leftarrow b_0'' = 0$
18:      $\mathcal{M}.con \leftarrow b_{127}^r = g + s_0'' + \mathbf{zg}$
19:      $\mathcal{M}.con \leftarrow s_{127}^r = f + \mathbf{zf}$
20:   **end for**
21:   $(\mathcal{M}, b_0', \ldots, b_{127}', s_0', \ldots, s_{127}', z) = \texttt{funcZ}(\mathcal{M}, b_0^R, \ldots, b_{127}^R, s_0^R, \ldots, s_{127}^R)$
22:   **for all** $i \in \{0, 1, \ldots, 127\}$ **do**
23:      $\mathcal{M}.con \leftarrow b_i' = 0$
24:      $\mathcal{M}.con \leftarrow s_i' = 0$
25:   **end for**
26:   $\mathcal{M}.con \leftarrow z = 1$
27:   **return** $\mathcal{M}$
28: **end procedure**

---

division trails, but only three initial properties can be feasible (see Table 4, where $x = (x_1, x_2, \ldots, x_{128})$ denotes the secret key). Moreover, all of them have even-number of trails, i.e., the superpoly shown in [12] is constant-0. Therefore, the cube attack against 184-round Grain-128AEAD is a zero-sum distinguisher.

6.3   Additional Constraints and Superpoly for 190 Rounds

Algorithm 5 evaluates funcZ, funcG, and funcF independently, and combines them. While this algorithm can enumerate all three-subset division trails, it includes many redundant trails. For example, let us consider that there are two propagations for one round from the fixed bitvector to fixed one. Then, considering such propagations is redundant because the number of three-subset division trails including such propagations in its inside is always even number. Therefore, we should remove such propagations from the model in advance to reduce the number of feasible three-subset division trails. We carefully checked three-subset division trails found in the attack against 184-round Grain-128AEAD. As a result, we find a frequently used (but redundant) propagation.

Table 4. Detailed results for superpoly against 184-round Grain-128AEAD.

Parity	# Trails	Monomial
0	4096	$x_{34}x_{39}x_{53}x_{62}x_{64}x_{81}x_{83}x_{84}x_{95}x_{125}$
0	4096	$x_{34}x_{39}x_{49}x_{53}x_{62}x_{64}x_{81}x_{83}x_{84}x_{95}x_{123}x_{127}x_{128}$
0	8192	$x_{23}x_{39}x_{48}x_{49}x_{53}x_{58}x_{59}x_{62}x_{64}x_{83}x_{84}x_{98}x_{118}x_{120}$

Property 1. In any round r, either $\mathbf{s}_0^r$ or $\mathbf{z}^r$ must be 0.

Proof. In round r, we assume that $\mathbf{s}_0^r = 1$ and $\mathbf{z}^r = 1$. The keystream bit $(\mathbf{z}^r = 1)$ can propagate to the rightmost bit of NFSR $(\mathbf{b}_{127}^{r+1})$ and the rightmost bit of LFSR $(\mathbf{s}_{127}^{r+1})$. The leftmost bit of the LFSR $(\mathbf{s}_0^r)$ can also propagate to the same two bits. Therefore, unless either of s_{127}^{r+1}, b_{127}^{r+1}, or $s_{127}^{r+1} \cdot b_{127}^{r+1}$ has monomial $s_0^r \cdot z^r$, such a propagation is infeasible. Clearly, s_{127}^{r+1} and b_{127}^{r+1} do not have such a monomial. Moreover, the monomial $s_0^r \cdot z^r$ is always canceled out in

$$
\begin{aligned}
s_{127}^{r+1} \cdot b_{127}^{r+1} &= (f^r + z^r) \cdot (g^r + z^r + s_0^r) \\
&= f^r \cdot g^r + f^r \cdot s_0^r + (f^r + g^r + 1 + s_0^r) \cdot z^r \\
&= f^r \cdot g^r + f^r \cdot s_0^r + (s_7^r + s_{38}^r + s_{70}^r + s_{81}^r + s_{96}^r + g^r + 1) \cdot z^r.
\end{aligned}
$$

$\square$

Property 1 is very simple and powerful. We just add the following constraint

$$
\mathcal{M}.con \leftarrow \mathbf{s}_0^r + \mathbf{z}^r \leq 1
$$

between the line 6 and 7 in Algorithm 5. We re-run Algorithm 2 by using the model generated by Algorithm 5 with the modification above. Then, $16,384$ trails become impossible, and there is no feasible solution.

Superpoly from 185 to 189 rounds. We showed that the 184-round attack is a zero-sum distinguisher and cannot recover any secret key bit. Similarly to the case of TRIVIUM, we expect that the number of rounds that we can attack can be improved. To attack more rounds, we use cube indices $I = \{1, 2, \ldots, 96\}$, where all IV bits are active. As a result, there is no feasible solution up to 189 rounds. In other words, we find zero-sum distinguishers from 185 to 189 rounds.

Superpoly for 190 rounds. From 190 rounds onwards, secret key bits can be involved. As a result, $7,621$ feasible three-subset division trails are enumerated, and $J[\mathbf{u}]$ in Algorithm 2 is non zero for $3,006$ different $\mathbf{u}$'s. Out of $3,006$ $\mathbf{u}$'s, there are $1,097$ $\mathbf{u}$'s whose $J[\mathbf{u}]$ is an odd number. In other words, the superpoly is represented as the sum of $1,097$ monomials. Interestingly, the recovered superpoly has completely different features of the one of TRIVIUM. While the superpoly of TRIVIUM is a very low-degree and simple Boolean function, the recovered superpoly for Grain128-AEAD has algebraic degree 21 and is a complicated Boolean function with no monomials of degree lower than 6. Since the Boolean function is too complicated to evaluate its weight theoretically, we experimentally evaluated the balancedness. We picked 2^{15} secret keys randomly and compute the output of the Boolean function. As a result, it is highly biased, and the fraction of keys that output 1 is about 0.032. Therefore, the information recovered from this superpoly is very small. Indeed, if the superpoly in the online phase evaluates to one, we gain almost 5 bit (i.e. $-\log_2(0.032)$) in an attack when filtering wrong keys. However, in the case where the superpoly evaluates to zero, we gain less than 0.04 bits (i.e. $-\log_2(1-0.032)$) in an attack. The average gain, given by the entropy, is only

$$-0.032 \log_2(0.032) - (1-0.032)\log_2(1-0.032) \approx 0.2$$

which limits the interest in this approach.

6.4 Towards Efficient Key-Recovery Attacks

To recover more bits of information, we use multiple cubes whose size decreases from 96 to 95. However, if the cube index misses one IV bit, the number of three-subset division trails increases. We need to pick appropriate non-cube indices, where the number of three-subset division trails does not expand to much. We were able to compute the representation of 15 superpolys p_j where the cube index set was $\{1..96\} \setminus j$ with

$$j \in J = \{27, 30, 31, 32, 34, 41, 44, 45, 46, 48, 58, 59, 64, 70, 72\}.$$

Those polynomials vary significantly in size (between 176 and 19, 925 monomials) but also share interesting properties. Again, due to their size, some of the properties can only be estimated experimentally.

Interestingly, all polynomials are highly biased toward zero and none of the polynomials involves all key bits. In particular none of the polynomials depends on the key bits

$$K_1, K_2, K_3, K_6 \text{ and } K_9.$$

Moreover, all polynomials can be evaluated rather efficiently on average. The details are given in Table 5. Note that the average total cost of evaluating the polynomials is an upper bound on the number of XORs and ANDs needed. This bound was derived using a time-memory tradeoff for the evaluation process, by fixing 14 key bits that appear frequently in all 15 polynomials. Fixing to all 2^{14} possible values resulted in $15 \cdot 2^{14}$ polynomials. Those polynomials are significantly simpler and simply counting the number of required AND and XOR operations in a trivial evaluation process resulted in the numbers in Table 5 that are sufficient for our attack. In particular, the average cost of evaluating all 15 polynomials together is smaller than 2^{12}, which is smaller than producing a single key stream bit with Grain128-AEAD reduced to 190 rounds.

Besides being highly unbalanced, the polynomials are also not independent when evaluated on random keys. In order to estimate how many wrong keys are

Table 5. Properties of the superpolys for Grain128-AEAD.

Poly	p_{27}	p_{30}	p_{31}	p_{32}	p_{34}	p_{41}	p_{44}	p_{45}	p_{46}	p_{48}	p_{58}	p_{59}	p_{64}	p_{70}	p_{72}
Nb. of ind. K_i	7	6	12	8	6	13	14	47	6	16	6	10	12	11	8
$Pr(p_j = 0)$	0.077	0.116	0.055	0.089	0.090	0.099	0.019	0.012	0.081	0.055	0.123	0.196	0.097	0.156	0.083
Av. cost	544	408	107	196	452	148	19	10	199	213	406	497	432	336	205

filtered on average, we estimated the entropy of $(p_{27}, \ldots, p_{72})$ when evaluated at uniformly random chosen keys. That is, for $v_j \in \{0, 1\}$ we estimated

$$\Pr((P_{27}, \ldots, P_{72}) = (v_{27}, \ldots, v_{72}))$$

for all 2^{15} possible outcomes. The distribution is still highly biased, in particular $\Pr(0, \ldots, 0) \approx 0.57$. However, the entropy, which was estimated using 2^{25} samples, increased to 5.03 which now makes the following attack possible.

1. The attacker evaluates in the online phase the values of the 15 superpolys for the given secret key.
2. The attacker guesses all key-bits except the bits K_1, K_2, K_3, K_6, K_9 and for each guess filters with the correct values of the superpolys given from the online phase.
3. For each guess that passes the filtering, the attacker runs through all possible values of K_1, K_2, K_3, K_6, K_9 and verifies the key against given key-stream.

The cost of the online phase is 15×2^{95} time and 2^{96} data, i.e. using all possible IV values for the given secret key.

In the second step, the number of guesses is 2^{128-5} and, due to the entropy, the average amount of not filtered guesses is $2^{128-5-5.03}$. As evaluating the polynomials is cheaper than evaluating Grain128-AEAD, the cost for this step is less than 2^{123} evaluations of Grain128-AEAD.

In the third step, the average cost is $2^5 \cdot 2^{128-5-5.03}$, i.e. less than 2^{123} evaluations of Grain128-AEAD as well. To conclude, the attack has an average time complexity of less than 2^{123} evaluations of Grain128-AEAD and a data complexity of 2^{96}. Note that this complexity is averaged over the given secret key. In particular, after the first step of the attack, the attacker already knows how efficient filtering will be in her particular case. For some keys filtering is significantly stronger. This observation might be further elaborated into a stronger attack for a smaller fraction of keys, i.e. a weak-key attack.

7   Conclusion

In this paper, we proposed a new modeling technique for the three-subset division property without unknown subset. Our technique is significant for the application to the cube attack. Unlike the previous experimental or theoretical cube attacks, our method does not need any assumption and can recover the actual superpoly in practical time. Our method leads to the best key-recovery attack on two of the most important stream ciphers.

Acknowledgement. The authors thank the anonymous Eurocrypt 2020 reviewers for careful reading and many helpful comments. Yonglin Hao is supported by National Key Research and Development Program of China (No. 2018YFA0306404). Gregor Leander is supported by the Deutsche Forschungsgemeinschaft (DFG, German Research Foundation) under Germany's Excellence Strategy - EXC 2092 CASA - 390781972. Qingju Wang is funded by the University of Luxembourg Internal Research Project (IRP) FDISC.

References

1. Knudsen, L., Wagner, D.: Integral cryptanalysis. In: Daemen, J., Rijmen, V. (eds.) FSE 2002. LNCS, vol. 2365, pp. 112–127. Springer, Heidelberg (2002). https://doi.org/10.1007/3-540-45661-9_9
2. Daemen, J., Knudsen, L., Rijmen, V.: The block cipher Square. In: Biham, E. (ed.) FSE 1997. LNCS, vol. 1267, pp. 149–165. Springer, Heidelberg (1997). https://doi.org/10.1007/BFb0052343
3. Lai, X.: Higher order derivatives and differential cryptanalysis. In: Blahut, R.E., Costello, D.J., Maurer, U., Mittelholzer, T. (eds.) Communications and Cryptography. SECS, vol. 276, pp. 227–233. Springer, Boston (1994). https://doi.org/10.1007/978-1-4615-2694-0_23
4. Todo, Y.: Structural evaluation by generalized integral property. In: Oswald, E., Fischlin, M. (eds.) EUROCRYPT 2015, Part I. LNCS, vol. 9056, pp. 287–314. Springer, Heidelberg (2015). https://doi.org/10.1007/978-3-662-46800-5_12
5. Todo, Y.: Integral cryptanalysis on full MISTY1. In: Gennaro, R., Robshaw, M. (eds.) CRYPTO 2015, Part I. LNCS, vol. 9215, pp. 413–432. Springer, Heidelberg (2015). https://doi.org/10.1007/978-3-662-47989-6_20
6. Sasaki, Y., Todo, Y.: New differential bounds and division property of LILLIPUT: block cipher with extended generalized Feistel network. In: Avanzi, R., Heys, H. (eds.) SAC 2016. LNCS, vol. 10532, pp. 264–283. Springer, Cham (2017). https://doi.org/10.1007/978-3-319-69453-5_15
7. Todo, Y., Morii, M.: Bit-based division property and application to SIMON family. In: Peyrin, T. (ed.) FSE 2016. LNCS, vol. 9783, pp. 357–377. Springer, Heidelberg (2016). https://doi.org/10.1007/978-3-662-52993-5_18
8. Sugio, N., Igarashi, Y., Kaneko, T., Higuchi, K.: New integral characteristics of KASUMI derived by division property. In: Choi, D., Guilley, S. (eds.) WISA 2016. LNCS, vol. 10144, pp. 267–279. Springer, Cham (2017). https://doi.org/10.1007/978-3-319-56549-1_23
9. Xiang, Z., Zhang, W., Bao, Z., Lin, D.: Applying MILP method to searching integral distinguishers based on division property for 6 lightweight block ciphers. In: Cheon, J.H., Takagi, T. (eds.) ASIACRYPT 2016, Part I. LNCS, vol. 10031, pp. 648–678. Springer, Heidelberg (2016). https://doi.org/10.1007/978-3-662-53887-6_24
10. Sun, L., Wang, W., Wang, M.: Automatic search of bit-based division property for ARX ciphers and word-based division property. In: Takagi, T., Peyrin, T. (eds.) ASIACRYPT 2017, Part I. LNCS, vol. 10624, pp. 128–157. Springer, Cham (2017). https://doi.org/10.1007/978-3-319-70694-8_5
11. Todo, Y., Isobe, T., Hao, Y., Meier, W.: Cube attacks on non-blackbox polynomials based on division property. In: Katz, J., Shacham, H. (eds.) CRYPTO 2017, Part III. LNCS, vol. 10403, pp. 250–279. Springer, Cham (2017). https://doi.org/10.1007/978-3-319-63697-9_9

12. Wang, Q., Hao, Y., Todo, Y., Li, C., Isobe, T., Meier, W.: Improved division property based cube attacks exploiting algebraic properties of superpoly. In: Shacham, H., Boldyreva, A. (eds.) CRYPTO 2018, Part I. LNCS, vol. 10991, pp. 275–305. Springer, Cham (2018). https://doi.org/10.1007/978-3-319-96884-1_10

13. Bernstein, D.J., et al.: GIMLI: a cross-platform permutation. In: Fischer, W., Homma, N. (eds.) CHES 2017. LNCS, vol. 10529, pp. 299–320. Springer, Cham (2017). https://doi.org/10.1007/978-3-319-66787-4_15

14. Banik, S., Pandey, S.K., Peyrin, T., Sasaki, Y., Sim, S.M., Todo, Y.: GIFT: a small present - towards reaching the limit of lightweight encryption. In: Fischer, W., Homma, N. (eds.) CHES 2017. LNCS, vol. 10529, pp. 321–345. Springer, Cham (2017). https://doi.org/10.1007/978-3-319-66787-4_16

15. Wang, Q., Liu, Z., Varıcı, K., Sasaki, Y., Rijmen, V., Todo, Y.: Cryptanalysis of reduced-round SIMON32 and SIMON48. In: Meier, W., Mukhopadhyay, D. (eds.) INDOCRYPT 2014. LNCS, vol. 8885, pp. 143–160. Springer, Cham (2014). https://doi.org/10.1007/978-3-319-13039-2_9

16. Hu, K., Wang, M.: Automatic search for a variant of division property using three subsets. In: Matsui, M. (ed.) CT-RSA 2019. LNCS, vol. 11405, pp. 412–432. Springer, Cham (2019). https://doi.org/10.1007/978-3-030-12612-4_21

17. Wang, S., Hu, B., Guan, J., Zhang, K., Shi, T.: MILP-aided method of searching division property using three subsets and applications. In: Galbraith, S.D., Moriai, S. (eds.) ASIACRYPT 2019, Part III. LNCS, vol. 11923, pp. 398–427. Springer, Cham (2019). https://doi.org/10.1007/978-3-030-34618-8_14

18. Dinur, I., Shamir, A.: Cube attacks on tweakable black box polynomials. In: Joux, A. (ed.) EUROCRYPT 2009. LNCS, vol. 5479, pp. 278–299. Springer, Heidelberg (2009). https://doi.org/10.1007/978-3-642-01001-9_16

19. Ye, C.D., Tian, T.: Revisit division property based cube attacks: key-recovery or distinguishing attacks? IACR Trans. Symm. Cryptol. **2019**(3), 81–102 (2019)

20. Fu, X., Wang, X., Dong, X., Meier, W.: A key-recovery attack on 855-round Trivium. In: Shacham, H., Boldyreva, A. (eds.) CRYPTO 2018, Part II. LNCS, vol. 10992, pp. 160–184. Springer, Cham (2018). https://doi.org/10.1007/978-3-319-96881-0_6

21. Hamann, M., Krause, M.: On stream ciphers with provable beyond-the-birthday-bound security against time-memory-data tradeoff attacks. Cryptogr. Commun. **10**(5), 959–1012 (2018). https://doi.org/10.1007/s12095-018-0294-5

22. Todo, Y., Isobe, T., Meier, W., Aoki, K., Zhang, B.: Fast correlation attack revisited - cryptanalysis on full Grain-128a, Grain-128, and Grain-v1. In: Shacham, H., Boldyreva, A. (eds.) CRYPTO 2018, Part II. LNCS, vol. 10992, pp. 129–159. Springer, Cham (2018). https://doi.org/10.1007/978-3-319-96881-0_5

23. Cannière, C.D., Preneel, B.: Trivium specifications. eSTREAM portfolio, Profile 2 (IIW) (2006)

24. Hao, Y., Jiao, L., Li, C., Meier, W., Todo, Y., Wang, Q.: Observations on the dynamic cube attack of 855-round TRIVIUM from Crypto '18. Cryptology ePrint Archive, Report 2018/972 (2018). https://eprint.iacr.org/2018/972

25. Fu, X., Wang, X., Dong, X., Meier, W., Hao, Y., Zhao, B.: A refinement of "a key-recovery attack on 855-round Trivium" from crypto 2018. Cryptology ePrint Archive, Report 2018/999 (2018). https://eprint.iacr.org/2018/999

26. Hell, M., Johansson, T., Meier, W., Sönnerup, J., Yoshida, H.: Grain-128AEAD: a lightweight AEAD stream cipher. Lightweight Cryptography (LWC) Standardization (2019)

27. Ågren, M., Hell, M., Johansson, T., Meier, W.: Grain-128a: a new version of Grain-128 with optional authentication. IJWMC **5**(1), 48–59 (2011)

Secret Sharing

Blackbox Secret Sharing Revisited: A Coding-Theoretic Approach with Application to Expansionless Near-Threshold Schemes

Ronald Cramer[1,2][✉] and Chaoping Xing[3][✉]

[1] CWI Amsterdam, Amsterdam, The Netherlands
cramer@cwi.nl
[2] Leiden University, Leiden, The Netherlands
cramer@math.leidenuniv.nl
[3] Shanghai Jiao Tong University, Shanghai, China
xingcp@sjtu.edu.cn

Abstract. A *blackbox* secret sharing (BBSS) scheme works in exactly the same way for all finite Abelian groups G; it can be instantiated for any such group G and *only* black-box access to its group operations and to random group elements is required. A secret is a single group element and each of the n players' shares is a vector of such elements. Share-computation and secret-reconstruction is by integer linear combinations. These do not depend on G, and neither do the privacy and reconstruction parameters t, r. This classical, fundamental primitive was introduced by Desmedt and Frankel (CRYPTO 1989) in their context of "threshold cryptography." The expansion factor is the total number of group elements in a full sharing divided by n. For threshold BBSS with t-privacy $(1 \leq t \leq n-1)$, $t+1$-reconstruction and arbitrary n, constructions with minimal expansion $O(\log n)$ exist (CRYPTO 2002, 2005).

These results are firmly rooted in number theory; each makes (different) judicious choices of orders in number fields admitting a vector of elements of very large length (in the number field degree) whose corresponding Vandermonde-determinant is sufficiently controlled so as to enable BBSS by a suitable adaptation of Shamir's scheme. Alternative approaches generally lead to very large expansion. The state of the art of BBSS has not changed for the last 17 years.

Our contributions are two-fold. (1) We introduce a novel, nontrivial, effective construction of BBSS based on *coding theory* instead of number theory. For threshold-BBSS we also achieve minimal expansion factor $O(\log n)$. (2) Our method is more versatile. Namely, we show, for the first time, BBSS that is *near-threshold*, i.e., $r - t$ is an arbitrarily small constant fraction of n, *and* that has expansion factor $O(1)$, i.e., individual share-vectors of *constant* length ("asymptotically expansionless"). Threshold can be concentrated essentially freely across full range. We also show expansion is minimal for near-threshold and that such BBSS cannot be attained by previous methods.

© International Association for Cryptologic Research 2020
A. Canteaut and Y. Ishai (Eds.): EUROCRYPT 2020, LNCS 12105, pp. 499–528, 2020.
https://doi.org/10.1007/978-3-030-45721-1_18

Our general construction is based on a well-known mathematical principle, the local-global principle. More precisely, we first construct BBSS over local rings through either Reed-Solomon or algebraic geometry codes. We then "glue" these schemes together in a dedicated manner to obtain a global secret sharing scheme, i.e., defined over the integers, which, as we finally prove using novel insights, has the desired BBSS properties. Though our main purpose here is advancing BBSS for its own sake, we also briefly address possible protocol applications.

Keywords: Foundations of secret sharing · Blackbox secret sharing

1   Introduction

This paper advances the state of the art in *blackbox* secret sharing (BBSS), a classical, fundamental primitive first studied by Desmedt and Frankel [14,15] in the late 1980s, motivated by their context of "threshold cryptography." A BBSS scheme works in exactly the same way for all finite Abelian groups G. I.e., it can be instantiated for any such group G and *only* black-box access to its group operations and to random group elements is required. The secret-space equals G (so the secret is a *single* group element) and the share-space for each of n players is a fixed finite product over G (so each share is a vector). Viewing G additively and using the basic fact that G may be viewed as a $\mathbb{Z}$-module,[1] each share is obtained by applying $\mathbb{Z}$-*linear forms*[2] on a vector consisting of secret and random group elements; likewise for secret-reconstruction from appropriate shares. Whether a given player set is reconstructing or gives privacy does not depend on structural information on G (e.g. access to its order), other than it being finite Abelian. This also holds for the integer coefficients of the forms in share computation and secret reconstruction. In this section, we first discuss the technical background of BBSS and its history. Then we overview our results and method. We also argue why our main claim cannot be achieved by previous methods. Finally, we briefly discuss possible protocol applications.

1.1   Background on BBSS

BBSS is conveniently formalized and elucidated mathematically by *Integer Span Programs* (ISP). The latter notion, introduced in [10], is not only sufficient for BBSS but also necessary; it captures exactly the principles laid out above. In a nutshell, an ISP is characterized by a positive integer e and $\mathbb{Z}$-submodules $V_1, \ldots, V_n \subset \mathbb{Z}^e$. Note that, by standard theory, any such submodule is free, i.e., has a basis. Let V_0 denote the $\mathbb{Z}$-module spanned by the "target vector" $\mu_e =$

---

[1] Briefly, "vectorspace axioms are satisfied except that scalars are defined over $\mathbb{Z}$ instead of a field."

[2] Owing to $\mathbb{Z}$-module structure, a form maps $(g_1, \ldots, g_m) \in G^m$ to $\sum_i \lambda_i g_i \in G$ for a fixed vector $(\lambda_1, \ldots, \lambda_m) \in \mathbb{Z}^m$.

$(1, 0, \ldots, 0) \in \mathbb{Z}^e$, i.e., V_0 consists of all its integer multiples.[3] For a nonempty subset $A \subset \{1, \ldots, n\}$ we write $V_A = \sum_{i \in A} V_i$, the $\mathbb{Z}$-span of the V_i's with $i \in A$. A set A is a *reconstructing set* if $V_0 \subset V_A$. It is a *privacy set* if there is a $\mathbb{Z}$-linear form $\phi_A : \mathbb{Z}^e \to \mathbb{Z}$ such that $\phi_A(V_A) \equiv 0$, whereas $\phi_A(V_0) = \mathbb{Z}$. The latter is equivalent to the condition $V_A \cap V_0 = \{0\}$.[4]

One may easily rephrase this definition in terms of matrices; this way one readily observes that a matrix whose rows are partitioned into n blocks each constituting a basis of a different space V_i can be used to define computation of shares by having the matrix act on a vector whose first coordinate is the secret and whose remaining ones are random group elements. Reconstruction is derived from the integer coefficients according to a span of the target vector. Privacy can be verified using the linear form in question, in a way familiar from schemes over finite fields.

Note that there is similarity with *Monotone Span Programs* or MSP [19], a notion due to Karchmer and Wigderson known to be intimately connected with linear secret sharing over finite fields, as first shown by Beimel [1]. In MSPs, the dividing line between the two types sets of sets is "to span or not to span the target vector." This is not the case for ISPs. The reconstruction condition is still equivalent to "the target vector being in the span." However, the privacy condition is *not* simply its negation; since we work over $\mathbb{Z}$ and not over a field it could be so that some nonzero multiple of the target vector is spanned but not the target vector itself. Indeed, write $V_A \cap V_0 = (a)\mu_e$ for some principal ideal (a) of the ring $\mathbb{Z}$ with $a \neq 0, \pm1$. Then choose, for instance, a prime number p dividing a and a prime number p' not dividing it. Now, if we take G as the cyclic group of order p, the set A is a privacy set, whereas, if we take G as the cyclic group of order p', it is a reconstructing set. In particular, the ISP definition is not just a verbatim translation of the MSP definition from finite fields to the integers. For more discussion, see [8,10].

The expansion factor in BBSS is the length of a full vector of n shares (i.e., the total number of group elements) divided by n. For threshold BBSS with t-privacy ($1 \leq t \leq n - 1$), $t + 1$-reconstruction and arbitrary positive n, Cramer and Fehr [10] show a construction that achieves expansion $O(\log n)$, which is minimal. This improved the $O(n)$ expansion from the earlier construction due to Desmedt and Frankel [14,15]. In [12], Cramer, Fehr and Stam prove that absolutely minimal expansion (up to an additive constant) can be achieved. For the lower bounds, please refer to [10,12].[5]

---

[3] In fact, any vector whose coordinates do not have a nontrivial common divisor may be taken as the target vector.

[4] The implication starting from the form-based definition is trivial. In the other direction, it follows e.g. using basic structural theory of finitely-generated modules over principal ideal domains, such as $\mathbb{Z}$.

[5] Note that the case $t = 0$ is trivial and that the case $t = n - 1$ is expansionless via "additive n-out-of-n secret sharing." Hence the restriction on t above. For those "interesting" t, the first step to lower bounds is the observation that threshold BBSS gives binary linear secret sharing for threshold access structures.

These results are firmly rooted in number theory. More precisely, each makes a judicious choice of orders in algebraic number fields[6] admitting a finite, large dedicated set of points that is sufficiently controlled so as to enable BBSS by a suitable adaptation of Shamir's secret sharing over finite fields. The choice of order, the control, and the exact way BBSS is realized all vary across these known results. In a nutshell, these methods all use "polynomials" whose coefficients are chosen in the tensor-product $R \otimes_{\mathbb{Z}} G$, where R is the order in question. The latter object is an R-module in a natural way. Thus, such a "polynomial" can be evaluated in a set of points in R. Getting a threshold BBSS in this way, mimicking Shamir's scheme to a certain degree, is down to a Vandermonde-determinant determined by these points satisfying one out of several possible convenient number-theoretical properties. The central issue in construction is then to find an infinite family of orders R such that $\mathbb{Z}$-rank of R tends to infinity and such that R admits a dedicated evaluation-point set constrained as indicated above that is very large compared to the $\mathbb{Z}$-rank of R, since the number of players n equals the cardinality of this set and the expansion factor equals the $\mathbb{Z}$-rank of R divided by n. In addition, care must be taken such that each positive number n of players can be accommodated.

In [14,15], this determinant attached to the evaluation-point set is required to be a *multiplicative unit* of R, so that the Lagrange Interpolation Theorem holds over R. This is best forced by using cyclotomic number fields. But the resulting expansion is $O(n)$. In [10], *two* evaluation sets are required whose attached determinants are *co-prime* in R. It is shown how to construct orders R admitting two such sets of cardinality 2^k where k is the $\mathbb{Z}$-rank of R. One of these sets can be taken simply as $\{1, \ldots, n\}$, the other being more intricate and depending on R. This gives minimal expansion $O(\log n)$. In [12], the two sets are reduced to a single one by requiring the attached determinant to be *primitive*, i.e., its only rational integers divisors are ± 1. It is shown that orders R of rank k exist that admit evaluation-point sets of cardinality 2^k. So expansion is minimal here too, in fact, better by an additive constant. The latter result, though, is not explicit and is significantly more intricate, mathematically. For a full treatment of threshold BBSS, please refer to [8]. There are alternative, more generic approaches. E.g., one can combine Benaloh-Leichter secret sharing [2] with Valiant's result on polynomial-size monotone Boolean formulas for threshold functions [28]. But this leads to very large expansion (but still polynomial in n). The state of the art of BBSS has not changed for the last 15 years.

1.2   Our Contributions

Our contributions here are two-fold.

1. We introduce a completely different, nontrivial effective construction of BBSS based on *coding theory* instead of number theory. For the threshold case we

---

[6] An order $\mathcal{O}$ in an algebraic number field K of degree k is a subring $\mathcal{O}$ of its ring of integers $\mathcal{O}_K$ such that $\mathcal{O}$ has finite index in $\mathcal{O}_K$ as a $\mathbb{Z}$-submodule, i.e., $|\mathcal{O}_K/\mathcal{O}|$ is finite. In particular, $\mathcal{O}$ has rank k as $\mathbb{Z}$-module, just as $\mathcal{O}_K$.

also achieve minimal expansion factor $O(\log n)$ as before. The threshold can be chosen freely.

2. Our general method is more *versatile* than previous methods. As an application *not* attainable by any previous method (as argued below), we demonstrate, for the first time, BBSS that is *near-threshold*, i.e., t-privacy and r-reconstruction are such that $r - t$ is an arbitrarily small constant fraction of n, *and* that achieves *expansion factor* $O(1)$, i.e., a constant number of group elements per share. Moreover, it is supported for arbitrary n and thresholds can be chosen essentially freely, for instance, concentrated around $n/2$. This result is asymptotically expansionless and minimal for near-threshold, as we also prove (see Main Theorem 1).

We now give an informal discussion why an expansionless, near-threshold BBSS cannot be fulfilled by previous methods. We restrict to the general approach from [10,12] based on "polynomial interpolation" involving number fields (since this approach gives exponentially smaller expansion anyway). Towards a contradiction, suppose, first, that BBSS as claimed above is achieved by evaluations of a *single* polynomial with coefficients in $R \otimes_{\mathbb{Z}} G$ (for some given R). Then the $\mathbb{Z}$-rank of R must be a constant c (equivalently, the number field in question has constant degree), since otherwise the $O(1)$ expansion claim is not met. We may assume there are at least n evaluation points in R used and each share corresponds to one or more (but at most a constant number of them) evaluations of a given polynomial.

Now fix a prime number p and an order R in a number field. Note that $|R/(p)| = p^c$ is also a constant. Suppose $n \gg p^c$. If we restrict the assumed BBSS work over $G = \mathbb{Z}/p\mathbb{Z}$ and consider that, *when taken modulo p*, the set of evaluation points used "collapses" to at most c distinct ones, this set can be partitioned into at most c "blocks" such that, within each block, polynomial evaluation gives the same result across the entire block. In other words, there is just "a constant number of evaluations that matter"; the others are always duplicates. Combining this with the fact that the assumed BBS ensures, in particular, that a full vector of shares determines the secret, there is in fact a *constant-sized* set of players that can reconstruct the secret jointly in case $G = \mathbb{Z}/p\mathbb{Z}$: a contradiction with the assumed parameters. Second, this argument extends to the case where various polynomials are used instead of just one[7] and where R may differ per polynomial. Also note that the argument does not depend on R being an order in a number field; it extends to any commutative ring R that has finite rank as a $\mathbb{Z}$-module, which exactly represents the minimal requirement on R for the BBSS paradigm from [10,12] to make sense anyway.

1.3 Our Method

Our general construction is based on a well-known mathematical principle, the local-global principle. More precisely, we first construct BBSS over local rings

---

[7] In [10], *two* polynomials are used, whereas in [12,14,15] there is a single one.

through either Reed-Solomon or algebraic geometry codes. We then "glue" these schemes together in a dedicated manner to obtain a global secret sharing scheme, i.e., defined over the integers, which, as we finally prove, has the desired BBSS properties.

In some more detail, we start from an observation exploited in [10] and earlier in [25]. Namely, a *weak* form of threshold BBSS is achievable simply by taking "polynomials" with coefficients in G and then evaluating in the integer points $0, 1, \ldots, n$. Defining $\Delta = \prod_{0 \leq i < j \leq n}(j - i)$, the free coefficient is taken as $\Delta \cdot s$, with $s \in G$ equal to the secret. The other coefficients are random in G. It is now straightforward to show that, using polynomials of degree $\leq t$ (with $1 \leq t < n$), there is t-privacy, and, in addition, there is $(t + 1)$-reconstruction not of the secret s itself but of a multiple $\Delta^2 \cdot s$, In [10], an order of rank $\log n$ is then hand-crafted that admits evaluation points $0, \alpha_1, \ldots, \alpha_n \in R$ such that, also by weak-BBSS with t-privacy, there is $(t + 1)$-reconstruction of the value $(\Delta')^2 \cdot s$, where Δ' is a Vandermonde determinant defined by the α_i's *and* such that Δ, Δ' are *coprime* in R. This leads to a "double-sharing" approach: by secret sharing a given secret independently according to each of these two weak-BBSS schemes, the secret can be reconstructed by a known linear combination over R (translated into linear combinations over $\mathbb{Z}$). This gives the desired BBSS. On a high level, we also follow this double-sharing approach, starting with weak-BBSS from polynomial-evaluation at integer points. However, our approach towards creating the second weak-BBSS, which, together with the first, should enforce the co-primality property, is completely different.

Let $P(n)$ denote the set of prime numbers p with $2 \leq p \leq n$. For the moment, fix n arbitrarily. For each $p \in P(n)$, we select an $\mathbb{F}_p$-linear secret sharing scheme with secret-space dimension 1 and "small" share-space dimension. We construct these schemes from linear codes as in [9], i.e., via codes with large distance as well as large dual distance (but, in the present case, without consideration of multiplicative properties). We also fix generator matrices for each, or, more precisely, monotone span programs. The privacy and reconstruction parameters are designed such that they match (sufficiently well) with the desired values t, r in each case. Note that this influences the constant in share-space dimension; e.g., if this constant was just 1, then this upperbounds the achievable r, t just on account of (dual-) distance bounds on binary linear codes.

Now, we glue these $|P(n)|$ schemes together in two steps: First, we apply *Chinese Remaindering* to the monotone span programs at hand, and second, we *arbitrarily lift* the result to the integers. Somewhat surprisingly, as a result, we obtain a weak-BBSS with t-privacy and r-reconstruction of a λ-multiple of the secret, where λ is an integer *coprime* with Δ. Indeed, this is by no means obvious since, at face value, this procedure does not even seem to account for behavior over groups whose order is (divisible by) a *power* of a prime in $P(n)$, a class of groups that is obviously finite for each n. But still we get around this issue thanks to novel, nontrivial ideas on lifting of linear secret sharing over finite fields to rings while preserving the relevant parameters. In the particular case of ours here, that means lifting schemes over $\mathbb{F}_p$ to schemes over $\mathbb{Z}/p^k\mathbb{Z}$; this is a key ingredient for making our local-global approach work, i.e., this allows to reduce the "global" problem to addressing, for each n, just a *finite* number of "local" problems.

As for recovering $\log n$ expansion for *threshold* BBSS, we may work with Shamir's scheme defined over a large enough extension of a prime field $\mathbb{F}_p$ with $p \in P(n)$ and turn it into a linear scheme over $\mathbb{F}_p$ in a standard way; simply "expand" extension field elements into coordinate-vectors over the base field, after selection of a basis; this turns out to work for our purposes. Since, in this case, we need threshold secret sharing over e.g. $\mathbb{F}_2$ in particular, it is clear that share-space dimension (over $\mathbb{F}_2$) will be $\log n$ in the worst case (as we go through $L(n)$). Note that the expansion achieved here matches exactly that of the number-theoretic approach from [10]. We do not necessarily say that the approach for threshold-BBSS in the present paper is conceptually/technically simpler than that of [10]: each feels "mathematically right" albeit seen from different standpoints. However, the result in [12], also number-theoretic and more intricate than [10], is still better by an *additive* constant.

Finally, we get to our claim on *expansionless, flexible near-threshold* BBSS, which is *not* attainable by previous methods as we have argued. We choose, for each prime p, linear secret sharing schemes over $\mathbb{F}_p$ with appropriate asymptotic properties. Here, asymptotic theory of linear codes comes into play here; asymptotic results from [9] show at once that all the necessary connections can be made. Indeed, by choosing a large enough *fixed* extension of a base field $\mathbb{F}_p$, one gets, asymptotically, that distance and dual distance can be concentrated around an arbitrary constant fraction of n, with the difference between distance and dual distance being an arbitrarily small constant fraction of n. This translates into similar properties for t-privacy and r-reconstruction in corresponding linear secret sharing schemes with share-space of constant dimension over the base field. As in the threshold case, schemes over extension fields are turned into schemes over the base field in a standard way.

It is for these reasons that we can achieve expansionless, flexible near-threshold BBSS. The gluing procedure is then by a form of diagonalization. I.e., index rows by the positive integers n and index the columns by the prime numbers. In location (n, p), we have a linear secret sharing scheme over $\mathbb{F}_p$ supporting n players and achieving the desired privacy and reconstruction. Then, for each n, we glue along the n-th row "up to the diagonal," i.e., up to location (n, p) where p is the largest prime $p \leq n$. Finally, for the compound BBSS to be explicit (poly-time) the underlying codes are required to be explicit. This means we need to resort to algebraic-geometric codes (AG). However, the latter cannot be taken off-the-shelf since we need to ensure that the compound BBSS works for each and every n and achieves the desired parameters. This leads us to handcraft the required AG-codes. In addition, we encounter several technical issues of parameter fine-tuning that have been suppressed in our overview for sake of brevity but that are still necessary for our approach.

1.4   Brief Remarks on Possible Protocol Applications

Though our primary purpose here is to advance the theoretical state of the art in BBSS, we briefly address some potential applications. Threshold-RSA [14] was eventually realized very efficiently without recourse to BBSS, exploiting specifics of RSA not generally present in cryptosystems over groups with secret of hard to compute order. Very briefly, "Shamir-sharing over the integers" can be used here for the purpose of practical threshold-RSA signatures [25]. Even though only reconstruction of a *multiple* of the secret can be guaranteed when doing so, this works for RSA if the constant scalar in this multiple is co-prime both to the public exponent and to the order of the (sub-group) of the "RSA-group" in question. The latter is by forcing existence of an easily accessible constant-index subgroup of the "RSA-group" whose order only has very large prime factors (implied by requiring prime factors of RSA-modulus to be Sophie Germain) and the former by requiring that the public exponent is a prime exceeding the number of players.

By applying our techniques for expansionless near-threshold BBSS to practical ranges of n (making some practical substitutions for the codes), one may, in principle remove the lower bound condition on the public exponent, with the benefit of rendering faster signature verification, while maintaining "practicality" and active security. In case of passive security only, the Sophie Germain requirement may also be removed. Note that, in the active case, the Sophie German condition facilitates the efficient zero knowledge proofs of correct "partial verification" in the style of Schnorr-proofs with exponentially large challenge space for exponentially small error probability in a single run. Without that condition one would have to resort to repetition of proofs supporting a 1-bit challenge space only (so error $1/2$ per run), leading to efficiency loss. However, using amortization techniques for zero knowledge [6], this effect can be neutralized if many statement are proven simultaneously. Thus, if many signatures are verified simultaneously, we may also remove the Sophie-Germain condition in the active case. Alternatively, we may thus also consider deploying these ideas towards improved threshold-RSA *decryption*. We suggest that this all merits further study.

Moreover, in [13], ISPs are shown to imply "integer linear secret sharing" with statistical privacy, by selecting secret and randomness from an appropriately large bounded range of integers instead of blackbox groups. Clearly, ISPs allow for full secret-reconstruction, not just a multiple. Known applications are to threshold cryptosystems based on class groups.[8] Also results also apply directly here. We believe there are other useful applications, for instance in MPC over the integers.[9] This may offer advantages for certain functions, compared to methods which emulate integer operations by first working over e.g. finite fields. But more research is needed still for this to be conclusive.

---

[8] Whereas these seemed out of fashion for some time, they appear to be making a comeback in the blockchain context presently.

[9] A topic which, surprisingly, has not seen much attention lately, especially given the surge in MPC research.

1.5   Organization of the Paper

In Sect. 2, we introduce monotone span programs and near-threshold black-box secret sharing schemes. We also show how to lift a monotone span programs modulo prime powers to a monotone span program over $\mathbb{Z}$. In Sect. 3, we show a lower bound on expansion factor on near-threshold black-box secret sharing schemes. This generalizes the lower bound on threshold black-box secret sharing schemes. Section 4 presents our gluing technique that glues a Vandermonde matrix with a generator matrix modulo an integer. Section 5 shows how to construct a generator matrix over $\mathbb{Z}$ that gives a linear code with both good minimum distance and dual minimum distance modulo every small prime p. The last section collects the results prepared in the previous sections to form our main result of this paper.

2   Monotone Span Programs and Near-Threshold Black-Box Secret Sharing Schemes

Throughout the paper, we denote by $[n]$ the set $\{1, 2, 3, \cdots, n\}$. We denote by $2^{[n]}$ the set of all subsets of $[n]$. Then $2^{[n]}$ has size 2^n.

2.1   Monotone Span Program

Monotone span programs (MSP for short) over finite fields were introduced by Karchmer and Wigderson [19]. Monotone span program is an efficient tool to construct linear secret sharing scheme (LSSS for short) for a given access structure. It is well known that there is a one-to-one correspondence between monotone span programs over finite fields with linear secret sharing schemes over finite fields (see e.g. [1,16]). Monotone span programs over rings (in particular over integers $\mathbb{Z}$) were introduced in [10,12] and it turns out that they have a similar correspondence with black-box secret sharing schemes. In addition, monotone span programs over rings are the basis for multi-party computation over black-box rings, as studied in [11]. In particular, the techniques of [7] for secure multiplication and VSS apply to this flavor of monotone span program as well.

Definition 1. The pair (Γ, Δ) with $\Gamma, \Delta \subseteq 2^{[n]}$ is called an access structure on $[n]$ if $\emptyset \in \Delta$, $[n] \in \Gamma$ and $\Gamma \cap \Delta = \emptyset$. Furthermore, it is called a monotone access structure if Γ is monotonously increasing and Δ is monotonously decreasing, i.e.,

(i) if $S_1 \in \Gamma$ and $S_1 \subseteq S_2$, then $S_2 \in \Gamma$;
(ii) if $T_1 \in \Delta$ and $T_2 \subseteq T_1$, then $T_2 \in \Delta$.

Let $t, r, n \in \mathbb{Z}$ with $0 < t < r < n$. Then $\mathfrak{R}_{t,r,n} = (\Delta_{t,n}, \Gamma_{r,n})$ is defined to be the access structure satisfying

(i) $\Delta_{t,n} = \{T \subseteq [n] : |T| \leq t\}$, and
(ii) $\Gamma_{r,n} = \{S \subseteq [n] : |S| \geq r\}$.

A monotone increasing set Γ can be efficiently described by the set Γ^- consisting of the minimal elements (sets) in Γ, i.e., the elements in Γ for which no proper subset is also in Γ. Similarly, the set Δ^+ consists of the maximal elements (sets) in Δ, i.e., the elements in Δ for which no proper superset is also in Δ. It is obvious that (Γ^-, Δ^+) generates a monotone access structure (Γ, Δ), i.e., Γ consists of subsets of $[n]$ containing an element of Γ^- and Δ consists of subsets of $[n]$ that are contained in an element of Δ^+.

Definition 2. A monotone access structure (Γ, Δ) is said to be complete if $\Gamma \cup \Delta = 2^{[n]}$. Thus, if $r = t + 1$, then $\mathfrak{R}_{t,r,n}$ is complete. In this case, we say that it is a threshold access structure and denote $\mathfrak{R}_{t,t+1,n}$ by $\mathfrak{R}_{t,n}$.

We provide necessary and sufficient conditions under which a (Γ, Δ)-scheme is a black-box secret sharing scheme for (Γ, Δ). This is a generalization of threshold monotone span programs over rings introduced in [10], where the latter was a generalization of monotone span program over finite fields introduced by Karchmer and Wigderson [19]. We will show that monotone span programs in this paper have a similar correspondence with black-box secret sharing schemes.

Let R be a ring and let (Γ, Δ) be a monotone access structure on $[n]$ and $M \in R^{h \times e}$ with $h \geq n$. We define a surjective function $\Psi : [h] \to [n]$ to group the rows of M. We say that "the j-th row is labelled by $\Psi(j)$" or "$\Psi(j)$ owns the j-th row." For any $S \subseteq [n]$, we write M_S to denote the submatrix obtained by keeping the rows M_i such that $\Psi(i) \in S$ (and not $i \in S$). Denote by h_S the cardinality $|\Psi^{-1}(S)|$. For any vectors $\mathbf{x}$ of length n, we define $\mathbf{x}_S$ analogously. Furthermore, for each $S \in \Gamma$, there exists a vector $\boldsymbol{\lambda}(S) \in R^{h_S}$ which is called a reconstruction vector. Denote by $\mathcal{R}$ the collection of reconstruction vectors. We denote by $\mathcal{B}$ the quadruple $(R, M, \Psi, \mathcal{R})$. Throughout this paper, all vectors are row vectors and we denote by $\mathbf{u}'$ the transpose of a vector $\mathbf{u}$.

Definition 3. A Monotone Span Program (MSP) $\mathcal{M}$ over a ring R is a quadruple $(R, M, \Psi, \boldsymbol{\mu}_e)$, where M is an $h \times e$ matrix over R with $n \leq h$, $\Psi : [h] \to [n]$ is a surjective function and $\boldsymbol{\mu}_e = (1, 0, 0, \ldots, 0) \in R^e$ is a vector that is called the target vector. The size of $\mathcal{M}$ is the number h of rows of M and is denoted as size$(\mathcal{M})$. If $R = \mathbb{Z}$, we call it an integer monotone span program. The expansion factor of $\mathcal{M}$ is defined to be the ratio h/n, where h is the number of rows of M.

Definition 4. Let R be a ring and let (Γ, Δ) be a monotone access structure on $[n]$. We say that a monotone span program $\mathcal{M} = (R, M, \Psi, \boldsymbol{\mu}_e)$ computes (Γ, Δ) if

(P1) for any $S \in \Gamma$, $\boldsymbol{\mu}_e \in \mathrm{im}(M_S')$, where M_S' is the transpose of M_S and $\mathrm{im}(M_S')$ stands for the row space of M_S; and

(P2) for any $T \in \Delta$, there exists a vector $\boldsymbol{\lambda} \in R^e$ with the first coordinate $\lambda_1 = 1$ such that $M_T \boldsymbol{\lambda}' = \mathbf{0}'$.

As noted in [10], if R is a field, then $\boldsymbol{\mu}_e \notin \mathrm{im}(M_S')$ implies that there exists a vector $\boldsymbol{\lambda} \in R^e$ with the first coordinate $\lambda_1 = 1$ such that $M_S \boldsymbol{\lambda}' = \mathbf{0}'$. If R is not a field this does not necessarily hold.

Using representations of monotone access structures as monotone Boolean formulas and using induction in a similar style as in [2], it is straightforward to verify that for every monotone access structure (Γ, Δ), there is an integer monotone span program that computes (Γ, Δ).

Lemma 1. *A monotone span program* $\mathcal{M} = (R, M, \Psi, \boldsymbol{\mu}_e)$ *computes* (Γ, Δ) *if and only if*

(R1) for any $S \in \Gamma$, *the equation* $\mathbf{x}M_S = \boldsymbol{\mu}_e$ *is solvable in R;*
(R2) for any $T \in \Delta$, *the equation* $\left(\begin{smallmatrix}\boldsymbol{\mu}_e\\M_T\end{smallmatrix}\right)\mathbf{x} = \boldsymbol{\mu}'_{h_T+1}$ *is solvable in R.*

Proof. It is clear that (P1) and (R1) are equivalent. To see the equivalence of (P2) and (R2), we note that $\boldsymbol{\mu}_e \cdot \boldsymbol{\lambda}' = 1$ implies that the first coordinate of $\boldsymbol{\lambda}$ is 1.

The above result converts a monotone span program $\mathcal{M} = (R, M, \Psi, \boldsymbol{\mu}_e)$ computing (Γ, Δ) to solvability of linear equations in R. If R is the integer ring, then we can reduce solvability of linear equations in $\mathbb{Z}$ to solvability of linear equations in $\mathbb{Z}_{p^\ell}$ for every prime p and integer $\ell \geq 1$.

Lemma 2. *Let* $N \in \mathbb{Z}^{m \times n}$ *and* $\mathbf{b} \in \mathbb{Z}^m$. *Then* $N\mathbf{x}' = \mathbf{b}'$ *is solvable over $\mathbb{Z}$ if and only if it is solvable over* $\mathbb{Z}_{p^\ell}$ *for all prime p and integer $\ell \geq 1$.*

Proof. The "only if" part is clear.

Now we prove the "if" part. By [10, Lemma 1], it is sufficient to show that $N\mathbf{x}' = \mathbf{b}'$ is solvable modulo k for every integer $k \geq 2$. Let k have the canonical factorization $k = \prod_{i=1}^{r} p_i^{e_i}$. Assume that $\mathbf{u}_i$ is a solution of $N\mathbf{x}' \equiv \mathbf{b}'$ (mod $p_i^{e_i}$). By the Chinese Remainder Theorem, we can find a vector $\mathbf{u} \in \mathbb{Z}_k$ such that $\mathbf{u} \equiv \mathbf{u}_i$ (mod $p_i^{e_i}$). This implies that $\mathbf{u}$ is a solution of $N\mathbf{x}' \equiv \mathbf{b}'$ (mod k).

Theorem 1. *Let* (Γ, Δ) *be a monotone access structure on* $[n]$. *Then* $\mathcal{M} = (\mathbb{Z}, M, \Psi, \boldsymbol{\mu}_e)$ *is a monotone span program computing* (Γ, Δ) *if and only if* $\mathcal{M}_{p^\ell} = (\mathbb{Z}_{p^\ell}, M, \Psi, \boldsymbol{\mu}_e)$ *is a monotone span program computing* (Γ, Δ) *for every prime p and integer $\ell \geq 1$, where M and $\boldsymbol{\mu}_e$ in $\mathcal{M}_p$ are viewed as a vector and a matrix modulo p^ℓ, respectively.*

Proof. Assume that $\mathcal{M} = (\mathbb{Z}, M, \Psi, \boldsymbol{\mu}_e)$ is a monotone span program computing (Γ, Δ). By taking modulo p^ℓ, we can easily show that $\mathcal{M}_p = (\mathbb{Z}_{p^\ell}, M, \Psi, \boldsymbol{\mu}_e)$ is a monotone span program computing (Γ, Δ) for every prime p and integer $\ell \geq 1$.

Now we prove the other direction. By Lemma 1, the conditions (R1) and (R2) are satisfied for $R = \mathbb{Z}_{p^\ell}$ for every prime p and integer $\ell \geq 1$. By Lemma 2, the conditions (R1) and (R2) are satisfied for $R = \mathbb{Z}$. By Lemma 1 again, $\mathcal{M} = (\mathbb{Z}, M, \Psi, \boldsymbol{\mu}_e)$ is a monotone span program computing (Γ, Δ).

This is an interesting mathematical result that obeys the local-global principle, also known as the Hasse principle. In mathematics (in particular number theory), the local-global principle says that a phenomenon is true globally if and only if it is true locally. A well-known example obeying this the local-global principle is the

Hasse-Minkowski theorem which states that the local-global principle holds for the problem of representing 0 by quadratic forms over the rational numbers. Of course, there are also some examples that do not obey the local-global principal. A counterexample by Ernst S. Selmer shows that the Hasse-Minkowski theorem cannot be extended to forms of degree 3 (see [21, pp. 250–258]).

Theorem 1 is a bridge to connect integer monotone span programs with monotone span programs over $\mathbb{Z}_{p^\ell}$. This in turns allows us to construct integer monotone span programs via monotone span programs over finite fields.

Theorem 2. *Let (Γ, Δ) be a monotone access structure on $[n]$. Let p be a prime and let $(\mathbb{Z}_p, M, \Psi)$ be a triple defined in Subsect. 2.1. If $M \in \mathbb{Z}_p^{h \times e}$ and*

(O1) for any $S \in \Gamma$, the $\mathbb{F}_p$-rank of M_S is e; and
(O2) for any $T \in \Delta$, the $\mathbb{F}_p$-rank of N_T is h_T, where N is the $h \times (e-1)$ matrix obtained from M by removing the first column,

Then for any integer $\ell \geq 1$, $(\mathbb{Z}_{p^\ell}, M^{(\ell)}, \Psi, \boldsymbol{\mu}_e)$ is a monotone span program computing (Γ, Δ), where $M^{(\ell)}$ is viewed as a lifting of M modulo p^ℓ, i.e., each entry a of M can be replaced by any element b satisfying $b \equiv a \pmod{p^\ell}$.

Proof. By Lemma 1, it is sufficient to show that the conditions (R1) and (R2) hold for the quadruple $(\mathbb{Z}_{p^\ell}, M^{(\ell)}, \Psi, \boldsymbol{\mu}_e)$. Let $S \in \Gamma$, then by (O1) the $\mathbb{F}_p$-rank of M_S is e, there is an $e \times e$ submatrix A of M_S such that $\det(A) \not\equiv 0 \mod p$. This implies that $A \pmod{p^\ell}$ is invertible. Thus, there exists a vector $\mathbf{u} \in \mathbb{Z}_{p^\ell}^e$ such that $\mathbf{u}A \equiv \boldsymbol{\mu}_e \pmod{p^\ell}$. Without loss of generality, we may assume that $M^{(\ell)} = \binom{A}{C}$ for some $(h-e) \times e$ matrix C over $\mathbb{F}_q$. Then $(\mathbf{u}, \mathbf{0})M^{(\ell)} = (\mathbf{u}, \mathbf{0})\binom{A}{C} = \mathbf{u}A \equiv \boldsymbol{\mu}_e \pmod{p^\ell}$. This proves (R1) for the quadruple $(\mathbb{Z}_{p^\ell}, M^{(\ell)}, \Psi, \boldsymbol{\mu}_e)$.

Let $M = (\mathbf{b}'|N)$. By (O2), for any $T \in \Delta$, the $\mathbb{F}_p$-rank of N_T is h_T. Hence, there is an $h_T \times h_T$ submatrix E of N_T such that $\det(E) \not\equiv 0 \mod p$. This implies that $E \pmod{p^\ell}$ is invertible. Thus, there exists a vector $\mathbf{v} \in \mathbb{Z}_{p^\ell}^{h_T}$ such that $E\mathbf{v}' \equiv -\mathbf{b}' \pmod{p^\ell}$. Without loss of generality, we may assume that $M_T^{(\ell)} = (\mathbf{b}'|E, F)$. Then $M_T^{(\ell)}(1, \mathbf{v}, \mathbf{0})' = (\mathbf{b}'|E, F)(1, \mathbf{v}, \mathbf{0})' = \mathbf{b} + E\mathbf{v}' = \mathbf{0} \pmod{p^\ell}$. This proves (R2) for the quadruple $(\mathbb{Z}_{p^\ell}, M^{(\ell)}, \Psi, \boldsymbol{\mu}_e)$.

We are interested in the smallest size of a monotone span program $\mathcal{M}$ computing (Γ, Δ). This is because this number determines the secret size (see Theorem 3).

Definition 5. For a given (Γ, Δ), denote by $\mathrm{msp}_R(\Gamma, \Delta)$ the smallest size of a monotone span program $\mathcal{M}$ over R computing (Γ, Δ). We also denote $\mathrm{msp}_{\mathbb{Z}}(\Gamma, \Delta)$ by $\mathrm{msp}(\Gamma, \Delta)$.

The main purposes of this paper are (i) to derive a lower bound on $\mathrm{msp}(\Gamma, \Delta)$; and more importantly (ii) to explicitly construct an MSP over $\mathbb{Z}$ with expansion factor achieving this lower bound up to a constant multiplicative factor.

2.2 Black-Box Secret Sharing Scheme

In this subsection, we will prove a one-to-one correspondence between black-box secret sharing schemes and integer monotone span programs. Now we introduce black-box secret sharing schemes.

Definition 6. Let (Γ, Δ) be a monotone access structure on $[n]$. A black-box secret sharing scheme (BBSSS for short) for (Γ, Δ) is a quadruple $\mathcal{B} = (\mathbb{Z}, M, \Psi, \mathcal{R})$ defined in Subsect. 2.1 satisfying the following requirement. Let G be an arbitrary finite Abelian group and $S \subseteq [n]$ be a non-empty set. For a uniformly distributed $s \in G, \mathbf{g} = (g_1, \cdots, g_e) \in G^e$ given that $g_1 = s$, define $\mathbf{s} = \mathbf{g}M' \in \mathbb{Z}^h$. Then:

(Q1) (Completeness) If $S \in \Gamma$, then $\boldsymbol{\lambda}(S) \cdot \mathbf{s}'_S = s$ with probability 1.
(Q2) (Privacy) If $T \in \Delta$, then $\mathbf{s}_T$ contains no Shannon information on s.

If $(\Gamma, \Delta) = \mathfrak{R}_{t,r,n}$, we say $\mathcal{B}$ is a near-threshold black-box secret sharing scheme with privacy t and reconstruction r. Furthermore, if $(\Gamma, \Delta) = \mathfrak{R}_{t,n}$, we say $\mathcal{B}$ is a threshold black-box secret sharing scheme.

In [10], it was proved that there is a one-to-one correspondence between threshold black-box secret sharing schemes and integer monotone span programs. We also note that [10] gives a characterization on threshold black-box secret sharing schemes.

Theorem 3. *Let (Γ, Δ) be a monotone access structure on $[n]$. Then there is a black-box secret sharing scheme $\mathcal{B} = (\mathbb{Z}, M, \Psi, \mathcal{R})$ for (Γ, Δ) if and only if there exists an integer monotone span program $\mathcal{M} = (\mathbb{Z}, M, \Psi, \boldsymbol{\mu}_e)$ computing (Γ, Δ).*

Proof. Assume that $\mathcal{M} = (\mathbb{Z}, M, \Psi, \boldsymbol{\mu}_e)$ is an integer monotone span program computing (Γ, Δ), i.e., the conditions (P1) and (P2) are given. Now we want to show that the conditions (Q1) and (Q2) are satisfied.

Let us fix a finite Abelian group G. Sample $s \in G$ uniformly at random and sample $\mathbf{g} = (s, g_2, \cdots, g_e)$ uniformly at random from $\{s\} \times G^{e-1}$. Lastly, let $\mathbf{s} = \mathbf{g}M'$. Let $S \in \Gamma$, by (P1), there exists a vector $\mathbf{u} \in \mathbb{Z}^{h_S}$ such that $\mathbf{u}M_S = \boldsymbol{\mu}_e$. This gives $s = \boldsymbol{\mu}_e \cdot \mathbf{g}' = (\mathbf{u}M_S) \cdot \mathbf{g}' = \mathbf{u} \cdot \mathbf{s}'_S$. To prove (Q2), we have to show that for any $T \in \Delta$ and any $s_1, s_2 \in G$, given a vector $\mathbf{g}_1 \in \mathbb{Z}^e$ with the first coordinate of $\mathbf{g}_1$ equal to s_1, there exists $\mathbf{g}_2$ such that s_2 is the first coordinate of $\mathbf{g}_2$ and $M_T\mathbf{g}'_1 = M_T\mathbf{g}'_2$. Let $\boldsymbol{\lambda} \in \mathbb{Z}^e$ with the first coordinate equal to 1 such that $M_T\boldsymbol{\lambda}' = \mathbf{0}'$. Put $\mathbf{g}_2 = \mathbf{g}_1 + (s_2 - s_1)\boldsymbol{\lambda}$. Then the first coordinate of $\mathbf{g}_2$ is s_2. Furthermore, we have $M_T\mathbf{g}'_2 = M_T(\mathbf{g}_1 + (s_2 - s_1)\boldsymbol{\lambda})' = M_T\mathbf{g}'_1 + (s_2 - s_1)M_T\boldsymbol{\lambda}' = M_T\mathbf{g}'_1$.

Now we prove the other direction. We prove one by one. For any $S \in \Gamma$, let $\boldsymbol{\lambda}(S) \in \mathcal{R}$. Choose a prime p such that p is bigger than the maximal absolute value of all entries of $\boldsymbol{\lambda}(S)M_S$. Set $G = \mathbb{Z}_p$ and let $\mathbf{g}_i \in G^e$ be the vector such that the ith position of $\mathbf{g}_i$ is 1 and the rest are 0. Then for $j \in [e]$, we have

$$\delta_{1,j} \equiv \boldsymbol{\lambda}(S)M_S\mathbf{g}'_i \pmod{p},$$

where $\delta_{1,j}$ is the Kronecker-delta function. Combining these e equations together, we obtain $\boldsymbol{\mu}_e \equiv \boldsymbol{\lambda}(S)M_S \pmod{p}$. As p is bigger than all entries of $\boldsymbol{\lambda}(S)M_S$, we get $\boldsymbol{\mu}_e = \boldsymbol{\lambda}(S)M_S \in \mathrm{im}(M)$.

Suppose that $T \in \Delta$. Recall that we want to show the existence of $\mathbf{v} = (1, v_2, \cdots, v_e) \in \mathbb{Z}^e$ such that $M_T \mathbf{v}' = \mathbf{0}'$. Let $M_T = (\mathbf{b}'|N_T)$, where $\mathbf{b}' \in \mathbb{Z}^{h_T}$ is the first column of M_T and $N_T \in \mathbb{Z}^{h_T \times (e-1)}$. Then the existence of such $\mathbf{v}$ is equivalent to the solvability of $-\mathbf{b}' = N_T \mathbf{x}$ in $\mathbb{Z}$. So by Lemma 2, to show that $-\mathbf{b}' = N_T \mathbf{x}$ is solvable over $\mathbb{Z}$, it is equivalent to showing that it is solvable modulo k for any integer $k \geq 2$.

Fix $k \geq 2$ and set $G = \mathbb{Z}_k$. Now for $T \in \Delta$, it follows from the privacy condition (Q2) that there exists $\mathbf{g}_1 \in \mathbb{Z}^e$ such that the first coordinate of $\mathbf{g}_1$ is $s - 1$ and $\mathbf{g}_1(M_T)' = \mathbf{g}(M_T)'$. Setting $\mathbf{v} = \mathbf{g} - \mathbf{g}_1$, Then the first coordinate of $\mathbf{v}$ is 1 and $M_T \mathbf{v}' = \mathbf{0}'$, i.e., $-\mathbf{b}' = N_T \mathbf{x}$ is solvable over $\mathbb{Z}_k$.

Definition 7. Let (Γ, Δ) be a monotone access structure on $[n]$. The expansion factor ϱ of a black-box secret sharing scheme $\mathcal{B} = (\mathbb{Z}, M, \Psi, \mathcal{R})$ for (Γ, Δ) is defined to be the ratio $\frac{h}{n}$, where h is the number of rows of M.

3   A Lower Bound on Expansion Factors

In this section, we are going to derive a lower bound on the expansion factor so that we know how far our construction of BBSSS is away from optimality. In literatures, some lower bounds have been derived (see [3,5]). For the sake of completeness, we derive a lower bound via a simple argument.

The idea is to obtain a lower bound on monotone span programs over finite fields $\mathbb{F}_p$ for primes p. As an integer monotone span program gives rise to a monotone span program modulo a prime with the same expansion factor, any lower bound on expansion factors of monotone span programs modulo primes is also a lower bound on integer monotone span programs. As one can expect, the worst lower bound on expansion factors of monotone span programs are from modulo 2. Thus, by deriving a lower bound on monotone span programs modulo 2 for the access structure $\mathfrak{R}_{t,r,n}$, we obtain a lower bound on the expansion factor of BBSSS.

Let write $\mathrm{msp}_2(\Gamma, \Delta)$ for $\mathrm{msp}_{\mathbb{F}_2}(\Gamma, \Delta)$. We first provide a lower bound on $\mathrm{msp}_2(\mathfrak{R}_{1,r,n})$.

Proposition 3. One has $\mathrm{msp}_2(\mathfrak{R}_{1,r,n}) \geq n \log \frac{n}{r-1}$.

Proof. Let $\mathcal{M} = (\mathbb{Z}_2, M, \Psi, \boldsymbol{\mu}_e)$ be a monotone span program computing $\mathfrak{R}_{1,r,n}$. For $M \in \mathbb{Z}_2^{h \times e}$, we write $M_i \in \mathbb{Z}_2^{h_i \times e}$ and h_i to represent $M_{\{i\}}$ and $h_{\{i\}}$, respectively. Since we are going to find a lower bound on h, we want to bound them when h_i is minimized. So we assume that all rows of M_i are $\mathbb{Z}_2$-linearly independent for any $1 \leq i \leq n$.

Define $H_0 = \{(0, v_2, \cdots, v_e) \in \mathbb{Z}_2^e\}$ and $H_1 = \{(1, v_2, \cdots, v_e) \in \mathbb{Z}_2^e\}$. Since $\{i\} \in \Delta(\mathfrak{R}_{1,r,n})$, there exists $\mathbf{c} \in \ker(M_i)$ with the first coordinate equal to 1, where $\ker(M_i)$ denotes the solution space of $M_i \mathbf{x}' = \mathbf{0}'$. Hence, $\ker(M_i) \cap H_1 \neq \emptyset$.

We claim that $|\ker(M_i) \cap H_0| = |\ker(M_i) \cap H_1| = 2^{e-1-h_i}$. Note that $\ker(M_i) \subseteq H_0 \cup H_1 = \mathbb{Z}_2^e$ and $|\ker(M_i)| = 2^{h_i}$. To prove our claim, it is sufficient to show that $|\ker(M_i) \cap H_0| = |\ker(M_i) \cap H_1|$. This is true as one can easily verify that $\mathbf{c} + \ker(M_i) \cap H_0 = |\ker(M_i) \cap H_1|$.

Let S be a subset of $[n]$ of size r, we have $S \in \Gamma(\mathfrak{R}_{1,r,n})$. Thus, $\boldsymbol{\mu}_e$ belongs to $\mathrm{im}(M_S')$. In other words, the first column of M_S is not a linear combination of the others. This implies that $\ker(M_S) \cap H_1 = \emptyset$. This means that for any $\mathbf{v} \in H_1$, it can appears in $\ker(M_i) \cap H_1$ for at most $(r-1)$ of $i \in S$. This gives the following inequality

$$(r-1)2^{e-1} = (r-1)|H_1| \geq \sum_{i=1}^{n} |\ker(M_i) \cap H_1| = \sum_{i=1}^{n} 2^{e-1-h_i},$$

i.e., $\sum_{i=1}^{n} 2^{-h_i} \leq r - 1$.

Recall that by the Log Sum Inequality, for any non-negative $a_1, \cdots, a_n$, $b_1, \cdots, b_n$, we have

$$\sum_{i=1}^{n} a_i \log \frac{a_i}{b_i} \geq a \log \frac{a}{b},$$

where $a = \sum_{i=1}^{n} a_i$ and $b = \sum_{i=1}^{n} b_i$. Let $a_i = 1$ and $b_i = 2^{-h_i}$. Then $a = n$ and $b = \sum_{i=1}^{n} 2^{-h_i} \leq r - 1$. Then

$$h = \sum_{i=1}^{n} h_i = \sum_{i=1}^{n} 1 \cdot \log \frac{1}{2^{-h_i}} \geq n \log \frac{n}{\sum_{i=1}^{n} 2^{-h_i}} \geq n \log \frac{n}{r-1}.$$

To find lower bounds on the expansion factor of the access structure $\mathfrak{R}_{t,r,n}$, let us consider the dual of $\mathfrak{R}_{t,r,n}$.

Definition 8. The dual (Γ^*, Δ^*) of a monotone access structure (Γ, Δ) on $[n]$ is defined by

(i) $\Delta^* = \{T \subseteq [1, n] : \bar{T} \in \Gamma\}$, where $\bar{T}$ is the complement of T, i.e., $(\bar{T}) = [n] \setminus T$.
(ii) $\Gamma^* = \{S \subseteq [1, n] : \bar{S} \in \Delta\}$.

It is easy to verify that (Γ^*, Δ^*) is a monotone access structure $[n]$ as long as (Γ, Δ) is.

Remark 1. One has $\mathfrak{R}_{t,r,n}^* = \mathfrak{R}_{n-r,n-t,n}$.

Lemma 4 (See [19]). *For any finite field $\mathbb{F}$ and monotone access structure (Γ, Δ), we have the equality $\mathrm{msp}_{\mathbb{F}}(\Gamma, \Delta) = \mathrm{msp}_{\mathbb{F}}(\Gamma^*, \Delta^*)$.*

Remark 2. It follows from Lemma 4 that $\mathrm{msp}_{\mathbb{F}}(\mathfrak{R}_{t,r,n}) = \mathrm{msp}_{\mathbb{F}}(\mathfrak{R}_{n-t,n-r,n})$. Thus, to find $\mathrm{msp}_{\mathbb{F}}(T_{t,r,n})$, we can always assume that $r \geq \frac{n-1}{2}$.

Theorem 4. *If $1 \leq t < r < n$, then $\mathrm{msp}_2(\mathfrak{R}_{t,r,n}) \geq n \log \frac{n+1}{2(r-t+1)}$.*

Proof. By Remark 2, we may assume that $r \geq \frac{n-1}{2}$. Consider any MSP $\mathcal{M} = (\mathbb{F}_2, M, \Psi, \epsilon)$ computing $\mathfrak{R}_{t,r,n}$. Without loss of generality, we may assume that $h_1 \leq h_2 \leq \cdots \leq h_n$. It is clear that $(M_1'|M_2'|\cdots|M_{r+1}')'$ is an MSP computing $\mathfrak{R}_{t,r,r+1}$. So we have $\sum_{i=1}^{r+1} h_i \geq \mathrm{msp}_2(\mathfrak{R}_{t,r,r+1})$. Note that for any $j > r+1, h_j \geq h_{r+1} \geq \frac{\mathrm{msp}_2(\mathfrak{R}_{t,r,r+1})}{r+1}$. Hence,

$$h = \sum_{i=1}^{r+1} h_i + \sum_{j=r+2}^{n} h_i \geq \mathrm{msp}_2(\mathfrak{R}_{t,r,r+1}) + \frac{n-(r+1)}{r+1}\mathrm{msp}_2(\mathfrak{R}_{t,r,r+1})$$

$$= \frac{n}{r+1}\mathrm{msp}_2(\mathfrak{R}_{t,r,r+1}).$$

This gives

$$\mathrm{msp}_2(\mathfrak{R}_{t,r,n}) \geq \frac{n}{r+1}\mathrm{msp}_2(\mathfrak{R}_{t,r,r+1}) = \frac{n}{r+1}\mathrm{msp}_2(\mathfrak{R}_{1,r+1-t,r+1})$$

$$\geq n\log\frac{r+1}{r-t+1} \geq n\log\frac{n+1}{2(r-t+1)}$$

and the proof is completed.

By considering modulo 2, we obtain the following lower bound.

Theorem 5. *For all integers r, t, n with $0 < t < r < n$, one has $\mathrm{msp}(\mathfrak{R}_{t,r,n}) \geq n \cdot \log\frac{n+1}{2(r-t+1)}$.*

Remark 3. It follows from [3,5] that, for all integers r, t, n with $0 < t < r < n$, one has

$$\mathrm{msp}(\mathfrak{R}_{t,r,n}) \geq \max\left\{n \cdot \log\frac{n-t+1}{r-t}, n \cdot \log\frac{r+1}{r-t}\right\} \geq n \cdot \log\frac{n+r-t+2}{2(r-t)}. \quad (1)$$

The lower bound in (1) is slightly better than the one given in Theorem 5.

4   Gluing Method

In Subsect. 2.1, we witnessed that an integer monotone span program obeys the local-global principle. Thus, given an access structure $\mathfrak{R}_{t,r,n}$, construction of an integer monotone span program computing $\mathfrak{R}_{t,r,n}$ is equivalent to construction of a monotone span program computing $\mathfrak{R}_{t,r,n}$ modulo every prime power. However, it is usually not easy to directly construct an integer monotone span program computing $\mathfrak{R}_{t,r,n}$ that is also a monotone span program computing $\mathfrak{R}_{t,r,n}$ modulo every prime power. On the other hand, it is much easier to develop a monotone span program computing $\mathfrak{R}_{t,r,n}$ modulo one given prime power. Thus, by the Chinese Remainder Theorem, for any given finite number n, we can lift monotone span programs computing $\mathfrak{R}_{t,r,n}$ modulo all prime $p \leq n$ to an integer monotone span program. The question is how to make it into an integer monotone span program modulo all prime $p > n$.

Our idea is to glue two integer monotone span programs, one is a monotone span program modulo primes $p \le n$ and other one modulo primes $p > n$. The first one can be obtained by lifting monotone span programs modulo every prime power $p \le n$. The other one can be constructed via an integer Vandermonde matrix. As a result, the integrated matrix gives an integer monotone span program that is also a monotone span program modulo every prime power. Hence, by the local-global principal, we obtain an integer monotone span program.

For positive integers $x_1, x_2, \ldots, x_n$, let us define the Vandermonde matrix

$$\Delta_i(x_1, x_2, \ldots, x_n) = \begin{pmatrix} x_1^i & x_1^{1+i} & x_1^{2+i} & \cdots & x_1^{n-1+i} \\ x_2^i & x_2^{1+i} & x_2^{2+i} & \cdots & x_2^{n-1+i} \\ \vdots & \vdots & \vdots & \vdots & \vdots \\ x_n^i & x_n^{1+i} & x_n^{2+i} & \cdots & x_n^{n-1+i} \end{pmatrix}.$$

We further denote by $\delta(x_1, x_2, \ldots, x_n)$ the determinant of $\Delta_1(x_1, x_2, \ldots, x_n)$, i.e., $\delta(x_1, x_2, \ldots, x_n) = \left(\prod_{i=1}^n x_i \right) \left(\prod_{1 \le i < j \le n} (x_j - x_i) \right)$. It is clear that every prime divisor of $\delta(x_1, x_2, \ldots, x_n)$ is at most $\max\{x_1, x_2, \ldots, x_n\}$. The matrix defined in the following lemma gives a threshold black-box secret sharing scheme modulo large primes.

Lemma 5. *Define the matrix*

$$L = \begin{pmatrix} 1 & 1 & 1 & \cdots & 1 \\ 2 & 2^2 & 2^3 & \cdots & 2^t \\ \vdots & \vdots & \vdots & \vdots & \vdots \\ n & n^2 & n^3 & \cdots & n^t \end{pmatrix} \in \mathbb{Z}^{n \times t}. \tag{2}$$

Then we have

(i) *For every subset T of $[n]$ of size t, the equation $\begin{pmatrix} 1 & \mathbf{0} \\ \delta \mathbf{1}' & L_T \end{pmatrix} \mathbf{x}' = \boldsymbol{\mu}'_{t+1}$ is solvable modulo p^ℓ for any prime $p > n$ and integer $\ell \ge 1$, where $\delta = \delta(1, 2, \ldots, n)$.*

(ii) *For every subset S of $[n]$ of size r with $r \ge t+1$, the equation $\mathbf{x}(\delta \mathbf{1}', L_S) = \boldsymbol{\mu}'_{t+1}$ is solvable modulo p^ℓ for all primes $p > n$ and integers $\ell \ge 1$.*

Proof. To prove part (i), we let $|T| = t$ with $T = \{i_1, i_2, \ldots, i_t\}$. Then the matrix L_T is in fact the matrix $\Delta_1(i_1, i_2, \ldots, i_t)$. As $\det(\Delta_1(i_1, i_2, \ldots, i_t)) = \delta(i_1, i_2, \ldots, i_t)$ is co-prime to p^ℓ for every prime $p > n$ and $\ell \ge 1$, we can find a matrix $A \in \mathbb{Z}^{t \times t}$ such that $\Delta_1(i_1, i_2, \ldots, i_s)A$ is the identity matrix I_t modulo p^ℓ, thus we have $\delta \mathbf{1}' \equiv \delta L_T A \mathbf{1}' \pmod{p^\ell}$, i.e., $(1, -\delta \mathbf{1} A') \in \mathbb{Z}_{p^\ell}^{t+1} \pmod{p^\ell}$ is a solution of $(\delta \mathbf{1}', \Delta_1(i_1, i_2, \ldots, i_t))\mathbf{x}' \equiv \mathbf{0}'$ modulo p^ℓ. Thus, it is also a solution of $\begin{pmatrix} 1 & \mathbf{0} \\ \delta \mathbf{1}' & L_T \end{pmatrix} \mathbf{x}' = \boldsymbol{\mu}'_{t+1}$ modulo p^ℓ.

Now let $|S| = r \ge t+1$ and denote $S = \{i_1, i_2, \ldots, i_r\}$. Then

$$(\delta \mathbf{1}', L_S) = \begin{pmatrix} \Delta^{(\delta)}(i_1, \ldots, i_{t+1}) \\ B \end{pmatrix}, \tag{3}$$

for a matrix B in $\mathbb{Z}^{(r-t-1)\times(t+1)}$, where $\Delta^{(\delta)}(i_1,\ldots,i_{t+1})$ is the matrix obtained from $\Delta_0(i_1,\ldots,i_{t+1})$ by multiplying δ to the first column. As $\Delta_0(i_1,\ldots,i_{t+1})$ is invertible modulo p^ℓ, $\Delta^{(\delta)}(i_1,\ldots,i_{t+1})$ is also invertible modulo p^ℓ. Hence, there is a solution $\mathbf{c} \in \mathbb{Z}_{p^\ell}^{t+1}$ of the equation $\mathbf{x}\Delta^{(\delta)}(i_1,i_2,\ldots,i_{t+1}) = \boldsymbol{\mu}_{t+1}$ modulo p^ℓ. Thus, $(\mathbf{c},\mathbf{0}) \in \mathbb{Z}^r$ is a solution of the equation $\mathbf{x}(\delta\mathbf{1}',L_S) \equiv \boldsymbol{\mu}_{t+1}$ modulo p^ℓ.

We now present our gluing method.

Theorem 6. *Let $N_i \in \mathbb{Z}^{m\times(l-1)}$ with $mt < l \leq mr$ be a matrix for $1 \leq i \leq n$. Let $\mathbf{c}_i \in \mathbb{Z}^m$. Put*

$$G = \begin{pmatrix} \mathbf{c}_1' & N_1 \\ \mathbf{c}_2' & N_2 \\ \vdots & \vdots \\ \mathbf{c}_n' & N_n \end{pmatrix}, \qquad N = \begin{pmatrix} N_1 \\ N_2 \\ \vdots \\ N_n \end{pmatrix}.$$

Suppose that for every prime $p \leq n$, every subset T of $[n]$ of size t and every subset S of $[n]$ of size r, the $\mathbb{Z}_p$-ranks of N_T and G_S are mt and l, respectively. Then there exists a monotone span program $\mathcal{M} = (\mathbb{Z}, M, \Psi, \boldsymbol{\mu}_{t+l})$ computing $\mathfrak{R}_{t,r,n}$ with $M \in \mathbb{Z}^{(m+1)n\times(t+l)}$. As a result, $\mathrm{msp}(\mathfrak{R}_{t,r,n}) \leq (m+1)n$.

Proof. Define the product

$$\rho_N = \prod_{S\subset[n],|S|=t} \left(\prod_{A\in\mathcal{M}_t(N_S),\det(A)\neq 0} \det(A) \right),$$

where $\mathcal{M}_t(N_S)$ stands for the set of $mt \times mt$ submatrices of N_S. By the given condition, we know that ρ_N is well defined and it is a nonzero integer. We write the above ρ_N into the product $\rho_N = \zeta_N \times \eta_N$ such that $\gcd(\zeta_N, \prod_{p\leq n} p) = 1$, and all prime divisors of η_N are less than or equal to n.

Define

$$M = \begin{pmatrix} \delta & \mathbf{0} & \mathbf{e}_1 \\ \zeta_N\mathbf{c}_1' & N_1 & \mathbf{0} \\ \hline \delta & \mathbf{0} & \mathbf{e}_2 \\ \zeta_N\mathbf{c}_2' & N_2 & \mathbf{0} \\ \hline \vdots & \vdots & \vdots \\ \hline \delta & \mathbf{0} & \mathbf{e}_n \\ \zeta_N\mathbf{c}_n' & N_n & \mathbf{0} \end{pmatrix}, \tag{4}$$

where $\delta = \delta(1,2,\ldots,n)$ and $\mathbf{e}_i = (i,i^2,\ldots,i^t)$ for $1 \leq i \leq n$. Let Ψ be the map splitting M into the blocks of (4). We claim that $\mathcal{M} = (\mathbb{Z}, M, \Psi, \boldsymbol{\mu}_{t+l})$ is an integer monotone span program computing $\mathfrak{R}_{t,r,n}$.

To prove privacy, by Lemma 1, it is sufficient to show that for every subset $T = \{i_1, i_2,\ldots,i_t\}$ of $[n]$ of size t and every prime power p^ℓ, the equation

$$\begin{pmatrix} \boldsymbol{\mu}_{t+l} \\ M_T \end{pmatrix}\mathbf{x}' \equiv \boldsymbol{\mu}'_{(m+1)t+1} \pmod{p^\ell} \tag{5}$$

has solutions in $\mathbb{Z}_{p^\ell}^{t+l}$. For $p \leq n$, we let L be the matrix defined in (2). Then $L_T = \Delta_1(i_1, i_2, \ldots, i_t)$. It is clear that one can find $D \in \mathbb{Z}^{t \times t}$ such that $L_T D \equiv \det(L_T) I_t \pmod{p^\ell}$. As $\det(L_T)$ is a divisor of δ, $(1, -\frac{\delta}{\det(L_T)} \mathbf{1} D')$ is a solution of the equation $\begin{pmatrix} 1 & \mathbf{0} \\ \delta \mathbf{1}' & L_T \end{pmatrix} \mathbf{x}' \equiv \boldsymbol{\mu}_t \pmod{p^\ell}$. On the other hand, it follows from the given condition that there exists an $mt \times mt$ submatrix A of N_T such that $\gcd(\det(A), p^\ell) = 1$. Then there exists an integer g such that $g \det(A) \equiv 1 \pmod{p^\ell}$. Without loss of generality, we may assume that $N_T = (A, B)$ with $B \in \mathbb{Z}^{mt \times (l-1-mt)}$. Let $H \in \mathbb{Z}_{p^\ell}^{mt \times mt}$ such that $AH = \det(A) I_{mt}$. Then $(1, -gcH', \mathbf{0})$ is a solution of the equation $\begin{pmatrix} 1 & \mathbf{0} \\ \mathbf{c}' & N_T \end{pmatrix} \mathbf{x}' = \begin{pmatrix} 1 & \mathbf{0} & \mathbf{0} \\ \mathbf{c}' & A & B \end{pmatrix} \mathbf{x}' = \boldsymbol{\mu}_l$ modulo p^ℓ, where $\mathbf{c} = \zeta_N(\mathbf{c}_{i_1}, \mathbf{c}_{i_2}, \ldots, \mathbf{c}_{i_t})$. In conclusion, the vector $(1, -gcH', \mathbf{0}, -\frac{\delta}{\det(L_T)} \mathbf{1} D')$ is a solution of (5).

If $p > n$, by Lemma 5 the equation $\begin{pmatrix} 1 & \mathbf{0} \\ \delta \mathbf{1}' & L_T \end{pmatrix} \mathbf{x}' \equiv \boldsymbol{\mu}'_{t+1} \pmod{p^\ell}$ has a solution $(1, \mathbf{u}) \in \mathbb{Z}^{t+1}$. On the other hand, by the given condition, there exists an $mt \times mt$ submatrix E of N_T such that $\det(E) \neq 0$. Without loss of generality, we may assume that $N_T = (E, F)$ with $F \in \mathbb{Z}^{mt \times (l-1-mt)}$. Assume that $e \geq 0$ is an integer such that $p^e | \det(E)$ and $p^{e+1} \nmid \det(E)$. Then by the definition of ζ_N, we have $p^e | \zeta_N$. Let $\zeta_N = p^e a$ and let $\det(E) = p^e b$ with $\gcd(b, p) = 1$. Then there exists an integer d such that $bd \equiv 1 \pmod{p^\ell}$. Let $C \in \mathbb{Z}_{p^\ell}^{mt \times mt}$ such that $AC = \det(E) I_{mt} = p^e b I_{mt}$. Hence, $(1, -ad\mathbf{v}C', \mathbf{0})$ is a solution of the equation $\begin{pmatrix} 1 & \mathbf{0} \\ \mathbf{c}' & N_S \end{pmatrix} \mathbf{x}' = \begin{pmatrix} 1 & \mathbf{0} & \mathbf{0} \\ \mathbf{c}' & E & F \end{pmatrix} \mathbf{x}' \equiv \boldsymbol{\mu}_{mt+1} \pmod{p^\ell}$, where $\mathbf{c} = \zeta_N(\mathbf{c}_{i_1}, \mathbf{c}_{i_2}, \ldots, \mathbf{c}_{i_t})$ and $\mathbf{v} = (\mathbf{c}_{i_1}, \mathbf{c}_{i_2}, \ldots, \mathbf{c}_{i_t})$. Thus, the vector $(1, -ad\mathbf{v}C', \mathbf{0}, \mathbf{u})$ is a solution of (5).

To prove reconstruction, by Lemma 1, it is sufficient to show that for every subset $S = \{i_1, i_2, \ldots, i_r\}$ of $[n]$ of size r and every prime power p^ℓ, the equation

$$\mathbf{x} M_S \equiv \boldsymbol{\mu}_{l+e} \pmod{p^\ell} \tag{6}$$

is solvable. If $p \leq n$, then $\mathbb{Z}_p$-rank of G_S is l. Without loss of generality, we may write $G_S = \begin{pmatrix} \mathbf{b}' & E \\ \mathbf{c}' & F \end{pmatrix}$ such that $(\mathbf{b}', E)$ is an $l \times l$ invertible matrix modulo p^ℓ. As ζ_N is co-prime with p, $(\zeta_N \mathbf{b}', E)$ is also an $l \times l$ invertible matrix modulo p^ℓ. Thus, there exists a vector $\mathbf{v} \in \mathbb{Z}^l$ such that $\mathbf{v} E \equiv \boldsymbol{\mu}_l \pmod{p^\ell}$. Hence, $(\mathbf{v}, \mathbf{0})$ is a solution of (6).

If $p > n$, let $S_1 = \{i_1, i_2, \ldots, i_{t+1}\} \subseteq S$. By Lemma 5, there is a vector $\mathbf{a} \in \mathbb{Z}_{p^\ell}^{t+1}$ such that $\mathbf{a}(\delta \mathbf{1}, L_{S_1}) \equiv \boldsymbol{\mu}_{t+1} \pmod{p^\ell}$. This implies that (6) is solvable modulo p^ℓ.

5   Lifting Codes over Prime Fields

As we have seen in the previous section, to construct a monotone span program, it is sufficient to construct a matrix G satisfying the conditions in Theorem 6. Our idea is to construct generator matrices over $\mathbb{Z}_p$ of the same size for every prime

p such that each generator matrix over $\mathbb{Z}_p$ satisfies the conditions in Theorem 6. Then we lift these matrices using the Chinese Remainder Theorem to obtain the desired matrix G in Theorem 6.

It has been known that linear secret sharing schemes with same secret and share spaces are equivalent to linear codes (see e.g. [4,20]).

Let us first review some notions from coding theory (see e.g. [22,23]) that are relevant to this work. Let $\mathbb{F}_q$ be a finite field of q elements. A q-ary linear code $\mathcal{C}$ of length n is an $\mathbb{F}_q$-subspace of $\mathbb{F}_q^n$. Then dimension of this code is defined to be the dimension of $\mathcal{C}$ as an $\mathbb{F}_q$-linear space. We denote by $[n,k]_q$ a q-ary linear code of length n and dimension k. In case there is no confusion, we just denote $[n,k]_q$ by $[n,k]$ or q-ary $[n,k]$-linear code. The (Euclidean) dual code of $\mathcal{C}$, denote by $\mathcal{C}^\perp$, is defined to be the set $\{\mathbf{x} \in \mathbb{F}_q : \langle \mathbf{c}, \mathbf{x} \rangle = 0 \text{ for all } \mathbf{c} \in \mathcal{C}\}$, where $\langle \cdot, \cdot \rangle$ is the Euclidean inner product. Then it is well known from linear algebra that $\mathcal{C}^\perp$ is a q-ary $[n, n-k]$-linear code. Apart from length and dimension, there is a third parameter d, called minimum distance which plays an important role in coding theory. We denote by $[n,k,d]_q$ a q-ary linear code of length n, dimension k and minimum distance d. We use $d^\perp$ to denote the minimum distance of the dual code. We also call $d^\perp$ the dual distance of $\mathcal{C}$. The distance d and dual distance $d^\perp$ are closely related to privacy and reconstruction of the linear secret sharing scheme arising from this code (see e.g. [4,20]).

For an $[n,k]_q$-linear code $\mathcal{C}$, a matrix G is called a generator matrix of $\mathcal{C}$ if the columns of G form an $\mathbb{F}_q$-basis of $\mathcal{C}$ (note that this is different from the usual definition in which rows of G form an $\mathbb{F}_q$-basis of $\mathcal{C}$). Thus, G has the size $n \times k$. A generator matrix of $\mathcal{C}^\perp$ is called a parity-check matrix of $\mathcal{C}$. Hence, H has size $n \times (n-k)$. It is clear that a linear code $\mathcal{C}$ is uniquely determined by either a generator matrix or a parity-check matrix. Therefore, all three parameters of a linear code $\mathcal{C}$ are completely determined by a generator matrix G or a parity-check matrix H. The length and dimension of $\mathcal{C}$ are determined by size of G or H in an obvious way. The following result shows how the minimum distance is determined by G or H.

Lemma 6 (see [22,29]). *Let $\mathcal{C}$ be a q-ary $[n,k]$-linear code with a generator matrix G or a parity-check matrix H. Then*

(i) *$\mathcal{C}$ has minimum distance d if and only if every $(n-d+1) \times k$ submatrix of G has rank k; and there is a $(n-d) \times k$ submatrix of G with rank less than k.*
(ii) *$\mathcal{C}$ has minimum distance d if and only if every $(d-1) \times (n-k)$ submatrix of H has rank $d-1$; and there is a $d \times (n-k)$ submatrix of H with rank less than d.*

In coding theory, there is a well-known propagation rule to construct new codes from given codes, called concatenation rule. Let $\mathcal{C}_1$ be a p^{k_0}-ary $[n_1, k_1, d_1]$-linear code and let $\mathcal{C}_0$ be a p-ary $[n_0, k_0, d_0]$-linear code. We fix an $\mathbb{F}_p$-isomorphism τ between $\mathbb{F}_{p^{k_0}}$ and $\mathcal{C}_0$. Then the concatenated code $\mathcal{C}$ is defined by $\{(\tau(c_1), \tau(c_2), \ldots, \tau(c_n)) : (c_1, c_2, \ldots, c_n) \in \mathcal{C}_1\}$. Furthermore, $\mathcal{C}$ is an $[n_0 n_1, k_0 k_1, \geq d_0 d_1]_p$-linear code (see e.g. [22]). However, usually $\mathcal{C}$ has small dual distance. In fact, the dual distance of $\mathcal{C}$ is at most the dual distance of $\mathcal{C}_0$. On the other hand, if $\mathcal{C}_0$ is the trivial code $\mathbb{F}_q^{k_0}$, then the dual distance of $\mathcal{C}$ is at least the dual distance of $\mathcal{C}_1$.

Fix an $\mathbb{F}_p$-basis $\gamma_1, \gamma_2, \ldots, \gamma_m$ of $\mathbb{F}_{p^m}$. Let $\beta_1, \beta_2, \ldots, \beta_m$ be an orthogonal basis of $\gamma_1, \gamma_2, \ldots, \gamma_m$, i.e, $\mathrm{Tr}(\gamma_i \beta_j) = \delta_{ij}$, where Tr is the trace map from $\mathbb{F}_{p^m}$ to $\mathbb{F}_p$ and where $\delta_{i,j}$ is the Kronecker-delta function. We define maps φ and ψ from $\mathbb{F}_{p^m}$ to $\mathbb{F}_p^m$ by setting $\varphi(\alpha) = (a_1, a_2, \ldots, a_m)$ if $\alpha = \sum_{i=1}^m a_i \gamma_i$ and $\psi(\alpha) = (b_1, b_2, \ldots, b_m)$ if $\alpha = \sum_{i=1}^m b_i \beta_i$, respectively. Then both maps are $\mathbb{F}_p$-isomorphisms from $\mathbb{F}_{p^m}$ to $\mathbb{F}_p^m$. Furthermore, we have $\langle \varphi(\alpha), \psi(\beta) \rangle = \mathrm{Tr}(\alpha\beta)$. We can extend these two $\mathbb{F}_p$-isomorphisms: $\mathbb{F}_{p^m}^n \to \mathbb{F}_p^{mn}$ by defining $\varphi(\alpha_1, \alpha_2, \ldots, \alpha_n) = (\varphi(\alpha_1), \varphi(\alpha_2), \ldots, \varphi(\alpha_n))$ and $\psi(\alpha_1, \alpha_2, \ldots, \alpha_n) = (\psi(\alpha_1), \psi(\alpha_2), \ldots, \psi(\alpha_n))$, respectively. Then they become $\mathbb{F}_p$-isomorphisms from $\mathbb{F}_{p^m}^n$ to $\mathbb{F}_p^{mn}$.

Lemma 7. *If $\mathcal{C}$ is a p^m-ary $[n, k, d]$-linear code with dual distance $d^\perp$. Then $\varphi(\mathcal{C})$ is a p-ary $[nm, km]$-linear code with distance at least d and dual distance at least $d^\perp$. Furthermore, the dual code of $\varphi(\mathcal{C})$ is $\psi(\mathcal{C}^\perp)$.*

Proof. $\varphi(\mathcal{C})$ (and $\psi(\mathcal{C}^\perp)$, respectively) is the concatenated code with the outer code $\mathcal{C}$ (and $\mathcal{C}^\perp$, respectively) and trivial inner code $\mathbb{F}_p^m$. Thus, $\varphi(\mathcal{C})$ is a p-ary linear code with the desired parameters. It remains to prove that $\varphi(\mathcal{C})^\perp$ is $\psi(\mathcal{C}^\perp)$.

Since the $\mathbb{F}_p$-dimension of $\varphi(\mathcal{C})^\perp$ is $nm - \dim_{\mathbb{F}_p} \varphi(\mathcal{C}) = nm - \dim_{\mathbb{F}_p} \mathcal{C} = nm - mk = \dim_{\mathbb{F}_p} \psi(\mathcal{C}^\perp)$, it is sufficient to show that codewords of $\varphi(\mathcal{C})$ and those of $\psi(\mathcal{C}^\perp)$ are orthogonal. Let $\mathbf{u} = (\varphi(\alpha_1), \varphi(\alpha_2), \ldots, \varphi(\alpha_n)) \in \varphi(\mathcal{C})$ with $(\alpha_1, \alpha_2, \ldots, \alpha_n) \in \mathcal{C}$. Let $\mathbf{v} = (\psi(\lambda_1), \psi(\lambda_2), \ldots, \psi(\lambda_n)) \subset \psi(\mathcal{C}^\perp)$ with $(\lambda_1, \lambda_2, \ldots, \lambda_n) \in \mathcal{C}^\perp$. Then the inner product of these vectors are

$$\langle \mathbf{u}, \mathbf{v} \rangle = \sum_{i=1}^n \langle \varphi(\alpha_i), \psi(\lambda_i) \rangle = \sum_{i=1}^n \mathrm{Tr}(\alpha_i \lambda_i) = \mathrm{Tr}\left(\sum_{i=1}^n \alpha_i \lambda_i\right) = 0.$$

This completes the proof.

Corollary 8. *Let $\mathcal{C}$ be a p^m-ary $[n, k, d]$-linear code with dual distance $d^\perp$. Let $(a_{ij})_{1 \le i \le n, 1 \le j \le k}$ be a generator matrix of $\mathcal{C}$. Then the matrix in $\mathbb{F}_p^{mn \times km}$ given below*

$$G = \begin{pmatrix} \varphi(\gamma_1 a_{11}) \ \varphi(\gamma_2 a_{11}) \ \cdots \ \varphi(\gamma_m a_{11}) & \cdots\cdots & \varphi(\gamma_1 a_{1k}) \ \varphi(\gamma_2 a_{1k}) \ \cdots \ \varphi(\gamma_m a_{1k}) \\ \varphi(\gamma_1 a_{21}) \ \varphi(\gamma_2 a_{21}) \ \cdots \ \varphi(\gamma_m a_{21}) & \cdots\cdots & \varphi(\gamma_1 a_{2k}) \ \varphi(\gamma_2 a_{2k}) \ \cdots \ \varphi(\gamma_m a_{2k}) \\ \vdots \quad\ \vdots \quad\ \vdots \quad\ \vdots & \vdots\ \vdots & \vdots \quad\ \vdots \quad\ \vdots \quad\ \vdots \\ \varphi(\gamma_1 a_{n1}) \ \varphi(\gamma_2 a_{n1}) \ \cdots \ \varphi(\gamma_m a_{n1}) & \cdots\cdots & \varphi(\gamma_1 a_{nk}) \ \varphi(\gamma_2 a_{nk}) \ \cdots \ \varphi(\gamma_m a_{nk}) \end{pmatrix}$$

$$(7)$$

is a generator matrix of $\varphi(\mathcal{C})$, where each $\varphi(\gamma_i a_{jl})$ is viewed as a column vector of length m. Furthermore, define Ψ to be the map from $[mn]$ to $[n]$ such that the first m numbers of $[mn]$ are mapped to 1 and the second m numbers of $[mn]$ are mapped to 2 and so on. Then

(i) *for any $S \subseteq [n]$ with $|S| \ge n - d + 1$, $\varphi(G_S)$ has $\mathbb{F}_p$-rank equal to mk;*

(ii) *for any $T \subseteq [n]$ with $|T| \le d^\perp - 1$, $\varphi(G_T)$ has $\mathbb{F}_p$-rank equal to mt, where $t = |T|$.*

Proof. It is clear that every column of G is a codeword of $\varphi(\mathcal{C})$. By Lemma 7, $\varphi(G)$ has dimension mk. Thus, to show that $\varphi(G)$ is a generator matrix of $\varphi(\mathcal{C})$, it is sufficient to show that all columns of $\varphi(\mathcal{C})$ are linearly independent. Let $\mathbf{g}_1', \mathbf{g}_2', \ldots, \mathbf{g}_k'$ be column vectors of G. We want to show that $\{\varphi(\gamma_i \mathbf{g}_j)\}_{1 \le i \le m, 1 \le j \le k}$ are $\mathbb{F}_p$-linearly independent. Suppose that $\sum_{i=1}^m \sum_{j=1}^k \lambda_{ij}$ $\varphi(\gamma_i \mathbf{g}_j) = \mathbf{0}$ for some $\lambda_{ij} \in \mathbb{F}_p$, i.e., $\varphi\left(\sum_{i=1}^m \sum_{j=1}^k \lambda_{ij} \gamma_i \mathbf{g}_j\right) = \mathbf{0}$. As φ is an isomorphism, we get $\sum_{i=1}^m \left(\sum_{j=1}^k \lambda_{ij} \gamma_i\right) \mathbf{g}_j = \mathbf{0}$. Since $\mathbf{g}_1, \mathbf{g}_2, \ldots, \mathbf{g}_k$ are $\mathbb{F}_{p^m}$-linearly independent, this forces that $\sum_{j=1}^k \lambda_{ij} \gamma_i = 0$ for $i = 1, 2, \ldots, k$. This gives $\gamma_{ij} = 0$ for all $1 \le i \le m$ and $1 \le j \le k$.

Now let $S \subseteq [n]$ with $|S| \ge n - d + 1$. Consider the new code $\mathcal{C}_1$ that is obtained from $\mathcal{C}$ by deleting $n - |S|$ positions at $i \in [n] \setminus S$. Then $\mathcal{C}_1$ is p^m-ary $[n - |S|, k, \ge d - n + |S|]$-linear code. By the first part of this lemma, we know that of $\varphi(G_S)$ is a generator matrix of $\varphi(\mathcal{C}_1)$. Hence, it has rank mk.

Let $T \subseteq [n]$ with $|T| \le d^{\perp} - 1$. If $\mathbf{u}_T \in \mathbb{F}_p^{mt}$ is a solution of $\mathbf{x}\varphi(G_T) = \mathbf{0}$. Then $(\mathbf{u}_T, \mathbf{0}_{[n] \setminus T})$ is a solution of $\mathbf{x}\varphi(G) = \mathbf{0}$. By Lemma 7, $(\mathbf{u}_T, \mathbf{0}_{[n] \setminus T})$ is a codeword in $\psi(\mathcal{C}^{\perp})$. Hence $\psi^{-1}(\mathbf{u}_T, \mathbf{0}_{[n] \setminus T})$ is a codeword of $\mathcal{C}^{\perp}$. As the Hamming weight of $\psi^{-1}(\mathbf{u}, \mathbf{0}_{[n] \setminus T})$ is at most $|T| \le d^{\perp} - 1$, we conclude that $\mathbf{u} = \mathbf{0}$. This implies that the $\mathbb{Z}_p$-rank of $\varphi(G_T')$ is mt. The proof is completed.

Given a matrix $A = (a_{ij})_{1 \le i \le n, 1 \le j \le k} \in \mathbb{F}_{p^m}^{n \times k}$, we denote by $\varphi(A)$ the matrix given in (7).

5.1   Reed-Solomon Codes

In this subsection, we are going to make use of Reed-Solomon codes to construct a matrix G satisfying the conditions of Theorem 6.

Let $m = \lceil \log n \rceil$. Then for any prime p, we have $n \le 2^m \le p^m$. Choose n distinct elements $\alpha_1, \alpha_2, \ldots, \alpha_n \in \mathbb{F}_{p^m}$. We denote by $\mathbb{F}_{p^m}[x]_{<t}$ the set of polynomials in $\mathbb{F}_{p^m}[x]$ of degree less than t. Then $\mathbb{F}_{p^m}[x]_{<t}$ is an $\mathbb{F}_{p^m}$-space of dimension t with a canonical basis $\{1, x, , x^2, \ldots, x^{t-1}\}$. A Reed-Solomon code is defined below

$$\mathcal{RS}[n, t] := \{(f(\alpha_i), f(\alpha_2), \ldots, f(\alpha_n)) : f \in \mathbb{F}_{p^m}[x]_{<t}\}.$$

The code $\mathcal{RS}[n, t]$ is a p^m-ary $[n, t]$-linear code with distance $d = n - t + 1$ and dual distance $d^{\perp} = t + 1$, respectively.

Fix an $\mathbb{F}_{p^m}$-basis $f_2, f_3, \ldots, f_{t+1}$ of $\mathbb{F}_{p^m}[x]_{<t}$. Extend this basis to an $\mathbb{F}_{p^m}$-basis $\{f_i\}_{i=1}^{t+1}$ of $\mathbb{F}_{p^m}[x]_{\le t}$. Define the matrix

$$A^{(p)} = \begin{pmatrix} f_1(\alpha_1) & f_2(\alpha_1) & f_3(\alpha_1) & \cdots & f_{t+1}(\alpha_1) \\ f_1(\alpha_2) & f_2(\alpha_2) & f_3(\alpha_2) & \cdots & f_{t+1}(\alpha_2) \\ \vdots & \vdots & \vdots & \vdots & \vdots \\ f_1(\alpha_n) & f_2(\alpha_n) & f_3(\alpha_n) & \cdots & f_{t+1}(\alpha_n) \end{pmatrix} \tag{8}$$

Then $A^{(p)}$ is a generator matrix of $\mathcal{RS}[n, t+1] = [n, n - t - 1]_{p^m}$.

Lemma 9. *Put $G^{(p)} = \varphi(A^{(p)})$. Then*

(i) *for any subset S of $[n]$ of size $t+1$, $G_S^{(p)}$ has $\mathbb{F}_p$-rank equal to $(t+1)m$; and*
(ii) *for any subset T of $[n]$ of size t, N_T has $\mathbb{F}_p$-rank mt, where N is obtained from $G^{(p)}$ by removing the first column from the left.*

Proof. As $A^{(p)}$ is a generator matrix of $\mathcal{RS}[n, t+1]$ whose distance is $n-t$, Part (i) directly follows from Corollary 8 (i). To prove Part (ii), we consider $B^{(p)}$ that is obtained from $A^{(p)}$ by removing the first column. Then $B^{(p)}$ is a generator matrix of $\mathcal{RS}[n, t]$ whose dual distance is $t+1$. By Corollary 8 (ii), $\varphi(B_T^{(p)})$ has $\mathbb{F}_p$-rank mt. Furthermore, $\varphi(B^{(p)})$ is in fact obtained from N_T by removing the first $m-1$ columns. As a result, N_T has $\mathbb{F}_p$-rank mt as well.

Corollary 10. *For any integer $n \geq 2$ and any integer t with $0 < t < n$, there exists a triple $(\mathbb{Z}, G, \Psi)$ defined in Subsect. 2.1 such that $G \in \mathbb{Z}^{nm \times (t+1)m}$ with $m \geq \lceil \log n \rceil$ and $|\Psi^{-1}(j)| = m$ for all $1 \leq j \leq n$ such that, for every prime $p \leq n$, if G is viewed a matrix modulo p, then*

(i) *for any subset S of $[n]$ of $t+1$, G_S has $\mathbb{F}_p$-rank equal to $(t+1)m$; and*
(ii) *for any subset T of $[n]$ of t, N_T has $\mathbb{F}_p$-rank mt, where N is obtained from G by removing the first column from the left.*

Proof. By Lemma 9, for every prime $p \leq n$, we can construct a matrix $G^{(p)} \in \mathbb{Z}^{nm \times (t+1)m}$ satisfying the two conditions in Lemma 9. By the Chinese Remainder Theorem, we can lift all $G^{(p)}$'s to one matrix $G \in \mathbb{Z}^{nm \times (t+1)m}$ such that $G \equiv G^{(p)} \pmod{p}$. Then G is the desired matrix.

5.2 Algebraic Geometry Codes

In the previous section, we made use of Reed-Solomon codes to construct a matrix G satisfying the conditions in Theorem 6. This would give a threshold BBSSS (see Theorem 7). However, in this case, the expansion factor h is $nm = n\lceil \log n \rceil$, i.e., the ratio is $\frac{h}{n} = \lceil \log n \rceil$ is unbounded. If we want to get a bounded ratio $\frac{h}{n}$, then the lower bound in Theorem 5 indicates that we have to use a near-threshold BBSSS. As in the case of linear secret sharing schemes, we can use algebraic geometry codes to get a bounded ratio $\frac{h}{n}$.

Let us first introduce an algebraic geometry codes very briefly. The reader may refer to the books [26,27] for the details on this topic. For convenience of the reader, we start with some background on global function fields over finite fields. The reader may refer to [24,26] for detailed background on function fields and algebraic-geometric codes.

For a prime power q, let $\mathbb{F}_q$ be the finite field of q elements. An algebraic function field over $\mathbb{F}_q$ in one variable is a field extension $F \supset \mathbb{F}_q$ such that F is a finite algebraic extension of $\mathbb{F}_q(x)$ for some $x \in F$ that is transcendental over $\mathbb{F}_q$. The field $\mathbb{F}_q$ is called the full constant field of F if the algebraic closure of $\mathbb{F}_q$ in F is $\mathbb{F}_q$ itself. Such a function field is also called a global function field. From now on, we always denote by $F/\mathbb{F}_q$ a function field F with the full constant field $\mathbb{F}_q$.

A discrete valuation of $F/\mathbb{F}_q$ is a map from F to $\mathbb{Z}\cup\{+\infty\}$ satisfying certain properties (see [26, Definition 1.19]). Then each discrete valuation ν from $F/\mathbb{F}_q$ to $\mathbb{Z}\cup\{+\infty\}$ defines a valuation ring $O = \{f \in F : \nu(f) \geq 0\}$ that is a local ring [26, Theorem 1.1.13]. The maximal ideal P of O is given by $P = \{f \in F : \nu(f) > 0\}$ and it is called a *place*. We denote the valuation ν and the local ring O corresponding to P by ν_P and O_P, respectively. The residue class field O_P/P, denoted by F_P, is a finite extension of $\mathbb{F}_q$. The extension degree $[F_P : \mathbb{F}_q]$ is called *degree* of P, denoted by $\deg(P)$. A place of degree one is called a *rational* place. For a nonzero function $z \in F$, the principal divisor of z is defined to be $\mathrm{div}(z) = \sum_{P \in \mathbb{P}_F} \nu_P(z)P$. The zero and pole divisors of z are defined to be $\mathrm{div}(z)_0 = \sum_{\nu_P(z)>0} \nu_P(z)P$ and $\mathrm{div}(z)_\infty = -\sum_{\nu_P(z)<0} \nu_P(z)P$, respectively. Then we have $\deg(\mathrm{div}(z)) = 0$, i.e, $\deg(\mathrm{div}(z)_0) = \deg(\mathrm{div}(z)_\infty)$. For two functions $f, g \in F$ and a place P, we have $\nu_P(f+g) \geq \min\{\nu_P(f), \nu_P(g)\}$ and the equality holds if $\nu_p(f) \neq \nu_P(g)$ (note that $\nu_P(0) = +\infty$). This implies that $f + g \neq 0$ if $\nu_P(f) \neq \nu_P(g)$.

If F is the rational function field $\mathbb{F}_q(x)$, then every discrete valuation of $F/\mathbb{F}_q$ is given by either ν_∞ or $\nu_{p(x)}$ for an irreducible polynomial $p(x)$, where ν_∞ is defined by $\nu_\infty(f/g) = \deg(g) - \deg(f)$ and $\nu_{p(x)}(f/g) = a - b$ with $p(x)^a || f$ and $p(x)^b || g$ for two nonzero polynomials $f, g \in \mathbb{F}_q[x]$. It is straightforward to verify that the degrees of places corresponding to ν_∞ and $\nu_{p(x)}$ are 1 and $\deg(p(x))$, respectively.

Let $\mathbb{P}_F$ denote the set of places of F. The divisor group, denoted by $\mathrm{Div}(F)$, is the free abelian group generated by all places in $\mathbb{P}_F$. An element $D = \sum_{P \in \mathbb{P}_F} n_P P$ of $\mathrm{Div}(F)$ is called a divisor of F, where $n_P = 0$ for almost all $P \in \mathbb{P}_F$. We denote n_p by $\nu_P(D)$. The support, denoted by $\mathrm{Supp}(\mathrm{D})$, of D is the set $\{P \in \mathbb{P}_F : n_P \neq 0\}$. Thus, $\mathrm{Supp}(\mathrm{D})$ of a divisor D is always a finite subset of $\mathbb{P}_F$. For a divisor D of $F/\mathbb{F}_q$, we define the Riemann-Roch space associated with D by

$$\mathcal{L}(D) := \{f \in F^* : \mathrm{div}(f) + D \geq 0\} \cup \{0\},$$

where F^* denotes the set of nonzero elements of F. Then $\mathcal{L}(D)$ is a finite dimensional space over $\mathbb{F}_q$ and its dimension $\dim_{\mathbb{F}_q} \mathcal{L}(D)$ is determined by the Riemann-Roch theorem which gives

$$\dim_{\mathbb{F}_q} \mathcal{L}(D) = \deg(D) + 1 - \mathfrak{g} + \dim_{\mathbb{F}_q} \mathcal{L}(W - D),$$

where $\mathfrak{g}$ is the genus of F and W is a canonical divisor of degree $2\mathfrak{g}-2$. Therefore, we always have that $\dim_{\mathbb{F}_q} \mathcal{L}(D) \geq \deg(D) + 1 - \mathfrak{g}$ and the equality holds if $\deg(D) \geq 2\mathfrak{g} - 1$ [26, Theorems 1.5.15 and 1.5.17].

Let p be a prime and let $n > l \geq 2$ be two integers. Let $F/\mathbb{F}_{p^m}$ be a function field with genus $\mathfrak{g}$ and $n + 1$ distinct $\mathbb{F}_{p^m}$-rational places $P_\infty, P_1, P_2, \ldots, P_n$. Define the ordered set $\mathcal{P} = \{P_1, P_2, \ldots, P_n\}$. Denote by $\mathcal{C}(lP_\infty, \mathcal{P})$ the algebraic geometric code defined by

$$\mathcal{C}(lP_\infty, \mathcal{P}) = \{(f(P_1), f(P_2), \ldots, f(P_n)) : f \in \mathcal{L}(lP_\infty)\}. \tag{9}$$

Lemma 11 (see [26, Theorem 2.2.4]). *Let* $\mathfrak{g} < k < n - \mathfrak{g}$. *Then* $\mathcal{C}((k + \mathfrak{g} - 1)P_\infty, \mathcal{P})$ *is a* p^m-*ary* $[n, k, \geq n - k - \mathfrak{g} + 1]$-*linear code and* $\mathcal{C}^\perp((t + 2\mathfrak{g} - 1)P_\infty, \mathcal{P})$ *is a* p^m-*ary* $[n, n - k, \geq k - \mathfrak{g} + 1]$-*linear code. Furthermore, the matrix*

$$
A = \begin{pmatrix}
f_1(P_1) & f_2(P_1) & f_3(P_1) & \cdots & f_k(P_1) \\
f_1(P_2) & f_2(P_2) & f_3(P_2) & \cdots & f_k(P_2) \\
\vdots & \vdots & \vdots & \vdots & \vdots \\
f_1(P_n) & f_2(P_n) & f_3(P_n) & \cdots & f_k(P_n)
\end{pmatrix} \tag{10}
$$

is a generator matrix of $\mathcal{C}((k + \mathfrak{g} - 1)P_\infty, \mathcal{P})$ *whenever* $f_1, f_2, \ldots, f_k$ *are a basis of* $\mathcal{L}((k + \mathfrak{g} - 1)P_\infty)$.

Similar to Corollary 10, we have the following result.

Lemma 12. *Let* $\mathfrak{g} < k < n - \mathfrak{g}$. *Let* $f_2, f_3, \ldots, f_{k-1}$ *be a* $\mathbb{F}_{p^m}$-*basis of* $\mathcal{L}((k + \mathfrak{g} - 2)P_\infty)$ *and let* $f_1, f_2, f_3, \ldots, f_{t+\mathfrak{g}+1}$ *be an* $\mathbb{F}_{p^m}$-*basis of* $\mathcal{L}((k + \mathfrak{g} - 1)P_\infty)$. *Let* A *be the matrix defined in* (10) *and put* $G^{(p)} = \varphi(A)$. *Furthermore, define* Ψ *to be the map from* $[mn]$ *to* $[n]$ *such that the first* m *numbers of* $[mn]$ *are mapped to* 1 *and the second* m *numbers of* $[mn]$ *are mapped to* 2 *and so on. Then*

(i) *for any subset* S *of* $[n]$ *of size at least* $k + \mathfrak{g}$, $G_S^{(p)}$ *has* $\mathbb{F}_p$-*rank equal to* $(t + \mathfrak{g} + 1)m$; *and*

(ii) *for any subset* T *of* $[n]$ *of size* t *with* $t \leq k - \mathfrak{g} - 1$, N_T *has* $\mathbb{F}_p$-*rank* mt, *where* N *is obtained from* $G^{(p)}$ *by removing the first column from the left.*

Proof. Note that A is a generator matrix of $\mathcal{L}((t + 2\mathfrak{g})P_\infty)$ with minimum distance at least $n - 2\mathfrak{g}$. Part (i) follows from Corollary 8.

Let B be the matrix of A obtained from A by removing the first column of A. Then B is a generator matrix of $\mathcal{C}((k + \mathfrak{g} - 2)P_\infty, \mathcal{P})$. By mimicking proof of Corollary 10(ii), we can Part (ii). $\blacksquare$

Corollary 13. *Let* $m \geq 2$ *be an even integer. Then for any integer* $n \geq 2$ *and any integer* k *with* $\frac{2(n+1)}{2^{m/2}-1} < k < n - \frac{2(n+1)}{2^{m/2}-1}$, *there exists a triple* $(\mathbb{Z}, G, \Psi)$ *defined in Subsect. 2.1 such that* $G \in \mathbb{Z}^{nm \times km}$ *and* $|\Psi^{-1}(j)| = m$ *for all* $1 \leq j \leq n$ *such that, for every prime* $p \leq n$, *if* G *is viewed as a matrix modulo* p, *then*

(i) *for any subset* S *of* $[n]$ *of size* r *with* $r \geq k + \frac{2(n+1)}{2^{m/2}-1}$, G_S *has* $\mathbb{F}_p$-*rank equal to* km; *and*

(ii) *for any subset* T *of* $[n]$ *of size* t *with* $t \leq k - \frac{2(n+1)}{2^{m/2}-1} - 1$, N_T *has* $\mathbb{F}_p$-*rank* mt, *where* N *is obtained from* G *by removing the first column from the left.*

Proof. If $p^m \geq n$, then the desired result follows from Corollary 10. Now we assume that $p^m < n$.

Define

$$
i(p, m, n) = \left\lceil \log_p \left(\frac{n}{p^m - 1} \right) \right\rceil. \tag{11}
$$

We claim that

$$p^{i(p,m,n)-1}(p^m - 1) < n \leq p^{i(p,m,n)}(p^m - 1). \tag{12}$$

To prove (12), it is sufficient to verify that $p^{i(p,m,n)-1} < \frac{n}{p^m-1} \leq p^{i(p,m,n)}$, i.e,
$i(p,m,n) - 1 < \log_p\left(\frac{n}{p^m-1}\right) \leq i(p,m,n)$ for all primes p.

Define

$$i(m,n) = \max_{p^m \leq n} p^{i(p,m,n)}(p^{m/2} + 1). \tag{13}$$

For $p^m \leq n$, we have

$$p^{i(p,m,n)}(p^{m/2} + 1) \leq p^{1+\log_p\left(\frac{n+1}{p^m-1}\right)}(p^{m/2} + 1) \leq p\left(\frac{n+1}{p^m - 1}\right)(p^{m/2} + 1)$$

$$= \frac{p(n+1)}{p^{m/2} - 1} \leq \frac{2(n+1)}{2^{m/2} - 1}.$$

For every p with $p^m \leq n$, by Lemma 14, there exists an algebraic function field $F/\mathbb{F}_{p^m}$ of genus $\mathfrak{g} \leq i(p,m,n)$ such that it has at least $n + 1$ distinct $\mathbb{F}_{p^m}$-rational points. We label these $n + 1$ pairwise distinct $\mathbb{F}_{p^m}$-rational points $P_\infty, P_1, P_2, \ldots, P_n$. Let $f_2, f_3, \ldots, f_{t+\mathfrak{g}+1}$ be a $\mathbb{F}_{p^m}$-basis of $\mathcal{L}((t + 2\mathfrak{g} - 1)P_\infty)$ and extend to a $\mathbb{F}_{p^m}$-basis $f_1, f_2, f_3, \ldots, f_{t+\mathfrak{g}+1}$ of $\mathcal{L}((t + 2\mathfrak{g})P_\infty)$. Let A be the matrix defined in (10) and put $G^{(p)} = \varphi(A)$.

By Corollary 13, for any subset S of $[n]$ or size r with $r \geq k + \frac{2(n+1)}{2^{m/2}-1} \geq k + \mathfrak{g}$, $G_S^{(p)}$ has $\mathbb{F}_p$-rank equal to km; and for any subset T of $[n]$ of size t with $t \leq k - \frac{2(n+1)}{2^{m/2}-1} - 1 \leq k - \mathfrak{g} - 1$, N_T has $\mathbb{F}_p$-rank mt. Now by the Chinese Remainder Theorem, we can lift all $G^{(p)}$ to a matrix $G \in \mathbb{Z}^{nm \times km}$ such that $G \equiv G^{(p)} \pmod{p}$. The desired result follows.

6   The Main Results

We are ready to state our final results by collecting some previous results.

Theorem 7. *For any $0 < t < n$, there is a threshold BBSSS over the access structure $\mathfrak{R}_{t,n}$ whose expansion factor ϱ satisfies $\log\frac{n+3}{2} \leq \varrho \leq 1 + \lceil\log n\rceil$.*

Proof. The lower bound follows from Remark 3 directly. By applying the matrix G obtained in Corollary 10 to Theorem 6, we obtain the desired upper bound.

The above upper bound is better than the one given in [10] by an additive constant and worse than the one given in [12] by an additive constant.

Theorem 8. *Let $m \geq 2$ be an even integer. Then for any integer $n \geq 2$ and any integer k with*

$$\frac{2(n+1)}{2^{m/2} - 1} < k < n - \frac{2(n+1)}{2^{m/2} - 1}, \quad r \geq k + \frac{2(n+1)}{2^{m/2} - 1}, \quad t \leq k - \frac{2(n+1)}{2^{m/2} - 1} - 1,$$

one has $\mathrm{msp}(\mathfrak{R}_{t,r,n}) \leq n(1+m)$. *As a result, for any* $0 < t < n - 2\left\lceil\frac{2(n+1)}{2^{m/2}-1}\right\rceil$
and r *with* $r = t + 2\left\lceil\frac{2(n+1)}{2^{m/2}-1}\right\rceil + 1$, *there is a near-threshold BBSSS over the access structure* $\mathfrak{R}_{t,r,n}$ *whose expansion factor* ϱ *satisfies*

$$\frac{m}{2} - 3 \approx \log\frac{n+1}{2(r-t)} \leq \varrho \leq m+1.$$

Proof. The lower bound on $\mathrm{msp}(\mathfrak{R}_{t,r,n})$ follows Theorem 5 directly. By applying the matrix G obtained in Corollary 13 to Theorem 6, we obtain the desired upper bound $\mathrm{msp}(\mathfrak{R}_{t,r,n})$.

An immediate consequence of Theorem 8 is the following result showing that our near-threshold black-box secret sharing schemes are expansionless.

MAIN THEOREM 1. *For any odd integer* $\varrho \geq 3$, *there exists a near-threshold BBSSS over the access structure* $\mathfrak{R}_{t,r,n}$ *with expansion factor* ϱ *and* $r - t = \exp(-O(\varrho))n$. *Furthermore, this is expansionless, i.e., every near-threshold BBSSS over the access structure* $\mathfrak{R}_{t,r,n}$ *with expansion factor* ϱ *must obey* $r - t = \exp(-\Omega(\varrho))n$.

Proof. The first part follows from Theorem 8, while the second part follows from Theorem 5.

Acknowledgments. We are grateful to Dr. Ivan Tjuawinata for his help on some preliminary part and several discussions. The work of Ronald Cramer was supported in part by ERC Advanced Grant No. 74079 (ALGSTRONGCRYPTO).

A   The Subfields of the Garcia-Stichtenoth Tower

In the original Garcia-Stichtenoth tower $\{E_i/\mathbb{F}_{p^m}\}_{i=1}^{\infty}$ (see [17,18]), the extension degree $[E_{i+1} : E_i] = p^m$ for all $i \geq 1$. However, in order to have a tower of slowly growing genus, we split each extension E_{i+1}/E_i into m extensions of degree p.

Lemma 14. *Let* m *be an even number and let* p *be a prime. Then there exists a function field family* $\{F_i/\mathbb{F}_{p^m}\}_{i=1}^{\infty}$ *such that, for every* $i \geq 1$, *the genus* $\mathfrak{g}(F_i)$ *is upper bounded by* $p^i(p^{m/2} + 1)$ *and the number* $N(F_i)$ *is lower bounded by* $p^i(p^m - 1)$.

Proof. Put $r = p^{m/2}$. Let $E_1 \subseteq E_2 \subseteq \ldots$ be the tower of global function fields over $\mathbb{F}_{p^m}$ constructed by Garcia and Stichtenoth [17], that is, $E_1 = \mathbb{F}_{p^m}(x_1)$ is a rational function field and $E_{n+1} = E_n(z_{n+1})$ for $n = 1, 2, \ldots$ with

$$z_{n+1}^r + z_{n+1} = x_n^{r+1} \quad \text{and} \quad x_{n+1} = \frac{z_{n+1}}{x_n}.$$

Then E_{n+1}/E_n is a Galois extension of degree r and $\mathrm{Gal}(E_{n+1}/E_n) \simeq \mathbb{Z}_p^{m/2}$ for each $n \geq 1$. Hence there exists a chain of fields

$$E_n = K_{n,0} \subset K_{n,1} \subset \ldots \subset K_{n,m/2} = E_{n+1}$$

such that $[K_{n,i+1} : K_{n,i}] = p$ for $0 \leq i \leq m/2 - 1$. From results in [17] we know that for all $n \geq 1$ we have

$$\mathfrak{g}(E_n) \leq r^n + r^{n-1}, \qquad N(E_n) \geq (p^m - 1)r^{n-1} + 1.$$

The last inequality implies

$$N(K_{n,i}) \geq \frac{N(E_{n+1})}{[E_{n+1} : K_{n,i}]} \geq p^i(p^m - 1)r^{n-1} + 1 \qquad \text{for } 0 \leq i \leq m/2.$$

Next we establish an upper bound for $\mathfrak{g}(K_{n,i})$. From [17] we know that for each place P of E_n that is ramified in the extension E_{n+1}/E_n we have $\nu_P(x_n) = -1$, and therefore we obtain $\nu_P(x_n^{r+1}) = -r - 1$. It follows that P is totally ramified in E_{n+1}/E_n. According to [17], the sum of the degrees of these places P is equal to $r^{\lfloor n/2 \rfloor}$, and so the same holds for the sum of the degrees of the places P' of $K_{n,i}$ that are ramified in $E_{n+1}/K_{n,i}$, where $0 \leq i \leq m/2 - 1$. For any such P' and the unique place P'' of E_{n+1} lying over it we have

$$d(P''|P') = (p^{m/2-i} - 1)(r + 2).$$

By combining these facts with the Hurwitz genus formula, we obtain

$$2\mathfrak{g}(E_{n+1}) - 2 = p^{m/2-i}(2\mathfrak{g}(K_{n,i}) - 2) + r^{\lfloor n/2 \rfloor}(r + 2)(p^{m/2-i} - 1)$$

for $0 \leq i \leq m/2$, and so

$$\mathfrak{g}(K_{n,i}) \leq \frac{p^i}{r}(\mathfrak{g}(E_{n+1}) - 1) - \frac{1}{2}r^{\lfloor n/2 \rfloor - 1}(r + 2)(r - p^i) + 1 \leq p^i(r^n + r^{n-1}).$$

Taking $\{F_i\}$ be the family $\{K_{0,0}, K_{0,1}, \ldots, K_{0,m/2}, K_{1,0}, K_{1,1}, \ldots, K_{1,m/2}, \ldots\}$ gives the desired result.

References

1. Beimel, A.: Secure schemes for secret sharing and key distribution. Ph.D. thesis, Technion, Haifa (1996)
2. Benaloh, J., Leichter, J.: Generalized secret sharing and monotone functions. In: Goldwasser, S. (ed.) CRYPTO 1988. LNCS, vol. 403, pp. 27–35. Springer, New York (1990). https://doi.org/10.1007/0-387-34799-2_3
3. Bogdanov, A., Guo, S., Komargodski, I.: Threshold secret sharing requires a linear size alphabet. In: Hirt, M., Smith, A. (eds.) TCC 2016. LNCS, vol. 9986, pp. 471–484. Springer, Heidelberg (2016). https://doi.org/10.1007/978-3-662-53644-5_18
4. Cascudo, I., Chen, H., Cramer, R., Xing, C.: Asymptotically good ideal linear secret sharing with strong multiplication over *any* fixed finite field. In: Halevi, S. (ed.) CRYPTO 2009. LNCS, vol. 5677, pp. 466–486. Springer, Heidelberg (2009). https://doi.org/10.1007/978-3-642-03356-8_28
5. Cascudo, I., Cramer, R., Xing, C.: Bounds on the threshold gap in secret sharing and its applications. IEEE Trans. Inf. Theory **59**(9), 5600–5612 (2013)

6. Cramer, R., Damgård, I., Keller, M.: On the amortized complexity of zero-knowledge protocols. J. Cryptol. **27**(2), 284–316 (2013). https://doi.org/10.1007/s00145-013-9145-x
7. Cramer, R., Damgård, I., Maurer, U.: General secure multi-party computation from any linear secret-sharing scheme. In: Preneel, B. (ed.) EUROCRYPT 2000. LNCS, vol. 1807, pp. 316–334. Springer, Heidelberg (2000). https://doi.org/10.1007/3-540-45539-6_22
8. Cramer, R., Damgård, I., Nielsen, J.B.: Secure Multiparty Computation and Secret Sharing. Cambridge University Press, Cmabridge (2015)
9. Chen, H., Cramer, R., Goldwasser, S., de Haan, R., Vaikuntanathan, V.: Secure computation from random error correcting codes. In: Naor, M. (ed.) EUROCRYPT 2007. LNCS, vol. 4515, pp. 291–310. Springer, Heidelberg (2007). https://doi.org/10.1007/978-3-540-72540-4_17
10. Cramer, R., Fehr, S.: Optimal black-box secret sharing over arbitrary Abelian groups. In: Yung, M. (ed.) CRYPTO 2002. LNCS, vol. 2442, pp. 272–287. Springer, Heidelberg (2002). https://doi.org/10.1007/3-540-45708-9_18
11. Cramer, R., Fehr, S., Ishai, Y., Kushilevitz, E.: Efficient multi-party computation over rings. In: Biham, E. (ed.) EUROCRYPT 2003. LNCS, vol. 2656, pp. 596–613. Springer, Heidelberg (2003). https://doi.org/10.1007/3-540-39200-9_37
12. Cramer, R., Fehr, S., Stam, M.: Black-box secret sharing from primitive sets in algebraic number fields. In: Shoup, V. (ed.) CRYPTO 2005. LNCS, vol. 3621, pp. 344–360. Springer, Heidelberg (2005). https://doi.org/10.1007/11535218_21
13. Damgård, I., Thorbek, R.: Linear integer secret sharing and distributed exponentiation. In: Yung, M., Dodis, Y., Kiayias, A., Malkin, T. (eds.) PKC 2006. LNCS, vol. 3958, pp. 75–90. Springer, Heidelberg (2006). https://doi.org/10.1007/11745853_6
14. Desmedt, Y., Frankel, Y.: Threshold cryptosystems. In: Brassard, G. (ed.) CRYPTO 1989. LNCS, vol. 435, pp. 307–315. Springer, New York (1990). https://doi.org/10.1007/0-387-34805-0_28
15. Desmedt, Y., Frankel, Y.: Perfect homomorphic zero-knowledge threshold schemes over any finite Abelian group. SIAM J. Discrete Math. **7**(4), 667–679 (1994)
16. Gál, A.: Combinatorial methods in Boolean function complexity. University of Chicago, Ph.D. thesis (1995)
17. Garcia, A., Stichtenoth, H.: A tower of Artin-Schreier extensions of function fields attaining the Drinfeld-Vladut bound. Invent. Math. **121**, 211–222 (1995)
18. Garcia, A., Stichtenoth, H.: On the asymptotic behavior of some towers of function fields over finite fields. J. Number Theory **61**, 248–273 (1996)
19. Karchmer, M., Wigderson, A.: On span programs. In: Proceedings of Structures in Complexity Theory 1993, pp. 102–111. IEEE Computer Society Press (1993)
20. Massey, J.L.: Minimal codewords and secret sharing. In: Proceedings of the 6th Joint Swedish-Russian Workshop on Information Theory, pp. 269–279 (1993)
21. Lang, S.: Survey of Diophantine Geometry. Springer, New York (1997)
22. Ling, S., Xing, C.: Coding Theory: A First Course. Cambridge University Press, Cambridge (2004)
23. van Lint, J.H.: Introduction to Coding Theory. Graduate Texts in Mathematics. Springer, Heidelberg (1999). https://doi.org/10.1007/978-3-642-58575-3
24. Niederreiter, H., Xing, C.P.: Rational Points on Curves over Finite Fields: Theory and Applications, LMS 285. Cambridge University Press, Cambridge (2001)
25. Shoup, V.: Practical threshold signatures. In: Preneel, B. (ed.) EUROCRYPT 2000. LNCS, vol. 1807, pp. 207–220. Springer, Heidelberg (2000). https://doi.org/10.1007/3-540-45539-6_15

26. Stichtenoth, H.: Algebraic Function Fields and Codes. Graduate Texts in Mathematics, vol. 254. Springer, Heidelberg (2009). https://doi.org/10.1007/978-3-540-76878-4
27. Tsfasman, M.A., Vlăduţ, S.G.: Algebraic-Geometric Codes. Kluwer, Amsterdam (1991)
28. Valiant, L.: Short monotone formulae for the majority function. J. Algorithms **5**(3), 363–366 (1984)
29. Xing, C., Yeo, S.L.: Construction of global function fields from linear codes and vice versa. Trans. Am. Math. Soc. **361**, 1333–1349 (2009)

Evolving Ramp Secret Sharing
with a Small Gap

Amos Beimel$^{(\boxtimes)}$ and Hussien Othman$^{(\boxtimes)}$

Department of Computer Science, Ben Gurion University, Beer Sheva, Israel
amos.beimel@gmail.com, hussien.othman@gmail.com

Abstract. Evolving secret-sharing schemes, introduced by Komargodski, Naor, and Yogev (TCC 2016b), are secret-sharing schemes in which there is no a-priory upper bound on the number of parties that will participate. The parties arrive one by one and when a party arrives the dealer gives it a share; the dealer cannot update this share when other parties arrive. Motivated by the fact that when the number of parties is known, ramp secret-sharing schemes are more efficient than threshold secret-sharing schemes, we study evolving ramp secret-sharing schemes. Specifically, we study evolving $(b(j), g(j))$-ramp secret-sharing schemes, where $g, b : \mathbb{N} \to \mathbb{N}$ are non-decreasing functions. In such schemes, any set of parties that for some j contains $g(j)$ parties from the first parties that arrive can reconstruct the secret, and any set such that for every j contains less than $b(j)$ parties from the first j parties that arrive cannot learn any information about the secret.

We focus on the case that the gap is small, namely $g(j) - b(j) = j^\beta$ for $0 < \beta < 1$. We show that there is an evolving ramp secret-sharing scheme with gap t^β, in which the share size of the j-th party is $\tilde{O}(j^{4 - \frac{1}{\log^2 1/\beta}})$. Furthermore, we show that our construction results in much better share size for fixed values of β, i.e., there is an evolving ramp secret-sharing scheme with gap $\sqrt{j}$, in which the share size of the j-th party is $\tilde{O}(j)$. Our construction should be compared to the best known evolving $g(j)$-threshold secret-sharing schemes (i.e., when $b(j) = g(j) - 1$) in which the share size of the j-th party is $\tilde{O}(j^4)$. Thus, our construction offers a significant improvement for every constant β, showing that allowing a gap between the sizes of the authorized and unauthorized sets can reduce the share size.

In addition, we present an evolving $(k/2, k)$-ramp secret-sharing scheme for a constant k (which can be very big), where any set of parties of size at least k can reconstruct the secret and any set of parties of size at most $k/2$ cannot learn any information about the secret. The share size of the j-th party in our construction is $O(\log k \log j)$. This is

This work was done while the first author was visiting Georgetown university, supported by NSF grant no. 1565387, TWC: Large: Collaborative: Computing Over Distributed Sensitive Data. The authors are also supported by ISF grant 152/17, by a grant from the Cyber Security Research Center at Ben-Gurion University of the Negev, and by the Frankel center for computer science. The second author is also supported by a scholarship from the Israeli Council For Higher Education.

A. Canteaut and Y. Ishai (Eds.): EUROCRYPT 2020, LNCS 12105, pp. 529–555, 2020.
https://doi.org/10.1007/978-3-030-45721-1_19

an improvement over the best known evolving k-threshold secret-sharing schemes in which the share size of the j-th party is $O(k \log j)$.

1   Introduction

In secret-sharing schemes (as in many cryptographic primitives) the number of parties is known in advance. If the number of parties is not known in advance, the dealer can assume an upper bound on this number. On one hand, if this upper bound is too pessimistic (e.g., very few parties are active), then the shares are unnecessarily large. On the other hand, if the upper bound is too optimistic and the number of parties exceeds the upper bound, then either new parties cannot join the system or the dealer needs to refresh the shares of all existing parties, which is very costly. Komargodski, Naor, and Yogev [14] suggested evolving secret-sharing schemes as a solution to this problem. In such schemes, there is no upper bound on the number of parties and the parties arrive one after the other. When a party arrives the dealer gives it a share; the dealer cannot update this share when other parties arrive.

Continuing our previous work [1], we consider evolving ramp secret-sharing schemes. In a traditional (b, g)-ramp secret-sharing schemes (with a fixed number of parties n, where $b < g \leq n$), sets of parties of size at least g should be able to reconstruct the secret, while sets of parties of size at most b should get no information on the secret.[1] There are no requirements on sets with more than b parties but less than g parties. Allowing a gap between b and g results in schemes that are more efficient than threshold secret-sharing schemes. Ramp secret-sharing schemes were first presented by Blakley and Meadows [4], and were used to construct efficient secure multiparty computation (MPC) protocols, starting in the work of Franklin and Yung [11]. In evolving (b, g)-ramp secret-sharing schemes (without an upper bound on the number of parties), g and b are non-decreasing functions $g, b : \mathbb{N} \to \mathbb{N}$ such that $b(j) < g(j)$ for every $j \in \mathbb{N}$, sets of parties that for some j contain at least $g(j)$ parties from the first j parties that arrive are authorized (i.e., should be able to reconstruct the secret), while sets of parties that for every j contain at most $b(j)$ parties from the first j parties that arrive are unauthorized (i.e., should get no information on the secret). Again, there are no requirements on sets that do not satisfy either of the requirements. In this work we investigate evolving ramp secret-sharing schemes, where the gap between g and b is small, e.g., $g(j) - b(j) = j^\beta$ for some constant β or $b(j) = k/2$ and $g(j) = k$ for some constant k.

Before presenting our results, we describe several results on evolving secret-sharing schemes. Komargodski, Naor, and Yogev [14] showed that every evolving access structure (i.e., collection of authorized sets) can be realized by a secret-sharing scheme, where the size of the share of the j-th party is 2^{j-1} (even if the dealer does not know the access structure in advance). They also

---

[1] The letters b and g stand for "bad" parties (that should not learn information about the secret) and "good" parties (that can reconstruct the secret).

showed evolving k-threshold secret-sharing schemes (where any set of k parties can reconstruct the secret), in which the share size of the j-th party is $(k-1)\log j + O(\log\log j)$. Komargodski and Paskin-Cherniavsky [15] considered evolving dynamic-threshold secret-sharing schemes in which the threshold is defined by a function $g : \mathbb{N} \to \mathbb{N}$; in such a scheme a set of parties is authorized if for some j the set contains at least $g(j)$ parties from the first j parties that arrive; all other parties are unauthorized. For every non-decreasing function $1 \le g(j) \le j$, they constructed an evolving $g(j)$-threshold secret-sharing scheme in which the share size of the j-th party is $O(j^4 \log j)$. As the number of parties is unbounded, this share size can be quite large. Beimel and Othman [1] constructed for any constants $0 < \alpha < \gamma < 1$ an evolving $(b(j) = \alpha j, g(j) = \gamma j)$-ramp secret-sharing scheme (i.e., the gap is a constant fraction of the parties) where the size of the share of the j-th party is $O(1)$.

Evolving ramp secret-sharing schemes with small gap are motivated due two reasons. First, they are step towards understanding the evolving dynamic threshold schemes, i.e., when the gap is 1. Second, it is a very interesting theoretical question to understand how the evolving ramp schemes behave as a function of the size of the gap. Namely, we know that when the gap is a constant fraction then the share size is $O(1)$ and when the gap is 1 the best share size of the j-th party is $\tilde{O}(j^4)$; understanding what the share size is in between these two extremes is a natural question.

1.1 Our Results

In this work we continue the investigation of evolving ramp secret-sharing schemes. We study the share size in ramp evolving secret-sharing schemes when the gap between $g(j)$ and $h(j)$ is small, i.e., $o(j)$. Can the share size be smaller than j^4 – the share size in the evolving threshold secret-sharing schemes of [15]? We give positive results when $g(j) - b(j) \le j^\beta$ for some constant β. We prove the following theorem:

Theorem 1.1. *For every constants $0 < \beta < 1$ and $0 < \gamma < 1$, there exists an evolving $(b(j) = \gamma j - j^\beta, g(j) = \gamma j)$-ramp secret-sharing scheme, where the share size of party p_j, for $j \in \mathbb{N}$, is*

$$O\left(j^{4 - O\left(\frac{1}{\log^2(1/\beta)}\right)} \log^2 j\right).$$

For $\beta \ge 1/2$, we prove the following better result.

Theorem 1.2. *Let $\beta > 0$ and $0 < \gamma \le 1$. There exists an evolving $(\gamma t - t^\beta, \gamma t)$-ramp secret-sharing scheme in which for every $j \in \mathbb{N}$ the share size of p_j is $O(j^{(1-\beta)/\beta} \log j)$.*

As instantiations of Theorem 1.2 we get:

- When $g(j) - b(j) = \frac{j}{\text{polylog}(j)}$, the share size in our scheme is polylog(j)
  (Theorem 1.2 with $\beta = 1 - \Theta(\frac{\log\log j}{\log j})$).

– When $g(j) - b(j) = \sqrt{j}$, the share size in our scheme is $\tilde{O}(j)$ (Theorem 1.2 with $\beta = 1/2$).

Thus, our constructions offer a significant improvement for a constant β compared to [15], showing that allowing a gap between $g(j)$ and $b(j)$ can reduce the share size in known evolving secret-sharing schemes compared to schemes in which there is no gap (i.e., $g(j) - b(j) = 1$).

In addition, we present a construction of evolving $(k/2, k)$-ramp secret-sharing schemes for a constant k (where any set of parties of size at least k can reconstruct the secret and any set of parties of size at most $k/2$ cannot learn any information about the secret). The share size of the j-th party in our construction is $O(\log k \log j)$. We prove the following theorem:

Theorem 1.3. *For every constant $k \in \mathbb{N}$, there exists an evolving $(k, k/2)$-ramp secret-sharing scheme, where the share size of party p_j, for $j \in \mathbb{N}$, is $O(\log k \log j)$.*

This is an improvement over the evolving k-threshold secret-sharing schemes of [14] in which the share size of the j-th party is $O(k \log j)$. Our result can be either seen as a first step in constructing improved evolving k-threshold secret-sharing schemes or as showing that for constant k evolving $(k/2, k)$-ramp secret-sharing schemes are more efficient.

1.2   Our Techniques

We next describe the ideas of our construction for an evolving $(b(j) = j/2 - j^\beta, g(j) = j/2)$-ramp secret-sharing scheme. We start in Sect. 3 by reducing the problem of realizing an evolving ramp secret-sharing scheme with an infinite number of parties to a problem of constructing secret-sharing realizing access structures with a finite number of parties. Specifically, for a given $t \in \mathbb{N}$, we define an access structure Γ_t containing the parties $\{p_{t^\beta}, \ldots, p_{2t}\}$. A set A whose maximal party is p_k should be able to reconstruct the secret in Γ_t if $k > t$ and $|A| > k/2 - t^\beta/2$. A set that should not learn any information on the secret in the evolving $(j/2 - j^\beta, j/2)$-ramp secret-sharing scheme, should not get any information on the secret in Γ_t. Given secret-sharing schemes realizing Γ_t, we construct an evolving $(j/2 - j^\beta, j/2)$-ramp secret-sharing scheme by executing a secret-sharing scheme realizing Γ_t for every t that is a power of 2. That is, for every $\ell \in \mathbb{N}$, when party p_{t^β} for $t = 2^\ell$ arrives, we share the secret by a secret-sharing scheme realizing Γ_t with parties $\{p_{t^\beta}, \ldots, p_{2t}\}$. When party p_j for $t^\beta \leq j \leq 2t$ arrives, we give p_j the share of p_j in the scheme realizing Γ_t (notice that p_j gets shares in the scheme for Γ_t for many values of t). The correctness of the scheme is explained by the fact that we "lose" at most t^β parties from the beginning; since we allow a gap of at most t^β parties, we will not miss any authorized set.

We present two constructions of secret-sharing schemes realizing the above access structure Γ_t. The first construction, described in Sect. 4, uses the so-called segments technique, where we have a sequence $n_0, n_1, \ldots, n_r$ of integers, where $t < n_0 < n_1 < \cdots < n_r \leq 2t$ and we share the secret among the parties $\{p_{t^\beta}, \ldots, p_{n_i}\}$ for every $0 \leq i \leq r$ using a threshold secret-sharing scheme, with an appropriate threshold. We choose the sequence of number of parties and thresholds so the correctness and security hold. This construction yields our best result when $\beta \geq 1/2$. For $\beta = 1/2$ we get an evolving secret-sharing scheme in which the share size of the j-th party is $O(j \log j)$.

Our second construction, described in Sect. 6, uses the so called tree technique (which also uses the segments technique). The tree technique was introduced in [15] (generalizing ideas of [14]). In the tree technique, we construct a tree, where for every edge in the tree we assign a set of consecutive parties and a weight. We define an access structure for this tree, where a set of parties A should be able to reconstruct the secret if there is a path from the root to a leaf such that for every edge in the path whose weight w the set A contains at least w parties from the set of parties assigned to the edge. In [15], an infinite tree is constructed with appropriate sets and weights such that the resulting scheme is an evolving $g(n)$-threshold secret-sharing scheme; in this scheme the share size of the j-th party is $\tilde{O}(j^4)$. Using the fact that we have a gap between b and g and our reduction to finite access structures, we can construct finite trees resulting in more efficient evolving secret-sharing schemes. For example, we optimize our construction for the evolving $(j/2 - j^{1/8}, j/2)$-ramp secret-sharing scheme, resulting in share size $\tilde{O}(j^{2.32})$ for the j-th party. For every $\beta < 1/2$ the share size of the j-th party in our evolving $(t/2 - t^\beta, t/2)$-ramp secret-sharing scheme is $O(j^{4 - \frac{1}{\log^2 1/\beta}} \log^2 j)$.

The results in Sect. 4 proves Theorem 1.2 only for a constant $\gamma \leq 1/2$. In Sect. 7, we prove Theorem 1.2 for any constant $\gamma > 0$. This is done by a reduction, where we use an evolving $(j/d - ((j/d\gamma)^\beta - 1), j/d)$-ramp secret-sharing scheme Π for any constant d to construct an evolving $(\gamma j - j^\beta, \gamma j)$-ramp secret-sharing scheme Π'. The reduction is simple, the share of the i-th party in Π' is the share of the $\lfloor \gamma dt \rfloor$-th party in Π. Verifying that the reduction is correct is quite easy (see proof of Theorem 7.1).

In Sect. 8, we construct an evolving $(k/2, k)$-ramp secret-sharing scheme in which the share size of the j-th party is $O(\log k \log j)$. The idea of the construction is as follows. We use the evolving k-threshold secret-sharing scheme of [14] as a building box. The secret-sharing scheme of [14] is recursive and its bottleneck is a procedure that shares k secrets $v_1, \ldots, v_k$ among a set of parties of size j, where each secret v_i is independently shared using an i-out-of-j threshold secret-sharing scheme. Since each sharing results in a share of size $\log j$, the total share of the j-th party is $k \log j$. For the ramp scheme, we use a similar procedure, however we use only $\log k$ threshold secret-sharing schemes, where for every $\ell \in \{0, \ldots, \log k\}$ we share $v_{2^\ell}, \ldots, v_{2^{\ell+1}-1}$ using a 2^ℓ-out-of-j threshold secret-sharing scheme. For the security of the scheme we observe that a set of size $k/2$ obtains less than k shares of the evolving k-threshold secret-sharing scheme, thus learns nothing about the secret. Since sharing k short secrets in a 2^ℓ-out-of-j threshold secret-sharing scheme requires only shares of size $\log j$, the share size in our scheme is $O(\log k \log j)$.

In Sect. 9, we analyze the share size in the schemes Π_{seg} and Π_{tree} – our schemes from Sect. 4 and Sect. 6 respectively. We prove that for $\beta > 1/2$ the share size in the scheme Π_{seg} is better than the share size in every implementation of Π_{tree}, that is, for $\beta > 1/2$ the best share size achievable using our schemes is $j^{(1-\beta)/\beta}$. Furthermore, we prove a weak lower bound of $\Omega(j)$ on the best share size in Π_{seg} and Π_{tree} for $\beta \leq 1/2$.

1.3   Previous Works

Secret-sharing schemes were introduced by Shamir [17] and Blakley [3] for threshold access structures, and by Ito, Saito, and Nishizeki for the general case [12]. Shamir's [17] and Blakley's [3] constructions are efficient both in the size of the shares and in the computation required for sharing and reconstruction. The size of the share in Shamir's scheme for sharing an ℓ-bit secret among n parties is $\max\{\ell, \log n\}$. Kilian and Nisan [13] proved a $\log(n - k + 2)$ lower bound on the share size for sharing a 1-bit secret for the k-out-of-n threshold access structure (see [7]). This lower bound implies that $\Omega(\log n)$ bits are necessary when k is not too close to n. Bogdanov, Guo, and Komargodski [5] proved that the lower bound of $\Omega(\log n)$ bits applies to any secret-sharing scheme realizing k-out-of-n threshold access structures for *every* $1 < k < n$. When $k = 1$ or $k = n$, schemes with share size of 1 are known.

Ramp secret-sharing schemes. Ramp secret-sharing schemes were presented by Blakley and Meadows [4]. For long enough secrets, they constructed a (b, g)-ramp secret-sharing scheme with share size $1/(g - b)$ times the size of the secret. Ramp schemes have found numerous applications in cryptography, including efficient secure multiparty computation (MPC) protocols (Franklin and Yung [11] and many follow-up works), broadcast encryption (Stinson and Wei [18]) and error decodable secret sharing (Martin, Paterson, and Stinson [16]). Cascudo, Cramer, and Xing [7] proved lower bounds on the share size in ramp secret-sharing schemes: If every set of size at least an can reconstruct the secret while every set of size at most bn cannot learn any information on the secret, then the length of the shares is at least $\log((1 - b)/(a - b))$. Bogdanov et al. [5] showed that for all $0 < b < a < 1$, in any ramp secret sharing the size of the shares is at least $\log(a/(a - b))$. On the positive side, Chen et al. [8] proved that for every $\epsilon > 0$ there is a ramp secret-sharing scheme with share size $O(1)$ in which every set of size at least $(1/2 + \epsilon)n$ can reconstruct the secret while every set of size at most $(1/2 - \epsilon)n$ cannot learn any information on the secret.

Evolving and online secret-sharing schemes. D'Arco et al. [10] constructed evolving k-threshold secret-sharing schemes, where the secret is reconstructed only with probability $p < 1$, however the share size is $O(1)$. Komargodski and Paskin-Cherniavsky [15] showed how to transform any evolving secret-sharing scheme to a *robust* scheme, where a shared secret can be recovered even if some parties hand-in incorrect shares. Cachin [6] and Csirmaz and Tardos [9] considered online secret sharing, which is similar to evolving secret-sharing schemes. As in evolving secret-sharing scheme, in on-line secret-sharing, parties can enroll in any time after the initialization, and the number of parties is unbounded. However, in the works on online secret-sharing, the number of authorized sets a party can join is bounded.

2   Preliminaries

In this section we present formal definitions of secret-sharing schemes and evolving secret-sharing schemes.

Notations. We denote the logarithmic function with base 2 by log. We use the notation $[n]$ to denote the set $\{1, 2, \ldots, n\}$. When we refer to a set of parties $A = \{p_{i_1}, p_{i_2}, \ldots, p_{i_t}\}$, we assume that $i_1 < i_2 < \cdots < i_t$.

2.1   Secret-Sharing Schemes

We next present the definition of secret-sharing schemes. Our definition is of non-perfect secret-sharing schemes, where some sets of parties can reconstruct the secret, some sets should not get any information on the secret, and there are no requirements on all other sets.

Definition 2.1 (Access structures). *Let $\mathcal{P} = \{p_1, \ldots, p_n\}$ be a set of parties. A collection $\Gamma \subseteq 2^{\{p_1, \ldots, p_n\}}$ is* monotone *if $B \in \Gamma$ and $B \subseteq C$ imply that $C \in \Gamma$. An* access structure *$\Gamma = (\Gamma_{\mathrm{YES}}, \Gamma_{\mathrm{NO}})$ is a pair of collections of sets such that $\Gamma_{\mathrm{YES}}, \Gamma_{\mathrm{NO}} \subseteq 2^{\{p_1, \ldots, p_n\}}$, the collections Γ_{YES} and $2^{\{p_1, \ldots, p_n\}} \setminus \Gamma_{\mathrm{NO}}$ are monotone, and $\Gamma_{\mathrm{YES}} \cap \Gamma_{\mathrm{NO}} = \emptyset$. Sets in Γ_{YES} are called* authorized, *and sets in Γ_{NO} are called* unauthorized. *The access structure is called an* incomplete access structure *if there is at least one subset of parties $A \subseteq \mathcal{P}$ such that $A \notin \Gamma_{\mathrm{YES}} \cup \Gamma_{\mathrm{NO}}$. Otherwise, it is called a* complete access structure.

Definition 2.2 (Secret-sharing schemes). *A secret-sharing $\Sigma = \langle \Pi, \mu \rangle$ over a set of parties $\mathcal{P} = \{p_1, \ldots, p_n\}$ with domain of secrets K is a pair, where μ is a probability distribution on some finite set R called the set of random strings and Π is a mapping from $K \times R$ to a set of n-tuples $K_1 \times K_2 \times \cdots \times K_n$ (the set K_j is called the* domain of shares *of p_j). A dealer distributes a secret $k \in K$ according to Σ by first sampling a random string $r \in R$ according to μ, computing a vector of shares $\Pi(k, r) = (s_1, \ldots, s_n)$, and privately communicating each share s_j to party p_j. For a set $A \subseteq \{p_1, \ldots, p_n\}$, we denote $\Pi_A(k, r)$ as the restriction of $\Pi(k, r)$ to its A-entries (i.e., the shares of the parties in A). The* size of the secret *is defined as $\log |K|$ and the* size of the share of party p_j *is defined as $\log |K_j|$.*

A secret-sharing scheme $\langle \Pi, \mu \rangle$ with domain of secrets K realizes an access structure $\Gamma = (\Gamma_{\mathrm{YES}}, \Gamma_{\mathrm{NO}})$ if the following two requirements hold:

CORRECTNESS. *The secret k can be reconstructed by any authorized set of parties. That is, for any set $B = \{p_{i_1}, \ldots, p_{i_{|B|}}\} \in \Gamma_{\mathrm{YES}}$, there exists a reconstruction function $\mathrm{Recon}_B : K_{i_1} \times \cdots \times K_{i_{|B|}} \to K$ such that for every secret $k \in K$ and every random string $r \in R$, $\mathrm{Recon}_B\left(\Pi_B(k, r)\right) = k$.*

SECURITY. *Every unauthorized set cannot learn anything about the secret from its shares. Formally, for any set $T \in \Gamma_{NO}$, every two secrets $a, b \in K$, and every possible vector of shares $\langle s_j \rangle_{p_j \in T}$,*

$$\Pr[\, \Pi_T(a, r) = \langle s_j \rangle_{p_j \in T} \,] = \Pr[\, \Pi_T(b, r) = \langle s_j \rangle_{p_j \in T} \,],$$

where the probability is over the choice of r from R at random according to μ.

Remark 2.3. For sets of parties $A \subseteq \mathcal{P}$ such that $A \notin \Gamma_{YES} \cup \Gamma_{NO}$ there are no requirements, i.e., they might be able to reconstruct the secret, they may have some partial information on the secret, or they may have no information on the secret.

Definition 2.4 (Threshold access structures). *Let $1 \le k \le n$. A k-out-of-n threshold access structure Γ over a set of parties $\mathcal{P} = \{p_1, \ldots, p_n\}$ is the complete access structure accepting all subsets of size at least k, that is, $\Gamma_{YES} = \{A \subseteq \mathcal{P} : |A| \ge k\}$ and $\Gamma_{NO} = \{A \subseteq \mathcal{P} : |A| < k\}$.*

The well known scheme of Shamir [17] for the k-out-of-n threshold access structure (based on polynomial interpolation) is an efficient threshold secret-sharing scheme, whose properties are summarized in the following claim.

Claim 2.5 (Shamir [17]). *For every $n \in N$ and $1 \le k \le n$, there is a secret-sharing scheme for secrets of size m realizing the k-out-of-n threshold access structure in which the share size is ℓ, where $\ell = \max\{m, \lceil \log(n+1) \rceil\}$.*

Definition 2.6 (Ramp secret-sharing schemes [4]). *Let $0 \le b < g \le n$. The (b, g)-ramp access structure over a set of parties $\mathcal{P} = \{p_1, \ldots, p_n\}$ is the incomplete access structure $\Gamma_{b,g} = (\Gamma_{YES}, \Gamma_{NO})$, where $\Gamma_{YES} = \{A \subseteq \mathcal{P} : |A| \ge g\}$ and $\Gamma_{NO} = \{A \subseteq \mathcal{P} : |A| \le b\}$. A (b, g)-ramp scheme with n parties is a secret-sharing scheme realizing $\Gamma_{b,g}$.*

Chen et al. [8] showed the existence of ramp secret-sharing schemes with share size $O(1)$.

Claim 2.7 (Chen et al. [8]). *For every constant $0 < \epsilon < 1/2$ there are integers ℓ and n_0 such that for every $n \ge n_0$ there is a $((1/2 - \epsilon)n, (1/2 + \epsilon)n)$-ramp secret-sharing scheme with n parties and share size ℓ.*

The next corollary, which can be found in [1], shows the existence of ramp secret-sharing schemes for any gap of $\Theta(n)$.

Corollary 2.8. *For every constants $0 < b < g < 1$ there are integers ℓ and n_0 such that for every $n \ge n_0$ there is a (b, g)-ramp secret-sharing scheme with n parties and share size ℓ.*

2.2 Secret Sharing for Evolving Access Structures

We proceed with the definition of an evolving access structure, introduced in [14].

Definition 2.9. (Evolving access structures). *Let* $\mathcal{P} = \{p_i\}_{i \in \mathbb{N}}$ *be an infinite set of parties. An evolving access structure* $\Gamma = (\Gamma_{\text{YES}}, \Gamma_{\text{NO}})$ *is a pair of collections of sets* $\Gamma_{\text{YES}}, \Gamma_{\text{NO}} \subset 2^{\mathcal{P}}$, *where each set in* $\Gamma_{\text{YES}} \cup \Gamma_{\text{NO}}$ *is finite and for every* $t \in \mathbb{N}$ *the collections* $\Gamma^t \triangleq (\Gamma_{\text{YES}} \cap 2^{\{p_1, \ldots, p_t\}}, \Gamma_{\text{NO}} \cap 2^{\{p_1, \ldots, p_t\}})$ *is an access structure as defined in Definition 2.1.*

Definition 2.10. (Evolving secret-sharing schemes). *Let* Γ *be an evolving access structure,* K *be a domain of secrets, where* $|K| \geq 2$, *and* $\{R^t\}_{t \in \mathbb{N}}, \{K^t\}_{t \in \mathbb{N}}$ *be two sequences of finite sets. An evolving secret-sharing scheme with domain of secrets* K *is a pair* $\Sigma = \langle \{\Pi^t\}_{t \in \mathbb{N}}, \{\mu^t\}_{t \in \mathbb{N}} \rangle$, *where, for every* $t \in \mathbb{N}$, μ^t *is a probability distribution on* R_t *and* Π^t *is a mapping* $\Pi^t : K \times R_1 \times \cdots \times R_t \to K_t$ *(this mapping returns the share of* p_j*).*

An evolving secret-sharing scheme $\Sigma = \langle \{\Pi^t\}_{t \in \mathbb{N}}, \{\mu^t\}_{t \in \mathbb{N}} \rangle$ *realizes* Γ *if for every* $t \in \mathbb{N}$ *the secret-sharing scheme* $\langle \mu^1 \times \cdots \times \mu^t, \Pi_t \rangle$, *where* $\Pi_t(k, (r_1, \ldots, r_k)) = \langle \Pi^1(k, r_1), \ldots, \Pi^t(k, r_1, \ldots, r_t) \rangle$, *is a secret-sharing scheme realizing* Γ^t *according to Definition 2.2.*

Definition 2.11. (Evolving ramp access structures). *For two non-decreasing functions* $b, g : \mathbb{N} \to \mathbb{N}$ *such that* $0 \leq b(t) < g(t) \leq t$ *for every* $t \in \mathbb{N}$, *the evolving* $(b(t), g(t))$-*ramp incomplete access structure is the evolving incomplete access structure* $\Gamma_{b(t), g(t)}$, *where for a set* A *whose maximum party is* p_t:

- *A is authorized if* $|A \cap \{p_1, \ldots, p_j\}| \geq g(j)$ *for some* $1 \leq j \leq t$,
- *A is unauthorized if* $|A \cap \{p_1, \ldots, p_j\}| \leq b(j)$ *for every* $1 \leq j \leq t$.

In other words, A is authorized in $\Gamma_{b(t), g(t)}$ if it is authorized in the $(b(j), g(j))$-ramp incomplete access structure for some $j \leq t$ and it is unauthorized in $\Gamma_{b(t), g(t)}$ if it is unauthorized in the $(b(j), g(j))$-ramp incomplete access structure for every $j \leq t$. In the above definition, there are no requirements on sets where $|A \cap \{p_1, \ldots, p_j\}| < g(j)$ for every j and $|A \cap \{p_1, \ldots, p_j\}| > b(j)$ for at least one j. We abuse notation and consider $g, b : \mathbb{N} \to \mathbb{R}$ (e.g., $g(t) = t/2$); in this case, we actually consider $\lceil g(t) \rceil$ and $\lfloor b(t) \rfloor$.

In the rest of the paper, the secret is taken from $\{0, 1\}$.

3 Reduction to an Access Structure with a Finite Number of Parties

Our goal is to construct an evolving $(\gamma t - f(t), \gamma t)$-ramp secret-sharing scheme for any constant $0 < \gamma < 1$ and some function $0 < f(t) \leq \gamma t$ such that $\gamma t - f(t)$ is non-decreasing. We show that to construct a ramp evolving secret-sharing scheme (with an unbounded number of parties) it suffices to construct a secret-sharing scheme for an access structure $\Gamma^f_{t, \rho, \gamma}$ with a finite number of parties.

The ramp evolving secret-sharing schemes we construct will use many copies of a scheme realizing $\Gamma^f_{t,\rho,\gamma}$ (for every t that is a power of 2). In the definition of $\Gamma^f_{t,\rho,\gamma}$, there is a parameter $0 < \rho \leq 1$. This parameter adds flexibility to our reductions and we use different values of ρ in our two constructions.

Definition 3.1. (The access structure $\Gamma^f_{t,\rho,\gamma}$). *Let $0 < \gamma < 1$ be a constant and $f : \mathbb{N} \to \mathbb{N}$ be a function such that $0 < f(j) < \gamma j$ for every $j \in \mathbb{N}$ and $\gamma t - f(t)$ is non-decreasing, let t be an integer, and let $0 < \rho \leq 1$. The incomplete access structure $\Gamma^f_{t,\rho,\gamma}$ over the set of parties $\{p_{\rho \cdot f(t)}, p_{\rho \cdot f(t)+1}, \ldots, p_{2t}\}$ is the following access structure, where for a set $A = \{p_{i_1}, \ldots, p_{i_k}\} \subseteq \{p_{\rho \cdot f(t)}, \ldots, p_{2t}\}$:*

– *if $i_j > t$ and $j \geq \gamma i_j - \gamma \rho \cdot f(t)$ for some $j \in [k]$, then A is authorized.*
– *If $j \leq \gamma i_j - f(i_j)$ for every $j \in [k]$, then A is unauthorized.*

Example 3.2. Consider the function $f(t) = \sqrt{t}$ and the access structure $\Gamma^{\sqrt{j}}_{t,1,1/2}$ whose parties are $\{p_{\sqrt{t}}, \ldots, p_{2t}\}$. Next we show examples of authorized and unauthorized subsets. The subset $A = \{p_{(t+\sqrt{t}+3)/2}, \ldots, p_{t+1}\}$ is authorized since it contains $(t+1)/2 - \sqrt{t}/2$ parties. The subset $B = \{p_{3t/2+1}, \ldots, p_{2t}\}$ is unauthorized for $t > 32$ since for every p_{i_j} in the set it holds that $i_j/2 - \sqrt{i_j} > 3t/4 - \sqrt{2t} \geq t/2 \geq j$. Notice that the unauthorized set B is bigger than the authorized set A. Such sets imply that realizing $\Gamma^f_{t,\rho,\gamma}$ is non-trivial.

Theorem 3.3. *Let $0 < \rho \leq 1$. If for every t there is a secret-sharing scheme $\Pi^f_{t,\rho,\gamma}$ realizing the access structure $\Gamma^f_{t,\rho,\gamma}$, where, for $\rho \cdot f(t) \leq j \leq t$, the size of the share of party p_j is $c_t(j)$, then the scheme $\Pi_{reduction}$, described in Fig. 1, realizes the evolving access structure $\Gamma_{\gamma t - f(t), \gamma t}$, where the size of the share of p_j is $\sum_{t : \exists_{i \in \mathbb{N}} t = 2^i \wedge \rho \cdot f(t) \leq j \leq 2t} c_t(j)$.*

The Scheme $\Pi_{reduction}$

– For every $\ell \in \mathbb{N}$ do:
  • Let $t = 2^\ell$
  • When party $p_{\rho \cdot f(t)}$ arrives, prepare the shares of $\Pi^f_{t,\rho,\gamma}$, denote these shares by $s_{t,\rho \cdot f(t)}, \ldots, s_{t,2t}$.
– The share of party p_j is $(s_{t,j})_{\{t : \exists_{i \in \mathbb{N}} t = 2^i \wedge \rho \cdot f(t) \leq j \leq 2t\}}$.

Fig. 1. The scheme $\Pi_{reduction}$ that realizes the evolving ramp access structure $\Gamma_{\gamma t - f(t), \gamma t}$, assuming a scheme $\Pi^f_{t,\rho,\gamma}$ realizing $\Gamma^f_{t,\rho,\gamma}$.

Proof. We first prove the correctness of the scheme $\Pi_{reduction}$. Consider a minimal authorized set $A = \{p_{i_1}, \ldots, p_{i_k}\}$ of $\Gamma_{\gamma t - f(t), \gamma t}$, thus, $k \geq \gamma i_k$. Let $\ell \in \mathbb{N}$ be the index such that $2^\ell < i_k \leq 2^{\ell+1}$ and let $t = 2^\ell$, thus, $t < i_k \leq 2t$.

As A is a minimal authorized set, it contains less than $\gamma\rho \cdot f(t)$ parties among the parties $\{p_1, \ldots, p_{\rho \cdot f(t)-1}\}$, i.e., it contains at least $\gamma i_k - \gamma\rho \cdot f(t)$ parties from $\{p_{\rho \cdot f(t)}, \ldots, p_{2t}\}$. This implies that A is authorized in $\Gamma^f_{t,\rho,\gamma}$ and the parties in A can reconstruct the secret from their shares in $\Pi^f_{t,\rho,\gamma}$.

We now prove the security of the scheme. Consider a set A that is unauthorized in $\Gamma_{\gamma t - f(t), \gamma t}$. By definition, it is unauthorized in all $\Gamma^f_{t,\rho,\gamma}$, thus, the parties in A have no information on the secret.

The share of p_j contains shares of $\Pi^f_{t,\rho,\gamma}$ for every value t such that t is a power of 2 and $\rho \cdot f(t) \leq j \leq 2t$, that is, the size of p_j's share is

$$\sum_{t\,:\,\exists_{i \in \mathbb{N}} t = 2^i \wedge \rho \cdot f(t) \leq j \leq 2t} c_t(j).$$

$\square$

For the case that $f(t) = t^\beta$ for some $0 < \beta < 1$, the reduction in Theorem 3.3 yields the following result.

Corollary 3.4. *Let $0 < \beta < 1$ be a constant and $c : \mathbb{N} \to \mathbb{N}$ be a function. If for every t there exists a scheme realizing $\Gamma^{f(t)=t^\beta}_{t,\rho,\gamma}$ where the size of the share of each party p_j, for $\rho t^\beta < j \leq 2t$, is $c(j)$, then there exists a scheme realizing $\Gamma_{\gamma t - t^\beta, \gamma t}$ in which the size of the share of each party p_j, for $j \in \mathbb{N}$, is $c(j) \log j$.*

Our main challenge in Sects. 4 to 6 is to construct efficient schemes realizing the access structure $\Gamma^f_{t,\rho,\gamma}$ for some parameter ρ.

Example 3.5. Consider the evolving $(t/4, t/2)$-ramp access structure, i.e., $f(t) = t/4$. In this case, $\Gamma^{f(t)=t/4}_{t,1,1/2}$ is an access structure over the parties $\{p_{t/4}, \ldots, p_{2t}\}$. A first attempt to realize $\Gamma^{f(t)=t/4}_{t,1,1/2}$ is to use one threshold secret-sharing scheme. This attempt fails since the set $\{p_{5t/8+1}, \ldots, p_{t+1}\}$ is an authorized set of size $\approx 3t/8$, while $\{p_{3t/2}, \ldots, p_{2t}\}$ is an unauthorized set of size $2t/4 = t/2$. To solve this problem, we use 4 threshold schemes. That is, to realize $\Gamma^{f(t)=t/4}_{t,1,1/2}$, for every $\alpha = 1, 2, 3, 4$, we share the secret s using a $(2+\alpha)t/8$-out-of-$(4+\alpha-1)t/4$ among the parties $\{p_{t/4}, \ldots, p_{t+\alpha t/4}\}$. In the next two paragraphs we prove that this scheme realizes $\Gamma^{f(t)=t/4}_{t,1,1/2}$.

Consider a minimal authorized set $A = \{p_{i_1}, \ldots, p_{i_k}\}$ of $\Gamma^{f(t)=t/4}_{t,1,1/2}$ and let α be such that $t + (\alpha-1)t/4 < i_k \leq t + \alpha t/4$. This set contains at least $i_k/2 - t/8 \geq (1 + (\alpha-1)/4)t/2 - t/8 = (2+\alpha)t/8$ parties from the set $\{p_{t/4}, \ldots, p_{t+\alpha t/4}\}$, thus it can reconstruct the secret.

Consider an unauthorized set A of $\Gamma^{f(t)=t/4}_{t,1,1/2}$. For every $\alpha = 1, 2, 3, 4$, it contains at most $(1+\alpha/4)t/4$ parties among the parties $\{p_{t/4}, \ldots, p_{t+\alpha t/4}\}$ (as such set contains at most a quarter of the parties ending at party $(1 + \alpha/4)t$). Since $(1 + \alpha/4)t/4 < (2+\alpha)t/8$, the parties in A cannot learn any information on the secret from each of the 4 schemes, thus, cannot learn any information on the secret.

The size of the share of party p_j in this scheme for $\Gamma_{t,1,1/2}^{f(t)=t/4}$ is $O(\log t) = O(\log j)$ (as this is the share size in Shamir's scheme). If instead of sharing the secret using a threshold secret-sharing scheme, we share the secret using a (non-evolving) $((1 + \alpha/4)t/4, (2 + \alpha)t/8)$-ramp secret-sharing scheme, the size of the share will be reduced to $O(1)$, by [8] (see Corollary 2.8). By Theorem 3.3, the size of the share of p_j in the evolving scheme realizing $\Gamma_{t/4,t/2}$ is the sum of the shares in the schemes realizing $\Gamma_{t,1,1/2}^{f(t)=t/4}$, where t is a power of two such that $t/4 < j < 2t$. Thus, the share size of p_j is $O(1)$.

4   First Scheme Realizing $\Gamma_{t,1,\gamma}^{f(t)}$: The Segments Technique

In this section we construct a simple scheme Π_{seg} realizing $\Gamma_{t,1,\gamma}^{f}$ for $0 < \gamma \leq 1/2$, proving Theorem 1.2 for $0 < \gamma \leq 1/2$. We analyze the share size of the evolving ramp scheme resulting by using Π_{seg} in $\Pi_{\text{reduction}}$ for a function $f(t) = t^\beta$ for some $\beta < 1$. For $\beta \geq 1/2$ this is our best scheme. For smaller values of β, the scheme presented in Sect. 6 is more efficient.

The scheme Π_{seg} is a generalization of the scheme presented in Example 3.5; we realize $\Gamma_{t,1,\gamma}^{f}$ using several threshold secret-sharing schemes on increasing segments of parties, where for larger segments we use larger thresholds. The scheme is described in Fig. 2.

The Scheme Π_{seg}

- For $\alpha = 1$ to $\lceil t/f(t) \rceil$,
  - Share s using Shamir's $(\lfloor \gamma(t + (\alpha - 2)f(t)) \rfloor + 1)$-out-of-$(t + (\alpha - 1)f(t))$ secret-sharing scheme among the parties $\{p_{f(t)}, \ldots, p_{t+\alpha f(t)}\}$; let $s_{\alpha,f(t)}, s_{\alpha,f(t)+1}, \ldots, s_{\alpha,t+\alpha f(t)}$ be the shares in this scheme.
- The share of p_j is $(s_{\alpha,j})_{\{\alpha:\alpha \geq \max\{1,(j-t)/f(t)\}\}}$.

Fig. 2. A scheme Π_{seg} realizing the access structure $\Gamma_{t,1,\gamma}^{f}$.

Lemma 4.1. *Let $0 < \gamma \leq 1/2$. The secret-sharing scheme Π_{seg}, described in Fig. 2, realizes the access structure $\Gamma_{t,1,\gamma}^{f}$ with share size $O(t/f(t) \log t)$.*

Proof. We start by proving the correctness of the scheme Π_{seg}. Consider a minimal authorized set $A = \{p_{i_1}, p_{i_2}, \ldots, p_{i_k}\}$ of $\Gamma_{t,1,\gamma}^{f}$ and let α be such that $t + (\alpha - 1)f(t) < i_k \leq t + \alpha f(t)$. Since A is a minimal authorized set,

$$|A| = k \geq \gamma i_k - \gamma f(t) > \gamma(t + (\alpha - 1)f(t)) - \gamma f(t) = \gamma(t + (\alpha - 2)f(t)).$$

Since $|A|$ is an integer,

$$|A| \geq \lfloor \gamma(t + (\alpha - 2)f(t)) \rfloor + 1.$$

By the construction, the parties in A can reconstruct the secret from the threshold scheme for the parties $\{p_{f(t)}, \ldots, p_{t+\alpha f(t)}\}$.

We continue by proving the security of the scheme. Consider an unauthorized set A. We show that for every α, the parties in A cannot learn any information about the secret from the threshold scheme for $\{p_{f(t)}, \ldots, p_{t+\alpha f(t)}\}$. Note that $f(t + \alpha f(t)) \geq f(t) \geq 2\gamma f(t)$. Since A is unauthorized, the number of parties in $A \cap \{p_{f(t)}, \ldots, p_{t+\alpha f(t)}\}$ is at most

$$\gamma(t + \alpha f(t)) - f(t + \alpha f(t)) \leq \gamma(t + \alpha f(t)) - 2\gamma f(t) = \gamma(t + (\alpha - 2)f(t)).$$

Thus, the parties in A cannot learn any information about the secret from the shares of each threshold scheme. As these schemes are executed with independent randomness, the parties in A cannot learn any information about the secret.

Finally, we analyze the share size of each party in the scheme. Each party gets at most $O(t/f(t))$ shares of Shamir's secret-sharing scheme with $O(t)$ parties; the size of each such share is $O(\log t)$. Thus, the total share size is $O(t/f(t) \log t)$. □

We next present two conclusions of Lemma 4.1.

Theorem 4.2. *For every constants $0 < \delta < \gamma \leq 1/2$, the evolving $(\delta t, \gamma t)$-ramp access structure can be realized by an evolving secret-sharing scheme with share size $O(1)$ for every party.*

Proof. Let $b = \gamma - \delta$. In this case $f(t) = bt$ and $\Gamma_{t,1,\gamma}^{f(t)=bt}$ is an access structure whose parties are $\{p_{bt}, \ldots, p_{2t}\}$. By Lemma 4.1, Π_{seg} realizes $\Gamma_{t,1,\gamma}^{f(t)=bt}$ with share size $O(\log t)$ (since b is constant). We next show how to reduce the share size to $O(1)$. By the construction, the secret is shared among the parties $\{p_{bt}, \ldots, p_{t+bt\alpha}\}$ for every $\alpha = 1$ to $\lceil 1/b \rceil$ by a $(\lfloor \gamma t(1 + b\alpha - 2b) \rfloor + 1)$-out-of-$(t + (\alpha - 1)bt)$ threshold secret-sharing scheme. However, in an unauthorized set there are at most $\delta(t + bt\alpha) = (\gamma - b)(t + bt\alpha) = \gamma t(1 + b\alpha - b/\gamma - b^2\alpha/\gamma) < \gamma t(1 + b\alpha - 2b)$ parties. Therefore, we can share the secret by a $(\gamma t(1 + b\alpha - b/\gamma - b^2\alpha/\gamma), \gamma t(1 + b\alpha - 2b) + 1)$-ramp secret-sharing scheme. By Corollary 2.8, we realize $\Gamma_{t,1,\gamma}^{f(t)=bt}$ with share size $O(1)$ for every party. By Theorem 3.3, the size of the share of p_j in the evolving scheme realizing $\Gamma_{\delta t, \gamma t}$ is the sum of the shares in the schemes realizing $\Gamma_{t,1,\gamma}^{f(t)=bt}$, where t is a power of two such that $\delta t < j < 2t$. There are $O(1)$ schemes. Thus, the share size of p_j is $O(1)$. □

The same result was proved in [1]. However, the analysis of the new scheme is much simpler than the one in [1]. We next prove Theorem 1.2 for $\gamma \leq 1/2$ (the case of $1/2 < \gamma \leq 1$ is obtained from the following lemma in Sect. 7).

Lemma 4.3. *For every $\beta > 0$ and $0 < \gamma \leq 1/2$, there exists an evolving $(\gamma t - t^\beta, \gamma t)$-ramp secret-sharing scheme in which for every $j \in \mathbb{N}$ the share size of p_j is $O(j^{(1-\beta)/\beta} \log j)$.*

Proof. Consider the scheme $\Pi_{\text{reduction}}$ with Π_{seg} as the scheme realizing $\Gamma_{t,1,\gamma}^{f(t)=t^\beta}$. By Lemma 4.1, the scheme Π_{seg} realizes $\Gamma_{t,1,\gamma}^{f(t)=t^\beta}$, where the share size of p_j is $c_t(j) = O(t^{1-\beta} \log t)$. Thus, by Theorem 3.3, $\Pi_{\text{reduction}}$ realizes the evolving ramp access structure $\Gamma_{\gamma t - t^\beta, \gamma t}$, where the share size of the party p_j is

$$\sum_{t \,:\, \exists_{i \in \mathbb{N}} t = 2^i \wedge t^\beta \leq j \leq 2t} c_t(j) = \sum_{t \,:\, \exists_{i \in \mathbb{N}} t = 2^i \wedge j/2 \leq t \leq j^{1/\beta}} c_t(j).$$

The largest value of t in the above sum is $j^{1/\beta}$ and $c_{j^{1/\beta}}(j) = O(j^{(1-\beta)/\beta} \log j)$; the second largest value of t in the above sum is $j^{1/\beta}/2$ and $c_{j^{1/\beta}/2}(j) = O(j^{(1-\beta)/\beta}/2^{1-\beta} \log j)$ and so on. Thus, the share size of p_j is a sum of a geometric sequence and is $O(j^{(1-\beta)/\beta} \log j)$. $\square$

5   Realizing Weighted Trees Access Structures

In this section, we review and generalize the tree technique introduced in [15] (generalizing ideas of [14]) in order to construct a scheme for the evolving majority access structure.

Next we overview and generalize the tree technique. In Sect. 6, we construct a specific tree that we use in our constructions.

5.1   A Secret Sharing Scheme Realizing Finite Trees

In this section, we define a complete access structure from a tree and show how to realize it. This scheme is a special case of the scheme realizing the connectivity access structure [2].

For a directed tree $T = (V, E)$, we define the following access structure. The edges in the tree represent the parties in the access structure. A set of edges is authorized if it contains a path from the root to a leaf, otherwise it is an unauthorized and should not learn any information on the secret.

We next describe a simple scheme Π_T realizing this tree. Let $k \in \{0,1\}$ be the secret. The share of each edge (u,v) is a bit $r_{u,v}$ computed as follows: if v is not a leaf, then it is a uniformly distributed random bit. Otherwise, if v is a leaf and $P = (v_0, v_1, \ldots, v_{n-1} = u, v_n = v)$ is the path from the root to v, then $r_{u,v} = \oplus_{i=0}^{n-2} r_{v_i, v_{i+1}} \oplus k$. To see that this scheme is correct, observe that the edges on a path can reconstruct the secret by computing the exclusive-or of the shares given to the parties (edges) of the path.

To see that this scheme is secure consider an unauthorized set, that is, a set of edges F not containing a path from s to a leaf. Define the set of nodes V_1 such that $v_i \in V_1$ if there exists a path from the root to v_i in (V, F). By definition,

$s \in V_1$ and V_1 does not contain leaves. Furthermore, for every $(v_i, v_j) \in F$ either both nodes v_i, v_j are in V_1 or both of them are not in V_1. Let $\{r_{i,j}\}_{(v_i,v_j) \in F}$ be a set of shares generated for the parties in F with a secret $k \in \{0, 1\}$, where $r_{i,j}$ is the share given to party (v_i, v_j). We next show that the same set of shares can be used to share the secret $k \oplus 1$. Complete the shares $\{r_{i,j}\}_{(v_i,v_j) \in F}$ of the parties in F to shares $\{r_{i,j}\}_{(v_i,v_j) \in E}$ of all the parties in the tree for the secret k. Consider the shares $r'_{i,j}$ such that $r'_{i,j} = r_{i,j} \oplus 1$ if $v_i \in V_1$ and $v_j \notin V_1$ and $r'_{i,j} = r_{i,j}$ otherwise. Notice that $r'_{i,j} = r_{i,j}$ for every $(v_i, v_j) \in F$. We claim that the shares $\{r'_{i,j}\}_{(v_i,v_j) \in E}$ are shares for the secret $k \oplus 1$. This is true since for any simple path $s = v_0, v_1, \ldots, v_{n-1}, v_n = v$ from the root to a leaf contains exactly one edge (v_i, v_{i+1}) such that $v_i \in V_1$ and $v_{i+1} \notin V_1$ and the exclusive or of the shares given to the parties (edges) on the path is $k \oplus 1$. As we describe a bijection between the shares of k and $k \oplus 1$, the probabilities of $\{r_{i,j}\}_{(v_i,v_j) \in F}$ given k and $k \oplus 1$ are equal, thus the security holds.

5.2   Secret-Sharing Schemes Realizing Finite Weighted Trees

Following [15], we describe an access structure for a finite directed weighted tree $T = (V, E)$, where each edge (u, v) has weight $w_{u,v}$. In addition, for each edge we assign a set of parties; informally, any set of at least $w_{u,v}$ parties among the parties assigned to an edge can reconstruct "the bit of the edge".

We remark that the tree used in [15] is infinite. However, since we allow a gap between the sizes of authorized and unauthorized sets, we can use a scheme realizing a finite tree.

Terminology: We use the following notations in our constructions.

- The i-th layer of the tree contains nodes of distance exactly i from the root.
- A node in the ith layer is identified by the sequence of weights assigned to the edges along the path from the root to that node; the node is denoted by $u_{w_1,w_2,\ldots,w_i}$, where $w_1, \ldots, w_i$ are the weights of the edges from the root to the node. That is, the root is u_ϵ and for every nodes $u_{w_1,w_2,\ldots,w_{i-1}}$ and $u_{w_1,w_2,\ldots,w_{i-1},w_i}$ in the $(i-1)$-th and i-th layers respectively there is an edge with weight w_i connecting them. We assume that for every node in the tree the weights of its outgoing edges are distinct, thus, the notation $u_{w_1,\ldots,w_i}$ uniquely identifies a node.
- We assign parties to each edge of the tree. That is, we consider a function $q : V \to \mathbb{N}$ such that $q(u_\epsilon)$ is the index of the first party in the scheme and for every $(u, v) \in E$ it holds that $q(v) > q(u)$, the parties $\{p_{q(u)+1}, \ldots, p_{q(v)}\}$ are assigned to the edge (u, v).

Definition 5.1. *Given a finite weighted tree $T = (V, E)$ with a weight function $w : E \to \mathbb{N}$ and a function $q : V \to \mathbb{N}$, let $u_{\max} = \max_{v \in V}\{q(v)\}$. We define the complete access structure $\Gamma_{T,w,q}$ with parties $\{p_{q(u_\epsilon)}, \ldots, p_{q(u_{\max})}\}$, where a set A is authorized in the access structure if and only if there exists a leaf $u_{w_1,\ldots,w_i}$ in the tree and a path*

$$(u_\epsilon, u_{w_1}), (u_{w_1}, u_{w_1,w_2}), \ldots, (u_{w_1,\ldots,w_{i-1}}, u_{w_1,\ldots,w_i})$$

such that $|A \cap \{p_{q(u_{w_1,\ldots,w_{j-1}})+1}, \ldots, p_{q(u_{w_1,\ldots,w_j})}\}| \geq w_j$ for every $1 \leq j \leq i$.

Given a finite weighted tree T, we construct a secret-sharing scheme, denoted by Π_{wt}, realizing $\Gamma_{T,w,q}$. We next informally describe Π_{wt}: we first share the secret using the scheme of Sect. 5.1. Then for every edge (u,v) we share the bit given to (u,v) by a threshold secret-sharing scheme among the parties assigned to the edge; the threshold used is the weight of the edge. The formal description of Π_{wt} appears in Fig. 3.

The Scheme Π_{wt}

- Run Π_T on the tree T. Denote the share given to an edge (u,v) by $r_{u,v}$, where if $w(e) = 0$ then $r_e = 0$ (instead of a random bit).
- For every edge $(v_{w_1,w_2,\ldots,w_{i-1}}, v_{w_1,w_2,\ldots,w_{i-1},w_i})$ such that $w_i > 0$, share the bit $r_{v_{w_1,w_2,\ldots,w_{i-1}},v_{w_1,w_2,\ldots,w_{i-1},w_i}}$ among the parties $\{p_{q(v_{w_1,w_2,\ldots,w_{i-1}})+1}, \ldots, p_{q(v_{w_1,w_2,\ldots,w_{i-1},w_i})}\}$ by a w_i-out-of-$\big(q(v_{w_1,w_2,\ldots,w_{i-1},w_i}) - q(v_{w_1,w_2,\ldots,w_{i-1}})\big)$ threshold secret-sharing scheme.

Fig. 3. The scheme Π_{wt} that realizes the access structure $\Gamma_{T,w,q}$.

Lemma 5.2. *The scheme Π_{wt} realizes $\Gamma_{T,w,q}$.*

Proof. Since we share the secret using Π_T, a set A can reconstruct the secret iff it can reconstruct the bits $r_{v_\epsilon,v_1}, r_{v_1,v_2}, \ldots, r_{v_{c-1},v_c}$ for some path $(v_\epsilon, \ldots, v_c)$ from the root to a leaf. Let $w_1, \ldots, w_c$ be the weights of the edges on this path. The bit r_{v_{j-1},v_j} is shared by a w_j-out-of-$(q(v_j) - q(v_{j-1}))$ threshold secret-sharing scheme among the parties $\{p_{q(v_{j-1})+1}, \ldots, p_{q(v_j)}\}$ and A can learn the bit r_{v_{j-1},v_j} if and only if $|A \cap \{p_{q(v_{j-1})+1}, \ldots, p_{q(v_j)}\}| \geq w_j$. $\qquad\square$

6 The Second Scheme Realizing $\Gamma^f_{t,1/2,\gamma}$: The Tree Technique

In this section, we prove Theorem 1.1. We show how to use the secret sharing for weighted trees described in Sect. 5 to realize $\Gamma^f_{t,1/2,\gamma}$, thus, to construct evolving ramp secret-sharing schemes. Our scheme Π_{tree} can be used for arbitrary functions $f(t)$, however to simplify the analysis of the share size, we only consider functions $f(t) = t^\beta$ for some constant $0 < \beta < 1$. In Fig. 4, we define a weighted tree T_{ramp}. The tree contains $n + 1$ layers for some constant n. The first n layers partition the parties $p_{f(t)/2}, \ldots, p_{t^\alpha}$ (for some $\alpha \leq 1$ as will be defined later) to n sets of consecutive parties, and the parties corresponding to edges from the $(i-1)$-th layer to the i-th layer are the parties from the i-th set. The $(n+1)$-th layer adds, for every node of layer n, edges as in the segment construction in Sect. 4 for the set of parties $p_{t^\alpha+1}, \ldots, p_{2t}$. We construct a scheme Π_{tree}:

- Execute Π_{wt} on T_{ramp}.

1. Parameters:
   - n: the number of layers in the tree (to be fixed later).
   - $q_0, q_1, q_2, \ldots, q_n$: $q_0 = \frac{f(t)}{2}$, $q_n \leq t$, $q_{n+1} = 2t$, where $q_1, q_2, \ldots, q_n$ will be chosen later.
   - Let $d_i = t + if(t)$ for $0 \leq i < \frac{t}{f(t)}$; $m = \lceil \frac{t}{f(t)} \rceil$ and $d_m = 2t$.
   - Let $W_i = \{0, \frac{\gamma f(t)}{2n}, \frac{2\gamma f(t)}{2n}, \ldots, \lfloor \frac{2nq_i}{\gamma f(t)} \rfloor \cdot \frac{\gamma f(t)}{2n}\}$ for $0 \leq i \leq n$.
2. Layer V_0 contains the root u_ϵ with $q(u_\epsilon) = q_0$.
3. For every $1 \leq i \leq n$, for each $u_{w_1, w_2, \ldots, w_{i-1}} \in V_{i-1}$ and $w_i \in W_i \cup \{\sum_{j=1}^{i-1} w_j\}$ such that $w_i \geq \sum_{j=1}^{i-1} w_j$, add the node $u_{w_1, w_2, \ldots, w_{i-1}, w_i - \sum_{j=1}^{i-1} w_j}$ in layer V_i, add the edge $(u_{w_1, w_2, \ldots, w_{i-1}}, u_{w_1, w_2, \ldots, w_{i-1}, w_i - \sum_{j=1}^{i-1} w_j})$ (with weight $w_i - \sum_{j=1}^{i-1} w_j$), and define $q(u_{w_1, \ldots, w_{i-1}, w_i}) = q_i$.
4. Add an additional layer V_{n+1}: For every $0 \leq i \leq \frac{t}{f(t)}$, for every $u_{w_1, w_2, \ldots, w_n} \in V_n$, add the node $u_{w_1, w_2, \ldots, w_n, w}$ to V_{n+1}, where $w = \lceil \gamma d_i - \sum_{i=1}^n w_i - \gamma f(t) \rceil$, add the edge $(u_{w_1, w_2, \ldots, w_n}, u_{w_1, w_2, \ldots, w_n, w})$, and define $q(u_{w_1, w_2, \ldots, w_n, w}) = d_{i+1}$.

Fig. 4. The weighted tree T_{ramp} used for realizing $\Gamma^f_{t,1/2,\gamma}$.

Lemma 6.1. *Let f be a function such that $f(t + f(t)) > f(t)$. The scheme Π_{tree} realizes the access structure $\Gamma^f_{t,1/2,\gamma}$.*

Proof. We start by proving the correctness of the scheme, that is, if $A = \{p_{i_1}, p_{i_2}, \ldots, p_{i_k}\}$ such that $t < i_k \leq 2t$ and $k \geq \gamma i_k - \frac{\gamma f(t)}{2}$, then A can reconstruct the secret. By Lemma 5.2, we need to prove that there is a path from the root to a leaf $u_{w_1, \ldots, w_{n+1}}$ such that

$$|A \cap \{p_{q(u_{w_1, \ldots, w_{i-1}})+1}, \ldots, p_{q(u_{w_1, \ldots, w_i})}\}| \geq w_i \tag{1}$$

for every $1 \leq i \leq n+1$. Let $z_i = |A \cap \{p_{q_{i-1}+1}, \ldots, p_{q_i}\}|$ for $1 \leq i \leq n$. We define the weights inductively. Assume that we defined $w_1, \ldots, w_{i-1}$ such that (1) holds for them. Let $w_i = \max\{w - \sum_{j=1}^{i-1} w_j : w \in W_i, w \leq \sum_{j=1}^{i-1} w_j + z_i\}$. By the construction of W_i, $w_i \geq z_i - \frac{\gamma}{2n} f(t)$. The path from the root to $u_{w_1, \ldots, w_n}$ satisfies (1) for every $1 \leq i \leq n$ and

$$\sum_{i=1}^n w_i \geq |A \cap \{p_{f(t)/2}, \ldots, p_{t^{\alpha_n}}\}| - \frac{\gamma f(t)}{2}. \tag{2}$$

Let j be the index such that $d_j < i_k \leq d_j + f(t)$ and let $w_{n+1} = \lceil \gamma d_j - \sum_{i=1}^{n} w_i - \gamma f(t) \rceil$. By the construction of T_{ramp} there is an edge between $u_{w_1,\ldots,w_n}$ and $u_{w_1,\ldots,w_n,w_{n+1}}$. To complete the proof of the correctness, we need to show that $|A \cap \{p_{t^{\alpha_n}+1}, \ldots, p_{d_j+f(t)}\}| \geq w_{n+1}$:

$$|A \cap \{p_{t^{\alpha_n}+1}, \ldots, p_{d_j+f(t)}\}| = |A| - |A \cap \{p_{f(t)/2}, \ldots, p_{t^{\alpha_n}}\}|$$

$$\geq \gamma i_k - \frac{\gamma f(t)}{2} - \left(\sum_{i=1}^{n} w_i + \frac{\gamma f(t)}{2} \right)$$

$$\geq \gamma d_j - \sum_{i=1}^{n} w_i - \gamma f(t).$$

Since $|A \cap \{p_{t^{\alpha_n}+1}, \ldots, p_{d_j+f(t)}\}|$ is an integer, $|A \cap \{p_{t^{\alpha_n}+1}, \ldots, p_{d_j+f(t)}\}| \geq \lceil \gamma d_j - \sum_{i=1}^{n} w_i - \gamma f(t) \rceil = w_{n+1}$.

We next prove the security of the scheme. Let A be an unauthorized set of $\Gamma_{t,1/2,\gamma}^{f}$. By Lemma 5.2, we need to prove that there is no path from the root to a leaf $u_{w_1,\ldots,w_{n+1}}$ such that

$$|A \cap \{p_{q_{w_1,\ldots,w_{i-1}+1}}, \ldots, p_{q_{w_1,\ldots,w_i}}\}| \geq w_i$$

for every $i = 1, \ldots, n+1$. Fix such a leaf $u_{w_1,\ldots,w_{n+1}}$ and let j be the index such that $w_{n+1} = \lceil \gamma d_j - \sum_{i=1}^{n} w_i - \gamma f(t) \rceil$ and $q(u_{w_1,\ldots,w_{n+1}}) = d_{j+1}$. Since A is unauthorized,

$$|A \cap \{p_{f(t)/2}, \ldots, p_{d_{j+1}}\}| \leq \gamma d_{j+1} - f(d_{j+1}) < \gamma d_{j+1} - f(t), \tag{3}$$

where the last inequality is implied by the assumption that $f(t + (j+1)f(t)) \geq f(t + f(t)) > f(t)$ for every t. If $|A \cap \{p_{q_{w_1,\ldots,w_{i-1}+1}}, \ldots, p_{q_{w_1,\ldots,w_i}}\}| < w_i$ for some $i = 1, \ldots, n$, then we are done. Otherwise,

$$|A \cap \{p_{t^{\alpha_n}+1}, \ldots, p_{d_{j+1}}\}| = |A \cap \{p_{f(t)/2}, \ldots, p_{d_{j+1}}\}| - |A \cap \{p_{f(t)/2}, \ldots, p_{t^{\alpha_n}}\}|$$

$$< (\gamma d_{j+1} - f(t)) - \sum_{i=1}^{n} w_i \quad \leq \quad w_{n+1}.$$

$\square$

6.1 Analysis of the Share Size

We next analyze the share size of the scheme Π_{tree} for a function $f(t) = t^\beta$ for some $0 < \beta < 1$. In this case, it would be convenient to write $q_0 = t^{\alpha_0}, q_1 = t^{\alpha_1}, \ldots, q_n = t^{\alpha_n}, q_{n+1} = 2t^{\alpha_{n+1}} = 2t$ (where $\alpha_{n+1} = 1$) and express the share size as a function of $\alpha_0, \ldots, \alpha_n, \alpha_{n+1}$.

Lemma 6.2. *Let* $q_0 = t^\beta/2$, $\alpha_0 = \beta, \alpha_{n+1} = 1, q_{n+1} = 2t$, *and let* n *and* $\alpha_1, \alpha_2, \ldots, \alpha_n, \alpha_n$ *be constants such that* $\beta < \alpha_1 < \alpha_2 < \cdots < \alpha_n \leq \alpha_{n+1} = 1$. *Denote* $q_i = t^{\alpha_i}$ *for* $i = 1, \ldots, n$. *For every* $1 \leq i \leq n+1$ *and* $q_{i-1} < j \leq q_i$, *the share size of the party* p_j *in* Π_{tree} *is* $O\left(j^{\frac{\sum_{\ell=1}^{i} \alpha_\ell - i\beta}{\alpha_{i-1}}} \log j \right)$.

Proof. The share of party p_j is composed of many shares of Shamir's threshold secret-sharing scheme with $O(t)$ parties; the size of each such share is $O(\log t)$. The number of shares of a threshold secret-sharing that party p_j gets is the number of edges between layer $i-1$ and layer i in T_{ramp}, i.e., the number of nodes in layer i in T_{ramp}; this number is bounded from above by

$$\prod_{\ell=1}^{i} |W_\ell| = \prod_{\ell=1}^{i} \frac{2nq_\ell}{\gamma f(t)} = \prod_{\ell=1}^{i} \frac{2n}{\gamma} t^{\alpha_\ell - \beta} = \left(\frac{2n}{\gamma}\right)^i \cdot t^{(\sum_{\ell=1}^{i} \alpha_\ell) - i\beta}.$$

This holds also for parties $p_{t^{\alpha_n}+1}, \ldots, p_{2t}$ by taking $\alpha_{n+1} = 1$ and $|W_{n+1}| = t^{1-\beta}$. As $n, i, \alpha_i = O(1)$, the total share size of p_j is $O\left(j^{\frac{\sum_{\ell=1}^{i} \alpha_\ell - i\beta}{\alpha_i - 1}} \log j\right)$. $\square$

By Theorem 3.3 and Lemma 6.2 we get the following lemma.

Lemma 6.3. *Let n and $\alpha_0, \alpha_1, \ldots, \alpha_n, \alpha_{n+1}$ be constants such that $\beta = \alpha_0 < \alpha_1 < \alpha_2 < \cdots < \alpha_n \leq \alpha_{n+1} = 1$. Define*

$$C = \max\left\{\frac{\sum_{\ell=1}^{i} \alpha_\ell - i\beta}{\alpha_{i-1}} : 1 \leq i \leq n+1\right\}.$$

Then, there is a secret-sharing scheme realizing $\Gamma_{t,1/2,\gamma}^{f(t)=t^\beta}$, where the size of the share of p_j, for $t^\beta/2 < j \leq 2t$, is $O(j^C \log j)$ and there is an evolving secret-sharing scheme realizing $\Gamma_{\gamma t - t^\beta, \gamma t}$, where the size of the share of p_j, for $j \in \mathbb{N}$, is $O(j^C \log^2 j)$.

In order to find the best share size, we should find the number of layers n and the values of $\alpha_1, \ldots, \alpha_n$ that minimize the above value C.

Example 6.4. Take $\alpha_0 = \beta$ and $\alpha_i = 2\alpha_{i-1}$ for $0 \leq i \leq \log 1/\beta$ and let i, j be such that $t^{\alpha_{i-1}} < j \leq t^{\alpha_i}$. In this case $n = \log(1/\beta)$. The share size of party p_j in the scheme realizing $\Gamma_{t,1/2,\gamma}^{f(t)=t^\beta}$ is $O(j^C \log j)$, where

$$C = \frac{\sum_{\ell=1}^{i} \alpha_\ell - i\beta}{\alpha_{i-1}} = \frac{\sum_{\ell=1}^{i} 2^\ell \beta - i\beta}{2^{i-1}\beta} = \frac{2^{i+1} - 1 - i}{2^{i-1}} \leq 4 - 2\beta \log(1/\beta),$$

where the last inequality is implied by the fact that $i \leq \log(1/\beta)$. By Corollary 3.4, this implies a scheme realizing the evolving access structure $\Gamma_{\gamma t - t^\beta, \gamma t}$ with share size $O(j^{4 - \beta \log(1/\beta)} \log^2 j)$. This should be compared to the secret-sharing scheme of [15], which realizes the dynamic majority access structure (i.e., $\Gamma_{t/2-1, t/2}$) with share size $\tilde{O}(j^4)$. Thus, our scheme improves on the scheme of [15] for every constant $\beta > 0$, showing that allowing a gap between the sizes of the authorized and unauthorized sets reduces the share size, in the best known schemes.

Our goal in the rest of the section is to find better choices of $\alpha_1, \ldots, \alpha_n, a_n$ that will reduce the share size. For $\beta = 1/8$ this is done in Example 6.6; similar optimization can be done for every fixed β. For general values of β this is done in Claim 6.8, where we care about the asymptotic dependency of the exponent in the share size on β.

Example 6.5. We next analyze the optimal share size that we can get by our scheme using one layer. We need to choose $\beta < \alpha_1 \leq 1$. By Lemma 6.2, the share size of the parties p_j where $t^\beta/2 \leq j \leq t^{\alpha_1}$ is $O(j^{\frac{\alpha_1-\beta}{\beta}} \log j)$, and the share size of the parties p_j where $t^{\alpha_1} < j \leq 2t$ is $O(j^{\frac{\alpha_1+1-2\beta}{\alpha_1}} \log j)$. We need to find α such that $\max\{\frac{\alpha_1-\beta}{\beta}, \frac{\alpha_1+1-2\beta}{\alpha_1}\}$ is minimized. The solution of this problem is when $\frac{\alpha_1-\beta}{\beta} = \frac{\alpha_1+1-2\beta}{\alpha_1}$ (since increasing α_1 will increase $\frac{\alpha_1-\beta}{\beta}$ and decrease $\frac{\alpha_1+1-2\beta}{\alpha_1}$), therefore, $\alpha_1 = \beta + \sqrt{\beta - \beta^2}$ and the exponent in the share size is $\sqrt{1/\beta - 1}$. Note that by using zero layers, the exponent in share size is $1/\beta - 1$. When $\beta > 1/2$ it holds that $1/\beta - 1 < \sqrt{1/\beta - 1}$, and zero layers are better in this case than one layer. When $\beta < 1/2$, one layer is better than zero layers.

Example 6.6. We present an upper bound for the share size that can be achieved by our construction for $\beta = \frac{1}{8}$. We get this upper bound for $n = 2$, that is, when $q_0 = \frac{t^{1/8}}{2}, q_1 = t^{\alpha_1}, q_2 = t^{\alpha_2}, q_3 = 2t$. We need to find α_1 and α_2. By Lemma 6.2, the share size of the parties p_j, where $t^{1/8}/2 \leq j \leq t^{\alpha_1}$, is $O(j^{\frac{\alpha_1-1/8}{1/8}} \log j)$, the share size of the parties p_j, where $t^{\alpha_1} < j \leq t^{\alpha_2}$, is $O(j^{\frac{\alpha_1+\alpha_2-2/8}{\alpha_1}} \log j)$, and the share size of the parties p_j, where $t^{\alpha_2} < j \leq 2t$, is $O(j^{\frac{\alpha_1+\alpha_2+1-3/8}{\alpha_2}} \log j)$. In order to find the an upper bound, we solve the following non-linear program.

> Minimize C subject to:
>
> $$\alpha_1 - 1/8 \leq C/8$$
> $$\alpha_2 + \alpha_1 - 2/8 \leq C\alpha_1$$
> $$1 + \alpha_1 + \alpha_2 - 3/8 \leq C\alpha_2$$
> $$1/8 < \alpha_1 < \alpha_2 \leq 1$$

A possible solution for this problem is $\alpha_1 = 0.413857, \alpha_2 = 0.792505$. In this case, $C = 2.310852$. However, we do not know if this solution is optimal.

Theorem 6.7. *There is an evolving secret-sharing scheme realizing the evolving access structure $\Gamma_{\gamma t - t^{1/8}, \gamma t}$, where the share size of party p_j is $O(j^{2.32} \log^2 j)$.*

Choosing the Parameters for the General case. In this subsection, we show how to choose good parameters for a general $0 < \beta < 1/2$. To minimize the share size, we need to minimize $\frac{\sum_{\ell=1}^{i} \alpha_\ell - i\beta}{\alpha_{i-1}}$. As the saving we aim to is bigger than $i\beta$, we will ignore this term and minimize $\frac{\sum_{\ell=1}^{i} \alpha_\ell}{\alpha_{i-1}} = \frac{\sum_{\ell=1}^{i-2} \alpha_\ell}{\alpha_{i-1}} + 1 + \frac{\alpha_i}{\alpha_{i-1}}$. In Example 6.4, we saw that if we take the values of α_i as a geometric sequence with common ratio 2, then we get an exponent slightly smaller than 4. If α_ℓ is much smaller than $2\alpha_{\ell-1}$ for many values on ℓ, then $\sum_{\ell=1}^{i-2} \alpha_\ell$ will be greater than α_{i-1} and the exponent in the share size will be larger than 4. On the other hand, if α_i is bigger than $2\alpha_{i-1}$, then $\frac{\alpha_{i-1}}{\alpha_i} > 2$ and, also in this case, the share size will be larger than 4. Thus, we take a sequence that is close to geometric sequence with common ratio 2.

Claim 6.8. *Let $\alpha_0 = \beta$ and $\alpha_i = (2 + \frac{1}{2i}) \cdot \alpha_{i-1}$ until the first n such that $\alpha_n \geq 1$ (and define $\alpha_n = 1$). Then, for every i*

$$\frac{\sum_{i=1}^{i} \alpha_\ell - i\beta}{\alpha_{i-1}} \leq \left(4 - O\left(\frac{1}{\log^2(1/\beta)} \right) \right).$$

Proof. Note that $\alpha_i > 2\alpha_{i-1}$, so $n \leq \log(1/\beta)$. Furthermore, for every $\ell \leq i$

$$\alpha_\ell = \frac{\alpha_i}{\left(2 + \frac{1}{2(\ell+1)} \right) \cdot \ldots \cdot \left(2 + \frac{1}{2i} \right)} \leq \frac{\alpha_i}{(2 + \frac{1}{2i})^{i-\ell}}.$$

Thus,

$$\sum_{\ell=1}^{i} \alpha_j \leq \sum_{\ell=1}^{i} \frac{\alpha_\ell}{\left(2 + \frac{1}{2i} \right)^{i-\ell}}$$

$$= \frac{\alpha_i}{\left(2 + \frac{1}{2i} \right)^{i}} \cdot \frac{\left(2 + \frac{1}{2i} \right)^{i+1} - \left(2 + \frac{1}{2i} \right)}{\left(1 + \frac{1}{2i} \right)}$$

$$\leq \alpha_i \left(2 + \frac{1}{2i} \right) \left(1 - \frac{1}{2i+1} \right).$$

For every $2 \leq i \leq n$,

$$\frac{\sum_{\ell=1}^{i} \alpha_\ell - i\beta}{\alpha_{i-1}} \leq \frac{\sum_{\ell=1}^{i-1} \alpha_\ell + \alpha_i}{\alpha_{i-1}}$$

$$\leq \left(2 + \frac{1}{2(i-1)} \right) \left(1 - \frac{1}{2(i-1)+1} \right) + \frac{\alpha_i}{\alpha_{i-1}}$$

$$\leq 4 - \frac{1}{2i(2i-1)}$$

$$\leq 4 - O\left(\frac{1}{\log^2(1/\beta)} \right),$$

where the last inequality is implied by the fact that $i \leq n \leq \log(1/\beta)$. Note that for $i = n+1$ it holds that $\frac{\alpha_n}{\alpha_{n-1}} = 1$ and therefore the inequality holds. $\square$

For example, for $\beta = 2^{-20}$ the exponent is less than $4 - 1/(40 \cdot 39) < 3.9994$. This should be compared to the simpler solution given in Example 6.4, where the exponent is $4 - 40/2^{20} > 3.99996$.

By Lemma 6.3 and Claim 6.8, we obtain our evolving ramp secret-sharing scheme, proving Theorem 1.1.

Remark 6.9. In our analysis in Sect. 6.1 we ignore the factor of $i\beta$ in the exponent in the share size. This implies that in our construction of T_{ramp} we can take $W_i = \{0, 1, \ldots, q_i\}$. The saving in this case, compared to the scheme of [15], stems from the fact that we take a collection of finite trees, where in each tree we ignore the first $f(t)/2$ parties.

7   Reduction Between Evolving Ramp Secret-Sharing Schemes

In this section we show how to construct an evolving secret-sharing scheme realizing $\Gamma_{\gamma t - t^\beta, \gamma t}$ for some constants γ, β from an evolving secret-sharing scheme realizing $\Gamma_{t/d - ((t/d\gamma)^\beta - 1), t/d}$ for a constant d such that $\gamma > 1/d$. This construction is used to prove Theorem 1.2 from Lemma 4.3.

Theorem 7.1. *Let $0 < \beta < 1$, $d \in \mathbb{N}$, and $1/d < \gamma < 1$ be constants, and let Π be a scheme that realizes the evolving ramp access structure $\Gamma_{t/d - ((\frac{t}{\gamma d})^\beta - 1), t/d}$ such that the length of the share of party p_j is $c(j)$. Then there is a scheme realizing the evolving ramp access structure $\Gamma_{\gamma t - t^\beta, \gamma t}$ such that the size of the share of party p_j is $c(\lfloor \gamma d j \rfloor)$.*

Proof. In Fig. 5 we describe the scheme Π' that realizes the evolving access structure $\Gamma_{\gamma t - t^\beta, \gamma t}$. Next we prove the correctness and security of this scheme as well as analyzing its share size.

The Scheme Π'

For every $j \in \mathbb{N}$:

1. Give party p_j the share of party $p_{\lfloor \gamma d j \rfloor}$ in Π.

Fig. 5. The scheme Π' that realizes the evolving access structure $\Gamma_{\gamma t - t^\beta, \gamma t}$.

First we observe that, as $\gamma d > 1$, for every $j > j'$, parties p_j and $p_{j'}$ in Π' get shares of parties $p_{\lfloor \gamma d j \rfloor}$ and $p_{\lfloor \gamma d j' \rfloor}$ in Π, respectively, such that $\lfloor \gamma d j \rfloor \geq \lfloor \gamma d (j' + 1) \rfloor \geq \lfloor (\gamma d j') + 1 \rfloor > \lfloor \gamma d j' \rfloor$, thus, the parties in Π' get shares of different parties in Π.

Correctness: Let $A = \{p_{i_1}, \ldots, p_{i_k}\}$ be a minimal authorized set, i.e., $|A| = k \geq \gamma i_k$. The parties in A get shares of parties in the set $\{p_1, \ldots, p_{\lfloor \gamma d i_k \rfloor}\}$ in Π and $|A| \geq \lfloor \gamma d i_k \rfloor / d$, thus they can reconstruct the secret.

Security: Let $A = \{p_{i_1}, \ldots, p_{i_k}\}$ be an unauthorized set. Thus, for every $1 \leq j \leq k$, parties $p_{i_1}, \ldots, p_{i_j}$ in Π' get shares of parties in the set $\{p_1, \ldots, p_{\lfloor \gamma di_j \rfloor}\}$, and

$$j \leq \gamma i_j - (i_j)^\beta \leq \frac{\lfloor \gamma di_j \rfloor + 1}{d} - \left(\frac{\lfloor \gamma di_j \rfloor}{\gamma d}\right)^\beta \leq \frac{\lfloor \gamma di_j \rfloor}{d} - \left(\left(\frac{\lfloor \gamma di_j \rfloor}{\gamma d}\right)^\beta - 1\right).$$

Thus, for every $1 \leq j \leq k$, parties $p_{i_1}, \ldots, p_{i_j}$ in Π' get shares of an unauthorized set in $\Gamma_{t/d - ((\frac{t}{\gamma d})^\beta - 1), t/d}$, and the parties $p_{i_1}, \ldots, p_{i_k}$ get no information about the secret.

Share size: Party p_j gets the share of party $p_{\lfloor \gamma dj \rfloor}$ in Π. Therefore, the share size of party p_j is $c(\lfloor \gamma dj \rfloor)$. $\qquad \square$

By applying the reduction of Theorem 7.1 to the scheme of Lemma 4.3, we obtain Theorem 1.2.

8   An Evolving $(k/2, k)$-Ramp Secret-Sharing Scheme

Komargodski et al. [14] presented an evolving secret-sharing scheme for the evolving k-threshold access structure for a constant k (i.e., the complete access structure containing all sets of size at least k). In their construction, the j th party's share size is $O(k \log j)$, we denote this construction by Π_0. An interesting open question is whether the dependency on k can be improved. We study a relaxation of the problem, namely evolving $(k/2, k)$-ramp secret-sharing for constant k; where every set that contains at least k parties can reconstruct the secret, and any set of size at most $k/2$ cannot learn any information about the secret. We require nothing regarding the sets of size greater than $k/2$ but smaller than k. We construct an evolving $(k/2, k)$-ramp secret-sharing scheme with share size $O(\log k \log j)$. In our construction, we use the scheme Π_0 of [14] as a building box.

In Fig. 6 we describe the scheme $\Pi_{k/2,k}$ that realizes the evolving $(k/2, k)$-threshold access structure. As in [14], we first partition the parties into sets, called generations, according to the order they arrive, where the i-th generation contains the parties $p_{2^{ki}}, \ldots, p_{2^{k(i+1)} - 1}$.

We use the following observation in order to analyze the share size in $\Pi_{k/2,k}$.

Observation 8.1. *Shamir's t-out-of-n secret-sharing scheme shares m different secrets $s_1, s_2, \ldots, s_m$ with sizes $\ell_1, \ldots, \ell_m$ among n parties using share size $\max\{\lceil \log(n+1) \rceil, \ell_1 + \ell_2 + \cdots + \ell_m\}$.*

Proof. We simply share the secret $s = s_0 \circ s_1 \circ \cdots \circ s_m$ by Shamir's secret-sharing scheme (where $\circ$ is the concatenation of string). $\qquad \square$

The Scheme $\Pi_{k/2,k}$

Let Π_0 be the evolving k-threshold scheme of [14].
When party $p_{2^{ki}}$ arrives, the dealer prepares shares for all the parties $\{p_{2^{ki}}, \ldots, p_{2^{k(i+1)}-1}\}$.

1. Generate the next k shares from the scheme Π_0. Denote these shares by $v_1^i, v_2^i, \ldots, v_k^i$.
2. For $\ell \in \{0, 1, \ldots, \log k\}$, share $v_{2^\ell}^i, \ldots, v_{2^{\ell+1}-1}^i$ by a 2^ℓ-out-of-$(2^{k(i+1)}-2^{ki})$ secret-sharing scheme among the parties $\{p_{2^{ki}}, \ldots, p_{2^{k(i+1)}-1}\}$. Denote this scheme by Π_ℓ^i. That is, the share v_1^i is shared with threshold 1 using Π_1^i, the shares v_2^i, v_3^i are shared with threshold 2 using Π_2^i, the shares $v_4^i, \ldots, v_7^i$ are shared with threshold 4 using Π_3^i, etc.

Fig. 6. The scheme $\Pi_{k/2,k}$ realizing the evolving $(k/2, k)$-access structure.

Theorem 8.2. *The scheme $\Pi_{k/2,k}$ realizes the evolving ramp access structure $\Gamma_{k/2,k}$ with share size $O(\log k \log j)$ for party p_j.*

Proof. Correctness: we show that any set of size at least k can reconstruct the secret. Let $A = \{p_{i_1}, p_{i_2}, \ldots, p_{i_k}\}$ be a minimal authorized set such that p_{i_k} is in the g-th generation, that is, $2^{kg} \le i_k \le 2^{k(g+1)} - 1$. For $1 \le j \le g$, let c_j be the number of of parties in A from the j-th generation. By the construction, c_j parties in generation j can reconstruct at least c_j shares from generation j (this is true since every v_ℓ^j is shared by threshold of at most ℓ). Therefore, the set A can reconstruct at least $\sum_{j=1}^k c_j = k$ shares of Π_0, thus, by the correctness of Π_0, the set A can reconstruct the secret.

Security: Let A be an unauthorized set of size at most $k/2$ ending in generation g. By the construction, c_j parties from the j-th generation can reconstruct at most $2c_j - 1$ shares from generation j (this is true since every v_ℓ^j is shared by threshold of at least $\lceil \ell/2 \rceil$), thus the set A can reconstruct at most $\sum_{j=1}^g (2c_j - 1) < k$ shares of Π_0. By the security of Π_0, the set A cannot learn any information about the secret.

Share size analysis: the share of party p_j in generation g is composed of the shares from the schemes Π_ℓ^i for every $\ell \in \{0, 1, \ldots, \log k\}$. The size of generation g is $2^{k(g+1)} - 2^{kg} \le 2^{kg} \cdot 2^k$. Party p_j is in the $\lfloor \frac{\log j}{k} \rfloor$-th generation. The log of the generation size of the generation of p_j is less than $kg + k \le \frac{k \log j}{k} + k = \log j + k$. The scheme Π_ℓ^i for every $0 \le \ell \le \log k$ requires share size $\max\{\log j + k, |v_{2^\ell}^g| + \cdots + |v_{2^{\ell+1}-1}^g|\}$ (by Observation 8.1). The shares $v_1^g, \ldots, v_k^g$ are generated from Π_0; recall that the share size of the n-th party in Π_0 is $k \log n$. By the construction, $k(g-1)$ shares from Π_0 were generated for the previous generations. Therefore,

$$|v_\ell^g| \le |v_k^g| \le k \log kg \le k \log k \frac{\log j}{k} = k \log \log j.$$

Thus, the share size in Π_ℓ^g is at most

$$\max\{\log j + k, 2^\ell \cdot k \log \log j\}.$$

The total share size is:

$$\sum_{\ell=0}^{\log k} \max\{\log j + k, 2^\ell \cdot k \log \log j\} \leq (\log k + 1)(\log j + k) + 2k^2 \log \log j.$$

$\square$

When $j > 2^{2k^2}$, the share size of p_j is $O(\log k \log j)$.

9 Properties of Optimal Choices of Parameters for the Tree Technique

In this section we show the limitations of the tree technique for $\beta \geq 1/2$. We also give an upper bound on the number of layers minimizing the share size in our scheme for general β.

9.1 The Share Size in Π_{tree}

In this subsection, we analyze the share size in Π_{tree} and prove that for $1/2 \leq \beta < 1$ the optimal share size is obtained when $n = 0$, i.e., it is $\Theta(j^{\frac{1-\beta}{\beta}})$.

Claim 9.1. *For every $\beta \geq 1/2$, the share size in Π_{tree} is $\Omega(j^{\frac{1-\beta}{\beta}})$ for at least one party p_j.*

Proof. Let $j = t^{\alpha_n} + 1$. By Lemma 6.2, the share size of the party p_j is $\Omega(j^C)$, where $C = \frac{1 + \sum_{\ell=1}^{n-1} \alpha_\ell + \alpha_n - \beta(n+1)}{\alpha_n}$. It holds that,

$$\sum_{\ell=1}^{n-1} \alpha_\ell = \alpha_n(C - \frac{1-\beta}{\beta}) + (n+1)\beta - \frac{2\beta-1}{\beta}\alpha_n - 1$$

$$\leq \alpha_n(C - \frac{1-\beta}{\beta}) + (n+1)\beta - (2\beta - 1) - n - 1$$

$$= \alpha_n(C - \frac{1-\beta}{\beta}) + (n-1)\beta,$$

where the inequality follows from the fact that $\alpha_n > \beta$ and $2\beta - 1 \geq 0$. As $\alpha_\ell > \beta$ for every $1 \leq \ell \leq n - 1$, we get that $\alpha_n(C - \frac{1-\beta}{\beta}) \geq \sum_{\ell=1}^{n-1} \alpha_\ell - (n-1)\beta \geq 0$, i.e., $C \geq \frac{1-\beta}{\beta}$.

$\square$

Remark 9.2. For every $n > 0$ and $\beta > 1/2$, Π_{tree} with n layers has shares greater than Π_{seg} (since, $\frac{2\beta-1}{\beta}\alpha_n > 2\beta - 1$ as $\alpha_n > \beta$).

Claim 9.3. *For every $\beta < 1/2$ there is at least one party p_j such that the share size of p_j in Π_{tree} is $\Omega(j)$.*

Proof. Let $j = t^{\alpha_n} + 1$. The share size of party p_j is $\Omega(j^{C'})$ where $C' = \frac{1 + \sum_{\ell=1}^{n-1} \alpha_\ell + \alpha_n - \beta(n+1)}{\alpha_n} \geq \frac{\alpha_n}{\alpha_n} = 1$ (since $\alpha_\ell \geq \beta$ for every $1 \leq \ell \leq n - 1$).

$\square$

9.2 Upper Bound on the Number of Layers in the Optimal Solution for Π_{tree}

In this section, we show that, for every $\beta < 1/2$, there exists a choice of the parameters $n, \alpha_1, \ldots, \alpha_n$ that minimizes the share size of Π_{tree} and the number of layers n is at most $O(\log(1/\beta))$.

Claim 9.4. *Let $n, \alpha_1, \ldots, \alpha_n$ be parameters for Π_{tree}. If the share size of party p_j, for every $j \in \mathbb{N}$, in Π_{tree} is less than j^4 and there exist indices $1 \leq i_1 < i_2 \leq n - 2$ such that $\alpha_{i_2} < 2\alpha_{i_1}$ and $\alpha_{i_1} \geq 2\beta$, then $i_2 \leq i_1 + 15$.*

Proof. By the assumption of the lemma, $\alpha_{i_1} - \beta \geq \alpha_{i_1} - 0.5\alpha_{i_1} = 0.5\alpha_{i_1}$. Recall that the the share size of party p_j where $j = t^{\alpha_{i_2}} + 1$ is greater than j^C, where $C = \frac{\sum_{\ell=1}^{i_2+1} \alpha_\ell - (i_2+1)\beta}{\alpha_{i_2}}$. We next analyze this expression, using the fact that $\alpha_\ell > \beta$ for $1 \leq \ell \leq i_1 - 1$ and $\alpha_\ell \geq \alpha_{i_1}$ for $\ell \geq i_1$.

$$\frac{\sum_{\ell=1}^{i_2+1} \alpha_\ell - (i_2+1)\beta}{\alpha_{i_2}} \geq \frac{\sum_{\ell=i_1}^{i_2+1}(\alpha_{i_1} - \beta)}{\alpha_{i_2}}$$

$$\geq \frac{\sum_{\ell=i_1}^{i_2+1} 0.5\alpha_{i_1}}{2\alpha_{i_i}}$$

$$\geq \frac{i_2 + 1 - i_1}{4}.$$

Since we assume that the exponent is at most 4, we obtain that $i_2 \leq i_1 + 15$. □

Lemma 9.5. *For every $\beta < 1/2$, there exists a choice of the parameters $n, \beta < \alpha_1 < \cdots < \alpha_n \leq 1$ that minimizes the share size in Π_{tree} and the number of layers n is at most $15 \log(1/\beta) + 2$.*

Proof. First, let i be the largest index such that $\alpha_i \leq 2\beta$. If $i \geq 2$, we consider the parameters $n-i+1, \alpha_i, \ldots, \alpha_n$ with $n-i+1$ layers. This choice of parameters can only decrease the share size of parties $p_{t^{\alpha_i}+1}, \ldots, p_{2t}$ (since $\alpha_1, \ldots, \alpha_{i-1} > \beta$). The share size of party p_j, where $t^\beta/2 \leq j \leq t^{\alpha_i}$, is $\tilde{O}(j^C)$ where $C = (\alpha_i - \beta)/\beta \leq 1$. By Claim 9.3, for every $\beta \leq 1/2$, the exponent of the share size is at least 1. Thus, $n - i + 1, \alpha_i, \ldots, \alpha_n$ is also optimal.[2]

Second, the optimal solution has exponent less than 4 (by our construction in Sect. 6.1). Thus, by Claim 9.4, for every $1 \leq \log(1/\beta)$, in the interval $2^d\beta + 1, \ldots, 2^{d+1}\beta$ there are at most 15 layers. Thus, the total number of layers is as most $15 \log(1/\beta) + 2$. □

References

1. Beimel, A., Othman, H.: Evolving ramp secret-sharing schemes. In: Catalano, D., De Prisco, R. (eds.) SCN 2018. LNCS, vol. 11035, pp. 313–332. Springer, Cham (2018). https://doi.org/10.1007/978-3-319-98113-0_17

---

[2] In fact, for every $\beta < 1/2$, it must hold that $\alpha_2 > \beta$, as the exponent in this case is greater than 1.

2. Benaloh, J., Rudich, S.: Private communication (1989)
3. Blakley, G.R.: Safeguarding cryptographic keys. In: AFIPS, p. 313 (1979)
4. Blakley, G.R., Meadows, C.: Security of ramp schemes. In: Blakley, G.R., Chaum, D. (eds.) CRYPTO 1984. LNCS, vol. 196, pp. 242–268. Springer, Heidelberg (1985). https://doi.org/10.1007/3-540-39568-7_20
5. Bogdanov, A., Guo, S., Komargodski, I.: Threshold secret sharing requires a linear size alphabet. In: Hirt, M., Smith, A. (eds.) TCC 2016. LNCS, vol. 9986, pp. 471–484. Springer, Heidelberg (2016). https://doi.org/10.1007/978-3-662-53644-5_18
6. Cachin, C.: On-line secret sharing. In: Boyd, C. (ed.) Cryptography and Coding 1995. LNCS, vol. 1025, pp. 190–198. Springer, Heidelberg (1995). https://doi.org/10.1007/3-540-60693-9_22
7. Cascudo Pueyo, I., Cramer, R., Xing, C.: Bounds on the threshold gap in secret sharing and its applications. IEEE Trans. Inf. Theory **59**, 5600–5612 (2013)
8. Chen, H., Cramer, R., Goldwasser, S., de Haan, R., Vaikuntanathan, V.: Secure computation from random error correcting codes. In: Naor, M. (ed.) EUROCRYPT 2007. LNCS, vol. 4515, pp. 291–310. Springer, Heidelberg (2007). https://doi.org/10.1007/978-3-540-72540-4_17
9. Csirmaz, L., Tardos, G.: On-line secret sharing. Des. Codes Cryptogr. **63**(1), 127–147 (2012)
10. D'Arco, P., De Prisco, R., De Santis, A., Pérez del Pozo, A., Vaccaro, U.: Probabilistic secret sharing. In: 43rd International Symposium on Mathematical Foundations of Computer Science (MFCS 2018). Leibniz International Proceedings in Informatics (LIPIcs), vol. 117, pp. 64:1–64:16 (2018)
11. Franklin, M.K., Yung, M.: Communication complexity of secure computation. In: STOC 1992, pp. 699–710 (1992)
12. Ito, M., Saito, A., Nishizeki, T.: Secret sharing schemes realizing general access structure. In: Proceedings of the Globecom 1987, pp. 56–64 (1987)
13. Kilian, J., Nisan, N.: Private communication (1990)
14. Komargodski, I., Naor, M., Yogev, E.: How to share a secret, infinitely. In: Hirt, M., Smith, A. (eds.) TCC 2016. LNCS, vol. 9986, pp. 485–514. Springer, Heidelberg (2016). https://doi.org/10.1007/978-3-662-53644-5_19
15. Komargodski, I., Paskin-Cherniavsky, A.: Evolving secret sharing: dynamic thresholds and robustness. In: Kalai, Y., Reyzin, L. (eds.) TCC 2017. LNCS, vol. 10678, pp. 379–393. Springer, Cham (2017). https://doi.org/10.1007/978-3-319-70503-3_12
16. Martin, K.M., Paterson, M.B., Stinson, D.R.: Error decodable secret sharing and one-round perfectly secure message transmission for general adversary structures. Cryptogr. Commun. **3**, 65–86 (2011)
17. Shamir, A.: How to share a secret. Commun. ACM **22**(11), 612–613 (1979)
18. Stinson, D.R., Wei, R.: An application of ramp schemes to broadcast encryption. Inform. Process. Lett. **69**, 131–135 (1999)

Lower Bounds for Leakage-Resilient Secret Sharing

Jesper Buus Nielsen[(✉)] and Mark Simkin[(✉)]

Aarhus University, Aarhus, Denmark
{jbn,simkin}@cs.au.dk

Abstract. Threshold secret sharing allows a dealer to split a secret into n shares such that any authorized subset of cardinality at least t of those shares efficiently reveals the secret, while at the same time any unauthorized subset of cardinality less than t contains no information about the secret. Leakage-resilience additionally requires that the secret remains hidden even if one is given a bounded amount of additional leakage from every share.

In this work, we study leakage-resilient secret sharing schemes and prove a lower bound on the share size and the required amount of randomness of any information-theoretically secure scheme. We prove that for any information-theoretically secure leakage-resilient secret sharing scheme either the amount of randomness across all shares or the share size has to be linear in n. More concretely, for a secret sharing scheme with p-bit long shares, ℓ-bit leakage per share, where $\widehat{t}$ shares uniquely define the remaining $n - \widehat{t}$ shares, it has to hold that

$$p \geq \frac{\ell(n - t)}{\widehat{t}} \ .$$

We use this lower bound to gain further insights into a question that was recently posed by Benhamouda et al. (CRYPTO'18), who ask to what extend existing regular secret sharing schemes already provide protection against leakage. The authors proved that Shamir's secret sharing is 1-bit leakage-resilient for reconstruction thresholds $t \geq 0.85n$ and conjectured that it is also 1-bit leakage-resilient for any other threshold that is a constant fraction of the total number of shares. We do not disprove their conjecture, but show that it is the best one could possibly hope for. Concretely, we show that for large enough n and any constant $0 < c < 1$ it holds that Shamir's secret sharing scheme is *not* leakage-resilient for $t \leq cn/\log n$.

In contrast to the setting with information-theoretic security, we show that our lower bound does not hold in the computational setting. That is, we show how to construct a leakage-resilient secret sharing scheme in the random oracle model that is secure against computationally bounded adversaries and violates the lower bound stated above.

J. B. Nielsen—Supported by the Independent Research Fund Denmark project BETHE and the Concordium Blockchain Research Center, Aarhus University, Denmark.
M. Simkin—Supported by the European Unions's Horizon 2020 research and innovation program under grant agreement No. 669255 (MPCPRO) and No. 731583 (SODA).

A. Canteaut and Y. Ishai (Eds.): EUROCRYPT 2020, LNCS 12105, pp. 556–577, 2020.
https://doi.org/10.1007/978-3-030-45721-1_20

1   Introduction

Threshold secret sharing, introduced by Shamir [Sha79] and Blakley [Bla79], is a fundamental building block in modern cryptography. It allows a dealer to split a secret into n shares such that any subset of cardinality at least t of those shares efficiently reveals the secret, while at the same time any subset of cardinality less than t contains no information about the secret in the information theoretic sense. Due to its computational simplicity, its strong privacy guarantees, and its information-theoretic security, it has found applications in various areas of cryptography ranging from secure multiparty computation [BGW88, CCD88, RB89] over threshold cryptography [Des88, DF90, Sho00] to attribute-based encryption [GPSW06, Wat11]. Stronger notions, like robust [RB89] and verifiable secret sharing [CGMA85] address the lack of authenticity in the original definition and prevent the participants or the dealer from tampering with the shares. All these classical notions of secret sharing have in common that they assume that any share is either fully corrupted or completely hidden from the adversary.

In contrast to these notions, a recent line of works [DP07, BGK14, GK18a, GK18b, ADN+18, KMS18, SV18, BS18] considers secret sharing in the context of side-channel attacks, where an adversary gets some form of restricted access to *all* shares. Generally, these works consider two types of adversaries. Active adversaries that may tamper with all shares and passive adversaries that may leak some bounded amount of information from each share. Constructing secret sharing schemes that remain secure in the presence of such powerful adversaries is a challenging task and, unsurprisingly, existing constructions are less efficient than regular secret sharing schemes in one way or another. Understanding what price one has to pay for such strong security guarantees is a foundational theoretical question and of significant practical importance when real-world resources are limited. While the efficiency of regular threshold secret sharing is well understood [BGK16], little is known about the price of additional security against side-channel attacks.

In this work, we focus on leakage-resilient secret sharing and we measure efficiency in terms of share size and the amount of randomness needed for secret sharing a value. The share size is an important measure to optimize, since it directly affects the efficiency of cryptographic primitives, like multiparty computation protocols, that are built on top of secret sharing. The celebrated BGW protocol [BGW88] for secure multiparty computation, for instance, exhibits a one-to-one correspondence between share size of the underlying secret sharing scheme and overall communication complexity of the protocol. That is, an increase of the share size by a factor of 2 directly translates to an increase of the overall communication complexity of the protocol by the same factor. The amount of randomness that cryptographic primitives require is an important measure to optimize for real-world applications. In research, it is often assumed that randomness is simply there when needed it, yet in reality it turns out to be a precious resource with limited availability. Generating good randomness is difficult and cryptographic primitives that required more randomness than what was available have led to devastating large-scale attacks [HDWH12].

1.1 Our Contribution

We prove that for any leakage-resilient secret sharing scheme with information-theoretic security either the amount of randomness across all shares or the share size has to be large.

Theorem 1 (Informal). *Let S be a t-out-of-n secret sharing scheme, let p be the bit length of each share, and let ℓ be the number of bits leaked from each share. If S is leakage-resilient against a computationally unbounded adversary and $\hat{t}$ shares uniquely define the remaining $n - \hat{t}$ shares, then*

$$p \geq \frac{\ell(n - t)}{\hat{t}}$$

For instance, for a $\mathcal{O}(1)$-out-of-n secret sharing scheme with 1-bit leakage, where $\mathcal{O}(1)$ shares uniquely define the remaining shares, the theorem tells us that the share size has to be *linear* in the number of shares. On the other hand, if we want the share size to be $o(n)$, then the theorem tells us that virtually *all* shares have to contain some independent, yet meaningful information[1].

We prove our lower bound by presenting a conceptually simple generic adversary, who breaks the leakage-resilience of any secret sharing scheme that violates our bound. More concretely, the adversary is given leakage from each share and its goal is to determine the secret value. The high-level idea behind our attack is to apply one separate uniformly random leakage function to each share. By correctness of a secret sharing scheme, we know that any two vectors of secret shares corresponding to two different secrets will always differ in at least $n-t+1$ positions. If the output of each leakage function is ℓ bits long, then two different shares produce the same leakage with probability $2^{-\ell}$. The smaller the threshold t, the larger the number of differing shares. The main observation behind our lower bound is that, with an increasing n, we quickly reach a point, where the leakage excludes all but one of the secrets that could have produced the given leakage.

We use our lower bound to gain further insights into an intriguing question that was recently posed by Benhamouda et al. [BDIR18], who ask to what extent existing regular secret sharing schemes already provide protection against leakage. Among other results, the authors show that Shamir's secret sharing scheme over a field $\mathbb{F}_{2^k}$ with small characteristic is not leakage-resilient. Specifically, the authors present an attack, which obtains one bit of the secret shared value from 1-bit leakage from each share. On the positive side, the authors show that t-out-of-n Shamir secret sharing over a prime order field $\mathbb{F}_q$ is 1-bit leakage-resilient if $t \geq 0.85n$. The authors leave it open to prove or disprove the leakage-resilience of Shamir secret sharing over $\mathbb{F}_q$ for other parameter ranges and conjecture:

Conjecture 1 ([BDIR18]). *Let $0 < c \leq 1$ be a constant and let $q \approx n$ be a prime. For large enough n, it holds that cn-out-of-n Shamir secret sharing over $\mathbb{F}_q$ is 1-bit leakage-resilient.*

---

[1] We will precise define what we mean by meaningful information in Sect. 3.1.

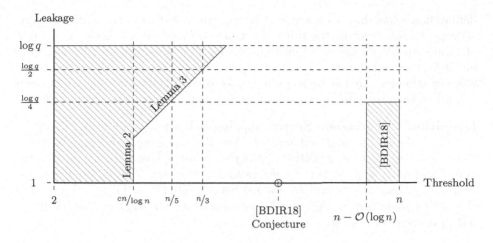

Fig. 1. Overview of our results on the leakage-resilience of Shamir's secret sharing over a prime order field $\mathbb{F}_q$ for an arbitrary number of parties n. The y-axis depicts the leakage per share in bits, the x-axis shows the reconstruction threshold. The red area indicates parameter ranges in which it is not leakage-resilient. The green area indicates parameter ranges where it is. The white area indicates parameter ranges, where we do not know anything. n is the number of parties, $\log q$ is the number of bits per share, and $0 < c < 1$ is an arbitrary, but fixed constant. (Color figure online)

We do not disprove their conjecture, but show that it is basically the best one could hope for. More concretely, we show that for a large enough n and any constant $0 < c < 1$ it holds that Shamir's secret sharing scheme is *not* leakage-resilient for $t \leq cn/\log n$. Our results regarding the leakage-resilience of Shamir's secret sharing scheme are illustrated in Fig. 1. Whereas the negative results above crucially rely on a computationally unbounded adversary, we also show that for the specific case of 2-out-of-n Shamir secret sharing there exists a computationally efficient attack.

Given the lower bound for information-theoretically secure secret sharing schemes, it may be natural to hope the same bound may apply to schemes that only need to be sure against a computationally bounded adversary. We show that this is not the case by presenting a leakage-resilient secret sharing scheme in the random oracle model that has a share size of $p = \mathcal{O}(n + \lambda + \ell)$ and is secure against any computationally bounded adversary that runs in time $\mathsf{poly}(\lambda)$. By setting, for instance, $\ell > n$ one can see that such a scheme violates our lower bound from above for sufficiently large n.

2 Preliminaries

For random variables V and W we use $V \approx_\epsilon W$ to denote that the distributions of V and W are at most ϵ apart in L_1 distance.

Our definition of threshold secret sharing follows the definition of Beimel [Bei11]. We additionally define a full reconstruction threshold $\hat{t}$, which defines how many shares are needed to reconstruct all shares of a particular secret sharing. In other words, the full reconstruction threshold $\hat{t}$ can also be seen as an upper bound on the total entropy among all shares of a secret sharing. In our definition and the remainder of the paper we assume perfectly correct secret sharing schemes. This is done for the sake of simplicity and all proofs easily extend to the case, where the reconstruction may fail with some probability.

Definition 1 (Threshold Secret Sharing Scheme). *Let* SHARE : $\{0,1\}^k \rightarrow$ $(\{0,1\}^p)^n$ *be an efficient randomized algorithm mapping k bit secrets into n shares each of length p. Let* REC : $(\{0,1\}^p)^n \rightarrow \{0,1\}^k$ *be a deterministic algorithm that maps a collection of t shares back to a secret. The notion generalises in a straight forward manner to schemes* SHARE : $\{0,1\}^k \rightarrow \prod_{i=1}^n \{0,1\}^{p_i}$, *where the shares possibly have different length. The pair* (SHARE, REC) *is called a t-out-of-n secret sharing if:*

1. **Perfect Correctness**: *Any t-out-of-n shares can be used to reconstruct the secret correctly. For any $x \in \{0,1\}^k$, for any set $T \subseteq [n]$ with $|T| \geq t$,*

$$\Pr[\text{REC}(\text{SHARE}(x)_T) = x] = 1$$

   where the probability is taken over the randomness of the sharing function and SHARE$(x)_T$ *denotes the restriction of the n shares produced by* SHARE(x) *to the ones identified by the set T.*
2. **Perfect Privacy**: *Less than t shares reveal no information about the underlying secret. More formally, for any two $x, y \in \{0,1\}^k$, any set $T \subseteq [n]$ with $|T| < t$,* SHARE$(x)_T$ *is identically distributed to* SHARE$(y)_T$.
3. **Full Reconstruction**: *A secret sharing scheme has $\hat{t}$-full-reconstruction if* SHARE(x) *can be computed from any subset* SHARE$(x)_T$ *with $|T| \geq \hat{t}$.*

The notion of Full Reconstruction is non-standard, but essential to our study. Leakage-resilient secret sharing schemes like [SV18] with very high leakage resilience all seem to use some notion of non-trivial correlated randomness which makes the full reconstruction threshold larger than the reconstruction threshold. To some extend our results will explain why this is the case. If you have a scheme with low full reconstruction threshold you get poor leakage resilience. So if you have a scheme with a low reconstruction threshold and good leakage resilience, then the full reconstruction threshold *must* be larger than the reconstruction threshold.

To model leakage-resilient secret sharing, we use the local leakage model as defined by Goyal and Kumar [GK18a] and Benhamouda et al. [BDIR18]. Intuitively, it allows the adversary to compute arbitrary independent leakage functions on all shares, which are only restricted in the size of their leakage output. For the sake of exposition, we split the definition in weak and regular local leakage-resilience. In weak local leakage-resilience the adversary is only given the output of the leakage functions. In regular local leakage-resilience, it is additionally given θ full shares. As such weak local leakage-resilience is a special case of regular local leakage-resilience for $\theta = 0$.

Definition 2 (Leakage Function). *We call* LEAK $= ($LEAK$_1, \ldots,$ LEAK$_n)$ *an ℓ-leakage function for* (SHARE, REC) *if* SHARE $: \{0,1\}^k \rightarrow \prod_{i=1}^{n} \{0,1\}^{p_i}$ *and* LEAK$_i : \{0,1\}^{p_i} \rightarrow \{0,1\}^{\ell}$. *For* $(\mathsf{sh}_1, \ldots, \mathsf{sh}_n) \leftarrow$ SHARE(s) *we define* $(b_1, \ldots, b_n) =$ LEAK$(\mathsf{sh}_1, \ldots, \mathsf{sh}_n)$ *by* $b_i =$ LEAK$_i(\mathsf{sh}_i)$.

Definition 3 (Weak Local Leakage-Resilience). *A secret sharing scheme* (SHARE, REC) *is said to be (ϵ, ℓ)-weakly-local-leakage-resilient (W-IND-LLR) if for every ℓ-leakage function vector* LEAK *and every pair of secrets $x, y \in \{0,1\}^k$ it holds that*

$$\text{LEAK}(\text{SHARE}(x)) \approx_\epsilon \text{LEAK}(\text{SHARE}(y)).$$

We also define leakage-resilience against a class of adversaries. Let B be a possibly randomized interactive algorithm. First the adversary outputs a pair of secrets (x_0, x_1) and a leakage function LEAK. *Then the game flips a uniformly random challenge bit c and inputs* LEAK(SHARE(x_c)) *to B. Then run B to get a guess $g \in \{0,1\}$. Let* $\mathsf{Adv}_B = 2|\Pr[g = c] - 1/2|$. *We say that* (SHARE, REC) *is (ϵ, ℓ)-weakly-local-leakage-resilient for a class $\mathcal{B}$ of adversaries if for all $B \in \mathcal{B}$ it holds that*

$$\mathsf{Adv}_B \leq \epsilon\,.$$

Definition 4 (Local Leakage-Resilience). *A secret sharing scheme* (SHARE, REC) *is said to be (ϵ, ℓ, θ)-local-leakage-resilient (IND-LLR) if for every ℓ-leakage function vector* LEAK, *for any set $T \subseteq [n]$ with $|T| < \theta$, and every pair of secrets $x, y \in \{0,1\}^k$ it holds that*

$$(\text{SHARE}(x)_T, \text{LEAK}(\text{SHARE}(x))) \approx_\epsilon (\text{SHARE}(y)_T, \text{LEAK}(\text{SHARE}(y)))\,.$$

We also add a one-way notion, which we will use for proving our lower bound. We will make the notion as weak as possible while still being meaningful, which makes our lower bound as strong as possible.

Definition 5 (Weak One-Way Local Leakage-Resilience). *We define what it means for a secret sharing scheme* (SHARE, REC) *to be ℓ-weakly one-way local-leakage-resilient (WOW-LLR). Let A be a possibly randomized interactive algorithm. Let $x \in \{0,1\}^k$ be a secret. The game* WOW$_A(x)$ *proceeds as follows. First the adversary outputs a leakage function* LEAK. *Then the game samples $(\mathsf{sh}_1, \ldots, \mathsf{sh}_n) \leftarrow$ SHARE(x) and we input* LEAK(SHARE(x)) *to A, who outputs a guess $y \in \{0,1\}^k \cup \{\bot\}$. The output of* WOW$_A(x)$ *is 1 if and only if $y = x$. We call A admissible if it always holds for all x that $y = x$ or $y = \bot$. We require that for all admissible A there exist x for which* $\Pr[\text{WOW}_A(x) = 1] < 1/2$.

Note that one-wayness is a very weak security notion, it only requires that all of the secret cannot be learned. Requiring that the adversary must only make guesses it knows are correct further weakens the notion, as it limits the set of adversaries, which in turn makes it easier to be WOW-LLR. We also weaken the notion by requiring only that $\Pr[\text{WOW}_A(x) = 1] < 1/2$, as opposed to requiring that $\Pr[\text{WOW}_A(x) = 1]$ is negligible. And finally we only require that (SHARE, REC) hides one x from the adversary, meaning that it might in principle be possible for A to recover almost all x with certainty. It seems hard to meaningfully further weaken the notion. Not surprisingly, W-IND-LLR implies WOW-LLR, but for completeness we prove a technical lemma to this effect.

Lemma 1. *Let* (SHARE, REC) *be a secret sharing scheme. If* (SHARE, REC) *is* $(1/2, \ell)$-*W-IND-LLR then* (SHARE, REC) *is* ℓ-*WOW-LLR.*

Proof. Assume that (SHARE, REC) is not WOW-LLR. This means that there exists an admissible A such that

$$\Pr[\text{WOW}_A(x) = 1] > 1/2$$

for all x. Now let B be W-IND-LLR adversary which first runs as follows. First pick x_0 and x_1 to be any distinct secrets. Run A to get a leakage function LEAK. Output (x_0, x_1) and LEAK. Get back

$$(b_1, \ldots, b_n) = \text{LEAK}(\text{SHARE}(x_c)) .$$

Input $(b_1, \ldots, b_n)$ to A and get back a guess y. If $y = \bot$, then output a uniform random guess g. Otherwise, since A is admissible we know that $y = x_c$ for $c = 0$ or $c = 1$. In that case, output $g = c$. We know that the probability that A guesses x_c is larger than $1/2$. So, clearly

$$\begin{aligned}
\text{Adv}_B &= 2|\Pr[g = c] - 1/2| \\
&\geq 2(1 \cdot \Pr[y \neq \bot] + 1/2 \cdot \Pr[y = \bot] - 1/2) \\
&> 2(1 \cdot 1/2 + 1/2 \cdot 1/2 - 1/2) \\
&= 1/2.
\end{aligned}$$

This implies that (SHARE, REC) is not $(1/2, \ell)$-W-IND-LLR.

2.1   Shamir's Secret Sharing

In t-out-of-n Shamir secret sharing [Sha79] the secrets and the shares come from a field $\mathbb{F}_q$, where q is usually chosen to be the smallest prime larger than n. Let $\alpha_1, \ldots, \alpha_n \in \mathbb{F}_q$ be distinct non-zero elements known to all parties. To share a secret $s \in \mathbb{F}_q$, the dealer picks a uniformly random polynomial P of degree $t - 1$ with $p(0) = s$. The share of party i is $\text{sh}_i = P(\alpha_i)$.

To reconstruct the secret, a sufficiently large subset of parties interpolates the polynomial P from their shares and evaluates the interpolated polynomial at position 0. Correctness follows from the fact that, in a field, any t points uniquely define a polynomial of degree $t - 1$. Privacy follows from the fact that for any $t - 1$ points any secret s is still possible and all secrets are equally likely.

3   Lower Bound

In this section we prove our main result.

Theorem 2. *Let $\mathcal{S} = (\text{SHARE}, \text{REC})$ be a t-out-of-n secret sharing scheme with $\hat{t}$-full-reconstruction. If $\mathcal{S}$ is ℓ-WOW-LLR and $\ell \geq 1$, then*

$$p \geq \frac{\ell(n - t)}{\hat{t}}.$$

Proof. We prove the theorem by exhibiting an explicit admissible adversary that breaks ℓ-WOW-LLR of any secret sharing scheme with a share size $p < \ell(n-t)/\hat{t}$. We provide an inefficient, randomized algorithm A that exactly recovers the secret shared value from the given leakage with probability at least $1/2$. Note that throughout the paper we give attacks succeeding with constant probability. It with be enough to present attacks succeeding with non-negligible probability. However, this does not seem to allow to strengthen our lower bounds.

The algorithm A proceeds as follows. Pick a random $\text{LEAK} = (\text{LEAK}_1, \ldots, \text{LEAK}_n)$ where each $\text{LEAK}_i : \{0,1\}^p \to \{0,1\}^\ell$ is an independent, uniformly random function mapping p-bit strings to ℓ-bit strings. Submit it to the leakage game and get back

$$(b_1, \ldots, b_n) = (\text{LEAK}_1(\text{sh}_1), \ldots, \text{LEAK}_n(\text{sh}_n)) ,$$

where

$$(\text{sh}_1, \ldots, \text{sh}_n) \leftarrow \text{SHARE}(s; r)$$

is a secret sharing of the secret s that the algorithm should try to recover. Now iterate over all secrets s' and randomizers r' and compute

$$(\text{sh}'_1, \ldots, \text{sh}'_n) \leftarrow \text{SHARE}(s'; r') .$$

Let

$$S = \{s' \mid \exists r : (b_1, \ldots, b_n) = (\text{LEAK}_1(\text{sh}'_1), \ldots, \text{LEAK}_n(\text{sh}'_n))\} .$$

This is the set of secrets s' which are consistent with the leakage $(b_1, \ldots, b_m)$. If $|S| > 1$, then output $\perp$. Otherwise, let $\{s\} = S$ and output s. Let succ be the event that the output is not $\perp$.

It is trivial to see that $s \in S$. Hence if $|S| = 1$, then indeed $S = \{s\}$. So when A does not output $\perp$, it outputs the correct secret s. Hence A is admissible.

We now prove that $\Pr[\text{succ}] \geq 1/2$. Let $(\text{sh}_1, \ldots, \text{sh}_n) \leftarrow \text{SHARE}(s; r)$ be the secret sharing of the secret that A is trying to guess and denote by $b_i \leftarrow \text{LEAK}_i(\text{sh}_i)$ the leakage from the i-th share. Let $(\text{sh}'_1, \ldots, \text{sh}'_n) \leftarrow \text{SHARE}(s'; r')$ be the secret sharing of some arbitrary but fixed secret s' with $s \neq s'$ and let $b'_i \leftarrow \text{LEAK}_i(\text{sh}'_i)$ be the corresponding leakage. By correctness of the secret sharing scheme, it is guaranteed that there exists a set $I \subseteq [n]$ with $|I| \geq n - t + 1$ such that $\text{sh}_i \neq \text{sh}'_i$ for all $i \in I$. So it clearly holds that

$$\Pr_{\text{LEAK}}[(b_1, \ldots, b_n) = (b'_1, \ldots, b'_n)] \leq 2^{-\ell(n-t+1)},$$

where the randomness is taken over a random LEAK.

Since each share is p bits long and since $\widehat{t}$ shares uniquely define any particular secret sharing, it follows that there exists at most a total of $2^{p\widehat{t}}$ possible secret sharings.

Let coll be the event that there exists any (s', r') with $s' \neq s$ such that $(b_1, \ldots, b_n) = (\text{LEAK}_1(\text{sh}'_1), \ldots, \text{LEAK}_n(\text{sh}'_n))$ when $(\text{sh}'_1, \ldots, \text{sh}'_n) \leftarrow \text{SHARE}(s'; r')$. By a union bound we get that

$$\Pr[\text{coll}] \leq 2^{p\widehat{t} - \ell(n-t+1)}$$
$$\Pr[\neg\text{coll}] \geq 1 - 2^{p\widehat{t} - \ell(n-t+1)} .$$

Observe that the event $\text{succ} = \neg\text{coll}$. If all secret sharings of all values $s' \neq s$ are inconsistent with the given leakage, then we can conclude that the secret shared value is s. For the probability of $\neg\text{coll}$ to be larger than $1/2$, it suffices that

$$1 - 2^{p\widehat{t} - \ell(n-t+1)} > 1/2$$
$$2^{p\widehat{t} - \ell(n-t+1)} < 1/2$$
$$p\widehat{t} - \ell(n-t+1) < -1$$
$$\ell(n-t+1) - 1 > p\widehat{t}$$
$$\frac{\ell(n-t+1) - 1}{\widehat{t}} > p$$

To prevent the attack described above, we therefore need that

$$\frac{\ell(n-t+1) - 1}{\widehat{t}} \leq p$$

has to hold. Finally, we observe that when $\ell \geq 1$, then $\ell(n-t+1) - 1 \geq \ell(n-t)$. ∎

As an immediate corollary of the theorem it follows that any secret sharing scheme, which only requires a constant number of shares for full reconstruction, has to have a share size that is linear in the number of shares if it wants to be leakage-resilient.

Corollary 1. *Let $\mathcal{S} = (\text{SHARE}, \text{REC})$ be a t-out-of-n secret sharing scheme with $\widehat{t}$-full-reconstruction, where t and $\widehat{t}$ are constants. If $\mathcal{S}$ is $(1/2, 1)$-W-IND-LLR, then its share size p is in $\Omega(n)$.*

When given some complete shares in addition to the leakage, then we obtain the following bound:

Theorem 3. *Let $\mathcal{S} = (\text{SHARE}, \text{REC})$ be a t-out-of-n secret sharing scheme with $\widehat{t}$-full-reconstruction. If $\mathcal{S}$ is $(1/2, \ell, \theta)$-IND-LLR, and $\ell \geq 1$, then*

$$p \geq \frac{\ell(n-t)}{\widehat{t} - \theta}.$$

Proof. The proof here is almost identical to the proof of Theorem 2. In addition to the leakage, we are now given θ complete shares. As before, let $(b_1, \ldots, b_n)$ and $(b'_1, \ldots, b'_n)$ be the leakage of some arbitrary, but fixed secret sharings $a = \text{SHARE}(s; r)$ and $a' = \text{SHARE}(s'; r')$ with $s \neq s'$. Let $T \subseteq [n]$ with $|T| < \theta$ be the subset of indices of shares that we get to see in addition to the leakage. We have already established that

$$\Pr[(b_1, \ldots, b_n) = (b'_1, \ldots, b'_n)] \leq 2^{-\ell(n-t+1)},$$

which implies

$$\Pr[(b_1, \ldots, b_n, a_T) = (b'_1, \ldots, b'_n, a'_T)] \leq 2^{-\ell(n-t+1)}.$$

Let us now consider the event coll that, for an arbitrary but fixed (s, r), there exists any (s', r') with $s' \neq s$ such that $(b_1, \ldots, b_n, a_T) = (b'_1, \ldots, b'_n, a'_T)$. There are at most $2^{p\hat{t}}$ possible secret sharings and at most $2^{p(\hat{t}-\theta)}$ possible secret sharings that match the shares a_T at the indices T. By a union bound we have

$$\Pr[\neg\text{coll}] \geq 1 - 2^{p(\hat{t}-\theta)-\ell(n-t+1)}.$$

For the probability of $\neg$coll to be larger than $1/2$ it thus suffices that

$$\frac{\ell(n-t+1)-1}{\hat{t}-\theta} > p.$$

To prevent the attack described above it must therefore hold that

$$\frac{\ell(n-t+1)-1}{\hat{t}-\theta} \leq p,$$

which for $\ell \geq 1$ is true if

$$\frac{\ell(n-t)}{\hat{t}-\theta} \leq p.$$

∎

3.1 A Lower Bound via Randomness Complexity

In this section we prove a lower bound via randomness complexity. To motivate it, consider the bound in Theorem 2 for the case $t = o(n)$. In this case we have that

$$p \geq \frac{\ell n}{\hat{t}}.$$

So, if we consider the relative leakage, then we have that

$$\frac{\ell}{p} \leq \frac{\hat{t}}{n}.$$

This means that to have a constant leakage rate[2], one still needs $\widehat{t} \in \Omega(n)$. That is, after having enough shares to reconstruct, there still needs to be randomness left in many of the other remaining shares. This explains existing constructions of leakage-resilient secret sharing schemes, where shares contain a lot more randomness than what is actually needed to get privacy against $t - 1$ parties.

However, the above theorem does not give a quantitative enough handle on this phenomenon. One could trivially get $\widehat{t} = n$ by adding an unused uniformly random bit to each share. But intuitively, this should not help against leakage-resilience. These bits are trivial in the sense that they could just be deleted. Neither should it help if we added a little bit of non-trivial randomness to the shares, as it could just be leaked. Below we prove a theorem which gets a better quantative handle of how much randomness there must be in the shares.

The following definition will be helpful in removing trivial randomness from consideration.

Definition 6. *Let $\mathcal{S} = (\text{SHARE}, \text{REC})$ be a t-out-of-n secret sharing scheme where share number i has length p_i. We call $\text{comp} = (\text{comp}_1, \ldots, \text{comp}_n)$ a compression of $\mathcal{S}$ if it holds for $i = 1, \ldots, n$ that $\text{comp}_i : \{0,1\}^{p_i} \to \{0,1\}^{q_i}$ and $q_i \le p_i$. Define $\text{SHARE}^{\text{comp}}$ by*

$$(\text{sh}'_1, \ldots, \text{sh}'_n) = \text{SHARE}^{\text{comp}}(s; r)$$

where

$$(\text{sh}_1, \ldots, \text{sh}_n) = \text{SHARE}(s; r)$$

and

$$(\text{sh}'_1, \ldots, \text{sh}'_n) = (\text{comp}_1(\text{sh}_1), \ldots, \text{comp}_n(\text{sh}_n)) \ .$$

We call a compression a correct compression of $\mathcal{S}$ if for some REC' it holds that $\mathcal{S}^{\text{comp}} = (\text{SHARE}^{\text{comp}}, \text{REC}')$ is again a t-out-of-n secret sharing scheme.

We now introduce a crude measure of the randomness complexity.

Definition 7. *Let $\mathcal{S} = (\text{SHARE}, \text{REC})$ be a t-out-of-n secret sharing scheme. Let*

$$\text{size}\,\mathcal{S} = |\{\text{SHARE}(s; r) | s \in \{0,1\}^k, r \in \{0,1\}^*\}| \ .$$

Let

$$\text{ran}\,\mathcal{S} = \log \min_{\text{comp}} \text{size}\,\mathcal{S}^{\text{comp}} \ ,$$

where the minimum is taken over all correct compressions of $\mathcal{S}$. We call a correct compression comp for $\mathcal{S}$ for which it holds that $\log_2 \text{size}\,\mathcal{S}^{\text{comp}} = \text{ran}\,\mathcal{S}$ a max-compression of comp.

Notice that the above measure is via max-entropy. This is a very crude notion of randomness, but for illustrating the phenomenon that a lot of randomness is left in each share, it works well and allows for a significantly simpler proof.

---

[2] The leakage rate is defined as the ratio between the number of bits leaked per share and the share size in bits.

Notice that if you secret share a random secret s using a random r, then you will hit all possible secret sharings with non-zero probability. So, the length of the random s and r must be *at least* $\mathrm{ran}\,\mathcal{S}$. So, if we can lower bound $\mathrm{ran}\,\mathcal{S}$, we also lower bounded the amount of randomness needed to sample a secret sharing.

To connect the randomness complexity to the above theorems, notice that if a secret sharing scheme $\mathcal{S}$ has share size p, then $\mathrm{ran}\,\mathcal{S} \leq \widehat{t}p$.

Theorem 4. *Let $\mathcal{S} = (\mathrm{SHARE}, \mathrm{REC})$ be a t-out-of-n secret sharing scheme with $\widehat{t}$-full-reconstruction. If $\mathcal{S}$ is $(1/2, \ell)$-weakly-leakage-resilient and $\ell \geq 1$, then*

$$\mathrm{ran}\,\mathcal{S} \geq \ell(n-t) .$$

Proof. We prove the theorem by showing a generic attack that breaks ℓ-WOW-LLR of any secret sharing scheme with $\mathrm{ran}\,\mathcal{S} < \ell(n-t)$. The adversary A proceeds as follows.

1. Let $\mathrm{comp} = (\mathrm{comp}_1, \dots, \mathrm{comp}_n)$ be a max-compression for $\mathcal{S} = (\mathrm{SHARE}, \mathrm{REC})$, where $\mathrm{comp}_i : \{0,1\}^{p_i} \to \{0,1\}^{q_i}$.
2. For $i = 1, \dots, n$, pick a uniformly random $\mathrm{LEAK}_i : \{0,1\}^{q_i} \to \{0,1\}^{\ell}$.
3. For $i = 1, \dots, n$, let $\mathrm{LEAK}_i' = \mathrm{LEAK}_i \circ \mathrm{comp}_i$.
4. Submit $\mathrm{LEAK}' = (\mathrm{LEAK}_1', \dots, \mathrm{LEAK}_n')$ to the WOW-LLR.
5. Get back $(b_1, \dots, b_n) = (\mathrm{LEAK}_1(\mathrm{comp}_1(\mathsf{sh}_1)), \dots, \mathrm{LEAK}_n(\mathrm{comp}_n(\mathsf{sh}_n)))$ where $(\mathsf{sh}_1, \dots, \mathsf{sh}_n) \leftarrow \mathrm{SHARE}(s; r)$ is a secret sharing of the secret s that the algorithm should try to recover.
6. Call $s' \in \{0,1\}^k$ consistent with $(b_1, \dots, b_n)$ if there exists r' such that

$$(b_1, \dots, b_n) = (\mathrm{LEAK}_1(\mathsf{sh}_1'), \dots, \mathrm{LEAK}_n(\mathsf{sh}_n'))$$

when

$$(\mathsf{sh}_1', \dots, \mathsf{sh}_n') \leftarrow \mathrm{SHARE}^{\mathrm{comp}}(s'; r') .$$

Compute

$$S = \{s' \in \{0,1\}^k \mid s' \text{ is consistent with } (b_1, \dots, b_n)\} .$$

7. If $|S| > 1$, then output $\bot$. Otherwise, let $\{s\} = S$ and output s.

Let succ be the event that the output is not $\bot$. It is trivial to see that $s \in S$. Hence if $|S| = 1$, then indeed $S = \{s\}$. So when A does not output $\bot$, it outputs the correct secret s and wins the WOW-LLR. We conclude the theorem by proving that $\Pr[\mathsf{succ}] \geq 1/2$.

Let $(\mathsf{sh}_1, \dots, \mathsf{sh}_n) \leftarrow \mathrm{SHARE}(s; r)$ be the secret sharing of the secret that A is trying to guess and denote by

$$b_i \leftarrow \mathrm{LEAK}_i(\mathrm{comp}_i(\mathsf{sh}_i))$$

the leakage from the i-th share. Let

$$(\mathsf{sh}_1', \dots, \mathsf{sh}_n') \leftarrow \mathrm{SHARE}^{\mathrm{comp}}(s'; r')$$

be the secret sharing of some arbitrary but fixed secret s' with $s \neq s'$ and let $b'_i \leftarrow \text{LEAK}_i(\text{sh}'_i)$ be the corresponding leakage. By correctness of comp we have that $(\text{SHARE}^{\text{comp}}, \text{REC})$ is correct. This guarantees that there exists a set $I \subseteq [n]$ with $|I| \geq n - t + 1$ such that $\text{sh}_i \neq \text{sh}'_i$ for all $i \in I$. So it clearly holds that

$$\Pr_{\text{LEAK}}[(b_1, \ldots, b_n) = (b'_1, \ldots, b'_n)] \leq 2^{-\ell(n-t+1)},$$

where the randomness is taken over a the random $(\text{LEAK}_1, \ldots, \text{LEAK}_n)$.

Let coll be the event that there exists any (s', r') with $s' \neq s$ such that $(b_1, \ldots, b_n) = (\text{LEAK}_1(\text{sh}'_1), \ldots, \text{LEAK}_n(\text{sh}'_n))$ when $(\text{sh}'_1, \ldots, \text{sh}'_n) \leftarrow \text{SHARE}^{\text{comp}}(s'; r')$. Observe that $\text{succ} = \neg\text{coll}$. By definition there are at most $2^{\text{ran}\,\mathcal{S}}$ possible secret sharings. So, by a union bound we get that

$$\Pr[\text{coll}] \leq 2^{\text{ran}\,\mathcal{S} - \ell(n-t+1)}$$

$$\Pr[\neg\text{coll}] \geq 1 - 2^{\text{ran}\,\mathcal{S} - \ell(n-t+1)}$$

$$1 - 2^{\text{ran}\,\mathcal{S} - \ell(n-t+1)} > 1/2$$

$$2^{\text{ran}\,\mathcal{S} - \ell(n-t+1)} < 1/2$$

$$\text{ran}\,\mathcal{S} - \ell(n-t+1) < -1$$

$$\ell(n-t+1) - 1 > \text{ran}\,\mathcal{S}$$

To prevent the attack described above, we therefore need that

$$\text{ran}\,\mathcal{S} \geq \ell(n-t+1) - 1 = \ell(n-t) + \ell - 1 \geq \ell(n-t) \,,$$

where we used that $\ell \geq 1$.   ■

To illustrate the theorem, consider a secret sharing scheme with constant threshold t, share size p, which tolerates leakage $\ell = (1 - o(1))p$. The theorem tells us that it *must* be the case that

$$\text{ran}\,\mathcal{S} \geq p(n-2) \approx pn \,.$$

So on average there are p bits of randomness in each share. In particular, after learning the constant number of shares needed to reconstruct, there is *still* about p bits of randomness left in each share that was not used for reconstructing. This quantifies that almost all randomness goes into achieving leakage-resilient and not into privacy of the secret sharing.

As another example, consider a secret sharing scheme with $t < cn$ for a constant $c < 1/2$ and $\ell = dp$ for a constant d. We get that

$$\text{ran}\,\mathcal{S} \geq \ell(1-c)n \,.$$

We have that

$$n - t = (1-c)n$$

and thus

$$\ell(n-t) = dp(1-c)n \,.$$

So after learning t shares of length p the average number of bits of randomness left per share is at least

$$\frac{dp(1-c)n - tp}{n-t} = \frac{dp(1-c)n - cnp}{(1-c)n} = p\frac{d(1-c)-c}{(1-c)} = p\left(d - \frac{c}{(1-c)}\right) .$$

So if

$$d > \frac{c}{(1-c)}$$

there is still randomness left in the shares.

4   Leakage-Resilience of Shamir's Secret Sharing

Benhamouda et al. [BDIR18] investigate the local leakage-resilience of Shamir's secret sharing. Among other results, the authors show that Shamir's scheme is not leakage-resilient if either the number of parties is constant or the secret sharing is done over a field with small characteristic. Using Fourier analytic techniques and additive combinatorics they show that t-out-of-n Shamir secret sharing is $(\mathsf{negl}(n), \lfloor \log q/4 \rfloor)$-W-IND-LLR in prime order fields $\mathbb{F}_q$, whenever $t = n - \mathcal{O}(\log n)$. In the recently published full version of the same paper[3], the authors further show that it is 1-bit leakage resilient for $t \approx 0.85n$. They leave it open to find other parameter ranges in which local leakage-resilience does or does not hold and postulate Conjecture 1, which was already stated in the introduction.

Our lower bound does not disprove Benhamouda et al.'s conjecture, but it does tell us how large n and thus the shares would have to be if the conjecture is indeed true. By plugging in the concrete parameters from the conjecture into Theorem 2, we get that

$$\frac{n-t}{t} \le p \Leftrightarrow \frac{n-cn}{cn} \le p \Leftrightarrow \frac{1-c}{c} \le p \Leftrightarrow \frac{1}{c} - 1 \le p$$

has to hold for the conjecture to be true. Since $p = \log q = \log n$ it follows that the share size has to be in $\Omega(1/c)$ and thus $n \in \Omega(2^{\frac{1}{c}})$.

Furthermore, using Theorem 2, we can show that Shamir's secret sharing is not local leakage-resilient for a large range of parameters. Concretely, we show that two natural strengthenings of Benhamouda et al.'s conjecture are not true. In Lemma 2 we consider a mildly smaller reconstruction threshold of $cn/\log n$. In Lemma 3 we consider a larger leakage. See Fig. 1 in the introduction for an overview of these results. A possible interpretation of these results is that the original conjecture of Benhamouda et al. is essentially the best one can hope for.

Lemma 2. *Let q be the smallest prime larger than n. Then for any constant $0 < c < 1$ and large enough n it holds that $(cn/\log n)$-out-of-n Shamir secret sharing over $\mathbb{F}_q$ is not $(1/2, 1)$-W-IND-LLR.*

---

[3] https://eprint.iacr.org/2019/653.

Proof. Via Theorem 2, we know that the adversary successfully breaks leakage-resilience, whenever

$$p < \frac{n-t}{t} = \frac{n}{t} - 1$$

Combining this inequality with the parameters from the stated theorem, we get that

$$p < \frac{\log n}{c} - 1$$

has to hold, which is true for any $0 < c < 1$ for large enough n, since $p = \log n$. ∎

Lemma 3. *Let q be the smallest prime larger than n. For any constant $0 < c < 1/2$ and any n, there exists a constant $0 < d < 1$, such that cn-out-of-n Shamir secret sharing over $\mathbb{F}_q$ is not $(1/2, d \log n)$-W-IND-LLR.*

Proof. For the attack from Theorem 2 to work we need that

$$\frac{\ell(n - cn)}{cn} > p \Leftrightarrow \frac{\ell(1 - c)}{c} > p \Leftrightarrow \ell > \frac{c}{1 - c} p$$

Since $p = \log n$, and $(1 - c) > c$, it follows that the inequality holds for any $\ell \geq \log n$ with any $d < c/1-c$. ∎

Lemma 3 provides an interesting insight into the relationship between the number of bits sufficient for reconstruction and the number of leaked bits sufficient for breaking local leakage-resilience. In general, cn-out-of-n Shamir secret sharing requires cn full shares and thus $cn \log n$ bits in total for reconstructing the secret[4]. Reconstruction can be seen as a form of structured leakage, where cn full shares are leaked. Lemma 3 shows that (inefficient) reconstruction is possible from unstructured leakage when the leakage is a small constant fraction larger than what is needed for reconstruction anyways, e.g. if $c = 1/5$, then we need $n/5 \log n$ bits for regular reconstruction and $n/4 \log n$ bits for reconstruction from the leakage.

4.1   An Efficient Attack for 2-Out-of-n Shamir Secret Sharing

All the results described above only apply to secret sharing schemes with information-theoretic security, since the proof of Theorem 2 relies on an adversary that can enumerate all possible secret sharings and thus runs in time at least exponential in the share size p. In the following, we show that for the specific case of 2-out-of-n Shamir secret sharing, we can break weak local leakage-resilience using only a single bit of leakage per share in a highly efficient manner. Our attack only requires $\mathcal{O}(n)$ field operations and does not depend on any particular properties of the underlying field.

---

[4] Over certain fields reconstruction can be performed with significantly fewer bits, but this approach does not work over general fields. See for example Guruswami and Wootters [GW16].

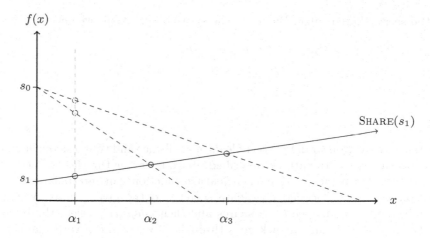

Fig. 2. Illustration of our efficient attack on 2-out-of-n Shamir secret sharing. The secret shared value is s_1 and the solid line represents the linear function that was used during the secret sharing. The dashed lines depict the linear functions that are interpolated from the shares under the assumption that the secret shared value is s_0. Two distinct incorrect points at $x = \alpha_1$ are extrapolated.

Theorem 5. *For any $\delta < 1 - 2^{-n}$, 2-out-of-n Shamir secret sharing over an arbitrary field $\mathbb{F}_q$ is not $(\delta, 1)$-W-IND-LLR. More concretely, there exists a distinguisher B that performs $\mathcal{O}(n)$ field operations and breaks weak local leakage-resilience with a success probability of $1 - 2^{-n-1}$.*

Proof. Let s_0 and s_1 be two arbitrary distinct secrets that are output by the adversary. Let f_1 be a uniformly random leakage function. For $2 \leq i \leq n$, we hardcode s_0, public values (α_1, α_i), and f_1 into the leakage function f_i. On input sh_i, the function f_i interpolates a linear function P_i between the points $(0, s_0)$ and $(\alpha_i, \mathsf{sh}_i)$. It outputs $f_1(P_i(\alpha_1))$. The adversary receives the leaked bits $b_1, \ldots, b_n$ and has to decide whether s_0 or s_1 was secret shared. If $b_1 = b_2 = \cdots = b_n$, then the adversary outputs guess $g = 0$. Otherwise it outputs $g = 1$.

Let us consider two cases. If s_0 was secret shared, then $(0, s_0)$ lies on a line with all shares and thus, for $2 \leq i \leq n$, each f_i interpolates the P that was initially used to compute the shares. Therefore, it holds that each $P_i(\alpha_1) = \mathsf{sh}_1$ and it follows that all leakage functions output the same bit $f_1(\mathsf{sh}_1)$. If s_1 was secret shared, then $(s_1, 0)$ does not lie on a line with the shares. It follows that, for each $2 \leq i \leq n$, f_i interpolates a distinct line P_i. All these lines intersect in $(s_1, 0)$ and therefore if follows that all $(P_i(\alpha_1), \alpha_1)$ are distinct. Since f_1 is a uniformly random function, we can conclude that the probability that $b_1 = b_2 = \cdots = b_n$ is 2^{-n}. A visual illustration of the reasoning above is depicted in Fig. 2. Let s_c

be the secret shared value. Based on the above observations we get

$$\mathsf{Adv}_B = 2|\Pr[g = c] - 1/2|$$
$$= 2(1 \cdot 1/2 + 1/2 \cdot (1 - 2^{-n}) - 1/2)$$
$$= 1 - 2^{-n}.$$

∎

Assuming a stronger definition of leakage-resilience and thus a stronger adversary, we can extent the attack described above to larger thresholds. The basic idea behind the attack is that each leakage function can interpolate a linear function using a hardcoded candidate secret and the given share. Assuming our adversary can first see $t - 2$ shares and then *adaptively* select the leakage-functions, then the same attack goes through in a straightforward manner for t-out-of-n Shamir secret sharing, because the adversary can hardcode $t - 2$ shares in addition to some candidate secret and let each leakage function interpolate a degree t polynomial.

Corollary 2. *For any $\delta < 1 - 2^{-n}$, t-out-of-n Shamir secret sharing over an arbitrary field $\mathbb{F}_q$ is not $(\delta, 1)$-W-IND-LLR against an distinguisher that sees $t - 2$ shares before choosing the leakage functions. In particular, there exists a distinguisher that performs $\mathcal{O}(n)$ field operations and breaks weak local leakage-resilience with a success probability of $1 - 2^{-n-1}$.*

5   Computational Leakage-Resilient Secret Sharing

A natural question is whether our lower bound from Sect. 3 also applies to computationally secure secret sharing schemes. In this section we answer this question in the negative by presenting a leakage-resilient secret sharing scheme, which violates our lower bound, in the random oracle model that is secure against computationally bounded adversaries.[5] More concretely we show:

Theorem 6. *Let λ be a security parameter. In the random oracle model there exists a $(\mathsf{negl}(\lambda), \ell)$-W-IND-LLR 2-out-of-$n$ secret sharing scheme $\mathcal{S} = (\mathrm{SHARE}, \mathrm{REC})$ for 1-bit secrets with share size $p = \mathcal{O}(\ell + \lambda + n)$ and full reconstruction threshold $\hat{t} = 2$ that is secure against computationally bounded adversaries that run in time $\mathsf{poly}(\lambda)$.*

---

[5] Note that our lower bound easily extends to information-theoretically secure secret sharing schemes in the random oracle model. And unbounded distinguisher can learn the entire RO, so the RO does not help more than an exponentially long, uniformly random, common reference string (CRS). Our lower bound clearly generalises to the case with a CRS, as it goes via counting the expected number of secret sharings consistent with a given leakage. This counting argument is not affect by a public CRS.

Remark 1. Note that, for instance for $\ell > n$ for sufficiently large n, such a secret sharing scheme violates the bound for information-theoretically secure schemes. For $\ell > n$ and $n > \lambda$ the share size is $p = \mathcal{O}(\ell + \lambda + n) = \mathcal{O}(\ell)$. And we have that the secret sharing scheme tolerates ℓ-bits of leakage from each share. When $\hat{t} = 2$ and information theoretic $(\mathsf{negl}(\lambda), \ell)$-W-IND-LLR 2-out-of-n would need to have share size $p \geq \frac{\ell(n-t)}{t} = \Theta(n\ell)$. So the computational version beats the information theoretic one by a factor n in share size.

Proof. For the sake of simplicity, assume we have access to the following multiple random oracles:

$$H_s : \{0,1\}^\lambda \to \{0,1\}^{2(\lambda+1)}$$

$$H_L : \{0,1\}^{\lambda + \lceil \log n \rceil} \to \{0,1\}^{\lambda + \ell}$$

$$H_R : \{0,1\}^{\lambda + \lceil \log n \rceil} \to \{0,1\}^\lambda$$

$$H_e : \{0,1\}^\lambda \to \{0,1\}^{\lambda + \ell}$$

We construct the secret sharing scheme for 1-bit secrets $m \in \{0,1\}$ from the theorem statement as follows.

SHARE(m;s):

1. Pick a seed $s \leftarrow \{0,1\}^\lambda$ uniformly at random.
2. Compute $s_1 \| s_2 = H_s(s)$.
3. Define linear function g over $\mathbb{Z}_{2^{(\lambda+1)}}$ through $g(1) = s_1$ and $g(2) = s_2$
4. Extrapolate $s_i = g(i)$ for $i = 0, \ldots, n$.
5. Compute $c = (s\|m) \oplus s_0$.
6. Compute $L_i = H_L(s\|i)$ and $R_i = H_R(s\|i)$ for $i = 1, \ldots, n$.
7. Compute $R_i' = H_e(R_i)$ for $i = 1, \ldots, n$.
8. Compute $e_{i,j} = s_i \oplus \langle L_i, R_j' \rangle$ for $i, j = 1, \ldots, n$ with $i \neq j$.
9. P_i's share sh_i is defined as $(L_i, R_i, \{e_{i,j}\}_{j=1,\ldots,n}, c)$.

Reconstruction works as follows.

REC($\mathsf{sh}_i, \mathsf{sh}_j$):

1. Compute $s_i = e_{i,j} \oplus \langle L_i, H_e(R_j) \rangle$ and $s_j = e_{j,i} \oplus \langle L_j, H_e(R_i) \rangle$.
2. Interpolate g from s_i and s_j and compute $s_0 = g(0)$.
3. Compute $(s\|m) = c \oplus s_0$ and return m.

It is easy to see that the proposed scheme is correct.

Note that besides learning m in reconstruction we also learn the seed s. From s we can recompute SHARE($m; s$). The full reconstruction threshold $\hat{t}$ is 2, since given access to the random oracles, m, and s, any two parties can compute all $L_i, R_i, e_{i,j}$, and thus all shares sh_i.

Since each party P_i holds exactly one L_i, one R_i, and $n-1$ bits $e_{i,j}$, it follows that the share size p is $(\ell + \lambda) + \lambda + (n-1) = \mathcal{O}(\ell + \lambda + n)$.

It is straight forward to see that SHARE is a secret sharing scheme with threshold 2. Assume we are given one share $(L_i, R_i, \{e_{i,j}\}_{j=1,\ldots,n}, c)$. We have to argue that the share leaks no information on m. There are two cases, the query case and the no-query case. In the query case, at some point a query of one of the following forms were made $H_R(s\|\cdot)$, $H_L(s\|\cdot)$, or $H_s(a)$. The non-query case is the complement.

If we are in the no-query case, then because we are in the random oracle model we can replace the secret sharing procedure with this one:

SHARE^2(m):

1. Pick a seed $s \leftarrow \{0,1\}^\lambda$ uniformly at random.
2. Sample uniformly random $s_1, s_2 \in \{0,1\}^{2(\lambda+1)}$.
3. Define linear function g over $\mathbb{Z}_{2^{(\lambda+1)}}$ through $g(1) = s_1$ and $g(2) = s_2$
4. Extrapolate $s_i = g(i)$ for $i = 0, \ldots, n$.
5. Compute $c = (s\|m) \oplus s_0$.
6. Sample uniformly random $L_i \in \{0,1\}^{\lambda+\ell}$ and $R_i \in \{0,1\}^\lambda$ for $i = 1, \ldots, n$.
7. Compute $R'_i = H_e(R_i)$ for $i = 1, \ldots, n$.
8. Compute $e_{i,j} = s_i \oplus \langle L_i, R'_j \rangle$ for $i,j = 1, \ldots, n$ with $i \neq j$.
9. P_i's share sh_i is defined as $(L_i, R_i, \{e_{i,j}\}_{j=1,\ldots,n}, c)$.

It is straight forward to see that for all $j \neq i$ we can replace $H_e(R_j)$ by a uniformly random string, as there is not enough information in sh_i to learn R_j and query H_e on this point. Namely, even if the adversary is given s_i, the values $\langle L_i, R'_j \rangle$ leaks at most one bit on R_j. This gives this hybrid:

SHARE^3(m):

1. Pick a seed $s \leftarrow \{0,1\}^\lambda$ uniformly at random.
2. Sample uniformly random $s_1, s_2 \in \{0,1\}^{2(\lambda+1)}$.
3. Define linear function g over $\mathbb{Z}_{2^{(\lambda+1)}}$ through $g(1) = s_1$ and $g(2) = s_2$
4. Extrapolate $s_i = g(i)$ for $i = 0, \ldots, n$.
5. Compute $c = (s\|m) \oplus s_0$.
6. Sample uniformly random $L_i \in \{0,1\}^{\lambda+\ell}$ and $R_i \in \{0,1\}^\lambda$ for i and let $R'_i = H_e(R_i)$.
7. Sample uniformly random $L_j \in \{0,1\}^{\lambda+\ell}$ and $R'_j \in \{0,1\}^{\lambda+\ell}$ for $j \neq i$.
8. Compute $e_{i,j} = s_i \oplus \langle L_i, R'_j \rangle$ for $i,j = 1, \ldots, n$ with $i \neq j$.
9. P_i's share sh_i is defined as $(L_i, R_i, \{e_{i,j}\}_{j=1,\ldots,n}, c)$.

Now given sh_i without $\{e_{i,j}\}_{j=1,\ldots,n}$ all the values $\langle L_i, R'_j \rangle$ are statistically close to uniformly random and independent. Hence we can jump to this hybrid:

SHARE^4(m):

1. Pick a seed $s \leftarrow \{0,1\}^\lambda$ uniformly at random.
2. Sample uniformly random $s_1, s_2 \in \{0,1\}^{2(\lambda+1)}$.
3. Define linear function g over $\mathbb{Z}_{2^{(\lambda+1)}}$ through $g(1) = s_1$ and $g(2) = s_2$
4. Extrapolate $s_i = g(i)$ for $i = 0, \ldots, n$.
5. Compute $c = (s\|m) \oplus s_0$.
6. Sample uniformly random $L_i \in \{0,1\}^{\lambda+\ell}$ and $R_i \in \{0,1\}^\lambda$ for i and let $R'_i = H_e(R_i)$.

7. Sample uniformly random $L_j \in \{0,1\}^{\lambda+\ell}$ and $R'_j \in \{0,1\}^{\lambda+\ell}$ for $j \neq i$.
8. Sample uniformly random bits $e_{i,j}$ for $i,j = 1,\ldots,n$ with $i \neq j$.
9. P_i's share sh_i is defined as $(L_i, R_i, \{e_{i,j}\}_{j=1,\ldots,n}, c)$

Now sh_i has no information on s_1 and s_2 and hence s_0 is uniformly random given sh_i. Therefore we can replace $c = (s\|m) \oplus s_0$ by a uniformly random value. At this point sh_i contains no information on m or s.

This sequence of indistinguishable hybrids shows that when we are in the no-query case, then sh_i is statistically close to independent from s and m, as desired. Note in particular that during an execution it holds until the point in time where we go into the query-case (because an oracle was queried on s for the first time) that sh_i is statistically close to independent of s. This means that to query an oracle on s the adversary has to guess close to λ bits of min-entropy on s. This happens with probability at most $2^{-\lambda}$. Therefore the query case happens with negligible probability. This concludes the proofs that SHARE is a secret sharing scheme with $t = 2$.

We then argue that the secret sharing scheme is leakage resilient against ℓ bits of leakage from each share. Here it is important that we are on the non-adaptive leakage case, where all leakage functions are picked before any leakage is seen. This ensures that when $\text{LEAK}_i((L_i, R_i, \{e_{i,j}\}_{j=1,\ldots,n}, c)$ is computed the leakage function has no information on s by the argument above that we are dealing with a secret sharing scheme with threshold $t = 2$. Hence by the sequence of hybrids above we see that R'_j is uniformly random in the view of LEAK_i as it did not query $H_e(R_j)$ except with negligible probability in polynomial time. Now notice that $\text{LEAK}_i((L_i, R_i, \{e_{i,j}\}_{j=1,\ldots,n}, c)$ will leave λ bits of min-entropy in R_i, as R_i has length $\ell + \lambda$ and the leakage is at most ℓ bits.

In guessing the values $\langle L_i, H_e(R_j) \rangle$ the adversary is therefore playing the following game.

GAME[1]: Pick $L_i \in \{0,1\}^{\ell+\lambda}$ uniformly at random. Ask for ℓ bits of leakage on L_i. Then be given R_j and try to guess $\langle L_i, H_e(R_j) \rangle$.

An adversary winning this game, can be modified to win the following game by programming that random oracle at R_j.

GAME[2]: Pick $L_i \in \{0,1\}^{\ell+\lambda}$ uniformly at random. Ask for ℓ bits of leakage on L_i. Then be given uniformly random $R'_j \in \{0,1\}^{\ell+\lambda}$ and try to guess $\langle L_i, R'_j \rangle$.

By the hard-core bit theorem, an adversary winning this game with non-negligible probability can guess L_i with non-negligible probability, a contradiction.

At this point the argument follows the one for secret sharing. We can first replace $\{e_{i,j}\}_{j=1,\ldots,n}$ by uniformly random values and then replace c by a uniformly random value. At this point there is no more information on m in the secret sharing.

Acknowledgements. We would like to thank Maciej Obremski for helpful discussions during the initial stages of this project.

References

[ADN+18] Aggarwal, D., et al.: Stronger leakage-resilient and non-malleable secret-sharing schemes for general access structures. Cryptology ePrint Archive, Report 2018/1147 (2018). https://eprint.iacr.org/2018/1147

[BDIR18] Benhamouda, F., Degwekar, A., Ishai, Y., Rabin, T.: On the local leakage resilience of linear secret sharing schemes. In: Shacham, H., Boldyreva, A. (eds.) CRYPTO 2018. LNCS, vol. 10991, pp. 531–561. Springer, Cham (2018). https://doi.org/10.1007/978-3-319-96884-1_18

[Bei11] Beimel, A.: Secret-sharing schemes: a survey. In: Chee, Y.M., et al. (eds.) IWCC 2011. LNCS, vol. 6639, pp. 11–46. Springer, Heidelberg (2011). https://doi.org/10.1007/978-3-642-20901-7_2

[BGK14] Boyle, E., Goldwasser, S., Kalai, Y.T.: Leakage-resilient coin tossing. Distrib. Comput. **27**(3), 147–164 (2014)

[BGK16] Bogdanov, A., Guo, S., Komargodski, I.: Threshold secret sharing requires a linear size alphabet. In: Hirt, M., Smith, A. (eds.) TCC 2016. LNCS, vol. 9986, pp. 471–484. Springer, Heidelberg (2016). https://doi.org/10.1007/978-3-662-53644-5_18

[BGW88] Ben-Or, M., Goldwasser, S., Wigderson, A.: Completeness theorems for non-cryptographic fault-tolerant distributed computation (extended abstract). In: 20th Annual ACM Symposium on Theory of Computing, pp. 1–10. ACM Press, May 1988

[Bla79] Blakley, G.R.: Safeguarding cryptographic keys, pp. 313–317. AFIPS Press (1979)

[BS18] Badrinarayanan, S., Srinivasan, A.: Revisiting non-malleable secret sharing. Cryptology ePrint Archive, Report 2018/1144 (2018). https://eprint.iacr.org/2018/1144

[CCD88] Chaum, D., Crépeau, C., Damgård, I.: Multiparty unconditionally secure protocols (extended abstract). In: 20th Annual ACM Symposium on Theory of Computing, pp. 11–19. ACM Press, May 1988

[CGMA85] Chor, B., Goldwasser, S., Micali, S., Awerbuch, B.: Verifiable secret sharing and achieving simultaneity in the presence of faults (extended abstract). In: 26th Annual Symposium on Foundations of Computer Science, pp. 383–395. IEEE Computer Society Press, October 1985

[Des88] Desmedt, Y.: Society and group oriented cryptography: a new concept. In: Pomerance, C. (ed.) CRYPTO 1987. LNCS, vol. 293, pp. 120–127. Springer, Heidelberg (1988). https://doi.org/10.1007/3-540-48184-2_8

[DF90] Desmedt, Y., Frankel, Y.: Threshold cryptosystems. In: Brassard, G. (ed.) CRYPTO 1989. LNCS, vol. 435, pp. 307–315. Springer, New York (1990). https://doi.org/10.1007/0-387-34805-0_28

[DP07] Dziembowski, S., Pietrzak, K.: Intrusion-resilient secret sharing. In: 48th Annual Symposium on Foundations of Computer Science, pp. 227–237. IEEE Computer Society Press, October 2007

[GK18a] Goyal, V., Kumar, A.: Non-malleable secret sharing. In: Diakonikolas, I., Kempe, D., Henzinger, M. (eds.) 50th Annual ACM Symposium on Theory of Computing, pp. 685–698. ACM Press, June 2018

[GK18b] Goyal, V., Kumar, A.: Non-malleable secret sharing for general access structures. In: Shacham, H., Boldyreva, A. (eds.) CRYPTO 2018. LNCS, vol. 10991, pp. 501–530. Springer, Cham (2018). https://doi.org/10.1007/978-3-319-96884-1_17

[GPSW06] Goyal, V., Pandey, O., Sahai, A., Waters, B.: Attribute-based encryption for fine-grained access control of encrypted data. In: Juels, A., Wright, R.N., De Capitani di Vimercati, S. (eds.) ACM CCS 2006: 13th Conference on Computer and Communications Security, pp. 89–98. ACM Press, October/November 2006. Available as Cryptology ePrint Archive Report 2006/309

[GW16] Guruswami, V., Wootters, M.: Repairing reed-solomon codes. In: Wichs, D., Mansour, Y. (eds.) 48th Annual ACM Symposium on Theory of Computing, pp. 216–226. ACM Press, June 2016

[HDWH12] Heninger, N., Durumeric, Z., Wustrow, E., Alex Halderman, J.: Mining your PS and QS: detection of widespread weak keys in network devices. In: Proceedings of the 21st USENIX Security Symposium, Bellevue, WA, USA, 8–10 August 2012, pp. 205–220 (2012)

[KMS18] Kumar, A., Meka, R., Sahai, A.: Leakage-resilient secret sharing. Cryptology ePrint Archive, Report 2018/1138 (2018). https://eprint.iacr.org/2018/1138

[RB89] Rabin, T., Ben-Or, M.: Verifiable secret sharing and multiparty protocols with honest majority (extended abstract). In: 21st Annual ACM Symposium on Theory of Computing, pp. 73–85. ACM Press, May 1989

[Sha79] Shamir, A.: How to share a secret. Commun. ACM 22(11), 612–613 (1979)

[Sho00] Shoup, V.: Practical threshold signatures. In: Preneel, B. (ed.) EUROCRYPT 2000. LNCS, vol. 1807, pp. 207–220. Springer, Heidelberg (2000). https://doi.org/10.1007/3-540-45539-6_15

[SV18] Srinivasan, A., Vasudevan, P.V.: Leakage resilient secret sharing and applications. Cryptology ePrint Archive, Report 2018/1154 (2018). https://eprint.iacr.org/2018/1154

[Wat11] Waters, B.: Ciphertext-policy attribute-based encryption: an expressive, efficient, and provably secure realization. In: Catalano, D., Fazio, N., Gennaro, R., Nicolosi, A. (eds.) PKC 2011. LNCS, vol. 6571, pp. 53–70. Springer, Heidelberg (2011). https://doi.org/10.1007/978-3-642-19379-8_4

Fault-Attack Security

FRIET: An Authenticated Encryption Scheme with Built-in Fault Detection

Thierry Simon[1,4(✉)], Lejla Batina[1], Joan Daemen[1(✉)], Vincent Grosso[1,2],
Pedro Maat Costa Massolino[1], Kostas Papagiannopoulos[1,5],
Francesco Regazzoni[3], and Niels Samwel[1]

[1] Digital Security Group, Radboud University, Nijmegen, The Netherlands
{lejla,joan,P.Massolino,k.papagiannopoulos,n.samwel}@cs.ru.nl
[2] CNRS/Univ. Lyon, Laboratoire Hubert Curien, UMR 5516, Saint-Etienne, France
vincent.grosso@univ-st-etienne.fr
[3] ALaRI, University of Lugano, Lugano, Switzerland
regazzoni@alari.ch
[4] STMicroelectronics Diegem, Diegem, Belgium
thierry.simon.13@gmail.com
[5] NXP Semiconductors Hamburg, Hamburg, Germany

Abstract. In this work we present a duplex-based authenticated encryption scheme FRIET based on a new permutation called FRIET-P. We designed FRIET-P with a novel approach for cryptographic permutations and block ciphers that takes fault-attack resistance into account and that we introduce in this paper.

In this method, we build a permutation f_C to be *embedded* in a larger one, f. First, we define f as a sequence of steps that all *abide* a chosen error-correcting code C, i.e., that map C-codewords to C-codewords. Then, we embed f_C in f by first encoding its input to an element of C, applying f and then decoding back from C. This last step detects a fault when the output of f is not in C.

We motivate the design of the permutation we use in FRIET and report on performance in soft- and hardware. We evaluate the fault-detection capabilities of the software and simulated hardware implementations with attacks. Finally, we perform a leakage evaluation. Our code is available at https://github.com/thisimon/Friet.git.

Keywords: Design of cryptographic primitives · Fault injection countermeasures · Side channel attack · Lightweight implementations

1 Introduction

Our daily routine relies on bank and transportation cards, car keys, phones and other mobile and embedded devices. Many of these should consume little energy and their continuous shrinking puts firm constraints on area and memory size.

These devices may be exposed to *side channel attacks* that exploits physical leakage such as response time, power consumption or electromagnetic radiation

© International Association for Cryptologic Research 2020
A. Canteaut and Y. Ishai (Eds.): EUROCRYPT 2020, LNCS 12105, pp. 581–611, 2020.
https://doi.org/10.1007/978-3-030-45721-1_21

to extract cryptographic keys or other secrets. Another vulnerability are fault injection attacks, where an attacker provokes faults in the cryptographic computation and uses the (faulty) outputs to recover the key. Side channel and fault injection attacks have led to an active research field where the main challenge is to come up with affordable and effective countermeasures.

The need for lightweight cryptography resistant to side channel and fault injection attacks has been partially addressed by the cryptographic community with many designs for (tweakable) block ciphers with small block sizes. The concept of building efficient (authenticated) encryption schemes from a cryptographic permutation such as proposed by the Bertoni et al. [7] has led to the emergence of several lightweight solutions. Despite their larger width, the overhead for permutation-based modes is smaller than that of block cipher-based modes and the total solution often takes significantly less resources than a block cipher-based solution.

At the primitive level, side channel attack countermeasures have been taken into account by adopting a round function of algebraic degree 2, ideal for masking. This includes the Keccak-f permutation, Ascon [18], Gimli [4] and Xoodoo [13].

1.1 Related Work

Here we mention some related previous works that are proposing certain modifications to crypto algorithms to defend against side channel and fault attacks. Intra-Instruction Redundancy [24] and Internal Redundancy Countermeasure [23] are generic countermeasures that can be applied to any cipher and they imply interleaving k copies of the plaintext with some fixed data. While the method can detect up to k faults, it is also quite expensive.

Some other approaches aim at combining resistance against both fault and side channel attacks. Schneider et al. [29] introduce a countermeasure for cryptographic hardware implementations that combines the concept of threshold implementation with an error detecting approach. Similarly to this, Reparaz et al. [27] propose a countermeasure that claims security against higher-order SCA, multiple-shot DFA and also combined attacks.

Craft [3] is a cipher designed to be used in conjunction with various linear codes which aims at implementations resistant against fault attacks. Craft differs from the approaches mentioned above because the technique is not applied to existing ciphers as an add-on, but takes into account fault attack resistance in the design phase.

Our approach goes one step further as we design a permutation for a specific linear code. This allows us to build the permutation from the most efficient step functions for that code, resulting in a very lightweight round function.

1.2 Our Contributions

The main contributions of this paper are our novel design method for ciphers with efficient fault-detecting implementations and the concrete authenticated encryption scheme FRIET implemented with a new permutation FRIET-P designed with our method. Moreover, we provide a design rationale for the permutation, performance evaluations in software and hardware including comparison with other relevant permutations, results of fault detection experiments and an evaluation of the impact of our method on leakage.

1.3 Organization of This Paper

The remainder of paper is organized as follows. In Sect. 2 we explain our method. The new authenticated encryption scheme FRIET is presented in Sect. 3 where we also discuss its properties and provide a security claim. The scheme is based on a permutation called FRIET-P and its embedding FRIET-PC that we present in Sect. 4. We provide rationale for the design choices in FRIET-PC in Sect. 5. Section 6 reports on our implementation results. In Sects. 7 and 8 we present fault resistance and leakage evaluation results respectively. Section 9 concludes the paper and gives directions for future work.

2 Code-Abiding Permutations

2.1 Permutations Abiding Some Error-Detecting Code

A (block) code C with *block length* n and *message length* k, with $k < n$, represents k-symbol messages with n-symbol codewords. The symbols belong to an alphabet whose size is denoted by α. The α^k codewords form a subset of the set of all α^n n-symbol vectors. With some abuse of notation, we denote the set of codewords by C. The Hamming distance between two codewords is the number of positions at which the corresponding symbols are different. The *distance d* of a code is the minimum of the Hamming distance over all pairs of its codewords. Often codes are characterized by their dimension parameters in the following notation: $[n, k, d]_\alpha$.

We can now define a code-abiding permutation.

Definition 1. *A permutation f on the set of n-symbol vectors is* code-abiding *for code C if $f(C) = C$.*

2.2 Protecting Against Faults by Permutation Embedding

As each codeword represents a message word, f induces a permutation over the space of all k-symbol vectors. We denote this permutation by f_C. We can express f_C as the composition of three steps: $f_C = \mathrm{dec}_C \circ f \circ \mathrm{enc}_C$ with enc_C encoding the k-symbol input as a n-symbol codeword in C and dec_C decoding the resulting n-symbol to a k-symbol output. We call f_C the *embedding* of f by C.

In general, the decoding dec_C of the output of f to a k-symbol message word can fail: it only succeeds if the output of f is in C. It follows that if there is a fault in the computation of f, it is likely that decoding fails. As a matter of fact, the probability that a random fault is undetected is α^{k-n}. Concretely, if f is y bits wider than f_C, this probability is 2^{-y}.

Hence, we can build a fault-resistant k-symbol permutation f_C by choosing a code C, designing a permutation f that abides C and embedding f_C in f by C. We call this design approach *code embedding*. Note that the datapath and key (or tweakey) schedule of block ciphers are also permutations and can therefore be designed with the code embedding approach.

2.3   Step Functions Abiding a Linear Code

The question is now: how do we choose a suitable code C and how do we define a permutation f that abides that code? The latter problem is the easier to break down: we define it as the iteration of a round function that abides C. That round function can in turn be defined as a sequence of steps that abide C.

We target permutations that can be efficiently implemented in hardware and in software using bitwise Boolean instructions and (cyclic) shifts. With this in mind, we target codes that are linear over $GF(2)$. In a linear $[n, k, d]_2$-code, a codeword satisfies $n - k$ linear binary equations, the so-called *parity* equations. Encoding simply consists in taking the k-bit message and appending $n - k$ bits so that the result satisfies the parity equations. We call the appended bits the *parity* bits. Decoding consists in verifying whether the n-bit vector satisfies the parity equations and if so, truncating to the first k bits. If the parity equations are not satisfied, decoding will return an error message.

We consider permutations having a state of b bits. To allow some flexibility in our choice of step functions, we apply a small code in parallel to parts of the state. We call those parts *slices*. Each slice is n bits wide and has $n - k$ bits of redundancy, i.e., its bits satisfy the $n - k$ parity equations. We denote the first k bits of a slice as its *native* part and its last $n - k$ bits as the parity part. We index the slices by j from 0 to $b/n - 1$ and denote their number b/n by ℓ, typically a power of two. Orthogonal to the slices, we partition the *state* in n equally sized *limbs*. A limb is an array of ℓ bits that are indexed by j from 0 to $\ell - 1$. In short, we arrange the b bits of the state in a two-dimensional array consisting of n limbs by ℓ slices. As a consequence, we call the first k limbs the native ones and the last $n - k$ limbs the parity ones.

We propose two types of step functions for the round function:

limb adaptation. This modifies a native limb, say with index j, by bitwise adding to it a function ϕ of the state. It also adds the function ϕ to each parity limb that depends on native limb j. This is code-abiding as each parity equation remains satisfied. This operation is not inherently invertible and care must be taken in the function ϕ and the part of the state it operates on. For fault detection it is important to freshly compute ϕ for every adapted limb. Indeed, if ϕ would be computed once for all adapted limbs, one fault in its computation could lead to an incorrect output that decodes successfully.

limb transposition. This is a re-ordering of the limbs, with a possible *correcting adaptation* to leave the parity equations invariant. We distinguish between *native* and *non-native* limb transpositions. In the former case, two native limbs swap and in the latter a native limb swaps places with a parity limb.

In many implementations, swapping two limbs as such has no cost: in software it can be dealt with at indexing level, in a combinatorial circuit in dedicated hardware, it is merely re-wiring. The correcting adaptation depends on the code C and the indices of the limbs being swapped. Typically, this cost is lower than the cost of a limb adaptation. For the simple code used in our permutation FRIET-P there is no correcting adaptation and in Appendix A, we give an example of a limb transposition that costs an additional bitwise limb addition.

A round function of a modern cipher consists of four types of operations. Each of these can be implemented with our two types of step functions:

- non-linearity, as in AES SubBytes [15], with limb adaptation with a non-linear function ϕ,
- mixing, as in AES MixColumns, with limb adaptation with a linear function ϕ and a non-native limb transposition,
- shuffling, as in ShiftRows, with native limb transposition,
- round constant (or key) addition, as in AES AddRoundKey, with limb adaptation where ϕ consists of a mere round constant or key.

2.4 Fault Detection Capacity of Code-Abiding Permutations

The protection offered by code embedding is that faults in the computation of the permutation are likely to lead to a decoding error. A decoding error implies that a fault occurred, but the converse is not necessarily true. If faults lead to an incorrect output that decodes successfully, we speak of *undetected faults*.

In order to analyze more precisely the fault detection capacity of code-abiding permutations, we use a single-limb fault model. A *single-limb fault*, also simply called *single fault*, is a fault that modifies the value of only one limb. If implemented correctly, a single fault in the computation of a code-abiding permutation is guaranteed to give a decoding error. To establish this, we analyze what happens when single faults are injected in a limb adaptation and transposition.

A limb transposition either involves no computation at all or a correcting adaptation. In the latter case a single fault would only modify the value of one parity limb, while leaving the native limbs unchanged. The corresponding parity equation would then be not satisfied and decoding would fail.

In a limb adaptation, fresh computations of ϕ are added to a native limb and one or more parity limbs. If the input of the limb adaptation is correct, it can only lead to an incorrect output that decodes successfully if at least d limbs are computed incorrectly, i.e. in the presence of d single faults, with d the distance of the code. At first sight, this is an argument for taking C with high distance d. However, this comes at a computational cost: limb adaptation adapts a single native limb at a cost that is a d-fold of that.

So far, we have only treated the case of a single step starting from a correct state. However, faults may be injected in different steps. As a fault in a single limb may, and typically will, propagate to other limbs, in principle a fault may be compensated by another fault some steps later and result in an erroneous state that decodes successfully. To prevent this, one may do intermediate checks of the parity equations in between the steps. However, the fault will typically propagate in a hard to predict way and compensating a fault becomes harder and harder as computation continues. This makes it an uninteresting attack path and we believe that intermediate parity checks are not worth their cost. Therefore, we think that a single parity check at the end of the permutation gives the best tradeoff between performances and fault detection.

Besides single faults, there are other types of faults that are not covered by the code embedding and must be countered with other means. For example, skipping a full step, round or number of rounds, will not lead to unsuccessful decoding. Another example are faults in the decoding operation itself, e.g., just faulting the reporting of the outcome from *false* to *true*. Clearly, implementations must have some redundancy in the control flow logic for the handling of the steps and the decoding operation. For an implementation to offer resistance against fault attacks, it must additionally have mechanisms to detect such faults.

A recently introduced type of fault attack, coined *statistical ineffective fault attacks* (SIFA) [17], can retrieve secrets even in the presence of fault checks. Here, one inject faults in repeated computations and the only information the attacker needs is the knowledge whether a fault occurred or not. Clearly, in the presence of a fault detection countermeasure such as code embedding, this information is available to the attacker. Using SIFA one can determine (secret) bits of the state if the probability that a fault occurs depends on their value. The simplest example is a fault in the computation of a multiplication in $GF(2)$, say $c = a \cdot b$ with a, b and c bits. Let us assume the adversary can inject faults in a. These faults will propagate to c if and only if $b = 1$. Such an attack would require knowledge of implementation details and on top of that the accurate injection of single-bit fault in a. However, using statistical techniques one can relax the latter requirement at the cost of more fault attempts. In Sect. 5.6 we present an architecture for a specific permutation that results in resistance against SIFA.

2.5   Our Approach: The Parity Check Code

Due to the fact that the computation cost of limb adaptation grows linearly with the distance of the code, we choose for the simple parity check code $[n, n-1, 2]_2$. This code has a single parity limb that is the sum of all $n - 1$ native limbs.

Adopting such a code simplifies limb adaptation and transpositions as follows:

- Limb adaptation modifies a limb and the parity limb. Its computation cost is twice as large as if it was computed on the native state alone.
- None of the $n!$ possible limb transpositions requires a correcting adaptation, as all limbs are in the (single) parity equation. Paradoxically, as a non-native limb transposition on the parity check code has no computation cost, it is cheaper to compute it than do the equivalent embedded mapping that requires $n - 2$ bitwise limb additions.

The primary goal of our approach is the guaranteed detection of any single-limb fault in the computation. The secondary goal is that it should be hard to enforce two or more compensating faults in the computation or in the registers. The easiest attack on limb adaptation would be to inject two compensating faults in the two ϕ computations. In this respect it is a good idea in software implementations to use different computation sequences and/or different registers so that the attacker has to induce two different faults for them to be compensating. For the same reason, in dedicated hardware implementations one shall not use the same combinatorial circuit for both ϕ. Instead of attacking the computation, an attacker could attack the registers and inject compensating faults on two limbs. To be successful, such attacks would require knowledge of the implementation details and the ability to inject faults very precisely.

The parity check code offers fault detection capabilities that are close to duplication. It detects any single-limb fault instead of any single fault, but not multiple faults. On the other hand, it can be implemented much more efficiently thanks to the cheap limb transpositions and uses less memory, since the state size increases only by $1/(n-1)$ instead of 2.

3 The Authenticated Encryption Scheme FRIET

We showcase the practicality of code embedding with a lightweight authenticated encryption (AE) scheme, called FRIET. It is permutation-based and uses SpongeWrap [7], a mode on top of the duplex [7] construction, similar to CAESAR candidate Ketje [8] NIST lightweight competition submissions Ascon [18], Gimli [4] and Xoodyak [11].

The permutation underlying our AE scheme is called FRIET-PC and it is the result of embedding a code on a permutation FRIET-P. We do not see FRIET (and FRIET-P) as the ultimate fault-attack resistant design but rather as a proof of concept, quite competitive with modern AE schemes (and permutations).

In this section we specify the mode and provide its security claim.

3.1 The Permutation AE Mode SpongeWrap

We adopt the AE mode proposed in the paper that introduced the duplex construction and its modes [7], namely SpongeWrap. SpongeWrap has the nice property that it supports AE in *sessions*. A session AE scheme converts sequences of messages, each consisting of (optional) associated data AD and plaintext P, both bit strings of arbitrary length, into a sequences of cryptograms, each consisting of possible associated data, ciphertext C (the enciphered plaintext) and a tag T. The session aspect is related to the tag T: this is not only computed on the associated data and ciphertext of its own cryptogram, but the full sequence of cryptograms that were generated since the start of the session. In other words, a session AE scheme is *stateful*. One can see session AE as support for intermediate tags.

Algorithm 1. SpongeWrap[f, ρ, τ], with permutation f, block length ρ and tag length τ.

Interface: $T \leftarrow$ start(K, D)
    $s \leftarrow 0^*$ (State s is a persistent data element during the session)
    absorb(K, none)
    absorb$(D, \text{encrypt})$
    $T \leftarrow$ squeeze(τ)
    return T

Interface: $(C, T) \leftarrow$ wrap(AD, P)
    absorb(AD, none)
    $C \leftarrow$ absorb$(P, \text{encrypt})$
    $T \leftarrow$ squeeze(τ)
    return (C, T)

Interface: $P \leftarrow$ unwrap(AD, C, T)
    absorb(AD, none)
    $P \leftarrow$ absorb$(C, \text{decrypt})$
    $T' \leftarrow$ squeeze(τ)
    if $(T' \neq T)$ **then return** error
    return P

Internal interface: $Y \leftarrow$ absorb(X, op) with op $\in \{\text{none}, \text{encrypt}, \text{decrypt}\}$
    Let $x[n]$ be X split in ρ-bit blocks, with $n > 0$ and last block possibly shorter
    $Y \leftarrow \epsilon$
    for all blocks of $x[n]$ **do**
        if (op $=$ none) **then** $b \leftarrow 0$ **else** $b \leftarrow 1$
        if (this is the last block) **then** $b \leftarrow b + 1$
        if op $=$ decrypt **then**
            temp $\leftarrow x[i] + (s$ truncated to $|x[i]|)$
            $Y \leftarrow Y \| \text{temp}$
            duplex$(\text{temp} \| b)$
        else if op $=$ encrypt **then**
            temp $\leftarrow x[i] + (s$ truncated to $|x[i]|)$
            $Y \leftarrow Y \| \text{temp}$
            duplex$(x[i] \| b)$
        else
            duplex$(x[i] \| b)$
    return Y

Internal interface: $Z \leftarrow$ squeeze(ℓ) with ℓ the requested length of the output Z
    $Z \leftarrow \epsilon$
    while $|Z| < \ell$ **do**
        $Z \leftarrow Z \| (s$ truncated to ρ bits)
        duplex(0)
    return Z truncated to ℓ bits

Internal interface: duplex(σ) with $|\sigma| \leq \rho$
    $s \leftarrow s + \sigma \| 1 \| 0^*$
    $s \leftarrow f(s)$

We do not take SpongeWrap [7] as such, but make three minor modifications. First, in the session startup we absorb a dedicated non-secret diversifier D that should be a nonce for sessions started with the same key K. Second, we have the session startup return a tag. Third, we allow for tag lengths longer than the sponge rate. We specify the SpongeWrap mode, with the duplex construction integrated, in Algorithm 1. Here, all parameters are arbitrary-length bit strings with $|X|$ denoting the length of a string X in bits.

SpongeWrap has a b-bit state, with b the width of the underlying permutation f. It has a *block length* ρ and all input strings are first split up into ρ-bit blocks, with the last block possibly shorter. Before a block is absorbed in the state, SpongeWrap appends a domain separation bit to indicate whether the next output will be used as keystream (1) or as tag or not at all (0). Then the block is padded with a single 1 followed by zeroes. The so-called *duplex rate r* is the size of the part of the state that is directly affected by absorbing, the *outer part*. Due to the domain separation bit and the first bit of the padding, we have $r = \rho + 2$. The remaining part of the state is called the *inner part* and its size is called the *capacity c*. We have $c = b - r = b - \rho - 2$.

The encryption of a message simply consists of splitting AD and P in blocks, padding each block, adding it to the state s and performing the permutation f. Concurrently, each plaintext block is encrypted by bitwise adding to it the outer part of the state at that point. Finally, SpongeWrap squeezes the tag T from the state with a (number of) duplex call(s). Decryption is very similar. After a message has been encrypted or decrypted, one can continue the session with more messages.

The state is initialized by absorbing first the key K and then the diversifier D. For confidentiality the couple (K, D) must be unique per session.

Because it uses the duplex construction, SpongeWrap lends itself quite well to the use of a code-embedded permutation f_C. Actually, we just have to instantiate duplex with the code-abiding permutation f and make some minor modifications:

- The state initialization must set the state to the codeword that encodes the all-0 vector. For linear codes, this is just the all-0 vector.
- When absorbing σ, it must first be converted to a valid codeword. If σ is one limb (as it turn out in Friet-PC), it suffices to (bitwise) add it to one limb and the parity limbs that depend on it.
- Before using the outer part of the state as tag or keystream, one must check whether the state is a valid codeword and return an error if not.

3.2   Exposure of Friet to Cryptanalysis and Side Channel Attacks

During a session, the outer state serves for in- and output and the inner state remains secret. A feature setting duplex apart from block cipher modes is the absence of a fixed key during operation. The state does depend on the key K, but evolves. Doing statistical (side channel) attacks, such as differential and linear cryptanalysis or DPA, require starting many sessions. If diversifier uniqueness is respected, these attacks are limited to absorbing of the diversifier D.

In typical use cases, FRIET would secure communication between devices that may both be accessible to attackers, such as IoT devices. We assume the two devices share a secret key K and can keep track of a session counter that serves as diversifier when a new session needs to be started. Whenever a session is started, one device (master) initiates the session and determines the session counter D and the other device (slave) follows and just must accept the session counter D. Consequently, the slave can be forced in starting a session multiple times with the same diversifier D. The slave can only be sure the session request comes from a valid device when verifying the session startup tag. If this tag is invalid, it can be a part of a denial of service attack, a statistical attack, or just corrupt due to a noisy communication channel. One typically offers protection against such attacks by having the slave keep track of two counters. The first of these two is the session counter and the slave only accepts session startup requests that have a higher session counter than any previously successful session. The second is a *session retry counter*. A successful session startup increments the session counter by 1 and resets the session retry counter to 0. An unsuccessful session startup just increments the session retry counter. If the session retry counter reaches some limit, the slave device refuses to use the key any longer. This limit shall be set to a value small enough to prevent an adversary to collect enough traces to conduct a statistical attack but large enough to still keep the session robust in the presence of noise communication.

Another attack vector on the slave device is a fault attack. In such an attack, an adversary forces a slave to start multiple sessions with the same diversifier D and injects faults in at least one of it. She can then mount a differential fault attacks to extract information about the secret inner state from a single faultless output and faulted ones. This is where our fault detection capability comes in. As soon as the slave device detects a fault, it will immediately abort the computation and with that the session.

3.3 Dimension Parameters and Security Claim for FRIET

The permutation in FRIET is called FRIET-PC and it has a width b of 384 bits, similar to the permutations Gimli [4] and Xoodoo [13].

A bound for the resistance of the keyed duplex construction against generic attacks was proven in [14] and it is mostly determined by the capacity c, the length of the key $k = |K|$ and the ability of an attacker to manipulate inputs.

Without access restrictions, and assuming $c > r$, the advantage of an attacker to distinguish the output of m keyed duplex instances from random bits, assuming the underlying permutation is randomly chosen, can be simplified to:

$$\frac{mN}{2^k} + \frac{MN}{2^c} , \tag{1}$$

with N the computational complexity and M the data complexity, expressed in the number of executions of FRIET-PC, respectively offline and online.

From this advantage and the tag length τ, the integrity and confidentiality security of SpongeWrap built on top of this duplex object follows immediately:

- Integrity is determined by forgery attacks, where forgery is the successful decryption of a cryptogram by a slave where the cryptogram was not created by the master. For generic attacks, this is upper bounded by (1) plus $q2^{-\tau}$ where q is the number of forgery attempts.
- Confidentiality is broken if keystream, i.e., keyed duplex output, can be predicted or successful decryption of a cryptogram by a slave where the cryptogram was not created by the master can be performed. For generic attacks, this is the same bound as for forgery.

In FRIET we choose a block length $\rho = 128$, implying a rate $r = \rho + 2 = 130$ and a capacity $c = b - r = 254$. We limit the key length to $k \geq 160$ and take as tag length $\tau = 128$. If we would assume that the underlying permutation FRIET-PC would be strong enough so that there are no attacks better than generic ones, we could just take as security claim (1) plus $q2^{-\tau}$. We take some safety margin by using in our claim a smaller value for the parameter c, namely $c = 192$.

Claim. The success probability of forgery or breaking confidentiality of FRIET is upper bounded by:

$$\frac{mN}{2^k} + \frac{MN}{2^{192}} + \frac{q}{2^{128}},$$

with m the number of instances under attack, N the computational complexity, M the data complexity, q the number of decryption attempts and k (≤ 160) the key length. We assume independent and uniformly random k-bit keys.

Clearly, this is a claim for 128-bit security. In our claim we assume that the adversary respects the nonce requirement for the diversifier and does not get access to deciphered ciphertext of cryptograms with an invalid tag.

3.4 Rationale for the Mode and Dimensions

After the publication of SpongeWrap, many variants were published with each specific advantages We opted for a slight SpongeWrap variant with large capacity for the following reasons. First, the bounds obtained in the security proofs assume ideal permutations and there may be better attacks that exploit specific properties of the permutation. The difference between claim capacity 192 and actual FRIET capacity 254 leaves safety margin. Second, in the duplex construction side channel leakage can be modeled as an increase of rate and hence a reduction of capacity. Also here this margin is advantageous.

4 Specification of the Permutations FRIET-PC and FRIET-P

In this section, we specify FRIET-P, the permutation implemented in FRIET. Besides, we specify FRIET-PC, its embedding by the linear code $[4, 3, 2]_2$ with parity bit the sum of the 3 native bits. As the propagation properties of FRIET-PC are most relevant, we introduce FRIET-PC first and FRIET-P second.

4.1   The Permutation FRIET-PC

FRIET-PC has width 384 and has a round function R_i operating on three limbs denoted as a, b and c. We index the bits of a limb by i ranging from 0 to 127. Limb a and the bits of limb b with indices 0 and 1 form the outer part. The nominal number of rounds is 24 and the round function R_i has 6 steps:

- two non-native limb transpositions τ_1 and τ_2,
- a round constant addition δ_i that is a limb adaptation,
- two mixing steps μ_1 and μ_2 that are limb adaptations,
- a non-linear step ξ, also a limb adaptation.

We specify the FRIET-PC permutation in Algorithm 2 using following notation:

- $x \oplus y$, the exclusive *or* (XOR) of limbs x and y,
- $x \wedge y$, the bitwise logical *AND* of limbs x and y,
- $x \lll n$, the cyclic shift to the left by offset n of limb x. We assume the bits with low indices at the right, so if $y \leftarrow x \lll n$, then $y_n = x_0$

The round constants are in Table 1 and the FRIET-PC round function Fig. 1.

Algorithm 2. FRIET-PC

Input: $a, b, c \in \{0, 1\}^{128}$
Output: $(a', b', c') \leftarrow$ FRIET-PC(a, b, c)
for Round index i from 0 to 23 **do**
$\quad (a, b, c) \leftarrow R_i(a, b, c)$
return (a, b, c)

Here R_i is specified by the following sequence of steps:

$$
\begin{aligned}
c \quad &\leftarrow c \oplus \mathrm{rc}_i & \delta_i \\
(a, b, c) &\leftarrow (a \oplus b \oplus c, c, a) & \tau_1 \\
b \quad &\leftarrow b \oplus (c \lll 1) & \mu_1 \\
c \quad &\leftarrow c \oplus (b \lll 80) & \mu_2 \\
(a, b, c) &\leftarrow (a, a \oplus b \oplus c, c) & \tau_2 \\
a \quad &\leftarrow a \oplus ((b \lll 36) \wedge (c \lll 67)) & \xi
\end{aligned}
$$

Table 1. Round constants rc_i in hexadecimal notation, omitting the leading zero digits

i	rc_i	i	rc_i	i	rc_i	i	rc_i	i	rc_i	i	rc_i
0	1111	4	101	8	1001	12	1	16	1110	20	1011
1	11100000	5	10110000	9	100000	13	110000	17	11010000	21	1100000
2	1101	6	110	10	100	14	111	18	1010	22	1100
3	10100000	7	11000000	11	10000000	15	11110000	19	1010000	23	10010000

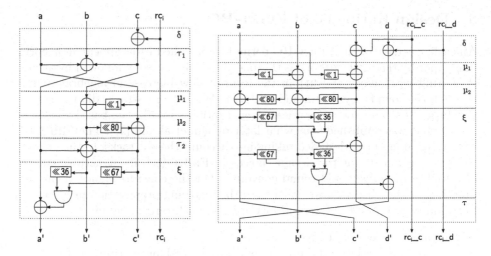

Fig. 1. Round of FRIET-PC   **Fig. 2.** Round of FRIET-P

4.2   The Round Function of Code-Abiding Permutation FRIET-P

We build a code-abiding permutation FRIET-P such that its embedding by the parity code $[4, 3, 2]_2$ is FRIET-PC. FRIET-P has width 512, i.e., 4 limbs.

We denote the parity limb d and after any step the parity equation $d = a \oplus b \oplus c$ should be satisfied. It is now straightforward to derive the round function of FRIET-P from the round specification in Algorithm 2 by substituting $(a \oplus b \oplus c)$ by d in limb transpositions steps and duplicating all limb adaptations in d. This results in:

$$
\begin{array}{lll}
c \leftarrow c \oplus \mathrm{rc}_i & d \leftarrow d \oplus \mathrm{rc}_i & \delta_i \\
(a, b, c, d) \leftarrow (d, c, a, b) & & \tau_1 \\
b \leftarrow b \oplus (c \lll 1) & d \leftarrow d \oplus (c \lll 1) & \mu_1 \\
c \leftarrow c \oplus (b \lll 80) & d \leftarrow d \oplus (b \lll 80) & \mu_2 \\
(a, b, c, d) \leftarrow (a, d, c, b) & & \tau_2 \\
a \leftarrow a \oplus ((b \lll 36) \wedge (c \lll 67)) & d \leftarrow d \oplus ((b \lll 36) \wedge (c \lll 67)) & \xi
\end{array}
$$

We transfer limb transpositions τ_1 and τ_2 to the end and merge them, yielding:

$$
\begin{array}{lll}
c \leftarrow c \oplus \mathrm{rc}_i & d \leftarrow d \oplus \mathrm{rc}_i & \delta_i \\
b \leftarrow b \oplus (a \lll 1) & c \leftarrow c \oplus (a \lll 1) & \mu_1 \\
a \leftarrow a \oplus (c \lll 80) & b \leftarrow b \oplus (c \lll 80) & \mu_2 \\
c \leftarrow c \oplus ((a \lll 67) \wedge (b \lll 36)) & d \leftarrow d \oplus ((a \lll 67) \wedge (b \lll 36)) & \xi \\
(a, b, c, d) \leftarrow (d, b, a, c) & & \tau
\end{array}
$$

This sequence of steps is depicted in Fig. 2 of the FRIET-P round function.

5   Design Rationale of FRIET-PC

An earlier version of the FRIET-PC permutation, called FRIT appeared on eprint in a paper by the same authors as this one [30]. This was soon followed by attacks exploiting weaknesses of FRIT in the form of slow increase of algebraic degree through the rounds, by Dobraunig et al. [19]. While these attacks did not assume the target use case of authenticated encryption in a duplex-based mode, an attack that was published somewhat later by Qin et al. did [25]. The FRIET-PC permutation has been designed taking into account these attacks. In this section, we give a rationale for the design choices in FRIET-PC: its structure, number of rounds, shift offsets and round constants. For the concrete choice of the step functions and their order, we considered the following propagation properties of iteration of the round function in forward and backward direction:

- increase in algebraic degree,
- diffusion properties: full diffusion and (strict) avalanche criterion ((S)AC),
- existence of exploitable invariants.

The non-native limb transpositions τ_1 and τ_2 are attractive, requiring no computation in FRIET-P while still achieving intra-slice mixing. Additionally, τ_1 shuffles the limbs between the rounds. To complement this, a very simple way to obtain mixing between slices consist in bitwise adding (XOR) to a limb the cyclic shift of another, as done by mixing steps μ_1 and μ_2. The simplest invertible non-linear function is the addition to a limb of the bitwise multiplication (AND) of two limbs. To avoid destructive intra-slice interaction with the limb transposition steps, we opted for integrating cyclic shifts in ξ. Finally, round constant addition δ_i breaks the shift-invariance of the round function.

Furthermore, all steps of the round function except τ_1 are involutions. As a consequence, the inverse round function is $\delta_i \circ \tau_1^{-1} \circ \mu_1 \circ \mu_2 \circ \tau_2 \circ \xi$. The similarity with the forward round function simplifies the analysis of the diffusion and algebraic properties of FRIET-PC in the backward direction.

We see FRIET-PC as a permutation dedicated for use in FRIET and hence its propagation analysis shall be seen in that light. Namely, an adversary does not have full access to the input and output of the FRIET-PC permutation in FRIET. She can only apply chosen or known inputs to the outer state and observe the outer part of the state at the output of FRIET-PC. For the input, in most attack scenario's the full input is secret and the adversary can only add (bitwise) a known or chosen value to the outer part of the state. If the implementation permits, the adversary can do this repeatedly for the same state and conduct statistical attacks or apply higher order differential techniques such as cube attacks [16]. In any case, she is limited to inject only $r = 130$ bits to the state or extract only 128 bits from it. Moreover, if the implementation of FRIET imposes that diversifier uniqueness is respected and does not release deciphered ciphertext prior to tag validation, the adversary's access is even much less. In our analysis we have anticipated the worst case.

5.1 Algebraic Degree

Permutations with low algebraic degree are vulnerable to attacks that make use of higher order differentials, such as cube attacks [16]. Therefore, it is important to verify that the algebraic degree of FRIET-PC and its inverse is not too small.

Let $f(r, x, i)$ be the Boolean function defined by the restriction of r rounds of FRIET-PC to output bit x_i, where $x \in \{a, b, c\}$ denotes the limb. This output bit can be expressed as a polynomial over $\mathbb{F}_2$ in the input bits of $f(r, x, i)$, which is the algebraic normal form (ANF) of the boolean function. The algebraic degree of $f(r, x, i)$ is defined as the degree of its ANF. Similarly, we define $f_{inv}(r, x, i)$ for r inverse rounds of FRIET-PC. We will study the algebraic degree of these Boolean functions in terms of the number of rounds r.

Both the round function and its inverse have algebraic degree 2. Hence the functions $f(r, x, i)$ and $f_{inv}(r, x, i)$ can have at most degree 2^r. Since limbs b and c are not modified by the linear operation ξ in the last round of the round-reduced FRIET-PC, $f(r, b, i)$ and $f(r, c, i)$ can be further bounded by 2^{r-1}. Moreover, as the round function is invertible, the maximum degree, irrespective of r, is 383.

These are just upper bounds and the actual algebraic degrees of $f(r, x, i)$ and $f_{inv}(r, x, i)$ can be lower. Indeed, the structure of the round function does not exclude possible cancellations in the terms of high degrees. The occurrence of such cancellations depends on the values of the cyclic offsets. If the resulting algebraic degree after $24 - \epsilon$ rounds is well below 130, then FRIET may be vulnerable to cube attacks. Here ϵ accounts for the 1 or possibly 2 rounds that may be skipped by carefully choosing the cube variables as in [31]. This is what happened in our previous design and was exploited in [19] and [25].

To avoid that, we verified that the theoretical upper bound on the degree for FRIET-PC and its inverse was satisfied up to 4 rounds by finding maximum degree monomials for all bit positions. For 5 rounds, we identified monomials of degree 32 for $f(5, a, 0)$ and $f_{inv}(5, a, 0)$ given respectively by

$b_9 b_{10} b_{12} b_{26} b_{27} b_{29} b_{40} b_{57} b_{59} b_{76} b_{77} b_{89} b_{106} b_{107} b_{110} b_{127} c_{16} c_{26} c_{27} c_{29} c_{43} c_{44} c_{46} c_{57} c_{74} c_{76} c_{93} c_{94} c_{106} c_{123}$
$c_{124} c_{127},$
$b_0 b_{27} b_{28} b_{29} b_{30} b_{45} b_{187} b_{59} b_{77} b_{78} b_{79} b_{106} b_{109} b_{123} b_{124} b_{125} c_{14} c_{28} c_{44} c_{46} c_{47} c_{48} c_{75} c_{78} c_{92} c_{93} c_{94} c_{97} c_{124} c_{125}$
$c_{126} c_{127}.$

We conclude from this analysis that it is extremely unlikely that FRIET is vulnerable to attacks using higher order differentials.

5.2 Diffusion Analysis

A property that is very informative about the vulnerability of a cryptographic primitive against structural distinguishers such as impossible differentials, integral cryptanalysis or truncated differentials is *diffusion*. We say a cryptographic permutation achieves *full diffusion* if every output bit depends on every input bit. Often one takes the rule of thumb that a permutation achieving full diffusion in r rounds is unlikely to have exploitable structural distinguishers covering more than $2r$ rounds. We evaluated FRIET-PC with respect to 3 avalanche-related diffusion metrics introduced in [13] by Daemen *et al.*.

Let $T : \mathbb{F}_2^b \to \mathbb{F}_2^b$ be a cryptographic primitive and Δ be an input difference of Hamming weight 1. Daemen *et al.* define the *avalanche probability vector* $P_{\Delta T}$ as the vector where component i is the probability that bit i of the output of T flips due to input difference Δ. They then propose the three following metrics:

Avalanche dependence. Number of output bits that may flip due to Δ:

$$D_{\mathrm{av}}(T, \Delta) = b - \sum_{i=0}^{b-1} \delta(P_{\Delta T}[i]),$$

with $\delta(x) = 1$ if $x = 0$ and 0 otherwise. Full diffusion means $D_{\mathrm{av}}(T, \Delta) = b$ for all choices of Δ.

Avalanche weight. Expected number of bits that flip due to Δ:

$$\overline{w}_{\mathrm{av}}(T, \Delta) = \sum_{i=0}^{n-1} P_{\Delta T}[i].$$

AC is satisfied if $\overline{w}_{\mathrm{av}}(T, \Delta) \approx b/2$ for all choices of Δ.

Avalanche entropy. The uncertainty about whether output bits flip due to input difference Δ:

$$H_{\mathrm{av}}(T, \Delta) = \sum_{i=0}^{n-1} (-P_{\Delta T}[i] \log_2(P_{\Delta T}[i]) - (1 - P_{\Delta T}[i]) \log_2(1 - P_{\Delta T}[i])).$$

SAC is satisfied if $H_{\mathrm{av}}(T, \Delta) \approx b$ for all choices of Δ.

Table 2 reports on the diffusion performance of round-reduced FRIET-PC and its inverse. We generated the avalanche probability vectors for these results from 250 000 random samples. We evaluated each metric on all 384 input differences Δ of Hamming weight 1 and, as is done for XOODOO in [13], we report on the worst-case values. From the table, one can observe that 8 rounds are needed for FRIET-PC and its inverse to exhibit the same behaviour as a random 384-bit permutation with respect to the three metrics, i.e. $D_{\mathrm{av}}(T, \Delta) = 384$, $\overline{w}_{\mathrm{av}}(T, \Delta) \approx 192$ and $H_{\mathrm{av}}(T, \Delta) \approx 384$. Note moreover that 7 rounds are enough to achieve full diffusion in the forward direction and 6 rounds in the inverse direction. This suggests that it will be very hard to find structural distinguishers over more than 14 rounds. Moreover, in FRIET the adversary has only access to 1/3 of the permutation's input and output greatly limiting the degrees of freedom when trying to exploit such distinguishers.

5.3   Invariant Attack

All round function steps except δ_i act uniformly on the limbs of the state. Let F be the round function with the round constant addition step δ_i removed. We observe that F satisfies the shift-invariance $F \circ \rho_k = \rho_k \circ F$, with $k \in \{0, \ldots, 127\}$ and where $\rho_k(a, b, c) = (a \lll k, b \lll k, c \lll k)$. The addition of round constants in step δ_i breaks these symmetries in the round function of FRIET-PC.

Table 2. Diffusion results

	Round	0	1	2	3	4	5	6	7	8
FRIET-PC	D_{av}	1	3	18	79	211	350	383	384	384
	$\overline{w}_{av}$	1.0	2.5	10.5	33.1	75.5	128.7	174.8	189.6	191.8
	H_{av}	0.0	1.0	12.2	62.2	161.7	298.0	374.3	383.7	384.0
FRIET-PC^{-1}	D_{av}	1	5	27	91	210	342	384	384	384
	$\overline{w}_{av}$	1.0	5.0	18.0	45.2	90.2	150.7	184.6	191.6	191.9
	H_{av}	0.0	0.0	18.0	71.0	175.3	304.1	378.6	384.0	384.0

Additionally, properly chosen round constants can defeat invariant attacks, including slide attacks, invariant subspace attacks and non-linear invariant attacks. As observed by Beierle *et al.* [2], both invariant subspace attacks and non-linear invariant attacks use a non-trivial invariant subspace of the linear layer. More formally, if we denote by λ the linear layer without the round constant addition and by D the set containing the bitwise differences (XOR) of the round constants, then the attacks require the existence of a non-trivial subspace V_D of $\mathbb{F}_2^b$ such that $D \subset V_D$ and $\lambda(V_D) \subset V_D$.

In the case of FRIET-P, we generated a sequence $(u_n)_{n \in \mathbb{N}}$ of 4-bit values from a Fibonacci linear-feedback shift register with polynomial $1 + x + x^4$ and initial state $u_0 = \text{0b1111}$. The round constant rc_i at round i is then obtained by setting its bits at indices $0, 4, 8$ and 12 according to u_i if i is even and at indices $16, 18, 20$ and 24 if i is odd. This particular choice allows for a very efficient bit-interleaved implementation of the round constant addition in software.

We verified with a simple SageMath [32] script that the smallest invariant subspace containing D is of maximal dimension, i.e., it equals the state space $\mathbb{F}_2^{384}$, a trivial invariant space. Remarkably, this holds true when the set D is reduced to the single difference between the two first round constants.

5.4   Choosing Shift Offsets

The round function has 4 shift offsets: One in each of μ_1 and μ_2 and two in ξ. With some abuse of notation we denote the shift offsets by μ_1, μ_2, ξ_1 and ξ_2. Because of FRIET-PC's shift invariance, we can fix μ_1 to 1 without loss of generality. Moreover, we can also choose $\xi_1 < \xi_2$ to reduce the number of possible 4-tuples to 2^{20}. In order to choose the 4 offsets, we ranked all possible 4-tuples following the avalanche dependence metric.

Testing all these offset combinations, we found that the best ones reach full diffusion after 6 rounds. From those we selected the one reaching degree 16 after 4 rounds, both forwards and backwards, with the best worst-case diffusion after 5 rounds. This gave the offset tuple $(\mu_1, \mu_2, \xi_1, \xi_2) = (1, 80, 36, 67)$ that we finally used in the FRIET-P round function.

5.5   Analysis of Differential and Linear Propagation

We conducted a couple of experiments to study the differential propagation and linear propagation in FRIET-PC. Concretely, we searched for low-weight trails on round-reduced FRIET-PC.

We first remind the reader of what differential and linear trails are, then characterize the differential and linear propagation through the non-linear step of the FRIET-PC round function and then report on our experiments.

Differential trails. An r-round differential trail $\mathbf{q}$ is a sequence of $r+1$ difference patterns $q_0, q_1, q_2, \ldots, q_r$ and its differential probability $\mathrm{DP}(\mathbf{q})$ is equal to the probability that input pair $(x, x + q_0)$ with x uniformly random will exhibit the sequence of differences through the rounds. Assuming that the conditions due to the round differentials are independent, $\mathrm{DP}(\mathbf{q})$ is the product of the probabilities of the round differentials (q_{i-1}, q_i). We have $\mathrm{DP}(\mathbf{q}) \approx \prod_i \mathrm{DP}(q_{i-1}, q_i)$. The weight of a differential $w(q_{i-1}, q_i)$ is usually defined by $\mathrm{DP}(q_{i-1}, q_i) = 2^{-w(q_{i-1}, q_i)}$ and the weight of a trail as the sum of the weight of its round differentials. It follows that in the round differential independence assumption we have $\mathrm{DP}(\mathbf{q}) \approx 2^{-w(\mathbf{q})}$.

We call input difference p and output difference q *compatible* if $\mathrm{DP}(p, q) > 0$. We now characterize the differential propagation properties of the FRIET-PC round function by splitting it into a linear layer λ and a non-linear layer. Clearly ξ is the only non-linear step and forms the non-linear layer, and we denote the remainder of the round function as λ. The weight of a round differential $(\lambda^{-1}(p), q)$ is equal to that of the differential (p, q) over ξ.

Linear trails. Besides studying the differential propagation probabilities, we also studied the input-output correlation properties. In other words, we tried to find linear trails on round-reduced FRIET-PC that exhibit high correlation contributions.

An r-round linear trail $\mathbf{q}$ is a sequence of $r + 1$ masks $q_0, q_1, \ldots, q_r$. The round correlation $C(q_i, q_{i+1})$ associated with two consecutive masks within a linear trail corresponds to the correlation between $q_i^T f(x)$ and $q_{i+1}^T x$ for all x, i.e. the correlation between the linear combination of the output bits of the round function whose coefficients are determined by mask q_i and the linear combination of the input bits of the round function whose coefficients are determined by mask q_{i+1}. Analogously to the differential probability, the correlation contribution of a trail $C(\mathbf{q})$ is the product of its round correlations. The correlation weight of a round correlation $w_C(q_i, q_{i+1})$ is then defined by $C^2(q_i, q_{i+1}) = 2^{-w_C(q_i, q_{i+1})}$ and the correlation weight of the trail by $w_C(\mathbf{q}) = \sum_i w_C(q_i, q_{i+1})$.

We say that an output mask q and an input mask p over a mapping are compatible if $C(p, q) > 0$. Clearly, the output mask q and the input mask p over the linear layer are compatible if and only if $q = \lambda^T(p)$ and the corresponding correlation weight is 0. It follows that the correlation weight of a round correlation $(q, (\lambda^T)^{-1}p)$ is given by that of the correlation (q, p) over ξ.

Propagation properties of ξ. Proposition 1 and its corollary characterize the behaviour of a differential over ξ.

Proposition 1. *A non-zero difference $p = (p_a, p_b, p_c)$ at the input and a non-zero difference $q = (q_a, q_b, q_c)$ at the output of ξ are compatible if*

$$q_b = p_b, \quad q_c = p_c, \quad (q_a \oplus p_a) \wedge ((p_b \lll 36) \vee (p_c \lll 67)) = 0.$$

Corollary 1. *The weight of a differential (p, q) over ξ is equal to $Hw(p_b \vee (p_c \lll 31))$ or equivalently $Hw(q_b \vee (q_c \lll 31))$, with Hw the Hamming weight.*

Proposition 2 and its corollary characterize the behaviour of a correlation over ξ.

Proposition 2. *A mask $q = (q_a, q_b, q_c)$ at the output and a mask $p = (p_a, p_b, p_c)$ at the input of ξ are compatible if*

$$q_a = p_a, \quad q_a \vee \left[(\overline{(q_b \lll 36) \oplus (q_b \lll 36)}) \wedge (\overline{(p_c \lll 67) \oplus (p_c \lll 67)}) \right] = 1.$$

Corollary 2. *The correlation weight of a correlation (p, q) over ξ is equal to $2Hw(p_a)$ or equivalently $2Hw(q_a)$.*

Trail experiments. Because an adversary can only access the outer state in FRIET, we restricted our analysis to differential trails with input differences in limb a and to linear trails starting from a mask $q_0 = (q_{0,a}, q_{0,b}, q_{0,c})$ such that $q_{0,a}$ has small Hamming weight and $q_{0,b} = q_{0,c} = 0$.

Table 3 provides the minimum weights for differential trails starting with 1, 2 and 3-bit differences/masks in limb a.

Table 3. Minimum weight of trails starting from an n-bit difference/mask in limb a

	differential				linear					
# Rounds	1	2	3	4	1	2	3	4	5	6
$n = 1$	4	10	18	29	2	4	6	12	22	36
$n = 2$	6	12	22	?	4	8	12	20	?	?
$n = 3$	8	14	?	?	6	8	14	?	?	?

Expanding from the minimum-weight 4-round trail starting from a 1-bit difference in limb a, we obtained a 6-round trail with weight 59 depicted in Table 4.

Expanding the minimum-weight 6-round linear trail starting from a 1-bit mask in limb a, we obtained a 8-round trail with weight 80 depicted in Table 5.

These preliminary results are quite promising and give us reasonable confidence that differential and linear cryptanalysis are no threat to FRIET.

Table 4. A 6-round differential trail for FRIET-PC, in the form of limb differences at the input of ξ in 6 successive rounds in hexadecimal notation and zeroes denoted as dots.

round	p_a	p_b	p_c	weight
0	1	.........2.................	.2	.........2................1	4
1	2	.........1.........2......		1	6
2	.........2................3	..2......4.........	.1......4	..2......5.........3......2	8
3	.........3.........2.....5	..1......4..2	.2	..3......6..2......1......3	11
4	...2......1.........3.....4	..4......b..1	.4..2...8	..5......a..3......2..2..5	15
5	...3.........2.....5.....9	..4..2...4	.a..1....	..6..2..c..1......b..3..4	15

Table 5. A 8-round linear trail for FRIET-PC in the form of masks at the output of ξ in the 8 successive rounds.

round	δ_a	δ_b	δ_c	weight
0	1			2
1	1	1	1	2
2	8		1	2
3	..............8..8.......1	8	........8..1	6
4	..............4..18..8......1	.........8......1	...1.......8..8.........1	10
5	....4..1........4..14..8..8...	........4..1...8	.......8.......4..18..8..1...1	14
6	8...c..14.......2...c.....18..1	...4..1........4.......8	...4..18.....14...4......8...	22
7	8.......c....16...a...8..1...1	8...8...4.......2..8......1...1	8..18..14.......2...c......1...1	22

5.6   Combined Resistance Against 1st Order DPA and SIFA

A straightforward FRIET-P implementation is vulnerable to SIFA [17] and SIFA-like attacks [28]. A realistic attack scenario would be the following. An adversary has access to the outer part of the state at a given time and can inject a fault during the computation of the permutation in order to recover some information on the inner part of the state. Provided that she can redo the attack multiple times on the same initial state, She could then try to inject a fault in the first round to modify one of the inputs of the AND operation in ξ. A bitflip in an input of a binary AND only propagates to its output if the other input is 1 and hence is only effective in that case. It can hence be simply be derived from the behavior of the fault-detection mechanism. Simulating probabilistic or less precise fault models such as, e.g., the random-AND fault model or a byte-based fault model would also yield exploitable results, although the adversary might need to profile the fault behavior of the device in advance with fault templates [28].

Figure 3 depicts an architecture for the FRIET round function offering resistance against first order DPA and SIFA, using countermeasures as introduced in [12]. This architecture can be used as the basis for dedicated hardware or a software implementation. It uses two-share masking, where the shares are indicated by subscripts 0 and 1, effectively duplicating each limb. We divide the round function processing in 4 algorithmic blocks that each operate on 4 limbs.

– α covers the linear steps μ_1 and μ_2, the addition of the round constants δ (at one side only), and the part of the non-linear step ξ that only takes input from a single share. The two α blocks operate on the two shares separately.
– β covers the part of the nonlinear step ξ that takes input from both shares. Each β block takes only a single share per limb.

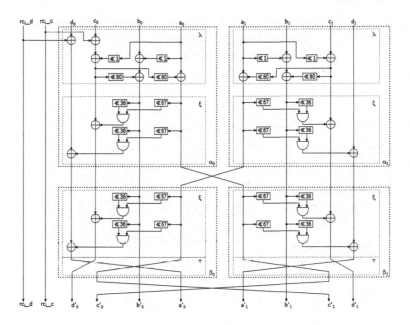

Fig. 3. Hardware architecture of FRIET secured against DPA and SIFA.

When instantiating this architecture in hard- or software, the main requirement is that the implementation must ensure that the computations of the blocks, and their internal variables, are kept separated from each other to avoid share recombination [1]. In hardware this can be achieved by hardwiring the 4 blocks in combinatorial logic and putting registers between the α and β layers, giving rise to a two-stage pipeline of the round functions. In software the four blocks will be executed serially and care must be taken to keep shares belonging to the same limb separated, e.g., not overwrite a register containing a_0 with a_1.

This results in resistance to first-order DPA and with it resistance against SIFA attacks that exploit faulty computations limited to a single block. Indeed, every block only takes a single share for each limb and hence the occurrence of a fault at the output of a block is independent of any native variable.

6   Implementation Results

In this section we discuss implementation specifics and we give results for dedicated hardware (FPGA and ASIC) and software (embedded ARM Cortex M4).

Although we envision FRIET to be implemented with the fault attack counter-measure in place, so by implementing FRIET-P and embedding FRIET-PC in it, for comparison purposes we also implemented FRIET with FRIET-PC directly. We refer to such an implementation as FRIET-C, where C stands for compact.

6.1   Hardware

We implemented FRIET and FRIET-C both in 2 versions, one with 1 round per clock cycle (1R), and another with 2 rounds per clock cycle (2R). We wrapped all 4 versions in a similar testing architecture and a full FRIET circuit as illustrated in Fig. 4.

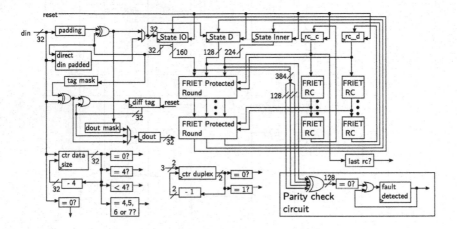

Fig. 4. Hardware architecture for FRIET.

The FRIET circuit has 5 registers: State_IO, State_D, State_Inner, rc_c and rc_d. The State_IO register holds the outer part of the state, State_Inner the inner part. The State_IO register is a circular shift register that loads 32 bits every clock cycle and has size 160 bits. The sponge rate is 130 and not 160 and thus the remaining 30 bits in State_IO register actually belong to the inner part that is supposedly in State_Inner. The State_D holds the parity limb. The rc_c and rc_d registers hold the round constants. The FRIET-C circuit differs from that of FRIET by the absence of registers State_D and rc_d.

The circuit communicates through a single 32-bit bus via a 3-field protocol: the command (4 bytes) encoding one of {reset, duplex-none, duplex-encrypt, duplex-decrypt, tag generate, tag verify}, the data length (4 bytes) and the data itself (variable). After receiving a command and data length, it takes 4 cycles to feed 16 bytes into the State_IO register. Then it performs the FRIET-P permutation, during which the circuit does not acknowledge the data in the "din" port. This takes 24 cycles int the 1R case and 12 in the 2R case.

When the circuit starts or receives a reset command, all state registers are reset with zeroes, thus satisfying the parity check. If the circuit receives data though the "din", then the new data is fed into State_IO and State_D simultaneously, keeping the parity unchanged. A dedicated circuit does a parity check every clock cycle for detecting faults. If it detects a fault, it sets a register "fault detected" to 1. We assume our circuit to be used with another circuit that monitors the state of this register and performs the appropriate action. During the design of the FRIET circuit, it was necessary to enforce the tools to not optimize the redundant part of the circuit.

Table 6 shows the hardware results for FRIET after place and route in FPGA and ASIC. We compare our results with Ketje-Sr from Guido Bertoni GitHub repository [6].

Table 6. Xilinx Virtex-7 xc7vx485tffg1761-3 and ASIC Nangate 45 nm standard cell results for Ketje Sr., FRIET, FRIET-C.

	FPGA				ASIC				
	Resources			Freq.	Throu.	Area	Freq.	Throu.	Power (μW)	
AE Scheme	Slice	LUT	FF	(MHz)	(Mb/s)	(GE)	(MHz)	(Mb/s)	static	dynamic
Ketje-Sr[6]	452	452	448	282	9037	9478	503	16096	161	2152
FRIET (1R)	251	905	494	410	1874	6943	508	2322	110	1724
FRIET-C (1R)	450	1653	628	399	1828	9253	508	2322	148	2226
FRIET (2R)	385	1401	493	391	3135	8890	508	4064	141	1737
FRIET-C (2R)	601	2258	628	366	2909	11100	508	4064	174	2245

6.2 Software

We implemented and benchmarked FRIET-PC and FRIET-P on an embedded ARM Cortex-M4 microcontroller.

The bitwise logical operations and cyclic shifts on the 128-bit limbs can be implemented very efficiently on the M4's 32-bit architecture using the technique of *bit interleaving* [5]. More precisely, we represent every 128-bit limb x as four 32-bit words x_0, x_1, x_2 and x_3 such that the word x_i contains the bits of x with indices congruent to i modulo 4. We also assume that input and output of the permutation are directly mapped to the bit-interleaved format in the state. The bit-interleaving representation offers two main advantages:

- The mixing steps, sum operations and the non-linear layer only require a single register as temporary variable. This allows computing FRIET-PC within the 14 registers that can be freely used.
- The mixing and non-linear steps combine bitwise logical operations with cyclic shifts. The *barrel shifter*, a feature of the Cortex M4, allows computing the shift operations alongside the bitwise Boolean instructions at no extra cost. This reduces the cost of a mixing step in FRIET-PC to 4 XOR operations and that of a non-linear step to 4 XOR and 4 AND operations.

The round constants were chosen such that they could be represented in bit-interleaved representation as the shift of an 8-bit value. As a consequence, the round constant addition consists in a single XOR operation for FRIET-PC and 2 XOR operations for FRIET-P. In FRIET-PC, the limb transposition takes 8 XOR instructions, while in FRIET-P it comes naturally for free. All in all, one round of FRIET-PC requires 29 XOR and 4 AND instructions and one round of FRIET-P takes 26 XOR, 8 AND and 4 load and store instructions because the 512-bit state does not fit into the registers. To further increase the performance, we fully unrolled the 24 rounds of the permutation. The FRIET-PC permutation takes 853 cycles and the FRIET-P permutation takes 1163. Hence in this implementation the code embedding results in an overhead of about 36% mostly due to the additional load and store instructions.

We compare our implementations in Table 7 with other permutations, ranked by decreasing cycles per byte per round ratio. We also provide the cycles per byte ratios. However, these results should be taken with a grain of salt as, the security margin taken in terms of the number of rounds and the amount of propagation achieved by a single round differs from one permutation to the other.

Table 7. Performance Comparison on Cortex-M3/M4

Permutation	Width (bits)	Rounds	Cycles/byte per round	Cycles/byte	Device
Xoodoo [13]	384	12	1.10	13.20	Cortex-M3
FRIET-P (this work)	384	24	1.01	24.23	Cortex-M4
Gimli [4]	384	24	0.91	21.81	Cortex-M3
FRIET-PC (this work)	384	24	0.74	17.78	Cortex-M4

7 Fault Resistance Evaluation

In this section we report on a number of experiments we conducted on implementations of FRIET to test the fault detection capability of our countermeasure.

7.1 Fault Attack on the Simulated Hardware Implementation

In this section we describe the simulation flow we used to evaluate the resistance against fault attacks of FRIET-P in hardware and the results we obtained. The flow we used for carrying out simulated attacks is implemented using standard electronic design automation commodities, and it is composed by a logic simulator (Modelsim 10.4d), a synthesis tool (Synopsys design compiler), and a number of custom made scripts. The routine to inject the faults is integrated into the logic simulator by means of dedicated test benches.

Resistance against fault attacks can be verified at different stages of the design flow. The first stage is called Register Transfer Level (RTL). At this level, it is possible only to examine the cycle-accurate behavior hardware circuit.

RTL does not map the circuit to a technological library that will compose the hardware and therefore information such as the exact delay of the circuit is not present yet. Still, verification at RTL allows confirming that injected faults can be effectively detected with granularity of a clock cycle. Furthermore, this level of simulation is independent from the target hardware platform.

The second stage is the netlist level. We carried out the synthesis using Synopsys Design Compiler as synthesis tool and the Nangate 45 nm open cell library as target technological library. Designs used in these experiments are obtained imposing a minimal area constraints to the design tool. The synthesis maps the RTL description on the gates of the technological library. After this step, we fully know the library gates that our circuit consists of and we have precise information about their delay. However, the results obtained at this stage are specific to the implementation and using a different technological libraries may lead to other conclusions.

We simulated fault injections by forcing a signal (or a set of signals) to a specific value, for a certain amount of time. With this approach, we simulated glitches injected with a minimum granularity of one bit (for instance, a single output of a flip flop or a single output of a gate) and a glitch minimal length equal to the time resolution of the simulation tool, which, in our case, was pico seconds. We randomly injected 500 000 single-bit glitch faults during the permutation execution on different signals of the design. We carried out the same analysis at RTL level and on the post-synthesis netlist.

In both cases the hardware cores under attack have been simulated till the completion of the permutation execution. All the faults we injected have been correctly detected. The results we obtained in simulation confirmed that all the single faults injected are indeed detected as expected by the hardware implementing FRIET-P, both at RTL level and after synthesis.

7.2   Fault Attack on the Software Implementation

Here we describe the setup that we use to evaluate the fault resistance of the permutation. We apply electro-magnetic fault injection, which is accomplished by emitting a short EM pulse from a specific position close to the target.

Figure 5 shows an overview of the setup. Our target is an STM32F407IG development board containing an ARM Cortex-M4F microcontroller. The xy-table moves a probe across the target with high precision. The VC Glitcher sends a signal so the probe will emit a pulse and it also controls a reset line, in case the pulse was too strong and the board is unable to respond. An oscilloscope is used together with a current probe to measure the power consumption in order to determine a time window where the fault should be injected.

We conducted an electro-magnetic fault injection experiment where we scanned the whole chip. We divided the surface of the chip in a 100 by 100 grid, injected 10 faults per position and repeated this 10 times. This resulted in a total of 1 000 000 faults. For the experiment, we focused on the last round. Table 8 shows the fault detection results of the experiment. Each fault has four possible outcomes:

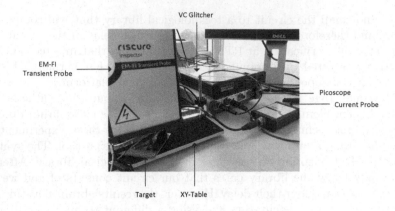

Fig. 5. The setup.

- Normal: no fault has occurred and the device behaves as expected,
- Reset: the EM pulse was too strong and the device was unable to respond so the device was reset,
- Undetected: a fault occurred that was not detected,
- Detected: a fault occurred that was detected.

Table 8. Experimental results of 1 000 000 glitches.

Result	Normal	Reset	Detected	Undetected
Number	860488	138916	596	0

The table shows that all faults are detected by our implementation. To achieve this, we added another countermeasure to the implementation. During preliminary experiments, we noticed in a handful of cases that a single glitch was able to modify bits from different words in the same bit-position. To counter this effect, we store the limbs in bit-interleaved format, where the 32-bit words representing limb b, c and d undergo a circular shift to the left by 1 bit for b, 2 bits for c and 3 bits for d. The rotated words in each limb ensure a glitch causing a fault in multiple words in the same bit position is still detected. During our fault resistance analysis we did not consider ineffective faults [9].

8   Side Channel Attack Evaluation

Many applications require protection against both fault injection and side channel attacks. The doubling of the ϕ function evaluations due to embedding suggests an increase in leakage. Regazzoni et al. [26] showed that, in the context of an AES S-box, various error detection mechanisms increase the vulnerability to power analysis attacks. Using a similar approach, Cojocar et al. [10] investigated the effect of instruction duplication and ineffective faults and their contribution to the overall side channel leakage. Both works note that standard side channel attacks, such as univariate correlation power analysis or even templates, are often unable to exploit the increase in leakage due to fault analysis countermeasures. In order to exploit this redundancy, horizontal attacks should be considered.

We investigate the impact of the code-abiding technique on the side channel attack vulnerability of FRIET-P with Soft Analytical Side Channel Attacks (SASCA) [33]. SASCA is a horizontal type of side channel attack based on the Belief Propagation (BP) algorithm [22]. The structure of SASCA allows exploitation of leakage of any instruction/gate and for our case it can also take advantage of the parity limb (up to XOR limitation studied in [20,21]).

Our SASCA evaluation has the following goals:

- Assess the increase in leakage between FRIET-PC and FRIET-P.
- Compare the side channel leakage of FRIET-P with that of a duplication FRIET-PC.

We simulate the leakage measurements of each 1-bit intermediate variable v using a Normal distribution $\mathcal{N}(v, \sigma^2)$, where the mean is the identity leakage function of the variable and the standard deviation σ is the same for all variables. The goal of the attack is to retrieve the value of bit b_0 of the initial state. Attacks are similar for other bits, and can be recovered with independent attacks in order to reduce computational cost of SASCA.

Figure 6 shows average success rate of simulated experiments for $SNR = 0.1$ in function of the number of traces used for the attack. Analyzing how fast the different success rates converge to 1, we can make three observations.

- BP converges to success rate 1 faster on FRIET-P than on FRIET-PC. Using SASCA we are able to observe and quantify the extra leakage penalty that is incurred by the fault-detecting extension.
- BP on FRIET-P converges slower than on duplicated FRIET-PC. Hence, our code-abiding leads to less exploitable leakage than duplication. As a result, considering side channel and fault injection attacks jointly, FRIET-P offers a better overall security level than duplicated FRIET-PC.
- We underline the need for such horizontal exploitation. The limited scope of standard techniques such as univariate correlation and templates can produce misleading results. Most forms of redundancy (such as the CRAFT/ FRIET-P error-detecting codes, the IIR method or duplication) can remain undetected without horizontal techniques that can cause extra leakage.

9   Conclusions and Future Work

We have presented a novel method to design cryptographic permutations and block ciphers such that they have efficient fault-detecting implementations by building code-abiding permutations and embedding a permutation in that. By a judicious choice of components, these permutations can be very lightweight,

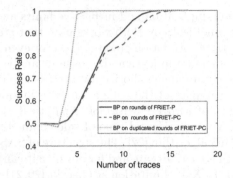

Fig. 6. Success rate of simulated SASCA

as demonstrated by our permutation FRIET-P that can be used to build an AE scheme FRIET offering 128 bits of claimed security. The result can compete with similar schemes that do not offer efficient protection against faults. We have evaluated the fault detection capabilities of FRIET-P in two instantiations and those results are very encouraging. As for the protection against side channel attacks, we only see a slight increase in leakage due to our embedding technique. All in all, this design method seems to be a very promising research avenue.

Acknowledgments. Joan Daemen is supported by the European Research Council under the ERC advanced grant agreement under grant ERC-2017-ADG Nr. 788980 ESCADA. Francesco Regazzoni received support from the European Union Horizon 2020 research and innovation program under CERBERO project (grant agreement number 732105). Lejla Batina and Pedro Maat C. Massolino were supported by the Technology Foundation STW (project 13499 - TYPHOON), from the Dutch government.

A   Design Strategy for a $[6, 3, 3]_2$-abiding Permutation

In this section, we discuss adapting the code embedding technique on a larger linear code. We focus on code $C = [6, 3, 3]_2$ and showcase the different limb transposition operations that a C-abiding permutation could take advantage of.

Let f_C be a C-abiding permutation on a state (a, b, c, d, e, f), with a, b, c native limbs and d, e, f parity limbs satisfying equations:

$$d = b + c, \quad e = a + c, \quad f = a + b.$$

Let's say that a native and a parity limb are *related* when both of them appear in the same parity equation. In particular, limb a is related to limbs e and f, but not to d. A native limb transposition then requires swapping two native limbs and the two parity limbs that are related to only one of the two native limbs involved. An example for such operation is given by $\pi(a, b, c, d, e, f) = (a, c, b, d, f, e)$. On the other hand, a non-native limb transposition requires swapping a native limb x

with a parity limb $x+y$ and bitwise add the other native limb y to the other parity limb related to x. An example for this is $\rho(a, b, c, d, e, f) = (e, b, c, d, a, f+c)$. Note that this the same computational cost of one bitwise addition as the associated embedded operation $\rho_C(a, b, c) = (a + c, b, c)$. By contrast, a limb adaptation operation requires three times as much computation as its embedded equivalent.

References

1. Balasch, J., Gierlichs, B., Grosso, V., Reparaz, O., Standaert, F.-X.: On the cost of lazy engineering for masked software implementations. In: Joye, M., Moradi, A. (eds.) CARDIS 2014. LNCS, vol. 8968, pp. 64–81. Springer, Cham (2015). https://doi.org/10.1007/978-3-319-16763-3_5

2. Beierle, C., Canteaut, A., Leander, G., Rotella, Y.: Proving resistance against invariant attacks: how to choose the round constants. In: Katz, J., Shacham, H. (eds.) CRYPTO 2017. LNCS, vol. 10402, pp. 647–678. Springer, Cham (2017). https://doi.org/10.1007/978-3-319-63715-0_22

3. Beierle, C., Leander, G., Moradi, A., Rasoolzadeh, S.: CRAFT: lightweight tweakable block cipher with efficient protection against DFA attacks. IACR ToSC 2019(1), 5–45 (2019). https://doi.org/10.13154/tosc.v2019.i1.5-45

4. Bernstein, D., et al.: Gimli 20190927, September 2019. http://csrc.nist.gov/CSRC/media/Projects/lightweight-cryptography/documents/round-2/spec-doc-rnd2/gimli-spec-round2.pdf

5. Bertoni, G., Daemen, J., Peeters, M., Assche, G.V., Keer, R.V.: Keccak implementation overview, May 2012. https://keccak.team/papers.html

6. Bertoni, G.: Ketje keyak vhdl. GitHub repository (2019). https://github.com/guidobertoni/KetjeKeyakVHDL

7. Bertoni, G., Daemen, J., Peeters, M., Van Assche, G.: Duplexing the sponge: single-pass authenticated encryption and other applications. In: Miri, A., Vaudenay, S. (eds.) SAC 2011. LNCS, vol. 7118, pp. 320–337. Springer, Heidelberg (2012). https://doi.org/10.1007/978-3-642-28496-0_19

8. Bertoni, G., Daemen, J., Peeters, M., Van Assche, G., Van Keer, R.: Caesar submission: Ketje v. 2 (2016)

9. Clavier, C.: Secret external encodings do not prevent transient fault analysis. In: Paillier, P., Verbauwhede, I. (eds.) CHES 2007. LNCS, vol. 4727, pp. 181–194. Springer, Heidelberg (2007). https://doi.org/10.1007/978-3-540-74735-2_13

10. Cojocar, L., Papagiannopoulos, K., Timmers, N.: Instruction duplication: leaky and not too fault-tolerant!. In: Eisenbarth, T., Teglia, Y. (eds.) CARDIS 2017. LNCS, vol. 10728, pp. 160–179. Springer, Cham (2018). https://doi.org/10.1007/978-3-319-75208-2_10

11. Daemen, J., Hoffert, S., Peeters, M., Assche, G.V., Keer, R.V.: Xoodyak, a lightweight cryptographic scheme, April 2018. http://csrc.nist.gov/CSRC/media/Projects/lightweight-cryptography/documents/round-2/spec-doc-rnd2/Xoodyak-spec-round2.pdf

12. Daemen, J., Dobraunig, C., Eichlseder, M., Gross, H., Mendel, F., Primas, R.: Protecting against statistical ineffective fault attacks. IACR ePrint Archive, Report 2019/536 (2019). https://eprint.iacr.org/2019/536

13. Daemen, J., Hoffert, S., Van Assche, G., Van Keer, R.: The design of Xoodoo and Xoofff. IACR ToSC 2018(4), 1–38 (2018). https://doi.org/10.13154/tosc.v2018.i4.1-38

14. Daemen, J., Mennink, B., Van Assche, G.: Full-state keyed duplex with built-in multi-user support. In: Takagi, T., Peyrin, T. (eds.) ASIACRYPT 2017. LNCS, vol. 10625, pp. 606–637. Springer, Cham (2017). https://doi.org/10.1007/978-3-319-70697-9_21

15. Daemen, J., Rijmen, V.: The Design of Rijndael. Springer, Heidelberg (2002). https://doi.org/10.1007/978-3-662-04722-4

16. Dinur, I., Shamir, A.: Cube attacks on tweakable black box polynomials. IACR ePrint Archive **2008**, 385 (2008)

17. Dobraunig, C., Eichlseder, M., Korak, T., Mangard, S., Mendel, F., Primas, R.: SIFA: exploiting ineffective fault inductions on symmetric cryptography. IACR TCHES **2018**(3), 547–572 (2018). https://doi.org/10.13154/tches.v2018.i3.547-572

18. Dobraunig, C., Eichlseder, M., Mendel, F., Schläffer, M.: Ascon v1. 2. Submission to the CAESAR Competition (2016)

19. Dobraunig, C., Eichlseder, M., Mendel, F., Schofnegger, M.: Algebraic cryptanalysis of variants of FRIT. In: Paterson, K.G., Stebila, D. (eds.) SAC 2019. LNCS, vol. 11959, pp. 149–170. Springer, Cham (2020). https://doi.org/10.1007/978-3-030-38471-5_7

20. Green, J., Roy, A., Oswald, E.: A systematic study of the impact of graphical models on inference-based attacks on AES. IACR ePrint Archive **2018**, 671 (2018)

21. Guo, Q., Grosso, V., Standaert, F.: Modeling soft analytical side-channel attacks from a coding theory viewpoint. IACR ePrint Archive **2018**, 498 (2018)

22. Kschischang, F.R., Frey, B.J., Loeliger, H.A.: Factor graphs and the sum-product algorithm. IEEE Trans. Inf. Theory **47**(2), 498–519 (2001)

23. Lac, B., Canteaut, A., Fournier, J.J.A., Sirdey, R.: Thwarting fault attacks using the internal redundancy countermeasure (IRC). IACR ePrint Archive **2017**, 910 (2017)

24. Patrick, C., Yuce, B., Ghalaty, N.F., Schaumont, P.: Lightweight fault attack resistance in software using intra-instruction redundancy. In: Avanzi, R., Heys, H. (eds.) SAC 2016. LNCS, vol. 10532, pp. 231–244. Springer, Cham (2017). https://doi.org/10.1007/978-3-319-69453-5_13

25. Qin, L., Dong, X., Jia, K., Zong, R.: Key-dependent cube attack on reduced Frit permutation in duplex-ae modes. IACR ePrint Archive **2019**, 170 (2019)

26. Regazzoni, F., Breveglieri, L., Ienne, P., Koren, I.: Interaction between fault attack countermeasures and the resistance against power analysis attacks. In: Joye, M., Tunstall, M. (eds.) Fault Analysis in Cryptography, pp. 257–272. Springer, Heidelberg (2012). https://doi.org/10.1007/978-3-642-29656-7_15

27. Reparaz, O., et al.: CAPA: the spirit of beaver against physical attacks. In: Shacham, H., Boldyreva, A. (eds.) CRYPTO 2018. LNCS, vol. 10991, pp. 121–151. Springer, Cham (2018). https://doi.org/10.1007/978-3-319-96884-1_5

28. Saha, S., Roy, D.B., Bag, A., Patranabis, S., Mukhopadhyay, D.: Breach the gate: Exploiting observability for fault template attacks on block ciphers. IACR ePrint Archive, Report 2019/937 (2019). https://eprint.iacr.org/2019/937

29. Schneider, T., Moradi, A., Güneysu, T.: ParTI – towards combined hardware countermeasures against side-channel and fault-injection attacks. In: Robshaw, M., Katz, J. (eds.) CRYPTO 2016. LNCS, vol. 9815, pp. 302–332. Springer, Heidelberg (2016). https://doi.org/10.1007/978-3-662-53008-5_11

30. Simon, T., et al.: Towards lightweight cryptographic primitives with built-in fault-detection. IACR ePrint Archive **2018**, 729 (2018)

31. Song, L., Guo, J., Shi, D., Ling, S.: New MILP modeling: improved conditional cube attacks on keccak-based constructions. In: Peyrin, T., Galbraith, S. (eds.) ASIACRYPT 2018. LNCS, vol. 11273, pp. 65–95. Springer, Cham (2018). https://doi.org/10.1007/978-3-030-03329-3_3
32. TS Developers: SageMath (2016)
33. Veyrat-Charvillon, N., Gérard, B., Standaert, F.-X.: Soft analytical side-channel attacks. In: Sarkar, P., Iwata, T. (eds.) ASIACRYPT 2014. LNCS, vol. 8873, pp. 282–296. Springer, Heidelberg (2014). https://doi.org/10.1007/978-3-662-45611-8_15

Fault Template Attacks on Block Ciphers Exploiting Fault Propagation

Sayandeep Saha[1]([✉]), Arnab Bag[1]([✉]), Debapriya Basu Roy[1,3],
Sikhar Patranabis[1,2], and Debdeep Mukhopadhyay[1]

[1] Department of Computer Science and Engineering,
Indian Institute of Technology, Kharagpur, Kharagpur, India
{sahasayandeep,arnabbag,debdeep}@iitkgp.ac.in
[2] Department of Computer Science, ETH Zurich, Zürich, Switzerland
sikhar.patranabis@inf.ethz.ch
[3] Technische Universität München, Munich, Germany
debapriya.basu-roy@tum.de

Abstract. Fault attacks (FA) are one of the potent practical threats to modern cryptographic implementations. Over the years the FA techniques have evolved, gradually moving towards the exploitation of device-centric properties of the faults. In this paper, we exploit the fact that activation and propagation of a fault through a given combinational circuit (i.e., observability of a fault) is data-dependent. Next, we show that this property of combinational circuits leads to powerful *Fault Template Attacks (FTA)*, even for implementations having dedicated protections against both power and fault-based vulnerabilities. The attacks found in this work are applicable even if the fault injection is made at the middle rounds of a block cipher, which are out of reach for most of the other existing fault analysis strategies. Quite evidently, they also work for a known-plaintext scenario. Moreover, the middle round attacks are entirely blind in the sense that no access to the ciphertexts (correct/faulty) or plaintexts are required. The adversary is only assumed to have the power of repeating an unknown plaintext several times. Practical validation over a hardware implementation of SCA-FA protected PRESENT, and simulated evaluation on a public software implementation of protected AES prove the efficacy of the proposed attacks.

Keywords: Fault attack · Fault propagation · Masking

1 Introduction

Implementation-based attacks are practical threats to modern cryptography. With the dramatic increase in the usage of embedded devices for IoT and mobile

D. B. Roy—Worked on this project during his stay at IIT Kharagpur.
S. Patranabis—Worked on this project during his stay at IIT Kharagpur.

Electronic supplementary material The online version of this chapter (https://doi.org/10.1007/978-3-030-45721-1_22) contains supplementary material, which is available to authorized users.

A. Canteaut and Y. Ishai (Eds.): EUROCRYPT 2020, LNCS 12105, pp. 612–643, 2020.
https://doi.org/10.1007/978-3-030-45721-1_22

applications, such attacks have become a real concern. Most of the modern embedded devices carry cryptographic cores and are physically accessible by the adversary. Therefore, suitable countermeasures are often implemented to protect the cryptographic computations from exploitation.

Side-channel attacks (SCA) [1] and Fault attacks (FA) [2,3] are the two most widely explored implementation attack classes till date. The main idea behind the first one is to passively exploit the operation dependency (simple-power-analysis) or data-dependency (differential/correlation power analysis) of the cryptographic computation to infer the secret key by measuring power or electromagnetic (EM) signals. In contrast, fault attacks are active in nature, as they work by corrupting the intermediate computation of the device in a controlled manner. Intentionally injected faults create a statistical bias in some of the intermediate computation states. Such bias is exploited by the adversary (either analytically or statistically) to reduce the entropy of the unknown key and thereby recovering the key [3].

The protection mechanisms found in modern devices mostly try to mitigate the two abovementioned classes of attacks. In this context, hardening the cipher algorithm itself with countermeasures is often preferred than the sensor and shield-based physical countermeasures. This is due to the fact that algorithm-level countermeasures are flexible in terms of usability. Moreover, they often provide provable security guarantees. Masking is the most prominent and widely deployed countermeasure so far, against passive SCA [4–7]. Masking is a class of techniques which implement secret sharing at the level of cryptographic circuits. Each cipher variable x is split into a certain number (say $d + 1$) of shares in masking which are statistically independent by their own, and also while considered in groups of size up to d. Each underlying function of the cipher is also shared into $d+1$ component functions (respecting the correctness) to process the shared variables. The order of protection d intuitively means that an adversary has to consider SCA leakages for $d + 1$ points, simultaneously, in order to gain some useful information about the intermediate computation. In the context of FA, detection-type countermeasures are the most common ones. The main principle of these FA countermeasures is to detect the presence of a fault via some redundant computation (time/space redundancy or information redundancy), and then react by either muting or randomizing the corrupted output [8,9]. Another alternative way is to avoid the explicit detection step altogether, and perform the computation in a way so that it gets deliberately randomized in the presence of an error in computation (infective countermeasure) [10].

Symmetric key primitives (such as block ciphers) are the most widely analyzed class of cryptographic constructs in the context of implementation-based attacks. Quite evidently, the current evaluation criteria for a block cipher design takes the overhead due to SCA and FA protections directly into account. In other words, countermeasures are nowadays becoming an essential part of a cipher. In practice, there exist proposals which judiciously integrate these two countermeasures for block ciphers [11]. Whether such hardened algorithms are actually secured or not is, however, a crucial question to be answered.

Recent developments in FA show that the answer to the above-mentioned question is negative. Although combined countermeasures are somewhat successful in throttling passive attacks, they often fall prey against active adversaries. In [12,13], it was shown that if an adversary has the power of injecting a sufficient number of faults, even the correct ciphertexts can be exploited for an attack. The attack in [12], also known as Statistical Ineffective Fault Analysis (SIFA), changed the widely regarded concept that fault attacks require faulty ciphertexts to proceed. Most of the existing FA countermeasures are based on this belief and thus were broken. In a slightly different setting, the so-called Persistent Fault Analysis (PFA) [14,15] presented a similar result. The main reason behind the success of SIFA and PFA is that they typically exploit the statistical bias in the event when a fault fails to alter the computation. However, this seemingly simple event can be exploited in several other ways, too, which may lead to more powerful attacks on protected implementations. Particularly, in this paper, we show that *once a fault is injected, whether it propagates to the output through the circuit or not is data-dependent.* This data dependency works as a source of information leakage which eventually leads towards the recovery of the secret even from protected cipher implementations. In contrast to SIFA or PFA, we do not require access to the correct/faulty ciphertexts. Our contributions in this paper are discussed below.

Our Contributions: In this paper, we propose a new attack strategy for protected implementations which exploits fundamental principles of digital gates to extract the secret. The main observation we exploit is that *the output observability of a fault, injected at one input of an AND gate depends on the values of the other inputs.* In general, the activation and propagation of a fault inside a circuit depends upon the value under process, which is indeed a side-channel leakage. Based on this simple observation we devise attacks which can break masking schemes of any arbitrary order, even if it is combined with FA countermeasures. *The strongest feature of this attack strategy is that it can enable attacks in the middle round of a cipher without requiring any explicit access to the ciphertexts even if they are correct. Just knowing whether the outcome of the encryption is faulty or not would suffice. The plaintexts are need not be known explicitly in all scenarios, but the adversary should be able to repeat a plaintext several times.* One should note that the attacks like SIFA require ciphertext access and are also not applicable to the middle rounds.[1]

The fault model utilized in this attack is similar to the one exploited for SIFA [12]. However, the exploitation methodology of the faults is entirely

---

[1] Several modern symmetric-key protocols do not expose the ciphertexts. One prominent example is the Message Authentication Codes (MAC) in certain application scenarios. Furthermore, for many existing Authenticated Encryption schemes, direct access to the plaintext is not available for the block ciphers used within the scheme. However, fixing the plaintext value may be achieved. Also, in real devices, the accessibility of plaintexts cannot be assumed in every scenario. One typical example is the shared root key usage in UMTS [16].

Table 1. Comparison of FTA with other competing attacks

Attack Algorithm	Breaks Masking?	Breaks Fault Countermeasure?	Requires Ciphertext Access?	Middle Round Attack?	Comments
SIFA	✓	✓	✓	✗	Breaks SCA-FA protection
PFA	✓	✓	✓	✗	Breaks SCA-FA protection
SEA	✗	✓	✗	✓	Masking is a countermeasure
BFA	✗	Not All	✗	✓	Masking is a countermeasure
FTA	✓	✓	✗	✓	Breaks SCA-FA protection

different from SIFA. While SIFA uses statistical analysis based on the correct ciphertexts, we propose a novel strategy based on *fault templates*. The Fault Template Attack strategy, abbreviated as FTA, efficiently exploits fault characteristics from different fault locations for constructing distinguishing fault patterns, which enable key/state recovery. In principle, FTA is closer to SCA than FAs, and hence, the evaluation of masking against this attack becomes essential.

The attacks proposed in this paper require multiple fault locations to extract the entire key. *Note that, we do not require multiple fault locations to be corrupted at the same time, but injections can be made one location at a time in different independent experiments.* The spatial and temporal control of the faults are practically feasible, *as we show by means of an EM fault injection setup in this paper.* In particular, we target a hardware implementation of PRESENT with first-order Threshold Implementation (TI) [17] for SCA protection, and duplication based FA protection. Although in our practical experiments, we target hardware implementations, similar faults can be generated for software as well. To establish this, we simulate the desired faults on a publicly available masked software implementation of AES augmented with an FA countermeasure and perform the key recovery for it. One advantage of FTA attack strategy is that an implementation similar to the target one can be extensively profiled before attack, and parameters for obtaining the desired faults can be identified.

The idea of FA without direct access to the plaintext and ciphertext has been explored previously. The closest to our proposal are the so-called Blind Fault Analysis (BFA) [18], the Safe-Error-Attack (SEA) [19] and the Fault Sensitivity Analysis (FSA) [20]. However, none of these attacks exploit the inherent circuit properties as we do in our case. *Finally, BFA and SEA can be throttled by masking, and FSA on masked implementations require timing information of the S-Boxes along with the faults.* The greatest advantage of our proposal lies at the point that our attacks are applicable for masking countermeasures even while combined with a state-of-the-art FA countermeasure. Although SIFA and

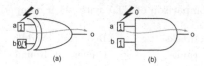

Fig. 1. Fault propagation: (a) XOR gate; (b) AND gate. The inputs for activation and propagation are in blue and the value of the stuck-at fault is in red. (Color figure online)

PFA work on masking, both of them require ciphertext access. The differences of our attack from other competing ones are summarized in Table 1.

In order to validate our idea both theoretically and practically, we choose the block cipher PRESENT as a test case [21]. This choice is motivated by that fact that PRESENT is a fairly well-analyzed design and also an ISO standard [22]. The choice of a lightweight cipher is also motivated by the fact that countermeasures are extremely crucial for such ciphers as they are supposed to be deployed on low cost embedded devices. However, the attacks are equally applicable to larger block ciphers like AES. Our validation on masked AES justifies this claim.

The rest of the paper is organized as follows. We begin by explaining the fundamental principles behind the attacks in Sect. 2 through interpretable examples. Feasibility of the attacks for unmasked but FA protected implementations are discussed in Sect. 3 taking PRESENT as an example. Attacks on combined countermeasures are proposed in Sect. 4 (on PRESENT), followed by a brief discussion on the practical evaluation of the attack in Sect. 5. We conclude the paper in Sect. 6. An extended version of this paper is available on eprint[2] providing further details on the practical experiments, and a brief discussion on the implication of FTA on state-of-the-art countermeasures.

2   The Fundamental Principle

2.1   Fault Activation and Propagation

The concept of fault activation and propagation is instrumental for structural fault testing of digital circuits. Almost every Automatic Test Pattern Generation (ATPG) algorithm relies on these two events. Consider a combinational circuit $\mathcal{C}$ and an internal net i in this circuit. The problem is to test if the net has been stuck at a value 0 or 1. A test pattern for exposing this fault to the output is required to perform the following two events in sequence:

1. **Fault Activation:** The test pattern is required to set the net i to value x such that i carries the complement of x (i.e., $\bar{x}$) in the presence of a fault and x, otherwise.
2. **Fault Propagation:** The test pattern has to ensure that the effect of the fault propagates to the output of the circuit $\mathcal{C}$.

---

[2] https://eprint.iacr.org/2019/937.

Both the activation and propagation events strongly depend upon the structure of the circuit graph, and the gates present in the circuit. However, understanding the fault activation and propagation property of each gate is the very first step to have an insight into the attacks we are going to propose. Let us first consider a linear 2-input XOR gate as shown in Fig. 1(a). Without loss of generality, we consider a stuck-at-0 fault at the input register a, while the input register b may take values independently. In order to activate the fault at a, one must set $a = 1$. The next step is to propagate the fault at the output. One may observe that setting the input b to either 0 or 1 will expose the fault at a to the output o. A similar phenomenon can be observed for an n-input XOR gate. This observation is summarized in the following statement:

Given an n-input XOR gate having an input set I, $(|I| = n)$, an output O, and a faulted input $i \in I$, the fault propagation to O does not depend upon the valuations of the subset $I \setminus \{i\}$.

An exactly opposite situation is observed for the nonlinear gates like AND/OR. For the sake of illustration, let us consider the two-input AND gate in Fig. 1(b). Here a stuck-at fault (either stuck-at-0 or stuck-at-1) at input register a can propagate to the output o if and only if the input b is set to the value 1^3. An input value of 1 for an AND gate is often referred to as *non-controlling value*[4]. The activation and propagation property of the AND gates, thus, can be stated as follows:

For an n-input AND gate with input set I, output O, and one faulty input $i \in I$, the fault propagation takes place if an only if every input in the subset $I \setminus \{i\}$ is set to its non-controlling value.

2.2 Information Leakage Due to Fault Propagation

Now we describe how information leaks due to the propagation of faults. Once again, we consider the AND and the XOR gate for our illustration. Let us assume that the gates are processing secret data and an active adversary $\mathcal{A}$ can only have the information whether the output is faulty or not. The adversary can, however, inject a stuck-at fault at one of the input registers of the gate[5]. We also consider that the adversary has complete knowledge about the type of the gate she is targeting. With this adversary model, now we can analyze the information leakage due to the presence of faults.

First, we consider the XOR gate. Without loss of generality, let us assume the fault to be stuck-at-0, and the injection point as a. Then the fault will propagate to the output whenever it gets activated. In other words, just by

---

[3] The fault activation takes place if a is set to 1 (stuck-at-0) or 0 (stuck-at 1).

[4] A controlling input value of a gate is defined as a value, which, if present for at least one input, sets the output of the gate to a known value. Non-controlling value is the complement of the controlling value.

[5] Although for simplicity we are considering stuck-at faults here, our arguments are also valid for single bit toggle faults, and later on, we show how such faults can be injected in an actual hardware.

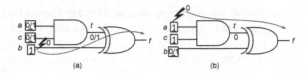

Fig. 2. Fault propagation through combinational circuits: (a) Injection at XOR gate input; (b) Injection at AND gate input. The inputs for activation and propagation are shown in blue and the nature of the stuck-at fault is shown in red. The propagated faulty intermediate value is shown in green. (Color figure online)

observing whether the output is faulty $\mathcal{A}$ can determine the value of a. More precisely, if the output is fault-free $a = 0$ and $a = 1$, otherwise.

The situation is slightly different in the case of AND gates. Here the output becomes faulty only if the fault is activated at a and b is set to its non-controlling value. In this case, the adversary can determine the values of both a and b. However, one should note that the fault will only propagate if both a and b are set to unity. For all other cases the output will remain uncorrupted and $\mathcal{A}$ cannot determine what value is being processed by the gate. Putting it in another way, the adversary can divide the value space of (a, b) into two equivalence classes. The first class contains values $(0, 0), (0, 1)(1, 0)$, whereas the second class contains only a single value $(1, 1)$. One should note that the intra-class values cannot be distinguished from each other.

One general trend in FA community is to quantify the leakage in terms of entropy loss. The same can be done here for both the gates. Without the fault the entropy of (a, b), denoted as $H((a, b))$, is 2. In the case of XOR gate, the entropy reduces after the first injection event. Depending on the value of the observable O_{f_1}, which we set to 1 if the fault is observed at the output (and 0, otherwise), the actual input value at the fault location can be revealed. More formally, we have $H((a, b)|O_{f_1} = 0) = 1$ and $H((a, b)|O_{f_1} = 1) = 1$. Therefore, the remaining entropy $H((a, b)|O_{f_1}) = \frac{1}{2} \times H((a, b)|O_{f_1} = 0) + \frac{1}{2} \times H((a, b)|O_{f_1} = 1) = 1$. In other words, the entropy of (a, b) reduces to 1 after one fault injection. The situation is slightly different in the case of AND gate. Here the remaining entropy can be calculated as $H((a, b)|O_{f_1}) = \frac{3}{4} \times \log_2 3 + \frac{1}{4} \times \log_2 1 = 1.18$. Although the leakage here is slightly less compared to the XOR gate, one should note that it is conditional on the non-faulty inputs of the gate too. In other words, partial information regarding both a and b are leaked, simultaneously. In contrast, XOR completely leaks one bit but does not leak anything about the other inputs.

As we shall show later in this paper, both AND and XOR gate leakages can be cleverly exploited to mount extremely strong FAs on block ciphers. In the next subsection, we extend the concept of leakage for larger circuits.

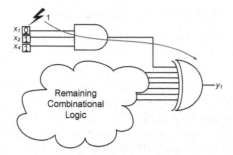

Fig. 3. Fault propagation through S-Box Polynomials. The input pattern causing the propagation is shown in blue. The stuck-at fault type is shown in red. (Color figure online)

2.3 Fault Propagation in Combinational Circuits

One convenient and general way of realizing different sub-operations of a block cipher is by means of algebraic expressions over $GF(2)$ also known as Algebraic Normal Form (ANF). For the sake of explanation, we also use ANF representation of the circuits throughout this paper. ANF representation is also common while implementing masking schemes. Therefore, a good starting point would be to analyze the effect of faults on an ANF expression. For example, let us consider the ANF expression $f = b + ca$ and its corresponding circuit in Fig. 2.[6] As in the previous case, we assume that the adversary $\mathcal{A}$ can only observe whether the output is faulty or not, but cannot observe the actual output of the circuit. Also, the inputs are not observable but can be kept fixed. With this setting the adversary injects a stuck-at-0 fault in b (see Fig. 2(a)). Now, since the input is fixed, a fault at the output would imply that $b = 1$. On the other hand, the output will be correct only if $b = 0$. The property of the XOR gate mentioned in the previous subsection ensures that the other input coming from the product term does not affect the recovery of the bit b. Similarly, one can recover the output of the product term ca.

Let us now consider recovery of the bits a and c, with the fault injected at a. From the properties of an AND gate, the fault will propagate to the wire t (see Fig. 2(b)) if and only if $c = 1$ and $a = 1$. This fault, on the other hand, will directly propagate to the output as the rest of the circuit only contain an XOR gate. However, from adversary's point of view, entropy reduction due to a non-faulty output is not very significant (non-faulty output may occur for (c, a) taking values $(0, 0)$, $(0, 1)$ and $(1, 0)$). Moreover, no further information is leaked even if the attacker now targets the input c with another fault. It may seem that the AND gates are not very useful as leakage sources. However, it is not true if we can somehow exploit the fact that it leaks information about more than one bits. The next subsection will elaborate the impact of this property on S-Boxes.

---

[6] Note that the "+" represents XOR operation here.

2.4   Propagation Characteristics of S-Boxes

The S-Boxes are one of the most common constituents of modern block ciphers. In most of the cases, they are the only non-linear function within a cipher. Mathematically, they are vectorial Boolean functions consisting of high degree polynomials over $GF(2)$. Such polynomials contain high degree monomials which are nothing but several bits AND-ed together. As a concrete example, we consider the S-Box polynomials for PRESENT as shown in Eq. (1). This S-Box has 4 input bits denoted as x_1, x_2, x_3, x_4 and 4 output bits y_1, y_2, y_3, y_4 (where x_1 and y_1 are the Most Significant Bits (MSB) and x_4 and y_4 are the Least Significant Bits (LSB)).

$$
\begin{aligned}
y_1 &= x_1 x_2 x_4 + x_1 x_3 x_4 + x_1 + x_2 x_3 x_4 + x_2 x_3 + x_3 + x_4 + 1 \\
y_2 &= x_1 x_2 x_4 + x_1 x_3 x_4 + x_1 x_3 + x_1 x_4 + x_1 + x_2 + x_3 x_4 + 1 \\
y_3 &= x_1 x_2 x_4 + x_1 x_2 + x_1 x_3 x_4 + x_1 x_3 + x_1 + x_2 x_3 x_4 + x_3 \\
y_4 &= x_1 + x_2 x_3 + x_2 + x_4
\end{aligned}
\tag{1}
$$

Let us consider the first polynomial in this system without loss of generality. Also, we consider a stuck-at-1 fault at x_1 during the computation of the first monomial $x_1 x_2 x_4$ in this polynomial. The exact location of this fault in the circuit is depicted in Fig. 3. Given this fault location, the fault propagates to the output only if $(x_1 = 0,\ x_2 = 1,\ x_3 = 0,\ x_4 = 1)$ or $(x_1 = 0,\ x_2 = 1,\ x_3 = 1,\ x_4 = 1)$. For the rest of the cases, the output remains unaltered. *Consequently, if the S-Box inputs are changing and the value is inaccessible for the adversary, she can still detect when the S-Box processes the input $(0, 1, 0, 1)$ or $(0, 1, 1, 1)$, as compared to other inputs.* In the next subsection, we shall show how this simple observation results in key leakage for an entire cipher.

3   Fault Observability Attacks

In this section, we describe how information leakage from gates eventually results in key leakage for so-called FA resilient block cipher implementations. For the sake of simplicity, we begin with implementations having redundancy-based detection-type FA countermeasures. Implementations having both masking and FA countermeasures will be considered in the subsequent sections. The detection-type FA countermeasures under consideration may use any form of redundancy (space, time or information redundancy) [8,9]. However, the attacks we are going to describe are equally applicable to any member of this classical countermeasure class. For the sake of simplicity, we, therefore, consider the most trivial form where the redundancy check happens at the end of the computation before outputting the ciphertexts.

3.1   Template-Based Fault Attacks

Before going to the actual attack instances, let us first describe our general attack strategy, which is based on constructing templates. Similar to the template attacks in SCA, fault template attacks also consist of two phases, namely:

Algorithm 1. *BUILD_TEMPLATE*

Input: Target Implementation C, Fault fl
Output: Template $\mathcal{T}$
   $\mathcal{T} := \emptyset$
   $w := $ GET_SBOX_SIZE()   ▷ Get the width of the S-Box
   for $(0 \leq k < 2^w)$ **do**   ▷ Vary one key word
      $F_t := \emptyset$
      for $(0 \leq p < 2^w)$ **do**   ▷ Vary one w-bit plaintext word
         $x := p \oplus k$
         $y_f := C(x)^{fl}$ ▷ Inject fault in one of the S-Boxes for each execution.
         $y_c := C(x)$
         if DETECT_FAULT(y_f, y_c) == 1 **then**   ▷ Fault detection function
            $F_t := F_t \cup \{1\}$
         else
              $F_t := F_t \cup \{0\}$
         end if
      end for
      $\mathcal{T} := \mathcal{T} \cup \{(F_t, k)\}$
   end for
   Return $\mathcal{T}$

Note that $C(x)$ (resp. $C(x)^{fl}$) is effectively $S(x+k)$ where $S(\cdot)$ is an S-Box. This is true for other template building algorithms as well in this paper

1. **Template Building (offline):** This is an offline phase where an implementation similar (preferably from the same device family) to the target is profiled extensively to construct an informed model for the attack. The aim of this informed modeling is to reason about some unknown directly in the online phase of the attack on the actual target, based on some observables from the online experiment[7]. Formally, a template $\mathcal{T}$ for fault attack can be represented as a mapping $\mathcal{T} : \mathcal{F} \to \mathcal{X}$, where an $a \in \mathcal{F}$ is constructed by computing some function on the observables (i.e. $a = \mathcal{G}(\mathcal{O})$). The location for a fault injection can be used as auxiliary information while computing the function from the observable set to the set $\mathcal{F}$. The range set $\mathcal{X}$ of the template $\mathcal{T}$ either represents a part of an intermediate state, (for example, the value of a byte/nibble) or a part of the secret key.

2. **Template Matching (online):** In this online phase, an implementation (identical to one profiled in the offline phase) with an unknown key is targeted with fault injection. The injection locations may be pre-decided from the template construction phase. The unknown is supposed to be discovered by first mapping the observables from this experiment to a member of the set $\mathcal{F}$ and then by finding out the corresponding value of the unknown from the set $\mathcal{X}$ using the template $\mathcal{T}$.

Unlike differential or statistical fault attacks, the key recovery algorithms in fault template attacks are fairly straightforward in general. The fault complexity of the attacks is comparable with that of the statistical fault attacks. However, one great advantage over statistical or differential fault attacks is that access to ciphertexts or plaintexts is not essential. The attacker only requires to

---

[7] The observable (denoted as $\mathcal{O}$), for example, can be the knowledge that whether the output of an encryption is faulty or not.

know whether the outcome is faulted or not. More precisely, FTA can target the middle rounds of block ciphers, which are otherwise inaccessible by statistical or differential attacks due to extensive computational complexity. Apart from that, the FTA differs significantly from all other classes of fault attacks in the way it exploits the leakage. While differential or statistical attacks use the bias in the state due to fault injection as a key distinguisher, template-based attacks directly recover the intermediate state values. From this aspect, this attack is closer to the SCA attacks. However, there are certain dissimilarities with SCA as well, in the sense that SCA template attacks try to model the noise from the target device and measurement equipment. In contrast, FTA goes beyond noise modeling and build templates over the fault characteristics of the underlying circuit.

Algorithm 2. *MATCH_TEMPLATE*

Input: Protected cipher with unknown key C_k, Fault fl, Template $\mathcal{T}$
Output: Set of candidate correct keys k_{cand}

$k_{cand} := \emptyset$ $\hspace{6cm}$ ▷ Set of candidate keys
$w := \texttt{GET\_SBOX\_SIZE}()$
$F_t := \emptyset$
for $(0 \leq p < 2^w)$ **do** $\hspace{3.5cm}$ ▷ Vary a single w bit word of the plaintext
$\hspace{0.5cm}\mathcal{O} := (C_k(p))^{fl}$ $\hspace{4cm}$ ▷ Inject fault for each execution
$\hspace{0.5cm}$**if** $(\mathcal{O} == 1)$ **then** $\hspace{4.5cm}$ ▷ Fault detected
$\hspace{1.5cm}F_t := F_t \cup \{1\}$
$\hspace{0.5cm}$**else**
$\hspace{1.5cm}F_t := F_t \cup \{0\}$
$\hspace{0.5cm}$**end if**
end for
$k_{cand} := k_{cand} \cup \{\mathcal{T}(F_t)\}$
Return k_{cand}

3.2 Attacks on Unmasked Implementations: Known Plaintext

In this subsection, we present the first concrete realization of FTA. The first attack we present requires the plaintexts to be known and controllable. However, explicit knowledge of the ciphertexts is not expected. The adversary is only provided with the information whether the outcome of an encryption is faulty or not. One practical example of such attack setup is a block-cipher based Message-Authentication Code (MAC), where the authentication tag might not be exposed to the adversary, but the correctness of the authentication is available. We also assume a stuck-at-1 fault model for simplicity. However, the attack also applies to stuck-at-0 and bit-flip models. For the sake of illustration, we mainly consider the PRESENT block cipher. The attack consists of two phases as detailed next.

Offline Phase – Template Building: Perhaps the most important aspect of the attacks we describe is the fault location. As elaborated in Sect. 2.4, leakage from the non-linear or the linear gates can be exploited. For this particular case we choose an AND gate for fault injection as in Sect. 2.4, respecting the fact that information regarding multiple bits are leaked, simultaneously. The same fault location as in Sect. 2.4 is utilized. *The observables, in this case, are the 0, 1 patterns, from the protected implementation where 0 represents a correct outcome and 1 represents a faulty outcome.* The domain set $\mathcal{F}$ of the template consists of patterns called *fault patterns* (denoted as F_t in the algorithm) constructed from the observables. The fault location, in this case, is fixed. The process of transforming the observables to fault patterns and then mapping them to the set $\mathcal{X}$ is outlined in Algorithm 1[8]. For each choice of the key nibble (which is a member from set $\mathcal{X}$), all 16 possible plaintext nibbles are fed to the S-Box equations according to a predefined sequence, and the stuck-at-1 fault is injected for each of the cases. Consequently, for each choice of the key nibble, one obtains a bit-string of 16 bits which is the desired fault pattern (F_t). The fault patterns are depicted in Table 2. It can be observed that corresponding to each fault pattern, there can be two candidate key suggestions. One should also note that changing the fault location might change the fault patterns and the mapping $\mathcal{T} : \mathcal{F} \rightarrow \mathcal{X}$.

Online Phase – Template Matching: The online phase of the attack is fairly straightforward. The attacker now targets an actual implementation (similar to that used in the template building phase) with an unknown key and constructs the fault patterns. The fault patterns are constructed for each S-Box at a time, by targeting the first round[9]. Next, the template is matched, and the key is recovered directly. The algorithm for the online phase is outlined in Algorithm 2 for each nibble/byte. Few intricacies associated with the attack are addressed in the following paragraphs.

Unique key recovery: The template used in the proposed attack reduces the entropy of each key nibble to 1-bit (that is, there are two choices per key nibble). The obvious question is whether the entropy can be reduced to zero or not. In other words, is it somehow possible to create a template which provides unique key suggestions for each fault pattern? The answer is negative for this particular example. This is because with the chosen fault (bit x_1 in the monomial $x_1x_2x_4$ of the first polynomial in Eq. (1)) location, no leakage happens for the variable x_3. In fact, there is no such location in the S-Box equations which can simultaneously leak information regarding all the bits. Therefore, one-bit uncertainty will always remain for the given template and for all other similar templates. However, the key can still be recovered uniquely if another template, corresponding to a different fault location, is utilized. The choice of this fault location should be such that it leaks about x_3. The main challenge in this context is to keep the number of injections as low as possible for the second template. Fortunately, it was observed that the second template can be constructed in a way so that it only

---

[8] Note that, in this attack in all our subsequent attacks, constructing the template for one S-Box is sufficient. The same template can be utilized for extracting all key nibbles of a round one by one.

[9] Extraction of round keys in a per-nibble/byte basis is done for all the attacks described in this paper.

Table 2. Template-1 for attacking the first round of PRESENT by varying the plaintext nibble. The black cells represent 1 (faulty output) and the gray cells represent 0 (correct output).

Table 3. Template-2 for attacking the first round of PRESENT. The black cells represent 1 (faulty output) and the gray cells represent 0 (correct output).

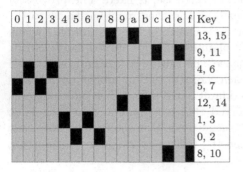

0	1	2	3	4	5	6	7	8	9	a	b	c	d	e	f	Key
								■	■							13, 15
													■	■		9, 11
■		■														4, 6
■	■															5, 7
							■	■								12, 14
			■		■											1, 3
			■	■												0, 2
														■	■	8, 10

0	Key
	2, 3, 6, 7, 10, 11, 14, 15
■	0, 1, 4, 5, 8, 9, 12, 13

requires a single fault injection. The trick is to corrupt a linear term x_3 in the same polynomial (The template is depicted in Table 3). Due to the activation-propagation property of the XOR gates, a single injection would reveal the value of the bit x_3. In practice, we take the intersection between the key suggestions obtained from two different templates and can identify the key uniquely. As a concrete example for why it works, consider the key suggestion (13, 15) from the first template. The second template will provide either of the two suggestion sets described in it. Now, since 13 and 15 only differ by the bit x_3, the suggestion set returned by template-2 is supposed to contain only one of 13 and 15. Hence taking the intersection of this second key suggestion set with the first one would uniquely determine the key.

Required number of faults: The proposed attack performs the key recovery in a nibble-wise manner. A straightforward application of Algorithm 2 for template matching here would require total 17 fault injections (16 for the first template matching and 1 for the second template matching) per nibble, and thus $17 \times 16 = 272$ fault injections for recovering the entire round key in the online phase. However, given the regularity of the fault patterns in template-1 (as shown in Table 2), the number of injections per nibble can be reduced further. Note that, each pattern consists of two faulty outputs (black cells in Table 2). *If we consider the first faulty outcome from each pattern, the index of them are unique per pattern.* In other words, if the index of the first faulty outcome in a pattern F_t is denoted as $Ind_1(F_t)$ then we have $\forall s, t, 0 \leq s, t \leq 7, s \neq t.\ Ind_1(F_s) \neq Ind_1(F_t)$. With this observation, the average number of injection for matching template-1 becomes 7.6, which is the expected value of $Ind_1(F_t)$'s for all F_t. In summary, with roughly $8 + 1 = 9$ fault injections on average, one can recover a key nibble. Another general trick for reducing the number of faults is to choose the highest degree monomial for injection so that the maximum number of bits can be leaked at once. The remaining bits can then be leaked by choosing lower degree terms and constructing templates for them. This trick reduces the number of key suggestions per pattern in a template. Moreover, we note that all fault locations within a single higher degree monomial are equivalent in terms of leakage. This fact gives extra flexibility while choosing the fault locations for an attack.

It should be observed that although the attack described in this subsection requires at most two fault locations to be corrupted to recover the key uniquely, the corruptions need not be simultaneous. In practice, one can run independent fault campaigns on the target implementation and combine the results to recover the key. A similar attack is also applicable for AES (see supplementary materiel in the extended version for a brief description of this attack). In the next subsection, we will explore the situations where the fault is injected at a middle round of the cipher. As we shall see, the attack methodology of our still allows the recovery of the key within reasonable computational and fault complexity.

3.3   Attacks on Unmasked Implementations: Middle Rounds

Classically FAs target the outer rounds of block ciphers. Attacking middle rounds are not feasible due to the extensive exhaustive search complexity involved, which becomes equal to the brute force complexity. However, the proposed template-based attack techniques do not suffer from this limitation. In this subsection, we shall investigate the feasibility of FTA on the middle rounds of a block cipher.

The main challenge in a middle round attack is that the round inputs are not accessible. Therefore, the attacks described in the last subsections cannot be directly applied in this context. However, template construction is still feasible. A single attack location, in this case, cannot provide sufficient exploitable leakage. The solution here is to corrupt multiple chosen locations and to construct a single template combining the information obtained. Unlike the previous case, where the plaintext was varying during the attack phase, in this case, it is required to

---

Algorithm 3. *BUILD_TEMPLATE_MIDDLE_ROUND*

Input: Target implementation C, Faults $fl_0, fl_1, ..., fl_h$
Output: Template $\mathcal{T}$

$\quad \mathcal{T} := \emptyset$
$\quad w := \text{GET\_SBOX\_SIZE}()$ $\qquad\qquad\qquad\qquad\qquad\qquad$ ▷ Get the width of the S-Box
$\quad \textbf{for } (0 \leq x < 2^w) \textbf{ do}$ $\qquad\qquad\qquad\qquad$ ▷ The key is known and fixed here and x is an
$\qquad\qquad\qquad\qquad\qquad\qquad\qquad\qquad\qquad\qquad$ intermediate S-Box input
$\qquad F_t := \emptyset$
$\qquad \textbf{for each } fl \in \{fl_0, fl_1,..., fl_h\} \textbf{ do}$
$\qquad\qquad y_f := C(x)^{fl}$ $\qquad\qquad\qquad$ ▷ Inject fault in one copy of the S-Box for each execution
$\qquad\qquad y_c := C(x)$
$\qquad\qquad \textbf{if } \text{DETECT\_FAULT}(y_f, y_c) \text{ == 1 then}$ $\qquad\qquad\qquad$ ▷ Fault detection function
$\qquad\qquad\qquad F_t := F_t \cup \{1\}$
$\qquad\qquad \textbf{else}$
$\qquad\qquad\qquad F_t := F_t \cup \{0\}$
$\qquad\qquad \textbf{end if}$
$\qquad \textbf{end for}$
$\qquad \mathcal{T} := \mathcal{T} \cup \{(F_t, x)\}$
$\quad \textbf{end for}$
$\quad \textbf{Return } \mathcal{T}$

Algorithm 4. *MATCH_TEMPLATE_MIDDLE_ROUND*

Input: Protected cipher with unknown key C_k, Faults $fl_0, fl_1, ..., fl_h$, Template $\mathcal{T}$
Output: Set of candidate correct states x_{cand}

    $x_{cand} := \emptyset$ ▷ Set of candidate states
    $w :=$ GET_SBOX_SIZE()
    $F_t := \emptyset$
    for each $fl \in \{fl_0, fl_1, ...fl_h\}$ **do**
        $\mathcal{O} := (C_k(p))^{fl}$ ▷ Inject fault for each execution
        if $(\mathcal{O} == 1)$ **then**   ▷ Fault detected
            $F_t := F_t \cup \{1\}$
        else
            $F_t := F_t \cup \{0\}$
        end if
    end for
    $x_{cand} := x_{cand} \cup \{\mathcal{T}(F_t)\}$
    Return x_{cand}

---

be kept fixed. Formally, the mapping from the set of observables to the set $\mathcal{F}$, in this case, is a function of fault locations. *Also, the range set $\mathcal{X}$ of the template, in this case, contains byte/nibble values from an intermediate state instead of keys (more precisely, the inputs of the S-Boxes).*

One aspect of this attack is to select the fault locations, which would lead to maximum possible leakage. In contrast to the previous attack, where corrupting the highest degree monomials leak the maximum number of bits, in this new attack we observe that linear monomials are better suited as fault locations. This is because linear monomials leak information irrespective of the value of their input or the other inputs of the S-Box, and as a result, the total number of fault injections would be minimized for them. Considering the example of PRESENT, one bit is leaked per fault location and hence 4 different locations have to be tried to extract a complete intermediate state nibble. The template building and the attack algorithm (in per S-Box basis) are outlined in Algorithm 3 and 4.

The template for the middle round attack on PRESENT is shown in Table 4, where each fl_i denotes a fault location. Since the linear terms are corrupted, each intermediate can be uniquely classified. In the online phase of the attack, the plaintext is held fixed. The specified fault locations are corrupted one at a time, and the fault patterns are constructed. An intermediate state can be recovered with this approach immediately (by applying the Algorithm 4 total 16 times). However, one should notice that recovering a single intermediate state does not allow the recovery of the round key. At least two consecutive states must be recovered for the actual key recovery. Fortunately, recovery of any state with the proposed attack strategy is fairly straightforward. Hence, one just need to recover the states corresponding to two consecutive rounds and extract one round of key in a trivial manner. In essence, the round key corresponding to any of the middle rounds can be recovered. The number of faults required for entire round key recovery is 128 in this case for PRESENT.

3.4   Discussion

The attack technique outlined for the middle rounds requires the fault to be injected at many different locations. Although the SEA attacks would also require a similar number of fault injections[10], as we show in the next section, the proposed attack strategy still works when masked implementations are targeted. This is clearly an advantage over SEA or BFA or as they are not applicable on masking implementations [18].

It is interesting to observe that a trade-off is involved regarding the required number of fault locations with the controllability of the plaintext. If the plaintext is known and can be controlled, the number of required fault locations are low. On the other hand, the number of different fault locations increases if the plaintext is kept fixed. This can be directly attributed to the leakage characteristics of the gates. The leakage from AND gates is more useful while its inputs are varying and it is exactly opposite for the XOR gates. It is worth mentioning that the middle round attacks can also be realized by corrupting several higher-order monomials in the S-Box polynomials. However, due to the relatively low leakage from AND gates for one fault, the number of injections required per location is supposed to be higher.

From the next section onward, we shall focus on attacking masked implementations. Although, masking is not meant for fault attack prevention, in certain cases it may aid the fault attack countermeasures [18]. The study on masking becomes more relevant in the present context because our attacks, in principle, are close to SCA attacks (in the sense that both tries to recover values of some intermediate state).

Table 4. Template for attacking the middle rounds of PRESENT. Here $fl_0 = x_1$ in polynomial of y_1, $fl_1 = x_3$ in polynomial of y_1, $fl_2 = x_4$ in polynomial of y_1, and $fl_3 = x_2$ in polynomial of y_4.

fl_0	fl_1	fl_2	fl_3	State		fl_0	fl_1	fl_2	fl_3	State
				0						8
				1						9
				2						a
				3						b
				4						c
				5						d
				6						e
				7						f

---

[10] In fact, one can perform the same attack at the key addition stages to recover the key directly.

4   Attack on Masked Implementations

Masking is a popular countermeasure for SCA attacks. Loosely speaking, masking implements secret sharing at the level of circuits. Over the years, several masking schemes have been proposed, the most popular one being the Threshold-Implementation (TI) [6]. For illustration purpose, in this work, we shall mostly use TI implementations.

Before going into the details of our proposed attack on masking, let us briefly comment on why SEA does not work on masking. Each fault injection in the SEA reveals one bit of information. However, each actual bit of a cipher is shared in multiple bits in the case of masking, and in order to recover the actual bit, all shares of the actual bit have to be recovered, simultaneously. Moreover, the mask changes at each execution of the cipher. Hence, even if a single bit is recovered with SEA, it becomes useless as the next execution of the cipher is suppose to change this bit with probability $\frac{1}{2}$. By the same argument, attacking linear terms in the masked S-Box polynomials would not work for key/state recovery, as attacking linear monomials typically imply faulting an XOR gate input. As an XOR gate only leaks about the faulted input bit, in this case, the attacker will end up recovering a uniformly random masked bit. **However, the FTA attack we propose next, works even while masks are unknown and varying randomly in each execution (such as in TI).** The only requirement is to repeat an unknown plaintext several times.

4.1   Leakage from Masking

Let us recall the unique property of AND gates that they leak about multiple bits, simultaneously. We typically exploit this property for breaching the security of masked implementations. To illustrate how the leakage happens, we start with a simple example. Consider the circuit depicted in Fig. 4, which corresponds to the first-order masked AND gate. The corresponding ANF equations are given as $q_0 = x_0 y_0 + r_{0,1}$ and $q_1 = x_1 y_1 + (r_{0,1} + x_0 y_1 + x_1 y_0)$. Here (q_0, q_1) represents the output shares and (x_0, x_1), (y_0, y_1) represent the input shares. *We assume that actual unmasked input to the gate (denoted as x and y) remains fixed. However, all the shares vary randomly due to the property of masking.* Consequently, all the inputs to the constituent gates of the masked circuit also vary randomly. Without loss of generality, let us now consider that a stuck-at-1 fault is induced at the input share x_0 during the computation of both the output shares. Now, from the ANF expression it can be observed that x_0 is AND-ed with y_0 and y_1 in two separate shares (i.e. $x_0 y_0$ in q_0 and $x_0 y_1$ in q_1). So, faulting x_0 would leak information about both y_0 and y_1. From the properties of the AND gate, the stuck-at-1 fault will propagate to the output only if $x_0 = 0$ and $y_i = 1$ with $i \in \{0, 1\}$. However, it should also be noted that if faults from both of the gates propagate simultaneously, then they (the faults) will cancel each other. The actual output of the masked AND circuit (i.e. $q_0 + q_1$) will be faulty only if one of the constituent AND gates propagate the fault effect. More specifically, the effective fault propagation requires either $(y_0 = 0, y_1 = 1)$ or $(y_0 = 1, y_1 = 0)$.

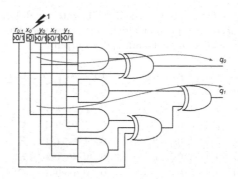

Fig. 4. Fault propagation through masked AND gate.

In summary, *the fault will propagate if and only if the actual unshared bit y ($y = y_0 + y_1$) equals to 1 and $x_0 = 0$. There will be no fault propagation if $y = 0$.* The fact is illustrated in the truth table at Table 5.

The above-mentioned observation establishes the fact that *a properly placed fault can leak the actual unshared input bits from a masked implementation.* This observation is sufficient for bypassing masking countermeasures as we shall show subsequently in this paper. However, to strongly establish our claim, we go through several examples before describing a complete attack algorithm.

4.2 Leakage from TI AND Gates

The second example of our involves a TI implemented AND gate. We specifically focus on a four-share realization of a first-order masked AND gate proposed in [6]. The ANF representation of the implementation is given as:

$$
\begin{aligned}
q_0 &= (x_2 + x_3)(y_1 + y_2) + y_1 + y_2 + y_3 + x_1 + x_2 + x_3 \\
q_1 &= (x_0 + x_2)(y_0 + y_3) + y_0 + y_2 + y_3 + x_0 + x_2 + x_3 \\
q_2 &= (x_1 + x_3)(y_0 + y_3) + y_1 + x_1 \\
q_3 &= (x_0 + x_1)(y_1 + y_2) + y_0 + x_0
\end{aligned}
\tag{2}
$$

Here (x_0, x_1, x_2, x_3), (y_0, y_1, y_2, y_3) and (q_0, q_1, q_2, q_3) represent the 4-shared inputs and output, respectively. Let us consider a fault injection at the input share x_3 which sets it to 0. An in-depth investigation of the ANF equations reveals that x_3 is multiplied with $y_1 + y_2$ and $y_0 + y_3$. The leakage due to this fault will reach the output only when $y_0 + y_1 + y_2 + y_3 = y = 1$. One may notice that x_3 also exists as linear monomial in the ANF expressions. However, the effect of this linear monomial gets canceled out in the computation of the actual output bit. Hence the fault effect of this linear term does not hamper the desired fault propagation. In essence, the TI AND gate is not secured against the proposed attack model.

TI AND gates are often utilized as constituents for Masked S-Boxes. One prominent example of this is a compact 4-bit S-Box from [23]. The circuit diagram of the S-Box is depicted in Fig. 5 with 4-shared TI gates. We specifically

Table 5. Output status for faulted masked AND gate for different input values. The variables x and y are used for representing the unshared variables (i.e. $x_0 + x_1 = x$ and $y_0 + y_1 = y$). C and F denote correct and faulty outputs.

x_0	x	y_0	y	$r_{0,1}$	C/F		x_0	x	y_0	y	$r_{0,1}$	C/F
0	0	0	0	0	C		0	0	0	0	1	C
0	0	0	1	0	F		0	0	0	1	1	F
0	1	0	0	0	C		0	1	0	0	1	C
0	1	0	1	0	F		0	1	0	1	1	F
0	0	1	1	0	F		0	0	1	1	1	F
0	0	1	0	0	C		0	0	1	0	1	C
0	1	1	1	0	F		0	1	1	1	1	F
0	1	1	0	0	C		0	1	1	0	1	C
1	1	0	0	0	C		1	1	0	0	1	C
1	1	0	1	0	C		1	1	0	1	1	C
1	0	0	0	0	C		1	0	0	0	1	C
1	0	0	1	0	C		1	0	0	1	1	C
1	1	1	1	0	C		1	1	1	1	1	C
1	1	1	0	0	C		1	1	1	0	1	C
1	0	1	1	0	C		1	0	1	1	1	C
1	0	1	0	0	C		1	0	1	0	1	C

target the highlighted AND gate in the structure, which is TI implemented. If we inject the same fault as we did for the TI AND gate example, the fault effect propagates to the output with the same probability as of the TI AND. This is because there is no non-linear gate in the output propagation path of this fault. As a result, we can conclude that even this S-Box leaks. It is worth mentioning that the choice of the target AND gate is totally arbitrary and, in principle, any of the TI AND gates depicted in the circuit can be targeted. One may also target the OR gate based on the same principle. However, the non-controlling input of OR being 1, the leakage will happen for the input value 0 instead of value 1.

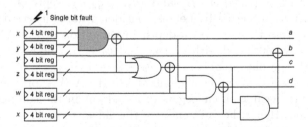

Fig. 5. Fault propagation through an S-Box having TI gates. Note that each constituent AND gate is 4-shared, and thus each wire and register are of 4-bit.

One important practical question is *how many of such desired fault locations may exist for a masked implementation*. It turns out there are plenty of such locations even for the simple TI AND gate implementation. It is apparent that any of the input shares from (x_0, x_1, x_2, x_3) or (y_0, y_1, y_2, y_3) can be faulted for causing leakage. In fact, changing the target input share will enable recovery of both x and y separately. Another point here is that *whether there will always exist such favorable situations where faulting a share will lead to the leakage of an unmasked bit*. We argue that it will always be the case because the output of any masking scheme must always satisfy the property of correctness. Putting it in a different way, the output of the masked AND gate must always result in $q = xy = (x_0 + x_1 + x_2 + x_3)(y_0 + y_1 + y_2 + y_3)$. Although shares are never supposed to be combined during the masked computation, ensuring correctness always requires that the monomials $x_3 y_0$ $x_3 y_1$, $x_3 y_2$ and $x_3 y_3$ are computed at some share during the masked computation (considering x_3 to be the fault location). Hence, irrespective of the masking scheme used, we are supposed to get fault locations which are exploitable for our purpose (i.e., leaks $(y_0 + y_1 + y_2 + y_3) = y$). Finding out such locations becomes even easier with our template-based setup where extensive profiling of the implementation is feasible for known key values.

So far we have discussed regarding the feasibility of leakage for masked AND gates, and S-Boxes constructed with masked gates. The obvious next step is to verify our claim for explicitly shared S-Boxes which we elaborate in the next subsection. As it will be shown, attacks are still possible for such S-Boxes.

4.3   Leakage from Shared S-Boxes

There are numerous examples of TI S-Boxes in the literature. For the sake of illustration, we choose the 4×4 S-Box from the GIFT block cipher [24]. For our purpose, we select the three-share TI implementation of this S-Box proposed in [25]. One should note that the GIFT S-Box is originally cubic. In order to realize a three-shared TI, the original S-Box function $S : GF(2)^4 \rightarrow GF(2)^4$ is broken into two bijective sub-functions $F : GF(2)^4 \rightarrow GF(2)^4$ and $G : GF(2)^4 \rightarrow GF(2)^4$, such that $S(X) = F(G(X))$. Both F and G are quadratic functions for which three-share TI is feasible. In [25], it was found that for the most optimized implementation in terms of Gate Equivalence (GE), F and G should be constructed as follows:

$$G(x_3, x_2, x_1, x_0) = (g_3, g_2, g_1, g_0) \qquad F(x_3, x_2, x_1, x_0) = (f_3, f_2, f_1, f_0)$$

$$g_3 = x_0 + x_1 + x_1 x_2 \qquad\qquad f_3 = x_1 x_0 + x_3$$

$$g_2 = 1 + x_2 \qquad\qquad (3)\quad f_2 = 1 + x_1 + x_2 + x_3 + x_3 x_0 \quad (4)$$

$$g_1 = x_1 + x_2 x_0 \qquad\qquad f_1 = x_0 + x_1$$

$$g_0 = x_0 + x_1 + x_1 x_0 + x_2 + x_3 \qquad f_0 = 1 + x_0$$

Here x_0 is denotes the LSB and x_3 is the MSB. Both G and F are shared into three functions each denoted as G_1, G_2, G_3 and F_1, F_2, F_3, respectively. Details of these shared functions can be found in [25]. For our current purpose,

Table 6. Output status for faulted masked AND gate for different input values with bit-flip fault. The variables x and y are used for representing the unshared variables (i.e. $x_0 + x_1 = x$ and $y_0 + y_1 = y$).

x_0	x	y_0	y	$r_{0,1}$	C/F
0	0	0	0	0	C
0	0	0	1	0	F
0	1	0	0	0	C
0	1	0	1	0	F
0	0	1	1	0	F
0	0	1	0	0	C
0	1	1	1	0	F
0	1	1	0	0	C
1	1	0	0	0	C
1	1	0	1	0	F
1	0	0	0	0	C
1	0	0	1	0	F
1	1	1	1	0	F
1	1	1	0	0	C
1	0	1	1	0	F
1	0	1	0	0	C

x_0	x	y_0	y	$r_{0,1}$	C/F
0	0	0	0	1	C
0	0	0	1	1	F
0	1	0	0	1	C
0	1	0	1	1	F
0	0	1	1	1	F
0	0	1	0	1	C
0	1	1	1	1	F
0	1	1	0	1	C
1	1	0	0	1	C
1	1	0	1	1	F
1	0	0	0	1	C
1	0	0	1	1	F
1	1	1	1	1	F
1	1	1	0	1	C
1	0	1	1	1	F
1	0	1	0	1	C

we only focus on the shares corresponding to the bit g_0 of G. The ANF equations corresponding to this bit are given as follows:

$$g_{10} = x_0^3 + x_1^3 + x_2^3 + x_3^3 + x_0^2 x_1^2 + x_0^2 x_1^3 + x_0^3 x_1^2$$
$$g_{20} = x_0^1 + x_1^1 + x_2^1 + x_3^1 + x_0^1 x_1^3 + x_0^3 x_1^1 + x_0^3 x_1^3 \tag{5}$$
$$g_{30} = x_0^2 + x_1^2 + x_2^2 + x_3^2 + x_0^1 x_1^1 + x_0^1 x_1^2 + x_0^2 x_1^1$$

Here $x_i = x_i^3 + x_i^2 + x_i^1$ for $i \in \{0, 1, 2, 3\}$, and $g_0 = g_{10} + g_{20} + g_{30}$.

We now search for suitable fault locations for our purpose. One such feasible location is x_0^2. One should observe that the leakage due to this fault injection actually depends upon $(x_1^1 + x_1^2 + x_1^3 + 1) = x_1 + 1$. Hence the fault propagation will take place in this case while x_1 is equal to zero. In a similar fashion, it can be shown that a fault injection at x_1^2 will leak the actual value of x_0. *One interesting observation here is that fault injection at any of the shares of an input bit x_i is equivalent to the injection at any other share of the same input. This is because all of them cause the leakage of the other unshared input bit associated.* This is, in fact, extremely useful from an attacker's point of view as she may select any one of them for leaking information.

4.4   Different Fault Models

So far, in this paper, we have mostly utilized stuck-at faults for all our illustrations. The attacks are equivalent for stuck-at-0 and stuck-at-1 fault models.

Interestingly, they are also equally applicable while the fault flips the value of the target bit. To show why it works, we recall the concept of fault activation and propagation described at the beginning of this work. Fault reaches the output of a gate from its input only while these two events are satisfied, simultaneously. Considering AND gates (and other non-linear gates), the fault activation depends on specific values at the target input for stuck-at faults (value 0 for stuck-at 1, and value 1 for stuck-at 0). However, for the bit-flip fault model, the fault is always active. In other words, in the case of stuck-at faults, the fault activation event happens with probability $\frac{1}{2}$, whereas, for bit-flip faults, it happens with probability 1. The fault propagation, however, still depends on the occurrence of a non-controlling value at other inputs of the gate. Hence, the main property we exploit for attacking masking schemes (that is, the fault propagation to the output depends on the value of unmasked bits) still holds for bit-flip fault models, and attacks are still feasible. In fact, it is found that the required number of injections become roughly half for bit-flip faults compared to stuck-at faults. In other words, in a noise-free scenario, one injection per fault location can recover the target unshared bit for bit-flip faults. To support our claim, we present the truth table corresponding to the simple first-order masked AND gate once again in Table 6, this time for a bit flip fault at x_0.

4.5 Template Attack on Masked PRESENT: Main Idea

In this subsection, we utilize the concepts developed in the previous subsections for attacking a complete block cipher implementation. A three-share TI implementation of PRESENT, with simple redundancy countermeasure, is considered for our experiments. As for the three-shared TI, we implemented the lightweight scheme proposed in [17]. Considering the fact that PRESENT S-Box is also cubic, it is first represented as a combination of two quadratic bijective mappings F and G. Each of these mappings is then converted to three-shared TI implementations. Generally, registers are used to interface the outputs of G and inputs of F. The implementation of the linear mappings is straightforward. For the sake of completeness, the keys are also masked. As for the fault countermeasure is concerned, we implemented the most common form of redundancy, where the redundancy check happens at the final stage just before outputting the ciphertext. Two separate copies of the masked PRESENT with different mask values are instantiated as two redundant branches of computation. Upon detection of a fault, the output is muted or randomized[11].

The three-shared ANF equations for F and G functions can be found in [17]. For our purpose, it is sufficient to focus only on the shared implementation of F, which is given below. For the sake of illustration, we first present the unshared version of F (Eq. (6)), and then the shares corresponding to it (Eq. (7)). Note that, in Eq. (6) x_0 denote the LSB and x_3 denote the MSB.

---

[11] Actually, our attacks do not depend on this choice and would equally apply for any detection-type countermeasure.

$$F(x_3, x_2, x_1, x_0) = (f_3, f_2, f_1, f_0)$$
$$f_3 = x_2 + x_1 + x_0 + x_3 x_0; f_2 = x_3 + x_1 x_0; f_1 = x_2 + x_1 + x_3 x_0; \quad (6)$$
$$f_0 = x_1 + x_2 x_0.$$

$$f_{10} = x_1^2 + x_2^2 x_0^2 + x_2^2 x_0^3 + x_2^3 x_0^2 \qquad f_{11} = x_2^2 + x_1^2 + x_3^2 x_0^2 + x_3^2 x_0^3 + x_3^3 x_0^2$$
$$f_{20} = x_1^3 + x_2^3 x_0^3 + x_2^1 x_0^3 + x_2^3 x_0^1 \qquad f_{21} = x_2^3 + x_1^3 + x_3^3 x_0^3 + x_3^1 x_0^3 + x_3^3 x_0^1 \quad (7)$$
$$f_{30} = x_1^1 + x_2^1 x_0^1 + x_2^1 x_0^2 + x_2^2 x_0^1 \qquad f_{31} = x_2^1 + x_1^1 + x_3^1 x_0^1 + x_3^1 x_0^2 + x_3^2 x_0^1$$

$$f_{12} = x_3^2 + x_1^2 x_0^2 + x_1^2 x_0^3 + x_1^3 x_0^2 \qquad f_{13} = x_2^2 + x_1^2 + x_0^2 + x_3^2 x_0^2 + x_3^2 x_0^3 + x_3^3 x_0^2$$
$$f_{22} = x_3^3 + x_1^3 x_0^3 + x_1^1 x_0^3 + x_1^3 x_0^1 \qquad f_{23} = x_2^3 + x_1^3 + x_0^3 + x_3^3 x_0^3 + x_3^1 x_0^3 + x_3^3 x_0^1$$
$$f_{32} = x_3^1 + x_1^1 x_0^1 + x_1^1 x_0^2 + x_1^2 x_0^1 \qquad f_{33} = x_2^1 + x_1^1 + x_0^1 + x_3^1 x_0^1 + x_3^1 x_0^2 + x_3^2 x_0^1$$

4.6 Middle Round Attacks

The most interesting question in the current context is how to attack the middle rounds of a cipher without direct access to the plaintexts or ciphertexts. The attacks in the first round with known plaintext will become trivial once the middle round attacks are figured out. Note that, *in all of these attacks (even for the known-plaintext case), we assume the plaintext to be fixed, whereas the masks vary randomly.* The attacker is only provided with the information whether the outcome is faulty or not, and nothing else. For the case of middle-round attacks, the value of the fixed plaintext is unknown to the adversary.

Template Construction: The very first step of the attack is template-building. The attacker is assumed to have complete knowledge of the implementation and key, and also can figure out suitable locations for fault injection. One critical question here is how many different fault locations will be required for the attack to happen. Let us take a closer look at this issue in the context of the shared PRESENT S-Box. Without loss of generality, let us assume the input share x_0^2 as the fault injection point during the computation of the shares (f_{10}, f_{20}, f_{30}). It is easy to observe that this fault leaks about the expression $(x_2^2 + x_2^3 + x_2^1) = x_2$. In a similar fashion the fault location x_0^2 during the computation of the shares (f_{11}, f_{21}, f_{31}) leaks about x_3; the location x_0^2 during the computation of the shares (f_{12}, f_{22}, f_{32}) leaks about x_1; and the location x_3^2 during the computation of (f_{13}, f_{23}, f_{33}) leaks about x_0. Consequently, we obtain the template shown in Table 7 for independent injections at these selected locations.

Algorithm 5. *BUILD_TEMPLATE_MASK*

Input: Masked cipher C, Faults $fl_0, fl_1, \cdots, fl_h$, Number of masked executions per input M
Output: Template $\mathcal{T}$
   $\mathcal{T} := \emptyset$
   $w :=$ GET_SBOX_SIZE()   ▷ Get the width of the S-Box
   for $(0 \leq x < 2^w)$ **do**
     $F_t := \emptyset$
     for each $fl \in \{fl_0, fl_1, \cdots, fl_h\}$ **do**
       $\mathcal{V} := \emptyset$
       for $m_{ind} \leq M$ **do**
         $m :=$ GEN_MASK()   ▷ Generate fresh mask for each execution
         $y_f := C(x, m)^{fl}$ ▷ Inject fault in one copy of the S-Box for each execution
         $m :=$ GEN_MASK()
         $y_c := C(x, m)$
         if DETECT_FAULT(y_f, y_c) == 1 **then**   ▷ Fault detection function
           $\mathcal{V} := \mathcal{V} \cup \{1\}$
         else
           $\mathcal{V} := \mathcal{V} \cup \{0\}$
         end if
       end for
       if $\mathcal{V} \sim \mathcal{D}_1$ **then**
         $F_t := F_t \cup \{1\}$
       else
         $F_t := F_t \cup \{0\}$
       end if
     end for
     $\mathcal{T} := \mathcal{T} \cup \{(F_t, x)\}$
   end for
   Return $\mathcal{T}$

The template construction algorithm is outlined in Algorithm 5. The aim is to characterize each S-Box input (denoted as x in the Algorithm 5) with respect to the fault locations. The plaintext nibble is kept fixed in this case during each fault injection campaign, while the mask varies randomly. One important observation at this point is that the fault injection campaign has to be repeated several times with different random mask for each valuation of an S-Box input. To understand why this is required, once again, we go back to the concept of fault activation and propagation. Let us consider any of the target fault locations; for example, x_0^2. The expression which leaks information is $(x_2^2 + x_2^3 + x_2^1)$. Now, for the fault to be activated in a stuck-at fault scenario, x_0^2 must take a specific value (0 or 1 depending on the fault). Since all the shared values change randomly at each execution of the cipher, we can expect that the fault activation happens with probability $\frac{1}{2}$ [12]. Once the fault is activated, the propagation happens depending on the value of the other input of the gate which actually causes the leakage. In order to let the fault activate, the injection campaigns have to run several times, corresponding to a specific fault location for both the template building and online attack stage. Given the activation probability of $\frac{1}{2}$, 2 executions (injections) with different valuations at x_0^2, would be required on average.

As a consequence of performing several executions of the cipher corresponding to one fault location, we are supposed to obtain a set of suggestions for the valuation of the bit to be leaked. For example, for two separate executions we

---

[12] For bit-flip faults the fault activation will happen with probability 1.

Table 7. Template for attacking TI PRESENT (middle round). The black cells indicate a faulty outcome and gray cells represent correct outcome.

$fl_0 = x_0^2$ (f_{10}, f_{20}, f_{30})	$fl_1 = x_0^2$ (f_{11}, f_{21}, f_{31})	$fl_2 = x_0^2$ (f_{12}, f_{22}, f_{32})	$fl_3 = x_3^2$ (f_{13}, f_{23}, f_{33})	State		$fl_0 = x_0^2$ (f_{10}, f_{20}, f_{30})	$fl_1 = x_0^2$ (f_{11}, f_{21}, f_{31})	$fl_2 = x_0^2$ (f_{12}, f_{22}, f_{32})	$fl_3 = x_3^2$ (f_{13}, f_{23}, f_{33})	State
⬛	⬛	⬛	⬜	0		⬛	⬜	⬜	⬛	8
⬛	⬛	⬜	⬜	1		⬛	⬜	⬜	⬜	9
⬜	⬛	⬛	⬛	2		⬜	⬜	⬛	⬜	a
⬜	⬜	⬛	⬛	3		⬜	⬜	⬜	⬛	b
⬜	⬛	⬜	⬜	4		⬜	⬛	⬜	⬜	c
⬜	⬜	⬜	⬜	5		⬜	⬜	⬜	⬜	d
⬛	⬜	⬜	⬜	6		⬜	⬜	⬛	⬜	e
⬛	⬛	⬜	⬛	7		⬛	⬜	⬜	⬛	f

may get two separate suggestions for the value of $(x_2^2 + x_2^3 + x_2^1)$. If the fault at x_0^2 is not activated, the suggestion will always be 0. However, if the fault is activated, the suggestion reflects the actual value of x_2. There is no way of understanding when the fault at x_0^2 gets activated. So, a suitable technique has to be figured out to discover the actual value of x_2 from the obtained set of values. Fortunately, the solution to this problem is simple. Let us consider the set of observables corresponding to a specific fault location as a random variable $\mathcal{V}$ taking values 0 or 1. The value of $\mathcal{V}$ is zero if no fault propagates to the output and 1, otherwise. Mathematically, $\mathcal{V}$ can be assumed as a Bernoulli distributed random variable. Now, it is easy to observe that *if the actual value to be leaked is 0, $\mathcal{V}$ will never take a value 1 (that is, the fault never propagates to the output)*. Therefore, the probability distribution of $\mathcal{V}$ for this case can be written as:

$$\mathcal{D}_0 : \mathbb{P}[\mathcal{V} = 0] = 1 \text{ and } \mathbb{P}[\mathcal{V} = 1] = 0 \tag{8}$$

If the value to be leaked is 1, the probability distribution of $\mathcal{V}$ becomes[13]:

$$\mathcal{D}_1 : \mathbb{P}[\mathcal{V} = 0] = \frac{1}{2} \text{ and } \mathbb{P}[\mathcal{V} = 1] = \frac{1}{2} \tag{9}$$

The template construction procedure becomes easy after the identification of these two distributions. *More precisely, if $\mathcal{V} \sim \mathcal{D}_0$ the corresponding location in the template takes a value 0. The opposite thing happens for $\mathcal{V} \sim \mathcal{D}_1$.*

---

[13] In the case of bit-flip faults $\mathcal{D}_1 : \mathbb{P}[\mathcal{V} = 0] = 0$ and $\mathbb{P}[\mathcal{V} = 1] = 1$, as the fault always gets activated in this case.

Algorithm 6. *MATCH_TEMPLATE_MASK*

Input: Protected cipher with unknown key C_k, Faults $fl_0, fl_1, \cdots, fl_h$, Template $\mathcal{T}$
Output: Set of candidate correct states x_{cand}

$\quad x_{cand} := \emptyset$ ▷ Set of candidate states
$\quad w := \text{GET\_SBOX\_SIZE}()$
$\quad F_t := \emptyset$
$\quad \textbf{for each } fl \in \{fl_0, fl_1, \cdots, fl_h\} \textbf{ do}$
$\quad\quad \mathcal{V} := \emptyset$
$\quad\quad \textbf{for } m_{ind} \leq M \textbf{ do}$
$\quad\quad\quad \mathcal{O} := (\overline{C_k}(P))^{fl}$ ▷ Inject fault for each masked execution
$\quad\quad\quad \textbf{if } (\mathcal{O} == 1) \textbf{ then}$ ▷ Fault detected
$\quad\quad\quad\quad \mathcal{V} := \mathcal{V} \cup \{1\}$
$\quad\quad\quad \textbf{else}$
$\quad\quad\quad\quad \mathcal{V} := \mathcal{V} \cup \{0\}$
$\quad\quad\quad \textbf{end if}$
$\quad\quad \textbf{end for}$
$\quad\quad \textbf{if } \mathcal{V} \sim \mathcal{D}_1 \textbf{ then}$
$\quad\quad\quad F_t := F_t \cup \{1\}$
$\quad\quad \textbf{else}$
$\quad\quad\quad F_t := F_t \cup \{0\}$
$\quad\quad \textbf{end if}$
$\quad \textbf{end for}$
$\quad x_{cand} := x_{cand} \cup \{\mathcal{T}(F_t)\}$
$\quad \textbf{Return } x_{cand}$

Online Phase: The online phase of the attack algorithm is outlined in Algorithm 6. Fundamentally it is similar to the template construction phase. We keep the plaintext fixed and run the fault campaigns at pre-decided locations. The templates are decided by observing the output distributions of the random variable $\mathcal{V}$ as described in the previous section. At the end of this step, one round of the cipher is recovered. In order to recover the complete round key, recovery of two consecutive rounds is essential. Recovery of another round is trivial with this approach, and therefore, a round key can be recovered uniquely.

Number of Faults: In the case of PRESENT, we use 4 fault locations, and each of them requires several fault injections with the mask changing randomly. The number of injections required for each of these locations depends upon the number of samples required to estimate the distribution of the variable $\mathcal{V}$ accurately. In ideal case, two fault injections on average should reveal the actual leakage for stuck-at faults. Experimentally, we found that 4–5 injections on average are required to reveal the actual distribution of $\mathcal{V}$[14]. The increased number is caused by the fact that an entire mask of 128-bit is generated randomly in our implementation and the activation of an injected fault happens with a slightly different probability than expected. Assuming, 5 injections required per fault location, the total number of fault requirements for a nibble becomes roughly 20. Therefore, around $32 \times 20 = 640$ faults are required to extract the entire round key of the PRESENT cipher (For bit-flip faults the count is 128 in a noise-free case.)[15]. Note that, in practical experiments, these numbers may rise

---

[14] For bit-flip faults, the number of injections per location is 1.
[15] Given the fact, that PRESENT uses an 80-bit master key, and 64-bit round keys, the remaining keyspace after one round key extraction would be of size 2^{16}, which is trivial to search exhaustively.

given the fact that some of the injections may be unsuccessful or the fault may hit wrong locations. In the next subsection, we show that the FTA is robust against such random noise in fault injection.

4.7   Handling Noisy Fault Injections

Noise in fault injection is a practical phenomenon. The primary sources of noise are the injection instruments and certain algorithmic features. The manifestation could be either a missed injection or injection at an undesired location. However, in both cases, the observable distribution may directly get affected. In this subsection, we investigate how noise in fault injection affects the attacks proposed in this work. For simplicity, here, we shall mainly consider the scenario where noise is random and uncorrelated with the actual information. A different noise scenario (where the noise is algorithmic and correlated with the signal), in the context of infective countermeasures, has been discussed in the supplementary material of the extended version.

The main reason behind the noise affecting the observable is that wherever a fault happens, it propagates to the output. As a result, the fault patterns for template matching cannot be constructed properly during the online phase. However, given the fact that a similar device is available for profiling in the offline phase, the noise distribution can be characterized quite efficiently, which eventually makes the attacks successful. As described in Sect. 4.6, for a specific fault location inside the S-Box the observable is a Bernoulli distributed random variable ($\mathcal{V}$). The random variable corresponding to the noisy version of this distribution is denoted as $\mathcal{V}'$. In order to make the attacks happen, we need to decide actual fault patterns by compensating the effect of noise. As already shown in Eq. (8), and (9), the noise-free distributions $\mathcal{D}_0$ and $\mathcal{D}_1$ only depend upon the leaked values. The main task there was to decide whether the noise-free random variable for the observable $\mathcal{V}$ is distributed according to $\mathcal{D}_0$ or $\mathcal{D}_1$.

Let us now characterize the noisy distribution. For convenience, let us define another random variable $\mathcal{V}_n$ denoting the distribution of the noise. The noisy random variable $\mathcal{V}'$ is then distributed as either of $\mathcal{D}_0'$ or $\mathcal{D}_1'$ defined as follows:

$$
\begin{aligned}
\mathcal{D}_0' : &P[\mathcal{V}' = 1] = p_{sig} \times P[\mathcal{V} = 1 | x = 0] + (1 - p_{sig}) \times P[\mathcal{V}_n = 1] \\
&P[\mathcal{V}' = 0] = 1 - P[\mathcal{V}' = 1]
\end{aligned}
\tag{10}
$$

and

$$
\begin{aligned}
\mathcal{D}_1' : &P[\mathcal{V}' = 1] = p_{sig} \times P[\mathcal{V} = 1 | x = 1] + (1 - p_{sig}) \times P[\mathcal{V}_n = 1] \\
&P[\mathcal{V}' = 0] = 1 - P[\mathcal{V}' = 1]
\end{aligned}
\tag{11}
$$

Here p_{sig} represents the signal probability, which can be characterized during the template building phase along with $\mathcal{V}_n$. The random variable x denotes the leaking intermediate (one component of the fault pattern). The decision making procedure for fault pattern recovery now can be stated as:

Decide the outcome (one component of the target fault pattern) to be 0 *(no fault propagation) if* $\mathcal{V}' \sim \mathcal{D}'_0$, *and to be* 1, *otherwise.*

Let us now try to see how the fault patterns can be recovered from the noisy distributions. The expected value $\mu_{\mathcal{V}_n}$ of $\mathcal{V}_n$ (which is nothing but $P[\mathcal{V}_n = 1]$) is normally distributed by Central Limit Theorem. This makes the mean of $\mathcal{D}'_0$ (denoted as $\mathcal{D}_{\mu_0}$) and $\mathcal{D}'_1$ ($\mathcal{D}_{\mu_1}$) normally distributed as well. In order to make the abovementioned decision process work with high confidence, both the means should be accurately estimated, and their distributions should overlap as less as possible. We now state our detection procedure for the fault patterns. Corresponding to each fault location, we perform the fault injection campaign for several different mask values and gather a sufficient number of observations for the noisy observable random variable $\mathcal{V}'$. The mean of $\mathcal{V}'$ is next estimated as $\mu_{\mathcal{V}'}$. In the next step, we estimate the probability of $\mu_{\mathcal{V}'}$ belonging to any of the two distributions $\mathcal{D}_{\mu_0}$ or $\mathcal{D}_{\mu_1}$. More precisely, we calculate the following:

$$P[\mathcal{D}_{\mu_0} \mid \mu_{\mathcal{V}'}] \text{ and } P[\mathcal{D}_{\mu_1} \mid \mu_{\mathcal{V}'}] \tag{12}$$

The outcome (one component of the target fault pattern) is assumed to take the value for which the probability is the highest.

In order to consider random noise distribution, here we set $P[\mathcal{V}_n = 1] = P[\mathcal{V}_n = 0] = 0.5$ (ref. Eq. (10) and (11)) without loss of generality. However, the proposed method also works for other noise distributions. Both signal probability p_{sig} and the noise distribution are considered to be known from the initial profiling and template building phase. In the online phase, the mean of the collected observables are calculated (per fault location), and its probability for belonging to any of $\mathcal{D}_{\mu_0}$ or $\mathcal{D}_{\mu_1}$ is calculated. The higher among these two probabilities give us the correct answer corresponding to that fault location. Once the entire fault pattern is recovered, the intermediate state can be found. It is observed that by increasing the number of injections per location at the online stage, it is possible to recover the desired states accurately even for very low signal values. Figure 6 presents the variation of fault injection count (per location) with the noise probability $(1 - p_{sig})$. Evidently, low signal probability requires a higher number of injections.

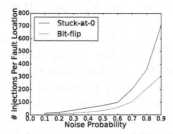

Fig. 6. Variation in number of injections with respect to noise probability. 100 independent experiments (with different key-plaintext pairs) have been performed for each probability value, and the median is plotted.

5 Practical Validation

The applicability of the proposed FTA attacks has been validated for both hardware and software implementations. Our first validation experiment performs the FTA attack on a hardware implementation of PRESENT having first-order TI [17] (and temporal redundancy-based fault detection) with Electromagnetic (EM) pulse-based fault injection. We found that EM-induced faults are precise enough to perform the FTA. Moreover, the EM injection does not require chip de-packaging and explicit access to the clock/voltage lines. Our target platform is an FPGA implementation of the protected PRESENT. We assume that the adversary has complete access to one of the FPGA implementations on which she can construct the fault templates. The target also belongs to the same FPGA family, and the configuration bit file of the design is the same one. The FTA attack we perform in this case is the one described in Sect. 4.6. In order to realize the desired faults, we target the internal registers situated at the inputs of the F function of the shared PRESENT S-Box.

The hardware experiment in this context is detailed in the supplementary material of the extended version. The faults injected in this experiment were bit faults targeted to precise locations within a register. One of the key observations is that **different bit locations within a register can be targeted by varying the fault injection parameters (especially the location of the EM probe over the target chip)**. Moreover, the generated faults are *repeatable* in the sense that they can induce the same fault effect arbitrary number of times at a given location with the injection parameters kept fixed. Indeed there are some noise during injection. However, the noise effect can be undone by increasing the number of observations at a specific location. During the profiling phase the noisy injections were detected assuming the knowledge of the key and masks, and the probability of the noise is estimated as the fraction of noisy injections among the total samples collected at a specific fault location. Perhaps the most crucial property of the fault injections is their *reproducability*. **By reproducability, we mean that the faults can be regenerated on another device from the same family with the same injection parameters found during the template-building phase.** This property has been validated practically in our experiments on FPGA platforms. Finally, we were able to perform complete key recovery from the hardware platform with 3150–3300 faults for different plaintext-key pairs.

The second example of ours performs simulated fault injection for a publicly available masked implementation of AES from [26], which uses Trichina Gates [27]. One should note that profiling of the target implementation to detect desired fault locations is an important factor in FTA attacks. This particular example demonstrates how to perform such profiling for a relatively less understood public implementation. The target implementation of ours is targeted for 32-bit Cortex M4 platform with Thumb-2 instruction set. Since the original implementation, in this case, lacks fault countermeasure, we added simple temporal redundancy, that is the cipher is executed multiple times, and the ciphertexts are matched before output. In all of our experiments, the observable is a string of $0, 1$ bits with its corresponding interpretations. Further details on this validation experiment can be found in the extended version of this paper.

6   Conclusion

Modern cryptographic devices incorporate special algorithmic tricks to throttle both SCA and FA. In this paper, we propose a new class of attacks which can efficiently bypass most of the state-of-the-art countermeasures against SCA and FA even if they are incorporated together. The attacks, abbreviated as FTA, are template-based and exploit the characteristics of basic gates under the influence of faults for information leakage. Although the fault model is similar to the SIFA attacks, the exploitation mechanism is entirely different from SIFA. Most importantly, FTA enables attacks on middle rounds of a protected cipher implementation, which is beyond the capability of SIFA or any other existing FA technique proposed so far. Middle round attacks without explicit knowledge of plaintexts and ciphertexts may render many well-known block cipher-based cryptographic protocols vulnerable. Practical validation of the attacks has been shown for an SCA-FA protected hardware implementation of PRESENT and a publicly available protected software implementation of AES. A comprehensive discussion on the impact of FTA over certain other classes of FA countermeasures is presented in the extended version of this paper.

Several future directions can be pointed out at this point to enhance FTA attacks. One feature of the current version of the attack is that it prefers bit faults. Although repeatable and reproducible bit faults are found to be practical, one potential future work could be to investigate if this requirement can be relaxed further. Another interesting exercise is to analyze the recently proposed SIFA [28] countermeasures. An FTA adversary, enhanced with the power of side channel analysis should be able to exploit some basic features of such countermeasures (such as correction operation) for potential information leakage. One future application would be to make these attacks work for secured public key implementations. Another potential future work is to figure out a suitable countermeasure against FTA attacks.

Acknowledgements. Debdeep Mukhopadhyay would like to acknowledge Synopsys Inc, USA (for partial support through the grant entitled "Formal Methods for Physical Security Verification of Cryptographic Designs Against Fault Attacks"), Defence Research and Development Organisation (DRDO), India (for partial support through the grant entitled, "Secure Resource-constrained Communication Framework for Tactical Networks using Physically Unclonable Functions"), and Department of Science and Technology (DST), Government of India (for partial support through the Swarnajayanti Fellowship grant).

References

1. Chari, S., Rao, J.R., Rohatgi, P.: Template attacks. In: Kaliski, B.S., Koç, K., Paar, C. (eds.) CHES 2002. LNCS, vol. 2523, pp. 13–28. Springer, Heidelberg (2003). https://doi.org/10.1007/3-540-36400-5_3

2. Boneh, D., DeMillo, R.A., Lipton, R.J.: On the importance of checking cryptographic protocols for faults. In: Fumy, W. (ed.) EUROCRYPT 1997. LNCS, vol. 1233, pp. 37–51. Springer, Heidelberg (1997). https://doi.org/10.1007/3-540-69053-0_4
3. Biham, E., Shamir, A.: Differential fault analysis of secret key cryptosystems. In: Kaliski, B.S. (ed.) CRYPTO 1997. LNCS, vol. 1294, pp. 513–525. Springer, Heidelberg (1997). https://doi.org/10.1007/BFb0052259
4. Ishai, Y., Sahai, A., Wagner, D.: Private circuits: securing hardware against probing attacks. In: Boneh, D. (ed.) CRYPTO 2003. LNCS, vol. 2729, pp. 463–481. Springer, Heidelberg (2003). https://doi.org/10.1007/978-3-540-45146-4_27
5. Reparaz, O., Bilgin, B., Nikova, S., Gierlichs, B., Verbauwhede, I.: Consolidating masking schemes. In: Gennaro, R., Robshaw, M. (eds.) CRYPTO 2015, Part I. LNCS, vol. 9215, pp. 764–783. Springer, Heidelberg (2015). https://doi.org/10.1007/978-3-662-47989-6_37
6. Nikova, S., Rechberger, C., Rijmen, V.: Threshold implementations against side-channel attacks and glitches. In: Ning, P., Qing, S., Li, N. (eds.) ICICS 2006. LNCS, vol. 4307, pp. 529–545. Springer, Heidelberg (2006). https://doi.org/10.1007/11935308_38
7. Gross, H., Mangard, S., Korak, T.: An efficient side-channel protected AES implementation with arbitrary protection order. In: Handschuh, H. (ed.) CT-RSA 2017. LNCS, vol. 10159, pp. 95–112. Springer, Cham (2017). https://doi.org/10.1007/978-3-319-52153-4_6
8. Guo, X., Mukhopadhyay, D., Jin, C., Karri, R.: Security analysis of concurrent error detection against differential fault analysis. J. Cryptogr. Eng. 5(3), 153–169 (2014). https://doi.org/10.1007/s13389-014-0092-8
9. Kulikowski, K., Karpovsky, M., Taubin, A.: Robust codes for fault attack resistant cryptographic hardware. In: FDTC, pp. 1–12 (2005)
10. Tupsamudre, H., Bisht, S., Mukhopadhyay, D.: Destroying fault invariant with randomization. In: Batina, L., Robshaw, M. (eds.) CHES 2014. LNCS, vol. 8731, pp. 93–111. Springer, Heidelberg (2014). https://doi.org/10.1007/978-3-662-44709-3_6
11. Schneider, T., Moradi, A., Güneysu, T.: ParTI – towards combined hardware countermeasures against side-channel and fault-injection attacks. In: Robshaw, M., Katz, J. (eds.) CRYPTO 2016, Part II. LNCS, vol. 9815, pp. 302–332. Springer, Heidelberg (2016). https://doi.org/10.1007/978-3-662-53008-5_11
12. Dobraunig, C., Eichlseder, M., Korak, T., Mangard, S., Mendel, F., Primas, R.: SIFA: exploiting ineffective fault inductions on symmetric cryptography. In: TCHES, pp. 547–572 (2018)
13. Dobraunig, C., Eichlseder, M., Gross, H., Mangard, S., Mendel, F., Primas, R.: Statistical ineffective fault attacks on masked AES with fault countermeasures. In: Peyrin, T., Galbraith, S. (eds.) ASIACRYPT 2018, Part II. LNCS, vol. 11273, pp. 315–342. Springer, Cham (2018). https://doi.org/10.1007/978-3-030-03329-3_11
14. Zhang, F., et al.: Persistent fault analysis on block ciphers. In: TCHES, pp. 150–172 (2018)
15. Pan, J., Zhang, F., Ren, K., Bhasin, S.: One fault is all it needs: breaking higher-order masking with persistent fault analysis. In: 2019 Design, Automation & Test in Europe Conference & Exhibition (DATE), pp. 1–6. IEEE (2019)
16. Niemi, V., Nyberg, K.: UMTS Security. Wiley, Hoboken (2006)
17. Poschmann, A., Moradi, A., Khoo, K., Lim, C.W., Wang, H., Ling, S.: Side-channel resistant crypto for less than 2,300 GE. J. Cryptol. 24(2), 322–345 (2011). https://doi.org/10.1007/s00145-010-9086-6

18. Korkikian, R., Pelissier, S., Naccache, D.: Blind fault attack against SPN ciphers. In: FDTC, pp. 94–103. IEEE (2014)

19. Yen, S.M., Joye, M.: Checking before output may not be enough against fault-based cryptanalysis. IEEE Trans. Comput. **49**(9), 967–970 (2000)

20. Li, Y., Sakiyama, K., Gomisawa, S., Fukunaga, T., Takahashi, J., Ohta, K.: Fault sensitivity analysis. In: Mangard, S., Standaert, F.-X. (eds.) CHES 2010. LNCS, vol. 6225, pp. 320–334. Springer, Heidelberg (2010). https://doi.org/10.1007/978-3-642-15031-9_22

21. Bogdanov, A., Knudsen, L.R., Leander, G., Paar, C., Poschmann, A., Robshaw, M.J.B., Seurin, Y., Vikkelsoe, C.: PRESENT: an ultra-lightweight block cipher. In: Paillier, P., Verbauwhede, I. (eds.) CHES 2007. LNCS, vol. 4727, pp. 450–466. Springer, Heidelberg (2007). https://doi.org/10.1007/978-3-540-74735-2_31

22. ISO/IEC 29192-2:2012: information technology-security techniques-lightweight cryptography-part 2: block ciphers. https://www.iso.org/standard/56552.html

23. Ullrich, M., De Canniere, C., Indesteege, S., Küçük, Ö., Mouha, N., Preneel, B.: Finding optimal bitsliced implementations of 4× 4-bit S-boxes. In: SKEW 2011 Symmetric Key Encryption Workshop, Copenhagen, Denmark, pp. 16–17 (2011)

24. Banik, S., Pandey, S.K., Peyrin, T., Sasaki, Y., Sim, S.M., Todo, Y.: GIFT: a small present. In: Fischer, W., Homma, N. (eds.) CHES 2017. LNCS, vol. 10529, pp. 321–345. Springer, Cham (2017). https://doi.org/10.1007/978-3-319-66787-4_16

25. Jati, A., Gupta, N., Chattopadhyay, A., Sanadhya, S.K., Chang, D.: Threshold implementations of GIFT : a trade-off analysis. IEEE Trans. Inf. Forensics Secur. **15**, 2110–2120 (2020)

26. Masked-AES-implementation. https://github.com/Secure-Embedded-Systems/Masked-AES-Implementation

27. Trichina, E.: Combinational logic design for AES subbyte transformation on masked data. IACR Cryptology ePrint Archive 2003/236 (2003)

28. Saha, S., Jap, D., Basu Roy, D., Chakraborty, A., Bhasin, S., Mukhopadhyay, D.: A framework to counter statistical ineffective fault analysis of block ciphers using domain transformation and error correction. IEEE Trans. Inf Forensics Secur. **15**, 1905–1010 (2020)

Security of Hedged Fiat–Shamir Signatures Under Fault Attacks

Diego F. Aranha[1]($\boxtimes$), Claudio Orlandi[2]($\boxtimes$), Akira Takahashi[2],
and Greg Zaverucha[3]

[1] Department of Engineering, DIGIT, Aarhus University, Aarhus, Denmark
dfaranha@eng.au.dk
[2] Department of Computer Science, DIGIT, Aarhus University, Aarhus, Denmark
{orlandi,takahashi}@cs.au.dk
[3] Microsoft Research, Redmond, USA
gregz@microsoft.com

Abstract. Deterministic generation of per-signature randomness has been a widely accepted solution to mitigate the catastrophic risk of randomness failure in Fiat–Shamir type signature schemes. However, recent studies have practically demonstrated that such de-randomized schemes, including EdDSA, are vulnerable to differential fault attacks, which enable adversaries to recover the entire secret signing key, by artificially provoking randomness reuse or corrupting computation in other ways. In order to balance concerns of both randomness failures and the threat of fault injection, some signature designs are advocating a "hedged" derivation of the per-signature randomness, by hashing the secret key, message, and a nonce. Despite the growing popularity of the hedged paradigm in practical signature schemes, to the best of our knowledge, there has been no attempt to formally analyze the fault resilience of hedged signatures.

We perform a formal security analysis of the fault resilience of signature schemes constructed via the Fiat–Shamir transform. We propose a model to characterize bit-tampering fault attacks, and investigate their impact across different steps of the signing operation. We prove that, for some types of faults, attacks are mitigated by the hedged paradigm, while attacks remain possible for others. As concrete case studies, we then apply our results to XEdDSA, a hedged version of EdDSA used in the Signal messaging protocol, and to Picnic2, a hedged Fiat–Shamir signature scheme in Round 2 of the NIST Post-Quantum standardization process.

1 Introduction

Deterministic Signatures and Fault Attacks. Some signature schemes require a fresh, secret random value per-signature, sometimes called a nonce. Nonce misuse is a devastating security threat intrinsic to these schemes, since the signing key can be computed after as few as two different messages are signed using the same value. The vulnerability can result from either programming mistakes attempting to implement non-trivial cryptographic standards, or faulty pseudo-random number generators. After multiple real-world implementations were found to

© International Association for Cryptologic Research 2020
A. Canteaut and Y. Ishai (Eds.): EUROCRYPT 2020, LNCS 12105, pp. 644–674, 2020.
https://doi.org/10.1007/978-3-030-45721-1_23

be surprisingly vulnerable to this attack [22,36] researchers and practitioners proposed deterministic signature schemes, such as EdDSA [16], as a counter-measure, in which per-signature randomness is derived from the message and secret key as a defense-in-depth mechanism. However, it has been shown that simple low-cost fault attacks during the computation of the derandomized sign-ing operation can leak the secret key by artificially provoking nonce reuse or by corrupting computation in other ways [3,7,9,68]. Recent papers have experimen-tally demonstrated the feasibility of these attacks [62,66,67]. Moreover, [23] and [64] extended such fault attacks to exploit deterministic lattice-based signature schemes among round two candidates of the NIST Post-Quantum Cryptography Standardization Process [2], where resistance to side-channel attacks is a design goal. Despite these attacks, deterministic signature generation is still likely a positive outcome in improving security, since fault attacks are harder to mount.

Fault Resilience of Hedged Signatures. In order to balance concerns of both nonce reuse and the threat of fault injection, some signature designs are advocating deriving the per-signature randomness from the secret key sk, message m, and a nonce n. The intention is to re-introduce some randomness as a countermea-sure to fault injection attacks, and gracefully handle the case of poor quality randomness, to achieve a middle-ground between fully-deterministic and fully-probabilistic schemes. We call constructions following this paradigm *hedged sig-natures.* Despite the growing popularity of the *hedged* paradigm in practical signature schemes (such as in XEdDSA, VXEdDSA [61], qTESLA [17], and Picnic2 [72]), to the best of our knowledge, there has been no attempt to for-mally analyze the fault resilience of hedged signatures in the literature. While the hedged construction intuitively mitigates some fault attacks that exploit the deterministic signatures, it does add a step where faults can be injected, and it has not been shown if faults to the hedging operation allow further attacks, potentially negating the benefit. Therefore, we set out to study the following question within the provable security methodology:

To what extent are hedged signatures secure against fault attacks?

Concretely, we study fault attacks in the context of signature schemes con-structed from identification schemes using the Fiat–Shamir transform [40]. We propose a formal model to capture the internal functioning of signature schemes constructed in the hedged paradigm, and characterize faults to investigate their impact across different steps of the signature computation.

We prove that for some types of faults, attacks are mitigated by the hedged paradigm, while for others, attacks remain possible. This provides important information when designing fault-tolerant implementations. We then apply our results to hedged EdDSA (called XEdDSA) and the Picnic2 post-quantum sig-nature scheme [72], both designed using the hedged construction. The XEdDSA scheme is used in the Signal protocol [27] which is in turn used by instant mes-saging services such as WhatsApp, Facebook Messenger and Skype.

Threat Model. We consider a weaker variant of the standard adversary assumed in the fault analysis literature [50], who is typically capable of injecting a fault into an arbitrary number of values. Our adversary is capable of injecting a single-bit fault each time a signature is computed. We further restrict the faults to be injected at the interfaces between the typical *commit, challenge, and response* phases of Fiat–Shamir signatures, i.e., only those function inputs and outputs can be faulted. This models transient faults injected into registers or memory cells, but does not fully capture persisting faults that permanently modify values in key storage, voltage glitches to skip instructions or micro-architectural attacks to modify executed instructions (such as RowHammer and variants [56]).

We argue that, even if our model does not capture *all* possible fault attacks, it provides a meaningful abstraction of a large class of fault attacks, and thus our analysis provides an important first step towards understanding the security of hedged signatures in the presence of faults. This way, designers and implementers can focus on protecting the portions of the attack surface that are detected as *most relevant* in practice. We observe that the effects of fault attacks found in the literature targeting deterministic signatures can be essentially characterized as simple bit-tampering faults on function input/output, even though some of actual experiments cause faults during computation [23]. Moreover, an abstract model is needed to prove general results, and the general functions common to all Fiat–Shamir signatures are a natural candidate for abstraction.

We consider two single-bit tampering functions to set or flip individual bits, respectively: $\texttt{flip\_bit}_i(x)$ to perform a logical negation of the i-th bit of x, and $\texttt{set\_bit}_{i,b}(x)$ to set the i-th bit of x to b. This captures both stuck-at and bit-flip fault injection attacks [51], introduced as data flows through the implementation. Such attacks are practically targeted at various components of the device, e.g., memory cells, processor registers, or data buses.

1.1   Our Contributions

A New Security Model for Analyzing Fault Attacks. We establish a formal security model tailored to Fiat–Shamir type signatures (hedged, deterministic or fully probabilistic). We survey the literature on fault attacks, showing that our model captures many practical attacks. As a first step, we abstract real-world hedged signature schemes, basing our formalization on Bellare and Tackmann's nonce-based signatures [15] and Bellare, Poettering and Stebila's de-randomized signatures [14]. We call this security notion *unforgeability under chosen message and nonce attacks* UF-CMNA. In this security experiment, when submitting a message to the signing oracle, the adversary may also choose the random input to the *hedged extractor*, a function that derives the per-signature randomness from a nonce, the secret key, and the message.

Then we extend UF-CMNA to include resilience to fault attacks. In this security experiment the adversary plays a game similar to the UF-CMNA game, but the signing oracle also allows the attacker to specify a fault to be applied to a specific part of the signing algorithm. We identify eleven different fault types that the adversary can apply to the signing algorithm, and we denote them by $f_0, \ldots, f_{10}$. For example, fault type f_1 applies $\texttt{set\_bit}$ or $\texttt{flip\_bit}$ to the secret key input to the hedged extractor. This notion is called *unforgeability under faults, chosen message and nonce attacks*, and is denoted F-UF-fCMNA where F is a set of fault types.

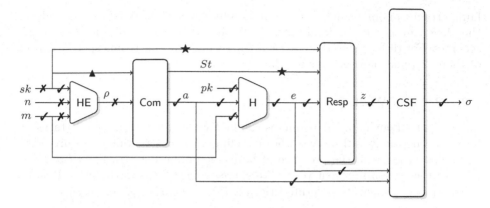

Fig. 1. Overview of our results for hedged Fiat–Shamir type signature schemes. ✓ indicates security against 1-bit fault on the corresponding wire value, and ✗ indicates an attack or counterexample. A ★ (resp. ▲) indicates that security only holds for the schemes derived from subset-revealing ID (resp. input-delayed ID) protocols. The function components HE, Com, H, Resp, and CSF stand for hedged extractor, commitment, hash function, response, and canonical serialization function, respectively (see Sects. 2 and 3 for the formal definitions).

Fault Resilience of Hedged Fiat–Shamir Signatures. We then prove that hedged Fiat–Shamir signature schemes are secure against attacks using certain fault types. Of the eleven fault types in our model, we found that the generic hedged Fiat–Shamir signature scheme is resilient to six of them (summarized in Fig. 1). As our model gives the attacker nearly full control of the RNG by default, our main results indicate that the hedged scheme can resist additional faults even in this (usually dire) scenario. The only constraint is that message-nonce pairs do not repeat as otherwise the scheme degenerates to a pure deterministic construction and attacks become trivial. When the underlying ID scheme has an additional property that we call *subset revealing*, the corresponding hedged signature scheme is secure against attacks that use eight of the eleven fault types. Overall, our results give a full characterization of which fault attacks are mitigated as intended by the hedged construction, and which fault attacks remain. Our conclusion is that hedging is never worse than the deterministic construction with respect to faults, plus it has the additional benefit of hedging against poor randomness.

Fault Resilience of XEdDSA and Picnic2. We use the Schnorr signature scheme throughout the paper as an example. As an application of our results, we show that hedged Schnorr resists attacks for six of the eleven fault types in our model. One implication is that the hedged scheme XEdDSA does provide better resistance to fault attacks than (deterministic) EdDSA. In particular, XEdDSA resists all fault injection attacks against EdDSA described in the literature that rely on nonce reuse without skipping nonce generation entirely [3,9,62,66,67]. We also show to what extent the Picnic2 signature scheme is secure against the fault attacks in our model. Because it is subset-revealing, resistance to eight of the eleven fault types is immediately established by our results for generic ID schemes. For the remaining three, we prove security for one (using specific details of Picnic2), and show attacks for the other two.

1.2   Related Work

To the best of our knowledge, ours is the first work considering fault attacks on hedged constructions. However, the modeling and construction of secure cryptographic schemes in the presence of faults or tampering attacks has received plenty of attention in recent years. We survey some of this work below. Related work on fault attacks to deterministic signature schemes is given in Sect. 2.3.

De-randomized and Hedged Constructions. Bellare and Tackmann [15] studied cryptography that is hedged against randomness failures. They also describe the "folklore construction", where the signing key and message to be signed are used to derive the per-signature randomness, and additional randomness may or may not be included in the derivation. Schnorr signatures with this construction have been analyzed by M'Raihi et al. [59]. A generic version of the folklore derandomization construction was proven UF-CMA secure by Bellare, Pottering and Stebila [14]. Other works on hedged cryptography include [65] and [11,12,19,47] when considering hedged public-key encryption in particular.

Fault Attacks and Tamper-Resilient Signatures. Tamper-resilient cryptography has received plenty of attention, both in the context of theoretical and practical cryptographic research, dating back at least to the early paper of Boneh, Demillo and Lipton [20] considering fault attacks on RSA signatures (here it is noted that some attacks fail when a random padding is used, since it ensures that the same message is never signed twice). Later Coron and Mandal [28] proved that RSA-PSS is protected against random faults, and Barthe et al. [10] extends this to non-random faults as well. All of the above works contain examples of how randomization improves the security of signature schemes against fault attacks (in a provable way).

Other early work includes Gennaro et al. [43] that provides an early framework for proving tamper resilience, and Ishai et al. [49] which proposes generic transformation for tamper-resilient circuits. In a later work by Faust et al. [39] a different and incomparable model was considered, which in particular guarantees security against tampering with *arbitrary* number of wires. We note that our model is similar to theirs since it also considers adversaries that are allowed to flip or reset each bit in the circuit. Similar ideas are also used in practice when considering fault resilient masking (e.g., [32]).

In our model the adversary is only allowed to tamper with part of the computation. Similar limitations have been considered before in the literature to circumvent impossibility results, in particular in the so called *split-state model* [35]. Several constructions have been proposed in this model including: non-malleable codes (Dziembowski, Pietrzak and Wichs [35]), signature schemes (Faonio et al. [37]), and more (Liu and Lysyanskaya [57]).

Other related work on tamper resilient signature schemes includes [6,31,38, 42]. Most of this previous work has focused on *constructing* novel tamper resilient signature schemes, or understanding the limits of tamper resilience, in theory. Instead, we focus on analyzing the tamper resilience of a popular transformation used in practice.

Related key attacks (RKA) can be seen as a special case of tampering. Bellare and Kohno [13] initiated the formal study of related-key attacks. Morita et al. [58] analyzed RKA security of Schnorr signatures.

Ineffective Fault Attacks (IFA) and Countermeasures. In this paper we consider not only `flip_bit` fault attacks, but also `set_bit` faults for the following reason. Clavier [26] proposed *ineffective fault attacks (IFA)*, in which the adversary forces a certain intermediate bit value to be stuck at 0 or 1, and tries to recover the secret internal state by observing whether the correct output is obtained (i.e., the injected fault was ineffective). IFA is very powerful, and works even if the target algorithm contains typical countermeasures against fault attacks, such as a correctness check after redundant operations [8] and the infective countermeasure [71]. IFA has been recently superseded by *statistical* ineffective fault attacks (SIFA) [33,34], that use statistical analysis to enable mounting IFA with low-precision bit-fixing, random or bit-flip faults. Daemen et al. [29] provided several practical countermeasures against SIFA, and their abstract adversarial model is close to ours in the sense that the adversaries are allowed to flip or set a single bit wire value in the circuit per query, though their security argument does not follow the provable security methodology.

Concurrent Work. An independent work by Fischlin and Günther [41] proposes a memory fault model for digital signatures and authenticated encryption. Their main result about a generic hedged signature scheme is two-fold: it is provably secure when the nonce is fully faulted, or when the message, nonce, and hedged extractor output are all differentially faulted in each signing query. The former essentially coincides with our Lemma 3, but with a different proof technique. For the latter, the outcome diverges because the adversarial power in our model is different in the following ways: 1. the adversary can locally inject a fault into *sk* as a hedged extractor input, 2. the adversary can inject a bit-fixing fault, not only a bit-flip (i.e., differential) fault, 3. the adversary has nearly full control over the nonce, instead of assuming nonces are randomly generated and subject to bit flips later on, but 4. the adversary cannot inject multi-bit faults into multiple variables in a query. We additionally consider fault attacks on other various intermediate values inside the signing operation. Our treatment is then more fine-grained and successfully captures typical existing attacks on deployed deterministic schemes (like attacks that fault the challenge hash), while [41] does not. The upside of the generic approach in [41] is that the result applies to more signature schemes.

$\mathsf{Gen}(1^\lambda)$	$\mathsf{Sign}(sk, m; \rho)$	$\mathsf{Verify}(pk, m, \sigma)$
$(pk, sk) \leftarrow \mathsf{IGen}(1^\lambda)$	$(a, St) \leftarrow \mathsf{Com}(sk; \rho)$	$(a, e, z) \leftarrow \mathsf{CDF}(\sigma, pk)$
return (pk, sk)	$e \leftarrow \mathsf{H}(a, m, pk)$	**return** $\mathsf{V}(a, e, z, pk) \overset{?}{=} 1$
	$z \leftarrow \mathsf{Resp}(sk, e, St)$	$\wedge\, \mathsf{H}(a, m, pk) \overset{?}{=} e$
$\mathsf{H}(x)$	$\sigma \leftarrow \mathsf{CSF}(a, e, z)$	
If $\mathrm{HT}[x] = \bot$:	**return** σ	
$\quad \mathrm{HT}[x] \leftarrow_\$ D_H$		
return $\mathrm{HT}[x]$		

Fig. 2. The Fiat–Shamir transform applied to canonical ID with serialization CSF, to construct the signature scheme $\mathbf{FS}[\mathsf{ID}, \mathsf{CSF}] = (\mathsf{Gen}, \mathsf{Sign}, \mathsf{Verify})$. The function $\mathsf{H} : \{0,1\}^* \to D_H$ is constructed with a cryptographic hash function which we model as a random oracle.

2 Preliminaries

Notation. The notation $|\cdot|$ denotes two quantities depending on the context: $|S|$ denotes the cardinality of a set S, and $|s|$ denotes the length of a bit string s. The notation $x \leftarrow_\$ X$ means that an element x is sampled from the set X uniformly at random. We often use the notation $[n]$ as a short hand for a set $\{1, \ldots, n\}$ where $n \in \mathbb{N}$. When we explicitly mention that an algorithm A is randomized, we use the notation $\mathsf{A}(x; \rho)$ meaning that it is executed on input x with random tape ρ. We also remark that if the lemmas/theorems are marked with "(informal)", then it means that asymptotic bounds are omitted. The full version [5] includes more rigorous statements for all of them.

Fiat–Shamir type Signature Schemes. This paper studies the robustness of Fiat–Shamir type signature schemes against fault attacks. The details of these algorithms appear in the full version. The Schnorr signature scheme [69] is one of the most well-known signature schemes using the Fiat–Shamir transform, and EdDSA and XEdDSA are essentially deterministic and hedged variants of Schnorr. The Picnic2 signature scheme [72] is constructed by applying the Fiat–Shamir transform to a three-round zero-knowledge proof system by Katz et al. [52], which follows so-called "MPC-in-the-head" paradigm [48]. The hedging strategy we study in this paper is recommended in its specification.

2.1 Definitions

In this subsection we recall several basic definitions related to digital signatures constructed from the identification protocols. Since this paper deals with Fiat–Shamir signatures, we always assume that the signing algorithm of digital signature schemes takes some randomness as input.

We now define a three-round public-coin identification protocol, the basis of Fiat–Shamir-type signatures. The definition below essentially follows the formalization of [54] unless explicitly stated.

Definition 1 (Canonical Identification Protocol). *A canonical identification protocol, denoted by a tuple of algorithms* $\mathsf{ID} = (\mathsf{IGen}, \mathsf{Com}, \mathsf{Resp}, \mathsf{V})$, *is a three-round protocol defined as follows:*

- $\mathsf{IGen}(1^\lambda)$, *where* λ *is a security parameter, outputs a key pair* (sk, pk). *In the context of identification protocols, pk and sk are sometimes called* statement *and* witness. *We assume that* IGen *defines a hard-relation, and that pk defines the parameters of the scheme including:* randomness space D_ρ, commitment space A, challenge space D_H *and* response space Z.
- Prover *invokes a committing algorithm* Com *on a secret key sk and randomness* $\rho \in D_\rho$ *as input, and outputs a commitment* $a \in A$ *and state* St.
- $\mathsf{Verifier}$ *samples a* challenge e *from the challenge space* $D_H \subseteq \{0,1\}^*$.
- Prover *executes a response algorithm* Resp *on* (sk, e, St) *to compute a response* $z \in Z \cup \{\bot\}$, *where* $\bot \notin Z$ *is a special symbol indicating failure. On top of this standard formalization, we further require that* Resp *returns* $\bot$ *whenever it receives a malformed challenge* $\tilde{e} \notin D_H$, *as such a simple sanity check is performed in most practical implementations.*
- $\mathsf{Verifier}$ *executes a verification algorithm* V *on* (a, e, z, pk) *as input, to output* 1 *(i.e., accept) or 0 (i.e., reject).*

We call a triple $(a, e, z) \in A \times D_H \times Z \cup \{\bot, \bot, \bot\}$ *a* transcript, *and it is said to be* valid *with respect to pk if* $\mathsf{V}(a, e, z, pk) = 1$. *We say that* ID *is* correct *if for every pair* (pk, sk) *output by* IGen, *for every* $\rho \in D_\rho$, *and for every transcript* (a, e, z) *from an honest execution of the protocol between* $\mathsf{Prover}(sk; \rho)$ *and* $\mathsf{Verifier}(pk)$, $\Pr[\mathsf{V}(a, e, z, pk) = 1] = 1$.

Remark. The response algorithm in the above definition does not explicitly take a commitment a as input. We decided to do so since a is generally not required to compute z, such as in the Schnorr identification scheme and, if needed, we assume that St contains a copy of a.

The following definition is adapted from [46, Chapter 6]. We explicitly differentiate three flavors of the special HVZK property depending on a level of indistinguishability, following the approach found in [44, Chapter 4]. Note that ϵ_{HVZK} below is equal to 0 for special *perfect* HVZK.

Definition 2 (Special c/s/p-HVZK). *Let* $\mathsf{ID} = (\mathsf{IGen}, \mathsf{Com}, \mathsf{Resp}, \mathsf{V})$ *be a canonical identification protocol.* ID *is said to be* special computational/statistical/perfect honest-verifier zero knowledge (special c/s/p-HVZK) *if there exists a probabilistic polynomial-time simulator* $\mathcal{M}$, *which on input pk and e outputs a transcript of the form* (a, e, z) *that is computationally/statistically/perfectly indistinguishable from a real transcript between an honest prover and verifier on common input pk. We also denote by* ϵ_{HVZK} *the upper bound on the advantage of all probabilistic polynomial-time distinguishing algorithms.*

In our security analysis of specific hedged-signature schemes in the presence of faults we will provide a concrete bound on the min-entropy of the associated ID scheme. But here we present a useful lemma stating that the commitment message a of any secure identification scheme must have high min-entropy. The lemma might be folklore but we were unable to find a reference to it, so we include it for completeness in the full version.

Lemma 1. *Let* ID *be a canonical identification protocol as in Definition 1, satisfying special-soundness and HVZK (as in Definition 2). Then, the min-entropy α of the commitment message a (given the public key) is at least $\alpha = \omega(\log(\lambda))$*

Definition 3 (Subset Revealing Identification Protocol). *Let* ID $=$ (IGen, Com, Resp, V) *be a canonical identification protocol. We say that* ID *is subset revealing if* ID *satisfies the following. (1) St is a set of c states $\{St_1, \ldots, St_c\}$, (2) Resp first derives an index set $I \subset [c]$ using only e as input, and outputs St_i for $i \in I$ as z, and (3) $|St|$ and $|D_H|$ are both polynomial in λ.*

Remark. Similar definitions were previously given by Kilian et al. [53] and Chailloux [24], where they make zero-knowledge or identification protocols simply reveal a subset of committed strings. Our definition generalizes their notion so that it can cover some protocols that reveal arbitrary values other than committed strings. Also notice that the Resp function of subset revealing ID schemes does not use sk at all. The above definition includes the Picnic2 identification protocol (discussed in more detail in Sect. 6), and many classic three-round public-coin zero-knowledge proof protocols, such as the ones for graph isomorphism, Hamilton graphs, and 3-colorable graphs [45]. We also emphasize that $|St|$ and $|D_H|$ need to be restricted for efficiency reasons – otherwise any identification protocol (including Schnorr) could be made subset revealing by simply precomputing (exponentially many) responses for every possible challenge and storing them in the state.

Serialization of Transcripts. For efficiency purposes, most Fiat-Shamir based signature schemes do not include the entire transcript of the identification protocol as part of the signature. Instead, redundant parts are omitted and recomputed during the verification phase. Different signature schemes omit different parts of the transcript: in some cases a is omitted and in others e is omitted. To capture this in our framework without loss of generality we introduce a *serialization* function that turns the transcript of an identification protocol into a signature.

Definition 4 (Canonical Serialization Function). *Let* ID $=$ (IGen, Com, Resp, V) *be a canonical identification protocol, and let pk be a public key output by IGen. We call a function CSF : $\{0,1\}^* \to \{0,1\}^*$ a canonical serialization function if CSF is efficiently computable and deterministic, and satisfies the following basic properties: (1) it is* valid, *meaning that there exists a corresponding de-serialization function CDF which satisfies the following: for any transcript $(a, e, z) \in A \times D_H \times Z \cup \{\bot, \bot, \bot\}$ such that V$(a, e, z, pk) = 1$, it holds that CDF(CSF$(a, e, z), pk) = (a, e, z)$, and (2) it is* sound with respect to invalid responses, *meaning that it returns $\bot$ upon receiving $z = \bot$ as input.*

Definition 5 (Fiat–Shamir Transform). The Fiat–Shamir transform, *denoted by* **FS**, *takes a canonical identification protocol* ID *and canonical serialization function* CSF *as input, and outputs a signature scheme* **FS**[ID, CSF] = (Gen, Sign, Verify) *defined in Fig. 2. For convenience, this paper refers to such schemes as* Fiat–Shamir *type signature schemes.*

Remarks. By construction, it holds that if ID is correct, then **FS**[ID, CSF] is a correct signature scheme. We assume ID is correct throughout the paper. In Fig. 2, the verification condition may appear redundant. However, the above definition allows us to capture several variations of the Fiat–Shamir transform. For instance, a type of Fiat–Shamir transform found in some papers e.g., Ohta–Okamoto [60] and Abdalla et al. [1] can be obtained by letting $CSF(a, e, z)$ output $\sigma := (a, z)$ and letting $CDF(\sigma, pk)$ call $e \leftarrow H(a, m, pk)$ inside to reconstruct the whole transcript. In contrast, if ID is commitment-recoverable [54], one can instantiate its serialization as follows: $CSF(a, e, z)$ outputs $\sigma := (e, z)$ and $CDF(\sigma, pk)$ calls $a \leftarrow Recover(pk, e, z)$ inside to reconstruct the transcript.

2.2 Relation Between UF-KOA Security and UF-CMA Security

The security notion *unforgeability against key-only attacks* (UF-KOA), is the same as UF-CMA, but with the restriction that the adversary is only given the public key, and no Sign oracle. The following result is a mild generalization of [55, Lemma 3.8]: the original lemma only covers perfect HVZK and does not include the serialization function which we use in this work. The proof is very similar to the original one and is provided in the full version. In Sect. 4, we extend this result, showing that for some signature schemes security against key-only attacks implies security against certain fault attacks.

Lemma 2 (UF-KOA → UF-CMA (informal)). *Let* ID *be a correct canonical identification protocol and* CSF *be a canonical serialization function for* ID. *Suppose* ID *is special c/s/p-HVZK and has α-bit min-entropy. If* FS := **FS**[ID, CSF] *is* UF-KOA *secure, then* FS *is* UF-CMA *secure in the random oracle model.*

2.3 Fault Attacks on Deterministic Fiat–Shamir Signatures

In recent years, several papers [3,9,62,66,67] presented differential fault attacks against deterministic Fiat–Shamir-type schemes. We present the conceptual overview of those previous attacks. A more detailed survey is given in the full version [5].

Special Soundness Attack (SSND). This type of attack exploits the *special soundness* property of the underlying canonical identification protocol. That is, there exists an efficient algorithm that extracts the witness sk corresponding to the statement pk, given two accepting transcripts (a, e, z) and (a, e', z'), where $e \neq e'$ [30]. Note in fact that it is easier to extract the secret key for an attacker than for a knowledge extractor in a proof of security, since the attacker can assume that the prover honestly follows the protocol while the special soundness property considers possibly cheating provers. SSND can be cheaply achieved by injecting a fault into commitment output, or hash input/output.

Large Randomness Bias Attack (LRB). This attack slightly modifies the randomness ρ to $\rho' = \rho + \Delta$ using, e.g., flip_bit fault. The attack highly relies on the deterministic property because the adversary knows that all signatures on the same message m use the same ρ, and if ρ is slightly perturbed by some sufficiently small Δ, he can find Δ with an exhaustive search. Then the adversary can recover the secret key by querying two deterministic signatures on the same message, which were computed using correlated randomness ρ and $\rho + \Delta$. LRB can be cheaply achieved by injecting a fault into the deterministic randomness derivation phase, or the randomness as response input.

3   Formal Treatment of Hedged Signatures

In this section, we give formal definitions for a hedged signature scheme and its security notion, based on Bellare–Tackmann's *nonce-based signatures* [15, §5] and Bellare–Poettering–Stebila's *de-randomized signatures* [14, §5.1]. Then we define our new security notion for hedged Fiat–Shamir signature schemes, which guarantees resilience against 1-bit faults on function inputs/outputs.

$\mathsf{HSign}(sk, m, n)$	$\mathsf{Exp}_{\mathsf{HSIG,HE}}^{\mathsf{UF\text{-}CMNA}}(\mathcal{A})$	$\mathsf{OHSign}(m, n)$
$\rho \leftarrow \mathsf{HE}(sk, (m, n))$	$M \leftarrow \emptyset; \mathrm{HET} \leftarrow \emptyset$	$\sigma \leftarrow \mathsf{HSign}(sk, m, n)$
$\sigma \leftarrow \mathsf{Sign}(sk, m; \rho)$	$(sk, pk) \leftarrow \mathsf{Gen}(1^\lambda)$	$M \leftarrow M \cup \{m\}$
return σ	$(m^*, \sigma^*) \leftarrow \mathcal{A}^{\mathsf{OHSign,HE}}(pk)$	**return** σ
	$v \leftarrow \mathsf{Verify}(m^*, \sigma^*)$	$\mathsf{HE}(sk', (m', n'))$
	return $(v = 1) \wedge m^* \notin M$	If $\mathrm{HET}[sk', m', n'] = \bot:$
		$\quad \mathrm{HET}[sk', m', n'] \leftarrow_\$ D_\rho$
		return $\mathrm{HET}[sk', m', n']$

Fig. 3. Hedged signature scheme $\mathsf{HSIG} = \mathbf{R2H}[\mathsf{SIG}, \mathsf{HE}] = (\mathsf{Gen}, \mathsf{HSign}, \mathsf{Verify})$ and UF-CMNA experiment. Key generation and verification are unchanged.

3.1   Security of Hedged Signature Schemes

We now consider a simple transformation **R2H**, which converts a randomized signature scheme to a so-called "hedged" one, and its security notion UF-CMNA (unforgeability against chosen message and nonce attacks). See Fig. 3 for the full details. Parts of the transformation appear in the literature independently, but by combining them, we can model the concrete hedged signature schemes of interest. We now describe the differences and similarities between **R2H** and the transformations that appeared in previous works.

On one hand, a hedged signing algorithm HSign takes a *nonce n* along with a message m, and derives the randomness $\rho \in D_\rho$ (of length ℓ_ρ bits) with a *hedged extractor* HE with $(sk, (m, n))$ as input. We do not specify how the nonces are generated here, but in practice they are the output of a pseudorandom number generator. As we will see soon, low entropy nonces do not really degrade the security of hedged signatures as long as the underlying randomized signature scheme is secure. The hedged construction we presented is essentially based on the approach taken in [15]. Note that HE is in practice a cryptographic hash function, that we will model as a random oracle.

On the other hand, we use the signing key sk as the key for the hedged extractor, whereas Bellare and Tackmann used a separately generated key (which they called the "seed"), that must be stored with sk. We chose to do so in order to model concrete hedged Fiat–Shamir type schemes, such as XEdDSA and Picnic2. In fact, the security of the deterministic construction that hashes sk and m to derive ρ (with no nonce) was formally treated by Bellare–Poettering–Stebila [14], and our security proof in the next section extends their result. Moreover, the signing oracle OHSign in our UF-CMNA experiment takes m and n as input adaptively chosen by the adversary $\mathcal{A}$. This can be regarded as the strongest instantiation of the oracle provided in [15], where nonces are derived via what they call a nonce generator (NG). Indeed, one of their results for nonce-based signatures (Theorem 5.1) does not impose any restrictions on NG, and it implicitly allows adversaries to fully control how the nonces are chosen in the signing oracle.

Now we formally define a security notion for hedged signature schemes, as a natural extension of the standard UF-CMA security definition. We also give a tweaked version of Theorem 4 in [14], where they only consider the signing oracle that doesn't take adversarially chosen nonces. Note that Lemma 3 applies to *any* secure signature schemes and hence it may be of independent interest. We present a proof in the full version [5] for completeness.

Definition 6 (UF-CMNA). *A hedged signature scheme* HSIG = (Gen, HSign, Verify) *is said to be* UF-CMNA *secure in the random oracle model, if for any probabilistic polynomial time adversary $\mathcal{A}$, its advantage*

$$\mathbf{Adv}_{\mathsf{HSIG,HE}}^{\mathsf{UF\text{-}CMNA}}(\mathcal{A}) := \Pr\left[\mathsf{Exp}_{\mathsf{HSIG,HE}}^{\mathsf{UF\text{-}CMNA}}(\mathcal{A}) = 1\right]$$

is negligible in security parameter λ, where $\mathsf{Exp}_{\mathsf{HSIG,HE}}^{\mathsf{UF\text{-}CMNA}}(\mathcal{A})$ is described in Fig. 3.

Lemma 3 (UF-CMA → UF-CMNA (informal)). *Let* SIG := (Gen, Sign, Verify) *be a randomized digital signature scheme, and let* HSIG := **R2H**[SIG, HE] = (Gen, HSign, Verify) *be the corresponding hedged signature scheme with* HE *modeled as a random oracle. If* SIG *is* UF-CMA *secure, then* HSIG *is* UF-CMNA *secure.*

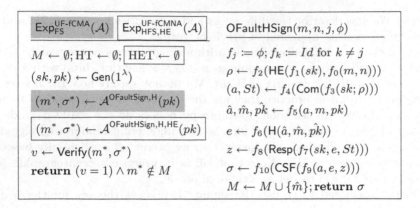

Fig. 4. UF-fCMNA and UF-fCMA security experiments and faulty signing oracles for both hedged (HFS) and plain (FS) Fiat–Shamir signature schemes. Id stands for the identity function. The function H and HE (not shown), are the same as in Figs. 2 and 3, respectively. The procedure OFaultSign(m, j, ϕ) (omitted) is the same as OFaultHSign, but the line assigning to ρ is replaced with $\rho \leftarrow_\$ D_\rho; \rho \leftarrow f_2(\rho)$.

3.2   Security of Hedged FS Type Signature Schemes Against Fault Adversaries

1-bit Transient Fault on Function Input/Output. To model transient fault attackers on data flow, recall that we consider the following 1-bit tampering functions: (1) $\texttt{flip\_bit}_i(x)$, which does a logical negation of the i-th bit of x, and $\texttt{set\_bit}_{i,b}(x)$, which sets the i-th bit of x to b. Using $\texttt{flip\_bit}_i(x)$ (for instance, with a random position i), we can model a typical bit-flip induced from fault injection to the memory cells, CPU register values, or data buses of the target device. Beyond faults, we also wish to capture the case in which the randomness has a 1-bit bias, which has been shown to be a serious threat for some Fiat–Shamir type signatures [4]. We can model this using $\texttt{set\_bit}_{i,b}$: when this function is applied to ρ, we can ensure that the first bit of ρ is "stuck" at zero by setting $i = 0$ and $b = 0$ to model 1-bit bias. Moreover, $\texttt{set\_bit}$ is a typical way to achieve so-called ineffective fault attacks [26,34]. Our formalization covers many fault attacks found in the surveyed literature (in the full version), as they rely only on low precision faults like random bit flips of the function input or output.

As a notable difference between our fault adversary model and actual attacks, some surveyed papers caused faults on several bits/bytes of function input or output when performing fault attack experiments. This is *not* to take advantage of multiple-bit faults, but rather because reliably causing a fault on a specific target memory cell is difficult in practical experiments. In fact, the attacks we classified as SSND and LRB can be achieved with uncontrolled 1-bit flip faults, and hence our model at least seems to capture the essence of previous attacks exploiting the deterministic nature of signing. A natural generalization is to allow set_bit to work on multiple bits, for example to model word faults, or word zeroing faults. We can also model stronger attacks that are uncommon in the literature, such as setting words to arbitrary values. However, we focus on 1-bit faults in this paper as a first attempt to perform the formal analyses. We leave the security analysis against multi-bit faults for future work. In the full version, we describe some more fault attacks that are not covered by our model, to illustrate the limitations of our analysis. Each of these issues makes an interesting direction for future work.

Equipping UF-CMNA *Adversaries with Faults.* Now we are ready to define security against fault adversaries using the above tampering functions. In Fig. 4, we give the modified hedged signing oracle OFaultHSign, which additionally takes a tampering function $\phi \in \{\texttt{set\_bit}_{i,b}, \texttt{flip\_bit}_i, Id\}$ and $j \in [0, 10]$ as input, where Id is the identity function. This way, the adversary can specify for each query the tampering function (ϕ) as well as the target input/output position (j) within the signing operation to be faulted. For example, when $j = 6$, ϕ is applied to the output of the hash function H, and when $j = 5$ it is applied to the input to H. The other positions are not faulted. Notice that we also allow the adversary to set $\phi := Id$ in arbitrary signing queries, so OFaultHSign includes the behavior of the non-faulty oracle OHSign as a special case. A generalization we considered but decided against, is allowing faults on multiple wire values per sign query. The combinatorial complexity of security analysis in this setting is daunting, and we did not find this to be relevant in practice, based on our survey of practical attacks.

Definition 7 (UF-fCMNA). *A hedged Fiat–Shamir signature scheme*

$$\mathsf{HFS} := \mathbf{R2H}[\mathbf{FS}[\mathsf{ID}, \mathsf{CSF}], \mathsf{HE}] = (\mathsf{Gen}, \mathsf{HSign}, \mathsf{Verify})$$

is said to be F-UF-fCMNA secure, if for any probabilistic polynomial time adversary $\mathcal{A}$ who makes queries to OFaultHSign with a fault function $f_j \in F \subseteq \{f_0, \ldots, f_{10}\}$ for each query (called F-adversary), its advantage

$$\mathbf{Adv}_{\mathsf{HFS},\mathsf{HE}}^{\mathsf{UF\text{-}fCMNA}}(\mathcal{A}) := \Pr\left[\mathsf{Exp}_{\mathsf{HFS},\mathsf{HE}}^{\mathsf{UF\text{-}fCMNA}}(\mathcal{A}) = 1\right]$$

is negligible in security parameter λ, where $\mathsf{Exp}_{\mathsf{HFS},\mathsf{HE}}^{\mathsf{UF\text{-}fCMNA}}(\mathcal{A})$ is described in Fig. 4.

In the next section, we also use the following intermediate security notion, which essentially guarantees the security of plain randomized Fiat–Shamir signature scheme against fault adversaries.

Definition 8 (UF-fCMA). *A Fiat–Shamir signature scheme*

$$\mathsf{FS} := \mathbf{FS}[\mathsf{ID}, \mathsf{CSF}] = (\mathsf{Gen}, \mathsf{Sign}, \mathsf{Verify})$$

is said to be F-UF-fCMA secure, if for any probabilistic polynomial time adversary $\mathcal{A}$ who makes queries to OFaultSign with a fault function $f_j \in F \subseteq \{f_2, \ldots, f_{10}\}$ per each query (called F-adversary), its advantage

$$\mathbf{Adv}_{\mathsf{FS}}^{\mathsf{UF\text{-}fCMA}}(\mathcal{A}) := \Pr\left[\mathsf{Exp}_{\mathsf{FS}}^{\mathsf{UF\text{-}fCMA}}(\mathcal{A}) = 1\right]$$

is negligible in security parameter λ, where $\mathsf{Exp}_{\mathsf{FS}}^{\mathsf{UF\text{-}fCMA}}(\mathcal{A})$ is described in Fig. 4.

Trivial Faults on the Root Input Wire Values. We remark the existence of two faults on the left most input wires in Fig. 1, which we do not explicitly consider in our model, but its (in)security can be proven trivially. First, faulting message m before it is loaded by the signing oracle can be regarded as a situation where the adversary queries a faulty message $\hat{m}$ to begin with, since the oracle stores $\hat{m}$ in M. Hence we can just treat such a query as one to non-faulty signing oracle (OSign). Second, the adversary could easily recover the entire secret key after roughly $|sk|$ signing queries by injecting set_bit faults to sk before it is loaded by the signing oracle, and the faulty secret key $\tilde{sk}$ is globally used throughout the signing operation: for example, if the most significant bit of sk is set to 0 at the very beginning of signing and its output still passed the verification, then the adversary can conclude that sk has 0 in the most significant bit with high probability. In doing so, the adversary iteratively recovers sk bit-by-bit if the fault is transient. The attack above is essentially a well-known impossibility result by Gennaro et al. [43] and such an attack can be practically achieved with ineffective faults. To overcome this issue, one would require an additional strict assumption on the upper-bound of faulty signing queries [31], or the signing algorithm needs to have some sophisticated features like self-destruct or key-updating mechanisms, which, however, are not yet widely implemented in real-world systems and are beyond the scope of this paper.

Winning Condition of Fault Adversaries. As described in Fig. 4, the UF-fCMNA experiment keeps track of possibly faulty messages $\hat{m}$ instead of queried messages m, and it does not regard σ^* as valid forgery if it verifies with $\hat{m}$ that $\mathcal{A}$ caused in prior queries. This may appear artificial, but we introduced this condition to rule out a trivial forgery "attack": if the experiment only keeps track of queried message m_i in i-th query, and adversaries target f_5 at m_i as hash input, they obtain a valid signature $\hat{\sigma}_i$ on message $\hat{m}_i$, yet $\hat{m}_i$ is not stored in a set of queried messages M. Hence the adversary can trivially win UF-fCMNA game by just submitting $(\hat{\sigma}_i, \hat{m}_i)$, which of course verifies. This is not an actual attack, since what $\mathcal{A}$ does there is essentially asking for a signature on $\hat{m}_i$ from the signing oracle, and hence outputting such a signature as forgery should not be considered as a meaningful threat.

Note that the OFaultHSign oracle in Fig. 4 stores all queried messages in the same set M, whether the adversary $\mathcal{A}$ decides to inject a fault (i.e., $\phi \in \{\text{set\_bit}_{i,b}, \text{flip\_bit}_i\}$) or not (i.e., $\phi := Id$), and so a forgery (m^*, σ^*) output by $\mathcal{A}$ is *not* considered valid even if m^* was only queried to OFaultHSign to obtain a faulty invalid signature. For some signature algorithms and fault types this is required; for example with Fiat–Shamir type signatures (derived from a commitment recoverable identification [54]), one can query OFaultHSign to get a signature (e, z) with a single bit-flip in z, and create a valid forgery by unflipping the bit.

Validity of Oracle Output. The signature output by OFaultHSign does not need to verify, but it may need to be well-formed in some way. Typically we show with a hybrid argument that OFaultHSign can be simulated without use of the private key, in a similar way to OHSign. In order for simulated outputs of OFaultHSign to be indistinguishable from real outputs, simulated signatures must be correctly distributed. In [10,28], the security proof shows that the faulty signature is statistically close to a value drawn from the uniform distribution, so OFaultHSign can output a random value. For the Fiat–Shamir type signature schemes we study this is not the case, for some fault types the real output of OFaultHSign verifies with an appropriately faulted hash function, and our proofs must take care to maintain these properties when simulating OFaultHSign.

4   Security of Hedged Signatures Against Fault Attacks

In this section we establish the (in)security of the class of hedged Fiat–Shamir signatures schemes. We give here a short overview of the main intuition behind the results in Table 1: f_0 faults (on the (message, nonce) pair which is input to the hedged-extractor) cannot be tolerated since they allow the adversary to get two signatures with the same randomness. On the other hand f_1 faults (on the secret key input to the hedged-extractor) can be tolerated since they do not significantly change the distribution input to the hedged-extractor. If the adversary faults the output of the hedged extractor (using f_2), we cannot prove security in general (and we can list concrete attacks e.g., against the Schnorr signature schemes), but we can prove security for the specific case of Picnic2, since the output of the hedged-extractor is not used directly, but is given as input to a PRG – thus the small bias is "absorbed" by PRG security. We remark that, while present, this attack is much less devastating than the large randomness bias LRB attack on deterministic schemes (described in Sect. 2.3). With the LRB attack, the adversary only needs two signatures to recover the full key, while the attack we will show on Schnorr signature requires a significant amount of faulty biased signatures as input in practice. This indicates that hedged constructions do, to some extent, mitigate the effect of faults on the synthetic randomness.

The hedged approach does not help when the adversary faults the input to the commitment function (via f_3), since in this case the adversary can attempt to set the bits of the secret key one at the time and check if the output signature is valid or not. Note that in some kinds of ID schemes like Schnorr (known as *input-delayed* protocols [25]) the secret key is not used in the commitment function. Faulting the input of the commitment function can still lead to insecurity, e.g., in Schnorr the adversary can bias the randomness, which in turns leads to a total break of the signature scheme. Next, the adversary can fault the output of the commitment function (via f_4): this leads to insecurity in general, e.g., in Schnorr this also leads to randomness bias. However, for a large class of ID schemes (which we call *subset-revealing*), including Picnic2, this fault does not lead to insecurity: intuitively either the adversary faults something that will be output as part of the response (which can easily be simulated by learning a non-faulty signature and then applying the fault on the result), or it is not part of the output and therefore irrelevant. Attacking the input or the output of the random oracle used to derive the challenge (f_5 and f_6) does not lead to insecurity, since the distribution of the random oracle does not change due to the fault (note that

Table 1. Summary of results for UF-fCMNA security of the hedged Fiat–Shamir type construction, for all fault types. ✓ indicates a proof of UF-fCMNA security, and ✗ indicates an attack or counterexample.

Fault type	ID is subset-revealing	ID not subset-revealing	XEdDSA	Picnic2
f_0	✗ Lemma 11		✗	✗
f_1	✓ Lemma 4		✓ Corollary 1	✓ Corollary 3
f_2	✗ Lemma 13		✗	✓ Lemma 19
f_3	✗ Lemma 12		✗	✗ Sect. 6
f_4	✓ Lemma 10	✗ Lemma 15	✗	✓ Corollary 3
f_5	✓ Lemma 7		✓ Corollary 1	
f_6	✓ Lemma 8			
f_7	✓ Lemma 9	✗ Lemma 14		
f_8, f_9, f_{10}	✓ Lemma 6			

this would not be the case for deterministic signatures, where this kind of fault would be fatal). Faults against the input of the response function (via f_7) can break non-subset revealing signatures (once again, we can show that this fault can be used to break Schnorr signatures), but do not help the adversary in the case of a subset-revealing signature like Picnic2: similar to the case of f_4 faults, we use the fact that if the response function only outputs subsets of its input, faulting part of the input either has no effect or can be efficiently simulated given a non-faulty signature. Similarly, faults against the output of the response function or the input/output of the serialization function (fault types f_8, f_9, f_{10}) can also be easily simulated from a non-faulty signature.

We expand this high-level intuition into full proofs by carefully measuring the concrete security loss in the reductions which is introduced by the different kind of faults. More precisely, we present a concrete reduction from UF-KOA to $\{f_1, f_4, \ldots, f_{10}\}$-UF-fCMNA security for schemes derived from subset-revealing ID schemes, and to $\{f_1, f_5, f_6, f_8, f_9, f_{10}\}$-UF-fCMNA when ID is non-subset-revealing. Our theorems generalize and adapt results from [14] and [55] without introducing significant additional concrete security loss. Then in Sect. 4.7, we describe attacks for the remaining fault types (f_0, f_2 and f_3), completely characterizing the security of generic **R2H**[**FS**[ID, CSF], HE] signature schemes for fault types $f_0, \ldots, f_{10}$.

4.1   Main Positive Result

Theorem 1 (UF-KOA → UF-fCMNA). *Let* ID *be a canonical identification protocol and* CSF *be a canonical serialization function for* ID. *Suppose* ID *satisfies the same properties as in Lemma 2 and it is subset revealing, and moreover, let us assume that* $\mathcal{A}$ *does not query the same* (m, n) *pair to* OFaultHSign *more than once. Then if* FS := **FS**[ID, CSF] *is UF-KOA secure,* HFS := **R2H**[FS, HE] *is* $\{f_1, f_4, \ldots, f_{10}\}$-UF-fCMNA *secure in the random oracle model. Concretely, given* $\{f_1, f_4, \ldots, f_{10}\}$-*adversary* $\mathcal{A}$ *against* HFS *running in time* t, *and making* *at most Q_s queries to* OFaultHSign, Q_h *queries to* H *and* Q_{he} *queries to* HE, *one can construct another adversary $\mathcal{B}$ against* FS *such that*

$$\mathbf{Adv}_{\mathsf{HFS,HE}}^{\mathsf{UF\text{-}fCMNA}}(\mathcal{A}) \leq 2 \cdot \left(\mathbf{Adv}_{\mathsf{FS}}^{\mathsf{UF\text{-}KOA}}(\mathcal{B}) + \frac{(Q_s + Q_h)Q_s}{2^{\alpha-1}} + Q_s \cdot \epsilon_{HVZK} \right),$$

where $\mathcal{B}$ makes at most Q_h queries to its hash oracle, and has running time t plus $Q_{he} \cdot |sk|$ invocations of Sign *and* Verify *of* FS. *Moreover, if we do not assume the subset-revealing property of* ID *and assume all the other conditions above, then we have that* HFS *is* $\{f_1, f_5, f_6, f_8, f_9, f_{10}\}$*-UF-fCMNA secure.*

Proof. The proof is two-fold. See Lemmas 4 and 5.

For the rest of this section we will assume that ID satisfies the properties in Lemma 2. As a first step, we give a reduction from UF-fCMA to UF-fCMNA security, and then we later give a reduction from UF-KOA to UF-fCMA. We observe that the UF-CMA-to-UF-CMNA reduction in Lemma 3 is mostly preserved, even in the presence of 1-bit faults on sk as a hedged extractor key. However, our proof shows that such a fault does affect the running time of the adversary because the reduction algorithm needs to go through all secret key candidates queried to random oracle *and* their faulty bit-flipped variants. We present a proof in the full version.

Lemma 4 (F-UF-fCMA $\rightarrow$ $F \cup \{f_1\}$-UF-fCMNA). *Suppose the fault adversary $\mathcal{A}$ does not query the same (m, n) pair to* OFaultHSign *more than once. If* FS := FS[ID, CSF] *is F-UF-fCMA secure, then* HFS := R2H[FS, HE] *is F'-UF-fCMNA secure in the random oracle model, where $F' = F \cup \{f_1\}$. Concretely, given an F'-adversary $\mathcal{A}$ against* HFS *running in time t, and making at most Q_s queries to* OFaultHSign, Q_h *queries to* H *and Q_{he} queries to* HE, *one can construct F-adversary $\mathcal{B}$ against* FS *such that*

$$\mathbf{Adv}_{\mathsf{HFS,HE}}^{\mathsf{UF\text{-}fCMNA}}(\mathcal{A}) \leq 2 \cdot \mathbf{Adv}_{\mathsf{FS}}^{\mathsf{UF\text{-}fCMA}}(\mathcal{B}),$$

where $\mathcal{B}$ makes at most Q_s queries to its signing oracle OFaultSign *and Q_h queries to its hash oracle, and has running time $t' \approx t + Q_{he} \cdot |sk|$.*

Remarks. Our reduction above crucially relies upon the assumption that adversaries are not allowed to query the same (m, n) pair. Without this condition, OFaultHSign must return a faulty signature derived from the same randomness ρ if the same (m, n) is queried twice, and thus one could not simulate it using OFaultSign as an oracle, since OFaultSign uses the fresh randomness even if queried with the same message m. In fact, by allowing the same (m, n) query the hedged construction HFS degenerates to a deterministic scheme and thus the SSND or LRB type fault attacks would become possible as we saw in Sect. 2.3. For the same reason, once we allow the adversaries to mount a fault f_0 on (m, n) right before HE is invoked during the signing query, the security is completely compromised. We will revisit this issue as a negative result in Lemma 11.

Lemma 5 (UF-KOA → UF-fCMA). *Suppose* ID *is subset revealing. If* FS $:=$ FS[ID, CSF] *is UF-KOA secure, then* FS *is* $\{f_4, \ldots, f_{10}\}$-*UF-fCMA secure in the random oracle model. Concretely, given* $\{f_4, \ldots, f_{10}\}$-*adversary* $\mathcal{A}$ *against* FS *running in time* t, *and making at most* Q_s *queries to* OFaultSign, Q_h *queries to* H, *one can construct another adversary* $\mathcal{B}$ *against* FS *such that*

$$\mathbf{Adv}_{\mathsf{FS}}^{\mathsf{UF\text{-}fCMA}}(\mathcal{A}) \leq \mathbf{Adv}_{\mathsf{FS}}^{\mathsf{UF\text{-}KOA}}(\mathcal{B}) + \frac{(Q_s + Q_h)Q_s}{2^{\alpha-1}} + Q_s \cdot \epsilon_{HVZK},$$

where $\mathcal{B}$ *makes at most* Q_h *queries to its hash oracle, and has running time* t. *If we do not assume the subset-revealing property of* ID *and assume all the other conditions above, then we have that* FS *is* $\{f_5, f_6, f_8, f_9, f_{10}\}$-*UF-fCMA secure.*

Proof. We obtain the results by putting together Lemmas 6 to 10 for FS derived from subset-revealing ID, and Lemmas 6 to 8 for FS derived from non-subset-revealing ID. The proofs for these lemmas appear in the full version.

Our proof extends the UF-KOA-to-UF-CMA reduction in [55]. We show that UF-KOA security of a randomized Fiat–Shamir signature scheme FS can be broken by a successful UF-fCMA adversary $\mathcal{A}$ by constructing an adversary $\mathcal{B}$ that uses $\mathcal{A}$ as a subroutine and simulates OFaultSign without using sk. We denote the random oracle and hash table in UF-fCMA experiment (resp. UF-KOA experiment) by H and HT (resp. H' and HT').

Preparation of Public Key. Upon receiving pk in the UF-KOA game, $\mathcal{B}$ forwards pk to $\mathcal{A}$.

Simulation of Random Oracle Queries. Upon receiving a random oracle query $H(a, m, pk)$ from $\mathcal{A}$, $\mathcal{B}$ forwards the input (a, m, pk) to its own random oracle (H' from the UF-KOA game) and provides $\mathcal{A}$ with the return value.

Simulation of Faulty Signing Queries. Suppose $\mathcal{A}$ chooses to use a fault function f_{j_i} in each faulty signing oracle query $i \in [Q_s]$. Then $\mathcal{B}$ answers i-th query by simulating the signature on m_i (or $\hat{m}_i$ if $\mathcal{A}$ chooses to apply f_5 to the message as hash input) using only pk as described in the lemma for f_{j_i}. Notice that the simulations are independent except they share the random oracle H and the set M storing (possibly faulty) queried messages. The hash input $(\hat{a}_i, \hat{m}_i, \hat{pk})$ in each signature simulation has at least $(\alpha - 1)$ bits of min-entropy (see the simulation in Lemma 7 in the full version). Because HT has at most $Q_h + Q_s$ existing entries, $\mathcal{B}$ fails to program the random oracle with probability at most $(Q_h + Q_s)/2^{\alpha-1}$ for each query. Moreover, $\mathcal{A}$ distinguishes the simulated signature from the one returned by the real signing oracle OFaultHSign with probability at most ϵ_{HVZK} for each query, since we use the special c/s/p-HVZK simulator $\mathcal{M}$ to derive a signature in every simulation.

Recalling that the number of signing queries is bounded by Q_s, and by a union bound, $\mathcal{A}$ overall distinguishes its simulated view from that in UF-fCMA game with probability at most

$$\frac{(Q_h + Q_s)Q_s}{2^{\alpha-1}} + Q_s \cdot \epsilon_{HVZK}.$$

Forgery. Suppose that at the end of the experiment $\mathcal{A}$ outputs its forgery (m^*, σ^*) that verifies and $m^* \notin M = \{\hat{m}_i : i \in [Q_s]\}$. (Recall from Fig. 4 that M stores possibly faulty messages $\hat{m}_i$ here instead of queried messages m_i, and thus $\mathcal{A}$ cannot win the game by simply submitting a signature on some faulty message that has been used for random oracle programming.) This means that the reconstructed transcript $(a^*, e^*, z^*) \leftarrow \mathsf{CDF}(\sigma^*, pk)$ satisfies

$$\mathsf{V}(a^*, e^*, z^*, pk) = 1 \quad \text{and} \quad \mathsf{H}(a^*, m^*, pk) = e^*.$$

Here we can guarantee that the $\mathrm{HT}[a^*, m^*, pk]$ has not been programmed by signing oracle simulation since m^* is fresh, i.e., $m^* \notin M$. Hence we ensure that $e^* = \mathrm{HT}[a^*, m^*, pk]$ has been directly set by $\mathcal{A}$, and $e^* = \mathrm{HT}'[a^*, m^*, pk]$ holds due to the hash query simulation. This implies (m^*, σ^*) is a valid forgery in the UF-KOA game as well.

4.2 Faulting Serialization Input/Output and Response Output

As a warm-up, we begin with the simplest analysis where faults do not have any meaningful impact on the signing oracle simulation. As we will show below, faulting with f_8, f_9 and f_{10} has no more security loss than the plain UF-KOA-to-UF-CMA reduction [55] does.

Lemma 6 (UF-KOA $\rightarrow$ $\{f_8, f_9, f_{10}\}$-UF-fCMA (informal)). *If* FS $:=$ **FS**[ID, CSF] *is* UF-KOA *secure, then* FS *is* $\{f_8, f_9, f_{10}\}$-UF-fCMA *secure in the random oracle model.*

Remark. As we briefly remarked after Definition 5, Lemma 6 holds for any instantiation of serialization as long as CSF and CDF are efficiently computable.

4.3 Faulting Challenge Hash Input

Recall that f_5 is the fault type that allows the attacker to fault the input (a, m, pk) to the hash function used to compute the challenge. Here we prove that randomized Fiat–Shamir signature schemes are secure against this type of fault attack, under the same conditions required for the plain UF-KOA-to-UF-CMA reduction [55]. Note that the proof of lemma below introduces a slight additional security loss compared to the plain UF-KOA-to-UF-CMA reduction because **set_bit** faults to the hash input increase the failure probability of random oracle programming.

Lemma 7 (UF-KOA $\rightarrow$ $\{f_5\}$-UF-fCMA (informal)). *If* FS $:=$ **FS**[ID, CSF] *is* UF-KOA *secure, then* FS *is* $\{f_5\}$-UF-fCMA *secure in the random oracle model.*

4.4 Faulting Challenge Hash Output

Recall that f_6 is the fault type that allows the attacker to fault the challenge hash function output, i.e., he can fault the bit string $e = \mathsf{H}(a, m, pk)$. We show that, unlike the fault with f_5, this type of fault does not introduce any additional loss in concrete security as long as the Resp function fails for invalid challenges outside the challenge space D_H.

Lemma 8 (UF-KOA $\rightarrow$ $\{f_6\}$-UF-fCMA (informal)). *If* FS $:=$ **FS**[ID, CSF] *is* UF-KOA *secure, then* FS *is* $\{f_6\}$-UF-fCMA *secure in the random oracle model.*

Remarks. The above lemma relies on the fact that faulty $\tilde{e}_i$ is necessarily a "well-formed" challenge. For example, the challenge in some subset-revealing schemes has a specific structure (e.g., a list of pairs (c_i, p_i) where the c_i are distinct, as in Picnic2). Computing Resp with a malformed challenge may cause σ to leak private information. This is why we required Definition 1 to have the condition that Resp validates $\tilde{e}_i \in D_h$ and otherwise returns $\bot$. This way, the signing algorithm does not leak information when a malformed challenge is input to the response phase, and eventually outputs $\bot$ as a signature because CSF is sound with respect to invalid response (see Definition 4).

Note that the proof can be generalized to the multi-bit fault setting. More specifically, the random oracle programming becomes unnecessary for output replacement faults (i.e., f_6 applies set_bit to every bit of e) because in that case the fault adversary would no longer be able to observe any relation between faulty $\tilde{e}_i$ and the original, unfaulty e.

4.5 Faulting Response Input

Next we prove the security against tampering function f_7, which lets an attacker fault the input (sk, e, St) to the Resp function. We only guarantee security assuming that the signature scheme is based on a subset revealing identification protocol (see Definition 3), and Resp and CSF make sure to rule out invalid challenge and response, respectively. As we will see in the next section, Picnic2 satisfies these additional properties.

Lemma 9 (UF-KOA $\rightarrow$ $\{f_7\}$-UF-fCMA (informal)). *Suppose* ID *is subset revealing. If* FS $:=$ **FS**[ID, CSF] *is* UF-KOA *secure, then* FS *is* $\{f_7\}$-UF-fCMA *secure in the random oracle model.*

Remark. Intuitively, subset revealing ID schemes are secure against faults on St because the adversary only obtains what they could have computed by changing non-faulty signatures by themselves. On the other hand, the Schnorr signature scheme is not secure against tampering with f_7 and we describe concrete fault attacks in Lemma 14.

As we remarked after Definition 3, one can consider a highly inefficient version of Schnorr signature that enumerates all possible responses in St and opens one of them. In doing so, the Resp function avoids any algebraic operations involving

sk and ρ, and we can mitigate the risk of faulty response input attacks described above. This countermeasure is of course impractical since the challenge space is too large, but it illustrates a concrete case where subset revealing ID schemes are more robust against fault attacks, in our model.

4.6   Faulting Commitment Output

Recall that a fault of type f_4 allows the attacker to fault the output of $\mathsf{Com}(sk; \rho)$, the commitment function in the first step of the ID scheme. Here we prove that randomized Fiat–Shamir signature schemes are secure against this type of fault attack, under the same conditions as ones in Lemma 9.

Lemma 10 (UF-KOA $\rightarrow$ $\{f_4\}$-UF-fCMA (informal)). *Suppose* ID *is subset revealing. If* FS $:=$ **FS**[ID, CSF] *is* UF-KOA *secure, then* FS *is* $\{f_4\}$-UF-fCMA *secure in the random oracle model.*

4.7   Negative Results

Here we show that fault attacks of type f_0, f_2 and f_3 are not mitigated by the hedged construction for an ID scheme with the same properties as in Theorem 1.

Lemma 11. *There exist canonical* ID *schemes such that* **R2H**[**FS**[ID, CSF], HE] *is* UF-CMNA-*secure, but not* $\{f_0\}$-UF-fCMNA *secure.*

Proof. We consider the Schnorr scheme that returns (e, z) as a signature for which **FS**[ID, CSF] is known to be UF-CMA secure and therefore **R2H**[**FS**[ID, CSF], HE] is UF-CMNA secure due to Lemma 3. Our $\{f_0\}$-adversary's strategy is as follows. The adversary first calls OFaultHSign with some (m, n) without fault (i.e., $\phi = Id$) to obtain a legitimate signature (e, z). Next, the adversary calls OFaultHSign with $\phi = \mathtt{flip\_bit}_i$, $j = 0$ and (m', n), where m' is identical to m except at the i-th bit. This way, it can fault m' back to m before the invocation of HE and hence the signature is derived from the same ρ as in the previous query, while the challenge and response are different since $e' = \mathsf{H}(a, m', pk)$ and $z = \rho + e' \cdot sk \mod q$. Hence we can recover sk with the SSND attack in Sect. 2.3 and break the scheme.

Lemma 12. *There exist canonical* ID *schemes such that* **R2H**[**FS**[ID, CSF], HE] *is* UF-CMNA-*secure, but not* $\{f_3\}$-UF-fCMNA *secure.*

Proof. We describe a simple attack that works for the Picnic ID scheme. Recall that f_3 is applied to input of $\mathsf{Com}(sk; \rho)$. When querying OFaultHSign, the attacker uses $\mathtt{set\_bit}$ to set the i-th bit of sk, denoted sk_i to 0, then observes whether the signature output is valid. If so, then the true value of sk_i is 0, and if not, then sk_i is one. By repeating this for each of the secret key bits, the entire key may be recovered. Some ID schemes may include internal checks and abort if some computations are detected to be incorrect relative to the public key, in this case the attacker checks whether OFaultHSign aborts.

Note that Lemma 12 only applies to ID schemes where sk is used by the Com function. For the Schnorr scheme and other so-called *input delayed protocols* [25], sk is only used by the Resp function. In this way subset-revealing ID schemes and input delayed ID schemes have the opposite behavior, since subset-revealing schemes do not use sk in the Resp function, but they must use it in the Com function.

The sensitivity of ephemeral randomness ρ in Schnorr-like schemes is well known, and once the attacker obtains sufficiently many biased signatures, the secret key can be recovered by solving the so-called *hidden number problem (HNP)* [21]. Previous works have shown that even a single-bit bias helps to recover sk by making use Bleichenbacher's solution to HNP [4,18]. However, the currently known algorithms for the HNP do not give an asymptotically efficient attack, they only reduce the concrete security of the scheme sufficiently to allow a practical attack on some parameter sets. For instance, with the current state-of-the-art algorithm based on Bleichenbacher's attack found in the literature [70, Theorem 2], one can practically break 1-bit biased signatures instantiated over 192-bit prime order groups, using $2^{29.6}$ signatures as input, and with $2^{29.6}$ space and $2^{59.2}$ time, which is tractable for computationally well-equipped adversaries as of today.

To attack Schnorr-like schemes with f_3, the adversary would instead target the randomness ρ to cause a single-bit bias in it, and this situation is essentially same as faulting with f_2. Such an attack would be also powerful enough to recover the entire signing key, which we describe below.

Lemma 13. *Relative to an oracle for the hidden number problem, there exist a non-subset revealing canonical* ID *scheme such that* **R2H[FS[ID, CSF], HE]** *is* UF-CMNA-*secure, but neither* $\{f_2\}$-UF-fCMNA *nor* $\{f_3\}$-UF-fCMNA *secure.*

Proof. We describe an attack that works for the Schnorr signature scheme. Recall that both f_2 and f_3 can tamper with ρ in Schnorr, as its St contains the randomness ρ. If f_2 or f_3 is set_bit and always targets at the most significant bit of ρ to fix its value, the attacker can introduce 1-bit bias in ρ.

Relative to an oracle for the HNP, the Schnorr scheme with unbiased ρ remains secure, however, the scheme with biased ρ is broken. We must assume here that the HNP oracle does not help an attacker break the Schnorr scheme with unbiased nonces (otherwise the Theorem is trivial). It is easy to see that the HNP with uniformly random nonces does not give a unique solution – the adversary is given a system of Q_s equations with $Q_s + 1$ unknowns, so a direct application of the HNP oracle does not help. However, there may be other ways to use the HNP oracle, so we must make the assumption.

For fault types f_7 and f_4, we have shown that **R2H[FS[ID, CSF], HE]** is secure assuming ID is subset-revealing. The following two lemmas give counterexamples when ID is not subset revealing, showing that canonical ID schemes are not generically secure for faults f_7 and f_4.

Lemma 14. *There exist non-subset-revealing canonical* ID *schemes such that* **R2H[FS[ID, CSF], HE]** *is* UF-CMNA-*secure, but not* $\{f_7\}$-UF-fCMNA *secure.*

Proof. We describe two attacks that work for the Schnorr signature scheme.

- If f_7 is set_bit and targeted at sk, the adversary can use the strategy of Lemma 12 to learn each bit of sk by checking whether the faulty signatures pass verification.
- If f_7 is flip_bit and targeted at the most significant bit of $St = \rho$, the adversary obtains (e, z') such that $z' = e \cdot sk + f_7(\rho)$, and he can recover the "faulty" commitment $a' = [f_7(\rho)]G$. Recall that the non-faulty commitment $a = [\rho]G$ satisfies $\mathsf{H}(a, m, pk) = e$, so the adversary can learn 1-bit of ρ by checking whether $\mathsf{H}(a' + [2^{\ell_\rho - 1}]G, m, pk) = e$ or $\mathsf{H}(a' - [2^{\ell_\rho - 1}]G, m, pk) = e$ holds, where ℓ_ρ is the bit length of ρ. Since we now have the most significant bit of ρ, we use the same argument as in Lemma 13 to show the scheme is vulnerable to fault attacks.

Lemma 15. *There exist non-subset-revealing canonical* ID *schemes such that* $\mathbf{R2H}[\mathbf{FS}[\mathsf{ID}, \mathsf{CSF}], \mathsf{HE}]$ *is* UF-CMNA-*secure, but not* $\{f_4\}$-UF-fCMNA *secure.*

Proof. Recall that f_4 is applied to (a, St), the output of Com. In the Schnorr signature scheme, St contains the per-signature ephemeral value ρ, which is the output of the hedged extractor. Therefore, the same attack as described in Lemma 14 for f_7-faults can be mounted with an f_4-fault.

5   Analysis of XEdDSA

In this section we apply the results of Sect. 4 to the XEdDSA signature scheme. The scheme is presented in the full version [5]. The associated ID scheme is the Schnorr ID scheme (denoted ID-Schnorr). Then we define Schnorr := $\mathbf{FS}[\mathsf{ID\text{-}Schnorr}, \mathsf{CSF}]$ and XEdDSA := $\mathbf{R2H}[\mathsf{Schnorr}, \mathsf{HE}]$, where CSF returns (a, z). We start by establishing some well-known properties of ID-Schnorr. Proof is given in the full version [5]. As noted in Sect. 2 ID-Schnorr is not subset-revealing.

Lemma 16. ID-Schnorr *is perfect HVZK (therefore* $\epsilon_{HVZK} = 0$*) and has* 2λ *bits of min-entropy.*

UF-KOA *Security* Let $\mathbf{Adv}_{\mathsf{Schnorr}}^{\mathsf{UF\text{-}KOA}}(\mathcal{A})$ be the (concrete) UF-KOA security of Schnorr against an adversary $\mathcal{A}$ running in time t. As non-hedged XEdDSA is identical to Schnorr in the UF-KOA setting, the concrete analysis for Schnorr of [55, Lemmas 3.5-3.7] and [63, Lemma 8] are applicable. We do not repeat those results here (as they are lengthy and don't add much to the present paper), but instead state our results in terms of $\mathbf{Adv}_{\mathsf{Schnorr}}^{\mathsf{UF\text{-}KOA}}(\mathcal{A})$. We can now apply the results of Sect. 4.

Corollary 1. *XEdDSA is* $\{f_1, f_5, f_6, f_8, f_9, f_{10}\}$-UF-fCMNA *secure.*

Proof. We've shown above that ID-Schnorr is perfect HVZK (so $\epsilon_{HVZK} = 0$) and has $\alpha = 2\lambda$ bits of min-entropy. Then we can apply Theorem 1, to obtain

$$\mathbf{Adv}_{\mathsf{XEdDSA}}^{\mathsf{UF\text{-}fCMNA}}(\mathcal{A}) \leq 2 \left(\mathbf{Adv}_{\mathsf{Schnorr}}^{\mathsf{UF\text{-}KOA}}(\mathcal{B}) + \frac{(Q_s + Q_h)Q_s}{2^{2\lambda - 1}} \right)$$

Remaining Fault Types. We now consider the faults of type f_0, f_2, f_3, f_4, and f_7 where we can't prove security. For each of these, we have given an attack elsewhere in the paper, for Schnorr signatures, but that also applies to XEdDSA. For type f_0 see Lemma 11, for types f_2 and f_3 see Lemma 13, for type f_4 see Lemma 15 and for type f_7 see Lemma 14.

6   Analysis of Picnic2

In this section we analyze the Picnic2 variant of the Picnic signature scheme using our formal model for fault attacks. Since Picnic is constructed from a subset-revealing ID scheme, more of the results from Sect. 4 apply, reducing our effort in this section. We use ID-Picnic2 to denote the ID scheme, and Picnic2 := **FS**[ID-Picnic2, CSF] and HS-Picnic2 := **R2H**[Picnic2, HE] to denote the randomized and hedged signature schemes. Proofs for this section, and details of the signature scheme are in the full version [5]. We begin with some general properties of Picnic2.

ID-Picnic2 Is a Subset-Revealing ID Scheme. Note that its St consists of $\{h_j, h'_j, \text{seed}^*_j, \{\hat{z}_{j,\alpha}\}, \text{state}_{j,i}, _{,j,i}, \text{msgs}_{j,i}\}_{j\in[M],i\in[n]}$ and Resp simply reveals a subset of it depending on a challenge $\mathcal{C}$ and $\mathcal{P}$.

The Picnic2 Specification Is an Instance of **R2H**. The specification recommends a hedging construction that is an instance of the **R2H** construction from Sect. 3. In this case, the salt and random seeds are derived deterministically from $sk\|m\|pk\|n$ where n is a 2λ-bit random value (acting as the nonce in the notation of Sect. 3). The function HE is instantiated with the SHA-3 based derivation function SHAKE. The security analysis in [72] applies to the randomized version of the signature scheme, so we must use Lemma 3 to establish UF-CMNA security of the hedged variant.

Lemma 17. *For security parameter* λ, *ID-Picnic2 has* $\alpha \geq 2\lambda + 256$ *bits of min-entropy.*

The next corollary shows that Picnic2 is secure against key-only attacks, and it follows from the unforgeability security proof of Picnic2 from [72].

Corollary 2. *The signature scheme* Picnic2 *is UF-KOA secure, when the hash functions* H_0, H_1, H_2 *and* G *are modeled as random oracles with* 2λ-*bit outputs, and key generation function* Gen *is* (t, ϵ_{OW})-*one-way.*

In particular, we have that

$$\mathbf{Adv}^{\text{UF-KOA}}_{\text{Picnic2}}(\mathcal{A}) \leq \frac{3Q_h^2}{2^{2\lambda}} + 2\epsilon_{OW} + \frac{Q_h}{2^\lambda} .$$

Lemma 18. ID-Picnic2 *is a special c-HVZK proof, under the following assumptions: the hash functions* H_0, H_1 *and* H_2 *are modeled as random oracles, and* *the PRG is* (t, ϵ_{PRG})*-secure. Simulated transcripts are computationally indistinguishable from real transcripts, and all polynomial-time distinguishing algorithms succeed with probability at most*

$$\epsilon_{HVZK} \leq (n+2)\tau \cdot \epsilon_{PRG} + \frac{q_0\tau + q_2 M}{2^\lambda}.$$

where q_0 *and* q_2 *are the number of queries to* H_0 *and* H_2, λ *is the security parameter, and* (M, n, τ) *are parameters of the scheme.*

We can now apply our results from Sect. 4.

Corollary 3. HS-Picnic2 *is* $\{f_1, f_4, \ldots, f_{10}\}$*-UF-fCMNA secure.*

Proof. Recall that by Corollary 2, Picnic2 is UF-KOA secure with

$$\mathbf{Adv}^{\mathsf{UF\text{-}KOA}}_{\mathsf{Picnic2}}(\mathcal{A}) \leq \frac{3Q_h{}^2}{2^{2\lambda}} + 2\epsilon_{OW} + \frac{Q_h}{2^\lambda}$$

and the min-entropy α is $2\lambda + 256$ as shown in Lemma 17.

We can apply Theorem 1, to obtain

$$\mathbf{Adv}^{\mathsf{UF\text{-}fCMNA}}_{\mathsf{HS\text{-}Picnic2}}(\mathcal{A}) \leq \frac{6Q_h{}^2}{2^{2\lambda}} + 4\epsilon_{OW} + \frac{2Q_h}{2^\lambda} + \frac{(Q_s + Q_h)Q_s}{2^{2\lambda+254}} + 2Q_s \cdot \epsilon_{HVZK},$$

where ϵ_{HVZK} is given in Theorem 18.

Fault type f_2 Recall that f_2 is a fault on ρ, the output of the hedged extractor. Intuitively, HS-Picnic2 is $\{f_2\}$-UF-fCMNA secure since ρ is not used directly, ρ is the list of seed^*_j values, which are used as input to a PRG when deriving the $\mathsf{seed}_{i,j}$ values. Applying a 1-bit fault to a seed^*_j value reduces the min-entropy by at most one bit, so only a small change to the security proof and analysis is required. Concretely we have:

Lemma 19. HS-Picnic2 *is* $\{f_2\}$*-UF-fCMNA secure.* $\mathbf{Adv}^{\mathsf{UF\text{-}fCMNA}}_{\mathsf{HS\text{-}Picnic2}}(\mathcal{A})$ *is the same as given in Corollary 3, except that* α *is reduced by 1.*

Fault type f_3 Recall that f_3 faults are applied to $\mathsf{Com}(f_3(sk; \rho))$. By setting bits of sk, the attacker can recover sk with an IFA.

7   Concluding Remarks

This paper explored the effects of bit-tampering fault attacks on various internal values in hedged Fiat–Shamir signing operations, within the provable security methodology. Our security model is general enough to capture a large class of signatures, but also fine-grained enough to cover existing attacks surveyed in Sect. 2.3. We remark, however, that there are several more advanced, yet practically relevant fault types that are not covered by our model: (1) faulting global parameters, (2) multiple bit and word faults, (3) faults within the Com and Resp functions, (4) multiple faults per signature query, and (5) persisting faults. A detailed discussion for each is given in the full version [5], to illustrate the limitations of our analysis. Each of these issues makes an interesting direction for future work.

Acknowledgments. This research was supported by: the Concordium Blockchain Research Center, Aarhus University, Denmark; the Carlsberg Foundation under the Semper Ardens Research Project CF18-112 (BCM); the European Research Council (ERC) under the European Unions's Horizon 2020 research and innovation programme under grant agreement No 803096 (SPEC); the Danish Independent Research Council under Grant-ID DFF-6108-00169 (FoCC). We thank anonymous reviewers for their valuable comments and suggestions.

References

1. Abdalla, M., An, J.H., Bellare, M., Namprempre, C.: From identification to signatures via the Fiat-Shamir transform: minimizing assumptions for security and forward-security. In: Knudsen, L.R. (ed.) EUROCRYPT 2002. LNCS, vol. 2332, pp. 418–433. Springer, Heidelberg (2002). https://doi.org/10.1007/3-540-46035-7_28
2. Alagic, G., et al.: Status report on the first round of the NIST post-quantum cryptography standardization process (2019)
3. Ambrose, C., Bos, J.W., Fay, B., Joye, M., Lochter, M., Murray, B.: Differential attacks on deterministic signatures. In: Smart, N.P. (ed.) CT-RSA 2018. LNCS, vol. 10808, pp. 339–353. Springer, Cham (2018). https://doi.org/10.1007/978-3-319-76953-0_18
4. Aranha, D.F., Fouque, P.-A., Gérard, B., Kammerer, J.-G., Tibouchi, M., Zapalow-icz, J.-C.: GLV/GLS decomposition, power analysis, and attacks on ECDSA signatures with single-bit nonce bias. In: Sarkar, P., Iwata, T. (eds.) ASIACRYPT 2014, Part I. LNCS, vol. 8873, pp. 262–281. Springer, Heidelberg (2014). https://doi.org/10.1007/978-3-662-45611-8_14
5. Aranha, D.F., Orlandi, C., Takahashi, A., Zaverucha, G.: Security of hedged Fiat-Shamir signatures under fault attacks. Cryptology ePrint Archive, Report 2019/956 (2019)
6. Austrin, P., Chung, K., Mahmoody, M., Pass, R., Seth, K.: On the impossibility of cryptography with tamperable randomness. Algorithmica **79**(4), 1052–1101 (2017)
7. Baert, M.: Ed25519 leaks private key if public key is incorrect #170. https://github.com/jedisct1/libsodium/issues/170
8. Bar-El, H., Choukri, H., Naccache, D., Tunstall, M., Whelan, C.: The sorcerer's apprentice guide to fault attacks. Proc. IEEE **94**(2), 370–382 (2006)
9. Barenghi, A., Pelosi, G.: A note on fault attacks against deterministic signature schemes. In: Ogawa, K., Yoshioka, K. (eds.) IWSEC 2016. LNCS, vol. 9836, pp. 182–192. Springer, Cham (2016). https://doi.org/10.1007/978-3-319-44524-3_11
10. Barthe, G., Dupressoir, F., Fouque, P.-A., Grégoire, B., Tibouchi, M., Zapalowicz, J.-C.: Making RSA-PSS provably secure against non-random faults. In: Batina, L., Robshaw, M. (eds.) CHES 2014. LNCS, vol. 8731, pp. 206–222. Springer, Heidelberg (2014). https://doi.org/10.1007/978-3-662-44709-3_12

11. Bellare, M., et al.: Hedged public-key encryption: how to protect against bad randomness. In: Matsui, M. (ed.) ASIACRYPT 2009. LNCS, vol. 5912, pp. 232–249. Springer, Heidelberg (2009). https://doi.org/10.1007/978-3-642-10366-7_14
12. Bellare, M., Hoang, V.T.: Resisting randomness subversion: fast deterministic and hedged public-key encryption in the standard model. In: Oswald, E., Fischlin, M. (eds.) EUROCRYPT 2015, Part II. LNCS, vol. 9057, pp. 627–656. Springer, Heidelberg (2015). https://doi.org/10.1007/978-3-662-46803-6_21
13. Bellare, M., Kohno, T.: A theoretical treatment of related-key attacks: RKA-PRPs, RKA-PRFs, and applications. In: Biham, E. (ed.) EUROCRYPT 2003. LNCS, vol. 2656, pp. 491–506. Springer, Heidelberg (2003). https://doi.org/10.1007/3-540-39200-9_31
14. Bellare, M., Poettering, B., Stebila, D.: From identification to signatures, tightly: a framework and generic transforms. In: Cheon, J.H., Takagi, T. (eds.) ASIACRYPT 2016, Part II. LNCS, vol. 10032, pp. 435–464. Springer, Heidelberg (2016). https://doi.org/10.1007/978-3-662-53890-6_15
15. Bellare, M., Tackmann, B.: Nonce-based cryptography: retaining security when randomness fails. In: Fischlin, M., Coron, J.-S. (eds.) EUROCRYPT 2016, Part I. LNCS, vol. 9665, pp. 729–757. Springer, Heidelberg (2016). https://doi.org/10.1007/978-3-662-49890-3_28
16. Bernstein, D.J., Duif, N., Lange, T., Schwabe, P., Yang, B.Y.: High-speed high-security signatures. J. Cryptogr. Eng. 2(2), 77–89 (2012). https://doi.org/10.1007/s13389-012-0027-1
17. Bindel, N., et al.: qTESLA. Technical report, National Institute of Standards and Technology. https://csrc.nist.gov/projects/post-quantum-cryptography/round-2-submissions
18. Bleichenbacher, D.: On the generation of one-time keys in DL signature schemes. Presentation at IEEE P1363 Working Group Meeting (2000)
19. Boldyreva, A., Patton, C., Shrimpton, T.: Hedging public-key encryption in the real world. In: Katz, J., Shacham, H. (eds.) CRYPTO 2017, Part III. LNCS, vol. 10403, pp. 462–494. Springer, Cham (2017). https://doi.org/10.1007/978-3-319-63697-9_16
20. Boneh, D., DeMillo, R.A., Lipton, R.J.: On the importance of checking cryptographic protocols for faults (extended abstract). In: Fumy, W. (ed.) EUROCRYPT 1997. LNCS, vol. 1233, pp. 37–51. Springer, Heidelberg (1997). https://doi.org/10.1007/3-540-69053-0_4
21. Boneh, D., Venkatesan, R.: Hardness of computing the most significant bits of secret keys in Diffie-Hellman and related schemes. In: Koblitz, N. (ed.) CRYPTO 1996. LNCS, vol. 1109, pp. 129–142. Springer, Heidelberg (1996). https://doi.org/10.1007/3-540-68697-5_11
22. Brengel, M., Rossow, C.: Identifying key leakage of bitcoin users. In: Bailey, M., Holz, T., Stamatogiannakis, M., Ioannidis, S. (eds.) RAID 2018. LNCS, vol. 11050, pp. 623–643. Springer, Cham (2018). https://doi.org/10.1007/978-3-030-00470-5_29
23. Bruinderink, L.G., Pessl, P.: Differential fault attacks on deterministic lattice signatures. IACR TCHES 2018(3), 21–43 (2018)
24. Chailloux, A.: Quantum security of the Fiat-Shamir transform of commit and open protocols. Cryptology ePrint Archive, Report 2019/699 (2019)
25. Ciampi, M., Persiano, G., Scafuro, A., Siniscalchi, L., Visconti, I.: Improved OR-composition of sigma-protocols. In: Kushilevitz, E., Malkin, T. (eds.) TCC 2016, Part II. LNCS, vol. 9563, pp. 112–141. Springer, Heidelberg (2016). https://doi.org/10.1007/978-3-662-49099-0_5

26. Clavier, C.: Secret external encodings do not prevent transient fault analysis. In: Paillier, P., Verbauwhede, I. (eds.) CHES 2007. LNCS, vol. 4727, pp. 181–194. Springer, Heidelberg (2007). https://doi.org/10.1007/978-3-540-74735-2_13
27. Cohn-Gordon, K., Cremers, C.J.F., Dowling, B., Garratt, L., Stebila, D.: A formal security analysis of the signal messaging protocol. In: EuroS&P, pp. 451–466. IEEE (2017)
28. Coron, J.-S., Mandal, A.: PSS is secure against random fault attacks. In: Matsui, M. (ed.) ASIACRYPT 2009. LNCS, vol. 5912, pp. 653–666. Springer, Heidelberg (2009). https://doi.org/10.1007/978-3-642-10366-7_38
29. Daemen, J., Dobraunig, C., Eichlseder, M., Gross, H., Mendel, F., Primas, R.: Protecting against statistical ineffective fault attacks. Cryptology ePrint Archive, Report 2019/536
30. Damgård, I.: On Σ-protocols. http://www.cs.au.dk/~ivan/Sigma.pdf
31. Damgård, I., Faust, S., Mukherjee, P., Venturi, D.: Bounded tamper resilience: how to go beyond the algebraic barrier. J. Cryptol. **30**(1), 152–190 (2015). https://doi.org/10.1007/s00145-015-9218-0
32. De Meyer, L., Arribas, V., Nikova, S., Nikov, V., Rijmen, V.: M&M: masks and macs against physical attacks. IACR TCHES **1**, 25–50 (2019)
33. Dobraunig, C., Eichlseder, M., Gross, H., Mangard, S., Mendel, F., Primas, R.: Statistical ineffective fault attacks on masked AES with fault countermeasures. In: Peyrin, T., Galbraith, S. (eds.) ASIACRYPT 2018, Part II. LNCS, vol. 11273, pp. 315–342. Springer, Cham (2018). https://doi.org/10.1007/978-3-030-03329-3_11
34. Dobraunig, C., Eichlseder, M., Korak, T., Mangard, S., Mendel, F., Primas, R.: SIFA: exploiting ineffective fault inductions on symmetric cryptography. IACR TCHES **3**, 547–572 (2018)
35. Dziembowski, S., Pietrzak, K., Wichs, D.: Non-malleable codes. J. ACM **65**(4), 20:1–20:32 (2018)
36. fail0verflow: Console hacking 2010 - PS3 epic fail. 27th Chaos Communications Congress (2010)
37. Faonio, A., Nielsen, J.B., Simkin, M., Venturi, D.: Continuously non-malleable codes with split-state refresh. In: Preneel, B., Vercauteren, F. (eds.) ACNS 2018. LNCS, vol. 10892, pp. 121–139. Springer, Cham (2018). https://doi.org/10.1007/978-3-319-93387-0_7
38. Faonio, A., Venturi, D.: Efficient public-key cryptography with bounded leakage and tamper resilience. In: Cheon, J.H., Takagi, T. (eds.) ASIACRYPT 2016, Part I. LNCS, vol. 10031, pp. 877–907. Springer, Heidelberg (2016). https://doi.org/10.1007/978-3-662-53887-6_32
39. Faust, S., Pietrzak, K., Venturi, D.: Tamper-proof circuits: how to trade leakage for tamper-resilience. In: Aceto, L., Henzinger, M., Sgall, J. (eds.) ICALP 2011, Part I. LNCS, vol. 6755, pp. 391–402. Springer, Heidelberg (2011). https://doi.org/10.1007/978-3-642-22006-7_33
40. Fiat, A., Shamir, A.: How to prove yourself: practical solutions to identification and signature problems. In: Odlyzko, A.M. (ed.) CRYPTO 1986. LNCS, vol. 263, pp. 186–194. Springer, Heidelberg (1987). https://doi.org/10.1007/3-540-47721-7_12
41. Fischlin, M., Günther, F.: Modeling memory faults in signature and authenticated encryption schemes. In: Jarecki, S. (ed.) CT-RSA 2020. LNCS, vol. 12006, pp. 56–84. Springer, Cham (2020). https://doi.org/10.1007/978-3-030-40186-3_4
42. Fujisaki, E., Xagawa, K.: Public-key cryptosystems resilient to continuous tampering and leakage of arbitrary functions. In: Cheon, J.H., Takagi, T. (eds.) ASIACRYPT 2016, Part I. LNCS, vol. 10031, pp. 908–938. Springer, Heidelberg (2016). https://doi.org/10.1007/978-3-662-53887-6_33

43. Gennaro, R., Lysyanskaya, A., Malkin, T., Micali, S., Rabin, T.: Algorithmic Tamper-Proof (ATP) security: theoretical foundations for security against hardware tampering. In: Naor, M. (ed.) TCC 2004. LNCS, vol. 2951, pp. 258–277. Springer, Heidelberg (2004). https://doi.org/10.1007/978-3-540-24638-1_15
44. Goldreich, O.: Foundations of Cryptography, vol. 1. Cambridge University Press, New York (2000)
45. Goldreich, O., Micali, S., Wigderson, A.: Proofs that yield nothing but their validity and a methodology of cryptographic protocol design (extended abstract). In: 27th FOCS, pp. 174–187. IEEE Computer Society Press (1986)
46. Hazay, C., Lindell, Y.: Efficient Secure Two-Party Protocols. ISC. Springer, Heidelberg (2010). https://doi.org/10.1007/978-3-642-14303-8
47. Huang, Z., Lai, J., Chen, W., Au, M.H., Peng, Z., Li, J.: Hedged nonce-based public-key encryption: adaptive security under randomness failures. In: Abdalla, M., Dahab, R. (eds.) PKC 2018, Part I. LNCS, vol. 10769, pp. 253–279. Springer, Cham (2018). https://doi.org/10.1007/978-3-319-76578-5_9
48. Ishai, Y., Kushilevitz, E., Ostrovsky, R., Sahai, A.: Zero-knowledge from secure multiparty computation. In: 39th ACM STOC, pp. 21–30. ACM Press (2007)
49. Ishai, Y., Prabhakaran, M., Sahai, A., Wagner, D.: Private circuits II: keeping secrets in tamperable circuits. In: Vaudenay, S. (ed.) EUROCRYPT 2006. LNCS, vol. 4004, pp. 308–327. Springer, Heidelberg (2006). https://doi.org/10.1007/11761679_19
50. Joye, M., Tunstall, M.: Fault analysis in cryptography, Information Security and Cryptography, vol. 147. Springer, Heidelberg (2012). https://doi.org/10.1007/978-3-642-29656-7
51. Karaklajic, D., Schmidt, J., Verbauwhede, I.: Hardware designer's guide to fault attacks. IEEE Trans. VLSI Syst. 21(12), 2295–2306 (2013)
52. Katz, J., Kolesnikov, V., Wang, X.: Improved non-interactive zero knowledge with applications to post-quantum signatures. In: ACM CCS 2018, pp. 525–537. ACM Press (2018)
53. Kilian, J., Micali, S., Ostrovsky, R.: Minimum resource zero-knowledge proofs (extended abstract). In: Brassard, G. (ed.) CRYPTO 1989. LNCS, vol. 435, pp. 545–546. Springer, New York (1990). https://doi.org/10.1007/0-387-34805-0_47
54. Kiltz, E., Lyubashevsky, V., Schaffner, C.: A concrete treatment of Fiat-Shamir signatures in the quantum random-oracle model. In: Nielsen, J.B., Rijmen, V. (eds.) EUROCRYPT 2018, Part III. LNCS, vol. 10822, pp. 552–586. Springer, Cham (2018). https://doi.org/10.1007/978-3-319-78372-7_18
55. Kiltz, E., Masny, D., Pan, J.: Optimal security proofs for signatures from identification schemes. In: Robshaw, M., Katz, J. (eds.) CRYPTO 2016, Part II. LNCS, vol. 9815, pp. 33–61. Springer, Heidelberg (2016). https://doi.org/10.1007/978-3-662-53008-5_2
56. Kim, Y., et al.: Flipping bits in memory without accessing them: an experimental study of DRAM disturbance errors. In: ISCA, pp. 361–372. IEEE Computer Society (2014)
57. Liu, F.-H., Lysyanskaya, A.: Tamper and leakage resilience in the split-state model. In: Safavi-Naini, R., Canetti, R. (eds.) CRYPTO 2012. LNCS, vol. 7417, pp. 517–532. Springer, Heidelberg (2012). https://doi.org/10.1007/978-3-642-32009-5_30
58. Morita, H., Schuldt, J.C.N., Matsuda, T., Hanaoka, G., Iwata, T.: On the security of the schnorr signature scheme and dsa against related-key attacks. In: Kwon, S., Yun, A. (eds.) ICISC 2015. LNCS, vol. 9558, pp. 20–35. Springer, Cham (2016). https://doi.org/10.1007/978-3-319-30840-1_2

59. M'Raïhi, D., Naccache, D., Pointcheval, D., Vaudenay, S.: Computational alternatives to random number generators. In: Tavares, S., Meijer, H. (eds.) SAC 1998. LNCS, vol. 1556, pp. 72–80. Springer, Heidelberg (1999). https://doi.org/10.1007/3-540-48892-8_6

60. Ohta, K., Okamoto, T.: On concrete security treatment of signatures derived from identification. In: Krawczyk, H. (ed.) CRYPTO 1998. LNCS, vol. 1462, pp. 354–369. Springer, Heidelberg (1998). https://doi.org/10.1007/BFb0055741

61. Perrin, T.: The XEdDSA and VXEdDSA Signature Schemes. Signalrevision 1. https://signal.org/docs/specifications/xeddsa/

62. Poddebniak, D., Somorovsky, J., Schinzel, S., Lochter, M., Rosler, P.: Attacking deterministic signature schemes using fault attacks. In: Euro S&P 2018, pp. 338–352. IEEE (2018)

63. Pointcheval, D., Stern, J.: Security arguments for digital signatures and blind signatures. J. Cryptol. 13(3), 361–396 (2000). https://doi.org/10.1007/s001450010003

64. Ravi, P., Jhanwar, M.P., Howe, J., Chattopadhyay, A., Bhasin, S.: Exploiting determinism in lattice-based signatures: practical fault attacks on pqm4 implementations of NIST candidates. In: Asia CCS 2019, pp. 427–440. ACM (2019)

65. Ristenpart, T., Yilek, S.: When good randomness goes bad: virtual machine reset vulnerabilities and hedging deployed cryptography. In: NDSS 2010. The Internet Society (2010)

66. Romailler, Y., Pelissier, S.: Practical fault attack against the Ed25519 and EdDSA signature schemes. In: FDTC 2017, pp. 17–24 (2017)

67. Samwel, N., Batina, L.: Practical fault injection on deterministic signatures: the case of EdDSA. In: Joux, A., Nitaj, A., Rachidi, T. (eds.) AFRICACRYPT 2018. LNCS, vol. 10831, pp. 306–321. Springer, Cham (2018). https://doi.org/10.1007/978-3-319-89339-6_17

68. Schmidt, B.: [curves] EdDSA specification. https://moderncrypto.org/mail-archive/curves/2016/000768.html

69. Schnorr, C.P.: Efficient signature generation by smart cards. J. Cryptol. 4(3), 161–174 (1991). https://doi.org/10.1007/BF00196725

70. Takahashi, A., Tibouchi, M., Abe, M.: New bleichenbacher records: fault attacks on qDSA signatures. IACR TCHES 3, 331–371 (2018)

71. Yen, S., Joye, M.: Checking before output may not be enough against fault-based cryptanalysis. IEEE Trans. Comput. 49(9), 967–970 (2000)

72. Zaverucha, G., et al.: Picnic. Technical report, National Institute of Standards and Technology. https://csrc.nist.gov/projects/post-quantum-cryptography/round-2-submissions

Succinct Proofs

Transparent SNARKs from DARK Compilers

Benedikt Bünz[1]($\boxtimes$), Ben Fisch[1]($\boxtimes$), and Alan Szepieniec[2]

[1] Stanford, Stanford, USA
{benedikt,bfisch}@cs.stanford.edu
[2] Nervos Foundation, Panama City, Panama

Abstract. We construct a new polynomial commitment scheme for univariate and multivariate polynomials over finite fields, with logarithmic size evaluation proofs and verification time, measured in the number of coefficients of the polynomial. The underlying technique is a *Diophantine Argument of Knowledge* (DARK), leveraging integer representations of polynomials and groups of unknown order. Security is shown from the strong RSA and the adaptive root assumptions. Moreover, the scheme does not require a trusted setup if instantiated with class groups. We apply this new cryptographic compiler to a restricted class of algebraic linear IOPs, which we call *Polynomial IOPs*, to obtain doubly-efficient public-coin interactive arguments of knowledge for any NP relation with succinct communication. With linear preprocessing, the online verifier's work is logarithmic in the circuit complexity of the relation.

There are many existing examples of Polynomial IOPs (PIOPs) dating back to the first PCP (BFLS, STOC'91). We present a generic compilation of any PIOP using our DARK polynomial commitment scheme. In particular, compiling the PIOP from PLONK (GWC, ePrint'19), an improvement on Sonic (MBKM, CCS'19), yields a public-coin interactive argument with quasi-linear preprocessing, quasi-linear (online) prover time, logarithmic communication, and logarithmic (online) verification time in the circuit size. Applying Fiat-Shamir results in a SNARK, which we call **Supersonic**.

Supersonic is also concretely efficient with 10 KB proofs and under 100 ms verification time for circuits with 1 million gates (estimated for 120-bit security). Most importantly, this SNARK is *transparent*: it does not require a trusted setup. We obtain zk-SNARKs by applying a hiding variant of our polynomial commitment scheme with zero-knowledge evaluations. Supersonic is the first complete zk-SNARK system that has both a practical prover time as well as asymptotically *logarithmic* proof size and verification time. The full version of the paper is available online [19].

1 Introduction

In recent years, there has been a surge of industry interest in verifiable outsourced computation [52] (such as trustless cloud computing) as well as zero-knowledge proofs. In particular, blockchains use efficient zero-knowledge proofs as a solution for balancing privacy and publicly-verifiable integrity: examples

© International Association for Cryptologic Research 2020
A. Canteaut and Y. Ishai (Eds.): EUROCRYPT 2020, LNCS 12105, pp. 677–706, 2020.
https://doi.org/10.1007/978-3-030-45721-1_24

include anonymous transactions in ZCash [5,37] and verifying Ethereum smart contracts over private inputs [27]. In these applications, zero-knowledge proofs are posted to the blockchain ledger as a part of transactions and nodes must verify many proofs in the span of a short period of time. Therefore, succinctness and fast verification are necessary properties for the deployment of such proof systems. Verifiable computation is also being explored as a scaling solution for blockhain transactions [20], and even as a way to entirely eliminate the need for maintaining historical blockchain data [40].

Following this pragmatic interest, there has also been a surge of research focused on obtaining proof systems with better concrete efficiency characteristics: *succinctness* (the proof size is sublinear in the original computation length T), *non-interactivity* (the proof is a single message), *prover-scalability* (proof generation time scales linearly or quasi-linearly in T), and *verifier-scalability* (verification time is sublinear in T). Proof systems that achieve all of these properties for general NP statements are called SNARGs ("succinct non-interactive arguments"). The proof is called an *argument* when it is only sound assuming the prover is computationally bounded, *i.e.*, *computationally sound* as opposed to statistically sound. Succinct statistically sound proofs are unlikely to exist [32].

Currently, there are numerous constructions that achieve different trade-offs between proof size, proof time, and verification time, but also under different *trust* models as well as cryptographic assumptions. Some constructions also achieve better efficiency by relying on a *preprocessing model* in which a one-time expensive setup procedure is performed in order to generate a compact verification key VK, which is later used to verify proof instances efficiently. Somewhat unfortunately, the best performing proof systems to date (considering proof size and verification time) require a *trusted* preprocessing. These are the pairing-based SNARKs extending from GGPR [6,9,31,35,47], which have been implemented in numerous libraries [6,16], and even deployed in live systems such as the ZCash [1] cryptocurrency. The trusted setup can be performed via *multi-party computation* (MPC) by a committee of parties, such that trust in only one of the parties is sufficient. This has been done on two occasions for the ZCash blockchain, involving elaborate "ceremonies" to engender public trust in the process [54].

A proof system is called *transparent* if it does not involve any trusted setup. Recent progress has yielded transparent proof systems for special types of computations: zk-STARKs [4] generate zero-knowledge proofs of size $O(\log^2 T)$ for a uniform computation[1], and the GKR protocol produces interactive proofs with communication $O(d \log T)$ for computations expressed as low-depth circuits of total size T and depth d [33]. In both cases, non-interactivity can be achieved in the random oracle model with the Fiat-Shamir heuristic [21,28]. These transparent proof systems perform significantly worse than SNARKs based on preprocessing. For computations expressed as an arithmetic circuit of 1-million

---

[1] A uniform computation is expressed as a RAM program P and a time bound T on the running time of the program. A uniform computation depends on the size of P's description but not on the time bound T.

gates, STARKs [4] report a proof size of 600 KB, whereas preprocessing SNARKs achieve 200 bytes [35]. Bulletproofs [13,18] is a transparent zero-knowledge proof system whose proofs are much smaller than those of STARK, but these proofs have a verification time that scales linearly in the size of the circuit; for an arithmetic circuit of one million gates the verification time is close to 1 min, more than 1,000 times more expensive than verifying a STARK proof for the same computation.

Another thread of research has produced proof systems that remove trust from the circuit preprocessing step, and instead have a *universal* (trusted) setup: a one-time trusted setup that can be reused for *any* computation [30,43,55]. All of these systems build SNARKs by combining an underlying reduction of circuit satisfiability to probabilistic testing of polynomials (with degree at most linear in the circuit size) together with *polynomial commitment schemes*. In a polynomial commitment scheme, a prover commits to a μ-variate polynomial f over $\mathbb{F}$ of total degree at most d with a message that is much smaller than sending all the coefficients of f. The prover can later produce a non-interactive argument that $f(z) = y$ for arbitrary $z \in \mathbb{F}^\mu$ and $y \in \mathbb{F}$. The trusted portion of the universal SNARK is entirely confined to the polynomial commitment scheme's setup. These constructions use variants of the Kate *et al.* commitment scheme for univariate polynomials [39], which requires a trusted setup.

1.1   Summary of Contributions

Following the observations of the recent universal SNARK constructions [30,43,55], SNARKs can be built from polynomial commitment schemes where all the trust is confined to the setup of the commitment scheme. The main technical contribution of our work is thus a new polynomial commitment scheme without trusted setup (*i.e.*, a transparent polynomial commitment scheme), which we can use to construct transparent SNARKs. The observation that transparent polynomial commitments imply transparent SNARKs was also implicit in the recent works that build transparent SNARKs from multi-round classical PCPs, and specifically interactive oracle proofs of proximity (IOPPs) [3]. As a secondary contribution, we present a framework that unifies all existing approaches to constructing SNARKs from polynomial commitments using the language of *interactive oracle proofs* (IOPs) [7,45]. We view polynomial commitment schemes as a compiler for *Polynomial IOPs*, and re-characterize the results of prior works as providing a variety of Polynomial IOPs for NP.

New polynomial commitment scheme. We construct a new polynomial commitment scheme for μ-multivariate polynomials of total degree d with optional zero-knowledge arguments of knowledge for correct evaluation that have $O(\mu \log d)$ size proofs and are verifiable in $O(\mu \log d)$ time. The commitment scheme requires a group of unknown order: two candidate instantiations are RSA groups and class groups of an imaginary quadratic order. Using RSA groups, we can apply the scheme to obtain universal preprocessing SNARKs with *constant-size* setup parameters, as opposed to the linear-size parameters

from previous attempts. Using class groups, we can remove the trusted setup
from trusted-setup SNARKs altogether, thereby making them *transparent*. Our
polynomial commitment scheme leverages the power of integer commitments
and *Diophantine Arguments of Knowledge* [42]; accordingly, we classify this tool
(and others of its kind) as a *DARK* proof system.

Polynomial IOP formalism. All SNARK constructions can be viewed as combining an underlying information-theoretic statistically-sound protocol with a
"cryptographic compiler" that transforms the underlying protocol into a succinct argument at the cost of computational soundness. We define a *Polynomial
IOP* as a refinement of algebraic linear IOPs [9,11,38], where in each round of
interaction the prover provides the verifier with oracle access to a multivariate
polynomial function of bounded degree. The verifier may then query this oracle
to evaluate the polynomial on arbitrary points of its choice. The existing universal and transparent SNARK constructions provide a variety of statistically-
sound Polynomial IOPs for circuit satisfiability (or RAM programs, in the case
of STARKs); these are then cryptographically compiled using some form of a
polynomial commitment, typically using Merkle trees or pairing groups.

The precise definition of Polynomial IOPs as a central and standalone notion
raises the question about its exact relation to other IOP notions. We present a
univariate Polynomial IOP for extracting an indicated coefficient of a polynomial. Furthermore, we present a univariate Polynomial IOP for proving that the
inner product between the coefficient vectors of two polynomials equals a given
value. This proof system is of independent interest. Together with an offline preprocessing phase during which the correctness of a multivariate polynomial is
ascertained, these two tools enable us to show that *any* algebraic linear IOP can
be realized with a multivariate Polynomial IOP.

Polynomial IOP compiler. We present a generic compilation of any public-
coin Polynomial IOP into a doubly-efficient public-coin interactive argument of
knowledge using an abstract polynomial commitment scheme. We prove that if
the commitment scheme's evaluation protocol has witness-extended emulation,
then the compiled interactive argument has this knowledge property as well.
If the commitment scheme is hiding and the evaluation is honest-verifier zero
knowledge (HVZK), then the compiled interactive argument is HVZK as well.
Finally, public-coin interactive arguments may be cryptographically compiled
into SNARKs using the Fiat-Shamir heuristic.

New SNARK without trusted setup. The main practical outcome of this
work is a new transparent proof system (Supersonic) for computations represented as arbitrary arithmetic circuits, obtained by cryptographically compiling
the Polynomial IOPs underlying Sonic [43], PLONK [30], and Marlin [22] using
the DARK polynomial commitment scheme. Supersonic improves the proof size
by an order of magnitude over STARKs without compromising on verification
time. For one million gates, Supersonic's proofs are just 7.8 KB and take around
75 ms to verify. Using the notation $O_\lambda(\cdot)$ to hide multiplicative factors dependent on the security parameter λ, STARKs have size and verification complexity

$O_\lambda(\log^2 T)$ whereas Supersonic has size and verification complexity $O_\lambda(\log T)$. (The additional multiplicative factors dependent on λ are actually better for Supersonic as well.) As a caveat, while the prover time in Supersonic is asymptotically on par with STARKs (*i.e.*, quasilinear in T), the concrete efficiency is much worse due to the use of heavy-weight "crypto operations" over 1200 bit class group elements in contrast to the light-weight FFTs and hash functions in STARKs. Furthermore, Supersonic is not quantum-secure due to its reliance on groups of unknown order, whereas STARKs are a candidate quantum-secure SNARK.

1.2   Related Work

Arguments based on hidden order groups. Fujisaki and Okamoto [29] proposed homomorphic integer commitment schemes based on the RSA group. They also provide protocols to prove that a list of committed integers satisfy modular polynomial equations as opening a commitment bit by bit. Damgård and Fujisaki [25] patched the soundness proof of that protocol and were the first to suggest using class groups of an imaginary quadratic order as a candidate group of unknown order. Lipmaa drew the link between zero-knowledge proofs constructed from integer commitment schemes and Diophantine complexity [42], coining the term *Diophantine Arguments of Knowledge*. Recently, Couteau *et al.* study protocols derived from integer commitments specifically in the RSA group to reduce the security assumptions needed; in the process they develop proofs for polynomial evaluation modulo a prime π that is not initially known to the verifier, in addition to a proof showing that an integer X lies in the range $[a, b]$ by showing that $1 + 4(X - a)(b - X)$ decomposes as the sum of 3 squares [24].

Pietrzak [44] developed an efficient proof of repeated squaring, *i.e.*, proving that $x^{2^T} = y$ with $O(\log T)$ proof size and verification time in order to build a conceptually simple verifiable delay function [10] based on the RSW time-lock puzzle [46]. Wesolowski [53] improves on this result by proposing a single-round protocol to prove correct repeated squaring in groups of unknown order with a constant size proof. Boneh *et al.* [12] observe that this protocol generalizes to arbitrary exponents (PoE) and develop a proof of knowledge of an integer exponent (PoKE), as well as a zero-knowledge variant. They use both PoE and PoKE to construct efficient accumulators and vector commitment schemes.

Transparent polynomial commitments. Whaby *et al.* constructed a transparent polynomial commitment scheme [51] for multilinear polynomials by combining a matrix commitment of Bootle *et al.* [14] with the inner-product argument of Bünz *et al.* [18]. For polynomials of degree d it has commitments of size $O(\sqrt{d})$ and evaluation arguments with $O(\sqrt{d})$ communication. Recently, Vlasov and Panarin [50], concurrently with Zhang *et al.* [56], show how to build a transparent polynomial commitment based on FRI (Fast Reed Solomon IOPP) [3]. The scheme has $O(\lambda)$ size commitments and evaluation arguments with $O(k \cdot \log^2 d)$ communication for repetition parameter k.

Polynomial IOP formalism. In concurrent work Chiesa *et al.* [22] introduce an information theoretic framework called *algebraic holographic proofs (AHP)*. They also show that with a polynomial commitment scheme an AHP can be compiled to a preprocessing SNARK. The AHP framework is essentially equivalent to our Polynomial IOP framework. In other concurrent work, Chiesa, Ojha, and Spooner show interesting connections between algebraic holographic proofs and recursive proof composition. In the same work, the authors develop an AHP-based transparent SNARK called Fractal [23].

2   Technical Overview

This technical overview provides an informal description of our key technical contribution: a polynomial commitment scheme with logarithmic evaluation proofs and verification time. The commitment scheme relies on four separate tools.

1. **Integer encoding of polynomials.** Given a univariate polynomial $f(X) \in \mathbb{Z}_p[X]$ the prover first encodes the polynomial as an integer. Interpreting the coefficients of $f(X)$ as integers in[2] $[0, p)$, define $\hat{f}(X)$ to be the *integer* polynomial with these coefficients. The prover computes $\hat{f}(q) \in \mathbb{Z}$ for some large integer $q \geq p$. This is an injective map from polynomials with bounded coefficients to integers and is also decodable: the coefficients of $f(q)$ can be recovered from the base-q expansion of $\hat{f}(q)$. For example, suppose that $f(X) = 2X^3 + 3X^2 + 4X + 1 \in \mathbb{Z}_5[X]$ and $q = 10$. Then the integer $\hat{f}(10) = 2341$ encodes the polynomial $f(X)$ because its coefficients appear in the decimal expansion of $\hat{f}(10)$.

   Note that this encoding is also additively homomorphic, assuming that q is sufficiently large. For example, let $g(X) = 4X^3 + 1X^2 + 3$ such that $\hat{g}(10) = 4103$. Then $\hat{f}(10) + \hat{g}(10) = 6444 = (\hat{g} + \hat{f})(10)$. The more homomorphic operations we want to permit, the larger q needs to be. The encoding additionally permits multiplication by polynomials ($\hat{f}(q) \cdot q^k$ is equal to the encoding of $f(X) \cdot X^k$).

2. **Succint integer commitments.** The integer $x \leftarrow \hat{f}(q)$ encoding a degree d polynomial $f(X)$ lies between q^d and q^{d+1}; in other words, its size is $(d + 1) \log_2 q$ bits. The prover commits to x using a *succinct* integer commitment scheme that is additively homomorphic. Specifically, we use exponentiation in a group $\mathbb{G}$ of unknown order: the commitment is the single group element $\mathbf{g}^x$ for a base element $\mathbf{g} \in \mathbb{G}$ specified in the setup. (Note that if the order n of $\mathbb{G}$ is known then this is not an integer commitment; $\mathbf{g}^x$ could be opened to any integer $x' \equiv x \bmod n$.)

3. **Evaluation protocol.** The evaluation protocol is an interactive argument to convince a verifier that C is an integer commitment to $\hat{f}(q)$ such that $f(z) = y$ at a provided point $z \in \mathbb{Z}_p$. The protocol must be *evaluation binding*: it should

---

[2] The choice to represent the coefficients by integers in $[0, p)$ optimizes for clarity, but later on we will in fact choose a balanced set of representatives, *i.e.*, $[-\frac{p-1}{2}; \frac{p-1}{2}]$.

be infeasible for the prover to succeed in arguing that $f(z) = y$ and $f(z) = y'$ for $y \neq y'$. The protocol should also be an *argument of knowledge*, which informally means that any prover who succeeds at any point x must "know" the coefficients of the committed f.

As a warmup, we first describe how a prover can efficiently convince a verifier that C is a commitment to an integer polynomial of degree at most d with bounded coefficients. Assume for now that $d = 2^k - 1$. The protocol uses a recursive divide-and-combine strategy. In each step we split $f(X)$ into two degree $d' = \lfloor \frac{d}{2} \rfloor$ polynomials $f_L(X)$ and $f_R(X)$. The left half $f_L(X)$ contains the first $d' + 1$ coefficients of $f(X)$ and the right half $f_R(X)$ the second, such that $f(X) = f_L(X) + X^{d'+1} f_R(X)$. The prover now commits to f_L and f_R by computing $C_L \leftarrow g^{\hat{f}_L(q)}$ and $C_R \leftarrow g^{\hat{f}_R(q)}$. The verifier checks the consistency of these commitments by testing $C_L C_R^{q^{d'+1}} = C$. The verifier then samples random $\alpha \in \mathbb{Z}_p$ and computes $C' \leftarrow C_L^\alpha C_R$, which is an integer commitment to $\alpha \hat{f}_L(q) + \hat{f}_R(q)$. The prover and verifier recurse on the statement that C' is a commitment to a polynomial of degree at most d', thus halving the "size" of the statement. After $\log_2(d + 1)$ rounds, the commitment C' exchanged between prover and verifier is a commitment to a polynomial of degree 0, *i.e.*, to a scalar $c \in \mathbb{Z}_p$. So C' is of the form $g^{\hat{c}}$ where $\hat{c}$ is some integer congruent to c modulo p. The prover sends $\hat{c}$ to the verifier directly. The verifier checks that $g^{\hat{c}} = C'$ and also that $\hat{c} < q$.[3]

To also show that $f(z) = y$ at a provided point z, the prover additionally sends $y_L = f_L(z) \bmod p$ and $y_R = f_R(z) \bmod p$ in each round. The verifier checks consistency with the claim, *i.e.*, that $y_L + z^{d'+1} y_R = y$, and also computes $y' \leftarrow \alpha y_L + y_R \bmod p$ to proceed to the next round. (The recursive claim is that C' commits to f' such that $f'(z) = y' \bmod p$.) In the final round of recursion, the value of the constant polynomial in z is the constant itself. So in addition to testing $C = g^{\hat{c}}$ and $\hat{c} < q$, the verifier also checks that $\hat{c} \equiv y \bmod p$.

4. **Outsourcing exponentiation for efficiency.** The evaluation protocol requires communicating only 2 group elements and 2 field elements per round. However, the verifier needs to check that $C_L C_R^{(q^{d'+1})} = C$, and naïvely performing the exponentiation requires $\Omega(d \cdot \log q)$ work. To reduce this workload, we employ a recent technique for proofs of exponentiation (PoE) in groups of unknown order due to Wesolowski [53] in which the prover computes this exponentiation and the verifier verifies it in essentially constant time. This outsourcing reduces the total verifier time (*i.e.*, of the entire protocol) to a quantity that is logarithmic in d.

3   Preliminaries

3.1   Assumptions

The cryptographic compilers make extensive use of groups of unknown order, *i.e.*, groups for which the order cannot be computed efficiently. Concretely, we

---

[3] In the full scheme, the verifier actually checks that $\hat{c} < B$ for a bound $B < q$ that depends on the field size p and the polynomial's maximum degree d.

require groups for which two specific hardness assumptions hold. First the Strong RSA Assumption [2] which roughly states that it is hard to take *arbitrary* roots of *random* elements. Secondly, the much newer Adaptive Root Assumption [53] which is the dual of the Strong RSA Assumption and states that it is hard to take *random* roots of *arbitrary* group elements. Both of these assumptions hold in generic groups of unknown order [12,26].

The r-strong RSA assumption as presented below is a parameterization on the Strong RSA assumption. For $r = 1$, our definition is identical to the standard Strong RSA Assumption. Higher values of r allows the adversary to take certain roots efficiently. For $r = 2$, the adversary is efficiently able to take square roots. In class groups of imaginary quadratic order taking square roots is easy. In rth order class groups taking rth roots is easy.

Assumption 1 (r-Strong RSA Assumption). *The r-Strong RSA Assumption states that an efficient adversary cannot compute ℓth roots for a given random group element, if ℓ not a power of r. Specifically, it holds for GGen if for any probabilistic polynomial time adversary $\mathcal{A}$:*

$$
\Pr \left[u^\ell = g \wedge \ell \neq r^k, k \in \mathbb{N} : \begin{array}{c} \mathbb{G} \leftarrow GGen(\lambda) \\ g \xleftarrow{\$} \mathbb{G} \\ (u, \ell) \in \mathbb{G} \times \mathbb{N} \leftarrow \mathcal{A}(\mathbb{G}, g) \end{array} \right] \leq \mathsf{negl}(\lambda) \ .
$$

Assumption 2 (Adaptive Root Assumption). *The Adaptive Root Assumption holds for GGen if there is no efficient adversary $(\mathcal{A}_0, \mathcal{A}_1)$ that succeeds in the following task. First, $\mathcal{A}_0$ outputs an element $\mathsf{w} \in \mathbb{G}$ and some st. Then, a random prime ℓ in Primes(λ) is chosen and $\mathcal{A}_1(\ell, \mathsf{st})$ outputs $\mathsf{w}^{1/\ell} \in \mathbb{G}$. For all efficient $(\mathcal{A}_0, \mathcal{A}_1)$:*

$$
\Pr \left[u^\ell = \mathsf{w} \neq 1 : \begin{array}{c} \mathbb{G} \xleftarrow{\$} GGen(\lambda) \\ (\mathsf{w}, \mathsf{st}) \xleftarrow{\$} \mathcal{A}_0(\mathbb{G}) \\ \ell \xleftarrow{\$} \mathsf{Primes}(\lambda) \\ u \leftarrow \mathcal{A}_1(\ell, \mathsf{st}) \end{array} \right] \leq \mathsf{negl}(\lambda).
$$

Groups of unknown order. We consider two candidate groups of unknown order. Both have their own upsides and downsides.

RSA Group. In the multiplicative group $\mathbb{Z}_n^*$ of integers modulo a product $n = p \cdot q$ of large primes p and q, computing the order of the group is as hard as factoring n. The Adaptive Root Assumption does not hold for $\mathbb{Z}_n^*$ because $-1 \in \mathbb{Z}_n^*$ can be easily computed and has order two. This can be resolved though by working instead in the quotient group $\mathbb{Z}_n^*/\langle -1 \rangle \cong \mathsf{QR}_n$. The downside of using an RSA group, or more precisely, the group of quadratic residues modulo an RSA modulus, is that this modulus cannot be generated in a publicly verifiable way without exposing the order, and thus requires a trusted setup.

Class Group. The class group of an imaginary quadratic order is defined as the quotient group of fractional ideals by principal ideals of an order of a number field $\mathbb{Q}(\sqrt{\Delta})$, with ideal multiplication. A class group $\mathcal{C}\ell(\Delta)$ is fully defined by its discriminant Δ, which needs to satisfy only public constraints such as $\Delta \equiv 1 \bmod 4$ and $-\Delta$ must be prime. As a result, Δ can be generated from public coins, thus obviating the need for a trusted setup. A group element can be represented by two integers strictly smaller (in absolute value) than $-\Delta$, which in turn is on the same order of magnitude as RSA group elements for a similar security level. We refer the reader to Buchmann and Hamdy's survey [17] and Straka's accessible blog post [49] for more details.

Working in $\mathcal{C}\ell(\Delta)$ does present an important difficulty: there is an efficient algorithm due to Gauss to compute square roots of arbitrary elements [15], and by repetition, arbitrary power of two roots. As a result, such class groups cannot be used to commit to integers but rather to *dyadic rationals*, which are rational numbers whose denominator is a power of two. Additionally, the standard Strong RSA Assumption is broken if computing square roots is easy. We therefore give a weakening of the Strong RSA assumption, called 2-Strong-RSA assumption, which is believed to still hold even if computing square roots is easy. The 2-Strong-RSA assumption assumes that computing non square roots is hard.

3.2 Interactive Arguments of Knowledge

Interactive arguments are *interactive proofs* [34] in which security holds only against a computationally bounded prover. In an interactive argument of knowledge for a relation $\mathcal{R}$, the prover convinces the verifier that it "knows" a witness w for a statement x such that $(x, w) \in \mathcal{R}$. In this paper, *knowledge* means that the argument has *witness-extended emulation*.

Definition 1 (Interactive Argument). *Let* $(\mathcal{P}, \mathcal{V})$ *denote a pair of PPT interactive algorithms and* **Setup** *denote a non-interactive setup algorithm that outputs public parameters* **pp** *given a security parameter. Both* $\mathcal{P}$ *and* $\mathcal{V}$ *have access to* **pp***. Let* $\langle \mathcal{P}(\mathsf{pp}, x, w), \mathcal{V}(\mathsf{pp}, x) \rangle$ *denote the output of* $\mathcal{V}$ *on input* x *after its interaction with* P*, who has witness* w*. The triple* (**Setup**, $\mathcal{P}, \mathcal{V}$) *is called an argument for relation* $\mathcal{R}$ *if for all non-uniform PPT adversaries* $\mathcal{A}$ *the following properties hold:*

- *Perfect Completeness.*

$$\Pr \left[\begin{array}{c} (x, w) \notin \mathcal{R} \text{ or} \\ \langle \mathcal{P}(\mathsf{pp}, x, w), \mathcal{V}(\mathsf{pp}, x) \rangle = 1 \end{array} : \begin{array}{c} \mathsf{pp} \leftarrow \mathsf{Setup}(1^\lambda) \\ (x, w) \leftarrow \mathcal{A}(\mathsf{pp}) \end{array} \right] = 1$$

- *Computational soundness.*

$$\Pr \left[\begin{array}{c} \forall w \ (x, w) \notin \mathcal{R} \text{ and} \\ \langle \mathcal{A}(\mathsf{pp}, x, \mathsf{st}), \mathcal{V}(\mathsf{pp}, x) \rangle = 1 \end{array} : \begin{array}{c} \mathsf{pp} \leftarrow \mathsf{Setup}(1^\lambda) \\ (x, \mathsf{st}) \leftarrow \mathcal{A}(\mathsf{pp}) \end{array} \right] \leq \mathsf{negl}(\lambda)$$

Definition 2 (Witness-extended emulation [36,41]). *Given a public-coin interactive argument tuple* (**Setup**, $\mathcal{P}, \mathcal{V}$) *and arbitrary prover algorithm* $\mathcal{P}^*$*, let* $\mathsf{Record}(\mathcal{P}^*, \mathsf{pp}, x, \mathsf{st})$ *denote the message transcript between* $\mathcal{P}^*$ *and* $\mathcal{V}$ *on shared* input x, *initial prover state* st, *and* pp *generated by* Setup. *Furthermore, let* $\mathcal{E}^{\mathsf{Record}(\mathcal{P}^*,\mathsf{pp},x,\mathsf{st})}$ *denote an machine* $\mathcal{E}$ *with a transcript oracle for this interaction that can be rewound to any round and run again on fresh verifier randomness. The tuple* (Setup, $\mathcal{P}, \mathcal{V}$) *has witness-extended emulation if for every deterministic polynomial time* $\mathcal{P}^*$ *there exists an expected polynomial time emulator* $\mathcal{E}$ *such that for all non-uniform polynomial time adversaries* $\mathcal{A}$ *the following condition holds:*

$$\Pr\left[\mathcal{A}(tr) = 1 : \begin{array}{c} \mathsf{pp} \leftarrow \mathsf{Setup}(1^\lambda) \\ (x,\mathsf{st}) \leftarrow \mathcal{A}(\mathsf{pp}) \\ tr \leftarrow \mathsf{Record}(\mathcal{P}^*,\mathsf{pp},x,\mathsf{st}) \end{array}\right] \approx$$

$$\Pr\left[\begin{array}{c} \mathcal{A}(tr) = 1 \text{ and} \\ tr \text{ accepting} \Rightarrow (x,w) \in \mathcal{R} \end{array} : \begin{array}{c} \mathsf{pp} \leftarrow \mathsf{Setup}(1^\lambda) \\ (x,\mathsf{st}) \leftarrow \mathcal{A}(\mathsf{pp}) \\ (tr,w) \leftarrow \mathcal{E}^{\mathsf{Record}(\mathcal{P}^*,\mathsf{pp},x,\mathsf{st})}(\mathsf{pp},x) \end{array}\right]$$

3.3   Commitment Schemes

In defining the syntax of the various protocols, we use the following convention with respect to public values (known to both the prover and the verifier) and secret ones (known only to the prover). In any list of arguments or returned tuple $(a,b,c;d,e)$ those variables listed before the semicolon are public, and those variables listed after it are secret. When there is no secret information, the semicolon is omitted.

Definition 3 (Commitment scheme). *A commitment scheme* Γ *is a tuple* $\Gamma = $ (Setup, Commit, Open) *of PPT algorithms where:*

- Setup$(1^\lambda) \to$ pp *generates public parameters* pp;
- Commit$(\mathsf{pp}; x) \to (c; r)$ *takes a secret message* x *and outputs a public commitment* c *and (optionally) a secret opening hint* r *(which might or might not be the randomness used in the computation).*
- Open$(\mathsf{pp}, c, x, r) \to b \in \{0,1\}$ *verifies the opening of commitment* c *to the message* x *provided with the opening hint* r.

A commitment scheme Γ *is* **binding** *if for all PPT adversaries* $\mathcal{A}$:

$$\Pr\left[b_0 = b_1 \neq 0 \wedge x_0 \neq x_1 : \begin{array}{c} \mathsf{pp} \leftarrow \mathsf{Setup}(1^\lambda) \\ (c,x_0,x_1,r_0,r_1) \leftarrow \mathcal{A}(\mathsf{pp}) \\ b_0 \leftarrow \mathsf{Open}(\mathsf{pp},c,x_0,r_0) \\ b_1 \leftarrow \mathsf{Open}(\mathsf{pp},c,x_1,r_1) \end{array}\right] \leq \mathsf{negl}(\lambda)$$

We now extend the syntax to polynomial commitment schemes. The following definition generalizes that of Kate *et al.* [39] to allow interactive evaluation proofs. It also stipulates that the polynomial's degree be an argument to the protocol, contrary to Kate *et al.* where the degree is known and fixed.

Definition 4 *(Polynomial commitment).* *A polynomial commitment scheme is a tuple of protocols* $\Gamma = $ (Setup, Commit, Open, Eval) *where* (Setup, Commit, Open) *is a binding commitment scheme for a message space* $R[X]$ *of polynomials over some ring* R, *and*

- $Eval(pp, c, z, y, d, \mu; f(X)) \rightarrow b \in \{0, 1\}$ *is an interactive public-coin protocol between a PPT prover $\mathcal{P}$ and verifier $\mathcal{V}$. Both $\mathcal{P}$ and $\mathcal{V}$ have as input a commitment c, points $z, y \in R$, and a degree d. The prover additionally knows the opening of c to a secret polynomial $f(X) \in R[X]$ with $\deg(f(X)) \leq d$. The protocol convinces the verifier that $f(z) = y$. In a multivariate extension of polynomial commitments, the input $\mu > 1$ indicates the number of variables in the committed polynomial and $z \in R^\mu$.*

*A polynomial commitment scheme is **correct** if an honest committer can successfully convince the verifier of any evaluation. Specifically, if the prover is honest then for all polynomials $f(X) \in R[X]$ and all points $z \in R$,*

$$
\Pr \left[b = 1 \ : \ \begin{array}{l} pp \leftarrow Setup(1^\lambda) \\ (c; r) \leftarrow Commit(pp, f(X)) \\ y \leftarrow f(z) \\ d \leftarrow \deg(f(X)) \\ b \leftarrow Eval(pp, c, z, y, d; f(X), r) \end{array} \right] = 1 \ .
$$

Knowledge soundness. Any successful prover in the Eval protocol must *know* a polynomial $f(X)$ such that $f(z) = y$ and c is a commitment to $f(X)$. More formally, since Eval is a public-coin interactive argument we define this knowledge property as a special case of witness-extended emulation (Definition 2).

Define the following NP relation given $pp \leftarrow Setup(1^\lambda)$:

$$
\mathcal{R}_{\mathsf{Eval}}(pp) = \left\{ \langle (c, z, y, d), (f(X), r) \rangle \ : \ \begin{array}{l} f \in R[X] \text{ and } \deg(f(X)) \leq d \text{ and } f(z) = y \\ \text{and } \mathsf{Open}(pp, c, f(X), r) = 1 \end{array} \right\}
$$

The correctness definition above implies that if $\Gamma = (\mathsf{Setup}, \mathsf{Commit}, \mathsf{Open}, \mathsf{Eval})$ is *correct* then Eval is a correct interactive argument for $\mathcal{R}_{\mathsf{Eval}}(pp)$, with overwhelming probability over the randomness of Setup. We say that Γ has **witness-extended emulation** if Eval has witness-extended emulation as an interactive argument for $\mathcal{R}_{\mathsf{Eval}}(pp)$.

3.4   Proofs of Exponentiation

Wesolowski [53] introduced a simple yet powerful proof of correct exponentiation ("PoE") in groups of unknown order. A prover can efficiently convince a verifier that a large exponentiation in such a group was done correctly. For instance, the prover wishes to convince the verifier that $w = u^x$ for known group elements $u, w \in \mathbb{G}$ and exponent $x \in \mathbb{Z}$, and the verifier wants to verify this with much less work than performing the exponentiation. To do this, the verifier samples a large enough prime ℓ at random and the prover provides him with $Q \leftarrow u^q$ where $q = \lfloor \frac{x}{\ell} \rfloor$. The verifier then simply computes the remainder $r \leftarrow (x \mod \ell)$ and checks that $Q^\ell u^r = w$. The protocol is an argument for the relation $\mathcal{R}_{\mathsf{PoE}} = \{ \langle (u, w, x), \varnothing \rangle \ : \ u^x = w \}$. The proof verification uses just $O(\lambda)$ group operations. When x is $x = q^d$ the verifier can compute $r \leftarrow x \mod \ell$ using just $\log(d)\ell$-bit multiplications.

PoE($\mathsf{u}, \mathsf{w}, x$) :

1. $\mathcal{V}$ samples $\ell \overset{\$}{\leftarrow} \text{Primes}(\lambda)$ and sends ℓ to $\mathcal{P}$
2. $\mathcal{P}$ computes quotient q and remainder r such that $x = q\ell + r$ and $r \in \{0, \ldots, \ell - 1\}$
3. $\mathcal{P}$ computes $\mathsf{Q} \leftarrow \mathsf{u}^q$ and sends it to $\mathcal{V}$
4. $\mathcal{V}$ computes $r \leftarrow (x \mod \ell)$ and checks that $\mathsf{Q}^\ell \mathsf{u}^r = \mathsf{w}$
5. **if** check passes **then return** 1 **else return** 0

Lemma 1 (PoE soundness [53]). *PoE is an argument system for Relation $\mathcal{R}_{PoE}$ with negligible soundness error, assuming the Adaptive Root Assumption (Assumption 2) holds for GGen.*

4 Polynomial Commitments from Groups of Unknown Order

4.1 Information-Theoretic Abstraction

Before we present our concrete polynomial commitment scheme based on groups of unknown order, we present the underlying information theoretic protocol that abstracts the concrete cryptographic instantiations. The purpose of this abstraction is two-fold: first, it provides an intuitive stepping stone from which presenting and studying the concrete cryptographic protocol is easier; and second, it opens the door to alternative cryptographic instantiations that provide the same interface but based on alternative hardness assumptions.

Let $[\![*]\!] : \mathbb{Z}_p[X] \to \mathbb{S}$ be a homomorphic commitment function that sends polynomials over a prime field to elements of some set $\mathbb{S}$. Moreover, let $\mathbb{S}$ be equipped with operations $* + * : \mathbb{S} \times \mathbb{S} \to \mathbb{S}$ and $* \cdot * : \mathbb{Z}_p[X] \times \mathbb{S} \to \mathbb{S}$ that accommodate two homomorphisms for $[\![*]\!]$:

- a *linear homomorphism*: $a \cdot [\![f(X)]\!] + b \cdot [\![g(X)]\!] = [\![af(X) + bg(X)]\!]$
- a *monomial homomorphism*: $X^d \cdot [\![f(X)]\!] = [\![X^d f(X)]\!]$.

For now, assume both prover and verifier have oracle access to the function $[\![*]\!]$ and to the operations $* \cdot *$ and $* + *$. (Later on, we will instantiate this commitment function using groups of unknown order and an encoding of polynomials as integers.)

The core idea of the evaluation protocol is to reduce the statement that is being proved from one about a polynomial $f(X)$ of degree d and its evaluation $y = f(z)$, to one about a polynomial $f'(X)$ of degree $d' = \lfloor \frac{d}{2} \rfloor$ and its evaluation $y' = f'(z)$. For simplicity, assume that $d + 1$ is a power of 2. The prover splits $f(X)$ into $f_L(X)$ and $f_R(X)$ such that $f(X) = f_L(X) + X^{d'+1} f_R(X)$ and such that both halves have degree at most d'. The prover obtains a random challenge $\alpha \in \mathbb{Z}_p$ from the verifier and proceeds to prove that $f'(X) = \alpha \cdot f_L(X) + f_R(X)$ has degree d' and that $f'(z) = y' = \alpha y_L + y_R$ with $y_L = f_L(z)$ and $y_R = f_R(z)$.

The proof repeats this reduction by using $f'(X), z, y'$ and d' as the input to the next recursion step. In the final step, $f(X) = f$ is a constant and the verifier checks that $f = y$.

The commitment function binds the prover to one particular polynomial for every commitment held by the verifier. In particular, at the start of every recursion step, the verifier is in possession of a commitment $[\![f(X)]\!]$ to $f(X)$. The prover provides commitments $[\![f_L(X)]\!]$ and $[\![f_R(X)]\!]$, and the verifier checks their soundness homomorphically by testing $[\![f(X)]\!] = [\![f_L(X)]\!] + X^{d'+1}[\![f_R(X)]\!]$. From these commitments, the verifier can also compute the commitment to $f'(X)$ homomorphically, via $[\![f'(X)]\!] = \alpha[\![f_L(X)]\!] + [\![f_R(X)]\!]$. In the last step, the verifier checks that the constant polynomial f matches the commitment by computing $[\![f]\!]$ outright.

4.2   Integer Polynomial Encoding

We propose using integer commitments in a group of unknown order as a concrete instantiation of the homomorphic commitment scheme required for the abstract protocol presented in Sect. 4.1. At the heart of our protocol is thus an encoding of integer polynomials with bounded coefficients as integers, which also has homomorphic properties. Any commitment scheme which is homomorphic over integer polynomials is automatically homomorphic over $\mathbb{Z}_p[X]$ polynomials as well (by reducing integer polynomials modulo p). Polynomials over $\mathbb{Z}_p[X]$ can be lifted to integer polynomials in a canonical way by choosing representatives in $[0, p)$. Therefore, from here on we will focus on building a homomorphic integer encoding of integer polynomials, and how to combine this with a homomorphic integer commitment scheme.

Strawman encoding. In order to encode integer polynomials over an odd prime field $\mathbb{F}_p$, we first lift them to the ring of polynomials over the integers by choosing representatives in $[0, p)$. In the technical overview (Sect. 2) we noted that a polynomial $f \in \mathbb{Z}[X]$ with positive coefficients bounded by q can be encoded as the integer $f(q)$. The coefficients of f can be recovered via the base q decomposition of $f(q)$. This encoding is an injective mapping from polynomials in $\mathbb{Z}[X]$ of degree at most d with positive coefficients less than q to the set $[0, q^{d+1})$. The encoding is also *partially* homomorphic. If f is encoded as $f(q)$ and g is encoded as $g(q)$ where coefficients of both g, f are less than $q/2$, then the base-q decomposition of $f(q) + g(q)$ gives back the polynomial $f + g$. By choosing a sufficiently large $q \gg p$ it is possible to perform several levels of homomorphic operations on encodings.

What goes wrong? Unfortunately, this simple encoding scheme does not quite work yet for the protocol outlined in Sect. 2. The homomorphic consistency checks ensure that if $[\![f_L(X)]\!]$ is a homomorphic integer commitment to the encoding of $f_L \in \mathbb{Z}[X]$, $[\![f_R(X)]\!]$ is a homomorphic integer commitment to the encoding of $f_R \in \mathbb{Z}[X]$, and both f_L, f_R are polynomials with $q/2$-bounded coefficients, then $[\![f(X)]\!]$ is an integer commitment to the encoding of $f_L + X^{d'} f_R$. (Moreover, if $f_L(z) = y_L \bmod p$ and $f_R(z) = y_R \bmod p$ then $f(z) = y_L + z^{d'} y_R \bmod p$).

However, the validity of $[\![f_L(X)]\!]$ and $[\![f_R(X)]\!]$ are never checked directly. The verifier only sees the opening of the commitment at the bottom level of recursion. If the intermediate encodings use integer polynomials with coefficients larger than $q/2$ the homomorphism is not preserved. Furthermore, even if $[\![f(X)]\!]$ is a commitment to $f^*(q)$ with positive q-bounded coefficients, an adversarial prover could find an integer polynomial g^* that does not have positive q-bounded coefficients such that $g^*(q) = f^*(q)$ and $g^* \not\equiv f^* \bmod p$ (*i.e.*, g^* with coefficients greater than q or negative coefficients). The prover could then commit to $g_L^*(q)$ and $g_R^*(q)$, and recurse on $\alpha g_L^*(q) + g_R^*(q)$ instead of $\alpha f_L^*(q) + f_R^*(q)$. This would be non-binding. (For example $f^*(X) = q-1$ and $g^*(X) = X-1$, or $f^*(X) = q+1$ and $g^*(X) = X+1$).

Inferring coefficient bounds. So what can the verifier infer from the opened commitment $[\![f']\!]$ at the bottom level of recursion? The opened commitment is an integer $f' = \alpha f_L + f_R$. From f', the verifier can infer a bound on the absolute value of the coefficients of the integer polynomial $f(X) = f_L + X f_R$, given that f_L and f_R were already committed in the second to last round. The bound holds with overwhelming probability over the randomness of $\alpha \in [0, p)$. This is reasoned as follows: if $f_0' \leftarrow \alpha_0 f_L + f_R$ and $f_1' \leftarrow \alpha_1 f_L + f_R$ such that $\max(|f_0'|, |f_1'|) < q/(2p)$ for some distinct $\alpha_0 \neq \alpha_1$, then $|f_L| \leq |f_1' - f_0'| < q/p$ and $|f_R| \leq |\alpha_0 f_1' - \alpha_1 f_0'| < q/2$. If no such pair exists, *i.e.* the bound only holds for a unique α, then there is a negligibly small probability $1/p$ that f' would have passed the bound check.

What about negative coefficients? As shown above, the verifier can infer a bound on the absolute values of f_L and f_R, but still cannot infer that f_L and f_R are both *positive* integers. Moreover, if $f_R > 0$ and $f_L < 0$, then it is still possible that $f_L + q f_R > 0$, and thus that there is a distinct $g \neq f$ with q-bounded positive coefficients such that $g(q) = f(q)$. For example, say $f_R = q/2$ and $f_L = -1$ then $f_L + q f_R = q^2/2 - 1$, and $\alpha f_L + f_R = q/2 - \alpha > 0$ for every $\alpha \in [0, p)$. Yet, also $q^2/2 - 1 = g(q)$ for $g(X) = (q/2 - 1)X + q - 1$.

Ensuring injectivity. How can we ensure the encoding scheme is injective over polynomials with either positive/negative coefficients bounded in absolute value? Fortunately, it is a fact that if $|f_L| < q/2$ and $|f_R| < q/2$ then at least one coefficient of g must be larger than $q/2$. In other words, if the prover had committed instead to f_L^* and f_R^* such that $g(X) = f_L^* + X f_R^*$ then the verifier could reject the opening of $\alpha \hat{f}_L^* + \hat{f}_R^*$ with overwhelming probability based on its size.

More generally, for every integer z in the range $B = (-\frac{q^{d+1}}{2}, \frac{q^{d+1}}{2})$ there is a unique degree (at most) d integer polynomial $h(X)$ with coefficients whose absolute values are bounded by $q/2$ such that $h(q) = z$. *We prove this elementary fact below and show how the coefficients of h can be recovered efficiently from z (Fact 1).* If the prover is committed to $h(q)$ at level i of the protocol, there is a unique pair of integers polynomial h_L and h_R with coefficients of absolute value bounded by $q/2$ such that $h_L(q) + q^{\frac{d+1}{2}} h_R(q) = h(q)$, and if the prover recurses on any other h_L^* and h_R^* with larger coefficients then the verifier's bound check at the bottom level of recursion will fail with overwhelming probability.

Final Encoding scheme. Let $\mathbb{Z}(b) := \{x \in \mathbb{Z} : |x| \leq b\}$ denote the set of integers with absolute value less than or equal to b. Define $\mathbb{Z}(b)[X] := \{f \in \mathbb{Z}[X] : ||f||_\infty \leq b\}$, the set of integer polynomials with coefficients from $\mathbb{Z}(b)$. (For a polynomial $g \in \mathbb{Z}[X]$ the norm $||g||_\infty$ is the maximum over the absolute values of all individual coefficients of g.)

- **Encoding.** For any integer q, the function $\mathsf{Enc} : \mathbb{Z}(b)[X] \to \mathbb{Z}$ maps $h(X) \mapsto h(q)$. A polynomial $f(X) \in \mathbb{Z}_p[X]$ is first mapped to $\mathbb{Z}(p/2)[X]$ by replacing each coefficient of f with its unique integer representative from $(-p/2, p/2)$ of the same equivalence class modulo p.
- **Decoding.** Decoding works as follows. Define the partial sum $S_k := \sum_{i=0}^{k} f_i q^i$ with $S_{-1} := 0$. Assuming $|f_i| < q/2$ for all i, observe that for any partial sum S_k we have $|S_k| < \frac{q^{k+1}}{2}$. Therefore, when $S_k < 0$ then $S_k \bmod q^{k+1} > q^{k+1}/2$ and when $S_k \geq 0$ then $S_k \bmod q^{k+1} < q^{k+1}/2$. This leads to a decoding strategy for recovering S_k from $y \in \mathbb{Z}$. The decode algorithm sets S_k to $y \bmod q^{k+1}$ if this value is less than $q^{k+1}/2$ and to $q^{k+1} - (y \bmod q^{k+1})$ otherwise. Two consecutive partial sums yield a coefficient of $f(X)$: $f_k = \frac{S_k - S_{k-1}}{q^k} \in \mathbb{Z}(b)$. These operations give rise to the following algorithm.

$\mathsf{Dec}(y \in \mathbb{Z})$:

1. **for each** k **in** $[0, \lfloor \log_q(|y|) \rfloor]$ **do:**
2. $S_{k-1} \leftarrow (y \bmod q^k)$
3.   **if** $S_{k-1} > q^k/2$ **then** $S_{k-1} \leftarrow q^k - S_{k-1}$ **end if**
4. $S_k \leftarrow (y \bmod q^{k+1})$
5.   **if** $S_k > q^{k+1}/2$ **then** $S_k \leftarrow q^{k+1} - S_k$ **end if**
6. $f_k \leftarrow (S_k - S_{k-1})/q^k$
7. **returen** $f(X) = \sum_{k=0}^{\lfloor \log_q(|y|) \rfloor} f_k X^k$

Fact 1. *Let q be an odd integer. For any z in the range $B = (-\frac{q^{d+1}}{2}, \frac{q^{d+1}}{2})$ there is a unique degree (at most) d integer polynomial $h(X)$ in $\mathbb{Z}(\frac{q-1}{2})[X]$ such that $h(q) = z$.*

4.3 Concrete Polynomial Commitment Scheme

We now instantiate the abstract homomorphic commitment function $[\![*]\!]$. To this end we sample a group of unknown order $\mathbb{G}$, and sample a random element $\mathbf{g}$ from this group. Lift the field polynomial $f(X) \in \mathbb{Z}_p[X]$ to an integer polynomial with bounded coefficients, *i.e.*, $\hat{f}(X) \in \mathbb{Z}(\frac{p-1}{2})[X]$ such that $\hat{f}(X) \bmod p = f(x)$. We encode $\hat{f}(X)$ as an integer by evaluating it at a "large enough" integer q. Finally we use exponentiation in $\mathbb{G}$ to commit to the integer. Therefore, $[\![f(X)]\!]$, corresponds to $\mathbf{g}^{\hat{f}(q)}$. This commitment function inherits the homomorphic properties of the integer encoding for a limited number of additions and multiplications-by-constant. The monomial homomorphism for X^d is achieved by raising the group element to the power q^d. To maintain consistency between the prover's witness polynomials and the verifier's commitments, the prover operates on polynomials with integer coefficients $\hat{f}(X), \hat{g}(X)$, etc., without ever reducing them modulo p.

The Setup, Commit and Open functionalities are presented formally below. Note that the scheme is parameterized by p and q.

- Setup(1^λ) : Sample $\mathbb{G} \xleftarrow{\$} GGen(\lambda)$ and $\mathbf{g} \xleftarrow{\$} \mathbb{G}$. Return $\mathsf{pp} = (\lambda, \mathbb{G}, \mathbf{g}, q)$.
- Commit($\mathsf{pp}; f(X) \in \mathbb{Z}_p[X]$) : Compute $\mathsf{C} \leftarrow \mathbf{g}^{\hat{f}(q)}$ and return $(\mathsf{C}; \hat{f}(X))$.
- Open($\mathsf{pp}, \mathsf{C}, f(X), \hat{f}(X)$) : Check that $\hat{f}(X) \in \mathbb{Z}(q/2)[X]$ and $\mathbf{g}^{\hat{f}(q)} = \mathsf{C}$ and $f(X) = \hat{f}(X) \bmod p$.

Evaluation protocol. Using the cryptographic compilation of the information theoretic protocol we get an Eval protocol with logarithmic communication. In every round, however, the verifier needs to check consistency between $[\![f_L(X)]\!], [\![f_R(X)]\!]$ and $[\![f(X)]\!]$. This is done by checking that $\mathsf{C}_L \cdot \mathsf{C}_R^{q^{d'+1}} = \mathsf{C}$. This naive check is highly inefficient as the exponent $q^{d'+1}$ has $O(d)$ bits. To resolve this inefficiency, we utilize a proof of exponentiation (PoE) [44,53] to outsource the computation to the prover. The PoE protocol is an argument that a large exponentiation in a group of unknown order was performed correctly. Wesolowski's PoE [53] is public coin, has constant communication and verification time, and is thus particularly well-suited here.

We now specify subtleties that were previously glossed over. First, we handle the case where $d+1$ is not a power of 2. Whenever $d+1$ is odd in the recursion, the polynomial is shifted by one degree—specifically, $f'(X) = Xf(X)$ and the protocol proceeds to prove that $f'(X)$ has degree bounded by $d' = d+1$ and evaluates to $y' = zy$ at z. The verifier obtains the matching commitment $\mathsf{C}' \leftarrow \mathsf{C}^q$.

Second, the coefficients of $f(X)$ grow by a factor of $\frac{p+1}{2}$ in every recursion step, but eventually the transmitted constant f has to be tested against some bound because if it is *too large* it should be rejected. However, the function interface provides no option to specify the allowable size of coefficients. We therefore define and use a subroutine EvalBounded, which takes an additional argument b and which proves, in addition to what Eval proves, that all coefficients f_i of $f(X)$ satisfy $|f_i| \leq b$. Importantly, b grows by a factor for $\frac{p+1}{2}$ in every recursion step. This subroutine is also useful if commitments were homomorphically combined prior to the execution of EvalBounded. The growth of these coefficients determines a lower bound on q: q should be *significantly* larger than b. Exactly which factor constitutes "significantly" is determined by the knowledge-soundness proof.

In the final round we check that the constant f satisfies $|f| \leq b$ and the protocol's correctness is guaranteed if $b = \frac{p-1}{2}(\frac{p+1}{2})^{\lceil \log_2(d+1) \rceil}$. However, q needs to be even larger than this value in order for extraction to work (and hence, for the proof of witness-extended emulation to go through). In RSA groups, where computing square roots is hard, we need $q > p^{2\log(d+1)+1}$; whereas in class groups where computing square roots is easy, we need $p^{3\log(d+1)+1}$. When this condition is satisfied, we can prove that the original committed polynomial has coefficients smaller than $\frac{q}{2}$. To avoid presenting two algorithms whose only difference is the one constant, we capture this constant explicitly in the variable $\varsigma_{p,d}$ and set its value depending on the context: $\varsigma_{p,d} = \begin{cases} p^{\log_2(d+1)} & \text{(in RSA groups)} \\ p^{2\log_2(d+1)} & \text{(in class groups)} \end{cases}$.

We now present the full, formal Eval protocol below.

$\mathsf{Eval}(\mathsf{pp}, \mathsf{C} \in \mathbb{G}, z \in \mathbb{Z}_p, y \in \mathbb{Z}_p, d \in \mathbb{N}; \tilde{f}(X) \in \mathbb{Z}_p[X]) : \,/\!/ \quad \tilde{f}(X) = \sum_{i=0}^d \tilde{f}_i X^i$

  1. $\mathcal{P}$ computes $f_i \in [-\frac{p-1}{2}, \frac{p-1}{2}]$ such that $f_i \equiv \tilde{f}_i \bmod p$ for all $i \in [0, d]$.

  2. $\mathcal{P}$ computes $f(X) \leftarrow \sum_{i=0}^d f_i \cdot X^i \in \mathbb{Z}(\frac{p-1}{2})[X] \subset \mathbb{Z}[X]$

  3. $\mathcal{P}$ and $\mathcal{V}$ run $\mathsf{EvalBounded}(\mathsf{pp}, \mathsf{C}, z, y, d, \frac{p-1}{2}; f(X))$

$\mathsf{EvalBounded}(\mathsf{pp}, \mathsf{C} \in \mathbb{G}, z \in \mathbb{Z}_p, y \in \mathbb{Z}_p, d \in \mathbb{N}, b \in \mathbb{Z}; f(X) \in \mathbb{Z}(b)[X])$

  1. **if** $d = 0$:

  2. $\mathcal{P}$ sends $f(X) \in \mathbb{Z}$ to the verifier. $/\!/\quad f = f(X)$ is a constant

  3. $\mathcal{V}$ checks that $b \cdot \varsigma_{p,d} < q /\!/ \quad \varsigma_{p,d} = O(p^{2\log(d)})$ (see Theorem 1 and 2)

  4. $\mathcal{V}$ checks that $|f| \leq b$

  5. $\mathcal{V}$ checks that $f \equiv y \bmod p$

  6. $\mathcal{V}$ checks that $\mathbf{g}^f = \mathsf{C}$

  7. $\mathcal{V}$ outputs 1 **if** all checks pass, 0 otherwise.

  8. **if** $d + 1$ is odd

  9. $d' \leftarrow d+1, \mathsf{C}' \leftarrow \mathsf{C}^q, y' \leftarrow y \cdot z \bmod p$ and $f'(X) \leftarrow X \cdot f(X)$.

 10. $\mathcal{P}$ and $\mathcal{V}$ run $\mathsf{EvalBounded}(\mathsf{pp}, \mathsf{C}', z, y', d', b; f'(X))$

 11. **else:** $/\!/\quad d \geq 1$ and $d+1$ is even

 12. $\mathcal{P}$ and $\mathcal{V}$ compute $d' \leftarrow \frac{d+1}{2} - 1$

 13. $\mathcal{P}$ computes $f_L(X) \leftarrow \sum_{i=0}^{d'} f_i \cdot X^i$ and $f_R(X) \leftarrow \sum_{i=0}^{d'} f_{d'+1+i} \cdot X^i$

 14. $\mathcal{P}$ computes $y_L \leftarrow f_L(z) \bmod p$ and $y_R \leftarrow f_R(z) \bmod p$

 15. $\mathcal{P}$ computes $\mathsf{C}_L \leftarrow \mathbf{g}^{f_L(q)}$ and $\mathsf{C}_R \leftarrow \mathbf{g}^{f_R(q)}$

 16. $\mathcal{P}$ sends $y_L, y_R, \mathsf{C}_L, \mathsf{C}_R$ to $\mathcal{V}$. $/\!/\quad$ See full version for an optimization

 17. $\mathcal{V}$ checks that $y = y_L + z^{d'+1} \cdot y_R \bmod p$, outputs 0 if check fails.

 18. $\mathcal{P}$ and $\mathcal{V}$ run $\mathsf{PoE}(\mathsf{C}_R, \mathsf{C}/\mathsf{C}_L, q^{d'+1}) /\!/\quad$ Showing that $\mathsf{C}_L \mathsf{C}_R^{(q^{d'+1})} = \mathsf{C}$

 19. $\mathcal{V}$ samples $\alpha \xleftarrow{\$} [-\frac{p-1}{2}, \frac{p-1}{2}]$ and sends it to $\mathcal{P}$

 20. $\mathcal{P}$ and $\mathcal{V}$ compute $y' \leftarrow \alpha y_L + y_R \bmod p, \mathsf{C}' \leftarrow \mathsf{C}_L^\alpha \mathsf{C}_R, b' \leftarrow b\frac{p+1}{2}$.

 21. $\mathcal{P}$ computes $f'(X) \leftarrow \alpha \cdot f_L(X) + f_R(X) \in \mathbb{Z}[X] /\!/\quad \deg(f'(X)) = d'$

 22. $\mathcal{P}$ and $\mathcal{V}$ run $\mathsf{EvalBounded}(\mathsf{pp}, \mathsf{C}', z, y', d', b'; f'(X))$

4.4   Security Analysis

Lemma 2. *The polynomial commitment scheme is binding for polynomials in $\mathbb{Z}(b)[X]$ for $b < q/2$ if either the Adaptive Root Assumption or the Strong RSA Assumption hold.*

Lemma 3. *The polynomial commitment scheme is correct for polynomials in* $\mathbb{Z}_p[X]$ *of degree at most* d *if* $q > p^{\lceil \log_2(d+1)\rceil+1}$.

All security proofs are in the full version of this paper [19, §A.1–§A.2]. Next is the main security theorem, which states that the evaluation protocol has witness-extended emulation. We start with a high-level intuitive overview where we also identify potential obstacles.

Proof idea. The goal is to construct an extractor by recursively computing $f(X)$ from $f'(X)$. In the final round the verifier receives f such that $|f| \leq b$, and therefore the extractor possesses this constant polynomial as well. Working backwards from here, the extractor uses rewinding in every step to find $f_L(X)$ and $f_R(X)$ and thereby finds $f(X) = f_L(X) + X^{d'+1}f_R(X)$. Specifically, in each round the extractor has $f'(X) = \alpha f_L(X) + f_R(X)$. Suppose the extractor also possesses $f''(X) = \alpha' f_L(X) + f_R(X)$. From $f'(X)$, $f''(X)$, α and α' it is easy to compute $f_L(X)$ and $f_R(X)$. The extractor then computes $f(X) = f_L(X) + X^{d'+1}f_R(X)$. A careful analysis shows that if the coefficients of $f'(X)$ are bounded by b then $f_L(X)$ and $f_R(X)$ must have coefficients bounded by $b \cdot p$ in absolute value. Using a similar analysis we can show that $f(z) \bmod p = y$ for the extracted polynomial $f(X)$.

This argument shows that there is an extractor algorithm $\mathcal{X}$ capable of extracting the witness $f(X)$ from a binary tree of accepting transcripts. Moreover, a tree-finding algorithm $\mathcal{T}$ can output such a tree by repeatedly rewinding the prover, running it with fresh verifier randomness each time, and recording the resulting transcripts. As a result, the Generalized Forking Lemma [14] applies and establishes that the protocol has witness-extended emulation.

The full proof takes into account the cryptographic compilation of the protocol using the integer encoding and the commitment scheme based on groups of unknown order. Additionally the full proof will need to support dyadic rationals because taking square roots is easy in class groups.

Theorem 1. *The polynomial commitment scheme for polynomials in* $\mathbb{Z}_p[X]$ *of degree at most* $d = \mathsf{poly}(\lambda)$, *instantiated using* $q > p^{2\lceil \log_2(d+1)\rceil+1}$ *and GGen, has witness extended emulation (Definition 2) if the Adaptive Root Assumption and the Strong RSA Assumption hold for GGen.*

Theorem 2. *Let GGen generate groups* $\mathbb{G}$ *of unknown order such that the order of* $\mathbb{G}$ *is odd, and such there exists a PPT algorithm for taking square roots in* $\mathbb{G}$. *The polynomial commitment scheme for polynomials in* $\mathbb{Z}_p[X]$ *of degree at most* $d = \mathsf{poly}(\lambda)$, *instantiated using* $q > p^{3\lceil \log_2(d+1)\rceil+1}$ *and GGen, has witness extended emulation (Definition 2) if the Adaptive Root Assumption and the 2-Strong RSA Assumption hold for GGen.*

The proof of Theorem 2 is nearly identical to the proof of Theorem 1 but the extracted polynomials are polynomials over the dyadic rationals and not over the integers. This requires the bound on q to be larger by a factor of $p^{\log(d+1)}$. Both proofs are presented in the full version of this paper [19, §A.3–§A.4].

4.5   Optimizations and Extensions

Out of space constraints, a number of interesting but non-essential sections are omitted. The full version of this paper [19] presents a range of optimizations for greater prover and verifier efficiency and smaller proof size. It also shows how to achieve extend the commitment to multivariate polynomials and shows how to make the commitment hiding with a ZK evaluation protocol.

4.6   Comparison

In Table 1 we give a comparison between different polynomial commitment schemes in the literature. In particular, we evaluate the size of the reference string ($|\mathsf{pp}|$), the prover and verifier time, as well as the size of the evaluation proof ($|\pi|$). Column 2 indicates whether the setup is transparent, *i.e.*, whether the reference string is structured. The symbol $\mathbb{G}_U$ denotes a group of unknown order, $\mathbb{G}_B$ a group with a bilinear map (pairing), and $\mathbb{G}_P$ a group with prime (and known) order. Furthermore, EXP refers to exponentiation of a λ bit number in these groups, and H is either the size of a hash output, or the time it takes to compute a hash, depending on context.

Note that even when precise factors are given, the numbers should be interpreted as estimates. For example we chose to not display smaller order terms. Note also that the prover time for the group based schemes could be brought down by a log factor when using multi-exponentiation techniques.

Table 1. Comparison table between different polynomial commitment schemes for an μ-variate polynomial of degree d.

Scheme	Transp.	$|\mathsf{pp}|$	Prover	Verifier	$|\pi|$
DARK *(this work)*	yes	$O(1)$	$O(d^\mu \mu \log(d))$ EXP	$3\mu \log(d)$ EXP	$2\mu \log(d)\, \mathbb{G}_U$
Based on Pairings	no	$d^\mu\, \mathbb{G}_B$	$O(d^\mu)$ EXP	μPairing	$\mu\, \mathbb{G}_B$
[14, $\sqrt{\cdot}$]	yes	$\sqrt{d^\mu}\mathbb{G}_P$	$O(d^\mu)$ EXP	$O(\sqrt{d^\mu})$ EXP	$O(\sqrt{d^\mu})\, \mathbb{G}_P$
Bulletproofs	yes	$2d^\mu\mathbb{G}_P$	$O(d^\mu)$ EXP	$O(d^\mu)$EXP	$2\mu \log(d)\, \mathbb{G}_P$
FRI ($\mu = 1$)[56]	yes	$O(1)$	$O(\lambda d)$ H	$O(\lambda \log^2(d))$ H	$O(\lambda \log^2(d))$ H

5   Transparent SNARKs via Polynomial IOPs

5.1   Algebraic Linear IOPs

An *interactive oracle proof (IOP)* [7,45] is a multi-round interactive PCP: in each round of an IOP the verifier sends a message to the prover and the prover responds with a polynomial length proof, which the verifier can query via random access. A t-round ℓ-query IOP has t rounds of interaction in which the verifier makes exactly ℓ queries in each round. Linear IOPs [11] are defined analogously except that in each round the prover sends a *linear* PCP [38], in which the prover sends a single proof vector $\boldsymbol{\pi} \in \mathbb{F}^m$ and the verifier makes *linear queries* to π. Specifically, the PCP gives the verifier access to an oracle that receives queries of the form $\mathbf{q} \in \mathbb{F}^m$ and returns the inner product $\langle \boldsymbol{\pi}, \mathbf{q} \rangle$.

Bitansky *et al.* [9] defined a linear PCP to be of *degree* (d_Q, d_V) if there is an explicit circuit of degree d_Q that derives the query vector from the verifier's random coins, and an explicit circuit of degree d_V that computes the verifier's decision from the query responses. In a multi-query PCP, d_Q refers to the maximum degree over all the independent circuits computing each query. Bitansky *et al.* called the linear PCP *algebraic* for a security parameter λ if it has degree $(\mathsf{poly}(\lambda), \mathsf{poly}(\lambda))$. The popular linear PCP based on *Quadratic Arithmetic Programs* (QAPs) implicit in the GGPR protocol [31] and follow-up works is an algebraic linear PCP with $d_Q \in O(m)$ and $d_V = 2$, where m is the size of the witness.

For the purposes of the present work, we are only interested in the algebraic nature of the query circuit and not the verifier's decision circuit. Of particular interest are linear PCPs where each query-and-response interaction corresponds to the evaluation of a fixed μ-variate degree d polynomial at a query point in $\mathbb{F}^\mu$. This description is equivalent to saying that the PCP is a vector of length $m = \binom{d+\mu}{\mu}$ and the query circuit is the vector of all μ-variate monomials of degree at most d (in some canonical order) evaluated at a point in $\mathbb{F}^\mu$. We call this a (μ, d) *Polynomial PCP* and define *Polynomial IOPs* analogously. As we will explain, we are interested in Polynomial PCPs where $\mu \ll m$ because we can cryptographically compile them into succinct arguments using polynomial commitments, in the same way that Merkle trees are used to compile classical (point) IOPs.

In general, evaluating the query circuit for a linear PCP requires $\Omega(m)$ work. However, a general "bootstrapping" technique can reduce the work for the verifier: the prover expands the verifier's random coins into a full query vector, and then provides the verifier with a second PCP demonstrating that this expansion was computed correctly. It may also help to allow the verifier to perform $O(m)$ work in a one-time preprocessing stage (for instance, to check the correctness of a PCP oracle), enabling it to perform sublinear "online" work when verifying arbitrary PCPs later. We call this a *preprocessing IOP*. In fact, we will see that any t-round (μ, d) algebraic linear IOP can be transformed into a $(t+1)$-round Polynomial IOP in which the verifier preprocesses (μ, d) Polynomial PCPs, at most one for each distinct query.

We recall the formal definition of public-coin linear IOPs as well an algebraic linear IOPs. Since we are not interested in the algebraic nature of the decision algorithm, we omit specifying the decision polynomial. From here onwards we use algebraic linear IOP as shorthand for algebraic *query* linear IOP.

Definition 5 (Public-coin linear IOP). *Let $\mathcal{R}$ be a binary relation and $\mathbb{F}$ a finite field. A t-round ℓ-query public-coin linear IOP for $\mathcal{R}$ over $\mathbb{F}$ with soundness error ϵ and knowledge error δ and query length $\mathbf{m} = (m_1, ..., m_t)$ consists of two stateful PPT algorithms, the prover $\mathcal{P}$, and the verifier $\mathcal{V} = (\mathcal{Q}, \mathcal{D})$, where the verifier consists in turn of a public deterministic query generator $\mathcal{Q}$ and a decision algorithm $\mathcal{D}$, that satisfy the following requirements:*

Protocol syntax. For each _ith_ round there is a prover state $\mathbf{st}_i^P$ and a verifier state $\mathbf{st}_i^V$. For any common input x and $\mathcal{R}$ witness w, at round 0 the states are $\mathbf{st}_0^P = (x, w)$ and $\mathbf{st}_0^V = x$. In the _ith_ round (starting at $i = 1$) the prover outputs a single[4] proof oracle $\mathcal{P}(\mathbf{st}_{i-1}^P) \rightarrow \boldsymbol{\pi}_i \in \mathbb{F}^{m_i}$. The verifier samples public random coins $coins_i \xleftarrow{\$} \{0,1\}^*$ and the query generator computes a query matrix from the verifier state and these coins: $\mathcal{Q}(\mathbf{st}_{i-1}^V, coins_i) \rightarrow \mathbf{Q}_i \in \mathbb{F}^{m_i \times \ell}$. The verifier obtains the linear oracle response vector $\boldsymbol{\pi}_i^\top \mathbf{Q}_i = \mathbf{a}_i \in \mathbb{F}^{1 \times \ell}$. The updated prover state is $\mathbf{st}_i^P \leftarrow (\mathbf{st}_{i-1}^P, \mathbf{Q}_i)$ and verifier state is $\mathbf{st}_i^V \leftarrow (\mathbf{st}_{i-1}^V, coins_i, \mathbf{a}_i)$ Finally, $\mathcal{D}(\mathbf{st}_t^V)$ returns 1 or 0.

(_Querying prior round oracles_: The syntax can be naturally extended so that in the _ith_ round the verifier may query any oracle, whether sent in the _ith_ round or earlier.)

Argument of Knowledge. As a proof system, $(\mathcal{P}, \mathcal{V})$ satisfies perfect completeness, soundness with respect to the relation $\mathcal{R}$ and with soundness error ϵ, and witness-extended emulation with respect $\mathcal{R}$ with knowledge error δ.

Furthermore, a linear IOP is **stateless** if for each $i \in [t]$, $\mathcal{Q}(\mathbf{st}_{i-1}^V, coins_i) = \mathcal{Q}(i, coins_i)$. It has **algebraic queries** if, additionally, for each $i \in [t]$, the map $coins_i \xmapsto{\mathcal{Q}(i,\cdot)} \mathbf{Q}_i \in \mathbb{F}^{m_i \times \ell}$ decomposes into two maps, $coins_i \xrightarrow{\mathcal{Q}_0(i,\cdot)} \boldsymbol{\Sigma}_i \xmapsto{\mathcal{Q}_1(i,\cdot)} \mathbf{Q}_i$, where $\boldsymbol{\Sigma}_i \in \mathbb{F}^{\mu_i \times \ell}$ is a matrix of $\mu_i < m_i$ rows and ℓ and $\mathcal{Q}_1(i, \cdot)$ is described by $\ell\mu_i$-variate polynomial functions of degree at most $d = \mathsf{poly}(\lambda)$: $\boldsymbol{p}_1, \ldots, \boldsymbol{p}_\ell : \mathbb{F}^{\mu_i} \rightarrow \mathbb{F}^{m_i}$ such that for all $k \in [\ell]$, $\boldsymbol{p}_k(\boldsymbol{\sigma}_{i,k}) = \mathbf{q}_{i,k}$, where $\boldsymbol{\sigma}_{i,k}$ and $\mathbf{q}_{i,k}$ denote the kth column of $\boldsymbol{\Sigma}_i$ and $\mathbf{Q}_i$, respectively.

We note that the separation into two maps $coins_i \xrightarrow{\mathcal{Q}_0(i,\cdot)} \boldsymbol{\Sigma}_i \xrightarrow{\mathcal{Q}_1(i,\cdot)} \mathbf{Q}_i$ subtly relaxes the definition of Bitansky _et al._ [9], which instead requires that $\mathbf{Q}_i$ be determined via $\boldsymbol{p}_1, \ldots, \boldsymbol{p}_\ell$ evaluated at a random $r \xleftarrow{\$} \mathbb{F}^{\mu_i}$. The [9] definition corresponds to the special case that $\mathcal{Q}_0(i, \cdot)$ samples a random element of $\mathbb{F}^{\mu_i}$ based on $coins_i$. The point is that $\mathcal{Q}_0$ can also do other computations that do not necessarily sample r uniformly, or even output a matrix rather than a vector. The separation into two steps is only meaningful when μ_i is smaller than m_i. The significance to SNARK constructions is that the query can be represented compactly as $\boldsymbol{\Sigma}_i$, and the prover will take advantage of the algebraic map $\mathcal{Q}_1(i, \cdot)$ to demonstrate that $\boldsymbol{\Sigma}_i$ was expanded correctly into $\mathbf{Q}_i$ and applied to the proof oracle π_i. We first present a standalone definition of Polynomial IOPs, and then explain how it is a special case of Algebraic Linear IOPs.

Definition 6 (Public coin Polynomial IOP). Let $\mathcal{R}$ be a binary relation and $\mathbb{F}$ a finite field. Let $\mathbf{X} = (X_1, \ldots, X_\mu)$ be a vector of μ indeterminates. A (μ, d) Polynomial IOP for $\mathcal{R}$ over $\mathbb{F}$ with soundness error ϵ and knowledge error

---

[4] The prover may also output more than one proof oracle per round, however this doesn't add any power since two proof oracles of the same size may be viewed as a single (concatenated) oracle of twice the length.

δ *consists of two stateful PPT algorithms, the* prover P, *and the* verifier V, *that satisfy the following requirements:*

Protocol syntax. For each ith round there is a prover state st_i^P *and a verifier state* st_i^V. *For any common input* x *and* R *witness* w, *at round 0 the states are* $st_0^P = (x, w)$ *and* $st_0^V = x$. *In the ith round (starting at* $i = 1$*) the prover outputs a single proof oracle* $P(st_{i-1}^P) \to \pi_i$, *which is a polynomial* $\pi_i(\mathbf{X}) \in \mathbb{F}[\mathbf{X}]$. *The verifier deterministically computes the query matrix* $\Sigma_i \in \mathbb{F}^{\mu \times \ell}$ *from its state and a string of public random bits* $coins_i \xleftarrow{\$} \{0,1\}^*$, *i.e,* $V(st_{i-1}^V, coins_i) \to \Sigma_i$. *This query matrix is interpreted as a list of* ℓ *points in* $\mathbb{F}^\mu$ *denoted* $(\sigma_{i,1}, \ldots, \sigma_{i,\ell})$. *The oracle* π_i *is queried on all points in this list, producing the response vector* $(\pi_i(\sigma_{i,1}), \ldots, \pi_\ell(\sigma_{i,\ell})) = \mathbf{a}_i \in \mathbb{F}^{1 \times \ell}$. *The updated prover state is* $st_i^P \leftarrow (st_{i-1}^P, \Sigma_i)$ *and verifier state is* $st_i^V \leftarrow (st_{i-1}^V, \Sigma_i, \mathbf{a}_i)$. *Finally,* $V(st_t^V)$ *returns 1 or 0.*

(Extensions: multiple and prior round oracles; various arity. The syntax can be naturally extended such that multiple oracles are sent in the ith round; that the verifier may query oracles sent in the ith round or earlier; or that some of the oracles are polynomials in fewer variables than μ.)

Argument of Knowledge. As a proof system, (P, V) *satisfies perfect completeness, soundness with respect to the relation* R *and with soundness error* ϵ, *and witness-extended emulation with respect* R *with knowledge error* δ.

Furthermore, a Polynomial IOP is **stateless** *if for each* $i \in [t]$, $V(st_{i-1}^V, coins_i) = V(i, coins_i)$.

Polynomial IOPs as a subclass of Algebraic Linear IOPs. In a Polynomial IOP, the two-step map $coins_i \xmapsto{V(i, \cdot)} (\sigma_{i,1}, \ldots, \sigma_{i,\ell}) \xmapsto{\mathbf{M}} (\mathbf{q}_{i,1}, \ldots, \mathbf{q}_{i,\ell})$ is a special case of the two-step map $coins_i \xmapsto{Q_0(i, \cdot)} \Sigma_i \xmapsto{Q_1(i, \cdot)} \mathbf{Q}_i$ in an algebraic linear IOP. Here $\mathbf{M} : \mathbb{F}^\mu \to \mathbb{F}^m$ represents the vector of monomials of degree at most d (in some canonical order) and the map associated with $\mathbf{M}$ is evaluation. Note that there are $m = \binom{\mu+d}{d}$ such monomials. Furthermore, for any $\mathbf{q}_{i,k}$, the inner product $\pi_i^T \mathbf{q}_{i,k}$ corresponds to the evaluation at $\sigma_{i,k}$ of the polynomial $\pi_i(\mathbf{X}) \in \mathbb{F}[\mathbf{X}]$, whose coefficient vector (in the same canonical monomial order) is equal to π_i.

5.2   Polynomial IOP Reductions

In this section we show that one can construct any algebraic linear IOP from a (multivariate) Polynomial IOP. This construction rests on two tools for univariate Polynomial IOPs. These tools are treated explicitly in the full version of this paper [19]. They can be realized with a small constant number of evaluations.

- *Coefficient queries.* The verifier verifies that an indicated coefficient of a polynomial oracle has a given value.
- *Inner products.* The verifier verifies that the inner product of the coefficient vectors of two polynomial oracles equals a given value.

Reducing algebraic linear IOPs to polynomial IOPs.

Theorem 3. *Any public-coin t-round stateless algebraic linear IOP can be implemented with a $t + 1$-round Polynomial IOP with preprocessing. Suppose the original ℓ-query IOP is (μ, d) algebraic with query length $(m_1, ..., m_t)$ then the resulting Polynomial IOP has for each $i \in [t]$: 2ℓ degree m_i univariate polynomial oracles, ℓ pre-processed multivariate oracles of degree d and $\mu + 1$ variables, ℓ degree $2m_i$ univariate polynomial oracles and 2ℓ degree $2m_i$ univariate polynomial oracles. There is exactly one query to each oracle on a random point in $\mathbb{F}$. The soundness loss of the transformation is $\mathsf{negl}(\lambda)$ for a sufficiently large field (i.e., whose cardinality is exponential in λ).*

We formally prove Theorem 3 in the full version of this paper [19]. Here we present the transformation without proof.

By definition of a (μ, d) algebraic linear IOP, in each ith round of the IOP there are ℓ query generation functions $\boldsymbol{p}_{i,1}, \ldots, \boldsymbol{p}_{i,\ell} : \mathbb{F}^\mu \to \mathbb{F}^{m_i}$, where each $\boldsymbol{p}_{i,k}$ is a vector whose jth component is a μ-variate degree-d polynomial $p_{i,k,j}$. These polynomials are applied to a seed matrix $\boldsymbol{\sigma}_{i,k} \in \mathbb{F}^\mu$ (which is identifiable with or derived from the verifier's ith round public-coin randomness $coins_i$); this evaluation produces $\boldsymbol{p}_{i,k}(\boldsymbol{\sigma}_{i,k}) = \mathbf{q}_{i,k} \in \mathbb{F}^{m_i}$ for all $k \in [\ell]$. The vectors $\mathbf{q}_{i,k}$ are the columns of the query matrix $\mathbf{Q}_i \in \mathbb{F}^{m_i \times \ell}$.

Preprocessed oracles. For each round i of the original algebraic linear IOP, the prover and verifier preprocess $(\mu + 1)$-variate degree-d polynomial oracles. For each $k \in [\ell]$, the vector of polynomials $\boldsymbol{p}_{i,k} = (p_{i,k,1}, \ldots, p_{i,k,m_i}) \in (\mathbb{F}[\mathbf{X}])^{m_i}$ with $\mathbf{X} = (X_1, \ldots, X_\mu)$ is encoded as a single polynomial in $\mu + 1$ variables as follows. Introduce a new indeterminate Z, and then define $\tilde{P}_{i,k}(\mathbf{X}, Z) := \sum_{j=1}^{m_i} p_{i,k,j}(\mathbf{X}) Z^j \in \mathbb{F}[\mathbf{X}, Z]$. The prover and verifier establish the oracle $\tilde{P}_{i,k}$, meaning that the verifier queries this oracle on enough points to be reassured that it is correct everywhere.

The transformed IOP. The original algebraic linear IOP is modified as follows.

- Wherever the original IOP prover sends an oracle $\boldsymbol{\pi}_i$ of length m_i, the new prover sends a degree $m_i - 1$ univariate polynomial oracle f_{π_i} whose coefficient vector is *the reverse* of $\boldsymbol{\pi}_i$.
- Wherever the original IOP verifier makes ℓ queries within a round to a particular proof oracle $\boldsymbol{\pi}_i$, where queries are defined by query matrix $\mathbf{Q}_i \in \mathbb{F}^{m_i \times \ell}$, consisting of column query vectors $(\mathbf{q}_{i,1}, ..., \mathbf{q}_{i,\ell})$, the new prover and verifier engage in the following interactive subprotocol for each $k \in [\ell]$ in order to replace the kth linear query $\langle \boldsymbol{\pi}_i, \mathbf{q}_{i,k} \rangle$:
  - Verifier: Run the original IOP verifier to get the public coin seed matrix $\boldsymbol{\Sigma}_i$ and send it to the prover.
  - Prover: Derive the query matrix $\mathbf{Q}_i$ from $\boldsymbol{\Sigma}_i$ using the polynomials $\boldsymbol{p}_{i,1}, \ldots, \boldsymbol{p}_{i,\ell}$. Send an oracle for the polynomial $F_{i,k}$ whose coefficient vector is $\mathbf{q}_{i,k}$.

- Verifier: Sample uniform random $\beta \xleftarrow{\$} \mathbb{F}$ and query both $F_{i,k}$ and $\tilde{P}_{i,k}$ (the kth preprocessed oracle for round i) at β in order to check that $F_{i,k}(\beta) = \tilde{P}_{i,k}(\sigma_{i,k}, \beta)$. If the check fails, abort and output 0.
- Prover: Compute $a_{i,k} = \langle \boldsymbol{\pi}, \mathbf{q}_{i,k} \rangle$ and send $a_{i,k}$ to the verifier.
- The prover and verifier run the inner product Polynomial IOP on the oracles $F_{i,k}$ and f_{π_i} to convince the verifier that $a_{i,k} = \langle \mathbf{q}_{i,k}, \boldsymbol{\pi}_i \rangle$. If the inner product subprotocol fails the verifier aborts and outputs 0.

If all substeps succeed, then the verifier obtains correct output of each oracle query; in other words, the responses are identical in the new and original IOP. These outputs are passed to the original verifier decision algorithm, which outputs 0 or 1.

5.3   Compiling Polynomial IOPs

Let $\Gamma = (\mathsf{Setup}, \mathsf{Commit}, \mathsf{Open}, \mathsf{Eval})$ be a multivariate polynomial commitment scheme. Given any t-round Polynomial IOP for $\mathcal{R}$ over $\mathbb{F}$, we construct an interactive protocol $\Pi = (\mathsf{Setup}, \mathcal{P}, \mathcal{V})$ as follows. For clarity in our explanation, Π consists of t *outer rounds* corresponding to the original IOP rounds and *subrounds* where subprotocols may add additional rounds of interaction between outer rounds.

- Setup: Run $\mathsf{pp} \leftarrow \mathsf{Setup}(1^\lambda)$
- In any round where the IOP prover sends a (μ, d) polynomial proof oracle $\boldsymbol{\pi} : \mathbb{F}^\mu \to \mathbb{F}$, in the corresponding *outer round* of Π, $\mathcal{P}$ sends the commitment $c_\pi \leftarrow \mathsf{Commit}(\mathsf{pp}; \boldsymbol{\pi})$
- In any round where the IOP verifier makes an *evaluation* query $\mathbf{z}$ to a (μ, d) polynomial proof oracle $\boldsymbol{\pi}$, in the corresponding *outer round* of Π, insert an interactive execution of $\mathsf{Eval}(\mathsf{pp}, c_\pi, \mathbf{z}, y, \mu, d; \boldsymbol{\pi})$ between $\mathcal{P}$ and $\mathcal{V}$, where $\boldsymbol{\pi}(\mathbf{z}) = y$.

If $\mathcal{V}$ does not abort in any of these subprotocols, then it receives a simulated IOP transcript of oracle queries and responses. It runs the IOP verifier decision algorithm on this transcript and outputs the result.

Theorem 4. *If the polynomial commitment scheme Γ has witness-extended emulation, and if the t-round Polynomial IOP for $\mathcal{R}$ has negligible knowledge error, then Π is a public-coin interactive argument for $\mathcal{R}$ that has witness-extended emulation.*

5.4   Concrete Instantiations

Several proof systems use Polynomial IOPs and our compiler can be applied to them. We present PLONK [30] here and discuss several other proof systems [4, 22, 31, 43, 48] in the full version [19].

Theorem 6 provides the main theoretical result of this work, tying together the new DARK polynomial commitment scheme (Theorem 1), the compilation of Polynomial IOPs into SNARKs with preprocessing using polynomial commitments (Theorem 4), and a concrete univariate Polynomial IOPs. To enable this tie-up, we re-characterize the result of PLONK in terms of Polynomial IOPs, making use of the coefficient query technique (Sect. 5.2) as necessary.

Theorem 5 (PLONK, [30]). *There is a 3-round HVZK Polynomial IOP with preprocessing for any NP relation $\mathcal{R}$ (with arithmetic complexity n) that makes 12 queries overall to 12 univariate degree n polynomial oracles. The total number of distinct query points is 2. The preprocessing verifier does $O(n)$ work to check 7 of the univariate degree n polynomials.*

Combining the PLONK Polynomial IOP with the new transparent polynomial compiler of Sect. 4 gives the following result. Analogous results are obtained by using Sonic [43] or Marlin [22] instead.

Theorem 6 (New Transparent zk-SNARK). *There exists an $O(\log n)$-round public-coin interactive argument of knowledge for any NP relation with arithmetic complexity n that has $O(\log n)$ communication, $O(\log n)$ "online" verification, quasilinear prover time, and a preprocessing step that is verifiable in quasilinear time. The argument of knowledge has witness-extended emulation assuming it is instantiated with a group $\mathbb{G}$ for which the Strong RSA Assumption, and the Adaptive Root Assumption hold.*

6   Evaluation

We now evaluate Supersonic, the trustless-setup SNARK built on the Polynomial IOPs underlying Sonic [43], PLONK [30], and Marlin [22] and compiled using our DARK polynomial commitment scheme. The commitment scheme has several useful batching properties. It is possible to evaluate k polynomials of degree at most d using only 2 group elements and $(k+1)$ field elements. To take advantage of this we delay the evaluation until the last step of the protocol. We present the proof size for both the compilation of Sonic, PLONK and Marlin in Table 2. We use 1600 bits as the size of class group elements and $\lambda = 120$. The security of 1600 bit class groups is believed to be equivalent to 3048bit RSA groups and have 120 bits of security [8, 17]. This leads to proof sizes of 16.5 KB for Sonic, 10.1 KB using PLONK and 12.3 KB using Marlin for circuits with $n = 2^{20}$ (one million) gates. Using 3048-bit RSA groups the proof sizes becomes 18.4 KB for the compilation of PLONK. If 100 bits of security suffice then a 1200 bit class group can be used and the compiled PLONK proofs are 7.8 KB for the same setting. In a 2048-bit RSA group this becomes 12.7 KB.

The comparison between the Polynomial IOPs is slightly misleading because n represents different indicators of complexity. Nevertheless this calculation shows that there are Polynomial IOPs that can be compiled using the DARK polynomial commitment scheme to SNARKs of roughly 10 KB in size. These numbers stand in contrast to STARKs which achieve proofs of 600 KB for computation of similar complexity [4]. We compare Supersonic to different other proof systems in Table 3. Supersonic is the only proof system with efficient verifier time, small proof sizes that does not require a trusted setup. Using $10\,\mu s$ per group operation[5], this gives a verification time of around 72 ms.

Table 2. Proof size for Supersonic. Column 2 says how many polynomials are committed to in the SRS (offline oracles) and how many are sent by the prover (online oracles). Column 3 states the number of distinct evaluation points. The proof size calculation uses $|\mathbb{Z}_p| = 120$ and $|\mathbb{G}| = 1600$ for $n = 2^{20}$ gates.

Polynomial IOP	Polynomials	Eval points	|SNARK|	Concrete size
Sonic [43]	12 in pp + 15	12	$(15 + 2\log_2(n))\mathbb{G}$ $+ (12 + 13\log_2(n))\mathbb{Z}_p$	15.3 KB
PLONK [30]	7 in pp + 7	2	$(7 + 2\log_2(n))\mathbb{G}$ $+ (2 + 3\log_2(n))\mathbb{Z}_p$	10.1 KB
Marlin [22]	9 in pp + 10	3	$(10 + 2\log_2(6n))\mathbb{G}$ $+ (3 + 4\log_2(6n))\mathbb{Z}_p$	12.3 KB

Table 3. Comparison table between different succinct arguments. In column order we compare on transparent setup, CRS size, prover and verifier time, asymptotic proof size and concrete proof for an NP relation with arithmetic complexity 2^{20}. Even when precise factors are given the numbers should be seen as estimates. For example, we chose to not display smaller order terms. The symbol $\mathbb{G}_U$ denotes an element in group of unknown order, $\mathbb{G}_B$ one in a group with a bilinear map (pairing), $\mathbb{G}_P$ one in a prime order group with known order. Furthermore, EXP refers to exponentiation of λ-bit numbers in these groups, and H is either the size of a hash output or the time it takes to compute a hash. The prover time for the group based schemes can be brought down by a log factor when using multi-exponentiation techniques.

Scheme	Transp.	|pp|	Prover	Verifier	$\|\pi\|$	$n = 2^{20}$
Supersonic	yes	$O(1)$	$O(n\log(n))$EXP	$3\log(n)$ EXP	$2\log(n)\,\mathbb{G}_U$	10.1 KB
PLONK [30]	no	$2n\,\mathbb{G}_B$	$O(n)$ EXP	1 Pairing	$O(1)\,\mathbb{G}_B$	720 b
Groth16 [35]	no	$2n\,\mathbb{G}_B$	$O(n)$ EXP	1 Pairing	$O(1)\,\mathbb{G}_B$	192 b
BP [18]	yes	$2n\,\mathbb{G}_P$	$O(n)$ EXP	$O(n)$ EXP	$2\log(n)\,\mathbb{G}_P$	1.7 KB
STARK	yes	$O(1)$	$O(\lambda T)$ H	$O(\lambda\log^2(T))$ H	$O(\lambda\log^2(T))$ H	600 KB

7 Conclusion

In this work we presented the DARK compiler: a polynomial commitment scheme from falsifiable assumptions in groups of unknown order with evaluation proofs that can be verified in logarithmic time. We also presented Polynomial IOPs, a

---

[5] The estimate comes from the recent Chia Inc. class group implementation competition. The competition used a larger 2048 bit discriminant but only performed repeated squaring. https://github.com/Chia-Network/vdfcontest2results.

unifying information-theoretical framework underlying the information theoretic foundation of several recent SNARK constructions. Polynomial IOPs can be compiled into a concrete SNARK using a polynomial commitment scheme and the Fiat-Shamir transform. We showed that applying the DARK compiler to recent Polynomial IOPs yields **the first trustless SNARKs (*i.e.*, with a transparent untrusted setup) that have practical proof sizes and verification times**. In particular, this is the first trustless/transparent SNARK construction that has asymptotically logarithmic verification time (ignoring the λ-dependent factors, which are comparable to λ-dependent factors in prior works). Finally, unlike all known SNARKs in bilinear groups, the construction does not require knowledge of exponent assumptions. Several important open questions remain:

- Our polynomial commitment scheme has prover time linear in the total number of coefficients, even for zero coefficients. Consequently for a sparse bivariate polynomial of degree d in each variable the prover time is quadratic in d. A sparse polynomial commitment scheme would directly enable an efficient compilation of simple information theoretic protocols such as QAPs.
- Asymptotically, Supersonic's prover time is on par with pairing-based SNARK constructions, however, a concrete implementation and performance comparison remains open.
- This work further motivates the study of class groups and groups of unknown order. In particular we rely on a recently introduced Adaptive Root Assumption.
- Our polynomial commitment scheme uses a simple underlying information theoretic protocol that could be compiled using a (partially) homomorphic commitment scheme over polynomials, or even another type of integer homomorphic commitment scheme. This leaves open whether there are different ways of instantiating our DARK compiler under different cryptographic assumptions.

Acknowledgements. We thank Dan Boneh for helpful discussions and comments. This work was supported by NSF, SGF, ONR, the Simons Foundation, the Nervos Foundation and the Findora Foundation.

References

1. Zcash. https://z.cash
2. Barić, N., Pfitzmann, B.: Collision-free accumulators and fail-stop signature schemes without trees. In: Fumy, W. (ed.) EUROCRYPT 1997. LNCS, vol. 1233, pp. 480–494. Springer, Heidelberg (1997). https://doi.org/10.1007/3-540-69053-0_33
3. Ben-Sasson, E., Bentov, I., Horesh, Y., Riabzev, M.: Fast reed-solomon interactive oracle proofs of proximity. In: Chatzigiannakis, I., Kaklamanis, C., Marx, D., Sannella, D. (eds.) ICALP 2018. LIPIcs, vol. 107, pp. 14:1–14:17. Schloss Dagstuhl, July 2018

4. Ben-Sasson, E., Bentov, I., Horesh, Y., Riabzev, M.: Scalable zero knowledge with no trusted setup. In: Boldyreva, A., Micciancio, D. (eds.) CRYPTO 2019, Part III. LNCS, vol. 11694, pp. 701–732. Springer, Cham (2019). https://doi.org/10.1007/978-3-030-26954-8_23

5. Ben-Sasson, E., et al.: Zerocash: decentralized anonymous payments from bitcoin. In: 2014 IEEE Symposium on Security and Privacy, pp. 459–474. IEEE Computer Society Press, May 2014

6. Ben-Sasson, E., Chiesa, A., Genkin, D., Tromer, E., Virza, M.: SNARKs for C: verifying program executions succinctly and in zero knowledge. In: Canetti, R., Garay, J.A. (eds.) CRYPTO 2013, Part II. LNCS, vol. 8043, pp. 90–108. Springer, Heidelberg (2013). https://doi.org/10.1007/978-3-642-40084-1_6

7. Ben-Sasson, E., Chiesa, A., Spooner, N.: Interactive oracle proofs. In: Hirt, M., Smith, A. (eds.) TCC 2016, Part II. LNCS, vol. 9986, pp. 31–60. Springer, Heidelberg (2016). https://doi.org/10.1007/978-3-662-53644-5_2

8. Biasse, J., Jacobson Jr., M.J., Silvester, A.K.: Security estimates for quadratic field based cryptosystems. CoRR abs/1004.5512 (2010). http://arxiv.org/abs/1004.5512

9. Bitansky, N., Chiesa, A., Ishai, Y., Paneth, O., Ostrovsky, R.: Succinct non-interactive arguments via linear interactive proofs. In: Sahai, A. (ed.) TCC 2013. LNCS, vol. 7785, pp. 315–333. Springer, Heidelberg (2013). https://doi.org/10.1007/978-3-642-36594-2_18

10. Boneh, D., Bonneau, J., Bünz, B., Fisch, B.: Verifiable delay functions. In: Shacham, H., Boldyreva, A. (eds.) CRYPTO 2018, Part I. LNCS, vol. 10991, pp. 757–788. Springer, Cham (2018). https://doi.org/10.1007/978-3-319-96884-1_25

11. Boneh, D., Boyle, E., Corrigan-Gibbs, H., Gilboa, N., Ishai, Y.: Zero-knowledge proofs on secret-shared data via fully linear PCPs. In: Boldyreva, A., Micciancio, D. (eds.) CRYPTO 2019, Part III. LNCS, vol. 11694, pp. 67–97. Springer, Cham (2019). https://doi.org/10.1007/978-3-030-26954-8_3

12. Boneh, D., Bünz, B., Fisch, B.: Batching techniques for accumulators with applications to IOPs and stateless blockchains. In: Boldyreva, A., Micciancio, D. (eds.) CRYPTO 2019, Part I. LNCS, vol. 11692, pp. 561–586. Springer, Cham (2019). https://doi.org/10.1007/978-3-030-26948-7_20

13. Bootle, J., Cerulli, A., Chaidos, P., Groth, J., Petit, C.: Efficient zero-knowledge arguments for arithmetic circuits in the discrete log setting. Cryptology ePrint Archive, Report 2016/263 (2016). http://eprint.iacr.org/2016/263

14. Bootle, J., Cerulli, A., Chaidos, P., Groth, J., Petit, C.: Efficient zero-knowledge arguments for arithmetic circuits in the discrete log setting. In: Fischlin, M., Coron, J.S. (eds.) EUROCRYPT 2016, Part II. LNCS, vol. 9666, pp. 327–357. Springer, Heidelberg (2016)

15. Bosma, W., Stevenhagen, P.: On the computation of quadratic 2-class groups. J. Theor. Nombr. **8**, 283–313 (1996)

16. Bowe, S.: Bellman zk-SNARKS library (2016). https://github.com/zkcrypto/bellman

17. Buchmann, J., Hamdy, S.: A survey on IQ cryptography. In: Public-Key Cryptography and Computational Number Theory, pp. 1–15 (2001)

18. Bünz, B., Bootle, J., Boneh, D., Poelstra, A., Wuille, P., Maxwell, G.: Bulletproofs: short proofs for confidential transactions and more. In: 2018 IEEE Symposium on Security and Privacy, pp. 315–334. IEEE Computer Society Press, May 2018

19. Bünz, B., Fisch, B., Szepieniec, A.: Transparent SNARKs from DARK compilers. Cryptology ePrint Archive, Report 2019/1229 (2019). https://eprint.iacr.org/2019/1229

20. Buterin, V.: ZK rollup (2016). https://ethresear.ch/t/on-chain-scaling-to-potentially-500-tx-sec-through-mass-tx-validation/3477
21. Canetti, R., et al.: Fiat-Shamir: from practice to theory. In: Charikar, M., Cohen, E. (eds.) 51st ACM STOC, pp. 1082–1090. ACM Press, June 2019
22. Chiesa, A., Hu, Y., Maller, M., Mishra, P., Vesely, N., Ward, N.: Marlin: preprocessing zkSNARKs with universal and updatable SRS. Cryptology ePrint Archive, Report 2019/1047 (2019). https://eprint.iacr.org/2019/1047
23. Chiesa, A., Ojha, D., Spooner, N.: Fractal: post-quantum and transparent recursive proofs from holography (2019). https://eprint.iacr.org/2019/1076
24. Couteau, G., Peters, T., Pointcheval, D.: Removing the strong RSA assumption from arguments over the integers. In: Coron, J.-S., Nielsen, J.B. (eds.) EUROCRYPT 2017, Part II. LNCS, vol. 10211, pp. 321–350. Springer, Cham (2017). https://doi.org/10.1007/978-3-319-56614-6_11
25. Damgård, I., Fujisaki, E.: A statistically-hiding integer commitment scheme based on groups with hidden order. In: Zheng, Y. (ed.) ASIACRYPT 2002. LNCS, vol. 2501, pp. 125–142. Springer, Heidelberg (2002). https://doi.org/10.1007/3-540-36178-2_8
26. Damgård, I., Koprowski, M.: Generic lower bounds for root extraction and signature schemes in general groups. In: Knudsen, L.R. (ed.) EUROCRYPT 2002. LNCS, vol. 2332, pp. 256–271. Springer, Heidelberg (2002). https://doi.org/10.1007/3-540-46035-7_17
27. Eberhardt, J.: Zokrates. https://zokrates.github.io/
28. Fiat, A., Shamir, A.: How to prove yourself: practical solutions to identification and signature problems. In: Odlyzko, A.M. (ed.) CRYPTO 1986. LNCS, vol. 263, pp. 186–194. Springer, Heidelberg (1987). https://doi.org/10.1007/3-540-47721-7_12
29. Fujisaki, E., Okamoto, T.: Statistical zero knowledge protocols to prove modular polynomial relations. In: Kaliski, B.S. (ed.) CRYPTO 1997. LNCS, vol. 1294, pp. 16–30. Springer, Heidelberg (1997). https://doi.org/10.1007/BFb0052225
30. Gabizon, A., Williamson, Z.J., Ciobotaru, O.: PLONK: permutations over lagrange-bases for oecumenical noninteractive arguments of knowledge. Cryptology ePrint Archive, Report 2019/953 (2019). https://eprint.iacr.org/2019/953
31. Gennaro, R., Gentry, C., Parno, B., Raykova, M.: Quadratic span programs and succinct NIZKs without PCPs. In: Johansson, T., Nguyen, P.Q. (eds.) EUROCRYPT 2013. LNCS, vol. 7881, pp. 626–645. Springer, Heidelberg (2013). https://doi.org/10.1007/978-3-642-38348-9_37
32. Goldreich, O., Vadhan, S., Wigderson, A.: On interactive proofs with a laconic prover. Comput. Complex. 11(1/2), 1–53 (2002)
33. Goldwasser, S., Kalai, Y.T., Rothblum, G.N.: Delegating computation: interactive proofs for muggles. In: Ladner, R.E., Dwork, C. (eds.) 40th ACM STOC, pp. 113–122. ACM Press, May 2008
34. Goldwasser, S., Micali, S., Rackoff, C.: The knowledge complexity of interactive proof-systems (extended abstract). In: 17th ACM STOC, pp. 291–304. ACM Press, May 1985
35. Groth, J.: On the size of pairing-based non-interactive arguments. In: Fischlin, M., Coron, J.-S. (eds.) EUROCRYPT 2016, Part II. LNCS, vol. 9666, pp. 305–326. Springer, Heidelberg (2016). https://doi.org/10.1007/978-3-662-49896-5_11
36. Groth, J., Ishai, Y.: Sub-linear zero-knowledge argument for correctness of a shuffle. In: Smart, N. (ed.) EUROCRYPT 2008. LNCS, vol. 4965, pp. 379–396. Springer, Heidelberg (2008). https://doi.org/10.1007/978-3-540-78967-3_22
37. Hopwood, D., Bowe, S., Hornby, T., Wilcox, N.: Zcash protocol specification (2019). https://zips.z.cash/protocol/protocol.pdf

38. Ishai, Y., Kushilevitz, E., Ostrovsky, R.: Efficient arguments without short PCPs (2007)
39. Kate, A., Zaverucha, G.M., Goldberg, I.: Constant-size commitments to polynomials and their applications. In: Abe, M. (ed.) ASIACRYPT 2010. LNCS, vol. 6477, pp. 177–194. Springer, Heidelberg (2010). https://doi.org/10.1007/978-3-642-17373-8_11
40. Labs, O.: Coda protocol (2018). https://codaprotocol.com/
41. Lindell, Y.: Parallel coin-tossing and constant-round secure two-party computation. In: Kilian, J. (ed.) CRYPTO 2001. LNCS, vol. 2139, pp. 171–189. Springer, Heidelberg (2001). https://doi.org/10.1007/3-540-44647-8_10
42. Lipmaa, H.: On diophantine complexity and statistical zero-knowledge arguments. In: Laih, C.-S. (ed.) ASIACRYPT 2003. LNCS, vol. 2894, pp. 398–415. Springer, Heidelberg (2003). https://doi.org/10.1007/978-3-540-40061-5_26
43. Maller, M., Bowe, S., Kohlweiss, M., Meiklejohn, S.: Sonic: zero-knowledge snarks from linear-size universal and updatable structured reference strings. Cryptology ePrint Archive, Report 2019/099 (2019). https://eprint.iacr.org/2019/099
44. Pietrzak, K.: Simple verifiable delay functions. In: 10th Innovations in Theoretical Computer Science Conference, ITCS 2019, San Diego, California, USA, 10–12 January 2019, pp. 60:1–60:15 (2019)
45. Reingold, O., Rothblum, G.N., Rothblum, R.D.: Constant-round interactive proofs for delegating computation. In: Wichs, D., Mansour, Y. (eds.) 48th ACM STOC, pp. 49–62. ACM Press, June 2016
46. Rivest, R., Shamir, A., Wagner, D.: Time-lock puzzles and timed-release crypto. MIT Technical report (1996)
47. Setty, S., Braun, B., Vu, V., Blumberg, A.J., Parno, B., Walfish, M.: Resolving the conflict between generality and plausibility in verified computation (2013)
48. Setty, S.: Spartan: efficient and general-purpose zkSNARKs without trusted setup. Cryptology ePrint Archive, Report 2019/550 (2019). https://eprint.iacr.org/2019/550
49. Straka, M.: Class groups for cryptographic accumulators (2019). https://www.michaelstraka.com/posts/classgroups/
50. Vlasov, A., Panarin, K.: Transparent polynomial commitment scheme with polylogarithmic communication complexity. Cryptology ePrint Archive, Report 2019/1020 (2019). https://eprint.iacr.org/2019/1020
51. Wahby, R.S., Tzialla, I., shelat, A., Thaler, J., Walfish, M.: Doubly-efficient zkSNARKs without trusted setup. In: 2018 IEEE Symposium on Security and Privacy, pp. 926–943. IEEE Computer Society Press, May 2018
52. Walfish, M., Blumberg, A.J.: Verifying computations without reexecuting them: from theoretical possibility to near practicality. Commun. ACM 58(2), 74–84 (2015)
53. Wesolowski, B.: Efficient verifiable delay functions. In: Ishai, Y., Rijmen, V. (eds.) EUROCRYPT 2019, Part III. LNCS, vol. 11478, pp. 379–407. Springer, Cham (2019). https://doi.org/10.1007/978-3-030-17659-4_13
54. Wilcox, Z.: The design of the ceremony (2016). https://z.cash/blog/the-design-of-the-ceremony.html
55. Xie, T., Zhang, J., Zhang, Y., Papamanthou, C., Song, D.: Libra: succinct zero-knowledge proofs with optimal prover computation. Cryptology ePrint Archive, Report 2019/317 (2019). https://eprint.iacr.org/2019/317
56. Zhang, J., Xie, T., Zhang, Y., Song, D.: Transparent polynomial delegation and its applications to zero knowledge proof. Cryptology ePrint Archive, Report 2019/1482 (2019). https://eprint.iacr.org/2019/1482

SPARKs: Succinct Parallelizable Arguments of Knowledge

Naomi Ephraim[1]($\boxtimes$), Cody Freitag[1]($\boxtimes$), Ilan Komargodski[2], and Rafael Pass[1]

[1] Cornell Tech, New York, NY 10044, USA
{nephraim,cfreitag,rafael}@cs.cornell.edu
[2] NTT Research, Palo Alto, CA 94303, USA
ilan.komargodski@ntt-research.ac.il

Abstract. We introduce the notion of a *Succinct Parallelizable Argument of Knowledge* (SPARK). This is an argument system with the following three properties for computing and proving a time T (non-deterministic) computation:

- The prover's (parallel) running time is $T + \text{polylog}\,T$. (In other words, the prover's running time is essentially T for large computation times!)
- The prover uses at most $\text{polylog}\,T$ processors.
- The communication complexity and verifier complexity are both $\text{polylog}\,T$.

While the third property is standard in succinct arguments, the combination of all three is desirable as it gives a way to leverage moderate parallelism in favor of near-optimal running time. We emphasize that even a factor two overhead in the prover's parallel running time is not allowed.

Our main results are the following, all for non-deterministic polynomial-time RAM computation. We construct (1) an (interactive) SPARK based solely on the existence of collision-resistant hash functions, and (2) a non-interactive SPARK based on any collision-resistant hash function and any SNARK with quasi-linear overhead (as satisfied by recent SNARK constructions).

1 Introduction

Interactive proof systems, introduced by Goldwasser, Micali and Rackoff [27], are one of the most fundamental concepts in theoretical computer science. Such systems consist of a prover who is able to convince a verifier of the validity of some statement if and only if it is true. The "if" direction is called *completeness* and the "only if" direction is called *soundness*. Proof systems where soundness is only guaranteed to hold for efficient (i.e., polynomial-time) provers are called *argument* systems.

We focus on *succinct* argument systems for NP: argument systems where the total communication is essentially independent of the size of the verification circuit of the language and even shorter than the statement. Since their introduction [12,31,34], succinct argument systems have drawn significant attention due

A. Canteaut and Y. Ishai (Eds.): EUROCRYPT 2020, LNCS 12105, pp. 707–737, 2020.
https://doi.org/10.1007/978-3-030-45721-1_25

to their appealing efficiency properties. Nowadays they are widely implemented and used in various systems, most notably in numerous blockchain platforms.

One aspect of such argument systems that has been the center of many recent works (e.g., [13,18,28,43] to name a few) is *prover efficiency*. Consider the application of succinct arguments to delegating (possibly non-deterministic) computation, where a prover performs some expensive computation and then uses a succinct argument to convince an efficient verifier the validity of the output. If computing the proof takes much longer than the computation (even, say, a multiplicative factor of two), this would cause a significant delay making the system useless in various realistic settings. This motivates the following question:

Is it possible to compute the proof in parallel
to the computation while incurring no additional delay?

SPARKs. In this work, we answer the above question affirmatively. We introduce succinct *parallelizable* arguments of knowledge (SPARKs) where the prover's running time is "essentially" optimal. More precisely, an interactive argument (P, V) is a SPARK if instances solvable in (non-deterministic) sequential time T can be proven with the following efficiency requirements (ignoring dependence on the security parameter or statement size):

- The prover's parallel time is $T + \mathrm{polylog}\,T$.[1] (In other words, the prover's running time is essentially T for large computations!)
- The total prover complexity is $T \cdot \mathrm{polylog}\,T$ and only uses $\mathrm{polylog}\,T$ parallel threads.
- The communication complexity and verifier complexity are $\mathrm{polylog}\,T$.

Note that the third property is standard for succinct arguments. The first two properties stipulate that the running time of a prover with only a moderate amount of parallel processors is optimal—even a factor two overhead in terms of a prover running time is not allowed. Without the first property, there are existing succinct arguments with time $T \cdot \mathrm{polylog}\,T$ using only a single processor (e.g., [7,10,28]). Without the second property, there are existing constructions with parallel time $T + \mathrm{polylog}\,T$ using roughly T processors (e.g., [7]).

1.1   Our Results

For our main theorem, we show the existence of SPARKs for NP based on the existence of collision-resistant hash functions. The formal theorem and full details are deferred to the full version of the paper.

Theorem 1.1 (Informal). *Assuming collision resistant hash functions, there exists a four-round SPARK for non-deterministic polynomial-time RAM computation.*

---

[1] Only the additive $\mathrm{polylog}\,T$ term is allowed to additionally depend on the security parameter or statement size.

If we additionally assume succinct non-interactive arguments of knowledge (SNARKs) where the prover's sequential running time is quasi-linear in the verification time, then we obtain non-interactive SPARKs. The formal theorem and full details are deferred to the full version of the paper.

Theorem 1.2 (Informal). *Assuming collision resistant hash functions and a SNARK for* NP *with a quasi-linear prover, there exists a non-interactive SPARK for non-deterministic polynomial-time RAM computation.*

Our results are obtained by a generic construction that assumes collision resistant hash functions and *any* succinct argument of knowledge for a specific NP language, where the prover's sequential running time is quasi-linear (i.e. $T \cdot \mathrm{polylog}\, T$ when using a single processor for T time computations), and results with a SPARK, where the prover's parallel time is essentially optimal. More precisely, we prove the following theorem.

Theorem 1.3 (Informal; see Theorem 5.6). *Assuming collision resistant hash functions, any succinct argument of knowledge for* NP *with a quasi-linear prover can be generically transformed into a SPARK for non-deterministic polynomial time RAM computation. Additionally, if the original succinct argument of knowledge is non-interactive, then so is the resulting SPARK.*

Applying the transformation to Kilian's protocol [31] instantiated with a quasi-linear size PCP [10, 19] yields a SPARK with poly-logarithmically many rounds. A simple modification to this transformation, when instantiated with Kilian's protocol, preserves the round complexity and yields Theorem 1.1. Theorem 1.2 follows by applying the above theorem to any SNARK where the prover has quasi-linear overhead (e.g., based on Micali's CS proofs [34] instantiated with a quasi-linear size PCP [10, 19]; see also [7, 28]).

Model of Computation. We define and build SPARKs for sequential RAM computations, whereas our construction of SPARKs is in the parallel RAM model. While the RAM model of computation is very expressive in theory, there is clearly not an exact one-to-one correspondence with real computers. For example, we do not take into account the performance of caches or other optimizations in modern processors that can easily result in additional overhead. As such, we view the results in this paper as showing a theoretical feasibility for practical implementations of SPARKs. We next briefly discuss and justify both the model of computation and the notion of time used in this work. For further details, see Sect. 3.1.

Recall that a RAM machine is a Turing machine with random access to its memory string. Between accesses, the machine applies some transition function to determine its next memory access. Each access is either a read or write, and we additionally assume that every time a process writes a value to a location in memory, it receives the previous value at that location. We define the running time of a RAM machine as the number of memory accesses it makes. For parallel RAM machines, we define the parallel running time as the number of "rounds" of memory accesses made by all processors, so if two processors access memory during the same logical round, we only count it as a single unit of parallel time. In other words, a SPARK proves a RAM computation that makes T sequential accesses in $T + \text{polylog}\, T$ rounds of parallel accesses.

Similar models have been used in other contexts for delegating RAM computation (see e.g., [28,29]), but they were much less sensitive to the model since they did not care about small multiplicative overheads. However, we believe that the above timing model we propose is reflective of real programs. For memory-intensive programs, our model captures the fact that memory accesses are practically the most time-consuming operations. For compute-intensive tasks, where the memory accesses are more sparse, it is only better that the overhead of a SPARK scales with the number of memory accesses and not the computation time itself.

1.2   Applications

SPARKs are a variant of succinct argument systems where the prover both computes and proves validity of the computation in parallel time which is essentially as efficient as possible. While our focus here is on establishing a theoretical feasibility result, we expect that our ideas may also be useful in practical constructions, which we leave for future work. Below we present applications of SPARKs.

Time-Tight Delegation of RAM Computation. In the problem of verifiable delegation of computation [26,29,39], there is a client who wishes to outsource an expensive computation M on an input x to a powerful yet untrusted server. The server should not only produce the output y but also a proof that the computation was done correctly.

A non-interactive SPARK directly gives a delegation protocol for sequential RAM computation. This is because SPARKs satisfy a "delayed-output" property—the output y of the computation need not be known to the SPARK prover or verifier in advance, as it is computed in parallel to the proof. Therefore, using a non-interactive SPARK, a server can perform a RAM computation as well as a proof with essentially no overhead over the sequential running time. Specifically, for T-time computations, the server runs in time $T + \text{polylog}\, T$ and uses at most $\text{polylog}\, T$ processors. We call delegation schemes with this property *time-tight*. Previously, the best that was known was where the server uses a single processor and runs in time $T \cdot \text{polylog}\, T$ [7,10,28], or where the server uses roughly T processors and runs in parallel time $T + \text{polylog}\, T$ [7].

Our time-tight delegation protocol also works for *non-deterministic* computations. For example, consider the case where a client wants to outsource a RAM computation over a large database (stored at the server) but only knows a hash of the database. The server can perform the computation while proving both that the output is correct and the database is consistent with the client's hash. Furthermore, if both the server and the client have agreed upon the hash at the beginning of the protocol, the running time depends only on the time of the RAM computation (otherwise, the server will need to prove that the initial database hashes to the correct value, which requires computing a hash over the whole database and will be expensive if the database is large).

Towards VDFs from Sequential Functions. Verifiable delay functions (VDFs) are functions that require some "long" time T to compute (where T is a parameter given to the function), yet the answer to the computation can be efficiently verified given a proof that can be jointly generated with the output (with only small overhead) [14,15,38,42]. The original work of Boneh et al. [14] suggests a theoretical construction of VDFs based on succinct non-interactive arguments (SNARGs) and any *iteratively sequential function* (ISF).[2] Other known constructions of VDFs [38,42] rely on the repeated squaring assumption—a concrete ISF.

Let us recall what ISFs are. A *sequential* function (SF) is a function that takes a long time to compute, even if one has many parallel processors. An ISF is the *iteration* of some round function and the assumption is that iterating the round function is the fastest way to evaluate the ISF, even if one has many parallel processors. Clearly, any VDF implies an SF and so any construction of VDFs will necessarily rely on such (but this is not the case for an ISF[3]). It is thus a very natural question whether we can get a VDF based on only SFs and SNARGs. Note that the construction of Boneh et al. [14] inherently relies on the iterated structure of the underlying sequential function.[4]

Towards answering this question, we observe that any non-interactive SPARK for computing and proving an SF implies a VDF: simply compute the non-interactive SPARK for the SF. If the SF does not require any parallelism to compute, then by our main theorem, any SF, SNARK (with quasi-linear overhead), and collision-resistant hash function imply a VDF. However, in general, a moderate amount of parallelism may help to speed up the computation of an SF, and thus for this application, we would require a SPARK for (moderately) parallel computation. We defer this extension of our main theorem to the full version.

In fact, one way to view our main construction is by improving existing techniques for constructing verifiable computation for iterated functions from

---

[2] Actually, their original construction relied on *incremental verifiable computation* [41], which exists based on SNARKs [12], and any ISF. In an updated version they show that actually SNARGs, along with ISFs, are sufficient.

[3] However, a *continuous* VDF [24] does imply an ISF.

[4] In the construction based on SNARGs and ISFs, they need to be able to "break" the computation of the function in various mid-points of the computation and the internal "state" in those locations has to be small for efficiency of the construction. In the construction based on SNARKs and ISFs, they rely on a *tight* construction of incremental verifiable computation but the number of parallel processors required for the latter is as large as the cost of a single step [8,12,36], and so many steps are needed.

SNARGs to arbitrary functions using SNARKs (and collision resistant hash functions). An interesting open question is how to construct verifiable computation for arbitrary functions from only SNARGs, rather than SNARKs.

Memory-Hard VDFs. A particularly appealing extension of the application above is to the existence of *memory-hard* VDFs. Recall that VDFs only guarantee that a long computation has been performed (and anyone can verify this publicly). It is very natural to require that not only a time-consuming computation was performed but also that the computation required many resources, for example, a large portion of the memory across time.

Clearly any VDF that is based on an ISF is not memory hard. The reason is that even if the basic round function is memory-hard, upon every iteration the memory consumption goes to 0! Since the VDF construction discussed above does not necessarily have to be instantiated with an ISF but rather any SF (and a SPARK for computing it), we can use a memory hard sequential function (e.g., [1–4,22,23]) and get a VDF where the computation not only takes a long time, but also requires large memory throughout. As above, this requires a SPARK for a memory hard function, which may require using more than one parallel processor, and as such we give this extension in the full version.

1.3   Related Work

Succinct Arguments with Efficient Provers. We elaborate on the existing succinct arguments that focus on prover efficiency. First, we recall that Kilian's succinct argument consists of a prover who commits to a PCP using a Merkle tree and locally opens a set of random locations specified by the verifier. As such, efficient PCP constructions immediately give rise to succinct arguments with an efficient prover. Specifically in [7,10], they show how to construct PCPs in quasi-linear time, which yield succinct arguments with a prover running in $T \cdot \mathrm{polylog}\, T$ time for T-time computations. In [7], they show how to construct a quasi-linear size PCP where every bit can be computed in $\mathrm{polylog}\, T$ depth given the transcript of the computation. This results in a succinct argument where the prover runs in parallel time $T + \mathrm{polylog}\, T$ using roughly T processors (as opposed to $\mathrm{polylog}\, T$ processors as required by SPARKs). Furthermore, the above arguments can be made non-interactive by applying the Fiat-Shamir transformation [25,34].

A different line of work has focused additionally on the prover's *space complexity*. Bitansky et al. [12] (following Valiant's [41] incrementally verifiable computation framework using recursive proof composition) construct complexity-preserving SNARKs, in which both the time and space of the underlying computation up to (multiplicative) polynomial factors in the security parameter. For the task of delegating deterministic T-time S-space computation, Holmgren and Rothblum [28] give a prover with $T \cdot \mathrm{polylog}\, T$ time and $S + o(S)$ space assuming sub-exponential LWE. We leave as future work the question of additionally reducing the prover's space complexity for SPARKs.

Tight VDFs. As we describe shortly in Sect. 2, our construction splits the computation into "chunks" and proves each of them in parallel. This idea is inspired by the recent transformations of Boneh et al. and Döttling et al. [14,20] in the context of verifiable delay functions (VDFs) [14,15]. Those works show how to use a VDF for an iterated sequential function where the honest evaluator has some overhead into a VDF where the honest evaluator uses multiple parallel processors and has essentially no parallel time overhead at all. However, iterated functions can be naturally split into chunks and so most of the technical difficulty in our work does not arise in that context. See Sect. 2 for more details.

IOPs. In an effort to bring down the quasi-linear overhead of PCPs, Ben-Sasson et al. [9] and Reingold et al. [39] introduced the concept of *interactive oracle proofs* (IOPs).[5] IOPs are a type of proof system that combines aspects of interactive proofs (IPs) and PCPs: in every round a prover sends a possibly long message but the verifier is allowed to read only a few bits. IOPs also generalize Interactive PCPs [30]. The most recent IOP is due to Ron-Zewi and Rothblum [40] (improving Ben-Sasson et al. [6]) and achieves nearly optimal overhead in proof length (i.e., a $1 + \epsilon$ factor for an arbitrary $\epsilon > 0$) and constant rounds and query complexity, however the prover's running time is some unspecified polynomial.

2   Technical Overview

In this section, we present the main techniques underlying our transformation from succinct arguments of knowledge with quasilinear overhead to SPARKs.

2.1   Warmup: SPARKs for Iterated Functions

Our starting point stems from the recent works of Boneh et al. and Döttling et al. [14,21]. For concreteness, we describe the setting of [14], which focuses on the simplified case of proving correctness of the output of an *iterated function* $g^{(T)}(x_0) = (g \circ \ldots \circ g)(x_0)$ for some $T \in \mathbb{N}$. Rather than proving that $g^{(T)}(x_0) = x_T$ directly, they split the computation into different sub-computations of geometrically decreasing size such that the proof for *every* sub-computation completes by time T.

To demonstrate this idea, suppose for simplicity that each iteration takes one unit of time to compute and that there is a succinct argument that can non-interactively prove any computation of k iterations of g in $2k$ additional time. Then, in order to prove that $g^{(T)}(x_0) = x_T$, they first perform $1/3$ of the computation to obtain $g^{(T/3)}(x_0) = x_{T/3}$ and then prove its correctness. Observe that $x_{T/3}$ can be computed in time $T/3$ and the proof can be generated in time $2T/3$ by assumption, so the proof that $g^{(T/3)}(x_0) = x_{T/3}$ completes by time T.

---

[5] To clarify notation, IOPs (introduced by [9]) are equivalent to the notion of Probabilistically Checkable Interactive Proofs (introduced concurrently and independently by [39]).

In parallel to proving that $g^{(T/3)}(x_0) = x_{T/3}$, they additionally compute and prove $1/3$ *of the remaining computation* (namely, that $g^{((T-T/3)/3)}(x_{T/3}) = x_{5T/9}$) in a separate parallel thread, which also will finish by time T. They continue in this fashion recursively until the remaining computation can be verified directly.

In this construction, the prover only needs to start at most $O(\log T)$ parallel computation threads and finishes in essentially parallel time T. The final proof consists of $O(\log T)$ proofs of the intermediate sub-computations. The verifier checks each proof for the sub-computations independently and accepts if all checks pass and the proposed inputs and outputs are consistent with each other. More generally, if the given non-interactive argument had α multiplicative overhead, the resulting number of threads needed would be $O(\alpha \cdot \log T)$. So, when the overhead is quasi-linear (i.e. $\alpha \in \text{polylog}\, T$), the resulting argument is still succinct.

2.2 Extending SPARKs to Arbitrary Computations

The focus of this work is extending the above example to handle arbitrary non-deterministic polynomial-time computation (possibly with a long output) which introduces many complications. Specifically, suppose we are given an statement (M, x, T) with witness w, where M is a RAM machine and we want to prove that $M(x, w)$ outputs some value y within T steps. We emphasize that our goal is to capture general non-deterministic, polynomial-time computation where the output y is not known in advance, so we would like to simultaneously compute y given (M, x, T) and w, and prove its correctness. Since M is a RAM machine, it has access to some (potentially large) memory $D \in \{0, 1\}^n$ where n consists of at most $2^{|x|}$ bits. To capture NP computation, we let the security parameter λ be roughly the input size $|x|$, and we let T be a arbitrary polynomial in λ. Let us try to employ the above strategy in this more general setting.

As M does not necessarily implement an iterated function, the first problem we encounter is that there is no natural way to split the computation into many sub-computations with small input and output. For intermediate statements, the naïve solution would be to prove that running the RAM machine M for k steps starting at some initial memory D_{start} results in final memory D_{final}. However, this is a problem because the size of the memory, n, may be large—perhaps even as large as the full running time T—so the intermediate statements we need to prove may be huge!

A natural attempt to mitigate this would be to instead provide a succinct commitment to the memory at the beginning and end of each sub-computation, and then have the prover additionally prove that it knows a memory string consistent with each commitment. Concretely, each sub-computation corresponding to k steps of computation would contain commitments $c_{\text{start}}, c_{\text{final}}$. The prover would show that there exist strings $D_{\text{start}}, D_{\text{final}}$ such that (1) $c_{\text{start}}, c_{\text{final}}$ are commitments to $D_{\text{start}}, D_{\text{final}}$, respectively, and (2) starting with memory D_{start} and running RAM machine M for k steps results in memory D_{final}. This seems like a step in the right direction, since the statement size for each sub-computation would only depend on the output size of the commitment and not the size of the memory. However, the prover's witness—and hence running time to prove each sub-computation—still scales linearly with the size of the memory in this approach. Therefore, the main challenge we are faced with is removing the dependence on the memory size in the witness of the sub-computations.

Using Local Updates. To overcome the above issues, we observe that in each sub-computation the prover only needs to prove that the transition from the initial commitment c_{start} to the final commitment c_{final} is consistent with k steps of computation done by M. At a high level, we do so by proving that there exists a sequence of k local updates to c_{start} which result in c_{final}. Then in order to verify a sub-computation corresponding to k steps, we can simply check the k local updates to the commitment of the memory, rather than checking the memory in its entirety. To formalize this idea, we rely on short commitments that allow for local updates which can be efficiently computed in parallel to the main computation. We call such commitments *concurrent locally updatable commitments*.

Given such commitments, will use a succinct argument of knowledge (P_{sARK}, V_{sARK}) for an NP language L_{upd} that corresponds to checking that a sequence of local updates are valid. Specifically, a statement $(M, x, k, c_{\mathsf{start}}, c_{\mathsf{final}}) \in L_{\mathsf{upd}}$ if and only if there exists a sequence of updates $u_1, \ldots, u_k$ such that, starting with short commitment c_{start}, running M on input x for k steps specifies the updates $u_1, \ldots, u_k$ that result in a commitment c_{final}. Then, as long as the updates are themselves succinct, the size of the witness scales only with the number of steps of the computation and not with the size of the memory.

In order to make the above approach work, we need locally updatable commitments that satisfy the following two properties:

1. Updates can be computed efficiently in parallel to the main computation.
2. Local updates can be verified as modifying at most a single location in the committed memory.

We next explain how we obtain the required commitments satisfying the above properties. We believe that this primitive and the techniques used to obtain it are of independent interest.

Concurrent Locally Updatable Commitments. Roughly speaking, a concurrent locally updatable commitment is a standard computationally binding string commitment scheme with a local update property which supports updating a single bit in the underlying message without re-committing to the whole message. For efficiency we additionally require that one can perform several local updates concurrently. For soundness, we require that no efficient adversary can find two different openings for the same location even if it is allowed to perform polynomially-many update operations. A formal definition appears in Sect. 4.

Our construction relies on Merkle trees [33] and hence can be instantiated with any collision resistant hash function. Recall that a Merkle tree uses a compressing hash function, which we assume for simplicity is given by $h\colon \{0,1\}^{2\lambda} \to \{0,1\}^{\lambda}$, and is obtained via a binary tree structure where nodes are associated with values. The leaves are associated with arbitrary values and each internal node is associated with a value that is the hash of the concatenation of its children's values.

It is well known that Merkle trees, when instantiated with a collision resistant hash function h, act as short commitments with local opening. The latter property enables proving claims about specific blocks in the input without opening the whole input, by revealing the *authentication path* from some input bit to the root (i.e. the hashes corresponding to sibling nodes along the path from the leaf to the root). Not only do Merkle trees have the local opening property, but the same technique allows for *local updates*. Namely, one can update the value of a specific bit in the input and compute the new root value without recomputing the whole tree (by updating the hashes along the authentication path of the bit). All of these local procedures cost time which is proportional to the depth of the tree, $\log n$, as opposed to the full memory n. We denote this update time as β (which may additionally depend polynomially on λ, for example, to compute the hash function at each level in the tree).

Let us see what happens when we use Merkle trees as our commitment. Recall that the Merkle tree contains the hash of the memory at every step of the computation, and we update its value after each such step. The latter operation, as mentioned above, takes β time. So even with local updates, using Merkle trees naïvely incurs a β delay for every update operation which implies a β *multiplicative* delay for the whole computation (which we want to avoid)! To handle this, we use a *pipelining* technique to perform the local updates in parallel.

Pipelining Local Updates. Consider two updates u_1 and u_2 that we want to apply to the current Merkle tree sequentially. We observe that since Merkle trees updates work "level by level," we can first update the first level of the tree (corresponding to the leaves) according to u_1. Then, update the second layer according to u_1 and *in parallel* update the first layer using u_2. Continuing in this fashion, we can update the third layer according to u_1 and in parallel update the second layer using u_2, and so on. The idea can be generalized to pipeline $u_1, \ldots, u_k$, so that the final update u_k completes after $(k-1) + \beta$ steps, and the memory is consistent with the Merkle tree given by performing update operations $u_1, \ldots, u_k$ sequentially. The implementation of this idea requires β additional parallel threads since the computation for at most β updates will overlap at a given time. A key point that allows us to pipeline these concurrent updates is that the operations at each level in the tree are data-independent in a standard Merkle tree. Namely, each processor can perform all of the reads/writes to a given level in the tree at a single time step, and the next processor can continue in the next time step without incurring any delay.

Ensuring Optimal Prover Run-Time. Using the above ingredients, we discuss how to put everything together to ensure optimal prover run-time. Concretely, suppose we have a concurrent locally updatable commitment where each update takes time β, and a succinct non-interactive argument of knowledge with $\alpha \in \text{polylog} \, T$ multiplicative overhead.

As discussed above, to prove that $M(x, w)$ output a value y in T steps, we split the computation into m sub-computations which all complete by time T. The ith sub-computation will consist of a "compute" phase, where we compute k_i steps of the total T computation steps, and a "proof" phase, where we use the succinct argument to prove correctness of those k_i steps. For the "compute" phase, recall that performing k_i steps of computation while also updating the commitment takes $k_i \cdot \beta$ total work. However, as described above, we can pipeline these updates so that the parallel time to compute these updates is only $(k_i - 1) + \beta$.

For the "proof" phase, recall that we that we use a succinct argument for the update language L_{upd} such that a statement $(M, x, k, c_{\text{start}}, c_{\text{final}}) \in L_{\text{upd}}$ if there exists a sequence of k updates such that (1) the updates are consistent with the computation of M and (2) applying these updates to c_{start} results in c_{final}. To compute the proofs in the desired amount of time, we need to set the values of k_i appropriately. As the total work to compute k_i steps with updates is $k_i \cdot \beta$, this implies that each proof takes at most $k_i \cdot \alpha \cdot \beta$ time. Therefore, the largest "chunk" of computation we can compute and prove by time T time is $T/(\alpha\beta + 1)$. For convenience, let $\gamma \triangleq \alpha\beta + 1$. Then, in the first sub-computation, we can compute and prove $k_1 = T/\gamma$ steps of computation. In each subsequent computation, we compute and prove a γ fraction of the remaining computation. Putting everything together, we get that $k_i = (T/\gamma) \cdot (1 - 1/\gamma)^{i-1}$ for $i \in [m-1]$ and then $k_m < \gamma$ is the number of remaining steps such that $\sum_{i=1}^{m} k_i = T$.

In Fig. 1 we show the structure of the compute and proof phases for all m sub-computations. We emphasize that the entire protocol completes within $T + \beta$ parallel time. As $\beta \in \text{polylog} \, T$, this implies that only have a small additive rather than multiplicative overhead. This is tight in the sense that computing the commitment for T steps of computation with updates takes $T + \beta$ time, so all of the proofs about the updates to the commitments are computed completely in parallel. Next, we note that we have a β gap between the time that the "compute" phase ends and the "proof" phase begins for a particular sub-computation. This is because we have to wait β additional time to finish computing the updates before we can start the proofs. However, we can immediately start computing the next sub-computation without waiting for the updates to complete. Lastly, the number of processors used in the protocol is β at all times in the constantly running "compute" phase which is additionally computing updates to the commitment in parallel. Then we have at most $m - 1$ additional processors for the proofs of the first $m - 1$ sub-computations. The last sub-computation, we don't have the prover compute the proof, and instead the prover will send the updates in the clear for the verifier to check directly.

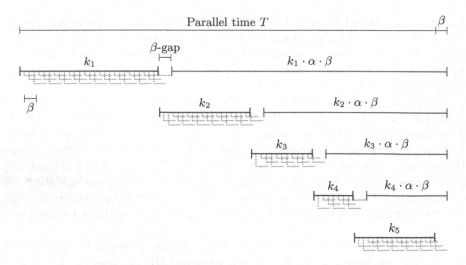

Fig. 1. The "compute" and "proof" phases for each of m sub-computations. For $i \in [m-1]$, the ith sub-computation consists of k_i steps, while pipelining updates which each take β time. After finishing all updates, the prover computes the proof which takes $k_i \cdot \alpha \cdot \beta$ time. In the final sub-computation, we send the updates to the verifier in the clear instead of giving a proof.

Computing the Initial Commitment. Before giving the full protocol, we address a final issue, which is for the prover to compute the commitment to the initial memory string. Specifically, the prover needs to commit to a string $D \in \{0,1\}^n$, which the RAM machine M assumes contains its inputs (x, w). Directly committing to the string $x || w$ would require roughly $|x| + |w|$ additional time, which could be as large as T. To circumvent the need to compute the initial commitment, we simply do not commit to the initial memory! Instead, we start with a commitment to an *uninitialized* memory that can be computed efficiently and allows each position to be initialized *exactly once* whenever it is first accessed. In Sect. 4, we discuss the full details of how we deal with this issue for our commitments.

2.3 Our SPARK Construction

We now summarize our full SPARK construction. Suppose that we have (1) a concurrent locally updatable commitment that starts as uninitialized where each update takes time β and (2) a succinct non-interactive argument of knowledge $(P_{\mathsf{sARK}}, V_{\mathsf{sARK}})$ for the update language L_{upd} with $\alpha \in \mathrm{polylog}\, T$ multiplicative overhead. Let $\gamma \triangleq \alpha\beta + 1$, as described above, which is the fraction of remaining computation done at each step. The protocol (P, V) for a statement (M, x, T) is as follows:

1. V samples public parameters pp for the commitment and sends them to P.

2. Using pp, P computes the commitment c_{start} for the uninitialized memory $D_{\mathsf{start}} = \perp^n$.

3. P computes T/γ steps of $M(x, w)$ while in parallel updating D_{start} and the corresponding local updates to $c_1 = c_{\mathsf{start}}$.

4. After completing the T/γ steps of the computation (but not necessarily completing all corresponding updates), P starts recursively computing and proving the remaining $T - T/\gamma$ steps in parallel.

5. Let $u_1, \ldots, u_{T/\gamma}$ be the current updates, which result in commitment c_1'. After computing the current updates, P uses $P_{\mathsf{sARK}}(u_1, \ldots, u_{T/\gamma})$ for language L_{upd} to prove that starting with commitment c_1, running M on input x for T/γ steps results in commitment c_1'.

6. P continues until there are at most γ steps of the computation. At this point, P computes the remaining steps and sends the corresponding updates to V in the clear to be verified directly.

7. After finishing the computation and all corresponding updates, P uses the final commitment to open the output y and give a proof of its correctness. V accepts if the proof certifying y verifies and V_{sARK} accepts all sub-protocols, which are consistent with each other.

Handling Interactive Protocols. The same transformation described above applies to interactive r-round succinct argument of knowledge. However, since the protocol is interactive, the prover starts an interactive protocol in order to prove that sub-computations were performed correctly. It is not necessarily the case that the messages in the various interactive arguments will be "synced" up, and so our transformation suffers from (at most) a polylog T factor increase in the round complexity. For specific underlying succinct argument, however, it may be the case that it is easy to synchronize the rounds in reduce the round complexity.

Security Proof and Argument of Knowledge Definition. We note that proving security in the above construction is somewhat non-trivial. The key issue is that we need to simultaneously extract witnesses from super logarithmically many *concurrent* or *parallel* arguments of knowledge, without causing a blow-up in the complexity of the resulting extractor. Towards resolving this issue, we introduce a new argument of knowledge definition, which (1) enables dealing with this issue in our proof of security, yet (2) is satisfied by known succinct arguments of knowledge for NP. We view this definition as an additional independent contribution. For more details, see Sect. 5.2.

3   Preliminaries

We defer some standard notation to the full version of the paper and instead focus on the necessary ingredients for our construction. We also defer the formal definition of succinct arguments of knowledge, as it is a natural analogue to the SPARK definition given in Sect. 5.2.

3.1   Random Access Memory

RAM computation consists of a machine M which keeps some local state state and has read/write access to memory $D \in (\{0,1\}^\lambda)^n$ (equivalent to the tape of a Turing machine). Here, λ is the security parameter and length of a word,[6] and $n \leq 2^\lambda$ is the number of words in memory used by M. When we write $M(x)$ to denote running M on input x, this means that M expects its initial memory D to be equal to $x||0^{n\lambda-|x|}$. The computation is defined using a function step, which has the following syntax:

$$(\mathsf{state}', \mathsf{op}, \ell, v^{\mathsf{wt}}) = \mathsf{step}(M, \mathsf{state}, v^{\mathsf{rd}}).$$

Specifically, step takes as input the description of the machine M, the current state state, and a word v^{rd} that was read in the last step from memory. Then, it outputs the next state state', the operation $\mathsf{op} \in \{\mathsf{rd}, \mathsf{wt}\}$ to do next, the next location $\ell \in [n]$ to access, and the word v^{wt} to write next if $\mathsf{op} = \mathsf{wt}$ (or $\perp$ if $\mathsf{op} = \mathsf{rd}$).

Using step, we can define each step of RAM computation to run step, and then either do a read or a write. We assume that each write operation returns the value in the memory location before the write. Formally, starting with an initially empty state state_0 and letting $b_0^{\mathsf{rd}} = \perp$, the ith step of computation for $i \geq 1$ is defined as:

1. Compute $(\mathsf{state}_i, \mathsf{op}_i, \ell_i, v_i^{\mathsf{wt}}) = \mathsf{step}(M, \mathsf{state}_{i-1}, v_{i-1}^{\mathsf{rd}})$.
2. If $\mathsf{op}_i = \mathsf{rd}$, let v_i^{rd} be the word in location ℓ_i of D.
3. If $\mathsf{op}_i = \mathsf{wt}$, let v_i^{rd} be the word at location ℓ_i in D and write v_i^{wt} to that location.

The computation halts when step outputs a special halting value with the output y of $M(x)$ written at the start of the memory, where we assume that M specifies its output length. Without loss of generality, we assume that the state size can hold $O(\log n)$ bits.

We also consider the parallel-RAM (PRAM) setting, where each step of the machine can potentially branch to multiple processors that have access to the same memory D. We formalize this by allowing step to output multiple values for $(\mathsf{state}', \mathsf{op}, \ell, v^{\mathsf{wt}})$, each associated with a process identifier specifying the process to continue the computation from that state. The computation halts when there are no running processors. We are in the exclusive-read exclusive-write (EREW) model, i.e., the most restrictive PRAM model, where if some process accesses a location (either a read or a write) in memory while another process accesses the same location (either a read or a write), there are no guarantees for the resulting effect. We also assume that n words in memory can be allocated and initialized to zeros for free.

---

[6] We note that the length of a word only needs to be greater than $\log n$, but can be as large as any fixed polynomial in λ. We set it to λ for simplicity.

(P)RAM Complexity. Each step of RAM computation is allowed to make a single access to memory. We think of step, which computes the transition function from state to state', as being implemented by an efficient CPU algorithm with access to a constant number of words. As a result, we define the running time of a RAM machine M as the number of accesses it makes to its working memory. For PRAM machines, each step of computation may make multiple parallel accesses to memory via different processors.

To model the complexity of a (P)RAM machine M, we consider two complexity measures: work and depth. Specifically, we let $\mathsf{work}_M(x)$ denote the total amount of computation done by all processors measured in steps (or equivalently memory accesses). When M is a non-deterministic machine, we denote this by $\mathsf{work}_M(x, w)$ where w is the witness. We let $\mathsf{depth}_M(x)$ (analogously, $\mathsf{depth}_M(x, w)$) denote the number of sequential steps until M halts, where steps that occur in parallel are counted as one step. For a (non-parallel) RAM machine, we simply denote its running time by $\mathsf{work}_M(x)$.

3.2 Universal and NP Relations

Next, we define a variant of the universal relation, introduced by [5]. For efficiency reasons, it will be helpful to define this relative to different computational models, so we give definitions for Turing machine computation and RAM machine computation.

Definition 3.1. *The universal relation for Turing machines $R_{\mathcal{U}}^{\mathsf{TM}}$ is the set of instance-witness pairs $((M, x, t, L, y), w)$ where M is a Turing machine such that $M(x, w)$ outputs y within t steps, and additionally $|y| \leq L$. We let $L_{\mathcal{U}}^{\mathsf{TM}}$ be the corresponding universal language. We similarly define $R_{\mathcal{U}}^{\mathsf{RAM}}$ and $L_{\mathcal{U}}^{\mathsf{RAM}}$ to the be universal relation and language, respectively, for RAM computation, where the given machine M is a RAM machine.*

Following [11,17], we define the NP relation R_c^{TM} as follows. For every $c \in \mathbb{N}$, we let $R_c^{\mathsf{TM}} \subseteq R_{\mathcal{U}}^{\mathsf{TM}}$ be a subset of the universal relation consisting of pairs $((M, x, t, L, y), w)$ where $t \leq |x|^c$. We let L_c^{TM} be the corresponding language. The relation R_c^{RAM} and language L_c^{RAM} are defined analogously for the case where M is a RAM machine.

The main difference between our definition and the standard universal relation of [5] is that we consider computation with long outputs y, and we also include an upper bound L on the length of y. We include y so as to have a definition which captures both deterministic and non-deterministic polynomial-time computation. A similar relation was given in [17] to define a canonical relation for P. Moreover, the universal relation of [5] is linear-time reducible to our definition above. With regards to L, we include this because in our main construction of SPARKs, the output y of the computation will not be known in advance. However, the complexity of the scheme inherently depends on L (as the output of the protocol is y).

Finally, we note that for a statement (M, x, y, L, t) with respect to RAM computation, we do not place any restriction on the length of the witness w.

Specifically, the machine M may only access t positions in w, but it could be the case that $|w|$ is significantly greater than t.

4   Concurrent Locally Updatable Commitment

In this section we define and construct a commitment that allows for local updates. Furthermore, we require that these local updates can be computed concurrently using multiple processors in a pipelined fashion (described in more detail below). We define our construction in the PRAM model.

For a security parameter $\lambda \in \mathbb{N}$, our commitment will be for strings D consisting of $n \le 2^\lambda$ words of length λ. It will also be helpful for us to capture the case when D is not defined at every location, that is, some words are set to $\bot$. To formalize this, below we define the notion of a partial string, which is simply a succinct way to represent strings over $(\{0,1\}^\lambda \cup \{\bot\})^n$.

Definition 4.1 (Partial string). *For any string $s \in (\{0,1\}^\lambda \cup \{\bot\})^*$ of words, we define the partial string D which represents s as follows. D is given by tuple (n, I, A), where n is the number of words (or $\bot$ elements) in s, $I \subseteq [n]$ is the set of non-$\bot$ locations in s, and $A \in \{0,1\}^{|I|}$ is the assignment to those indices. We let D_i denote the ith word in s.*

4.1   Concurrent Locally Updatable Commitment

Our commitment scheme C consists of algorithms with the following syntax:[7]

- $\mathsf{pp} \leftarrow \mathsf{C.Gen}(1^\lambda)$: A PPT algorithm that on input the security parameter λ, outputs a key pp.
- $(\mathsf{ptr}, \mathsf{com}) = \mathsf{C.Commit}(\mathsf{pp}, D)$: A deterministic algorithm that on input a key pp and a partial string $D = (n, I, A)$, outputs a pointer ptr to a location in memory and a string com.
- $(v, \pi) = \mathsf{C.Open}(\mathsf{pp}, \mathsf{ptr}, \ell)$: A read-only deterministic algorithm that on input a key pp, a pointer ptr, and a location $\ell \in [n]$, outputs a value $v \in \{0,1\}^\lambda \cup \{\bot\}$, and a proof π.
- $(\mathsf{com}, \tau) = \mathsf{C.Update}(\mathsf{pp}, \mathsf{ptr}, \ell, v)$: A deterministic algorithm that on input a key pp, a pointer ptr, a location $\ell \in [n]$, and a word $v \in \{0,1\}^\lambda$, outputs a commitment com and a proof τ.
- $b' = \mathsf{C.VerOpen}(\mathsf{pp}, \mathsf{com}, \ell, v, \pi)$: A deterministic algorithm that on input a key pp, a commitment com, a location $\ell \in [n]$, a value $v \in \{0,1\}^\lambda \cup \{\bot\}$, and a proof π, outputs a bit b'.
- $b' = \mathsf{C.VerUpd}(\mathsf{pp}, \mathsf{com}, \ell, v, \mathsf{com}', \tau)$: A deterministic algorithm that on input a key pp, a commitment com, a location $\ell \in [n]$, a word $v \in \{0,1\}^\lambda$, a commitment com', and a proof τ, outputs a bit b'.

---

[7] For simplicity, the only randomized algorithm in our definition is the key generation algorithm, and the rest are deterministic. However, with minor modifications to our main protocol, we could use a commitment where all algorithms may be randomized.

We require the following properties.

Definition 4.2 (Completeness). *Let $\lambda \in \mathbb{N}$, pp in the support of* C.Gen(1^λ), *and let $D = (n, I, A)$ be a partial string. For any $m \geq 0$, and $\ell_i \in [n]$, $v_i \in \{0,1\}^\lambda$ for $i \in [m]$, do the following:*

1. *Compute* $(\mathsf{ptr}, \mathsf{com}_0) = \mathsf{C.Commit}(\mathsf{pp}, D)$.
2. *For $i = 1, \ldots, m$, compute* $(\mathsf{com}_i, \tau_i) = \mathsf{C.Update}(\mathsf{pp}, \mathsf{ptr}, \ell_i, v_i)$.

Let D' be the partial string resulting from writing v_i to D_{ℓ_i} for $i = 1, \ldots, m$. Then, the following hold for any $\ell \in [n]$:

- **Open Completeness.** *Let $(v, \pi) = \mathsf{C.Open}(\mathsf{pp}, \mathsf{ptr}, \ell)$. Then,*

$$\mathsf{C.VerOpen}(\mathsf{pp}, \mathsf{com}_m, \ell, v, \pi) = 1 \ \wedge \ D'_\ell = v.$$

- **Update Completeness.** *For any $v \in \{0,1\}^\lambda$, let $(\mathsf{com}, \tau) = \mathsf{C.Update}(\mathsf{pp}, \mathsf{ptr}, \ell, v)$. It holds that*

$$\mathsf{C.VerUpd}(\mathsf{pp}, \mathsf{com}_m, \ell, v, \mathsf{com}, \tau) = 1.$$

Definition 4.3 (Soundness). *For all non-uniform PPT adversaries $\mathcal{A} = \{\mathcal{A}_\lambda\}_{\lambda \in \mathbb{N}}$, there exists a negligible function* negl *such that for all $\lambda \in \mathbb{N}$, it holds that*

$$\Pr\begin{bmatrix} \mathsf{C.VerOpen}(\mathsf{pp}, \mathsf{com}_0, \ell_0, v_0, \pi_0) = 1 \ \wedge \\ \forall i \in [m] : \mathsf{C.VerUpd}(\mathsf{pp}, \mathsf{com}_{i-1}, \ell_i, v_i, \mathsf{com}_i, \tau_i) = 1 \ \wedge \\ \mathsf{C.VerOpen}(\mathsf{pp}, \mathsf{com}_m, \ell_0, v, \pi) = 1 \ \wedge \\ v \neq v_j \end{bmatrix} \leq \mathsf{negl}(\lambda),$$

where j is the largest index with $\ell_j = \ell_0$, and the probability is over the choice of pp $\leftarrow$ C.Gen(1^λ) *and* $(m, \{(\mathsf{com}_i, \ell_i, v_i, \tau_i)\}_{i \in [m]}, \mathsf{com}_0, \ell_0, v_0, \pi_0, v, \pi) \leftarrow \mathcal{A}_\lambda(\mathsf{pp})$.

Lastly, we require the following efficiency properties, which at a high level say that any sequence of k updates can be computed (while opening the previous values) in a pipelined fashion with only additive overhead.

Definition 4.4 (Efficiency). *Let $\lambda \in \mathbb{N}$ and let $D = (n, I, A)$ be a partial string where $n \leq 2^\lambda$. We say that a concurrent locally updatable commitment satisfies efficiency if there exists a polynomial $\beta = \beta(\lambda, \log n)$ such that the following hold:*

- *The algorithms* C.Open, C.Update, C.VerOpen, *and* C.VerUpd *can each be computed with β work.*
- *Computing* C.Commit(pp, D) *can be done with $\beta \cdot (|I| + 1)$ work.*
- *For any key* pp, *pointer* ptr, *location $\ell \in [n]$, and word v, define $(\pi, \mathsf{com}, \tau)$ as follows:*
  - $(v', \pi) = \mathsf{C.Open}(\mathsf{pp}, \mathsf{ptr}, \ell)$
  - $(\mathsf{com}, \tau) = \mathsf{C.Update}(\mathsf{pp}, \mathsf{ptr}, \ell, v)$

There exists an algorithm OpenUpdate(pp, ptr, ℓ, v) *which outputs* $(v', \pi, \mathsf{com}, \tau)$, *such that k sequential calls to* OpenUpdate *can be computed with $k\beta$ work, which can be decoupled into depth $(k-1) + \beta$ using β processors.*

We say that a concurrent locally updatable commitment satisfies β-efficiency if the above hold with respect to a particular function β.

Remark 4.5. We emphasize that the completeness and soundness properties we give for concurrent locally updatable commitments must hold for any sequence of m "valid" local updates. At a high level, these notions stipulate that an opening will always give the correct value (with a proof) and that no adversary can find an opening for a value you wouldn't expect (based on the local updates). Furthermore, we require C.VerUpd to ensure that a local update a one location does not affect any other locations.

We note that our definition generalizes standard notions of completeness and position binding for vector commitments [16], as when there are no updates (i.e., $m = 0$), they are equivalent. Our definition also generalized the read and write security properties of other Merkle tree commitments, such as those in [29]. We note that it does not suffice to consider the properties to hold with respect to a single update (i.e., when $m = 1$). This is because our commitments keep state, so it may be the case that it internally keeps a counter and artificially breaks completeness or soundness after some $m > 1$ updates have occurred.

4.2 Construction

Before giving our construction, we discuss the building blocks we will be using.

Merkle Trees. Let $h: \{0,1\}^{2\lambda} \to \{0,1\}^{\lambda}$ be a compressing hash function. A Merkle tree [33] for a string $D \in \{0,1\}^{n\lambda}$ consists of a complete binary tree of $\log n + 1$ levels labelled $0, \ldots, \log n$ where level i consists of $n/2^i$ nodes. Each node is associated with a value in $\{0,1\}^{\lambda}$. The leaves at level 0 correspond to D, split into n blocks of length λ. The value of each node at level $i > 0$ is defined to be the hash (using h) of the concatenation of its children's values at level $i - 1$. The single node at level $\log n$ is referred to as the root or commitment of the Merkle tree.

An authentication path $\pi = (\pi_0, \ldots, \pi_{\log n - 1})$ for a leaf $i \in [n]$ consists of the values in the tree corresponding to the siblings of all nodes along the path from the leaf to the root, ordered from level 0 to $\log n - 1$. An authentication path $\pi = (\pi_0, \ldots, \pi_{\log n - 1})$ for a leaf i is said to be a valid opening for $v \in \{0,1\}^{\lambda}$ with respect to a commitment com if when hashing the value v at leaf i with π_0, hashing the resulting value with π_1, and so on for all values in π, the final value equals com. Whenever updating the value of a leaf i with block block, we additionally re-compute the hash values along the path to the root using its authentication path. The overall size needed to store the Merkle tree in memory is $2n\lambda$ bits.

Assuming the underlying hash function h is collision resistant, it is well known that a Merkle tree is a binding commitment to a fully defined string that allows for local opening and updates. Moreover, it is known that a standard Merkle tree satisfies the standard completeness and binding properties of a commitment.

In our construction, we will want to use a Merkle tree for values $v \in \{0,1\}^\lambda \cup \{\bot\}$. Therefore, we will use a Merkle tree for 2λ-bit values, so that we can uniquely encode each element of $\{0,1\}^\lambda \cup \{\bot\}$ as a string of length 2λ and each node in the Merkle tree corresponds to two consecutive words in memory.

Segment Tree. A segment tree is a data structure that provides a way for the prover to efficiently check if a range of indices in the partial string $D = (n, I, A)$ are $\bot$. To this end, we want to represent the set I (which will be constantly updated) in a way that allows us to check if $[i_1, i_2] \cap I = \emptyset$ in $O(\log n)$ time and independent of $|I|$ and $|i_2 - i_1|$.

To do so, we use a segment tree which mirrors the Merkle tree and consists of a complete binary tree with n leaves. Each node has an associated bit which is 1 if the corresponding node in the Merkle tree has been initialized and 0 otherwise. Every time a leaf in the Merkle tree is updated, we initialize all nodes in the tree along the path to the root, meaning we set the corresponding bits in the segment tree to 1. Then, if any node in the segment tree has a bit of 0, it guarantees that all indices corresponding to the leaves that are descendants of this node are $\bot$. This implies that for any range $[i_1, i_2]$, we can check if $[i_1, i_2] \cap I = \emptyset$ by checking the bits of $O(\log n)$ nodes in the tree that cover this range of indices. This data structure only requires $2n$ additional bits to store.

Our Construction. Let $\mathcal{H} = \{\mathcal{H}_\lambda\}_{\lambda \in \mathbb{N}}$ be a collision-resistant hash function family ensemble with $h \colon \{0,1\}^{4\lambda} \to \{0,1\}^{2\lambda}$ for each $h \in \mathcal{H}_\lambda$. Let $t_{\mathsf{hash}}(\lambda)$ be an upper bound on the running time of each $h \in \mathcal{H}_\lambda$. We also assume that we have a canonical, deterministic encoding of each value in $\{0,1\}^\lambda \cup \{\bot\}$ to 2λ-bit strings, denoted by $\mathsf{block}(v)$ for $v \in \{0,1\}^\lambda \cup \{\bot\}$, which can efficiently decoded (for example, we could represent $v \in \{0,1\}^\lambda$ as $v||0^\lambda$ and $\bot$ as $1^{2\lambda}$).

We now give our full concurrent updatable commitment construction $\mathsf{C} = (\mathsf{C.Gen}, \mathsf{C.Commit}, \mathsf{C.Open}, \mathsf{C.Update}, \mathsf{C.VerOpen}, \mathsf{C.VerUpd})$.

- $\mathsf{pp} \leftarrow \mathsf{C.Gen}(1^\lambda)$: Sample $h \leftarrow \mathcal{H}_\lambda$ and output $\mathsf{pp} = h$.
- $(\mathsf{ptr}, \mathsf{com}) = \mathsf{C.Commit}(\mathsf{pp}, D)$:
  1. Allocate $4n\lambda + 2n + 2\lambda \log n$ bits of memory at a pointer ptr, starting with a Merkle tree with n leaves at ptr, a corresponding segment tree at pointer $\mathsf{segtree}$, and $\log n$ extra blocks of size 2λ at pointer aux. We assume that all memory is initialized to 0.
  2. Define $\mathsf{dummy}(0) = \mathsf{block}(\bot)$. Let $h = \mathsf{pp}$, and for $j = 1, \ldots, \log n$, compute $\mathsf{dummy}(j) = h(\mathsf{dummy}(j-1)||\mathsf{dummy}(j-1))$ and write it to the next block of free memory at aux.
  3. Recall that $D = (n, I, A)$ specifies a set I of non-$\bot$ indices. For each location $\ell \in I$, run the update procedure defined below by $\mathsf{C.Update}(\mathsf{pp}, \mathsf{ptr}, \ell, D_\ell)$.
  4. Let com be the value of the root in ptr and output $(\mathsf{ptr}, \mathsf{com})$.
- $(v, \pi) = \mathsf{C.Open}(\mathsf{pp}, \mathsf{ptr}, \ell)$: Let $\mathsf{segtree}$ be the pointer to the segment tree in memory. For $j \in \{0, \ldots, \log(n) - 1\}$, let node_j be the ancestor of leaf ℓ at

level j and let sib_j be its sibling.

For each level $j = 0, \ldots, \log(n) - 1$:

1. Read node_j in ptr, and let its value be y_j.
2. Read node_j in $\mathsf{segtree}$, and if its value is 0, let $y_j = \mathsf{block}(\bot)$.
3. Read sib_j in ptr, and let its value be π_j.
4. Read sib_j in $\mathsf{segtree}$, and if its value is 0, set $\pi_j = \mathsf{dummy}(j)$.

Let $v \in \{0,1\}^\lambda \cup \{\bot\}$ be the value such that $y_0 = \mathsf{block}(v)$, or $\bot$ if there is no such value. Output (v, π) where $\pi = (\pi_0, \pi_1, \ldots, \pi_{\log(n)-1})$.

- $(\mathsf{com}, \tau) = \mathsf{C.Update}(\mathsf{pp}, \mathsf{ptr}, \ell, v)$: Let $\mathsf{segtree}$ be the pointer to the segment tree in memory. For $j \in \{0, \ldots, \log(n) - 1\}$, let node_j be the ancestor of leaf ℓ at level j and let sib_j be its sibling. Let $y_0 = \mathsf{block}(v)$.

For each level $j = 0, \ldots, \log(n) - 1$:

1. **Access Step.** Do the following in parallel:
   (a) Write y_j to node_j in ptr, and let $z_j \in \{0,1\}^{2\lambda}$ be the value overwritten at that location.[8]
   (b) Write 1 to node_j in $\mathsf{segtree}$.
   (c) Read sib_j in ptr, and let its value be π_j.
   (d) Read sib_j in $\mathsf{segtree}$, and if its value is 0, set $\pi_j = \mathsf{dummy}(j)$.
2. **Hash Steps.** Let y_{j+1} be the hash of the concatenation y_j and π_j (with the leftmost sibling first), using pp.

Let $v' \in \{0,1\}^\lambda \cup \{\bot\}$ be the value such that $z_0 = \mathsf{block}(v')$, or $\bot$ if there is no such value. Output (com, τ) where $\mathsf{com} = y_{\log n}$ and $\tau = v' \| (\pi_0, \pi_1, \ldots, \pi_{\log(n)-1})$.

- $b' = \mathsf{C.VerOpen}(\mathsf{pp}, \mathsf{com}, \ell, v, \pi)$: Verify that the authentication path π for leaf ℓ is valid for value $\mathsf{block}(v)$ with respect to com.
- $b' = \mathsf{C.VerUpd}(\mathsf{pp}, \mathsf{com}, \ell, v, \mathsf{com}', \tau)$: Output 1 if and only if the following hold:
  1. τ can be parsed as $v' \| \pi$ where $v' \in \{0,1\}^\lambda \cup \{\bot\}$ and π is an authentication path.
  2. $\mathsf{C.VerOpen}(\mathsf{pp}, \mathsf{com}, \ell, v', \pi) = 1$.
  3. $\mathsf{C.VerOpen}(\mathsf{pp}, \mathsf{com}', \ell, v, \pi) = 1$.

We now prove that our construction satisfies the completeness, soundness, and efficiency properties above assuming collision-resistant hash functions.

Theorem 4.6. *Assuming the existence of collision-resistant hash function families, there exists a concurrently updatable commitment scheme.*

We prove this theorem by showing that C, as described above, satisfies completeness, soundness, and efficiency. The proofs are deferred to the full version.

---

[8] Note that this is one place where we use the fact that writing to a location in memory returns the value being overwritten. We use this to put the value v' at leaf ℓ in the Merkle tree before the update into the update proof τ, which is used to verify that the commitment before the update and the commitment after the update only differ at one location.

5   Succinct Parallelizable Arguments of Knowledge

In this section, we define SPARKs and show how to construct them from any concurrent locally updatable commitment and succinct argument of knowledge with quasilinear overhead, for a specific NP language, defined in Sect. 5.1. More precisely, we construct a succinct argument system where the prover runs in optimal parallel time (i.e., depth). We define Succinct Parallelizable Arguments of Knowledge formally below, using the following syntax for interactive protocols. We denote by $\langle P(w), V \rangle$ the output of V in the interaction, which may be of arbitrary (polynomial) length. Furthermore, we let V output $\perp$ to indicate reject, and output $y \neq \perp$ to accept the output y.

Definition 5.1 (SPARK). *A Succinct Parallelizable Argument of Knowledge (SPARK) for a relation $R \subseteq R_{\mathcal{U}}^{\mathsf{RAM}}$ is a tuple of probabilistic interactive machines (P, V) where P is a PRAM machine, satisfying the following properties:*

- **Completeness:** *For every $\lambda \in \mathbb{N}$ and $((M, x, y, L, t), w) \in R$,*

$$\Pr\left[\langle P(w), V \rangle(1^\lambda, (M, x, t, L)) = y\right] = 1,$$

  where the probability is over the random coins of P and V.

- **Argument of Knowledge:** *There exists a probabilistic oracle machine $\mathcal{E}$ and a polynomial q such that for every non-uniform polynomial-time prover $P^\star = \{P_\lambda^\star\}_{\lambda \in \mathbb{N}}$, there exists a negligible function negl such that for every $\lambda \in \mathbb{N}$, $(M, x, t, L) \in \{0, 1\}^*$ with $|M, x, t| \leq \lambda$ and $L \leq \lambda$, and $z, s \in \{0, 1\}^*$, the following hold.*
  Let $P_{\lambda, z, s}^\star$ denote the machine $P_\lambda^\star$ with auxiliary input z and randomness s fixed, let V_r denote the verifier V using randomness $r \in \{0, 1\}^{\ell(\lambda)}$ where $\ell(\lambda)$ is a bound on the number of random bits used by $V(1^\lambda, \cdot)$. Then.
  1. *The expected running time of $\mathcal{E}^{P_{\lambda,z,s}^\star, V_r}(1^\lambda, (M, x, t, L))$ is bounded by $q(\lambda, t)$, where the expectation is over $r \leftarrow \{0, 1\}^{\ell(\lambda)}$ and the random coins of $\mathcal{E}$.*
  2. *It holds that*

$$\Pr\left[\begin{array}{l} r \leftarrow \{0, 1\}^{\ell(\lambda)} \\ y = \langle P_{\lambda, z, s}^\star, V_r \rangle(1^\lambda, (M, x, t, L)) \; : \; y \neq \perp \wedge ((M, x, y, L, t), w) \notin R \\ w \leftarrow \mathcal{E}^{P_{\lambda, z, s}^\star, V_r}(1^\lambda, (M, x, t, L)) \end{array}\right]$$
$$\leq \mathsf{negl}(\lambda).$$

- **Succinctness:** *There exist polynomials p and q such that for any $\lambda \in \mathbb{N}$ and $M, x, t, L \in \{0, 1\}^*$, it holds that*

$$\mathsf{work}_V(1^\lambda, (M, x, t, L)) \leq p(\lambda, |(M, x)|, L, \log t)$$

  and the length of the transcript produced in the interaction between $P(w)$ and V on common input $(1^\lambda, (M, x, t, L))$ is bounded by $q(\lambda, L, \log t)$.

- **Optimal prover depth:** *There exists a polynomial p such that for all $\lambda \in \mathbb{N}$ and $((M, x, t, L, y), w) \in R$, it holds that*

$$\mathsf{depth}_P(1^\lambda, (M, x, t, L), w) = t + p(\lambda, |(M, x)|, L, \log t)$$

and the total number of processors used by P is in $\mathrm{poly}(\lambda, L, \log t)$.

A SPARK for NP *is a uniformly computable ensemble* $\{(P_c, V_c)\}_{c \in \mathbb{N}}$ *where* (P_c, V_c) *is a SPARK for* R_c^{RAM}.

We next remark about some subtleties in our definition and compare to related notions.

Remark 5.2 (Delayed output). We note that our definition of SPARKs has a "delayed output" property where the prover picks the output of the protocol rather than it being known a priori to both the prover and verifier. For typical NP languages, this distinction is not important because the prover is always trying to prove that the relation outputs 1. However, for proving more general polynomial-time computation, the output may not be known in advance, so the prover must compute both the output and a proof.

Remark 5.3 (Execution by execution extraction). Since there may be many possible outputs y of the computation, it is very important that the extractor finds a witness for the actual output y that V accepts in the interaction. Morally, this definition should capture the fact that the prover actually knows a witness *for that output*, instead of a witness for an arbitrary output y' that the prover may never convince the verifier of. This is particularly relevant for NP relations, since when a prover convinces a verifier of an accepting witness (i.e., one where the relation outputs 1) it is not meaningful to extract a witness which makes the relation output 0. Note that it does not suffice to run the protocol and simply give the extractor y (and require the extractor to provide a witness for that output), as the malicious prover may only convince V of any particular y with small probability.

A similar challenge motivated the work on precise proofs of knowledge [35], where they defined arguments of knowledge where the extractor's behavior depended on a specific instance of the protocol.[9] To capture this, their extractor receives a uniformly sampled view of the prover in the protocol and extracts a consistent witness. In our definition above, we choose to give the extractor oracle access to the fixed prover *as well as* the verifier with fixed randomness which results in accepting a particular output y. This is akin to giving the extractor an interactive version of the view, while additionally making the extractor black-box in both the malicious prover and (fixed) verifier. As such, the extractor can emulate the interaction to deterministically figure out the output y it needs to extract for.

---

[9] They considered instances with different running times, whereas we consider instances with different outputs.

Remark 5.4 (On composition). It is often important for an argument of knowledge to be composable—that is, to be able to be used as a sub-protocol (possibly many times). Indeed, we require this for our transformation from arguments of knowledge to SPARKs. Often, the challenge with composing proofs of knowledge is obtaining the desired running time of the final extractor.

One definition which composes well is precise argument of knowledge [35]. As explained above, in that definition the extractor receives the prover's view in the protocol, and for *every* view, the running time of the extractor is a fixed polynomial (in the prover's running time on that view). However, this notion is quite strong, and hence is not known to hold for standard arguments of knowledge.

A more standard notion is witness-extended emulation [32], where the extractor is not given a view, but instead must output a uniformly distributed view of the verifier as well as a witness. Moreover, the extractor only needs to run in *expected* polynomial time, and may use rewinding. However, when this is used as a sub-protocol, the view picked by the extractor may not be compatible with the external view in the rest of the protocol.

To fix this issue, our definition essentially gives the extractor a uniformly sampled view, and we require that the extractor runs in expected polynomial time over the choice of the view. This can be seen as a relaxation of precise argument of knowledge, since it doesn't need to be efficient for every view, but also as a strengthening of witness-extended emulation, because the extractor must work on a given view, rather than being able to sample one itself.

Remark 5.5 (Standard arguments of knowledge). The definition we use for a succinct argument of knowledge (rather than SPARKs) can be obtained from the above definition by including y in the statement (as is standard for arguments) and making the necessary syntactic changes. The formal definition is deferred to the full version. We note that for succinct arguments of knowledge, the corresponding extraction definition is implied by the definition used in [37].

We our now ready to state our main result.

Theorem 5.6 *[Restatement of Theorem 1.3]. Suppose there exists a succinct argument of knowledge for NP with quasilinear overhead and a concurrent locally updatable commitment. Then, there exists a SPARK for NP.*

Next, we discuss some implications and details of this theorem. Then, to prove Theorem 5.6, we describe a helper language (Sect. 5.1) and then give the protocol (Sect. 5.2). We defer the proofs to the full version. We also discuss various extensions of the protocol in the full version.

The round complexity, prover's space complexity, and verifier's efficiency in the SPARK from the above theorem are all preserved from the underlying succinct argument up to $\mathrm{poly}(\lambda, |M, x|, L, \log t)$ factors. Furthermore, we observe that our SPARK has universal completeness, prover runtime, and succinctness, meaning that these three properties hold with respect to the universal relation $R_{\mathcal{U}}^{\mathsf{RAM}}$. Our soundness guarantee, however, requires knowing a polynomial upper bound on t, and as such we construct a protocol for R_c^{RAM} for each c such that

$t = |x|^c$. Alternatively, we could have achieved universal soundness by relying on a superpolynomial assumption on the soundness of the commitment scheme.

We can instantiate Theorem 5.6 with Kilian's 4-round succinct argument of knowledge [31], which exists assuming only collision resistant hash functions. Furthermore, we can instantiate the PCP used by Kilian's succinct argument with an efficient PCP (say [10] which has quasilinear prover running time and poly-logarithmic verifier running time). Since we already assume collision resistant hash functions for the commitment, this shows that we can achieve SPARKs for NP from collision resistance alone. Applying the transformation as specified, the round complexity of the resulting transformation would be $\text{poly}(\lambda, |M, x|, \log t)$. However, we can use the fact that for the standard implementation of Kilian (where the prover stores the entire PCP), the prover can compute the last two rounds in $\text{poly}(\lambda, \log t)$ time, so we can do the last two rounds of Kilian in parallel to reduce the round complexity to four. This gives Theorem 1.1. The full details of this modification are described in the full version.

By suitably modifying the SPARK definition to be non-interactive, and relying on any SNARK with quasi-linear overhead, the above transformation can be used to obtain a non-interactive SPARK. This gives Theorem 1.2, for which the formal details are also deferred to the full version.

5.1   The Update Language

For any $c \in \mathbb{N}$, we would like to give a SPARK for R_c^{RAM}. Let (M, x, y, L, t) be any statement in L_c^{RAM}, where M is a RAM program with access to a string $D \in \{0, 1\}^{n\lambda}$ in memory for $n \leq 2^\lambda$. To help with our construction, we define the language L_{upd} in Fig. 2. This language corresponds to k steps of a RAM computation where at each step we additionally update a commitment corresponding to the memory of M. Specifically, a statement

$$(M, x, k, \mathsf{pp}, \mathsf{state}_0, \mathsf{com}_0, v_0^{\mathsf{rd}}, \mathsf{state}_{\mathsf{final}}, \mathsf{com}_{\mathsf{final}}, v_{\mathsf{final}}^{\mathsf{rd}})$$

is in L_{upd} if there exists a sequence of k consistent updates starting at state state_0 and ending at $\mathsf{state}_{\mathsf{final}}$. The ith update specifies the commitment com_i after that step, the value v_i^{rd} read from memory during that step (if any), and proofs π_i, τ_i validating the operation (read or write) performed at that step.

The relation of this language is defined relative to the values given by $(\mathsf{state}_i, \mathsf{op}_i, \ell_i, v_i^{\mathsf{wt}}) = \mathsf{step}(M, \mathsf{state}_{i-1}, v_{i-1}^{\mathsf{rd}})$ for $i \in [k]$. The relation first checks that the final state state_k and commitment and com_k match those given by the statement. Then, for every step i, it checks (1) that the update from com_{i-1} to com_i is valid (using proof τ_i) and (2) in the case of a read operation, namely $\mathsf{op}_i = \mathsf{rd}$, there is a valid opening for com_{i-1} at position ℓ_i (using proof π_i). Specifically, this check guarantees that v_i^{rd} either already appeared in position ℓ_i in com_{i-1}, or that the position was $\bot$ before step i and was initialized correctly to v_i^{rd} in step i.

The key properties of this language are (1) the witness scales with the length of the computation and *not* the size of the memory, and (2) witnesses for consecutive L_{upd} computations can be merged into a single witness for a larger L_{upd}

Language L_{upd}:

Statement. $(M, x, k, \mathsf{pp}, \mathsf{state}_0, \mathsf{com}_0, v_0^{\mathsf{rd}}, \mathsf{state}_{\mathsf{final}}, \mathsf{com}_{\mathsf{final}}, v_{\mathsf{final}}^{\mathsf{rd}})$

Witness. $(u_1, \ldots, u_k)$, where $u_i = (\mathsf{com}_i, v_i^{\mathsf{prev}}, v_i^{\mathsf{rd}}, \pi_i, \tau_i)$ for all $i \in [k]$

Relation R_{upd}. Let $(\mathsf{state}_i, \mathsf{op}_i, \ell_i, v_i^{\mathsf{wt}}) = \mathsf{step}(M, \mathsf{state}_{i-1}, v_{i-1}^{\mathsf{rd}})$ for $i \in [k]$. Then, $(\mathsf{state}_k, \mathsf{com}_k, v_k^{\mathsf{rd}}) = (\mathsf{state}_{\mathsf{final}}, \mathsf{com}_{\mathsf{final}}, v_{\mathsf{final}}^{\mathsf{rd}})$ and for all $i \in [k]$ the following hold:

1. $\mathsf{C.VerUpd}(\mathsf{pp}, \mathsf{com}_{i-1}, \ell_i, v_i^{\mathsf{op}_i}, \mathsf{com}_i, \tau_i) = 1$.
2. $\mathsf{C.VerOpen}(\mathsf{pp}, \mathsf{com}_{i-1}, \ell_i, v_i^{\mathsf{prev}}, \pi_i) = 1$.
3. $v_i^{\mathsf{prev}} \in \{\bot, v_i^{\mathsf{rd}}\}$.
4. If $v_i^{\mathsf{prev}} = \bot$ and $\ell_i < |x|$, then $v_i^{\mathsf{rd}} = x_{\ell_i}$.

Fig. 2. A language for verifying k steps of a RAM computation M on input x from initial state state_0 to final state $\mathsf{state}_{\mathsf{final}}$.

computation. This allows us to prove that $(M, x, y, L, t) \in L_c^{\mathsf{RAM}}$ with witness w by splitting a proof that $M(x, w) = 1$ into proofs of many sub-computations, where the proof of each sub-computation will correspond to a statement in L_{upd}.

The Complexity of L_{upd}. Note that the language L_{upd} is a standard NP language. In particular, verifying that an instance-witness pair corresponding to k updates is in the relation for L_{upd} can be done by a circuit C with $|C| = k \cdot p(\lambda, |M, x|, \log n)$ for a polynomial p. Since we will only be using the succinct argument to prove statements in L_{upd}, we only need it to have quasi-linear overhead with respect to the circuit (or Turing Machine) complexity of this language.

5.2 The Protocol

Before defining our protocol in Figs. 3 and 4, we give an overview to introduce the necessary notation and emphasize certain aspects that were omitted for simplicity from the technical overview. Let $(P_{\mathsf{sARK}}, V_{\mathsf{sARK}})$ be the succinct argument of knowledge and let α be its prover efficiency. Let C be the concurrent locally updatable commitment and let β be its efficiency.

As mentioned in Sect. 5.1, to prove that $((M, x, y, L, t), w) \in R_c^{\mathsf{RAM}}$, we split the computation of $M(x, w)$ into m sub-computations in such a way that the proof of each sub-computation completes roughly by time t. The ith sub-computation consists of a "compute" phase, where we compute k_i steps of the total t steps of computation and maintain a commitment to the memory at each step, and a "proof" phase, where we use $(P_{\mathsf{sARK}}, V_{\mathsf{sARK}})$ to prove correctness of those k_i steps. For the "compute" phase, recall that performing k_i steps of computation while also updating the commitment takes $k_i \cdot \beta$ total work, yet computed in depth $(k_i - 1) + \beta$ using β processors by Theorem 4.6.

To complete the "proof" phase in the desired amount of time, suppose that the work of the prover in the interactive protocol $(P_{\mathsf{sARK}}, V_{\mathsf{sARK}})$ is bounded by a function α of the security parameter and total work of the computation (where we recall that the security parameter also upper bounds the statement size).

For any $k \leq t$ steps of computation, it will be convenient to consider $\alpha^\star$ to be an upper bound on the multiplicative overhead of computing a proof for a statement in L_{upd}. We define this formally below, but it can be roughly thought of as a value upper bounded by $\alpha(\lambda, \beta \cdot t)/(\beta \cdot t)$. Then, the largest number of steps of the computation that we can compute and prove and ensure we finish before time t is $k_1 = t/(\alpha^\star \cdot \beta + 1)$ steps. This is because it takes $k_1 + \beta$ steps to compute (with corresponding hash updates using β processors) and then can be proven in time $k_1 \cdot \alpha^\star \cdot \beta$. Put these together, computing and proving will finish roughly in time $t + \beta$. Furthermore, after computing the first k_1 steps, we can recursively carve out the next largest piece of computation we can finish in time t.

In general, let $\gamma \triangleq \alpha^\star \cdot \beta + 1$. The size of the ith sub-computation will be $k_i = (t/\gamma) \cdot (1 - 1/\gamma)^{i-1}$, which intuitively holds because at each sub-computation we are left with a $(1 - 1/\gamma)$ fraction of the total remaining computation. We continue recursively until the remaining computation is less than $\log \lambda$ steps, which the verifier can then compute directly given the witness, and thus in total recurse for $m = \gamma \log t$ steps. We formalize the above idea in Fig. 3 with the algorithm Compute-and-prove.

In the full protocol (formalized in Fig. 4), the verifier V first sends public parameters for the commitment (which alternatively could be part of a trusted common reference string in the non-interactive setting). The prover P then hashes an initially empty string (corresponding to uninitialized memory) and allocates memory to store the memory D for use when emulating M. M expects D to start with x and w. One way to achieve this would be for P to copy x, w to the start of D in $|x| + |w|$ time, but we want to avoid having P run in time depending on $|w|$ since this could be large. To resolve this, we instead have P translate all accesses to D that correspond to the witness to instead access its own memory where w is located. Because w is only needed to emulate M, if M overwrites the memory containing w, it will not cause any other issues for P. Finally, the prover P runs Compute-and-prove with V as discussed above. After proving all sub-computations, the prover sends the output y and a proof authenticating each word in y. Finally, V accepts if all sub-protocols are valid, the claimed statements are consistent with each other, and if the proofs of the claimed output are valid.

Parameters. For ease of readability for the protocol and corresponding proofs, we define the parameters and assumptions for the protocol with respect to $\lambda \in \mathbb{N}$, the relation R_c^{RAM}, and $M, x, t, L \in \{0, 1\}^*$ as follows:

- $\beta \triangleq \beta(\lambda, \log(n))$ is the efficiency of C.
- α is a function representing the prover efficiency of $(P_{\mathsf{sARK}}, V_{\mathsf{sARK}})$. For any security parameter Λ, machine and input of total length X, and time bound T, we assume that $\alpha(\Lambda, X, T)/T \in \mathrm{poly}(\Lambda, X, \log T)$ and is an increasing function in each of its inputs.

Compute-and-prove

Input: $T, \text{state}_0, \text{com}_0, v_0^{\text{rd}}$
Prover Input: Witness w, ptr
Hardcoded Values: $1^\lambda, M, x, \gamma, \text{pp}$
Protocol:

1. If $T \geq \gamma$, set $k = \lceil T/\gamma \rceil$, which will be the number of steps to compute, and otherwise set $k = T$.

2. P does the following for $i = 1, \ldots, k$:
   (a) Compute $(\text{state}_i, \text{op}_i, \ell_i, v_i^{\text{wt}}) = \text{step}(M, \text{state}_{i-1}, v_{i-1}^{\text{rd}})$.
   (b) If $\text{op}_i = \text{wt}$, update D with v_i^{wt} in location ℓ_i^{wt} and let v_i^{rd} be the value at that location that was overwritten.
   (c) If $\text{op}_i = \text{rd}$, let v_i^{rd} be the value at location ℓ_i in D.
   (d) Spawn a parallel process to compute $\text{OpenUpdate}(\text{pp}, \text{ptr}, \ell_i, v_i^{\text{op}_i})$ (specified by Definition 4.4) and let $(v_i^{\text{prev}}, \pi_i, \text{com}_i, \tau_i)$ be the output.

3. Without waiting Step 2d to halt, if $T \geq \gamma$, P spawns a process to run Compute-and-prove with V on input $(T - k, \text{state}_k, \text{com}_k, v_k^{\text{rd}})$.

4. Once step 2d halts, set $\text{statement} = (M, x, k, \text{pp}, \text{state}_0, \text{com}_0, v_0^{\text{rd}}, \text{state}_k, \text{com}_k, v_k^{\text{rd}})$ and $\text{wit} = ((\text{com}_1, v_1^{\text{prev}}, v_1^{\text{rd}}, \pi_1, \tau_1), \ldots, (\text{com}_k, v_k^{\text{prev}}, v_k^{\text{rd}}, \pi_k, \tau_k))$.

5. If $T \geq \gamma$, P spawns a process to run an interactive argument of knowledge with V to prove that $\text{statement} \in L_{\text{upd}}$ using $(P_{\text{sARK}}(\text{wit}), V_{\text{sARK}})$.

6. Otherwise, when $T < \gamma$, P sends wit to V, and V uses wit directly to verify that $\text{statement} \in L_{\text{upd}}$.

Fig. 3. A parallel algorithm, used in the SPARK in Fig. 4, that computes and proves T steps of RAM computation.

- $\alpha^\star \triangleq \alpha(\lambda, |M, x| + 6\lambda + \ell_{\text{Gen}}(\lambda) + \log t, t\beta)/(t\beta)$ is the worst-case multiplicative overhead of running P_{sARK} to prove a statement in L_{upd} corresponding to at most t steps of computation, where $\ell_{\text{Gen}}(\lambda)$ is the output length of $\text{C.Gen}(1^\lambda)$, and so $|M, x| + 6\lambda + \ell_{\text{Gen}}(\lambda) + \log t$ is an upper bound on the length of the L_{upd} statements. Note that $\alpha^\star$ is a function of λ, M, x, t, and β.
- $\gamma \triangleq \alpha^\star \cdot \beta + 1$ is the fraction of remaining computation done at each recursive call to Compute-and-prove. Note that γ is a function of λ, M, x, t, and β.

We formalize the protocol in Figs. 3 and 4. We prove Theorem 5.6, that this protocol is a SPARK by showing completeness, argument of knowledge, succinctness, and prover efficiency. The proofs are deferred to the full version.

Protocol $\Pi(1^\lambda, (M, x, t, L))$ for R_c^{RAM} between $P(w)$ and V:

1. V computes $\mathsf{pp} \leftarrow \mathsf{C.Gen}(1^\lambda)$ and $(*, \mathsf{com_{start}}) = \mathsf{C.Commit}(\mathsf{pp}, D_\perp)$, where where $D_\perp$ is the empty partial string. V sends pp to P.

2. Both parties compute γ (as in the parameters paragraph), initialize $\mathsf{state_{start}}$ as the initial (empty) state of M, and set $v_{\mathsf{start}}^{\mathsf{rd}} = \perp$.

3. P computes $(\mathsf{ptr}, \mathsf{com_{start}}) = \mathsf{C.Commit}(\mathsf{pp}, D_\perp)$. P additionally allocates memory for M, denoted D, and initialized to zeros (which we assume is free), and copies x to the start of the D. Whenever P needs to access a location ℓ in D that would correspond to the witness (i.e., $|x| < \ell < |x| + |w|$), it instead accesses the corresponding location in w in its own memory. For simplicity, when we write that P accesses a location in D, we implicitly assume it translates the location appropriately.

4. P and V run the sub-protocol $\mathsf{Compute\text{-}and\text{-}prove}(t, \mathsf{state_{start}}, \mathsf{com_{start}}, v_{\mathsf{start}}^{\mathsf{rd}})$. For $i \in [m]$, let Π_i be the ith sub-protocol proving $\mathsf{statement}_i :=$ $(M_i, x_i, k_i, \mathsf{pp}_i, \mathsf{state}_i, \mathsf{com}_i, v_i^{\mathsf{rd}}, \mathsf{state}_i', \mathsf{com}_i', v_i^{\mathsf{rd}\prime})$.

5. P computes $(y_i, \pi_{i,\mathsf{final}}) = \mathsf{C.Open}(\mathsf{pp}, \mathsf{ptr}, i)$ for $i \in [L']$ where $L' = \lceil L/\lambda \rceil$. Then, P sends $y = y_1 \| \dots \| y_{L'})$ and $\pi_{\mathsf{final}} = (\pi_{1,\mathsf{final}}, \dots, \pi_{L',\mathsf{final}})$ to V.

6. V outputs y if the following hold, and outputs $\perp$ otherwise:
   (a) V_{sARK} accepts in $\Pi_1, \dots, \Pi_{m-1}$ and V accepts in Π_m.
   (b) For all $i \in [m]$, it holds that $(M_i, x_i, \mathsf{pp}_i) = (M, x, \mathsf{pp})$.
   (c) $\sum_{i=1}^{m} k_i = t$ and $t \le |x|^c$.
   (d) $(\mathsf{state_{start}}, \mathsf{com_{start}}, v_{\mathsf{start}}^{\mathsf{rd}}) = (\mathsf{state}_1, \mathsf{com}_1, v_1^{\mathsf{rd}})$.
   (e) $(\mathsf{state}_i', \mathsf{com}_i', v_i^{\mathsf{rd}\prime}) = (\mathsf{state}_{i+1}, \mathsf{com}_{i+1}, v_{i+1}^{\mathsf{rd}})$ for all $i \in [m-1]$.
   (f) state_m' is a halting state, $|y| \le L$, and $\mathsf{C.VerOpen}(\mathsf{pp}, \mathsf{com}_m, i, y_i, \pi_{i,\mathsf{final}})$ accepts for all $i \in [L']$.

Fig. 4. A SPARK for R_c^{RAM}.

Acknowledgements. This work was supported in part by NSF Award SATC-1704788, NSF Award RI-1703846, AFOSR Award FA9550-18-1-0267, and by NSF Award DGE-1650441. This research is based upon work supported in part by the Office of the Director of National Intelligence (ODNI), Intelligence Advanced Research Projects Activity (IARPA), via 2019-19-020700006. The views and conclusions contained herein are those of the authors and should not be interpreted as necessarily representing the official policies, either expressed or implied, of ODNI, IARPA, or the U.S. Government. The U.S. Government is authorized to reproduce and distribute reprints for governmental purposes notwithstanding any copyright annotation therein.

References

1. Alwen, J., Blocki, J., Pietrzak, K.: Depth-robust graphs and their cumulative memory complexity. In: Coron, J.-S., Nielsen, J.B. (eds.) EUROCRYPT 2017. LNCS, vol. 10212, pp. 3–32. Springer, Cham (2017). https://doi.org/10.1007/978-3-319-56617-7_1

2. Alwen, J., Blocki, J., Pietrzak, K.: Sustained space complexity. In: Nielsen, J.B., Rijmen, V. (eds.) EUROCRYPT 2018. LNCS, vol. 10821, pp. 99–130. Springer, Cham (2018). https://doi.org/10.1007/978-3-319-78375-8_4
3. Alwen, J., Chen, B., Kamath, C., Kolmogorov, V., Pietrzak, K., Tessaro, S.: On the complexity of scrypt and proofs of space in the parallel random oracle model. In: Fischlin, M., Coron, J.-S. (eds.) EUROCRYPT 2016. LNCS, vol. 9666, pp. 358–387. Springer, Heidelberg (2016). https://doi.org/10.1007/978-3-662-49896-5_13
4. Alwen, J., Serbinenko, V.: High parallel complexity graphs and memory-hard functions. In: STOC, pp. 595–603. ACM (2015)
5. Barak, B., Goldreich, O.: Universal arguments and their applications. SIAM J. Comput. **38**(5), 1661–1694 (2008)
6. Ben-Sasson, E., Chiesa, A., Gabizon, A., Riabzev, M., Spooner, N.: Interactive oracle proofs with constant rate and query complexity. In: 44th International Colloquium on Automata, Languages, and Programming, ICALP, pp. 40:1–40:15 (2017)
7. Ben-Sasson, E., Chiesa, A., Genkin, D., Tromer, E.: On the concrete efficiency of probabilistically-checkable proofs. In: STOC, pp. 585–594. ACM (2013)
8. Ben-Sasson, E., Chiesa, A., Genkin, D., Tromer, E., Virza, M.: SNARKs for C: verifying program executions succinctly and in zero knowledge. In: Canetti, R., Garay, J.A. (eds.) CRYPTO 2013. LNCS, vol. 8043, pp. 90–108. Springer, Heidelberg (2013). https://doi.org/10.1007/978-3-642-40084-1_6
9. Ben-Sasson, E., Chiesa, A., Spooner, N.: Interactive oracle proofs. In: Hirt, M., Smith, A. (eds.) TCC 2016. LNCS, vol. 9986, pp. 31–60. Springer, Heidelberg (2016). https://doi.org/10.1007/978-3-662-53644-5_2
10. Ben-Sasson, E., Sudan, M.: Short PCPs with polylog query complexity. SIAM J. Comput. **38**(2), 551–607 (2008)
11. Bitansky, N., et al.: The hunting of the SNARK. J. Cryptol. **30**(4), 989–1066 (2017)
12. Bitansky, N., Canetti, R., Chiesa, A., Tromer, E.: From extractable collision resistance to succinct non-interactive arguments of knowledge, and back again. In: ITCS, pp. 326–349. ACM (2012)
13. Bitansky, N., Chiesa, A.: Succinct arguments from multi-prover interactive proofs and their efficiency benefits. In: Safavi-Naini, R., Canetti, R. (eds.) CRYPTO 2012. LNCS, vol. 7417, pp. 255–272. Springer, Heidelberg (2012). https://doi.org/10.1007/978-3-642-32009-5_16
14. Boneh, D., Bonneau, J., Bünz, B., Fisch, B.: Verifiable delay functions. In: Shacham, H., Boldyreva, A. (eds.) CRYPTO 2018. LNCS, vol. 10991, pp. 757–788. Springer, Cham (2018). https://doi.org/10.1007/978-3-319-96884-1_25
15. Boneh, D., Bünz, B., Fisch, B.: A survey of two verifiable delay functions. IACR Cryptology ePrint Archive 2018,712 (2018)
16. Catalano, D., Fiore, D.: Vector commitments and their applications. In: Kurosawa, K., Hanaoka, G. (eds.) PKC 2013. LNCS, vol. 7778, pp. 55–72. Springer, Heidelberg (2013). https://doi.org/10.1007/978-3-642-36362-7_5
17. Chung, K., Lin, H., Pass, R.: Constant-round concurrent zero knowledge from p-certificates. In: 54th Annual IEEE Symposium on Foundations of Computer Science, FOCS, pp. 50–59 (2013)
18. Costello, C., et al.: Geppetto: versatile verifiable computation. In: IEEE Symposium on Security and Privacy, pp. 253–270. IEEE Computer Society (2015)
19. Dinur, I.: The PCP theorem by gap amplification. J. ACM **54**(3), 12 (2007)
20. Döttling, N., Garg, S., Ishai, Y., Malavolta, G., Mour, T., Ostrovsky, R.: Trapdoor hash functions and their applications. IACR Cryptology ePrint Archive 2019,639 (2019)

21. Döttling, N., Garg, S., Malavolta, G., Vasudevan, P.N.: Tight verifiable delay functions. IACR Cryptology ePrint Archive 2019,659 (2019)
22. Dwork, C., Goldberg, A., Naor, M.: On memory-bound functions for fighting spam. In: Boneh, D. (ed.) CRYPTO 2003. LNCS, vol. 2729, pp. 426–444. Springer, Heidelberg (2003). https://doi.org/10.1007/978-3-540-45146-4_25
23. Dwork, C., Naor, M., Wee, H.: Pebbling and proofs of work. In: Shoup, V. (ed.) CRYPTO 2005. LNCS, vol. 3621, pp. 37–54. Springer, Heidelberg (2005). https://doi.org/10.1007/11535218_3
24. Ephraim, N., Freitag, C., Komargodski, I., Pass, R.: Continuous verifiable delay functions. IACR Cryptology ePrint Archive 2019,619 (2019)
25. Fiat, A., Shamir, A.: How to prove yourself: practical solutions to identification and signature problems. In: Odlyzko, A.M. (ed.) CRYPTO 1986. LNCS, vol. 263, pp. 186–194. Springer, Heidelberg (1987). https://doi.org/10.1007/3-540-47721-7_12
26. Goldwasser, S., Kalai, Y.T., Rothblum, G.N.: Delegating computation: interactive proofs for muggles. J. ACM 62(4), 27:1–27:64 (2015)
27. Goldwasser, S., Micali, S., Rackoff, C.: The knowledge complexity of interactive proof systems. SIAM J. Comput. 18(1), 186–208 (1989)
28. Holmgren, J., Rothblum, R.: Delegating computations with (almost) minimal time and space overhead. In: 59th IEEE Annual Symposium on Foundations of Computer Science, FOCS, pp. 124–135 (2018)
29. Kalai, Y., Paneth, O.: Delegating RAM computations. In: Hirt, M., Smith, A. (eds.) TCC 2016. LNCS, vol. 9986, pp. 91–118. Springer, Heidelberg (2016). https://doi.org/10.1007/978-3-662-53644-5_4
30. Kalai, Y.T., Raz, R.: Interactive PCP. In: Aceto, L., Damgård, I., Goldberg, L.A., Halldórsson, M.M., Ingólfsdóttir, A., Walukiewicz, I. (eds.) ICALP 2008. LNCS, vol. 5126, pp. 536–547. Springer, Heidelberg (2008). https://doi.org/10.1007/978-3-540-70583-3_44
31. Kilian, J.: A note on efficient zero-knowledge proofs and arguments. In: Proceedings of the Twenty-Fourth Annual ACM Symposium on Theory of Computing, pp. 723–732. ACM (1992)
32. Lindell, Y.: Parallel coin-tossing and constant-round secure two-party computation. J. Cryptol. 16(3), 143–184 (2003)
33. Merkle, R.C.: A certified digital signature. In: Brassard, G. (ed.) CRYPTO 1989. LNCS, vol. 435, pp. 218–238. Springer, New York (1990). https://doi.org/10.1007/0-387-34805-0_21
34. Micali, S.: Computationally sound proofs. SIAM J. Comput. 30(4), 1253–1298 (2000)
35. Micali, S., Pass, R.: Local zero knowledge. In: Proceedings of the 38th Annual ACM Symposium on Theory of Computing, Seattle, WA, USA, 21–23 May 2006, pp. 306–315 (2006)
36. Parno, B., Howell, J., Gentry, C., Raykova, M.: Pinocchio: nearly practical verifiable computation. Commun. ACM 59(2), 103–112 (2016)
37. Pass, R., Rosen, A.: Concurrent nonmalleable commitments. SIAM J. Comput. 37(6), 1891–1925 (2008)
38. Pietrzak, K.: Simple verifiable delay functions. In: 10th Innovations in Theoretical Computer Science Conference, ITCS, pp. 60:1–60:15 (2019)
39. Reingold, O., Rothblum, G.N., Rothblum, R.D.: Constant-round interactive proofs for delegating computation. In: 48th Annual ACM SIGACT Symposium on Theory of Computing, STOC, pp. 49–62 (2016)
40. Ron-Zewi, N., Rothblum, R.D.: Local proofs approaching the witness length. IACR Cryptology ePrint Archive 2019,1062 (2019)

41. Valiant, P.: Incrementally verifiable computation or proofs of knowledge imply time/space efficiency. In: Canetti, R. (ed.) TCC 2008. LNCS, vol. 4948, pp. 1–18. Springer, Heidelberg (2008). https://doi.org/10.1007/978-3-540-78524-8_1
42. Wesolowski, B.: Efficient verifiable delay functions. In: Ishai, Y., Rijmen, V. (eds.) EUROCRYPT 2019. LNCS, vol. 11478, pp. 379–407. Springer, Cham (2019). https://doi.org/10.1007/978-3-030-17659-4_13
43. Wu, H., Zheng, W., Chiesa, A., Popa, R.A., Stoica, I.: DIZK: a distributed zero knowledge proof system. In: USENIX Security Symposium, pp. 675–692. USENIX Association (2018)

Marlin: Preprocessing zkSNARKs
with Universal and Updatable SRS

Alessandro Chiesa[1(✉)], Yuncong Hu[1], Mary Maller[2], Pratyush Mishra[1(✉)],
Noah Vesely[1], and Nicholas Ward[1]

[1] UC Berkeley, Berkeley, USA
{alexch,yuncong_hu,pratyush,psi,npward}@berkeley.edu
[2] Ethereum Foundation, London, UK
mary.maller@ethereum.org

Abstract. We present a methodology to construct preprocessing zkSNARKs where the structured reference string (SRS) is universal and updatable. This exploits a novel use of *holography* [Babai et al., STOC 1991], where fast verification is achieved provided the statement being checked is given in encoded form.

We use our methodology to obtain a preprocessing zkSNARK where the SRS has linear size and arguments have constant size. Our construction improves on Sonic [Maller et al., CCS 2019], the prior state of the art in this setting, in all efficiency parameters: proving is an order of magnitude faster and verification is thrice as fast, even with smaller SRS size and argument size. Our construction is most efficient when instantiated in the algebraic group model (also used by Sonic), but we also demonstrate how to realize it under concrete knowledge assumptions. We implement and evaluate our construction.

The core of our preprocessing zkSNARK is an efficient *algebraic holographic proof* (AHP) for rank-1 constraint satisfiability (R1CS) that achieves linear proof length and constant query complexity.

1 Introduction

Succinct non-interactive arguments (SNARGs) are efficient certificates of membership in non-deterministic languages. Recent years have seen a surge of interest in zero-knowledge SNARGs of knowledge (zkSNARKs), with researchers studying constructions under different cryptographic assumptions, improvements in asymptotic efficiency, concrete performance of implementations, and numerous applications. The focus of this paper is *SNARGs in the preprocessing setting*, a notion that we motivate next.

When is fast verification possible? The size of a SNARG must be, as a minimum condition, sublinear in the size of the non-deterministic witness, and often is required to be even smaller (e.g., logarithmic in the size of the non-deterministic computation). The time to verify a SNARG would be, ideally, as fast as reading the SNARG. *This is in general too much to hope for, however.* The verification procedure must also read the *description* of the computation, in order know what statement is being verified. While there are natural

© International Association for Cryptologic Research 2020
A. Canteaut and Y. Ishai (Eds.): EUROCRYPT 2020, LNCS 12105, pp. 738–768, 2020.
https://doi.org/10.1007/978-3-030-45721-1_26

computations that have succinct descriptions (e.g., machine computations), in general the description of a computation could be as large as the computation itself, which means that the time to verify the SNARG could be asymptotically comparable to the size of the computation. This is unfortunate because there is a very useful class of computations for which we cannot expect fast verification: general circuit computations.

The preprocessing setting. An approach to avoid the above limitation is to design a verification procedure that has two phases: an offline phase that produces a short summary for a given circuit; and an online phase that uses this short summary to verify SNARGs that attest to the satisfiability of the circuit with different partial assignments to its input wires. Crucially, now the online phase could in principle be as fast as reading the SNARG (and the partial assignment), and thus sublinear in the circuit size. This goal was captured by *preprocessing SNARGs* [Gro10, Lip12, Gen+13, Bit+13], which have been studied in an influential line of works that has led to highly-efficient constructions that fulfill this goal (e.g., [Gro16]) and large-scale deployments in the real world that benefit from the online fast verification (e.g., [Zcash]).

The problem: circuit-specific SRS. The offline phase in efficient constructions of preprocessing SNARGS consists of sampling a structured reference string (SRS) that depends on the circuit that is being preprocessed. This implies that producing/validating proofs with respect to different circuits requires different SRSs. In many applications of interest, there is no single party that can be entrusted with sampling the SRS, and so real-world deployments have had to rely on cryptographic "ceremonies" [ZcashMPC] that use secure multi-party sampling protocols [Ben+15, BGG17, BGM17]. However, any modification in the circuit used in an application requires another cryptographic ceremony, which is unsustainable for many applications.

A solution: universal SRS. The above motivates preprocessing SNARGs where the SRS is *universal*, which means that the SRS supports any circuit up to a given size bound by enabling anyone, in an offline phase *after* the SRS is sampled, to publicly derive a circuit-specific SRS.[1] Known techniques to obtain a universal SRS from circuit-specific SRS introduce expensive overheads due to universal simulation [Ben+14a, Ben+14b]. Also, these techniques lead to universal SRSs that are not *updatable*, a property introduced in [Gro+18] that significantly simplifies cryptographic ceremonies. The recent work of Maller et al. [Mal+19] overcomes these shortcomings, obtaining the first efficient construction of a preprocessing SNARG with universal (and updatable) SRS. Even so, the construction in [Mal+19] is considerably more expensive than the state of the art for circuit-specific SRS [Gro16]. In this paper we ask: *can the efficiency gap between universal SRS and circuit-specific SRS be closed, or at least significantly reduced?*

---

[1] Even better than a universal SRS would be a URS (uniform reference string). However, achieving preprocessing SNARGs in the URS model with small argument size remains an open problem; see Sect. 1.2.

Concurrent work. A concurrent work [GWC19] studies the same question as this paper. See Sect. 1.2 for a brief discussion that compares the two works.

1.1 Our Results

In this paper we present MARLIN, a new preprocessing zkSNARK with universal (and updatable) SRS that improves on the prior state of the art [Mal+19, Sonic] in essentially all relevant efficiency parameters.[2] In addition to reducing argument size by several group and field elements and reducing time complexity of the verifier by over 3×, our construction overcomes the main efficiency drawback of [Mal+19, Sonic]: the cost of producing proofs. Indeed, our construction improves time complexity of the prover by over 10×, achieving prover efficiency comparable to the case of preprocessing zkSNARKs with *circuit-specific* SRS. In Fig. 1 we provide a comparison of our construction and [Mal+19, Sonic], including argument sizes for two popular elliptic curves; the table also includes the state of the art for circuit-specific SRS. We have implemented MARLIN in a Rust library,[3] and report evaluation results in Fig. 2.

Our zkSNARK is the result of several contributions that we deem of independent interest, summarized below.

(1) A new methodology. We present a general methodology to construct preprocessing SNARGs (and also zkSNARKs) where the SRS is universal (and updatable). Our methodology produces succinct *interactive* arguments that can be made non-interactive via the Fiat–Shamir transformation [FS86], and so below we focus on *preprocessing arguments with universal and updatable SRS*.

Our key observation is that the ability to preprocess a circuit in an offline phase is closely related to constructing "holographic proofs" [Bab+91], which means that the verifier does not receive the circuit description as an input but, rather, makes a small number of queries to an encoding of it. These queries are in addition to queries that the verifier makes to proofs sent by the prover. Moreover, in this paper we focus on the setting where the encoding of the circuit description consists of low-degree polynomials and also where proofs are themselves low-degree polynomials—this can be viewed as a requirement that honest and malicious provers are "algebraic". We call these *algebraic holographic proofs* (AHPs); see Sect. 4 for definitions.

We present a transformation that "compiles" any public-coin AHP into a corresponding preprocessing argument with universal (and updatable) SRS by using suitable polynomial commitments.

Theorem 1. *There is an efficient transformation that combines any public-coin AHP for a relation $\mathcal{R}$ and an extractable polynomial commitment scheme to*

---

[2] Maller et al. [Mal+19] discuss two variants of their protocol, a cheaper one for the "helped setting" and a costlier one for the "unhelped setting". The variant that is relevant to this paper is the latter one, because it is a preprocessing zkSNARK. (The former variant does not achieve succinct verification, and instead achieves a weaker guarantee that applies to proof batches.).

[3] https://github.com/scipr-lab/marlin.

construction	argument size over BN-256 (bytes)	argument size over BLS12-381 (bytes)
Sonic [Mal+19]	1152	1472
MARLIN [this work]	1088	1296
Groth16 [Gro16]	128	192

zkSNARK construction		sizes			time complexity			
		$\|ipk\|$	$\|ivk\|$	$\|\pi\|$	generator	indexer	prover	verifier
Sonic [Mal+19]	$\mathbb{G}_1$	$8M$	—	20	8 f-MSM(M)	4 v-MSM($3m$)	273 v-MSM(m)	7 pairings
	$\mathbb{G}_2$	$8M$	3	—	8 f-MSM(M)			
	$\mathbb{F}_q$	—	—	16	—	$O(m \log m)$	$O(m \log m)$	$O(\|\mathbf{x}\| + \log m)$
MARLIN [this work]	$\mathbb{G}_1$	$6M$	2	13	1 f-MSM($6M$)	9 v-MSM(m)	21 v-MSM(m)	2 pairings
	$\mathbb{G}_2$	—	2	—				
	$\mathbb{F}_q$	—	—	21	—	$O(m \log m)$	$O(m \log m)$	$O(\|\mathbf{x}\| + \log m)$
Groth16 [Gro16]	$\mathbb{G}_1$	$4n$	$O(\|\mathbf{x}\|)$	2	4 f-MSM(n)	N/A	4 v-MSM(n)	1 v-MSM($\|\mathbf{x}\|$)
	$\mathbb{G}_2$	n	$O(1)$	1	1 f-MSM(n)		1 v-MSM(n)	3 pairings
	$\mathbb{F}_q$	—	—	—	$O(m + n \log n)$		$O(m + n \log n)$	—

n: number of multiplication gates in the circuit
m: total number of (addition or multiplication) gates in the circuit
M: maximum supported circuit size (= number of addition and multiplication gates)

Fig. 1. Comparison of two preprocessing zkSNARKs with universal (and updatable) SRS: the prior state of the art and our construction. We include the current state of the art for circuit-specific SRS (in gray), for reference. Here $\mathbb{G}_1/\mathbb{G}_2/\mathbb{F}_q$ denote the number of elements or operations over the respective group/field; also, f-MSM(m) and v-MSM(m) denote fixed-base and variable-base multi-scalar multiplications (MSM) each of size m, respectively. The number of pairings that we report for Sonic's verifier is lower than that reported in [Mal+19] because we account for standard batching techniques for pairing equations.

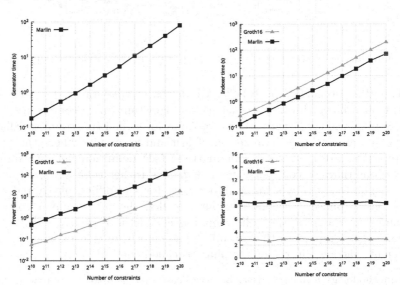

Fig. 2. Measured performance of MARLIN and [Gro16] over the BLS12-381 curve. We could not include measurements for [Mal+19, Sonic] because at the time of writing there is no working implementation of its unhelped variant.

obtain a public-coin preprocessing argument with universal SRS for the relation R. The transformation preserves zero knowledge and proof of knowledge of the underlying AHP. The SRS is updatable provided the SRS of the polynomial commitment scheme is.

The above transformation provides us with a *methodology* to construct preprocessing zkSNARKs with universal SRS (see Fig. 3). Namely, to improve the efficiency of preprocessing zkSNARKs with universal SRS it suffices to improve the efficiency of *simpler building blocks*: AHPs (an information-theoretic primitive) and polynomial commitments (a cryptographic primitive).[4]

The improvements achieved by our preprocessing zkSNARK (see Fig. 1) were obtained by following this methodology: we designed efficient constructions for each of these two building blocks (which we discuss shortly), combined them via Theorem 1, and then applied the Fiat–Shamir transformation [FS86].

Methodologies that combine information-theoretic probabilistic proofs and cryptographic tools have played a fundamental role in the construction of efficient argument systems. In the particular setting of preprocessing SNARGs, for example, the compiler introduced in [Bit+13] for *circuit-specific* SRS has paved the way towards current state-of-the-art constructions [Gro16], and also led to constructions that are plausibly post-quantum [Bon+17,Bon+18]. We believe that our methodology for universal SRS will also be useful in future work, and may lead to further efficiency improvements.

Fig. 3. Our methodology for constructing preprocessing SNARGs with universal SRS.

(2) An efficient AHP for R1CS. We design an algebraic holographic proof (AHP) that achieves linear proof length and constant query complexity, among other useful efficiency features. The protocol is for rank-1 constraint satisfiability (R1CS), a well-known generalization of arithmetic circuits where the "circuit description" is given by coefficient matrices (see definition below). Note that the relations that we consider consist of *triples* rather than *pairs*, because we need to split the verifier's input into a part for the offline phase and a part for the online phase. The offline input is called the *index*, and it consists of the coefficient matrices; the online input is called the *instance*, and it consists of a partial assignment to the variables. The algorithm that encodes the index (coefficient matrices) in the offline phase is called the *indexer*.

---

[4] The methodology also captures as a special case various folklore approaches used in prior works to construct *non*-preprocessing zkSNARKs via polynomial commitment schemes (see Sect. 1.2), thereby providing the first formal statement that clarifies what properties of algebraic proofs and polynomial commitment schemes are essential for these folklore approaches.

Definition 1 (informal). *The indexed relation* $\mathcal{R}_{R1CS}$ *is the set of triples* $(i, x, w) = ((\mathbb{F}, n, m, A, B, C), x, w)$ *where* $\mathbb{F}$ *is a finite field,* A, B, C *are* $n \times n$ *matrices over* $\mathbb{F}$*, each containing at most* m *non-zero entries, and* $z := (x, w)$ *is a vector in* $\mathbb{F}^n$ *such that* $Az \circ Bz = Cz$. *(Here "*$\circ$*" denotes the entry-wise product.)*

Theorem 2 (informal). *There exists a constant-round AHP for the indexed relation* $\mathcal{R}_{R1CS}$ *with linear proof length and constant query complexity. The soundness error is* $O(m/|\mathbb{F}|)$*, and the construction is a zero knowledge proof of knowledge. The arithmetic complexity of the indexer is* $O(m \log m)$*, of the prover is* $O(m \log m)$*, and of the verifier is* $O(|x| + \log m)$.

The literature on probabilistic proofs contains algebraic protocols that are holographic (e.g., [Bab+91] and [GKR15]) but *none achieve constant query complexity*, and so applying our methodology (Theorem 1) to these would lead to large argument sizes (many tens of kilobytes). These prior algebraic protocols rely on the multivariate sumcheck protocol applied to certain multivariate polynomials, which means that they incur sizable communication costs due to (a) the many rounds of the sumcheck protocol, and (b) the fact that applying the methodology would involve using multivariate polynomial commitment schemes that (for known constructions) lead to communication costs that are linear in the number of variables.

In contrast, our algebraic protocol relies on univariate polynomials and achieves constant query complexity, incurring small communication costs. Our algebraic protocol can be viewed as a "holographic variant" of the algebraic protocol for R1CS used in Aurora [Ben+19a], because it achieves an *exponential* improvement in verification time when the verifier is given a suitable encoding of the coefficient matrices.

(3) Extractable polynomial commitments. Polynomial commitment schemes, introduced in [KZG10], are commitment schemes specialized to work with univariate polynomials. The security properties in [KZG10], while sufficient for the applications therein, do not appear sufficient for standalone use, or even just for the transformation in Theorem 1. We propose a definition for polynomial commitment schemes that incorporates the functionality and security that we believe to suffice for standalone use (and in particular suffices for Theorem 1). Moreover, we show how to extend the construction of [KZG10] to fulfill this definition in the plain model under non-falsifiable knowledge assumptions, or via a more efficient construction in the algebraic group model [FKL18] under falsifiable assumptions. These constructions are of independent interest, and when combined with our transformation, lead to the first efficient preprocessing arguments with universal SRS under concrete knowledge assumptions, and also to the efficiency reported in Fig. 1.

We have implemented in a Rust library[5] the polynomial commitment schemes, and our implementation of MARLIN relies on this library. We deem this library of independent interest for other projects.

---

[5] https://github.com/scipr-lab/poly-commit.

1.2   Related Work

In this paper we study the goal of constructing preprocessing SNARGs with universal SRS, which achieve succinct verification regardless of the structure of the non-deterministic computation being checked. The most relevant prior work is Sonic [Mal+19], on which we improve as already discussed (see Fig. 1). The notion of updatable SRS was defined and achieved in [Gro+18], but with a less efficient construction.

Concurrent work. A concurrent work [GWC19] studies the same question as this paper, and also obtains efficiency improvements over Sonic [Mal+19]. Below is a brief comparison.

- We provide an implementation and evaluation of our construction, while [GWC19] do not. The estimated costs reported in [GWC19] suggest that an implementation may perform similarly to ours.
- Similarly to our work, [GWC19] extends the polynomial commitment in [KZG10] to support batching, and proves the extension secure in the algebraic group model. We additionally show how to prove security in the plain model under non-falsifiable knowledge assumptions, and consider the problem of enforcing different degrees for different polynomials (a feature that is not needed in [GWC19]).
- We show how to compile any algebraic holographic proof into a preprocessing argument with universal SRS, while [GWC19] focus on compiling a more restricted notion that they call "polynomial protocols".
- Our protocol natively supports R1CS, and can be viewed as a holographic variant of the algebraic protocol in [Ben+19a]. The protocol in [GWC19] natively supports a different constraint system, and involves a protocol that, similar to [Gro10], uses a permutation argument to attest that all variables in the same cycle of a permutation are equal (e.g., $(1)(2,3)(4)$ would require that the second and third entries are equal).

Preprocessing SNARGs with a URS. Setty [Set19] studies preprocessing SNARGs with a URS (uniform reference string), and describes a protocol that for n-gate arithmetic circuits and a chosen constant $c \geq 2$ achieves proving time $O_\lambda(n)$, argument size $O_\lambda(n^{1/c})$, and verification time $O_\lambda(n^{1-1/c})$. The protocol in [Set19] offers a tradeoff compared to our work: preprocessing with a URS instead of a SRS, at the cost of asymptotically larger argument size and verification time. The question of achieving processing with a URS while also achieving asymptotically small argument size and verification time remains open.

The protocol in [Set19] is obtained by combining the multivariate polynomial commitments of [Wah+18] and a modern rendition of the PCP in [Bab+91] (which itself can be viewed as the "bare bones" protocol of [GKR15] for circuits of depth 1). [Set19] lacks an analysis of concrete costs, and also does not discuss how to achieve zero knowledge beyond stating that techniques in other papers [Zha+17a, Wah+18, Xie+19] can be applied. Nevertheless, argument sizes would at best be similar to these other papers (tens of kilobytes), which is much larger than our argument sizes (in the SRS model).

We conclude by noting that the informal security proof in [Set19] appears insufficient to show soundness of the argument system, because the polynomial commitment scheme is only assumed to be binding but not also extractable (there is no explanation of where the witness encoded in the committed polynomial comes from). Our definitions and security proofs, if ported over to the multivariate setting, would fill this gap.

Non-preprocessing SNARGs for arbitrary computations. Checking arbitrary circuits without preprocessing them requires the verifier to read the circuit, so the main goal is to obtain small argument size. In this setting of non-preprocessing SNARGs for arbitrary circuits, constructions with a URS (uniform reference string) are based on discrete logarithms [Boo+16, Bün+18] or hash functions [Ame+17, Ben+19a], while constructions with a universal SRS (structured reference string) combine polynomial commitments and non-holographic algebraic proofs [Gab19]; all use random oracles to obtain non-interactive arguments.[6]

We find it interesting to remark that our methodology from Theorem 1 generalizes protocols such as [Gab19] in two ways. First, it formalizes the folklore approach of combining polynomial commitments and algebraic proofs to obtain arguments, identifying the security properties required to make this approach work. Second, it demonstrates how for algebraic *holographic* proofs the resulting argument enables preprocessing.

Non-preprocessing SNARGs for structured computations. Several works study SNARGs for structured computations. This structure enables fast verification *without* preprocessing. A line of works [Ben+17, Ben+19c, Ben+19b] combines hash functions and various interactive oracle proofs. Another line of works [Zha+17b, Zha+18, Zha+17a, Wah+18, Xie+19] combines multivariate polynomial commitments [PST13] and doubly efficient interactive proofs [GKR15]

While in this paper we study a different setting (*preprocessing* SNARGs for *arbitrary* computations), there are similarities, and notable differences, in the polynomial commitments used in our work and prior works. We begin by noting that the notion of "multivariate polynomial commitments" varies considerably across prior works, despite the fact that most of those commitments are based on the protocol introduced in [PST13].

- The commitments used in [Zha+17b, Zha+18] are required to satisfy extractability (a stronger notion than binding) because the security proof of the argument system involves extracting a polynomial encoding a witness. The commitment is a modification of [PST13] that uses knowledge commitments, a standard ingredient to achieve extractability under non-falsifiable assumptions in the plain model. Neither of these works consider hiding commitments as zero knowledge is not a goal for them.

---

[6] The linear verification time in most of the cited constructions can typically be partially mitigated via techniques that enable an untrusted party to help the verifier to check a batch of proofs for the same circuit faster than checking each proof individually (the linear cost in the circuit is paid only once per batch rather than once for each proof in the batch).

- The commitments used in [Zha+17a, Wah+18] must be compatible with the Cramer–Damgård transform [CD98] used in constructing the argument system. They consider a *modified setting* where the sender does not reveal the value of the commitment polynomial at a desired point but, instead, reveals a commitment to this value, along with a proof attesting that the committed value is correct. For this modified setting, they consider commitments that satisfy natural notions of extractability *and* hiding (achieving zero knowledge arguments is a goal in both papers). The commitments constructed in the two papers offer different tradeoffs. The commitment in [Zha+17a] is based on [PST13]: it relies on a SRS (structured reference string); it uses pairings; and for ℓ-variate polynomials achieves $O_\lambda(\ell)$-size arguments that can be checked in $O_\lambda(\ell)$ time. The commitment in [Wah+18] is inspired from [BG12] and [Bün+18]: it relies on a URS (uniform reference string); it does not use pairings; and for ℓ-variate *multilinear* polynomials and a given constant $c \geq 2$ achieves $O_\lambda(2^{\ell/c})$-size arguments that can be checked in $O_\lambda(2^{\ell-\ell/c})$ time.
- The commitments used in [Xie+19] are intended for the regular (unmodified) setting of commitment schemes where the sender reveals the value of the polynomial, because zero knowledge is later achieved by building on the algebraic techniques described in [CFS17]. The commitment definition in [Xie+19] considers binding and hiding, but not extractability. However, the given security analysis for the argument system does not seem to go through for this definition (there is no explanation of where the witness encoded in the committed polynomial comes from). Also, no commitment construction is provided in [Xie+19], and instead the reader is referred to [Zha+17a], which considers the modified setting described above.

In sum there are multiple notions of commitment and one must be precise about the functionality and security needed to construct an argument system. We now compare prior notions of commitments to the one that we use.

First, since in this paper we do not use the Cramer–Damgård transform for zero knowledge, commitments in the modified setting are not relevant. Instead, we achieve zero knowledge via *bounded independence* [Ben+16], and in particular we consider the familiar setting where the sender reveals evaluations to the committed polynomial. Second, prior works consider protocols where the sender commits to a polynomial in a single round, while we consider protocols where the sender commits to multiple polynomials of different degrees in each of several rounds. This multi-polynomial multi-round setting requires suitable extensions in terms of functionality (to enable batching techniques to save on argument size) and security (extractability and hiding need to be strengthened), which means that prior definitions do not suffice for us.

The above discrepancies have led us to formulate new definitions of functionality and security for polynomial commitments (as summarized in Sect. 2.2). We conclude by noting that, since in this paper we construct arguments that use *univariate* polynomials, our definitions are specialized to commitments for univariate polynomials. Corresponding definitions for multivariate polynomials can be obtained with straightforward modifications, and would strengthen definitions appearing in some prior works. Similarly, we fulfill the required definitions via natural adaptations of the univariate scheme of [KZG10], and analogous adaptations of the multivariate scheme of [PST13] would fulfill the multivariate analogues of these definitions.

2   Techniques

We discuss the main ideas behind our results. First we describe the two building blocks used in Theorem 1: AHPs and polynomial commitment schemes (described in Sects. 2.1 and 2.2 respectively). We describe how to combine these to obtain preprocessing arguments with universal SRS in Sect. 2.3. Next, we discuss constructions for these building blocks: in Sect. 2.4 we describe our AHP (underlying Theorem 2), and in Sect. 2.5 we describe our construction of polynomial commitments.

Throughout, instead of considering the usual notion of relations that consist of instance-witness pairs, we consider *indexed relations*, which consist of triples (i, x, w) where i is the index, x is the instance, and w is the witness. This is because i represents the part of the verifier input that is preprocessed in the offline phase (e.g., the circuit description) and x represents the part of the verifier input that comes in the online phase (e.g., a partial assignment to the circuit's input wires). The *indexed language* corresponding to an indexed relation $\mathcal{R}$, denoted $\mathcal{L}(\mathcal{R})$, is the set of pairs (i, x) for which there exists a witness w such that $(i, x, w) \in \mathcal{R}$.

2.1   Building Block: Algebraic Holographic Proofs

Interactive oracle proofs (IOPs) [BCS16, RRR16] are multi-round protocols where in each round the verifier sends a challenge and the prover sends an oracle (which the verifier can query). IOPs combine features of interactive proofs and probabilistically checkable proofs. *Algebraic holographic proofs* (AHPs) modify the notion of an IOP in two ways.

- *Holographic:* the verifier does not receive its input explicitly but, rather, has oracle access to a prescribed *encoding* of it. This potentially enables the verifier to run in time that is much faster than the time to read its input in full. (Our constructions will achieve this fast verification.)
- *Algebraic:* the honest prover must produce oracles that are low-degree polynomials (this restricts the completeness property), and all malicious provers must produce oracles that are low-degree polynomials (this relaxes the soundness property). The encoded input to the verifier must also be a low-degree polynomial.

Since in this paper we only work with *univariate* polynomials, our definitions focus on this case, but they can be modified in a straightforward way to be more general.

Informally, a (public-coin) AHP over a field $\mathbb{F}$ for an indexed relation $\mathcal{R}$ is specified by an indexer **I**, prover **P**, and verifier **V** that work as follows.

- *Offline phase.* The indexer **I** receives as input the index i to be preprocessed, and outputs one or more univariate polynomials over $\mathbb{F}$ encoding i.

– *Online phase.* For some instance x and witness w, the prover **P** receives
(i, x, w) and the verifier **V** receives x; **P** and **V** interact over some (in this
paper, constant) number of rounds, where in each round **V** sends a challenge
and **P** sends one or more polynomials; after the interaction, **V**(x) probabilistically queries the polynomials output by the indexer and the polynomials output by the prover, and then accepts or rejects. Crucially, **V** does *not* receive i
as input, but instead queries the polynomials output by **I** that encode i. This
enables the construction of verifiers **V** that run in time that is sublinear in |i|.

The completeness property states that for every $(i, x, w) \in \mathcal{R}$ the probability
that $\mathbf{P}(i, x, w)$ convinces $\mathbf{V}^{\mathbf{I}(i)}(x)$ to accept is 1. The soundness property states
that for every $(i, x) \notin \mathcal{L}(\mathcal{R})$ and *admissible* prover $\tilde{\mathbf{P}}$ the probability that $\tilde{\mathbf{P}}$
convinces $\mathbf{V}^{\mathbf{I}(i)}(x)$ to accept is at most a given soundness error ϵ. A prover is
"admissible" if the degrees of the polynomials it outputs fit within prescribed
degree bounds of the protocol. See Sect. 4 for details on AHPs.

2.2   Building Block: Polynomial Commitments

Informally, a *polynomial commitment scheme* [KZG10] allows a prover to produce a commitment c to a univariate polynomial $p \in \mathbb{F}[X]$, and later "open"
$p(X)$ at any point $z \in \mathbb{F}$, producing an *evaluation proof* π showing that the
opened value is consistent with the polynomial "inside" c at z. Turning this
informal goal into a useful definition requires some care, however, as we explain
below. In this paper we propose a set of definitions for polynomial commitment
schemes that we believe are useful for standalone use, and in particular suffice
as a building block for our compiler described in Sect. 2.3.

First, we consider constructions with strong efficiency requirements: the commitment c is much smaller than the polynomial p (e.g., c consists of a constant
number of group elements), and the proof π can be validated very fast (e.g., in
a constant number of cryptographic operations). These requirements not only
rule out natural constructions, but also imply that the usual binding property,
which states that an efficient adversary cannot open the same commitment to
two different values, does not capture the desired security. Indeed, even if the
adversary were to be bound to opening values of some function $f: \mathbb{F} \to \mathbb{F}$, it
may be that the function f is consistent with a polynomial whose degree is
higher than what was claimed. This means that a security definition needs to
incorporate guarantees about the degree of the committed function.[7]

Second, in many applications of polynomial commitments, an adversary produces multiple commitments to polynomials within a round of interaction and
across rounds of interaction. After this interaction, the adversary reveals values

---

[7] This consideration motivates the *strong correctness* property in [KZG10], which
states that *if* the adversary knows a polynomial that leads to the claimed commitment c then this polynomial has bounded degree. This notion, while sufficient
for the application in [KZG10], does not seem to suffice for standalone use because
there is no a priori guarantee that an adversary that can open values to a commitment knows a polynomial inside the commitment. In some sense, a knowledge
assumption is hidden in this hypothesis.

of all of these polynomials at one or more locations. This setting motivates a number of considerations. First, it is desirable to rely on a single set of public parameters for committing to multiple polynomials, even if the polynomials differ in degree. A construction such as that of [KZG10] can be modified in a natural way to achieve this is by committing both to the polynomial and its shift to the maximum degree, similarly to techniques used to bundle multiple low-degree tests into a single one [Ben+19a]. This modification needs to be addressed in any proof of security. Second, it would be desirable to batch evaluation proofs across different polynomials for the same location. Again, the construction in [KZG10] can support this, but one must argue that security still holds in this more general case.

The preceeding considerations require an extension of previous definitions and motivate our re-formulation of the primitive. Informally, a polynomial commitment scheme PC is a tuple of algorithms PC = (Setup, Trim, Commit, Open, Check). The setup algorithm PC.Setup takes as input a security parameter and maximum supported degree bound D, and outputs public parameters pp that contain the description of a finite field $\mathbb{F}$. The "trimming" algorithm PC.Trim then deterministically specializes these parameters for a given set of degree bounds and outputs a committer key ck and a receiver key rk. The sender can then invoke PC.Commit with input ck and a list of polynomials p with respective degree bounds d to generate a set of commitments c. Subsequently, the sender can use PC.Open to produce a proof π that convinces the receiver that the polynomials "inside" c respect the degree bounds d and, moreover, evaluate to the claimed set of values v at a given query set Q that specifies any number of evaluation points for each polynomial. The receiver can invoke PC.Check to check this proof.

The scheme PC is required to satisfy *extractability* and *efficiency* properties, and also, optionally, a *hiding* property. We outline these properties below, and provide detailed definitions in the full version.

Extractability. Consider an efficient sender adversary $\mathcal{A}$ that can produce a commitment c and degree bound $d \leq D$ such that, when asked for an evaluation at some point $z \in \mathbb{F}$, can produce a supposed evaluation v and proof π such that PC.Check accepts. Then PC is *extractable* if for every maximum degree bound D and every sender adversary $\mathcal{A}$ who can produce such commitments, there exists a corresponding efficient extractor $\mathcal{E}_{\mathcal{A}}$ that outputs a polynomial p of degree at most d that "explains" c so that $p(z) = v$. While for simplicity we have described the most basic case here, our definition considers adversaries and extractors who interact over multiple rounds, wherein the adversary may produce multiple commitments in each round and the extractor is required to output corresponding polynomials on a per-round basis (before seeing the query set, proof, or supposed evaluations).

In this work we rely on extractability to prove the security of our compiler (see Sect. 2.3); we do not know if weaker security notions studied in prior works, such as evaluation binding, suffice. More generally, we believe that extractability is a useful property that may be required across a range of other applications.

Efficiency. We require two notions of efficiency for PC. First, the time required to commit to a polynomial p and then to create an evaluation proof must be proportional to the degree of p, and not to the maximum degree D. (This ensures that the argument prover runs in time proportional to the size of the index.)

On the receiver's side, the commitment size, proof size, and time to verify an opening must be independent of the claimed degrees for the polynomials. (This ensures that the argument produced by our compiler is succinct.)

Hiding. The hiding property of PC states that commitments and proofs of evaluation reveal no information about the committed polynomial beyond the publicly stated degree bound and the evaluation itself. Namely, PC is *hiding* if there exists an efficient simulator that outputs simulated commitments and simulated evaluation proofs that cannot be distinguished from their real counterparts by any malicious distinguisher that only knows the degree bound and the evaluation.

Analogously to the case of extractability, we actually consider a more general definition that considers commitments to multiple polynomials within and across multiple rounds; moreover, the definition considers the case where some polynomials are designated as not hidden (and thus given to the simulator) because in our application we sometimes prefer to commit to a polynomial in a non-hiding way (for efficiency reasons).

2.3 Compiler: From AHPs to Preprocessing Arguments with Universal SRS

We describe the main ideas behind Theorem 1, which uses polynomial commitment schemes to compile any (public-coin) AHP into a corresponding (public-coin) preprocessing argument with universal SRS. In a subsequent step, the argument can be made non-interactive via the Fiat–Shamir transformation, and thereby obtain a preprocessing SNARG with universal SRS.

The basic intuition of the compiler follows the well-known framework of "commit to oracles and then open query answers" pioneered by Kilian [Kil92]. However, the commitment scheme used in our compiler leverages and enforces the algebraic structure of these oracles. While several works in the literature already take advantage of algebraic commitment schemes applied to algebraic oracles, our contribution is to observe that if we apply this framework to a holographic proof then we obtain a preprocessing argument.

Informally, first the argument indexer invokes the AHP indexer to generate polynomials, and then deterministically commits to these using the polynomial commitment scheme. Subsequently, the argument prover and argument verifier interact, each respectively simulating the AHP prover and AHP verifier. In each round, the argument prover sends succinct commitments to the polynomials output by the AHP prover in that round. After the interaction, the argument verifier declares its queries to the polynomials (of the prover and of the indexer). The argument prover replies with the desired evaluations along with an evaluation proof attesting to their correctness relative to the commitments.

This approach, while intuitive, must be proven secure. In particular, in the proof of soundness, we need to show that if the argument prover convinces the argument verifier with a certain probability, then we can find an AHP prover that convinces the AHP verifier with similar probability. This step is non-trivial: the AHP prover outputs polynomials, while the argument prover merely outputs succinct commitments and a few evaluations, which is much less information. In order to deduce the former from the latter requires *extraction*. This motivates considering polynomial commitment schemes that are extractable, in the sense described in Sect. 2.2. We do not know whether weaker security properties, such as the evaluation binding property studied in some prior works, suffice for proving the compiler secure.

The compiler outlined above is compatible with the properties of argument of knowledge and zero knowledge. Specifically, we prove that if the AHP is a proof of knowledge, then the compiler produces an argument of knowledge; also, if the AHP is (bounded-query) zero knowledge and the polynomial commitment scheme is hiding, then the compiler produces a zero knowledge argument.

See the full version for more details on the compiler.

2.4   Construction: An AHP for Constraint Systems

In prior sections we have described how we can use polynomial commitment schemes to compile AHPs into corresponding preprocessing SNARGs. In this section we discuss the main ideas behind Theorem 2, which provides an efficient AHP for the indexed relation corresponding to R1CS (see Definition 1). The preprocessing zkSNARK that we achieve in this paper (see Fig. 1) is based on this AHP.

Our protocol can be viewed as a "holographic variant" of the *non*-holographic algebraic proof for R1CS constructed in [Ben+19a]. Achieving holography involves designing a new sub-protocol that enables the verifier to evaluate low-degree extensions of the coefficient matrices at a random location. While in [Ben+19a] the verifier performed this computation in time $\text{poly}(|\mathbb{i}|)$ on its own, in our protocol the verifier performs it *exponentially faster*, in time $O(\log |\mathbb{i}|)$, by receiving help from the prover and having oracle access to the polynomials produced by the indexer. We introduce notation and then discuss the protocol.

Some notation. Consider an index $\mathbb{i} = (\mathbb{F}, n, m, A, B, C)$ specifying coefficient matrices, an instance $\mathbb{x} = x \in \mathbb{F}^*$ specifying a partial assignment to the variables, and a witness $\mathbb{w} = w \in \mathbb{F}^*$ specifying an assignment to the other variables such that the R1CS equation holds. The R1CS equation holds if and only if $Az \circ Bz = Cz$ for $z := (x, w) \in \mathbb{F}^n$. Below, we let H and K be prescribed subsets of $\mathbb{F}$ of sizes n and m respectively; we also let $v_H(X)$ and $v_K(X)$ be the vanishing polynomials of these two sets. (The vanishing polynomial of a set S is the monic polynomial of degree $|S|$ that vanishes on S, i.e., $\prod_{\gamma \in S}(X - \gamma)$.) We assume that both H and K are smooth multiplicative subgroups. This allows interpolation/evaluation over H in $O(n \log n)$ operations and also makes $v_H(X)$ computable in $O(\log n)$ operations (and similarly for K). Given an $n \times n$ matrix M with rows/columns indexed by elements of H, we denote by $\hat{M}(X, Y)$ the low-degree extension of M, i.e., the polynomial of individual degree less than n such that $\hat{M}(\kappa, \iota)$ is the (κ, ι)-th entry of M for every $\kappa, \iota \in H$.

A non-holographic starting point. We sketch a *non*-holographic protocol for R1CS with linear proof length and constant query complexity, inspired from [Ben+19a], that forms the starting point of our work. In this case the prover receives as input $(\mathbb{i}, \mathbb{x}, \mathbb{w})$ and the verifier receives as input $(\mathbb{i}, \mathbb{x})$. (The verifier reads the non-encoded index $\mathbb{i}$ because we are describing a non-holographic protocol.)

In the first message the prover **P** sends the univariate polynomial $\hat{z}(X)$ of degree less than n that agrees with the variable assignment z on H, and also sends the univariate polynomials $\hat{z}_A(X), \hat{z}_B(X), \hat{z}_C(X)$ of degree less than n that agree with the linear combinations $z_A := Az$, $z_B := Bz$, and $z_C := Cz$ on H. The prover is left to convince the verifier that the following two conditions hold:

(1) Entry-wise product: $\forall \kappa \in H$, $\hat{z}_A(\kappa)\hat{z}_B(\kappa) - \hat{z}_C(\kappa) = 0$.

(2) Linear relation: $\forall M \in \{A, B, C\}$, $\forall \kappa \in H$, $\hat{z}_M(\kappa) = \sum_{\iota \in H} M[\kappa, \iota]\hat{z}(\iota)$.

(The prover also needs to convince the verifier that $\hat{z}(X)$ encodes a full assignment z that is consistent with the partial assignment x, but we for simplicity we ignore this in this informal discussion.)

In order to convince the verifier of the first (entry-wise product) condition, the prover sends the polynomial $h_0(X)$ such that $\hat{z}_A(X)\hat{z}_B(X) - \hat{z}_C(X) = h_0(X)v_H(X)$. This polynomial equation is equivalent to the first condition (the left-hand side equals zero everywhere on H if and only if it is a multiple of H's vanishing polynomial). The verifier will check the equation at a random point $\beta \in \mathbb{F}$: it queries $\hat{z}_A(X), \hat{z}_B(X), \hat{z}_C(X), h_0(X)$ at β, evaluates $v_H(X)$ at β on its own, and checks that $\hat{z}_A(\beta)\hat{z}_B(\beta) - \hat{z}_C(\beta) = h_0(\beta)v_H(\beta)$. The soundness error is the maximum degree over the field size, which is at most $2n/|\mathbb{F}|$.

In order to convince the verifier of the second (linear relation) condition, the prover expects a random challenge $\alpha \in \mathbb{F}$ from the verifier, and then replies in a second message. For each $M \in \{A, B, C\}$, the prover sends polynomials $h_M(X)$ and $g_M(X)$ such that

$$r(\alpha, X)\hat{z}_M(X) - r_M(\alpha, X)\hat{z}(X) = h_M(X)v_H(X) + Xg_M(X)$$
$$\text{for}\quad r_M(Z, X) := \sum_{\kappa \in H} r(Z, \kappa)\hat{M}(\kappa, X)$$

where $r(Z, X)$ is a prescribed polynomial of individual degree less than n such that $(r(Z, \kappa))_{\kappa \in H}$ are n linearly independent polynomials. Prior work [Ben+19a] on checking linear relations via univariate sumchecks shows that this polynomial equation is equivalent, up to a soundness error of $n/|\mathbb{F}|$ over α, to the second condition.[8] The verifier will check this polynomial equation at the random point $\beta \in \mathbb{F}$: it queries $\hat{z}(X), \hat{z}_A(X), \hat{z}_B(X), \hat{z}_C(X), h_M(X), g_M(X)$ at β, evaluates $v_H(X)$ at β on its own, evaluates $r(Z, X)$ and $r_M(Z, X)$ at (α, β) on its own, and checks that $r(\alpha, \beta)\hat{z}_M(\beta) - r_M(\alpha, \beta)\hat{z}(\beta) = h_M(\beta)v_H(\beta) + \beta g_M(\beta)$. The additional soundness error is $2n/|\mathbb{F}|$.

---

[8] In particular, we are using the fact from [Ben+19a] that, given a multiplicative subgroup S of $\mathbb{F}$, a polynomial $f(X)$ sums to σ over S if and only if $f(X)$ can be written as $h(X)v_S(X) + Xg(X) + \sigma/|S|$ for some $h(X)$ and $g(X)$ with $\deg(g) < |S| - 1$.

The above is a simple 3-message protocol for R1CS with soundness error $\max\{2n/|\mathbb{F}|, 3n/|\mathbb{F}|\} = 3n/|\mathbb{F}|$ in the setting where the honest prover and malicious provers send polynomials of prescribed degrees, which the verifier can query at any location. The proof length (sum of all degrees) is linear in n and the query complexity is constant.

Barrier to holography. The verifier in the above protocol runs in time that is $\Omega(|i|) = \Omega(n+m)$. While this is inherent in the non-holographic setting (because the verifier must read i), we now discuss how exactly the verifier's computation depends on i. We shall later use this understanding to achieve an exponential improvement in the verifier's time when given a suitable encoding of i.

The verifier's check for the entry-wise product is $\hat{z}_A(\beta)\hat{z}_B(\beta) - \hat{z}_C(\beta) = h_0(\beta)v_H(\beta)$, and can be carried out in $O(\log n)$ operations *regardless* of the coefficient matrices contained in the index i. In other words, this check is efficient even in the non-holographic setting. However, the verifier's check for the linear relation is $r(\alpha, \beta)\hat{z}_M(\beta) - r_M(\alpha, \beta)\hat{z}(\beta) = h_M(\beta)v_H(\beta) + \beta g_M(\beta)$, which has a linear cost. Concretely, evaluating the polynomial $r_M(Z, X)$ at (α, β) requires $\Omega(n + m)$ operations.

In the holographic setting, a natural idea to reduce this cost would be to grant the verifier oracle access to the low-degree extension $\hat{M}$ for $M \in \{A, B, C\}$. This idea has two problems: the verifier *still* needs $\Omega(n)$ operations to evaluate $r_M(Z, X)$ at (α, β) and, moreover, the size of $\hat{M}$ is *quadratic* in n, which means that the encoding of the index i is $\Omega(n^2)$. We cannot afford such an expensive encoding in the offline preprocessing phase. We now describe how we overcome both of these problems, and obtain a holographic protocol.

Achieving holography. To overcome the above problems and obtain a holographic protocol, we rely yet again on the univariate sumcheck protocol. We introduce two additional rounds of interaction, and in each round the verifier learns that their verification equation holds provided the sumcheck from the next round holds. The last sumcheck will rely on polynomials output by the indexer, which the verifier knows are correct.

We address the first problem by letting the prover and verifier interact in an additional round, where we rely on an additional univariate sumcheck to reduce the problem of evaluating $r_M(Z, X)$ at (α, β) to the problem of evaluating $\hat{M}$ at (β_2, β) for a random $\beta_2 \in \mathbb{F}$. Namely, the verifier sends β to the prover, who computes

$$\sigma_2 := r_M(\alpha, \beta) = \sum_{\kappa \in H} r(\alpha, \kappa)\hat{M}(\kappa, \beta).$$

Then the prover replies with σ_2 and the polynomials $h_2(X)$ and $g_2(X)$ such that

$$r(\alpha, X)\hat{M}(X, \beta) = h_2(X)v_H(X) + Xg_2(X) + \sigma_2/n.$$

Prior techniques on univariate sumcheck [Ben+19a] tell us that this equation is equivalent to the polynomial $r(\alpha, X)\hat{M}(X, \beta)$ summing to σ_2 on H. Thus the verifier needs to check this equation at a random $\beta_2 \in \mathbb{F}$: $r(\alpha, \beta_2)\hat{M}(\beta_2, \beta) = h_2(\beta_2)v_H(\beta_2) + \beta_2 g_2(\beta_2) + \sigma_2/n$. The only expensive part of this equation for the verifier is computing the value $\hat{M}(\beta_2, \beta)$, which is problematic. Indeed, we have already noted that we cannot afford to simply let the verifier have oracle access to $\hat{M}$, because this polynomial has quadratic size (it contains a quadratic number of terms).

We address this second problem as follows. Let $u_H(X, Y) := \frac{v_H(X) - v_H(Y)}{X - Y}$ be the formal derivative of the vanishing polynomial $v_H(X)$, and note that $u_H(X, Y)$ vanishes on the square $H \times H$ except for on the diagonal, where it takes on the (non-zero) values $(u_H(a, a))_{a \in H}$. Moreover, $u_H(X, Y)$ can be evaluated at any point in $\mathbb{F} \times \mathbb{F}$ in $O(\log n)$ operations. Using this polynomial, we can write $\hat{M}$ as a sum of $m = |K|$ terms instead of $n^2 = |H|^2$ terms:

$$\hat{M}(X, Y) := \sum_{\kappa \in K} u_H(X, \hat{\text{row}}_M(\kappa)) \cdot u_H(Y, \hat{\text{col}}_M(\kappa)) \cdot \hat{\text{val}}_M(\kappa),$$

where $\hat{\text{row}}_M, \hat{\text{col}}_M, \hat{\text{val}}_M$ are the low-degree extensions of the row, column, and value of the non-zero entries in M according to some canonical order over K.[9]

This method of representing the low-degree extension of M suggests an idea: let the verifier have oracle access to the polynomials $\hat{\text{row}}_M, \hat{\text{col}}_M, \hat{\text{val}}_M$ and do *yet another* univariate sumcheck, but this time over the set K. The verifier sends β_2 to the prover, who computes

$$\sigma_3 := \hat{M}(\beta_2, \beta) = \sum_{\kappa \in K} u_H(\beta_2, \hat{\text{row}}_M(\kappa)) \cdot u_H(\beta, \hat{\text{col}}_M(\kappa)) \cdot \hat{\text{val}}_M(\kappa).$$

Then the prover replies with σ_3 and the polynomials $h_3(X)$ and $g_3(X)$ such that

$$u_H(\beta_2, \hat{\text{row}}_M(X)) u_H(\beta, \hat{\text{col}}_M(X)) \hat{\text{val}}_M(X) = h_3(X) v_K(X) + X g_3(X) + \sigma_3/m.$$

The verifier can then check this equation at a random $\beta_3 \in \mathbb{F}$, which only requires $O(\log m)$ operations.

The above idea *almost* works; the one remaining problem is that $h_3(X)$ has degree $\Omega(nm)$ (because the left-hand size of the equation has quadratic degree), which is too expensive for our target of a quasilinear-time prover. We overcome this problem by letting the prover run the univariate sumcheck protocol on the unique low-degree extension $\hat{f}(X)$ of the function $f: K \to \mathbb{F}$ defined as $f(\kappa) := u_H(\beta_2, \hat{\text{row}}_M(\kappa)) u_H(\beta, \hat{\text{col}}_M(\kappa)) \hat{\text{val}}_M(\kappa)$. Observe that $\hat{f}(X)$ has degree less than m. The verifier checks that $\hat{f}(X)$ and $u_H(\beta_2, \hat{\text{row}}_M(X)) u_H(\beta, \hat{\text{col}}_M(X)) \hat{\text{val}}_M(X)$ agree on K.

From sketch to protocol. In the above discussion we have ignored a number of technical aspects, such as proof of knowledge and zero knowledge (which are ultimately needed in the compiler if we want to construct a preprocessing zkSNARK). We have also not discussed time complexities of many algebraic steps, and we omitted discussion of how to batch multiple sumchecks into fewer ones, which brings important savings in argument size. For details, see our detailed construction in Sect. 5.

---

[9] Technicality: $\hat{\text{val}}(\kappa)$ actually equals the value divided by $u_H(\hat{\text{row}}_M(\kappa), \hat{\text{row}}_M(\kappa))$ $u_H(\hat{\text{col}}_M(\kappa), \hat{\text{col}}_M(\kappa))$.

2.5   Construction: Extractable Polynomial Commitments

We now sketch how to construct a polynomial commitment scheme that achieves the strong functionality and security requirements of our definition in Sect. 2.2. Our starting point is the $\mathsf{PolyCommit}_{\mathsf{DL}}$ construction of Kate et al. [KZG10], and then describe a sequence of natural and generic transformations that extend this construction to enable extractability, commitments to multiple polynomials, and the enforcement of per-polynomial degree bounds. In fact, once we arrive at a scheme that supports extractability for committed polynomials at a single point, our transformations build on this construction in a black box way to first support per-polynomial degree bounds, and then query sets that may request multiple evaluation points per polynomial. See the full version for details of these transformations.

Starting point: $\mathsf{PolyCommit}_{\mathsf{DL}}$. The setup phase samples a cryptographically secure bilinear group $(\mathbb{G}_1, \mathbb{G}_2, \mathbb{G}_T, q, G, H, e)$ and then samples a committer key ck and receiver key rk for a given degree bound D. The committer key consists of group elements encoding powers of a random field element β, namely, $\mathsf{ck} := \{G, \beta G, \ldots, \beta^D G\} \in \mathbb{G}_1^{D+1}$. The receiver key consists of the group elements $\mathsf{rk} := (G, H, \beta H) \in \mathbb{G}_1 \times \mathbb{G}_2^2$. Note that the SRS, which consists of the keys ck and rk, is updatable because the coefficients of group elements in the SRS are all monomials.

To commit to a polynomial $p \in \mathbb{F}_q[X]$, the sender computes $c := p(\beta)G$. To subsequently prove that the committed polynomial evaluates to v at a point z, the sender computes a witness polynomial $w(X) := (p(X) - p(z))/(X - z)$, and provides as proof a commitment to w: $\pi := w(\beta)G$. The idea is that the witness function w is a polynomial *if and only if* $p(z) = v$; otherwise, it is a rational function, and cannot be committed to using ck.

Finally, to verify a proof of evaluation, the receiver checks that the commitment and proof of evaluation are consistent. That is, it checks that the proof commits to a polynomial of the form $(p(X) - p(z))/(X - z)$ by checking the equality $e(c - vG, H) = e(\pi, \beta H - zH)$.

Achieving extractability. While the foregoing construction guarantees correctness of evaluations, it does not by itself guarantee that a commitment actually "contains" a suitable polynomial of degree at most D. We study two methods to address this issue, and thereby achieve extractability. One method is to modify the construction to use knowledge commitments [Gro10], and rely on a concrete knowledge assumption. The main disadvantage of this approach is that each commitment doubles in size. The other method is to move away from the plain model, and instead conduct the security analysis in the algebraic group model (AGM) [FKL18]. This latter method is more efficient because each commitment remains a single group element.

Committing to multiple polynomials at once. We enable the sender to simultaneously open multiple polynomials $[p_i]_{i=1}^n$ at the same point z as follows. Before generating a proof of evaluation for $[p_i]_{i=1}^n$, the sender requests from the receiver a random field element ξ, which he uses to take a random linear combination of the polynomials: $p := \sum_{i=1}^{n} \xi^i p_i$, and generates a proof of evaluation π for this polynomial p.

The receiver verifies π by using the fact that the commitments are additively homomorphic. The receiver takes a linear combination of the commitments and claimed evaluations, obtaining the combined commitment $c = \sum_{i=1}^{n} \xi^i c_i$ and evaluation $v = \sum_{i=1}^{n} \xi^i v_i$. Finally, it checks the pairing equations for c, π, and v.

Completeness of this check is straightforward, while soundness follows from the fact that if any polynomial does not match its evaluation, then the combined polynomial will not match its evaluation with high probability.

Enforcing multiple degree bounds. The construction so far enforces a single bound D on the degrees of all the polynomials p_i. To enforce a different degree bound d_i for each p_i, we require the sender to commit not only to each p_i, but also to "shifted polynomials" $p_i'(X) := X^{D-d_i} p_i(X)$. The proof of evaluation proves that, if p_i evaluates to v_i at z, then p_i' evaluates to $z^{D-d_i} v_i$.

The receiver checks that the commitment for each p_i' corresponds to an evaluation $z^{D-d_i} v_i$ so that, if z is sampled from a super-polynomial subset of $\mathbb{F}_q$, the probability that $\deg(p_i) \neq d_i$ is negligible. This trick is similar to the one used in [BS08, Ben+19a] to derive low-degree tests for specific degree bounds.

However, while sound, this approach is inefficient in our setting: the witness polynomial for p_i' has $\Omega(D)$ non-zero coefficients (instead of $O(d_i)$), and so constructing an evaluation proof for it requires $\Omega(D)$ scalar multiplications (instead of $O(d_i)$). To work around this, we instead produce a proof that the related polynomial $p_i^\star(X) := p_i'(X) - p_i(z) X^{D-d_i}$ evaluates to 0 at z. As we show in the full version, the witness polynomial for this claim has $O(d_i)$ non-zero coefficients, and so constructing the evaluation proof can be done in $O(d_i)$ scalar multiplications. Completeness is preserved because the receiver can check the correct evaluation of $p_i^\star$ by subtracting $p_i(z)(\beta^{D-d_i} \mathbb{G})$ from the commitment to the shifted polynomial p_i', thereby obtaining a commitment to $p_i^\star$, while security is preserved because $p_i'(z) = z^{D-d_i} v_i \iff p_i^\star(z) = 0$.

Evaluating at a query set instead of a single point. To support the case where the polynomials $[p_i]_{i=1}^n$ are evaluated at a set of points Q, the sender proceeds as follows. Say that there are k different points $[z_i]_{i=1}^k$ in Q. The sender partitions the polynomials $[p_i]_{i=1}^n$ into different groups such that every polynomial in a group is to be evaluated at the same point z_i. The sender runs PC.Open on each group, and outputs the resulting list of evaluation proofs.

Achieving hiding. To additionally achieve hiding, we follow the above blueprint, replacing PolyCommit$_{DL}$ with the hiding scheme PolyCommit$_{Ped}$ described in [KZG10].

3   Preliminaries

We denote by $[n]$ the set $\{1, \ldots, n\} \subseteq \mathbb{N}$. We use $\boldsymbol{a} = [a_i]_{i=1}^n$ as a short-hand for the tuple $(a_1, \ldots, a_n)$, and $[\boldsymbol{a}_i]_{i=1}^n = [[a_{i,j}]_{j=1}^m]_{i=1}^n$ as a short-hand for the tuple $(a_{1,1}, \ldots, a_{1,m}, \ldots, a_{n,1}, \ldots, a_{n,m})$; $|\boldsymbol{a}|$ denotes the number of entries in $\boldsymbol{a}$. If x is a binary string then $|x|$ denotes its bit length. If M is a matrix then $\|M\|$

denotes the number of nonzero entries in M. If S is a finite set then $|S|$ denotes its cardinality and $x \leftarrow S$ denotes that x is an element sampled at random from S. We denote by $\mathbb{F}$ a finite field, and whenever $\mathbb{F}$ is an input to an algorithm we implicitly assume that $\mathbb{F}$ is represented in a way that allows efficient field arithmetic. Given a finite set S, we denote by $\mathbb{F}^S$ the set of vectors indexed by elements in S. We denote by $\mathbb{F}[X]$ the ring of univariate polynomials over $\mathbb{F}$ in X, and by $\mathbb{F}^{<d}[X]$ the set of polynomials in $\mathbb{F}[X]$ with degree less than d.

We denote by $\lambda \in \mathbb{N}$ a security parameter. When we state that $n \in \mathbb{N}$ for some variable n, we implicitly assume that $n = \text{poly}(\lambda)$. We denote by $\text{negl}(\lambda)$ an unspecified function that is *negligible* in λ (namely, a function that vanishes faster than the inverse of any polynomial in λ). When a function can be expressed in the form $1 - \text{negl}(\lambda)$, we say that it is *overwhelming* in λ. When we say that $\mathcal{A}$ is an *efficient adversary* we mean that $\mathcal{A}$ is a family $\{\mathcal{A}_\lambda\}_{\lambda \in \mathbb{N}}$ of non-uniform polynomial-size circuits. If the adversary consists of multiple circuit families $\mathcal{A}_1, \mathcal{A}_2, \ldots$ then we write $\mathcal{A} = (\mathcal{A}_1, \mathcal{A}_2, \ldots)$.

Given two interactive algorithms A and B, we denote by $\langle A(x), B(y) \rangle(z)$ the output of $B(y, z)$ when interacting with $A(x, z)$. Note that this output could be a random variable. If we use this notation when A or B is a circuit, we mean that we are considering a circuit that implements a suitable next-message function to interact with the other party of the interaction.

3.1 Indexed Relations

An *indexed relation* $\mathcal{R}$ is a set of triples $(\mathbb{i}, \mathbb{x}, \mathbb{w})$ where $\mathbb{i}$ is the index, $\mathbb{x}$ is the instance, and $\mathbb{w}$ is the witness; the corresponding *indexed language* $\mathcal{L}(\mathcal{R})$ is the set of pairs $(\mathbb{i}, \mathbb{x})$ for which there exists a witness $\mathbb{w}$ such that $(\mathbb{i}, \mathbb{x}, \mathbb{w}) \in \mathcal{R}$. For example, the indexed relation of satisfiable boolean circuits consists of triples where $\mathbb{i}$ is the description of a boolean circuit, $\mathbb{x}$ is a partial assignment to its input wires, and $\mathbb{w}$ is an assignment to the remaining wires that makes the circuit to output 0. Given a size bound $\mathsf{N} \in \mathbb{N}$, we denote by $\mathcal{R}_\mathsf{N}$ the restriction of $\mathcal{R}$ to triples $(\mathbb{i}, \mathbb{x}, \mathbb{w})$ with $|\mathbb{i}| \leq \mathsf{N}$.

4 Algebraic Holographic Proofs

We define *algebraic holographic proofs* (AHPs), the notion of proofs that we use. For simplicity, the formal definition below is tailored to univariate polynomials, because our AHP construction is in this setting. The definition can be modified in a straightforward way to consider the general case of multivariate polynomials.

We represent polynomials through the coefficients that define them, as opposed to through their evaluation over a sufficiently large domain (as is typically the case in probabilistic proofs). This definitional choice is due to the fact that we will consider verifiers that may query the polynomials at any location in the field of definition. Moreover, the field of definition itself can be chosen from a given field family, and so we make the field an additional input to all algorithms; this degree of freedom is necessary when combining this component with polynomial commitment schemes. Finally, we consider the setting of *indexed relations* (see Sect. 3.1), where the verifier's input has two parts, the index and the instance; in the definition below, the verifier receives the index encoded and the instance explicitly.

Formally, an **algebraic holographic proof** (AHP) over a field family $\mathcal{F}$ for an indexed relation $\mathcal{R}$ is specified by a tuple

$$\mathsf{AHP} = (\mathsf{k}, \mathsf{s}, \mathsf{d}, \mathbf{I}, \mathbf{P}, \mathbf{V})$$

where $\mathsf{k}, \mathsf{s}, \mathsf{d} \colon \{0,1\}^* \to \mathbb{N}$ are polynomial-time computable functions and $\mathbf{I}, \mathbf{P}, \mathbf{V}$ are three algorithms known as the *indexer*, *prover*, and *verifier*. The parameter k specifies the number of interaction rounds, s specifies the number of polynomials in each round, and d specifies degree bounds on these polynomials.

In the offline phase ("0-th round"), the indexer $\mathbf{I}$ receives as input a field $\mathbb{F} \in \mathcal{F}$ and an index $\mathbb{i}$ for $\mathcal{R}$, and outputs $\mathsf{s}(0)$ polynomials $p_{0,1}, \ldots, p_{0,\mathsf{s}(0)} \in \mathbb{F}[X]$ of degrees at most $\mathsf{d}(|\mathbb{i}|, 0, 1), \ldots, \mathsf{d}(|\mathbb{i}|, 0, \mathsf{s}(0))$ respectively. Note that the offline phase does not depend on any particular instance or witness, and merely considers the task of encoding the given index $\mathbb{i}$.

In the online phase, given an instance $\mathbb{x}$ and witness $\mathbb{w}$ such that $(\mathbb{i}, \mathbb{x}, \mathbb{w}) \in \mathcal{R}$, the prover $\mathbf{P}$ receives $(\mathbb{F}, \mathbb{i}, \mathbb{x}, \mathbb{w})$ and the verifier $\mathbf{V}$ receives $(\mathbb{F}, \mathbb{x})$ and oracle access to the polynomials output by $\mathbf{I}(\mathbb{F}, \mathbb{i})$. The prover $\mathbf{P}$ and the verifier $\mathbf{V}$ interact over $\mathsf{k} = \mathsf{k}(|\mathbb{i}|)$ rounds.

For $i \in [\mathsf{k}]$, in the i-th round of interaction, the verifier $\mathbf{V}$ sends a message $\rho_i \in \mathbb{F}^*$ to the prover $\mathbf{P}$; then the prover $\mathbf{P}$ replies with $\mathsf{s}(i)$ oracle polynomials $p_{i,1}, \ldots, p_{i,\mathsf{s}(i)} \in \mathbb{F}[X]$. The verifier may query any of the polynomials it has received any number of times. A query consists of a location $z \in \mathbb{F}$ for an oracle $p_{i,j}$, and its corresponding answer is $p_{i,j}(z) \in \mathbb{F}$. After the interaction, the verifier accepts or rejects.

The function d determines which provers to consider for the completeness and soundness properties of the proof system. In more detail, we say that a (possibly malicious) prover $\tilde{\mathbf{P}}$ is **admissible** for AHP if, on every interaction with the verifier $\mathbf{V}$, it holds that for every round $i \in [\mathsf{k}]$ and oracle index $j \in [\mathsf{s}(i)]$ we have $\deg(p_{i,j}) \leq \mathsf{d}(|\mathbb{i}|, i, j)$. The honest prover $\mathbf{P}$ is required to be admissible under this definition.

We say that AHP has perfect completeness and soundness error ϵ if the following holds.

- **Completeness.** For every field $\mathbb{F} \in \mathcal{F}$ and index-instance-witness tuple $(\mathbb{i}, \mathbb{x}, \mathbb{w}) \in \mathcal{R}$, the probability that $\mathbf{P}(\mathbb{F}, \mathbb{i}, \mathbb{x}, \mathbb{w})$ convinces $\mathbf{V}^{\mathbf{I}(\mathbb{F}, \mathbb{i})}(\mathbb{F}, \mathbb{x})$ to accept in the interactive oracle protocol is 1.
- **Soundness.** For every field $\mathbb{F} \in \mathcal{F}$, index-instance pair $(\mathbb{i}, \mathbb{x}) \notin \mathcal{L}(\mathcal{R})$, and admissible prover $\tilde{\mathbf{P}}$, the probability that $\tilde{\mathbf{P}}$ convinces $\mathbf{V}^{\mathbf{I}(\mathbb{F}, \mathbb{i})}(\mathbb{F}, \mathbb{x})$ to accept in the interactive oracle protocol is at most ϵ.

The *proof length* l is the sum of all degree bounds in the offline and online phases, $\mathsf{l}(|\mathbb{i}|) := \sum_{i=0}^{\mathsf{k}(|\mathbb{i}|)} \sum_{j=1}^{\mathsf{s}(i)} \mathsf{d}(|\mathbb{i}|, i, j)$. The intuition for this definition is that in a probabilistic proof each oracle would consist of the evaluation of a polynomial over a domain whose size (in field elements) is linearly related to its degree bound, so that the resulting proof length would be linearly related to the sum of all degree bounds.

The *query complexity* q is the total number of queries made by the verifier to the polynomials. This includes queries to the polynomials output by the indexer and those sent by the prover.

All AHPs that we construct achieve the stronger property of *knowledge soundness* (against admissible provers), and optionally also *zero knowledge*. We define both of these properties below.

Knowledge soundness. We say that AHP has knowledge error ϵ if there exists a probabilistic polynomial-time extractor $\mathbf{E}$ for which the following holds. For every field $\mathbb{F} \in \mathcal{F}$, index i, instance x, and admissible prover $\tilde{\mathbf{P}}$, the probability that $\mathbf{E}^{\tilde{\mathbf{P}}}(\mathbb{F}, i, x, 1^{l(|i|)})$ outputs w such that $(i, x, w) \in \mathcal{R}$ is at least the probability that $\tilde{\mathbf{P}}$ convinces $\mathbf{V}^{\mathbf{I}(\mathbb{F}, i)}(\mathbb{F}, x)$ to accept minus ϵ. Here the notation $\mathbf{E}^{\tilde{\mathbf{P}}}$ means that the extractor $\mathbf{E}$ has black-box access to each of the next-message functions that define the interactive algorithm $\tilde{\mathbf{P}}$. (In particular, the extractor $\mathbf{E}$ can "rewind" the prover $\tilde{\mathbf{P}}$.) Note that since $\mathbf{E}$ receives the proof length $l(|i|)$ in unary, $\mathbf{E}$ has enough time to receive, and perform efficient computations on, polynomials output by $\tilde{\mathbf{P}}$.

Zero knowledge. We say that AHP has (perfect) zero knowledge with query bound b and query checker $\mathbf{C}$ if there exists a probabilistic polynomial-time simulator $\mathbf{S}$ such that for every field $\mathbb{F} \in \mathcal{F}$, index-instance-witness tuple $(i, x, w) \subset \mathcal{R}$, and $(b, \mathbf{C})$-query algorithm $\tilde{\mathbf{V}}$ the random variables $\mathrm{View}(\mathbf{P}(\mathbb{F}, i, x, w), \tilde{\mathbf{V}})$ and $\mathbf{S}^{\tilde{\mathbf{V}}}(\mathbb{F}, i, x)$, defined below, are identical. Here, we say that an algorithm is $(b, \mathbf{C})$-query if it makes at most b queries to oracles it has access to, and each query individually leads the checker $\mathbf{C}$ to output "ok".

- $\mathrm{View}(\mathbf{P}(\mathbb{F}, i, x, w), \tilde{\mathbf{V}})$ is the *view* of $\tilde{\mathbf{V}}$, namely, is the random variable $(r, a_1, \ldots, a_q)$ where r is $\mathbf{V}$'s randomness and $a_1, \ldots, a_q$ are the responses to $\tilde{\mathbf{V}}$'s queries determined by the oracles sent by $\mathbf{P}(\mathbb{F}, i, x, w)$.
- $\mathbf{S}^{\tilde{\mathbf{V}}}(\mathbb{F}, i, x)$ is the output of $\mathbf{S}(\mathbb{F}, i, x)$ when given straightline access to $\tilde{\mathbf{V}}$ ($\mathbf{S}$ may interact with $\tilde{\mathbf{V}}$, *without rewinding*, by exchanging messages with $\tilde{\mathbf{V}}$ and answering any oracle queries along the way), *prepended* with $\tilde{\mathbf{V}}$'s randomness r. Note that r could be of super-polynomial size, so $\mathbf{S}$ cannot sample r on $\tilde{\mathbf{V}}$'s behalf and then output it; instead, as in prior work, we restrict $\mathbf{S}$ to not see r, and prepend r to $\mathbf{S}$'s output.

A special case of interest. We **only consider** AHPs that satisfy the following properties.

- *Public coins:* AHP is *public-coin* if each verifier message to the prover is a uniformly random string of some prescribed length (or an empty string). All verifier queries can be postponed, without loss of generality, to a query phase that occurs after the interactive phase with the prover.
- *Non-adaptive queries:* AHP is *non-adaptive* if all of the verifier's query locations are solely determined by the verifier's randomness and inputs (the field $\mathbb{F}$ and the instance x).

Given these properties, we can view the verifier as two subroutines that execute in the query phase: a query algorithm $\mathbf{Q_V}$ that produces query locations based on the verifier's randomness, and a decision algorithm $\mathbf{D_V}$ that accepts or rejects based on the answers to the queries (and the verifier's randomness). In more detail, $\mathbf{Q_V}$ receives as input the field $\mathbb{F}$, the instance x, and randomness $\rho_1, \ldots, \rho_k, \rho_{k+1}$, and outputs a query set Q consisting of tuples $((i,j),z)$ to be interpreted as "query $p_{i,j}$ at $z \in \mathbb{F}$"; and $\mathbf{D_V}$ receives as input the field $\mathbb{F}$, the instance x, answers $(v_{((i,j),z)})_{((i,j),z) \in Q}$, and randomness $\rho_1, \ldots, \rho_k, \rho_{k+1}$, and outputs the decision bit.

While the above properties are not strictly necessary for the compiler that we describe in the full version, all "natural" protocols that we are aware of (including those that we construct in this paper) satisfy these properties, and so we restrict our attention to public-coin non-adaptive protocols for simplicity.

5   AHP for Constraint Systems

We construct an AHP for *rank-1 constraint satisfiability* (R1CS) that has linear proof length and constant query complexity. Below we define the indexed relation that represents this problem, and then state our result.

Definition 1 (R1CS indexed relation). *The indexed relation $\mathcal{R}_{R1CS}$ is the set of all triples*

$$(\mathbf{i}, \mathbf{x}, \mathbf{w}) = ((\mathbb{F}, H, K, A, B, C), x, w)$$

where $\mathbb{F}$ is a finite field, H and K are subsets of $\mathbb{F}$, A, B, C are $H \times H$ matrices over $\mathbb{F}$ with $|K| \geq \max\{\|A\|, \|B\|, \|C\|\}$, and $z := (x, w)$ is a vector in $\mathbb{F}^H$ such that $Az \circ Bz = Cz$.

Theorem 1. *There exists an AHP for the indexed relation $\mathcal{R}_{R1CS}$ that is a zero knowledge proof of knowledge with the following features. The indexer uses $O(|K| \log |K|)$ field operations and outputs $O(|K|)$ field elements. The prover and verifier exchange 7 messages. To achieve zero knowledge against b queries (with a query checker C that rejects queries in H), the prover uses $O((|K|+b) \log(|K|+b))$ field operations and outputs a total of $O(|H|+b)$ field elements. The verifier makes $O(1)$ queries to the encoded index and to the prover's messages, has soundness error $O((|K| + b)/|\mathbb{F}|)$, and uses $O(|x| + \log |K|)$ field operations.*

Remark 1 (restrictions on domains). Our protocol uses the univariate sumcheck of [Ben+19a] as a subroutine, and in particular inherits the requirement that the domains H and K must be additive or multiplicative subgroups of the field $\mathbb{F}$. For simplicity, in our descriptions we use multiplicative subgroups because we use this case in our implementation; the case of additive subgroups involves only minor modifications. Moreover, the arithmetic complexities for the indexer and prover stated in Theorem 1 assume that the domains H and K are "FFT-friendly" (e.g., they have smooth sizes); this is not a requirement, since in general the arithmetic complexities will be that of an FFT over the domains H and K. Note that we can assume without loss of generality that $|H| = O(|K|)$, for otherwise (if $|K| < |H|/3$) then are empty rows or columns across the matrices that we can drop and reduce their size. Finally, we assume that $|H| \leq |\mathbb{F}|/2$.

This section is organized as follows: in Sect. 5.1 we introduce algebraic notations and facts used in this section, and then in Sect. 5.2 we describe an AHP for checking linear relations. Due to space constraints, we describe how to use this latter AHP to construct our AHP for R1CS only in the full version.

Throughout we assume that H and K come equipped with bijections $\phi_H \colon H \to [|H|]$ and $\phi_K \colon K \to [|K|]$ that are computable in linear time. Moreover, we define the two sets $H[\leq k] := \{\kappa \in H : 1 \leq \phi_H(\kappa) \leq k\}$ and $H[> k] := \{\kappa \in H : \phi_H(\kappa) > k\}$ to denote the first k elements in H and the remaining elements, respectively. We can then write that $x \in \mathbb{F}^{H[\leq |x|]}$ and $w \in \mathbb{F}^{H[>|x|]}$.

5.1   Algebraic Preliminaries

Polynomial encodings. For a finite field $\mathbb{F}$, subset $S \subseteq \mathbb{F}$, and function $f \colon S \to \mathbb{F}$ we denote by $\hat{f}$ the (unique) univariate polynomial over $\mathbb{F}$ with degree less than $|S|$ such that $\hat{f}(a) = f(a)$ for every $a \in S$. We sometimes abuse notation and write $\hat{f}$ to denote *some* polynomial that agrees with f on S, which need not equal the (unique) such polynomial of smallest degree.

Vanishing polynomials. For a finite field $\mathbb{F}$ and subset $S \subseteq \mathbb{F}$, we denote by v_S the unique non-zero monic polynomial of degree at most $|S|$ that is zero everywhere on S; v_S is called the *vanishing polynomial* of S. If S is an additive or multiplicative coset in $\mathbb{F}$ then v_S can be evaluated in polylog($|S|$) field operations. For example, if S is a multiplicative subgroup of $\mathbb{F}$ then $v_S(X) = X^{|S|} - 1$ and, more generally, if S is a ξ-coset of a multiplicative subgroup S_0 (namely, $S = \xi S_0$) then $v_S(X) = \xi^{|S|} v_{S_0}(X/\xi) = X^{|S|} - \xi^{|S|}$; in either case, v_S can be evaluated in $O(\log|S|)$ field operations.

Derivative of vanishing polynomials. We rely on various properties of a bivariate polynomial u_S introduced in [Ben+19b]. For a finite field $\mathbb{F}$ and subset $S \subseteq \mathbb{F}$, we define
$$u_S(X, Y) := \frac{v_S(X) - v_S(Y)}{X - Y},$$
which is a polynomial of individual degree $|S| - 1$ because $X - Y$ divides $X^i - Y^i$ for any positive integer i. Note that $u_S(X, X)$ is the formal derivative of the vanishing polynomial $v_S(X)$. The bivariate polynomial $u_S(X, Y)$ satisfies two useful algebraic properties. First, the univariate polynomials $(u_S(X, a))_{a \in S}$ are linearly independent, and $u_S(X, Y)$ is their (unique) low-degree extension. Second, $u_S(X, Y)$ vanishes on the square $S \times S$ except for on the diagonal, where it takes on the (non-zero) values $(u_S(a, a))_{a \in S}$.

If S is an additive or multiplicative coset in $\mathbb{F}$, $u_S(X, Y)$ can be evaluated at any $(\alpha, \beta) \in \mathbb{F}^2$ in polylog($|S|$) field operations because in this case both v_S (and its derivative) can be evaluated in polylog($|S|$) field operations. For example, if S is a multiplicative subgroup then $u_S(X, Y) = (X^{|S|} - Y^{|S|})/(X - Y)$ and $u_S(X, X) = |S|X^{|S|-1}$, so both can be evaluated in $O(\log|S|)$ field operations.

Univariate sumcheck for subgroups. Prior work [Ben+19a] shows that, given a multiplicative subgroup S of $\mathbb{F}$, a polynomial $f(X)$ sums to σ over S if and only if $f(X)$ can be written as $h(X)v_S(X) + Xg(X) + \sigma/|S|$ for some $h(X)$ and $g(X)$ with $\deg(g) < |S| - 1$. This can be viewed as a univariate sumcheck protocol, and we shall rely on it throughout this section.

5.2   AHP for the Lincheck Problem

The *lincheck problem* for univariate polynomials considers the task of deciding whether two polynomials encode vectors that are linearly related in a prescribed way. In more detail, the problem is parametrized by a field $\mathbb{F}$, two subsets H and K of $\mathbb{F}$, and a matrix $M \in \mathbb{F}^{H \times H}$ with $|K| \geq \|M\| > 0$. Given oracle access to two low-degree polynomials $f_1, f_2 \in \mathbb{F}^{<d}[X]$, the problem asks to decide whether for every $a \in H$ it holds that $f_1(a) = \sum_{b \in H} M_{a,b} \cdot f_2(b)$, by asking a small number of queries to f_1 and f_2. The matrix M thus prescribes the linear relations that relate the values of f_1 and f_2 on H.

Ben-Sasson et al. [Ben+19a] solve this problem by reducing the lincheck problem to a sumcheck problem, and then reducing the sumcheck problem to low-degree testing (of univariate polynomials). In particular, this prior work achieves a 2-message algebraic *non-holographic* protocol that solves the lincheck problem with linear proof length and constant query complexity. In this section we show how to achieve a 6-message algebraic *holographic* protocol, again with linear proof length and constant query complexity. In Sect. 5.2.1 we describe the indexer algorithm, in Sect. 5.2.2 we describe the prover and verifier algorithms. In the full version we provide a diagram that summarizes the protocol, and provide completeness, soundness, and efficiency analyses.

5.2.1   Offline Phase: Encoding the Linear Relation

The indexer $\mathbf{I}$ for the lincheck problem receives as input a field $\mathbb{F}$, two subsets H and K of $\mathbb{F}$, and a matrix $M \in \mathbb{F}^{H \times H}$ with $|K| \geq \|M\|$. The non-zero entries of M are assumed to be presented in some canonical order (e.g., row-wise or column-wise). The output of $\mathbf{I}$ is three univariate polynomials $\hat{\text{row}}, \hat{\text{col}}, \hat{\text{val}}$ over $\mathbb{F}$ of degree less than $|K|$ such that the following polynomial is a low-degree extension of M:

$$\hat{M}(X, Y) := \sum_{\kappa \in K} u_H(X, \hat{\text{row}}(\kappa)) u_H(Y, \hat{\text{col}}(\kappa)) \hat{\text{val}}(\kappa). \tag{1}$$

The three aforementioned polynomials are the (unique) low-degree extensions of the three functions $\text{row}, \text{col}, \text{val}: K \to \mathbb{F}$ that respectively represent the row index, column index, and value of the non-zero entries of the matrix M. In more detail, for every $\kappa \in K$ with $1 \leq \phi_K(\kappa) \leq \|M\|$:

- $\text{row}(\kappa) := \phi_H^{-1}(t_\kappa)$ where t_κ is the row index of the $\phi_K(\kappa)$-th nonzero entry in M;
- $\text{col}(\kappa) := \phi_H^{-1}(t_\kappa)$ where t_κ is the column index of the $\phi_K(\kappa)$-th nonzero entry in M;
- $\text{val}(\kappa)$ is the value of the $\phi_K(\kappa)$-th nonzero entry in M, divided by $u_H(\text{row}(\kappa), \text{row}(\kappa)) u_H(\text{col}(\kappa), \text{col}(\kappa))$.

Also, $\mathsf{val}(\kappa)$ returns the element 0 for every $\kappa \in K$ with $\phi_K(\kappa) > \|M\|$, while $\mathsf{row}(\kappa)$ and $\mathsf{col}(\kappa)$ return an arbitrary element in H for such κ. The evaluation tables of these functions can be found in $O(|K|\log|H|)$ operations, from which interpolation yields the desired polynomials in $O(|K|\log|K|)$ operations.

Recall from Sect. 5.1 that the bivariate polynomial $u_H(X,Y)$ vanishes on the square $H \times H$ except for on the diagonal, where it takes on the (non-zero) values $(u_H(a,a))_{a \in H}$. By construction of the polynomials $\hat{\mathsf{row}}, \hat{\mathsf{col}}, \hat{\mathsf{val}}$, the polynomial $\hat{M}(X,Y)$ agrees with the matrix M everywhere on the domain $H \times H$. The individual degree of $\hat{M}(X,Y)$ is less than $|H|$. Thus, $\hat{M}$ is the unique low-degree extension of M.

We rewrite the polynomial $\hat{M}(X,Y)$ in a form that will be useful later:

Claim 1.

$$\hat{M}(X,Y) = \sum_{\kappa \in K} \frac{v_H(X)}{(X - \hat{\mathsf{row}}(\kappa))} \cdot \frac{v_H(Y)}{(Y - \hat{\mathsf{col}}(\kappa))} \cdot \hat{\mathsf{val}}(\kappa). \tag{2}$$

Proof. Note that $v_H(\hat{\mathsf{row}}(\kappa)) = v_H(\hat{\mathsf{col}}(\kappa)) = 0$ for every $\kappa \in K$ because $\hat{\mathsf{row}}(X)$ and $\hat{\mathsf{col}}(X)$ map K to H and v_H vanishes on H. Therefore:

$$\hat{M}(X,Y) = \sum_{\kappa \in K} u_H(X, \hat{\mathsf{row}}(\kappa)) \cdot u_H(Y, \hat{\mathsf{col}}(\kappa)) \cdot \hat{\mathsf{val}}(\kappa)$$

$$= \sum_{\kappa \in K} \frac{v_H(X) - v_H(\hat{\mathsf{row}}(\kappa))}{X - \hat{\mathsf{row}}(\kappa)} \cdot \frac{v_H(Y) - v_H(\hat{\mathsf{col}}(\kappa))}{Y - \hat{\mathsf{col}}(\kappa)} \cdot \hat{\mathsf{val}}(\kappa)$$

$$= \sum_{\kappa \in K} \frac{v_H(X)}{(X - \hat{\mathsf{row}}(\kappa))} \cdot \frac{v_H(Y)}{(Y - \hat{\mathsf{col}}(\kappa))} \cdot \hat{\mathsf{val}}(\kappa). \qquad \square$$

5.2.2 Online Phase: Proving and Verifying the Linear Relation

The prover $\mathbf{P}$ for the lincheck problem receives as input a field $\mathbb{F}$, two subsets H and K of $\mathbb{F}$, a matrix $M \in \mathbb{F}^{H \times H}$ with $|K| \geq \|M\|$, and two polynomials $f_1, f_2 \in \mathbb{F}^{<d}[X]$. The verifier $\mathbf{V}$ for the lincheck problem receives as input the field $\mathbb{F}$ and two subsets H and K of $\mathbb{F}$; $\mathbf{V}$ also has oracle access to the polynomials $\hat{\mathsf{row}}, \hat{\mathsf{col}}, \hat{\mathsf{val}}$ output by the indexer $\mathbf{I}$ invoked on appropriate inputs.

The protocol begins with a reduction from a lincheck problem to a sumcheck problem: $\mathbf{V}$ samples a random element $\alpha \in \mathbb{F}$ and sends it to $\mathbf{P}$. Indeed, letting $r(X,Y)$ denote the polynomial $u_H(X,Y)$, $\mathbf{P}$ is left to convince $\mathbf{V}$ that the following univariate polynomial sums to 0 on H:

$$q_1(X) := r(\alpha, X)f_1(X) - r_M(\alpha, X)f_2(X) \tag{3}$$

where $r_M(X,Y) := \sum_{\kappa \in H} r(X, \kappa)\hat{M}(\kappa, Y)$.

We rely on the univariate sumcheck protocol for this step: $\mathbf{P}$ sends to $\mathbf{V}$ the polynomials $g_1(X)$ and $h_1(X)$ such that $q_1(X) = h_1(X)v_H(X) + Xg_1(X)$. In order to check this polynomial identity, $\mathbf{V}$ samples a random element $\beta_1 \in \mathbb{F}$ with the intention of checking the identity at $X := \beta_1$. For the right-hand side, $\mathbf{V}$

queries g_1 and h_1 at β_1, and then evaluates $h_1(\beta_1)v_H(\beta_1)+\beta_1 g_1(\beta_1)$ in $O(\log|H|)$ operations. For the left-hand side, $\mathbf{V}$ queries f_1 and f_2 at β_1 and then needs to ask help from $\mathbf{P}$ to evaluate $r(\alpha, \beta_1)f_1(\beta_1) - r_M(\alpha, \beta_1)f_2(\beta_1)$. The reason is that while $r(\alpha, \beta_1)$ is easy to evaluate (it requires $O(\log|H|)$ operations), $r_M(\alpha, \beta_1) = \sum_{\kappa \in H} r(\alpha, \kappa)\hat{M}(\kappa, \beta_1)$ in general requires $\Omega(|H||K|)$ operations.

We thus rely on the univariate sumcheck protocol again. We define

$$q_2(X) := r(\alpha, X)\hat{M}(X, \beta_1) \tag{4}$$

$\mathbf{V}$ sends β_1 to $\mathbf{P}$, and then $\mathbf{P}$ replies with the sum $\sigma_2 := \sum_{\kappa \in H} r(\alpha, \kappa)\hat{M}(\kappa, \beta_1)$ and the polynomials $g_2(X)$ and $h_2(X)$ such that $q_2(X) = h_2(X)v_H(X) + Xg_2(X) + \sigma_2/|H|$. In order to check this polynomial identity, $\mathbf{V}$ samples a random element $\beta_2 \in \mathbb{F}$ with the intention of checking the identity at $X := \beta_2$. For the right-hand side, $\mathbf{V}$ queries g_2 and h_2 at β_2, and then evaluates $h_2(\beta_2)v_H(\beta_2) + \beta_2 g_2(\beta_2) + \sigma_2/|H|$ in $O(\log|H|)$ operations. To evaluate the left-hand side, however, $\mathbf{V}$ needs to ask help from $\mathbf{P}$. The reason is that while $r(\alpha, \beta_2)$ is easy to evaluate (it requires $O(\log|H|)$ operations), $\hat{M}(\beta_2, \beta_1)$ in general requires $\Omega(|K|)$ operations.

We thus rely on the univariate sumcheck protocol (yet) again: $\mathbf{V}$ sends β_2 to $\mathbf{P}$, and then $\mathbf{P}$ replies with the value $\sigma_3 := \hat{M}(\beta_2, \beta_1)$, which the verifier must check. Note though that we *cannot* use the sumcheck protocol directly to compute the sum obtained from Eq. (1):

$$\hat{M}(\beta_2, \beta_1) = \sum_{\kappa \in K} u_H(\beta_2, \hat{\mathrm{row}}(\kappa))u_H(\beta_1, \hat{\mathrm{col}}(\kappa))\hat{\mathrm{val}}(\kappa).$$

The reason is because the degree of the above addend, if we replace κ with an indeterminate, is $\Omega(|H||K|)$, which means that the degree of the polynomial h_3 sent as part of a sumcheck protocol also has degree $\Omega(|H||K|)$, which is not within our budget of an AHP with proof length $O(|H|+|K|)$. Instead, we make the minor modification that in the earlier rounds β_1 and β_2 are sampled from $\mathbb{F}\backslash H$ instead of $\mathbb{F}$, and we will leverage the sumcheck protocol to verify the equivalent (well defined) expression from Eq. (2):

$$\hat{M}(\beta_2, \beta_1) = \sum_{\kappa \in K} \frac{v_H(\beta_2)v_H(\beta_1)\hat{\mathrm{val}}(\kappa)}{(\beta_2 - \hat{\mathrm{row}}(\kappa))(\beta_1 - \hat{\mathrm{col}}(\kappa))}.$$

This may appear to be an odd choice, because if we replace κ with an indeterminate in the sum above, we obtain a rational function that is (in general) *not a polynomial*, and so does not immediately fit the sumcheck protocol. Nevertheless, we are still able to use the sumcheck protocol with it, as we now explain.

Define $f_3(X)$ to be the (unique) polynomial of degree less than $|K|$ such that

$$\forall \kappa \in K, \ f_3(\kappa) = \frac{v_H(\beta_2)v_H(\beta_1)\hat{\mathrm{val}}(\kappa)}{(\beta_2 - \hat{\mathrm{row}}(\kappa))(\beta_1 - \hat{\mathrm{col}}(\kappa))}. \tag{5}$$

The prover computes the polynomials $g_3(X)$ and $h_3(X)$ such that

$$f_3(X) = Xg_3(X) + \sigma_3/|K|,$$

$$h_3(X)v_K(X) = v_H(\beta_2)v_H(\beta_1)\hat{\mathsf{val}}(X) - (\beta_2 - \hat{\mathsf{row}}(X))(\beta_1 - \hat{\mathsf{col}}(X))f_3(X).$$

The first equation demonstrates that f_3 sums to σ_3 over K, and the second equation demonstrates that f_3 agrees with the correct addends over K. These two equations can be combined in a single equation that involves only $g_3(X)$ and $h_3(X)$:

$$h_3(X)v_K(X) = v_H(\beta_2)v_H(\beta_1)\hat{\mathsf{val}}(X)$$
$$- (\beta_2 - \hat{\mathsf{row}}(X))(\beta_1 - \hat{\mathsf{col}}(X))(Xg_3(X) + \sigma_3/|K|).$$

The prover thus only sends the two polynomials $g_3(X)$ and $h_3(X)$. In order to check this polynomial identity, $\mathbf{V}$ samples a random element $\beta_3 \in \mathbb{F}$ with the intention of checking the identity at $X := \beta_3$. Then $\mathbf{V}$ queries g_3, h_3, $\hat{\mathsf{row}}$, $\hat{\mathsf{col}}$, $\hat{\mathsf{val}}$ at β_3, and then evaluates $v_H(\beta_2)v_H(\beta_1)\hat{\mathsf{val}}(\beta_3) - (\beta_2 - \hat{\mathsf{row}}(\beta_3))(\beta_1 - \hat{\mathsf{col}}(\beta_3))(\beta_3 g_3(\beta_3) + \sigma_3/|K|) = h_3(\beta_3)v_K(\beta_3)$ in $O(\log|K|)$ operations.

If this third test passes then $\mathbf{V}$ can use the value σ_3 in place of $\hat{M}(\beta_2, \beta_1)$ to finish the second test. If this latter passes, $\mathbf{V}$ can in turn use the value σ_2 in place of $r_M(\alpha, \beta_1)$ to finish the first test.

Acknowledgments. This research was supported by: an Engineering and Physical Sciences Research Council grant (EP/N028104/1), a Google Faculty Award, the RISE-Lab at UC Berkeley, and donations from the Ethereum Foundation and the Interchain Foundation. The authors thank Dev Ojha and Nicholas Spooner for identifying and helping to fix an error in a prior version of our AHP for the lincheck problem.

References

[Ame+17] Ames, S., Hazay, C., Ishai, Y., Venkitasubramaniam, M.: Ligero: lightweight sublinear arguments without a trusted setup. In: CCS 2017 (2017)

[Bab+91] Babai, L., Fortnow, L., Levin, L.A., Szegedy, M.: Checking computations in polylogarithmic time. In: STOC 1991 (1991)

[BCS16] Ben-Sasson, E., Chiesa, A., Spooner, N.: Interactive oracle proofs. In: Hirt, M., Smith, A. (eds.) TCC 2016. LNCS, vol. 9986, pp. 31–60. Springer, Heidelberg (2016). https://doi.org/10.1007/978-3-662-53644-5_2

[BG12] Bayer, S., Groth, J.: Efficient zero-knowledge argument for correctness of a shuffle. In: Pointcheval, D., Johansson, T. (eds.) EUROCRYPT 2012. LNCS, vol. 7237, pp. 263–280. Springer, Heidelberg (2012). https://doi.org/10.1007/978-3-642-29011-4_17

[BGG17] Bowe, S., Gabizon, A., Green, M.: A multi-party protocol for constructing the public parameters of the Pinocchio zk-SNARK. ePrint Report 2017/602 (2017)

[BGM17] Bowe, S., Gabizon, A., Miers, I.: Scalable multi-party computation for zk-SNARK parameters in the random Beacon model. ePrint Report 2017/1050 (2017)

[Bit+13] Bitansky, N., Chiesa, A., Ishai, Y., Paneth, O., Ostrovsky, R.: Succinct non-interactive arguments via linear interactive proofs. In: Sahai, A. (ed.) TCC 2013. LNCS, vol. 7785, pp. 315–333. Springer, Heidelberg (2013). https://doi.org/10.1007/978-3-642-36594-2_18

[Bon+17] Boneh, D., Ishai, Y., Sahai, A., Wu, D.J.: Lattice-based SNARGs and their application to more efficient obfuscation. In: Coron, J.-S., Nielsen, J.B. (eds.) EUROCRYPT 2017. LNCS, vol. 10212, pp. 247–277. Springer, Cham (2017). https://doi.org/10.1007/978-3-319-56617-7_9

[Bon+18] Boneh, D., Ishai, Y., Sahai, A., Wu, D.J.: Quasi-optimal SNARGs via linear multi-prover interactive proofs. In: Nielsen, J.B., Rijmen, V. (eds.) EUROCRYPT 2018. LNCS, vol. 10822, pp. 222–255. Springer, Cham (2018). https://doi.org/10.1007/978-3-319-78372-7_8

[Boo+16] Bootle, J., Cerulli, A., Chaidos, P., Groth, J., Petit, C.: Efficient zero-knowledge arguments for arithmetic circuits in the discrete log setting. In: Fischlin, M., Coron, J.-S. (eds.) EUROCRYPT 2016. LNCS, vol. 9666, pp. 327–357. Springer, Heidelberg (2016). https://doi.org/10.1007/978-3-662-49896-5_12

[BS08] Ben-Sasson, E., Sudan, M.: Short PCPs with polylog query complexity. SIAM J. Comput. **38**(2), 551–607 (2008)

[Bün+18] Bünz, B., Bootle, J., Boneh, D., Poelstra, A., Wuille, P., Maxwell, G.: Bulletproofs: short proofs for confidential transactions and more. In: S&P 2018 (2018)

[CD98] Cramer, R., Damgård, I.: Zero-knowledge proofs for finite field arithmetic, or: can zero-knowledge be for free? In: Krawczyk, H. (ed.) CRYPTO 1998. LNCS, vol. 1462, pp. 424–441. Springer, Heidelberg (1998). https://doi.org/10.1007/BFb0055745

[CFS17] Chiesa, A., Forbes, M.A., Spooner, N.: A zero knowledge sumcheck and its applications. ePrint Report 2017/305 (2017)

[FKL18] Fuchsbauer, G., Kiltz, E., Loss, J.: The algebraic group model and its applications. In: Shacham, H., Boldyreva, A. (eds.) CRYPTO 2018. LNCS, vol. 10992, pp. 33–62. Springer, Cham (2018). https://doi.org/10.1007/978-3-319-96881-0_2

[FS86] Fiat, A., Shamir, A.: How to prove yourself: practical solutions to identification and signature problems. In: Odlyzko, A.M. (ed.) CRYPTO 1986. LNCS, vol. 263, pp. 186–194. Springer, Heidelberg (1987). https://doi.org/10.1007/3-540-47721-7_12

[Gab19] Gabizon, A.: Improved prover efficiency and SRS size in a Sonic-like system. ePrint Report 2019/601 (2019)

[Gen+13] Gennaro, R., Gentry, C., Parno, B., Raykova, M.: Quadratic span programs and succinct NIZKs without PCPs. In: Johansson, T., Nguyen, P.Q. (eds.) EUROCRYPT 2013. LNCS, vol. 7881, pp. 626–645. Springer, Heidelberg (2013). https://doi.org/10.1007/978-3-642-38348-9_37

[GKR15] Goldwasser, S., Kalai, Y.T., Rothblum, G.N.: Delegating computation: interactive proofs for muggles. JACM **62**(4), 1–64 (2015)

[Gro+18] Groth, J., Kohlweiss, M., Maller, M., Meiklejohn, S., Miers, I.: Updatable and universal common reference strings with applications to zk-SNARKs. In: Shacham, H., Boldyreva, A. (eds.) CRYPTO 2018. LNCS, vol. 10993, pp. 698–728. Springer, Cham (2018). https://doi.org/10.1007/978-3-319-96878-0_24

[Gro10] Groth, J.: Short pairing-based non-interactive zero-knowledge arguments. In: Abe, M. (ed.) ASIACRYPT 2010. LNCS, vol. 6477, pp. 321–340. Springer, Heidelberg (2010). https://doi.org/10.1007/978-3-642-17373-8_19

[Gro16] Groth, J.: On the size of pairing-based non-interactive arguments. In: Fischlin, M., Coron, J.-S. (eds.) EUROCRYPT 2016. LNCS, vol. 9666, pp. 305–326. Springer, Heidelberg (2016). https://doi.org/10.1007/978-3-662-49896-5_11

[GWC19] Gabizon, A., Williamson, Z.J., Ciobotaru, O.: PLONK: permutations over lagrange-bases for oecumenical noninteractive arguments of knowledge. ePrint Report 2019/953 (2019)

[Kil92] Kilian, J.: A note on efficient zero-knowledge proofs and arguments. In: STOC 1992 (1992)

[KZG10] Kate, A., Zaverucha, G.M., Goldberg, I.: Constant-size commitments to polynomials and their applications. In: Abe, M. (ed.) ASIACRYPT 2010. LNCS, vol. 6477, pp. 177–194. Springer, Heidelberg (2010). https://doi.org/10.1007/978-3-642-17373-8_11

[Lip12] Lipmaa, H.: Progression-free sets and sublinear pairing-based non-interactive zero-knowledge arguments. In: Cramer, R. (ed.) TCC 2012. LNCS, vol. 7194, pp. 169–189. Springer, Heidelberg (2012). https://doi.org/10.1007/978-3-642-28914-9_10

[Mal+19] Maller, M., Bowe, S., Kohlweiss, M., Meiklejohn, S.: Sonic: zero-knowledge SNARKs from linear-size universal and updateable structured reference strings. In: CCS 2019 (2019)

[PST13] Papamanthou, C., Shi, E., Tamassia, R.: Signatures of correct computation. In: Sahai, A. (ed.) TCC 2013. LNCS, vol. 7785, pp. 222–242. Springer, Heidelberg (2013). https://doi.org/10.1007/978-3-642-36594-2_13

[RRR16] Reingold, O., Rothblum, R., Rothblum, G.: Constant-round interactive proofs for delegating computation. In: STOC 2016 (2016)

[Set19] Setty, S.: Spartan: efficient and general-purpose zkSNARKs without trusted setup. ePrint Report 2019/550 (2019)

[Wah+18] Wahby, R.S., Tzialla, I., Shelat, A., Thaler, J., Walfish, M.: Doubly-efficient zkSNARKs without trusted setup. In: S&P 2018 (2018)

[Xie+19] Xie, T., Zhang, J., Zhang, Y., Papamanthou, C., Song, D.: Libra: succinct zero-knowledge proofs with optimal prover computation. In: Boldyreva, A., Micciancio, D. (eds.) CRYPTO 2019. LNCS, vol. 11694, pp. 733–764. Springer, Cham (2019). https://doi.org/10.1007/978-3-030-26954-8_24

[Zcash] Zcash. https://z.cash/

[ZcashMPC] The Zcash Ceremony. https://z.cash/blog/the-design-of-the-ceremony.html

[Zha+17a] Zhang, Y., Genkin, D., Katz, J., Papadopoulos, D., Papamanthou, C.: A zero-knowledge version of vSQL. ePrint Report 2017/1146 (2017)

[Zha+17b] Zhang, Y., Genkin, D., Katz, J., Papadopoulos, D., Papamanthou, C.: vSQL: verifying arbitrary SQL queries over dynamic outsourced databases. In: S&P 2017 (2017)

[Zha+18] Zhang, Y., Genkin, D., Katz, J., Papadopoulos, D., Papamanthou, C.: vRAM: faster verifiable RAM with program-independent preprocessing. In: S&P 2018 (2018)

[Ben+14a] Ben-Sasson, E., Chiesa, A., Tromer, E., Virza, M.: Scalable zero knowledge via cycles of elliptic curves. In: Garay, J.A., Gennaro, R. (eds.) CRYPTO 2014. LNCS, vol. 8617, pp. 276–294. Springer, Heidelberg (2014). https://doi.org/10.1007/978-3-662-44381-1_16

[Ben+14b] Ben-Sasson, E., Chiesa, A., Tromer, E., Virza, M.: Succinct non-interactive zero knowledge for a von Neumann architecture. In: USENIX Security 2014 (2014)

[Ben+15] Ben-Sasson, E., Chiesa, A., Green, M., Tromer, E., Virza, M.: Secure sampling of public parameters for succinct zero knowledge proofs. In: S&P 2015 (2015)

[Ben+16] Ben-Sasson, E., Chiesa, A., Gabizon, A., Virza, M.: Quasi-linear size zero knowledge from linear-algebraic PCPs. In: Kushilevitz, E., Malkin, T. (eds.) TCC 2016. LNCS, vol. 9563, pp. 33–64. Springer, Heidelberg (2016). https://doi.org/10.1007/978-3-662-49099-0_2

[Ben+17] Ben-Sasson, E., et al.: Computational integrity with a public random string from quasi-linear PCPs. In: Coron, J.-S., Nielsen, J.B. (eds.) EUROCRYPT 2017. LNCS, vol. 10212, pp. 551–579. Springer, Cham (2017). https://doi.org/10.1007/978-3-319-56617-7_19

[Ben+19a] Ben-Sasson, E., Chiesa, A., Riabzev, M., Spooner, N., Virza, M., Ward, N.P.: Aurora: transparent succinct arguments for R1CS. In: Ishai, Y., Rijmen, V. (eds.) EUROCRYPT 2019. LNCS, vol. 11476, pp. 103–128. Springer, Cham (2019). https://doi.org/10.1007/978-3-030-17653-2_4

[Ben+19b] Ben-Sasson, E., Chiesa, A., Goldberg, L., Gur, T., Riabzev, M., Spooner, N.: Linear-size constant-query IOPs for delegating computation. In: Hofheinz, D., Rosen, A. (eds.) TCC 2019. LNCS, vol. 11892, pp. 494–521. Springer, Cham (2019). https://doi.org/10.1007/978-3-030-36033-7_19

[Ben+19c] Ben-Sasson, E., Bentov, I., Horesh, Y., Riabzev, M.: Scalable zero knowledge with no trusted setup. In: Boldyreva, A., Micciancio, D. (eds.) CRYPTO 2019. LNCS, vol. 11694, pp. 701–732. Springer, Cham (2019). https://doi.org/10.1007/978-3-030-26954-8_23

FRACTAL: Post-quantum and Transparent Recursive Proofs from Holography

Alessandro Chiesa$^{(\boxtimes)}$, Dev Ojha, and Nicholas Spooner$^{(\boxtimes)}$

UC Berkeley, Berkeley, USA
{alexch,dojha,nick.spooner}@berkeley.edu

Abstract. We present a new methodology to efficiently realize recursive composition of succinct non-interactive arguments of knowledge (SNARKs). Prior to this work, the only known methodology relied on pairing-based SNARKs instantiated on cycles of pairing-friendly elliptic curves, an expensive algebraic object. Our methodology does not rely on any special algebraic objects and, moreover, achieves new desirable properties: it is *post-quantum* and it is *transparent* (the setup is public coin).

We exploit the fact that recursive composition is simpler for SNARKs with *preprocessing*, and the core of our work is obtaining a preprocessing zkSNARK for rank-1 constraint satisfiability (R1CS) that is post-quantum and transparent. We obtain this latter by establishing a connection between holography and preprocessing in the random oracle model, and then constructing a holographic proof for R1CS.

We experimentally validate our methodology, demonstrating feasibility in practice. (The full version of this work is available at https://ia.cr/2019/1076.)

Keywords: Succinct arguments · Holographic proofs · Recursive proof composition · Post-quantum cryptography

1 Introduction

Succinct non-interactive arguments (SNARGs) are cryptographic proofs for non-deterministic languages that are small and easy to verify. In the last few years, researchers from across multiple communities have investigated many aspects of SNARGs, including constructions under different cryptographic assumptions, improvements in asymptotic efficiency, concrete performance of implementations, and real-world applications. The focus of this paper is *recursive composition*, a notion that we motivate next.

Recursive composition. The time to validate a SNARG can be exponentially faster than the time to run the non-deterministic computation that it attests to, a property known as succinct verification. This exponential speedup raises an interesting prospect: could one produce a SNARG about a computation that involves validating prior SNARGs? Thanks to succinct verification, the time to run this (non-deterministic) computation would be essentially independent

© International Association for Cryptologic Research 2020
A. Canteaut and Y. Ishai (Eds.): EUROCRYPT 2020, LNCS 12105, pp. 769–793, 2020.
https://doi.org/10.1007/978-3-030-45721-1_27

of the time of the prior computations. This *recursive composition* of SNARGs enables *incrementally verifiable computation* [56] and *proof-carrying data* [18,30]. A critical technicality here is that, for recursive composition to work, the SNARG must be an *argument of knowledge*, i.e., a SNARK. This is because the security of a SNARG holds only against efficient adversaries, and the knowledge property ensures that prior SNARGs must have been efficiently produced, and so we can rely in turn on their security. A formal treatment of this can be found in [18], which discusses how the "strength" of a SNARG's knowledge property relates to how many recursions the SNARG supports.

Efficient recursion. Theory tells us that *any* succinct-verifier SNARK is recursively composable [18]. In practice, however, recursive composition is exceedingly difficult to realize efficiently. The reason is that, even if we have a SNARK that is concretely efficient when used "standalone", it is often prohibitively expensive to express the SNARK verifier's computation through the language supported by the SNARK. Indeed, while by now there are numerous SNARK constructions with remarkable concrete efficiency, *to date there is only a single efficient approach to recursion*. The approach, due to [15], uses pairing-based SNARKs with a special algebraic property discussed below.[1] This has enabled real-world applications such as Coda [51], a cryptocurrency that uses recursive composition to achieve strong scalability properties.

Limitations. The above efficient approach to recursion suffers from significant limitations.

- *It is pre-quantum.* Pairing-based SNARKs rely (at least) on the hardness of extracting discrete logarithms, and so are insecure against quantum attacks. Hence the approach of [15] is also insecure against quantum attacks. Devising an efficient *post-quantum* approach to recursion is an open problem.
- *It introduces toxic waste.* All known pairing-based SNARKs that can be used in the approach of [15] rely on a structured reference string (SRS). Sampling the SRS involves secret values (the "toxic waste") that must remain secret for security. Ensuring that this is the case in practice is difficult: the SRS must be sampled by some trusted party or via a cryptographic ceremony [1,12,21,22]. Devising an efficient *transparent* (toxic-waste free) approach to recursion is an open problem.
- *It uses expensive algebra.* The approach of [15] uses pairing-based SNARKs instantiated via *pairing-friendly cycles of elliptic curves*. Only a *single* cycle construction is known, *MNT cycles*; it consists of two prime-order elliptic curves, with embedding degrees 4 and 6 respectively. Curves in an MNT cycle must be much bigger than usual in order to compensate for the loss of security caused by the small embedding degrees. Moreover the fields that arise from MNT cycles are *imposed on applications* rather than being chosen depending on the needs of applications, causing additional performance

---

[1] A recent note sketches an alternative approach to recursion based on batch verification [23]. We omit a discussion of this note due to lack of sufficient detail (it does not provide definitions, full constructions, security arguments, or an efficiency analysis).

overheads. Attempts to find "better" cycles, without these limitations, have resulted in some negative results [26]. Indeed, finding *any other* cycles beyond MNT cycles is a challenging open problem.

1.1 Our Results

We present a new methodology for recursive composition that simultaneously overcomes all of the limitations discussed above. We experimentally validate our methodology, demonstrating feasibility in practice.

The starting point of our work is the observation that recursive composition is simpler when applied to a SNARG (of knowledge) that supports *preprocessing*, as we explain in Sect. 2.1. This property of a SNARG means that in an offline phase one can produce a short summary for a given circuit and then, in an online phase, one may use this short summary to verify SNARGs that attest to the satisfiability of the circuit with different partial assignments to its inputs. The online phase can be as fast as reading the SNARG (and the partial assignment), and in particular sublinear in the circuit size *even for arbitrary circuits*. Throughout, by "preprocessing SNARG" we mean a SNARG whose verifier runs in time *polylogarithmic* in the circuit size.[2]

Our methodology has three parts: (1) a transformation that maps any "holographic proof" into a preprocessing SNARG in the random oracle model; (2) a holographic proof for (rank-1) constraint systems, which leads to a correspond ing preprocessing SNARG; (3) a transformation that recurses any preprocessing SNARK (once the random oracle is heuristically instantiated via a cryptographic hash function).

We now summarize our contributions for each of these parts.

(1) From holographic proofs to preprocessing SNARGs. A probabilistic proof is *holographic* if the verifier does not receive the circuit description as an input but, rather, makes a small number of queries to an encoding of the circuit [7]. Recent work [27] has established a connection between holography and preprocessing (which we review in Sect. 1.2). The theorem below adds to this connection, by showing that interactive oracle proofs (IOPs) [14,52] that are holographic can be compiled into preprocessing SNARGs that are secure in the quantum random oracle model [20,28].

Theorem 1 (informal). *There is an efficient transformation that compiles any holographic IOP for a relation $\mathcal{R}$ into a preprocessing SNARG for $\mathcal{R}$ that is unconditionally secure in the random oracle model. If the IOP is a (honest-verifier) zero knowledge proof of knowledge then the transformation produces a zero knowledge SNARG of knowledge (zkSNARK). This extends to hold in the quantum random oracle model.*

---

[2] In contrast, *non*-preprocessing SNARGs can achieve fast verification *only for structured circuits*, because the verification procedure must at a minimum read the *description* of the circuit whose satisfiability it checks. The description of a circuit can be much smaller than the circuit itself only when the circuit has suitable structure, e.g., repeated sub-components in parallel or in series.

By applying Theorem 1 to known holographic proofs for non-deterministic computations (such as the PCP in [7] or the IPCP in [41]), we obtain the first transparent preprocessing SNARG and the first post-quantum preprocessing SNARG. Unfortunately, known holographic proofs are too expensive for practical use, because encoding the circuit is costly (as explained in Sect. 1.2). In this paper we address this problem by constructing an efficient holographic proof, discussed below.

We note that holographic proofs involve relations $\mathcal{R}$ that consist of *triples* rather than *pairs* because the statement being checked has two parts. One part is called the *index*, which is encoded in an offline phase by the *indexer* and this encoding is provided as an oracle to the verifier. The other part is called the *instance*, which is provided as an explicit input to the verifier. For example, the index may be a circuit description and the instance a partial assignment to its inputs. We refer to this notion as *indexed relations*.

(2) Efficient protocols for R1CS. We present a holographic IOP for rank-1 constraint satisfiability (R1CS), a standard generalization of arithmetic circuits where the "circuit description" is given by coefficient matrices. We describe the corresponding indexed relation.

Definition 1 (informal). *The indexed relation $\mathcal{R}_{\mathrm{R1CS}}$ is the set of triples $(\mathbb{i}, \mathbb{x}, \mathbb{w}) = ((\mathbb{F}, n, m, A, B, C), x, w)$ where $\mathbb{F}$ is a finite field, A, B, C are $n \times n$ matrices over $\mathbb{F}$, each containing at most m non-zero entries, and $z := (x, w)$ is a vector in $\mathbb{F}^n$ such that $Az \circ Bz = Cz$. (Here "$\circ$" denotes the entry-wise product.)*

Theorem 2 (informal). *There exists a public-coin holographic IOP for the indexed relation $\mathcal{R}_{\mathrm{R1CS}}$ that is a zero knowledge proof of knowledge with the following efficiency features. In the offline phase, the encoding of an index is computable in $O(m \log m)$ field operations and consists of $O(m)$ field elements. In the online phase, the protocol has $O(\log m)$ rounds, with the prover using $O(m \log m)$ field operations and the verifier using $O(|x| + \log m)$ field operations. Proof length is $O(m)$ field elements and query complexity is $O(\log m)$.*

The above theorem improves, in the holographic setting, on prior IOPs for R1CS (see Fig. 1): it offers an exponential improvement in verification time compared to the linear-time verification of [13], and it offers succinct verification for all coefficient matrices compared to only structured ones as in [11].

Armed with an efficient holographic IOP, we use our compiler to construct an efficient preprocessing SNARG in the random oracle model. The following theorem is obtained by applying Theorem 1 to Theorem 2.

Theorem 3 (informal). *There exists a preprocessing zkSNARK for R1CS that is unconditionally secure in the random oracle model (and the quantum random oracle model) with the following efficiency features. In the offline phase, anyone can publicly preprocess an index in time $O_\lambda(m \log m)$, obtaining a corresponding verification key of size $O_\lambda(1)$. In the online phase, the SNARG prover runs in time $O_\lambda(m \log m)$ and the SNARG verifier runs in time $O_\lambda(|x| + \log^2 m)$; argument size is $O_\lambda(\log^2 m)$.*

We have implemented the protocol underlying Theorem 3, obtaining the first efficient realization of a post-quantum transparent preprocessing zkSNARK.

For example, for a security level of 128 bits over a 181-bit prime field, arguments range from 80 kB to 200 kB for instances of up to millions of constraints. These argument sizes are two orders of magnitude bigger than *pre*-quantum *non*-transparent preprocessing zkSNARKs (see Sect. 1.2), and are 2× bigger that the state of the art in post-quantum transparent *non*-preprocessing zkSNARKs [13]. Our proving and verification times are comparable to prior work: proving takes several minutes, while verification takes several milliseconds *regardless of the constraint system*. (See the full version [29] for performance details.)

Besides its application to post-quantum transparent recursion, our preprocessing zkSNARK provides attractive benefits over prior constructions, as we discuss in Sect. 1.2.

Note that, when the random oracle in the construction is heuristically instantiated via an efficient cryptographic hash function (as in our implementation), the resulting preprocessing zkSNARK is in the uniform reference string (URS) model, which means that the system parameters consist of a uniformly random string of fixed size.[3] The term "transparent" refers to a construction in the URS model.

(3) Post-quantum transparent recursion. We obtain the first efficient realization of post-quantum transparent recursive composition for SNARKs. The cryptographic primitive that formally captures this capability is known as *proof carrying data* (PCD) [18,30], and so this is what we construct.

Theorem 4 (informal). *There is an efficient transformation that compiles any preprocessing SNARK in the URS model into a preprocessing PCD scheme in the URS model. Moreover, if the preprocessing SNARK is post-quantum secure then so is the preprocessing PCD scheme.*

The above transformation, which preserves the "transparent" property and post-quantum security, is where recursive composition occurs. For details, including the definition of PCD, see the full version [29].

Moreover, we provide an efficient implementation of the transformation in Theorem 4 applied to our implementation of the preprocessing zkSNARK from Theorem 3. The main challenge is to express the SNARK verifier's computation in as few constraints as possible, and in particular to design a constraint system for the SNARK verifier that on relatively small instances is smaller than the constraint system that it checks (thereby permitting arbitrary recursion depth). Via a combination of computer-assisted design and recent advances in algebraic hash functions, we achieve this threshold for all computations of at least 2 million constraints. Specifically, we can express a SNARK verifier checking 2 million constraints using only 1.7 million constraints, and this gap grows quickly with the computation size. *This is the first demonstration of post-quantum transparent recursive composition in practice.*

---

[3] We stress that this step is a heuristic due to well-known limitations to the random oracle methodology [24,40]. Investigating how to provably instantiate the random oracle for many natural constructions is an active research frontier.

	R1CS instances	holographic?	indexer time	prover time	verifier time	round complexity	proof length	query complexity
[13]	arbitrary	NO	N/A	$O(m + n \log n)$	$O(|\mathbb{x}| + m)$	$O(\log n)$	$O(n)$	$O(\log n)$
[11] †	semi-succinct	NO	N/A	$O(m + n \log n)$	$O(|\mathbb{x}| + \log n)$	$O(\log n)$	$O(n)$	$O(\log n)$
this work	arbitrary	YES	$O(m \log m)$	$O(m \log m)$	$O(|\mathbb{x}| + \log m)$	$O(\log m)$	$O(m)$	$O(\log m)$

Fig. 1. Comparison of IOPs for R1CS: two prior non-holographic IOPs, and our holographic IOP. Here n denotes the number of variables and m the number of non-zero coefficients in the matrices. †: The parameters stated for [11] reflect replacing the constant-query low-degree test in the construction with a concretely-efficient logarithmic-query low-degree test such as [9], to simplify comparison.

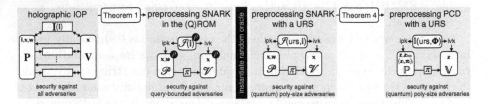

Fig. 2. Diagram of our methodology to recursive composition that is post-quantum and transparent.

1.2 Comparison with Prior Work

We provide a comparison with prior work in the three areas to which we contribute: holographic proofs (Sect. 1.2); preprocessing SNARGs (Sect. 1.2); and recursive composition of SNARKs (Sect. 1.2). We omit a general discussion of the now ample literature on SNARGs, and in particular do not discuss *non*-preprocessing SNARGs for structured computations (e.g., [10,57], and many others).

Prior holographic proofs. The verifier in a proof system cannot run in time that is sublinear in its input, because it must at a minimum read the input in order to know the statement being checked. Holographic proofs [7] avoid this limitation by considering a setting where the verifier does not receive its input explicitly but, instead, has query access to an encoding of it. The goal is then to verify the statement in time *sublinear* in its size; note that such algorithms are necessarily probabilistic.[4]

---

[4] The goal of sublinear verification via holographic proofs is similar to, but distinct from, the goal of sublinear verification via *proximity proofs* (as, e.g., studied in [17,33,35,46,53]). In this latter setting, the verifier has oracle access to an input that is *not* promised to be encoded and, in particular, cannot in general decide if the input is in the language without reading all of the input. To allow for sublinear verification without any promises on the input, the decision problem is relaxed: the verifier is only asked to decide if the input is in the language or *far* from any input in the language.

In Fig. 3 we compare the efficiency of prior holographic proofs and our holographic proof for the case of circuit satisfiability, where the input to the verifier is the description of an arbitrary circuit. There are two main prior holographic proofs in the literature. One is the PCP construction in [7], where it suffices for the verifier to query a few locations of a low-degree extension of the circuit description. Another one is the "bare bones" protocol in [41], which is a holographic IP for circuit *evaluation* that can be re-cast as a holographic IPCP for circuit *satisfaction*; the verifier relies on the low-degree extensions of functions that describe each layer of the circuit. The constructions in [7] and [41] are unfit for practical use as holographic proofs in Theorem 1, because encoding the circuit incurs a polynomial blowup due to the use of *multivariate* low-degree extensions (which yield encodings with inverse polynomial rate).

In the table we exclude the "algebraic holographic proof" of Marlin [27], because the soundness guarantee of such a proof is incompatible with Theorem 1.

Comparison with this work. Our holographic proof is the first to achieve efficient asymptotics not only for the prover and verifier, but also for the indexer, which is responsible for producing the encoding of the circuit.

	proof type	indexer time	prover time	verifier time
[7]	PCP	$\text{poly}(N)$	$\text{poly}(N)$	$\text{poly}(|x| + \log(N))$
[41]	IPCP	$\text{poly}(N)$	$\text{poly}(|w|) + O(N)$	$O(|x| + D \log W)$
this work	IOP	$O(N \log N)$	$O(N \log N)$	$O(|x| + \log N)$

Fig. 3. Comparison of holographic proofs for arithmetic circuit satisfiability. Here x denotes the known inputs, w the unknown inputs, and N the total number of gates; if the circuit is layered, D denotes circuit depth and W circuit width. Our Theorem 1 can be used to compile any of these holographic proofs into a preprocessing SNARG. (For better comparison with other works, [41] is stated as an IPCP for circuit satisfiability rather than as an IP for circuit evaluation; in the latter case, the prover time would be $O(N)$. The prover times for [41] incorporate the techniques for linear-time sumcheck introduced in [57].)

Prior preprocessing SNARGs. Prior works construct preprocessing SNARGs in a model where a trusted party samples, in a parameter setup phase, a structured reference string (SRS) that is proportional to circuit size. We summarize the main features of these constructions, distinguishing between the case of circuit-specific SRS and universal SRS.

- *Circuit-specific SRS:* a circuit is given as input to the setup algorithm, which samples a (long) proving key and a (short) verification key that can be used to produce and validate arguments for the circuit. Preprocessing SNARGs with circuit-specific SRS originate in [19,39,43,47], and have been studied in an influential line of work that has led to highly-efficient constructions (e.g., [44]) and large-scale deployments (e.g., [34]). They are obtained by combining linear interactive proofs and linear-only encodings. The argument sizes achievable in this setting are very small: less than 200 bytes.
- *Universal SRS:* a size bound is given as input to the setup algorithm, which samples a (long) proving key and a (short) verification key that can be used to produce and validate arguments for circuits within this bound. A public procedure can then be used to specialize both keys for arguments relative to the desired circuit. Preprocessing SNARGs with universal (and updatable) SRS were introduced in [45], and led to efficient constructions in [27,38,49]. They are obtained by combining "algebraic" holographic proofs (see below) and polynomial commitment schemes. The argument sizes currently achievable with universal SRS are bigger than with circuit-specific SRS: less than 1500 bytes.

Comparison with this work. Theorem 1 provides a methodology to obtain preprocessing SNARGs in the (quantum) random oracle model, which heuristically implies (by suitably instantiating the random oracle) preprocessing SNARGs that are post-quantum and transparent. Neither of these properties is achieved by prior preprocessing SNARGs. Theorem 1 also develops the connection between holography and preprocessing discovered in [27], which considers the case of holographic proofs where the completeness and soundness properties are restricted to "algebraic provers" (which output polynomials of prescribed degrees). We consider the case of general holographic proofs, where completeness and soundness are not restricted.

Moreover, our holographic proof (Theorem 2) leads to a preprocessing SNARG (Theorem 3) that, as supported by our implementation, provides attractive benefits over prior preprocessing SNARGs.

- Prior preprocessing SNARGs require cryptographic ceremonies to securely sample the long SRS, which makes deployments difficult and expensive. This has restricted the use of preprocessing SNARGs to proving relatively small computations, due to the prohibitive cost of securely sampling SRSs for large computations. This is unfortunate because preprocessing SNARGs could be useful for "scalability applications", which leverage succinct verification to efficiently check large computations (e.g., verifying the correctness of large batches of trades executed at a non-custodial exchange [8,55]). The transparent property of our preprocessing SNARG means that the long SRS is replaced with a fixed-size URS (uniform reference string). This simplifies deployments and enables scalability applications.
- Prior preprocessing SNARGs are limited to express computations over the prime fields that arise as the scalar fields of pairing-friendly elliptic curves.

Such fields are imposed by parametrized curve families that offer little flexibility for optimizations or applications. (Alternatively one can use the Cocks–Pinch method [37] to construct an elliptic curve with a desired scalar field, but the resulting curve is inefficient.)

In contrast, our preprocessing SNARG is easily configurable across a range of security levels, and supports most large prime fields and all large binary fields, which offers greater flexibility in terms of performance optimizations and customization for applications.

Remark 1 (weaker forms of preprocessing). Prior work proved recursive composition only for non-interactive arguments of knowledge with succinct verifiers [18]; this is the case for our definition of preprocessing SNARGs. In this paper we show that recursive composition is possible even when the verifier is merely *sublinear* in the circuit size, though the cost of each recursion is much steeper than in the polylogarithmic case.

This provides additional motivation to the study of preprocessing with sublinear verifiers, as recently undertaken by Setty [54]. In this latter work, Setty proposes a non-interactive argument in the URS (uniform reference string) model where, for n-gate arithmetic circuits and a chosen constant $c \geq 2$, proving time is $O_\lambda(n)$, argument size is $O_\lambda(n^{1/c})$, and verification time is $O_\lambda(n^{1-1/c})$.

Recursion for pairing-based SNARKs. The approach to recursive composition of [15] uses pairing-based (preprocessing) SNARKs based on pairing-friendly cycles of elliptic curves. This approach applies to constructions with circuit-specific SRS (e.g. [44]) *and* to those with universal SRS (e.g. [27,38,45,49]).

Informally, pairing-based SNARKs support languages that involve the satisfiability of constraint systems over a field that is *different* from the field used to compute the SNARK verifier — this restriction arises from the mathematics of the underlying pairing-friendly elliptic curve used to instantiate the pairing. This seemingly mundane fact has the regrettable consequence that expressing the SNARK verifier's computation in the language supported by the SNARK (to realize recursive composition) is unreasonably expensive due to this "field mismatch". To circumvent this barrier, prior work leveraged *two* pairing-based SNARKs where the field to compute one SNARK verifier equals the field of the language supported by the other SNARK, and vice versa. This condition enables each SNARK to efficiently verify the other SNARK's proofs.

These special SNARKs rely on pairing-friendly cycles of elliptic curves, which are pairs of pairing-friendly elliptic curves where the base field of one curve equals the scalar field of the other curve and vice versa. The only known construction is *MNT cycles*, which consist of two prime-order elliptic curves with embedding degrees 4 and 6 respectively. An MNT cycle must be much bigger than usual in order to compensate for the low security caused by the small embedding degrees. For example, for a security level of 128 bits, curves in an MNT cycle must be defined over a prime field with roughly 800 bits; this is over *three times* the 256 bits that suffice for curves with larger embedding degrees. These performance overheads can be significant in practice, e.g., Coda [51] is a project that has deployed MNT cycles in a product, and has organized a community challenge to speed up the proof generation for pairing-based SNARKs [32]. A natural approach to mitigate this problem would be to find "high-security" cycles (i.e., with higher embedding degrees) but to date little is known about pairing-friendly cycles beyond a few negative results [26].

Comparison with this work. The approach to recursion that we present in this paper is *not tied* to constructions of pairing-friendly cycles of elliptic curves. In particular, our approach scales gracefully across different security levels, and also offers more flexibility when choosing the desired field for an application. In addition, our approach is post-quantum and, moreover, uses a transparent (i.e., public-coin) setup.

On the other hand, our approach has two disadvantages. First, argument size is about 100 times bigger than the argument size achievable by cycle-based recursion. Second, the number of constraints needed to express the verifier's computation is about 45 times bigger than those needed in the case of cycle-based recursion (e.g., the verifier of [44] can be expressed in about 40,000 constraints). The vast majority of these constraints come from the many hash function invocations required to verify the argument.

Both of the above limitations are somewhat orthogonal to our approach and arguably temporary: the large proof size and many hash invocations come from the many queries required from current constructions of low-degree tests [9,16]. As the state of the art in low-degree testing progresses (e.g., to high-soundness constructions over large alphabets), both argument size and verifier size will also improve.

2   Techniques

We discuss the main ideas behind our results. In Sect. 2.1 we explain how preprocessing simplifies recursive composition. In Sect. 2.2 we describe our compiler from holographic IOPs to preprocessing SNARGs (Theorem 1). In Sect. 2.3 we describe our efficient holographic IOP (Theorem 2), and then in Sect. 2.4 we discuss the corresponding preprocessing SNARG (Theorem 3). In Sect. 2.5 we describe how to obtain post-quantum and transparent PCD (Theorem 4). In Sect. 2.6 we discuss our verifier circuit.

Recall that indexed relations consist of *triples* (i, x, w) where i is the index, x is the instance, and w is the witness. We use these relations because the statements being checked have two parts, the index i (e.g., a circuit description) given in an offline phase and the instance x (e.g., a partial input assignment) given in an online phase.

2.1   The Role of Preprocessing SNARKs in Recursive Composition

We explain why preprocessing simplifies recursive composition of SNARKs. For concreteness we consider the problem of incrementally proving the iterated application of a circuit $F: \{0,1\}^n \to \{0,1\}^n$ to an initial input $z_0 \in \{0,1\}^n$. We are thus interested in proving statements of the form "*given z_T there exists z_0 such that $z_T = F^T(z_0)$*", but wish to avoid having the SNARK prover check the correctness of all T invocations at once. Instead, we break the desired statement into T smaller statements "$\{z_i = F(z_{i-1})\}_{i=1}^T$ and then inductively prove them. Informally, for $i = 1, \ldots, T$, we produce a SNARK proof π_i for this statement:

> "*Given a counter i and claimed output z_i, there exists a prior output z_{i-1} such that $z_i = F(z_{i-1})$ and, if $i > 1$, there exists a SNARK proof π_{i-1} that attests to the correctness of z_{i-1}.*"

Formalizing this idea requires care, and in particular depends on how the SNARK achieves succinct verification (a prerequisite for recursive composition). There are two methods to achieve succinct verification.

(1) *Non-preprocessing SNARKs for structured computations.* The SNARK supports non-deterministic computations expressed as programs, i.e., it can be used to prove/verify statements of the form "given a program M, primary input $\mathbf{x}$, and time bound t, there exists an auxiliary input $\mathbf{w}$ such that M accepts $(\mathbf{x}, \mathbf{w})$ in t steps". (More generally, the SNARK could support any computation model for which the description of a computation can be significantly smaller than the size of the described computation.)

(2) *Preprocessing SNARKs for arbitrary computations.* The SNARK supports circuit satisfiability, i.e., it can be used to prove/verify statements of the form "given a circuit C and primary input $\mathbf{x}$, there exists an auxiliary input $\mathbf{w}$ such that $C(\mathbf{x}, \mathbf{w}) = 0$". Preprocessing enables the circuit C to be summarized into a short verification key ivk_C that can be used for succinct verification *regardless* of the structure of C. (More generally, the SNARK could support any computation model as long as preprocessing is possible.)

We compare the costs of recursive composition in these two cases, showing why the preprocessing case is cheaper. Throughout we consider SNARKs in the uniform reference string model, i.e., parameter setup consists of sampling a fully random string urs of size $\mathsf{poly}(\lambda)$ that suffices for proving/verifying any statement.

(1) Recursion without preprocessing. Let $(\mathcal{P}, \mathcal{V})$ be a *non*-preprocessing SNARK for non-deterministic program computations. In this case, recursion is realized via a program R, which depends on urs and F, that checks one invocation of the circuit F and the validity of a prior SNARK proof relative to the reference string urs. The program R is defined as follows:

Primary input: a tuple $\mathbf{x} = (M, i, z_i)$ consisting of the description of a program M, counter i, and claimed output z_i. (We later set $M := R$ to achieve recursion, as explained shortly.)

Auxiliary input: a tuple $\mathbf{w} = (z_{i-1}, \pi_{i-1})$ consisting of a previous output z_{i-1} and corresponding SNARK proof π_{i-1} that attests to its correctness.

Code: $R(\mathbf{x}, \mathbf{w})$ accepts if $z_i = F(z_{i-1})$ and, if $i > 1$, $\mathcal{V}(\mathsf{urs}, M, \mathbf{x}_{i-1}, t, \pi_{i-1}) = 1$ where $\mathbf{x}_{i-1} := (M, i - 1, z_{i-1})$ and t is a suitably chosen time bound.

The program R can be used to incrementally prove the iterated application of the circuit F. Given a tuple $(i - 1, z_{i-1}, \pi_{i-1})$ consisting of the current counter, output, and proof, one can use the SNARK prover to obtain the next tuple (i, z_i, π_i) by setting $z_i := F(z_{i-1})$ and computing the proof $\pi_i := \mathcal{P}(\mathsf{urs}, R, (R, i, z_i), t, \pi_i)$. Note that we have set $M := R$, so that (the description of) R is part of the primary input to R. A tuple (i, z_i, π_i) can then be verified by running the SNARK verifier, as $\mathcal{V}(\mathsf{urs}, R, (R, i, z_i), t, \pi_i)$.[5]

We refer the reader to [18] for details on how to prove the above construction secure. The aspect that we are interested to raise here is that the program R is tasked to simulate itself, essentially working as a universal machine. This means that every elementary operation of R, and in particular of F, needs to be simulated by R in its execution. This essentially means that the computation time of R, which dictates the cost of each proof composition, is at least a constant $c > 1$ times the size of $|F|$. *This multiplicative overhead on the size of the circuit F, while asymptotically irrelevant, is a significant overhead in concrete efficiency.*

(2) Recursion with preprocessing. We describe how to leverage preprocessing in order to avoid universal simulation, and in particular to avoid *any* multiplicative performance overheads in recursive composition. Intuitively, preprocessing provides a "cryptographic simplification" to the requisite recursion, by enabling us to replace the description of the computation with a succinct cryptographic commitment to it.

Let $(\mathcal{I}, \mathcal{P}, \mathcal{V})$ be a preprocessing SNARK for circuits. Recursion is realized via a circuit R that depends on urs and F, and checks one invocation of F and a prior proof. The circuit R is defined as follows:

Primary input: a tuple $\mathbb{x} = (\mathsf{ivk}, i, z_i)$ consisting of an index verification key ivk, counter i, and claimed output z_i. (We later set $\mathsf{ivk} := \mathsf{ivk}_R$ to achieve recursion.)

Auxiliary input: a tuple $\mathbb{w} = (z_{i-1}, \pi_{i-1})$ consisting of a previous output z_{i-1} and corresponding SNARK proof π_{i-1} that attests to its correctness.

Code: $R(\mathbb{x}, \mathbb{w})$ accepts if $z_i = F(z_{i-1})$ and, if $i > 1$, $\mathcal{V}(\mathsf{urs}, \mathsf{ivk}, \mathbb{x}_{i-1}, \pi_{i-1}) = 1$ where $\mathbb{x}_{i-1} := (\mathsf{ivk}, i - 1, z_{i-1})$.

The circuit R can be used for recursive composition as follows. In the offline phase, we run the indexer $\mathcal{I}$ on the circuit R, obtaining a long index proving key ipk_R and a short index verification key ivk_R that can be used to produce and validate SNARKs with respect to the circuit R. Subsequently, in the online

---

[5] The astute reader may notice that we could have applied the Recursion Theorem to the program R to obtain a new program R^* that has access to its own code, and thereby simplify primary inputs from triples $\mathbb{x} = (M, i, z_i)$ to pairs $\mathbb{x} = (i, z_i)$. This, however, adds unnecessary complexity. Indeed, here we can rely on the SNARK verifier to provide R with its own code as part of the primary input, obviating this extra step. (For reference, the Recursion Theorem states that for every program $A(x, y)$ there is a program $B(y)$ that computes $A(\langle B \rangle, y)$, where the angle brackets emphasize that the first argument is the description of the program B).

phase, one can use the prover $\mathcal{P}$ to go from a tuple $(i - 1, z_{i-1}, \pi_{i-1})$ to a new tuple (i, z_i, π_i) by letting $z_i := F(z_{i-1})$ and $\pi_i := \mathcal{P}(\mathsf{urs}, \mathsf{ipk}_R, (\mathsf{ivk}_R, i, z_i), \pi_i)$. Note that we have set $\mathsf{ivk} := \mathsf{ivk}_R$, so that the verification key ivk_R is part of the primary input to the circuit R. A tuple (i, z_i, π_i) can then be verified by running the SNARK verifier, as $\mathcal{V}(\mathsf{urs}, \mathsf{ivk}_R, (\mathsf{ivk}_R, i, z_i), \pi_i)$.

Crucially, the circuit R does *not* perform any universal simulation involving the circuit F, and in particular does not incur multiplicative overheads. Indeed, $|R| = |F| + |\mathcal{V}| = |F| + o(|F|)$. This was enabled by preprocessing, which let us provide the index verification key ivk_R as input to the circuit R.

In fact, preprocessing is *already* part of the efficient approach to recursive composition in [15]. There the preprocessing SNARK uses a structured, rather than uniform, reference string but the benefits of preprocessing are analogous (even when the reference string depends on the circuit or a bound on it).

In summary. Preprocessing SNARKs play an important role in efficient recursive composition. Our first milestone is post-quantum and transparent preprocessing SNARKs, which we then use to achieve post-quantum and transparent recursive composition.

2.2 From Holographic Proofs to Preprocessing with Random Oracles

We describe the main ideas behind Theorem 1, which provides a transformation that compiles any holographic IOP for an indexed relation $\mathcal{R}$ into a corresponding preprocessing SNARG for $\mathcal{R}$. For more details, see the full version [29].

Warmup: holographic PCPs. We first consider the case of PCPs, a special case of IOPs. Recall that the Micali transformation [50] compiles a (non-holographic) PCP into a (non-preprocessing) SNARG. We modify this transformation to compile a *holographic* PCP into a *preprocessing* SNARG, by using the fact that the SNARG verifier output by the Micali transformation invokes the PCP verifier as a black box.

In more detail, the main feature of a holographic PCP is that the PCP verifier does not receive the index as an explicit input but, rather, makes a small number of queries to an encoding of the index given as an oracle. If we apply the Micali transformation to the holographic PCP, we obtain a SNARG verifier that must answer queries by the PCP verifier to the encoded index. If we simply provided the index as an input to the SNARG verifier, then we cannot achieve succinct verification and so would not obtain a preprocessing SNARG. Instead, we let the SNARG indexer compute the encoded index, compute a Merkle tree over it, and output the corresponding root as an *index verification key* for the SNARG verifier. We can then have the SNARG prover extend the SNARG proof with answers to queries to the encoded index, certified by authentication paths relative to the index verification key. In this way the SNARG verifier can use the answers in the SNARG proof to answer the queries to the encoded index by the underlying PCP verifier.

This straightforward modification to the Micali transformation works: one can prove that if the soundness error of the holographic PCP is ϵ then the soundness error of the preprocessing SNARG is $t\epsilon + O(t^2 \cdot 2^{-\lambda})$ against t-query adversaries in the random oracle model. (A similar expression holds for quantum adversaries.)

General case: holographic IOPs. While efficient constructions of holographic PCPs are not known, in this paper we show how to construct an efficient holographic IOP (see Sect. 2.3). Hence we are actually interested in compiling holographic IOPs. In this case our starting point is the BCS transformation [14], which compiles a (non-holographic) IOP into a (non-preprocessing) SNARG. We adopt a similar strategy as above: we modify the BCS transformation to compile a *holographic* IOP into a *preprocessing* SNARG, using the fact that the SNARG verifier output by the BCS transformation invokes the IOP verifier as a black box. Indeed, the main feature of a holographic IOP is the fact that the IOP verifier makes a small number of queries to an encoding of the index given as an oracle. Therefore the SNARG indexer can output the Merkle root of the encoded index as an index verification key, which subsequently the SNARG verifier can use to authenticate answers about the encoded index claimed by the SNARG prover.

An important technical difference here is the fact that the soundness error of the resulting preprocessing SNARG is not related to the soundness error of the holographic IOP but, instead, to its *state-restoration soundness* (SRS) error, a stronger notion of soundness introduced in [14]. Namely, we prove that if the SRS error of the holographic PCP is $\epsilon_{\mathrm{sr}}(t)$ then the soundness error of the preprocessing SNARG is $\epsilon_{\mathrm{sr}}(t) + O(t^2 \cdot 2^{-\lambda})$. This phenomenon is inherited from the (unmodified) BCS transformation.

PoK and ZK. If the holographic IOP is a proof of knowledge, our transformation yields a preprocessing SNARG of knowledge (SNARK). If the holographic IOP is honest-verifier zero knowledge, the preprocessing SNARG is statistical zero knowledge. These features are inherited from the BCS transformation.

2.3 An Efficient Holographic Proof for Constraint Systems

We describe the main ideas behind Theorem 2, which provides an efficient construction of a holographic IOP for rank-1 constraint satisfiability (R1CS). See Definition 1 for the indexed relation representing this problem.

Our starting point: Marlin. Our construction borrows ideas from the *algebraic holographic proof* (AHP) underlying Marlin, a pairing-based zkSNARK due to [27]. An AHP is similar to a holographic IOP, except that the indexer and the prover (both honest and malicious) send *low-degree univariate polynomials* rather than evaluations of functions. The verifier may evaluate these polynomials at any point in the field.

To understand how AHPs and holographic IOPs differ, it is instructive to consider how one might construct a holographic IOP from an AHP. A natural approach is to construct the indexer and prover for the hIOP as follows: run the indexer/prover of the AHP, and whenever the indexer/prover outputs a polynomial, evaluate it and send this evaluation as the oracle. There are several issues with this approach. First, hIOPs require a stronger soundness guarantee: soundness must hold against malicious provers that send *arbitrary* oracles. Second, evaluating the polynomial requires selecting a set $L \subseteq \mathbb{F}$ over which to evaluate it. In general, since the verifier in the AHP may query any point in $\mathbb{F}$, we would need to take $L := \mathbb{F}$, which is prohibitively expensive for the indexer and prover if $\mathbb{F}$ is much larger than the instance size (as it often is, for both soundness and application reasons). Third, assuming that one manages to decouple L and $\mathbb{F}$, the soundness error of one invocation of the AHP will (at best) decrease with $1/|L|$ instead of $1/\mathbb{F}$, which requires somehow reducing the soundness error of the AHP to, say, $1/2^\lambda$, and simply re-running in parallel the AHP for $\lambda - \log|L|$ would be expensive in all relevant parameters.

The first issue could be resolved by composing the resulting protocol with a low-degree test. This introduces technicalities because we cannot hope to check that the oracle is exactly low-degree (as required in an AHP)—we can only check that the oracle is *close* to low-degree. The best way to resolve the second issue depends on the AHP itself, and would likely involve out-of-domain sampling [16]. Finally, resolving the third issue may not be possible in general (in fact, we do not see how resolve it for the AHP in Marlin).

These above issues show that, despite some similarities, there are markedly *different* design considerations on hIOPs versus AHPs. For this reason, while we will follow some of the ideas outlined above, we do not take the Marlin AHP as a black box. Instead, we will draw on the ideas underlying the Marlin AHP in order to build a suitable hIOP for this paper. Along the way, we also show how to reduce the round complexity of the Marlin AHP from 3 to 2, an ideas that we use to significantly improve the efficiency of our construction.

Aurora. The structure of our holographic IOP, like the Marlin AHP, follows the one of Aurora [13], an IOP for R1CS that we now briefly recall. Given an R1CS instance (A, B, C), the prover sends to the verifier f_z, the RS-encoding of a vector z, and three oracles f_A, f_B, f_C which are purportedly the RS-encodings of the three vectors Az, Bz, Cz respectively. The prover and verifier then engage in subprotocols to prove that (i) f_A, f_B, f_C are indeed encodings of Az, Bz, Cz, and (ii) $f_A \cdot f_B - f_C$ is an encoding of the zero vector.

Together these checks ensure that (A, B, C) is a satisfiable instance of R1CS. Testing (ii) is a straightforward application of known probabilistic checking techniques, and can be achieved with a logarithmic-time verifier. The primary challenge in the Aurora protocol (and protocols based on it) is testing (i).

In the Aurora protocol this is achieved via a reduction to univariate sumcheck, a univariate analogue of the [48] sumcheck protocol. Univariate sumcheck also has a logarithmic verifier, but the reduction itself runs in time linear in the number of nonzero entries in the matrices A, B, C. A key technical contribution of the Marlin AHP is showing how to shift most of the cost of the reduction to the indexer in order to reduce the online cost of verification to logarithmic, as we now explain.

Challenges. We describe the original lincheck protocol of [13], and explain why it is not holographic. The lincheck protocol, on input a matrix $M \in \mathbb{F}^{k \times k}$ and RS-encodings of vectors $\vec{x}, \vec{y} \in \mathbb{F}^k$, checks whether $\vec{x} = M\vec{y}$. It makes use of the following two facts: (i) for a vector of linearly-independent polynomials $\vec{u} \in \mathbb{F}[X]^k$ and any vectors $\vec{x}, \vec{y} \in \mathbb{F}^k$, if $\vec{x} \neq \vec{y}$ then the polynomials $\langle \vec{u}, \vec{x} \rangle$ and $\langle \vec{u}, \vec{y} \rangle$ are distinct, and so differ with high probability at a random $\alpha \in \mathbb{F}$, and (ii) for any matrix $M \in \mathbb{F}^{k \times k}$, $\langle \vec{u}, M\vec{y} \rangle = \langle \vec{u}M, \vec{y} \rangle$. The lincheck verifier sends a random $\alpha \in \mathbb{F}$ to the prover, and the prover then convinces the verifier that $\langle \vec{u}M, \vec{y} \rangle(\alpha) - \langle \vec{u}, \vec{x} \rangle(\alpha) = 0$ using the univariate sumcheck protocol.

This requires the verifier to evaluate the low-degree extensions of $\vec{u}_\alpha$ and $\vec{u}_\alpha M$ at a point $\beta \in \mathbb{F}$, where $\vec{u}_\alpha \in \mathbb{F}^k$ is obtained by evaluating each entry of $\vec{u}$ at α. This is equivalent to evaluating the bivariate polynomials $u(X, Y), u_M(X, Y) \in \mathbb{F}[X, Y]$, obtained respectively by extending $\vec{u}, \vec{u}M$ over Y, at a random point in $(\alpha, \beta) \in \mathbb{F}^2$. By choosing $\vec{u}$ appropriately, we can ensure that $u(X, Y)$ can be evaluated in logarithmic time [11]. But, without help from an indexer, evaluating $u_M(\alpha, \beta)$ requires time $\Omega(\|M\|)$.

A natural suggestion in the holographic setting is to have the indexer evaluate u_M over some domain $S \subseteq \mathbb{F} \times \mathbb{F}$, and make this evaluation part of the encoded index. This does achieve the goal of logarithmic verification time. Unfortunately, the degree of u_M in each variable is about k, and so even writing down the coefficients of u_M requires time $\Omega(k^2)$, which for sparse M is quadratic in $\|M\|$.

In the Marlin lincheck the indexer instead computes a certain *linear-size* (polynomial) encoding of M, which the verifier then uses in a multi-round protocol with the prover to evaluate u_M at its chosen point. Our holographic lincheck improves upon this protocol, reducing the number of rounds by one; we describe it next.

Our holographic lincheck. Recall from above that the lincheck verifier needs to check that $\langle \vec{u}, \vec{x} \rangle$ and $\langle \vec{u}M, \vec{y} \rangle$ are equal as polynomials in X. To do this, it will choose a random $\alpha \in \mathbb{F}$ and send it to the prover, then engage in the univariate sumcheck protocol to show that $\sum_h u(\alpha, h)\hat{x}(h) - u_M(\alpha, h)\hat{y}(h) = 0$, where $\hat{x}, \hat{y}$ are low-degree extensions of x and y.

To verify the above sum, the verifier must compute $u(\alpha, \beta)$ and $u_M(\alpha, \beta)$ for some $\beta \in \mathbb{F}$. The former can be computed in by the verifier in logarithmic time as discussed; for the latter, we ask the prover to help. Specifically, we show that $u_M \equiv \hat{M}^*$, the unique bivariate low-degree extension of a matrix M^* which can be computed in quasilinear time from M (and in particular has $\|M^*\| = \|M\|$). Hence to show that $u_M(\alpha, \beta) = \gamma$ the prover and verifier can engage in a holographic *matrix arithmetization* protocol for M^* to show that $\hat{M}^*(\alpha, \beta) = \gamma$. Marlin makes use of a similar matrix arithmetization protocol, but for M itself, with a subprotocol to compute u_M from $\hat{M}$, which is a cost that we completely eliminate. Another improvement is that for our matrix arithmetization protocol we can efficiently reduce soundness error even when using a low-degree test, due to its non-recursive use of the sumcheck protocol.

Matrix arithmetization. Our matrix arithmetization protocol is a holographic IOP for computing the low-degree extension of a matrix $M \in \mathbb{F}^{H \times H}$ (provided in the index). It is useful here to view M in its sparse representation as a map $\langle M \rangle \colon K \to H \times H \times \mathbb{F}$ for some $K \subseteq \mathbb{F}$, where if $\langle M \rangle(k) = (a, b, \gamma)$ for some $k \in K$ then $M_{a,b} = \gamma$, and $M_{a,b} = 0$ otherwise.

The indexer computes $\hat{\text{row}}, \hat{\text{col}}, \hat{\text{val}}$ which are the unique low-degree extensions of the functions $K \to \mathbb{F}$ induced by restricting $\langle M \rangle$ to its first, second, and third coordinates respectively, and outputs their evaluations over L. It is not hard to verify that

$$\hat{M}(\alpha, \beta) = \sum_{k \in K} L_{H, \hat{\text{row}}(k)}(\alpha) L_{H, \hat{\text{col}}(k)}(\beta) \hat{\text{val}}(k) \ ,$$

for any $\alpha, \beta \in \mathbb{F}$, where $L_{H,a}$ is the polynomial of minimal degree which is 1 on a and 0 on $H \setminus \{a\}$. In order to check this equation using the sumcheck protocol we must modify the right-hand side: the summand must be a polynomial which can be efficiently evaluated. To this end, we make use of the "unnormalized Lagrange" polynomial $u_H(X, Y) := (v_H(X) - v_H(Y))/(X - Y)$ from [11]. This polynomial has the property that for every $a, b \in H$, $u_H(a, b)$ is 0 if $a \neq b$ and nonzero if $a = b$; and it is easy to evaluate at every point in $\mathbb{F}$. By having the indexer renormalize $\hat{\text{val}}$ appropriately, we obtain

$$\hat{M}(X, Y) \equiv \sum_{k \in K} u_H(\hat{\text{row}}(k), \alpha) u_H(\hat{\text{col}}(k), \beta) \hat{\text{val}}(k).$$

We have made progress, but now the summand has quadratic degree: $\Omega(|H||K|)$ because we *compose* the polynomials u_H and $\hat{\text{row}}, \hat{\text{col}}$. Next we show how to remove this composition.

Observe that since the image of K under $\hat{\text{row}}, \hat{\text{col}}$ is contained in H, $v_H(\hat{\text{row}}(k)) = v_H(\hat{\text{col}}(k)) = 0$. Hence the rational function

$$\frac{v_H(\alpha)}{(\alpha - \hat{\text{row}}_{\langle M \rangle}(X))} \cdot \frac{v_H(\beta)}{(\beta - \hat{\text{col}}_{\langle M \rangle}(X))} \cdot \hat{\text{val}}_{\langle M \rangle}(X)$$

agrees with the summand on K; it is a rational extension of the summands. Moreover, the degrees of the numerator and denominator of the function are both $O(|K|)$. Now it remains to design a protocol to check the sum of a univariate rational function.

Rational sumcheck. Suppose that we want to check that $\sum_{k \in K} p(k)/q(k) = \gamma$, where p, q are low-degree polynomials. First, we have the prover send the (evaluation of the) unique polynomial f of degree $|K| - 1$ which agrees with p/q on K; that is, the unique low-degree extension of p/q viewed as a function from K to $\mathbb{F}$. We can use the *standard* univariate sumcheck protocol from [13] to test that $\sum_{k \in K} f(k) = \gamma$.

It then remains to check that f does indeed agree with p/q on K. This is achieved using standard techniques: if $p(k)/q(k) = f(k)$ for all $k \in K$, then $p(k) = q(k) \cdot f(k)$ for all $k \in K$ (at least if q does not vanish on K). Then $p - q \cdot f$ is a polynomial vanishing on K, and so is divisible by v_K. This can be checked using low-degree testing. Moreover, the degree of this equation is $\max(\deg(p), \deg(q) + |K|)$; in the matrix arithmetization protocol, this is $O(|K|)$.

Proof of knowledge and zero knowledge. Our full protocol for R1CS is a proof of knowledge, because when the verifier accepts with high enough probability it is possible to decode f_z into a satisfying assignment. We further achieve zero knowledge via techniques inherited from [13]. (Note that zero knowledge is not relevant for the matrix arithmetization protocol because the constraint matrices A, B, C are public.)

2.4   Post-quantum and Transparent Preprocessing

If we apply the compiler described in Sect. 2.2 (as captured in Theorem 1) to the efficient holographic proof for R1CS described in Sect. 2.3 (as captured in Theorem 2) then we obtain an efficient preprocessing zkSNARK for R1CS that is unconditionally secure in the (quantum) random oracle model (as captured in Theorem 3). We refer to the resulting construction as FRACTAL.

Implementation. We have implemented FRACTAL by extending the `libiop` library to support generic compilation of holographic proofs into preprocessing SNARGs, and then writing in code our holographic proof for R1CS. Our implementation supports a range of security levels and fields. (The only requirement on the field is that it contains certain smooth subgroups.) See the full version [29] for more details on the implementation.

Clearly, the security of our implementation relies on the random oracle methodology applied to preprocessing SNARGs produced by our compiler, namely, we assume that if we replace every call to the random oracle with a call to a cryptographic hash function then the resulting construction, which formally is in the URS model, inherits the relevant security properties that we proved in the (quantum) random oracle model.

Evaluation. We have evaluated FRACTAL, and its measured performance is consistent with asymptotic predictions. In particular, the polylogarithmic argument size and verification time quickly become smaller than native witness size and native execution time as the size of the checked computation increases.

We additionally compare the costs of FRACTAL to prior preprocessing SNARGs, finding that (a) our prover and verifier times are comparable to prior constructions; (b) argument sizes are larger than prior constructions (that have an SRS). The larger argument sizes of FRACTAL are nonetheless comparable with other post-quantum transparent *non*-preprocessing SNARGs. See the full version [29] for more details on evaluation.

2.5   Post-quantum and Transparent Recursive Composition

We summarize the ideas behind our contributions to recursive composition of SNARKs.

Proof-carrying data. Recursive composition is captured by a cryptographic primitive called *proof-carrying data* (PCD) [18,30], which will be our goal. Consider a network of nodes, where each node receives messages from other nodes, performs some local computation, and sends the result on. PCD is a primitive that allows us to check the correctness of such distributed computations by recursively producing proofs of correctness for each message. Here "correctness" is locally specified by a *compliance predicate* Φ, which takes as input the messages received by a node and the message sent by that node (and possibly some auxiliary local data). A distributed computation is then considered Φ-*compliant* if, for each node, the predicate Φ accepts the node's messages (and auxiliary local data).

PCD captures proving the iterated application of a circuit as in Sect. 2.1, in which case the distributed computation evolves along a path. PCD also captures more complex topologies, which is useful for supporting distributed computations on long paths (via "depth-reduction" techniques [18,56]) and for expressing dynamic distributed computations (such as MapReduce computations [31]).

From random oracle model to the URS model. While we have so far discussed constructions that are unconditionally secure in the (quantum) random oracle model, for recursion we now leave this model (by heuristically instantiating the random oracle with a cryptographic hash function) and start from preprocessing SNARKs in the URS model. The reason for this is far from mundane (and not motivated by implementation), as we now explain. The verifiers from Theorem 1 make calls to the random oracle, and therefore proving that the verifier has accepted would require using a SNARK that can prove the correctness of computations *in a relativized world where the oracle is a random function*. There is substantial evidence from complexity theory that such SNARKs do not exist (e.g., the PCP Theorem does not relativize with respect to a random oracle [25,36]). By instantiating the random oracle, all oracle calls can be "unrolled" into computations that do not involve oracle gates, and thus we can prove the the correctness of the resulting computation.[6] We stress that random oracles cannot be securely instantiated in the general case [24], and so we will assume that there is a secure instantiation of the random oracle for the preprocessing SNARKs produced via Theorem 1 (which, in particular, preserves proof of knowledge).

From SNARK to PCD. We prove that any preprocessing SNARK in the URS model can be transformed into a preprocessing PCD scheme in the URS model.[7] The construction realizes recursive composition by following the template given

---

[6] The necessity to instantiate the random oracle before recursion also arises in the first construction of incrementally verifiable computation [56]. One way to circumvent this difficulty is to consider oracles that are equipped with a public verification procedure [30], however this requires embedding a secret in the oracle, which does not lend itself to straightforward software realizations and so we do not consider this approach in this paper.

[7] Analogously to a SNARK, here *preprocessing* denotes the fact that the PCD scheme enables succinct verification regardless of the computation expressed by the compliance predicate Φ (as opposed to only for structured computations).

in Sect. 2.1, except that the compliance predicate Φ may expect multiple input messages. This construction simplifies that of [18] for preprocessing SNARKs in the SRS model: we do not need to rely on collision-resistant hash functions to shrink the verification key ivk because we require it to be succinct.[8]

Security against quantum adversaries. A key feature of our result is that we prove that if the SNARK is secure (i.e., is a proof of knowledge) against quantum adversaries then so is the resulting PCD scheme (i.e., it is also a proof of knowledge). Therefore, if we assume that FRACTAL achieves proof of knowledge against quantum adversaries when the random oracle is suitably instantiated, then by applying our result to FRACTAL we obtain a *post-quantum* preprocessing PCD scheme in the URS model.

We highlight here an important subtlety that arises when proving security against quantum adversaries. The proof of [18] makes use of the fact that, in the classical case, we may assume that the adversary is deterministic by selecting its randomness. This is not the case for quantum adversaries, since a quantum circuit can create its own randomness (e.g. by measuring a qubit in superposition). This means that we must be careful in defining the proof-of-knowledge property we require of the underlying SNARK. In particular, we must ensure that when we recursively extract proofs, these proofs are consistent with previously extracted proofs. When the adversary is deterministic, this is trivially implied by standard proof of knowledge; for quantum adversaries, it is not. We give a natural definition of proof of knowledge that suffices for the security reduction, and prove that it is realized by our SNARK construction (in the random oracle model).

2.6 The Verifier as a Constraint System

In order to recursively compose FRACTAL (the preprocessing zkSNARK discussed in Sect. 2.4), we need to express FRACTAL's verifier as a constraint system. The size of this constraint system is crucial because this determines the threshold at which recursive composition becomes possible. Towards this goal, we design and implement a constraint system that applies to a general class of verifiers, as outlined below. FRACTAL's verifier is obtained as an instantiation within this class. See the full version [29] for details.

Hash computations introduced by the compiler. Our compiler (Theorem 1) transforms any holographic IOP into a corresponding preprocessing SNARG, while preserving relevant zero knowledge or proof of knowledge properties. The preprocessing SNARG verifier makes a black-box use of the holographic IOP verifier, which means that we can design a *single* (parametrized) constraint system representing the transformation that works for *any* holographic IOP. All additional computations introduced by the compiler involve cryptographic hash functions (which

---

[8] In contrast, the verification key ivk in [18] is allowed to grow linearly with the public input to the circuit that it summarizes, and so recursion required replacing ivk with a short hash of it, and moving ivk to the witness of the recursion circuit.

heuristically instantiate the random oracle). In particular, there are two types of hash computations: (1) a hash chain computation used to derive the randomness for each round of the holographic IOP verifier, based on the Merkle roots provided by the preprocessing SNARG prover; and (2) verification of Merkle tree authentication paths in order to ensure the validity of the query answers provided by the preprocessing SNARG prover. We design generic constraint systems for both of these tasks. Since we are designing constraint systems it is more efficient to consider multiple hash functions specialized to work in different roles: a hash function to absorb inputs or squeeze outputs in the hash chain; a hash function to hash leaves of the Merkle tree; a many-to-one hash function for the internal nodes of the Merkle tree; and others.

Choice of hash function. While our implementation is generic with respect to the aforementioned hash functions (replacing any one of them with another would be a rather straightforward task), the choice of hash function is nonetheless critical for concrete efficiency as we now explain. Expressing standard cryptographic hash functions, such as from the SHA or Blake family, as a constraint system requires more than 20,000 constraints. While this is acceptable for certain applications, these costs are prohibitive for hash-intensive computations, as is the case for the verifiers output by our compiler. Fortunately, the last few years have seen exciting progress in the design of *algebraic hash functions* [2–4, 6, 42], which by design can be expressed via a small number of arithmetic constraints over large finite fields. While this is an active research front, and in particular no standards have been agreed upon, many of the proposed functions are *significantly cheaper* than prior ones, and their security analyses are promising. In this work we decide to use one of these as our choice of hash function (Rescue [4]). We do not claim that this is the "best" choice among the currently proposed ones. (In fact, we know how to achieve better results via a combination of different choices.) We merely make one choice that we believe to be reasonable, and in particular suffices to demonstrate the feasibility of our methodology in practice.

Holographic IOP computations. The constraint system that represents the holographic IOP verifier will, naturally, depend on the specific protocol that is provided as input to the compiler.

That said, all known efficient IOPs, holographic or otherwise, are obtained as the combination of two ingredients: (1) a low-degree test for the Reed–Solomon (RS) code; and (2) an RS-encoded IOP, which is a protocol where the verifier outputs a set of algebraic claims, known as rational constraints, about the prover's messages. Examples of IOPs that fall in this category include our holographic IOP for R1CS, as well as protocols for R1CS in [5, 11, 13] and for AIRs in [10].

We thus provide two constraint systems that target these two components. First, we provide a constraint system that realizes the FRI low-degree test [9], which is used in many efficient IOPs, including in our holographic IOP for R1CS. Second, we provide infrastructure to write constraint systems that express a desired RS-encoded IOP. This essentially entails specifying how many random elements the verifier should send in each round of the protocol, and then specifying constraints that express the rational constraints output by the verifier at the end of the RS-encoded IOP.

We then use the foregoing infrastructure to express the verifier of our holographic IOP for R1CS as a constraint system. We note that the very same generic infrastructure would make it straightforward to express the verifiers of other protocols with the same structure [5,10,11,13].

Remark 2 (succinct languages). We stress that our work in writing constraints for the verifier is restricted to non-uniform computation models such as R1CS (i.e., we are not concerned about the global structure of the constraint system). We do not claim to have an efficient way to express the same verifier via succinct languages such as AIR [10] or Succinct-R1CS [11]. Doing so remains a challenging open problem, that would open up additional opportunities in recursive composition of *non*-preprocessing SNARKs.

References

1. Abdolmaleki, B., Baghery, K., Lipmaa, H., Siim, J., Zając, M.: UC-secure CRS generation for NARKs. In: Buchmann, J., Nitaj, A., Rachidi, T. (eds.) AFRICACRYPT 2019. LNCS, vol. 11627, pp. 99–117. Springer, Cham (2019). https://doi.org/10.1007/978-3-030-23696-0_6
2. Albrecht, M.R., et al.: Algebraic cryptanalysis of STARK-friendly designs: application to MARVELlous and MiMC. IACR Cryptology ePrint Archive, Report 2019/419 (2019)
3. Albrecht, M.R., et al.: Feistel structures for MPC, and more. IACR Cryptology ePrint Archive, Report 2019/397 (2019)
4. Aly, A., Ashur, T., Ben-Sasson, E., Dhooghe, S., Szepieniec, A.: Design of symmetric-key primitives for advanced cryptographic protocols. IACR Cryptology ePrint Archive, Report 2019/426 (2019)
5. Ames, S., Hazay, C., Ishai, Y., Venkitasubramaniam, M.: Ligero: lightweight sublinear arguments without a trusted setup. In: Proceedings of the 24th ACM Conference on Computer and Communications Security, CCS 2017, pp. 2087–2104 (2017)
6. Ashur, T., Dhooghe, S.: MARVELlous: a STARK-friendly family of cryptographic primitives. IACR Cryptology ePrint Archive, Report 2018/1098 (2018)
7. Babai, L., Fortnow, L., Levin, L.A., Szegedy, M.: Checking computations in polylogarithmic time. In: Proceedings of the 23rd Annual ACM Symposium on Theory of Computing, STOC 1991, pp. 21–32 (1991)
8. Barry Whitehat: Rollup (2018). https://github.com/barryWhiteHat/roll_up
9. Ben-Sasson, E., Bentov, I., Horesh, Y., Riabzev, M.: Fast Reed-Solomon interactive oracle proofs of proximity. In: Proceedings of the 45th International Colloquium on Automata, Languages and Programming, ICALP 2018, pp. 14:1–14:17 (2018)
10. Ben-Sasson, E., Bentov, I., Horesh, Y., Riabzev, M.: Scalable zero knowledge with no trusted setup. In: Boldyreva, A., Micciancio, D. (eds.) CRYPTO 2019. LNCS, vol. 11694, pp. 701–732. Springer, Cham (2019). https://doi.org/10.1007/978-3-030-26954-8_23
11. Ben-Sasson, E., Chiesa, A., Goldberg, L., Gur, T., Riabzev, M., Spooner, N.: Linear-size constant-query IOPs for delegating computation. In: Hofheinz, D., Rosen, A. (eds.) TCC 2019. LNCS, vol. 11892, pp. 494–521. Springer, Cham (2019). https://doi.org/10.1007/978-3-030-36033-7_19

12. Ben-Sasson, E., Chiesa, A., Green, M., Tromer, E., Virza, M.: Secure sampling of public parameters for succinct zero knowledge proofs. In: Proceedings of the 36th IEEE Symposium on Security and Privacy, S&P 2015, pp. 287–304 (2015)
13. Ben-Sasson, E., Chiesa, A., Riabzev, M., Spooner, N., Virza, M., Ward, N.P.: Aurora: transparent succinct arguments for R1CS. In: Ishai, Y., Rijmen, V. (eds.) EUROCRYPT 2019. LNCS, vol. 11476, pp. 103–128. Springer, Cham (2019). https://doi.org/10.1007/978-3-030-17653-2_4. Full version available at https://eprint.iacr.org/2018/828
14. Ben-Sasson, E., Chiesa, A., Spooner, N.: Interactive oracle proofs. In: Hirt, M., Smith, A. (eds.) TCC 2016. LNCS, vol. 9986, pp. 31–60. Springer, Heidelberg (2016). https://doi.org/10.1007/978-3-662-53644-5_2
15. Ben-Sasson, E., Chiesa, A., Tromer, E., Virza, M.: Scalable zero knowledge via cycles of elliptic curves. In: Garay, J.A., Gennaro, R. (eds.) CRYPTO 2014. LNCS, vol. 8617, pp. 276–294. Springer, Heidelberg (2014). https://doi.org/10.1007/978-3-662-44381-1_16. Extended version at http://eprint.iacr.org/2014/595
16. Ben-Sasson, E., Goldberg, L., Kopparty, S., Saraf, S.: DEEP-FRI: sampling outside the box improves soundness (2019). eCCC TR19-044
17. Ben-Sasson, E., Goldreich, O., Harsha, P., Sudan, M., Vadhan, S.P.: Robust PCPs of proximity, shorter PCPs, and applications to coding. SIAM J. Comput. **36**(4), 889–974 (2006)
18. Bitansky, N., Canetti, R., Chiesa, A., Tromer, E.: Recursive composition and bootstrapping for SNARKs and proof-carrying data. In: Proceedings of the 45th ACM Symposium on the Theory of Computing, STOC 2013, pp. 111–120 (2013)
19. Bitansky, N., Chiesa, A., Ishai, Y., Paneth, O., Ostrovsky, R.: Succinct noninteractive arguments via linear interactive proofs. In: Sahai, A. (ed.) TCC 2013. LNCS, vol. 7785, pp. 315–333. Springer, Heidelberg (2013). https://doi.org/10.1007/978-3-642-36594-2_18
20. Boneh, D., Dagdelen, Ö., Fischlin, M., Lehmann, A., Schaffner, C., Zhandry, M.: Random oracles in a quantum world. In: Lee, D.H., Wang, X. (eds.) ASIACRYPT 2011. LNCS, vol. 7073, pp. 41–69. Springer, Heidelberg (2011). https://doi.org/10.1007/978-3-642-25385-0_3
21. Bowe, S., Gabizon, A., Green, M.: A multi-party protocol for constructing the public parameters of the Pinocchio zk-SNARK. Cryptology ePrint Archive, Report 2017/602 (2017)
22. Bowe, S., Gabizon, A., Miers, I.: Scalable multi-party computation for zk-SNARK parameters in the random beacon model. Cryptology ePrint Archive, Report 2017/1050 (2017)
23. Bowe, S., Grigg, J., Hopwood, D.: Halo: recursive proof composition without a trusted setup. Cryptology ePrint Archive, Report 2019/1021 (2019)
24. Canetti, R., Goldreich, O., Halevi, S.: The random oracle methodology, revisited. J. ACM **51**(4), 557–594 (2004)
25. Chang, R., Chari, S., Ranjan, D., Rohatgi, P.: Relativization: a revisionistic retrospective. Bull. Eur. Assoc. Theor. Comput. Sci. **47**, 144–153 (1992)
26. Chiesa, A., Chua, L., Weidner, M.: On cycles of pairing-friendly elliptic curves. SIAM J. Appl. Algebra Geom. **3**(2), 175–192 (2019). https://arxiv.org/abs/1803.02067
27. Chiesa, A., Hu, Y., Maller, M., Mishra, P., Vesely, N., Ward, N.: Marlin: preprocessing zkSNARKs with universal and updatable SRS. Cryptology ePrint Archive, Report 2019/1047 (2019)

28. Chiesa, A., Manohar, P., Spooner, N.: Succinct arguments in the quantum random oracle model. In: Hofheinz, D., Rosen, A. (eds.) TCC 2019. LNCS, vol. 11892, pp. 1–29. Springer, Cham (2019). https://doi.org/10.1007/978-3-030-36033-7_1. Available as Cryptology ePrint Archive, Report 2019/834

29. Chiesa, A., Ojha, D., Spooner, N.: Fractal: post-quantum and transparent recursive proofs from holography (full version of this work). Cryptology ePrint Archive, Report 2019/1076 (2019). https://ia.cr/2019/1076

30. Chiesa, A., Tromer, E.: Proof-carrying data and hearsay arguments from signature cards. In: Proceedings of the 1st Symposium on Innovations in Computer Science, ICS 2010, pp. 310–331 (2010)

31. Chiesa, A., Tromer, E., Virza, M.: Cluster computing in zero knowledge. In: Oswald, E., Fischlin, M. (eds.) EUROCRYPT 2015. LNCS, vol. 9057, pp. 371–403. Springer, Heidelberg (2015). https://doi.org/10.1007/978-3-662-46803-6_13

32. Coda: The SNARK Challenge (2019). https://coinlist.co/build/coda

33. Dinur, I., Reingold, O.: Assignment testers: towards a combinatorial proof of the PCP theorem. In: Proceedings of the 45th Annual IEEE Symposium on Foundations of Computer Science, FOCS 2004, pp. 155–164 (2004)

34. Electric Coin Company: Zcash Cryptocurrency (2014). https://z.cash/

35. Ergün, F., Kumar, R., Rubinfeld, R.: Fast approximate probabilistically checkable proofs. Inf. Comput. **189**(2), 135–159 (2004)

36. Fortnow, L.: The role of relativization in complexity theory. Bull. Eur. Assoc. Theor. Comput. Sci. **52**, 229–244 (1994)

37. Freeman, D., Scott, M., Teske, E.: A taxonomy of pairing-friendly elliptic curves. J. Cryptol. **23**(2), 224–280 (2010). https://doi.org/10.1007/s00145-009-9048-z

38. Gabizon, A., Williamson, Z.J., Ciobotaru, O.: PLONK: permutations over lagrangebases for oecumenical noninteractive arguments of knowledge. Cryptology ePrint Archive, Report 2019/953 (2019)

39. Gennaro, R., Gentry, C., Parno, B., Raykova, M.: Quadratic span programs and succinct NIZKs without PCPs. In: Johansson, T., Nguyen, P.Q. (eds.) EUROCRYPT 2013. LNCS, vol. 7881, pp. 626–645. Springer, Heidelberg (2013). https://doi.org/10.1007/978-3-642-38348-9_37

40. Goldwasser, S., Kalai, Y.T.: On the (in)security of the Fiat-Shamir paradigm. In: Proceedings of the 44th Annual IEEE Symposium on Foundations of Computer Science, FOCS 2003, pp. 102–113 (2003)

41. Goldwasser, S., Kalai, Y.T., Rothblum, G.N.: Delegating computation: interactive proofs for muggles. J. ACM **62**(4), 27:1–27:64 (2015)

42. Grassi, L., Kales, D., Khovratovich, D., Roy, A., Rechberger, C., Schofnegger, M.: Starkad and Poseidon: new hash functions for zero knowledge proof systems. IACR Cryptology ePrint Archive, Report 2019/458 (2019)

43. Groth, J.: Short pairing-based non-interactive zero-knowledge arguments. In: Abe, M. (ed.) ASIACRYPT 2010. LNCS, vol. 6477, pp. 321–340. Springer, Heidelberg (2010). https://doi.org/10.1007/978-3-642-17373-8_19

44. Groth, J.: On the size of pairing-based non-interactive arguments. In: Fischlin, M., Coron, J.-S. (eds.) EUROCRYPT 2016. LNCS, vol. 9666, pp. 305–326. Springer, Heidelberg (2016). https://doi.org/10.1007/978-3-662-49896-5_11

45. Groth, J., Kohlweiss, M., Maller, M., Meiklejohn, S., Miers, I.: Updatable and universal common reference strings with applications to zk-SNARKs. In: Shacham, H., Boldyreva, A. (eds.) CRYPTO 2018. LNCS, vol. 10993, pp. 698–728. Springer, Cham (2018). https://doi.org/10.1007/978-3-319-96878-0_24

46. Gur, T., Rothblum, R.D.: Non-interactive proofs of proximity. In: Proceedings of the 6th Innovations in Theoretical Computer Science Conference, ITCS 2015, pp. 133–142 (2015)
47. Lipmaa, H.: Progression-free sets and sublinear pairing-based non-interactive zero-knowledge arguments. In: Cramer, R. (ed.) TCC 2012. LNCS, vol. 7194, pp. 169–189. Springer, Heidelberg (2012). https://doi.org/10.1007/978-3-642-28914-9_10
48. Lund, C., Fortnow, L., Karloff, H.J., Nisan, N.: Algebraic methods for interactive proof systems. J. ACM **39**(4), 859–868 (1992)
49. Maller, M., Bowe, S., Kohlweiss, M., Meiklejohn, S.: Sonic: zero-knowledge SNARKs from linear-size universal and updateable structured reference strings. Cryptology ePrint Archive, Report 2019/099 (2019)
50. Micali, S.: Computationally sound proofs. SIAM J. Comput. **30**(4), 1253–1298 (2000). Preliminary version appeared in FOCS 1994
51. O(1) Labs: Coda Cryptocurrency (2017). https://codaprotocol.com/
52. Reingold, O., Rothblum, R., Rothblum, G.: Constant-round interactive proofs for delegating computation. In: Proceedings of the 48th ACM Symposium on the Theory of Computing, STOC 2016, pp. 49–62 (2016)
53. Rothblum, G.N., Vadhan, S.P., Wigderson, A.: Interactive proofs of proximity: delegating computation in sublinear time. In: Proceedings of the 45th ACM Symposium on the Theory of Computing, STOC 2013, pp. 793–802 (2013)
54. Setty, S.: Spartan: efficient and general-purpose zkSNARKs without trusted setup. Cryptology ePrint Archive, Report 2019/550 (2019)
55. StarkWare & 0x: StarkDEX (2019). https://www.starkdex.io/
56. Valiant, P.: Incrementally verifiable computation or proofs of knowledge imply time/space efficiency. In: Canetti, R. (ed.) TCC 2008. LNCS, vol. 4948, pp. 1–18. Springer, Heidelberg (2008). https://doi.org/10.1007/978-3-540-78524-8_1
57. Xie, T., Zhang, J., Zhang, Y., Papamanthou, C., Song, D.: Libra: succinct zero-knowledge proofs with optimal prover computation. In: Boldyreva, A., Micciancio, D. (eds.) CRYPTO 2019. LNCS, vol. 11694, pp. 733–764. Springer, Cham (2019). https://doi.org/10.1007/978-3-030-26954-8_24

Author Index

Aggarwal, Divesh I-343
Agrawal, Shweta I-13, I-110
Agrikola, Thomas II-96
Alagic, Gorjan III-759, III-788
Aranha, Diego F. I-644
Asharov, Gilad II-403
Auerbach, Benedikt III-475

Badrinarayanan, Saikrishna III-642
Bag, Arnab I-612
Bao, Zhenzhen II-641
Bardet, Magali III-64
Basu Roy, Debapriya I-612
Batina, Lejla I-581
Beimel, Amos I-529
Belaïd, Sonia III-311
Bellare, Mihir II-3, III-507
Beullens, Ward III-183
Bonnetain, Xavier II-493
Brakerski, Zvika I-79, II-551
Briaud, Pierre III-64
Bros, Maxime III-64
Bünz, Benedikt I-677

Castryck, Wouter II-523
Chiesa, Alessandro I-738, I-769
Cohen, Ran II-828
Coron, Jean-Sébastien III-342
Corrigan-Gibbs, Henry I-44
Couteau, Geoffroy III-442
Cramer, Ronald I-499

D'Anvers, Jan-Pieter III-3
Daemen, Joan I-581
Dagand, Pierre-Évariste III-311
Davis, Hannah II-3
de Boer, Koen II-341
Dinur, Itai I-405, II-433
Dodis, Yevgeniy I-313
Döttling, Nico I-79, II-551, II-768
Ducas, Léo II-341, II-608
Dulek, Yfke III-729
Dunkelman, Orr I-250, I-280

Ephraim, Naomi I-707, III-125
Esser, Andre III-94

Fehr, Serge II-341
Fernando, Rex III-642
Fisch, Ben I-677
Fischlin, Marc III-212
Flórez-Gutiérrez, Antonio I-221
Fouque, Pierre-Alain III-34
Freitag, Cody I-707, III-125
Fuchsbauer, Georg II-63

Gaborit, Philippe III-64
Galbraith, Steven II-608
Garay, Juan II-129, II-828
Garg, Ankit I-373
Garg, Sanjam I-79, II-373, II-768
Ghazi, Badih II-798
Ghoshal, Ashrujit II-33
Giacon, Federico III-475
Goldwasser, Shafi II-373
Gong, Junqing III-278
Goyal, Vipul III-668
Grassi, Lorenzo II-674
Greuet, Aurélien III-342
Grilo, Alex B. III-729
Grosso, Vincent I-581
Günther, Felix II-3
Guo, Chun II-641
Guo, Jian II-641

Hajiabadi, Mohammad II-768
Hao, Yonglin I-466
Harasser, Patrick III-212
Hazay, Carmit II-184, III-599
Heath, David III-569
Hofheinz, Dennis II-96
Hosoyamada, Akinori II-249
Hu, Yuncong I-738

Jain, Aayush I-141, III-642
Jain, Abhishek III-668

Janson, Christian   III-212
Jaques, Samuel   II-280
Jayanti, Siddhartha   II-159
Jeffery, Stacey   III-729
Jin, Zhengzhong   III-668

Kalai, Yael Tauman   I-373
Kastner, Julia   II-96
Katsumata, Shuichi   III-379, III-442
Keller, Nathan   I-250, I-280
Khurana, Dakshita   I-373, III-642
Kiayias, Aggelos   II-129
Kiltz, Eike   III-475
Kim, Sam   II-576
Kim, Seongkwang   I-435
Kirchner, Paul   III-34
Kogan, Dmitry   I-44
Kolesnikov, Vladimir   III-569
Komargodski, Ilan   I-707, II-403, III-125
Kuchta, Veronika   III-703

Lasry, Noam   I-250
Leander, Gregor   I-466
Lee, Byeonghak   I-435
Lee, Jooyoung   I-435
Li, Bao   III-538
Libert, Benoît   III-410
Lin, Huijia   III-247
Lin, Wei-Kai   II-403
Lombardi, Alex   III-620
Lüftenegger, Reinhard   II-674
Luo, Ji   III-247

Majenz, Christian   III-729, III-759, III-788
Malavolta, Giulio   I-79, III-668
Maller, Mary   I-738
Manohar, Nathan   I-141
Manurangsi, Pasin   II-798
Masny, Daniel   II-768
Massolino, Pedro Maat Costa   I-581
May, Alexander   III-94
Meier, Willi   I-466
Mercadier, Darius   III-311
Mishra, Pratyush   I-738
Morgan, Andrew   II-216
Mukhopadhyay, Debdeep   I-612
Musa, Saud Al   III-538

Naehrig, Michael   II-280
Naito, Yusuke   II-705
Nandi, Mridul   I-203
Nayak, Kartik   II-403
Naya-Plasencia, María   I-221, II-311
Neiger, Vincent   III-64
Nielsen, Jesper Buus   I-556
Nishimaki, Ryo   III-379

Obremski, Maciej   I-343
Ojha, Dev   I-769
Orlandi, Claudio   I-644
Ostrovsky, Rafail M.   II-129
Othman, Hussien   I-529

Pagh, Rasmus   II-798
Panagiotakos, Giorgos   II-129
Panny, Lorenz   II-523
Papagiannopoulos, Kostas   I-581
Pass, Rafael   I-707, II-216, III-125, III-599
Passelègue, Alain   III-410
Patranabis, Sikhar   I-612
Peikert, Chris   II-463
Pellet-Mary, Alice   I-110
Peserico, Enoch   II-403
Pinkas, Benny   II-739
Plouviez, Antoine   II-63
Polychroniadou, Antigoni   II-216
Prest, Thomas   II-608

Raghuraman, Srinivasan   II-159
Rechberger, Christian   II-674
Regazzoni, Francesco   I-581
Ribeiro, João   I-343
Rivain, Matthieu   III-311
Roetteler, Martin   II-280
Ronen, Eyal   I-280
Rossi, Mélissa   III-3
Rosulek, Mike   II-739
Rotaru, Dragos   II-674
Rotem, Lior   III-155
Ruatta, Olivier   III-64
Russell, Alexander   III-759, III-788

Saha, Sayandeep   I-612
Sahai, Amit   I-141, III-642
Sakzad, Amin   III-703

Samwel, Niels I-581
Sasaki, Yu II-249, II-705
Schaffner, Christian III-729
Schofnegger, Markus II-674
Schrottenloher, André II-311, II-493
Segev, Gil III-155
Seurin, Yannick II-63
Shahaf, Ido III-155
Shamir, Adi I-250, I-280
Shi, Elaine II-403
Silverberg, Alice I-3
Simkin, Mark I-556
Simon, Thierry I-581
Siniscalchi, Luisa I-343
Song, Fang III-788
Song, Ling II-641
Spooner, Nicholas I-769
Stehlé, Damien III-703
Steinfeld, Ron III-703
Stepanovs, Igors III-507
Sugawara, Takeshi II-705
Sun, Shi-Feng III-703
Szepieniec, Alan I-677

Takahashi, Akira I-644
Tessaro, Stefano II-33
Tibouchi, Mehdi III-34
Tillich, Jean-Pierre III-64
Todo, Yosuke I-466
Trieu, Ni II-739

Ünal, Akın I-169
Ursu, Bogdan III-442

Vaikuntanathan, Vinod I-313, III-620
Vasudevan, Prashant Nalini II-373
Velingker, Ameya II-798
Venkitasubramaniam, Muthuramakrishnan
    II-184, III-599
Vercauteren, Frederik II-523
Vesely, Noah I-738
Virdia, Fernando II-280, III-3
Visconti, Ivan I-343
Vyas, Nikhil II-159

Wallet, Alexandre III-34
Wang, Qingju I-466
Ward, Nicholas I-738
Wee, Hoeteck III-278, III-410
Weiss, Mor II-184
Wichs, Daniel I-313, II-768, III-620
Wintersdorff, Raphaël III-311
Wu, David J. III-410

Xing, Chaoping I-499

Yamada, Shota I-13, III-379
Yamakawa, Takashi III-379
Yanai, Avishay II-739
Yu, Wei III-538
Yu, Yang II-608, III-34

Zaverucha, Greg I-644
Zeitoun, Rina III-342
Zikas, Vassilis II-129, II-828

Printed in the United States
By Bookmasters